admirador *m*, **admiradora** *f* admirer

campeón *m*, **-ona** *f* champion

salvapantallas *m inv* INFOR screensaver

ronquido *m* snore; **ronquidos** *pl* snoring *sg*

enemigo 1 *adj* enemy *atr* **2** *m* enemy; **ser enemigo de** *fig* be opposed to, be against

lleno *adj* full (**de** of); *pared* covered (**de** with)

● Grammatical information

debatir ⟨3a⟩ **1** *v/t* debate, discuss **2** *v/i* struggle **3** *v/r* **debatirse**: **debatirse entre la vida y la muerte** fight for one's life

● Entries divided into grammatical categories

uva *f* BOT grape; **estar de mala uva** F be in a foul mood; **tener mala uva** F be a nasty piece of work F

fiambre *m* cold cut, *Br* cold meat; P (*cadaver*) stiff P

profiláctico 1 *adj* preventive, prophylactic *fml* **2** *m* condom

● Register labels

acomedido *adj L.Am.* obliging, helpful

acomedirse ⟨3l⟩ *v/r Méx* offer to help

residencial 1 *adj* residential **2** *f Arg, Chi* boarding house

sablear ⟨1a⟩ *v/t & v/i L.Am.* F scrounge (*a* from)

● Latin American Spanish

riñonera *f* fanny pack, *Br* bum bag

rotonda *f* traffic circle, *Br* roundabout

● British variants

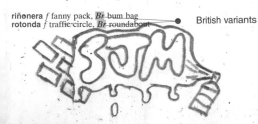

Langenscheidt
Pocket Dictionary

Spanish

Spanish – English
English – Spanish

edited by the
Langenscheidt editorial staff

Munich · Vienna

Compiled by LEXUS
with
José A. Gálvez · Roy Russell
Jane Goldie · Peter Terrell
Monica Tamariz-Martel Mirêlis · Rafael Alarcón Gaeta
Andrew Wilkes · Stephanie Parker
Mike Gonzalez

Activity section by Heather Bonikowski

© 2015 Langenscheidt GmbH & Co. KG, Munich

16020

Preface

This new dictionary of English and Spanish is a tool with 50,000 references for learners of the Spanish language at beginner's or intermediate level.

Thousands of colloquial and idiomatic expressions have been included. The user-friendly layout with all headwords in blue allows the user to have quick access to all the words, expressions and their translations.

Clarity of presentation has been a major objective. Is the *mouse* you need for your computer, for example, the same in Spanish as the *mouse* you don't want in the house? This dictionary is rich in sense distinctions like this – and in translation options tied to specific, identified senses.

Vocabulary needs grammar to back it up. In this dictionary you will find extra grammar information on Spanish conjugation and on irregular verb forms.

The additional activity section provides the user with an opportunity to develop language skills with a selection of engaging word puzzles. The games are designed specifically to improve vocabulary, spelling, grammar and comprehension in an enjoyable style.

Designed for a wide variety of uses, this dictionary will be of great value to those who wish to learn Spanish and have fun at the same time.

Contents

How to use the dictionary

To get the most out of your dictionary you should understand how and where to find the information you need. Whether you are yourself writing text in a foreign language or wanting to understand text that has been written in a foreign language, the following pages should help.

1. How and where do I find a word?

1.1 Spanish and English headwords. The word list for each language is arranged in alphabetical order and also gives irregular forms of verbs and nouns in their correct alphabetical order.

Sometimes you might want to look up terms made up of two separate words, for example **shooting star**, or hyphenated words, for example **absent-minded**. These words are treated as though they were a single word and their alphabetical ordering reflects this.

The only exception to this strict alphabetical ordering is made for English phrasal verbs - words like **go off, go out, go up**. These are positioned directly after their main verb (in this case **go**), rather than being scattered around in alphabetical positions.

Spanish words beginning with **ch** and **ll** are positioned in their alphabetical position in letters C and L. Words beginning with **ñ** are listed after N.

1.2 Spanish feminine headwords are shown as follows:

> **abogado** *m*, **-a** *f* lawyer
> **fumador** *m*, **fumadora** *f* smoker
> **bailarín** *m*, **-ina** *f* dancer
> **pibe** *m*, **-a** *f Rpl* F kid F
> **edil** *m*, **edila** *f* council(l)or

The feminine forms of these headwords are: **abogada, fumadora, bailarina, piba** and **edila**.

When a Spanish headword has a feminine form which translates differently from the masculine form, the feminine is entered as a separate headword in alphabetical order:

> **empresaria** *f* businesswoman; **empresa-**
> **rio** *m* businessman

1.3 Running heads

If you are looking for a Spanish or English word you can use the **running heads** printed in bold in the top corner of each page. The running head on the left tells you the *first* headword on the left-hand page and the one on the right tells you the *last* headword on the right-hand page.

1.4 How is the word spelt?

You can look up the spelling of a word in your dictionary in the same way as you would in a spelling dictionary. British spelling variants are marked *Br*.

2. How do I split a word?

Spanish speakers find English hyphenation very difficult. All you have to do with this dictionary is look for the bold dots between syllables. These dots show you where you can split a word at the end of a line but you should avoid having just one letter before or after the hyphen as in **a·mend** or **thirst·y**. In such cases it is better to take the entire word over to the next line.

3. Long dashes

In the Spanish-English part of the dictionary, when a headword is repeated in a phrase or compound with an altered form, a long dash is used:

> **escaso** *adj* … **-as posibilidades de** not
> much chance of, little chance of

Here **-as posibilidades** means **escasas posibilidades**.

4. What do the different typefaces mean?

4.1 All Spanish and English headwords and the Arabic numerals differentiating between parts of speech appear in **bold**:

> **neoyorquino 1** *adj* New York *atr* **2** *m*, **-a**
> New Yorker
> **splin·ter** ['splɪntər] **1** *n* astilla *f* **2** *v/i* astil-
> larse

4.2 Italics are used for:

a) abbreviated grammatical labels: *adj*, *adv*, *v/i*, *v/t* etc

b) gender labels: *m*, *f*, *mpl* etc

c) all the indicating words which are the signposts pointing to the correct translation for your needs:

> **sport·y** ['spɔːrtɪ] *adj person* deportista;
> *clothes* deportivo
> ◆ **work out 1** *v/t problem, puzzle* resol-
> ver; *solution* encontrar, hallar **2** *v/i at*
> *gym* hacer ejercicios; *of relationship etc*
> funcionar, ir bien
> **completo** *adj* complete; *autobús, teatro* full
> **grano** *m* grain; *de café* bean; *en la piel*
> pimple, spot

4.3 All phrases (examples and idioms) are given in **_secondary bold italics_**:

> **sym·pa·thet·ic** [sɪmpə'θetɪk] *adj* (*show-ing pity*) compasivo; (*understanding*) comprensivo; **_be sympathetic toward a person / an idea_** simpatizar con una persona / idea
> **salsa** *f* GASTR sauce; *baile* salsa; **_en su salsa_** *fig* in one's element

4.4 The normal typeface is used for the translations.

4.5 If a translation is given in italics, and not in the normal typeface, this means that the translation is more of an *explanation* in the other language and that an explanation has to be given because there just is no real equivalent:

> **'walk-up** *n apartamento en un edificio sin ascensor*
> **adobera** *f Méx type of mature cheese*

5. Stress

To indicate where to put the **stress** in English words, the stress marker appears before the syllable on which the main stress falls:

> **mo·tif** [moʊ'tiːf] motivo *m*
> **rec·ord**[1] ['rekɔːrd] *n* MUS disco *m*; SP *etc* récord *m*
> **re·cord**[2] [rɪ'kɔːrd] *v/t electronically* grabar; *in writing* anotar

Stress is shown either in the pronunciation or, if there is no pronunciation given, in the actual headword or compound itself:

> **'rec·ord hold·er** plusmarquista *m/f*

6. What do the various symbols and abbreviations tell you?

6.1 A solid blue diamond is used to indicate a phrasal verb:

> ◆ **call off** *v/t* (*cancel*) cancelar; *strike* desconvocar

6.2 A white diamond is used to divide up longer entries into more easily digested chunks of related bits of text:

> **de** *prp* ◇ *origen* from; **_de Nueva York_** from New York; **_de a_** from to ◇ *posesión* of; **_el coche de mi amigo_** my friend's car ◇ *material* (made) of; **_un anillo de oro_** a gold ring ◇ *contenido* of; **_un vaso de agua_** a glass of water ◇ *cualidad:* **_una mujer de 20 años_** a 20 year old woman ◇ *causa* with; **_temblaba de miedo_** she was shaking with fear …

6.3 The abbreviation F tells you that the word or phrase is used colloquially rather than in formal contexts. The abbreviation V warns you that a word or phrase is vulgar or taboo. Words or phrases labeled P are slang. Be careful how you use these words.

These abbreviations, F, V and P, are used both for headwords and phrases (placed after) and for the translations of headwords and phrases (placed after). If there is no such label given, then the word or phrase is neutral.

6.4 A colon before an English or Spanish word or phrase means that usage is restricted to this specific example (at least as far as this dictionary's translation is concerned):

> **catch-22** [kætʃtwentɪ'tuː]: *it's a catch-22 situation* es como la pescadilla que se muerde la cola
> **co·au·thor** [koʊnθər] ... **2** *v/t*: *co-author a book* escribir un libro conjuntamente
> **decantarse** ⟨1a⟩ *v/r*: *decantarse por* opt for

7. Does the dictionary deal with grammar too?

7.1 All English headwords are given a part of speech label:

> **tooth·less** ['tuːθlɪs] *adj* desdentado
> **top·ple** ['tɑːpl] **1** *v/i* derrumbarse **2** *v/t government* derrocar

But if a headword can only be used as a noun (in ordinary English) then no part of speech is given, since none is needed:

> '**tooth·paste** pasta *f* de dientes, dentífrico *m*

7.2 Spanish headwords have part of speech labels. Spanish gender markers are given:

> **barbacoa** *f* barbecue
> **bocazas** *m/f inv* F loudmouth F
> **budista** *m/f & adj* Buddhist

7.3 If an English translation of a Spanish adjective can only be used in front of a noun, and not after it, this is marked with *atr*:

> **bursátil** *adj* stock market *atr*
> **campestre** *adj* rural, country *atr*

7.4 If the Spanish, unlike the English, doesn't change form if used in the plural, this is marked with *inv*:

> **cortacircuitos** *m inv* circuit breaker
> **metrópolis** *f inv* metropolis

7.5 If the English, in spite of appearances, is not a plural form, this is marked with *nsg*:

> **bil·li·ards** ['bɪljərdz] *nsg* billar *m*
> **mea·sles** ['miːzlz] *nsg* sarampión *m*

English translations are given a *pl* or *sg* label (for plural or singular) in cases where this does not match the Spanish:

> **acciones** *pl* COM stock *sg*, *Br* shares
> **entarimado** *m* (*suelo*) floorboards *pl*

7.6 Irregular English plurals are identified:

> **the·sis** ['θiːsɪs] (*pl* **theses** ['θiːsiːz]) tesis
> *f inv*
> **thief** [θiːf] (*pl* **thieves** [θiːvz]) ladrón
> (-ona) *m(f)*
> **trout** [traʊt] (*pl* **trout**) trucha *f*

7.7 Words like **physics** or **media studies** have not been given a label to say if they are singular or plural for the simple reason that they can be either, depending on how they are used.

7.8 Irregular and semi-irregular verb forms are identified:

> **sim·pli·fy** ['sɪmplɪfaɪ] *v/t* (*pret & pp* **-ied**)
> simplificar
> **sing** [sɪŋ] *v/t & v/i* (*pret* **sang**, *pp* **sung**)
> cantar
> **la·bel** ['leɪbl] **1** *n* etiqueta *f* **2** *v/t* (*pret &*
> *pp* **-ed**, *Br* **-led**) *bags* etiquetar

7.9 Cross-references are given to tables of Spanish conjugations:

> **gemir** ⟨3l⟩ *v/i* moan, groan
> **esconder** ⟨2a⟩ **1** *v/t* hide, conceal ...

7.10 Grammatical information is provided on the prepositions you'll need in order to create complete sentences:

> **'switch·o·ver** *to new system* cambio *m* (*to*
> a)
> **sneer** [sniːr] **1** *n* mueca *f* desdeñosa **2** *v/i*
> burlarse (*at* de)
> **escindirse** ⟨3a⟩ *v/r* (*fragmentarse*) split
> (*en* into); (*segregarse*) break away (*de*
> from)
> **enviciarse** ⟨1b⟩ *v/r* get addicted (*con* to)

Abbreviations

and	&	y	electronics,	ELEC	electrónica,
see	→	véase	electronic		electrotecnia
registered	®	marca	engineering		
trademark		registrada	Spain	*Esp*	España
abbreviation	*abbr*	abreviatura	especially	*esp*	especialmente
abbreviation	*abr*	abreviatura	euphemistic	*euph*	eufemismo
adjective	*adj*	adjetivo	familiar,	F	familiar
adverb	*adv*	adverbio	colloquial		
agriculture	AGR	agricultura	feminine	*f*	femenino
anatomy	ANAT	anatomía	feminine noun	*fladj*	sustantivo
architecture	ARCHI	arquitectura	and adjective		femenino y
Argentina	*Arg*	Argentina			adjetivo
architecture	ARQUI	arquitectura	railroad	FERR	ferrocarriles
article	*art*	artículo	figurative	*fig*	figurativo
astronomy	AST	astronomía	financial	FIN	finanzas
astrology	ASTR	astrología	physics	FÍS	física
attributive	*atr*	atributivo	formal	*fml*	formal
motoring	AUTO	automóvil	photography	FOT	fotografía
civil aviation	AVIA	aviación	feminine plural	*fpl*	femenino
biology	BIO	biología			plural
Bolivia	*Bol*	Bolivia	feminine	*fsg*	femenino
botany	BOT	botánica	singular		singular
British English	*Br*	inglés	gastronomy	GASTR	gastronomía
		británico	geography	GEOG	geografía
Central	*C.Am.*	América	geology	GEOL	geología
America		Central	geometry	GEOM	geometría
chemistry	CHEM	química	grammatical	GRAM	gramática
Chile	*Chi*	Chile	historical	HIST	histórico
Colombia	*Col*	Colombia	humorous	*hum*	humorístico
commerce,	COM	comercio	IT term	INFOR	informática
business			interjection	*int*	interjección
comparative	*comp*	comparativo	interrogative	*interr*	interrogativo
computers,	COMPUT	informática	invariable	*inv*	invariable
IT term			ironic	*iron*	irónico
conjunction	*conj*	conjunción	ironic	*irón*	irónico
Southern Cone	*CSur*	Cono Sur	law	JUR	jurisprudencia
sports	DEP	deporte	Latin	*L.Am.*	América
contemptuous	*desp*	despectivo	America		Latina
determiner	*det*	determinante	law	LAW	jurisprudencia
Ecuador	*Ecuad*	Ecuador	linguistics	LING	lingüística
education	EDU	educación,	literary	*lit*	literario
(schools,		enseñanza	masculine	*m*	masculino
universities)		(sistema	masculine	*m/adj*	sustantivo
		escolar y	noun and		masculino y
		universitario)	adjective		adjetivo
electronics,	EL	electrónica,	nautical	MAR	navegación,
electronic		electrotecnia			marina
engineering			mathematics	MAT	matemáticas

mathematics	MATH	matemáticas	preterite (past tense)	*pret*	pretérito
medicine	MED	medicina	pronoun	*pron*	pronombre
meteorology	METEO	meteorología	preposition	*prp*	preposición
Mexico	Mex	México	psychology	PSI	psicología
Mexico	*Méx*	México	psychology	PSYCH	psicología
masculine and feminine	*m/f*	masculino y femenino	chemistry	QUÍM	química
masculine and feminine plural	*m/fpl*	masculino y femenino plural	radio	RAD	radio
			railroad	RAIL	ferrocarriles
military	MIL	militar	relative	*rel*	relativo
mineralogy	MIN	mineralogía	religion	REL	religión
motoring	MOT	automóvil	River Plate	*Rpl*	Río de la Plata
masculine plural	*mpl*	masculino plural	South America	S.Am.	América del Sur
music	MUS	música	singular	*sg*	singular
music	*MÚS*	música	someone	s.o.	alguien
mythology	MYTH	mitología	sports	SP	deporte
noun	*n*	sustantivo	Spain	*Span*	España
nautical	NAUT	navegación, náutica	something	*sth*	algo, alguna cosa
negative	*neg*	negativo	subjunctive	*subj*	subjuntivo
noun plural	*npl*	sustantivo plural	superlative	*sup*	superlativo
			bullfighting	TAUR	tauromaquia
noun singular	*nsg*	sustantivo singular	also	*tb*	también
			theater, theatre	TEA	teatro
ornithology	ORN	ornitología	technology	TÉC	técnica
oneself	o.s.	sí mismo	technology	TECH	técnica
popular, slang	P	popular	telecommunications	TELEC	telecomunicaciones
painting	PAINT	pintura	theater	THEA	teatro
Paraguay	*Parag*	Paraguay	typography, typesetting	TIP	tipografía
past participle	*part*	participio pasado	transportation	TRANSP	transportes
Peru	*Pe*	Perú	television	TV	televisión
pejorative	*pej*	peyorativo	vulgar	V	vulgar
photography	PHOT	fotografía	auxiliary verb	*v/aux*	verbo auxiliar
physics	PHYS	física	verb	*vb*	verbo
painting	PINT	pintura	Venezuela	*Ven*	Venezuela
plural	*pl*	plural	intransitive verb	*v/i*	verbo intransitivo
politics	POL	política	impersonal verb	*v/impers*	verbo impersonal
possessive	*pos*	posesivo	reflexive verb	*v/r*	verbo reflexivo
possessive	*poss*	posesivo	transitive verb	*v/t*	verbo transitivo
past participle	*pp*	participio pasado	West Indies	W.I.	Antillas
predicative usage	*pred*	predicativo	zoology	ZO	zoología
prefix	*pref*	prefijo			
preposition	*prep*	preposición			

The pronunciation of Spanish

Stress

1. If a word ends in a vowel, or in *n* or *s*, the penultimate syllable is stressed: **espada, biblioteca, hablan, telefonean, edificios**.
2. If a word ends in a consonant other than *n* or *s*, the last syllable is stressed: **dificultad, hablar, laurel, niñez**.
3. If a word is to be stressed in any way contrary to rules 1 and 2, an acute accent is written over the stressed vowel: **rubí, máquina, crímenes, carácter, continúa, autobús**.
4. **Diphthongs and syllable division**. Of the 5 vowels *a, e, o* are considered "strong" and *i* and *u* "weak":

   a) A combination of weak + strong forms a diphthong, the stress falling on the stronger element: **reina, baile, cosmonauta, tiene, bueno**.
   b) A combination of weak + weak forms a diphthong, the stress falling on the second element: **viuda, ruido**.
   c) Two strong vowels together remain two distinct syllables, the stress falling according to rules 1 and 2: **ma/estro, atra/er**.
   d) Any word having a vowel combination not stressed according to these rules has an accent: **traído, oído, baúl, río**.

Sounds

Since the pronunciation of Spanish is (unlike English) adequately represented by the spelling of words, Spanish headwords have not been given a phonetic transcription. The sounds of Spanish are described below.

The pronunciation described is primarily that of the educated Spaniard. But the main features of Latin American pronunciation are also covered.

Vowels

a   As in English *father*: **paz, pata**.

e   Like *e* in English *they* (but without the following sound of *y*): **grande, pelo**. A shorter sound when followed by a consonant in the same syllable, like *e* in English *get*: **España, renta**.

i   Like *i* in English *machine*, though somewhat shorter: **pila, rubí**.

o   As in English *November, token*: **solo, esposa**. A shorter sound when followed by a consonant in the same syllable, like *au* in English *fault* or the *a* in *fall*: **costra, omba**.

u   Like *oo* in English *food*: **pura, luna**. Silent after **q** and in **gue, gui**, unless marked with a dieresis (**antigüedad, argüir**).

y   When occurring as a vowel (in the conjunction **y** or at the end of a word), is pronounced like *i*.

Diphthongs

ai   like *i* in English *right*: **baile**, **vaina**.

ei   like *ey* in English *they*: **reina**, **peine**.

oi   like *oy* in English *boy*: **boina**, **oigo**.

au   like *ou* in English *bout*: **causa**, **audacia**.

eu   like the vowel sounds in English *may-you*, without the sound of the *y*:
      deuda, **reuma**.

Semiconsonants

i, y   like *y* in English *yes*: **yerno**, **tiene**; in some cases in *L.Am.* this *y* is pro-
       nounced like the *s* in English *measure*: **mayo**, **yo**.

u   like *w* in English *water*: **huevo**, **agua**.

Consonants

b, v   These two letters represent the same value in Spanish. There are two
       distinct pronunciations:
       1. At the start of a word and after *m* and *n* the sound is like English *b*:
          batalla, **ventaja**; **tromba**, **invierno**.
       2. In all other positions the sound is what is technically a "bilabial
          fricative". This sound does not exist in English. Go to say a *b* but
          do not quite bring your lips together: **estaba**, **cueva**, **de Vigo**.

c   1. *c* before *a*, *o*, *u* or a consonant is like English *k*: **café**, **cobre**.
       2. *c* before *e*, *i* is like English *th* in *thin*: **cédula**, **cinco**. In *L.Am.* this is
          pronounced like an English *s* in *chase*.

ch   like English ch in church: **mucho**, **chocho**.

d   Three distinct pronunciations:
       1. At the start of a word and after *l* and *n*, the sound is like English *d*:
          doy, **aldea**, **conde**.
       2. Between vowels and after consonants other than *l* and *n* the sound is
          relaxed and approaches English *th* in *this*: **codo**, **guardar**; in parts of
          Spain it is further relaxed and even disappears, particularly in the
          -ado ending.
       3. In final position, this type 2 is further relaxed or omitted altogether:
          usted, **Madrid**.

f   like English *f*: **fuero**, **flor**.

g   Three distinct pronunciations:

       1. Before *e* and *i* it is the same as the Spanish **j** (below): **coger**, **general.**
       2. At the start of a word and after *n*, the sound is that of English *g* in *get*:
          granada, **rango**.
       3. In other positions the sound is like 2 above, but much softer, the *g*
          almost disappearing: **agua**, **guerra**. N.B. In the group **gue**, **gui** the **u**
          is silent (**guerra**, **guindar**) unless marked with a dieresis (**antigüedad**,
          argüir). In the group **gua** all letters are sounded.

h   always silent: **honor**, **búho**.

j   A strong guttural sound not found in English, but like the *ch* in Scots *loch*, German *Achtung*: **jota**, **ejercer**.

k   like English *k*: **kilogramo**, **ketchup**.

l   like English *l*: **león**, **pala**.

ll   approximating to English *lli* in *million*: **millón**, **calle**. In *L.Am.* like the *s* in English *measure*.

m   like English *m*: **mano**, **como**.

n   like English *n*: **nono**, **pan**; except before **v**, when the group is pronounced like *mb*: **enviar**, **invadir**.

ñ   approximating to English *ni* in *onion*: **paño**, **ñoño**.

p   like English *p*: **Pepe**, **copa**.

q   like English *k*; always in combination with *u*, which is silent: **que**, **quiosco**.

r   a single trill stronger than any *r* in English, but like Scots *r*: **caro**, **querer**. Somewhat relaxed in final position. Pronounced like **rr** at the start of a word and after **l**, **n**, **s**: **rata**.

rr   strongly trilled: **carro**, **hierro**.

s   like *s* in English *chase*: **rosa**, **soso**. But before **b**, **d**, hard **g**, **l**, **m** and **n** it is like English *s* in *rose*: **desde**, **mismo**, **asno**. Before "impure **s**" in recent loan-words, an extra *e*-sound is inserted in pronunciation: **e-sprint**, **e-stand**.

t   like English *t*: **patata**, **tope**.

v   see *b*.

w   found in a few recent loan-words only and pronounced pretty much as the English *w*, but sometimes with a very slight *g* sound before it: **whisky**, **windsurf**. In one exceptional case it is pronounced like an English *v* or like Spanish **b** and **v**: **wáter**.

x   like English *gs* in *big sock*: **máximo**, **examen**. Before a consonant like English *s* in *chase*: **extraño**, **mixto**.

z   like English *th* in *thin*: **zote**, **zumbar**. In *L.Am.* like English *s* in *chase*.

The Spanish Alphabet

a	[ah]	g	[нeh]	m	['emeh]	rr	['erreh]	x	['ekees]
b	[beh]	h	['acheh]	n	['eneh]	s	['eseh]	y	[eegree-eh-ga]
c	[theh]	i	[ee]	ñ	['en-yeh]	t	[teh]	z	['theh-ta]
ch	[cheh]	j	['ḥota]	o	[oh]	u	[oo]		
d	[deh]	k	[ka]	p	[peh]	v	['ooveh]	н *is pronounced*
e	[eh]	l	['eleh]	q	[koo]	w	['ooveh	*as in the Scottish*
f	['ef-feh]	ll	['el-yeh]	r	['ereh]		doh-bleh]	*way of saying loch*

Written Spanish

I. Capitalization

The rules for capitalization in Spanish largely correspond to those for the English language. In contrast to English, however, adjectives derived from proper nouns are not capitalized (*americano* American, *español* Spanish).

II. Word division

Spanish words are divided according to the following rules:

1. If there is a **single consonant** between two vowels, the division is made between the first vowel and the consonant (*di-ne-ro, Gra-na-da*).

2. **Two consecutive consonants** may be divided (*miér-co-les, dis-cur-so*). If the second consonant is an *l* or *r*, however, the division comes before the two consonants (*re-gla, nie-bla; po-bre, ca-bra*). This also goes for *ch, ll* and *rr* (*te-cho, ca-lle, pe-rro*).

3. In the case of **three consecutive consonants** (usually including an *l* or *r*), the division comes after the first consonant (*ejem-plo, siem-pre*). If the second consonant is an *s*, however, the division comes after the *s* (*cons-tan-te, ins-ti-tu-to*).

4. In the case of **four consecutive consonants** (the second of these is usually an *s*), the division is made between the second and third consonants (*ins-tru-men-to*).

5. **Diphthongs** and **triphthongs** may not be divided (*bien, buey*). Vowels which are part of different syllables, however, may be divided (*frí-o, acre-e-dor*).

6. **Compounds**, including those formed with prefixes, are divided morphologically (*nos-otros, des-ali-ño, dis-cul-pa*).

III. Punctuation

In Spanish a comma is often placed after an adverbial phrase introducing a sentence (*sin embargo, todos los esfuerzos fueron inútiles* however, all efforts were in vain). A subsidiary clause beginning a sentence is also followed by a comma (*si tengo tiempo, lo haré* if I have time, I'll do it, **but:** *lo haré si tengo tiempo* I'll do it if I have time).

Questions and exclamations are introduced by an inverted question mark and exclamation point respectively, which immediately precedes the question or exclamation (*Dispense usted, ¿está en casa el señor Pérez?* Excuse me, is Mr. Pérez at home?; *¡Qué lástima!* What a shame!).

English pronunciation

Vowels

[ɑː]	*father*	['fɑːðər]
[æ]	*man*	[mæn]
[e]	*get*	[get]
[ə]	*about*	[ə'baut]
[ɜ]	*absurd*	[əb'sɜːrd]
[ɪ]	*stick*	[stɪk]
[iː]	*need*	[niːd]
[ɒː]	*in-laws*	['ɪnlɒːz]
[ɔː]	*more*	[mɔːr]
[ʌ]	*mother*	['mʌðər]
[ʊ]	*book*	[bʊk]
[uː]	*fruit*	[fruːt]

Diphthongs

[aɪ]	*time*	[taɪm]
[au]	*cloud*	[klaud]
[eɪ]	*name*	[neɪm]
[ɔɪ]	*point*	[pɔɪnt]
[ou]	*oath*	[ouθ]

Consonants

[b]	*bag*	[b] [æ]
[d]	*dear*	[dɪr]
[f]	*fall*	[fɔːl]
[g]	*give*	[gɪv]
[h]	*hole*	[houl]
[j]	*yes*	[jes]
[k]	*come*	[kʌm]
[l]	*land*	[lænd]
[m]	*mean*	[miːn]
[n]	*night*	[naɪt]
[p]	*pot*	[pɑːt]
[r]	*right*	[raɪt]
[s]	*sun*	[sʌn]
[t]	*take*	[teɪk]
[v]	*vain*	[veɪn]
[w]	*wait*	[weɪt]
[z]	*rose*	[rouz]
[ŋ]	*bring*	[brɪŋ]
[ʃ]	*she*	[ʃiː]
[tʃ]	*chair*	[tʃer]
[dʒ]	*join*	[dʒɔɪn]
[ʒ]	*leisure*	['liːʒər]
[θ]	*think*	[θɪŋk]
[ð]	*the*	[ðə]
[']	means that the following syllable is stressed: *ability* [ə'bɪlətɪ]

Part 1

Spanish-English
Dictionary

A

a *prp* ◇ *dirección* to; *al este de* to the east of; *a casa* home; *ir a la cama* / *al cine* go to bed / to the movies; *vamos a Bolivia* we're going to Bolivia; *voy a casa de Marta* I'm going to Marta's (house)

◇ *situación* at; *a la mesa* at the table; *al lado de* next to; *a la derecha* on the right; *al sol* in the sun; *a treinta kilómetros de Quito* thirty kilometers (*Br* kilometres) from Quito; *está a cinco kilómetros* it is five kilometers (*Br* kilometres) away

◇ *tiempo:* ¿*a qué hora llegas?* what time do you arrive?; *a las tres* at three o'clock; *estamos a quince de febrero* it's February fifteenth; *a los treinta años* at the age of thirty

◇ *modo:* *a la española* the Spanish way; *a mano* by hand; *a pie* on foot; *a 50 kilómetros por hora* at fifty kilometers (*Br* kilometres) an hour

◇ *precio:* ¿*a cómo* or *cuánto está?* how much is it?

◇ *objeto indirecto:* *dáselo a tu hermano* give it to your brother

◇ *objeto directo:* *vi a mi padre* I saw my father

◇ *en perífrasis verbal:* *empezar a* begin to; *jugar a las cartas* play cards; *a decir verdad* to tell the truth

◇ *para introducir pregunta:* ¿*a que no lo sabes?* I bet you don't know; *a ver ...* OK ..., right ...

ábaco *m* abacus

abadía *f* abbey

abajo 1 *adv situación* below, underneath; *en edificio* downstairs; *ponlo ahí abajo* put it down there, *el cajón de abajo siguiente* the drawer below; *último* the bottom drawer ◇ *dirección* down; *en edificio* downstairs; *cuesta abajo* downhill; *empuja hacia abajo* push down

◇ *con cantidades:* *de diez para abajo* ten or under, ten or below **2** *int:* ¡*abajo los traidores!* down with the traitors!

abalanzarse ⟨1f⟩ *v/i* rush *o* surge forward; *abalanzarse sobre algo* / *alguien* leap *o* pounce on sth/s.o.

abalear ⟨1a⟩ *v/t S. Am.* shoot

abandonar ⟨1a⟩ **1** *v/t lugar* leave; *objeto, a alguien* abandon; *a esposa, hijos* desert; *idea* give up, abandon; *actividad* give up **2** *v/r abandonarse* let o.s. go; *abandonarse a* abandon o.s. to

abanicar ⟨1g⟩ **1** *v/t* fan **2** *v/r* abanicarse *v/r* fan o.s.

abanico *m* fan; *fig* range; *abanico eléctrico Méx* electric fan

abaratar ⟨1a⟩ *v/t* reduce or lower the price of; *precio* reduce, lower

abarcar ⟨1g⟩ *v/t territorio* cover; *fig* comprise, cover; *L.Am. (acaparar)* hoard, stockpile; *el libro abarca desde ... hasta ...* the book covers the period from ... to ...; *abarcar con la vista* take in

abarrotado *adj* packed

abarrotar ⟨1a⟩ **1** *v/t lugar* pack; *L.Am.* COM buy up, stockpile **2** *v/r* abarrotarse *L.Am. del mercado* become glutted

abarrotes *mpl L.Am. (mercancías)* groceries; *(tienda de) abarrotes* grocery store, *Br* grocer's

abarrotería *f Méx, C.Am.* grocery store, *Br* grocer's

abarrotero *m*, *-a f Méx, C.Am.* storekeeper, shopkeeper

abastecer ⟨2d⟩ **1** *v/t* supply *(de* with) **2** *v/r* abastecerse stock up *(de* on *o* with)

abastecimiento *m* supply

abasto *m:* *no dan abasto* they can't cope *(con* with)

abatí *m Rpl* corn, *Br* maize; *Parag:* fermented maize drink

abatible *adj* collapsible, folding *atr*

abatido *adj* depressed

abatimiento *m* gloom

abatir ⟨3a⟩ *v/t edificio* knock *o* pull down; *árbol* cut down, fell; AVIA shoot *o* bring down; *fig* kill; *(deprimir)* depress

abdicación *f* abdication

abdicar ⟨1g⟩ *v/t* abdicate

abdomen *m* abdomen

abdominal *adj* abdominal

abdominales *mpl* sit-ups

abecedario *m* alphabet

abedul *m* birch

abeja *f* zo bee

abejorro *m* bumblebee

aberración *f* aberration

abertura *f* opening

abeto *m* fir (tree)

abiertamente *adv* openly

abierto 1 *part* → **abrir 2** *adj tb persona* open; *está abierto a nuevas ideas fig* he's open to new ideas

abigarrado *adj* multicolo(u)red

abismo *m* abyss; *fig* gulf

ablandar ⟨1a⟩ **1** *v/t tb fig* soften **2** *v/r*

ablandarse soften, get softer; *fig* relent

ablande *m Arg* AUTO running in

abnegación *f* self-denial

abnegado *adj* selfless

abocado *adj* doomed; *abocado al fracaso* doomed to failure, destined to fail

abochornar ⟨1a⟩ **1** *v/t* embarrass **2** *v/r* **abochornarse** feel embarrassed

abogacía *f* law

abogaderas *fpl L.Am.* F (*discusiones*) arguments

abogado *m*, **-a** *f* lawyer; *en tribunal superior* attorney, *Br* barrister; *no le faltaron abogados fig* there were plenty of people who defended him

abogar ⟨1h⟩ *v/i*: *abogar por alguien* defend; *algo* advocate

abolición *f* abolition

abolir ⟨3a⟩ *v/t* abolish

abollado *adj* dented

abolladura *f* dent

abollar ⟨1a⟩ *v/t* dent

abombado *adj S. Am.* F *comida* rotten, bad; F (*tonto*) dopey F

abombarse *S. Am. de comida* go off, go bad

abominable *adj* abominable

abominar ⟨1a⟩ *v/t* detest, loathe

abonado *m*, **-a** *f* subscriber; *a teléfono, gas, electricidad* customer; *a ópera, teatro* season-ticket holder

abonar ⟨1a⟩ **1** *v/t* COM pay; AGR fertilize; *Méx* pay on account; *abonar el terreno fig* sow the seeds **2** *v/r* **abonarse** *a espectáculo* buy a season ticket (*a* for); *a revista* take out a subscription (*a* to)

abono *m* COM payment; AGR fertilizer; *para espectáculo, transporte* season ticket

abordar ⟨1a⟩ *v/t* MAR board; *tema, asunto* broach, raise; *problema* tackle, deal with; *a una persona* approach

aborigen 1 *adj* native, indigenous **2** *m/f* native

aborrecer ⟨2d⟩ *v/t* loathe, detest

abortar ⟨1a⟩ **1** *v/i* MED espontáneamente miscarry; *de forma provocada* have an abortion **2** *v/t* *plan* foil

abortivo *adj aborto* atr; *píldora -a* abortion pill

aborto *m espontáneo* miscarriage; *provocado* abortion; *fig* F freak F; *tener un aborto* have a miscarriage

abotonar ⟨1a⟩ *v/t* button up

abra *f L.Am.* clearing

abrasador *adj* scorching (hot)

abrasar ⟨1a⟩ **1** *v/t* burn **2** *v/i del sol* burn, scorch; *de bebida, comida* be boiling hot **3** *v/r* **abrasarse**: *abrasarse de sed* F be parched F; *abrasarse de calor* F be sweltering F; *abrasarse de pasión lit* be aflame with passion *lit*

abrazar ⟨1f⟩ **1** *v/t* hug **2** *v/r* **abrazarse** embrace

abrazo *m* hug; *dar un abrazo a alguien* hug s.o., give s.o. a hug; *un abrazo en carta* best wishes; *más íntimo* love

abrebotellas *m inv* bottle opener

abrelatas *m inv* can opener, *Br tb* tin opener

abreviar ⟨1b⟩ *v/t* shorten; *palabra* abbreviate; *texto* abridge

abreviatura *f* abbreviation

abridor *m* bottle opener

abrigado *adj* warmly dressed

abrigar ⟨1h⟩ **1** *v/t* wrap up; *esperanzas* hold out; *duda* entertain **2** *v/r* **abrigarse** wrap up warm; *abrigarse del frío* (take) shelter from the cold

abrigo *m* coat; (*protección*) shelter; *ropa de abrigo* warm clothes; *al abrigo de* in the shelter of

abril *m* April

abrir ⟨3a; *part* **abierto**⟩ **1** *v/t* open; *túnel* dig; *grifo* turn on; *le abrió el apetito* it gave him an appetite **2** *v/i de persona* open up; *de ventana, puerta* open; *en un abrir y cerrar de ojos* in the twinkling of an eye **3** *v/r* **abrirse** open; *abrirse a algo fig* open up to sth; *abrirse paso entre* make one's way through

abrochar ⟨1a⟩ **1** *v/t* do up; *cinturón de seguridad* fasten **2** *v/r* **abrocharse** do up; *cinturón de seguridad* fasten; *tendremos que abrocharnos el cinturón* we'll have to tighten our belts

abrumador *adj* overwhelming

abrumar ⟨1a⟩ *v/t* overwhelm (*con* or *de* with); *abrumado de* or *con trabajo* snowed under with work

abrupto *adj terreno* rough; *pendiente* steep; *tono, respuesta* abrupt; *cambio* sudden

absentismo *m* absenteeism; *absentismo escolar* truancy

absolución *f* absolution

absolutamente *adv* absolutely; *no entendió absolutamente nada* he didn't understand a thing

absolutismo *m* absolutism

absoluto *adj* absolute; *en absoluto* not at all

absolver ⟨2h; *part* **absuelto**⟩ *v/t* JUR acquit; REL absolve

absorbente *adj* absorbent

absorber ⟨2a⟩ *v/t* absorb; (*consumir*) take; (*cautivar*) absorb

absorto *adj* absorbed (*en* in), engrossed (*en* in)

abstemio 1 *adj* teetotal **2** *m*, **-a** *f* teetotal-(l)er

abstención *f* abstention

abstenerse ⟨2l⟩ *v/r* refrain (**de** from); POL abstain

abstinencia *f* abstinence; **síndrome de abstinencia** MED withdrawal symptoms *pl*

abstracto *adj* abstract

abstraerse ⟨2p; *part* **abstraído**⟩ *v/r* shut o.s. off (**de** from)

abstraído 1 *adj* preoccupied; **abstraído en algo** engrossed in sth **2** *part* → **abstraerse**

absuelto *part* → **absolver**

absurdo 1 *adj* absurd **2** *m*: **es un absurdo que** it's absurd that

abuchear ⟨1a⟩ *v/t* boo

abucheo(s) *m* (*pl*) booing *sg*, boos *pl*

abuela *f* grandmother; F *persona mayor* old lady; **¡cuéntaselo a tu abuela!** F don't try to put one over on me! F, *Br* pull the other one! F

abuelo *m* grandfather; F *persona mayor* old man; **abuelos** grandparents

abultado *adj* bulging; *derrota* heavy

abultamiento *m* bulge

abultar ⟨1a⟩ *v/i* be bulky; **no abulta casi nada** it takes up almost no room at all

abundancia *f* abundance; **había comida en abundancia** there was plenty of food

abundante *adj* plentiful, abundant

abundar ⟨1a⟩ *v/i* be plentiful *o* abundant

aburguesarse ⟨1a⟩ *v/r desp* become bourgeois *o* middle class

aburrido *adj* (*que aburre*) boring; (*que se aburre*) bored; **aburrido de algo** bored *o* fed up F with sth

aburrimiento *m* boredom

aburrir ⟨3a⟩ **1** *v/t* bore **2** *v/r* **aburrirse** get bored; **aburrirse de algo** get bored *o* fed up F with sth; **aburrirse como una ostra** F get bored stiff F

abusado *adj Méx* F smart, clever; **¡abusado!** look out!

abusar ⟨1a⟩ *v/i*: **abusar de** *poder, confianza* abuse; *persona* take advantage of; **abusar del alcohol** drink too much; **abusar sexualmente de alguien** sexually abuse s.o.

abusivo *adj* JUR unfair

abuso *m* abuse; **abusos** *pl* **deshonestos** indecent assault *sg*

A.C. *abr* (= **antes de Cristo**) BC (= before Christ)

acá *adv* here; **de acá para allá** from here to there; **de entonces para acá** since then

acabado *m* finish

acabar ⟨1a⟩ **1** *v/t* finish **2** *v/i de persona* finish; *de función, acontecimiento* finish, end; **acabé haciéndolo yo** I ended up doing it myself; **acabar con** put an end to; *caramelos* finish off; *persona* destroy; **acabar de hacer algo** have just done sth; **va a acabar mal** F *persona* he'll come to no good; **esto va a acabar mal** F this is going to end badly **3** *v/r* **acabarse** *de actividad* finish, end; *de pan, dinero* run out; **se nos ha acabado el azúcar** we've run out of sugar; **¡se acabó!** that's that!

acacia *f* acacia

academia *f* academy; **academia de idiomas** language school; **academia militar** military academy

académico 1 *adj* academic **2** *m*, **-a** *f* academician

acalenturarse ⟨1a⟩ *v/r L.Am.* (*afiebrarse*) get a temperature *o* fever

acallar ⟨1a⟩ *v/t tb fig* silence

acalorarse ⟨1a⟩ *v/r* (*enfadarse*) get worked up; (*sofocarse*) get embarrassed

acampada *f* camp; **ir de acampada** go camping

acampar ⟨1a⟩ *v/i* camp

acantilado *m* cliff

acaparar ⟨1a⟩ *v/t* hoard, stockpile; *tiempo* take up; *interés* capture; (*monopolizar*) monopolize

acápite *m L.Am.* section; (*párrafo*) paragraph

acaramelado *adj fig* F lovey-dovey F

acariciar ⟨1b⟩ *v/t* caress; *perro* stroke; **acariciar una idea** *fig* contemplate an idea

acarrear ⟨1a⟩ *v/t* carry; *fig* give rise to, cause

acaso *adv* perhaps; **por si acaso** just in case

acatar ⟨1a⟩ *v/t* comply with, obey

acatarrarse ⟨1a⟩ *v/r* catch a cold

acaudalado *adj* wealthy, well-off

acceder ⟨2a⟩ *v/i* (*ceder*) agree (**a** to), accede (**a** to) *fml*; **acceder a** *lugar* gain access to; *cargo* accede to *fml*

accesible *adj* accessible

acceso *m tb* INFOR access; *de fiebre* attack, bout; *de tos* fit; **de difícil acceso** inaccessible

accesorio 1 *adj* incidental **2** *m* accessory

accidentado 1 *adj terreno, camino* rough; *viaje* eventful **2** *m*, **-a** *f* casualty

accidental *adj* (*no esencial*) incidental; (*casual*) chance *atr*

accidente *m* accident; (*casualidad*) chance; GEOG feature; **accidente de tráfico** *or* **de circulación** road traffic accident, RTA; **accidente laboral** industrial accident

acción *f* action; **acciones** *pl* COM stock *sg*, *Br* shares; **poner en acción** put into action

accionar ⟨1a⟩ *v/t* activate

accionista *m/f* stockholder, *Br* shareholder

acebo *m* holly

acechar ⟨1a⟩ *v/t* lie in wait for

acecho *m*: **al acecho** lying in wait

aceite *m* oil; **aceite de girasol / oliva** sunflower / olive oil; **aceite lubricante** lubricating oil

aceitera *f* TÉC oilcan; GASTR cruet

aceitoso *adj* oily

aceituna *f* olive

aceleración *f* acceleration

acelerador *m* accelerator

acelerar ⟨1a⟩ **1** *v/t motor* rev up; *fig* speed up; **aceleró el coche** she accelerated **2** *v/i* accelerate **3** *v/r* **acelerarse** *L.Am.* F (*enojarse*) lose one's cool

acelgas *fpl* BOT Swiss chard *sg*

acento *m* en ortografía, pronunciación accent; (*énfasis*) stress, emphasis; **poner el acento en** *fig* stress, emphasize

acentuar ⟨1e⟩ **1** *v/t* stress; *fig* accentuate, emphasize **2** *v/r* **acentuarse** become more pronounced

acepción *f* sense, meaning

aceptable *adj* acceptable

aceptación *f* acceptance; (*éxito*) success

aceptar ⟨1a⟩ *v/t* accept

acequia *f* irrigation ditch

acera *f* sidewalk, *Br* pavement; **ser de la otra acera, ser de la acera de enfrente** F be gay

acerca *adv*: **acerca de** about

acercar ⟨1g⟩ **1** *v/t* bring closer; **acercar a alguien a un lugar** give s.o. a ride (*Br* lift) somewhere **2** *v/r* **acercarse** approach; (*ir*) go; *de grupos, países* come closer together; *de fecha* draw near; **se acercó a mí** she came up to me *o* approached me; **acércate** come closer; **no te acerques a la pared** don't get close to the wall

acero *m* steel; **acero inoxidable** stainless steel

acertado *adj comentario* apt; *elección* good, wise; **estar muy acertado** be dead right

acertar ⟨1k⟩ **1** *v/t respuesta* get right; *al hacer una conjetura* guess **2** *v/i* be right; **acertar con algo** get sth right

acertijo *m* riddle, puzzle

achacar ⟨1g⟩ *v/t* attribute (**a** to)

achantarse ⟨1a⟩ *v/r* F keep quiet, keep one's mouth shut F

achaque *m* ailment

achatado *adj* flattened

achatarse ⟨1a⟩ *v/r* be flattened

achicharrar ⟨1a⟩ *v/t* **1** burn **2** *v/r* **achicharrarse** *fig* F roast F

achinado *adj L.Am.* oriental-looking

achinero *m C.Am.* vendedor peddler

achiquitarse ⟨1a⟩ *v/r L.Am.* become frightened *o* scared

achisparse ⟨1a⟩ *v/r* F get tipsy F

acholar ⟨1a⟩ *v/t S. Am.* embarrass

achuchar ⟨1a⟩ *v/t fig* F pester, nag

achuchón *m* F squeeze, hug; (*empujón*) push; **le dio un achuchón** *desmayo* she felt faint

achuras *fpl S. Am.* variety meat *sg*, *Br* offal *sg*

aciago *adj* fateful

acicalarse ⟨1a⟩ *v/r* get dressed up

acidez *f* acidity; **acidez de estómago** heartburn

ácido 1 *adj tb fig* sour, acid **2** *m* acid

acierto *m* idea good idea; *respuesta* correct answer; *habilidad* skill

aclamación *f* acclaim

aclamar ⟨1a⟩ *v/t* acclaim

aclaración *f* clarification

aclarar ⟨1a⟩ **1** *v/t* duda, problema clarify, clear up; *ropa, vajilla* rinse **2** *v/i de día* break, dawn; *del tiempo* clear up **3** *v/r* **aclararse**: **aclararse la voz** clear one's throat; **no me aclaro** F I don't understand; **por cansancio, ruido** etc I can't think straight

aclimatarse ⟨1a⟩ *v/r* acclimatize, become acclimatized

acné *m* acne

ACNUR *abr* (= **Alto Comisionado de las Naciones Unidas para los Refugiados**) UNHCR (= United Nations High Commission for Refugees)

acobardar ⟨1a⟩ **1** *v/t* daunt **2** *v/r* **acobardarse** get frightened, lose one's nerve

acodarse ⟨1a⟩ *v/r* lean (one's elbows) (**en** on)

acogedor *adj* welcoming; *lugar* cozy, *Br* cosy

acoger ⟨2c⟩ **1** *v/t* receive; *en casa* take in; **acoger con satisfacción** welcome, greet with satisfaction **2** *v/r* **acogerse**: **acogerse a algo** have recourse to sth

acogida *f* reception; **tener buena acogida** get a good reception, be well received

acojonar ⟨1a⟩ *v/t* V (*asustar*) scare the shit out of P; (*asombrar*) knock out F, blow away P **2** *v/r* **acojonarse** V be shit scared P

acolchado *adj Rpl* quilted

acolchonar ⟨1a⟩ v/t *Rpl* quilt

acomedido *adj L.Am.* obliging, helpful

acomedirse ⟨3l⟩ v/r *Méx* offer to help

acometer ⟨2a⟩ **1** v/t attack; *tarea, proyecto* undertake, tackle **2** v/i attack; **acometer contra algo** attack sth

acomodado *adj* well-off

acomodador *m* usher

acomodadora *f* usherette

acomodar ⟨1a⟩ v/t *(adaptar)* adapt; *a alguien* accommodate **2** v/r **acomodarse** make o.s. comfortable; *(adaptarse)* adapt **(a** to**)**

acompañamiento *m* accompaniment

acompañante *m/f* companion; MÚS accompanist

acompañar ⟨1a⟩ v/t *(ir con)* go with, accompany *fml*; *(permanecer con)* keep company; MÚS, GASTR accompany

acompaño *m C.Am. (reunión)* meeting

acomplejar ⟨1a⟩ **1** v/t: **acomplejar a alguien** give s.o. a complex **2** v/r **acomplejarse** get a complex

acondicionar ⟨1a⟩ v/t *un lugar* equip, fit out; *pelo* condition

acongojar ⟨1a⟩ v/t *lit* grieve *lit*, distress

aconsejable *adj* advisable

aconsejar ⟨1a⟩ v/t advise

acontecer ⟨2d⟩ v/i take place, occur

acontecimiento *m* event

acopio *m*: **hacer acopio de** gather, muster

acoplar ⟨1a⟩ **1** v/t *piezas* fit together **2** v/r **acoplarse** *de persona* fit in **(a** with**)**; *de nave espacial* dock **(a** with**)**; *de piezas* fit together

acorazado *adj* armo(u)red

acordar ⟨1m⟩ **1** v/t agree **2** v/r **acordarse** remember; **¿te acuerdas de él?** do you remember him?

acorde 1 *adj*: **acorde con** appropriate to, in keeping with **2** *m* MÚS chord

acordeón *m* accordion

acordeonista *m/f* accordionist

acordonar ⟨1a⟩ v/t cordon off

acorralar ⟨1a⟩ v/t *tb fig* corner

acortar ⟨1a⟩ **1** v/t shorten **2** v/i take a short cut **3** v/r **acortarse** get shorter

acosar ⟨1a⟩ v/t hound, pursue; *con preguntas* bombard **(con** with**)**

acosijar ⟨1a⟩ v/t *Méx* badger, pester

acoso *m fig* hounding, harassment; **acoso sexual** sexual harrassment

acostar ⟨1m⟩ **1** v/t put to bed **2** v/r **acostarse** go to bed; *(tumbarse)* lie down; **acostarse con alguien** go to bed with s.o., sleep with s.o.

acostumbrado *adj (habitual)* usual; **estar acostumbrado a algo** be used to sth

acostumbrar ⟨1a⟩ **1** v/t get used **(a** to**) 2** v/i: **acostumbraba a venir a este café todas las mañanas** he used to come to this café every morning **3** v/r acostumbrarse get used **(a** to**)**; **se acostumbró a levantarse temprano** he got used to getting up early

ácrata *m/f* & *adj* anarchist

acre *adj olor* acrid; *crítica* biting

acrecentar ⟨1k⟩ v/t increase **2** v/r **acrecentarse** increase, grow

acreditar ⟨1a⟩ **1** v/t *diplomático etc* accredit **(como** as**)**; *(avalar)* prove; *un documento que lo acredita como el propietario* a document that is proof of his ownership **2** v/r **acreditarse** acquire a good reputation

acreedor *m*, **acreedora** *f* creditor

acreencia *f L.Am.* credit

acribillar ⟨1a⟩ v/t: **acribillar a alguien a balazos** riddle s.o. with bullets; **acribillar a alguien a preguntas** bombard s.o. with questions

acrílico *m/adj* acrylic

acristalar ⟨1a⟩ v/t glaze

acróbata *m/f* acrobat

acrobático *adj* acrobatic; **vuelo acrobático** stunt flight

acta(s) *f (pl)* minutes *pl*

actitud *f (disposición)* attitude; *(posición)* position

activar ⟨1a⟩ v/t activate; *(estimular)* stimulate

actividad *f* activity

activista *m/f* POL activist

activo 1 *adj* active; **en activo** on active service; **población -a** labo(u)r force **2** *m* COM assets *pl*

acto *m (acción)*, TEA act; *ceremonia* ceremony; **acto sexual** sexual intercourse; **acto seguido** immediately afterward(s); **en el acto** instantly, there and then

actor *m* actor

actriz *f* actress

actuación *f* TEA performance; *(intervención)* intervention

actual *adj* present, current; *un tema muy actual* a very topical issue

actualidad *f* current situation; *en la actualidad* at present, presently; *(hoy en día)* nowadays; **actualidades** current affairs

actualizar ⟨1f⟩ v/t bring up to date, update

actualmente *adv* currently

actuar ⟨1e⟩ v/i *(obrar, ejercer)*, TEA act; MED work, act

acuarela *f* watercolo(u)r

acuario *m* aquarium

Acuario *m/f inv* ASTR Aquarius
acuático *adj* aquatic; *deporte acuático* water sport
acuchillar ⟨1a⟩ *v/t* stab
aciuciante *adj* pressing, urgent
acudir ⟨3a⟩ *v/i* come; *acudir a alguien* turn to s.o.; *acudir a las urnas* go to the polls
acueducto *m* aqueduct
acuerdo *m* agreement; *estar de acuerdo con* agree with; *llegar a un acuerdo, ponerse de acuerdo* come to *o* reach an agreement (*con* with); *de acuerdo con algo* in accordance with sth; *¡de acuerdo!* all right!, OK!
acumulación *f* accumulation
acumular ⟨1a⟩ **1** *v/t* accumulate **2** *v/r* acumularse accumulate
acunar ⟨1a⟩ *v/t* rock
acuñar ⟨1a⟩ *v/t monedas* mint; *término, expresión* coin
acuoso *adj* watery
acupuntura *f* acupuncture
acurrucarse ⟨1g⟩ *v/r* curl up
acusación *f* accusation
acusado *m*, **-a** *f* defendant
acusar ⟨1a⟩ *v/t* accuse (*de* of); JUR charge (*de* with); (*manifestar*) show; *acusar recibo de* acknowledge receipt of
acuse *m*: *acuse de recibo* acknowledg(e)ment
acusetas *m/f inv* S. Am. F tattletale F, Br tell-tale F
acusica *m/f* F tattletale F, Br tell-tale F
acústica *f* acoustics
adaptable *adj* adaptable
adaptación *f* adaptation; *adaptación cinematográfica* screen *o* movie version
adaptador *m* adaptor
adaptar ⟨1a⟩ **1** *v/t* adapt **2** adaptarse *v/r* adapt (*a* to)
A. de C. *abr* (= *año de Cristo*) AD (= Anno Domini)
adecentar ⟨1a⟩ *v/t* straighten up, tidy up
adecuadamente *adv* properly
adecuado *adj* suitable, appropriate
adecuar ⟨1d⟩ **1** *v/t* adapt (*a* to) **2** *v/r* adecuarse fit in (*a* with)
adefesio *m fig* F monstrosity F; *persona* freak F; *estar hecho un adefesio* look a sight
a. de J.C. *abr* (= *antes de Jesucristo*) BC (= before Christ)
adelantado *adj* advanced; *por adelantado* in advance; *ir adelantado de un reloj* be fast
adelantamiento *m* AUTO passing maneuver, Br overtaking manoeuvre
adelantar ⟨1a⟩ **1** *v/t mover* move forward;

reloj put forward; AUTO pass, Br overtake; *dinero* advance; (*conseguir*) achieve, gain **2** *v/i de un reloj* be fast; (*avanzar*) make progress; AUTO pass, Br overtake **3** *v/r* adelantarse *mover* move forward; (*ir delante*) go on ahead; *de estación, cosecha* be early; *de un reloj* gain; *se me adelantó* she beat me to it, she got there first
adelante *adv en espacio* forward; *seguir adelante* carry on, keep going; *¡adelante!* come in; *más adelante en tiempo* later on; *de ahora o de aquí en adelante* from now on; *salir adelante fig: de persona* succeed; *de proyecto* go ahead
adelanto *m tb* COM advance
adelfa *f* BOT oleander
adelgazante *adj* weight-reducing, slimming *atr*
adelgazar ⟨1f⟩ **1** *v/t* lose **2** *v/i* lose weight
ademán *m* gesture; *hacer ademán de* make as if to
además **1** *adv* as well, besides **2** *prp*: *además de* as well as
adentrarse ⟨1a⟩ *v/r*: *adentrarse en territorio* penetrate; *tema* go into
adentro **1** *adv* inside; *¡adentro!* get inside!; *mar adentro* out to sea; *adentro de L.Am.* inside **2** *mpl*: *para sus adentros* to oneself
adepto *m* follower; *fig* supporter
aderezar ⟨1f⟩ *v/t con especias* season; *ensalada* dress; *fig* liven up
adeudar ⟨1a⟩ *v/t* owe
adherente *adj* adhesive
adherir ⟨3i⟩ **1** *v/i* stick, adhere *fml* **2** *v/t* stick **3** *v/r* adherirse *a superficie* stick (*a* to), adhere (*a* to) *fml*; *adherirse a una organización* become a member of *o* join an organization; *adherirse a una idea* support an idea
adhesivo *m/adj* adhesive
adicción *f* addiction; *adicción a las drogas* drug addiction
adicional *adj* additional
adictivo *adj* addictive
adicto **1** *adj* addicted (*a* to); *ser adicto al régimen* be a supporter of the regime **2** *m*, **-a** *f* addict
adiestrar ⟨1a⟩ *v/t* train
adinerado *adj* wealthy
adiós **1** *int* goodbye, bye; *al cruzarse* hello **2** *m* goodbye; *decir adiós* say goodbye (*a* to)
aditivo *m* additive
adivinanza *f* riddle
adivinar ⟨1a⟩ *v/t* guess; *de adivino* foretell
adjetivo *m* adjective
adjudicar ⟨1g⟩ **1** *v/t* award **2** *v/r* adjudi-

carse win
adjuntar ⟨1a⟩ v/t enclose
adm. abr (= **administración**) admin (= administration)
administración f administration; de empresa etc management; (gobierno) administration, government; **administración pública** civil service
administrador m, **administradora** f administrator; de empresa etc manager
administrar ⟨1a⟩ v/t medicamento, sacramentos administer, give; empresa run, manage; bienes manage
administrativo 1 adj administrative **2** m, -a f administrative assistant
admirable adj admirable
admiración f admiration; **signo de admiración** exclamation mark
admirador m, **admiradora** f admirer
admirar ⟨1a⟩ **1** v/t admire; (asombrar) amaze **2** v/r **admirarse** be amazed (de at o by)
admisible adj admissible
admisión f admission; **derecho de admisión** right of admission
admitir ⟨3a⟩ v/t (aceptar) accept; (reconocer) admit
admón. abr (= **administración**) admin (= administration)
ADN m abr (= **ácido desoxirribonucleico**) DNA (= deoxyribonucleic acid)
adobar ⟨1a⟩ v/t GASTR marinate
adobera f Méx type of mature cheese
adobo m GASTR marinade
adoctrinar ⟨1a⟩ v/t indoctrinate
adolecer ⟨2d⟩ v/t suffer (**de** from)
adolescencia f adolescence
adolescente m/f adolescent
adonde adv where
adónde interr where
adopción f adoption
adoptar ⟨1a⟩ v/t adopt
adoptivo adj padres adoptive; hijo adopted
adoquín m paving stone
adorable adj lovable, adorable
adoración f adoration
adorar ⟨1a⟩ v/t love, adore; REL worship
adormecer ⟨2d⟩ **1** v/t make sleepy **2** v/r **adormecerse** doze off
adormidera f BOT poppy
adormilado adj sleepy
adormilarse ⟨1a⟩ v/r doze off
adornar ⟨1a⟩ v/t decorate
adorno m ornament; de Navidad decoration
adosar ⟨1a⟩ v/t: **adosar algo a algo** put sth (up) against sth
adquirir ⟨3i⟩ v/t acquire; (comprar) buy

adquisición f acquisition; **hacer una buena adquisición** make a good purchase
adquisitivo adj: **poder adquisitivo** purchasing power
adrede adv on purpose, deliberately
adrenalina f adrenaline
aduana f customs
aduanero 1 adj customs atr **2** m, -a f customs officer
aducir ⟨3o⟩ v/t razones, argumentos give, put forward; (alegar) claim
adueñarse ⟨1a⟩ v/r: **adueñarse de** take possession of
adulación f flattery
adular ⟨1a⟩ v/t flatter
adulón 1 adj S. Am. fawning **2** m, -ona f flatterer
adúltera f adulteress
adulterar ⟨1a⟩ v/t adulterate
adulterio m adultery; **cometer adulterio** commit adultery
adúltero 1 adj adulterous **2** m adulterer
adultez f adulthood
adulto 1 adj adult; **edad -a** adulthood **2** m, -a f adult
adusto adj paisaje harsh; persona stern, severe; L.Am. (inflexible) stubborn
adverbio m adverb
adversario m, -a f adversary, opponent
adverso adj adverse
advertencia f warning
advertir ⟨3i⟩ v/t warn (**de** about, of); (notar) notice
adyacente adj adjacent
aéreo adj air atr; vista, fotografía aerial; **compañía -a** airline
aerobic, aeróbic m aerobics
aerodinámico adj aerodynamic
aeroespacial adj aerospace atr
aerolínea f airline
aeromozo m, -a f L.Am. flight attendant
aeronáutico adj aeronautical
aeropuerto m airport
aerosol m aerosol
afable adj pleasant, affable
afamado adj famous
afán m (esfuerzo) effort; (deseo) eagerness; **sin afán de lucro** organización not-for-profit, non-profit (making)
afanar ⟨1a⟩ **1** v/i C.Am. (ganar dinero) make money **2** v/t C.Am. dinero make; Rpl F (robar) pinch F **3** v/r **afanarse** make an effort
afección f MED complaint, condition
afectado adj (afligido) upset (**por** by); (amanerado) affected
afectar ⟨1a⟩ v/t (producir efecto en) affect; (conmover) upset, affect; (fingir)

feign
afectivo *adj* emotional
afecto *m* affection; **tener afecto a alguien** be fond of s.o.
afectuoso *adj* affectionate
afeitada *f* shave
afeitado *m* shave
afeitadora *f* electric razor
afeitar ⟨1a⟩ **1** *v/t* shave; *barba* shave off **2** *v/r* **afeitarse** shave, have a shave
afeminado *adj* effeminate
aferrarse ⟨1k⟩ *v/r fig* cling (**a** to)
Afganistán Afghanistan
afianzar ⟨1f⟩ **1** *v/t fig* strengthen **2** *v/r* **afianzarse** become consolidated
afición *f* love (**por** of); (*pasatiempo*) pastime, hobby; **la afición** DEP the fans
aficionado 1 *adj*: **ser aficionado a** be interested in, *Br tb* be keen on **2** *m*, **-a** *f* enthusiast; **no profesional** amateur; **un partido de aficionados** an amateur game
aficionarse ⟨1a⟩ *v/r* become interested (**a** in)
afiebrarse ⟨1a⟩ *v/r L.Am.* develop a fever
afilado *adj* sharp
afilador *m* sharpener
afilalápices *m inv* pencil sharpener
afilar ⟨1a⟩ **1** *v/t* sharpen; *L.Am.* F (*halagar*) flatter, butter up F; *S. Am.* (*seducir*) seduce **2** *v/r* **afilarse** *S. Am.* F (*prepararse*) get ready
afiliarse ⟨1a⟩ *v/r*: **afiliarse a un partido** become a member of a party, join a party
afinar ⟨1a⟩ *v/t* MÚS tune; *punta* sharpen; *fig* perfect, fine-tune
afincarse ⟨1g⟩ *v/r* settle
afinidad *f* affinity
afirmación *f* statement; *declaración positiva* affirmation
afirmar ⟨1a⟩ *v/t* state, declare
afirmativo *adj* affirmative
afligido *adj* upset
afligir ⟨3c⟩ **1** *v/t* afflict; (*apenar*) upset; *L.Am.* F (*golpear*) beat up **2** *v/r* **afligirse** get upset
aflojar ⟨1a⟩ **1** *v/t nudo, tornillo* loosen; F *dinero* hand over **2** *v/i de tormenta* abate; *de viento, fiebre* drop **3** *v/r* **aflojarse** come o work loose
afluente *m* tributary
afmo. *abr* (= **afectísimo**): **su afmo** Yours truly
afónico *adj*: **está afónico** he has lost his voice
aforo *m* capacity
afortunado *adj* lucky, fortunate
afrecho *m Arg* bran
África Africa; **África del Sur** South Afri-

ca
africano 1 *adj* African **2** *m*, **-a** *f* African
afrodisíaco *m* aphrodisiac
afrontar ⟨1a⟩ *v/t* face (up to)
afuera *adv* outside
afueras *fpl* outskirts
agachar ⟨1a⟩ **1** *v/i* duck **2** *v/r* **agacharse** bend down; (*acuclillarse*) crouch down; *L.Am.* (*rendirse*) give in
agalla *f* zo gill; **tener agallas** F have guts F
agarrado *adj fig* F mean, stingy F
agarrar ⟨1a⟩ **1** *v/t* (*asir*) grab; *L.Am.* (*tomar*) take; *L.Am.* (*atrapar, pescar*), *resfriado* catch; *L.Am. velocidad* gather, pick up; **agarrar una calle** *L.Am.* go up o along a street **2** *v/i* (*asirse*) hold on; *de planta* take root; *L.Am. por un lugar* go; **agarró y se fue** he upped and went **3** *v/r* **agarrarse** (*asirse*) hold on; *L.Am. a golpes* get into a fight
agarrón *m Rpl* P (*pleito*) fight, argument; *L.Am.* (*tirón*) pull, tug
agarrotado *adj* stiff
agarrotarse ⟨1a⟩ *v/r de músculo* stiffen up; TÉC seize up
agasajar ⟨1a⟩ *v/t* fête
agazaparse ⟨1a⟩ *v/r* crouch (down); (*ocultarse*) hide
agencia *f* agency; **agencia inmobiliaria** real estate office, *Br* estate agency; **agencia de viajes** travel agency
agenciarse ⟨1b⟩ *v/r* F get hold of
agenda *f diario* diary; *programa* schedule; *de mitin* agenda
agente **1** *m* agent **2** *m/f* agent; **agente de cambio y bolsa** stockbroker; **agente de policía** police officer
ágil *adj* agile
agilidad *f* agility
agilizar ⟨1f⟩ *v/t* speed up
agitación *f* POL unrest
agitar ⟨1a⟩ **1** *v/t* shake; *brazos, pañuelo* wave; *fig* stir up **2** *v/r* **agitarse** become agitated o worked up
aglomeración *f de gente* crowd
aglomerar ⟨1a⟩ *v/t* pile up
aglutinar ⟨1a⟩ *v/t fig* bring together
agobiante *adj* oppressive
agobiar ⟨1b⟩ **1** *v/t de calor* oppress; *de problemas* get on top of, overwhelm **2** *v/r* **agobiarse** F feel overwhelmed
agobio *m*: **es un agobio** it's unbearable, it's a nightmare F
agolparse ⟨1a⟩ *v/r* crowd together
agonía *f* agony; **la espera fue una agonía** the wait was unbearable
agonizante *adj* dying
agonizar ⟨1f⟩ *v/i de persona* be dying; *de régimen* be crumbling

agujerear

agorero *adj* ominous

agosto *m* August; *hacer su agosto* F make a fortune

agotado *adj* (*cansado*) exhausted, worn out; (*terminado*) exhausted; (*vendido*) sold out

agotador *adj* exhausting

agotar ⟨1a⟩ **1** *v/t* (*cansar*) wear out, exhaust; (*terminar*) use up, exhaust **2** *v/r* **agotarse** (*cansarse*) get worn out, exhaust o.s.; (*terminarse*) run out, become exhausted; (*venderse*) sell out

agraciado *adj persona* attractive

agradable *adj* pleasant, nice

agradar ⟨1a⟩ *v/i*: *me agrada la idea* fml I like the idea; *nos agradaría mucho que ... fml* we would be delighted *o* very pleased if ...

agradecer ⟨2d⟩ *v/t*: *agradecer algo a alguien* thank s.o. for sth; *te lo agradezco* I appreciate it

agradecimiento *m* appreciation

agrado *m*: *ser del agrado de alguien* be to s.o.'s liking

agrandar ⟨1a⟩ **1** *v/t* make bigger **2** *v/r* **agrandarse** get bigger

agrario *adj* land *atr*, agrarian; *política* agricultural

agravar ⟨1a⟩ **1** *v/t* make worse, aggravate **2** *v/r* **agravarse** get worse, deteriorate

agravio *m* offense, *Br* offence

agredir ⟨3a⟩ *v/i* attack, assault

agregado *m*, **-a** *f en universidad* senior lecturer; *en colegio* senior teacher; POL attaché; *agregado cultural* cultural attaché

agregar ⟨1h⟩ *v/t* add

agresión *f* aggression

agresividad *f* aggression

agresivo *adj* aggressive

agresor *m*, **agresora** *f* aggressor

agreste *adj terreno* rough; *paisaje* wild

agriarse ⟨1b *or* 1c⟩ *v/r de vino* go sour; *de carácter* become bitter

agrícola *adj* agricultural, farming *atr*

agricultor *m*, **agricultora** *f* farmer

agricultura *f* agriculture

agridulce *adj* bittersweet

agriera *f* L.Am. heartburn

agrietarse ⟨1a⟩ *v/r* crack; *de manos, labios* chap

agringarse ⟨1h⟩ *v/r* L.Am. become Americanized

agrio *adj fruta* sour; *disputa, carácter* bitter

agrios *mpl* BOT citrus fruit *sg*

agropecuario *adj* farming *atr*, agricultural

agrupar ⟨1a⟩ **1** *v/t* group, put into groups

2 *v/r* **agruparse** gather

agua *f* water; *agua corriente* running water; *agua dulce* fresh water; *agua mineral* mineral water; *agua oxigenada* (hydrogen) peroxide; *agua potable* drinking water; *es agua pasada* it's water under the bridge; *está con el agua al cuello con problemas* he's up to his neck in problems F; *con deudas* he's up to his neck in debt F; *se me hace la boca agua* it makes my mouth water

aguas waters; *aguas pl residuales* effluent *sg*, sewage *sg*

aguacate *m* BOT avocado

aguacero *m* downpour

aguachento *adj CSur* watery

aguafiestas *m/f inv* partypooper F, killjoy

aguaitar ⟨1a⟩ *v/t S. Am.* spy on

aguamala *f S. Am.* jellyfish

aguamiel *f L.Am.* mixture of water and honey; *Méx* (*jugo de maguey*) agave sap

aguanieve *f* sleet

aguantar ⟨1a⟩ **1** *v/t un peso* bear, support; *respiración* hold; (*soportar*) put up with; *no lo puedo aguantar* I can't stand *o* bear it **2** *v/i* hang on, hold out **3** *v/r* **aguantarse** *contenerse* keep quiet; *me tuve que aguantar conformarme* I had to put up with it

aguante *m* patience; *física* stamina, endurance

aguar ⟨1a⟩ *v/t fiesta* spoil

aguardar ⟨1a⟩ **1** *v/t* wait for, await **2** *v/i* wait

aguardiente *m fruit-based alcoholic spirit*

aguarrás *m* turpentine, turps F

agualero *m*, **-a** *f S. Am.* water-seller

agudeza *f de voz, sonido* high pitch; MED intensity; (*perspicacia*) sharpness; *agudeza visual* sharp-sightedness

agudizar ⟨1f⟩ **1** *v/t un sentido* sharpen; *agudizar un problema* make a problem worse **2** *v/r* **agudizarse** MED get worse; *de un sentido* become sharper

agudo *adj* acute; (*afilado*) sharp; *sonido* high-pitched; (*perspicaz*) sharp

agüero *m* omen; *ser de mal agüero* be an ill omen

aguijón *m* zo sting; *fig* spur

águila *f* eagle; *¿águila o sol? Méx* heads or tails?; *ser un águila fig* be very sharp

aguilucho *m* eaglet

agüita *f L.Am.* F (*agua*) water; (*infusión*) infusion

aguja *f* needle; *de reloj* hand; *buscar una aguja en un pajar fig* look for a needle in a haystack

agujerear ⟨1a⟩ **1** *v/t* make holes in **2** *v/r* **agujerearse** develop holes

agujero *m* hole

agujetas *fpl* stiffness *sg*; **tener agujetas** be stiff

aguzar ⟨1f⟩ *v/t* sharpen; **aguzar el ingenio** sharpen one's wits; **aguzar el oído** prick up one's ears

ah *int* ah!

ahí *adv* there; **está por ahí** it's (somewhere) over there; *dando direcciones* it's that way

ahijada *f* goddaughter

ahijado *m* godson

ahínco *m* effort; **trabajar con ahínco** work hard

ahogado *adj* drowned

ahogar ⟨1h⟩ **1** *v/t* (*asfixiar*) suffocate; *en agua* drown; AUTO flood; *protestas* stifle **2** *v/r* **ahogarse** choke; (*asfixiarse*) suffocate; *en agua* drown; AUTO flood; **ahogarse en un vaso de agua** *fig* F get in a state over nothing

ahondar ⟨1a⟩ *v/i*: **ahondar en algo** go into sth in depth

ahora *adv* (*en este momento*) now; (*pronto*) in a moment; **ahora mismo** right now; **por ahora** for the present, for the time being; **ahora bien** however; **desde ahora, de ahora en adelante** from now on; **¡hasta ahora!** see you soon

ahorcar ⟨1g⟩ **1** *v/t* hang **2** *v/r* **ahorcarse** hang o.s.

ahorita *adv* L.Am. (*en este momento*) (right) now; *Méx, C.Am.* (*pronto*) in a moment; *Méx, C.Am.* (*hace poco*) just now

ahorrar ⟨1a⟩ **1** *v/t* save; **ahorrar algo a alguien** save s.o. (from) sth **2** *v/i* save (up) **3** *v/r* **ahorrarse** *dinero* save; *fig* spare o.s., save o.s.

ahorro *m* saving; **ahorros** *pl* savings; **caja de ahorros** savings bank

ahulado *m* C.Am., Méx oilskin

ahumar ⟨1a⟩ *v/t* smoke

ahuyentar ⟨1a⟩ **1** *v/t* scare off *o* away **2** *v/r* **ahuyentarse** L.Am. run away

AI *abr* (= *Amnistía Internacional*) AI (= Amnesty International)

airado *adj* angry

airbag *m* AUTO airbag

aire *m* air; **aire acondicionado** air-conditioning; **al aire libre** in the open air; **a mi aire** in my own way; **estar en el aire** *fig* F be up in the air F; **hace mucho aire** it is very windy

airear ⟨1a⟩ *v/t tb fig* air

airoso *adj*: **salir airoso de algo** do well in sth

aislado *adj* isolated

aislante 1 *adj* insulating, insulation *atr* **2** *m* insulator

aislar ⟨1a⟩ **1** *v/t* isolate; EL insulate **2** *v/r* **aislarse** cut o.s. off

ajardinado *adj* landscaped; **zona -a** area with parks and gardens

a. J.C. *abr* (= *antes de Jesucristo*) BC (= before Christ)

ajedrez *m* chess

ajeno *adj propiedad, problemas etc* someone else's; **me era totalmente ajeno** it was completely alien to me; **estar ajeno a** be unaware of, be oblivious to; **por razones -as a nuestra voluntad** for reasons beyond our control

ajete *m* BOT young garlic

ajetreo *m* bustle

ají *m* S. Am. chili, Br chilli

ajiaco *m* Col spicy potato stew

ajillo *m*: **al ajillo** with garlic

ajo *m* BOT garlic; **estar** *or* **andar en el ajo** F be in the know F

ajuar *m de novia* trousseau

ajustar ⟨1a⟩ **1** *v/t máquina etc* adjust; *tornillo* tighten; *precio* set; **ajustar cuentas** *fig* settle a score **2** *v/i* fit **3** *v/r* **ajustarse** *el cinturón* tighten; **ajustarse a algo** *fig* keep within sth; **ajustarse a la ley** comply with the law

ajuste *m*: **ajuste de cuentas** settling of scores

ajusticiar ⟨1b⟩ *v/t* execute

al *prp* **a** *y art* **el**; **al entrar** on coming in, when we / they etc came in

ala *f* wing; MIL flank; **ala delta** hang glider; **cortar las alas a alguien** clip s.o.'s wings

alabanza *f* acclaim

alabar ⟨1a⟩ *v/t* praise; acclaim

alacena *f* larder

alacrán *m* ZO scorpion

alambrada *f* wire fence

alambrar ⟨1a⟩ *v/t* fence

alambre *m* wire; **alambre de espino** *or* **de púas** barbed wire

álamo *m* BOT poplar; **álamo temblón** aspen

alarde *m* show, display; **hacer alarde de** make a show of

alardear ⟨1a⟩ *v/i* show off (*de* about)

alargador *m* TÉC extension cord, Br extension lead

alargar ⟨1h⟩ **1** *v/t* lengthen; *prenda* let down; *en tiempo* prolong; *mano, brazo* stretch out **2** *v/r* **alargarse** *de sombra, día* get longer, lengthen

alarido *m* shriek; **dar alaridos** shriek

alarma *f* (*mecanismo, miedo*) alarm; **dar la voz de alarma** raise the alarm

alarmante *adj* alarming

alarmar ⟨1a⟩ **1** *v/t* alarm **2** *v/r* **alarmarse** become alarmed

alba *f* dawn

albahaca *f* BOT basil

Albania Albania

albañil *m* bricklayer

albaricoque *m* BOT apricot

albatros *m inv* ZO albatross

albedrío *m*: **libre albedrío** free will

alberca *f* reservoir; *Méx* (swimming) pool

albergar ⟨1h⟩ *v/t* (*hospedar*) put up; (*contener*) house; *esperanzas* hold out

albergue *m* refuge, shelter; **albergue juvenil** youth hostel

albino *m*, **-a** *f* albino

albóndiga *f* meatball

albornoz *m* bathrobe

alborotador *m*, **alborotadora** *f* rioter

alborotar ⟨1a⟩ **1** *v/t* stir up; (*desordenar*) disturb **2** *v/i* make a racket **3** *v/r* **alborotarse** get excited; (*inquietarse*) get worked up

alboroto *m* commotion

álbum *m* album

alcachofa *f* BOT artichoke; *de ducha* shower head

alcalde *m*, **-esa** *f* mayor

alcalino *adj* alkaline

alcance *m* reach; *de arma etc* range; *de medida* scope; *de tragedia* extent, scale; **al alcance de la mano** within reach; **¿está al alcance de tu bolsillo?** can you afford it?; **dar alcance a alguien** catch up with s.o.; **poner al alcance de alguien** put within s.o.'s reach

alcancía *f* L.Am. piggy bank

alcantarilla *f* sewer; (*sumidero*) drain

alcanzar ⟨1f⟩ *v/t* a alguien catch up with; *lugar* reach, get to; *en nivel* reach; *cantidad* amount to; *objetivo* achieve **2** *v/i* en altura reach; *en cantidad* be enough; **alcanzar a oír / ver** manage to hear / see

alcaparra *f* BOT caper

alcayata *f* hook

alcázar *m* fortress

alce *m* ZO elk

alcista *adj en bolsa* rising, bull *atr*; **tendencia alcista** upward trend

alcoba *f* S. Am. bedroom

alcohol *m* alcohol; MED rubbing alcohol, *Br* surgical spirit; **alcohol de quemar** denatured alcohol, *Br* methylated spirits *sg*

alcoholemia *f* blood alcohol level; **prueba de alcoholemia** drunkometer test, *Br* Breathalyzer® test

alcohólico 1 *adj* alcoholic **2** *m*, **-a** *f* alcoholic

alcoholismo *m* alcoholism

alcornoque *m* BOT cork oak; **pedazo de alcornoque** F blockhead F

alcurnia *f* ancestry

aldea *f* (small) village

aleación *f* alloy

aleatorio *adj* random

aleccionar ⟨1a⟩ *v/t* instruct; (*regañar*) lecture

aledaños *mpl* surrounding area *sg*; *de ciudad* outskirts

alegador *adj* L.Am. argumentative

alegar ⟨1h⟩ **1** *v/t motivo, razón* cite; **alegar que** claim *o* allege that **2** *v/i* L.Am. (*discutir*) argue; (*quejarse*) moan, gripe

alegrar ⟨1a⟩ **1** *v/t* make happy; (*animar*) cheer up **2** *v/r* **alegrarse** cheer up; F *bebiendo* get tipsy; **alegrarse por alguien** be pleased for s.o. (**de** about)

alegre *adj* (*contento*) happy; *por naturaleza* happy, cheerful; F *bebido* tipsy

alegría *f* happiness

alejar ⟨1a⟩ **1** *v/t* move away **2** *v/r* **alejarse** move away (**de** from); *de situación, ámbito* get away (**de** from); **¡no te alejes mucho!** don't go too far away!

alelar ⟨1a⟩ *v/t* stupefy

aleluya *m* & *int* hallelujah

alemán 1 *m/adj* German **2** *m*, **-ana** *f* persona German

Alemania Germany

alentado *adj* L.Am. encouraged

alentar ⟨1k⟩ **1** *v/t* (*animar*) encourage; *esperanzas* cherish **2** *v/r* **alentarse** L.Am. get better

alergia *f* allergy

alérgico *adj* allergic (**a** to)

alerta 1 *adv*: **estar alerta** be on the alert **2** *f* alert; **dar la alerta** raise the alarm; **poner en alerta** alert

alertar ⟨1a⟩ *v/t* alert (**de** to)

aleta *f* ZO fin; *de buzo* flipper; *de la nariz* wing

aletargarse ⟨1h⟩ *v/r* feel lethargic

aletear ⟨1a⟩ *v/i* flap one's wings

alevosía *f* treachery

alfabético *adj* alphabetical

alfabetizar ⟨1f⟩ *v/t lista etc* put into alphabetical order; **alfabetizar a alguien** teach s.o. to read and write

alfabeto *m* alphabet

alfalfa *f* BOT alfalfa

alfanumérico *adj* alphanumeric

alfarero *m*, **-a** *f* potter

alfil *m* bishop

alfiler *m* pin; **alfiler de gancho** *Arg* safety pin; **no cabe un alfiler** *fig* F there's no room for anything else

alfiletero *m* (*cojín*) pincushion; (*estuche*) needlecase

alfombra f carpet; *más pequeña* rug

alfombrado m L.Am. carpeting, carpets pl

alfombrar ⟨1a⟩ v/t carpet

alfombrilla f mouse mat

alga f BOT alga; *marina* seaweed

álgebra f algebra

álgido adj fig decisive

algo 1 pron en frases afirmativas something; *en frases interrogativas o condicionales* anything; *algo es algo* it's something, it's better than nothing **2** adv rather, somewhat

algodón m cotton; *criado entre algodones* mollycoddled, pampered

alguacil m, **alguacilesa** f bailiff

alguien pron en frases afirmativas somebody, someone; *en frases interrogativas o condicionales* anybody, anyone

algún adj en frases afirmativas some; *en frases interrogativas o condicionales* any; *algún día* some day

alguno 1 adj en frases afirmativas some; *en frases interrogativas o condicionales* any; *no la influyó de modo alguno* it didn't influence her in any way; *¿has estado alguna vez en …?* have you ever been to …? **2** pron: persona someone, somebody; *algunos opinan que …* some people think that …; *alguno se podrá usar* objeto we'll be able to use some of them

alhaja f piece of jewel(le)ry; fig gem; *alhajas* jewelry sg

alhelí m BOT wallflower

aliado m, **-a** f ally

alianza f POL alliance; *(anillo)* wedding ring

aliarse ⟨1c⟩ v/r form an alliance *(con* with)

alias m inv alias

alicaído adj F down F

alicatar ⟨1a⟩ v/t tile

alicates mpl pliers

aliciente m *(estímulo)* incentive; *(atractivo)* attraction

alienar ⟨1a⟩ v/t alienate

alienígena m/f alien

aliento m breath; fig encouragement

aligerar ⟨1a⟩ v/t carga lighten; *aligerar el paso* quicken one's pace

alijo m MAR consignment

alimentación f *(dieta)* diet; *acción* feeding; EL power supply

alimentar ⟨1a⟩ **1** v/t tb TÉC, fig feed; EL power **2** v/i be nourishing **3** v/r alimentarse feed o.s.; *alimentarse de algo de* persona, *animal* live on sth; *de máquina* run on sth

alimento m *(comida)* food; *tiene poco alimento* it has little nutritional value; *alimentos dietéticos (de régimen)* slimming aids

alineación f DEP line-up

alinear ⟨1a⟩ **1** v/t align **2** v/r alinearse *(ponerse en fila)* line up; POL align o.s. *(con* with)

aliñar ⟨1a⟩ v/t dress

aliño m dressing

alioli m GASTR garlic mayonnaise

alisar ⟨1a⟩ v/t smooth

alistarse ⟨1a⟩ v/r MIL enlist

aliviar ⟨1b⟩ v/t alleviate, relieve

alivio m relief

allá adv de lugar (over) there; *allá por los años veinte* back in the twenties; *más allá* further on; *más allá de* beyond; *más allá* the hereafter; *allá él / ella* F that's up to him / her

allanamiento m: *allanamiento de morada* JUR breaking and entering

allanar ⟨1a⟩ v/t *(alisar)* smooth; *(aplanar)* level (out); *obstáculos* overcome

allegado m, **-a** f MIL relation, relative

allí adv there; *por allí* over there; *dando direcciones* that way; *¡allí está!* there it is!

alma f soul; *se me cayó el alma a los pies* F my heart sank; *llegar al alma* conmover move deeply; *herir* hurt deeply; *no se ve un alma* there isn't a soul to be seen; *lo siento en el alma* I am truly sorry

almacén m warehouse; *(tienda)* store, shop; *grandes almacenes* pl department store sg

almacenamiento m storage; *almacenamiento de datos* data storage

almacenar ⟨1a⟩ v/t tb INFOR store

almacenero m, **-a** f storekeeper, shopkeeper

almanaque m almanac

almeja f ZO clam

almenas fpl battlements

almendra f almond

almendro m almond tree

almíbar m syrup; *en almíbar* in syrup

almibarado adj fig syrupy

almidón m starch

almirante m admiral

almirez m mortar

almohada f pillow; *consultarlo con la almohada* sleep on it

almohadilla f small cushion; TÉC pad

almohadón m large cushion

almorranas fpl piles

almorzada f Méx lunch

almorzar ⟨1f & 1m⟩ v/i al mediodía have

lunch; *a media mañana* have a mid--morning snack **2** *v/t:* **almorzar algo al mediodía** have sth for lunch; *a media mañana* have sth as a mid-morning snack

almuerzo *m al mediodía* lunch; *a media mañana* mid-morning snack; **almuerzo de trabajo** working lunch

¿ **alo?** *L.Am.* hello?

alocado 1 *adj* crazy **2** *m, -a f* crazy fool

áloe *m* BOT aloe

alojamiento *m* accommodations *pl, Br* accommodation

alojar ⟨1a⟩ *v/t* accommodate **2** *v/r* **alojarse** stay (**en** in)

alojo *m L.Am.* → **alojamiento**

alondra *f* zo lark

alopecia *f* MED alopecia

alpaca *f animal, lana* alpaca

alpargata *f Esp* espadrille

alpinismo *m* mountaineering

alpinista *m/f* mountaineer, climber

alpiste *m* birdseed

alquilar ⟨1a⟩ *v/t de usuario* rent; *de dueño* rent out

alquiler *m acción: de coche etc* rental; *de casa* renting; *dinero* rental, *Br tb* rent; **alquiler de coches** car rental, *Br tb* car hire

alquitrán *m* tar

alrededor 1 *adv* around **2** *prp:* **alrededor de** around

alrededores *mpl* surrounding area *sg*

alta *f* MED discharge; **dar de alta** MED discharge; **darse de alta** *en organismo* register

altanero *adj* arrogant

altar *m* altar; **llevar al altar** marry

altavoz *m* loudspeaker

alteración *f* alteration

alterar ⟨1a⟩ **1** *v/t (cambiar)* alter; *a alguien* upset; **alterar el orden público** cause a breach of the peace **2** *v/r* **alterarse** get upset (**por** because of)

altercado *m* argument, altercation *fml*

alternar ⟨1a⟩ **1** *v/t* alternate; **alternar el trabajo con el descanso** alternate work and study **2** *v/i* mix **3** *v/r* **alternarse** alternate, take turns

alternativa *f* alternative

alternativo *adj* alternative

alterno *adj* alternate; **corriente -a** EL alternating current; **en días alternos** on alternate days

Alteza *f título* Highness

altibajos *mpl* ups and downs

altillo *m (desván)* attic; *en armario* top (part of the) closet

altiplano *m* high plateau

altisonante *adj* high-flown

altitud *f* altitude

altivo *adj* haughty

alto¹ 1 *adj persona* tall; *precio, número, montaña* high; **-as presiones** high pressure; **alto horno** blast furnace; **clase -a** high class; **en-a mar** on the high seas; **en voz -a** out loud **2** *adv volar, saltar* high; **hablar alto** speak loudly; **pasar por alto** overlook; **poner más alto** TV, RAD turn up; **por todo lo alto** ⊢ lavishly **3** *m (altura)* height; *Chi* pile

alto² *m* halt; *(pausa)* pause; **hacer un alto** stop; **alto el fuego** ceasefire, ¡alto! halt!

altoparlante *m L.Am.* loudspeaker

altozano *m* hillock

altramuz *m planta* lupin; *semilla* lupin seed

altruismo *m* altruism

altruista *adj* altruistic

altura *f* MAT height; MÚS pitch; AVIA altitude, height; GEOG latitude; **a estas alturas** by this time, by now; **estar a la altura de algo** be up to sth ⊢

alubia *f* BOT kidney bean

alucinación *f* hallucination

alucinado *adj* F gobsmacked F

alucinante *adj* F incredible

alucinar ⟨1a⟩ **1** *v/i* hallucinate **2** *v/t* F amaze

alucine *m:* **de alucine** F amazing

alucinógeno *m* hallucinogen

alud *m* avalanche

aludir ⟨3a⟩ *v/i:* **aludir a algo** allude to sth

aludido: **darse por aludido** take it personally

alumbrar ⟨1a⟩ **1** *v/t (dar luz a)* light (up) **2** *v/i* give off light

aluminio *m* aluminum, *Br* aluminium; **papel de aluminio** aluminum (*Br* aluminium) foil

alumno *m, -a f* student

alusión *f* allusion (**a** to); **hacer alusión a** refer to, allude to

aluvión *m* barrage

alza *f* rise; **en alza** en bolsa rising

alzado *m, -a f L.Am.* insurgent

alzar ⟨1f⟩ **1** *v/t barrera, brazo* lift, raise; *precios* raise **2** *v/r* **alzarse** rise; *en armas* rise up

alzo *m C.Am.* theft

a. m. *abr* (= *ante meridiem*) a. m. (= ante meridiem)

ama *f (dueña)* owner; **ama de casa** housewife, homemaker; **ama de llaves** housekeeper; **ama de leche** or **cría** *L.Am.* wetnurse

amabilidad *f* kindness

amable *adj* kind (**con** to)

amaestrar ⟨1a⟩ *v/t* train

amago *m* threat; **hizo amago de levantarse** she made as if to get up; **amago de infarto** minor heart attack

amainar ⟨1a⟩ *v/i de lluvia, viento* ease up, slacken off

amalgamar ⟨1a⟩ **1** *v/t fig* combine **2** *v/r* **amalgamarse** amalgamate

amamantar ⟨1a⟩ *v/t bebé* breastfeed; *cría* feed

amanecer ⟨2d⟩ *v/i* get light; *de persona* wake up **2** *m* dawn

amanerado *adj* affected

amante 1 *adj* loving; **es amante de la buena vida** he's fond of good living **2** *m/f en una relación* lover; **los amantes de la naturaleza** nature lovers

amañar ⟨1a⟩ *v/t* rig F; *partido* fix F

amapola *f* BOT poppy

amar ⟨1a⟩ *v/t* love

amargar ⟨1h⟩ **1** *v/t día, ocasión* spoil; **amargar a alguien** make s.o. bitter **2** *v/r* **amargarse** get bitter; **amargarse la vida** get upset

amargo *adj tb fig* bitter

amargura *f tb fig* bitterness

amarillento *adj* yellowish

amarillo *m/adj* yellow

amarrar ⟨1a⟩ *v/t L.Am. (atar)* tie

amasar ⟨1a⟩ *v/t pan* knead; *fortuna* amass

amatista *f* amethyst

amazona *f* horsewoman

amazónico *adj* GEOG Amazonian

Amazonas *el Amazonas* the Amazon

ambages *mpl:* **decirlo sin ambages** say it straight out

ámbar *m* amber; **el semáforo está en ámbar** the lights are yellow, *Br* the lights are at amber

ambición *f* ambition

ambicioso *adj* ambitious

ambidextro, ambidiestro *adj* ambidextrous

ambientador *m* air freshener

ambiental *adj* environmental

ambientar ⟨1a⟩ **1** *v/t película, novela* set **2** *v/r* **ambientarse** be set

ambiente 1 *adj:* **medio ambiente** environment; **temperatura ambiente** room temperature **2** *m (entorno)* environment; *(situación)* atmosphere

ambigüedad *f* ambiguity

ambiguo *adj* ambiguous

ámbito *m* area; *(límite)* scope

ambo *m Arg* two-piece suit

ambos, ambas 1 *adj* both **2** *pron* both (of us / you / them)

ambulancia *f* ambulance

ambulante 1 *adj* travel(l)ing; **venta ambulante** peddling, hawking **2** *m/f*

L.Am. (vendedor) street seller

ambulatorio 1 *adj* MED out-patient *atr* **2** *m* out-patient clinic

amedrentar ⟨1a⟩ *v/t* terrify

amén 1 *m* amen **2** *prp:* **amén de** as well as

amenaza *f* threat; **amenaza de bomba** bomb scare

amenazador *adj* threatening

amenazante *adj* threatening

amenazar ⟨1f⟩ **1** *v/t* threaten (**con, de** with) **2** *v/i:* **amenazar con** threaten to; **amenaza tempestad** there's a storm brewing

amenizar ⟨1f⟩ *v/t:* **amenizar algo** make sth more entertaining *o* enjoyable

ameno *adj* enjoyable

América America; **América del Norte** North America; **América del Sur** South America

americana *f* American (woman); *prenda* jacket

americano *m/adj* American

amerizar ⟨1f⟩ *v/i de nave espacial* splash down

ametralladora *f* machine gun

amianto *m* MIN asbestos

amígdala *f* ANAT tonsil

amigdalitis *f* MED tonsillitis

amigo 1 *adj* friendly; **ser amigo de algo** be fond of sth **2** *m, -a f* friend; **hacerse amigos** make friends

aminorar ⟨1a⟩ *v/t* reduce; **aminorar la marcha** slow down

amistad *f* friendship; **amistades** friends

amistosamente *adv* amicably

amistoso *adj* friendly; **partido amistoso** DEP friendly (game)

amnesia *f* amnesia

amnistía *f* amnesty

amo *m (dueño)* owner; HIST master

amoblado *S. Am.* **1** *adj* furnished **2** *m* furniture

amodorrarse ⟨1a⟩ *v/r* feel sleepy

amoldarse ⟨1a⟩ *v/r* adapt (**a** to)

amonestación *f* warning; DEP caution

amonestar ⟨1a⟩ *v/t reñir* reprimand; DEP caution

amoníaco, amoniaco *m* ammonia

amontonar ⟨1a⟩ **1** *v/t* pile up **2** *v/r* **amontonarse** *de objetos, problemas* pile up; *de gente* crowd together

amor *m* love; **amor mío** my love, darling; **amor propio** self-respect; **por amor al arte** *fig* just for the fun of it; **por amor de Dios** for God's sake; **hacer el amor** make love

amoral *adj* amoral

amoratado *adj* bruised

amordazar ⟨1f⟩ *v/t* gag; *animal, la prensa*

A

muzzle

amorfo *adj* shapeless

amoroso *adj* amorous

amortajar ⟨1a⟩ *v/t* shroud

amortiguador *m* AUTO shock absorber

amortiguar ⟨1i⟩ *v/t impacto* cushion; *sonido* muffle

amortizar ⟨1f⟩ *v/t* pay off; COM *bienes* charge off, *Br* write off

amotinarse ⟨1a⟩ *v/r* rebel

amp. *abr* (= *amperios*) amp (= amperes)

amparar ⟨1a⟩ **1** *v/t* protect; *(ayudar)* help **2** *v/r* **ampararse** seek shelter (*de* from), **ampararse en algo** seek protection in sth

amparo *m* protection; *(cobijo)* shelter; *al amparo de* under the protection of

ampliación *f de casa, carretera* extension; FOT enlargement; *ampliación de capital* COM increase in capital

ampliadora *f* FOT enlarger

ampliamente *adv* widely

ampliar ⟨1c⟩ **1** *v/t plantilla* increase; *negocio* expand; *plazo, edificio* extend; FOT enlarge **2** *v/r* **ampliarse** broaden

amplificador *m* amplifier

amplificar ⟨1g⟩ *v/t* amplify

amplio *adj casa* spacious; *gama, margen* wide; *falda* full

amplitud *f* breadth

ampolla *f* MED blister; *(botellita)* vial, *Br* phial

ampolleta *f Arg, Chi* light bulb

ampuloso *adj* pompous

amputación *f* amputation

amputar ⟨1a⟩ *v/t brazo, pierna* amputate

amueblar ⟨1a⟩ *v/t* furnish

amuermar ⟨1a⟩ *v/t* F bore

amuleto *m* charm

anabolizante *m* anabolic steroid

anacardo *m* BOT cashew

anaconda *f* ZO anaconda

anacoreta *m/f* hermit

anacrónico *adj* anachronistic

ánade *m* ZO duck

anagrama *m* anagram

anal *adj* anal

anales *mpl* annals

analfabeto 1 *adj* illiterate **2** *m*, **-a** *f* illiterate

analgésico 1 *adj* painkilling, analgesic **2** *m* painkiller, analgesic

análisis *m inv* analysis; *análisis de mercado* market research; *análisis de sangre* blood test; *análisis de sistemas* INFOR systems analysis

analista *m/f* analyst

analizar ⟨1f⟩ *v/t* analyze

analogía *f* analogy

analógico *adj* analog, *Br* analogue

análogo *adj* analogous

ananá(s) *m S. Am.* BOT pineapple

anarquía *f* anarchy

anárquico *adj* anarchic

anarquista 1 *adj* anarchist *atr* **2** *m/f* anarchist

anatema *m* anathema

anatomía *f* anatomy

anatómico *adj* anatomical; *asiento anatómico* AUTO anatomically designed seat

anca *f* haunch; *ancas pl de rana* GASTR frogs' legs

ancestral *adj* ancestral

ancho 1 *adj* wide, broad; *a sus -as* at ease, relaxed; *quedarse tan ancho* F carry on as if nothing had happened **2** *m* width; *ancho de vía* FERR gauge; *dos metros de ancho* two meters (*Br* metres) wide

anchoa *f* anchovy

anchura *f* width

anciana *f* old woman

anciano 1 *adj* old **2** *m* old man

ancla *f* MAR anchor

anclar ⟨1a⟩ *v/i* MAR anchor

andadas *fpl: volver a las andadas* F fall back into one's old ways

andador *m para bebé* baby walker; *para anciano* walker, Zimmer®

andamio *m* scaffolding

andanzas *fpl* adventures

andar ⟨1q⟩ **1** *v/i (caminar)* walk; *(funcionar)* work; *andando* on foot; *andar bien / mal* fig go well / badly; *andar con cuidado* be careful; *andar en algo (buscar)* rummage in sth; *andar tras algo* be after sth F; *andar haciendo algo* be doing sth; *¡anda!* come on! **2** *v/t* walk **3** *v/r* **andarse: andarse con bromas** kid around F

andas *fpl: llevar en andas* carry on one's shoulders

andén *m* platform; *L.Am.* sidewalk, *Br* pavement

Andes *mpl* Andes

andinismo *m L.Am.* mountaineering, climbing

andinista *m/f L.Am.* mountaineer, climber

andino *adj* Andean

Andorra Andorra

andrajoso *adj* ragged

andurriales *mpl: por estos andurriales* F around here

anécdota *f* anecdote

anegar ⟨1h⟩ **1** *v/t* flood **2** *v/r* **anegarse de** *campo, terreno* be flooded; *anegarse en llanto* dissolve into tears

anemia f MED an(a)emia
anémico adj an(a)emic
anestesia f MED an(a)esthesia
anestesiado adj an(a)esthetized, under F
anestesiar ⟨1b⟩ v/t an(a)esthetize
anexión f POL annexation
anexionar ⟨1a⟩ v/t POL annex
anexo 1 adj attached **2** m edificio annex,
Br annex(e)
anfeta F, **anfetamina** f MED amphetamine
anfibio m/adj amphibian
anfiteatro m TEA amphitheater, Br amphi-
theatre; de teatro dress circle
anfitrión m host
anfitriona f hostess
ánfora f L.Am. POL ballot box; HIST am-
phora
ángel m angel; **ángel custodio** or **de la
guarda** guardian angel
angelical adj angelic
angina f MED: **anginas** pl sore throat sg,
strep throat sg; **angina de pecho** angina
anglicano 1 adj Anglican **2** m, -a f Anglican
anglicismo m Anglicism
anglófono adj English-speaking
anglosajón 1 adj Anglo-Saxon **2** m, -ona
f Anglo-Saxon
angora f angora
angosto adj narrow
anguila f ZO eel
angula f ZO, GASTR elver
ángulo m MAT, fig angle
angustia f anguish
angustiado adj distraught
angustiante adj distressing
angustiar ⟨1b⟩ **1** v/t distress **2** v/r angustiarse (por over)
angustioso adj agonizing
anhelar ⟨1a⟩ v/t long for
anhelo m longing, desire (de for)
anhídrido m QUÍM anhydride; **anhídrido
carbónico** carbon dioxide
anidar ⟨1a⟩ v/i nest
anilla f ring; **cuaderno de anillas** ring
binder; **anillas** pl DEP rings
anillo m ring; **te viene como anillo al dedo** F it suits you perfectly
animación f liveliness; en películas animation; **hay mucha animación** it's very
lively
animado adj lively
animador m host; **animador turístico**
events organizer
animadora f hostess; DEP cheerleader
animal 1 adj animal atr; fig stupid **2** m tb
fig animal; **animal doméstico** mascota
pet; de granja domestic animal
animalada f: **decir / hacer una animala-**

da F say / do something nasty
animar ⟨1a⟩ **1** v/t cheer up; (alentar) encourage **2** v/r animarse cheer up
anímico adj mental; **estado anímico**
state of mind
ánimo m spirit; (coraje) encouragement;
estado de ánimo state of mind; **con ánimo de** with the intention of; **¡ánimo!**
cheer up!
animosidad f animosity
aniquilar ⟨1a⟩ v/t annihilate
anís m BOT aniseed; bebida anisette
aniversario m anniversary
ano m ANAT anus
anoche adv last night; **antes de anoche**
the night before last
anochecer ⟨2d⟩ **1** v/i get dark; **anocheció**
night fell, it got dark **2** m dusk
anodino adj anodyne; fig bland
anómalo adj anomalous
anonadar ⟨1a⟩ v/t: **anonadar a alguien**
take s.o. aback
anónimo 1 adj anonymous **2** m poison
pen letter
anorak m anorak
anorexia f MED anorexia
anoréxico adj anorexic
anormal adj abnormal
anotar ⟨1a⟩ v/t note down
anquilosarse ⟨1a⟩ v/r get stiff
ansia f yearning; (inquietud) anxiousness
ansiar ⟨1b⟩ v/t yearn for, long for
ansiedad f anxiety
ansioso adj anxious; **está ansioso por
verlos** he's longing to see them
anta f L.Am. zo tapir
antagonista m/f antagonist
antaño adv long ago
antártico adj Antarctic
Antártida Antarctica
ante[1] m suede; zo moose; Méx (postre)
egg and coconut dessert
ante[2] prp posición before; dificultad
faced with; **ante todo** above all
anteayer adv the day before yesterday
antebrazo m forearm
antecedente m precedent; **antecedentes
penales** previous convictions; **poner a
alguien en antecedentes** put s.o. in
the picture
antecesor m, **antecesora** f predecessor
antediluviano adj prehistoric hum
antelación f: **con antelación** in advance
antemano: **de antemano** beforehand
antena f de radio, televisión antenna, Br
aerial; zo antenna; **antena parabólica**
satellite dish
anteojos mpl binoculars
antepasado m, **-a** f ancestor

antepenúltimo *adj* third last

anteponer ⟨2r⟩ *v/t*: **anteponer algo a algo** put sth before sth

anteproyecto *m* draft

anterior *adj* previous, former

antes 1 *adv* before; **cuanto antes, lo antes posible** as soon as possible; **poco antes** shortly before; **antes que nada** first of all **2** *prp*: **antes de** before

antesala *f* lobby

antiadherente *adj* non-stick

antiaéreo *adj* anti-aircraft *atr*

antibala(s) *adj* bulletproof

antibelicista *adj* anti-war

antibiótico *m* antibiotic

anticiclón *m* anticyclone

anticipado *adj pago* advance *atr*; *elecciones* early; **por anticipado** in advance

anticipar ⟨1a⟩ **1** *v/t sueldo* advance; *fecha, viaje* move up, *Br* bring forward; *información, noticias* give a preview of **2** *v/r* **anticiparse** *de suceso* come early; **anticiparse a alguien** get there ahead of s.o.

anticonceptivo 1 *adj* contraceptive *atr* **2** *m* contraceptive

anticongelante *m* antifreeze

anticonstitucional *adj* unconstitutional

anticuado *adj* antiquated

anticuario *m* antique dealer

anticuerpo *m* BIO antibody

antideslizante *adj* non-slip

antidisturbios *adj*: **policía antidisturbios** riot police

antidoping *adj*: **control antidoping** dope test, drug test

antídoto *m* MED antidote; *fig* cure

antifaz *m* mask

antiguamente *adv* in the past

antigüedad *f* age; *en el trabajo* length of service; **antigüedades** antiques

antiguo *adj* old; *del pasado remoto* ancient; *su antiguo novio* her old *o* former boyfriend

antiinflamatorio *adj* MED anti-inflammatory

Antillas *fpl* West Indies

antílope *m* ZO antelope

antinatural *adj* unnatural

antinuclear *adj* anti-nuclear

antioxidante *m/adj* antioxidant

antipatía *f* antipathy, dislike

antipático *adj* disagreeable, unpleasant

antípodas *mpl* antipodes

antirreglamentario *adj* DEP *posición* offside; *una jugada -a* a foul

antirrobo *m* AUTO antitheft device

antisemitismo *m* anti-Semitism

antiséptico *m/adj* antiseptic

antisocial *adj* antisocial

antiterrorista *adj brigada* antiterrorist; **la lucha antiterrorista** the fight against terrorism

antítesis *f inv* antithesis

antojarse ⟨1a⟩ *v/r*: **se le antojó salir** he felt like going out; **se me antoja que ...** it seems to me that ...

antojo *m* whim; *de embarazada* craving; **a mi antojo** as I please

antología *f* anthology; **de antología** *fig* F fantastic, incredible F

antonomasia *f*: **por antonomasia** par excellence

antorcha *f* torch

antro *m* F dive F, dump F

antropófago *m*, **-a** *f* cannibal

antropología *f* anthropology

anual *adj* annual

anualidad *f* annual payment

anualmente *adv* yearly

anudar ⟨1a⟩ *v/t* knot

anular[1] ⟨1a⟩ *v/t* cancel; *matrimonio* annul; *gol* disallow

anular[2] *adj* ring-shaped; **dedo anular** ring finger

anunciante *m* COM advertiser

anunciar ⟨1b⟩ *v/t* announce; COM advertise

anuncio *m* announcement; *(presagio)* sign; COM advertisement; **anuncio luminoso** illuminated sign; **anuncios por palabras, pequeños anuncios** classified advertisements

anzuelo *m* (fish) hook; **morder** *or* **tragar el anzuelo** *fig* F take the bait

añadidura *f*: **por añadidura** in addition

añadir ⟨3a⟩ *v/t* add

añejo *adj* mature

añicos *mpl*: **hacer añicos** F smash to smithereens F

año *m* year; **año bisiesto** leap year; **año fiscal** fiscal year, *Br* financial year; **año luz** light year; **año nuevo** New Year; **¿cuándo cumples años?** when's your birthday?; **¿cuántos años tienes?** how old are you?; **a los diez años** at the age of ten; **los años veinte** the twenties

añorar ⟨1a⟩ *v/t* miss

aorta *f* ANAT aorta

apabullante *adj* overwhelming

apabullar ⟨1a⟩ *v/t* overwhelm

apacible *adj* mild-mannered

apaciguar ⟨1i⟩ **1** *v/t* pacify, calm down **2** *v/r* **apaciguarse** calm down

apadrinar ⟨1a⟩ *v/t* be godparent to; *político* support, back; *artista etc* sponsor; **apadrinar a la novia** give the bride away

apagado *adj fuego* out; *luz* off; *persona*

dull; *color* subdued

apagar ⟨1h⟩ 1 *v/t televisor, luz* turn off; *fuego* put out 2 *v/r* **apagarse** *de luz* go off; *de fuego* go out

apagón *m* blackout

apaisado *adj* landscape *atr*

apalabrar ⟨1a⟩ *v/t* agree (verbally)

apalancar ⟨1g⟩ 1 *v/t* lever 2 *v/r* **apalancarse** F settle

apalear ⟨1a⟩ *v/t* beat

apañar ⟨1a⟩ 1 *v/t* tidy up; *aparato* repair; *resultado* rig F, fix F; **estamos apañados** F we've had it F 2 *v/r* **apañárselas** manage; **apañárselas** manage, get by

apaño *m fig* F makeshift repair

aparador *m* sideboard; *Méx (escaparate)* shop window

aparato *m* piece of equipment; *doméstico* appliance; BIO, ANAT system; *de partido político* machine; **aparato respiratorio** respiratory system; **al aparato** TELEC speaking

aparatoso *adj* spectacular

aparcacoches *m inv* valet

aparcamiento *m* parking lot, *Br* car park; **aparcamiento subterráneo** underground parking garage, *Br* underground car park

aparcar ⟨1g⟩ 1 *v/t* park; *tema, proyecto* shelve 2 *v/r* park

aparearse ⟨1a⟩ *v/r* ZO mate

aparecer ⟨2d⟩ 1 *v/i* appear 2 *v/r* **aparecerse** turn up

aparejador *m*, **aparejadora** *f* architectural technician; *Br* quantity surveyor

aparejo *m*: **aparejos** *pl* **de pesca** fishing gear *sg*

aparentar ⟨1a⟩ *v/t* pretend; **no aparenta la edad que tiene** she doesn't look her age

aparente *adj (evidente)* apparent; *L.Am. (fingido)* feigned

aparentemente *adv* apparently

aparición *f* appearance; *(fantasma)* apparition; **hacer su aparición** make one's appearance

apariencia *f* appearance; **en apariencia** outwardly; **las apariencias engañan** appearances can be deceptive

apartado *m* section; **apartado de correos** PO box

apartamento *m* apartment, *Br* flat

apartamiento *m* separation; *L.Am. (apartamento)* apartment, *Br* flat

apartar ⟨1a⟩ 1 *v/t* separate; *para después* set o put aside; *de un sitio* move away (**de** from); **apartar a alguien de hacer algo** dissuade s.o. from doing sth 2 *v/r* **apartarse** move aside (**de** from); **apartarse**

del tema stray from the subject

aparte *adv* to one side; *(por separado)* separately; **aparte de** aside from, *Br* apart from; **punto y aparte** new paragraph

apasionado 1 *adj* passionate 2 *m/f* enthusiast

apasionante *adj* fascinating

apasionar ⟨1a⟩ *v/t* fascinate

apatía *f* apathy

apático *adj* apathetic

apdo. *abr (= apartado (de correos))* PO Box (= Post Office Box)

apearse ⟨1a⟩ *v/r* get off, alight *fml*; **apearse de algo** get off sth, alight from sth *fml*

apechugar ⟨1h⟩ *v/i*: **apechugar con algo** cope with sth

apego *m* attachment

apelación *f* JUR appeal

apelar ⟨1a⟩ *v/t tb* JUR appeal (**a** to)

apellidarse ⟨1a⟩ *v/r*: **¿cómo se apellida?** what's your / his / her surname?; **se apellida Ocaña** his / her surname is Ocaña

apellido *m* surname; **apellido de soltera** maiden name

apelmazarse ⟨1f⟩ *v/r de lana* get matted; *de arroz* stick together

apelotonarse ⟨1a⟩ *v/r* crowd together

apenado *adj* sad; *L.Am. (avergonzado)* ashamed; *L.Am. (incómodo)* embarrassed; *L.Am. (tímido)* shy

apenar ⟨1a⟩ 1 *v/t* sadden 2 *v/r* **apenarse** be upset *o* distressed; *L.Am. (avergonzarse)* be ashamed; *L.Am. (sentir incómodo)* be embarrassed; *L.Am. (ser tímido)* be shy

apenas 1 *adv* hardly, scarcely 2 *conj* as soon as

apéndice *m* appendix

apendicitis *f* MED appendicitis

apercibirse ⟨3a⟩ *v/r*: **apercibirse de algo** notice sth

apergaminado *adj fig* wrinkled

aperitivo *m comida* appetizer; *bebida* aperitif

apero *m utensilio* implement; *L.Am. (arneses)* harness; **aperos de labranza** farming implements

apertura *f* opening; FOT aperture; POL opening up

apesadumbrado *adj* heavy-hearted

apestar ⟨1a⟩ *v/t* stink out F 2 *v/i* reek (**a** of); **huele que apesta** it reeks

apestoso *adj* smelly

apetecer ⟨2d⟩ *v/i*: **me apetece ir a dar un paseo** I feel like going for a walk; **¿qué te apetece?** what do you feel like?

apetito *m* appetite

apetitoso *adj* appetizing

apiadarse ⟨1a⟩ *v/r* take pity (**de** on)

ápice *m*: **ni un ápice** *fig* not an ounce; **no ceder ni un ápice** *fig* not give an inch

apicultura *f* beekeeping

apilar ⟨1a⟩ *v/t* pile up

apiñarse ⟨1a⟩ *v/r* crowd together

apio *m* BOT celery

apisonadora *f* steamroller

aplacar ⟨1g⟩ *v/t hambre* satisfy; *sed* quench; *a alguien* calm down, placate *fml*

aplanar ⟨1a⟩ **1** *v/t* level, flatten; **aplanar las calles** *C.Am.*, *Pe* hang around the streets **2** *v/r* **aplanarse** *fig* (*descorazonarse*) lose heart

aplastante *adj* overwhelming; *calor* suffocating

aplastar ⟨1a⟩ *v/t th fig* crush

aplaudida *f L.Am.* applause

aplaudir ⟨3a⟩ **1** *v/i* applaud, clap **2** *v/t th fig* applaud

aplauso *m* round of applause

aplazamiento *m de visita*, *viaje* postponement

aplazar ⟨1f⟩ *v/t visita*, *viaje* put off, postpone; *Arg* fail

aplicación *f* application

aplicar ⟨1g⟩ **1** *v/t* apply; *sanciones* impose **2** *v/r* **aplicarse** apply o.s.

aplomo *m* composure, aplomb *fml*

apocalíptico *adj* apocalyptic

apócrifo *adj* apocryphal

apodar ⟨1a⟩ *v/t* nickname, call

apoderado *m* COM agent

apoderarse ⟨1a⟩ *v/r* **1** authorize **2** *v/r* **apoderarse** take possession *o* control (**de** of)

apodo *m* nickname

apogeo *m fig* height, peak; **estar en su apogeo** be at its height

apolillarse ⟨1a⟩ *v/r* get moth-eaten

apolítico *adj* apolitical

apología *f* defense, *Br* defence

apoltronarse ⟨1a⟩ *v/r* en un asiento settle down; *en trabajo*, *rutina* get into a rut

apoplejía *f* MED apoplexy; **ataque de apoplejía** MED stroke

aporrear ⟨1a⟩ *v/t* pound on

aportación *f* contribution; COM investment

aportar ⟨1a⟩ *v/t* contribute; **aportar pruebas** JUR provide evidence

apósito *m* dressing

aposta *adv* on purpose, deliberately

apostar ⟨1m⟩ **1** *v/t* bet (**por** on) **2** *v/i* bet; **apostar por algo** opt for sth **3** *v/r* **apostarse** bet; MIL position o.s.

apóstata *m/f* apostate

apóstol *m* apostle

apóstrofe, apóstrofo *m* apostrophe

apoteosis *f fig* climax

apoyar ⟨1a⟩ **1** *v/t* lean (**en** against), rest (**en** against); (*respaldar, confirmar*) support **2** *v/r* **apoyarse** lean (**en** on; **contra** against); *en persona* rely (**en** on); **¿en qué te apoyas para decir eso?** what are you basing that comment on?

apoyo *m fig* support

apreciable *adj* (*visible*) appreciable, noticeable; (*considerable*) considerable, substantial

apreciar ⟨1b⟩ *v/t* appreciate; (*sentir afecto por*) be fond of, think highly of

aprecio *m* respect

apremiar ⟨1b⟩ *v/t* press, put pressure on **2** *v/i*: **el tiempo apremia** time is pressing

aprender ⟨2a⟩ **1** *v/t* learn **2** *v/r* **aprenderse** learn; **aprenderse algo de memoria** learn sth (off) by heart

aprendiz *m*, **aprendiza** *f* apprentice, trainee

aprendizaje *m* apprenticeship

aprensión *f* (*miedo*) apprehension; (*asco*) squeamishness

apresar ⟨1a⟩ *v/t nave* seize; *ladrón, animal* catch, capture

aprestarse ⟨1a⟩ *v/r*: **aprestarse a** get ready to

apresurar ⟨1a⟩ **1** *v/t* hurry **2** *v/r* **apresurarse** hurry up; **apresurarse a hacer algo** hurry *o* rush to do sth

apretado *adj* tight; **iban muy apretados en el coche** they were very cramped *o* squashed in the car

apretar ⟨1k⟩ **1** *v/t botón* press; (*pellizcar, pinzar*) squeeze; *tuerca* tighten; **apretar el paso** quicken one's pace; **apretar los puños** clench one's fists **2** *v/i de ropa, zapato* be too tight **3** *v/r* **apretarse** squeeze *o* squash together; **apretarse el cinturón** *fig* tighten one's belt

apretón *m* squeeze; **apretón de manos** handshake

apretujar ⟨1a⟩ **1** *v/t* F squeeze, squash **2** *v/r* **apretujarse** F squash *o* squeeze together

aprieto *m* predicament

aprisa *adv* quickly

aprisionar ⟨1a⟩ *v/t fig* trap

aprobación *f* approval; *de ley* passing

aprobado *m* EDU pass

aprobar ⟨1m⟩ *v/t* approve; *comportamiento, idea* approve of; *examen* pass

apropiado *adj* appropriate, suitable

apropiarse ⟨1b⟩ *v/r*: **apropiarse de algo** take sth

aprovechado 1 *adj desp* opportunistic **2** *m*, **-a** *f desp* opportunist

aprovechar ⟨1a⟩ **1** v/t take advantage of; *tiempo, espacio* make good use of; **quiero aprovechar la ocasión para ...** I would like to take this opportunity to ... **2** v/i take the opportunity (**para** to); *¡que aproveche!* enjoy your meal! **3** v/r **aprovecharse** take advantage (**de** of)

aprovisionarse ⟨1a⟩ v/r stock up (**de** on)

aproximadamente adv approximately

aproximado adj approximate

aproximar ⟨1a⟩ **1** v/t bring closer **2** v/r **aproximarse** approach

aptitud f aptitude (**para** for), flair (**para** for)

apto adj suitable (**para** for); *para servicio militar* fit; EDU pass

apuesta f bet

apuesto adj handsome

apunado adj Pe, Bol suffering from altitude sickness

apunarse ⟨1a⟩ v/r S. Am. get altitude sickness

apuntador m, **apuntadora** f TEA prompter

apuntalar ⟨1a⟩ v/t *edificio* shore up; *fig* prop up

apuntar ⟨1a⟩ **1** v/t (*escribir*) note down, make a note of; TEA prompt; *en curso, para viaje etc* put down (**en, a** on; *para* for); *apuntar con el dedo* point at o to **2** v/i *con arma* aim **3** v/r **apuntarse** put one's name down (**para, en** o **a** for); *¡me apunto!* count me in!

apunte m note

apuñalar ⟨1a⟩ v/t stab

apurado adj L.Am. (*con prisa*) in a hurry; (*pobre*) short (of cash)

apurar ⟨1a⟩ **1** v/t *vaso* finish off; *a alguien* pressure, put pressure on **2** v/i Chi: *no me apura* I'm not in a hurry for it **3** v/r **apurarse** worry; L.Am. (*darse prisa*) hurry (up)

apuro m predicament, tight spot F; *vergüenza* embarrassment; L.Am. rush; *me da apuro* I'm embarrassed

aquejado adj: *estar aquejado de* be suffering from

aquel, aquella, aquellos, aquellas det singular that; plural those

aquél, aquélla, aquéllos, aquéllas pron singular that (one); plural those (ones)

aquello pron that

aquí adv en el espacio here; en el tiempo now; *desde aquí* from here; *por aquí* here

árabe 1 m/f & adj Arab **2** m idioma Arabic

Arabia Saudí Saudi Arabia

arado m plow, Br plough

arancel m tariff

arancelario adj tariff atr

arándano m blueberry

arandela f washer

araña f zo spider; *lámpara* chandelier

arañar ⟨1a⟩ v/t scratch

arañazo m scratch

arar ⟨1a⟩ v/t plow, Br plough

arbitraje m arbitration

arbitrar ⟨1a⟩ v/t en fútbol, boxeo referee; en tenis, béisbol umpire; en conflicto arbitrate

arbitrario adj arbitrary

árbitro m en fútbol, boxeo referee; en tenis, béisbol umpire; en conflicto arbitrator

árbol m tree; *árbol genealógico* family tree

arboleda f grove

arbusto m shrub, bush

arca f chest; *arca de Noé* Noah's Ark

arcada f MED: *me provocó arcadas* it made me retch o heave F

arcaico adj archaic

arce m BOT maple

arcén m shoulder, Br hard shoulder

archidiócesis f inv archdiocese

archipiélago m archipelago

archivador m filing cabinet

archivar ⟨1a⟩ v/t papeles, documentos file; asunto shelve

archivo m archive; INFOR file

arcilla f clay

arco m ARQUI arch; MÚS bow; L.Am. DEP goal; *arco iris* rainbow

arder ⟨2a⟩ v/i burn; estar muy caliente be exceedingly hot; *la reunión está que arde* F the meeting is about to erupt F

ardilla f zo squirrel

ardor m entusiasmo fervo(u)r; *ardor de estómago* heartburn

arduo adj arduous

área f; DEP *área de castigo* or *de penalty* penalty area; *área de descanso* pull-in (at the side of the road); *área de servicio* service area

arena f sand; *arenas pl movedizas* quicksand sg

arenga f morale-boosting speech; (*sermón*) harangue

arenque m herring

arepa f C.Am., Ven cornmeal roll

arete m L.Am. joya earring

Argelia Algeria

Argentina Argentina

argentino 1 adj Argentinian **2** m, -a f Argentinian

argolla f L.Am. ring

argot m slang

argucia f clever argument

argüir ⟨3g⟩ v/t & v/i argue

argumentar ⟨1a⟩ v/t argue

argumento m razón argument; de libro, película etc plot

árido adj arid, dry; fig dry

Aries m/f inv ASTR Aries

arisco adj unfriendly

aristocracia f aristocracy

aristócrata m/f aristocrat

aristocrático adj aristocratic

aritmética f arithmetic

arma f weapon; **arma blanca** knife; **arma de doble filo** or **de dos filos** fig two-edged sword; **arma de fuego** firearm; **alzarse en armas** rise up in arms

armada f navy

armadillo m zo armadillo

armado adj armed

armadura f armo(u)r

armamento m armaments pl

armar ⟨1a⟩ **1** v/t MIL arm; TÉC assemble, put together; **armar un escándalo** F kick up a fuss F, make a scene F **2** v/r **armarse** arm o.s.; **la que se va a armar** all hell will break loose F; **armarse de valor** pluck up courage

armario m closet; Br wardrobe; de cocina cabinet, Br cupboard

armazón f skeleton, framework

armisticio m armistice

armonía f harmony

armónica f harmonica, mouth organ

armonioso adj harmonious

armonizar ⟨1f⟩ **1** v/t harmonize; diferencias reconcile **2** v/i de color, estilo blend (con with); de persona get on (con with)

arnés m harness; para niños leading strings pl, Br leading reins pl

aro m hoop; L.Am. (pendiente) earring; **entrar** or **pasar por el aro** fig F bite the bullet, take the plunge

aroma m aroma; de flor scent

arpa f harp

arpía f harpy

arpón m harpoon

arquear ⟨1a⟩ v/t espalda arch; cejas raise

arqueología f arch(a)eology

arqueológico adj arch(a)eological

arqueólogo m, **-a** f arch(a)eologist

arquero m archer; L.Am. en fútbol goalkeeper

arquetipo m archetype

arquitectónico adj architectural

arquitecto m, **-a** f architect

arquitectura f architecture

arrabal m poor outlying area

arraigado adj entrenched

arraigar ⟨1h⟩ **1** v/i take root **2** v/r **arraigarse** de persona settle (**en** in); de costumbre, idea take root

arramblar ⟨1a⟩ v/t (destruir) destroy

arrancar ⟨1g⟩ **1** v/t planta, página pull out; vehículo start (up); (quitar) snatch **2** v/i de vehículo, máquina start (up); INFOR boot (up); Chi (huir) run away **3** v/r **arrancarse** Chi run away

arranque m AUTO starting mechanism; (energía) drive; (ataque) fit

arrasar ⟨1a⟩ **1** v/t devastate **2** v/i F be a big hit

arrastrar ⟨1a⟩ **1** v/t por el suelo, INFOR drag (**por** along); (llevarse) carry away **2** v/i por el suelo trail on the ground **3** v/r **arrastrarse** crawl; fig (humillarse) grovel (**delante de** to)

arrastre m: **estar para el arrastre** fig F be fit to drop F

arreada f Rpl round-up

arrebatar ⟨1a⟩ v/t snatch (**a** from)

arrebato m fit

arrebujarse ⟨1a⟩ v/r F wrap o.s. up; en cama snuggle up

arreciar ⟨1b⟩ v/t get worse; de viento get stronger

arrecife m reef

arredrarse ⟨1a⟩ v/r be intimidated (**ante** by)

arreglar ⟨1a⟩ **1** v/t (reparar) fix, repair; (ordenar) tidy (up); (solucionar) sort out; MÚS arrange; **arreglar cuentas** settle up; fig settle scores **2** v/r **arreglarse** get (o.s.) ready; de problema get sorted out; (apañarse) manage; **arreglárselas** manage

arreglo m (reparación) repair; (solución) solution; (acuerdo) arrangement, agreement; MÚS arrangement; **arreglo de cuentas** settling of scores; **con arreglo a** in accordance with; **esto no tiene arreglo** there's nothing to be done

arrellanarse ⟨1a⟩ v/r settle

arremangarse ⟨1h⟩ v/r roll up one's sleeves

arremeter ⟨2a⟩ v/i: **arremeter contra** charge (at); fig (criticar) attack

arremolinarse ⟨1a⟩ v/r mill around

arrendamiento m renting

arrendar ⟨1k⟩ v/t L.Am. (dar en alquiler) rent (out), let; (tomar en alquiler) rent; **se arrenda** for rent

arreo m Rpl driving, herding; (manada) herd

arrepentimiento m repentance; (cambio de opinión) change of heart

arrepentirse ⟨3i⟩ v/r be sorry; (cambiar de opinión) change one's mind; **arrepentirse de algo** regret sth

arrestar ⟨1a⟩ v/t arrest

arresto m arrest

arriba 1 *adv* ◇ *situación* up; *en edificio* upstairs; **ponlo ahí arriba** put it up there; **el cajón de arriba** *siguiente* the next drawer up, the drawer above; *último* the top drawer; **arriba del todo** right at the top
◇ *dirección* up; *en edificio* upstairs; **sigan hacia arriba** keep going up; **me miró de arriba abajo** *fig* she looked me up and down
◇ *con cantidades*: **de diez para arriba** ten or above **2** *int* long live
arribeño *m*, **-a** *f L.Am.* uplander, highlander
arribista *m/f* social climber
arriesgado *adj* adventurous
arriesgar ⟨1h⟩ **1** *v/t* risk **2** *v/r* **arriesgarse** take a risk; **arriesgarse a hacer algo** risk doing sth
arrimar ⟨1a⟩ **1** *v/t* move closer; **arrimar el hombro** F pull one's weight **2** *v/r* **arrimarse** move closer (**a** to)
arrinconar ⟨1a⟩ *v/t* (*acorralar*) corner; *libros etc* put away; *persona* cold-shoulder
arroba *f* INFOR 'at' symbol, @
arrodillarse ⟨1a⟩ *v/r* kneel (down)
arrogancia *f* arrogance
arrogante *adj* arrogant
arrojar ⟨1a⟩ **1** *v/t* (*lanzar*) throw; *resultado* produce; (*vomitar*) throw up **2** *v/r* **arrojarse** throw o.s.
arrollador *adj* overwhelming
arropar ⟨1a⟩ *v/t* wrap up; *fig* protect
arrope *m Rpl, Chi, Pe* fruit syrup
arroyo *m* stream; **sacar a alguien del arroyo** *fig* lift s.o. out of the gutter
arroz *m* rice; **arroz con leche** rice pudding
arruga *f* wrinkle
arrugar ⟨1h⟩ **1** *v/t* wrinkle; **2** *v/r* **arrugarse** *de piel, ropa* get wrinkled
arruinado *adj* ruined, broke F
arruinar ⟨1a⟩ **1** *v/t* ruin **2** *v/r* **arruinarse** be ruined
arrullo *m de paloma* cooing; *para niño* lullaby
arsenal *m* arsenal
arsénico *m* arsenic
art *abr* (= **artículo**) art. (= article)
art.° *abr* (= **artículo**) art. (= article)
arte *m* (*pl f*) art; **arte dramático** dramatic art; **bellas artes** *pl* fine arts *sg*; **malas artes** *pl* guile *sg*
artefacto *m* (*dispositivo*) device
arteria *f* artery
arterio(e)sclerosis *f* arteriosclerosis
artesana *f* craftswoman
artesanía *f* (handi)crafts *pl*
artesano *m* craftsman

Ártico *zona, océano* Arctic
articulación *f* ANAT, TÉC joint; *de sonidos* articulation
artículo *m de periódico*, GRAM, JUR article; COM product, item
artificial *adj* artificial
artillería *f* artillery; **artillería ligera / pesada** light / heavy artillery
artilugio *m aparato* gadget
artimaña *f* trick
artista *m/f* artist
artístico *adj* artistic
artritis *f* MED arthritis
arveja *f Rpl, Chi, Pe* BOT pea
arzobispo *m* archbishop
as *m tb fig* ace
asa *f* handle
asado 1 *adj* roast *atr* **2** *m* roast
asalariado *m*, **-a** *f* wage earner; *de empresa* employee
asaltante *m/f* assailant
asaltar ⟨1a⟩ *v/t persona* attack; *banco* rob
asalto *m a persona* attack (**a** on); *robo* robbery, raid; *en boxeo* round
asamblea *f reunión* meeting; *ente* assembly
asar ⟨1a⟩ **1** *v/t* roast; **asar a la parrilla** broil, *Br* grill **2** *v/r* **asarse** *fig* F be roasting F
ascender ⟨2g⟩ **1** *v/t a empleado* promote **2** *v/i de precios, temperatura etc* rise; *de montañero* climb; DEP, *en trabajo* be promoted (**a** to)
ascensión *f* ascent
ascenso *m de temperatura, precios* rise (**de** in); *de montaña* ascent; DEP, *en trabajo* promotion
ascensor *m* elevator, *Br* lift
ascético *adj* ascetic
asco *m* disgust; **me da asco** I find it disgusting; **¡qué asco!** how revolting o disgusting!
ascua *f* ember; **estar en** *or* **sobre ascuas** be on tenterhooks
asearse ⟨1a⟩ *v/r* wash up, *Br* have a wash
asediar ⟨1b⟩ *v/t tb fig* besiege
asedio *m* MIL siege, blockade; *a alguien* hounding
aseguradora *f* insurance company
asegurar ⟨1a⟩ **1** *v/t* (*afianzar*) secure; (*prometer*) assure; (*garantizar*) guarantee; COM insure **2** *v/r* **asegurarse** make sure
asentamiento *m* settlement
asentarse ⟨1k⟩ *v/r* settle
asentir ⟨3i⟩ *v/i* agree (**a** to), consent (**a** to); *con la cabeza* nod
aseo *m* cleanliness; (*baño*) restroom, toilet

aséptico *adj* aseptic

asequible *adj precio* affordable; *obra* accessible

aserrar ⟨1k⟩ *v/t* saw

aserrín *m L.Am.* sawdust

asesinar ⟨1a⟩ *v/t* murder; POL assassinate

asesinato *m* murder; POL assassination

asesino *m*, **-a** *f* murderer; POL assassin

asesor *m*, **asesora** *f* consultant, advisor, *Br* adviser; **asesor fiscal** financial advisor (*Br* adviser); **asesor de imagen** public relations consultant

asesorar ⟨1a⟩ *v/t* advise

asesoría *f* consultancy

asestar ⟨1a⟩ *v/t golpe* deal (**a** to), **me asestó una puñalada** he stabbed me

asfaltar ⟨1a⟩ *v/t* asphalt

asfalto *m* asphalt

asfixia *f* asphyxiation

asfixiante *adj* asphyxiating, suffocating

asfixiar ⟨1b⟩ **1** *v/t* asphyxiate, suffocate **2** *v/r* **asfixiarse** asphyxiate, suffocate

así 1 *adv* (*de este modo*) like this; (*de ese modo*) like that; **así no más** *S. Am.* just like that; **así pues** so; **así que** so; **así de grande** this big **2** *conj:* **así como** al igual que while, whereas

Asia Asia

asiático 1 *adj* Asian **2** *m*, **-a** *f* Asian

asiduidad *f* frequency; **con asiduidad con frecuencia** regularly

asiduo *adj* regular

asiento *m* seat; **tomar asiento** take a seat

asignación *f acción* allocation; *dinero* allowance

asignar ⟨1a⟩ *v/t* allocate; *persona, papel* assign

asignatura *f* subject

asilarse ⟨1a⟩ *v/r* take refuge, seek asylum

asilo *m* home, institution; POL asylum; **asilo de ancianos** old people's home

asimétrico *adj* asymmetrical

asimilar ⟨1a⟩ *v/t* assimilate

asimismo *adv* (*también*) also; (*igualmente*) in the same way, likewise

asistencia *f* (*ayuda*) assistance; *a lugar* tendance (**a** at); **asistencia en carretera** AUTO roadside assistance; **asistencia médica** medical care

asistenta *f* cleaner, cleaning woman

asistente *m/f* (*ayudante*) assistant; **asistente social** social worker; **los asistentes** those present

asistir ⟨3a⟩ **1** *v/t* help, assist **2** *v/i* be present; **asistir a una boda** attend a wedding

asma *f* asthma

asmático *adj* asthmatic

asno *m* ZO donkey; *persona* idiot

asociación *f* association

asociar ⟨1b⟩ **1** *v/t* associate; **asociar a alguien con algo** associate s.o. with sth **2** *v/r* **asociarse** team up (**con** with), go into partnership (**con** with); **asociarse a un grupo, club** become a member of

asolar ⟨1m⟩ *v/t* devastate

asoleada *f:* **pegarse una asoleada** *Bol, Pe* sunbathe

asomar ⟨1a⟩ **1** *v/t* put *o* stick out **2** *v/i* show **3** *v/r* **asomarse** lean out; **asomarse a** *or* **por la ventana** lean out of the window

asombrado *adj* amazed

asombrar ⟨1a⟩ *v/t* amaze, astonish **2** *v/r* **asombrarse** be amazed *o* astonished

asombro *m* amazement, astonishment

asombroso *adj* amazing

asomo *m:* **ni por asomo** no way

asorocharse ⟨1a⟩ *v/r Pe, Bol* get altitude sickness

aspecto *m de persona, cosa* look, appearance; (*faceta*) aspect; **tener buen aspecto** look good

áspero *adj superficie* rough; *sonido* harsh; *persona* abrupt

aspersor *m* sprinkler

aspiraciones *fpl* aspirations

aspirador *m*, **aspiradora** *f* vacuum cleaner

aspirante *m/f a cargo* candidate (**a** for); *a título* contender (**a** for)

aspirar ⟨1a⟩ **1** *v/t* suck up; *al respirar* inhale, breathe in **2** *v/i:* **aspirar a** aspire to

aspirina *f* aspirin

asqueado *adj* disgusted

asquear ⟨1a⟩ *v/t* disgust

asqueroso 1 *adj* (*sucio*) filthy; (*repugnante*) revolting, disgusting **2** *m*, **-a** *f* creep

asterisco *m* asterisk

astigmatismo *m* astigmatism

astilla *f* splinter; **astillas** *pl para fuego* kindling *sg;* **hacer astillas algo** *fig* smash sth to pieces

astillero *m* shipyard

astral *adj* astral

astringente *m/adj* astringent

astro *m* AST, *fig* star

astrología *f* astrology

astrólogo *m*, **-a** *f* astrologer

astronauta *m/f* astronaut

astronave *f* spaceship

astronomía *f* astronomy

astronómico *adj* astronomical

astrónomo *m*, **-a** *f* astronomer

astucia *f* shrewdness, astuteness

astuto *adj* shrewd, astute

asumir ⟨3a⟩ *v/t* assume; (*aceptar*) accept, come to terms with

asunto m matter; F (*relación*) affair; **asuntos exteriores** foreign affairs; **no es asunto tuyo** it's none of your business

asustar ⟨1a⟩ **1** v/t frighten, scare **2** v/r **asustarse** be frightened o scared

atacar ⟨1g⟩ v/t attack

atajar ⟨1a⟩ v/t check the spread of, contain; *L.Am. pelota* catch **2** v/i take a short cut

atajo m L.Am. short cut

atañer ⟨2f⟩ v/i concern

ataque m (*agresión*) attack; (*acceso*) fit; **ataque cardíaco** or **al corazón** MED heart attack; **le dio un ataque de risa** she burst out laughing

atar ⟨1a⟩ v/t tie (up); *fig* tie down

atardecer ⟨2d⟩ **1** v/i get dark **2** m dusk

atareado adj busy

atascar ⟨1g⟩ **1** v/t block **2** v/r **atascarse** de cañería get blocked; de mecanismo jam, stick; al hablar dry up

atasco m traffic jam

ataúd m coffin, casket

atemorizar ⟨1f⟩ v/t frighten

atención f attention; (*cortesía*) courtesy; **¡atención!** your attention, please!; **llamar la atención a alguien** tell s.o. off; *por ser llamativo* attract s.o.'s attention; **prestar atención** pay attention (**a** to)

atender ⟨2g⟩ **1** v/t a enfermo look after; en tienda attend to, serve **2** v/i pay attention (**a** to)

atenerse ⟨2l⟩ v/r: **atenerse a** normas abide by; consecuencias face, accept; **saber a qué atenerse** know where one stands

atentado m attack (**contra, a** on); **atentado terrorista** terrorist attack

atentamente adv attentively; en carta sincerely, Br Yours sincerely

atentar ⟨1k⟩ v/i: **atentar contra** vida make an attempt on; moral etc be contrary to

atento adj attentive; **estar atento a algo** pay attention to sth

atenuante adj JUR extenuating; **circunstancia atenuante** JUR extenuating circumstance

atenuar ⟨1e⟩ v/t lessen, reduce

ateo 1 adj atheistic **2** m, **-a** f atheist

aterciopelado adj tb fig velvety

aterido adj frozen

aterrador adj frightening

aterrar ⟨1a⟩ v/t terrify

aterrizaje m AVIA landing; **aterrizaje forzoso** or **de emergencia** emergency landing

aterrizar ⟨1f⟩ v/i land

aterrorizado adj terrified, petrified F

aterrorizar ⟨1f⟩ v/t terrify; (*amenazar*) terrorize

atestado adj overcrowded

atestiguar ⟨1i⟩ v/t JUR testify; fig bear witness to

atiborrarse ⟨1a⟩ v/r F stuff o.s. F (**de** with)

ático m piso top floor; apartamento top floor apartment (Br flat); (desván) attic

atinar ⟨1a⟩ v/i manage (**a** to); **no atinó con la respuesta correcta** she couldn't come up with the right answer

atípico adj atypical

atisbo m sign

atizar ⟨1f⟩ v/t fuego poke; pasiones stir up; **le atizó un golpe** she hit him

Atlántico m/adj: **el (océano) Atlántico** the Atlantic (Ocean)

atlas m inv atlas

atleta m/f athlete

atlético adj athletic

atletismo m athletics

atmo. abr (= atentísimo): **su atmo** Yours truly

atmósfera f atmosphere

atole m Méx flavored hot drink made with maize flour

atolladero m: **sacar a alguien del atolladero** fig F get s.o. out of a tight spot

atolondrado adj scatterbrained

atómico adj atomic

átomo m atom; **ni un átomo de** fig not an iota of

atónito adj astonished, amazed

atontar ⟨1a⟩ v/t make groggy o dopey; de golpe stun, daze; (*volver tonto*) turn into a zombie

atorar ⟨1a⟩ L.Am. **1** v/t cañería etc block (up) **2** v/r **atorarse** choke; de cañería etc get blocked (up)

atormentar ⟨1a⟩ v/t torment

atornillar ⟨1a⟩ v/t screw on

atorrante m Rpl, Chi F bum F, Br tramp; (*holgazán*) layabout

atosigar ⟨1h⟩ v/t pester

atrabancado adj Méx clumsy

atracar ⟨1g⟩ **1** v/t banco, tienda hold up; a alguien mug; Chi F make out with F, neck with Br F MAR dock

atracción f attraction

atraco m de banco, tienda robbery; de persona mugging

atracón m: **darse un atracón de** stuff o.s. with F

atractivo 1 adj attractive **2** m appeal, attraction

atraer ⟨2p⟩ v/t attract

atragantarse ⟨1a⟩ v/r choke (**con** on); **se**

le ha atragantado fig she can't stand o stomach him

atrancar ⟨1g⟩ **1** v/t *puerta* barricade **2** v/r **atrancarse** fig get stuck

atrapar ⟨1a⟩ v/t catch, trap

atrás adv *para indicar posición* at the back, behind; *para indicar movimiento* back; *años atrás* years ago o back; *hacia atrás* back, backwards; *quedarse atrás* get left behind

atrasado adj *en estudios, pago* behind (**en** in o with); *reloj* slow; *pueblo* backward; *ir atrasado de un reloj* be slow

atrasar ⟨1a⟩ **1** v/t *reloj* put back; *fecha* postpone, put back **2** v/i *de reloj* lose time

atraso m backwardness; COM **atrasos** arrears

atravesar ⟨1k⟩ v/t cross; *(perforar)* go through, pierce; *crisis* go through

atrevido adj daring

atreverse ⟨2a⟩ v/r dare

atribuir ⟨3g⟩ **1** v/t attribute (**a** to) **2** v/r **atribuirse** claim

atrincherarse ⟨1a⟩ v/r MIL dig o.s. in, entrench o.s.; *se atrincheró en su postura* fig he dug his heels in

atrocidad f atrocity

atrofiado adj atrophied

atrofiarse ⟨1b⟩ v/r atrophy

atropellar ⟨1a⟩ v/t knock down

atroz adj appalling, atrocious

ATS abr (= *ayudante técnico sanitario*) registered nurse

atte. abr (= *atentamente*) sincerely (yours)

atuendo m outfit

atufar ⟨1a⟩ v/t F stink out F

atún m tuna (fish)

aturdido adj in a daze

aturdir ⟨3a⟩ **1** v/t *de golpe, noticia* stun, daze; *(confundir)* bewilder, confuse **2** v/r **aturdirse** be stunned o dazed; *(confundirse)* be bewildered o confused

aturullar ⟨1a⟩ **1** v/t confuse **2** v/r **aturullarse** get confused

audacia f audacity

audaz adj daring, bold, audacious

audición f TEA audition; JUR hearing

audiencia f audience; JUR court; *índice de audiencia* TV ratings pl

audífono m *para sordos* hearing aid

audiovisual adj audiovisual

auditivo adj auditory; *problema* hearing atr

auditor m, **auditora** f auditor

auditoría f audit

auditorio m *(público)* audience; *sala* auditorium

auge m peak; *estar en auge* aumento be

enjoying a boom

augurar ⟨1a⟩ v/t *de persona* predict, foretell; *de indicio* augur

augurio m omen, sign; *un buen / mal augurio* a good / bad omen

aula f classroom; *en universidad* lecture hall, Br lecture theatre

aullido m howl

aumentar ⟨1a⟩ **1** v/t increase; *precio* increase, raise, put up **2** v/i *de precio, temperatura* rise, increase, go up

aumento m *de precios, temperaturas etc* rise (**de** in); increase (**de** in); *de sueldo* raise, Br rise; *ir en aumento* be increasing

aun adv even; *aun así* even so

aún adv *en oraciones no negativas* still; *en oraciones negativas* yet; *en comparaciones* even; *aún no* not yet

aunar ⟨1a⟩ v/t combine

aunque conj although, even though; + *subj* even if

auricular m *de teléfono* receiver; *auriculares* headphones, earphones

aurora f dawn; *aurora boreal* northern lights pl

auscultar ⟨1a⟩ v/t: *auscultar a alguien* listen to s.o.'s chest

ausencia f *de persona* absence; *no existencia* lack (**de** of); *brillaba por su ausencia* he was conspicuous by his absence

ausente adj absent

auspicio m sponsorship; *bajo los auspicios de* under the auspices of

austeridad f austerity

austero adj austere

austral adj southern

Australia Australia

australiano 1 adj Australian **2** m, -a f Australian

Austria Austria

austriaco 1 adj Austrian **2** m, -a f Austrian

auténtico adj authentic

autentificar ⟨1g⟩ v/t authenticate

autismo m autism

auto m JUR order; *L.Am.* AUTO car

autoadhesivo adj self-adhesive

autoayuda f self-help

autobiografía f autobiography

autobombo m F self-glorification

autobús m bus

autocaravana f camper van

autocontrol m self-control

autocrítica f self-criticism

autóctono adj indigenous, native

autodefensa f self-defense, Br self-defence

autodeterminación f self-determination

autodidacta 1 adj self-taught **2** m/f self-taught person

autoedición f desktop publishing, DTP

autoescuela f driving school

autoestima f self-esteem

autoestop m hitchhiking

autoestopista m/f hitchhiker

autógrafo m autograph

automático adj automatic

automatizar ⟨1f⟩ v/t automate

automedicación f self-medication

automóvil m car, automobile

automovilismo m driving

automovilista m/f motorist

autonomía f autonomy; **en España** autonomous region

autónomo adj autonomous

autopista f freeway, Br motorway; **autopista de la información** or **de la comunicación** INFOR information (super)highway

autopsia f post mortem, autopsy

autor m, **autora** f author; **de crimen** perpetrator

autoridad f authority

autoritario adj authoritarian

autorización f authority

autorizar ⟨1f⟩ v/t authorize

autorradio m car radio

autorretrato m self-portrait

autoservicio m supermarket; **restaurante** self-service restaurant

autostop m hitchhiking; **hacer autostop** hitch(hike)

autosuficiencia f self-sufficiency; **desp** smugness

autosuficiente adj self-sufficient; **desp** smug

autovía f divided highway, Br dual carriageway

auxiliar 1 adj auxiliary; **profesor** assistant **2** m/f assistant; **auxiliar f de vuelo** stewardess, flight attendant **3** ⟨1b⟩ v/t help

auxilio m help; **primeros auxilios** pl first aid sg

Av. abr (= **Avenida**) Ave (= Avenue)

aval m guarantee; **aval bancario** bank guarantee

avalancha f avalanche

avalar ⟨1a⟩ v/t guarantee; **fig** back

avance m advance

avanzado adj advanced

avanzar ⟨1f⟩ v/t move forward, advance **2** v/i advance, move forward; MIL advance (**hacia** on); **en trabajo** make progress

avaricia f avarice

avaro 1 adj miserly **2** m, -a f miser

avasallar ⟨1a⟩ v/t subjugate; **no dejes que te avasallen** fig don't let them push you around

Av.ᵈᵃ abr (= **Avenida**) Ave (= Avenue)

ave f bird; S. Am. (pollo) chicken; **ave de presa** or **de rapiña** bird of prey

avecinarse ⟨1a⟩ v/r approach

avejentar ⟨1a⟩ v/t age

avellana f BOT hazelnut

avellano m BOT hazel

avena f oats pl

avenida f avenue

avenirse ⟨3s⟩ v/r agree (**a** to)

aventajar ⟨1a⟩ v/t be ahead of

aventura f adventure; **riesgo** venture; **amorosa** affair

aventurar ⟨1a⟩ **1** v/t risk; **opinión** venture **2** v/r **aventurarse** venture; **aventurarse a hacer algo** venture to do sth

aventurero adj adventurous

avergonzar ⟨1n & 1f⟩ **1** v/t (aborchornar) embarrass; **le avergüenza** algo reprensible she's ashamed of it **2** v/r **avergonzarse** be ashamed (**de** of)

avería f TÉC fault; AUTO breakdown

averiarse ⟨1c⟩ v/r break down

averiguar ⟨1i⟩ v/t find out

aversión f aversion

avestruz m ZO ostrich; **del avestruz** política, táctica head-in-the-sand

aviación f aviation; MIL air force

avicultor m, **avicultora** f poultry farmer

avidez f eagerness

ávido adj eager (**de** for), avid (**de** for)

avinagrarse ⟨1a⟩ v/r de vino turn vinegary; **fig** become bitter o sour

avión m plane; **por avión** mandar una carta (by) airmail

avioneta f light aircraft

avisar ⟨1a⟩ v/t notificar let know, tell; **de peligro** warn; (llamar) call, send for

aviso m comunicación notice; (advertencia) warning; L.Am. (anuncio) advertisement; **hasta nuevo aviso** until further notice; **sin previo aviso** unexpectedly, without any warning

avispa f ZO wasp

avivar ⟨1a⟩ v/t fuego revive; **interés** arouse

avizor adj: **estar ojo avizor** be alert

axila f armpit

axioma m axiom

ay int de dolor ow!, ouch!; de susto oh!

ayer adv yesterday; **ayer por la mañana** yesterday morning

ayuda f help; **ayuda al desarrollo** development aid o assistance

ayudante m/f assistant

ayudar ⟨1a⟩ v/t help

ayunas: estoy en ayunas I haven't eaten anything
ayuno *m* fast
ayuntamiento *m* city council, town council; *edificio* city hall
azabache *m* MIN jet
azadón *m* mattock
azafata *f* flight attendant; **azafata de congresos** hostess
azafrán *m* BOT saffron
azalea *f* BOT azalea
azar *m* fate, chance; **al azar** at random
azorarse ⟨1a⟩ *v/r* be embarrassed
azotar ⟨1a⟩ *v/t con látigo* whip, flog; *con mano* smack; *de enfermedad, hambre* grip; *Méx puerta* slam
azote *m con látigo* lash; *con mano* smack;

fig scourge; **dar un azote a alguien** F smack s.o.
azotea *f* flat roof; **estar mal de la azotea** *fig* F be crazy F
azteca *m/f & adj* Aztec
azúcar *m* (*also f*) sugar; **azúcar glas** confectioner's sugar, *Br* icing sugar; **azúcar moreno** brown sugar
azucarero *m* sugar bowl
azucena *f* BOT Madonna lily
azufre *m* sulfur, *Br* sulphur
azul 1 *adj* blue; **azul celeste** sky-blue; **azul marino** navy(-blue) **2** *m* blue
azulejo *m* tile
azuzar ⟨1f⟩ *v/t.* **azuzar los perros a alguien** set the dogs on s.o.; *fig* egg s.o. on

B

B.A. *abr* (= **Buenos Aires**) Buenos Aires
baba *f* drool, dribble; **se le caía la baba** F he was drooling F (**con** over)
babear ⟨1a⟩ *v/i* dribble
babero *m* bib
Babia *f*: **estar en Babia** be miles away
babor *m* MAR port
babosa *f* zo slug
babosada *f* L.Am. F stupid thing to do / say
baboso *adj* L.Am. F stupid
baca *f* AUTO roof rack
bacalao *m* cod; **cortar el bacalao** F call the shots F
bache *m* pothole; *fig* rough patch
bachicha 1 *m/f Rpl, Chi desp* wop *desp* **2** *f Méx* cigarette stub
bachillerato *m Esp* high school leaver's certificate
bacón *m* bacon
bacteria *f* bacteria
bádminton *m* badminton
bafle *m* loudspeaker
bahía *f* bay
bailaor *m*, **bailaora** *f* flamenco dancer
bailar ⟨1a⟩ **1** *v/i* dance; *de zapato* be loose **2** *v/t* dance; **se lo bailó** *Méx* F he pinched F *o* swiped F it
bailarín *m*, **-ina** *f* dancer
baile *m* dance; *fiesta formal* ball; **baile de salón** ballroom dancing; **baile de San Vito** *fig* St. Vitus's dance

baja *f descenso* fall, drop; **estar de baja** (**por enfermedad**) be off sick; **bajas** MIL casualties
bajada *f* fall
bajar ⟨1a⟩ **1** *v/t voz, precio* lower; *escalera* go down; **bajar algo de arriba** get sth down **2** *v/i* go down; *de intereses* fall, drop **3** *v/r* **bajarse** get down; *de automóvil* get out (**de** of); *de tren, autobús* get off (**de** sth)
bajío *m* L.Am. lowland
bajo 1 *adj* low; *persona* short; **por lo bajo** at least **2** *m* MÚS bass; *piso* first floor, *Br* ground floor **3** *adv cantar, hablar* quietly, softly; *volar* low **4** *prp* under; **tres grados bajo cero** three degrees below zero
bajón *m* sharp decline; **dar un bajón** decline sharply, slump
bala *f* bullet; **como una bala** like lightning; **ni a bala** *L.Am.* F no way
balaceo *m L.Am.*, **balacera** *f L.Am.* shooting
balada *f* ballad
balance *m* COM balance
balancearse ⟨1a⟩ *v/r* swing, sway
balanza *f* scales *pl*; **balanza comercial** balance of trade; **balanza de pagos** balance of payments
balaustrada *f* balustrade
balazo *m* shot
balbucear ⟨1a⟩, **balbucir** ⟨3f; *defective*⟩ **1** *v/i* stammer; *de niño* babble **2** *v/t* stam-

mer

Balcanes *mpl* Balkans

balcánico *adj* Balkan

balcón *m* balcony

baldado *adj fig* F bushed F

balde *adv: de balde* for nothing; *en balde* in vain

baldosa *f* floor tile

balear ⟨1a⟩ *v/t L.Am.* shoot

baleo *m L.Am.* shooting

Baleares *fpl* Balearic Islands

baleárico *adj* Balearic

baliza *f* MAR buoy

ballena *f* ZO whale

ballet *m* ballet

balneario *m* spa

balón *m* ball

baloncesto *m* basketball

balonmano *m* handball

balonvolea *m* volleyball

balsa *f* raft; *como una balsa de aceite fig* like a mill pond

bálsamo *m* balsam

baluarte *m* stronghold; *persona* pillar, stalwart

balumba *f L.Am.* F heap, pile; F *(ruido)* noise, racket F

bambolearse ⟨1a⟩ *v/r* sway

bambolla *f L.Am.* F fuss

bambú *m* BOT bamboo

banal *adj* banal

banana *f L.Am., Rpl, Pe, Bol* banana

banca *f actividad* banking; *conjunto de bancos* banks *pl*; *en juego* bank; DEP, *Méx (asiento)* bench

bancal *m* terrace; *división de terreno* plot

bancario *adj* bank *atr*

bancarrota *f* bankruptcy; *estar en bancarrota* be bankrupt

banco *m* COM bank; *para sentarse* bench; *banco de arena* sand bank; *banco de datos* data bank

banda *f* MÚS, *(grupo)* band; *de delincuentes* gang; *(cinta)* sash; *en fútbol* touchline; *banda sonora* soundtrack

bandada *f de pájaros* flock

bandazo *m: dar bandazos de coche* swerve

bandeja *f* tray; *servir en bandeja* hand on a plate

bandera *f* flag; *(lleno) hasta la bandera* packed (out); *bajar la bandera de taxi* start the meter running

banderilla *f* TAUR banderilla *(dart stuck into bull's neck during bullfight)*

bandido *m*, -a *f* bandit

bando *m* edict; *en disputa* side

bandolero *m*, -a *f* bandit

banjo *m* MÚS banjo

banquero *m*, -a *f* banker

banqueta *f L.Am.* stool; *L.Am. (acera)* sidewalk, *Br* pavement; *banqueta trasera* AUTO back seat

banquete *m* banquet; *banquete de bodas* wedding reception

banquillo *m* JUR dock; DEP bench

bañadera *f Rpl (baño)* bath

bañador *m* swimsuit

bañar ⟨1a⟩ **1** *v/t de sol, mar* bathe; *a un niño, un enfermo* bathe, *Br* bath; GASTR coat (*con* with, *en* in) **2** *v/r* bañarse have a bath; *en el mar* go for a swim

bañera *f* (bath)tub, bath

bañista *m/f* swimmer

baño *m* bath; *en el mar* swim; *esp L.Am.* bathroom; TÉC plating; *baño de sangre* blood bath; *baño María* bain-marie

baptisterio *m* baptistry

baquiano *L.Am.* **1** *adj* expert *atr* **2** *m*, -a *f* guide

bar *m* bar

baraja *f* deck of cards

barandilla *f* handrail, banister

barata *f Méx* bargain counter; *(saldo)* sale

baratero *m*, -a *f Chi tendero* junk-shop owner

baratija *f* trinket

barato *adj* cheap

barba *f tb* BOT beard; *por barba* F a head, per person

barbacoa *f* barbecue

barbaridad *f* barbarity; *costar una barbaridad* cost a fortune; *decir barbaridades* say outrageous things; *¡qué barbaridad!* what a thing to say / do!

bárbaro **1** *adj* F tremendous, awesome F; *¡qué bárbaro!* amazing!, wicked! F **2** *m*, -a *f* F punk F

barbería *f* barber's shop

barbero *m* barber

barbilla *f* chin

barbitúrico *m* barbiturate

barbo *m pescado* barbel

barca *f* boat

barcaza *f* MAR barge

barco *m* boat; *más grande* ship; *barco de vela* sailing ship

baremo *m* scale

barniz *m para madera* varnish

barnizar ⟨1f⟩ *v/t* varnish

barómetro *m* barometer

barquero *m* boatman

barquillo *m* wafer; *Méx, C.Am.* ice-cream cone

barra *f de metal, en bar* bar; *de cortinas* rod; *barra de labios* lipstick; *barra de pan* baguette; *barra espaciadora* space-bar; *barra de herramientas* INFOR tool bar; **barra invertida** backslash

barraca f (*chabola*) shack; *de tiro* stand; *de feria* stall; *L.Am.* (*deposito*) shed; **barracas** pl *L.Am.* shanty town sg

barracón m MIL barrack room

barranco m ravine

barrena ⟨1a⟩ v/t drill

barrendero m, -a f street sweeper

barreno m drill hole

barreño m washing up bowl

barrer ⟨2a⟩ v/t sweep

barrera f barrier; **barrera del sonido** sound barrier

barriada f C.Am. (*barrio marginal*) slum, shanty town

barrial m *L.Am.* bog

barricada f barricade

barrida f *L.Am.* sweep; *L.Am.* (*redada*) police raid

barriga f belly; **rascarse la barriga** fig sit on one's butt F

barrigón adj F pudgy F

barril m barrel

barrio m neighbo(u)rhood, area; **barrio de chabolas** Esp shanty town; **irse al otro barrio** F kick the bucket P

barro m mud

barroco m/adj baroque

barrote m bar

bártulos mpl F things, gear sg F

barullo m uproar, racket

basar ⟨1a⟩ **1** v/t base (*en* on) **2** v/r **basarse** be based (*en* on)

báscula f scales

base f QUÍM, MAT, MIL base; **base de datos** INFOR database; **bases** de concurso etc conditions; **a base de** by dint of

básico adj basic

basílica f basilica

básquetbol m *L.Am.* basketball

bastante 1 adj enough; *número o cantidad considerable* plenty of; **quedan bastantes plazas** there are plenty of seats left **2** adv quite, fairly; **bebe bastante** she drinks quite a lot

bastar ⟨1a⟩ v/i be enough; **basta con uno** one is enough; **¡basta!** that's enough!

bastardo 1 adj bastard atr **2** m bastard

bastidor m: **entre bastidores** F behind the scenes

bastión m bastion

basto 1 adj rough, coarse **2** mpl: **bastos** (*en naipes*) suit in Spanish deck of cards

bastón m stick

basura f tb fig trash, Br rubbish; **cubo de la basura** trash can, Br rubbish bin

basural m *L.Am.* dump, Br tip

basurero m garbage collector, Br dustman

bata f robe, Br dressing gown; MED (white) coat; TÉC lab coat

batacazo m F bump

batalla f battle

batallón m battalion

batata f BOT sweet potato

bate m DEP bat

batería f MIL, EL, AUTO battery; MÚS drums, drum kit; **batería de cocina** set of pans; **aparcar en batería** AUTO parallel park

batido 1 adj camino well-trodden **2** m GASTR milkshake

batidora f mixer

batir ⟨3a⟩ v/t beat; *nata* whip; *récord* break

batismo m baptism, christening; **bautismo de fuego** baptism of fire

bautizar ⟨1f⟩ v/t baptize, christen; *barco* name; *vino* F water down

bautizo m baptism, christening

baya f berry

bayeta f cloth

bayoneta f bayonet

bayunco adj C.Am. P silly, stupid

baza f en naipes trick; fig trump card; **meter baza** F interfere

bazar m hardware and fancy goods store; *mercado* bazaar

bazo m ANAT spleen

bazofia f fig F load of trash F

beatífico adj beatific

beatitud f beatitude

beato 1 adj desp overpious **2** m, -a f desp over-pious person

bebé m baby

bebedor m, **bebedora** f drinker

beber ⟨2a⟩ **1** v/i & v/t drink **2** v/r **beberse** drink up

bebida f drink

beca f scholarship; (*del estado*) grant

becerro m calf

béchamel f GASTR béchamel (sauce)

bedel m porter

beige adj beige

béisbol m baseball

belén m nativity scene

belga m/f & adj Belgian

Bélgica Belgium

Belice Belize

belicista m/f warmonger

bélico adj war atr

beligerante adj belligerent

bellaco m, -a f rascal

belleza f beauty

bello adj beautiful

bellota f BOT acorn

bemol m MÚS flat; **mi bemol** E flat; **tener**

bemoles *fig* F be tricky F

bencina *f* benzine; *Pe*, *Bol* (*gasolina*) gas, *Br* petrol

bendecir ⟨3p⟩ *v/t* bless

bendición *f* blessing

bendito *adj* blessed

benefactor *adj* charitable

beneficencia *f* charity

beneficiar ⟨1b⟩ **1** *v/t* benefit; *Rpl* ganado slaughter **2** *v/r* **beneficiarse** benefit (*de*, *con* from)

beneficio *m* benefit; COM profit; *Rpl* slaughterhouse; *C.Am.* coffee-processing plant; *en beneficio de* in aid of

beneficioso *adj* beneficial

benéfico *adj* charity *atr*; *función -a* charity function *o* event

beneplácito *m* approval

benévolo *adj* benevolent, kind; (*indulgente*) lenient

bengala *f* flare

benigno *adj* MED benign

benjamín *m* youngest son

benjamina *f* youngest daughter

beodo *adj* drunk

berberecho *m* ZO cockle

berenjena *f* BOT egg plant, *Br* aubergine

berenjenal *m*: *meterse en un berenjenal* *fig* F get o.s. into a jam F

bermudas *mpl*, *fpl* Bermuda shorts

berrear ⟨1a⟩ *v/i* bellow; *de niño* bawl, yell

berrido *m* bellow; *de niño* yell

berrinche *m* F tantrum; *coger un berrinche* F throw a tantrum

berro *m* BOT watercress

berza *f* BOT cabbage

besamel *f* GASTR béchamel (sauce)

besar ⟨1a⟩ **1** *v/t* kiss **2** *v/r* **besarse** kiss

beso *m* kiss

bestia 1 *f* beast **2** *m/f fig* F brute F, swine F; *mujer* bitch F; *conducir a lo bestia* F drive like a madman

besugo *m* ZO bream; *fig* F idiot

betún *m* shoe polish

biberón *m* baby's bottle

Biblia *f* Bible

bibliografía *f* bibliography

biblioteca *f* library; *mueble* bookcase

bibliotecario *m*, **-a** *f* librarian

bicarbonato *m*: *bicarbonato (de sodio)* bicarbonate of soda, bicarb F

bíceps *mpl* biceps

bicho *m* bug, *Br tb* creepy-crawly; (*animal*) creature; *fig* F *persona* nasty piece of work; *¿qué bicho te ha picado?* what's eating you?

bici *f* F bike

bicicleta *f* bicycle; *ir o montar en bicicleta* go cycling; *bicicleta de montaña*

mountain bike

BID *abr* (= *Banco Interamericano de Desarollo*) IADB (= Inter-American Development Bank)

bidé *m* bidet

bidón *m* drum

bien 1 *m* good; *por tu bien* for your own good; *bienes pl* goods, property *o*; *bienes de consumo* consumer goods *o* durables; *bienes inmuebles* real estate *sg* **2** *adv* well; (*muy*) very; *más bien* rather; *o bien ... o ...* either ... or ...; *¡está bien!* it's OK!, it's alright!; *estoy bien* I'm fine, I'm OK; *¿estás bien aquí?* are you comfortable here?; *¡bien hecho!* well done!

bienestar *m* well-being

bienvenida *f* welcome; *dar la bienvenida a alguien* welcome s.o.

bienvenido *adj* welcome

bife *m Rpl* steak

bifocal *adj* bifocal

bifurcación *f* fork; *de línea férrea* junction

bifurcarse ⟨1g⟩ *v/r* fork

bigamia *f* bigamy

bigote *m* m(o)ustache; *bigotes de gato etc* whiskers

bikini *m* bikini

bilateral *adj* bilateral

bilingüe *adj* bilingual

bilis *f* bile; *fig* F bad mood

billar *m* billiards; *billar americano* pool

billete *m* ticket; *billete abierto* open ticket; *billete de autobús* bus ticket; *billete de banco* bill, *Br* banknote; *billete de ida*, *billete sencillo* one-way ticket, *Br* single (ticket); *billete de ida y vuelta* round-trip ticket, *Br* return (ticket)

billetera *f L.Am.*, **billetero** *m* billfold, *Br* wallet

billón *m* trillion

binario *adj* binary

bingo *m* bingo; *lugar* bingo hall

biodegradable *adj* biodegradable

biodiversidad *f* biodiversity

biografía *f* biography

biología *f* biology

biológico *adj* biological; AGR organic

biólogo *m*, **-a** *f* biologist

biombo *m* folding screen

biopsia *f* MED biopsy

bioquímica *f* biochemistry

bipartidismo *m* POL two-party system

biquini *m* bikini

birlar ⟨1a⟩ *v/t* F lift F, swipe F

birome *m Rpl* ballpoint (pen)

birria *f* F piece of junk F; *va hecha una birria* F she looks a real mess

bis *m* encore; *9 bis* 9A

bisabuela *f* great-grandmother

bisabuelo *m* great-grandfather

bisagra *f* hinge

biscote *m* rusk

bisexual *adj* bisexual

bisiesto *adj*: **año bisiesto** leap year

bisnieta *f* great-granddaughter

bisnieto *m* great-grandson

bisonte *m* zo bison

bisoñé *m* hairpiece, toupee

bisté, bistec *m* steak

bisturí *m* MED scalpel

bisutería *f* costume jewel(le)ry

bit *m* INFOR bit

bizco *adj* cross-eyed

bizcocho *m* sponge (cake)

blanca *f persona* white; MÚS half-note, *Br* minim; **estar sin blanca** *fig* F be broke F

blanco 1 *adj* white; (*sin escrito*) blank; **arma -a** knife **2** *m persona* white; (*diana*), *fig* target; **dar en el blanco** hit the nail on the head; **ser el blanco de todas las miradas** be the center (*Br* centre) of attention

blando *adj* soft

blanquear ⟨1a⟩ *v/t* whiten; *pared* whitewash; *dinero* launder

blanqueo *m* whitewashing; **blanqueo de dinero** money laundering

blanquillo *m Méx* egg

blasfemar ⟨1a⟩ *v/i* curse, swear; REL blaspheme

blasfemia *f* REL blasphemy

blindado *adj* armo(u)red; *puerta* reinforced; EL shielded

bloc *m* pad

blof *m L.Am.* bluff

bloque *m* block; POL bloc; **bloque de apartamentos** apartment building, *Br* block of flats; **en bloque** en masse

bloquear ⟨1a⟩ *v/t* block; DEP obstruct; (*atascar*) jam; MIL blockade; COM freeze

bloqueo *m* blockade

blusa *f* blouse

boa *f* zo boa constrictor

bobada *f* piece of nonsense

bobina *f* bobbin; FOT reel, spool; EL coil

bobo 1 *adj* silly, foolish **2** *m*, **-a** *f* fool

boca *f* mouth; **boca a boca** mouth to mouth; **boca de metro** subway entrance; **boca abajo** face down; **boca arriba** face up; **dejar con la boca abierta** leave open-mouthed; **se me hace la boca agua** my mouth is watering

bocacalle *f* side street

bocadillo *m* sandwich

bocado *m* mouthful, bite

bocana *f* river mouth

bocanada *f* mouthful; *de viento* gust

bocata *m* F → **bocadillo**

bocazas *m/f inv* F loudmouth F

boceto *m* sketch

bochar ⟨1a⟩ *v/t Rpl* F *en examen* fail, flunk F; *Méx* cold-shoulder, rebuff

bochinche *m Méx* uproar

bochorno *m* sultry weather; *fig* embarrassment

bocina *f* MAR, AUTO horn

bocio *m* MED goiter, *Br* goitre

boda *f* wedding

bodega *f* wine cellar; MAR, AVIA hold; *L.Am.* bar; *C.Am.*, *Pe*, *Bol* grocery store

bodeguero *m*, **-a** *f C.Am.*, *Pe*, *Ven* storekeeper

body *m prenda* body

bofetada *f* slap

bofetear ⟨1a⟩ *v/t L.Am.* slap

bofia *f* F cops *pl* F

boga *f*: **estar en boga** *fig* be in fashion

bogavante *m* zo lobster

bohemio 1 *adj* bohemian **2** *m*, **-a** *f* bohemian

bohío *m Cuba*, *Ven* hut

boicot *m* boycott

boicotear ⟨1a⟩ *v/t* boycott

boicoteo *m* boycotting

boina *f* beret

bojote *m L.Am.* *fig* bundle

bol *m* bowl

bola *f* ball; TÉC ball bearing; *de helado* scoop; F (*mentira*) fib F; **bola de nieve** snowball; **no dar pie con bola** get everything wrong

bolada *f L.Am.* throw; (*suerte*) piece of luck

bolado *m S. Am.* deal; *L. Am.* F (*mentira*) fib F

boleada *f Arg* hunt

boleador *m*, **boleadora** *f Méx* bootblack

boleadoras *fpl L.Am.* bolas

bolear ⟨1a⟩ **1** *v/i L.Am.* DEP have a knockabout **2** *v/t L.Am.* DEP bowl; *Rpl con boleadoras* bring down; *Méx zapatos* shine **3** *v/r* **bolearse** *Rpl* fall; (*aperarse*) get embarrassed

bolera *f* bowling alley

bolero 1 *m* MÚS bolero **2** *m/f Méx* F bootblack

boleta *f L.Am.* ticket; *L.Am.* (*pase*) pass, permit; *L.Am.* (*voto*) ballot paper

boletería *f L.Am.* ticket office; *en cine, teatro* box office

boletero *m*, **-a** *f L.Am.* ticket clerk; *en cine, teatro* box office employee

boletín *m* bulletin, report; **boletín de evaluación** report card; **boletín meteorológico** weather report

boleto *m L.Am.* ticket; **boleto de autobús** *L.Am.* bus ticket; **boleto de ida y**

vuelta L.Am., **boleto redondo** Méx round-trip ticket, Br return

boliche m AUTO jack; CSur grocery store, Br grocer's

bólido m fig racing car

bolígrafo m ball-point pen

bolillo m bobbin; Méx bread roll; **encaje de bolillos** handmade lace

Bolivia Bolivia

boliviano 1 adj Bolivian **2** m, -a f Bolivian

bollo m bun; (abolladura) bump

bolo m pin; C.Am., Méx christening present

bolos mpl bowling sg

bolsa f bag; COM stock exchange; L.Am. (bolsillo) pocket; **bolsa de agua caliente** hot-water bottle

bolsero m, -a f Méx F scrounger

bolsillo m pocket; **meterse a alguien en el bolsillo** F win s.o. over

bolso m purse; Br handbag

bolsón m Arg, Pe traveling bag, Br holdall

bomba f bomb; TÉC pump; S. Am. gas station; **bomba de relojería** time bomb; **caer como una bomba** fig F come as a bombshell; **pasarlo bomba** F have a great time

bombacha f Arg panties pl, Br tb knickers pl

bombacho m: **bombachos** pl, **pantalón bombacho** baggy pants pl

bombardear ⟨1a⟩ v/t bomb

bombero m, -a f firefighter; **llamar a los bomberos** call the fire department

bombilla f light bulb; Rpl metal straw for the mate gourd

bombillo m C.Am., Pe, Bol light bulb

bombita f Arg light bulb

bombo m MÚS bass drum; TÉC drum

bombón m chocolate; fig F babe F

bombona f cylinder

bonaerense 1 adj of Buenos Aires, Buenos Aires atr **2** m/f native of Buenos Aires

bonanza f fig boom, bonanza

bondad f goodness, kindness; **tenga la bondad de** please be so kind as to

bondadoso adj caring

bongo m L.Am. bongo

boniato m BOT sweet potato

bonito 1 adj pretty **2** m ZO tuna

bono m voucher; COM bond

bonsái m bonsai

boñiga f dung

boom m boom

boquerón m ZO anchovy

boquete m hole

boquiabierto adj fig F speechless

borbotón m: **salir a borbotones** de agua gush out; **hablaba a borbotones** fig it all came out in a rush; **hablar borbotón** burble, splutter

borda f MAR gunwale; **echar** or **tirar por la borda** throw overboard

bordado 1 adj embroidered **2** m embroidery

bordar ⟨1a⟩ v/t embroider; **bordar algo** fig do sth brilliantly

borde¹ adj F rude, uncouth

borde² m edge; **al borde de** fig on the verge o brink of

bordear ⟨1a⟩ v/t border

bordillo m curb, Br kerb

bordo m: **a bordo** MAR, AVIA on board

borona f corn, Br maize

borrachera f drunkenness; **agarrar una borrachera** get drunk

borrachería f Méx, Rpl → **borrachera**

borracho 1 adj drunk **2** m, -a f drunk

borrador m eraser; de texto draft; (boceto) sketch

borrar ⟨1a⟩ v/t erase; INFOR delete; pizarra clean; recuerdo blot out

borrasca f area of low pressure

borrego m ZO lamb; fig: persona sheep

borrico m, -a f donkey; fig dummy

borrón m blot; mancha extendida smudge; **hacer borrón y cuenta nueva** fig wipe the slate clean

borroso adj blurred, fuzzy

Bosnia Bosnia

bosque m wood; grande forest

bosquejo m sketch; fig outline

bostezar ⟨1f⟩ v/i yawn

bostezo m yawn

bota f boot; **bota de montar** riding boot; **ponerse las botas** fig F coin it F, rake it in F; (comer mucho) make a pig of o.s. F

botado L.Am. **1** adj (barato) dirt cheap **2** m, -a f abandoned child

botana f Méx snack

botánica f botany

botar ⟨1a⟩ **1** v/t MAR launch; pelota bounce; L.Am. (echar) throw; L.Am. (desechar) throw out; L.Am. (despedir) fire **2** v/i de pelota bounce

bote m (barco) boat; L.Am. (lata) can, Br tb tin; (tarro) jar; **pegar un bote** jump; **bote de la basura** Méx trash can, Br rubbish bin; **bote salvavidas** lifeboat; **chupar del bote** fig F line one's pockets F; **tener a alguien en el bote** F have s.o. in one's pocket F; **de bote en bote** packed out

botella f bottle

botijo m container with a spout for drinking from

botín m loot; calzado ankle boot

botiquín *m* medicine chest; *estuche* first-aid kit

botón *m en prenda*, TÉC button; BOT bud

botones *m inv en hotel* bellhop, bellboy

boutique *f* boutique

bóveda *f* vault

bovino *adj* bovine

boxeador *m*, **boxeadora** *f* boxer

boxear ⟨1a⟩ *v/i* box

boxeo *m* boxing

boya *f* buoy; *de caña* float

boyante *adj fig* buoyant

bragas *fpl* panties, *Br tb* knickers

bragueta *f* fly

bramido *m* roar, bellow

brandy *m* brandy

branquia *f* zo gill

brasa *f* ember; **a la brasa** GASTR char-broiled, *Br* char-grilled

brasero *m* brazier; *eléctrico* electric heater

Brasil Brazil

brasileño 1 *adj* Brazilian **2** *m*, **-a** *f* Brazilian

bravata *f* boast; *(amenaza)* threat

bravo *adj animal* fierce; *mar* rough, choppy; *persona* brave; *L.Am. (furioso)* angry; **¡bravo!** well done!; *en concierto etc* bravo!

bravucón *m*, **-ona** *f* F boaster, blowhard F

braza *f* breaststroke

brazalete *m* bracelet; *(banda)* armband

brazo *m* arm; *brazo de gitano* GASTR jelly roll, *Br* Swiss roll; *con los brazos abiertos* with open arms; *dar su brazo a torcer* give in

brebaje *m desp* concoction

brecha *f* breach; *fig* F gap; MED gash; *seguir en la brecha* F hang on in there F

brécol *m* broccoli

breva *f* BOT early fig; *no caerá esa breva fig* F no such luck!

breve *adj* brief; *en breve* shortly

brevedad *f* briefness, shortness

brevemente *adv* briefly

brozo *m* BOT heather

bribón *m*, **-ona** *f* rascal

bricolaje *m* do-it-yourself, DIY

brigada *f* MIL brigade; *en policía* squad

brillante 1 *adj* bright; *fig* brilliant **2** *m* diamond

brillar ⟨1a⟩ *v/i fig* shine

brillo *m* shine; *de estrella, luz* brightness; *dar or sacar brillo a algo* polish sth

brincar ⟨1g⟩ *v/i* jump up and down

brinco *m* F leap, bound; *dar brincos* jump

brindar ⟨1a⟩ **1** *v/t* offer **2** *v/i* drink a toast *(por* to)

brindis *m inv* toast

brío *m fig* F verve, spirit

brisa *f* MAR breeze

brisera *f L.Am.* windshield, *Br* windscreen

británico 1 *adj* British **2** *m*, **-a** *f* Briton, Brit F

broca *f* TÉC drill bit

brocha *f* brush

broche *m* brooch; *(cierre)* fastener; *L.Am. (pinza)* clothes pin

brocheta *f* skewer

brócoli *m* broccoli

broma *f* joke; *en broma* as a joke; *gastar bromas* play jokes; *tomar algo a broma* take sth as a joke

bromear ⟨1a⟩ *v/i* joke

bromista *m/f* joker

bronca *f* F telling off F; *Méx* F fight; *armar una bronca Méx* get into a fight; *echar bronca a alguien* F give s.o. a telling off, tell s.o. off

bronce *m* bronze

bronceado 1 *adj* tanned **2** *m* suntan

bronceador *m* suntan lotion

broncearse ⟨1a⟩ *v/r* get a tan

bronquitis *f* MED bronchitis

brotar ⟨1a⟩ *v/i* BOT sprout, bud; *fig* appear, arise

brote *m* BOT shoot; MED *fig* outbreak; *brotes de bambú* bamboo shoots; *brotes de soja* beansprouts

bruces: caer de bruces F fall flat on one's face

bruja *f* witch

brujo *m* wizard

brújula *f* compass

bruma *f* mist

bruñir ⟨3h⟩ *v/t* burnish, polish; *C.Am.* F *(molestar)* annoy

brusco *adj* sharp, abrupt; *respuesta, tono* brusque, curt

Bruselas Brussels

brutalidad *f* brutality

bruto 1 *adj* brutish; *(inculto)* ignorant; *(torpe)* clumsy; COM gross **2** *m*, **-a** *f* brute, animal

buceador *m*, **buceadora** *f* diver

bucear ⟨1a⟩ *v/i* dive; *fig* delve *(en* into)

bucólico *adj* bucolic

budista *m/f & adj* Buddhist

buen *adj* → **bueno**

buenaventura *f* fortune

bueno *adj* good; *(bondadoso)* kind; *(sabroso)* nice; *por las -as* willingly; *de -as a primeras* without warning; *ponerse bueno* get well; *¡bueno!* well!; *¿bueno? Méx* hello; *-a voluntad* goodwill; *¡-as!* hello!; *buenos días* good morning;

-as noches good evening; **-as tardes** good evening

buey m ZO ox

búfalo m ZO buffalo

bufanda f scarf; fig F perk

bufete m lawyer's office

buffet m GASTR buffet

bufón m buffoon, fool

buganvilla f BOT bougainvillea

buhardilla f attic, loft

búho m ZO owl

buitre m ZO vulture

bulbo m BOT bulb

bulevar m boulevard

Bulgaria Bulgaria

bulimia f MED bulimia

bulla f din, racket

bullicio m hubbub, din; (actividad) bustle

bullir ⟨3h⟩ v/i fig: de sangre boil; de lugar swarm, teem (**de** with)

bulo m F rumo(u)r

bulto m package; MED lump; en superficie bulge; (silueta) vague shape; (pieza de equipaje) piece of baggage

bumerán m boomerang

buque m ship; **buque de guerra** warship

burbuja f bubble

burdel m brothel

burdo adj rough

burgués 1 adj middle-class, bourgeois **2** m, **-esa** f middle-class person, member of the bourgeoisie

burguesía f middle class, bourgeoisie

burla f joke; (engaño) trick; **hacer burla de alguien** F make fun of s.o.

burlar ⟨1a⟩ **1** v/t F get round **2** v/r **burlarse** make fun (**de** of)

burlete m L.Am. draft excluder, Br draught excluder

buró m bureau

burocracia f bureaucracy

burócrata m/f bureaucrat

burocrático adj bureaucratic

burrada f fig F piece of nonsense; **hay una burrada** there's loads F; **costar una burrada** cost a packet F

burro m ZO donkey; **no ver tres en un burro** be as blind as a bat

bursátil adj stock market atr

bus m bus

busca 1 f search; **en busca de** in search of **2** m F pager

buscador m searcher; INFOR search engine

buscapersonas m inv pager

buscapleitos m/f inv troublemaker

buscar ⟨1a⟩ v/t search for, look for

búsqueda f search

busto m bust

butaca f armchair; TEA seat

butano m butane

butifarra f type of sausage

buzo m diver

buzón m mailbox, Br postbox; **buzón de voz** TELEC voicemail

byte m INFOR byte

C

C abr (= **Centígrado**) C (= Centigrade); (= **compañía**) Co. (= Company); c (= **calle**) St. (= Street); (= **capítulo**) ch. (= chapter)

cabal adj: **no estar en sus cabales** not be in one's right mind

cabalgar ⟨1h⟩ v/i ride

cabalgata f procession

caballa f ZO mackerel

caballada f Rpl: **decir / hacer una caballada** say / do sth stupid

caballería f MIL cavalry; (caballo) horse

caballero 1 adj gentlemanly, chivalrous **2** m hombre gentleman, man; hombre educado gentleman; HIST knight; trato sir; (**servicio de**) **caballeros** pl men's room, gents; **en tienda de ropa** menswear

caballeroso adj gentlemanly, chivalrous

caballito m: **caballito del diablo** ZO dragonfly; **caballito de mar** ZO seahorse; **caballitos** pl carousel sg, merry-go-round sg

caballo m horse; en ajedrez knight; **caballo balancín** rocking horse; **a caballo entre** halfway between; **montar** or **andar** Rpl **a caballo** ride (a horse); **me gusta montar a caballo** I like riding; **ir a caballo** go on horseback

cabaña f cabin

cabaret m cabaret

cabecear ⟨1a⟩ **1** v/i nod **2** v/t el balón head

cabecera f de mesa, cama head; de periódico masthead; de texto top

cabecero *m de cama* headboard

cabecilla *m/f* ringleader

cabello *m* hair

caber ⟨2m⟩ *v/i* fit; *caben tres litros* it holds three liters *o Br* litres; *cabemos todos* there's room for all of us; *no cabe duda fig* there's no doubt; *no me cabe en la cabeza* I just don't understand

cabestrillo *m* MED sling

cabeza *f* ANAT head; *cabeza de ajo* bulb of garlic; *cabeza (de ganado)* head (of cattle); *cabeza nuclear* nuclear warhead; *el equipo a la cabeza or en cabeza* the team at the top; *por cabeza* per head; *per persona*; *estar mal or no estar bien de la cabeza* F not be right in the head F **2** *m/f*: *cabeza de familia* head of the family; *cabeza de turco* scapegoat; *cabeza rapada* skinhead

cabezada *f*: *echar una cabezada* have a nap

cabezonería *f* pigheadedness

cabezota 1 *adj* pig-headed **2** *m/f* pig--headed person

cabida *f* capacity; *dar cabida a* hold

cabildo *m* POL council

cabina *f* cabin; *cabina telefónica* phone booth

cabizbajo *adj* dejected, downhearted

cable *m* EL cable; MAR line, rope; *echar un cable a alguien* give s.o. a hand

cabo *m* end; GEOG cape; MAR rope; MIL corporal; *al cabo de* after; *de cabo a rabo* F from start to finish; *atar cabos* F put two and two together F; *llevar a cabo* carry out

cabra *f* ZO goat; *estar como una cabra* F be nuts F

cabrear ⟨1a⟩ **1** *v/t* P bug F **2** *v/r cabrearse* P get mad F

cabriola *f*: *hacer cabriolas de niño* jump around

cabro *m* Chi boy; *cabro chico* Chi baby

cabrón *m* V bastard P, son of a bitch V

caca *f* F poop F, *Br* pooh F; *cosa mala* piece of trash F; *hacer caca* ⊦ poop F, *Br* do a pooh F

cacahuate *m* Méx peanut

cacahuete *m* peanut

cacalote *m* C.Am., Cuba, Méx crow

cacao *m* cocoa; *de labios* lip salve; *no valer un cacao* L.Am. fig F not be worth a bean F

cacatúa *f* ZO cockatoo

cacería *f* hunt

cacerola *f* pan

cachar ⟨1a⟩ *v/t* L.Am. (engañar) trick; L.Am. (sorprender) catch out; *¿me cachas?* Chi get it?

cacharro *m* pot; Méx, C.Am. F (*trasto*) piece of junk; Méx, C.Am. F *coche* junkheap; *lavar los cacharros* Méx, C.Am. wash the dishes

cachas *adj*: *estar cachas* F be a real hunk F

cachear ⟨1a⟩ *v/t* frisk

cachemira *f* cashmere

cachetada *f* L.Am. slap

cachete *m* cheek

cachetear ⟨1a⟩ *v/t* L.Am. slap

cachimba *f* pipe

cachivache *m* thing; *cachivaches pl* (*cosas*) things, stuff *sg* F; (*basura*) junk *sg*

cacho *m* F bit; *Rpl* (*cuerno*) horn; Ven, Col F (*marijuana*) joint F; *jugar al cacho* Bol, Pe play dice; *ponerle cachos a alguien* cheat on sb

cachondeo *m*: *estar de cachondeo* F be joking; *tomar a cachondeo* F take as a joke; *¡vaya cachondeo!* F what a laugh! F

cachondo *adj* F (*caliente*) horny F; (*gracioso*) funny

cachorro *m* ZO pup

cacique *m* chief; POL *local political boss*; *fig* F tyrant

cacle *m* Méx shoe

caco *m* F thief

cactus *m inv* BOT cactus

cada *adj considerado por separado* each; *con énfasis en la totalidad* every; *cada cosa en su sitio* everything in its place; *cada uno, cada cual* each one; *cada vez* every time, each time; *cada vez más* more and more, increasingly; *cada tres días* every three days; *uno de cada tres* one out of every three

cadáver *m* (dead) body, corpse

cadena *f* chain; *de perro* leash, *Br* lead; TV channel; *cadena perpetua* life sentence

cadencia *f* MÚS rhythm, cadence

cadera *f* hip

caducado *adj* out of date

caducar ⟨1g⟩ *v/i* expire

caducidad *f*: *fecha de caducidad* expiry date; *de alimentos, medicinas* use-by date

caer ⟨2o⟩ **1** *v/i* fall; *me cae bien / mal fig* I like / don't like him; *dejar caer algo* drop sth; *estar al caer* be about to arrive; *caer enfermo* fall ill; *caer en lunes* fall on a Monday; *¡ahora caigo! fig* now I get it! **2** *v/r caerse* fall (down)

café *m* coffee; (*bar*) café; *café con leche* white coffee; *café descafeinado* decaffeinated coffee; *café instantáneo* instant coffee; *café solo* black coffee

cafeína *f* caffeine

cafetera f coffee maker; *para servir* coffee pot

cafetería f coffee shop

cagar ⟨1h⟩ V **1** v/i have a shit P **2** v/r **cagarse** shit o.s. P; **cagarse de miedo** shit o.s. P

caguama f Méx (*tortuga*) turtle

caída f fall

caigo vb → **caer**

caimán m zo alligator; Méx, C.Am. útil monkey wrench

Cairo: **El Cairo** Cairo

caja f box; *de reloj, ordenador* case, casing; COM cash desk; *en supermercado* checkout; **caja de ahorros** savings bank; **caja de cambios** gearbox; **caja de caudales, caja fuerte** safe, strongbox; **caja de cerillas** matchbox; **caja de música** music box; **caja postal** post office savings bank; **caja registradora** cash register; **echar a alguien con cajas destempladas** F send s.o. packing

cajero m, **-a** f cashier; *de banco* teller; **cajero automático** ATM, Br tb cash point

cajeta f Méx caramel spread

cajón m drawer; L.Am. casket, coffin

cajuele f Méx AUTO trunk, Br boot

cal f lime

cala f cove

calabacín m BOT zucchini, Br courgette

calabaza f pumpkin; **dar calabazas a alguien** F *en examen* fail s.o., flunk s.o. F; *en relación* give s.o. the brush off F

calabozo m cell

calada f puff

calado adj soaked; **calado hasta los huesos** soaked to the skin

calamar m zo squid

calambre m EL shock; MED cramp

calamidad f calamity

calaña f desp sort, type

calar ⟨1a⟩ **1** v/t (*mojar*) soak; *techo, tela* soak through; *persona, conjura* see through **2** v/i *de zapato* leak; *de ideas, costumbres* take root; **calar hondo en** make a big impression on **3** v/r **calarse de motor** stall; **calarse hasta los huesos** get soaked to the skin

calato adj Chi, Pe naked

calavera f skull

calcar ⟨1g⟩ v/t trace

calceta f: **hacer calceta** knit

calcetín m sock

calcinado adj burnt

calcio m calcium

calcomanía f decal, Br transfer

calculador adj fig calculating

calculadora f calculator

calcular ⟨1a⟩ v/t tb fig calculate

cálculo m calculation; MED stone; **cálculo biliar** gallstone; **cálculo renal** kidney stone

caldear ⟨1a⟩ v/t warm up; *ánimos* inflame

caldera f boiler; Rpl, Chi kettle

calderilla f small change

caldero m (small) boiler

caldillo m Méx GASTR stock

caldo m GASTR stock; **caldo de cultivo** fig breeding ground

caldoso adj watery

calefacción f heating; **calefacción central** central heating

calefactor m heater

calendario m calendar; (*programa*) schedule

caléndula f BOT marigold

calentador m heater; **calentador de agua** water heater

calentamiento m: **calentamiento global** global warming

calentar ⟨1k⟩ **1** v/t heat (up); **calentar a alguien** fig provoke s.o. **2** v/i DEP warm up **3** v/r **calentarse** warm up; *fig: de discusión, disputa* become heated

calentura f fever

calibrar ⟨1a⟩ v/t gauge; fig weigh up

calibre m tb fig caliber, Br calibre

calidad f quality; **calidad de vida** quality of life; **en calidad de médico** as a doctor

cálido adj tb fig warm

caliente adj hot; F (*cachondo*) horny F; **en caliente** in the heat of the moment

calificable adj gradable

calificación f description; EDU grade, Br mark

calificar ⟨1g⟩ v/t describe, label (**de** as); EDU grade, Br mark

caligrafía f calligraphy

caliza f limestone

callado adj quiet

callar ⟨1a⟩ **1** v/i (*dejar de hablar*) go quiet; (*guardar silencio*) be quiet, keep quiet; **¡calla!** be quiet!, shut up! **2** v/t silence **3** v/r **callarse** (*dejar de hablar*) go quiet; (*guardar silencio*) be quiet, keep quiet; **callarse algo** keep sth quiet

calle f street; DEP lane; **echar a alguien a la calle** fig throw s.o out onto the street

callejón m alley; **callejón sin salida** blind alley; fig dead end

callo m callus; **callos** pl GASTR tripe sg

calma f calm

calmante 1 adj soothing **2** m MED sedative

calmar ⟨1a⟩ **1** v/t calm (down) **2** v/r **calmarse** calm down

calor m heat; fig warmth; **hace mucho calor** it's very hot; **tengo calor** I'm hot

caloría f calorie

calumnia f oral slander; por escrito libel

calumniar ⟨1b⟩ v/t oralmente slander; por escrito libel

caluroso adj hot; fig warm

calva f bald patch

calvario m fig calvary

calvicie f baldness

calvo 1 adj bald **2** m bald man

calzada f road (surface)

calzado m footwear

calzador m shoe horn

calzar ⟨1f⟩ **1** v/t zapato, bota etc put on; mueble, rueda wedge **2** v/r **calzarse** zapato, bota etc put on

calzón m DEP shorts pl; L.Am. de hombre shorts pl, Br (under)pants pl; L.Am. de mujer panties pl, Br tb knickers pl; **calzones** L.Am. shorts, Br (under)pants

calzoncillos mpl shorts, Br (under)pants

cama f bed; **cama de matrimonio** double bed; **hacer la cama** make the bed; **irse a la cama** go to bed

camaleón m chameleon

cámara f FOT, TV camera; (sala) chamber; **cámara de comercio e industria** chamber of commerce and industry; **a cámara lenta** in slow motion; **cámara de vídeo** video camera

camarada m/f comrade; de trabajo colleague, co-worker

camaradería f camaraderie, comradeship

camarera f waitress

camarero m waiter

camarógrafo m, -a f L.Am. camera operator

camarón m L.Am. ZO shrimp, Br prawn

camarote m MAR cabin

camarotero m L.Am. steward

cambalache m Arg F second-hand shop

cambiar ⟨1b⟩ **1** v/t change (por for); compra exchange (por for) **2** v/i change; **cambiar de lugar** change places; **cambiar de marcha** AUTO shift gear, Br change gear **3** v/r **cambiarse** change; **cambiarse de ropa** change (one's clothes)

cambio m change; COM exchange rate; **cambio climático** climate change; **cambio de marchas** AUTO gear shift, Br gear change; **cambio de sentido** U-turn; **a cambio de** in exchange for; **en cambio** on the other hand

camelia f BOT camellia

camello 1 m ZO camel **2** m/f F (vendedor de drogas) pusher F, dealer

camelo m F con F; (broma) joke

camilla f stretcher

caminar ⟨1a⟩ **1** v/i walk; fig move; **caminando** on foot **2** v/t walk

camino m (senda) path; (ruta) way; **a medio camino** halfway; **de camino a** on the way to; **por el camino** on the way; **abrirse camino** fig make one's way; **ir por buen / mal camino** fig be on the right / wrong track; **ponerse en camino** set out

camión m truck, Br tb lorry; Méx bus

camionero m, -a f truck driver, Br tb lorry driver; Méx bus driver

camioneta f van

camisa f shirt

camiseta f T-shirt

camisón m nightdress

camorra f F fight; **armar camorra** F cause trouble

campal adj: **batalla campal** pitched battle

campamento m camp

campana f bell; **campana extractora** extractor hood

campanada f chime; **dar la campanada** cause a stir

campanario m bell tower

campanazo m L.Am. warning

campanilla f small bell; ANAT uvula

campante adj: **tan campante** F as calm as anything F

campaña f campaign; **campaña electoral** election campaign

campechano adj down-to-earth

campeón m, -ona f champion

campeonato m championship; **de campeonato** F terrific F

campera f L.Am. jacket

campesino 1 adj peasant atr **2** m, -a f peasant

campestre adj rural, country atr

camping m campground, Br tb campsite

campo m DEP field; Br tb pitch; (estadio) stadium; Br tb ground; **el campo** (área rural) the country; **campo de batalla** battlefield; **campo de concentración** concentration camp; **campo de golf** golf course; **campo visual** MED field of vision; **a campo traviesa**, **campo a través** cross-country

campus m inv: **campus universitario** university campus

camuflaje m camouflage

camuflar ⟨1a⟩ v/t camouflage

cana f gray (Br grey) hair

Canadá Canada

canadiense m/f & adj Canadian

canal m channel; TRANSP canal

canalete m paddle

canalizar ⟨1f⟩ v/t channel

canalla m swine F, rat F

canalón m gutter

canapé *m* (*sofá*) couch; *para cama* base; GASTR canapé

Canarias *fpl* Canaries

canario 1 *adj* Canary *atr* **2** zo canary

canasta *f* basket; *juego* canasta

canastilla *f* (wrought-iron) gate

cancela *f* (wrought-iron) gate

cancelación *f* cancellation

cancelar ⟨1a⟩ *v/t* cancel; *deuda, cuenta* settle, pay

cáncer *m* MED, *fig* cancer; **Cáncer** *m/f inv* ASTR Cancer

cancerígeno *adj* carcinogenic

canceroso *adj* cancerous

cancha *f* DEP court; *L.Am. de fútbol* field, *Br tb* pitch; **cancha de tenis** tennis court; **¡cancha!** *Rpl* F gangway! F; **abrir** *or* **hacer cancha** *Rpl* make room

canchear ⟨1a⟩ *v/i L.Am.* climb

canciller *m* Chancellor; *S. Am. de asuntos exteriores* Secretary of State, *Br* Foreign Minister

canción *f* song; **siempre la misma canción** F the same old story F

candado *m* padlock

candela *f L.Am.* fire; **¿me das candela?** have you got a light?

candelabro *m* candelabra

candelero *m*: **estar en el candelero** *de persona* be in the limelight

candente *adj* red-hot; *tema* topical

candidato *m*, **-a** *f* candidate

candidatura *f* candidacy

cándido *adj* naive

candor *m* innocence; (*franqueza*) cando(u)r

canela *f* cinnamon

canelones *mpl* GASTR cannelloni *sg*

cangrejo *m* zo crab

canguro 1 *m* zo kangaroo **2** *m/f* F baby-sitter

caníbal 1 *adj* cannibal *atr* **2** *m/f* cannibal

canica *f* marble

caniche *m* poodle

canícula *f* dog days *pl*

canijo *adj* F puny

canilla *f L.Am.* faucet, *Br* tap

canillita *m/f Arg* newspaper vendor

canjear ⟨1a⟩ *v/t* exchange (**por** for)

canoa *f* canoe

canónico *adj* canonical

canónigo *m* canon

canonizar ⟨1f⟩ *v/t* canonize

cansado *adj* tired

cansancio *m* tiredness

cansar ⟨1a⟩ **1** *v/t* tire; (*aburrir*) bore **2** *v/r* **cansarse** get tired; (*aburrirse*) get bored; **cansarse de algo** get tired of sth

cantante *m/f* singer

cantar ⟨1a⟩ **1** *v/i* sing; *de delincuente*

squeal P **2** *v/t* sing **3** *m*: **ése es otro cantar** *fig* F that's a different story

cántaro *m* pitcher; **llover a cántaros** F pour (down)

cantautor *m*, **cantautora** *f* singer-songwriter

cante *m*: **cante hondo** *or* **jondo** flamenco singing

cantera *f* quarry

cantidad *f* quantity, amount; **había cantidad de** there was (*pl* were) a lot of

cantimplora *f* water bottle

cantina *f* canteen

canto[1] *m* singing; *de pájaro* song

canto[2] *m* edge; (*roca*) stone; **canto rodado** boulder; **darse con un canto en los dientes** count o.s. lucky

canturrear ⟨1a⟩ *v/t* sing softly

canutas: **las pasé canutas** F it was really tough F

caña *f* BOT reed; (*tallo*) stalk; *cerveza* small glass of beer; *L.Am.* straw; **muebles de caña** cane furniture; **caña de azúcar** sugar cane; **caña de pescar** fishing rod; **dar** *or* **meter caña a alguien** F wind s.o. up F; **¡dale caña!** F get off your butt! F

cañada *f* ravine; *L.Am.* (*arroyo*) stream

cáñamo *m* hemp; *L.Am.* marijuana plant

cañería *f* pipe

cañero *adj L.Am.* sugar-cane *atr*

caño *m* pipe; *de fuente* spout

cañón *m* HIST cannon; *antiaéreo, antitanque etc* gun; *de fusil* barrel; GEOG canyon **2** *adj* F great, fantastic F

cañonazo *m* gunshot

caoba *f* mahogany

caos *m* chaos

caótico *adj* chaotic

cap *abr* (= *capítulo*) ch. (= chapter)

capa *f* layer; *prenda* cloak; **capa de ozono** ozone layer; **capa de pintura** coat of paint

capacidad *f* capacity; (*aptitud*) competence; **capacidad de memoria** INFOR memory / storage capacity

capacitar ⟨1a⟩ *v/t* prepare; **capacitar alguien para hacer algo** qualify s.o. to do sth

capar ⟨1a⟩ *v/t* castrate

caparazón *m* zo shell

capataz *m* foreman

capataza *f* forewoman

capaz *adj* able (**de** to); **ser capaz de** be capable of

capcioso *adj*: **pregunta -a** trick question

capear ⟨1a⟩ *v/t temporal* weather

capellán *m* chaplain

capicúa adj: **número capicúa** reversible number

capilar 1 adj capillary atr; loción hair atr **2** m capillary

capilla f chapel; **capilla ardiente** chapel of rest

capirotada f Méx type of French toast with honey, cheese, raisins etc

capital 1 adj importancia prime; **pena capital** capital punishment **2** f de país capital **3** m COM capital

capitalismo m capitalism

capitalista 1 adj capitalist atr **2** m/f capitalist

capitán m captain

capitanear ⟨1a⟩ v/t captain

capitel m ARQUI capital

Capitolio m Capitol

capitulación f capitulation, surrender; (pacto) agreement

capitular ⟨1a⟩ v/i surrender, capitulate

capítulo m chapter

capó m AUTO hood, Br bonnet

capón m Rpl mutton

capota f AUTO top, Br hood

capote m cloak; MIL greatcoat

capotera f L.Am. coat stand

capricho m whim

caprichoso adj capricious

Capricornio m/f inv ASTR Capricorn

cápsula f capsule; **cápsula espacial** space capsule

captar ⟨1a⟩ v/t understand; RAD pick up; negocio take

capturar ⟨1a⟩ v/t capture

capucha f hood

capuchino m cappuccino

capullo m ZO cocoon; BOT bud

caqui 1 adj khaki **2** m BOT persimmon

cara f face; (expresión) look; fig nerve; **cara a algo** facing sth; **cara a cara** face to face; **de cara a** facing; fig with regard to; **dar la cara** face the consequences; **echar algo en cara a alguien** remind s.o. of sth; **tener cara dura** have a nerve; **tener buena / mala cara** de comida look good / bad; de persona look well / sick; **cara o cruz** heads or tails

carabinero m GASTR (large) shrimp, Br prawn; (agente de aduana) border guard

caracol m snail; **¡caracoles!** wow! F; enfado damn! F

caracola f ZO conch

carácter m character; (naturaleza) nature

característica f characteristic

característico adj characteristic (de of)

caracterizar ⟨1f⟩ **1** v/t characterize; TEA play (the part of) **2** v/r **caracterizarse** be characterized (**por** by)

caradura m/f F guy / woman with a nerve, Br cheeky devil F

carajillo m coffee with a shot of liquor

carajo m: **irse al carajo** F go down the tubes F

caramba int wow!; enfado damn! F

carambola f billar carom, Br cannon; **por** or **de carambola** F by sheer chance

caramelo m dulce candy, Br sweet; (azúcar derretida) caramel

carantoña f caress

caraqueño 1 adj of / from Caracas, Caracas atr **2** m, -a f native of Caracas

carátula f de disco jacket, Br tb sleeve; L.Am. de reloj face

caravana f (remolque) trailer, Br caravan; de tráfico queue of traffic, traffic jam; Méx (reverencia) bow

caray int F wow! F; enfado damn! F

carbón m coal

carboncillo m charcoal

carbonizar ⟨1f⟩ v/t char

carbono m QUÍM carbon

carburador m AUTO carburet(t)or

carburante m fuel

carca m/f & adj F reactionary

carcajada f laugh, guffaw; **reír a carcajadas** roar with laughter

carcajearse ⟨1a⟩ v/r have a good laugh (**de** at)

cárcel f prison

carcelero m, -a f warder, jailer

carcinoma f MED carcinoma

carcoma f ZO woodworm

carcomer ⟨2a⟩ **1** v/t eat away; fig: de envidia eat away at, consume **2** v/r **carcomerse**; **carcomerse de** fig be consumed with

cardamomo m BOT cardamom

cardenal m REL cardinal; (hematoma) bruise

cardíaco, cardiaco adj cardiac

cardinal adj cardinal; **número cardinal** cardinal number; **puntos cardinales** points of the compass, cardinal points

cardiólogo m, -a f cardiologist

cardo m BOT thistle

carecer ⟨2d⟩ v/i: **carecer de algo** lack sth

carencia f lack (**de** of)

carente adj: **carente de** lacking in

careta f mask

carga f load; de buque cargo; MIL, EL charge; (responsabilidad) burden; **carga explosiva** explosive charge; **carga fiscal** or **impositiva** tax burden; **ser una carga para alguien** be a burden to s.o.; **volver a la carga** return to the attack

cargado adj loaded (**de** with); aire stuffy; ambiente tense; café strong

cargamento *m* load

cargante *adj* F annoying

cargar ⟨1h⟩ **1** *v/t arma, camión* load; *batería, acusado* charge; COM charge (**en** to); *L.Am.* (*traer*) carry; *esto me carga L.Am.* P I can't stand this **2** *v/i* (*apoyarse*) rest (**sobre** on); (*fastidiar*) be annoying; **cargar con algo** carry sth; **cargar con la culpa** *fig* shoulder the blame; **cargar contra alguien** MIL, DEP charge (at) s.o. **3** *v/r* **cargarse con peso, responsabilidad** weigh o.s. down; F (*matar*) bump off F; F (*romper*) wreck F

cargo *m* position; JUR charge; **alto cargo** high-ranking position; *persona* high-ranking official; **a cargo de la madre** in the mother's care; **está a cargo de Gómez** Gómez is in charge of it; **hacerse cargo de algo** take charge of sth

cariarse ⟨1b⟩ *v/r* decay

Caribe *m* Caribbean

caribeño *adj* Caribbean

caricatura *f* caricature

caricaturizar ⟨1f⟩ *v/t* caricature

caricia *f* caress

caridad *f* charity

caries *f* MED caries

cariño *m* affection, fondness; **hacer cariño a alguien** *L.Am.* (*acariciar*) caress s.o.; (*abrazar*) hug s.o.; **¡cariño!** darling!; **con cariño** with love

cariñoso *adj* affectionate

carisma *m* charisma

carismático *adj* charismatic

caritativo *adj* charitable

cariz *m* look; **tomar mal cariz** start to look bad

carmín *m* **de labios** lipstick

carnaval *m* carnival

carne *f* meat; *de persona* flesh; **carne de gallina** *fig* goose bumps *pl*, *Br* gooseflesh; **carne picada** ground meat, *Br* mince; **de carne y hueso** flesh and blood; **sufrir algo en sus propias carnes** *fig* go through sth oneself

carné *m* → **carnet**

carnear ⟨1a⟩ *v/t L.Am.* slaughter

carnero *m* ram

carnet *m* card; **carnet de conducir** driver's license, *Br* driving licence; **carnet de identidad** identity card

carnicería *f* butcher's; *fig* carnage

carnicero *m*, **-a** *f* butcher

carnívoro *adj* carnivorous

carnoso *adj* fleshy

caro *adj* expensive, dear; **costar caro** *fig* cost dear

carozo *m* Chi, Rpl pit

carpa *f* **de circo** big top; ZO carp; *L.Am.*

para acampar tent; *L.Am. de mercado* stall

carpeta *f* file

carpintero *m* carpenter; *de obra* joiner; **pájaro carpintero** woodpecker

carpir ⟨3a⟩ *v/t L.Am.* hoe

carraspear ⟨1a⟩ *v/i* clear one's throat

carraspera *f* hoarseness

carrera *f* race; EDU degree course; *profesional* career; **carrera de armamento** arms race; **a las carreras** at top speed; *con prisas* in a rush; **hacer la carrera** F *de prostituta* turn tricks F; **carreras** *pl* **de coches** motor racing *sg*

carrerilla *f*: **tomar carrerilla** take a run up; **decir algo de carrerilla** reel sth off

carreta *f* cart

carrete *m* FOT (roll of) film; **carrete de hilo** reel of thread

carretera *f* highway, (main) road; **carretera de circunvalación** ring road

carretilla *f* wheelbarrow

carril *m* lane; **carril-bici** cycle lane; **carril-bus** bus lane

carrillo *m* cheek; **comer a dos carrillos** F stuff oneself F

carrito *m* cart, *Br* trolley; **carrito de bebé** buggy, *Br* pushchair

carro *m* cart; *L.Am.* car; *L.Am.* (*taxi*) taxi, cab; **carro de combate** tank; **carro-patrulla** *L.Am.* F patrol car

carrocería *f* AUTO bodywork

carroña *f* carrion

carruaje *m* carriage

carta *f* letter; GASTR menu; (*naipe*) playing card; (*mapa*) chart; **carta certificada** or **registrada** registered letter; **carta urgente** special-delivery letter; **a la carta** a la carte; **dar carta blanca a alguien** give s.o. carte blanche o a free hand; **poner las cartas boca arriba** *fig* put one's cards on the table; **tomar cartas en el asunto** intervene in the matter

cartearse ⟨1a⟩ *v/r* write to each other

cartel *m* poster; **estar en cartel** *de película, espectáculo* be on

cártel *m* cartel

cartelera *f* billboard; *de periódico* listings, entertainments section

cartera *f* wallet; (*maletín*) briefcase; COM, POL portfolio; *de colegio* knapsack, *Br* satchel; *L.Am.* purse, *Br* handbag; *mujer* mailwoman, *Br* postwoman

carterista *m/f* pickpocket

cartero *m* mailman, *Br* postman

cartílago *m* cartilage

cartilla *f* reader; *Méx* identity card; **cartilla de ahorros** savings book; **leerle a alguien la cartilla** F give s.o. a telling off F

cartógrafo *m*, **-a** *f* cartographer
cartón *m* cardboard; *de tabaco* carton; *cartón piedra* pap(i)er-mâché
cartuchera *f* cartridge belt
cartucho *m* *de arma* cartridge
cartulina *f* sheet of card; *cartulina roja* DEP red card
casa *f* house; *(hogar)* home; *en casa* at home; *como una casa* F huge F; *casa cuna* children's home; *casa de huéspedes* rooming house, *Br* boarding house; *casa matriz* head office; *casa de socorro* first aid post; *casa adosada, casa pareada* → **chalet**
casaca *f* cassock
casado *adj* married; *recién casado* newly-wed
casamentero *m*, **-a** *f* matchmaker
casar ⟨1a⟩ **1** *v/i fig* match (up); *casar con* go with **2** *v/r casarse* get married; *casarse con alguien* marry s.o.; *no casarse con nadie fig* refuse to compromise
cascabel *m* small bell
cascada *f* waterfall
cascado *adj voz* hoarse; F *persona* worn out F
cascanueces *m inv* nutcracker
cascar ⟨1g⟩ *v/t* crack; *algo quebradizo* break; *fig* F whack F; *cascarla* peg out F
cáscara *f de huevo* shell; *de naranja, limón* peel
cascarón *m* shell; *salir del cascarón* hatch (out)
cascarrabias *m inv* F grouch F
casco *m* helmet; *de barco* hull; *(botella vacía)* empty (bottle); *edificio* empty building; *de caballo* hoof; *de vasija* fragment; *casco urbano* urban area; *cascos azules* MIL blue berets, UN peace-keeping troops
cascote *m* piece of rubble
casera *f* landlady
casero 1 *adj* home-made; *comida* **-a** home cooking **2** *m* landlord
caseta *f* hut; *de feria* stall
casete *m (also f)* cassette
casi *adv* almost, nearly; *en frases negativas* hardly
casilla *f en formulario* box; *en tablero* square; *de correspondencia* pigeon hole; *S. Am.* post office box; *sacar a alguien de sus casillas* drive s.o. crazy
casino *m* casino
caso *m* case; *en caso de que, caso de* in the event that, in case of; *hacer caso* take notice; *ser un caso* F be a real case F; *no venir al caso* be irrelevant; *en todo caso* in any case, in any event; *en el peor de los casos* if the worst comes to

the worst; *en último caso* as a last resort
caspa *f* dandruff
caspiroleta *f S. Am.* eggnog
casquillo *m de cartucho* case; EL bulb holder; *L.Am.* horseshoe
cassette *m (also f)* cassette; *cassette virgen* blank cassette
casta *f* caste
castaña *f* chestnut; *sacar las castañas del fuego a alguien fig* F pull s.o.'s chestnuts out of the fire F
castaño 1 *adj color* chestnut, brown **2** *m* chestnut (tree); *color* chestnut, brown; *ya pasa de castaño oscuro* F it's gone too far, it's beyond a joke
castañuela *f* castanet; *estar como unas castañuelas* F be over the moon F
castellano *m* (Castilian) Spanish
castidad *f* chastity
castigar ⟨1h⟩ *v/t* punish
castigo *m* punishment
castillo *m* castle; *castillo de fuegos artificiales* firework display
castizo *adj* pure
casto *adj* chaste
castor *m* ZO beaver
castrar ⟨1a⟩ *v/t* castrate; *fig* emasculate
castrense *adj* army *atr*
casual *adj* chance *atr*
casualidad *f* chance, coincidence; *por* or *de casualidad* by chance
cataclismo *m* cataclysm, catastrophe
catalán 1 *adj* Catalan **2** *m*, **-ana** *f* Catalan
catalejo *m* telescope
catalizador *m* catalyst; AUTO catalytic converter
catalizar ⟨1f⟩ *v/t* catalyze
catalogar ⟨1h⟩ *v/t* catalog(ue); *fig* class
catálogo *m* catalog(ue)
catamarán *m* MAR catamaran
cataplasma *f* MED poultice; *fig: persona* bore
catapulta *f* slingshot, *Br* catapult
catapultar ⟨1a⟩ *v/t* catapult
catar ⟨1a⟩ *v/t* taste
catarata *f* GEOG waterfall; MED cataract
catarro *m* cold; *inflamación* catarrh
catástrofe *f* catastrophe
catastrófico *adj* catastrophic
cate *m* EDU F fail
catear ⟨1a⟩ *v/t* F flunk F
catecismo *m* catechism
catedral *f* cathedral; *una mentira como una catedral* F a whopping great lie F
catedrático *m*, **-a** *f* EDU head of department
categoría *f* category; *social* class; *fig: de local, restaurante* class; *(estatus)* standing; *actor de primera categoría* first-rate ac-

tor
categórico *adj* categorical
catequesis *f* catechism
catéter *m* MED catheter
catolicismo *m* (Roman) Catholicism
católico 1 *adj* (Roman) Catholic **2** *m*, **-a** *f* (Roman) Catholic
catorce *adj* fourteen
catre *m* bed
cauce *m* riverbed; *fig* channel; *volver a su cauce fig* get back to normal
caucho *m* rubber; *L.Am.* (*neumático*) tire, *Br* tyre
caudal *m de río* volume of flow; *fig* wealth
caudillo *m* leader
causa *f* cause; (*motivo*) reason; JUR lawsuit; *a causa de* because of
causante *m* cause
causar ⟨1a⟩ *v/t* cause
cáustico *adj tb fig* caustic
cautela *f* caution
cauteloso *adj* cautious
cauterizar ⟨1f⟩ *v/t* cauterize
cautivar ⟨1a⟩ *v/t fig* captivate
cautiverio *m*, **cautividad** *f* captivity
cautivo 1 *adj* captive **2** *m*, **-a** *f* captive
cauto *adj* cautious
cava *m* cava, sparkling wine
cavar ⟨1a⟩ *v/t* dig
caverna *f* cavern
cavernícola *m/f* caveman; *mujer* cavewoman
caviar *m* caviar
cavidad *f* cavity
cavilar ⟨1a⟩ *v/t* meditate on
cayó *vb* → *caer*
caza 1 *f actividad* hunting; *caza mayor / menor* big / small game; *andar a la caza de algo / alguien* be after sth/s.o. **2** *m* AVIA fighter
cazador *m* hunter
cazadora *f* hunter; *prenda* jacket
cazar ⟨1f⟩ **1** *v/t animal* hunt; *fig: información* track down; (*pillar, captar*) catch; *cazar un buen trabajo* get o.s. a good job **2** *v/i* hunt; *ir a cazar* go hunting
cazo *m* saucepan
cazuela *f* pan; *de barro, vidrio* casserole
cazurro *adj* stubborn; (*basto*) coarse; (*lento de entender*) dense F, thick F
c.c. *abr* (= *centímetro cúbico*) c.c. (= cubic centimeter)
c/c *abr* (= *cuenta corriente*) C/A (= checking account)
CD *m* (= *disco compacto*) CD (= compact disc); *reproductor* CD-player
CD-ROM *m* CD-ROM
cebada *f* barley
cebar ⟨1a⟩ **1** *v/t* fatten; *anzuelo* bait; TÉC

prime; *L.Am. mate* prepare **2** *v/r cebarse* feed (*en* on); *cebar con alguien* vent one's fury on s.o.
cebo *m* bait
cebolla *f* onion
cebra *f* zebra; *paso de cebra* crosswalk, *Br* zebra crossing
ceceo *m pronunciation of 's' with 'th' sound*
cecina *f* cured meat
cedazo *m* sieve
ceder ⟨2a⟩ **1** *v/t* give up; (*traspasar*) transfer, cede; *ceder el paso* AUTO yield, *Br* give way **2** *v/i* give way, yield; *de viento, lluvia* ease off
cedro *m* BOT cedar
cédula *f L.Am.* identity document
cegar ⟨1h & 1k⟩ *v/t* blind; *tubería* block
ceguera *f tb fig* blindness
ceja *f* eyebrow; *lo tiene entre ceja y ceja* F she can't stand him F
cejar ⟨1a⟩ *v/i* give up; *no cejar en* not let up in
celador *m*, **celadora** *f* orderly; *de cárcel* guard; *de museo* attendant
celda *f* cell
celebración *f* celebration
celebrar ⟨1a⟩ *v/t misa* celebrate; *reunión, acto oficial* hold; *fiesta* have, hold
célebre *adj* famous
celeste *adj* light blue, sky blue
celestial *adj* celestial; *fig* heavenly
celibato *m* celibacy
celo *m* zeal; (*cinta adhesiva*) Scotch® tape, *Br* Sellotape®; *en celo* ZO in heat; *celos pl* jealousy *sg*; *tener celos de* be jealous of
celofán *m* cellophane
celoso *adj* jealous (*de* of)
célula *f* cell
celular *adj* cellular
celulitis *f* cellulite
celulosa *f* cellulose
cementerio *m* cemetery
cemento *m* cement
cena *f* dinner; *más tarde* supper
cenagoso *adj* boggy
cenar ⟨1a⟩ **1** *v/t*: *cenar algo* have sth for dinner **2** *v/i* have dinner
cencerro *m* cowbell
cenicero *m* ashtray
cenit *m* AST zenith; *fig* peak
ceniza *f* ash; *cenizas* ashes
censo *m* census; *censo electoral* voting register, electoral roll
censura *f* censorship
censurar ⟨1a⟩ *v/t* censor; *tratamiento* condemn
cent *abr* (= *céntimo*) cent

centavo *m* cent

centellear ⟨1a⟩ *v/i* sparkle; *de estrella* twinkle

centena *f* hundred

centenar *m* hundred; *regalos a centenares* hundreds of gifts

centenario 1 *adj* hundred-year-old *atr* 2 *m* centennial, *Br* centenary

centeno *m* BOT rye

centígrado *adj* centigrade; *dos grados centígrados* two degrees centigrade

centímetro *m* centimeter, *Br* centimetre

céntimo *m* cent; *estar sin un céntimo* not have a red cent F

centinela *m/f* sentry; *de banda criminal* lookout

central 1 *adj* central; *(principal)* main, central 2 *f* head office; *central atómica or nuclear* nuclear power station; *central eléctrica* power station; *central telefónica* telephone exchange; *central térmica* thermal power station

centralismo *m* POL centralism

centralita *f* TELEC switchboard

centralizar ⟨1f⟩ *v/t* centralize

centrar ⟨1a⟩ 1 *v/t tb* DEP center, *Br* centre; *esfuerzos* focus (*en* on) 2 *v/r* centrarse concentrate (*en* on)

céntrico *adj* central

centrifugar ⟨1h⟩ *v/t* spin

centro *m* center, *Br* centre; *centro comercial* (shopping) mall, *Br* shopping centre; *centro urbano en señal* town center (*Br* centre)

Centroamérica Central America

centroamericano *adj* Central American

ceñido *adj* tight

ceñirse ⟨3h & 3l⟩ *v/r*: *ceñirse a algo fig* stick to sth

ceño *m*: *fruncir el ceño* frown

cepa *f de vid* stock

cepillar ⟨1a⟩ 1 *v/t* brush 2 *v/r* cepillarse brush; F *(comerse)* polish off F; F *(matar)* kill, knock off F

cepillo *m* brush; *cepillo de dientes* toothbrush

cera *f* wax

cerámica *f* ceramics

cerca[1] *f* fence

cerca[2] *adv* near, close; *de cerca* close up; *cerca de* near, close to; *(casi)* nearly

cercanía *f*: *tren de cercanías* suburban train

cercano *adj* nearby; *cercano a* close to, near to

cercar ⟨1g⟩ *v/t* surround; *con valla* fence in

cerciorarse ⟨1a⟩ *v/r* make sure (*de* of)

cerco *m* ring; *de puerta* frame; *L.Am.* fence; *poner cerco a* lay siege to

cerda *f animal* sow; *fig* F *persona* pig F; *de brocha* bristle

cerdo *m* hog, *Br* pig; *fig* F *persona* pig F

cereal *m* cereal; *cereales pl* (breakfast) cereal *sg*

cerebro *m* ANAT brain; *fig: persona* brains *sg*

ceremonia *f* ceremony

cereza *f* cherry

cerezo *m* cherry (tree)

cerilla *f* match

cernerse ⟨2g⟩ *v/r*: *cernerse sobre fig* hang over

cernícalo *m* ZO kestrel

cero *m* EDU zero, *Br tb* nought; *en fútbol etc* zero, *Br* nil; *en tenis* love; *bajo / sobre cero* below / above zero; *empezar desde cero fig* start from scratch; *vencer por tres a cero* win three-zero (*Br* nil)

cerrado *adj* closed; *persona* narrow-minded; *(tímido)* introverted; *cielo* overcast, *curva -a* tight curve

cerradura *f* lock; *ojo de la cerradura* keyhole

cerrajero *m*, *-a f* locksmith

cerrar ⟨1k⟩ 1 *v/t* close; *para siempre* close down; *tubería* block; *grifo* turn off; *cerrar con llave* lock 2 *v/i* close; *para siempre* close down 3 *v/r* cerrarse close; *de cielo* cloud over; *de persona* shut o.s. off (*a* from); *cerrarse de golpe* slam shut

cerrazón *f fig* narrow-mindedness

cerrero *adj L.Am. persona* rough

cerril *adj animal* wild; *(terco)* stubborn, pig-headed F; *(torpe)* F dense F

cerro *m* hill

cerrojo *m* bolt; *echar el cerrojo* bolt the door

certamen *m* competition

certeza *f* certainty

certidumbre *f* certainty

certificado 1 *adj carta* registered 2 *m* certificate

certificar ⟨1g⟩ *v/t* certify; *carta* register

cerval *adj*: *miedo cerval* terrible fear

cervecería *f* bar

cerveza *f* beer; *cerveza de barril or de presión* draft, *Br* draught (beer); *cerveza negra* stout; *cerveza rubia* lager; *fábrica de cerveza* brewery

cesante *adj Chi* unemployed, jobless; *dejar cesante a alguien* let s.o. go

cesar ⟨1a⟩ *v/i* stop; *no cesar de hacer algo* keep on doing sth; *sin cesar* non-stop

cesárea *f* MED C(a)esarean

cese *m* cessation

cesión *f* transfer

C

césped m lawn
cesta f basket; **cesta de la compra** shopping basket
cesto m large basket
C.F. abr (= **Club de Fútbol**) FC (= Football Club)
cfc abr (= **clorofluorocarbono**) CFC (= chlorofluorocarbon)
cg. abr (= **centigramo**) centigram
ch/ abr (= **cheque**) check
chabacano adj vulgar, tacky F
chabola f shack; **barrio de chabolas** shanty town
chacal m zo jackal
chacarero m, **-a** f Rpl, Chi smallholder, farmer
chacha f F shawl
chácharas fpl L.Am. junk sg, bits and pieces
chachi adj F great F
chacra f L.Am. AGR smallholding
chafar ⟨1a⟩ v/t squash; **cosa erguida** flatten; F **planes** etc ruin F
chaflán m corner
chal m shawl
chalado adj F crazy F (**por** about)
chalé m → **chalet**
chaleco m **de traje** waistcoat; **de sport** gilet, bodywarmer; **chaleco salvavidas** life vest; **chaleco antibalas** bulletproof vest
chalet m chalet; **chalet adosado** house sharing one or more walls with other houses; **chalet pareado** semi-detached house
chalupa f MAR small boat; Méx stuffed tortilla
chamaca f C.Am., Méx girl
chamaco m C.Am., Méx boy
chamarra f Méx (**saco**) (short) jacket
chamba f Méx F job
chambón m, **-ona** f Méx F clumsy idiot F
champán m, **champaña** f champagne
champiñón m BOT mushroom
champú m shampoo
chamuscar ⟨1g⟩ v/t scorch; **pelo** singe
chamusquina f: **oler a chamusquina** F smell fishy F
chance 1 m L.Am. chance; **dame chance** let me have a go **2** conj Méx perhaps, maybe
chanchería f L.Am. pork butcher's shop
chancho m L.Am. hog, Br pig; **carne** pork
chanchullo m F trick, scam F
chancla f thong, Br flip-flop; Méx, C.Am. (**zapato**) slipper
chancleta f thong, Br flip-flop; S. Am. F baby girl
chándal m tracksuit
changa f Rpl odd job

chango 1 adj Méx F sharp, smart **2** m, **-a** f Méx monkey
chanquetes mpl GASTR whitebait sg
chantaje m blackmail; **hacer chantaje a alguien** blackmail s.o.
chantajear ⟨1a⟩ v/t blackmail
chantajista m/f blackmailer
chanza f wisecrack
chao int bye
chapa f (**tapón**) cap; (**plancha**) sheet (of metal); (**insignia**) badge; AUTO bodywork
chapado adj plated; **chapado a la antigua** old-fashioned; **chapado en oro** gold-plated
chapar ⟨1a⟩ v/t plate; Arg, Pe catch
chaparro adj Méx small
chaparrón m downpour; fig F **de insultos** barrage
chapotear ⟨1a⟩ v/i splash
chapucero 1 adj shoddy, slapdash **2** m, **-a** f shoddy worker
chapurrear ⟨1a⟩ v/t: **chapurrear el francés** speak poor French
chapuza f (**trabajo mal hecho**) shoddy piece of work; (**trabajo menor**) odd job
chapuzón m dip; **darse un chapuzón** go for a dip
chaqué m morning coat
chaqueta f jacket; **chaqueta de punto** cardigan
chaquetero m, **-a** f F turncoat
chaquetón m three-quarter length coat
charango m Pe, Bol five string guitar
charca f pond
charco m puddle
charcutería f delicatessen
charla f chat; **organizada** talk
charlar ⟨1a⟩ v/i chat
charlatán 1 adj talkative **2** m, **-ana** f chatterbox
charol m patent leather; **zapatos de charol** patent leather shoes
charqui m L.Am. beef jerky
charro 1 adj desp garish, gaudy **2** m Méx (Mexican) cowboy
chasco m joke; **llevarse un chasco** be disappointed
chasis m inv AUTO chassis
chasquear ⟨1a⟩ v/t click; **látigo** crack
chasquido m click; **de látigo** crack
chatarra f scrap
chato adj nariz snub; L.Am. **nivel** low
chau int Rpl bye
chaucha f Rpl French bean
chaval m F kid F, boy
chavala f F kid F, girl
chavalo m C.Am. F kid F, boy
che int Rpl hey!, look!
checar ⟨1g⟩ v/t Méx check

checo 1 adj Czech **2** m, **-a** f Czech
chef m chef
chelo m MÚS cello
chepa f F hump; *subírsele a la chepa* get too familiar
cheque m check, Br cheque; *cheque cruzado* crossed check (Br cheque); *cheque sin fondos* bad check (Br cheque); *cheque de viaje* traveler's check, Br traveller's cheque
chequear ⟨1a⟩ v/t check; C.Am. equipaje check (in)
chequeo m MED check-up
chequera f checkbook, Br chequebook
chica f girl
chicha f L.Am. corn liquor; *no ser ni chicha ni limonada* F be neither one thing nor the other
chícharo m Méx pea
chiche adj C.Am. F (fácil) easy **2** m S. Am. (juguete) toy; (adorno) trinket
chichera f C.Am. jail
chichería f L.Am. bar selling corn liquor
chichón m bump
chicle m chewing gum
chico 1 adj small, little **2** m boy
chifa m Pe Chinese restaurant; (comida china) Chinese food
chifla f Méx whistling
chiflado adj F crazy F (por about), nuts F (por about)
chiflar ⟨1a⟩ v/t boo **2** v/i whistle; *me chifla ...* F I'm crazy about ... F
chile m chilli (pepper)
Chile Chile
chileno 1 adj Chilean **2** m, **-a** f Chilean
chillar ⟨1a⟩ v/i scream, shriek; de cerdo squeal
chillido m scream, shriek; de cerdo squeal
chillón 1 adj voz shrill; color loud **2** m, **-ona** f loudmouth
chilote m C.Am. baby corn
chimenea f chimney; de salón fireplace
chimichurri m Rpl hot sauce
chimpancé m zo chimpanzee
China China
china[1] f Chinese woman
china[2] f piedra small stone
chincheta f thumbtack, Br drawing pin
chinchorro m hammock
chinear ⟨1a⟩ v/t C.Am. niños look after
chingar ⟨1h⟩ v/t Méx V screw V, fuck V; *¡chinga tu madre!* screw you! V, fuck you! V; *no chingues* don't screw me around V
chino 1 adj Chinese **2** m Chinese man; idioma Chinese; *L.Am. desp* half-breed desp; *trabajo de chinos* F hard work; *me suena a chino* F it's all Chinese o double

Dutch to me F
chip m INFOR chip
chipirón m baby squid
chiquilla f girl, kid
chiquillo m boy, kid
chirimoya f BOT custard apple
chiringuito m beach bar
chiripa f: *de chiripa* F by sheer luck
chirona f: *en chirona* F in the can F, inside F
chirriar ⟨1c⟩ v/i squeak
chirrido m squeak
chisme m F bit of gossip; objeto doodad F, Br doodah F
chismografía f F gossip
chismorrear ⟨1a⟩ v/i F gossip
chismoso 1 adj gossipy **2** m, **-a** f F gossip
chispa f spark; (cantidad pequeña) spot; fig F wit
chispear ⟨1a⟩ v/i spark; fig sparkle; de lluvia spit
chistar ⟨1a⟩ v/i: *sin chistar* without saying a word
chiste m joke
chiva f L.Am. goat; C.Am., Col bus
chivarse ⟨1a⟩ v/r F rat F (a to)
chivato m, **-a** f stool pigeon F
chivo m zo kid; C.Am., Méx wages pl
chocante adj (sorprendente) startling; que ofende shocking; (extraño) odd; L.Am. (antipático) unpleasant
chocar ⟨1g⟩ v/t: *¡choca esos cinco!* P give me five! P, put it there! P **2** v/i crash (con, contra into), collide (con with); *chocarle a alguien* (sorprender) surprise s.o.; (ofender) shock s.o.; *me choca ese hombre* F that guy disgusts me; *chocar con un problema* come up against a problem
chocho adj F senile; *estar chocho con* dote on
choclo m Rpl corn, Br corn on the cob
chocolate m chocolate; F (hachís) hashish, hash F
chocolatina f chocolate bar
chófer, L.Am. chofer m driver
chollo m F bargain
cholo m L.Am. half-caste desp
chompa f S. Am. jumper, sweater
chop m L.Am. large beer
chopo m BOT poplar
choque m collision, crash; DEP, MIL clash; MED shock
chorizo m chorizo (spicy cured sausage); F thief; Rpl (filete) rump steak
chorlito m: *cabeza de chorlito* F featherbrain F
chorrada f F piece of junk; *decir chorradas* F talk garbage, Br talk rubbish

chorrear ⟨1a⟩ *v/i* gush out, stream; (*gotear*) drip

chorro *m* *líquido* jet, stream; *fig* stream; *C.Am.* faucet, *Br* tap

chovinista *m/f* chauvinist

choza *f* hut

chubasco *m* shower

chubasquero *m* raincoat

chuchería *f* knick-knack; (*golosina*) candy, *Br* sweet

chucho 1 *adj C.Am.* mean **2** *m* F (*perro*) mutt F, mongrel; *Chi* (*cárcel*) can F, prison

chueco *adj L.Am.* (*torcido*) twisted

chulería *f* bragging

chuleta *f* GASTR chop

chulo F 1 *adj* fantastic F, great F; *Méx* (*guapo*) attractive; (*presuntuoso*) cocky F **2** *m* pimp F

chumbera *f C.Am.* prickly pear

chumpipe *m C.Am.* turkey

chupa *f* jacket

chupado *adj* F (*delgado*) skinny F; (*fácil*) dead easy F; *L.Am.* F drunk

chupar ⟨1a⟩ *v/t* suck; (*absorber*) soak up **2** *v/r* **chuparse**: *chuparse algo* suck sth; *fig* F put up with sth; *chuparse los dedos* F lick one's fingers

chupete *m de bebé* pacifier, *Br* dummy; (*sorbete*) Popsicle®, *Br* ice lolly

chupi *adj* F great F, fantastic F

churrasco *m Rpl* steak

churro *m* fritter; (*chapuza*) botched job

chusma *f desp* rabble *desp*

chutar ⟨1a⟩ *v/i* DEP shoot; *esto va que chuta* F this is working out fine; *y vas que chutas* F and that's your lot!

chuzo *m Chi* F *persona* dead loss F; *caer chuzos de punta* F pelt down F

Cía. *abr* (= **Compañía**) Co. (= Company)

ciberespacio *m* cyberspace

cibernauta *m/f* Internet surfer

cibernética *f* cybernetics

cicatriz *f* scar

cicatrizar ⟨1f⟩ scar

cíclico *adj* cyclical

ciclismo *m* cycling

ciclista *m/f* cyclist

ciclo *m* cycle; *de cine* season

ciclomotor *m* moped

ciclón *m* cyclone

cicloturismo *m* bicycle touring

ciega *f* blind woman

ciego 1 *adj* blind; *a -as* blindly **2** *m* blind man

cielito *m Rpl* folk dance

cielo *m* sky; REL heaven; *ser un cielo* F be an angel F; *cielo raso* ceiling

ciempiés *m inv* ZO centipede

cien *adj* a *o* one hundred

ciencia *f* science; *ciencia ficción* science fiction; *a ciencia cierta* for certain, for sure

científico 1 *adj* scientific **2** *m*, *-a f* scientist

ciento *pron* a *o* one hundred; *cientos de* hundreds of; *el cinco por ciento* five percent

ciernes: *en ciernes* *fig* potential, in the making

cierre *m* fastener; *de negocio* closure; *cierre centralizado* AUTO central locking; *cierre relámpago* *L.Am.* zipper, *Br* zip

cierto *adj* certain; *hasta cierto punto* up to a point; *cierto encanto* a certain charm; *es cierto* it's true; *cierto día* one day; *por cierto* incidentally; *estar en lo cierto* be right

ciervo *m* ZO deer; *ciervo volante* ZO stag beetle

c.i.f. *abr* (= **costo, seguro y flete**) cif (= cost, insurance, freight)

cifra *f* figure

cigala *f* ZO crayfish

cigarra *f* ZO cicada

cigarrería *f L.Am.* shop selling cigarettes etc

cigarrillo *m* cigarette

cigarro *m* cigar; *L.Am.* cigarette

cigüeña *f* ZO stork

cigüeñal *m* AUTO crankshaft

cilantro *m* BOT coriander

cilindrada *f* AUTO cubic capacity

cilíndrico *adj* cylindrical

cilindro *m* cylinder

cima *f* summit; *fig* peak

cimarrón *adj L.Am.* animal wild; *esclavo* runaway; *mate cimarrón* *Arg* unsweetened maté

cimentar ⟨1k⟩ *v/t* lay the foundations of; *fig* base (*en* on)

cimientos *mpl* foundations

cinc *m* zinc

cincel *m* chisel

cinco 1 *adj* five **2** *m* five; *no tener ni cinco* F not have a red cent F

cincuenta *adj* fifty

cincuentón *m* man in his fifties

cincuentona *f* woman in her fifties

cine *m* movies *pl*, cinema

cineasta *m/f* film-maker

cinéfilo *m*, *-a f* movie buff

cinematográfico *adj* movie *atr*

cinético *adj* kinetic

cínico 1 *adj* cynical **2** *m*, *-a f* cynic

cinismo *m* cynicism

cinta *f* ribbon; *de música*, *vídeo* tape; *cinta adhesiva* adhesive tape; *cinta aislante* electrical tape, friction tape, *Br* insulating tape; *cinta métrica* tape measure; *cinta de vídeo* video tape

cintura *f* waist

cinturón *m* belt; *cinturón de seguridad* AUTO seatbelt

cíper *m Méx* zipper, *Br* zip

ciprés *m* BOT cypress

circo *m* circus

circuito *m* circuit; *corto circuito* EL short circuit

circulación *f* movement; FIN, MED circulation; AUTO traffic; *poner en circulación* put into circulation

circular 1 *adj* circular **2** ⟨1a⟩ *v/i* circulate; AUTO drive, travel; *de persona* move (along)

círculo *m* circle; *círculo vicioso* vicious circle

circuncisión *f* circumcision

circundante *adj* surrounding

circunferencia *f* circumference

circunscribir ⟨3a; *part* **circunscrito**⟩ *v/t* limit (*a* to)

circunscripción *f* POL electoral district, *Br* constituency

circunspecto *adj* circumspect, cautious

circunstancia *f* circumstance

circunstancial *adj* circumstantial

circunvalación *f*: *(carretera de) circunvalación* beltway, *Br* ring-road

cirio *m* candle; *armar or montar un cirio* F kick up a fuss F

ciruela *f* plum; *ciruela pasa* prune

cirugía *f* surgery; *cirugía estética* cosmetic surgery

cirujano *m*, **-a** *f* surgeon

cisco *m*: *hacer cisco* smash

cisne *m* ZO swan

cisterna *f de WC* cistern

cistitis *f* MED cystitis

cita *f* appointment; *de texto* quote, quotation

citar ⟨1a⟩ **1** *v/t a reunión* arrange to meet; *a juicio* summon; *(mencionar)* mention; *de texto* quote **2** *v/r citarse* arrange to meet

citología *f* smear test

cítrico *m* citrus fruit

ciudad *f* town; *más grande* city; *ciudad universitaria* university campus

ciudadano *m*, **-a** *f* citizen

cívico *adj* civic

civil *adj* civil; *casarse por lo civil* have a civil wedding

civilización *f* civilization

civismo *m* civility

cizaña *f*: *sembrar or meter cizaña* cause trouble

cl. *abr (= centilitro)* cl. (= centiliter)

clamar ⟨1a⟩ *v/i*: *clamar por algo* clamo(u)r for sth, cry out for sth

clamor *m* roar; *fig* clamo(u)r

clan *m* clan

clandestino *adj* POL clandestine, underground

claqué *m* tap-dancing

clara *f de huevo*; *bebida* beer with lemonade, *Br* shandy

claraboya *f* skylight

claridad *f* light; *fig* clarity

clarificar ⟨1g⟩ *v/t* clarify

clarinete *m* clarinet

clarividente *m/f* clairvoyant

claro *adj tb fig* clear; *color* light; *(luminoso)* bright; *salsa* thin; *¡claro!* of course!; *hablar claro* speak plainly

clase *f* class; *(variedad)* kind, sort; *clase particular* private class; *dar clase (s)* teach

clásico *adj* classical

clasificación *f* DEP league table

clasificar ⟨1g⟩ **1** *v/t* classify **2** *v/r clasificarse* DEP qualify

claudicar ⟨1g⟩ *v/i* give in

claustro *m* ARQUI cloister

claustrofobia *f* claustrophobia

cláusula *f* clause

clausurar ⟨1a⟩ *v/t acto oficial* close; *por orden oficial* close down

clavadiste *m/f Méx* diver

clavado *adj*: *ser clavado a alguien* be the spitting image of s.o.

clavar ⟨1a⟩ **1** *v/t* stick (*en* into); *clavos, estaca* drive (*en* into); *uñas* sink (*en* into); *clavar los ojos en alguien* fix one's eyes on s.o.; *clavar a alguien por algo* F overcharge s.o. for sth **2** *v/r clavarse: clavarse un cuchillo en la mano* stick a knife into one's hand

clave 1 *f* key; *en clave* in code **2** *adj (importante)* key

clavel *m* BOT carnation

clavícula *f* ANAT collarbone

clavija *f* EL pin

clavo *m de metal* nail; GASTR clove; *CSur* F *persona* dead loss F; *dar en el clavo* hit the nail on the head

claxon *m* AUTO horn

clemencia *f* clemency, mercy

clementina *f* BOT clementine

clérigo *m* priest, clergyman

clero *m* clergy

clic *m* INFOR click; *hacer clic en* click on

cliché *m* cliché

clienta, cliente *m/f de tienda* customer; *de empresa* client

clientela *f* clientele, customers *pl*

clima *m* climate

climatizado *adj* air-conditioned
climatizar ⟨1f⟩ *v/t* air-condition
clímax *m fig* climax
clínica *f* clinic
clínico *adj* clinical
clip *m para papeles* paperclip; *para el pelo* bobby pin, *Br* hairgrip
cloaca *f tb fig* sewer
clon *m* BIO clone
clonación *f* BIO cloning
clonar ⟨1a⟩ *v/t* clone
cloro *m* QUÍM chlorine
clóset *m L.Am.* closet, *Br* wardrobe
club *m* club; **club náutico** yacht club
cm *abr* (= *centímetro*) cm (= centimeter)
coacción *f* coercion
coaccionar ⟨1a⟩ *v/t* coerce
coagular ⟨1a⟩ **1** *v/t* coagulate; *sangre* clot **2** *v/r* **coagularse** coagulate; *de sangre* clot
coágulo *m* clot
coala *m* ZO koala
coalición *f* coalition
coaligarse ⟨1h⟩ *v/r tb* POL work together, join forces
coartada *f* JUR alibi
coba *f*: *dar coba a alguien* F soft-soap s.o. F
cobarde 1 *adj* cowardly **2** *m/f* coward
cobaya *m/f* guinea pig
cobertizo *m* shed
cobertor *m* (*manta*) blanket
cobertura *f* cover; TV *etc* coverage
cobija *f L.Am.* blanket
cobijar ⟨1a⟩ *v/t* give shelter to; (*acoger*) take in **2** *v/r* **cobijarse** take shelter
cobijo *m* shelter, refuge
cobra *f* ZO cobra
cobrador *m*, **cobradora** *f a domicilio* collector
cobrar ⟨1a⟩ **1** *v/t* charge; *subsidio, pensión* receive; *deuda* collect; *cheque* cash; *salud, fuerzas* recover; *importancia* acquire **2** *v/i* be paid, get paid; *vas a cobrar* F (*recibir un palo*) you're going to get it! F
cobre *m* copper
cobro *m* charging; *de subsidio* receipt; *de deuda* collection; *de cheque* cashing
coca *f* F *droga* coke F; *de coca Méx* free
cocacho *m S. Am.* F whack on the head F
cocada *f L.Am.* coconut cookie
cocaína *f* cocaine
cocainómano *m*, *-a f* cocaine addict
cocción *f* cooking; *en agua* boiling; *al horno* baking
cocer ⟨2b & 2h⟩ **1** *v/t* cook; *en agua* boil; *al horno* bake **2** *v/r* **cocerse** cook; *en agua* boil; *al horno* bake; *fig* F *de persona*

be roasting F
cochambroso *adj* F filthy
coche *m* car; *Méx* (*taxi*) cab, taxi; *coche de caballos* horse-drawn carriage; *co-che cama* sleeping car; *coche comedor L.Am.* dining car; *coche de línea* (long--distance) bus
cochecito *m*: *cochecito de niño* stroller, *Br* pushchair
cochera *f* garage; *de trenes* locomotive shed
cochina *f* sow; F *persona* pig F
cochino 1 *adj fig* filthy, dirty; (*asqueroso*) disgusting **2** *m* hog, *Br* pig; F *persona* pig F
cocido 1 *adj* boiled **2** *m* stew
cociente *m* quotient
cocina *f habitación* kitchen; *aparato* cooker, stove; *actividad* cooking; *cocina de gas* gas cooker *o* stove
cocinar ⟨1a⟩ **1** *v/t* cook; *fig* F plot **2** *v/i* cook
cocinero *m*, *-a f* cook
coco *m* BOT coconut; *monstruo* bogeyman F; *comer el coco a alguien* F softsoap s.o.; *más fuerte* brainwash s.o.
cocodrilo *m* crocodile
cocoliche *m Arg* pidgin Spanish
cocotazo *m L.Am.* F whack on the head F
cocotero *m* coconut palm
cóctel *m* cocktail; *cóctel Molotov* Molotov cocktail
cód *abr* (= *código*) code
codazo *m*: *darle a alguien un codazo* elbow s.o.
codearse ⟨1a⟩ *v/r*: *codearse con alguien* rub shoulders with s.o.
codicia *f* greed
codiciar ⟨1b⟩ *v/t* covet
codicioso *adj* greedy
codificado *adj* TV encrypted
código *m* code; *código de barras* COM barcode; *código postal* zip code, *Br* postcode
codo *m* ANAT elbow; *codo con codo fig* F side by side; *hablar por los codos* F talk nineteen to the dozen F
codorniz *f* ZO quail
coeficiente *m* coefficient
coetáneo *m*, *-a f* contemporary
coexistir ⟨3a⟩ *v/i* coexist (*con* with)
cofradía *f* fraternity; (*gremio*) guild
cofre *m de tesoro* chest; *para alhajas* jewel(le)ry box
coger ⟨2c⟩ **1** *v/t* (*asir*) take (hold of); *del suelo* pick up; *ladrón, enfermedad* catch; TRANSP catch, take; (*entender*) get; *L.Am.* V screw V **2** *v/i en un espacio* fit; *L.Am.* V screw V; *coger por la prime-*

ra a la derecha take the first right **3** v/r **cogerse** hold on (tight); *cogerse de algo* hold on to sth

cogorza f: *agarrar una cogorza* F get plastered F

cogote m F nape of the neck

cohabitar ⟨1a⟩ v/i live together, cohabit

cohecho m JUR bribery

coherencia f coherence

coherente adj coherent; *ser coherente con* be consistent with

cohesión f cohesion

cohete m rocket

cohibir ⟨3a⟩ v/t inhibit

COI abr (= *Comité Olímpico Internacional*) IOC (= International Olympic Committee)

coima f L.Am. bribe

coincidencia f coincidence

coincidir ⟨3a⟩ v/i coincide

coito m intercourse

cojear ⟨1a⟩ v/i de persona limp, hobble; de mesa, silla wobble

cojera f limp

cojín m cushion

cojo adj persona lame; mesa, silla wobbly

cojón m V ball V

cojonudo adj P awesome F, brilliant

col. abr (= *columna*) col. (= column)

col f cabbage; *col de Bruselas* Brussels sprout

cola¹ f (*pegamento*) glue

cola² f (*de animal*) tail; *de gente* line, Br queue; L.Am. F de persona butt F, Br bum F; *hacer cola* stand in line, Br queue; *estar a la cola* be in last place

colaboración f collaboration

colaborador m, **colaboradora** f collaborator; en periódico contributor

colaborar ⟨1a⟩ v/i collaborate

colación f: *traer* or *sacar a colación* bring up

colada f: *hacer la colada* do the laundry o washing

colado adj: *estar colado por alguien* F be nuts about s.o. F

colador m colander; para té etc strainer

colapsar ⟨1a⟩ **1** v/t paralyze; *colapsar el tráfico* bring traffic to a standstill **2** v/r *colapsarse* grind to a halt

colapso m collapse; *provocar un colapso en la ciudad* bring the city to a standstill

colar ⟨1m⟩ **1** v/t líquido strain; billete falso pass; *colar algo por la aduana* F smuggle sth through customs **2** v/i fig F: *no cuela* I'm not buying it F **3** v/r *colarse* F en un lugar get in; en una fiesta gatecrash; en una cola cut in line, Br push in

colcha f L.Am. bedspread

colchón m mattress; fig buffer

colchoneta f DEP mat; hinchable air bed

cole m F school

colección f collection

coleccionar ⟨1a⟩ v/t collect

coleccionista m/f collector

colecta f collection

colectivero m, **-a** f Arg bus driver

colectivo 1 adj collective **2** m L.Am. bus; Méx, C.Am. taxi

colega m/f colleague; F pal

colegiado m, **-a** f DEP referee

colegial m student, schoolboy

colegiala f student, schoolgirl

colegio m school; *colegio electoral* electoral college; *colegio profesional* professional institute

cólera 1 f anger; *montar en cólera* get in a rage **2** m MED cholera

colesterol m cholesterol

coleta f ponytail, *coletas* de pelo bunches

colgado adj: *dejar colgado a alguien* F let s.o. down

colgador m L.Am. hanger

colgante 1 adj hanging **2** m pendant

colgar ⟨1h & 1m⟩ **1** v/t hang; TELEC put down **2** v/i hang (*de* from); fig hang up **3** v/r *colgarse* hang o.s.; INFOR F lock up; *colgarse de algo* hang from sth; *colgarse de alguien* hang onto s.o.

colibrí m ZO hummingbird

cólico m MED colic

coliflor f cauliflower

colilla f cigarette end

colina f hill

colindante adj adjoining

colirio m MED eye drops pl

colisión f collision; fig clash

colisionar ⟨1a⟩ v/i collide (*con* with)

colitis f MED colitis

collar m necklace; para animal collar

colleras fpl Chi cuff links

colmar ⟨1a⟩ v/t deseos, ambición etc fulfill; *colmar un vaso* fill a glass to the brim; *colmar a alguien de elogios* heap praise on s.o.

colmena f beehive

colmillo m ANAT eye tooth; de perro fang; de elefante, rinoceronte tusk

colmo m: *¡es el colmo!* this is the last straw!; *para colmo* to cap it all

colocación f positioning, placing; (*trabajo*) position

colocar ⟨1g⟩ **1** v/t put, place; *colocar a alguien en un trabajo* get s.o. a job **2** v/r *colocarse* de persona position o.s.; *se colocó a mi lado* he stood next to me; *se colocaron en primer lugar* they

C

moved into first place

colofón m fig culmination

Colombia f Colombia

colombiano 1 adj Colombian **2** m, **-a** f Colombian

Colón Columbus

colonia f colony; **de viviendas** subdivision, Br estate; **perfume** cologne; **colonia de verano** summer camp

colonial adj colonial

colonización f colonization

colonizar ⟨1f⟩ v/t colonize

coloquial adj colloquial

coloquio m talk

color m colo(u)r; **color café** coffee-colo(u)red; L.Am. brown

colorado adj red

colorante m colo(u)ring

colorear ⟨1a⟩ v/t colo(u)r

colorete m blusher

colorido m colo(u)rs pl

colosal adj colossal

columna f column; **columna vertebral** ANAT spinal column

columnista m/f columnist

columpiar ⟨1b⟩ **1** v/t swing **2** v/r columpiarse swing

columpio m swing

colza f BOT rape

coma 1 f GRAM comma **2** m MED coma

comadre f L.Am. godmother

comadrear ⟨1a⟩ v/i F gossip

comadrona f midwife

comandante m MIL commander; **rango** major; AVIA captain

comarca f area

comba f jump rope, Br skipping rope; **jugar** or **saltar a la comba** jump rope, Br skip

combate m acción combat; MIL engagement; DEP fight; **fuera de combate** out of action

combatir ⟨3a⟩ v/t & v/i fight

combi m Méx minibus

combinación f combination; **prenda** slip; **hacer combinación** TRANSP change

combinar ⟨1a⟩ v/t combine

combustible m fuel

combustión f combustion

comedia f comedy

comedianta f actress

comediante m actor

comedido adj moderate

comedor m dining room

comején m termite

comensal m/f diner

comentar ⟨1a⟩ v/t comment on

comentario m comment; **comentario de texto** textual analysis; **comentarios** pl gossip sg

comentarista m/f commentator

comenzar ⟨1f & 1k⟩ v/t begin

comer ⟨2a⟩ **1** v/t eat; **a mediodía** have for lunch **2** v/i eat; **a mediodía** have lunch; **dar de comer a alguien** feed s.o. **3** v/r **comerse** tb fig eat up; **se comió una palabra** she missed out a word; **está para comértela** F she's really tasty F

comercial 1 adj commercial; **de negocios** business atr; **el déficit comercial** the trade deficit **2** m/f representative

comercializar ⟨1f⟩ v/t market, sell; desp commercialize

comerciante m/f trader; **comerciante al por menor** retailer

comercio m actividad trade; local store, shop; **comercio exterior** foreign trade

comestible 1 adj eatable, edible **2** m foodstuff; **comestibles** pl food sg

cometa 1 m comet **2** f kite

cometer ⟨2a⟩ v/t commit; error make

cometido m task

comezón f itch

cómic m comic

comicios mpl elections pl

cómico 1 adj comical **2** m, **-a** f comedian

comida f (comestibles) food; ocasión meal

comienzo m beginning

comillas fpl quotation marks, inverted commas

comino m BOT cumin; **me importa un comino** F I don't give a damn F

comisaría f precinct, Br police station

comisario m commissioner; **de policía** captain, Br superintendent

comisión f committee; **de gobierno** commission; (recompensa) commission

comité m committee

comitiva f retinue

como 1 adv as; **así como** as well as; **había como cincuenta** there were about fifty **2** conj if; **como si** as if; **como no bebas vas a enfermar** if you don't drink you'll get sick; **como no llegó, me fui solo** o since she didn't arrive, I went by myself

cómo adv how; **¿cómo estás?** how are you?; **¡cómo me gusta!** I really like it; **me gusta cómo habla** I like the way he talks; **¿cómo dice?** what did you say?; **¡cómo no!** Méx of course!

cómoda f chest of drawers

comodidad f comfort

comodín m en naipes joker

cómodo adj comfortable

comp. abr (= **compárese**) cf (= confer)

compacto adj compact

compadecer ⟨2d⟩ **1** v/t feel sorry for **2** v/r

compadecerse feel sorry (**de** for)
compadre *m L.Am.* F buddy F
compadrear ⟨1a⟩ *v/i Arg* F brag
compadrito *m Arg* F show-off
compaginar ⟨1a⟩ *v/t fig* combine
compañero *m*, **-a** *f* companion; *en una relación, un juego* partner; **compañero de trabajo** coworker, colleague; **compañero de clase** classmate
compañía *f* company; **hacer compañía a alguien** keep s.o. company
comparación *f* comparison; **en comparación con** in comparison with
comparado *adj*: **comparado con** compared with
comparar ⟨1a⟩ *v/t* compare
comparecencia *f JUR* appearance
comparecer ⟨2d⟩ *v/i* appear
compartir ⟨3a⟩ *v/t* share (**con** with)
compás *m MAT* compass; *MUS* rhythm; **al compás** to the beat
compasión *f* compassion
compatibilidad *f* compatibility
compatible *adj INFOR* compatible
compatriota *m/f* compatriot
compendio *m* summary
compenetrado *adj*: **están muy compenetrados** they are very much in tune with each other
compenetrarse ⟨1a⟩ *v/r*: **compenetrarse con alguien** reach a good understanding with s.o.
compensación *f* compensation
compensar ⟨1a⟩ **1** *v/t* compensate (**por** for) **2** *v/i fig* be worthwhile
competencia *f* (*habilidad*) competence; *entre rivales* competition; (*incumbencia*) area of responsibility, competency; **competencia desleal** unfair competition
competente *adj* competent
competición *f DEP* competition
competir ⟨3l⟩ *v/i* compete (**con** with)
competitivo *adj* competitive
compilar ⟨1a⟩ *v/t* compile
compinche *m/f* F buddy F; *desp* crony F
complacencia *f* (*placer*) pleasure; (*tolerancia*) indulgence
complacer ⟨2x⟩ *v/t* please
complaciente *adj* obliging, helpful
complejidad *f* complexity
complejo 1 *adj* complex **2** *m PSI* complex; **complejo de inferioridad** inferiority complex
complementar ⟨1a⟩ *v/t* complement
complemento *m* complement; *GRAM* complement, object; **complementos de moda** fashion accessories
completar ⟨1a⟩ *v/t* complete
completo *adj* complete; *autobús, teatro*

full; **por completo** completely
complicación *f* complication
complicado *adj* complicated
complicar ⟨1g⟩ **1** *v/t* complicate **2** *v/r* **complicarse** get complicated; **complicarse la vida** make things difficult for o.s.
cómplice *m/f* accomplice
complot *m* plot
componente *m* component
componer ⟨2r; *part* **compuesto** ⟩**1** *v/t* make up, comprise; *sinfonía, poema etc* compose; *algo roto* fix, mend **2** *v/r* **componerse** be made up (**de** of); *L.Am. MED* get better
comportamiento *m* behavio(u)r
comportarse ⟨1a⟩ *v/r* behave
composición *f* composition
compositor *m*, **compositora** *f* composer
compostura *f fig* composure
compota *f* compote
compra *f acción* purchase; (*cosa comprada*) purchase, buy; **ir de compras** go shopping
comprar ⟨1a⟩ *v/t* buy, purchase
compraventa *f* buying and selling
comprender ⟨2a⟩ *v/t* understand; (*abarcar*) include
comprensión *f* understanding; *de texto, auditiva* comprehension
comprensivo *adj* understanding
compresa *f* sanitary napkin, *Br* sanitary towel
compresión *f tb INFOR* compression
comprimido *m MED* pill
comprimir ⟨3a⟩ *v/t* compress
comprobación *f* check
comprobar ⟨1m⟩ *v/t* check; (*darse cuenta de*) realize
comprometer ⟨2a⟩ **1** *v/t* compromise; (*obligar*) commit **2** *v/r* **comprometerse** promise (**a** to); *a una causa* commit o.s.; *de novios* get engaged
comprometido *adj* committed; **estar comprometido en algo** be implicated in sth; **estar comprometido de novios** be engaged
compromiso *m* commitment; (*obligación*) obligation; (*acuerdo*) agreement; (*apuro*) awkward situation; **sin compromiso** COM without commitment; **soltero y sin compromiso** F footloose and fancy-free
compuesto 1 *part* → **componer 2** *adj* composed; **estar compuesto de** be composed of
compulsar ⟨1a⟩ *v/t* certify
compulsivo *adj PSI* compulsive
computación *f L.Am.* computer science

computadora f L.Am. computer; *computadora de escritorio* desktop (computer); *computadora personal* personal computer; *computadora portátil* laptop

computarizar ⟨1f⟩ v/t computerize

comulgar ⟨1h⟩ v/i take communion; *comulgar con alguien (en algo)* fig F think the same way as s.o. (on sth)

común adj common; *por lo común* generally

comuna f commune; L.Am. (*población*) town

comunicación f communication; TRANSP link

comunicado 1 adj connected; *el lugar está bien comunicado* the place has good transport links 2 m POL press release, communiqué

comunicar ⟨1g⟩ 1 v/t TRANSP connect, link; *comunicar algo a alguien* inform s.o. of sth 2 v/i communicate; TELEC busy, Br tb be engaged 3 v/r comunicarse communicate

comunidad f community; *comunidad autónoma* autonomous region

comunión f REL communion

comunismo m Communism

comunista m/f & adj Communist

comunitario adj POL EU atr, Community atr

con prp with; *voy con ellos* I'm going with them; *pan con mantequilla* bread and butter; *con todo eso* in spite of all that; *con tal de que* provided that, as long as; *con hacer eso* by doing that

conato m: *conato de violencia* minor outbreak of violence; *conato de incendio* small fire

cóncavo adj concave

concebir ⟨3l⟩ v/t conceive

conceder ⟨2a⟩ v/t concede; entrevista, permiso give; premio award

concejal m, concejala f council(l)or

concentración f concentration; de personas gathering

concentrar ⟨1a⟩ 1 v/t concentrate 2 v/r concentrarse concentrate (*en* on); de gente gather

concepto m concept; *en concepto de algo* COM (in payment) for sth; *bajo ningún concepto* on no account

concernir ⟨3i⟩ v/i concern; *en lo que concierne a X* as far as X is concerned

concertar ⟨1k⟩ v/t cita arrange; precio agree; esfuerzos coordinate

concesión f concession; COM dealership; *hacer concesiones* make concessions

concesionario m dealer

concha f zo shell

conchabar ⟨1a⟩ 1 v/t L.Am. trabajador hire 2 v/r conchabarse F plot

conciencia f conscience; *a conciencia* conscientiously; *con plena conciencia de* fully conscious of

concienciar ⟨1b⟩ v/t: *concienciar a alguien de algo* make s.o. aware of sth 2 v/r concienciarse realize (*de* sth)

concienzudo adj conscientious

concierto m MÚS concert; fig agreement

conciliador adj conciliatory

conciliar ⟨1b⟩ v/t reconcile; *conciliar el sueño* get to sleep

conciso adj concise

concluir ⟨3g⟩ v/t & v/i conclude

conclusión f conclusion; *en conclusión* in short

concretar ⟨1a⟩ 1 v/t specify; (*hacer concreto*) realize 2 v/r concretarse materialize; de esperanzas be fulfilled

concreto 1 adj specific; (*no abstracto*) concrete; *en concreto* specifically 2 m L.Am. concrete

concurrencia f audience; de circunstancias combination

concurrido adj crowded

concursante m/f competitor

concursar ⟨1a⟩ v/i compete

concurso m competition; COM tender

conde m count

condecoración f decoration

condecorar ⟨1a⟩ decorate

condena f JUR sentence; (*desaprobación*) condemnation

condenar ⟨1a⟩ v/t JUR sentence (*a* to); (*desaprobar*) condemn

condensación f condensation

condensado adj condensed

condensar ⟨1a⟩ 1 v/t condense; libro abridge 2 v/r condensarse condense

condesa f countess

condescendiente adj actitud accommodating; desp condescending

condición f condition; *a condición de que* on condition that; *estar en condiciones de* be in a position to

condimentar ⟨1a⟩ flavo(u)r

condimento m seasoning

condón m condom

cóndor m zo condor

conducir ⟨3o⟩ 1 v/t vehículo drive; (*dirigir*) lead (*a* to); EL, TÉC conduct 2 v/i drive; de camino lead (*a* to)

conducta f conduct, behavio(u)r

conducto m pipe; fig channel; *por conducto de* through

conductor m, conductora f driver; *conductor de orquesta* L.Am. conductor

condujo vb → conducir

conectar ⟨1a⟩ v/t connect, link; EL connect

conejillo m: **conejillo de Indias** tb fig guinea pig

conejo m rabbit

conexión f tb EL connection

confabularse ⟨1a⟩ v/r plot

confección f making; de vestidos dressmaking; de trajes tailoring

confeccionar ⟨1a⟩ v/t make

confederación f confederation

conferencia f lecture; (reunión) conference; TELEC long-distance call

conferenciante m/f lecturer

conferencista m/f L.Am. lecturer

conferir ⟨3i⟩ v/t award

confesar ⟨1k⟩ 1 v/t REL confess; delito confess to, admit 2 v/i JUR confess 3 v/r **confesarse** confess; (declararse) admit to being

confesión f confession

confeti m confetti

confiado adj trusting

confianza f confidence; **confianza en sí mismo** self-confidence; **de confianza** persona trustworthy; **amigo de confianza** good friend

confiar ⟨1c⟩ 1 v/t secreto confide (**a** to); **confiar algo a alguien** entrust s.o. with sth, entrust sth to s.o. 2 v/i trust (**en** in); (estar seguro) be confident (**en** of)

confidencia f confidence

confidencial adj confidential

configuración f configuration; INFOR set-up, configuration

configurar ⟨1a⟩ v/t shape; INFOR set up, configure

confinar ⟨1a⟩ v/t confine

confirmación f confirmation

confirmar ⟨1a⟩ v/t confirm

confiscar ⟨1g⟩ v/t confiscate

confitería f confectioner's

confitura f preserve

conflagración f conflagration; (guerra) war

conflicto m conflict

conformarse ⟨1a⟩ v/r make do (**con** with)

conforme 1 adj satisfied (**con** with) 2 prp: **conforme a** in accordance with

confortable adj comfortable

confrontación f confrontation

confundir ⟨3a⟩ 1 v/t confuse; (equivocar) mistake (**con** for) 2 v/r **confundirse** make a mistake; **confundirse de calle** get the wrong street

confusión f confusion

confuso adj confused

congelación f freezing; **congelación de precios / de salarios** price / wage freeze

congelado adj frozen

congelador m freezer

congelar ⟨1a⟩ 1 v/t freeze 2 v/r **congelarse** freeze

congeniar ⟨1b⟩ v/i get on well (**con** with)

congénito adj congenital

congestión f MED congestion; **congestión del tráfico** traffic congestion

congestionar ⟨1a⟩ v/t congest

congoja f anguish

congregar ⟨1h⟩ v/t bring together

congresal m/f L.Am., **congresista** m/f conference o convention delegate, conventioneer*

congreso m conference, convention; **Congreso** en EE.UU Congress; **congreso de los diputados** lower house of Spanish parliament

congrio m ZO conger eel

conjetura f conjecture

conjugar ⟨1h⟩ v/t GRAM conjugate; fig combine

conjunción f GRAM conjunction

conjuntivitis f MED conjunctivitis

conjunto 1 adj joint **2** m de personas, objetos collection; de prendas outfit; MAT set; **en conjunto** as a whole

conllevar ⟨1a⟩ v/t entail

conmemorar ⟨1a⟩ v/t commemorate

conmigo pron with me

conmoción f shock; (agitación) upheaval

conmocionar ⟨1a⟩ v/t shock

conmovedor adj moving

conmover ⟨2h⟩ 1 v/t move 2 v/r **conmoverse** be moved

conmutador m EL switch; L.Am. TELEC switchboard

connotación f connotation

cono m cone

conocer ⟨2d⟩ 1 v/t know; por primera vez meet; tristeza, amor etc experience, know; (reconocer) recognize; **dar a conocer** make known 2 v/r **conocerse** know one another; por primera vez meet one another; a sí mismo know o.s.; **se conoce que** it seems that

conocido 1 adj well-known **2** m, -a f acquaintance

conocimiento m knowledge; MED consciousness; **perder el conocimiento** lose consciousness

conquista f conquest

conquistar ⟨1a⟩ v/t conquer; persona win over

consabido adj usual

consagrar ⟨1a⟩ 1 v/t REL consecrate; (hacer famoso) make famous; vida devote 2 v/r **consagrarse** devote o.s. (**a** to)

consciente adj MED conscious; **conscien-**

te de aware of, conscious of

consecuencia f consequence; **a consecuencia de** as a result of; **en consecuencia** consequently

consecuente adj consistent

consecutivo adj consecutive; **tres años consecutivos** three years in a row

conseguir ⟨3l & 3d⟩ v/t get; *objetivo* achieve

consejero m, **-a** f adviser; COM director

consejo m piece of advice; **consejo de administración** board of directors; **consejo de ministros** grupo cabinet; *reunión* cabinet meeting

consenso m consensus

consentido adj spoilt

consentimiento m consent

consentir ⟨3i⟩ **1** v/t allow; *a niño* indulge **2** v/i: **consentir en algo** agree to sth

conserje m/f superintendent, *Br* caretaker

conserva f: **en conserva** canned, *Br* tinned; **conservas** pl canned (*Br* tinned) food sg

conservación f *de alimentos* preservation; *de edificios, especies* conservation

conservador adj conservative

conservante m preservative

conservar ⟨1a⟩ **1** v/t conserve; *alimento* preserve **2** v/r **conservarse** survive

conservatorio m conservatory

considerable adj considerable

consideración f consideration

considerar ⟨1a⟩ v/t consider

consigna f order; *de equipaje* baggage room, *Br* left-luggage

consigo pron with him / her; (*con usted, con ustedes*) with you; (*con uno*) with you, with one fml

consiguiente adj consequent; **por consiguiente** and so, therefore

consistencia f consistency

consistente adj consistent; (*sólido*) solid

consistir ⟨3a⟩ v/i consist (**en** of)

consola f INFOR console

consolar ⟨1m⟩ v/t console

consolidar ⟨1a⟩ **1** v/t consolidate **2** v/r **consolidarse** strengthen

consomé m GASTR consommé

consonancia f: **en consonancia con** in keeping with

consonante f consonant

consorte m/f spouse

conspiración f conspiracy

conspirar ⟨1a⟩ v/i conspire

constancia f constancy; **dejar constancia de** leave a record of

constante adj constant

constar ⟨1a⟩ v/i be recorded; **constar de**

consist of

constatación f verification

constatar ⟨1a⟩ v/t verify

constelación f AST constellation

consternar ⟨1a⟩ v/t dismay

constipado 1 adj: **estar constipado** have a cold **2** m cold

constiparse ⟨1a⟩ v/r get a cold

constitución f constitution

constituir ⟨3g⟩ v/t constitute, make up; *empresa, organismo* set up

construcción f construction; (*edificio*) building

construir ⟨3g⟩ v/t build, construct

consuelo m consolation

cónsul m/f consul

consulado m consulate

consulta f consultation; MED *local* office, *Br* surgery

consultar ⟨1a⟩ v/t consult

consultor m, **consultora** f consultant

consultoría f consultancy

consultorio m MED office, *Br* surgery

consumidor m, **consumidora** f COM consumer

consumir ⟨3a⟩ **1** v/t consume **2** v/r **consumirse** waste away

consumo m consumption; **de bajo consumo** economical

contabilidad f accountancy; **llevar la contabilidad** do the accounts

contable m/f accountant

contactar ⟨1a⟩ v/i: **contactar con alguien** contact s.o.

contacto m contact; AUTO ignition; **ponerse en contacto** get in touch (**con** with)

contado adj: **al contado** in cash

contador 1 m meter **2** m, **contadora** f *L.Am.* accountant

contagiar ⟨1b⟩ **1** v/t: **contagiar la gripe a alguien** give s.o. the flu; **nos contagió su entusiasmo** he infected us with his enthusiasm **2** v/r **contagiarse** become infected

contagioso adj contagious

contaminación f *de agua etc* contamination; *de río, medio ambiente* pollution

contaminar ⟨1a⟩ v/t contaminate; *río, medio ambiente* pollute

contar ⟨1m⟩ **1** v/t count; (*narrar*) tell **2** v/i count; **contar con** count on

contemplación f: **sin contemplaciones** without ceremony

contemplar ⟨1a⟩ v/t (*mirar*) look at, contemplate; *posibilidad* consider

contemporáneo 1 adj contemporary **2** m, **-a** f contemporary

contenedor m TRANSP container; **conte-**

convexo

nedor de basura dumpster, *Br* skip;
contenedor de vidrio bottle bank
contener ⟨2l⟩ **1** *v/t* contain; *respiración*
hold; *muchedumbre* hold back **2** *v/r* contenerse control o.s.
contenido *m* content
contentarse ⟨1a⟩ *v/r* be satisfied (**con**
with)
contento *adj* (*satisfecho*) pleased, (*feliz*)
happy
contestación *f* answer
contestador *m*: **contestador automático** TELEC answer machine
contestar ⟨1a⟩ **1** *v/t* answer, reply to **2** *v/i*
reply (**a** to), answer (**a** sth); *de forma insolente* answer back
contexto *m* context
contigo *pron* with you
contiguo *adj* adjoining, adjacent
continental *adj* continental
continente *m* continent
continuación *f* continuation; **a continuación** (*ahora*) now; (*después*) then
continuar ⟨1e⟩ **1** *v/t* continue **2** *v/i* continue; **continuar haciendo algo** continue *o*
carry on doing sth
continuidad *f* continuity
continuo *adj* (*sin parar*) continuous; (*frecuente*) continual
contorno *m* outline
contra *prp* against; **en contra de** against
contraataque *m* counterattack
contrabajo *m* double bass
contrabandista *m/f* smuggler
contrabando *m* contraband, smuggled
goods *pl*; *acción* smuggling; **hacer contrabando** smuggle; **pasar algo de contrabando** smuggle sth in
contracción *f* contraction
contraceptivo *m/adj* contraceptive
contradecir ⟨3p⟩ *v/t* contradict
contradicción *f* contradiction
contradictorio *adj* contradictory
contraer ⟨2p; *part* contraído⟩ **1** *v/t* contract, *músculo* tighten; **contraer matrimonio** marry **2** *v/r* contraerse contract
contraindicación *f* MED contraindication
contraluz *f*: **a contraluz** against the light
contrapartida *f* COM balancing entry; **como contrapartida** fig in contrast
contrapeso *m* counterweight
contraposición *f*: **en contraposición a**
in comparison to
contraproducente *adj* counterproduc-
tive
contrariedad *f* setback; (*disgusto*) annoyance
contrario **1** *adj* contrary; *sentido* opposite; *equipo* opposing; **al contrario,**

por el contrario on the contrary; **de lo
contrario** otherwise; **ser contrario a algo** be opposed to sth; **llevar la -a a alguien** contradict s.o. **2** *m*, -a *f* adversary,
opponent
contrarreloj *f* DEP time trial
contrarrestar ⟨1a⟩ *v/t* counteract
contraseña *f* password
contrastar ⟨1a⟩ *v/t* & *v/i* contrast (**con**
with)
contraste *m* contrast
contratar ⟨1a⟩ *v/t* contract; *trabajadores*
hire
contratiempo *m* setback
contrato *m* contract
contravenir ⟨3s⟩ *v/i* contravene
contribución *f* contribution; (*impuesto*)
tax
contribuir ⟨3g⟩ *v/t* contribute (**a** to)
contribuyente *m/f* taxpayer
contrincante *m/f* opponent
control *m* control, (*inspección*) check;
control remoto remote control
controlador *m*, controladora *f*: **controlador aéreo** air traffic controller
controlar ⟨1a⟩ **1** *v/t* control; (*vigilar*)
check **2** *v/r* controlarse control o.s.
controversia *f* controversy
contundente *adj* *arma* blunt; *fig*: *derrota*
overwhelming
contusión *f* MED bruise
convalecencia *f* convalescence
convaleciente *m/f* convalescent
convalidar ⟨1a⟩ *v/t* recognize
convencer ⟨2b⟩ *v/t* convince
convención *f* convention
convencional *adj* conventional
conveniencia *f* de hacer algo advisability;
hacer algo por conveniencia do sth in
one's own interest
conveniente *adj* convenient; (*útil*) useful;
(*aconsejable*) advisable
convenio *m* agreement
convenir ⟨3s⟩ **1** *v/t* agree **2** *v/i* be advisable; **no te conviene** it's not in your interest; **convenir a alguien hacer algo** be in
s.o.'s interests to do sth
conventillo *m* CSur tenement
convento *m* de monjes monastery; *de
monjas* convent
converger ⟨2c⟩ *v/i* converge
conversación *f* conversation
conversar ⟨1a⟩ *v/i* make conversation
conversión *f* conversion
convertible **1** *adj* COM convertible **2** *m*
L.Am. convertible
convertir ⟨3i⟩ **1** *v/t* convert **2** *v/r* convertirse: **convertirse en algo** turn into sth
convexo *adj* convex

convicción *f* conviction
convidar ⟨1a⟩ *v/t* invite (**a** to)
convincente *adj* convincing
convivencia *f* living together
convivir ⟨3a⟩ *v/i* live together
convocar ⟨1g⟩ *v/t* summon; *huelga* call; *oposiciones* organize
convocatoria *f* announcement; *de huelga* call
convoy *m* convoy
convulsión *f* convulsion; *fig* upheaval
conyugal *adj* conjugal
cónyuge *m/f* spouse
coña *f*: **decir algo de coña** F say sth as a joke; **darle la coña a alguien** F bug s.o. F; **¡ni de coña!** F no way! F
coñac *m* (*pl* ~s) brandy, cognac
coño *m* V cunt V
cooperación *f* cooperation
cooperar ⟨1a⟩ *v/i* cooperate
cooperativa *f* cooperative
coordinación *f* coordination
coordinar ⟨1a⟩ *v/t* coordinate
copa *f de vino etc* glass; DEP cup; **tomar una copa** have a drink; **copas** *pl* (*en naipes*) suit in Spanish deck of cards
copia *f* copy; **copia pirata** pirate copy
copiar ⟨1b⟩ *v/t* copy
copiloto *m/f* copilot
copioso *adj* copious
copla *f* verse; (*canción*) popular song
copo *m* flake; **copo de nieve** snowflake; **copos de maíz** cornflakes
copropietario *m*, -a *f* co-owner, joint owner
coquetear ⟨1a⟩ *v/i* flirt
coquetería *f* flirtatiousness
coqueto *adj* flirtatious; *lugar* pretty
coraje *m* courage; **me da coraje** *fig* F it makes me mad F
corajudo *adj L.Am.* brave
coral[1] *m* ZO coral
coral[2] *f* MÚS choir
Corán *m* Koran
coraza *f* cuirasse; ZO shell; *fig* shield
corazón *m* heart; *de fruta* core
corazonada *f* hunch
corbata *f* tie
corcho *m* cork
cordel *m* string
cordero *m* lamb
cordial *adj* cordial
cordillera *f* mountain range
cordón *m* cord; *de zapato* shoelace; **cordón umbilical** ANAT umbilical cord
cordura *f* sanity; (*prudencia*) good sense
Corea Korea
coreano 1 *adj* Korean 2 *m*, -a *f* Korean
coreografía *f* choreography

cormorán *m* ZO cormorant
cornada *f* TAUR goring
corneja *f* ZO crow
córner *m en fútbol* corner (kick)
corneta *f* MIL bugle
cornisa *f* ARQUI cornice
cornudo 1 *adj* horned 2 *m* cuckold
coro *m* MÚS choir; *de espectáculo, pieza musical* chorus; **a coro** together, in chorus
corona *f* crown; **corona de flores** garland
coronar ⟨1a⟩ *v/t* crown
coronario *adj* MED coronary
coronel *m* MIL colonel
coronilla *f* ANAT crown; **estoy hasta la coronilla** F I've had it up to here F
corotos *mpl L.Am.* F bits and pieces
corporación *f* corporation
corporal *adj placer, estética* physical; *fluido* body *atr*
corpulento *adj* solidly built
corral *m* farmyard
correa *f* lead; *de reloj* strap
corrección *f* correction; *en el trato* correctness
correcto *adj* correct; (*educado*) polite
corredizo *adj* sliding
corredor 1 *m*, corredora *f* DEP runner; COM agent; **corredor de bolsa** stockbroker 2 *m* ARQUI corridor
corregir ⟨3c & 3l⟩ *v/t* correct
correlación *f* correlation
correligionario *m*, -a *f*: **sus correligionarios republicanos** his fellow republicans
correntada *f L.Am.* current
correntoso *adj L.Am.* fast-flowing
correo *m* mail, *Br tb* post; **correos** *pl* post office *sg*; **correo aéreo** airmail; **correo electrónico** e-mail; **por correo** by mail; **echar al correo** mail, *Br tb* post
correr ⟨2a⟩ 1 *v/i* run; (*apresurarse*) rush; *de tiempo* pass; *de agua* run, flow; *correr con los gastos* pay the expenses; **a todo correr** at top speed 2 *v/t* run; *cortinas* draw; *mueble* slide, move; **correr la misma suerte** suffer the same fate 3 *v/r* **correrse** move; *de tinta* run
correspondencia *f* correspondence; FERR connection (**con** with)
corresponder ⟨2a⟩ *v/i*: **corresponder a alguien** *de bienes* be for s.o., be due to s.o.; *de responsabilidad* be up to s.o.; *de asunto* concern s.o.; *a un favor* repay s.o. (**con** with); **actuar como corresponde** do the right thing
correspondiente *adj* corresponding
corresponsal *m/f* correspondent
corretear ⟨1a⟩ *v/i* run around

corrida f: **corrida de toros** bullfight

corrido adj: **decir algo de corrido** fig say sth parrot-fashion

corriente 1 adj (actual) current; (común) ordinary; **corriente y moliente** F run-of-the-mill; **estar al corriente** be up to date **2** f EL, de agua current; **corriente de aire** draft, Br draught

corro m ring

corroborar ⟨1a⟩ v/t corroborate

corroer ⟨2za⟩ v/t corrode; fig eat up

corromper ⟨2a⟩ **1** v/t corrupt **2** v/r **corromperse** become corrupted

corrosión f corrosion

corrosivo adj corrosive; fig caustic

corrupción f decay; fig corruption; **corrupción de menores** corruption of minors

corrupto adj corrupt

corsetería f lingerie store

cortacésped m lawnmower

cortacircuitos m inv circuit breaker

cortada f L.Am. cut

cortado 1 adj cut; calle closed; leche curdled; persona shy; **quedarse cortado** be embarrassed **2** m coffee with a dash of milk

cortar ⟨1a⟩ **1** v/t cut; electricidad cut off; calle close **2** v/i cut **3** v/r **cortarse** cut o.s.; fig F get embarrassed; **cortarse el pelo** have one's hair cut

cortaúñas m inv nail clippers pl

corte[1] m cut; **corte de luz** power outage; **corte de pelo** haircut; **corte de tráfico** road closure; **me da corte** F I'm embarrassed

corte[2] f court; L.Am. JUR (law) court; **las Cortes** Spanish parliament

cortejar ⟨1a⟩ v/t court

cortés adj courteous

cortesía f courtesy

corteza f de árbol bark; de pan crust; de queso rind

cortina f curtain

corto adj short; **corto de vista** nearsighted; **ni corto ni perezoso** as bold as brass; **quedarse corto** fall short

cortocircuito m EL short circuit

corzo m ZO roe deer

cosa f thing; **como si tal cosa** as if nothing had happened; **decir a alguien cuatro cosas** give s.o. a piece of one's mind; **eso es otra cosa** that's another matter; **¿qué pasa? – poca cosa** what's new? – nothing much

coscorrón m bump on the head

cosecha f harvest

cosechar ⟨1a⟩ v/t harvest; fig gain, win

coser ⟨2a⟩ v/t sew; **ser coser y cantar** F

be dead easy F

cosmético m/adj cosmetic

cósmico adj cosmic

cosmonauta m/f cosmonaut

cosmopolita adj cosmopolitan

cosmos m cosmos

cosmovisión f L.Am. world view

cosquillas fpl: **hacer cosquillas a alguien** tickle s.o.; **tener cosquillas** be ticklish

cosquilleo m tickle

costa[1] f: **a costa de** at the expense of; **a toda costa** at all costs

costa[2] f GEOG coast

costado m side; **por los cuatro costados** fig throughout, through and through

costar ⟨1m⟩ **1** v/t en dinero cost; trabajo, esfuerzo etc take; **¿cuánto cuesta?** how much does it cost? **2** v/i en dinero cost; **me costó** it was hard work; **cueste lo que cueste** at all costs; **costar caro** fig cost dear

Costa Rica Costa Rica

costarricense m/f & adj Costa Rican

coste m → **costo**

costear ⟨1a⟩ v/t pay for

costero adj coastal

costilla f ANAT rib; GASTR sparerib

costo m cost; **costo de la vida** cost of living

costoso adj costly

costra f MED scab

costumbre f custom, de una persona habit; **de costumbre** usual

costura f sewing

costurear ⟨1a⟩ v/t L.Am. sew

cotarro m: **manejar el cotarro** F be the boss F

cotejar ⟨1a⟩ v/t compare

cotidiano adj daily

cotilla m/f F gossip

cotillear ⟨1a⟩ v/i F gossip

cotizado adj F quoted; fig sought-after

cotizar ⟨1f⟩ v/i de trabajador pay social security, Br pay National Insurance; de acciones, bonos be listed (a at); **cotizar en bolsa** be listed on the stock exchange

coto[1] m: **coto de caza** hunting reserve; **poner coto a algo** fig put a stop to sth

coto[2] m S. Am. MED goiter, Br goitre

cotorra f ZO parrot; F persona motormouth F

coyote m ZO coyote

coyuntura f situation; ANAT joint

C.P. abr (= **código postal**) zip code, Br post code

cráneo m ANAT skull, cranium

cráter m crater

creación f creation

creador *m*, **creadora** *f* creator
crear ⟨1a⟩ *v/t* create; *empresa* set up
creativo *adj* creative
crecer ⟨2d⟩ *v/i* grow
creces *fpl*: **con creces** *superar* with a comfortable margin; *pagar* with interest
creciente *adj* growing; *luna* waxing
crecimiento *m* growth
credencial *f* document
credibilidad *f* credibility
crédito *m* COM credit; *a crédito* on credit; *no dar crédito a sus oídos / ojos* F not believe one's ears / eyes
credo *m* REL, *fig* creed
crédulo *adj* credulous
creencia *f* belief
creer ⟨2e⟩ **1** *v/i* believe (*en* in) **2** *v/t* think; (*dar por cierto*) believe; *no creo que esté aquí* I don't think he's here; *¡ya lo creo!* F you bet! F **3** *v/r* *creerse: creerse que ...* believe that ...; *se cree muy lista* she thinks she's very clever
crema *f* GASTR cream
cremallera *f* zipper, *Br* zip; TÉC rack
crematorio *m* crematorium
cremoso *adj* creamy
crepe *f* GASTR crêpe, pancake
crepitar ⟨1a⟩ *v/i* crackle
crepúsculo *m tb fig* twilight
cresta *f* crest
cretino *m*, **-a** *f* F cretin F, moron F
creyente 1 *adj*: *ser creyente* REL believe in God **2** *m* REL believer
creyó *vb* → **creer**
cría *f acción* breeding; *de zorro, león* cub; *de perro* puppy; *de gato* kitten; *de oveja* lamb; *sus crías* her young
criada *f* maid
criado *m* servant
criar ⟨1c⟩ **1** *v/t niños* raise, bring up; *animales* breed **2** *v/r* *criarse* grow up
criatura *f* creature; F (*niño*) baby, child
crimen *m* crime
criminal *m/f & adj* criminal
crío *m*, **-a** *f* F kid F
criollo 1 *adj* Creole **2** *m*, **-a** *f* Creole
cripta *f* crypt
crisantemo *m* BOT chrysanthemum
crisis *f inv* crisis
crismas *m inv* Christmas card
crispar ⟨1a⟩ *v/t* irritate; *crisparle a alguien los nervios* get on s.o.'s nerves
cristal *m* crystal; (*vidrio*) glass; (*lente*) lens; *de ventana* pane; *cristal líquido* liquid crystal
cristalizar ⟨1f⟩ *v/i* crystallize; *de idea, proyecto* jell
cristianismo *m* Christianity
cristiano 1 *adj* Christian **2** *m*, **-a** *f* Christian

Cristo Christ
criterio *m* criterion; (*juicio*) judg(e)ment
crítica *f* criticism; *muchas críticas* a lot of criticism
criticar ⟨1g⟩ *v/t* criticize
crítico 1 *adj* critical **2** *m*, **-a** *f* critic
Croacia Croatia
crol *m* crawl
cromo *m* QUÍM chrome; (*estampa*) picture card, trading card
crónica *f* chronicle; *en periódico* report
crónico *adj* MED chronic
cronológico *adj* chronological
cronometrar ⟨1a⟩ *v/t* DEP time
cronómetro *m* stopwatch
croqueta *f* GASTR croquette
croquis *m inv* sketch
cross *m* DEP cross-country (running); *con motocicletas* motocross
cruce *m* cross; *de carreteras* crossroads *sg*; *cruce en las líneas* TELEC crossed line
crucero *m* cruise
crucial *adj* crucial
crucificar ⟨1g⟩ *v/t* crucify
crucifijo *m* crucifix
crucigrama *m* crossword
crudo 1 *adj alimento* raw; *fig* harsh **2** *m* crude (oil)
cruel *adj* cruel
cruento *adj* bloody
crujiente *adj* GASTR crunchy
crujir ⟨3a⟩ *v/i* creak; *al arder* crackle; *de grava* crunch
cruz *f* cross; *Cruz Roja* Red Cross
cruzar ⟨1f⟩ **1** *v/t* cross **2** *v/r* *cruzarse* pass one another; *cruzarse de brazos* cross one's arms; *cruzarse con alguien* pass s.o.
c.s.f. *abr* (= *costo, seguro, flete*) cif (= cost, insurance, freight)
cta, c.ta *abr* (= *cuenta*) A/C (= account)
cuaderno *m* notebook; EDU exercise book
cuadra *f* stable; *L.Am.* (*manzana*) block
cuadrado 1 *adj* square **2** *m* square; *al cuadrado* squared
cuadrilla *f* squad, team
cuadro *m* painting; (*grabado*) picture; (*tabla*) table; DEP team; *cuadro de mandos* or *de instrumentos* AUTO dashboard; *de* or *a cuadros* checked
cuádruple, cuadruplo *m* quadruple
cuajada *f* GASTR curd
cuajar ⟨1a⟩ *v/i de nieve* settle; *fig*: *de idea, proyecto etc* come together, jell F
cuajo *m*: *de cuajo* by the roots
cual 1 *pron rel*: *el cual, la cual etc cosa* which; *persona* who; *por lo cual* (and)

so **2** *adv* like

cuál *interr* which (one)

cualidad *f* quality

cualificar ⟨1g⟩ *v/t* qualify

cualquier *adj* any; *cualquier día* any day; *cualquier cosa* anything; *de cualquier modo* or *forma* anyway

cualquiera *pron persona* anyone, anybody; *cosa* any (one); *un cualquiera* a nobody; *¡cualquiera lo comprende!* nobody can understand it!

cuando 1 *conj* when; *condicional* if; *cuando quieras* whenever you want **2** *adv* when; *de cuando en cuando* from time to time; *cuando menos* at least

cuándo *interr* when

cuantía *f* amount, quantity; *fig* importance

cuantificar ⟨1g⟩ *v/t* quantify

cuantioso *adj* substantial

cuanto 1 *adj*: *cuanto dinero quieras* as much money as you want; *unos cuantos chavales* a few boys **2** *pron* all, everything; *se llevó cuanto podía* she took all o everything she could; *le dio cuanto necesitaba* he gave her everything she needed; *unas -as* a few; *todo cuanto* everything **3** *adv*: *cuanto antes, mejor* the sooner the better; *en cuanto* as soon as; *en cuanto a* as for

cuánto 1 *interr adj* how much; *pl* how many; *¿cuánto café?* how much coffee?; *¿cuántos huevos?* how many eggs? **2** *pron* how much; *pl* how many; *¿cuánto necesita Vd.?* how much do you need?; *¿cuántos ha dicho?* how many did you say?; *¿a cuánto están?* how much are they?; *¿a cuántos estamos?* what's the date today? **3** *exclamaciones*: *¡cuánta gente había!* there were so many people!; *¡cuánto me alegro!* I'm so pleased!

cuarenta *adj* forty

Cuaresma *f* Lent

cuartear ⟨1a⟩ **1** *v/t* cut up, quarter **2** *v/r* **cuartearse** crack

cuartel *m* barracks *pl*; *cuartel general* headquarters *pl*

cuartelazo *m L.Am.* military uprising

cuartilla *f* sheet of paper

cuarto 1 *adj* fourth **2** *m* (*habitación*) room; (*parte*) quarter; *cuarto de baño* bathroom; *cuarto de estar* living room; *cuarto de hora* quarter of an hour; *cuarto de kilo* quarter of a kilo; *de tres al cuarto* F third-rate; *las diez y cuarto* quarter past ten, quarter after ten; *las tres menos cuarto* a quarter to o of three

cuarzo *m* quartz

cuatro *adj* four; *cuatro gotas* F a few drops

cuatrocientos *adj* four hundred

cuba *f*: *estar como una cuba* F be plastered F

Cuba Cuba

cubano 1 *adj* Cuban **2** *m*, *-a f* Cuban

cubierta *f* MAR deck; AUTO tire, *Br* tyre

cubierto 1 *part* → *cubrir* **2** *m* piece of cutlery; *en la mesa* place setting; *cubiertos pl* cutlery *sg*

cubito *m*: *cubito de hielo* ice cube

cubo *m* cube; *recipiente* bucket; *cubo de la basura* *dentro* garbage can, *Br* rubbish bin; *fuera* garbage can, *Br* dustbin

cubrir ⟨3a; *part* **cubierto**⟩ **1** *v/t* cover (*de* with) **2** *v/r* **cubrirse** cover o.s.

cucaracha *f* ZO cockroach

cuchara *f* spoon; *meter su cuchara L.Am.* F stick one's oar in F

cucharada *f* spoonful

cucharilla *f* teaspoon

cucharón *m* ladle

cuchichear ⟨1a⟩ *v/i* whisper

cuchilla *f* razor blade

cuchillo *m* knife

cuclillas: *en cuclillas* squatting

cuco 1 *m* ZO cuckoo; *reloj de cuco* cuckoo clock **2** *adj* (*astuto*) sharp

cucurucho *m de papel etc* cone; *sombrero* pointed hat

cuece *vb* → *cocer*

cuelgo *vb* → *colgar*

cuello *m* ANAT neck; *de camisa etc* collar

cuelo *vb* → *colar*

cuenca *f* GEOG basin

cuenco *m* bowl

cuenta *f* (*cálculo*) sum; *de restaurante* check, *Br* bill; *com* account; *cuenta atrás* countdown; *cuenta bancaria* bank account; *cuenta corriente* checking account, *Br* current account; *más de la cuenta* too much; *caer en la cuenta* realize; *darse cuenta de algo* realize sth; *pedir cuentas a alguien* ask s.o. for an explanation; *perder la cuenta* lose count; *tener o tomar en cuenta* take into account; *corre por mi / su cuenta* I'll / he'll pay for it

cuentagotas *m inv* dropper

cuentakilómetros *m inv* odometer, *Br* mileometer

cuentista *m/f* story-teller; F (*mentiroso*) fibber F

cuento *m* (*short*) story; (*pretexto*) excuse; *cuento chino* F tall story F; *venir a cuento* be relevant

cuerda *f* rope; *de guitarra, violín* string;

dar cuerda al reloj wind the clock up; **dar cuerda a algo** fig F string sth out F; **cuerdas vocales** ANAT vocal chords
cuerdo adj sane; (sensato) sensible
cuerno m horn; de caracol feeler; **irse al cuerno** F fall through, be wrecked; **poner los cuernos a alguien** F be unfaithful to s.o.
cuero m leather; Rpl (fuete) whip; **en cueros** F naked
cuerpo m body; de policía force; **cuerpo diplomático** diplomatic corps sg; **a cuerpo de rey** like a king; **en cuerpo y alma** body and soul
cuervo m ZO raven, crow
cuesta f slope; **cuesta abajo** downhill; **cuesta arriba** uphill; **a cuestas** on one's back
cuestión f question; (asunto) matter, question; **en cuestión de ...** in a matter of ...
cuestionar ⟨1a⟩ v/t question
cuestionario m questionnaire
cueva f cave
cuidado m care; **¡cuidado!** look out!; **andar con cuidado** tread carefully; **me tiene sin cuidado** I could o Br couldn't care less; **tener cuidado** be careful
cuidadora f Méx nursemaid
cuidadoso adj careful
cuidar ⟨1a⟩ 1 v/t look after, take care of 2 v/i: **cuidar de** look after, take care of 3 v/r **cuidarse** look after o.s., take care of o.s.; **cuidarse de hacer algo** take care to do sth
culebra f ZO snake
culebrón m TV soap
culinario adj cooking atr, culinary
culminación f culmination
culminante adj: **punto culminante** peak, climax
culminar ⟨1a⟩ 1 v/i culminate (**en** in); fig reach a peak o climax 2 v/t finish
culo m V ass V, Br arse V; F butt F, Br bum F; **ser culo de mal asiento** fig F be restless, have ants in one's pants F
culpa f fault; **echar la culpa de algo a alguien** blame s.o. for sth; **por culpa de alguien** be s.o.'s fault; **tener la culpa** be to blame (**de** for)
culpabilidad f guilt
culpable 1 adj guilty 2 m/f culprit
culpar ⟨1a⟩ v/t: **culpar a alguien de algo** blame s.o. for sth
cultivar ⟨1a⟩ v/t AGR grow; tierra farm; fig cultivate
cultivo m AGR crop; BIO culture
culto 1 adj educated 2 m worship
cultura f culture

cultural adj cultural; **un nivel cultural muy pobre** a very poor standard of education
cumbre f tb POL summit
cumpleaños m inv birthday
cumplido m compliment; **no andarse con cumplidos** not stand on ceremony
cumplimentar ⟨1k⟩ v/t trámite carry out
cumplir ⟨3a⟩ **1** v/t orden carry out; promesa fulfill; condena serve; **cumplir diez años** reach the age of ten, turn ten 2 v/i: **cumplir con algo** carry sth out; **cumplir con su deber** do one's duty; **te invita sólo por cumplir** he's only inviting you out of politeness 3 v/r **cumplirse** de plazo expire
cúmulo m (montón) pile, heap
cuna f fig cradle
cundir ⟨3a⟩ v/i spread; (dar mucho de sí) go a long way
cuneta f ditch
cuñada f sister-in-law
cuñado m brother-in-law
cuota f share; de club, asociación fee
cupón m coupon
cúpula f dome; esp POL leadership
cura 1 m priest 2 f cure; (tratamiento) treatment; Méx, C.Am. F hangover; **tener cura** be curable
curado adj Méx, C.Am. F drunk
curandero m, -a f faith healer
curar ⟨1a⟩ **1** v/t tb GASTR cure; (tratar) treat; herida dress; pieles tan 2 v/i MED recover (**de** from) 3 v/r **curarse** MED recover; Méx, C.Am. F get drunk
curda f: **agarrarse una curda** F get plastered F
curiosidad f curiosity
curioso 1 adj curious; (raro) curious, odd, strange 2 m, -a f onlooker
curita f L.Am. Band-Aid®, Br Elastoplast®
currar ⟨1a⟩ v/i F work
currículum vitae m résumé, Br CV, Br curriculum vitae
curry m GASTR curry
cursi adj F persona affected
cursillo m short course
cursiva f italics pl
curso m course; **curso a distancia** or **por correspondencia** correspondence course; **en el curso de** in the course of
cursor m INFOR cursor
curtir ⟨3a⟩ v/t tan; fig harden
curva f curve
curvo adj curved
cúspide f de montaña summit; de fama etc height
custodia f JUR custody

custodiar ⟨1b⟩ *v/t* guard
cususa *f C.Am.* corn liquor
cutre *adj* F shabby, dingy

cuyo, -a *adj* whose
CV *m* resumé, *Br* CV

D

D

D. *abr* (= **Don**) Mr
Dª. *abr* (= **Doña**) Mrs
dactilar *adj* finger *atr*
dadivoso *adj* generous
dado[1] *m* dice
dado[2] **1** *part* → **dar 2** *adj* given; **ser dado a algo** be given to sth **3** *conj*: **dado que** since, given that
dalia *f* BOT dahlia
daltónico *adj* colo(u)r-blind
daltonismo *m* colo(u)r-blindness
dama *f* lady; **dama de honor** bridesmaid; (**juego de**) **damas** checkers *sg*, *Br* draughts *sg*
damasco *m* damask; *L.Am.* fruta apricot
damnificado 1 *adj* affected **2** *m*, **-a** *f* victim
danés 1 *adj* Danish **2** *m*, **-esa** *f* Dane
danza *f* dance
danzar ⟨1f⟩ *v/i* dance
dañar ⟨1a⟩ **1** *v/t* harm; *cosa* damage **2** *v/r* **dañarse** harm o.s.; *de un objeto* get damaged
dañino *adj* harmful; *fig* malicious
daño *m* harm; *a un objeto* damage; **hacer daño** hurt; **daños** *pl* damage *sg*; **daños y perjuicios** damages
dar ⟨1r; *part* **dado**⟩ **1** *v/t* give; *beneficio* yield; *luz* give off; *fiesta* give, have; **dar un golpe a** hit; **dar un salto / una patada / miedo** jump / kick / frighten; **el jamón me dió sed** the ham made me thirsty **2** *v/i*: **dame** give it to me, give me it; **dar a de ventana** look onto; **dar con algo** come across sth; **dar de comer a alguien** feed s.o.; **dar de beber a alguien** give s.o. something to drink; **dar de sí** *de material* stretch, give; **le dio por insultar a su madre** F she started insulting her mother; **¡qué más da!** what does it matter!; **da igual** it doesn't matter **3** *v/r* **darse** *de una situación* arise; **darse a algo** take to sth; **esto se me da bien** I'm good at this; **dárselas de algo** make o.s. out to be sth, claim to be sth
dardo *m* dart

datar ⟨1a⟩ *v/i*: **datar de** date from
dátil *m* BOT date
dato *m* piece of information; **datos** *pl* information *sg*, data *sg*; **datos personales** personal details
D.C. *abr* (= **después de Cristo**) AD (= Anno Domini)
dcho, dcha *abr* (= **derecho, derecha**) r (= right)
d. de J.C. *abr* (= **después de Jesucristo**) AD (= Anno Domini)
de *prp* ◇ *origen* from; **de Nueva York** from New York; **de ... a** from ... to
◇ *posesión* of; **el coche de mi amigo** my friend's car
◇ *material* (made) of; **un anillo de oro** a gold ring
◇ *contenido* of; **un vaso de agua** a glass of water
◇ *cualidad*: **una mujer de 20 años** a 20 year old woman
◇ *causa* with; **temblaba de miedo** she was shaking with fear
◇ *hora*: **de noche** at night, by night; **de día** by day
◇ *en calidad de* as; **trabajar de albañil** work as a bricklayer
◇ *agente* by; **de Goya** by Goya
◇ *condición* if; **de haberlo sabido** if I'd known
dé *vb* → **dar**
deambular ⟨1a⟩ *v/i* wander around
debajo 1 *adv* underneath **2** *prp*: (*por*) **debajo de** under; **un grado por debajo de lo normal** one degree below normal
debate *m* debate, discussion
debatir ⟨3a⟩ **1** *v/t* debate, discuss **2** *v/i* struggle **3** *v/r* **debatirse**: **debatirse entre la vida y la muerte** fight for one's life
deber 1 *m* duty; **deberes** *pl* homework *sg* **2** ⟨2a⟩ *v/t* owe **3** *v/i en presente* must, have to; *en pretérito* should have; *en futuro* (will) have to; *en condicional* should; **debe de tener quince años** he must be about 15 **4** *v/r* **deberse**: **deberse a** be due to, be caused by

debido 1 part → **deber 2** adj: **como es debido** properly; **debido a** owing to, on account of

débil adj weak

debilitar ⟨1a⟩ **1** v/t weaken **2** v/r **debilitarse** weaken, become weak; *de salud* deteriorate

debut m debut

década f decade

decadencia f decadence; *de un imperio* decline

decaer ⟨2o; part **decaído**⟩ v/i tb fig decline; *de rendimiento* fall off, decline; *de salud* deteriorate

decaído 1 part → **decaer 2** adj fig depressed, down F

decantarse ⟨1a⟩ v/r: **decantarse por** opt for

decapitar ⟨1a⟩ v/t behead, decapitate

decenio m decade

decente adj decent

decepción f disappointment

decepcionado adj disappointed

decepcionante adj disappointing

decepcionar ⟨1a⟩ v/t disappoint

decidido 1 part → **decidir 2** adj decisive; **estar decidido** be determined (**a** to)

decidir ⟨3a⟩ **1** v/t decide **2** v/r **decidirse** make up one's mind, decide

decimal adj decimal atr

décimo 1 adj tenth **2** m de lotería share of a lottery ticket

decir ⟨3p; part **dicho**⟩ **1** v/t say; (*contar*) tell; **querer decir** mean; **decir que sí** say yes; **decir que no** say no; **es decir** in other words; **no es rico, que digamos** let's say he's not rich; **¡no me digas!** you're kidding!; **¡quién lo diría!** who would believe it!; **se dice que ...** they say that ..., it's said that ... **2** v/i: **¡diga!**, **¡dígame!** *Esp* TELEC hello

decisión f decision; fig decisiveness

decisivo adj critical, decisive

declaración f declaration; **declaración de la renta** o **de impuestos** tax return; **prestar declaración** JUR testify, give evidence

declarar ⟨1a⟩ **1** v/t state; **bienes** declare; **declarar culpable** find guilty **2** v/i JUR give evidence **3** v/r **declararse** declare o.s.; *de incendio* break out; **declararse a alguien** declare one's love for s.o.

declinar ⟨1a⟩ v/t & v/i decline

declive m fig decline; **en declive** in decline

decodificador m → **descodificador**

decodificar ⟨1g⟩ v/t → **descodificar**

decolaje m L.Am. takeoff

decolar ⟨1a⟩ v/i L.Am. take off

decolorar ⟨1a⟩ v/t bleach

decoración f decoration

decorado m TEA set

decorador m, **decoradora** f: **decorador** (**de interiores**) interior decorator

decorar ⟨1a⟩ v/t decorate

decorativo adj decorative

decreciente adj decreasing, diminishing

decrépito adj decrepit

decretar ⟨1a⟩ v/t order, decree

decreto m decree

dedicación f dedication

dedicar ⟨1g⟩ **1** v/t dedicate; **esfuerzo** devote **2** v/r **dedicarse** devote o.s. (**a** to); **¿a qué se dedica?** what do you do (for a living)?

dedicatoria f dedication

dedillo m: **conocer algo al dedillo** F know sth like the back of one's hand; **saber algo al dedillo** F know sth off by heart

dedo m finger; **dedo del pie** toe; **dedo gordo** thumb; **dedo índice** forefinger; **no tiene dos dedos de frente** F he doesn't have much commonsense

deducción f deduction

deducir ⟨3o⟩ v/t deduce; COM deduct

defecar ⟨1g⟩ v/t defecate

defecto m defect; *moral* fault; INFOR default

defectuoso adj defective, faulty

defender ⟨2g⟩ **1** v/t defend **2** v/r **defenderse** defend o.s. (**de** against); fig F manage, get by; **defenderse del frío** ward off the cold

defenestrar ⟨1a⟩ v/t fig F oust

defensa 1 f JUR, DEP defense, Br defence; *L.Am.* AUTO fender, Br bumper; **defensas** MED defenses, Br defences **2** m/f DEP defender

defensivo adj defensive

defensor m, **defensora** f defender, champion; JUR defense counsel, Br defending counsel; **defensor del pueblo** en España ombudsman

deficiente 1 adj deficient; (*insatisfactorio*) inadequate **2** m/f handicapped person

déficit m deficit

definición f definition; **de alta definición** TV high definition

definir ⟨3a⟩ **1** v/t define **2** v/r **definirse** come down (**por** in favor of)

definitivo adj definitive; **respuesta** definite; **en -a** all in all

deforestación f deforestation

deformar ⟨1a⟩ v/t distort; MED deform

deforme adj deformed

defraudar ⟨1a⟩ v/t disappoint; (*estafar*)

defraud; *defraudar a Hacienda* evade taxes

defunción *f* death, demise *fml*

degenerar ⟨1a⟩ *v/i* degenerate (*en* into)

degollar ⟨1n⟩ *v/t* cut the throat of

degradante *adj* degrading

degradar ⟨1a⟩ **1** *v/t* degrade; MIL demote; PINT gradate **2** *v/r* **degradarse** demean o.s.

degustar ⟨1a⟩ *v/t* taste

dejadez *f* slovenliness; (*negligencia*) neglect

dejar ⟨1a⟩ **1** *v/t* leave; (*permitir*) let, allow; (*prestar*) lend; *beneficios* yield; *déjame en la esquina* drop me at the corner; *dejar para mañana* leave until tomorrow; *dejar caer algo* drop sth **2** *v/i*: *dejar de hacer algo* (*parar*) stop doing sth; *no deja de fastidiarme* he keeps (on) annoying me **3** *v/r* **dejarse** let o.s. go; *dejarse llevar* let o.s. be carried along

del *prp* de *y art* el

delantal *m* apron

delante *adv* in front; (*más avanzado*) ahead; (*enfrente*) opposite; *por delante* ahead; *se abrocha por delante* it does up at the front; *tener algo por delante* have sth ahead of *o* in front of one; *delante de* in front of; *el asiento de delante* the front seat

delantera *f* DEP forward line; *llevar la delantera* be ahead of, lead

delantero *m*, *-a f* DEP forward

delatar ⟨1a⟩ *v/t*: *delatar a alguien* inform on s.o.; *fig* give s.o. away

delegación *f* delegation; (*oficina*) local office; *delegación de Hacienda* tax office

delegado *m*, *-a f* delegate; COM representative

delegar ⟨1h⟩ *v/t* delegate

deleitar ⟨1a⟩ **1** *v/t* delight **2** *v/r* **deleitarse** take delight

deletrear ⟨1a⟩ *v/t* spell

delfín *m* ZO dolphin

delgado *adj* slim; *lámina, placa* thin

deliberado *adj* deliberate

deliberar ⟨1a⟩ *v/i* deliberate (*sobre* on)

delicadeza *f* gentleness; *de acabado, tallado* delicacy; (*tacto*) tact

delicado *adj* delicate

delicia *f* delight; *hacer las delicias de alguien* delight s.o.

delicioso *adj* delightful; *comida* delicious

delimitar ⟨1a⟩ *v/t* delimit

delincuente *m/f* criminal

delineante *m/f* draftsman, *Br* draughtsman; *mujer* draftswoman, *Br* draughtswoman

delinear ⟨1a⟩ *v/t* draft; *fig* draw up

delirar ⟨1a⟩ *v/i* be delirious; *¡tú deliras! fig* you must be crazy!

delirio *m* MED delirium; *tener delirio por el fútbol fig* be mad about soccer; *delirios de grandeza* delusions of grandeur

delito *m* offense, *Br* offence

demacrado *adj* haggard

demagógico *adj* demagogic

demanda *f* demand (*de* for); JUR lawsuit, claim

demandar ⟨1a⟩ *v/t* JUR sue

demás 1 *adj* remaining **2** *adv*: *lo demás* the rest; *los demás* the rest, the others; *por lo demás* apart from that

demasiado 1 *adj* too much; *antes de pl* too many; *demasiada gente* too many people; *hace demasiado calor* it's too hot **2** *adv antes de adj, adv* too; *con verbo* too much

demencia *f* MED dementia; *fig* madness; *demencia senil* MED senile dementia

demencial *adj fig* crazy, mad

demente 1 *adj* demented, crazy **2** *m/f* mad person

democracia *f* democracy

demócrata 1 *adj* democratic **2** *m/f* democrat

democrático *adj* democratic

demografía *f* demographics

demoler ⟨2h⟩ *v/t* demolish

demoniaco, demoníaco *adj* demonic

demonio *m* demon; *¡demonios!* F hell! F, damn! F

demora *f* delay; *sin demora* without delay

demorar ⟨1a⟩ **1** *v/i* stay on; *L.Am.* (*tardar*) be late; *no demores* don't be long **2** *v/t* delay **3** *v/r* **demorarse** be delayed; *¿cuánto se demora de Concepción a Santiago?* how long does it take to get from Concepción to Santiago?

demostración *f* proof; *de método* demonstration; *de fuerza, sentimiento* show

demostrar ⟨1m⟩ *v/t* prove; (*enseñar*) demonstrate; (*mostrar*) show

denegar ⟨1h & 1k⟩ *v/t* refuse

denigrante *adj* degrading; *artículo* denigrating

denigrar ⟨1a⟩ *v/t* degrade; (*criticar*) denigrate

denominación *f* name; *denominación de origen* guarantee of quality of a wine

denominador *m*: *denominador común fig* common denominator

denominar ⟨1a⟩ **1** *v/t* designate **2** *v/r* **denominarse** be called

denotar ⟨1a⟩ *v/t* show, indicate

densidad *f* density

denso adj bosque dense; fig weighty

dentadura f: **dentadura postiza** false teeth pl, dentures pl

dental adj dental

dentera f: **darle dentera a alguien** set s.o.'s teeth on edge

dentífrico m toothpaste

dentista m/f dentist

dentro 1 adv inside; **por dentro** inside; **de dentro** from inside **2 dentro de** en espacio in, inside; en tiempo in, within

denuncia f report; **poner una denuncia** make a formal complaint

denunciar ⟨1b⟩ v/t report; fig condemn, denounce

departamento m department; L.Am. (apartamento) apartment, Br flat

depender ⟨2a⟩ v/i depend (**de** on); **depender de alguien** en una jerarquía report to s.o.; **eso depende** that all depends

dependiente 1 adj dependent **2** m, -a f sales clerk, Br shop assistant

depilación f hair removal; con cera waxing; con pinzas plucking

depilar ⟨1a⟩ v/t con cera wax; con pinzas pluck

deplorar ⟨1a⟩ v/t deplore

deportar ⟨1a⟩ v/t deport

deporte m sport

deportista m/f sportsman; mujer sportswoman

depositar ⟨1a⟩ v/t tb fig put, place; dinero deposit (**en** in)

depósito m COM deposit; (almacén) store; de agua, AUTO tank; **depósito de cadáveres** morgue, Br mortuary

depravado adj depraved

depravar ⟨1a⟩ v/t deprave

depreciación f depreciation

depreciar ⟨1b⟩ **1** v/t lower the value of **2** v/r **depreciarse** depreciate, lose value

depredador 1 adj predatory **2** m ZO predator

depresión f MED depression

deprimente adj depressing

deprimir ⟨3a⟩ **1** v/t depress **2** v/r **deprimirse** get depressed

depuradora f purifier

depurar ⟨1a⟩ v/t purify; agua treat; POL purge

derecha f tb POL right; **la derecha** the right(-hand); **a la derecha** posición on the right; dirección to the right

derecho al lado right; (recto) straight; C.Am. fig straight, honest **2** adv straight **3** m (privilegio) right; JUR law; **del derecho** on the right side; **derecho de asilo** right to asylum; **derechos de autor** roy-

alties; **derechos humanos** human rights; **derecho de voto** right to vote; **no hay derecho** it's not fair, it's not right; **tener derecho a** have a right to **4** mpl: **derechos** fees; **derechos de inscripción** registration fee sg

derechura f straightness; C.Am., Pe (suerte) luck; **en derechura** straight away

deriva f: **ir a la deriva** MAR, fig drift

derivar ⟨1a⟩ **1** v/i derive (**de** from); de barco drift **2** v/r **derivarse** be derived (**de** from)

dermatólogo m, -a f dermatologist

derogar ⟨1h⟩ v/t repeal

derramar ⟨1a⟩ **1** v/t spill; luz, sangre shed; (esparcir) scatter **2** v/r **derramarse** spill; de gente scatter

derrame m MED: **derrame cerebral** stroke

derrapar ⟨1a⟩ v/i AUTO skid

derrengado adj exhausted

derretir ⟨3l⟩ **1** v/t melt **2** v/r **derretirse** melt; fig be besotted (**por** with)

derribar ⟨1a⟩ v/t edificio, persona knock down; avión shoot down; POL bring down

derrocar ⟨1g⟩ v/t POL overthrow

derrochador m, **derrochadora** f spendthrift

derrochar ⟨1a⟩ v/t waste; salud, felicidad exude, burst with

derroche m waste

derrota f defeat

derrotar ⟨1a⟩ v/t MIL defeat; DEP beat, defeat

derruir ⟨3g⟩ v/t edificio demolish

derrumbar ⟨1a⟩ **1** v/t knock down **2** v/r **derrumbarse** collapse, fall down; de una persona go to pieces

desabrido adj (soso) tasteless; persona surly; tiempo unpleasant

desabrochar ⟨1a⟩ v/t undo, unfasten

desacato m JUR contempt

desaceleración f deceleration

desacertado adj misguided

desaconsejar ⟨1a⟩ v/t advise against

desacreditado adj discredited

desacreditar ⟨1a⟩ v/t discredit

desactivar ⟨1a⟩ v/t bomba etc deactivate

desacuerdo m disagreement; **estar en desacuerdo con** disagree with

desafiar ⟨1c⟩ v/t challenge; peligro defy

desafinar ⟨1a⟩ v/i MÚS be out of tune

desafío m challenge; al peligro defiance

desafortunado adj unfortunate, unlucky

desagradable adj unpleasant, disagreeable

desagradar ⟨1a⟩ v/i: **me desagrada tener que ...** I dislike having to ...

desagradecido adj ungrateful; **una tarea -a** a thankless task desagrado *m* displeasure

desagravio *m* apology

desagüe *m* drain; *acción* drainage; (*cañería*) drainpipe

desahogar ⟨1h⟩ **1** *v/t sentimiento* vent **2** *v/r* desahogarse *fig* F let off steam F, get it out of one's system F

desahogo *m* comfort; **con desahogo** comfortably

desahuciar ⟨1b⟩ *v/t:* **desahuciar a alguien** declare s.o. terminally ill; (*inquilino*) evict s.o.

desairar ⟨1a⟩ *v/t* snub

desajustar ⟨1a⟩ *v/t tornillo, pieza* loosen; *mecanismo, instrumento* affect, throw out of balance

desajuste *m* disruption; COM imbalance

desalentar ⟨1k⟩ *v/t* discourage

desaliento *m* discouragement

desalinización *f* desalination

desaliñado *adj* slovenly

desalojar ⟨1a⟩ *v/t ante peligro* evacuate; (*desahuciar*) evict; (*vaciar*) vacate

desamparar ⟨1a⟩ *v/t:* **desamparar a alguien** abandon s.o.

desangelado *adj lugar* soulless

desangrarse ⟨1a⟩ *v/r* bleed to death

desanimar ⟨1a⟩ **1** *v/t* discourage, dishearten **2** *v/r* desanimarse become discouraged *o* disheartened

desánimo *m* discouragement

desapacible *adj* nasty, unpleasant

desaparecer ⟨2d⟩ **1** *v/i* disappear, vanish **2** *v/t L.Am.* disappear F

desaparecido *m*, -a *f L.Am.:* **un desaparecido** one of the disappeared

desaparición *f* disappearance

desapego *m* indifference; (*distancia*) distance, coolness

desapercibido *adj* unnoticed; **pasar desapercibido** go unnoticed

desaprensivo *adj* unscrupulous

desaprobar ⟨1m⟩ *v/t* disapprove of

desaprovechar ⟨1a⟩ *v/t oportunidad* waste

desarmado *adj* unarmed

desarmar ⟨1a⟩ *v/t* MIL disarm; TÉC take to pieces, dismantle

desarme *m* MIL disarmament

desarraigo *m fig* rootlessness

desarreglar ⟨1a⟩ *v/t* make untidy; *horario* disrupt

desarrollar ⟨1a⟩ **1** *v/t* develop; *tema* explain; *trabajo* carry out **2** *v/r* desarrollarse develop, evolve; (*ocurrir*) take place

desarrollo *m* development

desarticular ⟨1a⟩ *v/t banda criminal* break up; MED dislocate

desaseado *adj* F scruffy

desasirse ⟨3a⟩ *v/r* get free, free o.s.

desasosiego *m* disquiet, unease

desastre *m tb fig* disaster

desastroso *adj* disastrous

desatar ⟨1a⟩ **1** *v/t* untie; *fig* unleash **2** *v/r* desatarse *de animal, persona* get free; *de cordón* come undone; *fig* be unleashed, break out

desatascar ⟨1g⟩ *v/t* unblock

desatender ⟨2g⟩ *v/t* neglect; (*ignorar*) ignore

desatino *m* mistake

desatornillador *m esp L.Am.* screwdriver

desatornillar ⟨1a⟩ *v/t* unscrew

desatrancar ⟨1g⟩ *v/t cañería* unblock

desavenencia *f* disagreement

desaventajado *adj* unfavo(u)rable

desayunar ⟨1a⟩ *v/i* have breakfast **2** *v/t:* **desayunar algo** have sth for breakfast

desayuno *m* breakfast

desazón *f* (*ansiedad*) uneasiness, anxiety

desazonar ⟨1a⟩ *v/t* worry, make anxious

desbancar ⟨1g⟩ *v/t fig* displace, take the place of

desbandarse ⟨1a⟩ *v/r* disband; *de un grupo de personas* scatter

desbarajuste *m* mess

desbaratar ⟨1a⟩ *planes* ruin; *organización* disrupt

desbarrancar ⟨1g⟩ *L.Am.* **1** *v/t* push over the edge of a cliff **2** *v/r* desbarrancarse go over the edge of a cliff

desbocarse ⟨1g⟩ *v/r de un caballo* bolt

desbordante *adj energía, entusiasmo etc* boundless; **desbordante de** bursting with, overflowing with

desbordar ⟨1a⟩ **1** *v/t de un río* overflow, burst; *de un multitud* break through; *de un acontecimiento* overwhelm; *fig* exceed **2** *v/i* overflow **3** *v/r* desbordarse *de un río* burst its banks, overflow; *fig* get out of control

descabellado *adj:* **idea -a** F hare-brained idea F

descabellar ⟨1a⟩ *v/t* TAUR *kill with a knife--thrust in the neck*

descabello *m* fatal knife thrust

descafeinado *adj* decaffeinated; *fig* watered-down

descalabro *m* calamity, disaster

descalificar ⟨1g⟩ *v/t* disqualify

descalzarse ⟨1f⟩ *v/r* take one's shoes off

descalzo *adj* barefoot

descaminado *adj* fig misguided; **andar** *or* **ir descaminado** be on the wrong track

descamisado *adj* shirtless; *fig* ragged

descampado *m* open ground

descansar ⟨1a⟩ *v/i* rest, have a rest; **¡que descanses!** sleep well

descansillo _m_ landing

descanso _m_ rest; DEP half-time; TEA interval; **sin descanso** without a break

descapotable _m_ AUTO convertible

descarado _adj_ rude, impertinent

descarga _f_ EL, MIL discharge; _de mercancías_ unloading

descargar ⟨1h⟩ _v/t arma_, EL discharge; _fig: ira etc_ take out (**en, sobre** on); _mercancías_ unload; _de responsabilidad, culpa_ clear (**de** of)

descaro _m_ nerve

descarriado _adj:_ **ir descarriado** go astray

descarrilar ⟨1a⟩ _v/t_ derail

descartar ⟨1a⟩ _v/t_ rule out

descastado _adj_ cold, uncaring

descender ⟨2g⟩ **1** _v/i para indicar alejamiento_ go down, descend; _para indicar acercamiento_ come down, descend; _fig_ go down, decrease, diminish; **descender de** descend from **2** _v/t escalera_ go down; _para indicar acercamiento_ come down

descendiente 1 _adj_ descended **2** _m/f_ descendant

descenso _m de precio etc_ drop; _de montaña_, AVIA descent; DEP relegation; **la prueba de descenso** _en esquí_ the downhill (race _o_ competition)

descentralizar ⟨1f⟩ _v/t_ decentralize

descentrar ⟨1a⟩ _v/t fig_ shake

descifrar ⟨1a⟩ _v/t_ decipher; _fig_ work out

descodificación _f_ decoding

descodificador _m_ decoder

descodificar ⟨1g⟩ _v/t_ decode

descolgar ⟨1h & 1m⟩ **1** _v/t_ take down; _teléfono_ pick up **2** _v/r_ **descolgarse** _por una cuerda_ lower o.s.; _de un grupo_ break away

descollar ⟨1m⟩ _v/i_ stand out (**sobre** among)

descolonización _f_ decolonization

descolorido _adj_ faded; _fig_ colo(u)rless

descomponer ⟨2r; _part_ **descompuesto**⟩ **1** _v/t (dividir)_ break down; _(pudrir)_ cause to decompose; _L.Am. (romper)_ break **2** _v/r_ **descomponerse** _(pudrirse)_ decompose, rot; TÉC break down; _Rpl (emocionarse)_ break down (in tears); **se le descompuso la cara** he turned pale

descomposición _f_ breaking down; _putrefacción_ decomposition; _(diarrea)_ diarr(h)oea

descompuesto 1 _part_ → **descomponer 2** _adj alimento_ rotten; _cadáver_ decomposed; _persona_ upset; _L.Am._ tipsy; _L.Am. máquina_ broken down

descomunal _adj_ huge, enormous

desconcertar ⟨1k⟩ _v/t a persona_ disconcert

desconchado, desconchón _m_ place _where the paint is peeling; en porcelana_ chip

desconcierto _m_ uncertainty

desconectar ⟨1a⟩ **1** _v/t_ EL disconnect **2** _v/i fig_ switch off **3** _v/r_ **desconectarse** _fig_ lose touch (**de** with)

desconfiar ⟨1c⟩ _v/i_ be mistrustful (**de** of), be suspicious (**de** of)

descongelar ⟨1a⟩ _v/t comida_ thaw, defrost; _refrigerador_ defrost; _precios_ unfreeze

descongestionar ⟨1a⟩ _v/t_ MED unblock; **descongestionar el tráfico** relieve traffic congestion

desconocer ⟨2d⟩ _v/t_ not know

desconocido 1 _adj_ unknown **2** _m_, **-a** _f_ stranger

desconsiderado _adj_ inconsiderate

desconsolado _adj_ inconsolable

desconsuelo _m_ grief

descontado 1 _part_ → **descontar 2** _adj:_ **dar por descontado** take for granted; **por descontado** certainly

descontaminar ⟨1a⟩ _v/t_ decontaminate

descontar ⟨1m⟩ _v/t_ COM deduct, take off; _fig_ exclude

descontento 1 _adj_ dissatisfied **2** _m_ dissatisfaction

descontrol _m_ chaos

descontrolarse ⟨1a⟩ _v/r_ get out of control

desconvocar ⟨1g⟩ _v/t_ call off

descorazonar ⟨1a⟩ **1** _v/t_ discourage **2** _v/r_ **descorazonarse** get discouraged

descorchar ⟨1a⟩ _v/t botella_ uncork

descortés _adj_ impolite, rude

descoserse ⟨2a⟩ _v/r de costura, dobladillo etc_ come unstitched; _de prenda_ come apart at the seams

descosido _m:_ **como un descosido** F like mad F

descoyuntar ⟨1a⟩ _v/t_ dislocate

descremado _adj_ skimmed

describir ⟨3a; _part_ **descrito**⟩ _v/t_ describe

descripción _f_ description

descrito _part_ → **describir**

descuajaringarse ⟨1h⟩ _v/r_ F fall apart, fall to bits

descuartizar ⟨1f⟩ _v/t_ quarter

descubierto 1 _part_ → **descubrir 2** _adj_ uncovered; _persona_ bareheaded; _cielos_ clear; _piscina_ open-air; **al descubierto** in the open; **quedar al descubierto** be exposed **3** _m_ COM overdraft

descubrimiento _m_ discovery; _(revelación)_ revelation

descubrir ⟨3a; _part_ **descubierto**⟩ **1** _v/t_ discover; _poner de manifiesto_ uncover, reveal; _estatua_ unveil **2** _v/r_ **descubrirse**

take one's hat off; *fig* give o.s. away

descuento *m* discount; DEP stoppage time

descuerar ⟨1a⟩ *v/t L.Am.* skin; **descuerar a alguien** *fig* tear s.o. to pieces

descuidado *adj* careless

descuidar ⟨1a⟩ **1** *v/t* neglect **2** *v/i*: **¡descuida!** don't worry! **3** *v/r* **descuidarse** get careless; *en cuanto al aseo* let o.s. go; *(despistarse)* let one's concentration drop

descuido *m* carelessness; *(error)* mistake; *(omisión)* oversight; **en un descuido** *L.Am.* in a moment of carelessness

desde 1 *prp en el tiempo* since; *en el espacio* from; *en escala* from; **desde 1993** since 1993; **desde hace tres días** for three days; **desde ... hasta ...** from ... to ... **2** *adv*: **desde luego** of course; **desde ya** *Rpl* right away

desdén *m* disdain, contempt

desdeñable *adj* contemptible; **nada desdeñable** far from insignificant

desdeñar ⟨1a⟩ *v/t* scorn

desdibujado *adj* blurred

desdichado 1 *adj* unhappy; *(sin suerte)* unlucky **2** *m*, *-a f* poor soul

desdoblar ⟨1a⟩ *v/t* unfold; *(dividir)* split

desear ⟨1a⟩ *v/t* wish for; *suerte etc* wish; **¿qué desea?** what would you like?

desecar ⟨1g⟩ *v/t* dry

desechable *adj* disposable

desechar ⟨1a⟩ *v/t (tirar)* throw away; *(rechazar)* reject

desechos *mpl* waste sg

desembalar ⟨1a⟩ *v/t* unpack

desembarazarse ⟨1f⟩ *v/r*: **desembarazarse de** get rid of

desembarazo *m* ease

desembarcadero *m* MAR landing stage

desembarcar ⟨1g⟩ *v/i* disembark

desembocadura *f* mouth

desembocar ⟨1g⟩ *v/i* flow (**en** into); *de calle* come out (**en** into); *de situación* end (**en** in)

desembolsar ⟨1a⟩ *v/t* pay out

desembuchar ⟨1a⟩ *v/i fig* F spill the beans F, come out with it F

desempacar ⟨1g⟩ *v/t* unpack

desempaquetar ⟨1a⟩ *v/t* unwrap

desempatar ⟨1a⟩ *v/i* DEP, POL decide the winner

desempeñar ⟨1a⟩ *v/t deber, tarea* carry out; *cargo* hold; *papel* play

desempleado 1 *adj* unemployed **2** *m*, *-a f* unemployed person

desempleo *m* unemployment

desencadenar ⟨1a⟩ **1** *v/t fig* trigger **2** *v/r* **desencadenarse** *fig* be triggered

desencajarse ⟨1a⟩ *v/r de una pieza* come out; **se me ha desencajado la mandíbula** I dislocated my jaw

desencantado *adj fig* disenchanted (**con** with)

desencanto *m fig* disillusionment

desenchufar ⟨1a⟩ *v/t* EL unplug

desenfadado *adj* self-assured; *programa* light, undemanding

desenfocado *adj* FOT out of focus

desenfrenado *adj* frenzied, hectic

desenfreno *m* frenzy

desenfundar ⟨1a⟩ *v/t arma* take out, draw

desengañarse ⟨1a⟩ *v/r* become disillusioned (**de** with); *(dejar de engañarse)* stop kidding o.s.

desengaño *m* disappointment

desenlace *m* outcome, ending

desenmascarar ⟨1a⟩ *v/t fig* unmask, expose

desenredar ⟨1a⟩ *v/t* untangle; *situación confusa* straighten out, sort out

desenrollar ⟨1a⟩ *v/t* unroll

desenroscar ⟨1g⟩ *v/t* unscrew

desentenderse ⟨2g⟩ *v/r* not want to know (**de** about)

desentendido *adj*: **hacerse el desentendido** F pretend not to know

desentonar ⟨1a⟩ *v/i* MÚS go off key; **desentonar con** *fig* clash with; **decir algo que desentona** say sth out of place

desentrañar ⟨1a⟩ *v/t fig* unravel

desenvoltura *f fig* ease

desenvolverse ⟨2h; *part* **desenvuelto** ⟩ *v/r fig* cope

desenvuelto 1 *part* → **desenvolverse 2** *adj* self-confident

deseo *m* wish

desequilibrar ⟨1a⟩ *v/t* unbalance; **desequilibrar a alguien** throw s.o. off balance

desequilibrio *m* imbalance; **desequilibrio mental** mental instability

desertar ⟨1a⟩ *v/i* MIL desert

desertor *m*, **desertora** *f* deserter

desértico *adj* desert *atr*

desertización *f* desertification

desesperación *f* despair

desesperado *adj* in despair

desesperante *adj* infuriating, exasperating

desesperar ⟨1a⟩ **1** *v/t* infuriate, exasperate **2** *v/i* give up hope (**de** of), despair (**de** of) **3** *v/r* **desesperarse** get exasperated

desestabilizar ⟨1f⟩ *v/t* POL destabilize

desfachatez *f* impertinence

desfalco *m* embezzlement

desfallecer ⟨2d⟩ *v/i* faint

desfase *m fig* gap

desfavorable *adj* unfavo(u)rable

desfavorecer ⟨2d⟩ *v/t (no ser favorable)* not favo(u)r, be disadvantageous to; *de ropa etc* not suit

desfigurar ⟨1a⟩ *v/t* disfigure

desfiladero *m* ravine

desfilar ⟨1a⟩ *v/i* parade

desfile *m* parade; **desfile de modelos** *or* **de modas** fashion show

desfogarse ⟨1h⟩ *v/r fig* vent one's emotions

desforestación *f* deforestation

desgana *f* loss of appetite; **con desgana** *fig* reluctantly, half-heartedly

desgañitarse ⟨1a⟩ *v/r* F shout one's head off F

desgarbado *adj* F ungainly

desgarrador *adj* heartrending

desgarrar ⟨1a⟩ *v/t* tear up; *fig: corazón* break

desgastar ⟨1a⟩ *v/t* wear out; *defensas* wear down

desgaste *m* wear (and tear)

desglose *m* breakdown, itemization

desgracia *f* misfortune; *suceso* accident; **por desgracia** unfortunately

desgraciadamente *adv* unfortunately

desgraciado 1 *adj* unfortunate; *(miserable)* wretched **2** *m*, **-a** *f* wretch; *(sinvergüenza)* swine F

desgravar ⟨1a⟩ **1** *v/t* deduct **2** *v/i* be tax-deductible

desguazar ⟨1f⟩ *v/t* scrap

deshabitado *adj* uninhabited

deshacer ⟨2s; *part* **deshecho**⟩ **1** *v/t* undo; *maleta* unpack; *planes* wreck, ruin; **eso los obligó a deshacer todos sus planes** this forced them to cancel their plans **2** *v/r* **deshacerse** *de nudo de corbata, lazo etc* come undone; *de hielo* melt; **deshacerse de** get rid of

deshecho 1 *part* → **deshacer 2** *adj* F anímicamente devastated F; *de cansancio* beat F, exhausted

desheredar ⟨1a⟩ *v/t* disinherit

deshice *vb* → **deshacer**

deshidratar ⟨1a⟩ *v/t* dehydrate

deshielo *m* thaw

deshinchar ⟨1a⟩ **1** *v/t globo* deflate, let down **2** *v/r* **deshincharse** deflate, go down; *fig* lose heart

deshonesto *adj* dishonest

deshonra *f* dishono(u)r

deshonroso *adj* dishono(u)rable

deshora *f*: **a deshora (s)** at the wrong time

desidia *f* apathy, lethargy

desierto 1 *adj lugar* empty, deserted; **isla -a** desert island **2** *m* desert

designar ⟨1a⟩ *v/t* appoint, name; *lugar* select

designio *m* plan

desigual *adj* unequal; *terreno* uneven, irregular

desigualdad *f* inequality

desilusión *f* disappointment

desilusionado *adj* disappointed

desilusionar ⟨1a⟩ **1** *v/t* disappoint; *(quitar la ilusión)* disillusion **2** *v/r* **desilusionarse** be disappointed; *(perder la ilusión)* become disillusioned

desinfectante *m* disinfectant

desinfectar ⟨1a⟩ *v/t* disinfect

desinflar ⟨1a⟩ **1** *v/t globo, neumático* let the air out of, deflate **2** *v/r* **desinflarse** *de neumático* deflate; *fig* lose heart

desinformación *f* disinformation

desinhibir ⟨3a⟩ **1** *v/t*: **desinhibir alguien** get rid of s.o.'s inhibitions **2** *v/r* **desinhibirse** lose one's inhibitions

desintegrar ⟨1a⟩ **1** *v/t* cause to disintegrate; *grupo de gente* break up **2** *v/r* **desintegrarse** disintegrate; *de grupo de gente* break up

desinterés *m* lack of interest; *(generosidad)* unselfishness

desinteresado *adj* unselfish

desintoxicación *f* detoxification; **hacer una cura de desintoxicación** go into detox F, have treatment for drug / alcohol abuse

desistir ⟨3a⟩ *v/i* give up; **tuve que desistir de hacerlo** I had to stop doing it

deslealtad *f* disloyalty

desligar ⟨1h⟩ **1** *v/t* separate (*de* from); *fig persona* cut off (*de* from) **2** *v/r* **desligarse** *fig* cut o.s. off (*de* from)

desliz *m fig* F slip-up F

deslizar ⟨1f⟩ **1** *v/t* slide, run (*por* along); *idea, frase* slip in **2** *v/i* slide **3** *v/r* **deslizarse** slide

deslomarse ⟨1a⟩ *v/r fig* kill o.s.

deslucido *adj* tarnished; *colores* dull, drab

deslucir ⟨3f⟩ *v/t* tarnish; *fig* spoil

deslumbrante *adj* dazzling

deslumbrar ⟨1a⟩ **1** *v/t fig* dazzle **2** *v/r* **deslumbrarse** *fig* be dazzled

desmadre *m* F chaos

desmandarse ⟨1a⟩ *v/r de animal* break loose

desmantelar ⟨1a⟩ *v/t fortificación, organización* dismantle

desmañado *adj* clumsy

desmaquillar ⟨1a⟩ **1** *v/t* remove makeup from **2** *v/r* **desmaquillarse** remove one's makeup

desmarcarse ⟨1g⟩ *v/r* DEP lose one's

marker; **desmarcarse de** distance o.s. from

desmayarse ⟨1a⟩ v/r faint

desmayo m fainting fit; **sin desmayo** without flagging

desmedido adj excessive

desmelenarse ⟨1a⟩ v/r fig F let one's hair down F; (enfurecerse) hit the roof F

desmembrar ⟨1k⟩ v/t dismember

desmemoriado adj forgetful

desmentido m denial

desmentir ⟨3i⟩ v/t deny; **a alguien** contradict

desmenuzar ⟨1f⟩ v/t crumble up; fig break down

desmerecer ⟨2d⟩ **1** v/t not do justice to **2** v/i be unworthy (**con** of); **desmerecer de** not stand comparison with; **no desmerecer de** be in no way inferior to

desmesurado adj excessive

desmilitarización f demilitarization

desmitificar ⟨1g⟩ v/t demystify, demythologize

desmontar ⟨1a⟩ **1** v/t dismantle, take apart; tienda de campaña take down **2** v/i dismount

desmoralizado adj demoralized

desmoralizar ⟨1f⟩ v/t demoralize

desmoronamiento m tb fig collapse

desmoronarse ⟨1a⟩ v/r tb fig collapse

desnatado adj skimmed

desnaturalizado adj QUÍM denatured

desnivel m unevenness; entre personas disparity

desnivelar ⟨1a⟩ v/t upset the balance of

desnucarse ⟨1g⟩ v/r break one's neck

desnudar ⟨1a⟩ **1** v/t undress, fig fleece **2** v/r **desnudarse** undress

desnudo 1 adj naked; (sin decoración) bare **2** m PINT nude

desnutrición f undernourishment

desobedecer ⟨2d⟩ v/t disobey

desobediencia f disobedience

desobediente adj disobedient

desocupación f L.Am. unemployment

desocupado 1 adj apartamento vacant, empty; L.Am. sin trabajo unemployed **2** mpl: **los desocupados** the unemployed

desocupar ⟨1a⟩ v/t vacate

desodorante m deodorant

desoído part → **desoír**

desoír ⟨3q; part **desoído**⟩ v/t ignore, turn a deaf ear to

desolado adj desolate; fig griefstricken, devastated

desolar ⟨1m⟩ v/t tb fig devastate

desollar ⟨1m⟩ v/t skin

desorbitado adj astronomical; **con ojos**

desorbitados pop-eyed

desorden m disorder

desordenado adj untidy, messy F; fig disorganized

desordenar ⟨1a⟩ v/t make untidy

desorganización f lack of organization

desorganizado adj disorganized

desorientar ⟨1a⟩ **1** v/t disorient; (confundir) confuse **2** v/r **desorientarse** get disoriented, lose one's bearings; fig get confused

despabilado adj fig bright

despabilar ⟨1a⟩ **1** v/t wake up; **¡despabila!** get your act together! **2** v/r **despabilarse** fig get one's act together

despachar ⟨1a⟩ v/t **a persona, cliente** attend to; problema sort out; (vender) sell; (enviar) send, dispatch **2** v/i meet (**con** with) **3** v/r **despacharse** F polish off F; **despacharse a su gusto** speak one's mind

despacho m office; diplomático dispatch; **despacho de billetes** ticket office

despacio adv slowly; L.Am. (en voz baja) in a low voice

desparpajo m self-confidence

desparramar ⟨1a⟩ v/t scatter; líquido spill; dinero squander **2** v/r **desparramarse** spill; fig scatter

despavorido adj terrified

despecho m spite; **a despecho de** in spite of

despectivo adj contemptuous; GRAM pejorative

despedazar ⟨1f⟩ v/t tear apart

despedida f farewell; **despedida de soltero** stag party; **despedida de soltera** hen party

despedir ⟨3l⟩ **1** v/t see off; empleado dismiss; perfume give off; de jinete throw **2** v/r **despedirse** say goodbye (**de** to)

despegar ⟨1h⟩ **1** v/t remove, peel off **2** v/i AVIA, fig take off **3** v/r **despegarse** come unstuck (**de** from), come off (**de** sth); de persona distance o.s. (**de** from)

despegue m AVIA, fig take-off

despeinar ⟨1a⟩ v/t: **despeinar a alguien** muss s.o.'s hair

despejado adj cielo, cabeza clear

despejar ⟨1a⟩ **1** v/t clear; persona wake up **2** v/r **despejarse** de cielo clear up; fig wake o.s. up

despellejar ⟨1a⟩ v/t skin; **despellejar a alguien** fig tear s.o. to pieces

despenalizar ⟨1f⟩ v/t decriminalize

despensa f larder

despeñarse ⟨1a⟩ v/r throw o.s. off a cliff

desperdiciar ⟨1b⟩ v/t oportunidad waste

desperdicio *m* waste; **desperdicios** *pl* waste *sg*; **no tener desperdicio** be worthwhile

desperdigar ⟨1h⟩ *v/t* scatter

despertador *m* alarm (clock)

despertar ⟨1k⟩ **1** *v/t* wake, waken; *apetito* whet; *sospecha* arouse; *recuerdo* reawaken, trigger **2** *v/i* wake up **3** *v/r* **despertarse** wake (up)

despiadado *adj* ruthless

despido *m* dismissal

despierto *adj* awake; *fig* bright

despilfarrar ⟨1a⟩ *v/t* squander

despistado *adj* scatterbrained

despistarse ⟨1a⟩ *v/r* get distracted

despiste *m* distraction; **tener un despiste** become distracted

desplante *m*: **hacer un desplante a alguien** *fig* be rude to s.o.

desplazar ⟨1f⟩ **1** *v/t* move; (*suplantar*) take over from **2** *v/r* **desplazarse** travel

desplegar ⟨1h & 1k⟩ *v/t* unfold, open out; MIL deploy

despliegue *m* MIL deployment; **con gran despliegue de** *fig* with a great show of

desplomarse ⟨1a⟩ *v/r* collapse

desplome *m* collapse

despojar ⟨1a⟩ **1** *v/t* strip (**de** of) **2** *v/r* **despojarse**: **despojarse de** *prenda* take off

despojos *mpl* (*restos*) left-overs; (*desperdicios*) waste *sg*; *fig* spoils; *de animal* offal *sg*

desposeídos *mpl*: **los desposeídos** the dispossessed

déspota *m/f* despot

despotricar ⟨1g⟩ *v/i* F rant and rave F (**contra** about)

despreciar ⟨1b⟩ *v/t* look down on; *propuesta* reject

desprecio *m* contempt; (*indiferencia*) disregard; *acto* slight

desprender ⟨2a⟩ **1** *v/t* detach, separate; *olor* give off **2** *v/r* **desprenderse** come off; **desprenderse de** *fig* part with; **de este estudio se desprende que …** what emerges from the study is that …

despreocupación *f* indifference

despreocuparse ⟨1a⟩ *v/r* not worry (**de** about)

desprestigio *m* loss of prestige

desprevenido *adj* unprepared; **pillar** or L.Am. **agarrar desprevenido** catch unawares

desproporcionado *adj* disproportionate

despropósito *m* stupid thing

desprotegido *adj* unprotected

desprovisto *adj*: **desprovisto de** lacking in

después *adv* (*más tarde*) afterward, later;

seguido en orden next; **en el espacio** after; **yo voy después** I'm next; **después de** after; **después de todo** after all; **después de que se vaya** after he's gone

desquiciar ⟨1b⟩ **1** *v/t* fig drive crazy **2** *v/r* **desquiciarse** *fig* lose one's mind

desquitarse ⟨1a⟩ *v/r* get one's own back (**de** for)

desrielar ⟨1a⟩ *v/t* Chi derail

destacado *adj* outstanding

destacar ⟨1g⟩ **1** *v/i* stand out **2** *v/r* **destacarse** stand out (**por** because of); (*ser excelente*) be outstanding (**por** because of)

destajo *m*: **a destajo** piecework

destapar ⟨1a⟩ **1** *v/t* open, take the lid off; *fig* uncover **2** *v/r* **destaparse** take one's coat off; **en cama** kick off the bedcovers; *fig* strip (off)

destartalado *adj* *vehículo, casa* dilapidated

destello *m* *de estrella* twinkling; *de faros* gleam; *fig* brief period, moment

destemplarse ⟨1a⟩ *v/r* fig become unwell

desteñir ⟨3h & 3l⟩ **1** *v/t* discolo(u)r, fade **2** *v/r* **desteñirse** fade

desternillante *adj* F hilarious

desterrar ⟨1k⟩ *v/t* exile

destiempo *m*: **a destiempo** at the wrong moment

destierro *m* exile

destilar ⟨1a⟩ *v/t* distill; *fig* exude

destinar ⟨1a⟩ *v/t* *fondos* allocate (**para** for); *a persona* post (**a** to)

destino *m* fate; *de viaje etc* destination; **en el ejército etc** posting

destituir ⟨3g⟩ *v/t* dismiss

destornillador *m* screwdriver ·

destornillar ⟨1a⟩ *v/t* unscrew

destreza *f* skill

destrozar ⟨1f⟩ *v/t* destroy; *emocionalmente* shatter, devastate

destrozos *mpl* damage *sg*

destrucción *f* destruction

destruir ⟨3g⟩ *v/t* destroy; (*estropear*) ruin, wreck

desunir ⟨3a⟩ *v/t* divide

desuso *m* disuse; **caer en desuso** fall into disuse

desvaído *adj* *color, pintura* faded

desvalido *adj* helpless

desvalijar ⟨1a⟩ *v/t* rob; *apartamento* burglarize, burgle

desván *m* attic

desvanecimiento *m* MED fainting fit

desvarío *m* delirium; **desvaríos** ravings

desvelar ⟨1a⟩ **1** *v/t* keep awake; *secreto* reveal **2** *v/r* **desvelarse** stay awake; *fig* do one's best (**por** for)

desvelo *m* sleeplessness; **desvelos** efforts

desventaja f disadvantage

desventura f misfortune

desvergonzado adj shameless

desvergüenza f shamelessness

desvestir ⟨3l⟩ 1 v/t undress 2 v/r desvestirse get undressed, undress

desviar ⟨1c⟩ 1 v/t golpe deflect, parry; tráfico divert; río alter the course of; desviar la conversación change the subject; desviar la mirada look away; desviar a alguien del buen camino lead s.o. astray 2 v/r desviarse (girar) turn off; (bifurcarse) branch off; (apartarse) stray (de from)

desvincular ⟨1a⟩ 1 v/t dissociate (de from) 2 v/r desvincularse dissociate o.s. (de from)

desvío m diversion

detallar ⟨1a⟩ v/t explain in detail, give details of; COM itemize

detalle m detail; fig thoughtful gesture; al detalle retail

detección f detection

detectar ⟨1a⟩ v/t detect

detective m/f detective; detective privado private detective

detector m detector; detector de mentiras lie detector

detención f detention; orden de detención arrest warrant

detener ⟨2l⟩ 1 v/t stop; de policía arrest, detain 2 v/r detenerse stop

detenido 1 adj held up; (minucioso) detailed 2 m, -a f person under arrest

detenimiento m: con detenimiento thoroughly

detentar ⟨1a⟩ v/t hold

detergente m detergent

deteriorar ⟨1a⟩ 1 v/t damage 2 v/r deteriorarse deteriorate

deterioro m deterioration

determinado adj certain

determinar ⟨1a⟩ 1 v/t determine 2 v/r determinarse decide (a to)

detestar ⟨1a⟩ v/t detest

detonación f detonation

detonante m explosive; fig trigger

detonar ⟨1a⟩ 1 v/i detonate, go off 2 v/t detonate, set off

detractor m, detractora f detractor, critic

detrás adv behind; por detrás at the back; fig behind your / his etc back; detrás de behind; uno detrás de otro one after the other; estar detrás de algo fig be behind sth

detrimento m: en detrimento de to the detriment of

detritus m detritus

detuvo vb → detener

deuda f debt; estar en deuda con alguien fig be in s.o.'s debt, be indebted to s.o.

deudor m, deudora f debtor

devaluación f devaluation

devaluar ⟨1e⟩ v/t devalue

devanarse ⟨1a⟩ v/r: devanarse los sesos F rack one's brains F

devaneo m affair

devastar ⟨1a⟩ v/t devastate

devoción f tb fig devotion

devolver ⟨2h; part devuelto⟩ 1 v/t give back, return; fig: visita, saludo return; F (vomitar) throw up F 2 v/r devolverse L.Am. go back, return

devorar ⟨1a⟩ v/t devour

devuelto part → devolver

D.F. abr Méx (= Distrito Federal) Mexico City

dg. abr (= decigramo) decigram

di vb → dar

día m day; día de fiesta holiday; día festivo holiday; día hábil or laborable work day; poner al día update, bring up to date; a los pocos días a few days later; algún día, un día some day, one day; de día by day, during the day; de un día a or para otro from one day to the next; el día menos pensado when you least expect it; hace mal día tiempo it's a nasty day; hoy en día nowadays; todo el santo día all day long; todos los días every day; un día sí y otro no every other day; ya es de día it's light already; ¡buenos días! good morning

diabetes f diabetes

diabético 1 adj diabetic 2 m, -a f diabetic

diablesa f F she-devil

diablo m devil; un pobre diablo fig a poor devil; mandar a alguien al diablo tell s.o. to go to hell

diablura f prank, lark

diabólico adj diabolical

diadema f tiara; para el pelo hair-band

diáfano adj clear

diafragma m diaphragm

diagnosticar ⟨1g⟩ diagnose

diagnóstico 1 adj diagnostic 2 m diagnosis

diagonal 1 adj diagonal 2 f diagonal (line)

diagrama m diagram

dialecto m dialect

dialogar ⟨1h⟩ v/i talk (sobre about), discuss (sobre sth); (negociar) hold talks (con with)

diálogo m dialog(ue)

diamante m diamond

diametralmente adv: diametralmente

opuesto diametrically opposed

diámetro *m* diameter

diana *f* MIL reveille; (*blanco*) target; *para jugar a los dardos* dartboard; (*centro de blanco*) bull's eye; *dar en la diana* fig hit the nail on the head

diantre *int* F hell! F

diapositiva *f* FOT slide, transparency

diariero *m*, *-a f Arg* newspaper vendor

diario 1 *adj* daily 2 *m* diary; (*periódico*) newspaper; *a diario* daily

diarrea *f* MED diarrh(o)ea

dibujante *m/f* draftsman, *Br* draughtsman; *mujer* draftswoman, *Br* draughtswoman; *de viñetas* cartoonist

dibujar ⟨1a⟩ 1 *v/t* draw; *fig* describe 2 *v/r* **dibujarse** *fig* appear

dibujo *m* arte drawing; *ilustración* drawing, sketch; *estampado* pattern; *dibujos animados* cartoons; *película de dibujos animados* animation

diccionario *m* dictionary

dic.ᵉ *abr* (= *diciembre*) Dec. (= December)

dice *vb →* **decir**

díceres *mpl L.Am.* sayings

dicharachero *adj* chatty; (*gracioso*) witty

dicho 1 *part →* **decir** 2 *adj* said; *dicho y hecho* no sooner said than done; *mejor dicho* or rather 3 *m* saying

dichoso *adj* happy; F (*maldito*) damn F

diciembre *m* December

diciendo *vb →* **decir**

dictado *m* dictation

dictador *m*, **dictadora** *f* dictator

dictadura *f* dictatorship

dictaminar ⟨1a⟩ *v/t* state

dictar ⟨1a⟩ *v/t lección, texto* dictate; *ley* announce; *dictar sentencia* JUR pass sentence

didáctico *adj* educational

diecinueve *adj* nineteen

dieciocho *adj* eighteen

dieciséis *adj* sixteen

diecisiete *adj* seventeen

diente *m* tooth; *diente de ajo* clove of garlic; *diente de león* BOT dandelion; *poner los dientes largos a alguien* make s.o. jealous

diesel *m* diesel

diestro 1 *adj*: *a diestro y siniestro fig* Y left and right 2 *m* TAUR bullfighter

dieta *f* diet; *estar a dieta* be on a diet; *dietas* travel(l)ing expenses

dietético *adj* dietary

diez *adj* ten

diezmar ⟨1a⟩ *v/t* decimate

difamar ⟨1a⟩ *v/t* slander, defame; *por escrito* libel, defame

difamatorio *adj* defamatory

diferencia *f* difference; *a diferencia de* unlike; *con diferencia fig* by a long way

diferenciar ⟨1b⟩ 1 *v/t* differentiate 2 *v/r* **diferenciarse** differ (*de* from); *no se diferencian en nada* there's no difference at all between them

diferente *adj* different

diferido *adj* TV: *en diferido* prerecorded

difícil *adj* difficult

dificultad *f* difficulty; *poner dificultades* make it difficult

dificultar ⟨1a⟩ *v/t* hinder

difundir ⟨3a⟩ 1 *v/t* spread; (*programa*) broadcast 2 *v/r* **difundirse** spread

difunto 1 *adj* late 2 *m*, *-a f* deceased

difuso *adj idea, conocimientos* vague, sketchy

digerir ⟨3i⟩ *v/t* digest; F *noticia* take in

digestión *f* digestion

digital *adj* digital

digitalizar ⟨1f⟩ *v/t* INFOR digitalize

dígito *m* digit

dignarse ⟨1a⟩ *v/r* deign

dignidad *f* dignity

digno *adj* worthy; *trabajo* decent; *digno de mención* worth mentioning

digo *vb →* **decir**

digresión *f* digression

dije *vb →* **decir**

dilación *f*: *sin dilación* without delay

dilapidar ⟨1a⟩ *v/t* waste

dilatar ⟨1a⟩ 1 *v/t* dilate; (*prolongar*) prolong; (*aplazar*) postpone 2 *v/i Méx* (*tardar*) be late; *no me dilato* I won't be long

dilema *m* dilemma

diligencia *f* diligence; *vehículo* stagecoach; *diligencias* JUR procedures, formalities

diligente *adj* diligent

dilucidar ⟨1a⟩ *v/t* clarify

diluir ⟨3g⟩ *v/t* dilute

diluviar ⟨1b⟩ *v/i* pour down

diluvio *m* downpour; *fig* deluge

dimensión *f* dimension; *fig* size, scale; *dimensiones* measurements

diminutivo *m* diminutive

diminuto *adj* tiny, diminutive

dimisión *f* resignation

dimitir ⟨3a⟩ *v/t* resign

Dinamarca *f* Denmark

dinámico *adj fig* dynamic

dinamita *f* dynamite

dinastía *f* dynasty

dinero *m* money; *dinero en efectivo*, *dinero en metálico* cash

dinosaurio *m* dinosaur

dio *vb →* **dar**

Dios *m* God; *hazlo como Dios manda* do

it properly; **¡Dios mío!** my God!; **¡por Dios!** for God's sake!; **sabe Dios lo que dijo** God knows what he said

dios *m tb fig* god

diosa *f* goddess

diploma *m* diploma

diplomacia *f* diplomacy

diplomático 1 *adj* diplomatic **2** *m*, -a *f* diplomat

diputado *m*, -a *f* representative, *Br* Member of Parliament

dique *m* dike, *Br* dyke

dirá *vb* → **decir**

diré *vb* → **decir**

dirección *f tb* TEA, *de película* direction; COM management; POL leadership; *de coche* steering; *en carta* address; **en aquella dirección** that way; **dirección asistida** AUTO power steering; **dirección de correo electrónico** e-mail address

directiva *f* board of directors; POL executive committee

directivo 1 *adj* governing; COM managing **2** *m*, -a *f* COM manager

directo *adj* direct; **en directo** TV, RAD live

director 1 *adj* leading **2** *m*, **directora** *f* manager; EDU principal, *Br* head (teacher); TEA, *de película* director; **director de orquesta** conductor

directriz *f* guideline

dirigir ⟨3c⟩ **1** *v/t* TEA, *película* direct; COM manage, run; MÚS conduct; **dirigir una carta a** address a letter to; **dirigir una pregunta a** direct a question to **2** *v/r* **dirigirse** make, head (**a, hacia** for)

discapacidad *f* disability

discapacitado 1 *adj* disabled **2** *m*, -a *f* disabled person

discar ⟨1g⟩ *v/t L.Am.* TELEC dial

discernir ⟨3i⟩ *v/t* distinguish, discern

disciplina *f* discipline

disciplinar ⟨1a⟩ *v/t* discipline

discípulo *m*, -a *f* REL, *fig* disciple

disco *m* disk, *Br* disc; MÚS record; (*discoteca*) DEP discus; **disco compacto** compact disc; **disco duro**, *L.Am.* **disco rígido** INFOR hard disk

discordante *adj* discordant

discordia *f* discord; (*colección de discos*) record collection

discreción *f* discretion; **a discreción** *disparar* at will; **a discreción de** at the discretion of

discrepancia *f* discrepancy; (*desacuerdo*) disagreement

discrepar ⟨1a⟩ *v/i* disagree

discreto *adj* discreet

discriminación *f* discrimination

discriminar ⟨1a⟩ *v/t* discriminate against;

(*diferenciar*) differentiate

disculpa *f* apology

disculpar ⟨1a⟩ **1** *v/t* excuse **2** *v/r* **disculparse** apologize

discurrir ⟨3a⟩ *v/i de tiempo* pass; *de acontecimiento* pass off; (*reflexionar*) reflect (**sobre** on)

discurso *m* speech; *de tiempo* passage, passing

discusión *f* discussion; (*disputa*) argument

discutir ⟨3a⟩ **1** *v/t* discuss **2** *v/i* argue (**sobre** about)

diseminar ⟨1a⟩ *v/t* scatter; *fig* spread

disentir ⟨3i⟩ *v/i* disagree (**de** with)

diseñador *m*, **diseñadora** *f* designer

diseñar ⟨1a⟩ *v/t* design

diseño *m* design; **diseño gráfico** graphic design

disfraz *m para ocultar* disguise; *para fiestas* costume, fancy dress

disfrazarse ⟨1f⟩ *v/r para ocultarse* disguise o.s. (**de** as); *para divertirse* dress up (**de** as)

disfrutar ⟨1a⟩ **1** *v/t* enjoy **2** *v/i* have fun, enjoy o.s.; **disfrutar de buena salud** be in *o* enjoy good health

disgregarse ⟨1h⟩ *v/r* disintegrate

disgustar ⟨1a⟩ **1** *v/t* upset **2** *v/r* **disgustarse** get upset

disgusto *m*: **me causó un gran disgusto** I was very upset; **llevarse un disgusto** get upset; **a disgusto** unwillingly

disidente *m/f* dissident

disimular ⟨1a⟩ *v/t* disguise **2** *v/i* pretend

disimulo *m*: **con disimulo** unobtrusively

disipar ⟨1a⟩ **1** *v/t duda* dispel **2** *v/r* **disiparse** *de niebla* clear; *de duda* vanish

diskette *m* diskette, floppy (disk)

dislexia *f* dyslexia

dislocar ⟨1g⟩ *v/t* dislocate

disminución *f* decrease

disminuido 1 *adj* handicapped **2** *m*, -a *f* handicapped person; **disminuido físico** physically handicapped person

disminuir ⟨3g⟩ **1** *v/t gastos, costos* reduce, cut; *velocidad* reduce **2** *v/i* decrease, diminish

disociar ⟨1b⟩ *v/t* separate

disolvente *m* solvent

disolver ⟨1h; *part* **disuelto**⟩ *v/t* dissolve; *manifestación* break up

disparada *f L.Am.*: **a la disparada** in a rush

disparar ⟨1a⟩ **1** *v/t tiro, arma* fire; *foto* take; *precios* send up **2** *v/i* shoot, fire **3** *v/r* **dispararse** *de arma, alarma* go off; *de precios* rise dramatically, rocket F

disparatado *adj* absurd

disparate *m* F piece of nonsense; **es un disparate hacer eso** it's crazy to do that
disparo *m* shot
dispendio *m* waste
dispensar ⟨1a⟩ *v/t* dispense; *(recibimiento)* give; *(eximir)* excuse (**de** from)
dispensario *m* MED clinic
dispersar ⟨1a⟩ **1** *v/t* disperse **2** *v/r* **dispersarse** disperse
disperso *adj* scattered
displicente *adj* disdainful
disponer ⟨2r; *part* **dispuesto**⟩ **1** *v/t (arreglar)* arrange; *(preparar)* prepare; *(ordenar)* stipulate **2** *v/i*: **disponer de algo** have sth at one's disposal **3** *v/r* **disponerse** get ready (**a** to)
disponibilidad *f* COM availability
disponible *adj* available
disposición *f* disposition; *de objetos* arrangement; **disposición de ánimo** state of mind; **estar a disposición de alguien** be at s.o.'s disposal
dispositivo *m* device
dispuesto 1 *part* → **disponer 2** *adj* ready (**a** to)
disputa *f* dispute
disputar ⟨1a⟩ **1** *v/t* dispute; *partido* play **2** *v/i* argue (**sobre** about) **3** *v/r* **disputarse** compete for
disquería *f* L.Am. record store
disquete *m* INFOR diskette, floppy (disk)
disquetera *f* disk drive
distancia *f* tb fig distance
distanciarse ⟨1b⟩ *v/r* distance o.s. (**de** from)
distante *adj* tb fig distant
distar ⟨1a⟩ *v/i* be far (**de** from)
distinción *f* distinction; **a distinción de** unlike
distinguido *adj* distinguished
distinguir ⟨3d⟩ *v/t* distinguish (**de** from); *(divisar)* make out; *con un premio* hono(u)r
distintivo *m* emblem; MIL insignia
distinto *adj* different; **distintos** *(varios)* several
distorsión *f* distortion
distracción *f* distraction; *(descuido)* absent-mindedness; *(diversión)* entertainment; *(pasatiempo)* pastime; **por distracción** out of absent-mindedness
distraer ⟨2p; *part* **distraído**⟩ **1** *v/t* distract; **la radio la distrae** she enjoys listening to the radio **2** *v/r* **distraerse** get distracted; *(disfrutar)* enjoy o.s.
distraído 1 *part* → **distraer 2** *adj* absent-minded; *temporalmente* distracted
distribución *f* COM, *de película* distribution

distribuir ⟨3g⟩ *v/t* distribute; *beneficio* share out
distrito *m* district
disturbio *m* disturbance
disuadir ⟨3a⟩ *v/t* dissuade; POL deter; **disuadir a alguien de hacer algo** dissuade s.o. from doing sth
disuelto *part* → **disolver**
disuntiva *f* dilemma
diurético *adj* diuretic
diurno *adj* day *atr*
divagar ⟨1h⟩ *v/i* digress
diván *m* couch
diversidad *f* diversity
diversión *f* fun; *(pasatiempo)* pastime; **aquí no hay muchas diversiones** there's not much to do around here
diverso *adj* diverse; **diversos** several, various
divertido *adj* funny; *(entretenido)* entertaining
divertir ⟨3i⟩ **1** *v/t* entertain **2** *v/r* **divertirse** have fun, enjoy o.s.
dividendo *m* dividend
dividir ⟨3a⟩ *v/t* divide
divinamente *adv* fig wonderfully
divinidad *f* divinity
divino *adj* tb fig divine
divisa *f* currency; **divisas** *pl* foreign currency *sg*
divisar ⟨1a⟩ *v/t* make out
división *f* MAT, MIL, DEP division; **hubo división de opiniones** there were differences of opinion
divorciado 1 *adj* divorced **2** *m*, **-a** *f* divorcee
divorciarse ⟨1b⟩ *v/r* get divorced
divorcio *m* divorce
divulgación *f* spread
divulgar ⟨1h⟩ **1** *v/t* spread **2** *v/r* **divulgarse** spread
d. J.C. *abr* (= **después de Jesucristo**) A.D. (= Anno Domini)
dl. *abr* (= **decilitro**) deciliter
dm. *abr* (= **decímetro**) decimeter
dobladillo *m* hem
doblado *adj película* dubbed
doblaje *m* de película dubbing
doblar ⟨1a⟩ **1** *v/t* fold; *cantidad* double; *película* dub; MAR round; *pierna, brazo* bend; *en una carrera* pass, Br overtake; **doblar la esquina** go round *o* turn the corner **2** *v/i* turn; **doblar a la derecha** turn right **3** *v/r* **doblarse** bend; *fig* give in
doble 1 *adj* double; *nacionalidad* dual; **doble clic** *m* double click **2** *m*: **el doble** twice as much (**de** as); **el doble de gente** twice as many people; **dobles** *tenis* doubles **3** *m/f* en película double

doblegar ⟨1h⟩ *v/t fig*: *voluntad* break; *orgullo* humble

doblez 1 *m* fold **2** *f fig* deceit

doce *adj* twelve

docena *f* dozen

docente *adj* teaching *atr*

dócil *adj* docile

doctor, doctora *f* doctor; *doctor honoris causa* honorary doctor

doctorado *m* doctorate

doctrina *f* doctrine

documentación *f* documentation; *de una persona* papers

documental *m* documentary

documento *m* document; *documento nacional de identidad* national identity card

dogma *m* dogma

dogo *m* ZO mastiff

dólar *m* dollar

dolencia *f* ailment

doler ⟨2h⟩ *v/i tb fig* hurt; *me duele el brazo* my arm hurts; *le dolió que le mintieran fig* she was hurt that they had lied to her

dolor *m tb fig* pain; *dolor de cabeza* headache; *dolor de estómago* stomach-ache; *dolor de muelas* toothache

dolorido *adj* sore, aching; *fig* hurt

doloroso *adj tb fig* painful

domador *m*, **domadora** *f* tamer

domesticar ⟨1g⟩ *v/t* domesticate

doméstico 1 *adj* domestic, household *atr* **2** *m*, **-a** *f* servant

domiciliación *f de sueldo* credit transfer; *de pagos* direct billing, *Br* direct debit

domicilio *m* address; *repartir a domicilio* do home deliveries

dominante *adj* dominant; *desp* domineering

dominar ⟨1a⟩ **1** *v/t* dominate; *idioma* have a good command of **2** *v/i* dominate **3** *v/r* **dominarse** control o.s.

domingo *m* Sunday; *domingo de Ramos* Palm Sunday

dominguero *m*, **-a** *f* F weekender, Sunday tripper

dominical *adj* Sunday *atr*

dominicano GEOG **1** *adj* Dominican **2** *m*, **-a** *f* Dominican

dominio *m* control; *fig* command; *ser del dominio público* be in the public domain

dominó *m* dominoes *pl*

don¹ *m* gift; *don de gentes* way with people

don² *m* Mr; *don Enrique* Mr Sanchez *English uses the surname while Spanish uses the first name*

donación *f* donation; *donación de sangre* blood donation; *donación de órganos* organ donation

donante *m/f* donor; *donante de sangre* blood donor

donar ⟨1a⟩ *v/t sangre, órgano, dinero* donate

donativo *m* donation

doncella *f* maid

donde 1 *adv* where **2** *prp esp L.Am.*: *fui donde el médico* I went to the doctor's

dónde *interr* where; *¿de dónde eres?* where are you from?; *¿hacia dónde vas?* where are you going?

dondequiera *adv* wherever

doña *f* Mrs; *doña Estela* Mrs Sanchez *English uses the surname while Spanish uses the first name*

dopaje, doping *m* doping

dorada *f* ZO gilthead

dorado *adj* gold; *montura* gilt

dormido *adj* asleep; *quedarse dormido* fall asleep

dormir ⟨3k⟩ **1** *v/i* sleep; *(estar dormido)* be asleep **2** *v/t* put to sleep; *dormir a alguien* MED give s.o. a general an(a)esthetic **3** *v/r* **dormirse** go to sleep; *(quedarse dormido)* fall asleep; *(no despertarse)* oversleep; *no podía dormirme* I couldn't get to sleep

dormitorio *m* bedroom

dorso *m* back

dos *adj* two; *de dos en dos* in twos; *los dos* both; *anda con ojo con los dos* watch out for the pair of them; *cada dos por tres* all the time, continually

doscientos *adj* two hundred

dosificar ⟨1g⟩ *v/t* cut down on

dosis *f inv* dose

dotar ⟨1a⟩ *v/t equip* (*de* with); *fondos* provide (*de* with); *cualidades* endow (*de* with)

dote *f a novia* dowry; *tener dotes para algo* have a gift for sth

doy *vb* → *dar*

dpto. *abr* (= *departamento*) dept (= department)

Dr. *abr* (= *Doctor*) Dr (= Doctor)

Dra. *abr* (= *Doctora*) Dr (= Doctor)

dragar ⟨1h⟩ *v/t* dredge

dragón *m* dragon; MIL dragoon

drama *m* drama

dramático *adj* dramatic; *arte dramático* dramatic art

dramatizar ⟨1f⟩ *v/t* dramatize

drástico *adj* drastic

drenaje *m* drainage

droga *f* drug; *droga de diseño* designer drug

drogadicto 1 adj: *una mujer -a* a woman addicted to drugs **2** m, **-a** f drug addict
drogarse ⟨1h⟩ v/r take drugs
drogodependencia f drug dependency
droguería f store selling cleaning and household products
dromedario m zo dromedary
d.to abr (= *descuento*) discount
ducha f shower; *ser una ducha de agua fría* fig come as a shock
ducharse ⟨1a⟩ v/r have a shower, shower
duda f doubt; *sin duda* without doubt; *poner en duda* call into question
dudar ⟨1a⟩ **1** v/t doubt **2** v/i hesitate (*en* to)
dudoso adj doubtful; (*indeciso*) hesitant
duele vb → **doler**
duelo m grief; (*combate*) duel
duende m imp
dueño m, **-a** f owner
duermo vb → **dormir**
dulce 1 adj sweet; fig gentle **2** m candy, Br sweet
dulzura f tb fig sweetness
dumping m dumping
duna f dune

duo m MÚS duo
duodécimo adj twelfth
dúplex m duplex (apartment)
duplicado 1 adj duplicate; *por duplicado* in duplicate **2** m duplicate
duplicar ⟨1g⟩ v/t duplicate
duque m duke
duquesa f duchess
duración f duration
duradero adj lasting; *ropa, calzado* hard-wearing
durante prp indicando duración during; *indicando período* for; *durante seis meses* for six months
durar ⟨1a⟩ v/i last
duraznero m L.Am. BOT peach (tree)
durazno m L.Am. BOT peach
Durex® m Méx Scotch tape®, Br Sellotape®
duro 1 adj hard; *carne* tough; *clima*, fig harsh; *duro de oído* F hard of hearing; *ser duro de pelar* be a tough nut to crack **2** adv hard **3** m five peseta coin
DVD abr (= *Disco de Vídeo Digital*) DVD (= Digital Versatile o Video Disc)

E

E abr (= *este*) E (= East(ern))
e conj (*instead of y before words starting with i, hi*) and
ebanista m cabinetmaker
ébano m ebony
ebrio adj drunk
ebullición f: *punto de ebullición* boiling point
eccema m eczema
echar ⟨1a⟩ **1** v/t (*lanzar*) throw; (*poner*) put; *de un lugar* throw out; *humo* give off; *carta* mail, Br tb post; *lo han echado del trabajo* he's been fired; *echar abajo* pull down, destroy; *echar la culpa a alguien* blame s.o., put the blame on s.o.; *me echó 40 años* he thought I was 40 **2** v/i: *echar a* start to, begin to; *echar a correr* start o begin to run, start running **3** v/r *echarse* (*tirarse*) throw o.s.; (*tumbarse*) lie down; (*ponerse*) put on; *echarse a llorar* start o begin to cry, start crying
eclesiástico adj ecclesiastical, church atr
eclipsar ⟨1a⟩ v/t eclipse

eclipse m eclipse
eco m echo; *tener eco* fig make an impact
ecografía f (ultrasound) scan
ecología f ecology
ecológico adj ecological; *alimentos* organic
ecologista m/f ecologist
economato m co-operative store
economía f economy; *ciencia* economics; *economía de mercado* market economy; *economía sumergida* black economy
económico adj economic; (*barato*) economical
economista m/f economist
economizar ⟨1f⟩ v/t economize on, save
ecosistema m ecosystem
ecoturismo m ecotourism
ecuación f equation
ecuador m equator
Ecuador Ecuador
ecuánime adj (*sereno*) even-tempered; (*imparcial*) impartial

ecuatorial *adj* equatorial

ecuatoriano 1 *adj* Ecuadorean 2 *m*, -a *f* Ecuadorean

eczema *m* eczema

ed. *abr* (= **edición**) ed (= edition)

edad *f* age; **la Edad Media** the Middle Ages *pl*; **la tercera edad** the over 60s; **estar en la edad del pavo** to be at that awkward age; **a la edad de** at the age of; **¿qué edad tienes?** how old are you?

edición *f* edition

edificar ⟨1g⟩ *v/t* construct, build

edificio *m* building

edil *m*, edila *f* council(l)or

editar ⟨1a⟩ *v/t* edit; (*publicar*) publish

editor *m*, editora *f* editor

editorial 1 *m* editorial, leading article 2 *f* publishing company *o* house, publisher

edredón *m* eiderdown

educación *f* (*crianza*) upbringing; (*modales*) manners; **educación física** physical education, PE

educado *adj* polite, well-mannered; **mal educado** rude, ill-mannered

educar ⟨1g⟩ *v/t* educate; (*criar*) bring up; *voz* train

educativo *adj* educational

edulcorante *m* sweetener

EE. UU. *abr* (= **Estados Unidos**) US(A) (= United States (of America))

efectista *adj* theatrical, dramatic

efectivamente *adv* indeed

efectivo 1 *adj* effective; **hacer efectivo** COM cash 2 *m*: **en efectivo** (in) cash

efecto *m* effect; **efecto invernadero** greenhouse effect; **efectos secundarios** side effects; **en efecto** indeed, **surtir efecto** take effect, work

efectuar ⟨1e⟩ *v/t* carry out

efervescente *adj* effervescent; *bebida* carbonated, sparkling

eficacia *f* efficiency

eficaz *adj* (*efectivo*) effective; (*eficiente*) efficient

eficiencia *f* efficiency

eficiente *adj* efficient

efímero *adj* ephemeral, short-lived

efusivo *adj* effusive

egipcio 1 *adj* Egyptian 2 *m*, -a *f* Egyptian

Egipto *m* Egypt

ego *m* ego

egocéntrico *adj* egocentric, self-centered (*Br* -centred)

egoísmo *m* selfishness, egoism

egoísta 1 *adj* selfish, egoistic 2 *m/f* egoist

egresar ⟨1a⟩ *v/i* L.Am. *de universidad* graduate; *de colegio* graduate from high school, *Br* leave school

egreso *m* L.Am. graduation

eh *int para llamar atención* hey!; **¿eh?** eh?

eje *m* axis; *de auto* axle; *fig* linchpin

ejecución *f* (*realización*) implementation, carrying out; *de condenado* execution; MÚS performance

ejecutar ⟨1a⟩ *v/t* (*realizar*) carry out, implement; *condenado* execute; INFOR run, execute; MÚS play, perform

ejecutiva *f* executive

ejecutivo 1 *adj* executive; **el poder ejecutivo** POL the executive 2 *m* executive; **el Ejecutivo** the government

ejemplar 1 *adj* *alumno, padre etc* model *atr*, exemplary 2 *m de libro* copy; *de revista* issue; *animal, planta* specimen

ejemplo *m* example; **dar buen ejemplo** set a good example; **por ejemplo** for example

ejercer ⟨2b⟩ 1 *v/t cargo* practice, *Br* practise; *influencia* exert 2 *v/i de profesional* practice, *Br* practise; **ejerce de médico** he's a practicing (*Br* practising) doctor

ejercicio *m* exercise; COM fiscal year, *Br* financial year; **hacer ejercicio** exercise

ejercitar ⟨1a⟩ 1 *v/t músculo, derecho* exercise 2 *v/r* ejercitarse train; **ejercitarse en** practice, *Br* practise

ejército *m* army

ejido *m Méx* traditional rural communal farming unit

ejote *m* L.Am. green bean

el 1 *art* the 2 *pron*: **el de ...** that of ...; **el de Juan** Juan's; **el más grande** the biggest (one); **el que está ...** the one who is ...

él *pron sujeto* he; *cosa* it; *complemento* him; *cosa* it; **de él** his

elaborar ⟨1a⟩ *v/t* produce, make; *metal etc* work; *plan* devise, draw up

elasticidad *f* elasticity

elástico 1 *adj* elastic 2 *m* elastic; (*goma*) elastic band, *Br* rubber band

elección *f* choice

eleccionario *adj* L.Am. election *atr*, electoral

elecciones *fpl* election *sg*

elector *m* voter

electorado *m* electorate

electoral *adj* election *atr*, electoral

electricidad *f* electricity

electricista *m/f* electrician

eléctrico *adj luz, motor* electric; *aparato* electrical

electrocutar ⟨1a⟩ 1 *v/t* electrocute 2 *v/r* electrocutarse be electrocuted, electrocute o.s.

electrodo *m* electrode

electrodoméstico *m* electrical appliance

electrón *m* electron

electrónica *f* electronics

electrónico *adj* electronic
elefante *m* ZO elephant; **elefante marino** elephant seal, sea elephant
elegancia *f* elegance, stylishness
elegante *adj* elegant, stylish
elegantoso *adj L.Am.* F stylish, classy F
elegía *f* elegy
elegible *adj* eligible
elegir ⟨3c & 3l⟩ *v/t* choose; *por votación* elect
elemental *adj* (*esencial*) fundamental, essential; (*básico*) elementary, basic
elemento *m* element
elevado *adj* high; *fig* elevated
elevador *m* hoist; *L.Am.* elevator, *Br* lift
elevar ⟨1a⟩ **1** *v/t* raise **2** *v/r* **elevarse** rise; *de monumento* stand
eliminación *f* elimination; *de desperdicios* disposal
eliminar ⟨1a⟩ *v/t* eliminate; *desperdicios* dispose of
eliminatoria *f* DEP qualifying round, heat
élite *f* elite
elitista *adj* elitist
elixir *m* elixir; **elíxir bucal** mouthwash
ella *pron sujeto* she; *cosa* it; *complemento* her; *cosa* it; **de ella** her; **es de ella** it's hers
ellas *pron sujeto* they; *complemento* them; **de ellas** their; **es de ellas** it's theirs
ello *pron* it
ellos *pron sujeto* they; *complemento* them; **de ellos** their; **es de ellos** it's theirs
elocuente *adj* eloquent
elogiar ⟨1b⟩ *v/t* praise
elogio *m* praise
elote *m L.Am.* corncob; *granos* corn, *Br* sweetcorn
El Salvador El Salvador
eludir ⟨3a⟩ *v/t* evade, avoid
emanar ⟨1a⟩ **1** *v/i* emanate (**de** from) *fml; fig* stem (**de** from), derive (**de** from) **2** *v/t* exude, emit
emancipación *f* emancipation
emanciparse ⟨1a⟩ *v/r* become emancipated
embadurnar ⟨1a⟩ *v/t* smear (**de** with)
embajada *f* embassy
embajador *m*, **embajadora** *f* ambassador
embalaje *m* packing
embalar ⟨1a⟩ **1** *v/t* pack **2** *v/r* **embalarse** *de persona* get excited; **el coche se embaló** the car went faster and faster; **no te embales** don't go so fast
embalse *m* reservoir
embarazada 1 *adj* pregnant **2** *f* pregnant woman

embarazo *m* pregnancy; **interrupción del embarazo** termination, abortion
embarazoso *adj* awkward, embarrassing
embarcación *f* vessel, craft
embarcadero *m* wharf
embarcar ⟨1g⟩ **1** *v/t pasajeros* board, embark; *mercancías* load **2** *v/i* board, embark **3** *v/r* **embarcarse** *en barco* board, embark; *en avión* board; **embarcarse en** *fig* embark on
embargo *m* embargo; JUR seizure; **sin embargo** however
embarque *m* boarding; *de mercancías* loading
embarrancar ⟨1g⟩ *v/i* MAR run aground **2** *v/r* **embarrancarse** MAR run aground
embaucador 1 *adj* deceitful **2** *m*, **embaucadora** *f* trickster
embeberse ⟨2a⟩ *v/r* get absorbed *o* engrossed (**en** in)
embelesar ⟨1a⟩ *v/t* captivate
embestir ⟨3l⟩ **1** *v/t* charge **2** *v/i* charge (**contra** at)
emblema *m* emblem
embobar ⟨1a⟩ *v/t* fascinate
embolarse ⟨1a⟩ *v/r C.Am., Méx* F get plastered F
émbolo *m* TÉC piston
embolsar ⟨1a⟩ **1** *v/t* pocket **2** *v/r* **embolsarse** pocket
emborrachar ⟨1a⟩ **1** *v/t* make drunk, get drunk **2** *v/r* **emborracharse** get drunk
emborronar ⟨1a⟩ *v/t* blot, smudge
emboscada *f* ambush
embotar ⟨1a⟩ *v/t* blunt
embotellamiento *m* traffic jam
embotellar ⟨1a⟩ *v/t* bottle
embrague *m* AUTO clutch
embriagar ⟨1h⟩ *v/t fig* intoxicate
embriaguez *f* intoxication
embrión *m* embryo; **en embrión** in an embryonic state, in embryo
embrollo *m* tangle; *fig* mess, muddle
embromar ⟨1a⟩ *v/t Rpl* F (*molestar*) annoy
embrujar ⟨1a⟩ *v/t tb fig* bewitch
embrutecer ⟨2d⟩ **1** *v/t* brutalize **2** *v/r* **embrutecerse** become brutalized
embudo *m* funnel
embustero 1 *adj* lying **2** *m*, **-a** *f* liar
embutido *m* GASTR type of dried sausage
emergencia *f* emergency
emerger ⟨2c⟩ *v/i* emerge
emigración *f* emigration
emigrante *m* emigrant
emigrar ⟨1a⟩ *v/i* emigrate; ZO migrate
eminente *adj* eminent
emirato *m* emirate
emisario *m* emissary

emisión f emission; COM issue; RAD, TV broadcast

emisora f radio station

emitir ⟨3a⟩ v/t calor, sonido give out, emit; moneda issue; opinión express, give; veredicto deliver; RAD, TV broadcast; voto cast

emoción f emotion; ¡**qué emoción!** how exciting!

emocionado adj exciting

emocionante adj (excitante) exciting; (conmovedor) moving

emocionarse ⟨1a⟩ v/r get excited; (conmoverse) be moved

emotivo adj emotional; (conmovedor) moving

empacar ⟨1g⟩ **1** v/t & v/i L.Am. pack **2** v/r **empacarse** L.Am. (ponerse tozudo) dig one's heels in; tragar devour

empacharse ⟨1a⟩ v/r F get an upset stomach (**de** from); **empacharse de** fig overdose on

empacho m F upset stomach; fig bellyful F; **sin empacho** unashamedly

empadronar ⟨1a⟩ **1** v/t register **2** v/r **empadronarse** register

empalagoso adj sickly; fig sickly sweet, cloying

empalizada f palisade

empalmar ⟨1a⟩ **1** v/t connect, join **2** v/i connect (**con** with), join up (**con** with); de idea, conversación run o follow on (**con** from)

empanada f pie

empanadilla f pasty

empanar ⟨1a⟩ v/t coat in breadcrumbs

empantanarse ⟨1a⟩ v/r become swamped o waterlogged; fig get bogged down

empañado adj misty

empañar ⟨1a⟩ **1** v/t steam up, mist up; fig tarnish, sully **2** v/r **empañarse** de vidrio steam up, mist up

empapado adj soaked, dripping wet

empapar ⟨1a⟩ **1** v/t soak; (absorber) soak up; **2** v/r **empaparse** get soaked o drenched; **empaparse de algo** immerse o s. in sth

empapelar ⟨1a⟩ v/t wallpaper

empaque m presence; (seriedad) solemnity

empaquetar ⟨1a⟩ v/t pack

emparedado m sandwich

emparejar ⟨1a⟩ v/t personas pair off; calcetines match up

emparentado adj related

empastador m, **empastadora** f L.Am. bookbinder

empastar ⟨1a⟩ v/t muela fill; libro bind

empaste m filling

empatar ⟨1a⟩ v/i tie, Br draw; (igualar) tie the game, Br equalize

empate m tie, draw; **gol del empate** en fútbol equalizer

empecinarse ⟨1a⟩ v/r get an idea into one's head; **empecinarse en algo** insist on sth

empedernido adj inveterate, confirmed

empedrado m paving

empeine m instep

empellón m shove; **entró a empellones** he shoved his way in

empelotarse ⟨1a⟩ v/r L.Am. P take one's clothes off, strip off

empeñado adj (endeudado) in debt; **estar empeñado en hacer algo** be determined to do sth

empeñar ⟨1a⟩ **1** v/t pawn **2** v/r **empeñarse** (endeudarse) get into debt; (esforzarse) strive (**en** to), make an effort (**en** to); **empeñarse en hacer** obstinarse insist on doing, be determined to do

empeñero Méx **1** adj determined **2** m, -a f determined person

empeño m (obstinación) determination; (esfuerzo) effort; Méx fig pawn shop

empeñoso adj L.Am. hard-working

empeorar ⟨1a⟩ **1** v/t make worse **2** v/i deteriorate, get worse

empequeñecer ⟨2d⟩ v/t fig diminish

emperador m emperor; pez swordfish

emperatriz f empress

emperrarse ⟨1a⟩ v/r F: **emperrarse en hacer algo** have one's heart set on doing sth; **emperrarse con algo** set one's heart on sth

empezar ⟨1f & 1k⟩ **1** v/t start, begin **2** v/i start, begin; **empezar a hacer algo** start to do sth, start doing sth; **empezar por hacer algo** start o begin by doing sth

empiezo m S. Am. start, beginning

empinado adj steep

empinar ⟨1a⟩ v/t raise; **empinar el codo** F raise one's elbow F

empírico adj empirical

emplazamiento m site, location; JUR subpoena, summons

empleado 1 adj: **le está bien empleado** it serves him right **2** m, -a f employee; **-a de hogar** maid

emplear ⟨1a⟩ v/t (usar) use; persona employ

empleo m employment; (puesto) job; (uso) use; **modo de empleo** instructions for use pl, directions pl

emplomar ⟨1a⟩ v/t S. Am. fill

empobrecer ⟨2d⟩ **1** v/t impoverish, make poor **2** v/i become impoverished, become poor **3** v/r **empobrecerse** become impoverished, become poor

empobrecimiento *m* impoverishment

empollar ⟨1a⟩ *v/i* F cram F, *Br* swot F

empollón *m* F grind F, *Br* swot F

emporio *m L.Am.* almacén department store

empotrado *adj* built-in, fitted

empotrarse ⟨1a⟩ *v/r* crash (**contra** into)

emprendedor *adj* enterprising

emprender ⟨2a⟩ *v/t* embark on, undertake; **emprenderla con alguien** F take it out on s.o.

empresa *f* company; *fig* venture, undertaking; **empresa de trabajo temporal** temping agency

empresaria *f* businesswoman

empresarial *adj* business *atr*; **ciencias empresariales** business studies

empresario *m* businessman

empujar ⟨1a⟩ *v/t* push; *fig* urge on, spur on

empujón *m* push, shove; **salían a empujones** F they were pushing and shoving their way out

empuñar ⟨1a⟩ *v/t* grasp

emular ⟨1a⟩ *v/t* emulate

emulsión *f* emulsion

en *prp* (*dentro de*) in; (*sobre*) on; **en un mes** in a month; **en la mesa** on the table; **en inglés** in English; **en la calle** on the street, *Br tb* in the street; **en casa** at home; **en coche / tren** by car / train

enajenación *f* JUR transfer; **enajenación mental** insanity

enajenar ⟨1a⟩ *v/t* JUR transfer; (*trastornar*) drive insane

enamorado *adj* in love (**de** with)

enamorar ⟨1a⟩ *v/t*: **lo enamoró** she captivated him 2 *v/r* **enamorarse** fall in love (**de** with)

enano 1 *adj* tiny; *perro, árbol* miniature, dwarf *atr* 2 *m* dwarf; **trabajar como un enano** *fig* F work like a dog F

enarbolar ⟨1a⟩ *v/t* hoist, raise

encabezamiento *m* heading

encabezar ⟨1f⟩ *v/t* head; *movimiento, revolución* lead

encabritarse ⟨1a⟩ *v/r de caballo* rear up

encadenar ⟨1a⟩ 1 *v/t* chain (up); *fig* link *o* put together 2 *v/r* **encadenarse** chain oneself (**a** to)

encajar ⟨1a⟩ 1 *v/t piezas* fit; *golpe* take 2 *v/i* fit (**en** in; **con** with)

encaje *m* lace

encalado *m* whitewashing

encalar ⟨1a⟩ *v/t* whitewash

encallar ⟨1a⟩ *v/i* MAR run aground

encaminarse ⟨1a⟩ *v/r* set off (**a** for), head (**a** for); *fig* be aimed *o* directed (**a** at)

encandilar ⟨1a⟩ *v/t* dazzle

encantado *adj* (*contento*) delighted; *castillo* enchanted; **¡encantado!** nice to meet you

encantador *adj* charming

encantar ⟨1a⟩ *v/t*: **me / le encanta** I love / he loves it

encanto *m* (*atractivo*) charm; **como por encanto** as if by magic; **eres un encanto** you're an angel

encapricharse ⟨1a⟩ *v/r* fall in love (**de** with)

encapuchado *adj* hooded

encaramarse ⟨1a⟩ *v/r* climb

encarar ⟨1a⟩ *v/t* approach; *desgracia etc* face up to

encarcelar ⟨1a⟩ *v/t* put in prison, imprison

encarecer ⟨2d⟩ 1 *v/t* put up the price of, make more expensive 2 *v/r* **encarecerse** become more expensive; *de precios* increase, rise

encarecidamente *adv*: **le ruego encarecidamente que ...** I beg *o* urge you to ...

encargado *m*, *-a f* person in charge; *de un negocio* manager

encargar ⟨1h⟩ 1 *v/t* (*pedir*) order; **le encargué que me trajera ...** I asked him to bring me ... 2 *v/r* **encargarse** (*tener responsibilidad*) be in charge; **yo me encargo de la comida** I'll take care of *o* see to the food

encargo *m* job, errand; COM order; **¿te puedo hacer un encargo?** can I ask you to do something for me?; **hecho por encargo** made to order

encariñarse ⟨1a⟩ *v/r*: **encariñarse con alguien / algo** grow fond of s.o/sth, become attached to s.o/sth

encarnado *adj* red

encarnar ⟨1a⟩ *v/t cualidad etc* embody; TEA play

encarnizado *adj* bitter, fierce

encarrilar ⟨1a⟩ *v/t fig* direct, guide

encasillar ⟨1a⟩ *v/t* class, classify; (*estereotipar*) pigeonhole

encasquetar ⟨1a⟩ *v/t gorro etc* pull down; **me lo encasquetó** F he landed me with it F

encasquillarse ⟨1a⟩ *v/r de arma* jam

encauzar ⟨1f⟩ *v/t tb fig* channel

encefalopatía *f*: **encefalopatía espongiforme bovina** bovine spongiform encephalitis, BSE

encendedor *m* lighter

encender ⟨2g⟩ 1 *v/t fuego* light; *luz, televisión* switch on, turn on; *fig* inflame, arouse, stir up 2 *v/r* **encenderse** *de luz, televisión* come on

encendido 1 *adj luz, televisión* (switched) on; *fuego* lit; *cara* red **2** *m* AUTO ignition
encerado *m* blackboard
encerar ⟨1a⟩ *v/t* polish, wax
encerrar ⟨1k⟩ **1** *v/t* lock up, shut up; *(contener)* contain **2** *v/r* **encerrarse** shut o.s. up
encerrona *f tb fig* trap
encestar ⟨1a⟩ *v/i* score
encharcado *adj* flooded, waterlogged
enchicharse ⟨1a⟩ *v/r L.Am.* (*emborracharse*) get drunk; *Rpl* P (*enojarse*) get angry, get mad F
enchilada *f Méx* GASTR enchilada (*tortilla with a meat or cheese filling*)
enchiloso *adj C.Am., Méx* hot
enchufado *m*: **es un enchufado** F he has connections, he has friends in high places
enchufar ⟨1a⟩ *v/t* EL plug in
enchufe *m* EL *macho* plug; *hembra* socket; **tener enchufe** *fig* F have pull F, have connections F
enchufismo *m* string-pulling
encía *f* gum
enciclopedia *f* encyclop(a)edia
encierro *m protesta* sit-in; *de toros* bull running
encima *adv* on top; **encima de** on top of, on; **por encima de** over, above; **por encima de todo** above all; **lo ayudo, y encima se queja** I help him and then he goes and complains; **hacer algo muy por encima** do sth very quickly; **no lo llevo encima** I haven't got it on me; **ponerse algo encima** put sth on
encimera *f sábana* top sheet; *Esp mostrador* worktop
encina *f* BOT holm oak
encinta *adj* pregnant
enclaustrarse ⟨1a⟩ *v/r fig* shut o.s. away
enclave *m* enclave
enclenque 1 *adj* sickly, weak **2** *m/f* weakling
encoger ⟨2c⟩ **1** *v/t* shrink; *las piernas* tuck in **2** *v/i de material* shrink **3** *v/r* **encogerse** *de material* shrink; *fig: de persona* be intimidated, cower; **encogerse de hombros** shrug (one's shoulders)
encolar ⟨1a⟩ *v/t* glue, stick
encolerizarse ⟨1f⟩ *v/r* get angry
encomienda *f L.Am.* HIST grant of land and labor by colonial authorities after the Conquest
enconado *adj* fierce, heated
encontrar ⟨1m⟩ **1** *v/t* find **2** *v/r* **encontrarse** (*reunirse*) meet; (*estar*) be; **encontrarse con alguien** meet s.o., run into s.o.; **me encuentro bien** I'm fine, I feel fine

encontronazo *m* smash, crash
encorvar ⟨1a⟩ *v/t* hunch; *estantería* cause to buckle
encrespar ⟨1a⟩ **1** *v/t pelo* curl; *mar* make rough o choppy; *fig* arouse, inflame **2** *v/r* **encresparse** *del mar* turn choppy; *fig* become inflamed
encrucijada *f* crossroads; *fig* dilemma
encuadernar ⟨1a⟩ *v/t* bind
encuadrar ⟨1a⟩ *v/t en marco* frame; *en grupo* include, place
encuartelar ⟨1a⟩ *v/t L.Am.* billet
encubierto *part* → **encubrir**
encubrir ⟨3a; *part* **encubierto**⟩ *v/t delincuente* harbo(u)r; *delito* cover up, conceal
encuentro *m* meeting, encounter; DEP game; **salir** *or* **ir al encuentro de alguien** meet s.o., greet
encuerado *adj L.Am.* naked
encuesta *f* survey; (*sondeo*) (opinion) poll
encuestar ⟨1a⟩ *v/t* poll
encumbrarse ⟨1a⟩ *v/r fig* rise to the top
encurtidos *mpl* pickles
ende *adv*: **por ende** therefore, consequently
endeble *adj* weak, feeble
endémico *adj* endemic
endemoniado *adj* possessed; *fig* F terrible, awful
enderezar ⟨1f⟩ **1** *v/t* straighten out **2** *v/r* **enderezarse** straighten up, stand up straight; *fig* straighten o.s. out, sort o.s out
endeudarse ⟨1a⟩ *v/r* get (o.s.) into debt
endiablado *adj fig* (*malo*) terrible, awful; (*difícil*) tough
endibia *f* BOT endive
endilgar ⟨1h⟩ *v/t*: **me lo endilgó a mí** F he landed me with it F, **endilgar un sermón a alguien** F lecture s.o., give s.o. a lecture
endosar ⟨1a⟩ *v/t* COM endorse; **me lo endosó a mí** F she landed me with it F
endrina *f* BOT sloe
endrogarse ⟨1h⟩ *v/r Méx, C.Am.* get into debt
endulzar ⟨1f⟩ *v/t* sweeten; (*suavizar*) soften
endurecer ⟨2d⟩ **1** *v/t* harden; *fig* toughen up **2** *v/r* **endurecerse** harden, become harder; *fig* become harder, toughen up
enebro *m* BOT juniper
enema *m* MED enema
enemigo 1 *adj* enemy *atr* **2** *m* enemy; **ser enemigo de** *fig* be opposed to, be against
enemistarse ⟨1a⟩ *v/r* fall out

E

energético *adj crisis* energy *atr; alimento* energy-giving

energía *f* energy; **energía eólica** wind power; **energía nuclear** nuclear power, nuclear energy; **energía solar** solar power, solar energy

enérgico *adj* energetic; *fig* forceful, strong

energúmeno *m* lunatic; **ponerse hecho un energúmeno** go crazy F, blow a fuse F

ene. *abr* (= *enero*) Jan. (= January)

enero *m* January

enervar ⟨1a⟩ *v/t* irritate, get on the nerves of

enésimo *adj* nth; **por -a vez** for the umpteenth time

enfadado *adj* annoyed (**con** with); (*encolerizado*) angry (**con** with)

enfadar ⟨1a⟩ **1** *v/t* (*molestar*) annoy; (*encolerizar*) make angry, anger **2** *v/r* **enfadarse** (*molestarse*) get annoyed (**con** with); (*encolerizarse*) get angry (**con** with)

enfado *m* (*molestia*) annoyance; (*cólera*) anger

enfangarse ⟨1h⟩ *v/r* get muddy; **enfangarse en** *fig* get (o.s.) mixed up in

énfasis *m* emphasis; **poner énfasis en** emphasize, stress

enfático *adj* emphatic

enfermar ⟨1a⟩ **1** *v/t* drive crazy **2** *v/i* get sick, *Br tb* get ill

enfermedad *f* illness, disease

enfermería *f sala* infirmary, sickbay; *carrera* nursing

enfermero *m*, **-a** *f* nurse

enfermizo *adj* unhealthy

enfermo **1** *adj* sick, ill **2** *m*, **-a** *f* sick person

enfermoso *adj L.Am.* sickly, unhealthy

enfiestarse ⟨1a⟩ *v/r L.Am.* F party F, live it up F

enfocar ⟨1g⟩ *v/t cámara* focus; *imagen* get in focus; *fig: asunto* look at, consider

enfoque *m fig* approach

enfrentamiento *m* clash, confrontation

enfrentar ⟨1a⟩ **1** *v/t* confront, face up to **2** *v/r* **enfrentarse** DEP meet; **enfrentarse con alguien** confront s.o.; **enfrentarse a algo** face (up to) sth

enfrente *adv* opposite; **enfrente del colegio** opposite the school, across (the street) from the school

enfriar ⟨1c⟩ *v/t vino* chill; *algo caliente* cool (down); *fig* cool **2** *v/r* **enfriarse** (*perder calor*) cool down; (*perder demasiado calor*) get cold, go cold; *fig* cool, cool off; MED catch a cold, catch a chill

enfurecer ⟨2d⟩ **1** *v/t* infuriate, make furious **2** *v/r* **enfurecerse** get furious, get in-

to a rage **enfurecido** *adj* furious, enraged

enfurruñado *adj* F sulky

enfurruñarse ⟨1a⟩ *v/r* F go into a huff F

engalanar ⟨1a⟩ *v/t* decorate, deck

enganchar ⟨1a⟩ **1** *v/t* hook; F *novia, trabajo* land F **2** *v/r* **engancharse** get caught (**en** on); MIL sign up, enlist; **engancharse a la droga** F get hooked on drugs F

engañar ⟨1a⟩ *v/t* deceive, cheat; (*ser infiel a*) cheat on, be unfaithful to; **te han engañado** you've been had **2** *v/r* **engañarse** (*mentirse*) deceive o.s., kid o.s. F; (*equivocarse*) be wrong

engaño *m* (*mentira*) deception, deceit; (*ardid*) trick

engarzar ⟨1f⟩ *v/t joya* set

engatusar ⟨1a⟩ *v/t* F sweet-talk F

engendrar ⟨1a⟩ *v/t* father; *fig* breed, engender *fml*

engendro *m fig* eyesore

englobar ⟨1a⟩ *v/t* include, embrace *fml*

engordar ⟨1a⟩ **1** *v/t* put on, gain **2** *v/i de persona* put on weight, gain weight; *de comida* be fattening

engorrar ⟨1a⟩ *v/t Méx, W.I.* F annoy

engorroso *adj* tricky

engranaje *m* TÉC gears *pl; fig* machinery

engrasar ⟨1a⟩ *v/t* grease, lubricate

engrase *m* greasing, lubrication

engreído *adj* conceited

engrosar ⟨1m⟩ **1** *v/t* swell, increase **2** *v/i* put on weight, gain weight

engrudo *m* (flour and water) paste

engullir ⟨3h⟩ *v/t* bolt (down)

enhebrar ⟨1a⟩ *v/t* thread, string

enhiesto *adj lit persona* erect, upright; *torre, árbol* lofty

enhorabuena *f* congratulations *pl;* **dar la enhorabuena** congratulate (**por** on)

enigma *m* enigma

enigmático *adj* enigmatic

enjabonar ⟨1a⟩ *v/t* soap

enjambre *m tb fig* swarm

enjoyado *adj* bejewel(l)ed

enjuagar ⟨1h⟩ *v/t* rinse

enjugar ⟨1h⟩ *v/t deuda etc* wipe out; *líquido* mop up; *lágrimas* wipe away

enjuiciar ⟨1b⟩ *v/t* JUR institute proceedings against; *fig* judge

enlace *m* link, connection; **enlace matrimonial** marriage

enlatar ⟨1a⟩ *v/t* can, *Br tb* tin

enlazar ⟨1f⟩ **1** *v/t* link (up), connect; *L.Am. con cuerda* rope, lasso **2** *v/i de carretera* link up (**con** with); AVIA, FERR connect (**con** with)

enloquecer ⟨2d⟩ **1** *v/t* drive crazy *o* mad **2** *v/i* go crazy *o* mad enmarañar ⟨1a⟩ **1** v/t *pelo* tangle; *asunto* complicate, muddle **2** v/r **enmarañarse de pelo** get tangled; **enmarañarse en algo** get entangled o embroiled in sth

enmarcar ⟨1g⟩ v/t frame

enmascarar ⟨1a⟩ v/t hide, disguise

enmendar ⟨1k⟩ **1** v/t *asunto* rectify, put right; JUR, POL amend; **enmendarle la plana a alguien** find fault with what s.o. has done **2** v/r **enmendarse** mend one's ways

enmienda f POL amendment

enmicar ⟨1g⟩ v/t *L.Am.* laminate

enmudecer ⟨2d⟩ **1** v/t silence **2** v/i fall silent

ennoblecer ⟨2d⟩ v/t ennoble

enojado adj *L.Am.* angry

enojar ⟨1a⟩ **1** v/t (*molestar*) annoy; *L.Am.* (*encolerizar*) make angry **2** v/r **enojarse** *L.Am.* (*molestarse*) get annoyed; (*encolerizarse*) get angry

enojo m *L.Am.* anger

enojón adj *L.Am.* F irritable, touchy

enojoso adj (*delicado*) awkward; (*aburrido*) tedious, tiresome

enorgullecer ⟨2d⟩ **1** v/t make proud, fill with pride **2** v/r **enorgullecerse** be proud (**de** of)

enorme adj enormous, huge

enrarecido adj *aire* rarefied; *relaciones* strained

enredadera f BOT creeper, climbing plant

enredar ⟨1a⟩ **1** v/t tangle, get tangled; *fig* complicate, make complicated **2** v/i make trouble **3** v/r **enredarse** get tangled; *fig* complicated; **enredarse en algo** get mixed up o involved in sth

enredo m tangle; (*confusión*) mess, confusion; (*intriga*) intrigue; *amoroso* affair

enrevesado adj complicated, involved

enriquecer ⟨2d⟩ **1** v/t make rich; *fig* enrich **2** v/r **enriquecerse** get rich; *fig* be enriched

enrojecer ⟨2d⟩ **1** v/t turn red **2** v/i blush, go red

enrolarse ⟨1a⟩ v/r MIL enlist

enrollar ⟨1a⟩ **1** v/t roll up; *cable* coil; *hilo* wind; **me enrolla** F I like it, I think it's great **2** v/r **enrollarse** F *hablar* go on and on F; **se enrolló mucho con nosotros** (*se portó bien*) he was great to us; **¡no te enrolles!** F get to the point!; **enrollarse con alguien** *fig* F neck with s.o.

enroscar ⟨1g⟩ **1** v/t *tornillo* screw in; *cable, cuerda* coil **2** v/r **enroscarse** coil up

ensaimada f GASTR *pastry in the form of a spiral*

ensalada f GASTR salad

ensaladera f salad bowl

ensaladilla f: **ensaladilla rusa** GASTR Russian salad

ensalmo m: **como por ensalmo** as if by magic

ensalzar ⟨1f⟩ v/t extol, praise

ensamblar ⟨1a⟩ v/t assemble

ensanchar ⟨1a⟩ **1** v/t widen; *prenda* let out **2** v/r **ensancharse** widen, get wider; *de prenda* stretch

ensangrentar ⟨1k⟩ v/t stain with blood, cover with blood

ensañarse ⟨1a⟩ v/r show no mercy (**con** to)

ensartar ⟨1a⟩ **1** v/t *en hilo* string; *aguja* thread; *L.Am.* (*engañar*) trick, trap **2** v/r **ensartarse** *L.Am. en discusión* get involved, get caught up

ensayar ⟨1a⟩ v/t test, try (out); TEA rehearse

ensayo m TEA rehearsal; *escrito* essay; **ensayo general** dress rehearsal

enseguida adv immediately, right away

ensenada f inlet, cove

enseñanza f teaching; **enseñanza primaria** elementary education, *Br* primary education; **enseñanza secundaria** or **media** secondary education; **enseñanza superior** higher education

enseñar ⟨1a⟩ v/t (*dar clases*) teach; (*mostrar*) show

ensillar ⟨1a⟩ v/t saddle

ensimismarse ⟨1a⟩ v/r become lost in thought; *L.Am.* F get conceited o big-headed F

ensombrecer ⟨2d⟩ v/t cast a shadow over

ensordecedor adj deafening

ensuciar ⟨1b⟩ **1** v/t (get) dirty; *fig* sully, tarnish **2** v/r **ensuciarse** get dirty; *fig* get one's hands dirty

ensueño m: **de ensueño** *fig* fairy-tale *atr*, dream *atr*

entablar ⟨1a⟩ v/t strike up, start

entablillar ⟨1a⟩ v/t splint, put in a splint

entarimado m (*suelo*) floorboards *pl*; (*plataforma*) stage, platform

ente m (*ser*) being, entity; F (*persona rara*) oddball F; (*organización*) body

entejar ⟨1a⟩ v/t *L.Am.* tile

entender ⟨2g⟩ **1** v/t understand; **dar a entender a alguien** give s.o. to understand **2** v/i understand; **entender de algo** know about sth **3** v/r **entenderse** communicate; **a ver si nos entendemos** let's get this straight; **yo me entiendo** I know what I'm doing; **entenderse con alguien** get along with s.o., get on with s.o. **4** m: **a mi entender** in my opinion, to my mind

entendido **1** adj understood; **¿entendi-**

do? do you understand?, understood?;
tengo entendido que I gather *o* understand that **2** *m*, **-a** *f* expert, authority

entendimiento *m* understanding; *(inteligencia)* mind

enterado *adj* knowledgeable, well-informed; ***estar enterado de*** know about, have heard about; ***darse por enterado*** get the message, take the hint

enterarse ⟨1a⟩ *v/r* find out, hear *(de* about); ***¡para que te enteres!*** F so there! F; ***¡se va a enterar!*** F he's in for it! F

entereza *f* fortitude

enternecer ⟨2d⟩ *v/t* move, touch

entero 1 *adj (completo)* whole, entire; *(no roto)* intact, undamaged; ***por entero*** completely, entirely **2** *m (punto)* point

enterrar ⟨1k⟩ *v/t* bury; ***enterrar a todos*** *fig* outlive everybody

entidad *f* entity, body

entierro *m* burial; *(funeral)* funeral

entonar ⟨1a⟩ **1** *v/t* intone, sing; *fig* F perk up **2** *v/i* sing in tune **3** *v/r* **entonarse con bebida** get tipsy

entonces *adv* then; ***desde entonces*** since, since then; ***por entonces, en aquel entonces*** in those days, at that time

entornar ⟨1a⟩ *v/t puerta* leave ajar; *ojos* half close

entorno *m* environment

entorpecer ⟨2d⟩ *v/t* hold up, hinder; *paso* obstruct; *entendimiento* dull

entrada *f acción* entry; *lugar* entrance; *localidad* ticket; *pago* deposit, down payment; *de comida* starter; ***de entrada*** from the outset, from the start

entrañable *adj amistad* close, deep; *amigo* close, dear; *recuerdo* fond

entrañar ⟨1a⟩ *v/t* entail, involve

entrañas *fpl* entrails

entrar ⟨1a⟩ **1** *v/i para indicar acercamiento* to come in, enter; *para indicar alejamiento* go in, enter; *caber* fit; ***me entró frío / sueño*** I got cold / sleepy, I began to feel cold / sleepy; ***no me entra en la cabeza*** I can't understand it **2** *v/t para indicar acercamiento* bring in; *para indicar alejamiento* take in

entre *prp dos cosas, personas* between; *más de dos* among(st); *expresando cooperación* between; ***la relación entre ellos*** the relationship between them; ***entre nosotros*** among us; ***lo pagamos entre todos*** we paid for it among *o* between us

entreabierto 1 *part* → **entreabrir 2** *adj* half-open; *puerta* ajar

entreabrir ⟨3a; *part* **entreabierto** ⟩ *v/t* half-open

entreacto *m* TEA interval

entrecejo *m*: ***fruncir el entrecejo*** frown

entrecomillar ⟨1a⟩ *v/t* put in quotation marks

entrecortado *adj habla* halting; *respiración* difficult, labo(u)red

entrecot *m* entrecote

entredicho *m*: ***poner en entredicho*** call into question, question

entrega *f* handing over; *de mercancías* delivery; *(dedicación)* dedication, devotion; ***entrega a domicilio*** (home) delivery; ***entrega de premios*** prize-giving, presentation; ***hacer entrega de algo a alguien*** present s.o. with sth

entregar ⟨1h⟩ **1** *v/t* give, hand over; *trabajo, deberes* hand in; *mercancías* deliver; *premio* present **2** *v/r* **entregarse** give o.s. up; ***entregarse a*** *fig* devote o.s. to, dedicate o.s. to

entrelazar ⟨1f⟩ *v/t* interweave, intertwine

entremeses *mpl* GASTR appetizers, hors d'oeuvres

entremezclar ⟨1a⟩ **1** *v/t* intermingle, mix **2** *v/r* **entremezclarse** intermingle, mix

entrenador *m*, **entrenadora** *f* coach

entrenamiento *m* coaching

entrenar ⟨1a⟩ **1** *v/t* train **2** *v/r* **entrenarse** train

entrepierna *f* ANAT crotch

entresacar ⟨1g⟩ *v/t* extract, select

entresijos *mpl fig* details, ins and outs F

entresuelo *m* mezzanine; TEA dress circle

entretanto *adv* meanwhile, in the meantime

entretecho *m Arg, Chi* attic

entretener ⟨2l⟩ **1** *v/t (divertir)* entertain, amuse; *(retrasar)* keep, detain; *(distraer)* distract **2** *v/i* be entertaining **3** *v/r* **entretenerse** *(divertirse)* amuse o.s.; *(distraerse)* keep o.s. busy; *(retrasarse)* linger

entretenido *adj (divertido)* entertaining, enjoyable; ***estar entretenido*** *ocupado* be busy

entretenimiento *m* entertainment, amusement

entrevero *m S. Am. (lío)* mix-up, mess; *Chi (discusión)* argument

entrevista *f* interview

entrevistar ⟨1a⟩ **1** *v/t* interview **2** *v/r* **entrevistarse**: ***entrevistarse con alguien*** meet (with) s.o.

entristecer ⟨2d⟩ **1** *v/t* sadden **2** *v/r* **entristecerse** grow sad

entrometerse ⟨2a⟩ *v/r* meddle *(en* in)

entrometido 1 *part* → **entrometerse 2** *adj* meddling *atr*, interfering **3** *m* meddler, busybody entronizar ⟨1f⟩ v/t fig instal(l)

entumecer ⟨2d⟩ **1** v/t numb **2** v/r **entumecerse** go numb, get stiff

enturbiar ⟨1b⟩ v/t tb fig cloud

entusiasmado adj excited, delirious

entusiasmar ⟨1a⟩ v/t excite, make enthusiastic

entusiasmo m enthusiasm

entusiasta **1** adj enthusiastic **2** m/f enthusiast

enumerar ⟨1a⟩ v/t list, enumerate

enunciar ⟨1b⟩ v/t state

envalentonarse ⟨1a⟩ v/r become bolder o more daring; (insolentarse) become defiant

envanecerse ⟨2d⟩ v/r become conceited o vain

envasar ⟨1a⟩ v/t en botella bottle; en lata can; en paquete pack

envase m container; botella (empty) bottle; **envase de cartón** carton; **envase no retornable** nonreturnable bottle

envejecer ⟨2d⟩ **1** v/t age, make look older **2** v/i age, grow old

envejecimiento m aging, ageing

envenenar ⟨1a⟩ v/t tb fig poison

envergadura f AVIA wingspan; MAR breadth; fig magnitude, importance; **de gran** or **mucha envergadura** fig of great importance

enviado m, -a f POL envoy; de un periódico reporter, correspondent; **enviado especial** POL special envoy; de un periódico special correspondent

enviar ⟨1c⟩ v/t send

enviciarse ⟨1b⟩ v/r get addicted (con to)

envidia f envy, jealousy; **me da envidia** I'm envious o jealous; **tener envidia a alguien** or **de algo** envy s.o. sth

envidiar ⟨1b⟩ v/t envy; **envidiar a alguien por algo** envy s.o. sth

envidioso adj envious, jealous

envilecer ⟨2d⟩ **1** v/t degrade, debase **2** v/r **envilecerse** degrade o.s., debase o.s.

envío m shipment

enviudar ⟨1a⟩ v/i be widowed

envoltorio m wrapper

envoltura f cover, covering; de regalo wrapping; de caramelo wrapper

envolver ⟨2h; part envuelto⟩ **1** v/t wrap (up); (rodear) surround, envelop; (involucrar) involve; **envolver a alguien en algo** involve s.o. in sth **2** v/r **envolverse** wrap o.s. up; **envolverse en** fig become involved in

envuelto part → **envolver**

enyesado m plastering

enzarzarse ⟨1f⟩ v/r get involved (en in)

eólico adj wind atr

épico adj epic

epidemia f epidemic

epilepsia f MED epilepsy

epílogo m epilog(ue)

episcopal adj episcopal

episodio m episode

epistolar adj epistolary

epitafio m epitaph

época f time, period; parte del año time of year; GEOL epoch; **hacer época** be epoch-making

epopeya f epic, epic poem

equidad f fairness

equidistante adj equidistant

equilibrado adj well-balanced

equilibrar ⟨1a⟩ v/t balance

equilibrio m balance; FÍS equilibrium

equino adj equine

equinoccio m equinox

equipaje m baggage; **equipaje de mano** hand baggage

equipamiento m: **equipamiento de serie** AUTO standard features pl

equipar ⟨1a⟩ v/t equip (con with)

equiparar ⟨1a⟩ v/t put on a level (a o con with); **equiparar algo con algo** fig compare o liken sth to sth

equipo m DEP team; accesorios equipment; **equipo de música** or **de sonido** sound system

equitación f riding

equitativo adj fair, equitable

equivalente m/adj equivalent

equivaler ⟨2q⟩ v/i be equivalent (a to)

equivocación f mistake; **por equivocación** by mistake

equivocado adj wrong; **estar equivocado** be wrong, be mistaken

equivocar ⟨1g⟩ **1** v/t: **equivocar a alguien** make s.o. make a mistake **2** v/r **equivocarse** make a mistake; **te has equivocado** you are wrong o mistaken; **equivocarse de número** TELEC get the wrong number

equívoco **1** adj ambiguous, equivocal **2** m misunderstanding, (error) mistake

era f era

erección f erection

eres vb → **ser**

ergonómico adj ergonomic

erguir ⟨3n⟩ **1** v/t raise, lift; (poner derecho) straighten **2** v/r **erguirse de persona** stand up, rise; de edificio rise

erial m uncultivated land

erigir ⟨3c⟩ **1** v/t erect **2** v/r **erigirse: erigirse en** set o.s. up as

erizarse ⟨1f⟩ v/r de pelo stand on end

erizo m ZO hedgehog; **erizo de mar** ZO sea urchin

ermita *f* chapel

ermitaño 1 *m* ZO hermit crab **2** *m*, **-a** *f* hermit

erogación *f Méx, S. Am.* expenditure, outlay

erógeno *adj* erogenous

erosión *f* erosion

erosionar ⟨1a⟩ *v/t* GEOL erode

erótico *adj* erotic

erotismo *m* eroticism

erradicar ⟨1g⟩ *v/t* eradicate, wipe out

errante *adj* wandering

errar ⟨1l⟩ **1** *v/t* miss; ***errar el tiro*** miss **2** *v/i* miss; ***errar es humano*** to err is human

equivocarse be wrong, be mistaken

errata *f* mistake, error; *de imprenta* misprint

erre *f*: ***erre que erre*** F doggedly, stubbornly

erróneo *adj* wrong, erroneous

error *m* mistake, error; ***error de cálculo*** error of judg(e)ment

eructar ⟨1a⟩ *v/i* belch F, burp F

eructo *m* belch F, burp F

erudito 1 *adj* learned, erudite **2** *m* scholar

erupción *f* GEOL eruption; MED rash

esbelto *adj* slim, slender

esbozar ⟨1f⟩ *v/t* sketch; *idea, proyecto etc* outline

esbozo *m* sketch; *de idea, proyecto etc* outline

escabeche *m* type of marinade

escabroso *adj* rough; *problema* tricky; *relato* indecent

escabullirse ⟨3h⟩ *v/r* escape, slip away

escala *f tb* MÚS scale; AVIA stopover; ***escala de cuerda*** rope ladder; ***escala de valores*** scale of values; ***a escala*** to scale, life-sized

escalada *f* DEP climb, ascent; ***escalada de los precios*** increase in prices, escalation of prices

escalador *m*, **escaladora** *f* climber

escalafón *m fig* ladder

escalar ⟨1a⟩ **1** *v/t* climb, scale **2** *v/i* climb

escaldar ⟨1a⟩ *v/t* GASTR blanch; *manos* scald

escalera *f* stairs *pl*; staircase; ***escalera de caracol*** spiral staircase; ***escalera de incendios*** fire escape; ***escalera de mano*** ladder; ***escalera mecánica*** escalator

escalfar ⟨1a⟩ *v/t* poach

escalofriante *adj* horrifying

escalofrío *m* shiver

escalón *m* step; *de escalera de mano* rung

escalonar ⟨1a⟩ *v/t en tiempo* stagger; *terreno* terrace

escalope *m* escalope

escama *f* ZO scale; *de jabón, piel* flake

escamar ⟨1a⟩ **1** *v/t* scale, remove the scales from; *fig* make suspicious **2** *v/r* **escamarse** become suspicious

escamotear ⟨1a⟩ *v/t (ocultar)* hide, conceal; *(negar)* withhold

escampar ⟨1a⟩ *v/i* clear up, stop raining

escanciar ⟨1b⟩ *v/t fml* pour

escandalizar ⟨1f⟩ **1** *v/t* shock, scandalize **2** *v/r* **escandalizarse** be shocked

escándalo *m (asunto vergonzoso)* scandal; *(jaleo)* racket, ruckus; ***armar un escándalo*** make a scene

escandaloso *adj (vergonzoso)* scandalous, shocking; *(ruidoso)* noisy, rowdy

Escandinavia Scandinavia

escanear ⟨1a⟩ *v/t* scan

escáner *m* scanner

escaño *m* POL seat

escapar ⟨1a⟩ **1** *v/t* escape *(de* from); ***dejar escapar*** *oportunidad* pass up, let slip; *suspiro* let out, give **2** *v/r* **escaparse** *(huir)* escape *(de* from); *de casa* run away *(de* from); ***escaparse de situación*** get out of

escaparate *m* store window

escapatoria *f*: ***no tener escapatoria*** have no way out

escape *m de gas* leak; AUTO exhaust; ***salir a escape*** rush out

escarabajo *m* ZO beetle

escaramuza *f* skirmish

escarbadientes *m inv* toothpick

escarbar ⟨1a⟩ **1** *v/t tb fig* dig around *(en* in) **2** *v/t* dig around in

escarceos *mpl* forays, dabbling *sg*; ***escarceos amorosos*** romantic *o* amorous adventures

escarcha *f* frost

escardar ⟨1a⟩ *v/t* hoe

escarmentar ⟨1k⟩ **1** *v/t* teach a lesson to **2** *v/i* learn one's lesson; ***escarmentar en cabeza ajena*** learn from other people's mistakes

escarmiento *m* lesson; ***le sirvió de escarmiento*** it taught him a lesson

escarnio *m* ridicule, derision

escarola *f* endive, escarole

escarpado *adj* sheer, steep

escarpia *f* hook

escasear ⟨1a⟩ *v/i* be scarce, be in short supply

escasez *f* shortage, scarcity

escaso *adj recursos* limited; ***andar escaso de algo*** *falto* be short of sth; ***as posibilidades de*** not much chance of, little chance of; ***falta un mes escaso*** it's barely a month away

escatimar ⟨1a⟩ *v/t* be mean with, be very sparing with; ***no escatimar esfuerzos***

be unstinting in one's efforts, spare no effort

escayola f (plaster) cast

escayolar ⟨1a⟩ v/t put in a (plaster) cast

escena f scene; *escenario* stage; *entrar en escena* come on stage; *hacer una escena* fig make a scene

escenario m stage; fig scene

escénico adj stage atr

escenificar ⟨1g⟩ v/t stage

escepticismo m skepticism, Br scepticism

escéptico 1 adj skeptical, Br sceptical **2** m, -a f skeptic, Br sceptic

escindirse ⟨3a⟩ v/r (*fragmentarse*) split (*en* into); (*segregarse*) break away (*de* from)

escisión f (*fragmentación*) split; (*segregación*) break

esclarecer ⟨2d⟩ v/t throw o shed light on; *misterio* clear up

esclarecimiento m clarification; de misterio solving

esclavitud f slavery

esclavizar ⟨1f⟩ v/t enslave; fig tie down

esclavo m slave

esclerosis f MED: *esclerosis múltiple* multiple sclerosis

escoba f broom

escobilla f small brush; AUTO wiper blade

escocer ⟨2b & 2h⟩ v/i sting, smart; *todavía escuece la derrota* he's still smarting from the defeat

escocés 1 adj Scottish **2** m Scot, Scotsman

escocesa f Scot, Scotswoman

Escocia Scotland

escoger ⟨2c⟩ v/t choose, select

escogido adj select

escolar 1 adj school atr **2** m/f student

escolarización f education, schooling; *escolarización obligatoria* compulsory education

escolarizar ⟨1f⟩ v/t educate, provide schooling for

escolástico adj scholarly

escollera f breakwater

escollo m MAR reef; (*obstáculo*) hurdle, obstacle

escolta f **1** m/f motorista outrider; (*guardaespaldas*) bodyguard

escoltar ⟨1a⟩ v/t escort

escombros mpl rubble sg

esconder ⟨2a⟩ **1** v/t hide, conceal **2** v/r *esconderse* hide

escondidas fpl S. Am. hide-and-seek sg; *a escondidas* in secret, secretly

escondite m lugar hiding place; juego hide-and-seek

escondrijo m hiding place

escopeta f shotgun; *escopeta de aire comprimido* air gun, air rifle

escopetado adj: *salir escopetado* F shoot o dash off F

escopetazo m gunshot

escorbuto m scurvy

escoria f slag; desp dregs pl

Escorpio m/f inv ASTR Scorpio

escorpión m ZO scorpion

escotado adj low-cut

escote m neckline; de mujer cleavage

escotilla f MAR hatch

escozor m burning sensation, stinging; fig bitterness

escribir ⟨3a; part escrito⟩ v/t write; (*deletrear*) spell; *escribir a mano* hand-write, write by hand; *escribir a máquina* type

escrito 1 part → *escribir* **2** adj written; *por escrito* in writing **3** m document; *escritos* writings

escritor m, **escritora** f writer, author

escritorio m desk; *artículos de escritorio* stationery

escritura f writing; JUR deed; *Sagradas Escrituras* Holy Scripture

escrúpulo m scruple; *sin escrúpulos* unscrupulous

escrupuloso adj (*cuidadoso*) meticulous; (*honrado*) scrupulous; (*aprensivo*) fastidious

escrutar ⟨1a⟩ v/t scrutinize; *votos* count

escrutinio m de votos count; (*inspección*) scrutiny

escuadrón m squadron

escuálido adj skinny, emaciated

escucha f: *estar a la escucha* be listening out; *escuchas pl telefónicas* wire-tapping sg, Br tb phone-tapping sg

escuchar ⟨1a⟩ **1** v/t listen to o; L.Am. (*oír*) hear **2** v/i listen

escuchimizado adj F puny F, scrawny F

escudarse ⟨1a⟩ v/r fig hide (*en* behind)

escudería f stable

escudilla f bowl

escudo m arma shield; insignia badge; moneda escudo; *escudo de armas* coat of arms

escudriñar ⟨1a⟩ v/t (*mirar de lejos*) scan; (*examinar*) scrutinize

escuela f school; *escuela de comercio* business school; *escuela de idiomas* language school; *escuela primaria* elementary school, Br primary school

escuelero 1 adj L.Am. school atr **2** m, -a f L.Am. (*maestro*) teacher; Pe, Bol (*alumno*) student

escueto adj succinct, concise

escuincle *m/f Méx, C.Am.* F kid

esculpir ⟨3a⟩ *v/t* sculpt

escultor *m*, **escultora** *f* sculptor

escultura *f* sculpture

escupidera *f* spitoon; *L.Am.* chamber pot

escupir ⟨3a⟩ **1** *v/i* spit **2** *v/t* spit out

escupitajo *m* F gob of spit F

escurreplatos *m inv* plate rack

escurridizo *adj* slippery; *fig* evasive

escurridor *m* (*colador*) colander; (*escurreplatos*) plate rack

escurrir ⟨3a⟩ **1** *v/t ropa* wring out; *platos, verduras* drain **2** *v/i de platos* drain; *de ropa* drip-dry **3** *v/r* **escurrirse** *de líquido* drain away; (*deslizarse*) slip; (*escaparse*) slip away

escusado *m* bathroom

ese, esa, esos, esas *det singular* that; *plural* those

ése, ésa, ésos, ésas *pron singular* that (one); *plural* those (ones); **le ofrecí dinero pero ni por ésas** I offered him money but even that wasn't enough; **no soy de ésos que** I'm not one of those who

esencia *f* essence

esencial *adj* essential

esfera *f* sphere; **esfera de actividad** *fig* field *o* sphere (of activity)

esférico 1 *adj* spherical **2** *m* DEP F ball

esfinge *f* sphinx

esforzarse ⟨1f & 1m⟩ *v/r* make an effort, try hard

esfuerzo *m* effort; **hacer un esfuerzo** make an effort; **sin esfuerzo** effortlessly

esfumarse ⟨1a⟩ *v/r* F *tb fig* disappear

esgrima *f* fencing

esgrimir ⟨3a⟩ *v/t arma* wield; *fig: argumento* put forward, use

esguince *m* sprain

eslabón *m* link; **el eslabón perdido** the missing link

eslavo 1 *adj* Slavic, Slavonic **2** *m*, -a *f* Slav

eslogan *m* slogan

eslora *f* length

Eslovaquia Slovakia

Eslovenia Slovenia

esmalte *m* enamel; **esmalte de uñas** nail polish, nail varnish

esmerado *adj* meticulous

esmeralda *f* emerald

esmerarse ⟨1a⟩ *v/r* take great care (**en** over)

esmerilado *adj*: **cristal esmerilado** frosted glass

esmero *m* care; **con esmero** carefully

esmirriado *adj* F skinny F, scrawny F

esmoquin *m* tuxedo, *Br* dinner jacket

esnifar ⟨1a⟩ *v/t* F *pegamento* sniff F; *cocaína* snort F

esnob 1 *adj* snobbish **2** *m* snob

esnobismo *m* snobbishness

eso *pron* that; **en eso** just then, just at that moment; **eso mismo, eso es** that's it, that's the way; **a eso de las dos** at around two; **por eso** that's why; **¿y eso?** why's that?; **y eso que le dije que no se lo contara** and after I told him not to tell her

esotérico *adj* esoteric

espabilado *adj* (*listo*) bright, smart; (*vivo*) sharp, on the ball F

espabilar ⟨1a⟩ *v/t* (*quitar el sueño*) wake up, revive; **lo ha espabilado** (*avivado*) she's got him to wise up **2** *v/i* (*darse prisa*) hurry up, get a move on; (*avivarse*) wise up **3** *v/r* **espabilarse** *del sueño* wake oneself up; (*darse prisa*) hurry up, get a move on; (*avivarse*) wise up

espacial *adj cohete, viaje* space *atr*; FÍS, MAT spatial

espaciarse ⟨1a⟩ *v/r* become more (and more) infrequent

espacio *m* space; TV program, *Br* programme; **espacios verdes** green spaces; **espacio de tiempo** space of time; **espacio vital** living space

espacioso *adj* spacious, roomy

espada *f* sword; **espadas** *pl* (*en naipes*) suit in Spanish deck of cards; **estar entre la espada y la pared** be between a rock and a hard place

espadachín *m* skilled swordsman

espaguetis *mpl* spaghetti *sg*

espalda *f* back; **a espaldas de alguien** behind s.o.'s back; **de espaldas a** with one's back to; **por la espalda** from behind; **caerse de espaldas** fall flat on one's back; **no me des la espalda** don't sit with your back to me; **nadar a espalda** swim backstroke; **tener cubiertas las espaldas** *fig* keep one's back covered; **volver la espalda a alguien** *fig* turn one's back on s.o.

espaldarazo *m* slap on the back; (*reconocimiento*) recognition

espalderas *fpl* wall bars

espantajo *m* scarecrow; *fig* sight

espantapájaros *m inv* scarecrow

espantar ⟨1a⟩ **1** *v/t* (*asustar*) frighten, scare; (*ahuyentar*) frighten away, shoo away; F (*horrorizar*) horrify, appal(l) **2** *v/r* **espantarse** get frightened, get scared; F (*horrorizarse*) be horrified, be appal(l)ed

espanto *m* (*susto*) fright; *L.Am.* (*fantasma*) ghost; **nos llenó de espanto** *desagrado* we were horrified; **¡qué espanto!** how awful!; **de espanto** terrible

espantoso *adj* horrific, appalling; *para enfatizar* terrible, dreadful; *hace un calor espantoso* it's terribly hot, it's incredibly hot

España Spain

español 1 *adj* Spanish **2** *m idioma* Spanish **3** *m*, **-a** *f* Spaniard; *los españoles* the Spanish

esparadrapo *m* Band-Aid®, *Br* plaster

esparcimiento *m* relaxation

esparcir ⟨3b⟩ **1** *v/t papeles* scatter; *rumor* spread **2** *v/r esparcirse de papeles* be scattered; *de rumor* spread

espárrago *m* BOT asparagus; *espárrago triguero* wild asparagus; *¡vete a freír espárragos!* F get lost! F

espartano *adj* spartan

esparto *m* BOT esparto grass

espasmo *m* spasm

espátula *f* spatula; *en pintura* palette knife

especia *f* spice

especial *adj* special; *(difícil)* fussy; *en especial* especially

especialidad *f* specialty, *Br* speciality

especialista *m/f* specialist, expert; *en cine* stuntman; *mujer* stuntwoman

especializarse ⟨1f⟩ *v/r* specialize *(en* in)

especie *f* BIO species; *(tipo)* kind, sort

especiero *m* spice rack

especificar ⟨1g⟩ *v/t* specify

específico *adj* specific

espectacular *adj* spectacular

espectáculo *m* TEA show; *(escena)* sight; *dar el espectáculo* fig make a spectacle of o.s.

espectador *m*, **espectadora** *f en cine etc* member of the audience; DEP spectator; *(observador)* on-looker, observer

espectro *m* FÍS spectrum; *(fantasma)* ghost

especulación *f* speculation

especular ⟨1a⟩ *v/i* speculate

especulativo *adj* speculative

espejismo *m* mirage

espejo *m* mirror; *espejo retrovisor* rear-view mirror

espeleólogo *m* spelunker, *Br* pot-holer

espeluznante *adj* horrific, horrifying

espera *f* wait; *sala de espera* waiting room; *en espera de* pending; *estar a la espera de* be waiting for

esperanza *f* hope; *esperanza de vida* life expectancy

esperar ⟨1a⟩ **1** *v/t (aguardar)* wait for; *con esperanza* hope; *(suponer, confiar en)* expect **2** *v/i (aguardar)* wait

esperma *f* sperm

espesar ⟨1a⟩ **1** *v/t* thicken **2** *v/r espesarse* thicken, become thick

espeso *adj* thick; *vegetación, niebla* thick, dense

espesor *m* thickness

espesura *f* dense vegetation

espía *m/f* spy

espiar ⟨1c⟩ **1** *v/t* spy on **2** *v/i* spy

espiga *f* BOT ear, spike

espina *f de planta* thorn; *de pez* bone; *espina dorsal* spine, backbone; *dar mala espina a alguien* F make s.o. feel uneasy

espinacas *fpl* BOT spinach *sg*

espinazo *m* spine, backbone; *doblar el espinazo* fig *(trabajar mucho)* work o.s. into the ground; *(humillarse)* kowtow *(ante* to)

espinilla *f de la pierna* shin; *en la piel* pimple, spot

espinoso *adj* thorny, prickly; *fig* thorny, knotty

espionaje *m* spying, espionage

espiral 1 *adj* spiral *atr* **2** *f* spiral

espirar ⟨1a⟩ *v/t & v/i* exhale

espiritismo *m* spiritualism

espíritu *m* spirit

espiritual *adj* spiritual

espléndido *adj* splendid, magnificent; *(generoso)* generous

esplendor *m* splendo(u)r

espliego *m* lavender

espolear ⟨1a⟩ *v/t tb fig* spur on

espolvorear ⟨1a⟩ *v/t* sprinkle

esponja *f* sponge

esponjoso *adj bizcocho* spongy; *toalla* soft, fluffy

espónsor *m/f* sponsor

esponsorizar ⟨1f⟩ *v/t* sponsor

espontáneo *adj* spontaneous

esporádico *adj* sporadic

esposa *f* wife

esposas *fpl (manillas)* handcuffs *pl*

esposar ⟨1a⟩ *v/t* handcuff

esposo *m* husband

esprint *m* sprint

espuela *f* spur

espuerta *f: ganar dinero a espuertas* F make money hand over fist F

espuma *f* foam; *de jabón* lather; *de cerveza* froth; *espuma de afeitar* shaving foam; *espuma moldeadora* styling mousse

espumadera *f* slotted spoon, skimmer

espumarajo *m* froth, foam

espumilla *f* C.Am. GASTR meringue

espumoso *adj* frothy, foamy; *caldo* sparkling

esqueje *m* cutting

esquela *f aviso* death notice, obituary

esquelético *adj* skeletal

esqueleto *m* skeleton; *Méx, C.Am., Pe, Bol fig* blank form; **mover** *or* **menear el esqueleto** F dance

esquema *m (croquis)* sketch, diagram; *(sinopsis)* outline, summary

esquemático *adj* schematic, diagrammatic; *resumen* simplified

esquí *m tabla Wo* schematic, diagrammatic; **esquí de fondo** cross-country skiing; **esquí náutico** *o* **acuático** waterskiing

esquiador *m*, **esquiadora** *f* skier

esquiar ⟨1c⟩ *v/i* ski

esquilar ⟨1a⟩ *v/t* shear

esquilmar ⟨1a⟩ *v/t* overexploit; *a alguien* suck dry

esquina *f* corner

esquinazo *m Arg, Chi* serenade; **dar esquinazo a alguien** F give s.o. the slip F

esquirol *m/f* strikebreaker, scab F

esquite *m C.Am., Méx* popcorn

esquivar ⟨1a⟩ *v/t* avoid, dodge F

esquivo *adj (huraño)* unsociable; *(evasivo)* shifty, evasive

esquizofrenia *f* schizophrenia

esquizofrénico *adj* schizophrenic

esta *det* this

está *vb* → **estar**

estabilidad *f* stability

estabilizante *m* stabilizer

estabilizar ⟨1f⟩ *v/t* stabilize

estable *adj* stable

establecer ⟨2d⟩ **1** *v/t* establish; *negocio* set up **2** *v/r* **establecerse** *en lugar* settle; *en profesión* set up

establecimiento *m* establishment

establo *m* stable

estaca *f* stake

estacada *f: dejar a alguien en la estacada* F leave s.o. in the lurch

estación *f* station; *del año* season; **estación espacial** *or* **orbital** space station; **estación de invierno** *or* **invernal** winter resort; **estación de servicio** service station; **estación de trabajo** INFOR work station

estacional *adj* seasonal

estacionamiento *m* AUTO parking; *L.Am.* parking lot, *Br* car park

estacionar ⟨1a⟩ **1** *v/t* AUTO park **2** *v/r* **estacionarse** stabilize

estacionómetro *m Méx* parking meter

estadio *m* DEP stadium

estadística *f cifra* statistic; *ciencia* statistics

estado *m* state; MED condition; **estado civil** marital status; **estado de guerra** state of war; **en buen estado** in good condition; **el Estado** the State; **estado del bienestar** welfare state; **los Estados Unidos (de América)** the United States (of America)

estadounidense 1 *adj* American, US *atr* **2** *m/f* American

estafa *f* swindle, cheat

estafador *m*, **estafadora** *f* con artist F, fraudster

estafar ⟨1a⟩ *v/t* swindle, cheat (*a* out of), defraud (*a* of)

estalactita *f* stalactite

estalagmita *f* stalagmite

estallar ⟨1a⟩ *v/i* explode; *de guerra* break out; *de escándalo* break; **estalló en llanto** she burst into tears

estallido *m* explosion; *de guerra* outbreak

estamento *m* stratum, class

estampa *f de libro* illustration; *(aspecto)* appearance; REL prayer card

estampado *m tejido* patterned

estampar ⟨1a⟩ *v/t sello* put; *tejido* print; *pasaporte* stamp; **le estampó una bofetada en la cara** F she smacked him one F

estampido *m* bang

estampilla *f L.Am.* stamp

estancado *adj agua* stagnant; *fig* at a standstill

estancar ⟨1g⟩ **1** *v/t río* dam up, block; *fig* bring to a standstill **2** *v/r* **estancarse** stagnate; *fig* come to a standstill

estancia *f* stay; *Rpl* farm, ranch

estanciero *m, -a f Rpl* farmer, rancher

estanco **1** *adj* watertight **2** *m shop selling cigarettes etc*

estándar *m* standard

estandarizar ⟨1f⟩ *v/t* standardize

estandarte *m* standard, banner

estanque *m* pond

estante *m* shelf

estantería *f* shelves *pl*; *para libros* bookcase

estaño *m* tin

estar ⟨1p⟩ **1** *v/i* be; *¿está Javier?* is Javier in?; **estar haciendo algo** be doing sth; **estamos a 3 de enero** it's January 3rd; **el kilo está a cien pesetas** they're a hundred pesetas a kilo; **te estás grande** it's too big for you; **estar con alguien** agree with s.o.; *(apoyar)* support s.o.; **ahora estoy con Vd.** I'll be with you in just a moment; **estar a bien / mal con alguien** be on good / bad terms with s.o.; **estar de ocupación** work as, be; **estar en algo** be working on sth; **estar para hacer algo** be about to do sth; **no estar para algo** not be in a mood for sth; **estar por algo** be in favo(u)r of sth; **está por hacer** it hasn't been done yet; **estar sin dinero** have no money; **¿cómo está Vd.?** how are you?; **estoy mejor** I'm

(feeling) better; **¡ya estoy!** I'm ready!;
¡ya está! that's it! **2** v/r **estarse** stay; **estarse quieto** keep still
estárter m choke
estatal adj state atr
estático adj static
estatua f statue
estatura f height
estatutario adj statutory
estatuto m statute; **estatutos** articles of association
estatus m status
este¹ m east
este², **esta**, **estos**, **estas** det singular this; plural these
éste, **ésta**, **éstos**, **éstas** pron singular this (one); plural these (ones)
estela f MAR wake; AVIA, fig trail
estelar adj star atr
estepa f steppe
estera f mat
estercolero m dunghill, dung heap
estéreo adj stereo
estereofónico adj stereophonic
estereotipo m stereotype
estéril adj MED sterile; trabajo, esfuerzo etc futile
esterilidad f sterility
esterilizar ⟨1f⟩ v/t tb persona sterilize
esterilla f mat
esterlina adj: **libra esterlina** pound sterling
esternón m breast bone, sternum
estero m Rpl marsh
estertor m death rattle
esteticista m/f beautician
estético adj esthetic, Br aesthetic
estetoscopio m MED stethoscope
estibador m stevedore
estiércol m dung; (abono) manure
estilarse ⟨1a⟩ v/r be fashionable
estilista m/f stylist, de modas designer
estilo m style; **al estilo de** in the style of; **algo por el estilo** something like that; **son todos por el estilo** they're all the same
estilográfica f fountain pen
estima f esteem, respect; **tener a alguien en mucha estima** hold s.o. in high regard o esteem
estimación f (cálculo) estimate; (estima) esteem, respect
estimar ⟨1a⟩ v/t respect, hold in high regard; **estimo conveniente que** I consider it advisable to
estimulante 1 adj stimulating **2** m stimulant
estimular ⟨1a⟩ v/t stimulate; (animar) encourage

estímulo m stimulus; (incentivo) incentive
estío m lit summertime
estipular ⟨1a⟩ v/t stipulate
estirado adj snooty F, stuck-up F
estirar ⟨1a⟩ v/t stretch; (alisar) smooth out; dinero stretch, make go further; **estirar la pata** F kick the bucket F; **estirar las piernas** stretch one's legs
estirpe f stock
estival adj summer atr
esto pron this; **esto es** that is to say; **por esto** this is why; **a todo esto** (mientras tanto) meanwhile; (a propósito) incidentally
estofa f: **de baja estofa** desp low-class desp
estofado adj stewed
estofar ⟨1a⟩ v/t stew
estoico 1 adj stoic(al) **2** m, **-a** f stoic
estómago m stomach
estor m blind
estorbar ⟨1a⟩ **1** v/t (dificultar) hinder; **nos estorbaba** he was in our way **2** v/i get in the way
estorbo m hindrance, nuisance
estornino m zo starling
estornudar ⟨1a⟩ v/i sneeze
estornudo m sneeze
estoy vb → **estar**
estrado m platform
estrafalario adj F eccentric; ropa outlandish
estragón m BOT tarragon
estragos mpl devastation sg; **causar estragos entre** wreak havoc among
estrambótico adj F eccentric; ropa outlandish
estrangular ⟨1a⟩ v/t strangle
estraperlo m black market; **de estraperlo** on the black market
estratagema f stratagem
estrategia f strategy
estratégico adj strategic
estrato m fig stratum
estrechar ⟨1a⟩ **1** v/t ropa take in; mano shake; **estrechar entre los brazos** hug, embrace **2** v/r **estrecharse** narrow, get narrower
estrechez f fig hardship; **estrechez de miras** narrow-mindedness; **pasar estrecheces** suffer hardship
estrecho 1 adj narrow; (apretado) tight; amistad close; **estrecho de miras** narrow-minded **2** m strait, straits pl
estrella f tb de cine etc star; **estrella fugaz** falling star, shooting star; **estrella de mar** zo starfish; **estrella polar** Pole star
estrellar ⟨1a⟩ **1** v/t smash; **estrellar algo**

contra algo smash sth against sth; *estre-lló el coche contra un muro* he smashed the car into a wall **2** *v/r* **estrellarse** crash (*contra* into)

estrellón *m* Pe, Bol crash

estremecer ⟨2d⟩ **1** *v/t* shock, shake **F 2** *v/r* **estremecerse** shake, tremble; *de frío* shiver; *de horror* shudder

estrenar ⟨1a⟩ **1** *v/t ropa* wear for the first time, christen F; *objeto* try out, christen F; TEA, *película* premiere; *a estrenar* brand new **2** *v/r* **estrenarse** make one's debut

estreno *m* TEA, *de película* premiere; *de persona* debut; *estar de estreno* be wearing new clothes

estreñimiento *m* constipation

estrépito *m* noise, racket

estrés *m* stress

estresar ⟨1a⟩ *v/t*: *estresar alguien* cause s.o. stress, subject s.o. to stress

estría *f en piel* stretch mark

estribar ⟨1a⟩ *v/i*: *estribar en* stem from, lie in

estribillo *m* chorus, refrain

estribo *m* stirrup; *perder los estribos* fig fly off the handle F

estrictez *f S. Am.* strictness

estricto *adj* strict

estridente *adj* shrill, strident

estrofa *f* stanza, verse

estropajo *m* scourer

estropajoso *adj persona* wiry; *boca* dry; *camisa* scruffy

estropeado *adj (averiado)* broken

estropear ⟨1a⟩ **1** *v/t aparato* break; *plan* ruin, spoil **2** *v/r* **estropearse** break down; *de comida* go off, go bad; *de plan* go wrong

estructura *f* structure

estructurar ⟨1a⟩ *v/t* structure, organize

estruendo *m* racket, din

estrujar ⟨1a⟩ *v/t* F crumple up, scrunch up F; *trapo* wring out; *persona* squeeze, hold tightly

estuario *m* estuary

estuche *m* case, box

estuco *m* stuccowork

estudiante *m/f* student

estudiantil *adj* student *atr*

estudiar ⟨1b⟩ *v/t & v/i* study

estudio *m disciplina* study; *apartamento* studio, *Br* studio flat; *de cine, música* studio

estudioso *adj* studious

estufa *f* heater

estupefaciente *m* narcotic (drug)

estupefacto *adj* stupefied, speechless

estupendo *adj* fantastic, wonderful

estupidez *f cualidad* stupidity; *acción* stupid thing

estúpido 1 *adj* stupid **2** *m*, *-a f* idiot

estupor *m* astonishment, amazement; MED stupor

esturión *m* ZO sturgeon

estuve *vb* → *estar*

estuvo *vb* → *estar*

etapa *f* stage; *por etapas* in stages

etarra *m/f* member of ETA

etc *abr* (= *etcétera*) etc (= etcetera)

etcétera *m* etcetera, and so on; *y un largo etcétera de ...* and a long list of ..., and many other ...

etéreo *adj* ethereal

eternidad *f* eternity

eterno *adj* eternal; *la película se me hizo -a* the movie seemed to go on for ever

ética *f en filosofía* ethics; *comportamiento* principles *pl*

ético *adj* ethical

etimología *f* etymology

Etiopía Ethiopia

etiqueta *f* label; (*protocolo*) etiquette

etiquetar ⟨1a⟩ *v/t tb fig* label

étnico *adj* ethnic

eucalipto *m* BOT eucalyptus

eucaristía *f* Eucharist

eufemismo *m* euphemism

euforia *f* euphoria

eufórico *adj* euphoric

euro *m* euro

eurodiputado *m*, *-a f* MEP, member of the European Parliament

Europa Europe

europeísta *m/f* pro-European

europeo 1 *adj* European **2** *m*, *-a f* European

eusquera *m/adj* Basque

eutanasia *f* euthanasia

evacuación *f* evacuation

evacuar ⟨1d⟩ *v/t* evacuate

evadir ⟨3a⟩ **1** *v/t* avoid; *impuestos* evade **2** *v/r* **evadirse** *tb fig* escape

evaluación *f* evaluation, assessment; (*prueba*) test

evaluar ⟨1e⟩ *v/t* assess, evaluate

evangelio *m* gospel

evangelizar ⟨1f⟩ *v/t* evangelize

evaporación *f* evaporation

evaporar ⟨1a⟩ *v/r* evaporate; *fig* F vanish into thin air

evasión *f tb fig* escape; *evasión de capitales* flight of capital; *evasión fiscal* tax evasion

evasiva *f* evasive reply

evento *m* event

eventual *adj* possible; *trabajo* casual, temporary; *en el caso eventual de* in the

event of
eventualidad f eventuality
evidencia f evidence, proof; *poner en evidencia* demonstrate; *poner a alguien en evidencia* show s.o. up
evidente *adj* evident, clear
evitar ⟨1a⟩ *v/t* avoid; (*impedir*) prevent; *molestias* save; *no puedo evitarlo* I can't help it
evocar ⟨1g⟩ *v/t* evoke
evolución f BIO evolution; (*desarrollo*) development
evolucionar ⟨1a⟩ *v/t* BIO evolve; (*desarrollar*) develop
ex 1 *pref* ex- **2** *m/f* F ex F
exabrupto *m* sharp remark
exacerbar ⟨1a⟩ *v/t* exacerbate, make worse; (*irritar*) exasperate
exacto *adj medida* exact, precise; *informe* accurate; *¡exacto!* exactly!, precisely!
exageración f exaggeration
exagerado *adj* exaggerated
exagerar ⟨1a⟩ *v/t* exaggerate
exaltación f (*alabanza*) exaltation; (*entusiasmo*) agitation, excitement
exaltar ⟨1a⟩ *v/t* excite, get worked up
examen *m* test, exam; MED examination; (*análisis*) study; *examen de conducir* driving test
examinar ⟨1a⟩ **1** *v/t* examine **2** *v/r* **examinarse** take an exam
exasperar ⟨1a⟩ **1** *v/t* exasperate **2** *v/r* **exasperarse** get exasperated
excarcelar ⟨1a⟩ *v/t* release (from prison)
excavación f excavation
excavadora f digger
excavar ⟨1a⟩ *v/t* excavate; *túnel* dig
excedencia f extended leave of absence
excedente 1 *adj* surplus; *empleado* on extended leave of absence **2** *m* surplus
exceder ⟨2a⟩ **1** *v/t* exceed **2** *v/r* **excederse** go too far, get carried away
excelencia f excellence; *Su Excelencia la señora embajadora* Her Excellency the Ambassador; *por excelencia* par excellence
excelente *adj* excellent
excéntrico 1 *adj* eccentric **2** *m*, *-a* f eccentric
excepción f exception; *a excepción de* except for; *sin excepción* without exception
excepcional *adj* exceptional
excepto *prp* except
exceptuar ⟨1e⟩ *v/t* except; *exceptuando* with the exception of, except for
excesivo *adj* excessive
exceso *m* excess; *exceso de equipaje* excess baggage; *exceso de velocidad*

speeding; *en exceso* in excess, too much
excitación f excitement, agitation
excitante 1 *adj* exciting; *una bebida excitante* a stimulant **2** *m* stimulant
excitar ⟨1a⟩ **1** *v/t* excite; *sentimientos, sexualmente* arouse **2** *v/r* **excitarse** get excited; *sexualmente* become aroused
exclamación f exclamation
exclamar ⟨1a⟩ *v/t* exclaim
excluir ⟨3g⟩ *v/t* leave out (*de* of), exclude (*de* from); *posibilidad* rule out
exclusiva f *privilegio* exclusive rights *pl* (*de* to); *reportaje* exclusive
exclusivo *adj* exclusive
excomunión f excommunication
excremento *m* excrement
exculpar ⟨1a⟩ *v/t* exonerate
excursión f trip, excursion
excursionista *m/f* excursionist
excusa f excuse; *excusas* apologies
excusado *m* bathroom
excusar ⟨1a⟩ *v/t* excuse
execrable *adj* abominable, execrable *fml*
exención f exemption; *exención fiscal* tax exemption
exento *adj* exempt (*de* from); *exento de impuestos* tax-exempt, tax-free
exhalación f: *salir como una exhalación* *fig* rush *o* dash out
exhaustivo *adj* exhaustive
exhausto *adj* exhausted
exhibición f display, demonstration; *de película* screening, showing
exhibicionista *m/f* exhibitionist
exhibir ⟨3a⟩ **1** *v/t* show, display; *película* screen, show; *cuadro* exhibit **2** *v/r* **exhibirse** show o.s., let o.s. be seen
exhumar ⟨1a⟩ *v/t* exhume
exigencia f demand
exigente *adj* demanding
exigir ⟨3c⟩ *v/t* demand; (*requerir*) call for, demand; *le exigen mucho* they ask a lot of him
exiguo *adj* meager, *Br* meagre
exiliado 1 *adj* exiled, in exile *pred* **2** *m*, *-a* f exile
exiliar ⟨1a⟩ **1** *v/t* exile **2** *v/r* **exiliarse** go into exile
exilio *m* exile; *en el exilio* in exile
eximir ⟨3a⟩ *v/t* exempt (*de* from)
existencia f existence; (*vida*) life; *existencias* COM supplies, stocks
existencialista *m/f & adj* existentialist
existir ⟨3a⟩ *v/i* exist; *existen muchos problemas* there are a lot of problems
éxito *m* success; *éxito de taquilla* box-office hit; *tener éxito* be successful, be a success
exitoso *adj* successful

E

Exmo. *abr* (= *Excelentísimo*) Your / His Excellency

exonerar ⟨1a⟩ *v/t* exonerate; **exonerar a alguien de algo** exempt s.o. from sth

exorbitante *adj* exorbitant

exorcista *m/f* exorcist

exótico *adj* exotic

expandir ⟨3a⟩ **1** *v/t* expand **2** *v/r* expandirse expand; *de noticia* spread

expansión *f* expansion; (*recreo*) recreation

expatriarse ⟨1b⟩ *v/r* leave one's country

expectación *f* sense of anticipation

expectativa *f* (*esperanza*) expectation; **estar a la expectativa de algo** be waiting for sth; **expectativas** (*perspectivas*) prospects

expedición *f* expedition

expediente *m* file, dossier; (*investigación*) investigation, inquiry; **expediente académico** student record; **expediente disciplinario** disciplinary proceedings *pl*; **abrir un expediente a alguien** take disciplinary action against s.o.

expedir ⟨3l⟩ *v/t documento* issue; *mercancías* send, dispatch

expeditar ⟨1a⟩ *v/t L.Am.* (*apresurar*) hurry; (*concluir*) finish, conclude

expeditivo *adj* expeditious

expendedor *adj:* **máquina expendedora** vending machine

expendio *m L.Am.* store, shop

expensas *fpl:* **a expensas de** at the expense of

experiencia *f* experience

experimentado *adj* experienced

experimentar ⟨1a⟩ **1** *v/t* try out, experiment with **2** *v/i* experiment (**con** on)

experimento *m* experiment

experto 1 *adj* expert; **experto en hacer algo** expert o very good at doing sth **2** *m* expert (**en** on)

expiar ⟨1c⟩ *v/t* expiate, atone for

expirar ⟨1a⟩ *v/i* expire

explanada *f* open area; *junto al mar* esplanade

explayarse ⟨1a⟩ *v/r* speak at length; (*desahogarse*) unburden o.s.; (*distraerse*) relax, unwind; **explayarse sobre algo** expound on sth

explicación *f* explanation

explicar ⟨1g⟩ **1** *v/t* explain **2** *v/r* explicarse (*comprender*) understand; (*hacerse comprender*) express o.s.; **no me lo explico** I can't understand it, I don't get it F

explícito *adj* explicit

explorador *m*, **exploradora** *f* explorer; MIL scout

explorar ⟨1a⟩ *v/t* explore

explosión *f* explosion; **explosión demográfica** population explosion; **hacer explosión** go off, explode

explosionar ⟨1a⟩ *v/t & v/i* explode

explosivo *m/adj* explosive

explotación *f de mina, tierra* exploitation, working; *de negocio* running, operation; *de trabajador* exploitation

explotar ⟨1a⟩ **1** *v/t tierra, mina* work, exploit; *situación* take advantage of, exploit; *trabajador* exploit **2** *v/i* go off, explode; *fig* explode, blow a fuse F

expoliar ⟨1b⟩ *v/t* plunder, pillage

exponente *m* exponent

exponer ⟨2r; *part* **expuesto** ⟩ **1** *v/t idea, teoría* set out, put forward; (*revelar*) expose; *pintura, escultura* exhibit, show; (*arriesgar*) risk **2** *v/r* exponerse: **exponerse a algo** (*arriesgarse*) lay o.s. open to sth

exportación *f* export

exportar ⟨1a⟩ *v/t* export

exposición *f* exhibition

expresar ⟨1a⟩ **1** *v/t* express **2** *v/r* expresarse express o.s.

expresión *f* expression

expresivo *adj* expressive

expreso 1 *adj* express *atr;* **tren expreso** express (train) **2** *m* tren express (train); *café* espresso

exprimidor *m* lemon squeezer; *eléctrico* juicer

exprimir ⟨3a⟩ *v/t* squeeze; (*explotar*) exploit

ex profeso *adv* (*especialmente*) expressly; (*a propósito*) deliberately

expropiar ⟨1b⟩ *v/t* expropriate

expuesto *part* → **exponer**

expugnar ⟨1a⟩ *v/t* take by storm

expulsar ⟨1a⟩ *v/t* expel, throw out F; DEP expel from the game, *Br* send off

expulsión *f* expulsion; DEP sending off

exquisito *adj comida* delicious; (*bello*) exquisite; (*refinado*) refined

extasiarse ⟨1c⟩ *v/r* be enraptured, go into raptures

éxtasis *m tb droga* ecstasy

extender ⟨2g⟩ **1** *v/t brazos* stretch out; (*untar*) spread; *tela, papel* spread out; (*ampliar*) extend; **me extendió la mano** she held out her hand to me **2** *v/r* extenderse *de campos* stretch; *de influencia* extend; (*difundirse*) spread; (*durar*) last; *explayarse* go into detail

extendido 1 *part* → **extender 2** *adj costumbre* widespread; *brazos* outstretched; *mapa* spread out

extensión *f tb* TELEC extension; *superficie* expanse, area; **por extensión** by exten-

sion
extenso *adj* extensive, vast; *informe* lengthy, long
extenuar ⟨1e⟩ **1** *v/t* exhaust, tire out **2** *v/r* **extenuarse** exhaust o.s., tire o.s. out
exterior 1 *adj aspecto* external, outward; *capa* outer; *apartamento* overlooking the street; POL foreign; **la parte exterior del edificio** the exterior *o* the outside of the building **2** *m* (*fachada*) exterior, outside; *aspecto* exterior, outward appearance; **viajar al exterior** (*al extranjero*) travel abroad
exteriorizar ⟨1f⟩ *v/t* externalize
exterminar ⟨1a⟩ *v/t* exterminate, wipe out
externo 1 *adj aspecto* external, outward; *influencia* external, outside; *capa* outer; *deuda* foreign **2** *m*, **-a** *f* EDU *student who attends a boarding school but returns home each evening*, Br day boy / girl
extinción *f*: **en peligro de extinción** in danger of extinction
extinguidor *m L.Am.*: **extinguidor** (**de incendios**) (fire) extinguisher
extinguir ⟨3d⟩ **1** *v/t* BIO, ZO wipe out; *fuego* extinguish, put out **2** *v/r* **extinguirse** BIO, ZO become extinct, die out; *de fuego* go out; *de plazo* expire
extintor *m* fire extinguisher
extirpar ⟨1a⟩ *v/t* MED remove; *vicio* eradicate, stamp out
extorsión *f* extortion
extorsionar ⟨1a⟩ *v/t* extort money from
extra 1 *adj excelente* top quality; *adicional* extra; **horas extra** overtime; **paga extra** extra month's pay **2** *m/f de cine* extra **3** *m gasto* additional expense
extracto *m* extract; (*resumen*) summary; GASTR, QUÍM extract, essence; **extracto de cuenta** bank statement
extractor *m* extractor; **extractor de humos** extractor fan
extradición *f* extradition

extraditar ⟨1a⟩ *v/t* extradite
extraer ⟨2p⟩ *v/t* extract, pull out; *conclusión* draw
extrajudicial *adj* out-of-court
extralimitarse ⟨1a⟩ *v/r* go too far, exceed one's authority
extramatrimonial *adj* extramarital
extranjería *f*: **ley de extranjería** immigration laws *pl*
extranjero 1 *adj* foreign **2** *m*, **-a** *f* foreigner; **en el extranjero** abroad
extranjis: **de extranjis** F on the quiet F, on the sly F
extrañar ⟨1a⟩ **1** *v/t L.Am.* miss **2** *v/r* **extrañarse** be surprised (*de* at)
extraño 1 *adj* strange, odd **2** *m*, **-a** *f* stranger
extraordinario *adj* extraordinary
extrapolar ⟨1a⟩ *v/t* extrapolate
extrarradio *m* outlying districts *pl*, outskirts *pl*
extraterrestre *adj* extraterrestial, alien
extravagante *adj* outrageous
extravertido *adj* extrovert
extraviar ⟨1c⟩ **1** *v/t* lose, mislay **2** *v/r* **extraviarse** get lost, lose one's way
extremadamente *adv* extremely
extremado *adj* extreme
extremar ⟨1a⟩ *v/t* maximize
extremidad *f* end; **extremidades** extremities
extremista 1 *adj* extreme **2** *m/f* POL extremist
extremo 1 *adj* extreme **2** *m* extreme; *parte primera o última* end; *punto* point; **llegar al extremo de** reach the point of **3** *m/f*: **extremo derecho / izquierdo** DEP right / left wing; **en extremo** in the extreme
extrovertido *adj* extrovert
exuberante *adj* exuberant; *vegetación* lush
exultante *adj* elated
eyacular ⟨1a⟩ *v/t* ejaculate

F

fabada *f* GASTR *Asturian stew with pork sausage, bacon and beans*
fábrica *f* plant, factory
fabricación *f* manufacturing
fabricante *m* manufacturer, maker
fabricar ⟨1g⟩ *v/t* manufacture

fábula *f* fable; (*mentira*) lie
fabuloso *adj* fabulous, marvel(l)ous
facción *f* POL faction; **facciones** *pl* (*rasgos*) features
faceta *f* fig facet
facha 1 *f* look; (*cara*) face **2** *m/f desp* fas-

cist

fachada f tb fig façade
facial adj facial
fácil adj easy; **es fácil que** it's likely that
facilidad f ease; **con facilidad** easily; **tener facilidad para algo** have a gift for sth; **facilidades de pago** credit facilities, credit terms
facilitar ⟨1a⟩ v/t facilitate, make easier; (hacer factible) make possible; medios, dinero etc provide
factible adj feasible
factor m factor
factoría f esp L.Am. plant, factory
factura f COM invoice; de luz, gas etc bill
facturación f COM invoicing; (volumen de negocio) turnover; AVIA check-in
facturar ⟨1a⟩ v/t COM invoice, bill; volumen de negocio turn over; AVIA check in
facultad f faculty; (autoridad) authority
faena f task, job; **hacer una faena a alguien** play a dirty trick on s.o.
fagot m MÚS bassoon
faisán m ZO pheasant
faja f prenda interior girdle
fajarse ⟨1a⟩ v/r Méx, Ven F get into a fight
fajo m wad; de periódicos bundle
falacia f fallacy; (engaño) fraud
falange f ANAT phalange; MIL phalanx
falda f skirt; de montaña side
faldero m: **perro faldero** lap dog
falla f fault; de fabricación flaw
fallar ⟨1a⟩ v/i fail; (no acertar) miss; de sistema etc go wrong; JUR find (**en favor de** for; **en contra de** against); **fallar a alguien** let s.o. down 2 v/t JUR pronounce judg(e)ment in; pregunta get wrong; **fallar el tiro** miss
fallecer ⟨2d⟩ v/i pass away
fallecimiento m demise
fallo m mistake; TÉC fault; JUR judg(e)ment; **fallo cardiaco** heart failure
falsedad f falseness; (mentira) lie
falsificación f de moneda counterfeiting; de documentos, firma forgery
falsificar ⟨1g⟩ v/t moneda counterfeit; documento, firma forge, falsify
falso adj false; joyas fake; documento, firma forged; **jurar en falso** commit perjury
falta f (escasez) lack, want; (error) mistake; (ausencia) absence; en tenis fault; en fútbol foul; (tiro libre) free kick; **hacerle falta a alguien** foul s.o.; **falta de** lack of, shortage of; **sin falta** without fail; **buena falta le hace** it's about time; **echar en falta a alguien** miss s.o.; **hacer falta** be necessary
faltar ⟨1a⟩ v/i be missing; **falta una hora** there's an hour to go; **faltan 10 kilómetros** there are 10 kilometers to go; **sólo falta hacer la salsa** there's only the sauce to do; **faltar a** be absent from; **faltar a clase** miss class, be absent from class; **faltar a alguien** be disrespectful to s.o.; **faltar a su palabra** not keep one's word
falto adj: **falto de** lacking in, devoid of; **falto de recursos** short of resources
fama f fame; (reputación) reputation; **tener mala fama** have a bad reputation
familia f family; **sentirse como en familia** feel at home
familiar 1 adj family atr; (conocido) familiar; LING colloquial 2 m/f relation, relative
familiaridad f familiarity
familiarizarse ⟨1f⟩ v/r familiarize o.s. (**con** with)
famoso 1 adj famous 2 m, -a f celebrity
fan m/f fan
fanático 1 adj fanatical 2 m, -a f fanatic
fanatismo m fanaticism
fanfarrón 1 adj boastful 2 m, -ona f boaster
fanfarronear ⟨1a⟩ v/i boast, brag
fango m tb fig mud
fantasear ⟨1a⟩ v/i fantasize
fantasía f fantasy; (imaginación) imagination; **joyas de fantasía** costume jewel(l)ery
fantasma m ghost
fantástico adj fantastic
farándula f show business
fardar ⟨1a⟩ v/i: **fardar de algo** F boast about sth, show off about sth
fardo m bundle
faringitis f MED inflammation of the pharynx, pharyngitis
fariña f S. Am. manioc flour, cassava
farmacéutico 1 adj pharmaceutical 2 m, -a f pharmacist, Br chemist
farmacia f pharmacy, Br chemist's; estudios pharmacy; **farmacia de guardia** 24-hour pharmacist, Br emergency chemist
fármaco m medicine
farmacología f pharmacology
faro m MAR lighthouse; AUTO headlight, headlamp; **faro antiniebla** fog light
farol m lantern; (farola) streetlight, streetlamp; en juegos de cartas bluff
farola f streetlight, streetlamp
farolillo m: **ser el farolillo rojo** fig F be bottom of the league
farragoso adj texto dense
farrear ⟨1a⟩ v/i L.Am. F go out on the town F

farrista *adj L.Am.* F hard-drinking

farsa *f tb fig* farce

farsante *m/f* fraud, fake

fascículo *m* TIP instal(l)ment

fascinación *f* fascination

fascinante *adj* fascinating

fascinar ⟨1a⟩ *v/t* fascinate

fascismo *m* fascism

fascista *m/f & adj* fascist

fase *f* phase

fastidiar ⟨1b⟩ **1** *v/t* annoy; F (*estropear*) spoil **2** *v/r* **fastidiarse** grin and bear it

fastidio *m* annoyance; **¡qué fastidio!** what a nuisance!

fastuoso *adj* lavish

fatal **1** *adj* fatal; (*muy malo*) dreadful, awful **2** *adv* very badly

fatídico *adj* fateful

fatiga *f* tiredness, fatigue

fatigar ⟨1h⟩ **1** *v/t* tire **2** *v/r* **fatigarse** get tired

fatuo *adj* conceited; (*necio*) fatuous

fauces *fpl* ZO jaws

fauna *f* fauna

favor *m* favo(u)r; **a favor de** in favo(u)r of; **por favor** please; **hacer un favor** do a favo(u)r

favorecer ⟨2d⟩ *v/t* favo(u)r; *de ropa, color* suit

favoritismo *m* favo(u)ritism

favorito **1** *adj* favo(u)rite **2** *m*, **-a** *f* favo(u)rite

fax *m* fax; **enviar un fax a alguien** send s.o. a fax, fax s.o.

fayuca *f Méx* smuggling

fayuquero *m*, **-a** *f Méx* dealer in smuggled goods

F.C. *abr* (= *Fútbol Club*) FC (= Football Club)

fdo. *abr* (= *firmado*) signed

fe *f* faith (**en** in); **fe de erratas** errata

fealdad *f* ugliness

feb. *abr* (= *febrero*) Feb. (= February)

febrero *m* February

fecal *adj* f(a)ecal

fecha *f* date; **fecha límite de consumo** best before date; **fecha de nacimiento** date of birth

fechador *m Chi, Méx* postmark

fécula *f* starch

fecundación *f* fertilization; **fecundación in vitro** MED in vitro fertilization

fecundar ⟨1a⟩ *v/t* fertilize

fecundo *adj* fertile

federación *f* federation

federal *adj* federal

felicidad *f* happiness; **¡felicidades!** congratulations!

felicitación *f* letter of congratulations;

¡felicitaciones! congratulations!

felicitar ⟨1a⟩ *v/t* congratulate (**por** on)

felino *adj tb fig* feline

feliz *adj* happy; **¡feliz Navidad!** Merry Christmas!

felpa *f* towel(l)ing

felpudo *m* doormat

femenino **1** *adj* feminine; *moda, equipo* women's **2** GRAM feminine

femin(e)idad *f* femininity

feminismo *m* feminism

feminista *m/f & adj* feminist

fenomenal **1** *adj* F fantastic F, phenomenal F **2** *adv*: **lo pasé fenomenal** F I had a fantastic time F

fenómeno **1** *m* phenomenon; *persona* genius **2** *adj* F fantastic F, great F

feo **1** *adj* ugly; *fig* nasty **2** *m*: **hacer un feo a alguien** F snub s.o.

féretro *m* casket, coffin

feria *f* COM fair; *L.Am.* (*mercado*) market; *Méx* (*calderilla*) small change; **feria de muestras** trade fair

feriado **1** *adj L.Am.*: **día feriado** (public) holiday **2** *m L.Am.* (public) holiday; **abierto feriados** open on public holidays

ferial **1** *adj*: **recinto ferial** fairground **2** *m* fair

fermentación *f* fermentation

fermentar ⟨1a⟩ *v/t* ferment

fermento *m* ferment

ferocidad *f* ferocity

feroz *adj* fierce; (*cruel*) cruel

férreo *adj tb fig* iron *atr*; **del ferrocarril** rail *atr*

ferretería *f* hardware store

ferrocarril *m* railroad, *Br* railway

ferrocarrilero *m L.Am.* railroad *o Br* railway worker

ferroviario *adj* rail *atr*

ferry *m* ferry

fértil *adj* fertile

fertilidad *f* fertility

fertilizante *m* fertilizer

ferviente *adj fig* fervent

fervor *m* fervo(u)r

festejar ⟨1a⟩ *v/t persona* wine and dine; *L.Am.* celebrate

festejo *m* celebration; **festejos** festivities

festín *m* banquet

festival *m* festival; **festival cinematográfico** film festival

festividad *f* feast; **festividades** festivities

festivo *adj* festive

fetal *adj* fetal

fetiche *m* fetish

fétido *adj* fetid

feto *m* fetus

feudal adj feudal

feudo m fig domain

FF. AA. abr (= **fuerzas armadas**) armed forces

FF. CC. abr (= **ferrocarriles**) railroads

fiable adj trustworthy; *datos, máquina* etc reliable

fiambre m cold cut, Br cold meat; P (*cadáver*) stiff P

fiambrera f lunch pan, Br lunch box

fiambrería f L.Am. delicatessen

fianza f deposit; JUR bail; **bajo fianza** on bail

fiar ⟨1c⟩ 1 v/i give credit 2 v/r **fiarse**: **fiarse de alguien** trust s.o.; **no me fío** I don't trust him / them *etc*

fiasco m fiasco

fibra f en tejido, alimento fiber, Br fibre; **fibra óptica** optical fiber (Br fibre); **fibra de vidrio** fiberglass, Br fibreglass

fibroso adj fibrous

ficción f fiction

ficha f file card, index card; en juegos de mesa counter; en un casino chip; en damas checker, Br draught; en ajedrez man, piece; TELEC token

fichar ⟨1a⟩ 1 v/t DEP sign; JUR open a file on 2 v/i DEP sign (**por** for)

fichero m file cabinet, Br filing cabinet; INFOR file

ficticio adj fictitious

fidedigno adj reliable

fidelidad f fidelity

fideo m noodle

fiebre f fever; (*temperatura*) temperature; **fiebre del heno** hay fever

fiel 1 adj faithful; (*leal*) loyal 2 mpl: **los fieles** REL the faithful pl

fieltro m felt

fiera f wild animal; **ponerse hecho una fiera** F go wild F

fiero adj fierce

fierro m L.Am. iron

fiesta f festival; (*reunión social*) party; (*día festivo*) public holiday; **estar de fiesta** be in a party mood

fifí m L.Am. P afeminado sissy F

figura f figure; (*estatuilla*) figurine; (*forma*) shape; *naipes* face card, Br picture card; **tener buena figura** have a good figure

figurado adj figurative; **sentido figurado** figurative sense

figurar ⟨1a⟩ 1 v/i appear (**en** in); **aquí figura como ...** she appears o is down here as ... 2 v/r **figurarse** imagine; **¡figúrate!** just imagine!

fijar ⟨1a⟩ 1 v/t fix; *cartel; fecha, objetivo* set; *residencia* establish; *atención*

focus 2 v/r **fijarse** (*establecerse*) settle; (*prestar atención*) pay attention (**en** to); **fijarse en algo** (*darse cuenta*) notice sth

fijo adj fixed; *trabajo* permanent; *fecha* definite

fila f line, Br queue; de asientos row; **en fila india** in single file; **filas** MIL ranks

filatelia f philately, stamp collecting

filete m GASTR fillet

filial 1 adj filial 2 f COM subsidiary

Filipinas fpl Philippines

film(e) m movie, film

filmación f filming, shooting

filmar ⟨1a⟩ v/t film, shoot

filo m edge; de navaja cutting edge; **al filo de las siete** fig around 7 o'clock

filología f philology; **filología hispánica** EDU Spanish language and literature

filólogo m, -a f philologist

filón m vein, seam; fig goldmine

filoso adj L.Am. sharp

filosofía f philosophy

filosófico adj philosophical

filósofo m, -a f philosopher

filtración f leak

filtrar ⟨1a⟩ 1 v/t filter; *información* leak 2 v/r **filtrarse** filter (**por** through); de agua, información leak

filtro m filter

fin m end; (*objetivo*) aim, purpose; **fin de semana** weekend; **a fines de mayo** at the end of May; **al fin y al cabo** at the end of the day, after all; **en fin** anyway

final f/adj final

finalidad f purpose, aim

finalista 1 adj: **las dos selecciones finalistas** the two teams that reached the final 2 m/f finalist

finalización f completion

finalizado adj complete

finalizar ⟨1f⟩ v/t & v/i end, finish

finalmente adv eventually

financiación f funding

financiar ⟨1b⟩ v/t finance, fund

financista m/f L.Am. financier

finanzas fpl finances

finca f (*bien inmueble*) property; L.Am. (*granja*) farm

fingido adj false

fingir ⟨3c⟩ 1 v/t feign fml; **fingió no haberlo oído** I pretended I hadn't heard 2 v/r **fingirse**: **fingirse enfermo** pretend to be ill, feign illness fml

finlandés 1 adj Finnish 2 m, -esa f Finn

Finlandia Finland

fino adj calidad fine; libro, tela thin; (*esbelto*) slim; modales, gusto refined; *sentido de humor* subtle

firma f signature; *acto* signing; COM firm

firmamento *m* firmament

firmar ⟨1a⟩ *v/t* sign

firme *adj* firm; *(estable)* steady; **en firme** COM firm

fiscal **1** *adj* tax *atr*, fiscal **2** *m/f* district attorney, *Br* public prosecutor

fisgar ⟨1h⟩ *v/i* F snoop F; **fisgar en algo** snoop around in sth

fisgón *m*, -ona *f* snoop

fisgonear ⟨1a⟩ *v/i* F snoop around F (**en** in)

física *f* physics

físico **1** *adj* physical **2** *m*, -a *f* physicist **3** *m de una persona* physique

fisiología *f* physiology

fisión *f* fission

fisioterapeuta *m/f* physical therapist, *Br* physiotherapist

fisioterapia *f* physical therapy, *Br* physiotherapy

fisonomía *f* features *pl*

fisura *f* crack; MED fracture

flác(c)ido *adj* flabby

flaco *adj* thin; **punto flaco** weak point

flacuchento *adj* *L.Am.* F skinny

flagelar ⟨1a⟩ *v/t* flagellate

flagrante *adj* flagrant; **en flagrante delito** red-handed, in flagrante delicto

flamante *adj* *(nuevo)* brand-new

flamenco **1** *adj* MÚS flamenco **2** *m* MÚS flamenco; ZO flamingo

flan *m* crème caramel

flanco *m* flank

flaquear ⟨1a⟩ *v/i* weaken; *de entusiasmo* flag

flaqueza *f* fig weakness

flash *m* FOT flash

flato *m* MED stitch

flatulencia *f* MED flatulence

flauta *f* flute; *Méx* fried taco; **flauta dulce** recorder; **flauta travesera** (transverse) flute

flautista *m/f* flautist

flecha *f* arrow

flechazo *m* fig love at first sight

flecos *mpl* fringe *sg*

flema *f* fig phlegm

flemático *adj* phlegmatic

flemón *m* MED gumboil

flequillo *m del pelo* fringe

fletar ⟨1a⟩ *v/t* charter; *(embarcar)* load

flete *m* *L.Am.* freight, cost of transport

fletero *adj* *L.Am.* hire *atr*, charter *atr*

flexibilidad *f* flexibility

flexible *adj* flexible

flexión *f* *en gimnasia* push-up, *Br* press-up; *de piernas* squat; *de la voz* inflection

flexionar ⟨1a⟩ **1** *v/t* flex **2** *v/r* **flexionarse** bend

flexo *m* desk lamp

flipar ⟨1a⟩ *v/i*: **le flipa el cine** P he's mad about the movies F

flirtear ⟨1a⟩ *v/i* flirt (**con** with)

flojo *adj* loose, *café*, *argumento* weak; COM *actividad* slack; *novela*, *redacción* poor; *L.Am.* lazy

flojera *f* *L.Am.* laziness; **me da flojera** I can't be bothered

flor *f* flower

flora *f* flora

florear ⟨1a⟩ **1** *v/t* decorate with flowers; *Méx (halagar)* flatter, compliment **2** *v/i* flower, bloom

florecer ⟨2d⟩ *v/i* BOT flower. bloom; *de negocio, civilización etc* flourish

floreciente *adj* flourishing

florero *m* vase

florista *m/f* florist

floristería *f* florist's, flower shop

flota *f* fleet

flotación *f* flotation

flotador *m* float

flotar ⟨1a⟩ *v/i* float

flote MAR: **a flote** afloat

fluctuación *f* fluctuation

fluctuar ⟨1e⟩ *v/i* fluctuate

fluidez *f* fluidity

fluido **1** *adj* fluid; *tráfico* free-flowing; *lenguaje* fluent **2** *m* fluid

fluir ⟨3g⟩ *v/i* flow

flujo *m* flow

fluorescente **1** *adj* fluorescent **2** *m* strip light

fluvial *adj* river *atr*

FM *abr* (= **frecuencia modulada**) FM (= frequency modulation)

FMI *abr* (= **Fondo Monetario Internacional**) IMF (= International Monetary Fund)

fobia *f* phobia

foca *f* ZO seal

foco *m* focus; TEA, TV spotlight; *de infección* center, *Br* centre; *de incendio* seat; *L.Am.* *(bombilla)* lightbulb; *de auto* headlight; *de calle* streetlight

fofo *adj* flabby

fogata *f* bonfire

fogoso *adj* fiery, ardent

foie-gras *m* foie gras

folclore *m* folklore

fólico *adj*: **ácido fólico** folic acid

folio *m* sheet (of paper)

folklore *m* folklore

follaje *m* foliage

folleto *m* pamphlet

follón *m* argument; *(lío)* mess; **armar un follón** kick up a fuss

fomentar ⟨1a⟩ *v/t* foster; COM promote; *re-*

belión foment, incite

fomento *m* COM promotion

fonda *f L.Am.* cheap restaurant; (*pensión*) boarding house

fondear ⟨1a⟩ **1** *v/t* MAR anchor **2** *v/r* **fondearse** *L.Am.* get rich

fondero *m*, **-a** *f L.Am.* restaurant owner

fondista *m/f* DEP long-distance runner

fondo *m* bottom; *de sala, cuarto* etc back; *de pasillo* end; (*profundidad*) depth; PINT, FOT background; (*colección*) collection; COM fund; **fondo de inversión** investment fund; **fondo de pensiones** pension fund; **Fondo Monetario Internacional** International Monetary Fund; **fondos** *pl* money sg, funds; **tiene buen fondo** he's got a good heart; **en el fondo** deep down; **tocar fondo** *fig* reach bottom

fonética *f* phonetics

fontanería *f* plumbing

fontanero *m* plumber

footing *m* DEP jogging; **hacer footing** go jogging, jog

forastero 1 *adj* foreign **2** *m*, **-a** *f* outsider, stranger

forcejear ⟨1a⟩ *v/i* struggle

forcejeo *m* struggle

forense 1 *adj* forensic **2** *m/f* forensic scientist

forestación *f* afforestation

forestal *adj* forest *atr*

forestar ⟨1a⟩ *v/t L.Am.* afforest

forjar ⟨1a⟩ *v/t* metal forge

forma *f* form; (*apariencia*) shape; (*manera*) way; **de todas formas** in any case, anyway; **estar en forma** be fit

formación *f* formation; (*entrenamiento*) training; **formación profesional** vocational training

formal *adj* formal; *niño* well-behaved; (*responsable*) responsible

formalizar ⟨1f⟩ *v/t* formalize; *relación* make official

formar ⟨1a⟩ **1** *v/t* form; (*educar*) educate **2** *v/r* **formarse** form

formatear ⟨1a⟩ *v/t* INFOR format

formato *m* format

formidable *adj* huge; (*estupendo*) tremendous

fórmula *f* formula

formular ⟨1a⟩ *v/t teoría* formulate; *queja* make, lodge

formulario *m* form

fornicar ⟨1g⟩ *v/i* fornicate

fornido *adj* well-built

foro *m* forum

forofo *m*, **-a** *f* F fan

forrado *adj prenda* lined; *libro* covered;

fig F loaded F

forraje *m* fodder

forrar 1 *v/t prenda* line; *libro, silla* cover **2** *v/r* **forrarse** F make a fortune F

forro *m de prenda* lining; *de libro* cover

fortalecer ⟨2d⟩ **1** *v/t tb fig* strengthen **2** *v/r* **fortalecerse** strengthen

fortaleza *f* strength of character; MIL fortress

fortificar ⟨1g⟩ *v/t* MIL fortify

fortuito *adj* chance *atr*, accidental

fortuna *f* fortune; (*suerte*) luck; **por fortuna** fortunately, luckily

forzar ⟨1f & 1m⟩ *v/t* force; (*violar*) rape

forzoso *adj aterrizaje* forced

forzudo *adj* brawny

fosa *f* pit; (*tumba*) grave; **fosa común** common grave; **fosas nasales** nostrils

fósforo *m* QUÍM phosphorus; *L.Am.* (*cerilla*) match

fósil 1 *adj* fossilized **2** *m* fossil

foso *m* ditch; TEA, MÚS pit; *de castillo* moat

foto *f* photo

fotocopia *f* photocopy

fotocopiadora *f* photocopier

fotocopiar ⟨1a⟩ *v/t* photocopy

fotogénico *adj* photogenic

fotografía *f* photography

fotografiar ⟨1c⟩ *v/t* photograph

fotógrafo *m*, **-a** *f* photographer

FP *f* (= **formación profesional**) vocational training

frac *m* tail coat

fracasado 1 *adj* unsuccessful **2** *m*, **-a** *f* loser

fracasar ⟨1a⟩ *v/i* fail

fracaso *m* failure

fracción *f* fraction; POL faction

fraccionamiento *m L.Am.* (housing) project, *Br* estate

fraccionar ⟨1a⟩ *v/t* break up; FIN pay in instal(l)ments

fractura *f* MED fracture

fracturar ⟨1a⟩ *v/t* MED fracture

fragancia *f* fragrance

frágil *adj* fragile

fragmentar ⟨1a⟩ *v/t* fragment

fragmento *m* fragment; *de novela, poema* excerpt, extract

fraguar ⟨1i⟩ *v/t* forge; *plan* devise; *complot* hatch

fraile *m* friar, monk

frambuesa *f* raspberry

francés 1 *adj* French **2** *m* Frenchman; *idioma* French

francesa *f* Frenchwoman

Francia France

franco *adj* (*sincero*) frank; (*evidente*) dis-

tinct, marked; COM free
francotirador *m* sniper
franela *f* flannel
franja *f* fringe; *de tierra* strip
franquear ⟨1a⟩ *v/t carta* pay the postage on; *camino, obstáculo* clear
franqueo *m* postage
franqueza *f* frankness
franquicia *f* (*exención*) exemption; COM franchise
frasco *m* bottle
frase *f* phrase; (*oración*) sentence; **frase hecha** set phrase
fraternal *adj* brotherly
fraternidad *f* brotherhood, fraternity
fraternizar ⟨1f⟩ *v/i* POL fraternize
fraude *m* fraud
fraudulento *adj* fraudulent
frazada *f L.Am.* blanket
frecuencia *f* frequency; **frecuencia modulada** RAD frequency modulation; **con frecuencia** frequently
frecuentar ⟨1a⟩ *v/t* frequent
frecuente *adj* frequent; (*común*) common
frecuentemente *adv* often, frequently
fregadero *m* sink
fregar ⟨1h & 1k⟩ *v/t platos* wash; *el suelo* mop; *L.Am.* F bug F
fregón 1 *adj* annoying **2** *m L.Am.* F nuisance, pain in the neck F
fregona *f* mop; *L.Am.* F nuisance, pain in the neck F
freidora *f* deep fryer
freidura *f* frying
freír ⟨3m; *part* **frito**⟩ *v/t* fry; F (*matar*) waste P
frenada *f esp L.Am.*: **dar una frenada** F slam the brakes on, hit the brakes F
frenar ⟨1a⟩ **1** *v/i* AUTO brake **2** *v/t fig* slow down; *impulsos* check
frenazo *m*: **pegar** *or* **dar un frenazo** F slam the brakes on, hit the brakes F
frenesí *m* frenzy
frenético *adj* frenetic
freno *m* brake; **freno de mano** parking brake, *Br* handbrake
frente 1 *f* forehead **2** *m* MIL, METEO front; **de frente** *colisión* head-on; **de frente al grupo** *L.Am.* facing the group; **hacer frente a** face up to **3** *prp*: **frente a** opposite
fresa *f* strawberry
fresco 1 *adj cold; pescado etc* fresh; *persona* F fresh F, *Br* cheeky F **2** *m, -a f*: **¡eres un fresco!** F you've got nerve! F, *Br* you've got a cheek! **3** *m* fresh air; *C.Am.* fruit drink
frescor *m* freshness
frescura *f* freshness; (*frío*) coolness; *fig*

nerve
fresno *m* BOT ash tree
fresón *m* strawberry
frialdad *f tb fig* coldness
fricción *f* TÉC, *fig* friction
friccionar ⟨1a⟩ *v/t* rub
friega *f L.Am.* F hassle F, drag F
frígido *adj* MED frigid
frigorífico 1 *adj* refrigerated **2** *m* fridge
frijol *m*, **frijol** *m L.Am.* bean
frío 1 *adj tb fig* cold **2** *m* cold; **tener frío** be cold
friolento *L.Am.*, **friolero** *adj*: **es friolento** he feels the cold
fritar ⟨1a⟩ *v/t L.Am.* fry
frito 1 *part* → **freír 2** *adj* fried **3** *mpl*: **fritos** fried food *sg*
fritura *f* fried food
frívolo *adj* frivolous
frondoso *adj* leafy
frontal *adj* frontal; *ataque etc* head-on; (*delantero*) front *atr*
frontera *f* border
fronterizo *adj* border *atr*
frontón *m* DEP pelota; *cancha* pelota court
frotar ⟨1a⟩ *v/t* rub
fructífero *adj* fruitful, productive
frugal *adj persona* frugal
fruncir ⟨3b⟩ *v/t material* gather; **fruncir el ceño** frown
frustración *f* frustration
frustrante *adj* frustrating
frustrar ⟨1a⟩ **1** *v/t* frustrate; *plan* thwart **2** *v/t* **frustrarse** fail
fruta *f* fruit
frutal 1 *adj* fruit *atr* **2** *m* fruit tree
frutería *f* fruit store, *Br* greengrocer's
frutilla *f S. Am.* strawberry
fruto *m tb fig* fruit; *nuez, almendra etc* nut; **frutos secos** nuts
fucsia *adj* fuchsia
fue *vb* → **ir, ser**
fuego *m* fire; **¿tienes fuego?** do you have a light?; **fuegos artificiales** fireworks; **pegar** *or* **prender fuego a** set fire to
fuel(-oil) *m* fuel oil
fuelle *m* bellows *pl*
fuente *f* fountain; *recipiente* dish; *fig* source
fuera 1 *vb* → **ir, ser 2** *adv* outside; (*en otro lugar*) away; (*en otro país*) abroad; **por fuera** on the outside; **¡fuera!** get out! **3** *prp*: **fuera de** outside; **¡sal fuera de aquí!** get out of here!; **está fuera del país** he's abroad, he's out of the country
fuero *m*: **en el fuero interno** deep down
fuerte 1 *adj* strong; *dolor* intense; *lluvia* heavy; *aumento* sharp; *ruido* loud; *fig* P incredible F **2** *adv* hard **3** *m* MIL fort

fuerza f strength; (*violencia*) force; EL power; **fuerza aérea** air force; **fuerza de voluntad** willpower; **fuerzas armadas** armed forces; **fuerzas de seguridad** security forces; **a fuerza de ...** by (dint of)

fuese vb → **ir, ser**

fuete m L.Am. whip

fuga f escape; *de gas, agua* leak; **darse a la fuga** flee

fugarse ⟨1h⟩ v/r run away; *de la cárcel* escape

fugaz adj fig fleeting

fugitivo 1 adj runaway atr **2** m, -a f fugitive

fui vb → **ir, ser**

fuimos vb → **ir, ser**

fulano m so-and-so

fulgor m brightness

fulgurante adj fig dazzling

fulminante adj sudden

fulminar ⟨1a⟩ v/t: **lo fulminó un rayo** he was killed by lightning; **fulminar a alguien con la mirada** look daggers at s.o. F

fumador m, **fumadora** f smoker

fumar ⟨1a⟩ **1** v/t smoke **2** v/i smoke; **prohibido fumar** no smoking **3** v/r **fumarse** smoke; **fumarse una clase** F skip a class F

fumigar ⟨1h⟩ v/t fumigate

función f purpose, function; *en el trabajo* duty; TEA performance; **en función de** according to

funcional adj functional

funcionamiento m working

funcionar ⟨1a⟩ v/i work; **no funciona** out of order

funcionario m, **-a** f government employee, civil servant

funda f cover; *de gafas* case; *de almohada* pillowcase

fundación f foundation

fundador m, **fundadora** f founder

fundamental adj fundamental

fundamentalismo m fundamentalism

fundamentalista m/f fundamentalist

fundamentalmente adv essentially

fundamento m foundation; **fundamen-**

tos (*nociones*) fundamentals

fundar ⟨1a⟩ **1** v/t fig base (**en** on) **2** v/r **fundarse** be based (**en** on)

fundición f smelting; (*fábrica*) foundry

fundir ⟨3a⟩ **1** v/t *hielo* melt; *metal* smelt; COM merge **2** v/r **fundirse** melt; *de bombilla* fuse; *de plomos* blow; COM merge; *L.Am. fig: de empresa* go under

fúnebre adj funeral atr; fig: *ambiente* gloomy

funeral m funeral

funeraria f funeral parlo(u)r, Br undertaker's

funesto adj disastrous

funicular m funicular; (*teleférico*) cable car

furcia f P whore P

furgón m van; FERR boxcar, Br goods van; **furgón de equipajes** baggage car, Br luggage van

furgoneta f van

furia f fury; **ponerse hecho una furia** go into a fury o rage

furibundo adj furious

furioso adj furious

furor m: **hacer furor** fig be all the rage F

furtivo adj furtive

fuselaje m fuselage

fusible m EL fuse

fusil m rifle

fusilar ⟨1a⟩ v/t shoot; fig F (*plagiar*) lift F

fusión f FÍS fusion; COM merger

fusionar ⟨1a⟩ **1** v/t COM merge **2** v/r **fusionarse** merge

fusta f riding crop

fútbol m soccer, Br football; **fútbol americano** football, Br American football; **fútbol sala** five-a-side soccer (Br football)

futbolín m Foosball®, table football

futbolista m/f soccer player, Br footballer, Br football player

fútil adj trivial

futre m Chi dandy

futuro 1 adj future atr **2** m future

futurólogo m, **-a** f futurologist

G

g. *abr* (= **gramo** (**s**)) gr(s) (= gram(s))
gabardina *f prenda* raincoat; *material* gabardine
gabinete *m* (*despacho*) office; *en una casa* study; POL cabinet; *L.Am. de médico* office, *Br* surgery
gacela *f* ZO gazelle
gaceta *f* gazette
gachas *fpl* porridge *sg*
gachupín *m Méx desp* Spaniard
gacilla *f C.Am.* safety pin
gafas *fpl* glasses; **gafas de sol** sunglasses
gafe 1 *adj* jinxed **2** *m* jinx **3** *m/f*: **es un gafe** he's jinxed
gaita *f* MÚS bagpipes *pl*
gajes *mpl*: **gajes del oficio** *iron* occupational hazard
gajo *m* segment
gala *f* gala; **traje de gala** formal dress
galante *adj* gallant
galápago *m* ZO turtle
galardonar ⟨1a⟩ *v/t*: **fue galardonado con ...** he was awarded ...
galaxia *f* galaxy
galería *f* gallery; **galería de arte** art gallery
Gales Wales
galés Welsh
galgo *m* greyhound
gallera *f L.Am.* cockpit
galleta *f* cookie, *Br* biscuit
gallina 1 *f* hen **2** *m* F chicken
gallinazo *m L.Am.* turkey buzzard
gallo *m* rooster, *Br* cock
galón *m adorno* braid; MIL stripe; *medida* gallon
galope *m* gallop
galpón *m L.Am.* large shed; *W.I.* HIST slave quarters *pl*
gama *f* range
gamba *f* ZO GASTR shrimp, *Br* prawn
gamberro *m*, **-a** *f* troublemaker
gamín *m*, **-ina** *f Col* street kid
gamo *m* ZO fallow deer
gamonal *m Pe, Bol desp* chief
gamuza *f* chamois
gana *f*: **de mala gana** unwillingly, grudgingly; **no me da la gana** I don't want to; **... me da ganas de ...** makes me want to; **tener ganas de (hacer) algo** feel like (doing) sth
ganadería *f* stockbreeding
ganadero *m*, **-a** *f* stockbreeder
ganado *m* cattle *pl*

ganador *m* winner
ganancia *f* profit
ganar ⟨1a⟩ **1** win; *mediante el trabajo* earn **2** *v/i mediante el trabajo* earn; (*vencer*) win; (*mejorar*) improve **3** *v/r* **ganarse** *a alguien* win over; **ganarse la vida** earn one's living
ganchillo *m* crochet
gancho *m* hook; *L.Am., Arg fig* F sex-appeal; **hacer gancho** L.Am. (*ayudar*) lend a hand; **tener gancho** F *de un grupo, una campaña* be popular; *de una persona* have that certain something
gandul *m* lazybones *sg*
gandulear ⟨1a⟩ *v/i* F loaf around F
ganga *f* bargain
gangrena *f* MED gangrene
gángster *m* gangster
ganso *m* goose; *macho* gander
garabatear ⟨1a⟩ *v/i & v/t* doodle
garabato *m* doodle
garaje *m* garage
garantía *f* guarantee
garantizar ⟨1f⟩ *v/t* guarantee
garapiña *f Cuba, Méx* pineapple squash
garbanzo *m* BOT chickpea
garbo *m al moverse* grace
gardenia *f* BOT gardenia
garete *m*: **irse al garete** *fig* F go to pot F
garfio *m* hook
gargajo *m* piece of phlegm
garganta *f* ANAT throat; GEOG gorge
gargantilla *f* choker
gárgaras *fpl*: **hacer gárgaras** gargle
garito *m* gambling den
garra *f* claw; *de ave* talon; **caer en las garras de alguien** *fig* fall into s.o.'s clutches; **tener garra** F be compelling
garrafa *f* carafe
garrafal *adj error etc* terrible
garrapata *f* ZO tick
garrote *m palo* club, stick; *tipo de ejecución* garrotte
garúa *f L.Am.* drizzle
garuar ⟨1e⟩ *v/i L.Am.* drizzle
garzón *m Rpl* (*mesero*) waiter
garza *f* ZO heron
gas *m* gas; **gas natural** natural gas; **gases** *pl* MED gas *sg*, wind *sg*; **con gas** sparkling, carbonated; **sin gas** still
gasa *f* gauze
gaseosa *f* lemonade
gasfitero *m Pe, Bol* plumber
gasoducto *m* gas pipeline

gasoil, gasóleo m oil; *para motores diesel* tic F, great F

gasolina f gas, Br petrol

gasolinera f gas station, Br petrol station

gastar ⟨1a⟩ **1** v/t *dinero* spend; *energía, electricidad etc* use; (*llevar*) wear; (*desperdiciar*) waste; (*desgastar*) wear out; **¿qué número gastas?** what size do you take?, what size are you? **2** v/r **gastarse** *dinero* spend; *gasolina, agua* run out of; *pila* run down; *ropa, zapatos* wear out

gasto m expense

gastronomía f gastronomy

gata f (female) cat; *Méx* servant, maid; **a gatas** F on all fours; **andar a gatas** F crawl

gatear ⟨1a⟩ v/i crawl

gatillo m trigger

gato m cat; AUTO jack; **aquí hay gato encerrado** F there's something fishy going on here F; **cuatro gatos** a handful of people

gaucho m Rpl gaucho

gaviota f (sea)gull

gay 1 adj gay **2** m gay (man)

gazpacho m gazpacho (*cold soup made with tomatoes, peppers, garlic etc*)

gel m gel

gelatina f gelatin(e); GASTR Jell-O®, Br jelly

gélido adj icy

gema f gem

gemelo 1 adj twin atr; **hermano gemelo** twin brother **2** mpl: **gemelos** twins; *de camisa* cuff links; (*prismáticos*) binoculars

gemido m moan, groan

Géminis m/f inv ASTR Gemini

gemir ⟨3l⟩ v/i moan, groan

gen m gene

genealógico adj: **árbol genealógico** family tree

generación f generation

generador m EL generator

general 1 adj general; **en general** in general; **por lo general** usually, generally **2** m general

generalización f generalization

generalizar ⟨1f⟩ **1** v/t spread **2** v/i generalize **3** v/r **generalizarse** spread

generalmente adv generally

generar ⟨1a⟩ v/t generate

género m (*tipo*) type; *de literatura* genre; GRAM gender; COM goods pl, merchandise

generosidad f generosity

generoso adj generous

genética f genetics

genético adj genetic

genial adj brilliant; F (*estupendo*) fantas-

genialidad f brilliance

genio m talento, *persona* genius; (*carácter*) temper; **tener mal genio** be bad-tempered

genital adj genital

genitales mpl genitals

genocidio m genocide

gente f people pl; L.Am. (*persona*) person

gentileza f kindness; **por gentileza de** by courtesy of

gentío m crowd

genuino adj genuine, real

geografía f geography

geográfico adj geographical

geología f geology

geológico adj geological

geólogo m, -a f geologist

geometría f geometry

geométrico adj geometric(al)

geranio m BOT geranium

gerente m/f manager

geriatría f geriatrics sg

germen m germ

germinar ⟨1a⟩ v/i tb fig germinate

gerundio m GRAM gerund

gestación f gestation

gesticular ⟨1a⟩ v/i gesticulate

gestión f management; **gestiones** pl (*trámites*) formalities, procedure sg

gestionar ⟨1a⟩ v/t *trámites* take care of; *negocio* manage

gesto m *movimiento* gesture; (*expresión*) expression

gestoría f Esp agency offering clients help with official documents

gigante 1 adj giant atr **2** m giant

gilipollas m/f inv P jerk P

gilipollez f Esp V bullshit V

gimnasia f gymnastics; **hacer gimnasia** do exercises

gimnasio m gym

gimnasta m/f gymnast

gimotear ⟨1a⟩ v/i whine, whimper

ginebra f gin

ginecólogo m, -a f gyn(a)ecologist

gin-tonic m gin and tonic, G and T F

gira f tour

girar ⟨1a⟩ **1** v/i (*dar vueltas, torcer*) turn; *alrededor de algo* revolve; fig (*tratar*) revolve (**en torno a** around) **2** v/t COM transfer

girasol m BOT sunflower

giro m turn; GRAM idiom; **giro postal** COM money order

gis m L.Am. chalk

gitano 1 adj gypsy atr **2** m, -a f gypsy

glacial adj icy

granel

glaciar *m* glacier
glándula *f* ANAT gland
global *adj* (*de todo el mundo*) global; *visión, resultado* overall; *cantidad* total
globo *m* aerostático, *de niño* balloon; *terrestre* globe; *globo terráqueo* globe
gloria *f* glory; (*delicia*) delight; *estar en la gloria* be in seventh heaven
gloriado *m* Pe, Bol, Ecuad type of punch
glorieta *f* traffic circle, Br roundabout
glorioso *adj* glorious
glosario *m* glossary
glotón **1** *adj* greedy **2** *m*, -ona *f* glutton
glucosa *f* glucose
gnomo *m* gnome
gobernador *m* governor
gobernante *m* leader
gobernar ⟨1k⟩ *v/t & v/i* rule, govern
gobierno *m* government
goce *m* pleasure, enjoyment
gofre *m* waffle
gol *m* DEP goal
goleador *m* DEP (goal)scorer
golf *m* DEP golf
golfista *m/f* golfer
golfo **1** *m* GEOG gulf **2** *m*, -a *f* good-for--nothing; *niño* little devil
Golfo de México *m* Gulf of Mexico
golondrina *f* ZO swallow
golosina *f* candy, Br sweet
goloso *adj* sweet-toothed
golpe *m* knock, blow; *golpe de Estado* coup d'état; *de golpe* suddenly; *no da golpe* F she doesn't do a thing
golpear ⟨1a⟩ *v/t cosa* bang, hit; *persona* hit
goma *f* (*caucho*) rubber; (*pegamento*) glue; (*banda elástica*) rubber band; F (*preservativo*) condom, rubber P; *C.Am.* F (*resaca*) hangover; *goma (de borrar)* eraser; *goma espuma* foam rubber
gomina *f* hair gel
gominola *f* jelly bean
góndola *f* Chi bus
gong *m* gong
gordinflón *m*, -ona *f* F fatso F
gordo **1** *adj* fat; *me cae gordo* F I can't stand him; *se va a armar la -a* all hell will break loose F **2** *m*, -a *f* fat person **3** *m* premio jackpot
gorila *m* ZO gorilla
gorjeo *m de pájaro* chirping, warbling; *de niño* gurgling
gorra *f* cap; *de gorra* F for free F
gorrino *m* fig pig
gorrión *m* ZO sparrow
gorro *m* cap; *estar hasta el gorro de algo* F be fed up to the back teeth with sth F

gorrón *m*, -ona *f* F scrounger
gorronear ⟨1a⟩ *v/t & v/i* F scrounge F
gota *f* drop; *ni gota* F *de cerveza, leche etc* not a drop; *de pan* not a scrap
gotear ⟨1a⟩ *v/i* drip; *filtrarse* leak
gotera *f* leak; (*mancha*) stain
gotero *m* MED drip; *L.Am.* (eye)dropper
gozar ⟨1f⟩ *v/i* (*disfrutar*) enjoy o.s.; *gozar de* (*disfrutar de*) enjoy; (*poseer*) have, enjoy
gozo *m* (*alegría*) joy; (*placer*) pleasure
grabación *f* recording
grabado *m* engraving
grabadora *f* tape recorder
grabar ⟨1a⟩ *v/t* record, video *etc* record; PINT, *fig* engrave
gracia *f*: *tener gracia* (*ser divertido*) be funny; (*tener encanto*) be graceful; *me hace gracia* I think it's funny, it makes me laugh; *no le veo la gracia* I don't think it's funny; *dar las gracias a alguien* thank s.o.; *gracias* thank you
grácil *adj* dainty
gracioso *adj* funny
gradas *fpl* DEP stands, grandstand *sg*
graderío *m* stands *pl*
grado *m* degree; *de buen grado* with good grace, readily
graduación *f* TÉC *etc* adjustment; *de alcohol* alcohol content; EDU graduation; MIL rank
gradual *adj* gradual
gradualmente *adv* gradually
graduarse ⟨1e⟩ *v/r* graduate, get one's degree
gráfica *f* graph
gráfico **1** *adj* graphic; *artes -as* graphic arts **2** *m* MAT graph; INFOR graphic
gragea *f* tablet, pill
grajo *m* ZO rook
Gral. *abr* (= *General*) Gen (= General)
gramática *f* grammar
gramatical *adj* grammatical
gramo *m* gram
gran short form of *grande* before a noun
granada *f* BOT pomegranate; *granada de mano* MIL hand grenade
granangular *m* wide-angle lens
granate *adj* dark crimson
Gran Bretaña Great Britain
grande **1** *adj* big; *a lo grande* in style **2** *m/f* L.Am. (*adulto*) grown-up, adult; (*mayor*) eldest; *pasarlo en grande* F have a great time
grandeza *f* greatness
grandiosidad *f* grandeur
grandioso *adj* impressive, magnificent
granel *m*: *vender a granel* COM sell in bulk; *había comida a granel* F there

was loads of food F

granero *m* granary

granito *m* granite

granizada *f* hailstorm

granizado *m type of soft drink made with crushed ice*

granizar ⟨1f⟩ *v/i* hail

granizo *m* hail

granja *f* farm

granjearse ⟨1a⟩ *v/r* win, earn

granjero *m*, **-a** *f* farmer

grano *m* grain; *de café* bean; *en la piel* pimple, spot; **ir al grano** get (straight) to the point

granuja *m* rascal

grapa *f* staple

grapadora *f* stapler

grapar ⟨1a⟩ *v/t* staple

grasa *f* BIO, GASTR fat; *lubricante, suciedad* grease

grasiento *adj* greasy, oily

graso *adj* greasy; *carne* fatty

gratificación *f* gratification

gratificar ⟨1g⟩ *v/t* reward

gratinar ⟨1a⟩ *v/t* cook au gratin

gratis *adj & adv* free

gratitud *f* gratitude

gratuito *adj* free

grava *f* gravel

gravar ⟨1a⟩ *v/t* tax

grave *adj* serious; *tono* grave, solemn; *nota* low; *voz* deep; **estar grave** be seriously ill

gravedad *f* seriousness, gravity; Fís gravity

gravemente *adv* seriously

gravilla *f* grave

Grecia *f* Greece

gremio *m* HIST guild; *fig* F *(oficio manual)* trade; *(profesión)* profession

griego 1 *adj* Greek **2** *m*, **-a** *f* Greek

grieta *f* crack

grifo *m adj* Méx F high **2** *m* faucet, *Br* tap; *Pe (gasolinera)* gas station, *Br* petrol station

grillo *m* ZO cricket

grima *f*: **me da grima** *Esp de ruido, material etc* it sets my teeth on edge; *de algo asqueroso* it gives me the creeps F; **en grima** *Pe* alone

gringo *m L.Am. desp* gringo *desp*, foreigner

gripe *f* flu, influenza

gris *adj* gray, *Br* grey

gritar ⟨1a⟩ *v/t & v/i* shout, yell

griterío *m* shouting

grito *m* cry, shout; **a grito pelado** at the top of one's voice; **pedir algo a gritos** F be crying out for sth

grosella *f* redcurrant

grosero 1 *adj* rude **2** *m*, **-a** *f* rude person

grosor *m* thickness

grotesco *adj* grotesque

grúa *f* crane; AUTO wrecker, *Br* breakdown truck

grueso *adj* thick; *persona* stout

grulla *f* ZO crane

grumo *m* lump

gruñido *m* grunt; *de perro* growl

gruñir ⟨3h⟩ *v/i (quejarse)* grumble, moan F; *de perro* growl; *de cerdo* grunt

gruñón 1 *adj* F grumpy **2** *m*, **-ona** *f* F grouch F

grupo *m* group

gruta *f* cave; *artificial* grotto

guacamol, guacamole *m* guacamole

guachimán *m Chi* watchman

guacho 1 *adj S. Am. (sin casa)* homeless; *(huérfano)* orphaned **2** *m*, **-a** *f S. Am. sin casa* homeless person; *(huérfano)* orphan

guadaño *m Cuba, Méx* small boat

guagua *f W.I., Ven, Canaries* bus; *Pe, Bol, Chi (niño)* baby

guajolote *m Méx, C.Am.* turkey

guanaco 1 *adj L.Am.* F dumb F, stupid **2** *m* ZO guanaco **3** *m*, **-a** *f persona* idiot

guantazo *m* slap

guante *m* glove

guantera *f* AUTO glove compartment

guapo *adj hombre* handsome, good-looking; *mujer* beautiful; *S. Am.* gutsy

guaracha *f W.I.* street band

guarache → **huarache**

guarapo *m L.Am. alcoholic drink made from sugar cane and herbs*

guarda *m/f* keeper; **guarda jurado** security guard

guardabosques *m/f inv* forest ranger

guardacostas *m inv* coastguard vessel

guardaespaldas *m/f inv* bodyguard

guardameta *m/f* DEP goalkeeper

guardar ⟨1a⟩ *v/t* keep; *poner en un lugar* put (away); *recuerdo* have; *apariencias* keep up; INFOR save; **guardar silencio** remain silent, keep silent **2** *v/r* **guardarse** keep; **guardarse de** refrain from

guardarropa *m* checkroom, *Br* cloakroom; *(ropa, armario)* wardrobe

guardería *f* nursery

guardia 1 *f* guard; **de guardia** on duty; **bajar la guardia** *fig* lower one's guard **2** *m/f* MIL guard; *(policía)* police officer; **guardia civil** *Esp* civil guard; **guardia de seguridad** security guard; **guardia de tráfico** traffic warden

guardián 1 *adj*: **perro guardián** guard dog **2** *m*, **-ana** *f* guard; *fig* guardian guarecer ⟨2d⟩ **1** v/t shelter **2** v/r guarecerse shelter, take shelter (**de** from)

guarida f zo den; **de personas** hideout

guarnición f GASTR accompaniment; MIL garrison

guaro m C.Am. sugar-cane liquor

guarro **1** adj F sucio filthy **2** m tb fig F pig

guarura m Méx (guardaespaldas) bodyguard; F (gamberro) thug

guasa f L.Am. joke; **de guasa** as a joke

guaso **1** adj S. Am. rude **2** m Chi peasant

guata f L.Am. F paunch

Guatemala Guatemala

guatemalteco **1** adj Guatemalan **2** m, -a f Guatemalan

guatón adj L.Am. F pot-bellied, big-bellied

guay int Esp F cool F, neat F

guayaba f L.Am. BOT guava

guayabera f Méx, C.Am., W.I. loose embroidered shirt

gubernamental adj governmental, government atr

guepardo m ZO cheetah

güero **1** adj Méx, C.Am. fair, light-skinned **2** m, -a f Méx, C.Am. blond(e)

guerra f war; **guerra civil** civil war; **guerra fría** cold war; **guerra mundial** world war; **dar guerra a alguien** F give s.o. trouble

guerrero **1** adj warlike **2** m warrior

guerrilla f guerillas pl

guerrillero m guerilla

gueto m ghetto

guevear v/i → huevear

guevón → huevón

guía **1** m/f guide; **guía turístico** tourist guide **2** f libro guide (book); **guía telefónica** or **de teléfonos** phone book

guiar ⟨1c⟩ **1** v/t guide **2** v/r guiarse: **guiarse por** follow

guijarro m pebble

guillotina f guillotine

güinche m L.Am. winch, pulley

guinda **1** adj L.Am. purple **2** f fresca morello cherry; **en dulce** glacé cherry

guindilla f GASTR chil(l)i

guiñar ⟨1a⟩ v/t: **le guiñó un ojo** she winked at him

guiño m wink

guión m de película script; GRAM corto hyphen; largo dash

guionista m/f scriptwriter

guiri m Esp P (light-skinned) foreigner

guirnalda f garland

guisante m pea

guisar ⟨1a⟩ v/t GASTR stew, casserole

guiso m GASTR stew, casserole

guitarra f guitar

guitarrista m/f guitarist

gula f gluttony

gusano m worm

gustar ⟨1a⟩ v/i: **me gusta viajar** I like to travel, I like travelling; **¿te gusta el ajo?** do you like garlic?; **no me gusta** I don't like it

gusto m taste; (placer) pleasure; **a gusto** at ease; **con mucho gusto** with pleasure; **de buen gusto** in good taste, tasteful; **de mal gusto** in bad taste, tasteless; **da gusto ...** it's a pleasure ...; **mucho** or **tanto gusto** how do you do

gutural adj guttural

H

ha vb → haber

haba f broad bean; **en todas partes se cuecen habas** it's the same the world over

Habana: **La Habana** Havana

habanero m, -a f citizen of Havana

habano m Havana (cigar)

haber ⟨2k⟩ **1** v/aux have; **hemos llegado** we've arrived; **he de levantarme pronto** I have to o I've got to get up early; **de haberlo sabido** if I'd known; **has de ver** Méx you ought to see it **2** v/impers:

hay there is sg, there are pl; **hubo un incendio** there was a fire; **¿qué hay?**, Méx **¿qué hubo?** how's it going?, what's happening?; **hay que hacerlo** it has to be done; **no hay de qué** not at all, don't mention it; **no hay más que decir** there's nothing more to be said **3** m asset; pago fee; **tiene en su haber 50.000 ptas** she's 50,000 pesetas in credit

habichuela f kidney bean

hábil adj skilled; (capaz) capable; (astuto) clever, smart

habilidad f skill; (*capacidad*) ability; (*astucia*) cleverness

habilitar ⟨1a⟩ v/t *lugar* fit out; *persona* authorize

habitación f room; (*dormitorio*) bedroom; **habitación doble / individual** double / single room

habitante m/f inhabitant

habitar ⟨1a⟩ v/i live (**en** in)

hábitat m habitat

hábito m tb REL habit; (*práctica*) knack; **colgar los hábitos** *fig de sacerdote* give up the priesthood

habitual 1 adj usual, regular **2** m/f regular

habituar ⟨1e⟩ **1** v/t: **habituar a alguien a algo** get s.o. used to sth **2** v/r **habituarse: habituarse a algo** get used to sth

habla f speech; **¡al habla!** TELEC speaking; **quedarse sin habla** *fig* be speechless

hablada f *L.Am.* piece of gossip; **habladas** pl gossip sg

hablador adj talkative; *Méx* boastful

habladurías fpl gossip sg

hablante m/f speaker

hablar ⟨1a⟩ **1** v/i speak; (*conversar*) talk; **hablar claro** *fig* say what one means; **hablar con alguien** talk to s.o., talk with s.o.; **hablar de** *de libro etc* be about, deal with; **hablar por hablar** talk for the sake of it; **¡ni hablar!** no way! **2** v/r **hablarse** speak to one another; **no se hablan** they're not speaking (to each other)

hacendado 1 adj land-owing **2** m, -a f land-owner

hacendoso adj hardworking

hacer ⟨2s; *part* **hecho**⟩ **1** v/t (*realizar*) do; (*elaborar, crear*) make; **¡haz algo!** do something!; **hacer una pregunta** ask a question; **¡qué le vamos a hacer!** that's life; **no hace más que quejarse** all he does is complain; **le hicieron ir** they made him go; **tengo que hacer los deberes** I have to do my homework **2** v/i: **haces bien / mal en ir** you are doing the right / wrong thing by going; **me hace mal** it's making me ill; **esto hará de mesa** de objeto this will do as a table; **hacer como que** or **como si** act as if; **no hace** *L.Am.* it doesn't matter; **se me hace qué** *L.Am.* it seems to me that **3** v/impers: **hace calor / frío** it's hot / cold; **hace tres días** three days ago; **hace mucho (tiempo)** a long time ago; **desde hace un año** for a year **4** v/r **hacerse** *traje* make; *casa* build o.s.; (*cocinarse*) cook; (*convertirse, volverse*) get, become; **hacerse viejo** get old; **hacerse de noche** get dark; **se hace tarde** it's getting late; **hacerse el sordo / el tonto** pretend to

be deaf / stupid; **hacerse a algo** get used to sth; **hacerse con algo** get hold of sth

hacha f ax, *Br* axe; **ser un hacha para algo** F be brilliant at sth

hachís m hashish

hacia prp toward; **hacia adelante** forward; **hacia abajo** down; **hacia arriba** up; **hacia atrás** back(ward); **hacia las cuatro** about four (o'clock)

Hacienda f *ministerio* Treasury Department, *Br* Treasury; *oficina* Internal Revenue Service, *Br* Inland Revenue

hacienda f *L.Am.* (*granja*) ranch, estate

hacinar ⟨1a⟩ v/t stack

hada f fairy

haga vb → **hacer**

hago vb → **hacer**

Haití Haiti

hala int come on!; *sorpresa* wow!

halagar ⟨1h⟩ v/t flatter

halago m flattery

halar ⟨1a⟩ v/t *L.Am.* haul, pull

halcón m zo falcon

halitosis f MED halitosis, bad breath

hall m hall

hallar ⟨1a⟩ **1** v/t find; (*descubrir*) discover; *muerte, destino* meet **2** v/r **hallarse** be; (*sentirse*) feel

hallazgo m find; (*descubrimiento*) discovery

halógeno adj halogen

halterofilia f DEP weight-lifting

hamaca f hammock; (*tumbona*) deck chair; *L.Am.* (*mecedora*) rocking chair

hamacar ⟨1g⟩ v/t *L.Am.* swing

hamaquear ⟨1a⟩ v/t *L.Am.* swing

hambre f hunger; **morirse de hambre** *fig* be starving; **pasar hambre** be starving

hambriento adj *tb fig* hungry (**de** for)

hambruna f famine

hamburguesa f GASTR hamburger

hamburguesería f hamburger bar

hampa f underworld

hámster m zo hamster

hangar m hangar

haragán m, -ana f shirker

harapo m rag

haré vb → **hacer**

harina f flour

harinoso adj floury

hartar ⟨1a⟩ **1** v/t: **hartar a alguien con algo** tire s.o. with sth; **hartar a alguien de algo** give s.o. too much of sth **2** v/r **hartarse** get sick (**de** of) F, get tired (**de** of); (*llenarse*) stuff o.s. (**de** with)

harto 1 adj fed up F; (*lleno*) full (up); **había hartos pasteles** there were cakes in abundance; **hace harto frío** *L.Am.* it's

very cold; **estar harto de algo** be sick of sth F, be fed up with sth F **2** *adv* very much; *delante del adjetivo* extremely; **me gusta harto** *L.Am.* F I like it a lot
hartón 1 *adj L.Am.* greedy **2** *m:* **darse un hartón de algo** overdose on sth
has *vb* → **haber**
hasta *prp* until, till; **llegó hasta Bilbao** he went as far as Bilbao; **hasta ahora** so far; **hasta aquí** up to here; **¿hasta cuándo?** how long?; **hasta que** until; **¡hasta luego!** see you (later); **¡hasta la vista!** see you (later) **2** *adv* even
hastiar ⟨1c⟩ *v/t* tire; (*aburrir*) bore
hastío *m* boredom
hatajo *m* bunch
hato *m L.Am.* bundle
hay *vb* → **haber**
haya 1 *vb* → **haber 2** *f* BOT beech
haz 1 *m* bundle; *de luz* beam **2** *vb* → **hacer**
hazaña *f* achievement
hazmerreír *m* fig F laughing stock
he *vb* → **haber**
hebilla *f* buckle
hechicero 1 *adj* bewitching, captivating **2** *m* sorcerer; *de tribu* witch-doctor
hechizado *adj* spellbound
hechizar ⟨1f⟩ *v/t* fig bewitch, captivate
hechizo *m* spell, charm
hecho 1 *part* → *hacer*; **hecho a mano** hand-made; **¡bien hecho!** well done!; **muy hecho** *carne* well-done **2** *adj* finished; **un hombre hecho y derecho** a fully grown man **3** *m* fact; **de hecho** in fact
hectárea *f* hectare (*10,000 sq m*)
hedor *m* stink, stench
helada *f* frost
heladera *f Rpl* fridge
heladería *f* ice-cream parlo(u)r
helado 1 *adj* frozen; *fig* icy; **quedarse helado** be stunned **2** *m* ice cream
helar ⟨1k⟩ **1** *v/t* freeze **2** *v/i* freeze; **anoche heló** there was a frost last night **3** *v/r* **helarse** *tb* fig freeze
helecho *m* BOT fern
hélice *f* propeller
helicóptero *m* helicopter
hematoma *m* bruise
hembra *f* ZO, TÉC female
hemiplejía *f* MED hemiplegia
hemisferio *m* hemisphere
hemofilia *f* MED h(a)emophilia
hemorragia *f* MED h(a)emorrhage, bleeding
hemorroides *fpl* MED h(a)emorrhoids, piles
hendidura *f* crack
heno *m* hay

hepatitis *f* MED hepatitis
herbicida *m* herbicide, weed-killer
herboristería *f* herbalist
hercúleo *adj* Herculean
heredar ⟨1a⟩ *v/t* inherit (**de** from)
heredera *f* heiress
heredero *m* heir
hereditario *adj* hereditary
hereje *m* heretic
herencia *f* inheritance
herida *f de arma* wound; (*lesión*) injury; *mujer* wounded woman; *mujer lesionada* injured woman
herido 1 *adj de arma* wounded; (*lesionado*) injured **2** *m de bala* wounded man; (*lesionado*) injured man
herir ⟨3i⟩ *v/t con arma* wound; (*lesionar*) injure; *fig* (*ofender*) hurt
hermana *f* sister
hermanastra *f* stepsister
hermanastro *m* stepbrother
hermano *m* brother
hermético *adj* airtight, hermetic; *fig: persona* inscrutable
hermoso *adj* beautiful
hernia *f* MED hernia
héroe *m* hero
heroico *adj* heroic
heroína *f mujer* heroine; *droga* heroin
heroinómano *m*, **-a** *f* heroin addict
herpes *m* MED herpes
herradura *f* horseshoe
herramienta *f* tool
hervidero *m* fig hotbed
hervido *m S. Am.* stew
hervir ⟨3i⟩ **1** *v/i* boil; *fig* swarm, seethe (**de** with) **2** *v/t* boil
heterodoxo *adj* unorthodox
heterogéneo *adj* heterogeneous
hez *f* scum, dregs *pl*
hibernar ⟨1a⟩ *v/i* hibernate
híbrido 1 *adj* hybrid *atr* **2** *m* hybrid
hice *vb* → **hacer**
hicimos *vb* → **hacer**
hidratante *adj* moisturizing; **crema hidratante** moisturizing cream
hidratar ⟨1a⟩ *v/t* hydrate; *piel* moisturize
hidrato *m:* **hidrato de carbono** carbohydrate
hidráulico *adj* hydraulic
hidroavión *m* seaplane
hidroeléctrico *adj* hydroelectric
hidrógeno *m* hydrogen
hiedra *f* BOT ivy
hielo *m* ice; **romper el hielo** *fig* break the ice
hiena *f* ZO hyena
hierba *f* grass; **mala hierba** weed
hiere *vb* → **herir**

hierro *m* iron
hierve *vb* → **hervir**
hígado *m* liver; **ser un hígado** *C.Am.*,
Méx F be a pain in the butt F
higiene *f* hygiene
higiénico *adj* hygienic
higo *m* BOT fig
higuera *f* BOT fig tree
hija *f* daughter
hijastra *f* stepdaughter
hijastro *m* stepson
hijo *m* son; **hijos** children *pl*; **hijo de puta**
P son of a bitch V, bastard P; **hijo único**
only child
hilachos *mpl Méx* rags
hilera *f* row, line
hilo *m* thread; **hilo dental** dental floss; **sin
hilos** TELEC cordless; **colgar** or **pender
de un hilo** *fig* hang by a thread; **perder
el hilo** *fig* lose the thread
himno *m* hymn; **himno nacional** national
anthem
hincapié *m*: **hacer hincapié** put special
emphasis (**en** on)
hincar ⟨1g⟩ **1** *v/t* thrust, stick (**en** into);
hincar el diente F sink one's teeth (**en**
into) **2** *v/r* **hincarse**: **hincarse de rodillas** kneel down
hincha *m* F fan, supporter
hinchado *adj* swollen
hinchar ⟨1a⟩ **1** *v/t* inflate, blow up; *Rpl* P
annoy **2** *v/r* **hincharse** MED swell; *fig*
stuff o.s (**de** with); (*mostrarse orgulloso*)
swell with pride
hinchazón *f* swelling
hiperactivo *adj* hyperactive
hipermercado *m* hypermarket
hipertensión *f* MED high blood pressure,
hypertension
hipertexto *m* hypertext
hípico *adj* equestrian; **concurso hípico**
show-jumping event; **carrera -a** horse
race
hipnosis *f* hypnosis
hipnotizar ⟨1f⟩ *v/t* hypnotize
hipo *m* hiccups *pl*, hiccoughs *pl*; **quitar el
hipo** F take one's breath away
hipocondríaco 1 *adj* hypochondriac **2** *m*,
-a *f* hypochondriac
hipocresía *f* hypocrisy
hipócrita 1 *adj* hypocritical **2** *m/f* hypo-
crite
hipódromo *m* racetrack
hipopótamo *m* ZO hippopotamus
hipoteca *f* COM mortgage
hipotecar ⟨1g⟩ *v/t* COM mortgage; *fig* compromise
hipótesis *f* hypothesis
hipotético *adj* hypothetical

hispánico *adj* Hispanic
hispano 1 *adj* (*español*) Spanish; (*hispanohablante*) Spanish-speaking; *en
EE.UU.* Hispanic **2** *m*, **-a** *f* (*español*)
Spaniard; (*hispanohablante*) Spanish
speaker; *en EE.UU.* Hispanic
hispanohablante *adj* Spanish-speaking
histeria *f* hysteria
histérico *adj* hysterical
historia *f* history; (*cuento*) story; **una historia de drogas** F some drugs business;
déjate de historias F stop making excuses
historiador *m*, **historiadora** *f* historian
historial *m* record
histórico *adj* historical; (*importante*) his-
toric
historieta *f* anecdote; (*viñetas*) comic
strip
hito *m* tb *fig* milestone
hizo *vb* → **hacer**
Hnos. *abr* (= **Hermanos**) Bros (= Brothers)
hobby *m* hobby
hocico *m* snout; **de perro** muzzle
hockey *m* field hockey, *Br* hockey; **hockey sobre hielo** hockey, *Br* ice hockey
hogar *m* *fig* home
hogareño *adj* home *atr*; **persona** home-
-loving
hoguera *f* bonfire
hoja *f* BOT leaf; **de papel** sheet; **de libro**
page; **de cuchillo** blade; **hoja de afeitar**
razor blade; **hoja de cálculo** INFOR
spreadsheet
hojalata *f* tin
hojaldre *m* GASTR puff pastry
hojear ⟨1a⟩ *v/t* leaf through, flip through
hola *int* hello, hi F
Holanda Holland
holandés 1 *adj* Dutch **2** *m* Dutchman
holandesa *f* Dutchwoman
holding *m* holding company
holgado *adj* loose, comfortable; **estar
holgado de tiempo** have time to spare
holgazán *m* idler
holgazanear ⟨1a⟩ *v/i* laze around
holgura *f* ease; **de ropa** looseness; TÉC
play; **vivir con holgura** live comfortably
hollín *m* soot
holocausto *m* holocaust
hombre *m* man; **el hombre** (*la humanidad*) man, mankind; **hombre lobo** were-
wolf; **hombre de negocios** businessman; **hombre rana** frogman; **¡claro,
hombre!** you bet!, sure thing!; **¡hombre,
qué alegría!** that's great!
hombro *m* shoulder; **hombro con hombro** shoulder to shoulder; **encogerse**

de hombros shrug (one's shoulders)
homenaje m homage; **rendir homenaje a alguien** pay tribute to s.o.
homeopatía f hom(o)eopathy
homicidio m homicide
homogéneo adj homogenous
homologación f approval; de título, diploma official recognition
homólogo m, **-a** f counterpart, opposite number
homosexual m/f & adj homosexual
hondo adj deep
Honduras Honduras
hondureño 1 adj Honduran **2** m, **-a** f Honduran
honesto adj hono(u)rable, decent
hongo m fungus
honor m hono(u)r; **en honor a** in hono(u)r of; **hacer honor a** live up to; **palabra de honor** word of hono(u)r
honorarios mpl fees
honra f hono(u)r; **¡a mucha honra!** I'm hono(u)red
honradez f honesty
honrado adj honest
hora f hour; **horas** pl **extraordinarias** overtime sg; **hora local** local time; **hora punta** rush hour; **a la hora de ... fig** when it comes to ...; **a última hora** at the last minute; **¡ya era hora!** about time too!; **tengo hora con el dentista** I have an appointment with the dentist; **¿qué hora es?** what time is it?
horario m schedule, Br timetable; **horario comercial** business hours pl; **horario flexible** flextime, Br flexitime; **horario de trabajo** (working) hours pl
horca f gallows pl
horcajadas fpl: **a horcajadas** astride
horchata f drink made from tiger-nuts
horda f horde
horizontal adj horizontal
horizonte m horizon
hormiga f ant
hormigón m concrete; **hormigón armado** reinforced concrete
hormigueo m pins and needles pl
hormiguero m ant hill; **la sala era un hormiguero de gente** the hall was swarming with people
hormona f hormone
hornilla f ring
horno m oven; de cerámica kiln; **alto horno** blast furnace
horóscopo m horoscope
horqueta f L.Am. de camino fork
horquilla f para pelo hairpin
horrendo adj horrendous
horrible adj horrible, dreadful

horripilante adj horrible
horror m horror; (**a** of); **tener horror a** be terrified of; **me gusta horrores** I like it a lot; **¡qué horror!** how awful!
horrorizar ⟨1f⟩ v/t horrify
horroroso adj terrible; (de mala calidad) dreadful; (feo) hideous
hortaliza f vegetable
hortensia f BOT hydrangea
hortera 1 f adj tacky F **2** m/f F tacky person F
horterada f F tacky thing F; **es una horterada** it's tacky F
horticultor m, **horticultora** f horticulturist
horticultura f horticulture
hosco adj sullen
hospedaje m accommodations pl, Br accommodation; **dar hospedaje a alguien** put s.o. up
hospedarse ⟨1a⟩ v/r stay (**en** at)
hospital m hospital
hospitalario adj hospitable; MED hospital atr
hospitalidad f hospitality
hospitalizar ⟨1f⟩ v/t hospitalize
hostal m hostel
hostelera f landlady
hostelería f hotel industry
hostelero 1 adj hotel atr **2** m landlord
hostia f REL host; P (golpe) sock F, wallop F; **¡hostias!** P Christ! P
hostigar ⟨1h⟩ v/t pester; MIL harass; caballo whip
hostil adj hostile
hostilidad f hostility
hotel m hotel
hotelero m, **-a** f hotelier
hoy adv today; **de hoy** of today; **los padres de hoy** today's parents, parents today; **de hoy en adelante** from now on; **por hoy** for today; **hoy por hoy** at the present time; **hoy en día** nowadays
hoya f hole; de tumba grave; GEOG plain; S. Am. river basin
hoyo m hole; (depresión) hollow
hoyuelo m dimple
hoz f sickle
huachafo adj Pe (cursi) affected, pretentious
huarache m Méx rough sandal
huayno m Pe, Bol Andean dance rhythm
hubo vb → **haber**
hucha f money box
hueco 1 adj hollow; (vacío) empty; fig: persona shallow **2** m gap; (agujero) hole; de ascensor shaft
huele vb → **oler**
huelga f strike; **huelga de celo** work-to-

rule; **huelga general** general strike; **huelga de hambre** hunger strike; **declararse en huelga, ir a la huelga** go on strike

huelguista *m/f* striker

huella *f* mark; *de animal* track; **huellas dactilares** finger prints

huelo *vb* → *oler*

huérfano **1** *adj* orphan *atr* **2** *m*, -a *f* orphan

huero *adj fig* empty; *L.Am.* blond

huerta *f* truck farm, *Br* market garden

huerto *m* kitchen garden; **llevar a alguien al huerto** F put one over on s.o. F

huesear ⟨1a⟩ *v/i C.Am.* beg

huesillo *m S. Am.* sun-dried peach

hueso *m* bone; *de fruta* pit, stone; *persona* tough nut; *Méx* F cushy number F; *Méx* F (*influencia*) influence, pull F; **hueso duro de roer** *fig* F hard nut to crack F; **estar en los huesos** be all skin and bone

huésped *m/f* guest

huesudo *adj* bony

huevas *fpl* roe *sg*

huevear ⟨1a⟩ *v/i Chi* P mess around F

huevo *m* egg; P (*testículo*) ball V; **huevo duro** hard-boiled egg; **huevo escalfado** poached egg; **huevo frito** fried egg; **huevo pasado por agua** soft-boiled egg; **huevos revueltos** scrambled eggs; **un huevo de** P a load of F

huevón *m*, -ona *f Chi* P idiot; *L.Am.* F (*flojo*) idler F

huida *fpl* flight, escape

huir ⟨3g⟩ *v/i* flee, escape (**de** from); **huir de algo** avoid sth

hulado *m C.Am., Méx* rubberized cloth

hule *m* oilcloth; *L.Am.* (*caucho*) rubber

humanidad *f* humanity; **humanidades** humanities

humanismo *m* humanism

humanitario *adj* humanitarian

humanizar ⟨1f⟩ *v/t* humanize

humano *adj* human

humareda *f* cloud of smoke

humear ⟨1a⟩ *v/i con humo* smoke; *con vapor* steam

humedad *f* humidity; *de una casa* damp (-ness)

humedecer ⟨2d⟩ *v/t* dampen

húmedo *adj* humid; *toalla* damp

humildad *f* humility

humilde *adj* humble; (*sin orgullo*) modest; *clase social* lowly

humillación *f* humiliation

humillante *adj* humiliating

humillar ⟨1a⟩ *v/t* humiliate

humita *f S. Am.* meat and corn paste wrapped in leaves

humo *m* smoke; (*vapor*) steam; **tener muchos humos** F be a real bighead F

humor *m* humo(u)r; **estar de buen / mal humor** be in a good / bad mood; **sentido del humor** sense of humo(u)r

humorista *m/f* humo(u)rist; (*cómico*) comedian

humus *m* GASTR hummus

hundido *adj fig: persona* depressed

hundir ⟨3a⟩ **1** *v/t* sink; *fig: empresa* ruin, bring down; *persona* devastate **2** *v/r* hundirse sink; *fig: de empresa* collapse; *de persona* go to pieces

húngaro **1** *adj* Hungarian **2** *m*, -a *f* Hungarian

Hungría Hungary

huracán *m* hurricane

huraño *adj* unsociable

hurgar ⟨1h⟩ **1** *v/i* rummage (**en** in) **2** *v/r* hurgarse: **hurgarse la nariz** pick one's nose

hurón *m* ZO ferret

hurtadillas *fpl*: **a hurtadillas** furtively

hurtar ⟨1a⟩ *v/t* steal

hurto *m* theft

husmear ⟨1a⟩ *v/i* F nose around F (**en** in)

huy *int sorpresa* wow!; *dolor* ouch!

huyo *vb* → *huir*

I+D *abr* (= *investigación y desarrollo*) R&D (= research and development)

iba *vb* → *ir*

ibérico *adj* Iberian

iberoamericano *adj* Latin American

iceberg *m* iceberg

icono *m tb* INFOR icon

ida *f* outward journey; (*billete de*) **ida y vuelta** round trip (ticket), *Br* return (ticket)

idea *f* idea; **hacerse a la idea de que ...** get used to the idea that ...; **no tener ni**

idea not have a clue
ideal *m/adj* ideal
idealista 1 *adj* idealistic **2** *m/f* idealist
idear *v/t* ⟨1a⟩ think up, come up with
idéntico *adj* identical
identidad *f* identity
identificación *f* identification
identificar ⟨1g⟩ **1** *v/t* identify **2** *v/r* **identificarse** identify o.s.
ideología *f* ideology
idílico *adj* idyllic
idilio *m* idyll; *(relación amorosa)* romance
idioma *m* language
idiota 1 *adj* idiotic **2** *m/f* idiot
idiotez *f* stupid thing to say / do
ido 1 *part* → **ir 2** *adj* *(chiflado)* nuts F; **estar ido** be miles away F
idolatrar ⟨1a⟩ *v/t tb fig* worship
ídolo *m tb fig* idol
idóneo *adj* suitable
iglesia *f* church
ignominioso *adj* ignominious
ignorancia *f* ignorance
ignorante *adj* ignorant
ignorar ⟨1a⟩ *v/t* not know, not be aware of; **ignoro cómo sucedió** I don't know how it happened
igual 1 *adj* *(idéntico)* same *(a, que* as); *(proporcionado)* equal *(a* to); *(constante)* constant; **al igual que** like, the same as; **me da igual** I don't mind **2** *m/f* equal; **no tener igual** have no equal
igualado *adj* even
igualar ⟨1a⟩ **1** *v/t precio, marca* equal, match; *(nivelar)* level off; **igualar algo** MAT make sth equal *(con, a* to) **2** *v/i* DEP tie the game, *Br* equalize
igualdad *f* equality; **igualdad de oportunidades** equal opportunities
igualitario *adj* egalitarian
igualmente *adv* equally
iguana *f* zo iguana
ilegal *adj* illegal
ilegible *adj* illegible
ilegítimo *adj* unlawful; *hijo* illegitimate
ileso *adj* unhurt
ilícito *adj* illicit
ilimitado *adj* unlimited
Ilmo. *abr* (= **ilustrísimo**) His / Your Excellency
ilógico *adj* illogical
iluminación *f* illumination
iluminar ⟨1a⟩ *v/t edificio, calle etc* light, illuminate; *monumento* light up, illuminate; *fig* light up
ilusión *f* illusion; *(deseo, esperanza)* hope
ilusionarse ⟨1a⟩ *v/r* get one's hopes up; *(entusiasmarse)* get excited *(con* about)
ilustración *f* illustration

ilustrar ⟨1a⟩ *v/t* illustrate; *(aclarar)* explain
ilustre *adj* illustrious
imagen *f tb fig* image; **ser la viva imagen de** be the spitting image of
imaginable *adj* imaginable
imaginación *f* imagination
imaginar ⟨1a⟩ **1** *v/t* imagine **2** *v/r* **imaginarse** imagine; **¡ya me lo imagino!** I can just imagine it!
imaginativo *adj* imaginative
imán *m* magnet
imbatible *adj* unbeatable
imbécil 1 *adj* stupid **2** *m/f* idiot, imbecile
imbecilidad *f* stupidity; **¡qué imbecilidad decir eso!** what a stupid thing to say!
imitación *f* imitation
imitar ⟨1a⟩ *v/t* imitate
impaciencia *f* impatience
impacientar ⟨1a⟩ **1** *v/t* make impatient **2** *v/r* **impacientarse** lose (one's) patience
impaciente *adj* impatient
impactar ⟨1a⟩ *v/t* hit; *(impresionar)* have an impact on
impacto *m tb fig* impact; **impacto de bala** bullet wound; **impacto ecológico** ecological
impar *adj número* odd
imparcial *adj* impartial
imparcialidad *f* impartiality
impasible *adj* impassive
impávido *adj* fearless, undaunted
impecable *adj* impeccable
impedimento *m* impediment
impedir ⟨3l⟩ *v/t* prevent; *(estorbar)* impede
imperante *adj* ruling; *fig* prevailing
imperar ⟨1a⟩ *v/i* rule; *fig* prevail
imperativo 1 *adj* GRAM imperative; *obligación* pressing **2** *m* GRAM imperative
imperdible *m* safety pin
imperdonable *adj* unpardonable, unforgivable
imperfecto *m/adj* imperfect
imperial *adj* imperial
imperio *m* empire
imperioso *adj necesidad* pressing; *persona* imperious
impermeable 1 *adj* waterproof **2** *m* raincoat
impersonal *adj* impersonal
impertérrito *adj* unperturbed, unmoved
impertinente 1 *adj* impertinent **2** *m/f*: **¡eres un impertinente!** you've got nerve! F, *Br* you've got a cheek! F
ímpetu *m* impetus
impetuoso *adj* impetuous
implacable *adj* implacable

implemento *m* implement

implicar ⟨1g⟩ *v/t* mean, imply; (*involucrar*) involve; *en un delito* implicate (*en* in)

implícito *adj* implicit

implorar ⟨1a⟩ *v/t* beg for

imponente *adj* impressive, imposing; F terrific

imponer ⟨2r⟩ **1** *v/t* impose; *miedo, respeto* inspire; *impuesto* impose, levy **2** *v/i* be imposing *o* impressive **3** *v/r* **imponerse** (*hacerse respetar*) assert o.s.; DEP win; (*prevalecer*) prevail; (*ser necesario*) be imperative; *imponerse una tarea* set o.s. a task

importación *f* import, importation; *artículo* import

importancia *f* importance; *dar importancia a* attach importance to; *darse importancia* give o.s. airs; *tener importancia* be important

importante *adj* important

importar ⟨1a⟩ *v/i* matter; *no importa* it doesn't matter; *eso a ti no te importa* that's none of your business; *¿qué importa?* what does it matter?; *¿le importa …?* do you mind …?

importe *m* amount; (*coste*) cost

importuno *adj* inopportune;

imposibilitar ⟨1a⟩ *v/t*: *imposibilitar algo* make sth impossible, prevent sth

imposible *adj* impossible

impostor *m*, **impostora** *f* impostor

impotencia *f* impotence, helplessness; MED impotence

impotente *adj* helpless, powerless, impotent; MED impotent

impreciso *adj* imprecise

impredecible *adj* unpredictable

impregnar ⟨1a⟩ *v/t* saturate (*de* with); TÉC impregnate (*de* with)

imprenta *f taller* printer's; *arte, técnica* printing; *máquina* printing press

imprescindible *adj* essential; *persona* indispensable

impresión *f* impression; *acto* printing; (*tirada*) print run; *la sangre le da impresión* he can't stand the sight of blood

impresionante *adj* impressive

impresionar ⟨1a⟩ *v/t*: *impresionarle a alguien* impress s.o.; (*conmover*) move s.o.; (*alterar*) shock s.o.

impresionismo *m* impressionism

impreso *m* form; *impresos pl* printed matter *sg*

impresora *f* INFOR printer; *impresora de chorro de tinta* inkjet (printer); *impresora de inyección de tinta* inkjet (printer); *impresora láser* laser (printer)

imprevisible *adj* unpredictable

imprevisto 1 *adj* unforeseen, unexpected **2** *m* unexpected event

imprimir ⟨3a⟩ *v/t tb* INFOR print; *fig* transmit

improbable *adj* unlikely, improbable

improcedente *adj* improper

improductivo *adj* unproductive

impropio *adj* inappropriate

improvisar ⟨1a⟩ *v/t* improvise

improviso *adj*: *de improviso* unexpectedly

imprudencia *f* recklessness, rashness

imprudente *adj* reckless, rash

impuesto *m* tax; *impuesto sobre el valor añadido* sales tax, *Br* value-added tax; *impuesto sobre la renta* income tax

impugnar ⟨1a⟩ *v/t* challenge

impulsar ⟨1a⟩ *v/t* TÉC propel; COM boost

impulsivo *adj* impulsive

impulso *m* impulse; (*empuje*) impetus; COM boost; *fig* urge, impulse; *tomar impulso* take a run up

impunidad *f* impunity

impureza *f* impurity

imputar ⟨1a⟩ *v/t* attribute

inacabable *adj* endless, never-ending

inaccesible *adj* inaccessible

inaceptable *adj* unacceptable

inactivo *adj* inactive

inadaptado *adj* maladjusted

inadecuado *adj* inadequate

inadmisible *adj* inadmissible

inadvertido *adj*: *pasar inadvertido* go unnoticed

inagotable *adj* inexhaustible

inaguantable *adj* unbearable

inalámbrico 1 *adj* TELEC cordless **2** *m* TELEC cordless telephone

inamovible *adj* immovable

inanición *f* starvation

inapreciable *adj* (*valioso*) priceless; (*insignificante*) negligible

inasequible *adj objetivo* unattainable; *precio* prohibitive

inaudito *adj* unprecedented

inauguración *f* official opening, inauguration

inaugurar ⟨1a⟩ *v/t* (officially) open, inaugurate

inca *m/f & adj* HIST Inca

incalculable *adj* incalculable

incalificable *adj* indescribable

incandescente *adj* incandescent

incansable *adj* tireless

incapacidad *f* disability; (*falta de capacidad*) inability; (*ineptitud*) incompetence

incapacitar ⟨1a⟩ *v/t* JUR disqualify

incapaz *adj* incapable (*de* of)

incautarse ⟨1a⟩ v/r: **incautarse de** seize
incauto *adj* unwary
incendiar ⟨1b⟩ **1** v/t set fire to **2** v/r incendiarse burn
incendio *m* fire; **incendio forestal** forest fire
incentivo *m* incentive
incertidumbre *f* uncertainty
incesante *adj* incessant
incesto *m* incest
incidencia *f* (*efecto*) effect; (*frecuencia*) incidence; (*incidente*) incident
incidente *m* incident
incidir ⟨3a⟩ v/i: **incidir en** (*afectar*) have an effect on, affect; (*recalcar*) stress; **incidir en un error** make a mistake
incienso *m* incense
incierto *m* uncertain
incineración *f* de cadáver cremation
incinerador *m* incinerator
incinerar ⟨1a⟩ v/t incinerate; *cadáver* cremate
incipiente *adj* incipient
incitante *adj* provocative
incitar ⟨1a⟩ v/t incite
inclemencia *f* del tiempo inclemency
inclinación *f* inclination; *de un terreno* slope; *muestra de respeto* bow; *fig* tendency
inclinar ⟨1a⟩ v/t tilt; **inclinar la cabeza** nod (one's head); **me inclina a creer que ...** it makes me think that ... **2** v/r inclinarse bend (down); *de un terreno* slope; *desde la vertical* lean; *en señal de respeto* bow; **inclinarse a** *fig* tend to, be inclined to
incluido *prp* inclusive
incluir ⟨3g⟩ v/t include
inclusive *adv* inclusive
incluso *adv, prp & conj* even
incógnita *f* unknown factor; MAT unknown (quantity)
incógnito *adj*: **de incógnito** incognito
incoherente *adj* incoherent
incombustible *adj* fireproof
incomodidad *f* uncomfortableness; (*fastidio*) inconvenience
incómodo *adj* uncomfortable; (*fastidioso*) inconvenient
incomparable *adj* incomparable
incompatibilidad *f* incompatibility
incompatible *adj tb* INFOR incompatible
incompetencia *f* incompetence
incompetente *adj* incompetent
incompleto *adj* incomplete
incomprendido *adj* misunderstood
incomprensible *adj* incomprehensible
incomunicado *adj* isolated, cut off; JUR in solitary confinement

inconcebible *adj* inconceivable
incondicional *adj* unconditional;
inconexo *adj* unconnected
inconfesable *adj* shameful
inconfundible *adj* unmistakable
incongruente *adj* incongruous
inconsciencia *f* MED unconsciousness; (*desconocimiento*) lack of awareness, unawareness; (*irreflexión*) thoughtlessness
inconsciente *adj* MED unconscious; (*ignorante*) unaware; (*irreflexivo*) thoughtless
inconsecuente *adj* inconsistent
inconsistente *adj* flimsy, weak
inconsolable *adj* inconsolable
inconstante *adj* fickle
incontable *adj* uncountable
incontinencia *f* MED incontinence
incontrolable *adj* uncontrollable
inconveniente **1** *adj* (*inoportuno*) inconvenient; (*impropio*) inappropriate **2** *m* (*desventaja*) drawback, disadvantage; (*estorbo*) problem; **no tengo inconveniente** I don't mind
incordiar ⟨1b⟩ v/t annoy
incordio *m* nuisance
incorporar ⟨1a⟩ **1** v/t incorporate **2** v/r incorporarse sit up; **incorporarse a** MIL join
incorrecto *adj* incorrect, wrong; *comportamiento* impolite
incorregible *adj* incorrigible
incorruptible *adj* incorruptible
incredulidad *f* disbelief, incredulity
incrédulo *adj* incredulous
increíble *adj* incredible
incrementar ⟨1a⟩ **1** v/t increase **2** v/r incrementarse increase
incremento *m* growth
incriminar ⟨1a⟩ v/t incriminate
incruento *adj* bloodless
incrustar ⟨1a⟩ **1** v/t incrust (**de** with) **2** v/r incrustarse de la suciedad become ingrained
incubación *f* incubation
incubadora *f* incubator
incubar ⟨1a⟩ v/t incubate
incuestionable *adj* unquestionable
inculcar ⟨1g⟩ v/t instil(l) (**en** in)
inculpar ⟨1a⟩ v/t JUR accuse;
inculto *adj* ignorant, uneducated
incultura *f* ignorance, lack of education
incumbencia *f* responsibility, duty; **no es de mi incumbencia** it's not my responsibility
incumplimiento *m* non-fulfillment (**de** of), non-compliance (**de** with)
incumplir ⟨3a⟩ v/t break
incurable *adj* incurable

incurrir ⟨3a⟩ v/i: **incurrir en un error** make a mistake; **incurrir en gastos** incur costs

incursión f MIL raid; fig foray

indagar ⟨1h⟩ v/i investigate

indecente adj indecent; película obscene

indecisión f indecisiveness

indeciso adj undecided; por naturaleza indecisive

indefenso adj defenseless, Br defenceless

indefinidamente adv indefinitely

indefinido adj (impreciso) vague; (ilimitado) indefinite

indemnización f compensation

indemnizar ⟨1f⟩ v/t compensate (**por** for)

independencia f independence

independentismo m POL pro-independence movement

independiente adj independent

independizarse ⟨1f⟩ v/r become independent

indescriptible adj indescribable

indeseable adj undesirable

indestructible adj indestructible

indeterminado adj indeterminate; (indefinido) indefinite

India: **la India** India

indiada f L.Am. group of Indians

indicación f indication; (señal) sign; **indicaciones** para llegar directions; (instrucciones) instructions

indicado adj (adecuado) suitable; **lo más / menos indicado** the best / worst thing; **hora -a** specified time

indicador m indicator

indicar ⟨1g⟩ v/t show, indicate; (señalar) point out; (sugerir) suggest

índice m index; **dedo índice** index finger; **índice de precios al consumo** consumer price index, Br retail price index

indicio m indication, sign; (vestigio) trace

indiferencia f indifference

indiferente adj indifferent; (irrelevante) immaterial

indígena 1 adj indigenous, native 2 m/f native

indigente adj destitute

indigestión f indigestion

indigesto adj indigestible

indignación f indignation

indignado adj indignant

indignar ⟨1a⟩ 1 v/t: **indignar a alguien** make s.o. indignant 2 v/r **indignarse** become indignant

indigno adj unworthy (**de** of)

indio 1 adj Indian 2 m, -a f Indian; **hacer el indio** F clown around F, play the fool F

indirecta f insinuation; (sugerencia) hint

indirecto adj indirect

indiscreción f indiscretion, lack of discretion; (declaración) indiscreet remark

indiscreto adj indiscreet

indiscriminado adj indiscriminate

indiscutible adj indisputable

indispensable adj indispensable

indisponerse ⟨2r⟩ v/r become unwell; **indisponerse con alguien** fall out with s.o.

indisposición f indisposition

indispuesto adj indisposed, unwell

indistinto adj forma indistinct, vague; noción vague; sonido faint

individual adj individual; cama, habitación single

individualismo m individualism

individualista m/f individualist

individuo m individual

indivisible adj indivisible

indocumentado adj: **un hombre indocumentado** a man with no identity papers

índole f nature

indolente adj lazy

indoloro adj painless

indómito adj indomitable

Indonesia Indonesia

inducir ⟨3o⟩ v/t (persuadir) lead, induce (**a** to); EL induce

indudable adj undoubted

indudablemente adv undoubtedly

indulgente adj indulgent

indultar ⟨1a⟩ v/t pardon

indulto m pardon

indumentaria f clothing

industria f industry; (esfuerzo) industriousness, industry

industrial 1 adj industrial 2 m/f industrialist

industrializar ⟨1f⟩ 1 v/t industrialize 2 v/r industrializarse industrialize

inédito adj unpublished; fig unprecedented

ineficacia f inefficiency; de un procedimiento ineffectiveness

ineficaz adj inefficient; procedimiento ineffective

ineficiencia f inefficiency

ineficiente adj inefficient

ineludible adj unavoidable

inepto 1 adj inept, incompetent 2 m, -a f incompetent fool

inequívoco adj unequivocal

inercia f inertia

inerte adj fig lifeless; FÍS inert

inesperado adj unexpected

inestabilidad f instability

inestable adj unstable; tiempo unsettled

inestimable adj invaluable

inevitable adj inevitable

inexacto *adj* inaccurate
inexcusable *adj* inexcusable
inexistente *adj* non-existent
inexperto *adj* inexperienced
inexplicable *adj* inexplicable
infalible *adj* infallible
infame *adj* vile, loathsome; (*terrible*) dreadful
infancia *f* infancy
infantería *f* MIL infantry
infantil *adj* children's *atr*; *naturaleza* childlike; *desp* infantile, childish
infarto *m* MED heart attack
infección *f* MED infection
infeccioso *adj* infectious
infectar ⟨1a⟩ **1** *v/t* infect **2** *v/r* **infectarse** become infected
infecundo *adj* infertile
infeliz 1 *adj* unhappy, miserable **2** *m/f* poor devil
inferior 1 *adj* inferior (*a* to); *en el espacio* lower (*a* than) **2** *m/f* inferior
inferioridad *f* inferiority
inferir ⟨3i⟩ *v/t* infer (*de* from); *daño* do, cause (*a* to)
infernal *adj ruido* infernal; (*muy malo*) diabolical
infertilidad *f* infertility
infestar ⟨1a⟩ *v/t* infest; (*invadir*) overrun
infidelidad *f* infidelity
infiel 1 *adj* unfaithful **2** *m/f* unbeliever
infierno *m* hell
infiltrar ⟨1a⟩ *v/r*: **infiltrarse en** infiltrate; *de agua* seep into
infinidad *f*: **infinidad de** countless
infinitivo *m* GRAM infinitive
infinito 1 *adj* infinite **2** *m* infinity
inflación *f* COM inflation; *tasa de inflación* inflation rate
inflacionista *adj* inflationary
inflamable *adj* flammable
inflamación *f* MED inflammation
inflamar ⟨1a⟩ **1** *v/t tb fig* inflame **2** *v/r* **inflamarse** MED become inflamed
inflar ⟨1a⟩ **1** *v/t* inflate **2** *v/r* **inflarse** swell (up); *fig* F get conceited
infligir ⟨3c⟩ *v/t* inflict
inflexible *adj fig* inflexible
influencia *f* influence; *tener influencias* have contacts
influenciar ⟨1b⟩ *v/t* influence
influir ⟨3g⟩ *v/i*: **influir en alguien / algo** influence s.o./sth, have an influence on s.o./sth
influjo *m* influence
influyente *adj* influential
infografía *f* computer graphics *pl*
información *f* information; (*noticias*) news *sg*

informal *adj* informal; *persona* unreliable
informar ⟨1a⟩ **1** *v/t* inform (*de, sobre* about) **2** *v/r* **informarse** find out (*de, sobre* about)
informática *f* information technology
informático 1 *adj* computer *atr* **2** *m*, *-a f* IT specialist
informativo 1 *adj* informative; *programa* news *atr* **2** *m* TV, RAD news *sg*
informatizar ⟨1f⟩ *v/t* computerize
informe 1 *adj* shapeless **2** *m* report; *informes* (*referencias*) references
infracción *f* offense, *Br* offence
infraestructura *f* infrastructure
in fraganti *adv* F in the act F
infrahumano *adj* subhuman
infrarrojo *adj* infra-red
infravalorar ⟨1a⟩ *v/t* undervalue
infrecuente *adj* infrequent
infringir ⟨3c⟩ *v/t* JUR infringe, violate
infructuoso *adj* fruitless
infundado *adj* unfounded, groundless
infundir ⟨3a⟩ *v/t* inspire; *terror* instil(l); *sospechas* arouse
infusión *f* infusion; *de tila, manzanilla* tea
ingeniarse ⟨1b⟩ *v/r*: **ingeniárselas para** manage to
ingeniería *f* engineering
ingeniero *m*, *-a f* engineer
ingenio *m* ingenuity; (*aparato*) device; *ingenio azucarero* L.Am. sugar refinery
ingenioso *adj* ingenious
ingenuidad *f* naivety
ingenuo 1 *adj* naive **2** *m*, *-a f* naive person, sucker F
ingerir ⟨3i⟩ *v/t* swallow
Inglaterra England
ingle *f* groin
inglés 1 *adj* English **2** *m* Englishman; *idioma* English
inglesa *f* Englishwoman
ingrato *adj* ungrateful; *tarea* thankless
ingrediente *m* ingredient
ingresar ⟨1a⟩ **1** *v/i*: **ingresar en** *en universidad* go to; *en asociación, cuerpo* join; *en hospital* be admitted to **2** *v/t cheque* pay in, deposit
ingreso *m* entry; *en una asociación* joining; *en hospital* admission; COM deposit; *ingresos pl* income *sg*; *examen de ingreso* entrance exam
inhabitable *adj* uninhabitable
inhalar ⟨1a⟩ *v/t* inhale
inherente *adj* inherent
inhibición *f* inhibition; JUR disqualification
inhibir ⟨3a⟩ *v/t* inhibit
inhóspito *adj* inhospitable
inhumano *adj* inhuman

iniciación f initiation

inicial f/adj initial

iniciar ⟨1b⟩ v/t initiate; *curso* start, begin

iniciativa f initiative; **tomar la iniciativa** take the initiative

inicio m start, beginning

inigualable adj incomparable; *precio* unbeatable

inimaginable adj unimaginable

inimitable adj inimitable

ininteligible adj unintelligible

ininterrumpido adj uninterrupted

injerencia f interference

injertar ⟨1a⟩ v/t graft

injerto m graft

injuriar ⟨1b⟩ v/t insult

injusticia f injustice

injustificado adj unjustified

injusto adj unjust

inmaculado adj immaculate

inmaduro adj immature

inmediaciones fpl immediate area sg (**de** of), vicinity sg (**de** of)

inmediatamente adv immediately

inmediato adj immediate; **de inmediato** immediately

inmejorable adj unbeatable

inmenso adj immense

inmersión f immersion; *de submarino* dive

inmerso adj fig immersed (**en** in)

inmigración f immigration

inmigrante m/f immigrant

inmigrar ⟨1a⟩ v/i immigrate

inminente adj imminent

inmiscuirse ⟨3g⟩ v/r meddle

inmobiliaria f realtor's office, Br estate agency

inmoderado adj excessive, immoderate

inmoral adj immoral

inmoralidad f immorality

inmortal adj immortal

inmóvil adj *persona* motionless; *vehículo* stationary

inmovilizar ⟨1f⟩ v/t immobilize

inmueble m building

inmundo adj filthy

inmune adj immune

inmunidad f MED, POL immunity

inmunizar ⟨1f⟩ v/t immunize

inmutarse ⟨1a⟩ v/r: **no inmutarse** not bat an eyelid; **sin inmutarse** without batting an eyelid

innato adj innate, inborn

innecesario adj unnecessary

innegable adj undeniable

innovación f innovation

innumerable adj innumerable, countless

inocencia f innocence

inocente adj innocent

inocuo adj harmless, innocuous; *película* bland

inodoro m toilet

inofensivo adj inoffensive, harmless

inoficioso adj L.Am. (*inútil*) useless

inolvidable adj unforgettable

inopia f: **estar en la inopia** F (*distraído*) be miles away F; (*alejado de la realidad*) be on another planet F

inoportuno adj inopportune; (*molesto*) inconvenient

inorgánico adj inorganic

inoxidable adj: **acero inoxidable** stainless steel

inquietar ⟨1a⟩ **1** v/t worry **2** v/r **inquietarse** worry, get worried o anxious

inquietud f worry, anxiety; *intelectual* interest

inquilino m tenant

inquisitivo adj inquisitive

insaciable adj insatiable

insatisfacción f dissatisfaction

insatisfactorio adj unsatisfactory

insatisfecho adj dissatisfied

inscribir ⟨3a⟩ **1** v/t (*grabar*) inscribe; *en lista, registro* register, enter; *en curso, concurso* enrol(l); register **2** v/r **inscribirse en un curso** enrol(l), register; *en un concurso* enter

inscripción f inscription; *en lista, registro* registration, entry; *en curso, concurso* enrol(l)ment, registration;

insecticida m insecticide

insecto m insect

inseguro adj insecure; *estructura* unsteady; (*peligroso*) dangerous, unsafe

inseminación f insemination; **inseminación artificial** artificial insemination

insensato adj foolish

insensible adj insensitive (**a** to)

inseparable adj inseparable

insertar ⟨1a⟩ v/t insert

inservible adj useless

insidia f treachery; **actuar con insidia** act treacherously

insignia f insignia

insignificante adj insignificant

insinuante adj suggestive

insinuar ⟨1e⟩ **1** v/t insinuate **2** v/r **insinuarse**: **insinuarse a alguien** make advances to s.o.

insípido adj insipid

insistencia f insistence

insistir ⟨3a⟩ v/i insist; **insistir en hacer algo** insist on doing sth; **insistir en algo** stress sth

insociable adj unsociable

insolación f MED sunstroke

insolente *adj* insolent
insólito *adj* unusual
insolvente *adj* insolvent
insomnio *m* insomnia
insondable *adj* unfathomable
insonorizar ⟨1f⟩ *v/t* soundproof
insoportable *adj* unbearable, intolerable
insospechado *adj* unexpected
inspección *f* inspection
inspeccionar ⟨1a⟩ *v/t* inspect
inspector *m*, **inspectora** *f* inspector
inspiración *f* inspiration; MED inhalation
inspirar ⟨1a⟩ *v/t* inspire; MED inhale
instalación *f acto* installation; ***instalaciones deportivas*** sports facilities
instalar ⟨1a⟩ **1** *v/t* instal(l); (*colocar*) put; *un negocio* set up **2** *v/r* **instalarse en un sitio** instal(l) o.s.
instancia *f* JUR petition; (*petición por escrito*) application; ***a instancias de*** at the request of
instantáneo *adj* immediate, instantaneous
instante *m* moment, instant; ***al instante*** right away, immediately
instar ⟨1a⟩ *v/t* urge, press
instaurar ⟨1a⟩ *v/t* establish
instigar ⟨1h⟩ *v/t* incite (**a** to)
instinto *m* instinct
institución *f* institution
instituto *m* institute; *Esp* high school, *Br* secondary school; ***instituto de belleza*** beauty salon; ***instituto de educación secundaria*** high school, *Br* secondary school
instrucción *f* education; (*formación*) training; MIL drill; INFOR instruction, statement; JUR hearing; ***instrucciones de uso*** instructions, directions (for use)
instructor *m*, **instructora** *f* instructor
instruido *adj* educated
instruir ⟨3g⟩ *v/t* educate; (*formar*) train; JUR *pleito* hear
instrumental 1 *adj* instrumental **2** *m* MED instruments *pl*
instrumento *m* instrument; (*herramienta*) tool, instrument; *fig* tool; ***instrumento musical*** musical instrument
insubordinación *f* insubordination
insubordinarse ⟨1a⟩ *v/r* **con un superior** be insubordinate; (*rebelarse*) rebel
insuficiente 1 *adj* insufficient, inadequate **2** *m* EDU *nota* fail
insufrible *adj* insufferable
insulina *f* insulin
insulso *adj* bland, insipid
insultada *f L.Am.* (*insultos*) string of insults
insultar ⟨1a⟩ *v/t* insult

insulto *m* insult
insumiso *m person who refuses to do military service*
insuperable *adj* insurmountable
insurrección *f* insurrection
insustancial *adj conferencia* lightweight; *estructura* flimsy
intachable *adj* faultless
intacto *adj* intact; (*sin tocar*) untouched
integración *f* integration
integral *adj* complete; *alimento* whole
integrar ⟨1a⟩ *v/t* integrate; *equipo* make up
íntegro *adj* whole, entire; ***un hombre íntegro*** *fig* a man of integrity
intelectual *m/f & adj* intellectual
inteligencia *f* intelligence
inteligente *adj* intelligent
inteligible *adj* intelligible
intemperie *f*: ***a la intemperie*** in the open air
intempestivo *adj* untimely
intención *f* intention; ***doble or segunda intención*** ulterior motive
intencionado *adj* deliberate
intendente *m Rpl* military governor; (*alcalde*) mayor
intensidad *f* intensity; (*fuerza*) strength
intensificar ⟨1g⟩ **1** *v/t* intensify **2** *v/r* **intensificarse** intensify
intensivo *adj* intensive
intenso *adj* intense; (*fuerte*) strong
intentar ⟨1a⟩ *v/t* try, attempt
intento *m* attempt, try; *Méx* (*intención*) aim
interacción *f* interaction
interactivo *adj* interactive
intercalar ⟨1a⟩ *v/t* insert
intercambiar ⟨1a⟩ *v/t* exchange, swap
intercambio *m* exchange, swap
interceder ⟨2a⟩ *v/i* intercede (**por** for)
interceptar ⟨1a⟩ *v/t tb* DEP intercept
intercesión *f* intercession
interés *m tb* COM interest; *desp* self-interest; ***sin interés*** interest free; ***intereses*** (*bienes*) interests
interesante *adj* interesting
interesar ⟨1a⟩ **1** *v/t* interest **2** *v/r* **interesarse**: ***interesarse por*** take an interest in
interface, **interfaz** *f* INFOR interface
interferencia *f* interference
interferir ⟨3i⟩ **1** *v/t* interfere with **2** *v/i* interfere (**en** in)
interino *adj* substitute *atr*, replacement *atr*; (*provisional*) provisional, acting *atr*
interior 1 *adj* interior; *bolsillo* inside *atr*; COM, POL domestic **2** *m* interior; DEP inside-forward; ***en su interior*** *fig* inwardly
interiorista *m/f* interior designer

interjección *f* GRAM interjection

interlocutor *m*, **interlocutora** *f* speaker; *mi interlocutor* the person I was talking to

intermediario *m* COM intermediary, middle-man

intermedio 1 *adj nivel* intermediate; *tamaño* medium; *calidad* average, medium **2** *m* intermission

interminable *adj* interminable, endless

intermitente 1 *adj* intermittent **2** *m* AUTO turn signal, *Br* indicator

internacional *adj* international

internado *m* boarding school

internarse ⟨1a⟩ *v/r:* **internarse en** go into

internauta *m/f* INFOR Internet user, Net surfer

Internet *f* INFOR Internet

interno 1 *adj* internal; POL domestic, internal **2** *m*, **-a** *f* EDU boarder; (*preso*) inmate; MED intern, *Br* houseman

interpelar ⟨1a⟩ *v/t* question

interplanetario *adj* interplanetary

interpolar ⟨1a⟩ *v/t* insert, interpolate *fml*

interponerse ⟨2r⟩ *v/r* intervene

interpretación *f* interpretation; TEA performance (*de* as)

interpretar ⟨1a⟩ *v/t* interpret; TEA play

intérprete *m/f* interpreter

interrogación *f* interrogation; *signo de interrogación* question mark

interrogante 1 *adj* questioning **2** *m* (*also f*) question; *fig* question mark, doubt

interrogar ⟨1h⟩ *v/t* question; *de policía* interrogate, question

interrogatorio *m* questioning, interrogation

interrumpir ⟨3a⟩ **1** *v/t* interrupt; *servicio* suspend; *reunión, vacaciones* cut short, curtail **2** *v/i* interrupt

interrupción *f* interruption; *de servicio* suspension; *de reunión, vacaciones* curtailment; *sin interrupción* non-stop

interruptor *m* EL switch

intersección *f* intersection

intervalo *m tb* MÚS interval; (*espacio*) gap

intervención *f* intervention; *en debate, congreso* participation; *en película, espectáculo* appearance; MED operation

intervenir ⟨3s⟩ **1** *v/i* intervene; *en debate, congreso* take part, participate; *en película, espectáculo* appear **2** *v/t* TELEC tap; *contrabando* seize; MED operate on

intestino *m* intestine

intimar ⟨1a⟩ *v/i* (*hacerse amigos*) become friendly (*con* with); (*tratar*) mix (*con* with)

intimidad *f* intimacy; (*lo privado*) privacy; *en la intimidad* in private

intimidar ⟨1a⟩ *v/t* intimidate

íntimo *adj* intimate; (*privado*) private; *somos íntimos amigos* we're close friends

intolerable *adj* intolerable, unbearable

intolerante *adj* intolerant

intoxicación *f* poisoning

intranquilidad *f* unease; (*nerviosismo*) restlessness

intranquilo *adj* uneasy; (*nervioso*) restless

intransferible *adj* non-transferable

intransigente *adj* intransigent

intransitable *adj* impassable

intransitivo *adj* GRAM intransitive

intrascendente *adj* unimportant

intravenoso *adj* MED intravenous

intrépido *adj* intrepid

intriga *f* intrigue; *de novela* plot

intrigante 1 *adj* scheming; (*curioso*) intriguing **2** *m/f* schemer

intrigar ⟨1h⟩ **1** *v/t* (*interesar*) intrigue **2** *v/i* plot, scheme

intrincado *adj* intricate

intrínseco *adj* intrinsic

introducción *f* introduction; *acción de meter* insertion; INFOR input

introducir ⟨3o⟩ **1** *v/t* introduce; (*meter*) insert; INFOR input **2** *v/r:* **introducirse**: *introducirse en* get into; *introducirse en un mercado* gain access to *o* break into a market

intromisión *f* interference

introvertido *adj* introverted

intruso *m* intruder

intuición *f* intuition

intuir ⟨3g⟩ *v/t* sense

intuitivo *adj* intuitive

inundación *f* flood

inundadizo *adj L.Am.* prone to flooding

inundar ⟨1a⟩ *v/t* flood

inusitado *adj* unusual, uncommon

inusual *adj* unusual

inútil 1 *adj* useless; MIL unfit **2** *m/f:* **es un inútil** he's useless

inutilidad *f* uselessness

inutilizar ⟨1f⟩ *v/t:* **inutilizar algo** render sth useless

inútilmente *adv* uselessly

invadir ⟨3a⟩ *v/t* invade; *de un sentimiento* overcome

invalidar ⟨1a⟩ *v/t* invalidate

invalidez *f* disability

inválido 1 *adj persona* disabled; *documento, billete* invalid **2** *m*, **-a** *f* disabled person

invasión *f* MIL invasion

invasor *m*, **invasora** *f* invader

invencible *adj* invincible; *miedo* insur-

mountable
invención f invention
inventar ⟨1a⟩ v/t invent
inventario m inventory
invento m invention
inventor m inventor
invernada f Rpl winter pasture
invernadero m greenhouse
invernal adj winter atr
inverosímil adj unlikely
inversión f reversal; COM investment
inverso adj opposite; *orden* reverse; **a la -a** the other way round
inversor m, **inversora** f investor
invertebrado m invertebrate
invertir ⟨3i⟩ v/t reverse; COM invest (**en** in)
investigación f investigation; EDU, TÉC research; **investigación y desarrollo** research and development
investigador m, **investigadora** f researcher
investigar ⟨1h⟩ v/t investigate; EDU, TÉC research
inviable adj nonviable
invidente m/f blind person
invierno m winter
inviolable adj inviolable
invisible adj invisible
invitación f invitation
invitado m, -a f guest
invitar ⟨1a⟩ v/t invite (**a** to); (*convidar*) treat (**a** to)
invocar ⟨1g⟩ v/t invoke
involucrar ⟨1a⟩ v/t involve (**en** in)
involuntario adj involuntary
invulnerable adj invulnerable
inyección f MED, AUTO injection
inyectar ⟨1a⟩ v/t tb TÉC inject
IPC abr (= **índice de precios al consumo**) CPI (= consumer price index), Br RPI (= retail price index)
ir ⟨3t⟩ **1** v/i go (**a** to); **ir a pie** walk, go on foot; **ir en avión** fly; **¡ya voy!** I'm coming!; **ir a por algo** go and fetch sth; **ir bien / mal** go well / badly; **iba de amarillo / de uniforme** she was wearing yellow/a uniform; **van dos a dos** DEP the score is two all, **¿de qué va la película?** what's the movie about?; **¡qué va!** you must be joking! F; **¡vamos!** come on!; **¡vaya!** well! 2 v/aux: **va a llover** it's going to rain; **ya voy comprendiendo** I'm beginning to understand; **ir para viejo** be getting old **3** v/r **irse** go (away), leave; **¡vete!** go away!; **¡vámonos!** let's go
ira f anger
Irak Iraq, Irak
Irán Iran
iraní m/f & adj Iranian

iraquí m/f & adj Iraqi, Iraki
iris m inv ANAT iris; **arco iris** rainbow
Irlanda Ireland
irlandés 1 adj Irish **2** m Irishman
irlandesa f Irishwoman
ironía f irony
irónico adj ironic
irracional adj tb MAT irrational
irradiar ⟨1b⟩ v/t radiate; MED irradiate
irreal adj unreal
irrealizable adj unattainable; *proyecto* unfeasible
irreconciliable adj irreconcilable
irrecuperable adj irretrievable
irrefutable adj irrefutable
irregular adj irregular; *superficie* uneven
irregularidad f irregularity; **de superficie** unevenness
irrelevante adj irrelevant
irremediable adj fig irremediable
irreparable adj irreparable
irreprochable adj irreproachable
irresistible adj irresistible
irrespetuoso adj disrespectful
irresponsable adj irresponsible
irreverente adj irreverent
irreversible adj irreversible
irrevocable adj irrevocable
irrigar ⟨1h⟩ v/t MED, AGR irrigate
irrisorio adj laughable, derisory
irritación f tb MED irritation
irritante adj tb MED irritating
irritar ⟨1a⟩ **1** v/t tb MED irritate **2** v/r **irritarse** get irritated
irrompible adj unbreakable
irrumpir ⟨3a⟩ v/i burst in
irrupción f: **hacer irrupción en** burst into
Isla f island
islam m Islam
islámico adj Islamic
islamismo m Islam
isleño 1 adj island atr **2** m, -a f islander
Israel Israel
israelí m/f & adj Israeli
Italia Italy
italiano 1 adj Italian **2** m, -a f Italian
itinerario m itinerary
ITV abr Esp (= **inspección técnica de vehículos**) compulsory annual test of motor vehicles of a certain age, Br MOT
IVA abr (= **impuesto sobre el valor añadido**) sales tax, Br VAT (= value-added tax)
izar ⟨1f⟩ v/t hoist
izdo., izda abr (= **izquierdo, izquierda**) l (= left)
izquierda f tb POL left; **por la izquierda** on the left
izquierdo adj left

J

jabalí *m* zo wild boar
jabalina *f* javelin
jabón *m* soap; **jabón de afeitar** shaving soap
jabonera *f* soap dish
jabonoso *adj* soapy
jacinto *m* hyacinth
jactancia *f* boasting
jactancioso *adj* boastful
jactarse ⟨1a⟩ *v/r* boast (**de** about), brag (**de** about)
jacuzzi *m* jacuzzi®
jade *m* MIN jade
jadear ⟨1a⟩ *v/i* pant
jadeo *m* panting
jaguar *m* zo jaguar
jalar ⟨1a⟩ **1** *v/t L.Am.* pull; *con esfuerza* haul; *(atraer)* attract; *Méx* F *(dar aventón)* give a ride *o Br* lift to; **¿te jala el arte?** *Méx* do you feel drawn to art? **2** *v/i L.Am.* pull; *(trabajar mucho)* work hard; *Méx* F *(tener influencia)* have pull F; **jalar hacia** F head toward; **jalar para la casa** F clear off home **3** *v/r* **jalarse** *Méx (irse)* go, leave; F *(emborracharse)* get plastered F
jalea *f* jelly; **jalea real** royal jelly
jaleo *m (ruido)* racket, uproar; *(lío)* mess, muddle; **armar jaleo** F kick up a fuss F
jalón *m* pull; **dar un jalón a algo** pull sth; **de un jalón** *Méx fig* in one go
jalonar ⟨1a⟩ *v/t* fig mark out
Jamaica Jamaica
jamás *adv* never; **jamás te olvidaré** I'll never forget you; **¿viste jamás algo así?** did you ever see anything like it?; **nunca jamás** never ever; **por siempre jamás** for ever and ever
jamón *m* ham; **jamón de York** cooked ham; **jamón serrano** cured ham; **¡y un jamón!** F *(¡no!)* no way! F; *(¡bromeas!)* come off it! F
jangada *f S. Am.* F dirty trick
Japón *m* Japan
japonés **1** *adj* Japanese **2** *m*, **-esa** *f* Japanese
jaque *m* check; **jaque mate** checkmate; **dar jaque a** checkmate
jaqueca *f* MED migraine
jarabe *m* syrup; *Méx* type of folk dance
jardín *m* garden; **jardín botánico** botanic(al) gardens; **jardín de infancia** kindergarten

jardinería *f* gardening
jardinero *m*, **-a** *f* gardener
jarra *f* pitcher, *Br* jug; **en jarras** with hands on hips
jarro *m* pitcher, *Br* jug; **un jarro de agua fría** *fig* a total shock, a bombshell
jarrón *m* vase
jauja *f*: **¡esto es jauja!** this is the life!
jaula *f* cage
jauría *f* pack
jazmín *m* BOT jasmine
J.C. *abr* (= **Jesucristo**) J.C. (= Jesus Christ)
jefatura *f* headquarters; *(dirección)* leadership; **jefatura de policía** police headquarters
jefe *m*, **-a** *f de departamento, organización* head; *(superior)* boss; POL leader; *de tribu* chief; **jefe de cocina** (head) chef; **jefe de estado** head of state
jengibre *m* BOT ginger
jeque *m* sheik
jerarquía *f* hierarchy
jerez *m* sherry
jerga *f* jargon; *(argot)* slang
jeringa *f* MED syringe
jeringuilla *f* MED syringe; **jeringuilla desechable** *or* **de un solo uso** disposable syringe
jeroglífico *m* hieroglyphic; *rompecabezas* puzzle
jersey *m* sweater
Jesucristo *m* Jesus Christ
Jesús *m* Jesus; **¡Jesús!** good grief!; *por estornudo* bless you!
jet **1** *m* AVIA jet **2** *f*: **jet (set)** jet set
jeta *f* F face, mug F; **¡qué jeta tiene!** F he's got nerve! F, *Br* what a cheek! F
jibia *f* zo cuttlefish
jícara *f Méx* drinking bowl
jícaro *m L.Am.* BOT calabash
jilguero *m* zo goldfinch
jilote *m C.Am., Méx* young corn
jineta *f* zo civet
jinete *m* rider; *en carrera* jockey
jirafa *f* zo giraffe
jitomate *m Méx* tomato
JJ.OO *abr* (= **Juegos Olímpicos**) Olympic Games
jocoso *adj* humorous, joking
joder ⟨2a⟩ **1** *v/i* V screw, fuck V **2** *v/t* V *(follar)* screw V, fuck V; *(estropear)* screw up V, fuck up V; *L.Am.* F *(fastidiar)* annoy, irritate; **¡¡joder!!** V fuck! V; **me jode**

un montón V it really pisses me off P

jolgorio m F partying F

jolín int wow! F, jeez! F

jornada f (working) day; *distancia* day's journey; **media jornada** half-day; **jornada laboral** work day; **jornada partida** split shift

jornal m day's wage

jornalero m, **-a** f day labo(u)rer

joroba f hump; *fig* pain F, drag F

jorobado *adj* hump-backed; *fig* F in a bad way F

jorobar ⟨1a⟩ v/t F (*molestar*) bug F; *planes* ruin

jorongo m Méx poncho

jota f *letter* 'j'; **no saber ni jota** F not have a clue F

joven 1 *adj* young 2 m/f young man; *mujer* young woman; **los jóvenes** young people

jovial *adj* cheerful

joya f jewel; *persona* gem; **joyas** pl jewelry sg, Br jewellery sg

joyería f jewel(l)ery store, Br jeweller's

joyero 1 m, **-a** f jewel(l)er 2 m jewelry (Br jewellery) box

juanete m MED bunion

jubilación f retirement; **jubilación anticipada** early retirement

jubilado 1 *adj* retired 2 m, **-a** f retiree, Br pensioner

jubilar ⟨1a⟩ 1 v/t retire; (*desechar*) get rid of 2 v/r *jubilarse* retire; *C.Am.* play hooky, play truant

júbilo m jubilation

jubiloso *adj* jubilant

judaísmo m Judaism

judía f BOT bean; **judía verde** green bean, runner bean

judicial *adj* judicial

judío 1 *adj* Jewish 2 m, **-a** f Jew

judo m DEP judo

juego m game; *acción* play; *por dinero* gambling; (*conjunto de objetos*) set; **juego de azar** game of chance; **juego de café** coffee set; **juego de manos** conjuring trick; **juego de mesa** board game; **juego de rol** role-playing game; **juego de sociedad** game; **Juegos Olímpicos** Olympic Games; **estar en juego** fig be at stake; **fuera de juego** DEP offside; **hacer juego con** go with, match

juerga f F partying F; **irse de juerga** F go out on the town F, go out partying F

jueves m inv Thursday

juez m/f judge; **juez de línea** en fútbol assistant referee; *en fútbol americano* line judge

jueza f → **juez**

jugada f play, Br move; *en ajedrez* move; **hacerle una mala jugada a alguien** play a dirty trick on s.o.

jugador m, **jugadora** f player

jugar ⟨1o⟩ 1 v/t play 2 v/i play; *con dinero* gamble; **jugar al baloncesto** play basketball 3 v/r **jugarse** risk; **jugarse la vida** risk one's life; **jugársela a alguien** do the dirty on s.o.

jugarreta f F dirty trick F

jugo m juice; **sacar jugo a algo** get the most out of sth

jugoso *adj* tb fig juicy

juguete m toy

juguetear ⟨1a⟩ v/i play

juicio m judg(e)ment; JUR trial; (*sensatez*) sense; (*cordura*) sanity; **a mi juicio** in my opinion; **estar en su juicio** be in one's right mind; **perder el juicio** lose one's mind

julio m July

junco m BOT reed

jungla f jungle

junio m June

júnior *adj* tb DEP junior

junta f POL (regional) government; *militar* junta; COM board; (*sesión*) meeting; TÉC joint; **junta directiva** board of directors; **junta general anual** annual general meeting

juntar ⟨1a⟩ 1 v/t put together; *gente* gather together; *bienes* collect, accumulate 2 v/r **juntarse** (*reunirse*) meet, assemble; *de pareja: empezar a salir* start going out; *empezar a vivir juntos* move in together; *de caminos, ríos* meet, join; **juntarse con alguien** *socialmente* mix with s.o.

junto 1 *adj* together 2 *prp:* **junto a** next to, near; **junto con** together with

juntura f TÉC joint

jupa f *C.Am., Méx* fig F head, nut F

jurado m JUR jury

juramento m oath; **bajo juramento** under oath

jurar ⟨1a⟩ v/i swear

jurídico *adj* legal

jurisdicción f jurisdiction

jurisprudencia f jurisprudence

justamente *adv* fairly; (*precisamente*) precisely

justicia f justice; **la justicia** (*la ley*) the law; **hacer justicia a** do justice to

justificable *adj* justifiable

justificación f tb TIP justification

justificante m *de pago* receipt; *de ausencia, propiedad* certificate

justificar ⟨1g⟩ v/t tb TIP justify; *mala conducta* justify, excuse

justo *adj* just, fair; (*exacto*) right, exact;

lo justo just enough; *¡justo!* right!, exactly!
juvenil *adj* youthful
juventud *f* youth

juzgado 1 *part* → **juzgar 2** *m* court
juzgar ⟨1h⟩ *v/t* JUR try; (*valorar*) judge; *considerar* consider, judge; *a juzgar por* to judge by, judging by

K

kárate *m* DEP karate
kayak *m* DEP kayak
ketchup *m* ketchup
kg. *abr* (= *kilogramo*) kg (= kilogram)
kilo *m* kilo; *fig* F million
kilogramo *m* kilogram, *Br* kilogramme
kilómetro *m* kilometer, *Br* kilometre

kiosco *m* kiosk
kiwi *m* BOT kiwi (fruit)
kleenex® *m* kleenex, tissue
km. *abr* (= *kilómetro*) km (= kilometer)
km./h. *abr* (= *kilómetros por hora*) kph (= kilometers per hour)
kv. *abr* (= *kilovatio*) kw (= kilowatt)

L

la 1 *art* the **2** *pron complemento directo sg* her; *a usted* you; *algo* it; *la que está embarazada* the one who is pregnant; *la más grande* the biggest (one); *dame la roja* give me the red one
laberinto *m* labyrinth, maze
labia *f*: *tener mucha labia* have the gift of the gab
labio *m* lip
labor *f* work; (*tarea*) task, job; *hacer labores* do needlework; *no estar por la labor* F not be enthusiastic about the idea
laborable *adj*: *día laborable* workday
laboral *adj* labo(u)r *atr*
laboratorio *m* laboratory, lab F
laborioso *adj* laborious; *persona* hardworking
labrador *m* farm labo(u)rer, farm worker
labranza *f* de la tierra cultivation
labrar ⟨1a⟩ *v/t tierra* work; *piedra* carve
labriego *m* farm labo(u)rer, farm worker
laca *f* lacquer; *para el cabello* hairspray; *laca de uñas* nail varnish *o* polish
lacear ⟨1a⟩ *v/t Rpl* lasso
lacio *adj* limp; *pelo* lank
lacónico *adj* laconic
lacra *f* scar; *L.Am.* (*llaga*) sore; *la corrupción es una lacra social* corruption is a

blot on society
lacre *m* sealing wax
lacrimógeno *adj fig* tear-jerking
lactancia *f* lactation
lácteo *adj*: *Vía Láctea* Milky Way; *productos lácteos* dairy products
ladear ⟨1a⟩ *v/t* tilt
ladera *f* slope
ladino 1 *adj* cunning, sly **2** *m C.Am. Indian who has become absorbed into white culture*
lado *m* side; (*lugar*) place; *al lado* nearby; *al lado de* beside, next to; *de lado* sideways; *ir por otro lado* go another way; *por un lado ... por otro lado* on the one hand ... on the other hand; *hacerse a un lado* *fig* stand aside
ladrar ⟨1a⟩ *v/i* bark
ladrillo *m* brick
ladrón *m* thief
lagartija *f* ZO small lizard
lagarto *m* ZO lizard
lago *m* lake
lágrima *f* tear
laguna *f* lagoon; *fig* gap
laico *adj* lay
lamentable *adj* deplorable
lamentablemente *adv* regretfully

lamentar ⟨1a⟩ **1** v/t regret, be sorry about; *muerte* mourn **2** v/r lamentarse complain (*de* about)

lamento m whimper; *por dolor* groan

lamer ⟨2a⟩ v/t lick

lámina f sheet

lámpara f lamp; *lámpara halógena* halogen lamp; *lámpara de pie* floor lamp, *Br* standard lamp

lamparón m F grease mark

lana f wool, *Méx* P dough F; *pura lana virgen* pure new wool

lancha f launch; *lancha fueraborda* outboard

langosta f zo *insecto* locust; *crustáceo* spiny lobster

langostino m zo king prawn

languidecer ⟨2d⟩ v/i languish

lánguido adj languid

lanza f lance

lanzadera f shuttle; *lanzadera espacial* space shuttle

lanzado **1** adj fig go-ahead; *es muy lanzado con las chicas* he's not shy with girls **2** part → lanzar

lanzamiento m MIL, COM launch; *lanzamiento de disco / de martillo* discus / hammer (throw); *lanzamiento de peso* shot put

lanzar ⟨1f⟩ **1** v/t throw; *cohete, producto* launch; *bomba* drop **2** v/r lanzarse throw o.s. (*en* into); (*precipitarse*) pounce (*sobre* on); *lanzarse a hacer algo* rush into doing sth

lapa f zo limpet

lapicera f Rpl, Chi (ballpoint) pen; *lapicera fuente* L.Am. fountain pen

lapicero m automatic pencil, *Br* propelling pencil

lápida f memorial stone

lapidario adj memorable

lápiz m pencil; *lápiz de ojos* eyeliner; *lápiz labial* or *de labios* lipstick; *lápiz óptico* light pen

lapso m de tiempo space, period

lapsus m inv slip; *tener un lapsus* have a momentary lapse

larga f: *poner la* (*s*) *larga* (*s*) put the headlights on full beam; *dar largas a alguien* F put s.o. off

largar ⟨1h⟩ **1** v/t drive away **2** v/r largarse F clear off o out F

largo **1** adj long; *persona* tall; *a la -a* in the long run; *a lo largo del día* throughout the day; *a lo largo de la calle* along the street; *¡largo!* F scram! F; *esto va para largo* this will take some time; *pasar de largo* go (straight) past **2** m length

largometraje m feature film

larguero m DEP crossbar

laringe f larynx

laringitis f MED laryngitis

larva f zo larva

las **1** art fpl the **2** pron complemento directo pl them; *a ustedes* you; *llévate las que quieras* take whichever ones you want; *las de ...* those of ...; *las de Juan* Juan's; *las que llevan falda* the ones o those that are wearing dresses

lasaña f GASTR lasagne

lascivo adj lewd

láser m laser; *rayo láser* laser beam

lástima f pity, shame; *me da lástima no usarlo* it's a shame o pity not to use it; *¡qué lástima!* what a pity o shame!

lastimar ⟨1a⟩ **1** v/t (*herir*) hurt **2** v/r lastimarse hurt o.s.

lastimoso adj pitiful; (*deplorable*) shameful

lastre m ballast; fig burden

lata f can, *Br tb* tin; fig F drag F, pain F, *dar la lata* ⊢ be a drag F o a pain F

latente adj latent

lateral **1** adj side attr; *cuestiones laterales* side issues **2** m DEP: *lateral derecho / izquierdo* right / left back

latería f L.Am. tin works

latero m, -a f L.Am. tinsmith

latido m beat

latifundio m large estate

latigazo m lash; (*chasquido*) crack

látigo m whip

latín m Latin

latino adj Latin

Latinoamérica Latin America

latinoamericano **1** adj Latin American **2** m, -a f Latin American

latir ⟨3a⟩ v/i beat

latitud f GEOG latitude

latón m brass

laucha f S. Am. mouse

laurel m BOT laurel; *dormirse en los laureles* fig rest on one's laurels

lava f lava

lavable adj washable

lavabo m washbowl

lavada f L.Am. wash

lavado m washing; *lavado de cerebro* fig brainwashing

lavadora f washing machine

lavamanos m inv L.Am. → lavabo

lavanda f BOT lavender

lavandería f laundry

lavaplatos m inv dishwasher; L.Am. sink

lavar ⟨1a⟩ **1** v/t wash; *lavar los platos* wash the dishes; *lavar la ropa* do the laundry, *Br tb* do the washing; *lavar en seco* dry-clean **2** v/i (*lavar los platos*) do the dishes; *de detergente* clean **3** v/r **lavarse** wash up, *Br* have a wash; *lavarse los dientes* brush one's teeth; *lavarse las manos* wash one's hands; *yo me lavo las manos* fig I wash my hands of it

lavarropas *m inv L.Am.* washing machine

lavavajillas *m inv líquido* dishwashing liquid, *Br* washing-up liquid; *electrodoméstico* dishwasher

laxante *m/adj* MED laxative

laxo *adj* relaxed; *(poco estricto)* lax

lazada *f* bow

lazarillo *m* guide; *perro lazarillo* seeing eye dog, *Br* guide dog

lazo *m* knot; *de adorno* bow; *para atrapar animales* lasso

le *pron sg complemento indirecto* (to) him; *(a ella)* (to) her; *(a usted)* (to) you; *(a algo)* (to) it; *complemento directo* him; *(a usted)* you

leal *adj* loyal

lealtad *f* loyalty

lección *f* lesson; *esto le servirá de lección* that will teach him a lesson

lechar ⟨1a⟩ v/t *L.Am. (ordeñar)* milk

leche *f* milk; *leche condensada* condensed milk; *leche entera* whole milk; *leche en polvo* powdered milk; *estar de mala leche* P be in a foul mood; *tener mala leche* P be out to make trouble

lechería *f* dairy

lechero 1 *adj* dairy *atr* **2** *m* milkman

lecho *m tb de río* bed

lechón *m* suckling pig

lechuga *f* lettuce; *ser más fresco que una lechuga* F have a lot of nerve

lechuza *f* zo barn-owl; *Cuba, Méx* P hooker F

lectivo *adj: día lectivo* school day

lector *m*, **~a** *f* reader

lectura *f* reading

leer ⟨2e⟩ v/t read

legado *m* legacy; *persona* legate

legal *adj* legal; *fig* F *persona* great F, terrific F

legalidad *f* legality

legalizar ⟨1f⟩ v/t legalize

legaña *f: tener legañas en los ojos* have sleep in one's eyes

legar ⟨1h⟩ v/t leave

legendario *adj* legendary

legible *adj* legible

legión *f* legion

legislación *f* legislation

legislar ⟨1a⟩ v/i legislate

legislativo *adj* legislative

legislatura *f cuerpo* legislature; *periodo* term of office

legitimar ⟨1a⟩ v/t justify; *documento* authenticate

legítimo *adj* legitimate; *(verdadero)* authentic

lego *adj* lay *atr*; *fig* ignorant

legua *f: se ve a la legua* fig F you can see it a mile off F; *hecho* it's blindingly obvious F

legumbre *f* BOT pulse

leída *f L.Am.* reading

lejanía *f* distance; *en la lejanía* in the distance

lejano *adj* distant

lejía *f* bleach

lejos 1 *adv* far, far away; *Navidad queda lejos* Christmas is a long way off; *a lo lejos* in the distance; *ir demasiado lejos* fig go too far, overstep the mark; *llegar lejos* fig go far **2** *prp: lejos de* far from

lele *adj C.Am.* stupid

lema *m* slogan

lencería *f* lingerie

lengua *f* tongue; *lengua materna* mother tongue; *con la lengua fuera* fig with one's tongue hanging out; *irse de la lengua* let the cat out of the bag; *sacar la lengua a alguien* stick one's tongue out at s.o.; *lo tengo en la punta de la lengua* it's on the tip of my tongue

lenguado *m* zo sole

lenguaje *m* language; *lenguaje de programación* INFOR programming language

lenguaraz *adj* foul-mouthed

lengüeta 1 *f de zapato* tongue **2** *adj: ser lengüeta S. Am.* F be a gossip

lenitivo *m* balm

lente *m* lens; *lentes de contacto* contact lenses, contacts

lentes *mpl L.Am.* glasses

lenteja *f* BOT lentil

lentejuela *f* sequin

lentillas *fpl* contact lenses

lentitud *f* slowness

lento *adj* slow; *a fuego lento* on a low heat

leña *f* (fire)wood; *echar leña al fuego* fig add fuel to the fire

leñador *m* woodcutter

leño *m* log

Leo *m/f inv* ASTR Leo

león *m* zo lion; *L.Am.* puma; *león marino* sealion

leona *f* lioness

leonera *f* lion's den; *jaula* lion's cage; *Rpl, Chi* fig F *habitación desordenada etc* pigsty F; *L.Am.* F *para prisioneros* bullpen F, *Br* communal cell for holding prisoners temporarily

leopardo *m* zo leopard
leotardo *m de gimnasta* leotard; **leotardos** tights, *Br* heavy tights
lépero *adj C.Am., Méx* coarse
lerdo *adj* (*torpe*) slow(-witted)
les *pron pl complemento indirecto* (to) them; (*a ustedes*) (to) you; *complemento directo* them; (*a ustedes*) you
lesbiana *f* lesbian
lesión *f* injury
lesionado *adj* injured
lesionar ⟨1a⟩ *v/t* injure
letal *adj* lethal
letanía *f* litany
letárgico *adj* lethargic
letra *f* letter; *de canción* lyrics *pl*; **letra de cambio** COM bill of exchange; **letra de imprenta** block capital; **letra mayúscula** capital letter; **al pie de la letra** word for word
letrero *m* sign
letrina *f* latrine
leucemia *f* MED leuk(a)emia
levadura *f* yeast
levantamiento *m* raising; (*rebelión*) rising; *de embargo* lifting
levantar ⟨1a⟩ **1** *v/t* raise; *bulto* lift (up); *del suelo* pick up; *edificio, estatua* put up, erect; *embargo* lift; **levantar sospechas** arouse suspicion; **¡levanta los ánimos!** cheer up!; **levantar la voz** raise one's voice **2** *v/r* **levantarse** get up; (*ponerse de pie*) stand up; *de un edificio, una montaña* rise; *en rebelión* rise up
levante *m* east
levar ⟨1a⟩ *v/t:* **levar anclas** weigh anchor
leve *adj* slight; *sonrisa* faint
levedad *f* lightness
levitar ⟨1a⟩ *v/i* levitate
léxico *m* lexicon
ley *f* law; **con todas las de la ley** fairly and squarely
leyenda *f* legend
leyendo *vb* → **leer**
leyó *vb* → **leer**
liana *f* BOT liana, creeper
liar ⟨1c⟩ **1** *v/t* tie (up); *en papel* wrap (up); *cigarillo* roll; *persona* confuse **2** *v/r* **liarse de una persona** get confused; **liarse a hacer algo** get tied up doing sth; **liarse con alguien** F get involved with s.o.
Líbano Lebanon
libélula *f* zo dragonfly
liberación *f* release; *de un país* liberation
liberal *adj* liberal
liberalización *f* liberalization
liberalizar ⟨1f⟩ *v/t* liberalize
liberar ⟨1a⟩ **1** *v/t* (set) free, release; *país* liberate; *energía* release **2** *v/r* **liberarse**:

liberarse de algo free o.s. of sth
libertad *f* freedom, liberty; **libertad bajo fianza** JUR bail; **libertad condicional** JUR probation; **dejar a alguien en libertad** release s.o., let s.o. go
libertinaje *m* licentiousness
Libia Libya
líbido *f* libido
libio(-a) *m/f & adj* Libyan
libra *f* pound; **libra esterlina** pound (sterling)
Libra *m/f inv* ASTR Libra
librar ⟨1a⟩ **1** *v/t* free (**de** from); *cheque* draw; *batalla* fight **2** *v/i:* **libro los lunes** I have Mondays off **3** *v/r* **librarse: librarse de algo** get out of sth; **de buena nos hemos librado** F that was lucky
libre *adj* free; *tiempo* spare, free; **eres libre de** you're free to
librecambio *m* free trade
librera *f* bookseller
librería *f* book store
librero *m* bookseller; *L.Am. mueble* bookcase
libreta *f* notebook; **libreta de ahorros** bankbook, passbook
libro *m* book; **libro de bolsillo** paperback (book); **libro de cocina** cookbook, cookery book; **libro de familia** booklet recording family births, marriages and deaths; **libro de reclamaciones** complaints book
licencia *f* permit, license, *Br* licence; (*permiso*) permission; MIL leave; **licencia (de manejar o conducir)** L.Am. driver's license, *Br* driving licence; **tomarse demasiadas licencias** take liberties
licenciado *m*, **-a** *f* graduate
licenciar ⟨1b⟩ **1** *v/t* MIL discharge **2** *v/r* **licenciarse** graduate; MIL be discharged
licenciatura *f* EDU degree
liceo *m* L.Am. high school, *Br* secondary school
licitación *f* L.Am. bidding
licitador *m*, **licitadora** *f* L.Am. bidder
licitar ⟨1a⟩ *v/t* L.Am. *en subasta* bid for
lícito *adj* legal; (*razonable*) fair, reasonable
licor *m* liquor, *Br* spirits *pl*
licuado *m* Méx fruit milkshake
licuadora *f* blender
licuar ⟨1d⟩ *v/t* blend, liquidize
líder *m/f* leader **2** *adj* leading
liderar ⟨1a⟩ *v/t* lead
liderazgo *m* leadership
lidia *f* bullfighting
lidiar ⟨1b⟩ **1** *v/i fig* do battle, struggle **2** *v/t* *toro* fight
liebre *f* zo hare

lienzo *m* canvas

liga *f* POL, DEP league; *de medias* garter

ligamento *m* ANAT ligament

ligar ⟨1h⟩ **1** *v/t* bind; (*atar*) tie **2** *v/i*: *ligar con* F pick up F

ligereza *f* lightness; (*rapidez*) speed; *de movimiento* agility; *de carácter* shallowness, superficiality

ligero 1 *adj* (*de poco peso*) light; (*rápido*) rapid, quick; *movimiento* agile, nimble; (*leve*) slight; *ligero de ropa* scantily clad; *a la -a* (*sin pensar*) lightly, casually; *tomar algo a la -a* not take sth seriously **2** *adv* quickly

ligón *m* F: *es un ligón* he's a real Don Juan F

ligue *m* F: *estar de ligue* be on the pick-up F; *be on the pull* F

liguero *m* garter belt, *Br* suspender belt

lija *f*: *papel de lija* sandpaper

lijar ⟨1a⟩ *v/t* sand

lila *f* BOT lilac

lima *f* file; BOT lime; *lima de uñas* nail file

limar ⟨1a⟩ *v/t* file; *fig* polish

limitado 1 *adj* limited **2** *part* → **limitar**

limitar ⟨1a⟩ **1** *v/t* limit **2** *v/i*: *limitar con* border on **3** *v/r* *limitarse* limit *o* restrict o.s. (*a* to)

límite 1 *m* limit; (*línea de separación*) boundary; *límite de velocidad* speed limit **2** *adj*: *situación límite* life-threatening situation

limítrofe *adj* neighbo(u)ring

limón *m* lemon

limonada *f* lemonade

limosna *f*: *una limosna, por favor* can you spare some change?

limpiabotas *m/f inv* bootblack

limpiacristales *m inv* window cleaner

limpiada *f* L.Am. clean

limpiamanos *m inv* L.Am. hand towel

limpiaparabrisas *m inv* AUTO windshield wiper, *Br* windscreen wiper

limpiar ⟨1b⟩ *v/t* clean; *con un trapo* wipe; *fig* clean up; *limpiar a alguien* F clean s.o. out F

limpieza *f* *estado* cleanliness; *acto* cleaning; *limpieza general* spring cleaning; *limpieza en seco* dry-cleaning; *hacer la limpieza* do the cleaning

limpio *adj* clean; (*ordenado*) neat, tidy; *político* honest; *gana $5.000 limpios al mes* he takes home $5,000 a month; *quedarse limpio* S. Am. F be broke F; *sacar algo en limpio* *fig* make sense of sth

limusina *f* limousine

linaje *m* lineage

lince *m* ZO lynx; *ojos* or *vista de lince* *fig* eyes like a hawk

linchar ⟨1a⟩ *v/t* lynch

lindar ⟨1a⟩ *v/i*: *lindar con algo* adjoin sth; *fig* border on sth

lindo *adj* lovely; *de lo lindo* a lot, a great deal

línea *f* line; *línea aérea* airline; *mantener la línea* watch one's figure; *de primera línea* *fig* first-rate; *tecnología de primera línea* state-of-the-art technology; *entre líneas* *fig* between the lines

lineal *adj* linear

linfático *adj* lymphatic

lingote *m* ingot; *lingote de oro* gold bar

lingüista *m/f* linguist

lingüística *f* linguistics

lingüístico *adj* linguistic

linier *m* DEP assistant referee, linesman

lino *m* linen; BOT flax

linterna *f* flashlight, *Br* torch

lío *m* bundle; (*desorden*) mess; F (*jaleo*) fuss; *lío amoroso* F affair; *estar hecho un lío* be all confused; *hacerse un lío* get into a muddle; *meterse en líos* get into trouble

liposucción *f* MED liposuction

lipotimia *f* MED blackout

liquen *m* BOT lichen

liquidación *f* COM *de cuenta, deuda* settlement; *de negocio* liquidation; *liquidación total* clearance sale

liquidar ⟨1a⟩ *v/t* *cuenta, deuda* settle; COM *negocio* wind up, liquidate; *existencias* sell off; F (*matar*) liquidate F, bump off F

liquidez *f* COM liquidity

líquido 1 *adj* liquid; COM net **2** *m* liquid

lira *f* lira

lírico *adj* lyrical

lirio *m* BOT lily

lirón *m* ZO dormouse; *dormir como un lirón* *fig* sleep like a log

lisiado 1 *adj* crippled **2** *m* cripple

liso *adj* smooth; *terreno* flat; *pelo* straight; (*sin adornos*) plain; *-a y llanamente* plainly and simply

lisonja *f* flattery

lista *f* list; *lista de boda* wedding list; *lista de espera* waiting list; *pasar lista* take the roll call, *Br* call the register

listado *m* INFOR printout

listín *m*: *listín* (*telefónico*) phone book

listo *adj* (*inteligente*) clever; (*preparado*) ready; *pasarse de listo* F try to be too smart F

listón *m* *de madera* strip; DEP bar; *poner el listón muy alto* *fig* set very high standards

lisura *f* Rpl, Pe curse, swearword

litera f bunk; _de tren_ couchette

literal adj literal

literario adj literary

literatura f literature

litigante m/f & adj JUR litigant

litigar ⟨1h⟩ v/i JUR go to litigation

litigio m lawsuit

litografía f lithography

litoral 1 adj coastal **2** m coast

litro m liter, Br litre

liturgia f REL liturgy

liviano adj light; _(de poca importancia)_ trivial

lívido adj pale

llaga f ulcer; _poner o meter el dedo en la llaga_ put one's finger on it

llama f flame; zo llama

llamada f call; _en una puerta_ knock; _en timbre_ ring; _llamada a cobro revertido_ collect call; _llamada de auxilio_ distress call

llamado m _L.Am_ call

llamador m (door) knocker

llamamiento m call; _hacer un llamamiento a algo_ call for sth

llamar ⟨1a⟩ **1** v/t call; TELEC call, Br tb ring **2** v/t TELEC call, Br tb ring; _llamar a la puerta_ knock at the door; _con timbre_ ring the bell; _el fútbol no me llama nada_ football isn't appeal to them in the slightest **3** v/r llamarse be called; _¿cómo te llamas?_ what's your name?

llamarada f flare-up

llamativo adj eyecatching; _color_ loud

llamón adj _Méx_ moaning

llano 1 adj terreno level; _trato_ natural; _persona_ unassuming **2** m flat ground

llanta f wheel rim; _C.Am., Méx (neumático)_ tire, Br tyre

llanto m sobbing

llanura f plain

llave f key; _para tuerca_ wrench, Br tb spanner; _llave de contacto_ AUTO ignition key; _llave inglesa_ TÉC monkey wrench; _llave de paso_ stop cock; _llave en mano_ available for immediate occupancy; _bajo llave_ under lock and key; _cerrar con llave_ lock

llavero m key ring

llegada f arrival

llegar ⟨1h⟩ **1** v/i arrive; _(alcanzar)_ reach; _la comida no llegó para todos_ there wasn't enough food for everyone; _me llega hasta las rodillas_ it comes down to my knees; _el agua me llegaba a la cintura_ the water came up to my waist; _llegar a saber_ find out; _llegar a ser_ get to be; _llegar a viejo_ live to a ripe old age **2** v/r llegarse: _llégate al vecino_ F run over

to the neighbo(u)r's

llenar ⟨1a⟩ **1** v/t fill; _impreso_ fill out _o_ in **2** v/i be filling **3** v/r llenarse fill up; _me he llenado_ I have had enough (to eat)

lleno adj full _(de_ of); _pared_ covered _(de_ with); _de lleno_ fully

llevadero adj bearable

llevar ⟨1a⟩ **1** v/t take; _ropa, gafas_ wear; _ritmo_ keep up; _llevar a alguien en coche_ drive s.o., take s.o. in the car; _llevar dinero encima_ carry money; _llevar las de perder_ be likely to lose; _me lleva dos años_ he's two years older than me; _llevo ocho días aquí_ I've been here a week; _llevo una hora esperando_ I've been waiting for an hour **2** v/i lead _(a_ to) **3** v/r llevarse take; _susto, sorpresa_ get; _llevarse bien / mal_ get on well / badly; _se lleva el color rojo_ red is fashionable

llorar ⟨1a⟩ v/i cry, weep

lloriquear ⟨1a⟩ v/i snivel, whine

lloro m weeping, crying

llorón 1 adj _ser llorón_ be a crybaby F **2** m F crybaby F

llovedera f _L.Am.,_ **llovedero** m _L.Am._ rainy season

llover ⟨2h⟩ v/i rain; _llueve_ it is raining

llovizna f drizzle

lloviznar ⟨1a⟩ v/i drizzle

llueve vb → **llover**

lluvia f rain; _Rpl (ducha)_ shower; _lluvia ácida_ acid rain

lluvioso adj rainy

lo 1 art sg the; _lo bueno_ the good thing; _no sabes lo difícil que es_ you don't know how difficult it is **2** pron sg: _a él_ him; _a usted_ you; _algo_ it; _lo sé_ I know **3** pron rel sg: _lo que_ what; _lo cual_ which

loable adj praiseworthy, laudable

lobo m wolf; _lobo marino_ seal; _lobo de mar_ fig sea dog

lóbrego adj gloomy

lóbulo m lobe; _lóbulo de la oreja_ earlobe

loca f madwoman

locador m _S. Am._ landlord

local 1 adj local **2** m premises pl; _local comercial_ commercial premises pl

localidad f town; TEA seat

localización f location

localizar ⟨1f⟩ v/t locate; _incendio_ contain, bring under control

loción f lotion

loco 1 adj mad, crazy; _a lo loco_ F _(sin pensar)_ hastily; _es para volverse loco_ it's enough to drive you mad _o_ crazy **2** m madman

locomoción f locomotion; _medio de locomoción_ means of transport

locomotora f locomotive

locro *m S. Am.* stew of meat, corn and potatoes

locuaz *adj* talkative, loquacious *fml*

locución *f* phrase

locura *f* madness; *es una locura* it's madness

locutor *m*, **locutora** *f* RAD, TV presenter

locutorio *m* TELEC phone booth

lodazal *m* quagmire

lodo *m* mud

lógica *f* logic

logística *f* logistics

lógico *adj* logical

logopeda *m/f* speech therapist

logotipo *m* logo

logrado *adj* excellent

lograr ⟨1a⟩ *v/t* achieve; (*obtener*) obtain; *lograr hacer algo* manage to do sth; *lograr que alguien haga algo* (manage to) get s.o. to do sth

logrero *m L.Am.* F profiteer

logro *m* achievement

loma *f L.Am.* small hill

lombriz *f*: *lombriz de tierra* earthworm

lomo *m* back; GASTR loin; *a lomos de burro* on a donkey

lona *f* canvas

loncha *f* slice

lonche *m L.Am.* afternoon snack

lonchería *f L.Am.* diner, luncheonette

londinense 1 *adj* London *atr* **2** *m/f* Londoner

Londres London

longaniza *f* type of dried sausage

longevidad *f* longevity

longevo *adj* long-lived

longitud *f* longitude; (*largo*) length

longitudinal *adj* longitudinal

lonja *f de pescado* fish market; (*loncha*) slice

loquera *f L.Am.* F shrink F; *enfermera* psychiatric nurse

loquero *m L.Am.* F *persona* shrink F; *enfermero* psychiatric nurse; (*manicomio*) mental hospital, funny farm F

loro *m* parrot; *estar al loro* F (*enterado*) be clued up F, be on the ball F

los *mpl* **1** *art* the **2** *pron complemento directo pl* them; *a ustedes* you; *llévate los que quieras* take whichever ones you want; *los de ...* those of ...; *los de Juan* Juan's; *los que juegan* the ones *o* those that are playing

losa *f* flagstone

lote *m en reparto* share, part; *L.Am.* (*solar*) lot

lotería *f* lottery

loto 1 *m* BOT lotus **2** *f* F lottery

loza *f* china

lozano *adj* healthy-looking

lubina *f* ZO sea bass

lubri(fi)cación *f* lubrication

lubri(fi)cante 1 *adj* lubricating **2** *m* lubricant

lubri(fi)car ⟨1g⟩ *v/t* lubricate

lucero *m* bright star; (*Venus*) Venus

lucha *f* fight, struggle; DEP wrestling; *lucha libre* DEP all-in wrestling

luchador **1** *adj espíritu* fighting **2** *m*, **luchadora** *f* fighter

luchar ⟨1a⟩ *v/i* fight (*por* for)

lúcido *adj* lucid, clear

luciérnaga *f* ZO glow-worm

lucimiento *m* (*brillo*) splendo(u)r; *le ofrece oportunidades de lucimiento* it gives him a chance to shine

lucio *m* ZO pike

lucir ⟨3f⟩ **1** *v/i* shine; *L.Am.* (*verse bien*) look good **2** *v/t ropa, joya* wear **3** *v/r lucirse tb irón* excel o.s., surpass o.s.

lucrativo *adj* lucrative

lucro *m* profit; *afán de lucro* profit-making; *sin ánimo de lucro* non-profit (making), not-for-profit

ludopatía *f* compulsive gambling

luego 1 *adv* (*después*) later; *en orden, espacio* then; *L.Am.* (*en seguida*) right now; *luego luego Méx* straight away; *¡desde luego!* of course!; *¡hasta luego!* see you (later) **2** *conj* therefore; *luego que L.Am.* after

lugar *m* place; *lugar común* cliché; *en lugar de* instead of; *en primer lugar* in the first place, first(ly); *fuera de lugar* out of place; *yo en tu lugar* if I were you, (if I were) in your place; *dar lugar a* give rise to; *tener lugar* take place

lúgubre *adj* gloomy

lujo *m* luxury

lujoso *adj* luxurious

lujuria *f* lust

lujurioso *adj* lecherous

lumbago *m* MED lumbago

lumbre *f* fire

lumbrera *f* genius

luminoso *adj* luminous; *lámpara, habitación* bright

luna *f* moon; *de tienda* window; *de vehículo* windshield, *Br* windscreen; *luna de miel* honeymoon; *luna llena / nueva* full / new moon; *media luna L.Am.* GASTR croissant; *estar en la luna* F have one's head in the clouds F

lunar 1 *adj* lunar **2** *m en la piel* mole; *de lunares* spotted, polka-dot

lunático *adj* lunatic

lunes *m inv* Monday

luneta *f*: *luneta térmica* AUTO heated

windshield, *Br* heated windscreen
lunfardo *m Arg* slang used in Buenos Aires
lupa *f* magnifying glass; *mirar algo con lupa fig* go through sth with a fine tooth-comb
lustrabotas *m/f inv L.Am.* bootblack
lustrador *m*, **lustradora** *f L.Am.* bootblack
lustrar ⟨1a⟩ *v/t* polish
lustre *m* shine; *fig* luster, *Br* lustre; *dar lustre a fig* give added luster (*Br* lustre) to
lustro *m* period of five years

lustroso *adj* shiny
luto *m* mourning; *estar de luto por alguien* be in mourning for s.o.
luxación *f* MED dislocation
luz *f* light; *luz trasera* AUTO rear light; *luces de carretera* or *largas* AUTO full o main beam headlights; *luces de cruce* or *cortas* AUTO dipped headlights; *luz verde tb fig* green light; *arrojar luz sobre algo fig* shed light on s.th.; *dar a luz* give birth to; *salir a la luz fig* come to light; *a todas luces* evidently, clearly; *de pocas luces fig* F dim F, not very bright

M

m *abr* (= *metro*) m (= meter); (= *minuto*) m (= minute)
macabro 1 *adj* macabre **2** *m*, **-a** *f* ghoul
macaco *m* zo macaque
macana *f L.Am.* billyclub, *Br* truncheon; F (*mentira*) lie, fib F; *hizo / dijo una macana* he did / said something stupid; *¡qué macana! Rpl* P what a drag!
macanear ⟨1a⟩ *v/t L.Am.* (*aporrear*) beat
macanudo *S. Am.* F great F, fantastic F
macarra 1 *m* P pimp **2** *adj* F: *ser macarra* be a bastard P
macarrones *mpl* macaroni *sg*
macedonia *f*: *macedonia de frutas* fruit salad
macerar ⟨1a⟩ *v/t* GASTR soak
maceta *f* flowerpot
macetero *m* flowerpot holder; *L.Am.* flowerpot
machacar ⟨1g⟩ *v/t* crush; *fig* thrash
machete *m* machete
machismo *m* male chauvinism
machista 1 *adj* sexist **2** *m* sexist, male chauvinist
macho 1 *adj* male; (*varonil*) tough; *desp* macho **2** *m* male; *apelativo* F man F, *Br* mate F; *L.Am.* (*plátano*) banana
macizo 1 *adj* solid; *estar macizo* F be a dish F **2** *m* GEOG massif; *macizo de flores* flower bed
macuto *m* backpack
madeja *f* hank
madera *f* wood; *tener madera de* have the makings of
maderera *f* timber merchant

madero *m* P cop P
madrastra *f* step-mother
madre 1 *f* mother; *madre soltera* single mother; *dar en la madre a alguien* F hit s.o. where it hurts; *¡me vale madre! Méx* V I don't give a fuck! V **2** *adj Méx*, *C.Am.* F great F, fantastic
madreselva *f* BOT honeysuckle
Madrid Madrid
madriguera *f* (*agujero*) burrow; (*guarida*) *tb fig* den
madrileño 1 *adj* of / from Madrid, Madrid *atr* **2** *m*, **-a** *f* native of Madrid
madrina *f* godmother
madrugada *f* early morning; (*amanecer*) dawn; *de madrugada* in the small hours
madrugador *m*, **madrugadora** *f* early riser
madrugar ⟨1h⟩ *v/i L.Am.* (*quedar despierto*) stay up till the small hours; (*levantarse temprano*) get up early
madurar ⟨1a⟩ **1** *v/t fig*: *idea* think through **2** *v/i de persona* mature; *de fruta* ripen
madurez *f* maturity; *edad* middle age; *de fruta* ripeness
maduro *adj mentalmente* mature; *de edad* middle-aged; *fruta* ripe
maestría *f* mastery; *Méx* EDU master's (degree)
maestro 1 *adj* master *atr* **2** *m*, **-a** *f* EDU teacher; MÚS maestro
mafia *f* mafia
mafioso 1 *adj* mafia *atr* **2** *m* mafioso, gangster
magdalena *f* cupcake, *Br tb* fairy cake

magia *f tb fig* magic
mágico *adj* magic
magisterio *m* teaching profession
magistrado *m* judge
magistral *adj* masterly
magnanimidad *f* magnanimity
magnánimo *adj* magnanimous
magnate *m* magnate, tycoon
magnesio *m* magnesium
magnético *adj* magnetic
magnetofón *m* tape recorder
magnífico *adj* wonderful, magnificent
magnitud *f* magnitude
magnolia *f* BOT magnolia
mago *m tb fig* magician; **los Reyes Magos** the Three Wise Men, the Three Kings
magrear ⟨1a⟩ *v/t* feel up F
Magreb Maghreb
magro *adj carne* lean
magulladura *f* bruise
magullar ⟨1a⟩ *v/t* bruise
magullón *m* L.Am. bruise
mahometano 1 *adj* Muslim **2** *m*, -a *f* Muslim
mahonesa *f* mayonnaise
maillot *m* DEP jersey
maíz *m* corn
majada *f* CSur flock of sheep
majaderear ⟨1a⟩ L.Am. F **1** *v/t* bug F **2** *v/i* keep going on F
majadería *f*: **decir / hacer una majadería** say / do something stupid
majadero 1 *adj* idiotic, stupid **2** *m*, -a *f* idiot
majareta *adj* F nutty F, screwy F
majestad *f* majesty
majestuoso *adj* majestic
majo *adj* F nice; (*bonito*) pretty
mal 1 *adj* → **malo 2** *adv* badly; **¡mal que bien** one way or the other; **¡menos mal!** thank goodness!; **ponerse a mal con alguien** fall out with s.o.; **tomarse algo a mal** take sth badly **3** *m* MED illness; **el mal menor** the lesser of two evils
malabar *m/adj*: (*juegos*) **-es** *pl* juggling *sg*
malabarista *m/f* juggler
malacrianza *f* L.Am. rudeness
malaria *f* MED malaria
malcriadez *f* L.Am. bad upbringing
malcriado *adj* spoilt
malcrianza *f* L.Am. rudeness
malcriar ⟨1c⟩ *v/t* spoil
maldad *f* evil; **es una maldad hacer eso** it's a wicked thing to do
maldecir ⟨3p⟩ **1** *v/i* curse; **maldecir de alguien** speak ill of s.o. **2** *v/t* curse
maldición *f* curse

maldito *adj* F damn F; **¡-a sea!** (god)damn it!
maleante *m/f* & *adj* criminal
malecón *m* breakwater
maleducado *adj* rude, bad-mannered
maleficio *m* curse
maléfico *adj* evil
malentendido *m* misunderstanding
malestar *m* MED discomfort; *social* unrest
maleta *f* bag, suitcase; *L.Am.* AUTO trunk, *Br* boot; **hacer la maleta** pack one's bags
maletero *m* trunk, *Br* boot
maletín *m* briefcase
malévolo *adj* malevolent
maleza *f* undergrowth
malformación *f* MED malformation
malgastar ⟨1a⟩ *v/t* waste
malgenioso *adj* Méx bad-tempered
malhablado *adj* foul-mouthed
malhechor *m*, **malhechora** *f* criminal
malherir ⟨3i⟩ *v/t* hurt badly
malhumorado *adj* bad-tempered
malicia *f* (*mala intención*) malice; (*astucia*) cunning, slyness; **no tener malicia** F be very naïve
malicioso *adj* (*malintencionado*) malicious; (*astuto*) cunning, sly
maligno *adj* harmful; MED malignant
malinchismo *m* Méx treason
malla *f* mesh; *Rpl* swimsuit
malo 1 *adj* bad; *calidad* poor; (*enfermo*) sick, ill; **por las buenas o por las -as** whether he / she etc likes it or not; **por las -as** by force; **lo malo es que** unfortunately; **ponerse malo** fall ill **2** *m hum* bad guy, baddy F
malogrado *adj muerto* dead before one's time
malograr ⟨1a⟩ **1** *v/t* waste; *trabajo* spoil, ruin **2** *v/r* **malograrse** fail; *de plan* come to nothing; *fallecer* die before one's time; *S. Am.* (*descomponerse*) break down; (*funcionar mal*) go wrong
maloliente *adj* stinking
malparado *adj*: **quedar** *or* **salir malparado de algo** come out badly from sth
malpensado *adj*: **ser malpensado** have a nasty mind
malsano *adj* unhealthy
malsonante *adj* rude
malta *f* malt
maltratar ⟨1a⟩ *v/t* mistreat
maltrato *m* abuse, harsh words *pl*
maltrecho *adj* weakened, diminished; *cosa* damaged
malva *adj* mauve
malvado *adj* evil
malversación *f*: **malversación de fondos** embezzlement

malversar ⟨1a⟩ v/t embezzle
Malvinas: las Malvinas the Falklands, the Falkland Islands
malvivir ⟨3a⟩ v/i scrape by
mamá f mom, Br mum
mama f breast
mamadera f L.Am. feeding bottle
mamar ⟨1a⟩ v/i suck; **dar de mamar** (breast)feed
mamarracho m: **vas hecho un mamarracho** F you look a mess F
mamífero m mammal
mamila f Méx feeding bottle
mamografía f MED mammography
mamón 1 adj Méx P cocky 2 m P bastard P
mamona f P bitch P
mamotreto m F libro hefty tome
mampara f screen
mamporro m F punch
mampostería f masonry
maná m fig manna
manada f herd; **de lobos** pack
manantial m spring
manar ⟨1a⟩ v/i flow
manatí m zo manatee
manaza f: **ser un manazas** F be ham-handed F
mancebo m youth
Mancha: Canal de la Mancha English Channel
mancha f (dirty) mark; **de grasa, sangre etc** stain
manchar ⟨1a⟩ 1 v/t get dirty; **de grasa, sangre etc** stain 2 v/r **mancharse** get dirty
mancillar ⟨1a⟩ v/t fig sully
manco adj **de mano** one-handed; **de brazo** one-armed
mancornas fpl Pe, Bol cufflinks
mancuernas fpl C.Am. cufflinks
mandamás m inv F big shot F
mandado m Méx, C.Am.: **los mandados** pl the shopping sg
mandamiento m order; JUR warrant; REL commandment
mandar ⟨1a⟩ 1 v/t order; (enviar) send; **a mí no me manda nadie** nobody tells me what to do; **mandar hacer algo** have sth done 2 v/i be in charge; **¿mande?** Méx can I help you?; Méx TELEC hallo?; **(¿cómo?)** what did you say?, excuse me?
mandarina f mandarin (orange)
mandatario m leader; **primer mandatario** Méx President
mandato m order; POL mandate
mandíbula f ANAT jaw; **reírse a mandíbula batiente** F laugh one's head off F
mandioca f cassava

mando m command; **alto mando** high command; **mando a distancia** TV remote control; **tablero de mandos** AUTO dashboard
mandolina f MÚS mandolin
mandón adj F bossy
manecilla f hand
manejable adj easy to handle; **automóvil** maneuverable, Br manoeuvrable
manejar ⟨1a⟩ 1 v/t handle; **máquina** operate; L.Am. AUTO drive 2 v/i L.Am. AUTO drive 3 v/r **manejarse** manage, get by
manejo m handling; **de una máquina** operation
manera f way; **esa es su manera de ser** that's the way he is; **maneras** manners; **lo hace a su manera** he does it his way; **de manera que** so (that); **de ninguna manera** certainly not; **no hay manera** de it is impossible to; **de todas maneras** anyway, in any case
manga f sleeve; **manga de riego** hosepipe; **en mangas de camisa** in shirtsleeves; **sin mangas** sleeveless; **sacarse algo de la manga** fig make up sth; **traer algo en la manga** F have sth up one's sleeve
manganeso m manganese
mangar ⟨1h⟩ v/t swipe F, pinch F
mangle m BOT mangrove
mango m BOT mango; CSur F (dinero) dough F, cash; **estoy sin un mango** CSur F I'm broke F, I don't have a bean F
mangonear ⟨1a⟩ 1 v/i F boss people around; (entrometerse) meddle 2 v/t: **mangonear a alguien** boss s.o. around
manguera f hose(pipe)
maní m S. Am. peanut
manía f (costumbre) habit, mania; (antipatía) dislike; (obsesión) obsession; **manía persecutoria** persecution complex; **tiene sus -s** she has her little ways; **tener manía a alguien** F have it in for s.o. F
maníaco m maniac
maniatar ⟨1a⟩ v/t: **maniatar a alguien** tie s.o.'s hands
maniático adj F fussy
manicomio m lunatic asylum
manicura f manicure; **hacerse la manicura** have a manicure
manido adj fig clichéd, done to death F
manifestación f de gente demonstration; (muestra) show; (declaración) statement
manifestante m/f demonstrator
manifestar ⟨1k⟩ 1 v/t (demostrar) show; (declarar) declare, state 2 v/r **manifestarse** demonstrate
manifiesto 1 adj clear, manifest; **poner**

de manifiesto make clear **2** *m* manifesto

manigua *f* W.I. thicket, bush

manija *f* L.Am. (*asa*) handle

manillar *m* handlebars *pl*

maniobra *f* maneuver, *Br* manoeuvre; **hacer maniobras** maneuver, *Br* manoeuvre

maniobrar ⟨1a⟩ *v/i* maneuver, *Br* manoeuvre

manipulación *f* manipulation; (*manejo*) handling

manipular ⟨1a⟩ *v/t* manipulate; (*manejar*) handle

maniquí 1 *m* dummy **2** *m/f* model

manirroto 1 *adj* extravagant **2** *m*, **-a** *f* spendthrift

manisero *m*, **-a** *f* W.I., S. Am. peanut seller

manitas *fpl*: **ser un manitas** be handy

manito *m* Méx pal, buddy

manivela *f* handle

manjar *m* delicacy

mano 1 *f* hand; **mano de obra** labo(u)r, manpower; **mano de pintura** coat of paint; **¡manos arriba!** hands up!; **a mano derecha / izquierda** on the right/left; **atar las manos a alguien** *fig* tie s.o.'s hands; **de segunda mano** second-hand; **echar una mano a alguien** give s.o. a hand; **estar a manos** L.Am. F be even, be quits; **hecho a mano** handmade; **poner la mano en el fuego** *fig* swear to it; **poner manos a la obra** get down to work; **se le fue la mano con** *fig* he overdid it with; **tener a mano** have to hand; **traerse algo entre manos** be plotting sth **2** *m* Méx F pal, buddy F

manojo *m* handful; **manojo de llaves** bunch of keys; **manojo de nervios** *fig* bundle of nerves

manopla *f* mitten

manosear ⟨1a⟩ *v/t fruta* handle; *persona* F grope F

manotazo *m* slap

manotear ⟨1a⟩ **1** *v/t Arg, Méx* grab **2** *v/i Arg, Méx* wave one's hands around

mansalva *f*: **a mansalva** in vast numbers; *bebida, comida* in vast amounts

mansedumbre *f* docility; *de persona* mildness

mansión *f* mansion

manso *adj* docile; *persona* mild

manta *f* blanket; **tirar de la manta** *fig* uncover the truth

manteca *f* fat; *Rpl* butter; **manteca de cacao** cocoa butter; **manteca de cerdo** lard

mantel *m* tablecloth; **mantel individual** table mat

mantelería *f* table linen; **una mantelería** a set of table linen

mantención *f* L.Am. → **manutención**

mantener ⟨2l⟩ **1** *v/t* (*sujetar*) hold; *techo etc* hold up; (*preservar*) keep; *conversación, relación* have; *económicamente* support; (*afirmar*) maintain **2** *v/r* **mantenerse** (*sujetarse*) be held; *económicamente* support o.s.; *en forma* keep

mantenimiento *m* maintenance; *económico* support; **gimnasia de mantenimiento** gym

mantequilla *f* butter

mantequillera *f* L.Am. butter dish

mantilla *f de bebé* shawl; **estar en mantillas** *fig* F be in its infancy

mantuvo *vb* → **mantener**

manual *m/adj* manual

manualidades *fpl* handicrafts

manubrio *m* handle; S. Am. handlebars *pl*

manufacturar ⟨1a⟩ *v/t* manufacture

manuscrito 1 *adj* handwritten **2** *m* manuscript

manutención *f* maintenance

manzana *f* apple; *de casas* block; **manzana de la discordia** *fig* bone of contention

manzanilla *f* camomile tea

manzano *m* apple tree

maña *f* skill; **darse o tener maña para** be good at; **tiene muchas mañas** L.Am. she's got lots of tricks up her sleeve F

mañana 1 *f* morning; **por la mañana** in the morning; **mañana por la mañana** tomorrow morning; **de la mañana a la noche** from morning until night; **de la noche a la mañana** *fig* overnight; **esta mañana** this morning; **muy de mañana** very early (in the morning) **2** *adv* tomorrow; **pasado mañana** the day after tomorrow

mañanita *f* shawl

mañero *adj Rpl* (*animal: terco*) stubborn; (*nervioso*) skittish, nervous

mañoso *adj* skil(l)ful; L.Am. *animal* stubborn

mapa *m* map; **mapa de carreteras** road map

mapache *m* raccoon

mapamundi *m* map of the world

maqueta *f* model

maquillador *m*, **maquilladora** *f* make-up artist

maquillaje *m* make-up

maquillar ⟨1a⟩ **1** *v/t* make up **2** *v/r* **maquillarse** put on one's make-up

máquina *f* machine; FERR locomotive; C.Am., W.I. car; **máquina de afeitar** (electric) shaver; **máquina de coser**

sewing machine; **máquina de fotos** camera; **máquina recreativa** arcade game; **pasar algo a máquina** type sth; **a toda máquina** at top speed

maquinaciones *fpl* scheming *sg*

maquinador 1 *adj* scheming **2** *m*, **maquinadora** *f* schemer

maquinal *adj fig* mechanical

maquinar ⟨1a⟩ *v/t* plot

maquinaria *f* machinery

maquinilla *f*: **maquinilla de afeitar** razor; **maquinilla eléctrica** electric razor

maquinista *m/f* FERR engineer, *Br* train driver

mar *m* (*also f*) GEOG sea; **sudaba a mares** *fig* F the sweat was pouring off him F; **llover a mares** *fig* F pour, bucket down F; **alta mar** high seas *pl*; **la mar de bien** (*muy bien*) really well

maraca *f* MÚS maraca

maraña *f de hilos* tangle; (*lío*) jumble

marasmo *m fig* stagnation

maratón *m* (*also f*) marathon

maratoniano *adj* marathon *atr*

maravilla *f* marvel, wonder; BOT marigold; **de maravilla** marvellously, wonderfully; **a las mil maravillas** marvellously, wonderfully

maravillar ⟨1a⟩ **1** *v/t* amaze, astonish **2** *v/r* **maravillarse** be amazed *o* astonished (**de** at)

maravilloso *adj* marvellous, wonderful

marca *f* mark; COM brand; **marca registrada** registered trademark; **de marca** brand-name *atr*

marcador *m* DEP scoreboard

marcaje *m* DEP marking

marcapasos *m inv* MED pacemaker

marcar ⟨1g⟩ *v/t* mark; *número de teléfono* dial; *gol* score; *res* brand; *de termómetro, contador etc* read, register

marcha *f* (*salida*) departure; (*velocidad*) speed; (*avance*) progress; MIL march; AUTO gear; DEP walk; **marcha atrás** AUTO reverse (gear); **a marchas forzadas** *fig* flat out; **a toda marcha** at top speed; **hacer algo sobre la marcha** do sth as one goes along; **ponerse en marcha** get started, get going; **tener mucha marcha** F be very lively

marchante *m L.Am.* regular customer

marchar ⟨1a⟩ **1** *v/i* (*progresar*) go; (*funcionar*) work; (*caminar*) walk; MIL march **2** *v/r* **marcharse** leave, go

marchitarse ⟨1a⟩ *v/r* wilt

marchito *adj* withered

marcial *adj* martial; **artes marciales** martial arts

marciano *m* Martian

marco *m moneda* mark; *de cuadro, puerta* frame; *fig* framework

marea *f* tide; **marea alta** high tide; **marea baja** low tide; **marea negra** oil slick

mareado *adj* dizzy

marear ⟨1a⟩ **1** *v/t* make feel nauseous, *Br* make feel sick; *fig* (*confundir*) confuse **2** *v/r* **marearse** feel nauseous, *Br* feel sick

marejada *f* heavy sea

maremoto *m* tidal wave

mareo *m* seasickness

marfil *m* ivory

margarina *f* margarine

margarita *f* BOT daisy

margen *m tb fig* margin; **al margen de eso** apart from that; **mantenerse al margen** keep out

marginación *f* marginalization

marginal *adj* marginal

marginar ⟨1a⟩ *v/t* marginalize

mariachi 1 *m* mariachi band **2** *m/f* mariachi player

marica *m* F fag P, *Br* poof P

maricón *m* P fag P, *Br* poof P

marido *m* husband

marihuana *f* marijuana

marimacho *m* F butch woman

marimba *f Rpl* MÚS marimba

marina *f* navy; **marina mercante** merchant navy

marinar ⟨1a⟩ *v/t* GASTR marinade

marinero 1 *adj* sea *atr* **2** *m* sailor

marino 1 *adj brisa* sea *atr*; *planta, animal* marine; **azul marino** navy blue **2** *m* sailor

marioneta *f tb fig* puppet

mariposa *f* butterfly

mariquita *f* ladybug, *Br* ladybird

marisco *m* seafood

marisma *f* salt marsh

marítimo *adj* maritime

marketing *m* marketing

marmita *f* pot, pan

mármol *m* marble

marmota *f*: **dormir como una marmota** F sleep like a log

marqués *m* marquis

marquesa *f* marchioness

marquesina *f* marquee, *Br* canopy

marranada *f* F dirty trick

marrano 1 *adj* filthy **2** *m* hog, *Br* pig; F *persona* pig F

marras *adv*: **el ordenador de marras** the darned computer F

marrón *m/adj* brown

marroquinería *f* leather goods

Marruecos Morocco

marta *f* ZO marten

Marte *m* AST Mars

martes *m inv* Tuesday

martillero *m S. Am.* auctioneer

martillo *m* hammer; *martillo neumático* pneumatic drill

martín *m*: *martín pescador* zo kingfisher

mártir *m/f* martyr

martirio *m tb fig* martyrdom

martirizar ⟨1f⟩ *v/t tb fig* martyr

marzo *m* March

mas *conj* but

más 1 *adj* more **2** *adv comp* more; *sup* most; mat plus; *más grande / pequeño* bigger / smaller; *el más grande / pequeño* the largest / smallest; *trabajar más* work harder; *más bien* rather; *más que, más de lo que* more than; *más o menos* more or less; *¿qué más?* what else?; *no más L.Am.* → *nomás*; *por más que* however much; *sin más* without more ado; *más lejos* further

masa *f* mass; gastr dough; *pillar a alguien con las manos en la masa* F catch s.o. red-handed

masacrar ⟨1a⟩ *v/t* massacre

masacre *f* massacre

masaje *m* massage

masajista *m/f* masseur; *mujer* masseuse

mascar ⟨1g⟩ **1** *v/t* chew **2** *v/i L.Am.* chew tobacco

máscara *f* mask

mascarilla *f* mask; *cosmética* face pack

mascota *f* mascot; *animal doméstico* pet

masculino *adj* masculine

mascullar ⟨1a⟩ *v/t* mutter

masificación *f* overcrowding

masilla *f* putty

masita *f L.Am. small sweet cake or bun*

masivo *adj* massive

masón *m* mason

masoquismo *m* masochism

masoquista 1 *adj* masochistic **2** *m/f* masochist

máster *m* master's (degree)

masticación *f* chewing

masticar ⟨1g⟩ *v/t* chew

mástil *m* mast; *de tienda* pole

mastín *m* zo mastiff

mastodóntico *adj* colossal, enormous

mastuerzo *m* bot cress

masturbarse ⟨1a⟩ *v/r* masturbate

mata *f* bush

matadero *m* slaughterhouse

matador *m* taur matador

matanza *f de animales* slaughter; *de gente* slaughter, massacre

matar ⟨1a⟩ **1** *v/t* kill; *ganado* slaughter **2** *v/r matarse* kill o.s.; *morir* be killed; *matarse a trabajar* work o.s. to death

matarratas *m* rat poison

matasanos *m/f inv* F quack F

matasellos *m inv* postmark

mate 1 *adj* matt **2** *m en ajedrez* mate; *L.Am.* (*infusión*) maté

matear ⟨1a⟩ **1** *v/t CSur* checkmate **2** *v/i L.Am.* drink maté

matemáticas *fpl* mathematics

matemático 1 *adj* mathematical **2** *m*, -a *f* mathematician

materia *f* matter; (*material*) material; (*tema*) subject; *materia prima* raw material; *en materia de* as regards

material *m/adj* material

materialismo *m* materialism

materializar ⟨1f⟩ *v/t*: *materializar algo* make sth a reality

maternal *adj* maternal

materno *adj* maternal

matinal *adj* morning *atr*

matero *m*, -a *f L.Am.* maté drinker

matiz *m de ironía* touch; *de color* shade

matizar ⟨1f⟩ *v/t comentarios* qualify

matón *m* bully; (*criminal*) thug

matorral *m* thicket

matrícula *f* auto license plate, *Br* numberplate; edu enrol(l)ment, registration

matricular ⟨1a⟩ **1** *v/t* register **2** *v/r matricularse* edu enrol(l), register

matrimonial *adj* marriage *atr*, marital

matrimonio *m* marriage; *boda* wedding

matriz *f* matrix; anat womb

matrona *f* (*comadrona*) midwife

matutino *adj* morning *atr*

maullar ⟨1a⟩ *v/i* miaow

maullido *m* miaow

mausoleo *m* mausoleum

máxima *f* maxim

máxime *adv* especially

máximo *adj* maximum

mayo *m* May

mayonesa *f* gastr mayonnaise

mayor 1 *adj comp*: *en tamaño* larger, bigger; *en edad* older; *en importancia* greater; *ser mayor de edad* be an adult; *al por mayor* com wholesale **2** *adj sup*: *el mayor en edad* the oldest *o* eldest; *en tamaño* the largest *o* biggest; *en importancia* the greatest; *los mayores* adults; *la mayor parte* the majority

mayordomo *m* butler

mayoreo *m*: *vender al mayoreo Méx* sell wholesale

mayoría *f* majority; *alcanzar la mayoría de edad* come of age; *la mayoría de* the majority of, most (of); *en la mayoría de los casos* in the majority of cases, in most cases

mayorista *m/f* wholesaler

mayoritario *adj* majority *atr*

mayúscula *f* capital (letter), upper case letter

melocotón

mazamorra *f* S. Am. kind of porridge made from corn

mazapán *m* marzipan

mazmorra *f* dungeon

mazo *m* mallet

mazorca *f* cob

me *pron pers complemento directo* me; *complemento indirecto* (to) me; *reflexivo* myself; *me dio el libro* he gave me the book, he gave the book to me

mear ⟨1a⟩ F **1** *v/i* pee F **2** *v/r* **mearse** pee o.s. F; *mearse de risa* wet o.s. (laughing) F

meca *f fig* mecca

mecachis *int* F blast! F

mecánica *f* mechanics

mecánico 1 *adj* mechanical **2** *m*, **-a** *f* mechanic

mecanismo *m* mechanism

mecanizar ⟨1f⟩ *v/t* mechanize

mecanógrafo *m*, **-a** *f* typist

mecanografiar ⟨1c⟩ *v/t* type

mecate *m* Méx string, cord

mecedora *f* rocking chair

mecenas *m inv* patron, sponsor

mecer ⟨2b⟩ **1** *v/t* rock **2** *v/r* **mecerse** rock

mecha *f* wick; *de explosivo* fuse; *del pelo* highlight; Méx F fear

mechero *m* cigarette lighter

mechón *m de pelo* lock

medalla *f* medal

medallista *m/f* medal(l)ist

media *f* stocking; *medias pl* pantyhose *pl*, Br tights *pl*

mediación *f* mediation

mediado *adj*: *a mediados de junio* mid-June, halfway through June

mediador *m*, **mediadora** *f* mediator

mediana *f* AUTO median strip, Br central reservation

mediano *adj* medium, average

medianoche *f* midnight

mediante *prp* by means of

mediar ⟨1b⟩ *v/i* mediate

mediático *adj* media *atr*

medicación *f* medication

medicamento *m* medicine, drug

medicina *f* medicine

medicinal *adj* medicinal

médico 1 *adj* medical **2** *m/f* doctor; *médico de cabecera or de familia* family physician, Br GP, Br general practitioner; *médico de urgencia* emergency doctor

medida *f* measurement; *acto* measurement; *(grado)* extent; *hecho a medida* made to measure; *a medida que* as; *tomar medidas fig* take measures o steps

medidor *m* S. Am. meter

medieval *adj* medi(a)eval

medio 1 *adj* half; *tamaño* medium; *(de promedio)* average; *las tres y -a* half past three, three-thirty **2** *m* environment; *(centro)* middle, *(manera)* means; *medio ambiente* environment; *por medio de* by means of; *en medio de* in the middle of; *medios dinero* means, resources; *medios de comunicación* or *de información* (mass) media; *medios de transporte* means of transport **3** *adv* half; *hacer algo a -as* half do sth; *ir a -as* go halves; *día por medio* L.Am. every other day; *quitar de en medio algo* F move sth out of the way

medioambiental *adj* environmental

mediocre *adj* mediocre

mediodía *m* midday; *a mediodía* (*a las doce*) at noon, at twelve o'clock; (*a la hora de comer*) at lunchtime

medir ⟨3l⟩ **1** *v/t* measure **2** *v/i*: *mide 2 metros de ancho / largo / alto* it's 2 meters (*o Br* metres) wide / long / tall

meditación *f* meditation

meditar ⟨1a⟩ **1** *v/t* ponder **2** *v/i* meditate

Mediterráneo *m/adj*: (*mar*) *Mediterráneo* Mediterranean (Sea)

médium *m/f* medium

médula *f* marrow; *médula espinal* spinal cord; *hasta la médula fig* through and through, to the core

medusa *f* zo jellyfish

megafonía *f* public-address o PA system

megáfono *m* bullhorn, Br loud-hailer

megalomanía *f* megalomania

mejicano 1 *adj* Mexican **2** *m*, **-a** *f* Mexican

Méjico Mexico; Méx DF Mexico City

mejilla *f* cheek

mejillón *m* zo mussel

mejor *adj comp* better; *el mejor sup* best; *lo mejor* the best thing; *lo mejor posible* as well as possible; *a lo mejor* perhaps, maybe; *tanto mejor* all the better

mejora *f* improvement

mejorana *f* BOT marjoram

mejorar ⟨1a⟩ **1** *v/t* improve **2** *v/i* improve; *¡que te mejores!* get well soon!

mejoría *f* improvement

mejunje *m desp* concoction

melancolía *f* melancholy

melancólico *adj* gloomy, melancholic

melena *f* long hair; *de león* mane

melindroso *adj* affected

mella *f*: *hacer mella en alguien* have an effect on s.o., affect s.o.

mellado *adj* gap-toothed

mellizo 1 *adj* twin *atr* **2** *m*, **-a** *f* twin

melocotón *m* peach

M

melocotonero *m* peach tree

melodía *f* melody

melodrama *m* melodrama

melón *m* melon

membrana *f* membrane

membrillo *m* quince; *dulce de membrillo* quince jelly

memela *f* *Méx* corn tortilla

memo 1 *adj* F dumb F **2** *m*, -a *f* F idiot

memorable *adj* memorable

memoria *f tb* INFOR memory; (*informe*) report; *de memoria* by heart; *memorias* (*biografía*) memoirs

memorizar ⟨1f⟩ *v/t* memorize

mención *f*: *hacer mención de* mention

mencionar ⟨1a⟩ *v/t* mention

mendigar ⟨1h⟩ *v/t* beg for

mendigo *m* beggar

menear ⟨1a⟩ **1** *v/t* shake; *las caderas* sway; *menear la cola* wag its tail **2** *v/r* menearse fidget

menestra *f* vegetable stew

mengano *m*, -a *f* F so-and-so F

menguante *adj* decreasing, diminishing; *luna* waning

menguar ⟨1i⟩ *v/i* decrease, diminish; *de la luna* wane

meningitis *f* MED meningitis

menopausia *f* MED menopause

menor *adj comp* less; *en tamaño* smaller; *en edad* younger; *ser menor de edad* be a minor; *al por menor* COM retail; *el menor sup*: *en tamaño* the smallest; *en edad* the youngest; *el número menor* the lowest number

menos 1 *adj en cantidad* less; *en número* fewer **2** *adv comp en cantidad* less; *sup en cantidad* least; MAT minus; *es menos guapa que Ana* she is not as pretty as Ana; *tres menos dos* three minus two; *a menos que* unless; *al menos, por lo menos* at least; *echar de menos* miss; *eso es lo de menos* that's the least of it; *ni mucho menos* far from it; *son las dos menos diez* it's ten of two, it's ten to two

menoscabar ⟨1a⟩ *v/t autoridad* diminish; (*dañar*) harm

menospreciar ⟨1b⟩ *v/t* underestimate; (*desdeñar*) look down on

mensaje *m* message

mensajero *m* courier

menstruación *f* menstruation

menstruar ⟨1h⟩ *v/i* menstruate

mensual *adj* monthly

mensualidad *f* monthly instal(l)ment, monthly payment

mensualmente *adv* monthly

menta *f* BOT mint

mental *adj* mental

mentalidad *f* mentality

mentalizar ⟨1f⟩ **1** *v/t*: *mentalizar a alguien* make s.o. aware **2** *v/r* mentalizarse mentally prepare o.s.

mente *f* mind

mentecato 1 *adj* F dim F **2** *m* F fool

mentir ⟨3i⟩ *v/i* lie

mentira *f* lie

mentiroso 1 *adj*: *ser muy mentiroso* tell a lot of lies **2** *m*, -a *f* liar

mentón *m* chin

mentor *m* mentor

menú *m tb* INFOR menu; *menú de ayuda* help menu

menudencias *fpl Méx* giblets

menudeo *m* L.Am. retail trade

menudo 1 *adj* small; *¡a suerte!* fig F lucky devil!; *¡-as vacaciones!* irón F some vacation!; *a menudo* often **2** *m* L.Am. small change; *menudos* GASTR giblets

meñique *m*/*adj*: (*dedo*) *meñique* little finger

meollo *m* fig heart

mercader *m* trader

mercadería *f* L.Am. merchandise

mercadillo *m* street market

mercado *m* market; *Mercado Común* Common Market; *mercado negro* black market

mercadotecnia *f* marketing

mercancía *f* merchandise

mercantil *adj* commercial

merced *f*: *estar a merced de alguien* be at s.o.'s mercy

mercenario *m*/*adj* mercenary

mercería *f* notions *pl*, *Br* haberdashery

MERCOSUR *abr* (= *Mercado Común del Sur*) Common Market including Argentina, Brazil, Paraguay and Uruguay

mercurio *m* mercury

merecer ⟨2d⟩ *v/t* deserve; *no merecer la pena* it's not worth it

merecido *m* just deserts *pl*

merendar ⟨1k⟩ **1** *v/t*: *merendar algo* have sth as an afternoon snack **2** *v/i* have an afternoon snack

merengue *m* GASTR meringue

meridiano *m*/*f* meridian

meridional 1 *adj* southern **2** *m* southerner

merienda *f* afternoon snack

mérito *m* merit

merluza *f* zo hake; *agarrar una merluza* fig F get plastered F

mermar ⟨1a⟩ **1** *v/t* reduce **2** *v/i* diminish

mermelada *f* jam

mero 1 *adj* mere; *el mero jefe Méx* F the big boss **2** *m* zo grouper

merodear ⟨1a⟩ v/i loiter
mes m month
mesa f table; mesa redonda fig round table; poner / quitar la mesa set / clear the table
mesera f L.Am. waitress
mesero m L.Am. waiter
meseta f plateau
mesilla, mesita f: mesilla (de noche) night stand, Br bedside table
mesón m traditional restaurant decorated in rustic style
mestizo m person of mixed race
mesura f: con mesura in moderation
meta f en fútbol goal; en carrera finishing line; fig (objetivo) goal, objective
metabolismo m metabolism
metafísica f metaphysics
metáfora f metaphor
metal m metal
metálico 1 adj metallic 2 m: en metálico (in) cash
metalúrgico adj metallurgical
metamorfosis f inv transformation, metamorphosis
medura f: medura de pata F blunder
meteorito m meteorite
meteorológico adj weather atr, meteorological; pronóstico meteorológico weather forecast
meteorólogo m, -a f meteorologist
meter ⟨2a⟩ 1 v/t gen put (en in, into); (involucrar) involve (en in); meter a alguien en un lío get s.o. into a mess 2 v/r meterse: meterse en algo get into sth, (involucrarse) get involved in sth, get mixed up in sth; meterse con alguien pick on s.o.; meterse de administrativo get a job in admin; ¿dónde se ha metido? where has he got to?
meticuloso adj meticulous
metido adj involved; L.Am. F nosy F; estar muy metido en algo be very involved in sth
metódico adj methodical
método m method
metomentodo m/f F busybody F
metralleta f sub-machine gun
métrico adj metric
metro m medida meter, Br metre; para medir rule; transporte subway, Br underground
metrópolis f inv metropolis
metropolitano adj metropolitan
mexicano 1 adj Mexican 2 m, -a Mexican
México Mexico; Méx DF Mexico City
mezcal m Méx mescal
mezcla f sustancia mixture; de tabaco, café etc blend; acto mixing; de tabaco, café

etc blending
mezclar ⟨1a⟩ 1 v/t mix; tabaco, café etc blend; mezclar a alguien en algo get s.o. mixed up o involved in sth 2 v/r mezclarse mix; mezclarse en algo get mixed up o involved in sth
mezquinar ⟨1a⟩ v/t L.Am. skimp on
mezquino adj mean
mezquita f mosque
mg. abr (= miligramo) mg (= milligram)
mi, mis adj pos my
mí pron me; reflexivo myself; ¿y a mí qué? so what?, what's it to me?
michelín m F spare tire, Br spare tyre
mico m ZO monkey
micro m or f Chi bus
microbio m microbe
microbús m minibus
microchip m (micro)chip
microfilm(e) m microfilm
micrófono m microphone; micrófono oculto bug
microondas m inv microwave
microordenador m microcomputer
microprocesador m microprocessor
microscópico adj microscopic
microscopio m microscope
mide vb → medir
miedo m fear (a of); dar miedo be frightening; me da miedo la oscuridad I'm frightened of the dark; tener miedo de que be afraid that; por miedo a for fear of; de miedo F great F, awesome F
miedoso adj timid; ¡no seas tan miedoso! don't be scared!
miel f honey
miembro m member; (extremidad) limb, member fml
mientras 1 conj while; mientras que whereas 2 adv: mientras tanto in the meantime, meanwhile
miércoles m inv Wednesday
mierda f P shit P, crap P; una mierda de película a crap movie P; ¡una mierda! no way! P
miga f de pan crumb; migas crumbs; hacer buenas / malas migas fig F get on well / badly
migraña f MED migraine
migratorio adj migratory
mijo m BOT millet
mil adj thousand
milagro m miracle; de milagro miraculously, by a miracle
milagroso adj miraculous
milano m ZO kite
milenio m millennium
mili f F military service
milicia f militia

M

milico *m S. Am. desp* soldier
milímetro *m* millimeter, *Br* millimetre
militante *m/f & adj* militant
militar 1 *adj* military 2 *m* soldier; *los militares* the military 3 ⟨1a⟩ *v/i* POL: *militar en* be a member of
milla *f* mile
millar *m* thousand
millón *m* million; *(mil millones)* billion
millonario *m* millionaire
milpa *f Méx, C.Am.* corn, *Br* maize; *terreno* cornfield, *Br* field of maize
mimar ⟨1a⟩ *v/t* spoil, pamper
mimbre *m* BOT willow; *muebles pl de mimbre* wicker furniture *sg*
mímica *f* mime
mimo *m* TEA mime
mimosa *f* BOT mimosa
mimoso *adj*: *ser mimoso* be cuddly
mina *f* MIN mine; *Rpl* F broad F, *Br* bird F; *mina antipersonal* MIL antipersonnel mine
minar ⟨1a⟩ *v/t* mine; *fig* undermine
mineral *m/adj* mineral
minería *f* mining
minero 1 *adj* mining 2 *m* miner
miniatura *f* miniature
minifalda *f* miniskirt
minimizar ⟨1f⟩ *v/t* minimize
mínimo 1 *adj* minimum; *como mínimo* at the very least 2 *m* minimum
minino *m* F puss F, pussy (cat) F
ministerio *m* POL department; *ministerio de Asuntos Exteriores*, *L.Am.* ministerio de Relaciones Exteriores State Department, *Br* Foreign Office; *ministerio de Hacienda* Treasury Department, *Br* Treasury; *ministerio del Interior* Department of the Interior, *Br* Home Office
ministro *m*, -a *f* minister; *ministro del Interior* Secretary of the Interior, *Br* Home Secretary; *primer ministro* Prime Minister
minoría *f* minority
minorista COM 1 *adj* retail *atr* 2 *m/f* retailer
minoritario *adj* minority *atr*
mintió *vb* → *mentir*
minucia *f* minor detail
minucioso *adj* meticulous, thorough
minúscula *f* small letter, lower case letter
minúsculo *adj* tiny, minute
minusvalía *f* disability
minusválido 1 *adj* disabled 2 *m*, -a *f* disabled person; *los minusválidos* the disabled
minutero *m* minute hand
minuto *m* minute
mío, mía *pron* mine; *el mío / la -a* mine

miope *adj* near-sighted, short-sighted
miopía *f* near-sightedness, short-sightedness
mira *f*: *con miras a* with a view to
mirada *f* look; *echar una mirada* take a look (*a* at)
mirador *m* viewpoint
mirar ⟨1a⟩ 1 *v/t* look at; *(observar)* watch; *L.Am.* (ver) see; *¿qué miras desde aquí?* what can you see from here? 2 *v/i* look; *mirar al norte de una ventana etc* face north; *mirar por la ventana* look out of the window
mirilla *f* spyhole
mirlo *m* ZO blackbird
misa *f* REL mass
misántropo *m* misanthropist
miserable *adj* wretched
miseria *f* poverty; *fig* misery
misericordia *f* mercy, compassion
mísero *adj* wretched; *sueldo* miserable
misil *m* missile
misión *f* mission
misionero *m*, -a *f* missionary
mismo 1 *adj* same; *lo mismo que* the same as; *yo mismo* I myself; *da lo mismo* it doesn't matter, it's all the same; *me da lo mismo* I don't care, it's all the same to me 2 *adv*: *aquí mismo* right here; *ahora mismo* right now, this very minute
misógino *adj* misogynistic
misterio *m* mystery
misterioso *adj* mysterious
místico *adj* mystic(al)
mitad *f* half; *(= mitad del camino)* halfway; *a mitad de la película* halfway through the movie; *a mitad de precio* half-price
mítico *adj* mythical
mitigar ⟨1h⟩ *v/t* mitigate; *ansiedad, dolor etc* ease
mitin *m* POL meeting
mito *m* myth
mitología *f* mythology
mixto *adj* mixed; *comisión* joint
mm. *abr (= milímetro)* mm (= millimeter)
mobiliario *m* furniture
mochila *f* backpack
mochilero *m*, -a *f* backpacker
mochuelo *m* ZO little owl
moción *f* POL motion; *moción de confianza* /censura vote of confidence / no confidence
moco *m*: *tener mocos* have a runny nose
mocoso *m*, -a *f* F snotty-nosed kid F
moda *f* fashion; *de moda* fashionable, in fashion; *estar pasado de moda* be out of fashion
modales *mpl* manners

modalidad f form; DEP discipline; **modalidad de pago** method of payment
modelar ⟨1a⟩ v/t model
modelismo m model making
modelo 1 m model 2 m/f **persona** model
módem m INFOR modem
moderado 1 adj moderate 2 m, -a f moderate
moderador m, **moderadora** f TV presenter
moderar ⟨1a⟩ **1** v/t moderate; *impulsos* control, restrain; *velocidad, gastos* reduce; *debate* chair **2** v/r **moderarse** control o.s., restrain o.s.
modernización f modernization
modernizar ⟨1f⟩ v/t modernize
moderno adj modern
modestia f modesty; **modestia aparte** though I say so myself
modesto adj modest
módico adj precio reasonable
modificación f modification
modificar ⟨1g⟩ v/t modify
modista m/f dressmaker; *diseñador* fashion designer
modo m way; **a modo de** as; **de modo que** so that; **de ningún modo** not at all; **en cierto modo** in a way o sense; **de todos modos** anyway
modorra f drowsiness
módulo m module
mofarse ⟨1a⟩ v/r: **mofarse de** make fun of
mofeta f ZO skunk
mofletes mpl chubby cheeks
mogollón m F (discusión) argument; **mogollón de** F loads of F
moho m mo(u)ld
moisés m inv Moses basket
mojado adj (húmedo) damp, moist; (empapado) wet
mojar ⟨1a⟩ **1** v/t (humedecer) dampen, moisten; (empapar) wet; galleta dunk, dip **2** v/r **mojarse** get wet
mojigato 1 adj prudish 2 m, -a f prude
mojón m tb fig milestone
molar ⟨2h⟩ **1** v/t: **me mola ese tío** P I like the guy a lot **2** v/i P be cool F
molcajete m Méx, C.Am. (mortero) grinding stone
molde m mo(u)ld; *para bizcocho* (cake) tin; **romper moldes** fig break the mo(u)ld
moldear ⟨1a⟩ v/t mo(u)ld
moldura f ARQUI mo(u)lding
mole 1 f mass 2 m Méx mole (spicy sauce made with chilies and tomatoes)
molécula f molecule
moler ⟨2h⟩ v/t grind; fruta mash; **carne**

molida ground meat, Br mince; **moler a alguien a palos** fig beat s.o. to a pulp
molestar ⟨1a⟩ **1** v/t bother, annoy; (doler) trouble; **no molestar** do not disturb **2** v/r **molestarse** get upset; (ofenderse) take offense (Br offence); (enojarse) get annoyed; **molestarse en hacer algo** take the trouble to do sth
molestia f nuisance; **molestias** pl MED discomfort sg
molesto adj annoying; (incómodo) inconvenient
molestoso adj L.Am. annoying
molido adj F bushed F
molinillo m: **molinillo de café** coffee grinder o mill
molino m mill; **molino de viento** windmill
mollera f F head; **duro de mollera** F pigheaded F
molusco m ZO mollusk, Br mollusc
momento m moment; **al momento** at once; **por el momento, de momento** for the moment
momia f mummy
momificar ⟨1g⟩ v/t mummify
monada f: **su hija es una monada** her daughter is lovely; **¡qué monada!** how lovely!
monaguillo m altar boy
monarca m monarch
monarquía f monarchy
monasterio m monastery
mondadientes m inv toothpick
mondar ⟨1a⟩ **1** v/t peel; árbol prune **2** v/r **mondarse: mondarse de risa** F split one's sides laughing
mondongo m tripe
moneda f coin; (divisa) currency
monedero m change purse, Br purse
monetario adj monetary
monigote m rag doll; F (tonto) idiot
monitor[1] m TV, INFOR monitor
monitor[2] m, **monitora** f (profesor) instructor
monja f nun
monje m monk
mono 1 m ZO monkey; *prenda* coveralls pl, Br boilersuit 2 adj pretty, cute
monógamo adj monogamous
monólogo m monolog(ue)
monopatín m skateboard
monopolio m monopoly
monopolizar ⟨1f⟩ v/t tb fig monopolize
monosílabo adj monosyllabic
monotonía f monotony
monótono adj monotonous
monovolumen m AUTO minivan, Br people carrier, MPV

M

monsergas *fpl*: *déjate de monsergas* F stop going on F

monstruo *m* monster; (*fenómeno*) phenomenon

monstruosidad *f* eyesore, monstrosity

monstruoso *adj* monstrous

monta *f*: *de poca monta* unimportant

montacargas *m inv* hoist

montada *f L.Am.* mounted police

montaje *m* TÉC assembly; *de película* editing; TEA staging; *fig* F con F

montante *m* COM total

montaña *f* mountain; *montaña rusa* rollercoaster

montañero *m*, **-a** *f* mountaineer

montañismo *m* mountaineering

montañoso *adj* mountainous

montaplatos *m inv* dumb waiter

montar ⟨1a⟩ **1** *v/t* TÉC assemble; *tienda* put up; *negocio* set up; *película* edit; *caballo* mount; *montar la guardia* mount guard **2** *v/i*: *montar en bicicleta* ride a bicycle; *montar a caballo* ride a horse

monte *m* mountain; (*bosque*) woodland

montículo *m* mound

montón *m* pile, heap; *ser del montón* *fig* be average, not stand out; *montones de* F piles of F, loads of F

montura *f de gafas* frame

monumento *m* monument

moño *m* bun

moqueta *f* (wall-to-wall) carpet

mora *f* BOT *de zarza* blackberry; *de morera* mulberry

morada *f* dwelling

morado *adj* purple; *pasarlas -as* F have a rough time

moral 1 *adj* moral **2** *f* (*moralidad*) morals *pl*; (*ánimo*) morale

moraleja *f* moral

moralidad *f* morality

moralista *m/f* moralist

moratón *m* bruise

moratoria *f* moratorium

morbo *m* F perverted kind of pleasure

morboso *adj* perverted

morcilla *f* blood sausage, *Br* black pudding

mordaz *adj* biting

mordaza *f* gag

morder ⟨2h⟩ *v/t* bite

mordida *f Méx* F bribe

mordisco *m* bite

mordisquear ⟨1a⟩ *v/t* nibble

morena *f* ZO moray eel

moreno *adj pelo, piel* dark; (*bronceado*) tanned

morera *f* BOT white mulberry tree

moretón *m L.Am.* bruise

morfina *f* morphine

morfología *f* morphology

moribundo *adj* dying

morir ⟨3k; *part* *muerto*⟩ **1** *v/i* die (*de* of); *morir de hambre* die of hunger, starve to death **2** *v/r* **morirse** die; *morirse de* *fig* die of; *morirse por* *fig* be dying for

morisco *adj* Moorish

mormón *m* Mormon

moro 1 *adj* North African **2** *m* North African; *no hay moros en la costa* F the coast is clear

morocho *adj S. Am. persona* dark

moronga *f C.Am., Méx* blood sausage, *Br* black pudding

morralla *f Méx* small change

morriña *f* homesickness

morro *m* ZO snout; *tener mucho morro* F have a real nerve

morrongo *m* F pussycat F

morsa *f* ZO walrus

mortaja *f* shroud; *L.Am.* cigarette paper

mortal 1 *adj* mortal; *accidente, herida* fatal; *dosis* lethal **2** *m/f* mortal

mortalidad *f* mortality

mortalmente *adv* fatally

mortero *m* *tb* MIL mortar

mortífero *adj* lethal

mortificar ⟨1g⟩ **1** *v/t* torment **2** *v/r* **mortificarse** *fig* distress o.s.; *Méx* (*apenarse*) be embarrassed *o* ashamed

mosaico *m* mosaic

mosca *f* fly; *por si las moscas* F just to be on the safe side

moscada *adj*: *nuez moscada* nutmeg

moscardón *m* hornet

Moscú Moscow

mosquear ⟨1a⟩ **1** *v/t Esp* F rile **2** *v/r* **mosquearse** F get hot under the collar F; (*sentir recelo*) smell a rat F

mosquitero *m* mosquito net

mosquito *m* mosquito

mostaza *f* mustard

mosto *m* grape juice

mostrador *m* counter; *en bar* bar; *mostrador de facturación* check-in desk

mostrar ⟨1m⟩ **1** *v/t* show **2** *v/r* **mostrarse**: *mostrarse contento* seem happy

mota *f* speck; *en diseño* dot

mote *m* nickname; *S. Am.* boiled corn *o* *Br* maize

motel *m* motel

motín *m* mutiny; *en una cárcel* riot

motivación *f* motivation

motivar ⟨1a⟩ *v/t* motivate

motivo *m* motive, reason; MÚS, PINT motif; *con motivo de* because of

moto *f* motorcycle, motorbike; *moto acuática* *or* *de agua* jet ski

motocicleta f motorcycle

motociclismo m motorcycle racing

motociclista m/f motorcyclist

motocross m motocross

motor m engine; eléctrico motor

motora f motorboat

motorista m/f motorcyclist

motosierra f chain saw

motriz adj motor

mover ⟨2h⟩ 1 v/t move; (agitar) shake; (impulsar, incitar) drive 2 v/r moverse move; ¡muévete! get a move on! F, hurry up!

movida f F scene

móvil 1 adj mobile 2 m TELEC cellphone, Br mobile (phone)

movilidad f mobility

movilizar ⟨1f⟩ v/t mobilize

movimiento m movement; COM, fig activity

moza f girl; camarera waitress

mozo 1 adj: en mis años mozos in my youth 2 m boy; camarero waiter

mucama f Rpl maid

mucamo m Rpl servant

muchacha f girl

muchachada f Arg group of youngsters

muchacho m boy

muchedumbre f crowd

mucho 1 adj cantidad a lot of, lots of; esp neg much; no tengo mucho dinero I don't have much money; muchos a lot of, lots of many; esp neg many; no tengo muchos amigos I don't have many friends; tengo mucho frío I am very cold; es mucho coche para mí it's too big a car for me 2 adv a lot; esp neg much; no me gustó mucho I didn't like it very much; ¿dura / tarda mucho? does it last / take long?; como mucho at the most; ni mucho menos far from it; por mucho que however much 3 pron a lot, much; muchos a lot of people, many people

muda f de ropa change of clothes

mudanza f de casa move

mudarse ⟨1a⟩ v/r: mudarse de casa move house; mudarse de ropa change (one's clothes)

mudo adj mute; letra silent

mueble m piece of furniture

mueca f de dolor grimace; hacer muecas make faces

muela f tooth; ANAT molar; muela del juicio wisdom tooth

muelle m TÉC spring; MAR wharf

muérdago m BOT mistletoe

muerde vb → morder

muere vb → morir

muermo m fig F boredom; ser un muermo fig F be a drag F

muerte f death; de mala muerte fig F lousy F, awful F

muerto 1 part → morir 2 adj dead 3 m, -a f dead person

muestra f sample; (señal) sign; (exposición) show

muestrario m collection of samples

mueve vb → mover

mugir ⟨3c⟩ v/i moo

mugre f filth

mugriento adj filthy

mugroso adj dirty

mujer f woman; (esposa) wife

mujeriego m womanizer

mújol m zo gray o Br grey mullet

mula f mule; Méx trash, Br rubbish

mulato m mulatto

muleta f crutch; TAUR cape

mullido adj soft

mullir ⟨3h⟩ v/t almohada plump up

multa f fine

multar ⟨1a⟩ v/t fine

multicine m multiscreen

multicolor adj multicolo(u)red

multilateral adj multilateral

multimedia f/adj multimedia

multimillonario m multimillionaire

multinacional f multinational

múltiple adj multiple

multiplicación f multiplication

multiplicar ⟨1g⟩ 1 v/t multiply 2 v/r multiplicarse multiply

múltiplo m MAT multiple

multipropiedad f timeshare

multitud f crowd, multitud de thousands of

multitudinario adj mass atr

multiuso adj multipurpose

mundano adj society atr; REL wordly

mundial 1 adj world atr 2 m: el mundial de fútbol the World Cup

mundo m world; el otro mundo the next world; nada del otro mundo nothing out of the ordinary; todo el mundo everybody, everyone

munición f ammunition

municipal adj municipal

municipio m municipality

muñeca f doll; ANAT wrist

muñeco m doll; fig puppet; muñeco de nieve snowman

muñón m MED stump

mural adj wall atr 2 m mural

muralla f de ciudad wall

murciélago m zo bat

murga f: dar la murga a alguien F bug s.o. F

M

murió vb → **morir**
murmullo m murmur
murmurar ⟨1a⟩ v/i hablar murmur; *criticar* gossip
muro m wall
musa f muse
musaraña f zo shrew; **pensar en las musarañas** F daydream
muscular adj muscular
músculo m muscle
musculoso adj muscular
museo m museum; *de pintura* art gallery
musgo m BOT moss
música f music

musical m/adj musical
músico m, -a f musician
musitar ⟨1a⟩ v/i mumble
muslo m thigh
mustio adj withered; *fig* down F
musulmán 1 adj Muslim 2 m, -ana f Muslim
mutilado m, -a f disabled person
mutilar ⟨1a⟩ v/t mutilate
mutualidad f benefit society, *Br* friendly society
mutuo adj mutual
muy adv very; (*demasiado*) too; **muy valorado** highly valued

N, Ñ

N abr (= **norte**) N (North(ern))
nabo m 1 adj *Arg* F dumb F 2 m turnip
nácar m mother-of-pearl
nacatamal m *C.Am.*, *Méx* meat, rice and corn in a banana leaf
nacer ⟨2d⟩ v/i be born; *de un huevo* hatch; *de una planta* sprout; *de un río, del sol* rise; (*surgir*) arise (**de** from)
naciente adj *país*, *gobierno* newly formed; *sol* rising
nacimiento m birth; *de Navidad* crèche, nativity scene
nación f nation
nacional adj national
nacionalidad f nationality
nacionalismo m nationalism
nacionalización f COM nationalization
nacionalizar ⟨1f⟩ 1 v/t COM nationalize; *persona* naturalize 2 v/r **nacionalizarse** become naturalized
naco m *Col* purée
nada 1 pron nothing; **no hay nada** there isn't anything; **¡nada de eso!** F you can put that idea out of your head; **nada más** nothing else; **nada menos que** no less than; **lo dices como si nada** you talk about it as if it was nothing; **¡de nada!** you're welcome, not at all; **no es nada** it's nothing 2 adv not at all; **no ha llovido nada** it hasn't rained 3 f nothingness
nadador m, nadadora f swimmer
nadar ⟨1a⟩ v/i swim
nadería f trifle
nadie pron nobody, no-one; **no había nadie** there was nobody there, there wasn't

anyone there
nado: **atravesar a nado** swim across
nafta f *Arg* gas(oline), *Br* petrol
naftalina f naphthalene
nailon m nylon
naipe m (playing) card
nalga f buttock
nana f lullaby; *Rpl* F (*abuela*) grandma
napias fpl F schnozzle sg F, *Br* hooter sg F
naranja 1 f orange; **media naranja** F (*pareja*) other half 2 adj orange
naranjada f orangeade
naranjo m orange tree
narciso m BOT daffodil
narcótico m/adj narcotic
narcotráfico m drug trafficking
nariz f nose; **¡narices!** F nonsense!; **estar hasta las narices de algo** F be sick of sth F, be up to here with sth F; **meter las narices en algo** F stick one's nose in sth F
narración f narration
narrador m, narradora f narrator
narrar ⟨1a⟩ v/t: **narrar algo** tell the story of sth
nasal adj nasal
nata f cream; **nata montada** whipped cream
natación f swimming
natal adj native; **ciudad natal** city of one's birth, home town
natalidad f birthrate
natillas fpl custard sg
nativo m, -a f native
nato adj born
natural 1 adj natural; **ser natural de** come

from; **es natural** it's only natural **2** *m:* **fruta al natural** fruit in its own juice

naturaleza *f* nature

naturalidad *f* naturalness

naturalmente *adv* naturally

naturista 1 *adj* nudist, naturist; *medicina natural* **2** *m/f* nudist, naturist

naufragar ⟨1h⟩ *v/i* be shipwrecked; *fig* fail

naufragio *m* shipwreck

náufrago 1 *adj* shipwrecked **2** *m,* **-a** *f* shipwrecked person

náuseas *fpl* nausea *sg*

nauseabundo *adj* nauseating

náutico *adj* nautical

navaja *f* knife

navajazo *m* knife wound, slash

navajero *m:* **le asaltó un navajero** he was attacked by a man with a knife

naval *adj* naval

nave *f* ship; *de iglesia* nave; **nave espacial** spacecraft

navegación *f* navigation; **navegación a vela** sailing

navegador *m* INFOR browser

navegante *m/f* navigator

navegar ⟨1h⟩ **1** *v/i* sail; *por el aire, espacio* fly; **navegar por la red** *or* **por Internet** INFOR surf the Net **2** *v/t* sail

Navidad *f* Christmas

navideño *adj* Christmas *atr*

navío *m* ship

nazi *m/f* & *adj* Nazi

nazismo *m* Nazi(i)sm

N. B. *abr* (= *nótese bien*) NB (= *nota bene*)

neblina *f* mist

nebuloso *adj* *fig* hazy, nebulous

necesario *adj* necessary

neceser *m* toilet kit, *Br* toilet bag

necesidad *f* need; (*cosa esencial*) necessity; *de primera necesidad* essential; *en caso de necesidad* if necessary; **hacer sus -es** F relieve o.s.

necesitado *adj* needy

necesitar ⟨1a⟩ *v/t* need

necio *adj* brainless

necrológica *f* obituary

nefasto *adj* harmful

negación *f* negation; *de acusación* denial

negar ⟨1h & 1k⟩ **1** *v/t* *acusación* deny; (*no conceder*) refuse **2** *v/r* **negarse** refuse (*a* to)

negativa *f* refusal; *de acusación* denial

negativo 1 *adj* negative **2** *m* FOT negative

negligencia *f* JUR negligence

negociable *adj* negotiable

negociación *f* negotiation; **negociaciones** talks

negociador *m,* **negociadora** *f* negotiator

negociante *m/f* businessman; *mujer* businesswoman; *desp* money-grubber

negociar ⟨1b⟩ *v/t* negotiate

negocio *m* business; (*trato*) deal

negra *f* black woman; MÚS quarter note, *Br* crotchet; *L.Am.* (*querida*) honey, dear

negrita *f* bold

negro 1 *adj* black; **estar negro** F be furious **2** *m* black man; *L.Am.* (*querido*) honey, dear

nena *f* F little girl, kid F

nene *m* F little boy, kid F

nenúfar *m* BOT water lily

neón *m* neon

neocelandés *m,* **-esa** *f* New Zealander

neón *m* neon

neoyorquino 1 *adj* New York *atr* **2** *m,* **-a** *f* New Yorker

nepotismo *m* nepotism

nervio *m* ANAT nerve

nerviosismo *m* nervousness

nervioso *adj* nervous, **ponerse nervioso** get nervous; (*agitado*) get agitated; **poner a alguien nervioso** get on s.o.'s nerves

neto *adj* COM net

neumático 1 *adj* pneumatic **2** *m* AUTO tire, *Br* tyre

neumonía *f* MED pneumonia

neurocirujano *m,* **-a** *f* brain surgeon

neurólogo *m,* **-a** *f* neurologist

neurosis *f inv* neurosis

neurótico *adj* neurotic

neutral *adj* neutral

neutralidad *f* neutrality

neutralizar ⟨1f⟩ *v/t* neutralize

neutro *adj* neutral

nevada *f* snowfall

nevar ⟨1k⟩ *v/i* snow

nevazón *f* *Arg, Chi* snowstorm

nevera *f* refrigerator, fridge; **nevera portátil** cooler

nevería *f Méx, C.Am.* ice-cream parlo(u)r

nevero *m* snowdrift

nexo *m* link; GRAM connective

ni *conj* neither; *ni ... ni* neither ... nor; *ni siquiera* not even; *no di ni una* I made a real mess of things

Nicaragua Nicaragua

nicaragüense *m/f* & *adj* Nicaraguan

nicho *m* niche

nicotina *f* nicotine; *bajo en nicotina* low in nicotine

nido *m* nest

niebla *f* fog

nieta *f* granddaughter

nieto *m* grandson; **nietos** grandchildren

nieva *vb* → **nevar**

nieve *f* snow; *Méx* water ice, sorbet

nihilismo m nihilism
nimiedad f triviality
nimio adj trivial
ningún adj → **ninguno**
ninguno adj no; **no hay -a razón** there's no reason why, there isn't any reason why
niña f girl; forma de cortesía young lady
niñato m, **-a** f brat
niñera f nanny
niñería f: **una niñería** a childish thing
niñez f childhood
niño 1 adj young; desp childish **2** m boy; forma de cortesía young man; **niños** children pl; **niño de pecho** infant
níquel m nickel
níspero m BOT loquat
nítido adj clear; imagen sharp
nitrógeno m nitrogen
nitroglicerina f nitroglycerin
nivel m level; (altura) height; **nivel del mar** sea level; **nivel de vida** standard of living
nivelar ⟨1a⟩ v/t level
nixtamal m Méx, C.Am. dough from which corn tortillas are made
n.º abr (= número) No. (= number)
no adv no; para negar verbo not; **no entiendo** I don't understand, I do not understand; **no te vayas** don't go; **no bien** as soon as; **no del todo** not entirely; **ya no** not any more; **no más** L.Am. → **nomás; así no más** L.Am. just like that; **te gusta, ¿no?** you like it, don't you?; **te ha llamado, ¿no?** he called you, didn't he?; **¿a que no?** I bet you don't/can't etc
nobiliario adj noble
noble m/f & adj noble
nobleza f nobility
noche f night; **de noche, por la noche** at night; **de la noche a la mañana** fig overnight; **¡buenas noches!** saludo good evening; despedida good night
Nochebuena f Christmas Eve
nochecita f L.Am. evening
nochero m L.Am. night watchman
Nochevieja f New Year's Eve
noción f notion
nocivo adj harmful
noctámbulo m, **-a** f sleepwalker
nocturno adj night atr; ZO nocturnal; **clase -a** evening class
nogal m BOT walnut
nómada 1 adj nomadic **2** m/f nomad
nomás adv L.Am. just, only; **llévaselo nomás** just take it away; **nomás llegue, te avisaré** as soon as he arrives, I'll let you know; **siga nomás** just carry on; **nomás lo vio, echó a llorar** as soon as she saw him she started to cry

nombramiento m appointment
nombrar ⟨1a⟩ v/t mention; para un cargo appoint
nombre m name; GRAM noun; **nombre de pila** first name; **no tener nombre** fig be inexcusable
nomenclatura f nomenclature
nomeolvides f inv BOT forget-me-not
nómina f pay slip
nominal adj nominal
nominar ⟨1a⟩ v/t nominate
non adj odd
nono adj ninth
nopal m L.Am. BOT prickly pear
nor(d)este m northeast
noria f de agua waterwheel; en feria ferris wheel
norma f standard; (regla) rule, regulation
normal adj normal
normalidad f normality
normalizar ⟨1f⟩ v/t standardize
normativa f rules pl, regulations pl
noroeste m northwest
norte m north
Norteamérica North America
norteamericano 1 adj North American **2** m, **-a** f North American
norteño 1 adj northern **2** m, **-a** f northerner
Noruega Norway
noruego 1 adj Norwegian **2** m, **-a** f Norwegian
nos pron complemento directo us; complemento indirecto (to) us; reflexivo ourselves; **nos dio el dinero** he gave us the money, he gave the money to us
nosotros, nosotras pron we; complemento us; **ven con nosotros** come with us; **somos nosotros** it's us
nostalgia f nostalgia; por la patria homesickness
nostálgico adj nostalgic
nota f tb MÚS note; EDU grade, mark; **nota a pie de página** footnote; **tomar nota de algo** make a note of sth
notable adj remarkable, notable
notar ⟨1a⟩ v/t notice; (sentir) feel; **hacer notar algo a alguien** point sth out to s.o.; **se nota que** you can tell that; **hacerse notar** draw attention to o.s.
notaría f notary's office
notario m, **-a** f notary
noticia f piece of news; en noticiario news story, item of news; **noticias** pl news sg
noticiario m RAD, TV news sg
notificación f notification
notificar ⟨1g⟩ v/t notify
notorio adj famous, well-known
novatada f practical joke

novato *m*, **-a** *f* beginner, rookie F

novecientos *adj* nine hundred

novedad *f* novelty; *cosa* new thing; (*noticia*) piece of news; *acontecimiento* new development; *llegar sin novedad* arrive safely

novedoso *adj* novel, new; *invento* innovative

novela *f* novel; *novela negra* crime novel; *novela rosa* romantic novel

novelista *m/f* novelist

noveno *adj* ninth

noventa *adj* ninety

novia *f* girlfriend; *el día de la boda* bride

noviazgo *m* engagement

noviembre *m* November

novillada *f* bullfight featuring novice bulls

novillero *m* novice (bullfighter)

novillo *m* zo young bull; *vaca* heifer; *hacer novillos* F play hooky F, play truant

novio *m* boyfriend; *el día de la boda* bridegroom; *los novios* the bride and groom; (*recién casados*) the newly-weds

nube *f* cloud; *estar en las nubes* fig be miles away; *estar por las nubes* fig F be incredibly expensive

nublado 1 *adj* cloudy, overcast **2** *m* storm cloud

nublarse ⟨1a⟩ *v/r* cloud over

nuboso *adj* cloudy

nuca *f* nape of the neck

nuclear *adj* nuclear

núcleo *m* nucleus; *de problema* heart

nudillo *m* knuckle

nudista *m/f* nudist; *playa nudista* nudist beach

nudo *m* knot; *se me hace un nudo en la garganta* I get a lump in my throat

nuera *f* daughter-in-law

nuestro 1 *adj pos* our **2** *pron* ours

nueva *f lit* piece of news

nuevamente *adv* again

Nueva York New York

Nueva Zelanda New Zealand

nueve *adj* nine

nuevo *adj* new; (*otro*) another; *de nuevo* again

nuez *f* BOT walnut; ANAT Adam's apple

nulidad *f* nullity; *fig* F dead loss F

nulo *adj* null and void; F *persona* hopeless; (*inexistente*) non-existent, zero

núm. *abr* (= *número*) No. (= number)

numerar ⟨1a⟩ *v/t* number

numérico *adj* numerical; *teclado numérico* numeric keypad, number pad

número *m* number; *de publicación* issue; *de zapato* size; *número complementario* en lotería bonus number; *número secreto* PIN (number); *en números rojos* fig in the red; *montar un número* F make a scene

numeroso *adj* numerous

numismática *f* numismatics

nunca *adv* never; *nunca jamás* or *más nunca* never again; *más que nunca* more than ever

nupcial *adj* wedding *atr*

nutria *f* zo otter

nutrición *f* nutrition

nutrido *adj fig* large

nutriente *m* nutrient

nutrir ⟨3a⟩ *v/t* nourish; *fig: esperanzas* cherish

nutritivo *adj* nutritious, nourishing

nylon *m* nylon

ñandú *m* zo rhea

ñandutí *m* Parag type of lace

ñapa *f* S. Am. extra, bonus; *le di dos de ñapa* I threw in an extra two

ñato *adj* Rpl snub-nosed

ñeque *m* S. Am. strength; *de ñeque* F gutsy F; *tener mucho ñeque* F have a lot of guts F

ñoñería *f* feebleness F, wimpish behavio(u)r F

ñoño 1 *adj* feeble F, wimpish F **2** *m*, **-a** *f* drip F, wimp F

ñu *m* zo gnu

O

O *abr* (= *oeste*) W (= West(ern))

o *conj* or; *o … o* either … or; *o sea* in other words

oasis *m inv* oasis

obcecación *f* obstinacy

obcecarse ⟨1g⟩ *v/r* stubbornly insist

obedecer ⟨2d⟩ **1** *v/t* obey **2** *v/i* obey; *de una máquina* respond; *obedecer a* fig be due to

obediencia *f* obedience

obediente adj obedient
obelisco m obelisk
obesidad f obesity
obeso adj obese
obispo m bishop
objeción f objection; **objeción de conciencia** conscientious objection
objetar ⟨1a⟩ v/t object; **tener algo que objetar** have any objection 2 v/i become a conscientious objector
objetividad f objectivity
objetivo 1 adj objective **2** m objective; MIL target; FOT lens
objeto m object; **con objeto de** with the aim of
objetor m, **objetora** f objector; **objetor de conciencia** conscientious objector
oblicuo adj oblique, slanted
obligación f obligation, duty; COM bond
obligar ⟨1h⟩ v/t: **obligar a alguien** oblige o force s.o. (**a** to); **de una ley** apply to s.o.
obligatorio adj obligatory, compulsory
obnubilar ⟨1a⟩ v/t cloud
oboe m MÚS oboe
obra f work; **obras** pl de construcción building work sg; **en la vía pública** road works; **obra de arte** work of art; **obra maestra** masterpiece; **obra de teatro** play
obraje m Méx butcher's
obrar ⟨1a⟩ v/i act
obrero 1 adj working **2** m, **-a** f worker
obsceno adj obscene
obsequiar ⟨1b⟩ v/t: **obsequiar a alguien con algo** present s.o. with sth
obsequio m gift
obsequioso adj attentive
observación f observation; JUR observance
observador 1 adj observant **2** m, **observadora** f observer
observar ⟨1a⟩ v/t observe; (advertir) notice, observe; (comentar) remark, observe
observatorio m observatory
obsesión f obsession
obsesionar ⟨1a⟩ **1** v/t obsess **2** v/r **obsesionarse** become obsessed (**con** with)
obsesivo adj obsessive
obsoleto adj obsolete
obstaculizar ⟨1f⟩ v/t hinder, hamper
obstáculo m obstacle
obstante: no obstante nevertheless
obstetra m/f obstetrician
obstetricia f obstetrics
obstinación f obstinacy
obstinado adj obstinate
obstinarse ⟨1a⟩ v/r insist (**en** on)
obstrucción f obstruction, blockage

obstruir ⟨3g⟩ v/t obstruct, block
obtener ⟨2l; part **obtuvo**⟩ v/t get, obtain fml
obturador m shutter
obtuvo vb → **obtener**
obvio adj obvious
oca f goose
ocasión f occasion; (oportunidad) chance, opportunity; **con ocasión de** on the occasion of; **de ocasión** COM cut-price, bargain atr; **de segunda mano** second-hand, used
ocasional adj occasional
ocasionar ⟨1a⟩ v/t cause
ocaso m del sol setting; de un imperio, un poder decline
occidental 1 adj western **2** m/f Westerner
occidente m west
OCDE abr (= **Organización de Cooperación y Desarrollo Económico**) OECD (= Organization for Economic Cooperation and Development)
océano m ocean
oceanógrafo m, **-a** f oceanographer
ocelote m ZO ocelot
ochenta adj eighty
ocho adj eight
ochocientos adj eight hundred
ocio m leisure time, free time; desp idleness
ociosear ⟨1a⟩ v/i S. Am. laze around
ocioso adj idle
ocre m/adj ocher, Br ochre
oct.ᵉ abr (= **octubre**) Oct. (= October)
octavilla f leaflet
octavo 1 adj eighth **2** m eighth; DEP **octavos de final** last 16
octógono m octagon
octubre m October
ocular adj eye atr
oculista m/f ophthalmologist
ocultación f concealment
ocultar ⟨1a⟩ v/t hide, conceal
ocultismo m occult
oculto adj hidden; (sobrenatural) occult
ocupación f tb MIL occupation; (actividad) activity
ocupado adj busy; asiento taken
ocupante m/f occupant
ocupar ⟨1a⟩ **1** v/t espacio take up, occupy; (habitar) live in, occupy; obreros employ; periodo de tiempo spend, occupy; MIL occupy **2** v/r **ocuparse: ocuparse de** deal with; (cuidar de) look after
ocurrencia f occurrence; (chiste) quip, funny remark
ocurrir ⟨3a⟩ v/i happen, occur; **se me ocurrió** it occurred to me, it struck me
odiar ⟨1b⟩ v/t hate

odio *m* hatred, hate

odioso *adj* odious, hateful

odisea *f fig* odyssey

odontólogo *m* odontologist

OEA *abr* (= *Organización de los Estados Americanos*) OAS (= Organization of American States)

oeste *m* west

ofender ⟨2a⟩ **1** *v/t* offend **2** *v/r* **ofenderse** take offense (*por* at)

ofensa *f* insult

ofensiva *f* offensive

ofensivo *adj* offensive

oferta *f* offer; *oferta pública de adquisición* takeover bid

oficial **1** *adj* official **2** *m/f* MIL officer

oficialista *adj* L.Am. pro-government

oficina *f* office; *oficina de correos* post office; *oficina de empleo* employment office; *oficina de turismo* tourist office

oficinista *m/f* office worker

oficio *m trabajo* trade

oficioso *adj* unofficial

ofimática *f* INFOR office automation

ofrecer ⟨2d⟩ **1** *v/t* offer **2** *v/r* **ofrecerse** volunteer, offer one's services (*de* as); (*presentarse*) appear; *¿qué se le ofrece?* what can I do for you?

ofrecimiento *m* offer

ofrenda *f* offering

oftalmólogo *m*, *-a f* ophthalmologist

ofuscar ⟨1g⟩ *v/t tb fig* blind

ogro *m tb fig* ogre

oída *f*: *conocer algo de oídas* have heard of sth

oído *m* hearing; *hacer oídos sordos* turn a deaf ear; *ser todo oídos fig* be all ears

oigo *vb* → *oír*

oír ⟨3q⟩ *v/t tb* JUR hear; (*escuchar*) listen to; *¡oye!* listen!, hey! F; *como quien oye llover*, *salió sin él* he turned a deaf ear and went off without it

OIT *abr* (= *Organización Internacional de Trabajo*) ILO (= International Labor Organization)

ojal *m* buttonhole

ojalá *int*: *¡ojalá!* let's hope so; *¡ojalá venga!* I hope he comes; *¡ojalá tuvieras razón!* I only hope you're right

ojeada *f* glance; *echar una ojeada a alguien* glance at s.o.

ojeras *fpl* bags under the eyes

ojo *m* ANAT eye; *¡ojo!* watch out!, mind! F; *ojo de la cerradura* keyhole; *a ojo* roughly; *andar con ojo* F keep one's eyes open F; *costar un ojo de la cara* F cost an arm and a leg F; *no pegar ojo* F not sleep a wink F

ojota *f C.Am.*, *Méx* sandal

okupa *m/f Esp* F squatter

ola *f* wave; *ola de calor* heat wave; *ola de frío* cold spell

oleada *f fig* wave, flood

oleaje *m* swell

óleo *m* oil

oleoducto *m* (oil) pipeline

oler ⟨2i⟩ **1** *v/i* smell (*a* of) **2** *v/t* smell **3** *v/r*: *me huelo algo fig* there's something fishy going on, I smell a rat

olfatear ⟨1a⟩ *v/t* smell

olfato *m* sense of smell; *fig* nose

olimpíada, olimpiada *f* Olympics *pl*

olímpico *adj* Olympic

olisquear ⟨1a⟩ *v/t* sniff

oliva *f* BOT olive

olivo *m* olive tree

olla *f* pot; *olla exprés* or *a presión* pressure cooker

olmo *m* BOT elm

olor *m* smell; *agradable* scent; *olor corporal* body odo(u)r, BO

oloroso *adj* scented

OLP *abr* (= *Organización para la Liberación de Palestina*) PLO (= Palestine Liberation Organization)

olvidadizo *adj* forgetful

olvidar ⟨1a⟩ **1** *v/t* forget **2** *v/r* **olvidarse**: *olvidarse de algo* forget sth

olvido *m* oblivion

ombligo *m* ANAT navel

OMC *abr* (= *Organización Mundial de Comercio*) WTO (= World Trade Organization)

omisión *f* omission

omiso *adj*: *hacer caso omiso de algo* ignore sth

omitir ⟨3a⟩ *v/t* omit, leave out

omnipotente *adj* omnipotent

omóplato, omoplato *m* ANAT shoulder blade

OMS *abr* (= *Organización Mundial de la Salud*) WHO (= World Health Organization)

once *adj* eleven

oncología *f* MED oncology

onda *f* wave; *estar en la onda* F be with it F; *¿qué onda? Méx* F what's happening? F

ondulado *adj* wavy; *cartón* corrugated

ONG *abr* (= *Organización no Gubernamental*) NGO (= non-governmental organization)

onomatopeya *f* onomatopœia

ONU *abr* (= *Organización de las Naciones Unidas*) UN (= United Nations)

onza *f* ounce

OPA *abr* (= *oferta pública de adquisición*) takeover bid

opaco *adj* opaque

opción *f* option, choice; (*posibilidad*) chance

opcional *adj* optional

OPEP *abr* (= **Organización de Países Exportadores de Petróleo**) OPEC (= Organization of Petroleum Exporting Countries)

ópera *f* MÚS opera; **ópera prima** first work

operación *f* operation

operador *m*, operadora *f* TELEC, INFOR operator; **operador turístico** tour operator

operar ⟨1a⟩ **1** *v/t* MED operate on; *cambio* bring about **2** *v/i* operate; COM do business (**con** with) **3** *v/r* **operarse** MED have an operation (**de** on); *de un cambio* occur

operario *m*, -a *f* operator, operative

operativo **1** *adj* operational; **sistema operativo** INFOR operating system **2** *m* L.Am. operation

opereta *f* MÚS operetta

opinar ⟨1a⟩ **1** *v/t* think (**de** about) **2** *v/i* express an opinion

opinión *f* opinion; **la opinión pública** public opinion; **en mi opinión** in my opinion

opio *m* opium

opíparo *adj* sumptuous

oponente *m/f* opponent

oponer ⟨2r; *part* **opuesto**⟩ **1** *v/t resistencia* put up (**a** to), offer (**a** to); *razón, argumento* put forward (**a** against) **2** *v/r* **oponerse** be opposed (**a** to); (*manifestar oposición*) object (**a** to)

oporto *m* port

oportunidad *f* opportunity

oportunista **1** *adj* opportunistic **2** *m/f* opportunist

oportuno *adj* timely; *momento* opportune; *respuesta, medida* suitable, appropriate

oposición *f* POL opposition; **oposiciones** official entrance exams

opresión *f* oppression

opresor **1** *adj* oppressive **2** *m*, opresora *f* oppressor

oprimir ⟨3a⟩ *v/t* oppress; *botón* press; *de zapatos* be too tight for

optar ⟨1a⟩ *v/i* (*elegir*) opt (**por** for); **optar a** be in the running for; **optar por hacer algo** opt to do sth

optativo *adj* optional

óptica *f* optician's; FÍS optics; *fig* point of view

óptico **1** *adj* optical **2** *m*, -a *f* optician

optimismo *m* optimism

optimista **1** *adj* optimistic **2** *m/f* optimist

optimizar ⟨1f⟩ *v/t* optimize

óptimo *adj* ideal

opuesto **1** *part* → **oponer 2** *adj* opposite; *opinión* contrary

opulencia *f* opulence

opuso *vb* → **oponer**

oquedad *f* cavity

oración *f* REL prayer; GRAM sentence

orador *m*, oradora *f* orator

oral *adj* oral; **prueba de inglés oral** English oral (exam)

orangután *m* ZO orangutan

orar ⟨1a⟩ *v/i* pray (**por** for)

oratoria *f* oratory

órbita *f* orbit; **colocar** *or* **poner en órbita** put into orbit

orca *f* ZO killer whale

órdago *m*: **de órdago** F terrific F

orden **1** *m* order; **orden del día** agenda; **por orden alfabético** in alphabetical order; **poner en orden** tidy up **2** *f* (*mandamiento*) order; **¡a la orden!** yes, sir; **por orden de** by order of, on the orders of

ordenado *adj* tidy

ordenador *m* INFOR computer; **ordenador de escritorio** desktop (computer); **ordenador personal** personal computer; **ordenador portátil** portable (computer), laptop; **asistido por ordenador** computer aided

ordenanza **1** *f* by-law **2** *m* office junior, gofer F; MIL orderly

ordenar ⟨1a⟩ *v/t habitación* tidy up; *alfabéticamente* arrange; (*mandar*) order

ordeñar ⟨1a⟩ *v/t* milk

ordinario *adj* ordinary; *desp* vulgar; **de ordinario** usually, ordinarily

orégano *m* BOT oregano

oreja *f* ear; **aguzar las orejas** L.Am. prick one's ears up; **ver las orejas al lobo** *fig* F wake up to the danger

orejeras *fpl* earmuffs

orfanato *m* orphanage

orfebrería *f* goldsmith / silversmith work

orfelinato *m* orphanage

orgánico *adj* organic

organigrama *m* flow chart; *de empresa* organization chart, tree diagram

organillo *m* barrel organ

organismo *m* organism; POL agency, organization; **organismo modificado genéticamente** genetically modified organism

organización *f* organization; **Organización de Cooperación y Desarrollo Económico** Organization for Economic Cooperation and Development; **Organización de las Naciones Unidas** United Nations; **Organizacíon de los Estados Americanos** Organization of American

States; *Organización del Tratado del Atlántico Norte* North Atlantic Treaty Organization; *Organización de Países Exportadores de Petróleo* Organization of Petroleum Exporting Countries; *Organización Internacional de Trabajo* International Labor Organization; *Organización Mundial de Comercio* World Trade Organization; *Organización Mundial de la Salud* World Health Organization; *Organización para la Liberación de Palestina* Palestine Liberation Organization

organizador 1 *adj* organizing **2** *m*, organizadora *f* organizer; *organizador personal* personal organizer

organizar ⟨1f⟩ **1** *v/t* organize **2** *v/r* organizarse *de persona* organize one's time

órgano *m* MÚS, ANAT, *fig* organ

orgasmo *m* orgasm

orgía *f* orgy

orgullo *m* pride

orgulloso *adj* proud (*de* of)

orientación *f* orientation; (*ayuda*) guidance; *sentido de la orientación* sense of direction

orientador *m*, **orientadora** *f* counsel(l)or

oriental 1 *adj* oriental, eastern **2** *m/f* Oriental

orientar ⟨1a⟩ **1** *v/t* (*aconsejar*) advise; *orientar algo hacia algo* turn sth toward sth **2** *v/r* orientarse get one's bearings; *de una planta* turn (*hacia* toward)

oriente *m* east; *Oriente* Orient; *Oriente Medio* Middle East; *Extremo* or *Lejano Oriente* Far East

orificio *m* hole; *en cuerpo* orifice

origen *m* origin; *dar origen a* give rise to

originalidad *f* originality

originar ⟨1a⟩ **1** *v/t* give rise to **2** *v/r* originarse originate; *de un incendio* start

originario *adj* original; (*nativo*) native (*de* of)

orilla *f* shore; *de un río* bank

orina *f* urine

orinal *m* urinal

orinar ⟨1a⟩ *v/i* urinate

oriundo *adj* native (*de* to)

ornamental *adj* ornamental

ornitología *f* ornithology

ornitólogo *m*, **-a** *f* ornithologist

oro *m* gold; *guardar como oro en paño con mucho cariño* treasure sth; *con mucho cuidado* guard sth with one's life; *prometer el oro y el moro* promise the earth; *oros* (*en naipes*) suit in Spanish deck of cards

orondo *adj* fat; *fig* smug

oropéndola *f* ZO golden oriole

orquesta *f* orchestra

orquestar ⟨1a⟩ *v/t fig* orchestrate

orquídea *f* BOT orchid

ortiga *f* BOT nettle

ortodoncia *f* MED orthodontics

ortodoxo *adj* orthodox

ortografía *f* spelling

ortopédico 1 *adj* orthop(a)edic **2** *m*, **-a** *f* orthop(a)edist

oruga *f* ZO caterpillar; TÉC (caterpillar) track

orujo *m* liquor made from the remains of grapes

orzuelo *m* MED styc

os *pron complemento directo* you; *complemento indirecto* (to) you; *reflexivo* yourselves; *os lo devolveré* I'll give you it back, I'll give it back to you

osa *f* AST: *Osa Mayor* Great Bear; *Osa Menor* Little Bear

osadía *f* daring; (*descaro*) audacity

osamenta *f* bones *pl*

osar ⟨1a⟩ *v/i* dare

oscilación *f* oscillation; *de precios* fluctuation

oscilar ⟨1a⟩ *v/i* oscillate; *de precios* fluctuate

oscurecer ⟨2d⟩ **1** *v/t* darken; *logro, triunfo* overshadow **2** *v/i* get dark **3** *v/r* oscurecerse darken

oscuridad *f* darkness

oscuro *adj* dark; *fig* obscure; *a -as* in the dark

óseo *adj* bone *atr*

osezno *m* cub

osito *m*: *osito de peluche* teddy bear

oso *m* bear; *oso hormiguero* anteater; *oso panda* panda; *oso polar* polar bear

ostensible *adj* obvious

ostentación *f* ostentation; *hacer ostentación de* flaunt

ostentar ⟨1a⟩ *v/t* flaunt; *cargo* hold

ostentoso *adj* ostentatious

osteoporosis *f* MED osteoporosis

ostra *f* ZO oyster; *¡ostras!* ⊢ hell! F

ostrero *m* ZO oyster-catcher

OTAN *abr* (= *Organización del Tratado del Atlántico Norte*) NATO (= North Atlantic Treaty Organization)

otitis *f* MED earache

otoño *m* fall, *Br* autumn

otorgar ⟨1h⟩ *v/t* award; *favor* grant

otorrino F, **otorrinolaringólogo** *m* MED ear, nose and throat o ENT specialist

otro 1 *adj* (*diferente*) another; *con el, la* other; *otros* other; *otros dos libros* another two books **2** *pron* (*adicional*) another (one); (*persona distinta*) someone *o* somebody else; *(cosa distinta)* another one; a different one; **otros** others; **entre otros** among others **3** *siguiente*: **¡hasta -a!** see you soon **4** *pron recíproco*: **amar el uno al otro** love one another

ovación *f* ovation

ovacionar ⟨1a⟩ *v/t* cheer, give an ovation to

ovalado *adj* oval

óvalo *m* oval

ovario *m* ANAT ovary

oveja *f* sheep; **oveja negra** *fig* black sheep

overol *m Méx* overalls *pl*, *Br* dungarees *pl*

ovillo *m* ball; **hacerse un ovillo** *fig* curl up (into a ball)

ovino 1 *adj* sheep *atr* **2** *m* sheep; **ovinos** sheep *pl*

OVNI *abr* (= **objeto volante no identificado**) UFO (= unidentified flying object)

ovulación *f* ovulation

óvulo *m* egg

oxidado *adj* rusty

oxidar ⟨1a⟩ **1** *v/t* rust **2** *v/r* **oxidarse** rust, go rusty

óxido *m* QUÍM oxide; *(herrumbre)* rust

oxigenarse ⟨1a⟩ *v/r fig* get some fresh air

oxígeno *m* oxygen

oye *vb* → **oír**

oyendo *vb* → **oír**

oyente *m/f* listener

oyó *vb* → **oír**

ozono *m* ozone; **capa de ozono** ozone layer

P

pabellón *m* pavilion; *edificio* block; MÚS bell; MAR flag

pachanga *f*: **ir de pachanga** *Méx, W.I., C.Am.* F go on a spree F

pachocha *L.Am.*, **pachorra** *f* F slowness

pachucho *adj* MED F poorly

paciencia *f* patience

paciente *m/f* & *adj* patient

pacificador *m*, **pacificadora** *f* peace-maker

pacificar ⟨1g⟩ *v/t* pacify

pacífico 1 *adj* peaceful; *persona* peaceable; **el océano Pacífico** the Pacific Ocean **2** *m*: **el Pacífico** the Pacific

pacifista 1 *adj* pacifist *atr* **2** *m/f* pacifist

paco *m*, **-a** *f L.Am.* F *(policía)* cop F

pacotilla *f*: **de pacotilla** third-rate, lousy F

pacotillero *m*, **-a** *f L.Am.* street vendor

pactar ⟨1a⟩ **1** *v/t* agree; **pactar un acuerdo** reach (an) agreement **2** *v/i* reach (an) agreement

pacto *m* agreement, pact

padecer ⟨2d⟩ **1** *v/t* suffer **2** *v/i* suffer; **padecer de** have trouble with

padrastro *m* step-father

padre *m* father; REL Father; **de padre y muy señor mío** terrible; **padres** parents; **¡qué padre!** *Méx* F brilliant!

padrenuestro *m* Lord's Prayer

padrillo *m Rpl* stallion

padrino *m en bautizo* godfather; *(en boda)* man who gives away the bride

padrón *m* register of local inhabitants

paella *f* GASTR paella

pág. *abr* (= **página**) p. (= page)

paga *f* pay; *de niño* allowance, *Br* pocket money

pagado *adj* paid

pagano *adj* pagan

pagar ⟨1h⟩ **1** *v/t* pay; *compra, gastos, crimen* pay for; *favor* repay; **¡me las pagarás!** you'll pay for this! **2** *v/i* pay; **pagar a escote** F go Dutch F

pagaré *m* IOU

página *f* page; **página web** web page; **páginas amarillas** yellow pages

pago *m* payment; *Rpl (quinta)* piece of land; **pago al contado** *o* **en efectivo** payment in cash; **en pago de** in payment for; **por estos pagos** F in this neck of the woods F

país *m* country; **país en vías de desarrollo** developing country; **los Países Bajos** the Netherlands

paisaje *m* landscape

paisano *m*: **de paisano** MIL in civilian clothes; *policía* in plain clothes

paja *f* straw; **hacerse una paja** V jerk off V

pajar *m* hayloft

pajarería *f* pet shop

pajarita *f corbata* bow tie; *de papel* paper bird

pájaro *m* bird; *fig* ugly customer F, nasty piece of work F; **pájaro carpintero**

woodpecker; *matar dos pájaros de un tiro* kill two birds with one stone

Pakistán Pakistan

pakistaní *m/f & adj* Pakistani

pala *f* spade; *raqueta* paddle; *para servir* slice; *para recoger* dustpan

palabra *f tb fig* word; *palabra de honor* word of hono(u)r; *bajo palabra* on parole; *en una palabra* in a word; *tomar la palabra* speak

palabrota *f* swearword

palacete *m* small palace

palaciego *adj* palace *atr*

palacio *m* palace; *palacio de deportes* sports center (*Br* centre); *palacio de justicia* law courts

paladar *m* palate

palanca *f* lever; *palanca de cambios* AUTO gearshift, *Br* gear lever; *tener palanca Méx fig* F have pull F *o* clout F

palangana *f* plastic bowl for washing dishes, *Br* washing-up bowl

palanganear ⟨1a⟩ *v/i S. Am.* show off

palangre *m* trawl line

palanqueta *f* crowbar

palco *m* TEA box

palenque *m L.Am.* cockpit (*in cock fighting*)

Palestina Palestine

palestino 1 *adj* Palestinian **2** *m*, *-a f* Palestinian

palestra *f* arena; *salir or saltar a la palestra fig* hit the headlines

paleta *f* PINT palette; TÉC trowel

paletilla *f* GASTR shoulder

paleto F 1 *adj* hick *atr* F, provincial **2** *m*, *-a f* hick F, *Br* yokel F

paliar ⟨1b⟩ *v/t* alleviate; *dolor* relieve

paliativo *m/adj* palliative

palidecer ⟨2d⟩ *v/i de persona* turn pale

palidez *f* paleness

pálido *adj* pale

palillo *m para dientes* toothpick; *para comer* chopstick

palique *m*: *estar de palique* F have a chat

paliza 1 *f* beating; (*derrota*) thrashing F, drubbing F; (*pesadez*) drag F **2** *m/f* F drag F

palma *f* palm; *dar palmas* clap (one's hands)

palmada *f* pat; (*manotazo*) slap

palmar ⟨1a⟩ *v/t*: *palmarla* P kick the bucket F

palmera *f* BOT palm tree; (*dulce*) heart-shaped pastry

palmito *m* BOT palmetto; GASTR palm heart; *fig* F attractiveness

palmo *m* hand's breadth; *palmo a palmo* inch by inch

palo *m de madera etc* stick; MAR mast; *de*

portería post, upright; *palo de golf* golf club; *palo mayor* MAR mainmast; *a medio palo L.Am.* F half-drunk; *a palo seco* whisky straight up; *ser un palo L.Am.* F be fantastic; *de tal palo tal astilla* a chip off the old block F

paloma *f* pigeon; *blanca* dove; *paloma mensajera* carrier pigeon

palomar *m* pigeon loft

palometa *f* ZO *pez* pompano

palomilla *f C.Am.*, *Méx* F gang

palomita *f Méx* checkmark, *Br* tick; *palomitas pl de maíz* popcorn *sg*

palpable *adj fig* palpable

palpar ⟨1a⟩ *v/t con las manos* feel, touch; *fig* feel

palpitación *f* palpitation

palpitante *adj corazón* pounding; *cuestión* burning

palpitar ⟨1a⟩ *v/i del corazón* pound; *Rpl fig* have a hunch F, have a feeling

palta *f S. Am.* BOT avocado

palto *m S. Am.* jacket

paludismo *m* MED malaria

palurdo 1 *adj* F hick *atr* F, provincial **2** *m*, *-a f* F hick F, *Br* yokel F

pamela *f* picture hat

pampa *f* GEOG pampa, prairie; *a la pampa Rpl* in the open

pamplinas *fpl* nonsense *sg*

pan *m* bread; *un pan* a loaf; *pan francés L.Am.* French bread; *pan integral* wholemeal bread; *pan de molde* sliced bread; *pan de barra* French bread; *pan rallado* breadcrumbs *pl*; *pan tostado* toast; *ser pan comido* F be easy as pie F

pana *f* corduroy

panacea *f* panacea

panadería *f* baker's shop

panadero *m*, *-a f* baker

panal *m* honeycomb

Panamá Panama; *el Canal de Panamá* the Panama Canal; *Ciudad de Panamá* Panama city

panameño 1 *adj* Panamanian **2** *m*, *-a f* Panamanian

pancarta *f* placard

panceta *f* belly pork

páncreas *m inv* ANAT

panda *m* ZO panda

pandereta *f* tambourine

pandilla *f* group; *de delincuentes* gang

panecillo *m* (bread) roll

panel *m tb grupo de personas* panel; *panel solar* solar panel

panela *f L.Am.* brown sugar loaf

panera *f* bread basket

panfleto *m* pamphlet

pánico m panic; **sembrar el pánico** spread panic

panocha, panoja f ear

panoli adj F dopey F

panorama m panorama

panorámico adj: **vista -a** panoramic view

panqueque m L.Am. pancake

pantalla f TV, INFOR screen; de lámpara shade; **pequeña pantalla** fig small screen

pantalón m, **pantalones** mpl pants pl, Br trousers pl; **llevar los pantalones** fig F wear the pants (Br trousers) F

pantano m reservoir

panteón m pantheon

pantera f ZO panther

pantomima f pantomime

pantorrilla f ANAT calf

pantufla f slipper

panty m pantyhose pl, Br tights pl

panza f de persona belly

pañal m diaper, Br nappy

paño m cloth; **paño de cocina** dishtowel

pañuelo m handkerchief; **el mundo es un pañuelo** fig F it's a small world

papa 1 m Pope **2** f L.Am. potato

papá m F pop F, dad F; **papás** L.Am. parents; **Papá Noel** Santa Claus

papada f double chin

papagayo m ZO parrot

papal 1 adj papal **2** m L.Am. potato field

papalote m Méx kite

papanatas m/f inv F dope F, dimwit F

paparruchas fpl F baloney sg F

papaya f BOT papaya

papel m paper; trozo piece of paper; TEA, fig role; **papel de aluminio** foil; **papel de envolver** wrapping paper; **papel de regalo** giftwrap; **papel higiénico** toilet paper o tissue; **papel reciclado** recycled paper; **perder los papeles** lose control; **ser papel mojado** fig not be worth the paper it's written on

papelada f L.Am. farce

papeleo m paperwork

papelera f wastepaper basket

papelería f stationer's shop

papelero m L.Am. F muddle, mess

papeleta f de rifa raffle ticket; fig chore; **papeleta de voto** ballot paper

paperas fpl MED mumps

papilla f para bebés baby food; para enfermos puree; **hacer papilla a alguien** F beat s.o. to a pulp F

papista adj: **ser más papista que el papa** hold extreme views

paquete m package, parcel; de cigarrillos packet; F en moto (pillion) passenger

Paquistán Pakistan

paquistaní m/f & adj Pakistani

par 1 f par; **es bella a la par que inteligente** she is beautiful as well as intelligent, she is both beautiful and intelligent **2** m pair; **abierto de par en par** wide open; **un par de** a pair of

para prp for ◊ dirección toward(s); **ir para** head for; **va para directora** she's going to end up as manager

◊ tiempo for; **listo para mañana** ready for tomorrow; **para siempre** forever; **diez para las ocho** L.Am. ten of eight, ten to eight

◊ finalidad: **lo hace para ayudarte** he does it (in order) to help you; **para que** so that; **¿para qué te marchas?** what are you leaving for?; **para mí** for me; **lo heredó todo para morir a los 30** he inherited it all, only to die at 30

parabólica f satellite dish

parabrisas m inv AUTO windshield, Br windscreen

paracaídas m inv parachute

paracaidista m/f parachutist; MIL paratrooper

parachoques m inv AUTO fender, Br bumper

parada f stop; **parada de autobús** bus stop; **parada de taxis** taxi rank

paradero m whereabouts sg; L.Am. → **parada**

parado 1 adj unemployed; L.Am. (de pie) standing (up); **salir bien / mal parado** come off well / badly **2** m, **-a** f unemployed person

paradoja f paradox

paradójico adj paradoxical

parador m Esp parador (state-run luxury hotel)

parafernalia f F paraphernalia

parafina f kerosene, Br paraffin

paraguas m inv umbrella

Paraguay Paraguay

paraguayo 1 adj Paraguayan **2** m, **-a** f Paraguayan

paraíso m paradise; **paraíso fiscal** tax haven

paralelismo m parallel

paralelo m/adj parallel

parálisis f tb fig paralysis

paralítico 1 adj paralytic **2** m, **-a** f person who is paralyzed

paralización f tb fig paralysis

paralizar ⟨1f⟩ v/t MED paralyze; actividad bring to a halt; país, economía paralyze, bring to a standstill

parámetro m parameter

paramilitar adj paramilitary

parangón m: **sin parangón** incomparable

paranoia f paranoia

paranoico 1 adj MED paranoid **2** m, -a f MED person suffering from paranoia

paranormal adj paranormal

parapente m hang glider; *actividad* hang gliding

parapeto m parapet

parapléjico 1 adj MED paraplegic **2** m, -a f paraplegic

parar ⟨1a⟩ **1** v/t stop; *L.Am.* (*poner de pie*) stand up **2** v/i stop; *en alojamiento* stay; *parar de llover* stop raining; *ir a parar* end up **3** v/r **pararse** stop; *L.Am.* (*ponerse de pie*) stand up

pararrayos m inv lightning rod

parásito m parasite

parcela f lot, *Br* plot

parchar ⟨1a⟩ v/t *L.Am.* patch; (*arreglar*) repair

parche m patch

parcial adj (*partidario*) bias(s)ed

pardo 1 adj *color* dun; *L.Am. desp* half--breed desp, *Br tb* half-caste desp **2** m *color* dun; *L.Am. desp* half-breed desp

parecer 1 m opinion, view; *al parecer* apparently **2** ⟨2d⟩ v/i seem, look; *me parece que* I think (that), it seems to me that; *me parece bien* it seems fine to me, *¿qué te parece?* what do you think? **3** v/r **parecerse** resemble each other; *parecerse a alguien* resemble s.o.

parecido 1 adj similar **2** m similarity

pared f wall; *subirse por las paredes* F hit the roof F

pareja f (*conjunto de dos*) pair; *en una relación* couple; *de una persona* partner; *de un objeto* other one

parejo adj *L.Am. suelo* level, even; *andar parejos* be neck and neck; *llegaron parejos* they arrived at the same time

paréntesis m inv parenthesis; *fig* break; *entre paréntesis fig* by the way

pareo m wrap-around skirt

parida f P stupid thing to say / do

pariente m/f relative

paripé m: *hacer el paripé* F put on an act F

parir ⟨3a⟩ **1** v/i give birth **2** v/t give birth to

París Paris

parisino 1 adj Parisian **2** m, -a f Parisian

parka f parka

parking m parking lot, *Br* car park

parlamentario 1 adj parliamentary **2** m, -a f member of parliament

parlamento m parliament

parlanchín adj chatty

parlante m *L.Am.* loudspeaker

parlotear ⟨1a⟩ v/i chatter

parmesano m/adj Parmesan

paro m unemployment; *estar en paro* be unemployed; *paro cardíaco* cardiac arrest

parodia f parody

parpadear ⟨1a⟩ v/i blink

parpadeo m blinking

párpado m eye lid

parque m park; *para bebé* playpen; *parque de atracciones* amusement park; *parque de bomberos* fire station; *parque nacional* national park; *parque natural* nature reserve; *parque temático* theme park

parqué m → **parquet**

parquear ⟨1a⟩ v/t *L.Am.* park

parquet m parquet

parquímetro m parking meter

parra f (grape) vine

párrafo m paragraph

parranda f: *andar or irse de parranda* go out on the town F

parricidio m parricide

parrilla f broiler, *Br* grill; *a la parrilla* broiled, *Br* grilled

parrillada f *L.Am.* barbecue

párroco m parish priest

parroquia f REL parish; COM clientele, customers pl

parsimonia f parsimony

parte 1 m report; *parte meteorológico* weather report; *dar parte a alguien* inform s.o. **2** f *trozo* part; JUR party; *alguna parte* somewhere; *ninguna parte* nowhere; *otra parte* somewhere else; *de parte de* on behalf of; *en parte* partly; *en or por todas partes* everywhere; *la mayor parte de* the majority of, most of; *por otra parte* moreover; *estar de parte de alguien* be on s.o.'s side; *formar parte de* form part of; *tomar parte en* take part in

participación f participation

participante m/f participant

participar ⟨1a⟩ **1** v/t *una noticia* announce **2** v/i take part (*en* in), participate (*en* in)

participio m GRAM participle

partícula f particle

particular 1 adj *clase, propiedad* private; *asunto* personal; (*específico*) particular; (*especial*) peculiar; *en particular* in particular **2** m (*persona*) individual; *particulares* particulars

particularidad f peculiarity

partida f *en juego* game; (*remesa*) consignment; *documento* certificate; *partida de nacimiento* birth certificate

partidario 1 adj: *ser partidario de* be in favo(u)r of **2** m, -a f supporter

P

partidismo *m* partisanship

partido *m* POL party; DEP game; **sacar partido de** take advantage of; **tomar partido** take sides

partir ⟨3a⟩ **1** *v/t* (*dividir, repartir*) split; (*romper*) break open, split open; (*cortar*) cut **2** *v/i* (*irse*) leave; **a partir de hoy** (starting) from today; **a partir de ahora** from now on; **partir de** *fig* start from **3** *v/r* **partirse** (*romperse*) break; **partirse de risa** F split one's sides laughing F

partitura *f* MÚS score

parto *m* birth; *fig* creation

parvulario *m* kindergarten

pasa *f* raisin

pasable *adj* passable

pasada *f con trapo* wipe; *de pintura* coat; **de pasada** in passing; **¡qué pasada!** F that's incredible!

pasadizo *m* passage

pasado **1** *adj tiempo* last; **el lunes pasado** last Monday; **pasado de moda** old-fashioned **2** *m* past

pasaje *m* (*billete*) ticket; MÚS, *de texto* passage

pasajero **1** *adj* temporary; *relación* brief **2** *m*, -a *f* passenger

pasamano(s) *m* handrail

pasamontañas *m inv* balaclava (helmet)

pasaporte *m* passport

pasar ⟨1a⟩ **1** *v/t* pass; *el tiempo* spend; *un lugar* go past; *frontera* cross; *problemas, dificultades* experience; AUTO (*adelantar*) pass, *Br* overtake; *una película* show; **para pasar el tiempo** (in order) to pass the time; **pasar la mano por** run one's hand through; **pasarlo bien** have a good time **2** *v/i* (*suceder*) happen; *en juegos* pass; **pasar de alguien** F not want anything to do with s.o.; **paso de coger el teléfono** F I can't be bothered to pick up the phone; **pasé a visitarla** I dropped by to see her; **pasar de moda** go out of fashion; **pasar por** go by; **pasé por la tienda** I stopped off at the shop; **pasar por aquí** come this way; **dejar pasar** *oportunidad* miss; **hacerse pasar por** pass o.s. off as; **pasaré por tu casa** I'll drop by your house; **¡pasa!** come in; **¿qué pasa?** what's happening?, what's going on?; **¿qué te pasa?** what's the matter?; **pase lo que pase** whatever happens, come what may **3** *v/r* **pasarse** *tb fig* go too far; *del tiempo* pass, go by; (*usar el tiempo*) spend; *de molestia, dolor* go away; **pasarse al enemigo** go over to the enemy; **se le pasó llamar** he forgot to call

pasarela *f* catwalk

pasatiempo *m* pastime

Pascua *f* Easter; **¡felices Pascuas!** Merry Christmas!

pase *m tb* DEP, TAUR pass; *en el cine* showing; **pase de modelos** fashion show

pasear ⟨1a⟩ **1** *v/t* take for a walk; (*exhibir*) show off **2** *v/i* walk **3** *v/r* **pasearse** walk

paseo *m* walk; **paseo marítimo** seafront; **dar un paseo** go for a walk; **mandar a alguien a paseo** *fig* F tell s.o. to get lost

pasillo *m* corridor; *en avión, cine* aisle

pasión *f* passion

pasividad *f* passivity

pasivo *adj* passive

pasmar ⟨1a⟩ *v/t* amaze, astonish

paso *m* step; (*manera de andar*) walk; (*ritmo*) pace, rate; *de agua* flow; *de tráfico* movement; (*cruce*) crossing; *de tiempo* passing; (*huella*) footprint; **paso a nivel** grade crossing, *Br* level crossing; **paso de peatones** crosswalk, pedestrian crossing; **a este paso** *fig* at this rate; **de paso** on the way; **estar de paso** be passing through

pasta *f sustancia* paste; GASTR pasta; P (*dinero*) dough P; **pasta de dientes** toothpaste; **pastas de té** type of cookie (*Br* biscuit)

pastel *m* GASTR cake; *pintura, color* pastel

pastelería *f* cake shop

pastelero *m*, -a *f* pastry cook

paste(u)rizar ⟨1f⟩ *v/t* pasteurize

pastilla *f* tablet; *de jabón* bar; **a toda pastilla** F at top speed F, flat out F

pasto *m* (*hierba*) grass; **a todo pasto** F for all one is worth F

pastor *m* shepherd; REL pastor; **pastor alemán** German shepherd

pata[1] *m/f Pe* F pal F, buddy F

pata[2] *f* leg; **a cuatro patas** on all fours; **meter la pata** F put one's foot in it F; **tener mala pata** F be unlucky

patada *f* kick; **dar una patada** kick

patalear ⟨1a⟩ *v/i* stamp one's feet; *fig* kick and scream

patata *f* potato; **patatas fritas** *de sartén* French fries, *Br* chips; *de bolsa* chips, *Br* crisps

patatús *m*: **le dio un patatús** F he had a fit F

paté *m* paté

patear ⟨1a⟩ *v/t & v/i L.Am. de animal* kick

patentar ⟨1a⟩ *v/t* patent

patente **1** *adj* clear, obvious **2** *f* patent; *L.Am.* AUTO license plate, *Br* number-plate

paternidad *f* paternity, fatherhood

paterno *adj* paternal

patético *adj* pitiful

patíbulo *m* scaffold

patilla *f de gafas* arm; **patillas** *barba* sideburns

patín *m* skate; **patín** *(de ruedas)* **en línea** rollerblade®, in-line skate

patinador *m*, **patinadora** *f* skater

patinaje *m* skating; **patinaje artístico** figure skating; **patinaje sobre hielo** ice-skating; **patinaje sobre ruedas** roller-skating

patinar ⟨1a⟩ *v/i* skate

patinazo *m* skid; *fig* F blunder; **dar un patinazo** skid

patinete *m* scooter

patio *m* courtyard, patio; **patio de butacas** TEA orchestra, *Br* stalls *pl*

pato *m* ZO duck; **pagar el pato** F take the rap F, *Br* carry the can F

patojo *adj Chi* F squat

patológico *adj* pathological

patoso *adj* clumsy

patraña *f* homeland

patria *f* homeland

patriarca *m* patriarch

patrimonio *m* heritage; **patrimonio artístico** artistic heritage

patriota *m/f* patriot

patriótico *adj* patriotic

patriotismo *m* patriotism

patrocinador *m*, **patrocinadora** *f* sponsor

patrocinar ⟨1a⟩ *v/t* sponsor

patrocinio *m* sponsorship

patrón *m (jefe)* boss; REL patron saint; *para costura* pattern; *(modelo)* standard; MAR skipper

patrona *f (jefa)* boss; REL patron saint

patronal employers *pl*

patrulla *f* patrol

patrullar ⟨1a⟩ *v/t* patrol

patrullero *m* patrolman

paulatino *adj* gradual

pausa *f* pause; *en una actividad* break; MÚS rest; **pausa publicitaria** commercial break

pausado *adj* slow, deliberate

pauta *f* guideline; **marcar la pauta** set the guidelines

pavimento *m* pavement, *Br* road surface

pavo *m* 1 *adj L.Am.* F stupid 2 *m* ZO turkey; **pavo real** peacock

pavonearse ⟨1a⟩ *v/r* boast *(de* about)

pavor *m* terror; **me da pavor** it terrifies me

payada *f Rpl* improvized ballad

payador *m Rpl* gaucho singer

payasadas *fpl* antics; **hacer payasadas** fool *o* clown around

payaso *m* clown

paz *f* peace; **dejar en paz** leave alone

pe: **de pe a pa** F from start to finish

PC *abr (= Partido Comunista)* CP (= Communist Party)

P.D. *abr (= posdata)* PS (= postscript)

peaje *m* *dinero, lugar* toll

peatón *m* pedestrian

peatonal *adj* pedestrian *atr*

pebete *m*, **-a** *f Rpl* F kid F

peca *f* freckle

pecado *m* sin

pecador *m*, **pecadora** *f* sinner

pecaminoso *adj* sinful

pecar ⟨1g⟩ *v/i* sin; **pecar de ingenuo / generoso** be very naive / generous

pecera *f* fish tank, aquarium

pecho *m (caja torácica)* chest; *(mama)* breast; **tomar algo a pecho** take sth to heart

pechuga *f* GASTR breast; *L.Am. fig* F *(cadura)* nerve F

pooooo *adj* freckled

pectoral *adj* ANAT pectoral

peculiar *adj* peculiar, odd; *(característico)* typical

peculiaridad *f (característica)* peculiarity

pedagogía *f* education

pedagogo *m*, **-a** *f* teacher

pedal *m* pedal

pedalear ⟨1a⟩ *v/i* pedal

pedante 1 *adj* pedantic; *(presuntuoso)* pretentious **2** *m/f* pedant; *(presuntuoso)* pretentious individual

pedantería *f* pedantry; *(presunción)* pretentiousness

pedazo *m* piece, bit; **pedazo de bruto** F blockhead F; **hacer pedazos** F smash to bits F

pederasta *m* pederast

pedestal *m* pedestal

pediatra *m/f* p(a)ediatrician

pedicura *f* pedicure

pedicuro *m*, **-a** *f* pedicurist, *Br* chiropodist

pedido *m* order

pedigrí *m* pedigree

pedigüeño *m*, **-a** *f* person who is always asking to borrow things, moocher F

pedir ⟨3l⟩ **1** *v/t* ask for; *(necesitar)* need; *en bar, restaurante* order; **me pidió que no fuera** he asked me not to go **2** *v/i mendigar* beg; *en bar, restaurante* order

pedo *m* 1 *adj* drunk **2** *m* F fart F; **agarrarse un pedo** F get plastered F; **tirarse** *or* **echar un pedo** F fart F

pedorreta *f* F Bronx cheer F, *Br* raspberry F

pedrada *f* blow with a stone; **me dio una pedrada en la cabeza** he hit me over the head with a stone

pedregal m stony ground

pedregoso adj stony

Pedro m: **como Pedro por su casa** fig F as if he / she owned the place

pega f F snag F, hitch F; **poner pegas** raise objections

pegadizo adj catchy

pegado adj (adherido) stuck (**a** to); **estar pegado a** (cerca de) be right up against; **estar pegado a alguien** fig follow s.o. around, be s.o.'s shadow

pegajoso adj sticky; fig: persona clingy

pegamento m glue

pegar ⟨1h⟩ **1** v/t (golpear) hit; (adherir) stick, glue; bofetada, susto, resfriado give; **pegar un grito** shout; **no me pega la gana** Méx F I don't feel like it **2** v/i (golpear) hit; (adherir) stick; del sol beat down; (armonizar) go (together) **3** v/r **pegarse** resfriado catch; acento pick up; susto give o.s.; **pegarse un golpe / un tiro** hit / shoot o.s.; **pegársela a alguien** F con s.o.

pegatina f sticker

pegote m F (cosa fea) eyesore

peinado m hairstyle

peinador m, **peinadora** f L.Am. hairdresser

peinar ⟨1a⟩ **1** v/t tb fig comb; **peinar a alguien** comb s.o.'s hair **2** v/r **peinarse** comb one's hair

peine m comb

p. ej. abr (= por ejemplo) e.g. (= exempli gratia, for example)

Pekín Beijing

pela f F peseta

peladero m L.Am. vacant lot

peladilla f sugared almond

pelado adj peeled; fig bare; F (sin dinero) broke F

pelar ⟨1a⟩ **1** v/t manzana, patata etc peel; **hace un frío que pela** F it's freezing F **2** v/r **pelarse** (cortarse el pelo) have a haircut; Rpl F (chismear) gossip

pelazón f C.Am. backbiting

peldaño m step

pelea f fight

pelear ⟨1a⟩ **1** v/i fight **2** v/r **pelearse** fight

pelele m puppet

peleón adj argumentative; **vino peleón** F jug wine, Br plonk F

peletería f furrier's

peliagudo adj tricky

pelícano m zo pelican

película f movie, film; FOT film; **película del Oeste** Western; **de película** F awesome F, fantastic F

peligrar ⟨1a⟩ v/i be at risk

peligro m danger; **correr peligro** be in danger; **poner en peligro** endanger, put at risk

peligroso adj dangerous

pelillo m: **¡pelillos a la mar!** fig F let's bury the hatchet

pelín: **un pelín** F a (little) bit

pelirrojo adj red-haired, red-headed

pellejo m de animal skin, hide; **salvar el pellejo** fig F save one's (own) skin F

pellizcar ⟨1g⟩ v/t pinch

pellizco m pinch; **un buen pellizco** F a tidy sum F

pelma **1** adj annoying **2** m/f pain F

pelmazo m, **-a** f F pain F

pelo m de persona, de perro hair; de animal fur; **tiene el pelo muy largo** he has very long hair; **sin pelo** F (sin preparación) unprepared; **montar a pelo** ride bareback; **por los pelos** F by a whisker F, by the skin of one's teeth F; **tomar el pelo a alguien** F pull s.o.'s leg F

pelota **1** f ball; **pelotas** F nuts F, balls F; **en pelotas** P stark naked; **hacer la pelota a alguien** suck up to s.o. F **2** m/f F creep F

pelotazo m: **rompió el cristal de un pelotazo** he smashed the window with a ball

pelotero m, **-a** f L.Am. (base)ball player

pelotón m MIL squad; DEP bunch, pack

peluca f wig

peluche m soft toy; **oso de peluche** teddy bear

peludo adj persona hairy; animal furry

peluquearse ⟨1a⟩ v/r L.Am. get one's hair cut

peluquería f hairdresser's

peluquero m, **-a** f hairdresser

peluquín m toupee, hairpiece

pelusa f fluff

pelvis f inv ANAT pelvis

pena f (tristeza) sadness, sorrow; (congoja) grief, distress; (lástima) pity; JUR sentence; **pena capital** death penalty, capital punishment; **pena de muerte** death penalty; **no vale** or **no merece la pena** it's not worth it; **¡qué pena!** what a shame o pity!; **a duras penas** with great difficulty; **me da pena** L.Am. I'm ashamed

penal adj penal; **derecho penal** criminal law

penalidad f fig hardship

penalización f acción penalization; DEP penalty

penalizar ⟨1f⟩ v/t penalize

penalty m DEP penalty

penca **1** adj Chi soft, weak **2** f L.Am. (nopal) leaf of the prickly pear plant

pendejada *f L.Am.* stupid thing to do
pendejo 1 *m* (*pelea*) fight 2 *m*, -a *f L.Am.* F dummy F
pendenciero *adj* troublemaker
pendiente 1 *adj* unresolved, unfinished; *cuenta* unpaid 2 *m* earring 3 *f* slope
pendón 1 *adj* swinging F 2 *m*, -ona *f* F swinger F
péndulo *m* pendulum
pene *m* ANAT penis
penetración *f* penetration
penetrante *adj mirada* penetrating; *sonido* piercing; *frío* bitter; *herida* deep; *análisis* incisive
penetrar ⟨1a⟩ *v/i* penetrate; (*entrar*) enter; *de un líquido* seep in
penicilina *f* penicillin
península *f* peninsula; *península Ibérica* Iberian Peninsula
penique *m* penny
penitencia *f* penitence
penitenciado *m L. Am.* prisoner, convict
penitenciario *adj* penitentiary *atr*, prison *atr*
penoso *adj* distressing; *trabajo* laborious
pensamiento *m* thought; BOT pansy
pensar ⟨1k⟩ 1 *v/t* think about; (*opinar*) think; *¡ni pensarlo!* don't even think about it 2 *v/i* think (*en* about)
pensativo *adj* thoughtful
pensión *f hotel* rooming house, *Br* guesthouse; *dinero* pension; *pensión alimenticia* child support, *Br* maintenance; *pensión completa* American plan, *Br* full board
pensionista *m/f* pensioner
pentagrama *m* MÚS stave
pentatlón *m* DEP pentathlon
penúltimo *adj* penultimate
penumbra *f* half-light
penuria *f* shortage (*de* of); (*pobreza*) poverty
peña *f* crag, cliff; (*roca*) rock; F *de amigos* group, circle
peñasco *m* boulder
peñón *m*: *el Peñón de Gibraltar* the Rock of Gibraltar
peón *m en ajedrez* pawn; *trabajador* labo(u)rer
peor *adj comp* worse; *de mal en peor* from bad to worse
pepa *f L.Am.* (*semilla*) seed; *soltar la pepa* F spill the beans
pepinillo *m* gherkin
pepino *m* cucumber; *me importa un pepino* F I don't give a damn F
pepita *f* pip

one
pequinés *m* ZO Pekinese, Peke F
pera *f* pear
peral *m* pear tree
perca *f pez* perch
percance *m* mishap
percatarse ⟨1a⟩ *v/r* notice; *percatarse de algo* notice sth
percebe *m* ZO barnacle
percepción *f* perception; COM *acto* receipt
percha *f* coat hanger; *gancho* coat hook
perchero *m* coat rack
percibir ⟨3a⟩ *v/t* perceive; COM *sueldo* receive
percusión *f* MÚS percussion
perdedor *m*, perdedora *f* loser
perder ⟨2g⟩ 1 *v/t objeto* lose; *tren, avión etc* miss; *el tiempo* waste 2 *v/i* lose; *echar a perder* ruin; *echarse a perder de alimento* go bad 3 *v/r* perderse get lost
perdición *f* downfall
pérdida *f* loss
perdido *adj* lost; *ponerse perdido* get filthy
perdigón *m* pellet
perdiz *f* ZO partridge
perdón *m* pardon; REL forgiveness; *pedir perdón* say sorry, apologize; *¡perdón!* sorry
perdonar ⟨1a⟩ *v/t* forgive; JUR pardon; *perdonar algo a alguien* forgive s.o. sth; *¡perdone!* sorry; *perdone, ¿tiene hora?* excuse me, do you have the time?
perdurar ⟨1a⟩ *v/i* endure
perecedero *adj* perishable
perecer ⟨2d⟩ *v/i* perish
peregrinación *f* pilgrimage
peregrinar ⟨1a⟩ *v/i* go on a pilgrimage
peregrino *m*, -a *f* pilgrim
perejil *m* BOT parsley
perenne *adj* BOT perennial
perentorio *adj* (*urgente*) urgent, pressing; (*apremiante*) peremptory
pereza *f* laziness
perezoso 1 *adj* lazy 2 *m* ZO sloth
perfección *f* perfection; *a la perfección* perfectly, to perfection
perfeccionamiento *m* perfecting
perfeccionar ⟨1a⟩ *v/t* perfect
perfeccionista *m/f* perfectionist
perfecto *adj* perfect
pérfido *adj* treacherous
perfil *m* profile; *de perfil* in profile, from the side
perforación *f* puncture
perforadora *f* punch
perforar ⟨1a⟩ *v/t* pierce; *calle* dig up
perfumar ⟨1a⟩ *v/t* perfume
perfume *m* perfume

perfumería f perfume shop
pergamino m parchment
pergenio m, **-a** f Rpl F kid F
pericia f expertise
pericote m Chi, Pe zo large rat
periferia f periphery; **de ciudad** outskirts pl
perilla f goatee; **me viene de perilla** F that'll be very useful; **tu visita me viene de perilla** F you've come at just the right time
perímetro m perimeter
periódico 1 adj periodic **2** m newspaper
periodismo m journalism
periodista m/f journalist
período, periodo m period
peripecia f adventure
periquete m: **en un periquete** F in a second, in no time F
periquito m zo budgerigar
periscopio m periscope
perito 1 adj expert **2** m, **-a** f expert; COM **en seguros** loss adjuster
perjudicar ⟨1g⟩ v/t harm, damage
perjudicial adj harmful, damaging
perjuicio m harm, damage; **sin perjuicio de** without affecting
perjurio m perjury
perla f pearl; **nos vino de perlas** F it suited us fine F
permanecer ⟨2d⟩ v/i remain, stay
permanente 1 adj permanent **2** f perm
permeable adj permeable
permisible adj permissible
permisivo adj permissive
permiso m permission; **documento** permit; **permiso de conducir** driver's license, Br driving licence; **permiso de residencia** residence permit; **con permiso** excuse me; **estar de permiso** be on leave
permitir ⟨3a⟩ **1** v/t permit, allow **2** v/r permitirse afford; **permitirse el lujo de** permit o.s. the luxury of
pernicioso adj harmful
pernoctar ⟨1a⟩ v/i spend the night
pero 1 conj but **2** m flaw, defect; **no hay peros que valgan** no excuses
perogrullada f platitude
peronismo m Peronism
peronista m/f Peronist
perorata f F lecture
perpendicular adj perpendicular
perpetrar ⟨1a⟩ v/t **crimen** perpetrate, commit
perpetuar ⟨1e⟩ v/t perpetuate
perpetuidad f: **a perpetuidad** in perpetuity
perpetuo adj fig perpetual

perplejidad f perplexity
perplejo adj puzzled, perplexed
perra f dog; **el perro y la perra** the dog and the bitch; **perras** F pesetas
perrera f kennels pl
perrería f F dirty trick
perrito m: **perrito caliente** GASTR hot dog
perro m dog; **perro callejero** stray; **perro guardián** guard dog; **perro lazarillo** seeing eye dog, Br guide dog; **perro pastor** sheepdog; **llevarse como el perro y el gato** fig fight like cat and dog; **hace un tiempo de perros** F the weather is lousy F
persecución f pursuit; (acoso) persecution
perseguidor m, **perseguidora** f persecutor
perseguir ⟨3l & 3d⟩ v/t pursue; **delincuente** look for; (molestar) pester; (acosar) persecute
perseverancia f perseverance
perseverar ⟨1a⟩ v/i persevere (**en** with)
persiana f blind
pérsico adj Persian
persignarse ⟨1a⟩ v/r cross o.s.
persistente adj persistent
persistir ⟨3a⟩ v/i persist
persona f person; **quince personas** fifteen people
personaje m TEA character; **famoso** celebrity
personal 1 adj personal **2** m personnel, staff
personalidad f personality
personalizar ⟨1f⟩ v/t personalize
personificar ⟨1g⟩ v/t personify, embody
perspectiva f perspective; fig point of view; **perspectivas** pl outlook sg, prospects
perspicacia f shrewdness, perspicacity
persuadir ⟨3a⟩ v/t persuade
persuasión f persuasion
persuasivo adj persuasive
pertenecer ⟨2d⟩ v/i belong (**a** to)
pertenencias fpl belongings
pértiga f pole; **salto con pértiga** DEP pole vault
pertinaz adj persistent; (terco) obstinate
pertinente adj relevant, pertinent
pertrechos mpl MIL equipment sg
perturbar ⟨1a⟩ v/t disturb; **reunión** disrupt
Perú Peru
peruano 1 adj Peruvian **2** m, **-a** f Peruvian
perversión f perversion
perverso adj perverted
pervertido m, **-a** f pervert
pervertir ⟨3i⟩ v/t pervert

pesa f para balanza weight; DEP shot; C.Am., W.I. butcher's shop
pesadez f fig drag F
pesadilla f nightmare
pesado 1 adj objeto heavy; libro, clase etc tedious, boring; trabajo tough **2** m, -a f bore; **¡qué pesado es!** F he's a real pain F
pésame m condolences pl
pesar ⟨1a⟩ **1** v/t weigh **2** v/i be heavy; (influir) carry weight; fig weigh heavily (**sobre** on); **me pesa tener que informarle ...** I regret to have to inform you ... **3** m sorrow; **a pesar de** in spite of, despite
pesca f actividad fishing; (peces) fish pl
pescadería f fish shop
pescadero m, -a f fishmonger
pescadilla f pez whiting
pescado m GASTR fish
pescador m fisherman
pescar ⟨1g⟩ **1** v/t un pez, resfriado etc catch; (intentar tomar) fish for; trabajo, marido etc land **2** v/i fish
pescuezo m neck
pese: pese a despite
pesero m L.Am. minibus; Méx (collective) taxi
peseta f peseta
pesetero adj F money-grubbing F
pesimismo m pessimism
pesimista 1 adj pessimistic **2** m/f pessimist
pésimo adj sup awful, terrible
peso m weight; moneda peso; **de peso** fig weighty
pesquero 1 adj fishing atr **2** m fishing boat
pesquisa f investigation
pestaña f eyelash
pestañear ⟨1a⟩ v/i flutter one's eyelashes; **sin pestañear** fig without batting an eyelid
peste f MED plague; F olor stink F; **echar pestes** F curse and swear
pesticida m pesticide
pestilente adj foul-smelling
pestillo m (picaporte) door handle; (cerradura) bolt
petaca f para tabaco tobacco pouch; para bebida hip flask; C.Am. F insecto ladybug, Br ladybird
pétalo m petal
petanca f type of bowls
petardo 1 m firecracker **2** m, -a f F nerd F
petate m kit bag; L.Am. F en el suelo mat
petición f request; **a petición de** at the request of
petirrojo m ZO robin
petiso L.Am. **1** m, -a f F shorty F **2** m pony

peto m bib; **pantalón de peto** overalls pl, Br dungarees pl
petrificado adj petrified
petróleo m oil, petroleum
petrolero 1 adj oil atr **2** m MAR oil tanker
petrolífero adj oil atr
petroquímica f petrochemical
petulante adj smug
peyorativo adj pejorative
pez m ZO fish; **pez espada** swordfish; **pez gordo** F big shot F; **estar pez en algo** F be clueless about sth F
pezón m nipple
pezuña f ZO hoof
piadoso adj pious
pianista m/f pianist
piano m piano; **piano de cola** grand piano
piar ⟨1c⟩ v/i tweet, chirrup
PIB abr (= producto interior bruto) GDP (= gross domestic product)
pibe m, -a f Rpl F kid F
picada f de serpiente bite; de abeja sting; L.Am. para comer snacks pl, nibbles pl; Rpl (camino) path
picadero m escuela riding school
picado 1 adj diente decayed; mar rough, choppy; carne ground, Br minced; verdura minced, Br finely chopped; fig offended **2** m MAR dive; **caer en picado de precios** nosedive, plummet
picadora f en cocina mincer
picadura f de reptil, mosquito bite; de avispa sting; tabaco cut tobacco
picaflor m L.Am. ZO hummingbird; fig womanizer
picante 1 adj hot, spicy; chiste risqué **2** m hot spice
picaporte m door handle
picar ⟨1g⟩ **1** v/t de mosquito, serpiente bite; de avispa sting; de ave peck; carne grind, Br mince; verdura mince, Br finely chop; TAUR jab with a lance; (molestar) annoy; la curiosidad pique **2** v/i tb fig take the bait; L.Am. de la comida be hot; (producir picor) itch; del sol burn
picardía f (astucia) craftiness, slyness; (travesura) mischievousness; Méx (taco, palabrota) swearing, swearwords pl
pícaro adj persona crafty, sly; comentario mischievous
picarón m Méx, Chi, Pe (buñuelo) fritter
picatoste m piece of fried bread
picha f V prick V
pichicato m Pe, Bol F coke P
pichincha f L.Am. bargain
pichón m L.Am. ORN chick; F (novato) rookie F
Picio: más feo que Picio F as ugly as sin F

P

picnic *m* (*pl ~s*) picnic

pico *m* zo beak; F (*boca*) mouth; *de montaña* peak; *herramienta* pickax(e); *a las tres y pico* some time after three o'clock; *cerrar el pico* F shut one's mouth F

picor *m* itch

picota *f* bigarreau (*type of sweet cherry*)

picotazo *m* peck

picotear ⟨1a⟩ *v/t* peck

pido *vb* → pedir

pie *m* foot; *de estatua, lámpara* base; *a pie* on foot; *de pie* standing; *no tiene ni pies ni cabeza* it doesn't make any sense at all, I can't make head nor tail of it

piedad *f* pity; (*clemencia*) mercy

piedra *f tb* MED stone; *piedra preciosa* precious stone; *quedarse de piedra fig* F be stunned

piel *f de persona, fruta* skin; *de animal* hide, skin; (*cuero*) leather; *abrigo de pieles* fur coat

pienso[1] *vb* → pensar

pienso[2] *m* animal feed

pierdo *vb* → perder

pierna *f* leg; *dormir a pierna suelta* sleep like a log

pieza *f de un conjunto*, MÚS piece; *de aparato* part; TEA play; (*habitación*) room; *pieza de recambio* spare (part); *quedarse de una pieza* F be amazed

pifia *f* F (*error*) booboo F; *Chi, Pe, Rpl* defect

pigmento *m* pigment

pigmeo *m, -a f* pigmy

pijama *m* pajamas *pl*, *Br* pyjamas *pl*

pijo 1 *adj* posh 2 *m* V (*pene*) prick V 3 *m, -a f* F *persona* rich kid F

pila *f* EL battery; (*montón*) pile; (*fregadero*) sink

pilar *m tb fig* pillar

píldora *f* pill

pileta *f Rpl* sink; (*alberca*) swimming pool

pillaje *m* pillage

pillar ⟨1a⟩ *v/t* (*tomar*) seize; (*atrapar*) catch; (*atropellar*) hit; *chiste* get

pillo 1 *adj* mischievous 2 *m, -a f* rascal

pilón *m Méx*: *me dio dos de pilón* he gave me two extra

pilotar ⟨1a⟩ *v/t* AVIA fly, pilot; AUTO drive; MAR steer

piloto *m* AVIA, MAR pilot; AUTO driver; EL pilot light; *piloto automático* autopilot

piltrafa *f*: *piltrafas* rags; *estar hecho una piltrafa fig* be a total wreck F

pimentón *m* paprika

pimienta *f* pepper

pimiento *m* pepper; *me importa un pimiento* F I couldn't care less F

pimpón *m* ping-pong

PIN *m* PIN

pinar *m* pine forest

pincel *m* paintbrush

pinchadiscos *m/f* F disc jockey, DJ

pinchar ⟨1a⟩ 1 *v/t* prick; AUTO puncture; TELEC tap; F (*molestar*) bug F, needle F; *pincharle a alguien* MED give s.o. a shot 2 *v/i* prick; AUTO get a flat tire, *Br* get a puncture 3 *v/r* pincharse *con aguja etc* prick o.s.; F (*inyectarse*) shoot up F; *se nos pinchó una rueda* we got a flat (tire) *o Br* a puncture

pinchazo *m herida* prick; *dolor* sharp pain; AUTO flat (tire), *Br* puncture; F flop F

pinche[1] *m* cook's assistant

pinche[2] *adj Méx* F rotten F; *C.Am., Méx* (*tacaño*) tight-fisted

pincho *m* GASTR bar snack

pingajo *m* F rag

ping-pong *m* ping-pong

pingüino *m* zo penguin

pino *m* BOT pine; *hacer el pino* do a handstand

pinol(e) *m C.Am., Méx* cornstarch, *Br* cornflour; *L.Am.* roasted corn

pinta *f aspecto* looks *pl*; *tener buena pinta fig* look inviting

pintalabios *m* lipstick

pintar ⟨1a⟩ 1 *v/t* paint; *no pintar nada fig* F not count 2 *v/r* pintarse put on one's makeup

pintor *m*, pintora *f* painter; *pintor (de brocha gorda)* (house) painter

pintoresco *adj* picturesque

pintura *f sustancia* paint; *obra* painting

pinza *f clothes* pin, *Br* clothes peg; zo claw; *pinzas* tweezers; *L.Am.* (*alicates*) pliers

piña *f del pino* pine cone; *fruta* pineapple

piñón *m* BOT pine nut; TÉC pinion

piojo *m* zo louse; *piojos pl* lice *pl*

piola *f L.Am.* cord, twine

piolín *m Arg* cord, twine

pionero 1 *adj* pioneering 2 *m, -a f tb fig* pioneer

pipa *f* pipe; *pipas semillas* sunflower seeds; *pasarlo pipa* F have a great time

pipí *m* F pee F; *hacer pipí* F pee F

pipiolo *m C.Am., Méx* F kid F; *pipiolos pl C.Am.* F (*dinero*) cash *sg*

pique *m* resentment; (*rivalidad*) rivalry; *irse a pique fig* go under, go to the wall

piqueta *f herramienta* pickax(e); *en cámping* tentpeg

piquete *m* POL picket

pirado *adj* F crazy F

piragua *f* canoe

piragüista *m/f* DEP canoeist

pirámide *f* pyramid

piraña *f* zo piranha

pirarse ⟨1a⟩ *v/r* F (*marcharse*) clear off F; *pirarse por alguien* F lose one's head over s.o. F

pirata *m/f* pirate; *pirata informático* hacker

piratear ⟨1a⟩ *v/t* INFOR pirate

pirenaico *adj* Pyrenean

Pirineos *mpl* Pyrenees

pirómano *m*, **-a** *f* pyromaniac; JUR arsonist

piropo *m* compliment

pirotécnico *adj* fireworks *atr*

piruleta *f*, **pirulí** *m* lollipop

pis *m* F pee F; *hacer pis* F have a pee F

pisada *f* footstep; *huella* footprint

pisapapeles *m* paperweight

pisar ⟨1a⟩ *v/t* step on; *uvas* tread; *fig (maltratar)* walk all over; *idea* steal; *pisar a alguien* step on s.o.'s foot

piscifactoría *f* fish farm

piscina *f* swimming pool

Piscis *m/f inv* ASTR Pisces

piso *m* apartment, *Br* flat; (*planta*) floor

pisotear ⟨1a⟩ *v/t* trample

pista *f* track, trail; (*indicio*) clue; *de atletismo* track; *pista de aterrizaje* AVIA runway; *pista de baile* dance floor; *pista de tenis / squash* tennis / squash court; *seguir la pista a alguien* be on the trail of s.o.

pistacho *m* BOT pistachio

pisto *m* GASTR *mixture of tomatoes, peppers etc cooked in oil*; *C.Am.*, *Méx* F (*dinero*) cash, dough F

pistola *f* pistol

pistón *m* piston

pitada *f* (*abucheo*) whistle; *S. Am. de cigarillo* puff

pitar ⟨1a⟩ **1** *v/i* whistle; *con bocina* beep, hoot; *L.Am. (fumar)* smoke; *salir pitando* F dash off F **2** *v/t* (*abuchear*) whistle at; *penalti*, *falta etc* call, *Br* blow for; *silbato* blow

pitazo *m* L.Am. whistle

pitear ⟨1a⟩ *v/i* L.Am. blow a whistle

pitido *m* whistle; *con bocina* beep, hoot

pitillo *m* cigarette; *hecho a mano* roll-up

pito *m* whistle; (*bocina*) horn; *me importa un pito* F I don't give a hoot F

pitón *m* zo python

pitonisa *f* fortune-teller

pitorrearse ⟨1a⟩ *v/r*: *pitorrearse de alguien* F make fun of s.o.

pivot *m* en baloncesto center, *Br* centre

piyama *m* L.Am. pajamas *pl*, *Br* pyjamas *pl*

pizarra *f* blackboard; *piedra* slate

pizca *f* pinch; *Méx* AGR harvest; *ni pizca de* not a bit of

pizza *f* pizza

placa *f* (*lámina*) sheet; (*plancha*) plate; (*letrero*) plaque; *Méx* AUTO license plate, *Br* number plate; *placa madre* INFOR motherboard; *placa* (*dental*) plaque; *placa de matrícula* AUTO license plate, *Br* number plate

placer ⟨2x⟩ **1** *v/i* please; *siempre hace lo que le place* he always does as he pleases **2** *m* pleasure

plácido *adj* placid

plaga *f* AGR pest; MED plague; *fig* scourge; (*abundancia*) glut

plagado *adj* infested; (*lleno*) full; *plagado de gente* swarming with people

plagiar ⟨1b⟩ *v/t* plagiarize; *L.Am.* (*secuestrar*) kidnap

plagio *m* plagiarism

plan *m* plan

plana *f*: *primera plana* front page

plancha *f* *para planchar* iron; *en cocina* broiler, *Br* grill; *de metal* sheet; F (*metedura de pata*) goof F; *a la plancha* GASTR broiled, *Br* grilled

planchar ⟨1a⟩ *v/t* iron; *Méx* F (*dar plantón*) stand up F; *L.Am.* (*lisonjear*) flatter

planeador *m* glider

planear ⟨1a⟩ **1** *v/t* plan **2** *v/i* AVIA glide

planeta *m* planet

planetario *m* planetarium

planificación *f* planning; *planificación familiar* family planning

planificar ⟨1g⟩ *v/t* plan

plano 1 *adj* flat **2** *m* ARQUI plan; *de ciudad* map; *en cine* shot; MAT plane; *fig* level

planta *f* BOT plant; (*piso*) floor; *planta del pie* sole of the foot

plantación *f* plantation

plantado *adj*: *dejar a alguien plantado* F stand s.o. up F

plantar ⟨1a⟩ **1** *v/t* *árbol etc* plant; *tienda de campaña* put up; *plantar a alguien* F stand s.o. up F **2** *v/r* *plantarse* put one's foot down

planteamiento *m* *de problema* posing; (*perspectiva*) approach

plantear ⟨1a⟩ *v/t* *dificultad*, *problema* pose, create; *cuestión* raise

plantel *m* (*equipo*) team; *L.Am.* staff

plantilla *f* *para zapato* insole; (*personal*) staff; DEP squad; *para cortar*, INFOR template

plantón *m*: *dar un plantón a alguien* F stand s.o. up F

plasma *m* plasma

plasmar ⟨1a⟩ *v/t* (*modelar*) shape; *fig* (*representar*) express

plasta 1 *m/f* F pain F, drag F **2** *adj*: *ser plasta* F be a pain *o* drag F

plástica *f* EDU handicrafts

plástico *m* plastic

plastificado *adj* laminated

plastificar ⟨1g⟩ *v/t documento* laminate

plastilina *f* Plasticine®

plata *f* silver; *L.Am.* F (*dinero*) cash, dough F

plataforma *f tb* POL platform; *plataforma petrolífera* oil rig

platal *m L.Am.* fortune

plátano *m* banana

plateado *adj Méx* wealthy

plática *f Méx* chat, talk

platicar ⟨1g⟩ **1** *v/t L.Am.* tell **2** *v/i Méx* chat, talk

platillo *m*: *platillo volante* flying saucer; *platillos* MÚS cymbals

platino *m* platinum

plato *m* plate; GASTR dish; *plato principal* main course; *plato preparado / precocinado* ready meal; *plato sopero / hondo* soup dish; *pagar los platos rotos* F carry the can F

plató *m de película* set; TV studio

platónico *adj* platonic

platudo *adj Chi* rich

plausible *adj* plausible

playa *f* beach; *playa de estacionamiento L.Am.* parking lot, *Br* car park

playeras *fpl* canvas shoes

playo *adj Rpl* shallow

plaza *f* square; (*vacante*) job opening, *Br* vacancy; *en vehículo* seat; *de trabajo* position; *plaza de toros* bull ring

plazo *m* period; (*pago*) instal(l)ment; *a corto / largo plazo* in the short / long term; *a plazos* in instal(l)ments

plebiscito *m* plebiscite

plegable *adj* collapsible, folding

plegar ⟨1h & 1k⟩ **1** *v/t* fold (up) **2** *v/r plegarse* *fig* submit (*a* to)

plegaria *f* prayer

pleito *m* JUR lawsuit; *fig* dispute; *poner un pleito a alguien* sue s.o.

pleno 1 *adj* full; *en pleno día* in broad daylight **2** *m* plenary session

pliego *vb* → *plegar* **2** *m* (*hoja de papel*) sheet (of paper); (*carta*) sealed letter *o* document

pliegue *m* fold, crease

plomería *f Méx* plumbing

plomero *m Méx* plumber

plomo *m* lead; EL fuse; *fig* F drag F; *sin plomo* AUTO unleaded

pluma *f* feather; *para escribir* fountain pen

plumaje *m* plumage

plumero *m para limpiar* feather duster; *CSur para maquillaje* powder puff; *vérsele el plumero a alguien* *fig* F see what s.o. is up to F

plumífero *m* F down jacket

plural 1 *adj* plural **2** *m* GRAM plural

pluralismo *m* POL pluralism

pluriempleo *m* having more than one job

plus *m* bonus

plusmarquista *m/f* record holder

plusvalía *f* COM capital gain

plutonio *m* QUÍM plutonium

pluviosidad *f* rainfall

PNB *abr* (= *producto nacional bruto*) GNP (= gross national product)

P.º *abr* (= *Paseo*) Ave (= Avenue)

p.o. *abr* (= *por orden*) p. p. (per procurationem, by proxy)

población *f gente* population; (*ciudad*) city, town; (*pueblo*) village; *Chi* shanty town

poblado 1 *adj* populated; *barba* bushy; *poblado de* *fig* full of **2** *m* (*pueblo*) settlement

poblador *m*, **pobladora** *f Chi* shanty town dweller

poblar ⟨1m⟩ *v/t* populate

pobre 1 *adj económicamente, en calidad* poor **2** *m/f* poor person; *los pobres* the poor

pobreza *f* poverty

pocilga *f* pigpen

pócima *f* concoction

poción *f* potion

poco 1 *adj sg* little, not much; *pl* few, not many; *un poco de* a little; *unos pocos* a few **2** *adv* little; *trabaja poco* he doesn't work much; *ahora se ve muy poco* it's seldom seen now; *estuvo poco por aquí* he wasn't around much; *poco conocido* little known; *poco a poco* little by little; *dentro de poco* soon, shortly; *hace poco* a short time ago, not long ago; *por poco* nearly, almost; *¡a poco no lo hacemos!* *Méx* don't tell me we're not doing it; *de a poco me fui tranquilizando Rpl* little by little I calmed down **3** *m*: *un poco* a little, a bit

podar ⟨1a⟩ *v/t* AGR prune

poder ⟨2t⟩ **1** *v/aux capacidad* can, be able to; *permiso* can, be allowed to; *posibilidad* may, might; *no pude hablar con ella* I wasn't able to talk to her; *¿puedo ir contigo?* can *o* may I come with you?; *¡podías habérselo dicho!* you could have *o* you might have told him **2** *v/i*: *poder con* (*sobreponerse a*) manage, cope with; *me puede* he can beat me; *es franco a más no poder* F he's as frank as they come F; *comimos a más no poder* F we ate to bursting point F; *no puedo más* I can't take any more, I've had enough; *puede ser* perhaps, maybe; *puede que* perhaps, maybe; *¿se puede?* can I come in?, do you mind if I come in? **3** *m tb* POL power; *en poder de alguien* in s.o.'s hands

poderoso *adj* powerful

podio *m* podium

podólogo *m*, **-a** *f* MED podiatrist, *Br* chiropodist

podrido *adj tb fig* rotten

poema *m* poem

poesía *f género* poetry; (*poema*) poem

poeta *m/f* poet

poético *adj* poetic

poetisa *f* poet

polaco 1 *adj* Polish **2** *m*, **-a** *f* Pole

polar *adj* polar

polea *f* TÉC pulley

polémica *f* controversy

polémico *adj* controversial

polen *m* BOT pollen

poleo *m* BOT pennyroyal

polera *f Chi* turtle neck (sweater)

poli *m/f* F cop F; *la poli* F the cops *pl* F

policía 1 *f* police **2** *m/f* police officer, policeman; *mujer* police officer, policewoman

policíaco, policiaco *adj* detective *atr*

policial *adj* police *atr*

polideportivo *m* sports center, *Br* sports centre

poliéster *m* polyester

polifacético *adj* versatile, multifaceted

poligamia *f* polygamy

políglota *m/f* polyglot

polígono *m* MAT polygon; *polígono industrial* industrial zone, *Br* industrial estate

polilla *f* ZO moth

polio *f* MED polio

poliomielitis *f* MED poliomyelitis

política *f* politics

políticamente *adv*: *políticamente correcto* politically correct

político 1 *adj* political **2** *m*, **-a** *f* politician

póliza *f* policy; *póliza de seguros* insurance policy

polizón *m/f* stowaway

polla *f* V prick V, cock V

pollera *f L.Am.* skirt

pollería *f* poulterer's

pollito *m* chick

pollo *m* ZO, GASTR chicken

polluelo *m* ZO chick

polo *m* GEOG, EL pole; *prenda* polo shirt; DEP polo; *Polo Norte* North Pole; *Polo Sur* South Pole

polola *f Chi* girlfriend

pololear ⟨1a⟩ *v/i Chi* be going steady

pololo *m Chi* boyfriend

Polonia Poland

polución *f* pollution; *polución atmosférica* air pollution, atmospheric pollution

polucionar ⟨1a⟩ *v/t* pollute

polvo *m* dust; *en química, medicina etc* powder; *polvos pl de talco* talcum powder *sg*; *echar un polvo* V have a screw V; *estar hecho polvo* F be all in F

pólvora *f* gunpowder

polvorín *m almacén* magazine; *fig* powder keg

polvorón *m* GASTR *type of small cake*

pomada *f* cream

pomelo *m* BOT grapefruit

pómez *f*: *piedra pómez* pumice stone

pomo *m* doorknob

pompa *f* pomp; *pompa de jabón* bubble; *pompas pl fúnebres ceremonia* funeral ceremony *sg*; *establecimiento* funeral parlo(u)r *sg*

pomposo *adj* pompous

pómulo *m* ANAT cheekbone

pon *vb* → **poner**

ponchadura *f Méx* flat, *Br* puncture

ponchar ⟨1a⟩ *v/t L.Am.* puncture **2** *v/r* **poncharse** *Méx* get a flat *o Br* puncture

ponche *m* punch

poncho *m* poncho; *pisarse el poncho S. Am.* be mistaken

ponderación *f mesura* deliberation; *en estadísticas* weighting

ponencia *f* presentation; EDU paper

poner ⟨2r; *part* **puesto** ⟩ **1** *v/t* put; (*añadir*) put in; RAD, TV turn on, switch on; *la mesa* set; *ropa* put on; *telegrama* send; (*escribir*) put down; *en periódico, libro etc* say; *negocio* set up; *huevos* lay; *poner a alguien furioso* make s.o. angry; *ponerle a alguien con alguien* TELEC put s.o. through to s.o.; *ponerle una multa a alguien* fine s.o.; *pongamos que* let's suppose *o* assume that **2** *v/r* **ponerse** *ropa* put on; *ponte en el banco* go and sit on the bench; *se puso ahí* she stood over there; *dile que se ponga* TELEC tell her to come to the phone; *ponerse palido* turn pale; *ponerse furioso* get angry; *ponerse enfermo* become *o* fall ill; *ponerse a* start to

pongo[1] *vb* → **poner**

pongo[2] *m Pe* indentured Indian laborer

poni *m* ZO pony

poniente *m* west

pontífice *m* pontiff; *sumo pontífice*

Pope

ponzoñoso *adj* poisonous

pop 1 *adj* pop; *música pop* pop music 2 *m* pop

popa *f* MAR stern

popular *adj* popular; (*del pueblo*) folk *atr*; *barrio* lower-class

popularidad *f* popularity

popularizar ⟨1f⟩ *v/t* popularize

póquer *m* poker

por *prp* ◇ *motivo* for, because of; *lo hizo por amor* she did it out of love; *luchó por sus ideales* he fought for his ideals ◇ *medio* by; *por avión* by air; *por correo* by mail, *Br tb* by post ◇ *tiempo*: *por un segundo* L.Am. for a second; *por la mañana* in the morning ◇ *movimiento*: *por la calle* down the street; *por un tunel* through a tunnel; *por aquí* this way ◇ *posición aproximada* around, about; *está por aquí* it's around here (somewhere) ◇ *cambio*: *por cincuenta pesos* for fifty pesos ◇ *otros usos*: *por hora* an *o* per hour; *dos por dos* two times two; *¿por qué?* why?; *el motivo por el cual o por el que ...* the reason why ...

porcelana *f* porcelain, china; *de porcelana* porcelain *atr*, china *atr*

porcentaje *m* percentage

porche *f* porch

porción *f* portion

pordiosero *m*, -a *f* beggar

porfiar ⟨1c⟩ *v/i* insist (*en* on)

pormenor *m* detail

porno 1 *adj* porn *atr* 2 *m* porn

pornografía *f* pornography

pornográfico *adj* pornographic

poro *m* pore

poroso *adj* porous

poroto *m Rpl*, *Chi* bean; *porotos verdes* L.Am. green beans

porque *conj* because; *porque sí* just because

porqué *m* reason

porquería *f* (*suciedad*) filth; F *cosa de poca calidad* piece of trash F

porra *f* baton; (*palo*) club; *¡vete a la porra!* F go to hell! F

porrazo *m*: *darle un porrazo a alguien* F hit s.o.; *darse o pegarse un porrazo* crash (*contra* into)

porro *m* F joint F

porrón *m* container from which wine is poured straight into the mouth

portaaviones *m inv* aircraft carrier

portada *f* TIP front page; *de revista* cover; ARQUI front

portafolios *m inv* briefcase

portal *m* foyer; (*entrada*) doorway

portaligas *m inv Arg*, *Chi* garter belt, *Br* suspender belt

portarse ⟨1a⟩ *v/r* behave

portátil *adj* portable

portavoz *m/f* spokesman; *mujer* spokeswoman

portazo *m*: *dar un portazo* F slam the door

porte *m* (*aspecto*) appearance, air; (*gasto de correo*) postage

portento *m* wonder; *persona* genius

porteño *Arg* 1 *adj* of Buenos Aires, Buenos Aires *atr* 2 *m*, -a *f* native of Buenos Aires

portería *f* reception; *casa* superintendent's apartment, *Br* caretaker's flat; DEP goal

portero *m* doorman; *de edificio* superintendent, *Br* caretaker; DEP goalkeeper; *portero automático* intercom, *Br* entryphone

portón *m* large door

Portugal Portugal

portugués 1 *m/adj* Portuguese 2 *m*, -esa *f persona* Portuguese

porvenir *m* future

posada *f C.Am.*, *Méx* Christmas party; (*fonda*) inn

posar ⟨1a⟩ 1 *v/t mano* lay, place (*sobre* on); *posar la mirada en* gaze at 2 *v/r posarse de ave, insecto*, AVIA land

posavasos *m inv* coaster

posdata *f* postscript

poseer ⟨2e⟩ *v/t* possess; (*ser dueño de*) own, possess

posesión *f* possession; *tomar posesión* (*de un cargo*) POL take up office

posguerra *f* postwar period

posibilidad *f* possibility

posibilitar ⟨1a⟩ *v/t* make possible

posible *adj* possible; *en lo posible* as far as possible; *hacer todo lo posible* do everything possible; *es posible que ...* perhaps ...

posición *f tb* MIL, *fig* position; *social* standing, status

positivo *adj* positive

posmoderno *adj* postmodern

poso *m* dregs *pl*

posología *f* dosage

posponer ⟨2r; *part* pospuesto⟩ *v/t* postpone

pospuesto *part* → *posponer*

posta *f*: *a posta* on purpose

postal 1 *adj* mail *atr*, postal 2 *f* postcard

poste *m* post

póster *m* poster

postergar ⟨1a⟩ *v/t* postpone

posteridad *f* posterity

posterior *adj* later, subsequent; (*trasero*) rear *atr*, back *atr*

postizo **1** *adj* false **2** *m* hairpiece

postor *m* bidder; *al mejor postor* to the highest bidder

postrar ⟨1a⟩ **1** *v/t*: *la gripe lo postró* he was laid up with flu **2** *v/r* postrarse prostrate o.s.

postre *m* dessert; *a la postre* in the end

postular ⟨1a⟩ *v/t hipótesis* put forward, advance

póstumo *adj* posthumous

postura *f tb fig* position

pos(t)venta *adj inv* after-sales *atr*

potable *adj* drinkable; (*fig* F) passable; *agua potable* drinking water

potaje *m* GASTR stew

potasio *m* potassium

potencia *f* power; *en potencia* potential

potencial *m/adj* potential

potenciar ⟨1b⟩ *v/t fig* foster, promote

potentado *m*, *-a f* tycoon

potente *adj* powerful

potestad *f* authority; *patria potestad* parental authority

potingue *m* F *desp* lotion, cream

potro *m* ZO colt

pozo *m* well; MIN shaft; *Rpl* pothole; *un pozo sin fondo fig* a bottomless pit

pozol *m C.Am.* corn liquor

pozole *m Méx* corn stew

práctica *f* practice

practicar ⟨1g⟩ *v/t* practice, *Br* practise; *deporte* play; *practicar la equitación / la esgrima* ride / fence

práctico *adj* practical

pradera *f* prairie, grassland

prado *m* meadow

pragmático *adj* pragmatic

pragmatismo *m* pragmatism

pral. *abr* (= *principal*) first

preámbulo *m* preamble

prebenda *f* sinecure

precalentamiento *m* DEP warm-up

precario *adj* precarious

precaución *f* precaution; *tomar precauciones* take precautions

precavido *adj* cautious

precedente **1** *adj* previous **2** *m* precedent

preceder ⟨2a⟩ *v/t* precede

preceptivo *adj* compulsory, mandatory

preciado *adj* precious

preciarse ⟨1b⟩ *v/r*: *cualquier fontanero que se precie ...* any self-respecting plumber ...

precinto *m* seal

precio *m* price; *precio de venta al público* recommended retail price

preciosidad *f*: *esa casa / chica es una preciosidad* that house / girl is gorgeous o beautiful

precioso *adj* (*de valor*) precious; (*hermoso*) beautiful

preciosura *f L.Am.* F → *preciosidad*

precipicio *m* precipice

precipitación *f* (*prisa*) hurry, haste; *precipitaciones* rain *sg*

precipitado *adj* hasty, sudden

precipitarse ⟨1a⟩ *v/r* rush; *fig* be hasty

precisamente *adv* precisely

precisión *f* precision

preciso *adj* precise, accurate; *ser preciso* be necessary

preconcebido *adj* preconceived

precoz *adj* early; *niño* precocious

precursor *m*, precursora *f* precursor, forerunner

predecesor *m*, predecesora *f* predecessor

predecir ⟨3p; *part* predicho ⟩ *v/t* predict

predestinar ⟨1a⟩ *v/t* predestine

predicado *m* predicate

predicador *m*, predicadora *f* preacher

predicar ⟨1g⟩ *v/t* preach; *predicar con el ejemplo* F practice (*Br* practise) what one preaches

predicción *f* prediction, forecast

predicho *part* → *predecir*

predilecto *adj* favo(u)rite

predisponer ⟨2r⟩ *v/t* prejudice

predisposición *f tb* MED predisposition; (*tendencia*) tendency; *una predisposición en contra de* a prejudice against

predispuesto *adj* predisposed (*a* to)

predominante *adj* predominant

predominar ⟨1a⟩ *v/t* predominate

preeminente *adj* preeminent

preescolar *adj* preschool

preestreno *m* preview

preexistente *adj* pre-existing

prefabricado *adj* prefabricated

prefacio *m* preface, foreword

preferencia *f* preference

preferente *adj* preferential

preferible *adj* preferable (*a* to); *es preferible que ...* it's better if ...

preferido **1** *part* → *preferir* **2** *adj* favo(u)rite

preferir ⟨3i⟩ *v/t* prefer

prefijo *m* prefix; TELEC area code, *Br* dialling code

pregonar ⟨1a⟩ *v/t* proclaim, make public

pregunta *f* question

preguntar ⟨1a⟩ **1** *v/t* ask **2** *v/i* ask; *preguntar por algo* ask about sth; *preguntar*

P

por alguien *paradero* ask for s.o.; *salud etc* ask about s.o. **3** *v/r* **preguntarse** wonder

prehistoria *f* prehistory
prehistórico *adj* prehistoric
prejuicio *m* prejudice
prelavado *m* prewash
preliminar 1 *adj* preliminary; DEP qualifying **2** *m L.Am.* qualifier
preludio *m* prelude
premamá *adj* maternity *atr*
prematrimonial *adj* premarital
prematuro 1 *adj* premature **2** *m*, **-a** *f* premature baby
premeditado *adj* premeditated
premeditación *f* premeditation; **con premeditación** deliberately
premiado 1 *adj* prizewinning **2** *m*, **-a** *f* prizewinner
premiar 〈1b〉 *v/t* award a prize to
premio *m* prize
premisa *f* premise
premonición *f* premonition
premura *f* haste
prenatal *adj* prenatal
prenda *f* item of clothing, garment; *garantía* security; *en juegos* forfeit; **no soltar prenda** not say a word (**sobre** about)
prender 〈2a; *part* **preso** 〉 *v/t a fugitivo* capture; *sujetar* pin up; *L.Am. fuego* light; *L.Am. luz* switch on, turn on; **prender fuego a** set fire to **2** *v/i de planta* take; *(empezar a arder)* catch; *de moda* catch on
prendería *f Esp* pawnbroker's, pawn shop
prensa *f* press; **prensa amarilla** gutter press
prensar 〈1a〉 *v/t* press
preñado *adj* pregnant
preocupación *f* worry, concern
preocupado *adj* worried (**por** about), concerned (**por** about)
preocupante *adj* worrying
preocupar 〈1a〉 *v/t* worry, concern **2** *v/r* **preocuparse** worry (**por** about); **preocuparse de** *(encargarse)* look after, take care of
preparación *f* preparation; *(educación)* education; *para trabajo* training
preparado *adj* ready, prepared
preparador *m*, **preparadora** *f*: **preparador físico** trainer
preparar 〈1a〉 **1** *v/t* prepare, get ready **2** *v/r* **prepararse** get ready (**para** for), prepare o.s. (**para** for); *de tormenta, crisis* be brewing
preparativos *mpl* preparations
preponderante *adj* predominant

preposición *f* preposition
prepotente *adj* arrogant
prerrogativa *f* prerogative
presa *f* *(dique)* dam; *(embalse)* reservoir; *(víctima)* prey; *L.Am. para comer* bite to eat
presagio *m* omen, sign; *(premonición)* premonition
prescindir 〈3a〉 *v/i*: **prescindir de** *(privarse de)* do without; *(omitir)* leave out, dispense with; *(no tener en cuenta)* disregard
prescribir 〈3a; *part* **prescrito** 〉 *v/i* JUR prescribe
prescrito *part* → **prescribir**
presencia *f* presence; **buena presencia** smart appearance
presenciar 〈1b〉 *v/t* witness; *(estar presente a)* attend, be present at
presentación *f* presentation; COM launch; *entre personas* introduction
presentador *m*, **presentadora** *f* TV presenter
presentar 〈1a〉 **1** *v/t* present; *a alguien* introduce; *producto* launch; *solicitud* submit **2** *v/r* **presentarse** *en sitio* show up; *(darse a conocer)* introduce o.s.; *a examen* take; *de problema, dificultad* arise; *a elecciones* run
presente 1 *adj*: **tener algo presente** bear sth in mind; **¡presente!** here! **2** *m tiempo* present **3** *m/fpl*: **los presentes** those present
presentimiento *m* premonition
presentir 〈3i〉 *v/t* foresee; **presiento que vendrá** I have a feeling he'll come
preservar 〈1a〉 *v/t* protect
preservativo *m* condom
presidencia *f* presidency; *de compañía* presidency, *Br* chairmanship; *de comité* chairmanship
presidencial *adj* presidential
presidente *m*, **-a** *f* president; *de gobierno* premier, prime minister; *de compañía* president, *Br* chairman, *Br mujer* chairwoman; *de comité* chair
presidiario *m*, **-a** *f* prisoner
presidir 〈3a〉 *v/t* be president of; *reunión* chair, preside over
presión *f* pressure; **presión sanguínea** blood pressure
presionar 〈1a〉 *v/t botón* press; *fig* put pressure on, pressure
preso 1 *part* → **prender 2** *m*, **-a** *f* prisoner
prestación *f* provision; **prestación social sustitutoria** MIL community service in lieu of military service
prestado *adj*: **dejar prestado algo** lend sth; **pedir prestado algo** borrow sth

prestamista *m/f* moneylender

préstamo *m* loan; *préstamo bancario* bank loan

prestar ⟨1a⟩ *v/t dinero* lend; *ayuda* give; *L.Am.* borrow; *prestar atencíon* pay attention

prestidigitador *m*, **prestidigitadora** *f* conjurer

prestigio *m* prestige

prestigioso *adj* prestigious

presumido *adj* conceited; *(coqueto)* vain

presumir ⟨3a⟩ **1** *v/t* presume **2** *v/i* show off; *presumir de algo* boast *o* brag about sth; *presume de listo* he thinks he's very clever

presuntamente *adv* allegedly

presunto *adj* alleged, suspected

presuntuoso *adj* conceited

presuponer ⟨2r; *part* **presupuesto**⟩ *v/t* assume

presupuesto 1 *part* → **presuponer 2** *m* POL budget

presuroso *adj* hurried

pretencioso *adj* pretentious

pretender ⟨2a⟩ *v/t*: *pretendía convencerlos* he was trying to persuade them

pretendiente *m de mujer* suitor

pretensión *f L.Am. (arrogancia)* vanity; *sin pretensiones* unpretentious

pretérito *m* GRAM preterite

pretextar ⟨1a⟩ *v/t* claim

pretexto *m* pretext

prevalecer ⟨2d⟩ *v/t* prevail (*sobre* over)

prevaricación *f* corruption

prevención *f* prevention

prevenido 1 *part* → **prevenir 2** *adj* well-prepared

prevenir ⟨3s⟩ *v/t* prevent; *(avisar)* warn (*contra* against)

preventivo *adj* preventive, preventative

prever ⟨2v; *part* **previsto**⟩ *v/t* foresee

previo *adj* previous; *sin previo aviso* without (prior) warning

previsible *adj* foreseeable

previsión *f (predicción)* forecast; *(preparación)* foresight

previsor *adj* farsighted

previsto 1 *part* → **prever 2** *adj* foreseen, expected; *tener previsto* have planned

prieto *adj L.Am.* dark-skinned

prima *f de seguro* premium; *(pago extra)* bonus

primacía *f* supremacy, primacy; *(prioridad)* priority

primario *adj* primary

primavera *f* spring; BOT primrose

primer *adj* first

primera *f* first class; AUTO first gear; *a la primera* first-time; *de primera* F first-

-class, first-rate

primerizo *adj* inexperienced, green F; *madre* new, first-time

primero 1 *adj* first; *primeros auxilios pl* first aid *sg* **2** *m*, *-a f* first (one) **3** *adv* first

primitivo *adj* primitive; *(original)* original

primo *m*, *-a f* cousin

primogénito 1 *adj* first **2** *m*, *-a f* first child

primordial *adj* fundamental

primoroso *adj* exquisite

princesa *f* princess

principal *adj* main, principal; *lo principal* the main *o* most important thing

príncipe *m* prince

principiante 1 *adj* inexperienced **2** *m/f* beginner

principio *m* principle; *en tiempo* beginning; *a principios de abril* at the beginning of April; *en principio* in principle

pringar ⟨1h⟩ **1** *v/t ensuciar* get greasy; *fig* F get involved (*en* in) **2** *v/r* **pringarse** get greasy; *fig* F get mixed up (*en* in)

pringoso *adj* greasy

pringue *f* greasy

prioridad *f* priority

prioritario *adj* priority *atr*

prisa *f* hurry, rush; *darse prisa* hurry (up); *tener prisa* be in a hurry *o* rush

prisión *f* prison, jail

prisionero 1 *adj* captive **2** *m*, *-a f* prisoner

prismáticos *mpl* binoculars

priva *f Esp* F booze F

privacidad *f* privacy

privación *f acción* deprivation; *sufrir privaciones* sufffer privation(s) *o* hardship

privado 1 *part* → **privar 2** *adj* private

privar ⟨1a⟩ **1** *v/t*: *privar a alguien de algo* deprive s.o. of sth **2** *v/r* **privarse** deprive o.s.; *privarse de algo* deprive o.s. of sth, go without sth

privatización *f* privatization

privatizar ⟨1f⟩ *v/t* privatize

privilegiado *adj* privileged; *(excelente)* exceptional

privilegio *m* privilege

pro 1 *prp* for, in aid of; *en pro de* for **2** *m* pro; *los pros y los contras* the pros and cons

proa *f* MAR bow

probabilidad *f* probability

probable *adj* probable, likely; *es probable que venga* she'll probably come

probador *m* fitting room

probar ⟨1m⟩ **1** *v/t teoría* test, try out; *(comer un poco de)* taste, try; *(comer por primera vez)* try **2** *v/i* try; *probar a hacer* try doing **3** *v/r* **probarse** try on

probeta *f* test tube

problema *m* problem

problemático *adj* problematic

procedencia *f* origin, provenance

proceder ⟨2a⟩ **1** *v/i* come (*de* from); (*actuar*) proceed; (*ser conveniente*) be fitting; **proceder a** proceed to; **proceder contra alguien** initiate proceedings against s.o. **2** *m* conduct

procedimiento *m* procedure, method; JUR proceedings *pl*

procesado *m*, -a *f* accused, defendant

procesador *m* INFOR processor; **procesador de textos** word processor

procesamiento *m*: **procesamiento de textos** word processing

procesar ⟨1a⟩ *v/t* INFOR process; JUR prosecute

procesión *f* procession

proceso *m* process; JUR trial; **proceso de datos / textos** INFOR data / word processing

proclamar ⟨1a⟩ *v/t* proclaim

proclive *adj* given (*a* to)

procrear ⟨1a⟩ *v/i* breed, procreate *fml*

procurar ⟨1a⟩ *v/t* try; **procura no llegar tarde** try not to be late

prodigar ⟨1h⟩ **1** *v/t* be generous with **2** *v/r* **prodigarse** (*aparecer*) be seen in public

prodigio *m* wonder, miracle; *persona* prodigy

prodigioso *adj* prodigious

pródigo *adj* (*generoso*) generous; (*derrochador*) extravagant

producción *f* production

producir ⟨3o⟩ **1** *v/t* produce; (*causar*) cause **2** *v/r* **producirse** happen, occur; **se produjo un ruido tremendo** there was a tremendous noise

productividad *f* productivity

productivo *adj* productive; *empresa* profitable

producto *m* product; **producto interior bruto** gross domestic product; **producto nacional bruto** gross national product

productor *m*, productora *f* producer

produjo *vb* → **producir**

produzco *vb* → **producir**

proeza *f* feat, exploit

profana *f* laywoman

profanar ⟨1a⟩ *v/t* defile, desecrate

profano **1** *adj fig* lay *atr* **2** *m* layman

profecía *f* prophecy

profesar ⟨1a⟩ *v/t* REL profess; *fig* feel, have

profesión *f* profession

profesional *m/f* & *adj* professional

profesor *m*, profesora *f* teacher; *de universidad* professor, *Br* lecturer

profesorado *m* faculty, *Br* staff *pl*

profeta *m* prophet

profetizar ⟨1f⟩ *v/t* prophesy

profiláctico **1** *adj* preventive, prophylactic *fml* **2** *m* condom

prófugo *m*, -a *f* JUR fugitive

profundidad *f* depth

profundizar ⟨1f⟩ *v/i*: **profundizar en algo** go into sth in depth

profundo *adj* deep; *pensamiento, persona* profound

profuso *adj* abundant, plentiful

programa *m* program, *Br* programme; INFOR program; EDU syllabus; **programa de estudios** curriculum

programación *f* RAD, TV programs *pl*, *Br* programmes; INFOR programming

programador *m*, programadora *f* programmer

programar ⟨1a⟩ *v/t* *aparato* program, *Br* programme; INFOR program; (*planear*) schedule

progresar ⟨1a⟩ *v/i* progress, make progress

progresista *m/f* & *adj* progressive

progresivo *adj* progressive

progreso *m* progress

prohibición *f* ban (*de* on)

prohibido *adj* forbidden

prohibir ⟨3a⟩ *v/t* forbid; *oficialmente* ban

prohibitivo *adj precio* prohibitive

prójimo *m* fellow human being

prole *f* offspring

proletario **1** *adj* proletarian **2** *m*, -a *f* proletarian

proliferación *f* proliferation

proliferar ⟨1a⟩ *v/t* proliferate

prolífico *adj* prolific

prolijo *adj* long-winded; (*minucioso*) detailed

prólogo *m* preface

prolongado *adj* prolonged, lengthy

prolongar ⟨1h⟩ **1** *v/t* extend, prolong **2** *v/r* **prolongarse** go *o* carry on; *en espacio* extend

promedio *m* average

promesa *f* promise

prometedor *adj* bright, promising

prometer ⟨2a⟩ **1** *v/t* promise **2** *v/r* **prometerse** get engaged

prometida *f* fiancée

prometido **1** *part* → **prometer 2** *adj* engaged **3** *m* fiancé

prominente *adj* prominent

promiscuidad *f* promiscuity

promiscuo *adj* promiscuous

promoción *f* promotion; EDU year

promocionar ⟨1a⟩ *v/t* promote

promotor *m*, promotora *f* promoter; **promotor inmobiliario** developer

promover ⟨2h⟩ *v/t* promote; (*causar*) provoke, cause

promulgar ⟨1h⟩ *v/t ley* promulgate

pronombre *m* GRAM pronoun

pronosticar ⟨1g⟩ *v/t* forecast

pronóstico *m* MED prognosis; **pronóstico del tiempo** weather forecast

pronto 1 *adj* prompt **2** *adv (dentro de poco)* soon; *(temprano)* early; **de pronto** suddenly; **tan pronto como** as soon as

pronunciación *f* pronunciation

pronunciar ⟨1b⟩ *v/t* pronounce; *(decir)* say; **pronunciar un discurso** give a speech

propaganda *f* advertising; POL propaganda

propagar ⟨1h⟩ **1** *v/t* spread **2** *v/r* **propagarse** spread

propano *m* propane

proparse ⟨1a⟩ *v/r* go too far

propenso *adj* prone (**a** to); **ser propenso a hacer** be prone to do, have a tendency to do

propiciar ⟨1b⟩ *v/t (favorecer)* promote; *(causar)* bring about

propicio *adj* favo(u)rable

propiedad *f* property

propietario *m*, **-a** *f* owner

propina *f* tip

propinar ⟨1a⟩ *v/t golpe, paliza* give

propio *adj* own; *(característico)* characteristic (**de** of), typical (**de** of); *(adecuado)* suitable (**para** for); **la -a directora** the director herself

proponer ⟨2r; *part* **propuesto** ⟩ *v/t* propose, suggest

proporción *f* proportion

proporcional *adj* proportional

proporcionar ⟨1a⟩ *v/t* provide, supply; *satisfacción* give

proposición *f* proposal, suggestion

propósito *m (intención)* intention; *(objetivo)* purpose; **a propósito** on purpose; *(por cierto)* by the way

propuesto *part* → **proponer**

propuesta *f* proposal

propugnar ⟨1a⟩ *v/t* advocate

propulsar ⟨1a⟩ *v/t* TÉC propel; *fig* promote

propulsor *m (motor)* engine

prórroga *f* DEP overtime, *Br* extra time

prorrogar ⟨1h⟩ *v/t plazo* extend

prorrumpir ⟨3a⟩ *v/i* burst (**en** into)

prosa *f* prose

prosaico *adj* mundane, prosaic

proseguir ⟨3d & 3l⟩ **1** *v/t* carry on, continue **2** *v/i* continue (**con** with)

proselitismo *m* proselytism

prospecto *m* directions for use *pl*; *de propaganda* leaflet

prosperar ⟨1a⟩ *v/i* prosper, thrive

prosperidad *f* prosperity

próspero *adj* prosperous, thriving

próstata *f* prostate

prostíbulo *m* brothel

prostitución *f* prostitution

prostituirse ⟨3g⟩ *v/r* prostitute o.s.

prostituta *f* prostitute

prostituto *m* male prostitute

protagonista *m/f personaje* main character; *actor, actriz* star; *de una hazaña* hero; *mujer* heroine

protagonizar ⟨1f⟩ *v/t* star in, play the lead in; *incidente* play a leading role in

protección *f* protection

proteger ⟨2c⟩ *v/t* protect (**de** from)

proteína *f* protein

protésico *m*, **-a** *f*: **protésico dental** dental technician

prótesis *f* prosthesis

protesta *f* protest

protestante *m/f* Protestant

protestar ⟨1a⟩ **1** *v/t* protest **2** *v/i (quejarse)* complain (**por, de** about); *(expresar oposición)* protest (**contra, por** about, against)

protocolo *m* protocol

prototipo *m* TÉC prototype

protuberancia *f* protuberance

prov. *abr* (= **provincia**) province

provecho *m* benefit; **¡buen provecho!** enjoy (your meal); **sacar provecho de** benefit from

proveedor *m*, **proveedora** *f* supplier; **proveedor de (acceso a) Internet** Internet Service Provider, ISP

proveer ⟨2e; *part* **provisto** ⟩ *v/t* supply; **proveer a alguien de algo** supply s.o. with sth

provenir ⟨3s⟩ *v/i* come (**de** from)

proverbio *m* proverb

providencia *f* providence

provincia *f* province

provincial *adj* provincial

provinciano 1 *adj* provincial **2** *m*, **-a** *f* provincial

provisional *adj* provisional

provisiones *fpl* provisions

provisto 1 *part* → **proveer 2** *adj*: **provisto de** equipped with

provocación *f* provocation

provocador *adj* provocative

provocar ⟨1g⟩ *v/t* cause; *al enfado* provoke; *sexualmente* lead on; **¿te provoca un café?** *S. Am.* how about a coffee?

provocativo *adj* provocative

proxeneta *m* pimp

proxenetismo *m* procuring

proximidad *f* proximity

próximo *adj (siguiente)* next; *(cercano)* near, close

P

proyección f MAT, PSI projection; *de película* showing

proyectar ⟨1a⟩ v/t project; *(planear)* plan; *película* show; *sombra* cast

proyectil m missile

proyecto m plan; *trabajo* project; **proyecto de ley** bill; **tener en proyecto hacer algo** plan to do sth

proyector m projector

prudencia f caution, prudence

prudente adj careful, cautious

prueba f tb TIP proof; JUR piece of evidence; DEP event; EDU test; **a prueba de bala** bulletproof; **poner algo a prueba** put sth to the test

P.S. abr (= *postscriptum (posdata)*) PS (= postscript)

pseudo... pref pseudo-

pseudónimo m pseudonym

psicoanálisis f (psycho)analysis

psicoanalista m/f (psycho)analyst

psicodélico adj psychedelic

psicología f psychology

psicológico adj psychological

psicólogo m, -a f psychologist

psicópata m/f psychopath

psicosis f inv psychosis

psicoterapia f psychotherapy

psiquiatra m/f psychiatrist

psiquiatría f psychiatry

psiquiátrico adj psychiatric

psíquico adj psychic

pta abr (= *peseta*) peseta

ptas abr (= *pesetas*) pesetas

púa f ZO spine, quill; MÚS plectrum, pick

pub m bar

pubertad f puberty

publicación f publication

publicar ⟨1g⟩ 1 v/t publish 2 v/r publicarse come out, be published

publicidad f *(divulgación)* publicity; COM advertising; *(anuncios)* advertisements pl

publicista m/f advertising executive

publicitario 1 adj advertising atr 2 m, -a f advertising executive

público 1 adj public; *escuela* public, Br state 2 m public; TEA audience; DEP spectators pl, crowd

pucho m S. Am. P cigarette butt, Br fag end F; **no valer un pucho** be completely worthless

pude vb → **poder**

púdico adj modest

pudín m pudding

pudo vb → **poder**

pudor m modesty

pudrir ⟨3a⟩ 1 v/t rot 2 v/r **pudrirse** rot; **pudrirse de envidia** be green with envy

pueblerino m, -a f hick desp

pueblero m, -a f L.Am. villager; *de pueblo más grande* townsman; *mujer* townswoman

pueblo m village; *más grande* town

puedo vb → **poder**

puente m bridge; **hacer puente** have a day off between a weekend and a public holiday

puenting m bungee jumping

puerco 1 adj dirty; *fig* filthy F 2 m ZO pig; **puerco espín** porcupine

puericultura f childcare

puerro m BOT leek

puerta f door; *en valla* gate; DEP goal; **puerta de embarque** gate

puerto m MAR port; GEOG pass

Puerto Rico Puerto Rico

puertorriqueño 1 adj Puerto Rican 2 m, -a f Puerto Rican

pues conj well; *fml (porque)* as, since; **pues bien** well; **¡pues sí!** of course!

puesta f: **puesta a punto** tune-up; **puesta de sol** sunset

puestero m, -a f L.Am. stall holder

puesto 1 part → **poner** 2 m lugar place; *en mercado* stand, stall; MIL post; **puesto (de trabajo)** job 3 conj: **puesto que** since, given that

pugnar ⟨1a⟩ v/i fight (*por* for; *por hacer* to do)

puja f *(lucha)* struggle; *en subasta* bid

pujar ⟨1a⟩ v/i *(luchar)* struggle; *en subasta* bid

pulcro adj immaculate

pulga f ZO flea; **tener malas pulgas** fig F be bad-tempered

pulgada f inch

pulgar m thumb

pulimentar ⟨1a⟩ v/t polish

pulir ⟨3a⟩ v/t polish

pulla f gibe

pulmón m lung

pulmonía f MED pneumonia

pulpa f pulp

pulpería f L.Am. mom-and-pop store, Br corner shop

pulpero m, -a f S. Am. storekeeper, shopkeeper

púlpito m pulpit

pulpo m ZO octopus

pulque m Méx pulque *(alcoholic drink made from cactus)*

pulquería f Méx pulque bar

pulsación f beat; *al escribir a máquina* key stroke

pulsar ⟨1a⟩ v/t *botón, tecla* press

pulsera f bracelet

pulso m pulse; *fig* steady hand; **tomar el pulso a alguien** take s.o.'s pulse; **tomar**

el pulso a algo *fig* take the pulse of sth
pulular ⟨1a⟩ *v/i* mill around
pulverizador *m* spray
pulverizar ⟨1f⟩ *v/t* spray; (*convertir en polvo*) pulverize, crush
puma *m* zo puma, mountain lion
puna *f L.Am.* GEOG high Andean plateau; MED altitude sickness
pundonor *m* pride
punitivo *adj* punitive
punta *f* tip; (*extremo*) end; *de lápiz*, GEOG point; *L.Am.* (*grupo*) group; **sacar punta a** sharpen
puntada *f* stitch
puntapié *m* kick
puntera *f* toe
puntería *f* aim
puntero 1 *adj* leading **2** *m* pointer
puntiagudo *adj* pointed, sharp
puntilla *f:* **de puntillas** on tippy-toe, *Br* on tiptoe
puntilloso *adj* particular, punctilious *fml*
punto *m* point, *señal* dot; *signo de punctuación* period, *Br* full stop; **en costura**, *sutura* stitch; **dos puntos** colon; **punto muerto** AUTO neutral; **punto de vista** point of view; **punto y coma** semicolon; **a punto** (*listo*) ready; (*a tiempo*) in time; **de punto** knitted; **en punto** on the dot; **estar a punto de** be about to; **hacer punto** knit; **hasta cierto punto** up to a point; **empresa** *f* **punto.com** dot.com (company)
puntuación *f* punctuation; DEP score; EDU grade, mark
puntual *adj* punctual
puntualidad *f* punctuality
puntualizar ⟨1f⟩ *v/t* (*señalar*) point out; (*aclarar*) clarify
punzada *f* sharp *o* stabbing pain
punzante *adj* stinging
puñado *m* handful
puñal *m* dagger
puñalada *f* stab wound
puñeta *f:* **¡puñeta(s)!** F for heaven's sake! F; **hacer la puñeta a alguien** F give s.o. a

hard time F
puñetazo *m* punch; **dar un puñetazo** punch
puño *m* fist; *de camisa* cuff; *de bastón*, *paraguas* handle
pupa *f en labio* cold sore; **hacerse pupa** *lenguaje infantil* hurt o.s.
pupila *f* pupil
pupitre *m* desk
pupusa *f L.Am.* filled dumpling
purasangre *m* thoroughbred
puré *m* purée; *sopa* cream; **puré de patatas** *or* **papas** *L.Am.* mashed potatoes
pureza *f* purity
purga *f* POL purge
purgante *m/adj* laxative, purgative
purgatorio *m* REL purgatory
purificación *f* purification
purificar ⟨1g⟩ *v/t* purify
purista *m/f* purist
puritano 1 *adj* puritanical **2** *m*, **-a** *f* puritan
puro 1 *adj* pure; *casualidad, coincidencia* sheer; *Méx* (*único*) sole, only; **la -a verdad** the honest truth; **te sirven la -a comida** *Méx* they just serve food **2** *m* cigar
púrpura *f* purple
pus *m* pus
puse *vb* → **poder**
pusilánime *adj* fainthearted
puso *vb* → **poder**
puta *f* P whore P
putada *f* P dirty trick; **¡qué putada!** shit! P
putear ⟨1a⟩ *v/t L.Am.* P swear at; **putear alguien** *Esp* give s.o. a hard time, make life difficult for s.o.
puto *adj* P goddamn F, *Br* bloody F; **de puta madre** P great F, fantastic F
putrefacción *f* putrefaction
puzzle *m* jigsaw (puzzle)
PVC *abr* (= **cloruro de polivinilo**) PVC (= polyvinyl chloride)
P.V.P. *abr* (= **precio de venta al público**) RRP (= recommended retail price)
pza. *abr* (= **plaza**) sq (= square)

Q

q.e.p. d. *abr* (= *que en paz descanse*)
RIP (= requiescat in pace)

que 1 *pron rel sujeto: persona* who, that;
cosa which, that; *complemento: persona*
that, whom *fml; cosa* that, which; *el coche que ves* the car you can see, the car
that *o* which you can see; *el que* the one
that **2** *conj* that; *lo mismo que tú* the
same as you; *¡que entre!* tell him to
come in; *¡que descanses!* sleep well;
¡que sí! I said yes; *¡que no!* I said no;
es que ... the thing is ...; *yo que tú* if
I were you

qué 1 *adj & pron interr* what; *¿qué pasó?*
what happened?; *¿qué día es?* what day
is it?; *¿qué vestido prefieres?* which
dress do you prefer? **2** *adj & pron int:*
¡qué moto! what a motorbike!; *¡qué
de flores!* what a lot of flowers! **3** *adv:*
¡qué alto es! he's so tall!; *¡qué bien!*
great!

quebrada *f L.Am.* stream

quebradero *m:* **quebraderos de cabeza**
F headaches

quebradizo *adj* brittle

quebrado 1 *adj* broken **2** *m* MAT fraction

quebrantahuesos *m inv* ZO lammergeier

quebrantar ⟨1a⟩ *v/t ley, contrato* break

quebrar ⟨1k⟩ **1** *v/t* break **2** *v/i* COM go
bankrupt **3** *v/r quebrarse* break

quedar ⟨1a⟩ **1** *v/i* (*permanecer*) stay; *en
un estado* be; (*sobrar*) be left; *quedó
sin resolver* it wasn't sorted out, it
wasn't sorted out; *te queda bien / mal
de estilo* it suits you / doesn't suit you;
de talla it fits you / doesn't fit you; *quedar cerca* be nearby; *quedar con alguien* F arrange to meet (with) s.o.; *quedar en algo* agree to sth; *¿queda mucho
tiempo?* is there much time left? **2** *v/r*
quedarse stay; *quedarse ciego* go
blind; *quedarse con algo* keep sth;
me quedé sin comer I ended up not eating

quehaceres *mpl* tasks

queja *f* complaint

quejarse ⟨1a⟩ *v/r* complain (*a* to; *de*
about)

quejica *adj* F whining F

quejido *m* moan, groan

quejumbroso *adj* moaning

quemado *adj* burnt; *Méx* (*desvirtuado*)
discredited; *quemado por el sol* sun-
burnt; *oler a quemado* smell of burning

quemadura *f* burn

quemar ⟨1a⟩ **1** *v/t* burn; *con agua* scald; F
recursos use up; F *dinero* blow F **2** *v/i* be
very hot **3** *v/r* **quemarse** burn o.s.; *de tostada, papeles* burn; *fig* burn o.s. out; *Méx*
(*desvirtuarse*) become discredited

quena *f S. Am.* Indian flute

quepo *vb* → *caber*

queque *m L.Am.* cake

querella *f* JUR lawsuit

querellarse ⟨1a⟩ *v/r* JUR bring a lawsuit
(*contra* against)

querer ⟨2u⟩ *v/t* (*desear*) want; (*amar*)
love; *querer decir* mean; *sin querer* un-
intentionally; *quisiera ...* I would like ...

querido 1 *part* → *querer* **2** *adj* dear **3** *m,* -a
f darling

queroseno *m* kerosene

queso *m* cheese; *queso para untar*
cheese spread; *queso rallado* grated
cheese

quicio *m:* *sacar de quicio a alguien* F
drive s.o. crazy F

quid *m:* *el quid de la cuestión* the nub of
the question

quiebra *f* COM bankruptcy

quien *pron rel sujeto* who, that; *objeto*
who, whom *fml,* that; *no soy quien para
hacerlo* I'm not the right person to do it

quién *pron* who; *¿quién es?* who is it?;
¿de quién es este libro? whose is this
book?, who does this book belong to?

quienquiera *pron* whoever

quiero *vb* → *querer*

quieto *adj* still; *¡estáte quieto!* keep still!

quijotesco *adj* quixotic

quilate *m* carat

quilla *f* keel

quimera *f* pipe dream

química *f* chemistry

químico 1 *adj* chemical **2** *m,* -a *f* chemist

quimioterapia *f* MED chemotherapy

quimono *m* kimono

quincalla *f* junk

quince *adj* fifteen

quincena *f* two weeks, *Br* fortnight

quiniela *f* lottery where the winners are de-
cided by soccer results

quinientos *adj* five hundred

quinina *f* quinine

quinquenio *m* five-year period

quinta *f* MIL draft, *Br* call-up; *es de mi quinta* he's my age
quinteto *m* MÚS quintet
quinto 1 *adj* fifth **2** *m* MIL conscript
quiosco *m* kiosk; *quiosco de prensa* newsstand, *Br* newsagent's
quiosquero *m*, **-a** *f* newspaper vendor
quirófano *m* operating room, *Br* operating theatre
quiromancia, quiromancía *f* palmistry
quirúrgico *adj* surgical
quise *vb* → **querer**
quisiera *vb* → **querer**
quiso *vb* → **querer**
quisque F: *todo quisque* everyone and his brother F, *Br* the world and his wife F

quisquilla *f* ZO shrimp
quisquilloso *adj* touchy
quiste *m* MED cyst
quitaesmalte *m* nail varnish remover
quitamanchas *m inv* stain remover
quitar ⟨1a⟩ **1** *v/t ropa* take off, remove; *obstáculos* remove; *quitar algo a alguien* take sth (away) from s.o.; *quitar la mesa* clear the table **2** *v/i*: ¡*quita*! get out of the way! **3** *v/r* **quitarse** *ropa, gafas* take off; (*apartarse*) get out of the way; *quitarse algo/a alguien de encima* get rid of s.o./sth; ¡*quítate de en medio*! F get out of the way!
quizá(s) *adv* perhaps, maybe
quórum *m* quorum

R

rabadilla *f* ANAT coccyx
rábano *m* BOT radish; *me importa un rábano* F I don't give a damn F
rabia *f* MED rabies *sg*; *dar rabia a alguien* make s.o. mad; *tener rabia a alguien* have it in for s.o.
rabiar ⟨1b⟩ *v/i*: *rabiar de dolor* be in agony; *hacer rabiar a alguien* fig F jerk s.o.'s chain F, pull s.o.'s leg F; *rabiar por* be dying for
rabieta *f* tantrum
rabino *m* rabbi
rabo *m* tail
rabioso *adj* MED rabid; *fig* furious
rabón *adj* L.Am. *animal* short-tailed
rácano *adj* F stingy F, mean
racha *f* spell
racial *adj* racial
racimo *m* bunch
ración *f* share; (*porción*) serving, portion
racional *adj* rational
racionalizar ⟨1f⟩ *v/t* rationalize
racionamiento *m* rationing
racionar ⟨1a⟩ *v/t* ration
racismo *m* racism
racista *m/f & adj* racist
radar *m* radar
radiación *f* radiation
radiactividad *f* radioactivity
radiactivo *adj* radioactive
radiador *m* radiator
radiante *adj* radiant
radiar ⟨1b⟩ *v/t* radiate

radical *m/f & adj* radical
radicalismo *m* radicalism
radicar ⟨1g⟩ *v/i* stem (*en* from), lie (*en* in)
radio 1 *m* MAT radius; QUÍM radium; *L.Am.* radio; *en un radio de* within a radius of; *radio de acción* range **2** *f* radio; *radio despertador* clock radio
radioaficionado *m* radio ham
radiocasete *m* radio cassette player
radiodifusión *f* broadcasting
radiofónico *adj* radio *atr*
radiografía *f* X-ray
radiografiar ⟨1c⟩ *v/t* X-ray
radiología *f* radiology
radiólogo *m*, **-a** *f* radiologist
radiotaxi *m* radio taxi
radiotelegrafista *m/f* radio operator
radioyente *m/f* listener
ráfaga *f* gust; *de balas* burst
rafting *m* rafting
ragú *m* GASTR ragout
raído *adj* threadbare
rail, raíl *m* rail
raíz *f* root; *raíz cuadrada /cúbica* MAT square / cube root; *a raíz de* as a result of; *echar raíces de persona* put down roots
raja *f* (*rodaja*) slice; (*corte*) cut; (*grieta*) crack
rajar ⟨1a⟩ **1** *v/t fruta* cut, slice; *cerámica* crack; *neumático* slash **2** *v/i* F gossip **3** *v/r* **rajarse** fig F back out F

R

rajatabla: *a rajatabla* strictly, to the letter
ralentí *m*: *al ralentí* AUTO idling; FOT in slow motion
ralentizar ⟨1f⟩ *v/t* slow down
rallador *m* grater
rallar ⟨1a⟩ *v/t* GASTR grate
rally(e) *m* rally
rama *f* branch; POL wing; *andarse por las ramas* beat about the bush
ramificación *f* ramification
ramo *m* COM sector; *ramo de flores* bunch of flowers
rampa *f* ramp; *rampa de lanzamiento* launch pad
ramplón *adj* vulgar
rana *f* ZO frog
ranchera *f* typical Mexican song
ranchero *adj*: *canción -a* romantic ballad; *música -a* music of northern Mexico **2** *m* L.Am. rancher
rancho *m* Méx small farm; L.Am. (*barrio de chabolas*) shanty town
rancio *adj* rancid; *fig* ancient
rango *m* rank; *de alto rango* high-ranking
ranking *m* ranking
ranura *f* slot
rapapolvo *m* F telling-off F
rapar ⟨1a⟩ *v/t pelo* crop
rapaz 1 *adj* predatory; *ave rapaz* bird of prey **2** *m*, *-a* f F kid F
rape *m pescado* anglerfish; *al rape pelo* cropped
rapidez *f* speed, rapidity
rápido 1 *adj* quick, fast **2** *m* rapids *pl*
rapiña *f* pillage
raptar ⟨1a⟩ *v/t* kidnap
rapto *m* kidnap
raptor *m*, **raptora** *f* kidnapper
raqueta *f* racket
raquítico *adj fig* rickety
rareza *f* scarcity, rarity
raro *adj* rare
ras *m*: *a ras de tierra* at ground level
rasante *adj vuelo* low
rasca *f* L.Am.: *pegarse una rasca* F get plastered F
rascacielos *m inv* skyscraper
rascado *adj* L.Am. F plastered F
rascar ⟨1g⟩ *v/t* scratch; *superficie* scrape, scratch
rasero *m*: *medir por el mismo rasero* treat equally
rasgado *adj boca* wide; *ojos rasgados* almond-shaped eyes
rasgar ⟨1h⟩ *v/t* tear (up)
rasgo *m* feature; *a grandes rasgos* broadly speaking
rasguño *m* MED scratch
raso 1 *adj* flat, level; *soldado raso* pri-

vate **2** *m material* satin; *al raso* in the open air
raspa *f* fishbone; L.Am. F (*reprimanda*) telling-off
raspado *m* Méx water ice
raspadura *f* scrape
raspar ⟨1a⟩ **1** *v/t* scrape; *con lija* sand **2** *v/i* be rough
rastra *f*: *entrar a rastras* drag o.s. in, crawl in
rastreador *adj*: *perro rastreador* tracker dog
rastrear ⟨1a⟩ **1** *v/t persona* track; *bosque, zona comb* **2** *v/i* rake
rastrero *adj* mean, low
rastrillo *m* rake
rastro *m* flea market; (*huella*) trace; *desaparecer sin dejar rastro* vanish without trace
rastrojo *m* stubble
rasurar ⟨1a⟩ *v/t* shave
rata *f* ZO rat
ratero *m*, *-a* f petty thief
raticida *m* rat poison
ratificar ⟨1g⟩ *v/t* POL ratify
rato *m* time, while; *ratos libres* spare time *sg*; *al poco rato* after a short time *o* while; *todo el rato* all the time; *un buen rato* a good while, a pretty long time; *pasar el rato* pass the time; *he pasado un buen / mal rato* I've had a great / an awful time
ratón *m* ZO, INFOR mouse
ratonera *f* mouse trap
raudal *m*: *tienen dinero a raudales* they've got loads of money F
raudo *adj* swift
raya *f* GRAM dash; ZO ray; *de pelo* part, Br parting; *a or de rayas* striped; *pasarse de la raya* overstep the mark, go too far
rayado *adj disco, superficie* scratched
rayano *adj* bordering (*en* on)
rayar ⟨1a⟩ **1** *v/t* scratch; (*tachar*) cross out **2** *v/i* border (*en* on), verge (*en* on)
rayo *m* FÍS ray; METEO (bolt of) lightning; *rayo láser* laser beam; *rayo X* X-ray; *rayos ultravioleta* ultraviolet rays
raza *f* race; *de animal* breed
razón *f* reason; *a razón de precio* at; *dar la razón a alguien* admit that s.o. is right; *entrar en razón* see sense; *perder la razón* lose one's mind; *tener razón* be right
razonable *adj precio* reasonable
razonamiento *m* reasoning
razonar ⟨1a⟩ *v/i* reason
RDSI *abr* (= *Red Digital de Servicios Integrados*) ISDN (= Integrated Services Digital Network)

reacción *f* reaction (*a* to); *avión a reacción* jet (aircraft)

reaccionar ⟨1a⟩ *v/i* react (*a* to)

reaccionario 1 *adj* reactionary **2** *m*, -a *f* reactionary

reacio *adj* reluctant (*a* to)

reactivación *f* COM revival, upturn

reactivar ⟨1a⟩ *v/t* COM revive

reactor *m* reactor; (*motor*) jet engine

reafirmar 1 *v/t* reaffirm **2** *v/r* reafirmarse: *reafirmarse en idea* reassert

reajuste *m* adjustment; *reajuste ministerial* POL cabinet reshuffle

real *adj* (*regio*) royal; (*verdadero*) real

realeza *f* royalty

realidad *f* reality; *en realidad* in fact, in reality

realismo *m* realism

realista 1 *adj* realistic **2** *m/f* realist

realización *f* fulfil(l)ment; RAD, TV production

realizador *m*, **realizadora** *f* de película director; RAD, TV producer

realizar ⟨1f⟩ **1** *v/t tarea* carry out; RAD, TV produce; COM realize **2** *v/r* realizarse de *persona* fulfil(l) o.s.

realquilar ⟨1a⟩ *v/t* sublet

realzar ⟨1f⟩ *v/t* highlight

reanimación *f* revival

reanimar ⟨1a⟩ *v/t* revive

reanudación *f* resumption

reanudar ⟨1a⟩ *v/t* resume

reaparecer ⟨2d⟩ *v/i* reappear

reaparición *f* reappearance

reaseguro *m* reinsurance

rebaja *f* reduction; *rebajas de verano / invierno* summer / winter sale

rebajar ⟨1a⟩ **1** *v/t precio* lower, reduce; *mercancías* reduce **2** *v/r* rebajarse lower o.s., humble o.s.

rebanada *f* slice

rebanar ⟨1a⟩ *v/t* slice

rebañar ⟨1a⟩ *v/t*: *rebañar algo* wipe sth clean

rebaño *m* flock

rebasar ⟨1a⟩ *v/t Méx* AUTO pass; *Br* overtake

rebatir ⟨3a⟩ *v/t razones* rebut, refute

rebeca *f* cardigan

rebeco *m* ZO chamois

rebelarse ⟨1a⟩ *v/r* rebel

rebelde 1 *adj* rebel *atr* **2** *m/f* rebel

rebeldía *f* rebelliousness

rebelión *f* rebellion

reblandecer ⟨2d⟩ *v/t* soften

rebobinar ⟨1a⟩ *v/t* rewind

rebosar ⟨1a⟩ *v/i* overflow

rebotar ⟨1a⟩ **1** *v/t* bounce; (*disgustar*) annoy **2** *v/i* bounce, rebound

rebote *m* bounce; *de rebote* on the rebound

rebozar ⟨1f⟩ *v/t* GASTR coat

rebuscado *adj* over-elaborate

rebuznar ⟨1a⟩ *v/i* bray

recado *m* errand; *Rpl* (*arnés*) harness; *dejar un recado* leave a message

recaída *f* MED relapse

recalar ⟨1a⟩ *v/i* MAR put in (*en* at), call (*en* at)

recalcar ⟨1g⟩ *v/t* stress, emphasize

recalcitrante *adj* recalcitrant

recalentar ⟨1k⟩ *v/t comida* warm *o* heat up

recámara *f* de arma de fuego chamber; *L.Am.* (*dormitorio*) bedroom

recambio *m* COM spare part

recapacitar ⟨1a⟩ *v/t* think over, reflect on

recapitular ⟨1a⟩ *v/t* recap

recargar ⟨1h⟩ *v/t batería* recharge; *reci piente* refill; *recargar un 5%* charge 5% extra

recargo *m* surcharge

recatado *adj* modest; (*cauto*) cautious

recato *m* modesty; (*prudencia*) caution

recauchutar ⟨1a⟩ *v/t neumáticos* retread

recaudación *f acción* collection; *cantidad* takings *pl*

recaudar ⟨1a⟩ *v/t impuestos, dinero* collect

recaudo *m*: *poner a buen recaudo* put in a safe place

recelo *m* mistrust

recepción *f en hotel* reception

recepcionista *m/f* receptionist

receptivo *adj* receptive

receptor *m* receiver

recesión *f* recession

receta *f* GASTR recipe; *receta médica* prescription

recetar ⟨1a⟩ *v/t* MED prescribe

recetario *m* recipe book

rechazar ⟨1f⟩ *v/t* reject; MIL repel

rechazo *m* rejection

rechinar ⟨1a⟩ *v/i* creak, squeak

rechistar ⟨1a⟩ *v/i* protest; *sin rechistar* F without a murmur, without complaining

rechoncho *adj* F dumpy F

rechupete: *de rechupete* F delicious

recibidor *m* entrance hall

recibimiento *m* reception

recibir ⟨3a⟩ *v/t* receive

recibo *m* (*sales*) receipt

reciclable *adj* recyclable

reciclado, reciclaje *m* recycling

reciclar ⟨1a⟩ *v/t* recycle

recién *adv* newly; *L.Am.* (*hace poco*) just; *recién casados* newly-weds; *recién nacido* newborn; *recién pintado* wet paint; **recién llegamos** we've only just arrived

reciente *adj* recent

recinto *m* premises *pl*; *área* grounds *pl*

recio *adj* sturdy, tough

recipiente *m* container

recíproco *adj* reciprocal

recital *m* recital

recitar ⟨1a⟩ *v/t* recite

reclamación *f* complaint; POL claim, demand

reclamar ⟨1a⟩ **1** *v/t* claim, demand **2** *v/i* complain

reclame *m* *L.Am.* advertisement

reclamo *m* lure

reclinable *adj:* **asiento reclinable** reclining seat

reclinar ⟨1a⟩ **1** *v/t* rest **2** *v/r* **reclinarse** lean, recline (**contra** against)

recluir ⟨3g⟩ *v/t* imprison, confine

reclusión *f* JUR imprisonment, confinement

recluso *m,* **-a** *f* prisoner

recluta *m/f* recruit

reclutar ⟨1a⟩ *v/t tb* COM recruit

recobrar ⟨1a⟩ **1** *v/t* recover **2** *v/r* **recobrarse** recover (**de** from)

recogedor *m* dustpan

recogepelotas *m/f inv* ball boy; *niña* ball girl

recoger ⟨2c⟩ **1** *v/t* pick up, collect; *habitación* tidy up; AGR harvest; (*mostrar*) show **2** *v/r* **recogerse** go home

recogida *f* collection; **recogida de basuras** garbage collection, *Br* refuse collection; **recogida de equipajes** baggage reclaim

recolectar ⟨1a⟩ *v/t* AGR harvest, bring in

recomendación *f* recommendation

recomendar ⟨1k⟩ *v/t* recommend

recompensa *f* reward

recompensar ⟨1a⟩ *v/t* reward

recomponer ⟨2r; *part* **recompuesto** ⟩ *v/t* mend

reconciliación *f* reconciliation

reconciliar ⟨1b⟩ **1** *v/t* reconcile **2** *v/r* **reconciliarse** make up (**con** with), be reconciled (**con** with)

recóndito *adj* remote

reconfortar ⟨1a⟩ *v/t* comfort

reconocer ⟨2d⟩ *v/t* recognize; *errores* admit, acknowledge; *área* reconnoiter, *Br* reconnoitre; MED examine

reconocimiento *m* recognition; *de error* acknowledg(e)ment; MED examination, check-up; MIL reconnaissance

reconquista *f* reconquest

reconquistar ⟨1a⟩ *v/t* reconquer

reconsiderar ⟨1a⟩ *v/t* reconsider

reconstrucción *f* reconstruction

reconstruir ⟨3g⟩ *v/t fig* reconstruct

reconvenir ⟨3s⟩ *v/i* JUR counterclaim

reconversión *f* COM restructuring

recopilación *f* compilation

recopilar ⟨1a⟩ *v/t* compile

récord 1 *adj* record(-breaking) **2** *m* record

recordar ⟨1m⟩ *v/t* remember, recall; **recordar algo a alguien** remind s.o. of sth

recordatorio *m* reminder

recorrer ⟨2a⟩ *v/t distancia* cover, do; *a pie* walk; *territorio, país* go around, travel around; *camino* go along, travel along

recorrido *m* route; DEP round

recortar ⟨1a⟩ *v/t* cut out; *fig* cut

recorte *m fig* cutback; **recorte de periódico** cutting, clipping; **recorte salarial** salary cut

recostarse ⟨1m⟩ *v/r* lie down

recoveco *m* nook, cranny; *en camino* bend

recrearse ⟨1a⟩ *v/r* amuse o.s.

recreativo *adj* recreational; **juegos recreativos** amusements

recreo *m* recreation; EDU recess, *Br* break

recriminar ⟨1a⟩ *v/t* reproach

recrudecerse ⟨2d⟩ *v/r* intensify

recta *f* DEP straight; **recta final** *tb fig* home straight

rectángulo *m* rectangle

rectificar ⟨1g⟩ *v/t* correct, rectify; *camino* straighten

rectitud *f* rectitude, probity

recto *adj* straight; (*honesto*) honest

rector *m* rector, *Br* vice-chancellor

rectorado *m* rector's office, *Br* vice-chancellor's office

recuadro *m* TIP inset, box

recubierto *part* → **recubrir**

recubrir ⟨3a; *part* **recubierto** ⟩ *v/t* cover (**de** with)

recuento *m* count; **recuento de votos** recount

recuerdo *m* memory; **da recuerdos a Luís** give my regards to Luís

recuperación *f tb fig* recovery

recuperar ⟨1a⟩ **1** *v/t tiempo* make up; *algo perdido* recover **2** *v/r* **recuperarse** recover (**de** from)

recurrir ⟨3a⟩ **1** *v/t* JUR appeal against **2** *v/i:* **recurrir a** resort to, turn to

recurso *m* JUR appeal; *material* resource; **recursos humanos** human resources; **recursos naturales** natural resources

red *f* net; INFOR, *fig* network; *caer en las redes de fig* fall into the clutches of; **Red Digital de Servicios Integrados** Integrated Services Digital Network

redacción *f* writing; *de editorial* editorial

department; EDU essay

redactar ⟨1a⟩ *v/t* write, compose

redactor *m*, **redactora** *f* editor

redada *f* raid

redentor *m*, **redentora** *f* COM redeemer; *el Redentor* REL the Savio(u)r

redoble *m* MÚS (drum)roll

redomado *adj* F total, out-and-out

redonda *f*: *a la redonda* around, round about

redondear ⟨1a⟩ *v/t para más* round up; *para menos* round down; (*rematar*) round off

redondo *adj* round; *negocio* excellent; *caer redondo* flop down

reducción *f* reduction; MED setting

reducido *adj precio* reduced; *espacio* small, confined

reducir ⟨3o⟩ **1** *v/t* reduce (*a* to); MIL overcome **2** *v/r* **reducirse** come down (*a* to)

reducto *m* redoubt

redujo *vb* → *reducir*

redundancia *f* tautology

redundar ⟨1a⟩ *v/i* have an impact (*en* on)

reeditar ⟨1a⟩ *v/t* republish, reissue

reelegir ⟨3c & 3l⟩ *v/t* re-elect

reembolsar ⟨1a⟩ *v/t* refund

reembolso *m* refund; *contra reembolso* collect on delivery, *Br* cash on delivery, COD

reemplazar ⟨1f⟩ *v/t* replace

reencarnación *f* REL reincarnation

reestructurar ⟨1a⟩ *v/t* restructure

refacción *f* L.Am. *de edificio* refurbishment; AUTO spare part

referencia *f* reference; *hacer referencia a* refer to, make reference to; *referencias* COM references

referéndum *m* referendum

referente *adj*: *referente a* referring to, relating to

referirse ⟨3i⟩ *v/r* refer (*a* to)

refilón *m*: *mirar de refilón* glance at

refinado *adj* tb fig refined

refinar ⟨1a⟩ *v/t* TÉC refine

refinería *f* TÉC refinery

reflector *m* reflector; EL spotlight

reflejar ⟨1a⟩ **1** *v/t* tb fig reflect **2** *v/r* **reflejarse** be reflected

reflejo *m* reflex; *imagen* reflection

reflexión *f* fig reflection, thought

reflexionar ⟨1a⟩ *v/t* reflect on, ponder

reflexivo *adj* GRAM reflexive

reflotar ⟨1a⟩ *v/t* COM refloat

reforestar ⟨1a⟩ *v/t* reforest

reforma *f* reform; *reformas pl* (*obras*) refurbishment *sg*; (*reparaciones*) repairs

reformador *m*, **reformadora** *f* reformer

reformar ⟨1a⟩ **1** *v/t* reform; *edificio* refur-

bish; (*reparar*) repair **2** *v/r* **reformarse** mend one's ways, reform

reformatorio *m* reform school, reformatory

reformista 1 *adj* reformist, reform *atr* **2** *m/f* reformer

reforzar ⟨1f & 1m⟩ *v/t* reinforce; *vigilancia* increase, step up

refrán *m* saying

refrenar ⟨1a⟩ *v/t* restrain, contain

refrescante *adj* refreshing

refrescar ⟨1g⟩ **1** *v/t* tb fig refresh; *conocimientos* brush up **2** *v/i* cool down **3** *v/r* **refrescarse** cool down

refresco *m* soda, *Br* soft drink

refriega *f* MIL clash, skirmish

refrigerador *m* refrigerator

refrigerar ⟨1a⟩ *v/t* refrigerate

refrigerio *m* snack

refuerzo *m* reinforcement; *refuerzos* MIL reinforcements

refugiado *m*, *-a* *f* refugee

refugiarse ⟨1b⟩ *v/r* take refuge

refugio *m* refuge

refulgente *adj* dazzling

refunfuñar ⟨1a⟩ *v/i* grumble

refutar ⟨1a⟩ *v/t* refute

regadera *f* watering can; *Méx* (*ducha*) shower; *estar como una regadera* F be nuts F

regadío *m*: *tierra de regadío* irrigated land

regalar ⟨1a⟩ *v/t*: *regalar algo a alguien* give sth to s.o., give s.o. sth

regaliz *m* BOT licorice, *Br* liquorice

regalo *m* gift, present

regañadientes: *a regañadientes* reluctantly

regañar ⟨1a⟩ **1** *v/t* tell off **2** *v/i* quarrel

regañina *f* F telling off

regar ⟨1h & 1k⟩ *v/t* water; AGR irrigate

regata *f* regatta

regatear ⟨1a⟩ *v/t* DEP get past, dodge; *no regatear esfuerzos* spare no effort

regazo *m* lap

regenerar ⟨1a⟩ *v/t* regenerate

regente *m/f* regent

regidor 1 *adj* governing, ruling **2** *m*, **regidora** *f* TEA stage manager

régimen *m* POL regime; MED diet; *estar a régimen* be on a diet

regimiento *m* MIL regiment

regio *adj* regal, majestic; *S. Am.* F (*estupendo*) great F, fantastic F

región *f* region

regional *adj* regional

regionalismo *m* regionalism

regir ⟨3l & 3c⟩ **1** *v/t* rule, govern **2** *v/i* apply, be in force **3** *v/r* **regirse** be guided

(*por* by)

registrar ⟨1a⟩ **1** *v/t* register; *casa* search **2** *v/r* **registrarse** be recorded; *se registró un máximo de 45°C* a high of 45°C was recorded

registro *m* register; *de casa* search; *registro civil* register of births, marriages and deaths

regla *f* (*norma*) rule; *para medir* ruler; MED period; *por regla general* as a rule

reglamentar ⟨1a⟩ *v/t* regulate

reglamentario *adj* regulation *atr*

reglamento *m* regulation

regocijarse ⟨1a⟩ *v/r* rejoice (*de* at), take delight (*de* in)

regocijo *m* delight

regodearse ⟨1a⟩ *v/r* gloat (*con* over), delight (*en* in)

regresar ⟨1a⟩ **1** *v/i* return **2** *v/t Méx* return, give back **3** *v/r* **regresarse** *L.Am.* return

regreso *m* return

regüeldo *m* F belch

reguero *m* trail; *como un reguero de pólvora fig* like wildfire

regulación *f* regulation; *de temperatura* control

regular 1 *adj sin variar* regular; (*común*) ordinary; (*habitual*) regular, normal; (*no muy bien*) so-so **2** ⟨1a⟩ *v/t* TÉC regulate; *temperatura* control

regularidad *f* regularity

regularizar ⟨1f⟩ *v/t* regularize

regusto *m* aftertaste

rehabilitación *f* MED, *fig* rehabilitation; ARQUI restoration

rehabilitar ⟨1a⟩ *v/t* ARQUI restore

rehacer ⟨2s; *part* **rehecho** ⟩ *v/t película, ropa, cama* remake; *trabajo, ejercicio* redo; *casa, vida* rebuild

rehén *m* hostage

rehice *vb* → **rehacer**

rehizo *vb* → **rehacer**

rehogar ⟨1h⟩ *v/t* GASTR fry

rehuir ⟨3g⟩ *v/t* shy away from

rehusar ⟨1a⟩ *v/t* refuse, decline

reimprimir ⟨3a⟩ *v/t* reprint

reina *f* queen

reinado *m* reign

reinante *adj tb fig* reigning

reinar ⟨1a⟩ *v/i tb fig* reign

reincidente 1 *adj* repeat **2** *m/f* repeat offender

reincidir ⟨3a⟩ *v/i* reoffend

reincorporarse ⟨1a⟩ *v/r* return (*a* to)

reino *m tb fig* kingdom; *el Reino Unido* the United Kingdom

reinserción *f*: *reinserción social* social rehabilitation

reinsertar ⟨1a⟩ *v/t* rehabilitate

reinstaurar ⟨1a⟩ *v/t* bring back

reintegrarse ⟨1a⟩ *v/r* return (*a* to)

reintegro *m* (*en lotería*) prize in the form of a refund of the stake money

reír ⟨3m⟩ **1** *v/i* laugh **2** *v/r* **reírse** laugh (*de* at)

reiterar ⟨1a⟩ *v/t* repeat, reiterate

reivindicación *f* claim

reivindicar ⟨1g⟩ *v/t* claim; *reivindicar un atentado* claim responsibility for an attack

reja *f* AGR plowshare, *Br* ploughshare; (*barrote*) bar, railing; *meter entre rejas fig* F put behind bars

rejilla *f* FERR luggage rack

rejuvenecer ⟨2d⟩ *v/t* rejuvenate

relación *f* relationship; *relaciones públicas* pl public relations, PR *sg*

relacionado *adj* related (*con* to)

relacionarse ⟨1a⟩ *v/r* be connected (*con* to), be related (*con* to)

relajación *f* relaxation

relajante *adj* relaxing

relajar ⟨1a⟩ **1** *v/t* relax **2** *v/r* **relajarse** relax

relajo *m* C.Am., *Méx* uproar

relamerse ⟨2a⟩ *v/r* lick one's lips

relámpago *m* flash of lightning; *viaje relámpago* flying visit

relatar ⟨1a⟩ *v/t* tell, relate

relatividad *f* relativity

relativo *adj* relative; *relativo a* regarding, about

relato *m* short story

relax *m* relaxation

releer ⟨2e⟩ *v/t* reread

relegar ⟨1h⟩ *v/t* relegate

relevante *adj* relevant

relevar ⟨1a⟩ *v/t* MIL relieve; *relevar a alguien de algo* relieve s.o. of sth

relevo *m* MIL change; (*sustituto*) relief, replacement; *carrera de relevos* relay (race); *tomar el relevo de alguien* take over from s.o., relieve s.o.

relicario *m* shrine

relieve *m* relief; *poner de relieve* highlight

religión *f* religion

religiosa *f* nun

religioso 1 *adj* religious **2** *m* monk

relinchar ⟨1a⟩ *v/i* neigh

reliquia *f* relic

rellano *m* landing

rellenar ⟨1a⟩ *v/t* fill; GASTR *pollo, pimientos* stuff; *formulario* fill out, fill in

relleno 1 *adj* GASTR *pollo, pimientos* stuffed; *pastel* filled **2** *m tb en cojín* stuffing; *en pastel* filling

reloj *m* clock; *de pulsera* watch, wristwatch; *reloj de pared* wall clock; *reloj de sol* sundial

relojería *f* watchmaker's

relojero *m*, -a *f* watchmaker

reluciente *adj* sparkling, glittering

remanso *m* backwater; *remanso de paz* *fig* haven of peace

remar ⟨1a⟩ *v/i* row

remarcar ⟨1g⟩ *v/t* stress, emphasize

rematar ⟨1a⟩ **1** *v/t* finish off; *L.Am.* com auction **2** *v/i en fútbol* shoot

remate *m L.Am.* com auction, sale; *en fútbol* shot; *ser tonto de remate* be a complete idiot

remediar ⟨1b⟩ *v/t* remedy; *no puedo remediarlo* I can't do anything about it

remedio *m* remedy; *sin remedio* hopeless; *no hay más remedio que ...* there's no alternative but to ...

rememorar ⟨1a⟩ *v/t* remember

remendar ⟨1k⟩ *v/t con parche* patch; *(zurcir)* darn

remesa *f (envío)* shipment, consignment; *L.Am. dinero* remittance

remezón *m L.Am.* earth tremor

remiendo *m (parche)* patch; *(zurcido)* darn

remilgado *adj* fussy, finicky

reminiscencia *f* reminiscence

remiso *adj* reluctant (*a* to)

remite *m en carta* return address

remitente *m/f* sender

remitir ⟨3a⟩ **1** *v/t* send, ship; *en texto* refer (*a* to) **2** *v/i* MED go into remission; *de crisis* ease (off)

remo *m pala* oar; *deporte* rowing

remodelar ⟨1a⟩ *v/t* redesign, remodel

remojar ⟨1a⟩ *v/t* soak; *L.Am.* F *acontecimiento* celebrate

remojo *m: poner a* or *en remojo* leave to soak

remojón *m* drenching, soaking; *darse un remojón* go for a dip

remolacha *f* beet, *Br* beetroot; *remolacha azucarera* sugar beet

remolcador *m* tug

remolcar ⟨1g⟩ *v/t* AUTO, MAR tow

remolino *m de aire* eddy; *de agua* whirlpool

remolón *m*, -ona *f* F slacker; *hacerse el remolón* slack (off)

remolque *m* AUTO trailer

remontarse ⟨1a⟩ *v/r en el tiempo* go back (*a* to)

remonte *m* ski lift

remorder ⟨2h⟩ *v/t: me remuerde la conciencia* I have a guilty conscience

remordimiento *m* remorse

remoto *adj* remote; *no tengo ni la más -a*

idea I haven't the faintest idea

remover ⟨2h⟩ *v/t (agitar)* stir; *L.Am. (destituir)* dismiss; *C.Am., Méx (quitar)* remove

remplazar *v/t* → *reemplazar*

remuneración *f* remuneration

remunerar ⟨1a⟩ *v/t* pay

renacentista *adj* Renaissance *atr*

renacer ⟨2d⟩ *v/i fig* be reborn

Renacimiento *m* Renaissance

renacuajo *m* ZO tadpole; F *persona* shrimp F

renal *adj* ANAT renal, kidney *atr*

rencilla *f* fight, argument

rencor *m* resentment; *guardar rencor a alguien* bear s.o. a grudge

rencoroso *adj* resentful

rendición *f* surrender

rendija *f* crack; *(hueco)* gap

rendimiento *m* performance; FIN yield; *(producción)* output

rendir ⟨3l⟩ **1** *v/t honores* pay, do; *beneficio* produce, yield **2** *v/i* perform **3** *v/r rendirse* surrender

renegado **1** *adj* renegade *atr* **2** *m* renegade

renegar ⟨1h & 1k⟩ *v/i: renegar de alguien* disown s.o.; *renegar de algo* renounce sth

renegrido *adj* blackened

RENFE *abr* (= *Red Nacional de Ferrocarriles Españoles*) Spanish rail operator

renglón *m* line; *a renglón seguido* immediately after

rengo *adj* CSur lame

renguear ⟨1a⟩ *v/i* CSur limp, walk with a limp

reno *m* ZO reindeer

renombre *m: de renombre* famous, renowned

renovación *f* renewal

renovador *adj: las fuerzas renovadoras* the forces of renewal

renovar ⟨1m⟩ *v/t* renew

renta *f* income; *de casa* rent; *renta per cápita* income per capita

rentabilidad *f* profitability

rentable *adj* profitable

rentar ⟨1a⟩ *v/t (arrendar)* rent out; *(alquiler)* rent; *carro* hire

renuente *adj* reluctant, unwilling

renunciar ⟨1b⟩ *v/i: renunciar a tabaco, alcohol etc* give up; *puesto* resign; *demanda* drop

reñir ⟨3h & 3l⟩ **1** *v/t* tell off **2** *v/i* quarrel, fight F

reo *m*, -a *f* accused

reojo: *de reojo* out of the corner of one's eye

repantigarse ⟨1h⟩ v/r lounge, sprawl

reparación f repair; fig reparation

reparar ⟨1a⟩ **1** v/t repair **2** v/i: **reparar en algo** notice sth

reparo m: **poner reparos a** find problems with; **no tener reparos en** have no reservations about

repartición f S. Am. department

repartidor m delivery man

repartir ⟨3a⟩ v/t (dividir) share out, divide up; productos deliver

reparto m (división) share-out, distribution; TEA cast; **reparto a domicilio** home delivery

repasar ⟨1a⟩ v/t trabajo go over again; EDU revise

repecho m steep slope

repelente 1 adj fig repellent, repulsive; F niño horrible **2** m repellent

repelús m: **dar repelús a alguien** F give s.o. the creeps F

repente: **de repente** suddenly

repentino adj sudden

repercusión f fig repercussion

repercutir ⟨3a⟩ v/i have repercussions (**en** on)

repertorio m TEA, MÚS repertoire

repetición f repetition

repetido adj repeated

repetir ⟨3l⟩ **1** v/t repeat **2** v/i de comida repeat **3** v/r **repetirse** happen again

repetitivo adj repetitive

repipi adj F (afectado) affected; **es tan repipi** niño he's such a know-it-all F

repisa f shelf

replantear ⟨1a⟩ v/t pregunta, problema bring up again

replegarse ⟨1h & 1k⟩ v/r MIL withdraw

repleto adj full (**de** of)

réplica f replica

replicar ⟨1g⟩ v/t reply

repoblar ⟨1m⟩ v/t repopulate

repollo m BOT cabbage

reponerse ⟨2r; part **repuesto**⟩ v/r recover (**de** from)

reportaje m story, report

reportero m, **-a** f reporter; **reportero gráfico** press photographer

reposacabezas m inv AUTO headrest

reposar ⟨1a⟩ v/i rest; de vino settle

reposera f L.Am. lounger

reposición f TEA revival; TV repeat

reposo m rest

repostar ⟨1a⟩ v/i refuel

repostería f pastries pl

reprender ⟨2a⟩ v/t scold, tell off

represa f dam; (embalse) reservoir

represalia f reprisal

representación f representation; TEA performance; **en representación de** on behalf of

representante m/f tb COM representative

representar ⟨1a⟩ v/t represent; obra put on, perform; papel play; **representar menos años** look younger

represión f repression

reprimenda f reprimand

reprimir ⟨3a⟩ v/t tb PSI repress

reprobar ⟨1m⟩ v/t condemn; L.Am. EDU fail

reprochar ⟨1a⟩ v/t reproach

reproche m reproach

reproducción f BIO reproduction

reproducir ⟨3o⟩ **1** v/t reproduce **2** v/r **reproducirse** BIO reproduce, breed

reptil m ZO reptile

república f republic

republicano 1 adj republican **2** m, **-a** f republican

repudiar ⟨1b⟩ v/t fml repudiate; herencia renounce

repuesto 1 part → **reponerse 2** m spare part, replacement; **de repuesto** spare

repugnancia f disgust, repugnance

repugnante adj disgusting, repugnant

repugnar ⟨1a⟩ v/t disgust, repel

repulsión f repulsion

repulsivo adj repulsive

repuse vb → **reponerse**

reputación f reputation

requerir ⟨3i⟩ v/t require; JUR summons

requesón m cottage cheese

requetebién adv F really well, brilliantly F

réquiem m requiem

requisar ⟨1a⟩ v/t Arg, Chi MIL requisition

requisito m requirement

res f L.Am. bull; **carne f de res** beef; **reses** pl cattle pl

resaca f MAR undertow, undercurrent; de beber hangover

resaltar ⟨1a⟩ **1** v/t highlight, stress **2** v/i ARQUI jut out; fig stand out

resarcirse ⟨3b⟩ v/r make up (**de** for)

resbaladizo adj slippery; fig tricky

resbalar ⟨1a⟩ v/i slide; fig slip (up)

resbalón m slip; fig F slip-up

resbaloso adj L.Am. slippery

rescatar ⟨1a⟩ v/t persona, animal rescue, save; bienes save

rescate m de peligro rescue; en secuestro ransom

rescindir ⟨3a⟩ v/t cancel; contrato terminate

rescisión f cancellation; de contrato termination

reseco adj (seco) parched; (flaco) skinny

resentimiento m resentment

resentirse ⟨3i⟩ v/r get upset; de rendi-

miento, calidad suffer; **resentirse de algo** suffer from the effects of sth
reseña *f de libro etc* review
reseñar ⟨1a⟩ *v/t* review
reserva **1** *f* reservation; **reserva natural** nature reserve; **sin reservas** without reservation **2** *m/f* DEP reserve
reservar ⟨1a⟩ **1** *v/t (guardar)* set aside, put by; *billete* reserve **2** *v/r* **reservarse** save o.s. (**para** for)
resfriado **1** *adj:* **estar resfriado** have a cold **2** *m* cold
resfriarse ⟨1c⟩ *v/r* catch cold
resfrío *m L.Am.* cold
resguardar ⟨1a⟩ **1** *v/t* protect (**de** from) **2** *v/r* **resguardarse** protect o.s. (**de** from)
resguardo *m* COM counterfoil
residencia *f* residence; **residencia de ancianos** *or* **para la tercera edad** retirement home
residencial **1** *adj* residential **2** *f Arg, Chi* boarding house
residente **1** *adj* resident **2** *m/f* resident
residir ⟨3a⟩ *v/i* reside; **residir en** *fig* lie in
residual *adj* residual; *(de desecho)* waste *atr*
residuo *m* residue; **residuos** waste *sg*
resignación *f actitud* resignation
resignarse ⟨1a⟩ *v/r* resign o.s. (**a** to)
resina *f* resin
resistencia *f* resistance; EL, TÉC resistor
resistir ⟨3a⟩ **1** *v/i* resist; *(aguantar)* hold out **2** *v/t tentación* resist; *frío, dolor* stand, bear **3** *v/r* **resistirse** be reluctant (**a** to)
resolución *f actitud* determination, decisiveness; *de problema* solution (**de** to); JUR ruling
resolver ⟨2h; *part* **resuelto**⟩ **1** *v/t problema* solve **2** *v/r* **resolverse** decide (**a** to; **por** on)
resonar ⟨1m⟩ *v/i* echo
resoplar ⟨1a⟩ *v/i* snort
resorte *m* spring
respaldar ⟨1a⟩ *v/t* back, support
respaldo *m de silla* back; *fig* backing, support
respectar ⟨1a⟩ *v/i:* **por lo que respecta a …** as regards …, as far as … is concerned
respectivo *adj* respective
respecto *m:* **al respecto** on the matter; **con respecto a** regarding, as regards
respetable *adj* respectable
respetar ⟨1a⟩ *v/t* respect
respeto *m* respect
respetuoso *adj* respectful
respiración *f* breathing; **estar con respiración asistida** MED be on a respirator
respirar ⟨1a⟩ *v/t & v/i* breathe

respiratorio *adj* respiratory
respiro *m fig* breather, break
resplandeciente *adj* shining
resplandor *m* shine, gleam
responder ⟨2a⟩ **1** *v/t* answer **2** *v/i:* **responder a** answer, reply to; MED respond to; *descripción* fit, match; *(ser debido a)* be due to
responsabilidad *f* responsibility
responsabilizarse ⟨1f⟩ *v/r* take responsibility (**de** for)
responsable **1** *adj* responsible (**de** for) **2** *m/f* person responsible (**de** for); **los responsables del crimen** those responsible for the crime
respuesta *f (contestación)* reply, answer; *fig* response
resquebrajar ⟨1a⟩ **1** *v/t* crack **2** *v/r* **resquebrajarse** crack
resquicio *m* gap
resta *f* MAT subtraction
restablecer ⟨2d⟩ **1** *v/t* re-establish **2** *v/r* **restablecerse** recover
restablecimiento *m* re-establishment; *de enfermo* recovery
restante **1** *adj* remaining **2** *m/fpl:* **los / las restantes** *pl* the rest *pl*, the remainder *pl*
restar ⟨1a⟩ **1** *v/t* subtract; **restar importancia a** play down the importance of **2** *v/i* remain, be left
restauración *f* restoration
restaurante *m* restaurant
restaurar ⟨1a⟩ *v/t* restore
restituir ⟨3g⟩ *v/t* restore; *en cargo* reinstate
resto *m* rest, remainder; **los restos mortales** the (mortal) remains
restregar ⟨1h & 1k⟩ *v/t* scrub
restricción *f* restriction
restringir ⟨3c⟩ *v/t* restrict, limit
resucitar ⟨1a⟩ **1** *v/t* resuscitate; *fig* revive **2** *v/i de persona* rise from *o* come back from the dead
resuello *m* puffing, heavy breathing
resuelto **1** *part →* **resolver 2** *adj* decisive, resolute
resultado *m* result; **sin resultado** without success
resultar ⟨1a⟩ *v/i* turn out; **resultar caro** prove expensive, turn out to be expensive, **resulta que …** it turns out that …
resumen *m* summary; **en resumen** in short
resumir ⟨3a⟩ *v/t* summarize
resurgir ⟨3c⟩ *v/i* reappear, come back
resurrección *f* REL resurrection
retaguardia *f* MIL rearguard
retahíla *f* string
retar ⟨1a⟩ *v/t* challenge; *Rpl (regañar)*

scold, tell off

retardar ⟨1a⟩ v/t delay

retazo m fig snippet, fragment

retención f MED retention; de persona detention; **retención fiscal** tax deduction

retener ⟨2l⟩ v/t dinero etc withhold, deduct; persona detain, hold

reticencia f reticence

reticente adj reticent

retintín m: **con retintín** F sarcastically

retirada f MIL retreat, withdrawal

retirado adj (jubilado) retired; (alejado) remote, out-of-the-way

retirar ⟨1a⟩ 1 v/t take away, remove; acusación, dinero withdraw 2 v/r retirarse MIL withdraw

retiro m lugar retreat

reto m challenge; Rpl (regañina) scolding, telling-off

retobado adj L.Am. unruly

retocar ⟨1g⟩ v/t FOT retouch, touch up; (acabar) put the finishing touches to

retomar ⟨1a⟩ v/t: **retomar algo** fig take sth up again

retoque m FOT touching-up; (acabado) finishing touch

retorcer ⟨2b & 2h⟩ v/t twist

retorcido adj fig twisted

retorcijón m stomach cramp

retórica f rhetoric

retornar ⟨1a⟩ v/i return

retorno m return

retortijón m cramps pl, Br stomach cramp

retozar ⟨1f⟩ v/i frolic, romp

retractar ⟨1a⟩ v/t retract, withdraw

retraer ⟨2p; part retraído ⟩ 1 v/t retract 2 v/r retraerse withdraw

retraído 1 part → **retraer 2** adj withdrawn

retransmisión f RAD, TV transmission, broadcast

retransmitir ⟨3a⟩ v/t transmit, broadcast

retrasado 1 part → **retrasar 2** adj tren, entrega late; con trabajo, pagos behind; **está retrasado en clase** he's lagging behind in class; **retrasado mental** mentally handicapped

retrasar ⟨1a⟩ 1 v/t hold up; reloj put back; reunión postpone, put back 2 v/i de reloj lose time; en los estudios be behind 3 v/r retrasarse (atrasarse) be behind; de reloj lose time; con trabajo, pagos get behind

retraso m delay; **ir con retraso** be late

retratar ⟨1a⟩ v/t FOT take a picture of; fig depict

retrato m picture; **retrato-robot** composite photo, E-Fit®

retrete m bathroom

retribución f salary

retroactivo adj retroactive

retroceder ⟨2a⟩ v/i go back, move back; fig back down

retroceso m fig backward step

retrógrado adj retrograde

retroproyector m overhead projector

retrospectiva f retrospective

retrovisor m AUTO rear-view mirror; **retrovisor exterior** wing mirror

retumbar ⟨1a⟩ v/i boom

retuve vb → **retener**

reuma, reúma m MED rheumatism

reunificación f POL reunification

reunión f meeting; de amigos get-together

reunir ⟨3a⟩ 1 v/t personas bring together; requisitos meet, fulfil(l); datos gather (together) 2 v/r reunirse meet up, get together; COM meet

reutilizar ⟨1f⟩ v/t re-use

revalorizar ⟨1f⟩ 1 v/t revalue 2 v/r revalorizarse appreciate (**en** by), increase in value (**en** by)

revaluar vb → **revalorizar**

revancha f revenge

revelación f revelation

revelado m development

revelar ⟨1a⟩ v/t FOT develop

reventa f resale

reventar ⟨1k⟩ 1 v/i burst; **lleno a reventar** full to bursting 2 v/t puerta etc break down 3 v/r reventarse burst; **se reventó a trabajar** fig he worked his butt off F

reventón m AUTO blowout

reverberar ⟨1a⟩ v/i de sonido reverberate

reverencia f reverence; saludo: de hombre bow; de mujer curtsy

reverendo m REL reverend

reversible adj ropa reversible

reverso m reverse, back

revés m setback; tenis backhand; **al o del revés** back to front; **con el interior fuera** inside out

revestir ⟨3l⟩ v/t TÉC cover (**de** with); **revestir gravedad** be serious

revisación f L.Am. check-up

revisada f L.Am. → **revisión**

revisar ⟨1a⟩ v/t check, inspect

revisión f check, inspection; AUTO service; **revisión técnica** roadworthiness test, Br MOT (test); **revisión médica** check-up

revisor m, **revisora** f FERR (ticket) inspector

revista f magazine; **pasar revista a** MIL inspect, review; fig review

revivir ⟨3a⟩ 1 v/i revive 2 v/t relive

revocar ⟨1g & 1m⟩ v/t pared render; JUR revoke

revolcarse ⟨1g & 1m⟩ v/r roll around

revolcón m tumble; F de amantes roll in the hay F

revolotear ⟨1a⟩ v/t flutter
revoltijo, revoltillo m mess, jumble
revoltoso adj niño naughty
revolución f revolution
revolucionario 1 adj revolutionary **2** m, -a f revolutionary
revólver m revolver
revolver ⟨2h; part **revuelto** ⟩ **1** v/t GASTR stir; estómago turn; (desordenar) mess up **2** v/i rummage (**en** in) **3** v/r **revolverse del tiempo** worsen
revuelo m stir
revuelto 1 part → **revolver 2** adj mar rough; gente restless
rey m king
reyerta f fight
rezagarse ⟨1h⟩ v/r drop back, fall behind
rezar ⟨1f⟩ **1** v/t oración say **2** v/i pray; de texto say
rezo m prayer
rezongar ⟨1h⟩ v/i grumble
rezumar ⟨1a⟩ v/t & v/i ooze
ría 1 vb → **reír 2** f estuary
riachuelo m stream
riada f flood
ribera f shore, bank
riberano L.Am. **1** adj L.Am. coastal; de río riverside atr **2** m, -a f person who lives by the sea / river
ribereño de bordering (on)
rica f rich woman
rico 1 adj rich; comida delicious; F niño cute, sweet; **rico en vitaminas** rich in vitamins **2** m rich man; **nuevo rico** nouveau riche
ridiculizar ⟨1f⟩ v/t ridicule
ridículo 1 adj ridiculous **2** m ridicule; **hacer el ridículo, quedar en ridículo** make a fool of o.s.
ríe vb → **reír**
riego 1 vb → **regar 2** m AGR irrigation; **riego sanguíneo** blood flow
rien vb → **reír**
rienda f rein; **dar rienda suelta a** give free rein to
riesgo m risk; **a riesgo de** at the risk of; **correr el riesgo** run the risk (**de** of)
riesgoso adj L.Am. risky
rifa f raffle
rifar ⟨1a⟩ **1** v/t raffle **2** v/r **rifarse** fig fight over
rifle m rifle
rige vb → **regir**
rigidez f rigidity; de carácter inflexibility; fig strictness
rígido adj rigid; carácter inflexible; fig strict
rigor m rigo(u)r
riguroso adj rigorous, harsh

rima f rhyme
rimar ⟨1a⟩ v/i rhyme (**con** with)
rimbombante adj ostentatious
rímel m mascara
rincón m corner
rinde vb → **rendir**
rinoceronte m ZO rhino, rhinoceros
riña f quarrel, fight
riñe vb → **reñir**
riñón m ANAT kidney; **costar un riñón** F cost an arm and a leg F
riñonera f fanny pack, Br bum bag
río 1 m river; **río abajo / arriba** up / down river; **el Río de la Plata** the River Plate **2** vb → **reír**
rioplatense adj of / from the River Plate area, River Plate atr
riqueza f wealth
risa f laugh; **risas** pl laughter sg; **dar risa** be funny; **morirse de risa** kill o.s. laughing; **tomar algo a risa** treat sth as a joke
ristra f string
risueño adj cheerful
rítmico adj rhythmic(al)
ritmo m rhythm; de desarrollo rate, pace
rito m rite
ritual m/adj ritual
rival m/f rival
rivalidad f rivalry
rivalizar ⟨1f⟩ v/i: **rivalizar con** rival
rizado adj curly
rizar ⟨1f⟩ **1** v/t curl **2** rizarse v/r curl
rizo m curl
robar ⟨1a⟩ v/t persona, banco rob; objeto steal; naipe take, pick up
roble m BOT oak
robo m robbery; en casa burglary
robot m robot; **robot de cocina** food processor
robótica f robotics
robustecer ⟨2d⟩ **1** v/t strengthen **2** v/r **robustecerse** become stronger
robusto adj robust, sturdy
roca f rock
roce m fig friction; **tener roces con** come into conflict with
rociar ⟨1c⟩ v/t spray
rocín m F nag
rocío m dew
rock m MÚS rock
rococó adj rococo
rocódromo m climbing wall
rocoto m S. Am. hot red pepper
rodaballo m ZO turbot
rodaja f slice
rodaje m de película shooting, filming; AUTO breaking in, Br running in
rodapié m baseboard, Br skirting board
rodar ⟨1m⟩ **1** v/i roll; de coche go, travel (**a**

at); **sin rumbo fijo** wander **2** v/t película shoot; AUTO break in, Br run in

rodear ⟨1a⟩ **1** v/t surround **2** v/r **rodearse** surround o.s. (**de** with)

rodeo m detour; **con caballos y vaqueros** etc rodeo; **andarse con rodeos** beat about the bush; **hablar sin rodeos** speak plainly, not beat about the bush

rodilla f knee; **de rodillas** kneeling, on one's knees; **hincarse** or **ponerse de rodillas** kneel (down)

rodillo m rolling pin; TÉC roller

rododendro m BOT rhododendron

roedor m rodent

roer ⟨2za⟩ v/t gnaw; fig eat into

rogar ⟨1h & 1m⟩ v/t ask for; (*implorar*) beg for, plead for; **hacerse de rogar** play hard to get

rojizo adj reddish

rojo 1 adj red; **al rojo vivo** red hot **2** m color red **3** m, **-a** f POL red, commie F

rol m role

rollizo adj F chubby

rollo m FOT roll; fig F drag F; **buen / mal rollo** F good / bad atmosphere; **¡qué rollo!** F what a drag! F

Roma Rome

romance m romance

románico m/adj Romanesque

romano 1 adj Roman **2** m, **-a** f Roman

romántico 1 adj romantic **2** m, **-a** f romantic

rombo m rhombus

romero m BOT rosemary

rompecabezas m puzzle

rompehielos m inv icebreaker

romper ⟨2a; part **roto**⟩ **1** v/t break; (*hacer añicos*) smash; **tela**, **papel** tear **2** v/i break; **romper a** start to; **romper con alguien** break up with s.o. **3** v/r **romperse** break

rompopo m C.Am., Méx bebida eggnog

ron m'rum

roncar ⟨1g⟩ v/i snore

roncha f MED bump, swelling

ronco adj hoarse; **quedarse ronco** go hoarse

ronda f round

rondar ⟨1a⟩ **1** v/t patrol; **me ronda una idea** I have an idea going around in my head **2** v/i F hang around

ronquido m snore; **ronquidos** pl snoring sg

ronronear ⟨1a⟩ v/i de gato purr

roña f grime

roñoso adj grimy, grubby

ropa f clothes pl; **ropa de cama** bedclothes pl; **ropa interior** underwear; **ropa íntima** L.Am. underwear

ropero m closet, Br wardrobe

rosa 1 adj pink **2** f BOT rose; **fresco como una rosa** fresh as a daisy; **ver algo de color de rosa** see sth through rose-col-o(u)red glasses

rosado 1 adj pink; **vino** rosé **2** m rosé

rosal m rosebush

rosario m REL rosary; fig string

rosbif m GASTR roast beef

rosca f TÉC thread; GASTR F pastry similar to a donut

rosco m GASTR pastry similar to a donut; **no comerse un rosco** P not get anywhere

roscón m GASTR large ring-shaped cake

rosquilla f pastry similar to a donut

rosticería f L.Am. type of deli that sells roast chicken

rostro m face

rotación f rotation

rotisería f L.Am. deli, delicatessen

roto 1 part → **romper 2** adj pierna etc broken; (*hecho añicos*) smashed; **tela**, **papel** torn **3** m, **-a** f Chi one of the urban poor

rotonda f traffic circle, Br roundabout

rotoso adj Rpl F scruffy

rotulador m fiber-tip, Br fibre-tip, felt-tip

rótulo m sign

rotundo adj fig categorical

rotura f breakage; **una rotura de cadera** MED a broken hip

rozadura f chafing, rubbing

rozagante adj healthy

rozar ⟨1f⟩ **1** v/t rub; (*tocar ligeramente*) brush; (*hecho añicos*) smashed; fig **tela**, **papel** rub; **3** v/r **rozarse** wear

rte. abr (= **remitente**) sender

ruana f Ecuad poncho

rubéola, **rubéola** f MED German measles sg

rubí m ruby

rubicundo adj ruddy

rubio adj blond; **tabaco rubio** Virginia tobacco

ruborizarse ⟨1f⟩ v/r go red, blush

rúbrica f heading; **de firma** flourish

rubro m L.Am. category, heading

rudeza f roughness

rudimentario adj rudimentary

rudo adj rough

rueda f wheel; **rueda dentada** cogwheel; **rueda de prensa** press conference; **rueda de recambio** spare wheel

ruedo m TAUR bullring

ruego **1** vb → **rogar 2** m request

rufián m rogue

rugby m rugby

rugido m roar

rugir ⟨3c⟩ v/i roar

rugoso *adj superficie* rough
ruido *m* noise; ***hacer ruido*** make a noise; ***mucho ruido y pocas nueces*** all talk and no action
ruidoso *adj* noisy
ruin *adj* despicable, mean; (*tacaño*) mean, miserly
ruina *f* ruin; ***llevar a alguien a la ruina*** *fig* bankrupt s.o.
ruiseñor *m zo* nightingale
ruleta *f* roulette
ruletero *m Méx* cab *o* taxi driver
rulo *m* roller
rumbeador *m Rpl* tracker
rumbear ⟨1a⟩ *v/i L.Am.* head (*para* for)
rumbo *m* course; ***tomar rumbo a*** head for; ***perder el rumbo*** *fig* lose one's way

rumboso *adj* lavish
rumiar ⟨1b⟩ *v/t fig* ponder
rumor *m* rumo(u)r
rumorearse ⟨1a⟩ *v/r* be rumo(u)red
rupestre *adj*: ***pintura rupestre*** cave painting
ruptura *f de relaciones* breaking off; *de pareja* break-up
rural 1 *adj* rural **2** *m Rpl* station wagon, *Br* estate car, ***rurales** Méx* (rural) police
Rusia Russia
ruso 1 *adj* Russian **2** *m*, **-a** *f* Russian
rústico *adj* rustic
ruta *f* route
rutina *f* routine
rutinario *adj* routine *atr*

S

S *abr* (*= sur*) S (*= South(ern)*)
S.A. *abr* (*= sociedad anónima*) inc (*= incorporated*), *Br* plc (*= public limited company*)
sábado *m* Saturday
sábana *f* sheet; ***sábana ajustable*** fitted sheet
sabana *f* savanna(h)
sabandija *f* bug, creepy-crawly
sabañón *m* chilblain
sabelotodo *m* F know-it-all F, *Br* know-all F
saber ⟨2n⟩ **1** *v/t* know (*de* about); ***saber hacer algo*** know how to do sth, be able to do sth; ***no lo supe hasta más tarde*** I didn't find out till later; ***hacer saber algo a alguien*** let s.o. know sth; ***¡qué sé yo!*** who knows?; ***que yo sepa*** as far as I know; ***sabérselas todas*** F know every trick in the book **2** *v/i* taste (*a* of); ***me sabe a quemado*** it tastes burnt to me; ***me sabe mal*** *fig* it upsets me **3** *m* knowledge, learning
sabiduría *f* wisdom; (*conocimientos*) knowledge
sabiendas *fpl*: ***a sabiendas*** knowingly; ***a sabiendas que*** knowing full well that
sabio 1 *adj* wise; (*sensato*) sensible **2** *m*, **-a** *f* wise person; (*experto*) expert
sabiondo *m*, **-a** *f* know- it-all F, *Br* know-all F
sablazo *m*: ***dar un sablazo a alguien*** F

scrounge money off s.o.
sable *m* saber, *Br* sabre
sablear ⟨1a⟩ *v/t & v/i L.Am.* F scrounge (*a* from)
sabor *m* flavo(u)r, taste; ***dejar mal sabor de boca*** *fig* leave a bad taste in the mouth
saborear ⟨1a⟩ *v/t* savo(u)r; *fig* relish
sabotaje *m* sabotage
saboteador *m*, **saboteadora** *f* saboteur
sabotear ⟨1a⟩ *v/t* sabotage
sabroso *adj* tasty; *fig* juicy; *L.Am.* (*agradable*) nice, pleasant
sabrosura *f L.Am.* tasty dish
sabueso *m fig* sleuth
sacacorchos *m inv* corkscrew
sacamuelas *m inv desp* F dentist
sacapuntas *m inv* pencil sharpener
sacar ⟨1g⟩ **1** *v/t* take out, *mancha* take out, remove; *información* get; *disco, libro* bring out; *fotocopias* make; ***sacar a alguien a bailar*** ask s.o. to dance; ***sacar algo en claro*** (*entender*) make sense of sth; ***sacar de paseo*** take for a walk **2** *v/r* **sacarse** *L.Am. ropa* take off
sacarina *f* saccharin(e)
sacerdote *m* priest
sacerdotisa *f* priestess
saciar ⟨1b⟩ *v/t fig* satisfy, fulfill
saciedad *f*: ***repetir algo hasta la saciedad*** *fig* repeat sth time and again, repeat sth ad nauseam

S

saco *m* sack; *L.Am.* jacket; **saco de dormir** sleeping bag; **entrar a saco en** F burst into, barge into F

sacramento *m* sacrament

sacrificar ⟨1g⟩ **1** *v/t* sacrifice; (*matar*) slaughter **2** *v/r* **sacrificarse** make sacrifices (*por* for)

sacrificio *m* sacrifice

sacrilegio *m* sacrilege

sacristán *m* sexton

sacristía *f* vestry

sacudida *f* shake, jolt; EL shock

sacudir ⟨3a⟩ **1** *v/t tb* fig shake; F *niño* beat, wallop **2** *v/r* **sacudirse** shake off, shrug off; **sacudirse alguien (de encima)** get rid of s.o.

sádico 1 *adj* sadistic **2** *m*, **-a** *f* sadist

sadismo *m* sadism

safari *m* safari; **safari fotográfico** photographic safari

sagaz *adj* shrewd, sharp

Sagitario *m/f inv* ASTR Sagittarius

sagrado *adj* sacred, holy

sagrario *m* tabernacle

Sahara Sahara

sainete *m* TEA short farce, one-act play

sal 1 *f* salt; **sal común** cooking salt; **sal marina** sea salt **2** *vb* → **salir**

sala *f* room, hall; *de cine* screen; JUR court room; **sala de embarque** AVIA departure lounge; **sala de espera** waiting room; **sala de estar** living room; **sala de fiestas** night club; **sala de sesiones** *or* **de juntas** boardroom

saladero *m L.Am.* meat / fish salting factory

salado *adj* salted; (*con demasiada sal*) salty; (*no dulce*) savo(u)ry; *fig* funny, witty; *C.Am., Chi, Rpl* F pric(e)y F

salamandra *f* ZO salamander

salamanquesa *f* ZO gecko

salami *m* salami

salar ⟨1a⟩ **1** *v/t* add salt to, salt; *para conservar* salt **2** *m Arg* salt mine

salarial *adj* salary *atr*

salario *m* salary; **salario base** basic wage; **salario mínimo** minimum wage

salazón *f* salted fish / meat; **en salazón** salt *atr*

salchicha *f* sausage

salchichón *m* type of spiced sausage

saldar ⟨1a⟩ *v/t disputa* settle; *deuda* settle, pay; *géneros* sell off

saldo *m* COM balance; (*resultado*) result; **saldo acreedor** credit balance; **saldo deudor** debit balance; **de saldo** reduced, on sale

saldré *vb* → **salir**

salero *m* salt cellar; *fig* wit

saleroso *adj* funny, witty

salga *vb* → **salir**

salgo *vb* → **salir**

salida *f* exit, way out; TRANSP departure; *de carrera* start; **salida de emergencia** emergency exit; **salida de tono** ill-judged remark

saliente *adj* projecting, protruding; *presidente* retiring, outgoing

salir ⟨3r⟩ **1** *v/i* leave, go out; (*aparecer*) appear, come out; **salir de** (*ir fuera de*) leave, go out of; (*venir fuera de*) leave, come out of; (*dejar*) leave, go out of; s.o.: **salir a 1000 pesetas** cost 1000 pesetas; **salir bien / mal** turn out well / badly; **el dibujo no me sale** FI can't get this drawing right; **no me salió el trabajo** I didn't get the job; **salir con alguien** date s.o., go out with s.o.; **salir perdiendo** end up losing **2** *v/r* **salirse** *de líquido* overflow; (*dejar*) leave; **salirse de la carretera** leave the road, go off the road; **salirse con la suya** get what one wants

salitre *m* saltpeter, *Br* saltpetre

saliva *f* saliva; **tragar saliva** hold one's tongue

salmo *m* psalm

salmón *m* ZO salmon; **color salmón** salmon

salmonete *m* ZO red mullet

salmuera *f* pickle, brine

salobre *adj* salt; (*con demasiada sal*) salty

salomónico *adj* just, fair

salón *m* living room; **salón de actos** auditorium, hall; **salón de baile** dance hall; **salón de belleza** beauty parlo(u)r, beautician's

salpicadera *f Méx* AUTO fender, *Br* mudguard

salpicadero *m* AUTO dash(board)

salpicadura *f* stain

salpicar ⟨1g⟩ *v/t* splash, spatter (*con* with); *fig* sprinkle, pepper

salpicón *m* GASTR *vegetable salad with chopped meat or fish*

salpimentar ⟨1k⟩ *v/t* season (with salt and pepper)

salsa *f* GASTR sauce; *baile* salsa; **en su salsa** *fig* in one's element

salsera *f* sauce boat

saltamontes *m inv* ZO grasshopper

saltar ⟨1a⟩ **1** *v/i* jump, leap; **saltar a la vista** fig be obvious, be clear; **saltar sobre** pounce on; **saltar a la comba** jump rope, *Br* skip **2** *v/t valla* jump **3** *v/r* **saltarse** (*omitir*) miss, skip

saltear ⟨1a⟩ *v/t* GASTR sauté

saltimbanqui *m* acrobat

salto *m* leap, jump; **salto de agua** waterfall; **salto de altura** high jump; **salto de longitud** long jump; **salto mortal** somersault

saltón *adj*: **ojos saltones** bulging eyes

salubridad *f L.Am.* health; **Salubridad** *L.Am.* Department of Health

salud *f* health; **¡(a tu) salud!** cheers!

saludable *adj* healthy

saludar ⟨1a⟩ *v/t* say hello to, greet; MIL salute

saludo *m* greeting; MIL salute; **saludos en carta** best wishes

salva *f*: **salva de aplausos** round of applause

salvación *f* REL salvation

salvado *m* bran

salvador *m* REL savio(u)r

salvadoreño 1 *adj* Salvador(e)an 2 *m*, -a *f* Salvador(e)an

salvaguardar ⟨1a⟩ *v/t* safeguard, protect

salvajada *f* atrocity, act of savagery; **decir una salvajada** say something outrageous

salvaje 1 *adj* wild; (*bruto*) brutal 2 *m/f* savage

salvajismo *m* savagery

salvamanteles *m inv* table mat

salvamento *m* rescue; **buque de salvamento** life boat

salvapantallas *m inv* INFOR screensaver

salvar ⟨1a⟩ 1 *v/t* save; *obstáculo* get round, get over 2 *v/r* **salvarse** escape, get out

salvavidas *m inv* life belt

salvedad *f* (*excepción*) exception

salvo 1 *adj*: **estar a salvo** be safe (and sound); **ponerse a salvo** reach safety 2 *adv* & *prp* except, save; **salvo error u omisión** errors and omissions excepted

sambenito *m*: **le han colgado el sambenito de vago** F they've got him down as idle F

sambumbia *f L.Am.* watery drink

San *adj* Saint

sanar ⟨1a⟩ 1 *v/t* cure 2 *v/i de persona* get well, recover; *de herida* heal

sanatorio *m* sanitarium, clinic

sanción *f* JUR penalty, sanction

sancionar ⟨1a⟩ *v/t* penalize; (*multar*) fine

sancocho *m W.I.* type of stew

sandalia *f* sandal

sándalo *m* BOT sandalwood

sandez *f* nonsense; **decir sandeces** talk nonsense

sandía *f* watermelon

sandunga *f* F wit

sandunguero *adj L.Am.* F witty

sandwich *m* tostado toasted sandwich; *L.Am. sin tostar* sandwich

saneamiento *m* cleaning up; COM restructuring, rationalization

sanear ⟨1a⟩ *v/t* clean up; COM restructure, rationalize

sangrar ⟨1a⟩ 1 *v/t* **sangrar a alguien** *fig* F sponge off s.o. 2 *v/i* bleed

sangre *f* blood; **sangre fría** *fig* calmness, coolness; **a sangre fría** *fig* in cold blood; **no llegará la sangre al río** it won't come to that, it won't be that bad

sangría *f* GASTR sangria

sangriento *adj* bloody

sangrigordo *adj Méx* tedious, boring

sanguijuela *f* ZO leech

sanguinario *adj* bloodthirsty

sanidad *f* health

sanitario *adj* (public) health *atr*

sanitarios *mpl* bathroom fittings

sano *adj* healthy; **sano y salvo** safe and well; **cortar por lo sano** take drastic measures

sanseacabó: **y sanseacabó** F and that's that F

santa *f* Saint

santiamén *m*: **en un santiamén** F in an instant

santidad *f*: **Su Santidad** His Holiness

santiguarse ⟨1i⟩ *v/r* cross o.s., make the sign of the cross

santo 1 *adj* holy 2 *m* saint; **santo y seña** F password; **¿a santo de qué?** F what on earth for? F; **no es santo de mi devoción** F I don't like him very much

santuario *m* fig sanctuary

santurrón *m*, **-ona** *f* sanctimonious person

saña *f* viciousness

sapo *m* ZO toad; **echar sapos y culebras** *fig* curse and swear

saque *m en tenis* serve; **saque de banda** *en fútbol* throw-in; **saque de esquina** corner (kick); **tener buen saque** F have a big appetite

saquear ⟨1a⟩ *v/t* sack, ransack

sarampión *m* MED measles

sarao *m* party

sarape *m Méx* poncho, blanket

sarcasmo *m* sarcasm

sarcástico *adj* sarcastic

sarcófago *m* sarcophagus

sardina *f* sardine; **como sardinas en lata** like sardines

sargento *m* sergeant

sarna *f* MED scabies

sarnoso *adj* scabby

sarpullido *m* MED rash

sarro *m* tartar

sarta *f* string, series

S

sartén f frying pan; **tener la sartén por el mango** fig be the boss, be in the driving seat

sastra f tailor(ess)

sastre m tailor

satán, satanás m Satan

satánico adj satanic

satélite m satellite; **ciudad satélite** satellite town

satén, satín m satin

sátira f satire

satírico adj satirical

satirizar ⟨1f⟩ v/t satirize

satisfacción f satisfaction

satisfacer ⟨2s; part **satisfecho** ⟩ v/t satisfy; requisito, exigencia meet, fulfil(l); deuda settle, pay off

satisfactorio adj satisfactory

satisfecho 1 part → **satisfacer 2** adj satisfied; (lleno) full; **darse por satisfecho** be satisfied (**con** with)

saturar ⟨1a⟩ v/t saturate

sauce m BOT willow; **sauce llorón** weeping willow

saúco m BOT elder

saudí m/f & adj Saudi

saudita m/f Saudi

sauna f sauna

savia f sap

saxofón, saxófono m saxophone, sax F

sazón f: **a la sazón** at that time

sazonar ⟨1a⟩ v/t GASTR season

scooter m motor scooter

se ◇ pron complemento indirecto: a él (to) him; a ella (to) her; a usted, ustedes (to) you; a ellos (to) them; **se lo daré** I will give it to him / her / you / them ◇ reflexivo: con él himself; con ella herself; cosa itself; con usted yourself; con ustedes yourselves; con ellos themselves; **se vistió** he got dressed, he dressed himself; **se lavó las manos** she washed her hands; **se abrazaron** they hugged each other ◇ oración impersonal: **se cree** it is thought; **se habla español** Spanish spoken

sé vb → **saber**

sea vb → **ser**

sebo m grease, fat

secador m: **secador (de pelo)** hair dryer

secadora f dryer

secar ⟨1g⟩ **1** v/t dry **2** v/r **secarse** dry

sección f section

secesión f POL secession

seco adj dry; fig persona curt, brusque; **parar en seco** stop dead

secreción f secretion

secretaria f secretary; **secretaria de dirección** executive secretary

secretaría f secretary's office; de organización secretariat

secretario m tb POL secretary

secreter m mueble writing desk

secretismo m secrecy

secreto 1 adj secret **2** m secret; **un secreto a voces** an open secret; **en secreto** in secret

secta f sect

sectario adj sectarian

sectarismo m sectarianism

sector m sector

secuaz m/f follower

secuela f MED after-effect

secuencia f sequence

secuencial adj INFOR sequential

secuestrador m, **secuestradora** f kidnapper

secuestrar ⟨1a⟩ v/t barco, avión hijack; persona abduct, kidnap

secuestro m de barco, avión hijacking; de persona abduction, kidnapping; **secuestro aéreo** hijacking

secundar ⟨1a⟩ v/t support, back

secundario adj secondary

sed f tb fig thirst; **tener sed** be thirsty

seda f silk; **como una seda** F as smooth as silk

sedal m fishing line

sedante m sedative

sede f de organización headquarters; de acontecimiento site; **sede social** head office

sedentario adj sedentary

sedición f sedition

sediento adj thirsty; **estar sediento de** fig thirst for

sedimentar ⟨1a⟩ v/t deposit

sedimento m sediment

sedoso adj silky

seducción f seduction; (atracción) attraction

seducir ⟨3o⟩ v/t seduce; (atraer) attract; (cautivar) captivate, charm

seductor 1 adj seductive; (atractivo) attractive; oferta tempting **2** m seducer

seductora f seductress

segadora f reaper, harvester

segar ⟨1h & 1k⟩ v/t reap, harvest

seglar adj secular, lay atr

segmento m segment

segregación f segregation; **segregación racial** racial segregation

segregar ⟨1h⟩ v/t segregate

seguida f: **en seguida** at once, immediately

seguido 1 adj consecutive, successive; **ir todo seguido** go straight on **2** adv

sentimental

L.Am. often, frequently

seguidor *m*, **seguidora** *f* follower, supporter

seguimiento *m* monitoring

seguir ⟨3l & 3d⟩ **1** *v/t* follow; **seguir a alguien** follow s.o. **2** *v/i* continue, carry on; **sigue enfadado conmigo** he's still angry with me; **seguir haciendo algo** go on doing sth, continue to do sth

según 1 *prp* according to; **según él** according to him **2** *adv* it depends

segunda *f*: **de segunda** *fig* second-rate

segundero *m* second hand

segundo *m/adj* second

seguridad *f* safety; *contra crimen* security; *(certeza)* certainty; **Seguridad Social** *Esp* Social Security

seguro 1 *adj* safe; *(estable)* steady; *(cierto)* sure; **es seguro** *(cierto)* it's a certainty; **seguro de sí mismo** self-confident, sure of o.s. **2** *adv* for sure **3** *m* COM insurance; *de puerta, coche* lock; *L.Am. (imperdible)* safety pin; **poner el seguro** lock the door; **ir sobre seguro** be on the safe side

seis *adj* six

seiscientos *adj* six hundred

seísmo *m* earthquake

selección *f* selection; **selección nacional** DEP national team

seleccionador *m*, **seleccionadora** *f* DEP: **seleccionador nacional** national team manager

seleccionar ⟨1a⟩ *v/t* choose, select

selectividad *f en España* university entrance exam

selecto *adj* select, exclusive

sellar ⟨1a⟩ *v/t* seal

sello *m* stamp; *fig* hallmark; **sello discográfico** record label

selva *f (bosque)* forest; *(jungla)* jungle

semáforo *m* traffic light

semana *f* week; **Semana Santa** Holy Week, Easter

semanal *adj* weekly

semanario *m* weekly

semblante *m* face

sembrado *m* sown field

sembrar ⟨1k⟩ *v/t* sow; *fig: pánico, inquietud etc* spread

semejante 1 *adj* similar; **jamás he oído semejante tontería** I've never heard such nonsense **2** *m* fellow human being, fellow creature

semejanza *f* similarity

semejarse ⟨1a⟩ *v/r* look alike, resemble each other

semen *m* BIO semen

semental *m toro* stud bull; *caballo* stallion

semestre *m* six-month period; EDU semester

semicírculo *m* semicircle

semiconductor *m* EL semiconductor

semifinal *f* DEP semifinal

semilla *f* seed

seminario *m* seminary

seminarista *m* seminarian

semítico *adj* Semitic

sémola *f* semolina

senado *m* senate

senador *m*, **senadora** *f* senator

sencillez *f* simplicity

sencillo 1 *adj* simple **2** *m L.Am.* small change

senda *f* path, track

senderismo *m* trekking, hiking

senderista *m/f* walker, hiker

sendero *m* path, track

sendos, **-as** *adj pl*: **les entregó sendos diplomas** he presented each of them with a diploma

senil *adj* senile

seno *m tb fig* bosom; **senos** breasts

sensación *f* feeling, sensation; **causar sensación** *fig* cause a sensation

sensacional *adj* sensational

sensacionalista *adj* sensationalist

sensatez *f* good sense

sensato *adj* sensible

sensibilidad *f* feeling; *(emotividad)* sensitivity

sensibilizar ⟨1f⟩ *v/t* make aware (**sobre** of)

sensible *adj* sensitive; *(apreciable)* appreciable, noticeable

sensiblero *adj* sentimental, schmaltzy F

sensor *m* sensor

sensorial *adj* sensory

sensual *adj* sensual

sensualidad *f* sensuality

sentada *f* sit-down

sentado *adj* sitting, seated; **dar por sentado** *fig* take for granted, assume

sentar ⟨1k⟩ **1** *v/t fig* establish, create; **sentar las bases** lay the foundations, pave the way **2** *v/i*: **sentar bien a alguien** *de comida* agree with s.o.; **le sienta bien esa chaqueta** that jacket suits her, she looks good in that jacket **3** *v/r* **sentarse** sit down

sentencia *f* JUR sentence

sentenciar ⟨1b⟩ *v/t* JUR sentence

sentido *m* sense; *(significado)* meaning; **sentido común** common sense; **sentido del humor** sense of humo(u)r; **perder / recobrar el sentido** lose / regain consciousness

sentimental *adj* emotional; **ser senti-**

mental be sentimental
sentimentalismo *m* sentiment
sentimiento *m* feeling; ***lo acompaño en el sentimiento*** my condolences
sentir 1 *m* feeling, opinion 2 ⟨3i⟩ *v/t* feel; *(percibir)* sense; ***lo siento*** I'm sorry 3 *v/r*
sentirse feel; *L.Am. (ofenderse)* take offense, *Br* take offence
seña *f* gesture, sign; ***me hizo una seña para que entrara*** he gestured to me to go in; ***señas*** *pl* address *sg*; ***hacer señas*** wave
señal *f* signal; *fig* sign, trace; COM deposit, down payment; ***en señal de*** as a token of, as a mark of
señalado *adj* special
señalar ⟨1a⟩ *v/t* indicate, point out
señalizar ⟨1f⟩ *v/t* signpost
Señor *m* Lord
señor 1 *m* gentleman, man; *trato* sir; *escrito* Mr; ***el señor López*** Mr López; ***los señores López*** Mr and Mrs López
señora *f* lady, woman; *trato* ma'am, *Br* madam; *escrito* Mrs, Ms; ***la señora López*** Mrs López; ***mi señora*** my wife; ***señoras y señores*** ladies and gentlemen
señoría *f*: ***su señoría*** your Hono(u)r
señorial *adj* lordly, noble
señorita *f* young lady, young woman; *tratamiento* miss; *escrito* Miss; ***la señorita López*** Ms López, Miss López
señuelo *m* decoy
sepa *vb* → *saber*
separación *f* separation; ***separación de bienes*** JUR division of property
separado *adj* separated; ***por separado*** separately
separar ⟨1a⟩ 1 *v/t* separate 2 *v/r* ***separarse*** separate, split up F
separatismo *m* separatism
separatista *m/f & adj* separatist
sepia *f* ZO cuttlefish
sept.ᵉ *abr* (= ***septiembre***) Sept. (= September)
septentrional *adj* northern
septiembre *m* September
séptimo *adj* seventh
sepulcro *m* tomb
sepultar ⟨1a⟩ *v/t* bury
sepultura *f* burial; *(tumba)* tomb; ***dar sepultura a alguien*** bury s.o.
sequedad *f* fig curtness
sequía *f* drought
séquito *m* retinue, entourage
ser ⟨2w; *part* **sido**⟩ 1 *v/i* be; ***ser de Sevilla*** be from Seville; ***ser de madera / plata*** be made of wood / silver; ***es de Juan*** it's Juan's, it belongs to Juan; ***ser para*** be for; ***a no ser que*** unless;

¡eso es! exactly!, that's right!; ***es que ...*** the thing is ...; ***es de esperar*** it's to be hoped; ***¿cuánto es?*** how much is it?; ***¿qué es de ti?*** how's life?, how're things?; ***o sea*** in other words 2 *m* being
Serbia Serbia
serenarse ⟨1a⟩ *v/r* calm down; *del tiempo* clear up
serenata *f* MÚS serenade
serenidad *f* calmness, serenity
sereno 1 *m*: ***dormir al sereno*** sleep outdoors 2 *adj* calm, serene
serial *m* TV, RAD series
serie *f* series; ***fuera de serie*** out of this world, extraordinary
seriedad *f* seriousness
serio *adj* serious; *(responsable)* reliable; ***en serio*** seriously
sermón *m* sermon
sermonear ⟨1a⟩ *v/i* preach
seropositivo *adj* MED HIV positive
serpentina *f* streamer
serpiente *f* ZO snake; ***serpiente de cascabel*** rattlesnake
serranía *f* mountainous region
serrar ⟨1k⟩ *v/t* saw
serrín *m* sawdust
serrucho *m* handsaw
servicial *adj* obliging, helpful
servicio *m* service; ***servicios*** *pl* restroom *sg*, *Br* toilets; ***servicio doméstico*** domestic service; ***servicio militar*** military service; ***servicio pos(t)venta*** after-sales service; ***servicio de atención al cliente*** customer service; ***estar de servicio*** be on duty
servidor *m* INFOR server
servil *adj* servile
servilismo *m* servility
servilleta *f* napkin, serviette
servilletero *m* napkin ring
servir ⟨3l⟩ 1 *v/t* serve 2 *v/i* be of use; ***¿para qué sirve esto?*** what is this (used) for?; ***no servir de nada*** be no use at all 3 *v/r* ***servirse*** help o.s.; *comida* help oneself to
servodirección power steering
sésamo *m* sesame
sesenta *adj* sixty
sesgar ⟨1h⟩ *v/t* slant, skew
sesión *f* session; *en cine, teatro* show, performance
sesionar ⟨1a⟩ *v/i* L.Am. be in session
seso *m* ANAT brain; *fig* brains *pl*, sense; ***sesos*** GASTR brains
set *m* tenis set
seta *f* BOT mushroom; *venenosa* toadstool
setecientos *adj* seven hundred
setenta *adj* seventy

seto *m* hedge

s.e.u.o. *abr* (= *salvo error u omisión*) E & OE (= errors and omissions excepted)

seudónimo *m* pseudonym

severo *adj* severe

sevillanas *fpl* folk dance from Seville

sexismo *m* sexism

sexista *m/f* & *adj* sexist

sexo *m* sex

sexto *adj* sixth

sexual *adj* sexual

sexualidad *f* sexuality

sexy *adj inv* sexy

shock *m* MED shock

si *conj* if; *si no* if not; *como si* as if; *por si* in case; *me pregunto si vendrá* I wonder whether he'll come

sí *adv* yes 2 *pron tercera persona: singular masculino* himself; *femenino* herself; *cosa, animal* itself; *plural* themselves; *usted* yourself; *ustedes* yourselves; *por sí solo* by himself / itself, on his / its own

siamés *adj* Siamese

sibarita *m* bon vivant, epicure

Siberia Siberia

sicario *m* hired assassin

Sicilia Sicily

SIDA *abr* (= *síndrome de inmunidad deficiente adquirida*) Aids (= acquired immune-deficiency syndrome)

sidecar *m* sidecar

sideral *adj viajes* space *atr*; *espacio sideral* outer space

siderurgia *f* iron and steel making

sido *part* → *ser*

sidra *f* cider

siembra *f* sowing

siempre *adv* always; *siempre que* providing that, as long as; *lo de siempre* the same old story; *para siempre* for ever

sien *f* ANAT temple

siendo *vb* → *ser*

siento *vb* → *sentir*

sierra *f* saw; GEOG mountain range

siesta *f* siesta, nap; *dormir la siesta* have a siesta *o* nap

siete *adj* seven

sífilis *f* MED syphilis

siga *vb* → *seguir*

sigilo *m* secrecy, stealth

sigiloso *adj* stealthy

sigla *f* abbreviation, acronym

siglo *m* century; *hace siglos o un siglo que no le veo fig* I haven't seen him in a long long time

signatario *m*, -a *f* signatory

significado *m* meaning

significar ⟨1g⟩ *v/t* mean, signify

significativo *adj* meaningful, significant

signo *m* sign; *signo de admiración* exclamation mark; *signo de interrogación* question mark; *signo de puntuación* punctuation mark

sigo *vb* → *seguir*

siguiente 1 *adj* next, following 2 *pron* next (one)

sílaba *f* syllable

silbar ⟨1a⟩ *v/i* & *v/t* whistle

silbato *m* whistle

silbido *m* whistle

silenciador *m* AUTO muffler, *Br* silencer

silencio *m* silence; *en silencio* in silence, silently

silencioso *adj* silent

silicio *m* QUÍM silicon

silicona *f* silicone

silla *f* chair; *silla de montar* saddle; *silla de ruedas* wheelchair

sillín *m* saddle

sillón *m* armchair, easy chair

silueta *f* silhouette

silvestre *adj* wild

silvicultura *f* forestry

simbiosis *f* symbiosis

simbolismo *m* symbolism

simbolizar ⟨1f⟩ *v/t* symbolize

símbolo *m* symbol

simétrico *adj* symmetrical

similar *adj* similar

similitud *f* similarity

simio *m* ZO ape

simpatía *f* warmth, friendliness

simpático *adj* nice, lik(e)able

simpatizante *m/f* sympathizer, supporter

simpatizar ⟨1f⟩ *v/i* sympathize

simple 1 *adj* simple; (*mero*) ordinary 2 *m* simpleton

simplicidad *f* simplicity

simplificar ⟨1g⟩ *v/t* simplify

simplista *adj* simplistic

simposio *m* symposium

simulación *f* simulation

simulacro *m* (*cosa falsa*) pretense, *Br* pretence, sham; (*simulación*) simulation; *simulacro de incendio* fire drill

simulador *m* simulator

simular ⟨1a⟩ *v/t* simulate

simultanear ⟨1a⟩ *v/t*: *simultanear dos cargos* hold two positions at the same time

simultáneo *adj* simultaneous

sin *prp* without; *sin que* without; *sin preguntar* without asking

sinagoga *f* synagogue

sinceridad *f* sincerity

sincero *adj* sincere

síncope *m* MED blackout

sincronizar ⟨1f⟩ *v/t* synchronize

S

sindical *adj* (labor, *Br* trade) union *atr*

sindicalismo *m* (labor, *Br* trade) union movement

sindicalista *m/f* (labor, *Br* trade) union member

sindicato *m* (labor, *Br* trade) union

síndrome *m* syndrome

sinfín *m*: **un sinfín de ...** no end of ...

sinfonía *f* MÚS symphony

singular 1 *adj* singular; *fig* outstanding, extraordinary **2** *m* GRAM singular

siniestro 1 *adj* sinister **2** *m* accident; (*catástrofe*) disaster

sinnúmero *m*: **un sinnúmero de** no end of

sino 1 *m* fate **2** *conj* but; (*salvo*) except; **no cena en casa, sino en el bar** he doesn't have dinner at home, he has it in the bar

sinónimo 1 *adj* synonymous **2** *m* synonym

sinopsis *f inv* synopsis

sinsentido *m* nonsense

sintaxis *f* syntax

síntesis *f inv* synthesis; (*resumen*) summary

sintético *adj* synthetic

sintetizador *m* MÚS synthesizer

síntoma *m* symptom

sintonía *f melodía* theme tune, signature tune; RAD tuning, reception; **estar en la sintonía de** RAD be tuned to

sintonizar ⟨1f⟩ **1** *v/t* radio tune in **2** *v/i fig* be in tune (**con** with)

sinuoso *adj* winding

sinusitis *f* MED sinusitis

sinvergüenza *m/f* swine; **¡qué sinvergüenza!** (*descarado*) what a nerve!

siquiera *adv*: **ni siquiera** not even; **siquiera bebe algo** *L.Am.* at least have a drink

sirena *f* siren; MYTH mermaid

Siria Syria

sirve *vb* → **servir**

sirvienta *f* maid

sirviente *m* servant

sisar ⟨1a⟩ *v/t* F pilfer

sísmico *adj* seismic

sistema *m* system; **sistema operativo** operating system

sistemático *adj* systematic

sitiar ⟨1b⟩ *v/t* surround, lay siege to

sitio *m* place; (*espacio*) room; **hacer sitio** make room; **en ningún sitio** nowhere; **sitio web** web site

situación *f* situation

situar ⟨1e⟩ **1** *v/t* place, put **2** *v/r* **situarse** be

S.L. *abr* (= **sociedad limitada**) Ltd (= limited)

slip *m* underpants *pl*

s/n *abr* (= **sin número**) not numbered

sobaco *m* armpit

sobar ⟨1a⟩ *v/t* handle, finger; F *sexualmente* grope F

soberanía *f* sovereignty

soberano *m*, **-a** *f* sovereign

soberbia *f* pride, arrogance

soberbio *adj* proud, arrogant; *fig* superb

sobornar ⟨1a⟩ *v/t* bribe

soborno *m* bribe

sobra *f* surplus, excess; **hay de sobra** there's more than enough; **sobras** leftovers

sobradamente *adv conocido* well

sobrar ⟨1a⟩ *v/t*: **sobra comida** there's food left over; **me sobró pintura** I had some paint left over; **sobraba uno** there was one left

sobre 1 *m* envelope **2** *prp* on; **sobre esto** about this; **sobre las tres** about three o'clock; **sobre todo** above all, especially

sobrecargar ⟨1h⟩ *v/t* overload

sobrecargo *m* AVIA chief flight attendant; MAR purser

sobrecoger ⟨2c⟩ *v/t* (*asustar*) strike fear into; (*impresionar*) have an effect on

sobredosis *f inv* overdose

sobrehumano *adj* superhuman

sobremesa *f*: **de sobremesa** afternoon *atr*

sobrenatural *adj* supernatural

sobrenombre *m* nickname

sobrentenderse ⟨2g⟩ *v/r*: **se sobrentiende de que ...** needless to say, ...

sobrepasar ⟨1a⟩ **1** *v/t* exceed, surpass; **me sobrepasa en altura** he is taller than me **2** *v/r* **sobrepasarse** go too far

sobrepeso *m* excess weight

sobreponerse ⟨2r; *part* **sobrepuesto**⟩ *v/r*: **sobreponerse a** overcome, get over

sobrepuesto *part* → **sobreponerse**

sobresaliente *adj* outstanding, excellent

sobresalir ⟨3r⟩ *v/t* stick out, protrude; *fig* excel; **sobresalir entre** stand out among

sobresaltar ⟨1a⟩ **1** *v/t* startle **2** *v/r* **sobresaltarse** jump, start

sobresalto *m* jump, start

sobreseer ⟨2e⟩ *v/t* JUR dismiss

sobrestimar ⟨1a⟩ *v/t* overestimate

sobresueldo *m* bonus

sobrevalorar ⟨1a⟩ *v/t* overrate

sobrevenir ⟨3s⟩ *v/i* happen; *de guerra* break out

sobrevivir ⟨3a⟩ *v/i* survive

sobrevolar ⟨1m⟩ *v/t* fly over

sobriedad *f* soberness; *de comida, decoración* simplicity; (*moderación*) restraint

sobrina *f* niece

sobrino *m* nephew

sobrio *adj* sober; *comida, decoración* simple; *(moderado)* restrained

socarrón *adj* sarcastic, snide F

socavar ⟨1a⟩ *v/t tb fig* undermine

socavón *m* hollow

sociable *adj* sociable

social *adj* social

socialismo *m* socialism

socialista *m/f & adj* socialist

sociedad *f* society; **sociedad anónima** public corporation, *Br* public limited company; **sociedad de consumo** consumer society

socio *m*, **-a** *f* de club, asociación etc member; COM partner

sociología *f* sociology

socorrer ⟨2a⟩ *v/t* help, assist

socorrista *m/f* life guard

socorro *m* help, assistance; **¡socorro!** help!

soda *f* soda (water)

sodio *m* sodium

sofá *m* sofa

sofisticación *f* sophistication

sofisticado *adj* sophisticated

sofocante *adj* suffocating

sofocar ⟨1g⟩ **1** *v/t* suffocate; *incendio* put out **2** *v/r* **sofocarse** *fig* get embarrassed; *(irritarse)* get angry

sofoco *m fig* embarrassment

sofreír ⟨3m⟩ *v/t* sauté

sofrito *m* GASTR mixture of fried onions, peppers etc

software *m* INFOR software

soga *f* rope; **estar con la soga al cuello** be in big trouble F

sois *vb* → **ser**

soja *f* soy, *Br* soya

sol *m* sun; **hace sol** it's sunny; **tomar el sol** sunbathe

solamente *adv* only

solapa *f* lapel

solar *m* vacant lot

solariego *adj*: **casa -a** family seat

solario, solárium *m* solarium

soldado *m/f* soldier

soldador *m* welder

soldadura *f* welding, soldering

soldar ⟨1m⟩ *v/t* weld, solder

soleado *adj* sunny

soledad *f* solitude, loneliness

solemne *adj* solemn

soler ⟨2h⟩ *v/i*: **soler hacer algo** usually do sth; **suele venir temprano** he usually comes early; **solía visitarme** he used to visit me

solera *f* traditional character

solfeo *m* (tonic) sol-fa

solicitante *m/f* applicant

solicitar ⟨1a⟩ *v/t* request; *empleo, beca* apply for

solícito *adj* attentive

solicitud *f* application, request

solidaridad *f* solidarity

solidario *adj* supportive, understanding

solidarizarse ⟨1f⟩ *v/r*: **solidarizarse con alguien** support s.o., back s.o.

solidez *f* solidity; *fig* strength

sólido *adj* solid; *fig* sound

solista *m/f* soloist

solitaria *f* zo tapeworm

solitario 1 *adj* solitary; *lugar* lonely **2** *m* solitaire, *Br* patience; **actuó en solitario** he acted alone

soliviantar ⟨1a⟩ **1** *v/t* incite, stir up **2** *v/r* **soliviantarse** rise up, rebel

sollozar ⟨1f⟩ *v/i* sob

sollozo *m* sob

solo *adj* single; **estar solo** be alone; **sentirse solo** feel lonely; **un solo día** a single day; **a solas** alone, by o.s.; **por sí solo** by o.s.

sólo *adv* only, just

solomillo *m* GASTR sirloin

solsticio *m* solstice

soltar ⟨1m⟩ **1** *v/t* let go of; *(librar)* release, let go; *olor* give off **2** *v/r* **soltarse** free o.s.; **soltarse a andar / hablar** begin o start to walk / talk

soltera *f* single o unmarried woman

soltero 1 *adj* single, not married **2** *m* bachelor, unmarried man

solterona *f desp* old maid

soltura *f* fluency, ease

soluble *adj* soluble

solución *f* solution

solucionar ⟨1a⟩ *v/t* solve

solventar ⟨1a⟩ *v/t* resolve, settle

solvente *adj* solvent

somanta *f* F beating

sombra *f* shadow; **a la sombra de un árbol** in the shade of a tree; **a la sombra de** *fig* under the protection of; **sombra de ojos** eye shadow

sombrero *m* hat; **sombrero de copa** top hat

sombrilla *f* sunshade, beach umbrella

sombrío *adj fig* somber; *Br* sombre

someter ⟨2a⟩ **1** *v/t* subject; **someter algo a votación** put sth to the vote **2** *v/r* **someterse** yield (**a** to); *al ley* comply (**a** with); *(rendirse)* give in (**a** to); **someterse a tratamiento** undergo treatment

somier *m* bed base

somnífero *m* sleeping pill

somnolencia *f* sleepiness, drowsiness

somnoliento *adj* sleepy, drowsy

S

somos *vb* → **ser**

son[1] *m* sound; *al son de* to the sound of; *en son de paz* in peace

son[2] *vb* → **ser**

sonado *adj* F famous, well-known

sonajero *m* rattle

sonámbulo *m* sleep-walker

sonar ⟨1m⟩ **1** *v/i* ring out; *sonar a* sound like; *me suena esa voz* I know that voice, that voice sounds familiar **2** *v/r* **sonarse**: *sonarse* (*la nariz*) blow one's nose

sonata *f* MÚS sonata

sonda *f* MED catheter; *sonda espacial* space probe

sondaje *m* L.Am. poll, survey

sondear ⟨1a⟩ *v/t* fig survey, poll

sondeo *m*: *sondeo* (*de opinión*) survey, (opinion) poll

soneto *m* sonnet

sonido *m* sound

soniquete *m* droning

sonreír ⟨3m⟩ *v/i* smile

sonriente *adj* smiling

sonrisa *f* smile

sonrojar ⟨1a⟩ **1** *v/t*: *sonrojar a alguien* make s.o. blush **2** *v/r* **sonrojarse** blush

sonrojo *m* blush

sonsacar ⟨1g⟩ *v/t*: *sonsacar algo* worm sth out of (*a* of), wheedle sth out (*a* of)

sonso *adj* L.Am. F silly

soñador 1 *adj* dreamy **2** *m* dreamer

soñar ⟨1m⟩ **1** *v/t* dream (*con* about) **2** *v/i* dream; *¡ni soñarlo!* dream on! F

soñolencia *f* → **somnolencia**

soñoliento *adj* → **somnoliento**

sopa *f* soup; *estar hecho una sopa* F be sopping wet; *hasta en la sopa* F all over the place F

sopapo *m* F smack, slap

sopera *f* soup tureen

sopesar ⟨1a⟩ *v/t* fig weigh up

sopetón *m*: *de sopetón* unexpectedly

soplar ⟨1a⟩ **1** *v/i* del viento blow **2** *v/t* vela blow out; *polvo* blow away; *soplar algo a la policía* tip the police off about sth

soplete *m* welding torch

soplo *m*: *en un soplo* F in an instant

soplón *m* F informer, stool pigeon F

soponcio *m*: *le dio un soponcio* F he passed out

sopor *m* drowsiness, sleepiness

soporífero *adj* soporific

soportal *m* porch

soportar ⟨1a⟩ *v/t* fig put up with, bear; *no puedo soportar a José* I can't stand José

soporte *m* support, stand; *soporte lógico* INFOR software; *soporte físico* INFOR hardware

soprano MÚS **1** *m* soprano **2** *m/f* soprano

sorber ⟨2a⟩ *v/t* sip

sorbete *m* sorbet; C.Am. ice cream

sorbetería *f* C.Am. ice-cream parlo(u)r

sorbo *m* sip

sordera *f* deafness

sórdido *adj* sordid

sordo 1 *adj* deaf **2** *m*, *-a f* deaf person; *hacerse el sordo* turn a deaf ear

sordomudo 1 *adj* deaf and dumb **2** *m*, *-a f* deaf-mute

sorna *f* sarcasm; *con sorna* sarcastically, mockingly

sorocharse ⟨1a⟩ *v/r* Pe, Bol get altitude sickness

soroche *m* Pe, Bol altitude sickness

sorprendente *adj* surprising

sorprender ⟨2a⟩ *v/t* surprise

sorpresa *f* surprise; *de* or *por sorpresa* by surprise

sortear ⟨1a⟩ *v/t* draw lots for; *obstáculo* get round

sorteo *m* (*lotería*) lottery, (prize) draw

sortija *f* ring

sortilegio *m* spell, charm

SOS *m* SOS

sosa *f* QUÍM: *sosa cáustica* caustic soda

sosegado *adj* calm

sosegarse ⟨1h & 1k⟩ *v/r* calm down

sosería *f* insipidity, dullness

sosiego *m* calm, quiet

soslayo *adj*: *de soslayo* sideways

soso 1 *adj* tasteless, insipid; *fig* dull **2** *m*, *-a f* stick-in-the-mud F

sospecha *f* suspicion

sospechar ⟨1a⟩ **1** *v/t* suspect **2** *v/i* be suspicious; *sospechar de alguien* suspect someone

sospechoso 1 *adj* suspicious **2** *m*, *-a f* suspect

sostén *m* brassiere, bra; fig pillar, mainstay

sostener ⟨2l⟩ **1** *v/t* familia support; *opinión* hold **2** *v/r* **sostenerse** support o.s.; *de pie* stand up; *en el poder* stay, remain

sota *f* naipes jack

sotana *f* REL cassock

sótano *m* basement, Br cellar

soterrar ⟨1k⟩ *v/t* bury

soviético *adj* Soviet

soy *vb* → **ser**

soya *f* L.Am. soy, Br soya

spot *m* TV commercial

spray *m* spray

sprint *m* sprint

squash *m* DEP squash

Sr. *abr* (= *señor*) Mr

S

Sra. *abr* (= **señora**) Mrs
Sres. *abr* (= **Señores**) Messrs (= Messieurs)
Srta. *abr* (= **Señorita**) Miss
stand *m* COM stand
stock *m* COM stock; **tener en stock** have in stock
su, sus *adj pos*: *de él* his; *de ella* her; *de cosa* its; *de usted, ustedes* your; *de ellos* their; *de uno* one's
suave *adj* soft, smooth; *sabor, licor* mild
suavidad *f* softness, smoothness; *de sabor, licor* mildness
suavizante *m de pelo, ropa* conditioner
suavizar ⟨1f⟩ *v/t tb fig* soften
subacuático *adj* underwater
subalterno 1 *adj* subordinate **2** *m*, **-a** *f* subordinate
subasta *f* auction; **sacar a subasta** put up for auction
subastar ⟨1a⟩ *v/t* auction (off)
subcampeón *m* DEP runner-up
subconsciente *m/adj* subconscious
subcontrata(ción) *f* subcontracting
subdesarrollado *adj* underdeveloped
subdesarrollo *m* underdevelopment
subdirector *m*, **subdirectora** *f* deputy manager
súbdito *m* subject
subestimar ⟨1a⟩ *v/t* underestimate
subida *f* rise, ascent; **subida de los precios** rise in prices
subido 1 *part* → **subir 2** *adj*: **subido de tono** *fig* risqué, racy
subir ⟨3a⟩ **1** *v/t cuesta, escalera* go up, climb; *montaña* climb; *objeto* raise, lift; *intereses, precio* raise **2** *v/i para indicar acercamiento* come up; *para indicar alejamiento* go up; *de precio* rise, go up; *a un tren, autobús* get on; *a un coche* get in **3** *v/r* **subirse** go up; *a un árbol* climb
súbito *adj*: **de súbito** suddenly, all of a sudden
subjetivo *adj* subjective
subjuntivo *m* GRAM subjunctive
sublevar ⟨1a⟩ **1** *v/t* incite to revolt; *fig* infuriate, get angry **2** *v/r* **sublevarse** rise up, revolt
sublimación *f fig* sublimation
sublime *adj* sublime, lofty
subliminal *adj* subliminal
submarinismo *m* scuba diving
submarinista *m/f* scuba diver
submarino 1 *adj* underwater **2** *m* submarine
subnormal *adj* subnormal
subordinado 1 *adj* subordinate **2** *m*, **-a** *f* subordinate
subproducto *m* by-product

subrayar ⟨1a⟩ *v/t* underline; *fig* underline, emphasize
subrepticio *adj* surreptitious
subsanar ⟨1a⟩ *v/t* put right, rectify
subsidiario *adj* subsidiary
subsidio *m* welfare, *Br* benefit; **subsidio de paro** *or* **desempleo** unemployment compensation (*Br* benefit)
subsistencia *f* subsistence, survival; *de pobreza, tradición* persistence
subsistir ⟨3a⟩ *v/i* live, survive; *de pobreza, tradición* live on, persist
subte *m Rpl* subway, *Br* underground
subterfugio *m* subterfuge
subterráneo 1 *adj* underground **2** *m L.Am.* subway, *Br* underground
subtítulo *m* subtitle
suburbio *m* slum area
subvención *f* subsidy
subvencionar ⟨1a⟩ *v/t* subsidize
subversivo *adj* subversive
subyacente *adj* underlying
subyugar ⟨1h⟩ *v/t* subjugate
succionar ⟨1a⟩ *v/t* suck
sucedáneo *m* substitute
suceder ⟨2a⟩ *v/i* happen, occur; **suceder a** follow; **¿qué sucede?** what's going on?
sucesión *f* succession; **sucesión al trono** succession to the throne
sucesivo *adj* successive; **en lo sucesivo** from now on
suceso *m* event
sucesor *m*, **sucesora** *f* successor
suciedad *f* dirt
sucio *adj tb fig* dirty
suculento *adj* succulent
sucumbir ⟨3a⟩ *v/i* succumb, give in
sucursal *f* COM branch
sudaca *m/f desp* South American
sudadera *f* sweatshirt
Sudáfrica South Africa
sudafricano 1 *adj* South African **2** *m*, **-a** *f* South African
Sudamérica South America
sudamericano 1 *adj* South American **2** *m*, **-a** *f* South American
sudar ⟨1a⟩ *v/i* sweat
sudario *m* REL shroud
sudeste *m* southeast
sudoeste *m* southwest
sudor *m* sweat
sudoración *f* perspiration
sudoroso *adj* sweaty
Suecia Sweden
sueco 1 *adj* Swedish **2** *m*, **-a** *f* Swede; **hacerse el sueco** F pretend not to hear, act dumb F
suegra *f* mother-in-law

S

suegro *m* father-in-law

suela *f de zapato* sole

sueldo *m* salary

suelo *m en casa* floor; *en el exterior* earth, ground; AGR soil; *estar por los suelos* F be at rock bottom F

suelto 1 *adj* loose, free; *un pendiente suelto* a single earring; *andar suelto* be at large **2** *m* loose change

sueño *m (estado de dormir)* sleep; *(fantasía, imagen mental)* dream; *tener sueño* be sleepy

suero *m* MED saline solution; *sanguíneo* blood serum

suerte *f* luck; *por suerte* luckily; *echar a suertes* toss for, draw lots for; *probar suerte* try one's luck

suertero *m*, **-a** *f L.Am.* F, **suertudo** *m*, **-a** *f L.Am.* F lucky devil F

suéter *m* sweater

suficiente 1 *adj* enough, sufficient **2** *m* EDU pass

sufragar ⟨1h⟩ *v/t* COM meet, pay

sufragio *m*: *sufragio universal* universal suffrage

sufrimiento *m* suffering

sufrir ⟨3a⟩ **1** *v/t fig* suffer, put up with **2** *v/i* suffer (*de* from)

sugerencia *f* suggestion

sugerir ⟨3i⟩ *v/t* suggest

sugestionar ⟨1a⟩ *v/t* influence

sugestivo *adj* suggestive

suicida 1 *adj* suicidal **2** *m/f* suicide victim

suicidarse ⟨1a⟩ *v/r* commit suicide

suicidio *m* suicide

suite *f* suite

Suiza Switzerland

suizo 1 *adj* Swiss **2** *m*, **-a** *f* Swiss **3** *m* GASTR *sugar topped bun*

sujetador *m* brassiere, bra

sujetapapeles *m inv* paperclip

sujetar ⟨1a⟩ *v/t* hold (down), keep in place; *(sostener)* hold

sujeto 1 *adj* secure **2** *m* individual; GRAM subject

sulfurarse ⟨1a⟩ *v/r fig* F blow one's top F

suma *f* sum; *en suma* in short

sumamente *adv* extremely, highly

sumar ⟨1a⟩ **1** *v/t* add; *5 y 6 suman 11* 5 and 6 make 11 **2** *v/i* add up **3** *v/r* sumarse: *sumarse a* join

sumario *m* summary; JUR indictment

sumergir ⟨3c⟩ **1** *v/t* submerge, immerse **2** *v/r* sumergirse *fig* immerse o.s. (*en* in), throw o.s. (*en* into)

sumidero *m* drain

suministrar ⟨1a⟩ *v/t* supply, provide

suministro *m* supply

sumir ⟨3a⟩ **1** *v/t fig* plunge, throw (*en* in-

to) **2** *v/r* sumirse *fig* sink (*en* into)

sumisión *f* submission

sumiso *adj* submissive

sumo *adj* supreme; *con sumo cuidado* with the utmost care; *a lo sumo* at the most

suntuoso *adj* sumptuous

supe *vb* → *saber*

supeditar ⟨1a⟩ *v/t* make conditional (*a* upon)

súper *adj* F super F, great F

superable *adj* surmountable

superación *f* overcoming, surmounting

superar ⟨1a⟩ **1** *v/t persona* beat; *límite* go beyond, exceed; *obstáculo* overcome, surmount **2** *v/r* superarse surpass o.s., excel o.s.

superávit *m* surplus

superchería *f* trick, swindle

superdotado *adj* gifted

superficial *adj* superficial, shallow

superficialidad *f* superficiality, shallowness

superficie *f* surface

superfluo *adj* superfluous

superior 1 *adj* upper; *en jerarquía* superior; *ser superior a* be superior to **2** *m* superior

superiora *f* REL Mother Superior

superioridad *f* superiority

superlativo *adj* superlative

supermercado *m* supermarket

superpoblación *f* overpopulation

superponer ⟨2r⟩ *v/t* superimpose

superpotencia *f* POL superpower

superpuesto *adj* superimposed

supersónico *adj* supersonic

superstición *f* superstition

supersticioso *adj* superstitious

supervisar ⟨1a⟩ *v/t* supervise

supervisor *m*, **supervisora** *f* supervisor

supervivencia *f* survival

superviviente 1 *adj* surviving **2** *m/f* survivor

suplantar ⟨1a⟩ *v/t* replace, take the place of

suplementario *adj* supplementary

suplemento *m* supplement

suplente *m/f* substitute, stand-in

súplica *f* plea

suplicar ⟨1g⟩ *v/t cosa* plead for, beg for; *persona* beg

suplicio *m fig* torment, ordeal

suplir ⟨3a⟩ *v/t carencia* make up for; *(sustituir)* substitute

supo *vb* → *saber*

suponer ⟨2r; *part* supuesto⟩ *v/t* suppose, assume

suposición *f* supposition

supositorio *m* MED suppository
supremacía *f* supremacy
supremo *adj* supreme
supresión *f* suppression; *de impuesto, ley* abolition; *de restricción* lifting; *de servicio* withdrawal
suprimir ⟨3a⟩ *v/t* suppress; *ley, impuesto* abolish; *restricción* lift; *servicio* withdraw; *puesto de trabajo* cut
supuesto 1 *part* → **suponer 2** *adj* supposed, alleged; **por supuesto** of course **3** *m* assumption
sur *m* south
surco *m* AGR furrow
sureño *adj* southern
surf(ing) *m* surfing
surfista *m/f* surfer
surgir ⟨3c⟩ *v/i fig* emerge; *de problema* come up; *de agua* spout
surrealismo *m* surrealism
surtido 1 *adj* assorted; **bien surtido** COM well stocked **2** *m* assortment, range
surtidor *m*: **surtidor de gasolina or de nafta** gas pump, *Br* petrol pump
surtir ⟨3a⟩ **1** *v/t* supply; **surtir efecto** have the desired effect **2** *v/i* spout **3** *v/r* **surtirse** stock up (**de** with)
susceptible *adj* touchy; **ser susceptible de mejora** leave room for improvement
suscitar ⟨1a⟩ *v/t* arouse; *polémica* generate; *escándalo* provoke
suscribir ⟨3a; *part* **suscrito** ⟩ **1** *v/t* subscribe to **2** *v/r* **suscribirse** subscribe
suscripción *f* subscription
suscriptor *m*, **suscriptora** *f* subscriber
suscrito *part* → **suscribir**
suspender ⟨2a⟩ **1** *v/t* empleado, *alumno* suspend; *objeto* hang; *reunión* adjourn;

examen fail **2** *v/i* EDU fail
suspense *m fig* suspense
suspensión *f* suspension
suspenso 1 *adj* **alumnos suspensos** students who have failed; **en suspenso** suspended **2** *m* fail
suspensores *mpl L.Am.* suspenders, *Br* braces
suspicacia *f* suspicion
suspicaz *adj* suspicious
suspirar ⟨1a⟩ *v/i* sigh; **suspirar por algo** yearn for sth, long for sth
suspiro *m* sigh
sustancia *f* substance
sustancial *adj* substantial
sustantivo *m* GRAM noun
sustentar ⟨1a⟩ *v/t* sustain; *familia* support; *opinión* maintain
sustento *m* means of support
sustitución *f* substitution
sustituir ⟨3g⟩ *v/t*: **sustituir X por Y** replace X with Y, substitute Y for X
sustituto *m* substitute
susto *m* fright, scare; **dar** *or* **pegar un susto a alguien** give s.o. a fright
sustraer ⟨2p; *part* **sustraído** ⟩ *v/t* subtract, take away; (*robar*) steal
sustraído *part* → **sustraer**
susurrar ⟨1a⟩ *v/t* whisper
susurro *m* whisper
sutil *adj fig* subtle
sutileza *f fig* subtlety
suyo, suya *pron pos*: *de él* his; *de ella* hers; *de usted, ustedes* yours; *de ellos* theirs; **los suyos** his / her etc folks, his / her etc family; **hacer de las -as** get up to one's old tricks; **salirse con la -a** get one's own way

T

tabaco *m* tobacco
tábano *m* ZO horsefly
tabarra *f*: **dar la tabarra a alguien** F bug s.o. F
taberna *f* bar
tabernero *m* bar owner, *Br* landlord; (*camarero*) bartender
tabique *m* partition, partition wall
tabla *f de madera* board, plank; PINT panel; (*cuadro*) table; **tabla de multiplicar** multiplication table; **tabla de planchar**

ironing board; **tabla de surf** surf board; **acabar** *or* **quedar en tablas** end in a tie
tablero *m* board, plank; *de juego* board; **tablero de mandos** *or* **de instrumentos** AUTO dashboard
tableta *f*: **tableta de chocolate** chocolate bar
tablón *m* plank; **tablón de anuncios** bulletin board, *Br* notice board
tabú *m* taboo
tabulador *m* *tb* INFOR tab key

taburete *m* stool

tacañería *f* F miserliness, stinginess F

tacaño 1 *adj* F miserly, stingy F **2** *m*, **-a** *f* F miser F, tightwad F

tacha *f* flaw, blemish; *sin tacha* beyond reproach

tachadura *f* crossing-out

tachar ⟨1a⟩ *v/t* cross out

tacho *m* *Rpl* (*papelera*) wastepaper basket; *en la calle* garbage can, *Br* litter basket

tachón *m* crossing-out

tachuela *f* thumbtack, *Br* drawing pin

tácito *adj* tacit

taciturno *adj* taciturn

taco *m* F (*palabrota*) swear word; *L.Am.* heel; GASTR taco (*filled tortilla*)

tacón *m* de zapato heel; *zapatos de tacón* high-heeled shoes

táctica *f* tactics *pl*

táctico *adj* tactical

tacto *m* (sense of) touch; *fig* tact, discretion

TAE *abr* (= *tasa anual efectiva*) APR (= annual percentage rate)

tahona *f* bakery

tahúr *m* gambler, card-sharp F

taita *m* *S. Am.* F dad, pop F; *S. Am.* (*abuelo*) grandfather

tajada *f* GASTR slice; *agarrar una tajada* F get drunk; *sacar tajada* take a cut F

tajamar *m* *S. Am.* (*dique*) dike

tajante *adj* categorical

tajo *m* cut

tal 1 *adj* such; *no dije tal cosa* I said no such thing; *el gerente era un tal Lucas* the manager was someone called Lucas **2** *adv*: *tal como* such as; *dejó la habitación tal cual la encontró* she left the room just as she found it; *tal para cual* two of a kind; *tal vez* maybe, perhaps; *¿qué tal?* how's it going?; *¿que tal la película?* what was the movie like?; *con tal de que* + *subj* as long as, provided that

tala *f* de árboles felling

taladrar ⟨1a⟩ *v/t* drill

taladro *m* drill

talante *m* (*genio, humor*) mood; *un talante bonachón* a kindly nature; *de mal talante* in a bad mood

talar ⟨1a⟩ *v/t* árbol fell, cut down

talco *m* talc, talcum; *polvos de talco* talcum powder

talego *m* P 1000 pesetas

talento *m* talent

talismán *m* talisman

talla *f* size; (*estatura*) height; *C.Am.* F (*mentira*) lie; *dar la talla* *fig* make the grade

tallar ⟨1a⟩ *v/t* carve; *piedra preciosa* cut

tallarín *m* noodle

taller *m* workshop; *taller mecánico* AUTO repair shop; *taller de reparaciones* repair shop

tallo *m* BOT stalk, stem

talón *m* ANAT heel; COM stub; *talón de Aquiles* *fig* Achilles' heel; *pisar los talones a alguien* be hot on s.o.'s heels

talonario *m*: *talonario de cheques* check book, *Br* cheque book

tamal *m* *Méx, C.Am.* tamale (*meat wrapped in a leaf and steamed*)

tamaño 1 *adj*: *tamaño fallo / problema* such a great mistake / problem **2** *m* size

tambalearse ⟨1a⟩ *v/r* stagger, lurch; *de coche* sway

tambarria *f* *C.Am., Pe, Bol* F party

también *adv* also, too, as well; *yo también* me too; *él también dice que ...* he also says that ...

tambo *m* *Rpl* dairy farm; *Méx type of large container*

tambor *m* drum; *persona* drummer

tamborilear ⟨1a⟩ *v/i* drum with one's fingers

tamiz *m* sieve

tampoco *adv* neither; *él tampoco va* he's not going either

tampón *m* tampon; *de tinta* ink-pad

tan *adv* so; *tan ... como ...* as ... as ...; *tan sólo* merely

tanatorio *m* funeral parlo(u)r

tanda *f* series, batch; (*turno*) shift; *L.Am.* (commercial) break; *tanda de penaltis* DEP penalty shootout

tanga *m* tanga

tangente *f* MAT tangent; *salir or irse por la tangente* F sidestep the issue, duck the question F

tangible *adj* *fig* tangible

tango *m* tango

tanque *m* *tb* MIL tank

tantear ⟨1a⟩ *v/t* feel; (*calcular a ojo*) work out roughly; *situación* size up; *persona* sound out; (*probar*) try out; *tantear el terreno* *fig* see how the land lies

tantito *adv* *Méx* a little

tanto 1 *pron* so much; *igual cantidad* as much; *un tanto* a little; *tantos pl* so many *pl*; *igual número* as many; *tienes tanto* you have so much; *no hay tantos como ayer* there aren't as many as yesterday; *a las -as de la noche* in the small hours **2** *adv* so much; *igual cantidad* as much; *periodo* so long; *tardó tanto como él* she took as long as him; *tanto mejor* so much the better; *no es para tanto* it's not such a big deal; **estar al tanto** be informed (**de** about); **por lo tanto** therefore, so **3** *m* point; **tanto por ciento** percentage

tapa *f* lid; **tapa dura** hardback

tapacubos *m inv* AUTO hub cap

tapadera *f* lid; *fig* front

tapadillo *m*: **de tapadillo** on the sly

tapado *m* Arg, Chi coat

tapar ⟨1a⟩ **1** *v/t* cover; *recipiente* put the lid on **2** *v/r* **taparse** wrap up; **taparse los ojos** cover one's eyes

taparrabo *m* loincloth

tapete *m* tablecloth; **poner algo sobre el tapete** bring sth up for discussion

tapia *f* wall; **más sordo que una tapia** as deaf as a post

tapicería *f* upholstery

tapicero *m*, -a *f* upholsterer

tapioca *f* tapioca

tapir *m* tapir

tapiz *m* tapestry

tapizar ⟨1f⟩ *v/t* upholster

tapón *m* top, cap; *de baño* plug; *de tráfico* traffic jam

taponar ⟨1a⟩ *v/t* block; *herida* swab

tapujo *m*: **sin tapujos** openly

taquicardia *f* MED tachycardia

taquigrafía *f* shorthand

taquilla *f* ticket office; TEA box-office; *C.Am.* (*bar*) small bar

taquillero **1** *adj cantante* popular; **una película -a** a hit movie, a box-office hit **2** *m*, -a *f* ticket clerk

tara *f* defect

tarado *adj* F stupid, dumb F

tarántula *f* ZO tarantula

tararear ⟨1a⟩ *v/t* hum

tardar ⟨1a⟩ *v/i* take a long time; **tardamos dos horas** we were two hours overdue *o* late; **¡no tardes!** don't be late; **a más tardar** at the latest; **¿cuánto se tarda ...?** how long does it take to ...?

tarde **1** *adv* late; **tarde o temprano** sooner or later **2** *f hasta las 5 ó 6* afternoon; *desde las 5 ó 6* evening; **¡buenas tardes!** good afternoon / evening; **por la tarde** in the afternoon / evening; **de tarde en tarde** from time to time

tardón *adj* F slow; (*impuntual*) late

tarea *f* task, job; **tareas** *pl* **domésticas** housework *sg*

tarifa *f* rate; *de tren* fare; **tarifa plana** flat rate

tarima *f* platform; **suelo de tarima** wooden floor

tarjeta *f* card; **tarjeta amarilla** DEP yellow card; **tarjeta de crédito** credit card; **tarjeta de embarque** AVIA boarding card;

tarjeta de sonido INFOR sound card; **tarjeta de visita** (business) card; **tarjeta gráfica** INFOR graphics card; **tarjeta inteligente** smart card; **tarjeta monedero** electronic purse; **tarjeta postal** postcard; **tarjeta roja** DEP red card; **tarjeta telefónica** phone card

tarro *m* jar; P (*cabeza*) head

tarta *f* cake; *plana* tart; **tarta helada** ice--cream cake

tartamudear ⟨1a⟩ *v/i* stutter, stammer

tartamudez *f* stuttering, stammering

tartamudo **1** *adj* stuttering, stammering; **ser tartamudo** stutter, stammer **2** *m*, -a *f* stutterer, stammerer

tartera *f* lunch box

tarugo *m* F blockhead

tarumba F crazy F; **volverse tarumba** go crazy

tasa *f* rate; (*impuesto*) tax; **tasa de desempleo** *or* **paro** unemployment rate

tasar ⟨1a⟩ *v/t* fix a price for; (*valorar*) assess

tasca *f* F bar

tata *m L.Am.* F (*abuelo*) grandpa F

tatarabuela *f* great-great-grandmother

tatarabuelo *m* great-great-grandfather

tataranieta *f* great-great-granddaughter

tataranieto *m* great-great-grandson

tate *int* F (*ahora caigo*) oh I see; (*cuidado*) look out!

tatuaje *m* tattoo

taurino *adj* bullfighting *atr*

Tauro *m/f inv* ASTR Taurus

tauromaquia *f* bullfighting

taxi *m* cab, taxi

taxista *m/f* cab *o* taxi driver

taza *f* cup; *del wáter* bowl

tazón *m* bowl

te *pron directo* you; *indirecto* (to) you; *reflexivo* yourself

té *m* tea

teatral *adj fig* theatrical

teatro *m tb fig* theater, *Br* theatre

tebeo *m* children's comic

techar ⟨1a⟩ *v/t* roof

techo *m* ceiling; (*tejado*) roof; **techo solar** AUTO sun-roof; **los sin techo** the homeless; **tocar techo** *fig* peak

tecla *f* key

teclado *m* MÚS, INFOR keyboard

teclear ⟨1a⟩ *v/t* key

técnica *f* technique

técnico **1** *adj* technical **2** *m/f* technician; *de televisor, lavadora etc* repairman

tecnología *f* technology; **alta tecnología** hi-tech; **tecnología punta** state-of-the--art technology, leading-edge technology

tecolote *m Méx, C.Am.* (*búho*) owl

T

tedio *m* tedium
tedioso *adj* tedious
teja *f* roof tile; **a toca teja** in hard cash
tejado *m* roof
tejanos *mpl* jeans
tejemanejes *mpl* F scheming *sg*, plotting *sg*
tejer ⟨2a⟩ **1** *v/t* weave; *(hacer punto)* knit; F *intriga* devise **2** *v/i* L.Am. F plot, scheme
tejido *m* fabric; ANAT tissue
tejo *m* BOT yew; **tirar a alguien los tejos** F hit on s.o., come on to s.o. F
tejón *m* ZO badger
Tel. *abr* (= **teléfono**) Tel. (= telephone)
tela *f* fabric, material; **tela de araña** spiderweb; **poner en tela de juicio** call into question; **hay tela para rato** F there's a lot to be done
telar *m* loom
telaraña *f* spiderweb
tele *f* F TV, *Br* telly F
telearrastre *m* drag lift
telebanca *f* telephone banking
telecabina *f* cable car
telecomedia *f* sitcom
telecompra *f* home shopping
telecomunicaciones *fpl* telecommunications
telediario *m* TV (television) news *sg*
teledirigido *adj* remote-controlled
teléf. *abr* (= **teléfono**) tel. (= telephone)
teleférico *m* cable car
telefilm(e) *m* TV movie
telefonear ⟨1a⟩ *v/t & v/i* call, phone
telefonema *m* L.Am. (phone) message
telefónico *adj* (tele)phone *atr*
teléfono *m* (tele)phone; **teléfono inalámbrico** cordless (phone); **teléfono móvil** cellphone, *Br* mobile (phone)
telégrafo *m* telegraph
telegrama *m* telegram
telemando *m* remote control
telemática *f* data comms
telenovela *f* soap (opera)
teleobjetivo *m* FOT telephoto lens
telepatía *f* telepathy
telescópico *adj* telescopic
telescopio *m* telescope
teleserie *f* (television) series
telesilla *f* chair lift
telespectador *m*, **telespectadora** *f* (television) viewer
telesquí *m* drag lift
teletexto *m* teletext
teletienda *f* home shopping
teletrabajo *m* teleworking
teletrabajador *m*, **teletrabajadora** *f* teleworker

televidente *m/f* (television) viewer
televisar ⟨1a⟩ *v/t* televise
televisión *f* television; **televisión por cable** cable (television); **televisión digital** digital television; **televisión de pago** pay-per-view television; **televisión vía satélite** satellite television
televisivo *adj* television *atr*
televisor *m* TV, television (set); **televisor en color** color TV
télex *m* telex
telón *m* TEA curtain; **el telón de acero** POL the Iron Curtain; **telón de fondo** *fig* backdrop, background
telonero *m*, **-a** *f* supporting artist
tema *m* subject, topic; MÚS, *de novela* theme
temario *m* syllabus
temático *adj* thematic
temblar ⟨1k⟩ *v/i* tremble, shake; *de frío* shiver
temblor *m* trembling, shaking; *de frío* shivering; L.Am. *(terremoto)* earthquake; **temblor de tierra** earth tremor
tembloroso *adj* trembling, shaking; *de frío* shivering
temer ⟨2a⟩ **1** *v/t* be afraid of **2** *v/r* **temerse** be afraid; **me temo que no podrá venir** I'm afraid he won't be able to come; **temerse lo peor** fear the worst
temerario *adj* rash, reckless
temeridad *f* rashness, recklessness
temible *adj* terrifying
temor *m* fear
témpano *m* ice floe
temperamento *m* temperament
temperante *adj Méx* teetotal
temperatura *f* temperature
tempestad *f* storm
tempestuoso *adj tb fig* stormy
templado *adj* warm; *clima* temperate; *fig* moderate, restrained
templanza *f* restraint
templar ⟨1a⟩ *v/t ira, nervios etc* calm
templo *m* temple
temporada *f* season; **una temporada** a time, some time
temporal 1 *adj* temporary **2** *m* storm
temporizador *m* timer
tempranear ⟨1a⟩ *v/i* L.Am. get up early
temprano *adj & adv* early
ten *vb* → **tener**
tenacidad *f* tenacity
tenaz *adj* determined, tenacious
tenaza *f* pincer, claw; **tenazas** pincers; *para las uñas* pliers
tendedero *m* clotheshorse, airer
tendencia *f* tendency; *(corriente)* trend
tendencioso *adj* tendentious

tender ⟨2g⟩ **1** v/t *ropa* hang out; *cable* lay; *le tendió la mano* he held out his hand to her **2** v/i: *tender a* tend to **3** v/r *tenderse* lie down

tenderete *m* stall

tendero *m*, -a *f* storekeeper, shopkeeper

tendido *m* EL: *tendido eléctrico* power lines *pl*

tendón *m* ANAT tendon; *tendón de Aquiles* Achilles' tendon

tenebroso *adj* dark, gloomy

tenedor *m* fork

tener ⟨2l⟩ **1** v/t have; *tener 10 años* be 10 (years old); *tener un metro de ancho / largo* be one metre (*Br* meter) wide / long; *tener que madrugar* I must get up early, I have to o I've got to get up early; *tengo ¿esas tenemos?* so that's how it is, eh? **2** v/r *tenerse* stand up; *fig* stand firm; *se tiene por atractivo* he thinks he's attractive

lenga *vb* → **tener**

tengo *vb* → **tener**

tenia *f* ZO tapeworm

teniente *m/f* MIL lieutenant

tenis *m* tennis; *tenis de mesa* table tennis

tenista *m/f* tennis player

tenor *m* MÚS tenor; *a tenor de* along the lines of

tenorio *m* lady-killer

tensar ⟨1a⟩ v/t tighten; *músculo* tense, tighten

tensión *f* tension; EL voltage; MED blood pressure

tenso *adj* tense; *cuerda, cable* taut

tentación *f* temptation

tentáculo *m* ZO, *fig* tentacle

tentador *adj* tempting

tentar ⟨1k⟩ v/t tempt, entice

tentativa *f* attempt

tentempié *m* F snack

tenue *adj* faint

teñir ⟨3h & 3l⟩ v/t dye; *fig* tinge

teología *f* theology

teorema *m* theorem

teoría *f* theory; *en teoría* in theory

tequila *m* tequila

terapeuta *m/f* therapist

terapéutico *adj* therapeutic

terapia *f* therapy

tercer *adj* third; *Tercer Mundo* Third World

tercermundista *adj* Third-World *atr*

tercero *m/adj* third

terciarse ⟨1b⟩ v/r *de oportunidad* come up

tercio *m* third

terciopelo *m* velvet

terco *adj* stubborn

tergiversar ⟨1a⟩ v/t distort, twist

termas *fpl* hot springs

térmico *adj* heat *atr*

terminación *f* GRAM ending

terminal **1** *m* INFOR terminal **2** *f* AVIA terminal; *terminal de autobuses* bus station

terminante *adj* categorical

terminar ⟨1a⟩ **1** v/t end, finish **2** v/i end, finish; (*parar*) stop **3** v/r *terminarse* run out; (*finalizar*) come to an end; *se ha terminado la leche* we've run out of milk, the milk's all gone

término *m* end, conclusion; (*palabra*) term; *término municipal* municipal area; *por término medio* on average; *poner término a algo* put an end to sth

terminología *f* terminology

termita *f* ZO termite

termo *m* thermos® (flask)

termómetro *m* thermometer

termostato *m* thermostat

ternera *f* calf; GASTR veal

ternero *m* calf

terno *m* CSur suit

ternura *f* tenderness

terracota *f* terracotta

terraplén *m* embankment

terrateniente *m/f* landowner

terraza *f* terrace; (*balcón*) balcony; (*café*) sidewalk café

terremoto *m* earthquake

terrenal *adj* earthly, worldly

terreno *m* land; *fig* field; *un terreno* a plot o piece of land; *terreno de juego* DEP field

terrestre *adj animal* land *atr; transporte* surface *atr; la atmósfera terrestre* the earth's atmosphere

terrible *adj* terrible, awful

territorial *adj* territorial

territorio *m* territory

terrón *m* lump, clod; *terrón de azúcar* sugar lump

terror *m* terror

terrorífico *adj* terrifying

terrorismo *m* terrorism

terrorista **1** *adj* terrorist *atr* **2** *m/f* terrorist

terso *adj* smooth

tertulia *f* TV debate, round table discussion

tertuliar ⟨1b⟩ v/i *L.Am.* get together for a discussion

tesina *f* dissertation

tesis *f inv* thesis

tesitura *f* situation

tesón *m* tenacity, determination

tesorero *m*, -a *f* treasurer

T

tesoro *m* treasure; *tesoro público* treasury

test *m* test

testa *f* head

testaferro *m* front man

testamento *m* JUR will

testarudez *f* stubbornness

testarudo *adj* stubborn

testículo *m* ANAT testicle

testificar ⟨1g⟩ **1** *v/t* (*probar, mostrar*) be proof of; *testificar que* JUR testify that, give evidence that **2** *v/i* testify, give evidence

testigo 1 *m/f* JUR witness; *testigo de cargo* witness for the prosecution; *testigo ocular* or *presencial* eye witness **2** *m* DEP baton

testimonio *m* testimony, evidence

teta *f* F boob F; ZO teat, nipple

tétanos *m* MED tetanus

tetera *f* teapot

tetilla *f de hombre* nipple

tetina *f de biberón* teat

tetrabrik® *m* carton

tétrico *adj* gloomy

textil 1 *adj* textile *atr* **2** *mpl*: *textiles* textiles

texto *m* text

textual *adj* textual

textura *f* texture

tez *f* complexion

ti *pron* you; *reflexivo* yourself; *¿y a ti qué te importa?* so what?, what's it to you?

tía *f* aunt; F (*chica*) girl, chick F; *¡tía buena!* F hey gorgeous! F

tianguis *m* Méx, C.Am. market

tibio *adj* tb fig lukewarm

tiburón *m* ZO, fig F shark

tic *m* MED tic

ticket *m* (*sales*) receipt

tictac *m* tick-tock

tiempo *m* time; (*clima*) weather; GRAM tense; *tiempo libre* spare time, free time; *tiempo real* INFOR real time; *a tiempo* in time; *a un tiempo, al mismo tiempo* at the same time; *antes de tiempo llegar* ahead of time, early; *celebrar victoria* too soon; *con tiempo* in good time, early; *desde hace mucho tiempo* for a long time; *hace buen / mal tiempo* the weather's fine / bad; *hace mucho tiempo* a long time ago

tienda *f* store, shop; *tienda de campaña* tent; *ir de tiendas* go shopping

tiene *vb* → **tener**

tientas *fpl*: *andar a tientas* fig feel one's way

tiento *m*: *con tiento* fig carefully

tierno *adj* soft; *carne* tender; *pan* fresh; *persona* tender-hearted

tierra *f* land; *materia* soil, earth; (*patria*) native land, homeland; *la Tierra* the earth; *tierra firme* dry land, terra firma; *echar por tierra* ruin, wreck

tieso *adj* stiff, rigid

tiesto *m* flower pot

tifón *m* typhoon

tifus *m* MED typhus

tigre *m* ZO tiger; *L.Am.* puma; *L.Am.* (*leopardo*) jaguar

tigresa *f* tigress

tijeras *fpl* scissors

tila *f* lime blossom tea

tildar ⟨1a⟩ *v/t*: *tildar a alguien de* fig brand s.o. as

tilde *f* accent; *en ñ* tilde

tilín *m*: *me hizo tilín* F I took an immediate liking to her

timador *m*, **timadora** *f* cheat

timar ⟨1a⟩ *v/t* cheat

timba *f* F gambling den

timbal *m* MÚS kettle drum

timbre *m de puerta* bell; *Méx* (postage) stamp

timidez *f* shyness, timidity

tímido *adj* shy, timid

timo *m* confidence trick, swindle

timón *m* MAR, AVIA rudder

tímpano *m* ANAT eardrum

tina *f* large jar; *L.Am.* (*bañera*) (bath)tub

tinglado *m* fig F mess

tinieblas *fpl* darkness *sg*

tino *m* aim, marksmanship; (*sensatez*) judg(e)ment; *con mucho tino* wisely, sensibly

tinta *f* ink; *de buena tinta* fig on good authority; *medias tintas* fig half measures

tinte *m* dye; fig veneer, gloss

tinterillo *m L.Am.* F shyster F

tintero *m* inkwell; *dejarse algo en el tintero* leave sth unsaid

tintin(e)ar ⟨1a⟩ *v/t* jingle

tinto *adj*: *vino tinto* red wine

tintorería *f* dry cleaner's

tío *m* uncle; F (*tipo*) guy F; F *apelativo* pal F

tiovivo *m* carousel, merry-go-round

típico *adj* typical (*de* of)

tipo *m* type, kind; F *persona* guy F; COM rate; *tipo de cambio* exchange rate; *tipo de interés* interest rate; *tener buen tipo* be well built; *de mujer* have a good figure

tipográfico *adj* typographic(al)

tíquet, tiquete *m L.Am.* receipt

tiquismiquis *m/f* F fuss-budget F, Br fusspot F

tira *f* strip; *la tira de* F loads of F, masses of F; *tira y afloja* fig give and take

tonelada

tirabuzón *m* curl; *(sacacorchos)* cork-screw

tirachinas *m inv* slingshot, *Br* catapult

tirada *f* TIP print run; *de una tirada* in one go

tiradero *m Méx* dump

tirado *adj* P *(barato)* dirt-cheap F; *estar tirado* F *(fácil)* be a walkover F *o* a piece of cake F

tiradores *mpl Arg* suspenders, *Br* braces

tiranía *f* tyranny

tirano 1 *adj* tyrannical **2** *m*, **-a** *f* tyrant

tirante 1 *adj* taut, *fig* tense **2** *m* strap; *tirantes* suspenders, *Br* braces

tirantez *f fig* tension

tirar ⟨1a⟩ **1** *v/t* throw; *edificio*, *persona* knock down; *(volcar)* knock over; *basura* throw away; *dinero* waste, throw away F; TIP print; F *en examen* fail **2** *v/i* pull, attract; *(disparar)* shoot; *tirar a* tend toward; *tirar a conservador* have conservative tendencies; *tirar de algo* pull sth; *ir tirando* F get by, manage **3** *v/r* *tirarse* throw o.s.; F *tiempo* spend; *tirarse a alguien* P screw s.o. P

tirita *f* MED Bandaid®, *Br* plaster

tiritar ⟨1a⟩ *v/i* shiver

tiro *m* shot; MÚS play; *tiro al blanco* target practice; *al tiro* CSur F at once, right away; *de tiros largos* F dressed up; *ni a tiros* F for love nor money; *le salió el tiro por la culata* F it backfired on him; *le sentó como un tiro* F he needed it like a hole in the head F

tirón *m* tug, jerk; *de un tirón* at a stretch, without a break

tiroteo *m* shooting

tirria *f*: *tener tirria a alguien* F have it in for s.o. F

tisana *f* herbal tea

títere *m* tb *fig* puppet; *no dejar títere con cabeza* F spare no-one

titiritero *m*, **-a** *f* acrobat

titubear ⟨1a⟩ *v/i* waver, hesitate

titubeo *m* wavering, hesitation

titular *m* de periódico headline

titularse ⟨1a⟩ *v/r* be entitled

título *m* title; *universitario* degree; JUR title; COM bond; *tener muchos títulos* be highly qualified; *a título de* as; *títulos de crédito* credits

tiza *f* chalk

tiznar ⟨1a⟩ *v/t* blacken

tizón *m* ember

tlapalería *f Méx* hardware store

TLC *abr* (= *Tratado de Libre Comercio*) NAFTA (= North American Free Trade Agreement)

toalla *f* towel; *tirar or arrojar la toalla fig*

throw in the towel

toallero *m* towel rail

tobillo *m* ankle

tobogán *m* slide

tocadiscos *m inv* record player

tocado *adj*: *estar tocado fig* F be crazy F

tocador *m* dressing-table

tocante: *en lo tocante a ...* with regard to ...

tocar ⟨1g⟩ **1** *v/t* touch; MÚS play **2** *v/i* L.Am. *a la puerta* knock (on the door); L.Am. *(sonar la campanita)* ring the doorbell; *te toca jugar* it's your turn **3** *v/r* *tocarse* touch

tocateja: *a tocateja* in hard cash

tocayo *m*, **-a** *f* namesake

tocino *m* bacon

tocólogo *m*, **-a** *f* obstetrician

todavía *adv* still, yet; *todavía no ha llegado* he still hasn't come, he hasn't come yet; *todavía no* not yet

todo 1 *adj* all; *todos los domingos* every Sunday; *-a la clase* the whole *o* the entire class **2** *adv* all; *estaba todo sucio* it was all dirty; *con todo* all the same; *del todo* entirely, absolutely **3** *pron* all, everything; *pl* everybody, everyone; *ir a por -as* go all out

todoterreno *m* AUTO off-road *o* all-terrain vehicle

toldo *m* awning; L.Am. Indian hut

tolerancia *f* tolerance

tolerar ⟨1a⟩ *v/t* tolerate

toma *f* FOT shot, take; *toma de conciencia* realization; *toma de corriente* outlet, socket; *toma de posesión* POL taking office

tomado *adj Méx* F *(borracho)* drunk

tomadura *f*: *tomadura de pelo* F joke

tomar ⟨1a⟩ **1** *v/t* take; *decisión* make, take; *bebida*, *comida* have; *tomarla con alguien* F have it in for s.o. F; *tomar el sol* sunbathe; *¡toma!* here (you are); *toma y daca* give and take **2** *v/i* L.Am. drink; *tomar por la derecha* turn right **3** *v/r* *tomarse* take; *comida*, *bebida* have; *se lo tomó a pecho* he took it to heart

tomate *m* tomato

tomavistas *m inv* movie camera, cine camera

tomillo *m* BOT thyme

tomo *m* volume, tome; *un timador de tomo y lomo* F an out-and-out conman

ton *m*: *sin ton ni son* for no particular reason

tonada *f* song

tonalidad *f* tonality

tonel *m* barrel, cask

tonelada *f peso* ton

T

tónica f tonic

tónico m MED tonic

tonificar ⟨1g⟩ v/t tone up

tono m MÚS, MED, PINT tone

tontería f fig stupid o dumb F thing; **tonterías** pl nonsense sg

tonto **1** adj silly, foolish **2** m, -a f fool, idiot; **hacer el tonto** play the fool; **hacerse el tonto** act dumb F

top m prenda top

topacio m MIN topaz

toparse ⟨1a⟩ v/r: **toparse con alguien** bump into s.o., run into s.o.

tope m limit; pieza stop; Méx en la calle speed bump; **pasarlo a tope** F have a great time; **estar hasta los topes** F be bursting at the seams F

tópico m cliché, platitude

topo m ZO mole

toque m: **toque de queda** MIL, fig curfew; **dar los últimos toques** put the finishing touches (**a** to)

toquilla f shawl

tórax m ANAT thorax

torbellino m whirlwind

torcer ⟨2b & 2h⟩ **1** v/t twist; (doblar) bend; (girar) turn **2** v/i turn; **torcer a la derecha** turn right **3** v/r torcerse twist, bend; fig go wrong; **torcerse un pie** sprain one's ankle

torcido adj twisted, bent

toreador m esp L.Am. bullfighter

torear ⟨1a⟩ **1** v/i fight bulls **2** v/t fight; fig dodge, sidestep

toreo m bullfighting

torera f: **saltarse algo a la torera** F flout sth, disregard sth

torero m bullfighter

tormenta f storm

tormento m torture

tornado m tornado, twister F

tornarse ⟨1a⟩ v/r triste, difícil etc become

torneo m competition, tournament

tornillo m screw; con tuerca bolt; **le falta un tornillo** F he's got a screw loose F

torniquete m turnstile; MED tourniquet

torno m de alfarería wheel; **en torno a** around, about

toro m bull; **ir a los toros** go to a bullfight; **coger al toro por los cuernos** take the bull by the horns

toronja f L.Am. grapefruit

torpe adj clumsy; (tonto) dense, dim

torpedo m MIL torpedo

torpeza f clumsiness; (necedad) stupidity

torre f tower; **torre de control** AVIA control tower

torrencial adj torrential

torrente m fig avalanche, flood

torrezno m GASTR fried rasher of bacon

tórrido adj torrid

torrija f GASTR French toast

torta f cake; plana tart; F slap

tortazo m F crash; (bofetada) punch

tortícolis m MED crick in the neck

tortilla f omelette; L.Am. tortilla

tortillera f V dyke F, lesbian

tortuga f ZO tortoise; marina turtle; **a paso de tortuga** fig at a snail's pace

tortuoso adj fig tortuous

tortura f tb fig torture

torturar ⟨1a⟩ v/t torture

tos f cough

tosco adj fig rough, coarse

toser ⟨2a⟩ v/i cough

tostada f piece of toast

tostado adj (moreno) brown, tanned

tostador m toaster

tostar ⟨1m⟩ **1** v/t toast; café roast; al sol tan **2** v/r tostarse tan, get brown

tostón m F bore

total **1** adj total, complete; **en total** altogether, in total **2** m whole; **un total de 50 personas** a total of 50 people

totalidad f totality

totalitario adj totalitarian

tóxico adj toxic

toxicómano m, -a f drug addict

toxina f toxin

tozudo adj obstinate

trabajador **1** adj hard-working **2** m, trabajadora f worker; **trabajador eventual** casual worker

trabajar ⟨1a⟩ **1** v/i work **2** v/t work; tema, músculos work on

trabajo m work; **trabajo en equipo** team work; **trabajo temporal** temporary work; **trabajo a tiempo parcial** part-time work

trabajoso adj hard, laborious

trabalenguas m inv tongue twister

trabar ⟨1a⟩ **1** v/t conversación, amistad strike up **2** v/r trabarse get tangled up

trabucarse ⟨1g⟩ v/r get all mixed up

tracción f TÉC traction; **tracción delantera/ trasera** front / rear-wheel drive

tractor m tractor

tradición f tradition

tradicional adj traditional

traducción f translation

traducir ⟨3o⟩ v/t translate

traductor m, traductora f translator

traer ⟨2p; part traído⟩ **1** v/t bring; **traer consigo** involve, entail; **este periódico la trae en portada** this newspaper carries it on the front page **2** v/r traerse: **este asunto se las trae** F it's a very tricky

matter
traficante *m* dealer
traficar ⟨1g⟩ *v/i* deal (**en** in)
tráfico *m* traffic; **tráfico de drogas** drug trafficking, drug dealing
tragaperras *f inv* slot machine
tragar ⟨1h⟩ **1** *v/t* swallow; **no lo trago** I can't stand him *o* bear him **2** *v/r* **tragarse** *tb fig* F swallow
tragedia *f* tragedy
trágico *adj* tragic
tragicomedia *f* tragicomedy
trago *m* mouthful; F *bebida* drink; **de un trago** in one gulp; **pasar un mal trago** *fig* have a hard time
tragón *adj* greedy
traición *f* treachery, betrayal
traicionar ⟨1a⟩ *v/t* betray
traidor 1 *adj* treacherous **2** *m*, **traidora** *f* traitor
traido *part* → **traer**
traigo *vb* → **traer**
tráiler *m* trailer
traje 1 *m* suit; **traje de baño** swimsuit **2** *vb* → **traer**
trajín *m* hustle and bustle
trajo *vb* → **traer**
trama *f* (*tema*) plot
tramar ⟨1a⟩ *v/t complot* hatch
tramitar ⟨1a⟩ *v/t documento*: *de persona* apply for; *de banco etc* process
trámite *m* formality
tramo *m* section, stretch; *de escaleras* flight
trampa *f* trap; (*truco*) scam F, trick; **hacer trampas** cheat
trampilla *f* trapdoor
trampolín *m* diving board
tramposo *m*, **-a** *f* cheat, crook
tranca *f*: **llevaba una tranca increíble** F he was wasted F *o* smashed F; **a trancas y barrancas** with great difficulty
trancazo *m* F dose of flu
trance *m* (*momento difícil*) tough time; **en trance** in a trance
tranquilidad *f* calm, quietness
tranquilizante *m* tranquilizer, *Br* tranquilliser
tranquilizar ⟨1f⟩ *v/t*: **tranquilizar a alguien** calm s.o. down
tranquillo *m*: **coger el tranquillo de algo** F get the hang of sth F
tranquilo *adj* calm, quiet; **¡tranquilo!** don't worry; **déjame tranquilo** leave me alone
transacción *f* COM deal, transaction;
transar ⟨1a⟩ *v/i L.Am.* (*ser vendido*) sell out
transatlántico 1 *adj* transatlantic **2** *m* liner

transbordador *m* ferry; **transbordador espacial** space shuttle
transbordo *m*: **hacer transbordo** TRANSP transfer, change
transcendental *adj fig* momentous
transcurrir ⟨3a⟩ *v/i de tiempo* pass, go by
transcurso *m* course; *de tiempo* passing
transeúnte *m/f* passer-by
transexual *m/f* transsexual
transferencia *f* COM transfer
transformación *f* transformation
transformador *m* EL transformer
transformar ⟨1a⟩ *v/t* transform
transfronterizo *adj* cross-border
tránsfuga *m/f* POL defector
transfusión *f*: **transfusión de sangre** blood transfusion
transgénico *adj* genetically modified
transgredir ⟨3a⟩ *v/t* infringe
transición *f* transition
transigir ⟨3c⟩ *v/i* compromise, make concessions
transistor *m* transistor
transitivo *adj* GRAM transitive
tránsito *m* COM transit; *L.Am.* (*circulación*) traffic
translúcido *adj* translucent
transmisión *f* transmission; **transmisión de datos** data transmission; **enfermedad de transmisión sexual** sexually transmitted disease
transmitir ⟨3a⟩ *v/t* spread; RAD, TV broadcast, transmit
transparencia *f para proyectar* transparency, slide
transparente *adj* transparent
transpiración *f* perspiration
transpirar ⟨1a⟩ *v/i* perspire
transplantar ⟨1a⟩ *v/t* transplant
transportar ⟨1a⟩ *v/t* transport
transporte *m* transport
tranvía *m* streetcar, *Br* tram
trapecio *m* trapeze
trapecista *m/f* trapeze artist(e)
trapiche *m CSur* sugar mill *o* press
trapicheo *m* F shady deal F
trapo *m* viejo rag; *para limpiar* cloth; **trapos** F clothes
trapujear ⟨1a⟩ *v/t & v/i C.Am.* smuggle
tráquea *f* ANAT windpipe, trachea
traqueteo *m* rattle, clatter
tras *prp en el espacio* behind; *en el tiempo* after
trasero 1 *adj* rear *atr*, back *atr* **2** *m* F butt F, *Br* rear end F
trasiego *m fig* bustle
trasladar ⟨1a⟩ **1** *v/t* move; *trabajador* transfer **2** *v/r* **trasladarse** move (**a** to);

se traslada Méx: en negocio under new management

traslado m move; de trabajador transfer; **traslado al aeropuerto** airport transfer

trasluz m: **al trasluz** against the light

trasnochar ⟨1a⟩ v/i (acostarse tarde) go to bed late, stay up late; (no dormir) stay up all night; L.Am. stay overnight, spend the night

traspapelar ⟨1a⟩ v/t mislay

traspasar ⟨1a⟩ v/t (atravesar) go through; COM transfer

traspié m trip, stumble; **dar un traspié** fig slip up, blunder

trasplantar ⟨1a⟩ v/t AGR, MED transplant

trasplante m AGR, MED transplant

trastada f F prank, trick; **hacer trastadas** get up to mischief

traste m: **irse al traste** F fall through, go down the tubes F

trastero m lumber room

trasto m desp piece of junk; persona good-for-nothing

trastornar ⟨1a⟩ v/t upset; (molestar) inconvenience

trastorno m inconvenience; MED disorder

tratado m esp POL treaty; **Tratado de Libre Comercio** North American Free Trade Agreement

tratamiento m treatment; **tratamiento de datos / textos** INFOR data / word processing

tratar ⟨1a⟩ **1** v/t treat; (manejar) handle; (dirigirse a) address (**de** as); gente come into contact with; tema deal with **2** v/i: **tratar con alguien** deal with s.o.; **tratar de** (intentar) try to **3** v/r **tratarse:** ¿**de qué se trata?** what's it about?

trato m de prisionero, animal treatment; COM deal; **malos tratos** pl ill treatment sg, abuse sg.; **tener trato con alguien** have dealings with s.o.; **¡trato hecho!** it's a deal

trauma m trauma

traumatizar ⟨1f⟩ v/t traumatize

traumatólogo m, **-a** f trauma specialist, traumatologist

través m: **a través de** through

travesaño m en fútbol crossbar

travesía f crossing

travesti m transvestite, drag artist

travesura f bit of mischief, prank

travieso adj niño mischievous

trayecto m journey; **10 dólares por trayecto** 10 dollars each way

trayectoria f fig course, path

trazar ⟨1f⟩ v/t (dibujar) draw; ruta plot, trace; (describir) outline, describe

trazo m line

trébol m BOT clover

trece adj thirteen; **mantenerse** or **seguir en sus trece** stand firm, not budge

trecho m stretch, distance

tregua f truce, cease-fire; **sin tregua** relentlessly

treinta adj thirty

tremebundo adj horrendous, frightening

tremendo adj awful, dreadful; éxito, alegría tremendous

tren m FERR train; **tren de alta velocidad** high speed train; **tren de lavado** car wash; **vivir a todo tren** F live in style; **estar como un tren** F be absolutely gorgeous

trenca f duffel coat

trenza f plait

trepa m F socialmente social climber; en el trabajo careerist

trepar ⟨1a⟩ v/i climb (**a** up), scale (**a** sth)

tres adj three

trescientos adj three hundred

tresillo m living-room suite, Br three-piece suite

treta f trick, ploy

triángulo m triangle

tribu f tribe

tribuna f grandstand

tribunal m court; **Tribunal Supremo** Supreme Court

tributo m tribute; (impuesto) tax

triciclo m tricycle

tricotar ⟨1a⟩ v/i knit

trifulca f F brawl, punch-up F

trigo m wheat

trillado adj fig hackneyed, clichéd

trillar ⟨1a⟩ v/t AGR thresh

trillizos mpl triplets

trillón m quintillion, Br trillion

trimestral adj quarterly

trimestre m quarter; escolar semester, Br term

trinar ⟨1a⟩ v/i trill, warble; **está que trina** fig F he's fuming F, he's hopping mad F

trincar ⟨1g⟩ v/t F criminal catch

trinchera f MIL trench

trineo m sled, sleigh

trino m trill, warble

trío m trio

tripa f F belly F, gut F; **hacer de tripas corazón** fig pluck up courage

triple m: **el triple que el año pasado** three times as much as last year

triplicar ⟨1g⟩ v/t triple, treble

trípode m tripod

tripulación f AVIA, MAR crew

tripular ⟨1a⟩ v/t man

triquiñuela f F dodge F, trick

tris *m*: *estuvo en un tris de caerse* F she came within an inch of falling

triste *adj* sad

tristeza *f* sadness

triturar ⟨1a⟩ *v/t* grind

triunfador 1 *adj* winning **2** *m*, **triunfadora** *f* winner, victor

triunfar ⟨1a⟩ *v/i* triumph, win

triunfo *m* triumph, victory; *en naipes* trump

trivial *adj* trivial

triza *f*: *hacer trizas* F *jarrón* smash to bits; *papel*, *vestido* tear to shreds

trocear ⟨1a⟩ *v/t* cut into pieces, cut up

troche: *había errores a troche y moche* F there were mistakes galore F

trofeo *m* trophy

troglodita *m/f* cave-dweller

troj(e) *f Arg* granary

trola *f* F fib

trolebús *m* trolley bus

tromba *f*: *tromba de agua* downpour

trombón *m* MÚS trombone

trombosis *f* MED thrombosis

trompa 1 *adj* F wasted F **2** *f* MÚS horn; ZO trunk

trompazo *m L.Am.* F whack F; *darse un trompazo con algo* F bang into sth

trompearse ⟨1a⟩ *L.Am.* F fight, lay into each other F

trompeta *f* MÚS trumpet

trompetista *m/f* MÚS trumpeter

trompicón *m*: *a trompicones* in fits and starts

trompo *m* spinning top

trona *f* high chair

tronar ⟨1m⟩ *v/i* thunder

troncha *f S. Am.* slice, piece

tronchante *adj* F sidesplitting

troncharse ⟨1a⟩ *v/r*: *troncharse de risa* F split one's sides laughing

tronco *m* trunk; *cortado* log; *dormir como un tronco* sleep like a log

trono *m* throne

tropa *f* MIL (*soldado raso*) ordinary soldier; *tropas* troops

tropel *m*: *en tropel* in a mad rush; *salir en tropel* pour out

tropezar ⟨1f & 1k⟩ *v/i* trip, stumble

tropical *adj* tropical

trópico *m* tropic

tropiezo *m fig* setback

tropilla *f L.Am.* herd

trotar ⟨1a⟩ *v/i fig* gad around

trote *m* trot; *ya no estoy para esos trotes* I'm not up to it any more

trozo *m* piece

trucha *f* ZO trout

truco *m* trick; *coger el truco a algo* F get the hang of sth F

truculento *adj* horrifying

trueno *m* thunder

trueque *m* barter

trufa *f* BOT truffle

truhán *m* rogue

Tte. *abr* (= *Teniente*) Lieut. (= Lieutenant)

tú *pron sg* you; *tratar de tú* address as 'tu'

tu, **tus** *adj pos* your

tuberculosis *f* MED TB, tuberculosis

tubería *f* pipe

tubo *m* tube; *tubo de escape* AUTO exhaust (pipe); *por un tubo* F an enormous amount

tucán *m* ZO toucan

tuerca *f* TÉC nut

tulipán *m* BOT tulip

tullido *m* cripple

tumba *f* tomb, grave

tumbar ⟨1a⟩ **1** *v/t* knock down **2** *v/r* tumbarse lie down

tumbo *m* tumble; *ir dando tumbos* stagger along

tumbona *f* (sun) lounger

tumor *m* MED tumo(u)r

tumulto *m* uproar

tuna *f Méx fruta* prickly pear

tunda *f* F beating

tundra *f* GEOG tundra

túnel *m* tunnel; *túnel de lavado* car wash

Túnez Tunisia

túnica *f* tunic

tuntún: *decir algo al buen tuntún* say sth off the top of one's head

tupé *m* F quiff

tupido *adj pelo* thick; *vegetación* dense, thick

turbante *m* turban

turbar ⟨1a⟩ **1** *v/t* (*emocionar*) upset; *paz*, *tranquilidad* disturb; (*avergonzar*) embarrass **2** *v/r* turbarse (*emocionarse*) get upset; *de paz*, *tranquilidad* be disturbed; (*avergonzarse*) get embarrassed

turbina *f* turbine

turbio *adj* cloudy, murky; *fig* shady, murky

turbo *m* turbo

turbulencia *f* turbulence

turbulento *adj* turbulent

turco 1 *adj* Turkish **2** *m*, **-a** *f* Turk

turismo *m* tourism; *automóvil* sedan, *Br* saloon (car); *turismo rural* tourism in rural areas

turista *m/f* tourist

turístico *adj* tourist *atr*

turnarse ⟨1a⟩ *v/r* take it in turns

turno *m* turn; *turno de noche* night shift; *por turnos* in turns

T

turquesa f piedra preciosa turquoise; **azul turquesa** turquoise

Turquía Turkey

turrón m nougat

turulato adj F stunned, dazed

tute m: **darse un tute** F work like a dog F, slave F

tutear ⟨1a⟩ v/t address as 'tu'

tutiplén: había comida a tutiplén F there was loads o masses to eat F

tutor m, **tutora** f EDU tutor

tuve vb → **tener**

tuvo vb → **tener**

tuyo, tuya pron pos yours; **los tuyos** your folks, your family

TV abr (= **televisión**) TV (= television)

U

u conj (instead of **o** before words starting with o) or

ubicación f L.Am. location; (localización) finding

ubicado adj located, situated

ubicar ⟨1g⟩ **1** v/t L.Am. place, put; (localizar) locate **2** v/r **ubicarse** be located, be situated; **en un empleo** get a job

ubicuo adj ubiquitous

ubre f udder

UCI abr (= **Unidad de Cuidados Intensivos**) ICU (= Intensive Care Unit)

Ud. pron → **usted**

Uds. pron → **usted**

UE abr (= **Unión Europea**) EU (= European Union)

ufano adj conceited; (contento) proud

ujier m usher

úlcera f MED ulcer

ulcerarse ⟨1a⟩ v/r MED become ulcerous, ulcerate

ulterior adj subsequent

últimamente adv lately

ultimar ⟨1a⟩ v/t finalize; L.Am. (rematar) finish off

ultimátum m ultimatum

último adj last; (más reciente) latest; piso top atr; **-as noticias** latest news sg; **por último** finally; **está en las -as** he doesn't have long (to live)

ultra m POL right-wing extremist

ultraderecha f POL extreme right

ultrajante adj outrageous; palabras insulting

ultrajar ⟨1a⟩ v/t outrage; (insultar) insult

ultraje m outrage; (insulto) insult

ultraligero m AVIA microlight

ultramarinos mpl groceries; **tienda de ultramarinos** grocery store, Br grocer's (shop)

ultramoderno adj ultramodern

ultranza: a ultranza for all one is worth; **un defensor a ultranza de algo** an ardent defender of sth

ultrasónico adj ultrasonic

ultrasonido m ultrasound

ultratumba f: **la vida de ultratumba** life beyond the grave

ultravioleta f adj ultraviolet

ulular ⟨1a⟩ v/i de viento howl; de búho hoot

umbilical adj ANAT umbilical

umbral m fig threshold; **en el umbral de** fig on the threshold of

umbrío adj shady

un, una art a; antes de vocal y h muda an; **unos coches / pájaros** some cars / birds

unánime adj unanimous

unanimidad f unanimity; **por unanimidad** unanimously

unción f fig unction

ungir ⟨3c⟩ v/t REL anoint

ungüento m ointment

únicamente adv only

único adj only; (sin par) unique; **es único** it's unique; **hijo único** only child; **lo único que ...** the only thing that ...

unicornio m MYTH unicorn

unidad f MIL, MAT unit; (cohesión) unity; **unidad de cuidados intensivos, unidad de vigilancia intensiva** MED intensive care unit; **unidad de disco** INFOR disk drive; **unidad monetaria** monetary unity

unido adj united; **una familia -a** a close-knit family

unificación f unification

unificar ⟨1g⟩ v/t unify

uniformar ⟨1a⟩ v/t fig standardize

uniforme 1 adj uniform; superficie even **2** m uniform

unilateral *adj* unilateral
unión *f* union; *Unión Europea* European Union
unir ⟨3a⟩ **1** *v/t* join; *personas* unite; *características* combine (*con* with); *ciudades* link **2** *v/r* **unirse** join together; *unirse a* join
unisex *adj* unisex
unísono *adj*: *al unísono* in unison
unitario *adj* unitary; *precio unitario* unit price
universal *adj* universal
universidad *f* university; *universidad a distancia* university correspondence school, *Br* Open University
universitario **1** *adj* university *atr* **2** *m*, *-a f* (*estudiante*) university student
universo *m* universe
uno **1** *pron* one; *es la -a* it's one o'clock; *me lo dijo uno* someone *o* somebody told me; *uno a uno, uno por uno, de uno en uno* one by one; *no dar ni -a* F not get anything right; *unos cuantos* a few, some; *unos niños* some children; *-as mil pesetas* about a thousand pesetas **2** *m* one; *el uno de enero* January first, the first of January
untar ⟨1a⟩ *v/t* spread; *untar a alguien* F (*sobornar*) grease s.o.'s palm
untuoso *adj* fig oily
uña *f* ANAT nail; ZO claw; *defenderse con uñas y dientes* fig F fight tooth and nail; *ser uña y carne* *personas* be extremely close
uperisado *adj*: *leche -a* UHT milk
uranio *m* uranium
urbanidad *f* civility
urbanismo *m* city planning, *Br* town planning
urbanización *f* (*urban*) development; (*colonia*) housing development, *Br* housing estate
urbanizar ⟨1f⟩ *v/t terreno* develop
urbano *adj* urban; (*cortés*) courteous; *guardia urbano* local police officer
urbe *f* city
urdir ⟨3a⟩ *v/t complot* hatch
urea *f* urea
uretra *f* ANAT urethra
urgencia *f* urgency; (*prisa*) haste; MED emergency; *urgencias* *pl* emergency room *sg*, *Br* casualty *sg*

urgente *adj* urgent
urgir ⟨3c⟩ *v/i* be urgent
urinario *m* urinal
urna *f* urn; *urna electoral* ballot box
urólogo *m* MED urologist
urraca *f* ZO magpie
URSS *abr* (= *Unión de las Repúblicas Socialistas Soviéticas*) USSR (= Union of Soviet Socialist Republics)
urticaria *f* MED hives
Uruguay Uruguay
uruguayo **1** *adj* Uruguayan **2** *m*, *-a f* Uruguayan
usado *adj* (*gastado*) worn; (*de segunda mano*) second hand
usar ⟨1a⟩ **1** *v/t* use; *ropa, gafas* wear **2** *v/i*: *listo para usar* ready to use **3** *v/r* **usarse** be used
uso *m* use; (*costumbre*) custom; *obligatorio el uso de casco* helmets must be worn; *en buen uso* still in use
usted *pron* you; *tratar de usted* address as 'usted'; *ustedes* *pl* you; *de usted / ustedes* your; *es de usted / ustedes* it's yours
usual *adj* common, usual
usuario *m*, *-a f* INFOR user
usufructo *m* JUR usufruct
usura *f* usury
usurero *m*, *-a f* usurer
usurpar ⟨1a⟩ *v/t* usurp
utensilio *m* tool; *de cocina* utensil; *utensilios* *pl* equipment *sg*; *utensilios* *pl* *de pesca* fishing tackle *sg*
útero *m* ANAT uterus
útil **1** *adj* useful **2** *m* tool; *útiles* *pl* *de pesca* fishing tackle *sg*
utilidad *f* usefulness
utilitario **1** *adj* functional, utilitarian **2** *m* AUTO compact
utilitarismo *m* utilitarianism
utilización *f* use
utilizar ⟨1f⟩ *v/t* use
utopía *f* utopia
utópico *adj* utopian
uva *f* BOT grape; *estar de mala uva* F be in a foul mood; *tener mala uva* F be a nasty piece of work F
UVI *abr* (= *Unidad de Vigilancia Intensiva*) ICU (= Intensive Care Unit)
úvula *f* ANAT uvula

V

va *vb* → **ir**

vaca *f* cow; GASTR beef; **vaca lechera** dairy cow; **vaca marina** manatee, sea cow; **mal** or **enfermedad de las vacas locas** F mad cow disease F

vacaciones *fpl* vacation *sg*, Br holiday *sg*; **de vacaciones** on vacation, Br on holiday

vacante 1 *adj* vacant, empty **2** *f* job opening, position, Br vacancy; **cubrir una vacante** fill a position

vaciar ⟨1b⟩ **1** *v/t* empty **2** *v/r* **vaciarse** empty

vacilación *f* hesitation

vacilante *adj* unsteady; *(dubitativo)* hesitant

vacilar ⟨1a⟩ **1** *v/i* hesitate; *de fe, resolución* waver; *de objeto* wobble, rock; *de persona* stagger; *Méx* F *(divertirse)* have fun **2** *v/t* F make fun of

vacío 1 *adj* empty **2** *m* FÍS vacuum; *fig espacio* void; **vacío de poder** power vacuum; **vacío legal** loophole; **dejar un vacío** *fig* leave a gap; **envasado al vacío** vacuum packed; **hacer el vacío a alguien** *fig* ostracize s.o.

vacuna *f* vaccine

vacunación *f* vaccination

vacunar ⟨1a⟩ *v/t* vaccinate

vacuno *adj* bovine; **ganado vacuno** cattle *pl*

vacuo *adj fig* vacuous

vadear ⟨1a⟩ *v/t río* ford; *dificultad* get around

vado *m* ford; *en la calle* entrance ramp; **vado permanente** *letrero* keep clear

vagabundear ⟨1a⟩ *v/i* drift around

vagabundo 1 *m perro* stray **2** *m*, **-a** *f* hobo, Br tramp

vagancia *f* laziness, idleness

vagar ⟨1h⟩ *v/i* wander

vagido *m de bebe* cry

vagina *f* ANAT vagina

vago *adj (holgazán)* lazy; *(indefinido)* vague; **hacer el vago** laze around

vagón *m de carga* wagon; *de pasajeros* car, Br coach; **vagón restaurante** dining car, Br tb restaurant car

vaguear ⟨1a⟩ *v/i* laze around

vaguedad *f* vagueness

vahído *m* MED dizzy spell

vaho *m (aliento)* breath; *(vapor)* steam

vaina *f* BOT pod; *S. Am.* F drag F

vainilla *f* vanilla

vais *vb* → **ir**

vaivén *m* to-and-fro, swinging; **vaivenes** *fig* ups and downs

vajilla *f* dishes *pl*; *juego* dinner service, set of dishes

vale *m* voucher, coupon

valedero *adj* valid

valentía *f* bravery

valer ⟨2q⟩ **1** *v/t* be worth; *(costar)* cost **2** *v/i de billete, carné* be valid; *(estar permitido)* be allowed; *(tener valor)* be worth; *(servir)* be of use; **no valer para algo** be no good at sth; **más vale caro** it's more expensive; **sus consejos me valieron de mucho** his advice was very useful to me; **más vale ...** it's better to ...; **más te vale ...** you'd better ...; **¡vale!** okay, sure **3** *v/r* **valerse** manage (by o.s.); **valerse de** make use of

valeriana *f* BOT valerian

valeroso *adj* valiant

valga *vb* → **valer**

valgo *vb* → **valer**

valía *f* worth

validar ⟨1a⟩ *v/t* validate

validez *f* validity

válido *adj* valid

valiente *adj* brave; *irón* fine

valija *f (maleta)* bag, suitcase, Br tb case; **valija diplomática** diplomatic bag

valioso *adj* valuable

valla *f* fence; DEP, *fig* hurdle; **valla publicitaria** billboard, Br hoarding; **carrera de vallas** DEP hurdles

vallado *m* fence

vallar ⟨1a⟩ *v/t* fence in

valle *m* valley

valor *m* value; *(valentía)* courage; **valor añadido**, L.Am. **valor agregado** value added; **valor nominal** *de acción* nominal value; *de título* par value; **objetos de valor** valuables; **valores** COM securities

valoración *f (tasación)* valuation

valorar ⟨1a⟩ *v/t* value *(en* at); *(estimar)* appreciate, value

vals *m* waltz

valuar ⟨1e⟩ *v/t* value

válvula *f* ANAT, EL valve; **válvula de escape** *fig* safety valve

vampiro *m fig* vampire

van *vb* → **ir**

vanagloriarse ⟨1b⟩ *v/r* boast *(de* about), brag *(de* about)

vandálico *adj* destructive

vandalismo *m* vandalism
vándalo *m*, -a *f* vandal
vanguardia *f* MIL vanguard; *de vanguardia fig* avant-garde
vanidad *f* vanity
vanidoso *adj* conceited, vain
vano *adj* futile, vain; *en vano* in vain
vapor *m* vapo(u)r; *de agua* steam; *cocinar al vapor* steam
vaporizar ⟨1f⟩ **1** *v/t* vaporize **2** *v/r* vaporizarse vaporize
vaporoso *adj* vaporous; *fig: vestido* gauzy, filmy
vapulear ⟨1a⟩ *v/t* beat up
vapuleo *m* beating
vaquería *f* dairy
vaquero **1** *adj tela* denim; *pantalones vaqueros* jeans **2** *m* cowboy, cowhand
vaquilla *f* heifer
vara *f* stick; TÉC rod; (*bastón de mando*) staff
varapalo *m* Γ (*contratiempo*) hitch Γ, setback
variable *adj* variable; *tiempo* changeable
variación *f* variation
variado *adj* varied
variar ⟨1c⟩ **1** *v/t* vary; (*cambiar*) change **2** *v/i* vary; (*cambiar*) change; *para variar* for a change
varice *f* MED varicose vein
varicela *f* MED chickenpox
variedad *f* variety; *variedades pl* vaudeville *sg*, Br variety *sg*
variopinto *adj* varied, diverse
varios *adj* several
varita *f*: *varita mágica* magic wand
variz *f* varicose vein
varón *m* man, male
varonil *adj* manly, virile
vas *vb* → *ir*
vasallo *m* vassal
vasco **1** *adj* Basque; *País Vasco* Basque country **2** *m idioma* Basque **3** *m*, -a *f* Basque
Vascongadas *fpl* Basque country *sg*
vascuence *m* Basque
vascular *adj* ANAT vascular
vasectomía *f* MED vasectomy
vaselina *f* Vaseline®
vasija *f* container, vessel
vaso *m* glass; ANAT vessel
vasto *adj* vast
Vaticano *m* Vatican
vaticinar ⟨1a⟩ *v/t* predict, forecast
vaticinio *m* prediction, forecast
vatio *m* EL watt
vaya **1** *vb* → *ir* **2** *int* well!
V.° B.° *abr* (= *visto bueno*) approved, OK
Vd. *pron* → *usted*

Vds. *pron* → *usted*
ve *vb* → *ir, ver*
vea *vb* → *ver*
vecindad *f* Méx poor area
vecindario *m* neighbo(u)rhood
vecino **1** *adj* neighbo(u)ring **2** *m*, -a *f* neighbo(u)r
vedado *m*: *vedado de caza* game reserve
vedar ⟨1a⟩ *v/t* ban, prohibit
vedette *f* star
vegetación *f* vegetation
vegetal **1** *adj* vegetable, plant *atr* **2** *m* vegetable
vegetar ⟨1a⟩ *v/i fig* vegetate
vegetariano **1** *adj* vegetarian **2** *m*, -a *f* vegetarian
vehemente *adj* vehement
vehículo *m tb* vehicle; MED carrier
veinte *m/adj* twenty
veintena *f* twenty; *aproximadamente* about twenty
vejación *f* humiliation
vejar ⟨1a⟩ *v/t* humiliate
vejestorio *m* F old fossil F, old relic F
vejez *f* old age
vejiga *f* ANAT bladder
vela *f para alumbrar* candle; DEP sailing; *de barco* sail; *a toda vela* flat out F, all out F; *estar a dos velas* F be broke F; *pasar la noche en vela* stay up all night
velada *f* evening
velador *m* L.Am. *lámpara* bedlamp, Br bedside light; *Chi mueble* nightstand, Br bedside table
velar ⟨1a⟩ *v/i*: *velar por algo* look after sth
velatorio *m* wake
velcro® *m* Velcro
veleidad *f* fickleness
velero *m* MAR sailing ship
veleta **1** *f* weathervane **2** *m/f fig* weathercock
vello *m* (body) hair
velo *m* veil
velocidad *f* speed; (*marcha*) gear
velódromo *m* velodrome
veloz *adj* fast, speedy
ven *vb* → *venir*
vena *f* ANAT vein; *le dio la vena y lo hizo* F she just upped and did it F; *estar en vena* F be on form
venado *m* ZO deer
vencedor **1** *adj* winning **2** *m*, *vencedora f* winner
vencejo *m* ZO swift
vencer ⟨2b⟩ **1** *v/t* defeat; *fig* (*superar*) overcome **2** *v/i* win; COM *de plazo etc* expire

vencido adj: *darse por vencido* admit defeat, give in; *a la tercera va la -a* third time lucky

vencimiento m expiration, Br expiry; *de bono* maturity

venda f bandage

vendaje m MED dressing

vendar ⟨1a⟩ v/t MED bandage, dress; *vendar los ojos a alguien* blindfold s.o.

vendaval m gale

vendedor m, **vendedora** f seller

vender ⟨2a⟩ **1** v/t sell; *fig (traicionar)* betray **2** v/r **venderse** sell o.s.; *venderse al enemigo* sell out to the enemy

vendimia f grape harvest

vendimiar ⟨1b⟩ v/t *uvas* harvest, pick

vendré vb → **venir**

veneno m poison

venenoso adj poisonous

venerable adj venerable

venerar ⟨1a⟩ v/t venerate, worship

venéreo adj MED venereal

venezolano 1 adj Venezuelan **2** m, **-a** f Venezuelan

Venezuela Venezuela

venga vb → **venir**

venganza f vengeance, revenge

vengar ⟨1h⟩ **1** v/t avenge **2** v/r **vengarse** take revenge (*de* on; *por* for)

vengativo adj vengeful

vengo vb → **venir**

venir ⟨3s⟩ **1** v/i come; *venir de España* come from Spain; *venir bien* be convenient; *venir mal* be inconvenient; *le vino una idea* an idea occurred to him; *viene a ser lo mismo* it comes down to the same thing; *el año que viene* next year; *¡venga!* come on; *¿a qué viene eso?* why do you say that? **2** v/r **venirse**: *venirse abajo* collapse; *fig: de persona* fall apart, go to pieces

venta f sale; *venta por correo or por catálogo* mail order; *venta al detalle or al por menor* retail; *en venta* for sale

ventaja f advantage; DEP *en carrera, partido* lead; *ventaja fiscal* tax advantage

ventajoso adj advantageous

ventana f window; *ventana de la nariz* nostril

ventanilla f AVIA, AUTO, FERR window; MAR porthole

ventilación f ventilation

ventilador m fan

ventilar ⟨1a⟩ v/t air; *fig: problema* talk over; *opiniones* air

ventisca f blizzard

ventosa f ZO sucker

ventosidad f wind, flatulence

ventrílocuo m ventriloquist

veo vb → **ver**

ver ⟨2v; *part* visto⟩ **1** v/t see; *televisión* watch; JUR *pleito* hear; L.Am. *(mirar)* look at; *está por ver* it remains to be seen; *no puede verla fig* he can't stand the sight of her; *no tiene nada que ver con* it doesn't have anything to do with; *¡a ver!* let's see; *¡hay que ver!* would you believe it!; *ya veremos* we'll see **2** v/i L.Am. *(mirar)* look; *ve aquí dentro* L.Am. look in here **3** v/r *verse* see o.s.; *(encontrarse)* see one another; *¡habráse visto!* would you believe it!; *¡se las verá conmigo!* F he'll have me to deal with!

veranear ⟨1a⟩ v/i spend the summer vacation *o* Br holidays

veraniego adj summer atr

verano m summer

veras f: *de veras* really, truly

verbal adj GRAM verbal

verbena f *(fiesta)* party

verbo m GRAM verb

verborrea f desp verbosity

verdad f truth; *a decir verdad* to tell the truth; *de verdad* real, proper; *no te gusta, ¿verdad?* you don't like it, do you?; *vas a venir, ¿verdad?* you're coming, aren't you?; *es verdad* it's true, it's the truth

verdadero adj true; *(cierto)* real

verde 1 adj green; *fruta* unripe; F *chiste* blue, dirty; *viejo verde* dirty old man; *poner verde a alguien* F criticize s.o. **2** m green; *los verdes* POL the Greens

verdoso adj greenish

verdugo m executioner

verdulería f fruit and vegetable store, Br greengrocer's

verdura f: **verdura(s)** *(hortalizas)* greens pl, *(green)* vegetables pl

vereda f S. Am. sidewalk, Br pavement; *meter alguien en vereda fig* put s.o. back on the straight and narrow, bring s.o. into line

veredicto m JUR, fig verdict

verga f rod

vergel m orchard

vergonzoso adj disgraceful, shameful; *(tímido)* shy

vergüenza f shame; *(escándalo)* disgrace; *me da vergüenza* I'm embarrassed; *es una vergüenza* it's a disgrace; *no sé cómo no se te cae la cara de vergüenza* you should be ashamed (of yourself)

vericuetos mpl fig twists and turns

verídico adj true

verificar ⟨1g⟩ v/t verify

verja f railing; *(puerta)* iron gate

vermú, vermut *m* vermouth
verosímil *adj* realistic; (*creíble*) plausible
verruga *f* wart
versado *adj* well-versed (**en** in)
versar ⟨1a⟩ *v/i*: **versar sobre** deal with, be about
versátil *adj* fickle; *artista* versatile
versículo *m* verse
versión *f* version; **en versión original película** original language version
verso *m* verse
vértebra *f* ANAT vertebra
vertedero *m* dump, tip
verter ⟨2g⟩ *v/t* dump; (*derramar*) spill; *fig: opinión* voice
vertical *adj* vertical
vertido *m* dumping; **vertidos** *pl* waste *sg*
vertiente *f* L.Am. (*cuesta*) slope; (*lado*) side
vertiginoso *adj* dizzy; (*rápido*) frantic
vértigo *m* MED vertigo; **darle a alguien vértigo** make s.o. dizzy
vesícula *f* blister; **vesícula biliar** ANAT gall-bladder
vespa® *f* motorscooter
vestíbulo *m de casa* hall; *de edificio público* lobby
vestido *m* dress; L.Am. *de hombre* suit
vestigio *m* vestige, trace
vestir ⟨3l⟩ **1** *v/t* dress; (*llevar puesto*) wear **2** *v/i* dress; **vestir de negro** wear black, dress in black; **vestir de uniforme** wear a uniform **3** *v/r* **vestirse** get dressed; (*disfrazarse*) dress up; **vestirse de algo** wear sth
vestuario *m* DEP locker room; TEA wardrobe
veta *f* MIN vein
vetar ⟨1a⟩ *v/t* POL veto
veterano **1** *adj* veteran; (*experimentado*) experienced **2** *m*, **-a** *f* veteran
veterinario **1** *adj* veterinary **2** *m*, **-a** *f* veterinarian, vet
veto *m* veto
vetusto *adj* ancient
vez *f* time; **a la vez** at the same time; **a su vez** for his / her part; **cada vez que** every time that; **de vez en cuando** from time to time; **en vez de** instead of; **érase una vez** once upon a time, there was; **otra vez** again; **tal vez** perhaps, maybe; **una vez** once; **a veces** sometimes; **muchas veces** (*con frecuencia*) often; **hacer las veces de** *objeto* serve as; *de persona* act as
vi *vb* → **ver**
vía 1 *f* FERR track; **vía estrecha** FERR narrow gauge; **darle vía libre a alguien** give s.o. a free hand; **por vía aérea** by air; **en**

vías de *fig* in the process of **2** *prp* via
viable *adj plan, solución* viable, feasible
viaducto *m* viaduct
viajante *m/f* sales rep
viajar ⟨1a⟩ *v/i* travel
viaje *m* trip, journey; **viaje organizado** package tour; **viaje de ida** outward journey; **viaje de ida y vuelta** round trip; **viaje de novios** honeymoon; **viaje de vuelta** return journey
viajero *m*, **-a** *f* travel(l)er
viario *adj* road *atr*; **educación -a** instruction in road safety
víbora *f tb fig* viper
vibración *f* vibration
vibrante *adj fig* exciting
vibrar ⟨1a⟩ *v/t* vibrate
vicaría *f* pastor's house, vicarage; **pasar por la vicaría** F get married in church
vicecónsul *m* vice-consul
vicepresidente *m*, **-a** *f* POL vice-president; COM vice-president, *Br* deputy chairman
vicerrector *m* vice-rector
viceversa *adv*: **y viceversa** and vice versa
viciado *adj* air stuffy
viciarse ⟨1b⟩ *v/r* fall into bad habits
vicio *m* vice; **pasarlo de vicio** F have a great time F
vicioso *adj* vicious; (*corrompido*) depraved
vicisitudes *fpl* ups and downs
víctima *f* victim
victimar ⟨1a⟩ *v/t* L.Am. kill
victoria *f* victory; **cantar victoria** claim victory
victorioso *adj* victorious
vicuña *f* ZO vicuna
vid *f* vine
vida *f* life; *esp* TÉC life span; **de por vida** for life; **en mi vida** never (in my life); **ganarse la vida** earn a living; **hacer la vida imposible a alguien** make s.o.'s life impossible; **vida mía** my love
vidente *m/f* seer, clairvoyant
vídeo *m* video
videocámara *f* video camera
videocas(s)et(t)e *m* video cassette
videoclip *m* pop video
videoconferencia *f* video conference
videojuego *m* video game
videotex(to) *m* videotext
vidriera *f* L.Am. shop window
vidrio *m* L.Am. glass; (*ventana*) window
vieira *f* ZO scallop
vieja *f* old woman
viejo 1 *adj* old **2** *m* old man; **mis viejos** F my folks F
viendo *vb* → **ver**
viene *vb* → **venir**

V

viento *m* wind; *viento en popa* *fig* F splendidly; *contra viento y marea* *fig* come what may; *hacer viento* be windy; *proclamar a los cuatro vientos* *fig* shout from the rooftops

vientre *m* belly

viernes *m inv* Friday; *Viernes Santo* Good Friday

Vietnam Vietnam

vietnamita *adj & m/f* Vietnamese

viga *f* beam, girder

vigente *adj legislación* in force

vigésimo *adj* twentieth

vigilante 1 *adj* watchful, vigilant **2** *m* *L.Am.* policeman; *vigilante nocturno* night watchman; *vigilante jurado* security guard

vigilar ⟨1a⟩ **1** *v/i* keep watch **2** *v/t* watch; *a un preso* guard

vigor *m* vigo(u)r; *en vigor* in force

vigoroso *adj* vigorous

vil *adj* vile, despicable

vilipendiar ⟨1b⟩ *v/t* insult, vilify *fml*; *(despreciar)* revile

villa *f* town

villancico *m* Christmas carol

villano 1 *adj* villainous **2** *m*, *-a f* villain

vilo: *en vilo* in the air; *fig* in suspense, on tenterhooks; *levantar en vilo* lift off the ground; *tener a alguien en vilo* *fig* keep s.o. in suspense *o* on tenterhooks

vinagre *m* vinegar

vinagrera *f* vinegar bottle; *S. Am.* *(indigestión)* indigestion; *vinagreras pl* cruet *sg*

vinagreta *f* vinaigrette

vincha *f S. Am.* hairband

vinculante *adj* binding

vincular ⟨1a⟩ *v/t* link (*a* to); *(comprometer)* bind

vínculo *m* link; *fig (relación)* tie, bond

vindicar ⟨1g⟩ *v/t* vindicate

vine *vb* → *venir*

vinícola *adj región, país* wine-growing *atr*; *industria* wine-making *atr*

viniendo *vb* → *venir*

vinicultura *f* wine-growing

vino 1 *m* wine; *vino blanco* white wine; *vino de mesa* table wine; *vino tinto* red wine **2** *vb* → *venir*

viña *f* vineyard

viñatero *m*, *-a f S. Am.* wine grower

viñedo *m* vineyard

viñeta *f* TIP vignette

vio *vb* → *ver*

viola *f* MÚS viola

violación *f* rape; *de derechos* violation

violador *m*, *violadora f* rapist

violar ⟨1a⟩ *v/t* rape

violencia *f* violence

violentar ⟨1a⟩ *v/t puerta* force; *(incomodar)* embarrass

violento *adj* violent; *(embarazoso)* embarrassing; *persona* embarrassed

violeta 1 *f* BOT violet **2** *m/adj* violet

violín *m* violin

violinista *m/f* violinist

violonc(h)elo *m* cello

VIP *m* VIP

viperino *adj* malicious; *lengua -a* sharp tongue

viral *adj* viral

virar ⟨1a⟩ *v/t* MAR, AVIA turn

virgen 1 *adj* virgin; *cinta* blank; *lana virgen* pure new wool **2** *f* virgin

virginidad *f* virginity

Virgo *m/f inv* ASTR Virgo

virguería *f*: *hace virguerías* P he's a whizz F

vírico *adj* viral

viril *adj* virile, manly

virtual *adj* virtual

virtud *f* virtue; *en virtud de* by virtue of

virtuoso 1 *adj* virtuous **2** *m*, *-a f* virtuoso

viruela *f* MED smallpox

virulento *adj* MED, *fig* virulent

virus *m inv* MED virus; *virus informático* computer virus

viruta *f* shaving

visa *f L.Am.* visa

visado *m* visa

víscera *f* vision, sight; *fig* vision; *(opinión)* ~

vísceras *fpl* guts, entrails

visceral *adj fig* gut *atr*, visceral

viscoso *adj* viscous

visera *f de gorra* peak; *de casco* visor

visibilidad *f* visibility

visible *adj* visible; *fig* evident, obvious

visillo *m* sheer, *Br* net curtain

visión *f* vision, sight; *fig* vision; *(opinión)* view; *tener visión de futuro* be forward looking

visita *f* visit; *visita a domicilio* house call; *visita guiada* guided tour; *hacer una visita a alguien* visit s.o.

visitante 1 *adj* visiting; DEP away **2** *m/f* visitor

visitar ⟨1a⟩ *v/t* visit

vislumbrar ⟨1a⟩ *v/t* glimpse

visos *mpl*: *tener visos de* show signs of

visón *m* ZO mink

víspera *f* eve; *en vísperas de* on the eve of

vista *f* (eye)sight; JUR hearing; *vista cansada* MED tired eyes; *a la vista* COM at sight, on demand; *a primera vista* at first sight; *con vistas a* with a view to; *en vista de* in view of; *hasta la vista* bye!, see you!; *hacer la vista gorda* *fig* F turn a blind eye; *tener vista para algo fig* have a good eye for sth; *volver la vista atrás tb fig* look back

vistazo *m* look; *echar un vistazo a* take a (quick) look at

viste *vb* → *ver, vestir*

visto 1 *part* → *ver* **2** *adj*: *está bien visto* it's the done thing; *está mal visto* it's not done, it's not the done thing; *está visto que* it's obvious that; *por lo visto* apparently **3** *m* check(mark), *Br* tick; *dar el visto bueno* give one's approval

vistoso *adj* eye-catching

visual *adj* visual

visualizar ⟨1f⟩ *v/t* visualize; *en pantalla* display

vital *adj* vital; *persona* lively

vitalicio *adj* life *atr*, for life; *renta -a* life annuity

vitalidad *f* vitality, liveliness

vitamina *f* vitamin

viticultor *m*, **viticultura** *f* wine grower

vítores *mpl* cheers, acclaim *sg*

vitorear ⟨1a⟩ *v/t* cheer

vítreo *adj* vitreous

vitrificar ⟨1g⟩ *v/t* vitrify

vitrina *f* display cabinet; *L.Am.* shop window

vitrocerámica *f* ceramic hob

vituperar ⟨1a⟩ *v/t* condemn

viuda *f* widow

viudedad *f* widowhood; *pensión de viudedad* widow's pension

viudo 1 *adj* widowed **2** *m* widower; *quedarse viudo* be widowed

viva *int* hurrah!; *¡viva el rey!* long live the king!

vivaz *adj* bright, sharp

vivencia *f* experience

víveres *mpl* provisions

vívido *adj* vivid

vivienda *f* housing; *(casa)* house

vivir ⟨3a⟩ **1** *v/t* live through, experience **2** *v/i* live; *vivir de algo* live on sth

vivo *adj* alive; *color* bright; *ritmo* lively; *fig* F sharp, smart

vocabulario *m* vocabulary

vocación *f* vocation

vocal 1 *m/f* member **2** *f* vowel

vocalista *m/f* vocalist

vocalizar ⟨1f⟩ *v/i* vocalize

voceador *m*, **voceadora** *f Méx* newspaper vendor

vocerío *m* uproar

vocero *m*, **-a** *f esp L.Am.* spokesperson

vociferar ⟨1a⟩ *v/i* shout

vodka *m* vodka

volador *adj* flying

volandas: *en volandas fig* in the air

volante 1 *adj* flying **2** *m* AUTO steering wheel; *de vestido* flounce; MED referral (slip)

volar ⟨1m⟩ **1** *v/i* fly; *fig* vanish **2** *v/t* fly; *edificio* blow up

volátil *adj tb fig* volatile .

volatilizarse ⟨1f⟩ *v/r fig* vanish into thin air

volcán *m* volcano

volcánico *adj* volcanic

volcar ⟨1g & 1m⟩ **1** *v/t* knock over; *(vaciar)* empty; *barco, coche* overturn **2** *v/i de coche, barco* overturn **3** *v/r volcarse* tip over; *volcarse por alguien* F bend over backwards for s.o., go out of one's way for s.o.; *volcarse en algo* throw o.s. into sth

volea *f tenis* volley

voleibol *m* volleyball

voleo *m*: *a voleo* at random

voley-playa *m* beach volleyball

voltaje *m* EL voltage

voltear ⟨1a⟩ **1** *v/t L.Am. (invertir)* turn over; *Rpl (tumbar)* knock over; *voltear el jersey* turn the sweater inside out; *voltear la cabeza* turn one's head **2** *v/i* roll over; *de campanas* ring out

voltereta *f* somersault

voltio *m* EL volt

voluble *adj* erratic, unpredictable

volumen *m* TIP, MÚS, RAD volume; *volumen de negocios* COM turnover

voluntad *f* will; *buena / mala voluntad* good / ill will

voluntario 1 *adj* volunteer **2** *m*, *-a f* volunteer

voluntarioso *adj* willing, enthusiastic

voluptuoso *adj* voluptuous

volver ⟨2h; *part* **vuelto** ⟩ **1** *v/t página, mirada etc* turn (*a* to; *hacia* toward); *volver loco* drive crazy **2** *v/i return; *volver a hacer algo* do sth again **3** *v/r* volverse turn round; *volverse loco* go crazy

vomitar ⟨1a⟩ **1** *v/t* throw up; *lava* hurl, throw out **2** *v/i* throw up, be sick; *tengo ganas de vomitar* I feel nauseous, *Br* I feel sick

vómito *m* MED vomit

vorágine *f (remolino)* whirlpool; *fig* whirl

voraz *adj* voracious; *incendio* fierce

vos *pron pers sg Rpl, C.Am., Ven* you

vosotros, vosotras *pron pers pl* you

votación *f* vote, ballot

votar ⟨1a⟩ **1** *v/t (aprobar)* vote **2** *v/i* vote

voto *m* POL vote; *voto en blanco* spoiled ballot paper

voy *vb* → *ir*

voz *f* voice; *fig* rumo(u)r; *voz activa / pa-*

siva GRAM active / passive voice; *a media voz* in a hushed voice, in a low voice; *a voz en grito* at the top of one's voice; *en voz alta* aloud; *en voz baja* in a low voice; *correr la voz* spread the word; *llevar la voz cantante* fig call the tune, call the shots; *no tener voz ni voto* fig not have a say; *voz en off* voice-over
vuelco 1 vb → *volcar* **2** m: *dar un vuelco* fig take a dramatic turn; *me dio un vuelco el corazón* my heart missed a beat
vuelo 1 vb → *volar* **2** m flight; *vuelo chárter* charter flight; *vuelo nacional* domestic flight; *al vuelo coger, cazar* in mid-air; *una falda con vuelo* a full skirt

vuelta f return; *en carrera* lap; *vuelta de carnero* L.Am. half-somersault; *vuelta al mundo* round-the- world trip; *a la vuelta* on the way back; *a la vuelta de la esquina* fig just around the corner; *dar la vuelta* llave etc turn; *dar media vuelta* turn round; *dar una vuelta* go for a walk; *dar cien vueltas a alguien* F be a hundred times better than s.o. F
vuelto 1 part → *volver* **2** m L.Am. change
vuelvo vb → *volver*
vuestro 1 adj pos your **2** pron yours
vulgar adj vulgar, common; *abundante* common
vulgaridad f vulgarity
vulgo m lower classes pl
vulnerable adj vulnerable

W

w. abr (= *watio*) w (= watt)
walkman m personal stereo
wáter m bathroom, toilet
waterpolo m DEP water polo

WC abr WC
whisky m whiskey, Br whisky
windsurf(ing) m wind-surfing
windsurfista m/f windsurfer

X, Y

xenofobia f xenophobia
xilófono m MÚS xylophone
y conj and
ya adv already; (*ahora mismo*) now; *¡ya! incredulidad* oh, yeah!, sure!; *comprensión* I know, I understand; *asenso* OK, sure; *al terminar* finished!, done!; *ya no vive aquí* he doesn't live here any more, he no longer lives here; *ya que* since, as; *ya lo sé* I know; *ya viene* she's coming now; *¿lo puede hacer? – ¡ya lo creo!* can she do it? - you bet!; *ya ... ya ...* either ... or ...
yacaré m L.Am. ZO cayman
yacer ⟨2y⟩ v/i lie
yacimiento m MIN deposit
yanqui m/f Yankee
yapa f L.Am. bit extra (for free); Pe, Bol

(*propina*) tip
yate m yacht
yaya f grandma
yayo m grandpa
yedra f BOT ivy
yegua f ZO mare
yema f yolk; *yema del dedo* fingertip
yendo vb → *ir*
yerba f L.Am. grass; *yerba mate* maté
yerbatero m, -a f Rpl herbalist
yerno m son-in-law
yeso m plaster
yo pron I; *soy yo* it's me; *yo que tú* if I were you
yodo m iodine
yoga m yoga
yogur m yog(h)urt
yonqui m/f F junkie

yuca f BOT yucca
yugo m yoke
Yugoslavia Yugoslavia
yugoslavo 1 adj Yugoslav(ian) **2** m, **-a** f Yugoslav(ian)

yugular adj ANAT jugular
yute m jute
yuxtaposición f juxtaposition
yuyo m L.Am. weed

Z

zacatal m C.Am., Méx pasture
zacate m C.Am., Méx fodder
zafarse ⟨1a⟩ v/r get away (**de** from); (soltarse) come undone; **zafarse de algo** (evitar) get out of sth
zafio adj coarse
zafiro m sapphire
zaga f: **ir a la zaga** bring up the rear
zalamero 1 adj flattering; empalagoso syrupy, sugary **2** m, **-a** f flatterer, sweet talker
zamba f Arg (baile) Argentinian folkdance
zambomba f MÚS type of drum
zambullirse ⟨3h⟩ v/r dive (**en** into); fig throw o.s. (**en** into), immerse o.s. (**en** in)
zamparse ⟨1a⟩ v/r F wolf down F
zanahoria f carrot
zancada f stride
zancadilla f fig obstacle; **poner** or **echar la zancadilla a alguien** trip s.o. up
zancudo m L.Am. mosquito
zángano m zo drone; fig F lazybones sg
zanja f ditch
zanjar ⟨1a⟩ v/t fig problemas settle; dificultades overcome
zapatería f shoe store, shoe shop
zapatero m, **-a** f shoemaker; **zapatero remendón** shoe mender
zapatilla f slipper; de deporte sneaker, Br trainer
Zapatista m/f Méx member or supporter of the Zapatista National Liberation Army
zapato m shoe
zapear ⟨1a⟩ v/i TV F channel hop
zapeo, zapping m TV F channel hopping
zarandear ⟨1a⟩ v/t shake violently, buffet;

zarandear a alguien fig give s.o. a hard time
zarpa f paw
zarpar ⟨1a⟩ v/i MAR set sail (**para** for)
zarza f BOT bramble
zarzamora f BOT blackberry
zarzuela f MÚS type of operetta
zascandilear ⟨1a⟩ v/i mess around
zigzaguear ⟨1a⟩ v/i zigzag
zinc m zinc
zócalo m baseboard, Br skirting board
zodíaco, zodiaco m AST zodiac
zona f area, zone
zoncería f L.Am. F stupid thing
zonzo adj L.Am. F stupid
zoo m zoo
zoológico 1 adj zoological **2** m zoo
zoom m FOT zoom
zopilote m L.Am. zo turkey buzzard
zorra f zo vixen; P whore P
zorro 1 adj sly, crafty **2** m zo fox; fig old fox
zozobrar ⟨1a⟩ v/i MAR overturn; fig go under
zueco m clog
zulo m hiding place
zumba f L.Am., Méx (paliza) beating
zumbar ⟨1a⟩ **1** v/i buzz; **me zumban los oídos** my ears are ringing o buzzing **2** v/t golpe, bofetada give
zumbido m buzzing
zumo m juice
zurcir ⟨3b⟩ v/t calcetines darn; chaqueta, pantalones patch
zurdo 1 adj left-handed **2** m, f left-hander
zurrar ⟨1a⟩ v/t TÉC tan; **zurrar a alguien** F tan s.o.'s hide F

Activity & Reference Section

The following section contains three parts, each of which will help you in your learning:

Games and puzzles to help you learn to use this dictionary and practice your Spanish-language skills. You'll learn about the different features of this dictionary and how to look something up effectively.

Basic words and expressions to reinforce your learning and help you master the basics.

A short grammar reference to help you use the language correctly.

Using Your Dictionary

Using a bilingual dictionary is important if you want to speak, read or write in a foreign language. Unfortunately, if you don't understand the symbols in your dictionary or the format of the entries, you'll make mistakes.

What kind of mistakes? Think of some of the words you know in English that sound or look alike. For example, think about the word *ring*. How many meanings can you think of for this word, *ring*? Try to list at least three.

a. _____

b. _____

c. _____

Now look up *ring* in the English side of the dictionary. There are nine Spanish words that correspond to the single English word *ring*. Some of these Spanish words are listed below in scrambled form.

Unscramble the jumbled Spanish words, then draw a line connecting each Spanish word with of the appropriate English meaning.

Spanish jumble	English meanings
1. ROSNA	a. a circle around something
2. LONAIL	b. the action of a bell or telephone (to ring)
3. ATSPI	c. jewelry worn on the finger
4. NOOT	d. the boxing venue
5. GNRI	e. one of the venues at a circus
6. LÍCCURO	f. the ring or tone of someone's voice

With so many Spanish words, each meaning something different, you must be careful to choose the right one. Using the wrong definition can obscure your meaning. Imagine the bizarre and misleading sentences you would make if you never looked beyond the first definition.

For example:

The boxer wearily entered the circle.

She always wore the circle left to her by her grandmother.

I was waiting for the phone circle when there was a knock at the door.

If you choose the wrong definition, you simply won't be understood. Mistakes like these are easy to avoid, once you know what to look for when using your dictionary. The following pages will review the structure of your bilingual dictionary and show you how to pick the right word when you use it. Read the tips and guidelines, then complete the puzzles and exercises to practice what you have learned.

Identifying Headwords

If you are looking for a single word in the dictionary, you simply look for that word's location in alphabetical order. However, if you are looking for a phrase, or an object that is described by several words, you will have to decide which word to look up.

Two-word terms are listed by their first word. If you are looking for the Spanish equivalent of *shooting star*, you will find it under *shooting*.

So-called phrasal verbs in English are found in a block under the main verb. The phrasal verbs *go ahead*, *go back*, *go off*, *go on*, *go out*, and *go up* are all found in a block after *go*.

Idiomatic expressions are found under the key word in the expression. The phrase *give someone a ring*, meaning to call someone, is found in the entry for *ring*.

Feminine headwords that are variants of a masculine headword and share a meaning with the masculine word will be found in alphabetical order with their masculine counterpart. In Spanish a male lawyer is called an **abogado** and a female lawyer is an **abogada**. Both of the words are found in alphabetical order under the masculine form, **abogado**.

Find the following words and phrases in your bilingual dictionary. Identify the headword under which you should look for each. Then, try to find all of the headwords in the word-search puzzle on the next page.

1. in the middle of
2. be in shock
3. break in
4. dog
5. bring up
6. string someone along
7. be in jeopardy
8. get away with it

9. that's a relief
10. take advantage of
11. bailarín
12. tan pronto como
13. sin duda
14. colgar de un hilo
15. menos mal

z	h	r	u	o	v	ó	l	x	q	r	e	r	p	o	u	j	k
u	g	c	d	u	a	v	c	l	x	f	í	u	c	t	e	c	i
í	a	e	z	ó	v	c	d	e	ñ	u	i	a	j	l	j	k	u
m	e	q	t	b	a	h	g	l	w	a	o	á	e	p	i	r	y
e	é	w	c	i	o	a	p	f	m	l	r	g	o	h	r	e	s
k	n	k	b	g	t	y	z	o	i	u	n	i	p	b	s	h	f
c	f	ñ	i	n	g	b	s	h	z	i	d	r	a	a	i	g	e
í	s	e	a	d	n	r	f	e	r	e	a	á	r	i	y	n	t
u	e	v	o	l	u	e	r	t	a	e	l	d	d	l	o	o	r
s	d	e	n	u	m	a	s	ó	m	s	e	z	y	a	e	t	y
a	h	d	s	o	i	k	b	r	i	n	g	w	o	r	l	m	s
ñ	e	o	d	q	m	i	d	d	l	e	j	d	l	í	r	a	q
b	d	g	c	o	r	g	l	e	y	d	n	i	o	n	u	l	l
e	z	g	n	k	z	w	a	c	s	u	n	s	e	i	e	a	f
l	w	y	u	f	v	é	ó	o	i	d	a	i	l	q	r	t	g
c	é	f	g	i	r	a	m	l	o	a	c	e	d	u	i	á	a
a	n	r	y	t	e	i	s	e	g	p	r	o	n	t	o	a	w
u	ñ	a	c	a	s	n	e	l	e	h	s	e	s	g	r	d	ó

Alphabetization

The entries in a bilingual dictionary are in alphabetical order. They are ordered from A to Z for each language. If words begin with the same letter or letters, they are alphabetized from A to Z using the first unique letter in each word.

Practice alphabetizing the following words. Rewrite the words in alphabetical order, using the space provided below. Next to each word also write the number that is associated with it. Then follow that order to connect the dots on the next page. Not all of the dots will be used, only those whose numbers appear in the word list.

universo	1	fecha	48
sueño	2	hasta	57
ciudad	3	calle	59
escuela	4	repente	60
nos	7	hoy	62
aquí	8	bastante	65
entender	9	mágico	74
disfraz	10	mañana	75
cuchillo	15	vida	76
jamás	16	algo	77
lente	17	zapato	77
tiempo	20	marrón	79
boleta	21	pie	81
nadie	23	otro	82
dulce	27	miel	84
más	30	lavaplatos	86
corazón	41	gritar	87
piel	42	miedo	93
así	44	flor	95
silla	45	despacio	99
llover	46		

¿Qué país ve Ud.?

Spelling

Like any dictionary, a bilingual dictionary will tell you if you have spelled a word right. But how can you look up a word if you don't know how to spell it? Though it may be time consuming, the only way to check your spelling with a dictionary is to take your best guess, or your best guesses, and look to see which appears in the dictionary.

Practice checking your spelling using the words below. Each group includes one correct spelling and three incorrect spellings. Look up the words and cross out the misspelled versions (the ones you do not find in the dictionary). Rewrite the correct spelling in the blanks on the next page. When you have filled in all of the blanks, use the circled letters to reveal a mystery message.

1. esfara	esfera	esfira	esfura
2. devisa	deviza	divisa	diviza
3. mendir	mentir	mindir	mintir
4. viata	viota	viuda	viuta
5. abagado	apagedo	apagado	apadato
6. paor	peor	pior	pour
7. mammeca	manmeca	mandeca	manteca
8. jarbín	jardén	jardín	jartiín
9. corana	corena	corona	coruna

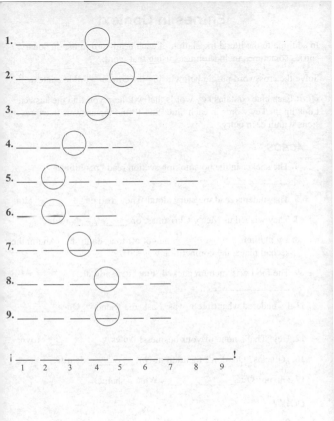

Entries in Context

In addition to the literal translation of each headword in the dictionary, entries sometimes include phrases using that word.

Solve the crossword puzzle below using the correct word in context.

Hint: Each clue contains key words that will help you find the answer. Look up the key words in each clue. You'll find the answers in expressions within each entry.

ACROSS

4. The sticker in the no smoking section read "**prohibido** _____."

5. The students read the story aloud. They read **en** _____ **alta**.

7. They wished us Merry Christmas, or _____ **Navidad**.

8. **En primer** _____, he got off to a rough start. And in the second place, the competition was stiff.

9. The food was vacuum packed. **Fue envasado al** _____.

11. I wondered what time it was; I asked a friend, "**¿Qué** _____ **es?**"

12. Hey! That's none of your business! **No es** _____ **tuyo.**

16. ¿Gracias? Oh, don't mention it. **No** _____ **de qué.**

17. Oh, no! **Qué** _____. What a shame!

DOWN

1. She had lost her lighter, so she asked her friend for a light, "**¿Tienes** _____**?**"

2. It's pouring rain! **Está lloviendo a** _____.

3. He plans to be in the lead soon. **Va a estar en** _____.

5. Do you dine out once in a while? Sure, **de** _____ **en cuando.**

6. Tonight she will pick out her clothes and pack her bags (**hacer la
_____**). Tomorrow she is leaving on vacation.

10. They have open-air seating on the patio, if you'd prefer to dine **al
_____ libre**.

11. _____ **en día** (nowadays), many women have careers. This
may not have been the case for previous generations.

13. The weather is nice. It's sunny out. **Hace _____.**

14. Good night. ¡**Buenas _____!** See you again tomorrow.

15. You wonder if it is worth all the trouble? I think so. **En mi
opinion, vale la _____.**

Word Families

Some English words have several related meanings that are represented by different words in Spanish. These related meanings belong to the same word family and are grouped together under a single English headword. Other words, while they look the same, do not belong to the same word family. These words are written under a separate headword.

Think back to our first example, *ring*. The translations **círculo**, **anillo**, and **pista** all refer to related meanings of *ring* in English. They are all circular things, though in different contexts. **Timbrazo**, **dar un telefonazo a alguien**, and **sonar**, however, refer to a totally different meaning of *ring* in English: the sound a bell or phone makes.

The word family for circles, with all of its nuanced Spanish translations, is grouped together under *ring¹*. The word family for sounds is grouped together under *ring²*.

Study the lists of words below. Each group includes three Spanish translations belonging to one word family, and one Spanish translation of an identical-looking but unrelated English word. Eliminate the translation that is not in the same word family as the others. Then rewrite the misfit word in the corresponding blanks. When you have filled in all of the blanks, use the circled letters to reveal a bonus message.

Hint: Look up the Spanish words to find out what they mean. Then look up those words in the English-Spanish side of your dictionary to find the word family that contains the Spanish words.

1. encender	iluminar	ligero	luz
2. atasco	aprieto	embutir	mermelada
3. a juego	fósforo	igualar	partida
4. estampilla	patear	sello	timbre
5. anillo	cuadrilátero	pista	timbrazo

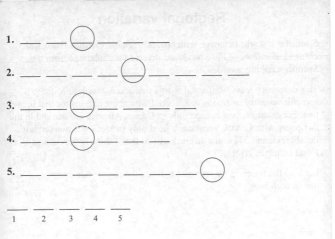

1. ___ ___ ⊖ ___ ___ ___ ___

2. ___ ___ ___ ___ ⊖ ___ ___ ___ ___ ___

3. ___ ___ ⊖ ___ ___ ___ ___ ___ ___

4. ___ ___ ⊖ ___ ___ ___ ___ ___ ___ ___

5. ___ ___ ___ ___ ___ ___ ___ ___ ⊖ ___

___ ___ ___ ___ ___
1   2   3   4   5

Regional variation

Spanish is a world language with several regional variants. Historical change and influence have produced diverse vocabularies across the Spanish-speaking world.

This dictionary leaves universal words unmarked. Words specific to a particular country or region are marked with abbreviations for that location. For example, words used only in Central America are marked in the dictionary with **C.Am**. Vocabulary used only in Mexico is marked with the abbreviation **Méx**, and so forth. A full list of these abbreviations is found on pages 10–11.

Look up the following words and indicate the regional or country affiliation in each box.

carro	majada	tuna	pelazón	abarrotes
afanar	papa	rebasar	terno	abalear
choclo	ñapa	corotos	chichera	chompa
chicha	frutilla	huachafo	egreso	okupa
plática	vecindad	hilachos	mañero	guanaco

If this puzzle were a BINGO card, which country or region would win?

_____

Running Heads

Running heads are the words printed in blue at the top of each page. The running head on the left tells you the first headword on the left-hand page. The running head on the right tells you the last headword on the right-hand page. All the words that fall in alphabetical order between the two running heads appear on those two dictionary pages.

Look up the running head on the page where each headword appears, and write it in the space provided. Then unscramble the jumbled running heads and match them with what you wrote.

Headword	Running head	Jumbled running head
1. apenas	APAGAR	FOLOCNÓ
2. bombilla		CILIMO
3. cómodo		ÍTFICNOPE
4. famoso		SUTOJ
5. joven		MOOSS
6. magia		RAAGAP
7. minuto		OOPCA
8. oreja		CEHILBO
9. polvo		DARALSATR
10. sorna		NEIVE
11. transición		GIAAM
12. vetusto		CAHFAAD

Parts of Speech

In Spanish and English, words are categorized into different **parts of speech**. These labels tell us what function a word performs in a sentence. In this dictionary, the part of speech is given before a word's definition.

Nouns are things. **Verbs** describe actions. **Adjectives** describe nouns in sentences. For example, the adjective *pretty* tells you about the noun *girl* in the phrase *a pretty girl*. **Adverbs** also describe, but they modify verbs, adjectives, and other adverbs. The adverb *quickly* tells you more about how the action is carried out in the phrase *ran quickly*.

Prepositions specify relationships in time and space. They are words such as *in, on, before,* or *with*. **Articles** are words that accompany nouns. Words like *the* and *a* or *an* modify the noun, marking it as specific or general, and known or unknown

Conjunctions are words like *and, but,* and *if* that join phrases and sentences together. **Pronouns** take the place of nouns in a sentence.

The following activity uses words from the dictionary in a Sudoku-style puzzle. In Sudoku puzzles, the numbers 1 to 9 are used to fill in grids. All digits 1 to 9 must appear, but cannot be repeated, in each square, row, and column.

In the following puzzles, you are given a set of words for each part of the grid. Look up each word to find out its part of speech. Then arrange the words within the square so that, in the whole puzzle, you do not repeat any part of speech within a column or row.

Hint: If one of the words given in the puzzle is a noun, then you know that no other nouns can be put in that row or column of the grid. Use the process of elimination to figure out where the other parts of speech can go.

Let's try a small puzzle first. You will use the categories noun *n*, verb *v*, adjective *adj*, and preposition *prp* to solve this puzzle. The sections are numbered from top left to bottom right.

Part 1

a, beber, cocina, **correcto**

Part 2

de, **donación**, escapar, espartano

Part 3

en, huelga, inferior, jugar

Part 4

lotería, **montar**, móvil, para

	correcto		
			donación
		montar	
en			

Now try a larger puzzle. For this puzzle, you will use the categories noun *n*, verb *v*, adjective *adj*, preposition *prp*, article *art*, and pronoun *pron*. The sections are numbered from top left to bottom right.

Part 1

antiguo, **ascensor**, **batir**, la, él, en

Part 2

charla, dócil, **educar**, ella, entre, los

Part 3

cierto, con, cola, **descansar**, **nosotros**, una

Part 4

cultura, **exclusivo**, ellos, leer, sin, un

Part 5

a, diferente, ejercer, ejemplo, **las**, **yo**

Part 6

de, el, familia, mantener, marinero, **Usted**

		batir	charla		
ascensor					educar
	descansar			cultura	
una	nosotros			exclusivo	
a		las			Usted
		yo	de		

Gender

Spanish nouns belong to one of two groups: feminine or masculine. A noun's gender is indicated in an entry after the headword or pronunciation with **m** for masculine, **f** for feminine, and **m/f** if the same form of the word can be used for a man or a woman.

In some cases, the masculine and feminine forms of one word mean two different things. For example, the masculine **un partido** means *a political party*. The feminine **una partida** means *a game or match*. The gender associated with each meaning follows the headword in the dictionary entry.

Look up the words in the grids below. Circle the feminine words. Put an **X** through the masculine words.

pie	persona	mano
distrito	huracán	computadora
lengua	jamón	disco

naranja	saco	manzana
estrella	mesa	objeto
miel	miedo	tren

gorro	océano	estación
escalera	onda	sirena
sabor	policía	lobo

Think of these as tic-tac-toe grids. Does masculine or feminine win more matches?

Adjectives

Adjectives in Spanish change form to agree in gender and number with the noun they modify. In many cases, the feminine form ends in −a, and the masculine form ends in −o. An −s is added to make the plural for either gender. Some adjectives have irregular forms, in this case, the irregular forms are written out after the headword.

Use the dictionary to determine whether the nouns in the following phrases are masculine or feminine, singular or plural. Then write in the correct inflected form of the adjective. Check your answers against the word search. The correct forms are found in the puzzle.

1. a difficult exam   un examen _____

2. a tall woman   una mujer _____

3. an important message   un mensaje _____

4. secondary school   la escuela _____

5. the red cars   los carros _____

6. an unforgettable picnic   un picnic _____

7. a beautiful girl   una chica _____

8. a romantic song   una canción _____

9. the first time   la _____ vez

10. two Peruvian monuments   dos monumentos _____

11. a heavy backpack   una mochila _____

t	r	v	g	m	l	u	o	b	p	o	á	o	a	e	l	é	ó
f	e	á	i	f	í	n	l	ú	b	i	s	ú	t	u	é	n	i
k	p	a	i	c	o	b	v	m	h	e	a	i	l	ú	q	a	r
p	r	c	b	ú	g	m	s	i	t	p	e	r	u	a	n	o	s
g	i	b	o	u	m	c	é	a	ñ	e	ú	w	e	k	s	g	u
q	m	i	n	r	d	e	c	y	o	d	i	g	í	f	k	e	é
á	e	s	i	d	o	i	e	á	c	z	i	b	e	m	f	o	b
n	r	á	t	á	t	s	i	e	u	e	ú	f	i	o	n	d	e
n	a	ó	a	n	u	é	i	a	ú	ú	p	l	í	u	t	i	ó
u	s	e	á	p	í	j	e	a	c	r	v	m	c	c	o	u	í
í	é	m	o	p	e	s	a	d	a	e	l	j	e	é	i	à	d
p	o	c	i	t	s	e	c	u	n	d	a	r	i	a	u	l	v
r	u	o	a	b	e	a	l	t	a	é	a	o	g	h	g	é	e
r	o	v	á	p	k	s	x	p	h	a	r	w	g	a	h	g	a
é	w	ó	i	d	o	u	e	i	m	p	o	r	t	a	n	t	e
é	s	u	z	j	e	v	c	g	u	o	á	ú	o	i	é	v	u
v	o	n	o	i	e	n	i	z	é	e	i	v	u	h	o	k	í
p	z	r	i	n	o	l	v	i	d	a	b	l	e	b	p	l	v
i	s	c	f	a	i	p	e	t	k	ó	i	f	é	e	a	g	u
é	e	e	d	í	v	c	i	o	s	é	h	s	r	r	f	z	é

Verbs

Verbs are listed in the dictionary in their infinitive form. To use the verb in a sentence, you must conjugate it and use the form that agrees with the sentence's subject.

Most verbs fall into categories with other verbs that are conjugated in the same way. In the verb appendix of this dictionary, you will find an example of each category, along with conjugations of common irregular verbs.

For this puzzle, conjugate the given verbs in the present tense. Use the context and the subject pronoun to determine the person and number of the form you need. The correct answer fits in the crossword spaces provided.

Hint: The verb class code given in the verb's dictionary entry tells you which model conjugation to follow.

ACROSS

2. Los jugadores _____ Cubanos, de la Habana. **ser**

4. Yo _____ el periódico por la mañana. **leer**

5. Los sábados, yo _____ con mi familia. **descansar**

8. Yo tengo un gato, y él _____ un perro. **tener**

9. Tú _____ a la fiesta ¿verdad? **ir**

11. Nosotros _____ al cine. **ir**

13. Mis hijos _____ mucho la televisión. **mirar**

14. Yo _____ siempre las llaves. **perder**

15. Carlos _____ la maleta antes de ir de vacaciones. **hacer**

16. Tú _____ visitar Machu Picchu? **querer**

17. ¿Ustedes _____ una palabra en el diccionario? **buscar**

18. Machu Picchu _____ en el Perú. **estar**

DOWN

1. Nosotros _____ cuando habla el profesor. **comprender**

3. Los amigos _____ algo en la cafetería antes de comer. **beber**

6. Los alumnos _____ de la clase a las tres. **salir**

7. Yo _____ por lo menos ocho horas por noche. **dormir**

9. Nosotros siempre _____ a Sudamérica. **viajar**

10. El equipo argentino _____ el partido. **ganar**

12. Ella _____ la puerta cuando llega a casa. **cerrar**

When you are reading Spanish, you face a different challenge. You see a conjugated verb in context and need to determine what its infinitive is in order to understand its meaning.

For the next puzzle, you will see conjugated verbs in the sentences. Figure out which verb the conjugated form represents, and write the infinitive (the headword form) in the puzzle.

ACROSS

3. Martín y Anita **llegaron** a las ocho.

5. ¿Por qué no **viene** a la fiesta tu novio?

7. ¡**Ganamos**!

10. Quiero que Ustedes **hagan** la tarea.

11. Las hojas **caen** en el otoño.

13. El chico **esconde** los caramelos.

15. No entiendo lo que **dices**.

16. Rita **cumple** diez años mañana.

18. Sofia **compartió** su bocadillo con sus amigos.

19. ¿Qué te **parece** el libro?

DOWN

1. No **volvimos** a casa.

2. Los alumnos **dieron** el examen.

4. A los niños les **gustan** mucho los videojuegos.

6. Ellos **hablaban** siempre con los amigos.

8. Las mujeres **prepararon** la cena.

9. Que yo **sepa**, está bien.

12. **Tomas** el sol en la playa.

14. El gato **se duerme** en el sillón.

16. Los abuelos **comieron** en casa.

17. El se **murió**.

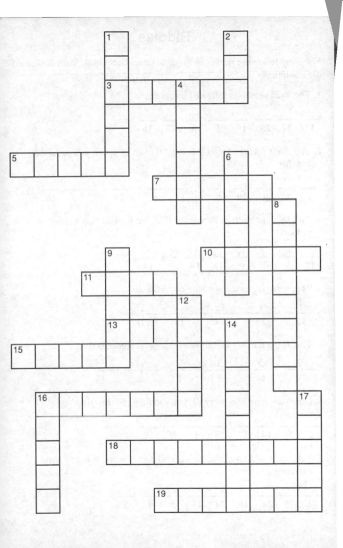

Riddles

Solve the following riddles in English. Give the Spanish word for the riddle's solution.

1. This cold season is followed by spring.

$\overline{}\ \overline{}\ \overline{}\ \overline{}\ \overline{}\ \overline{}\ \overline{}\ \overline{}$
15 27 25 15 5 6 27 16

2. You don't want to forget this type of clothing when you go to the beach.

$\overline{}\ \overline{}\ \overline{}\ \overline{}\ \overline{}\quad\overline{}\ \overline{}\quad\overline{}\ \overline{}\ \overline{}\ \overline{}$
1 6 9 20 5   13 5   28 9 7 16

3. This thing protects you from the rain, but it's bad luck to open it indoors!

p   a   r   a   g   u   a   s
17 9   6   9   14 14 9   10

4. This adjective is the opposite of "difficult."

f   a   c   i   l
12 29 24 15 18

5. This is the number that follows three and precedes five.

c   u   a   t   r   o
24 14 9   1   6   16

6. If you are injured or very ill, you should go to this place.

$\overline{}\ \overline{}\ \overline{}\ \overline{}\ \overline{}\ \overline{}\ \overline{}\ \overline{}$
2 16 10 17 15 1 9 18

7. This mode of transportation has only two wheels. It is also good exercise!

$\overline{}\ \overline{}\ \overline{}\ \overline{}\ \overline{}\ \overline{}\ \overline{}\ \overline{}\ \overline{}$
28 15 24 15 24 18 5 1 5

8. This large mammal lives in the ocean.

$\overline{\text{28}}$ $\overline{\text{9}}$ $\overline{\text{18}}$ $\overline{\text{18}}$ $\overline{\text{5}}$ $\overline{\text{27}}$ $\overline{\text{9}}$

9. This person is your mother's mother.

$\overline{\text{9}}$ $\overline{\text{28}}$ $\overline{\text{14}}$ $\overline{\text{9}}$ $\overline{\text{18}}$ $\overline{\text{9}}$

10. There are twelve of these in a year.

$\overline{\text{26}}$ $\overline{\text{5}}$ $\overline{\text{10}}$

11. Wearing this in the car is a safety precaution.

$\overline{\text{24}}$ $\overline{\text{15}}$ $\overline{\text{27}}$ $\overline{\text{1}}$ $\overline{\text{14}}$ $\overline{\text{6}}$ $\overline{\text{30}}$ $\overline{\text{27}}$ $\overline{\text{13}}$ $\overline{\text{5}}$

$\overline{\text{10}}$ $\overline{\text{5}}$ $\overline{\text{11}}$ $\overline{\text{14}}$ $\overline{\text{6}}$ $\overline{\text{15}}$ $\overline{\text{13}}$ $\overline{\text{9}}$ $\overline{\text{13}}$

12. Snow White bit into this red fruit and fell into a long slumber.

$\overline{\text{26}}$ $\overline{\text{9}}$ $\overline{\text{27}}$ $\overline{\text{22}}$ $\overline{\text{9}}$ $\overline{\text{27}}$ $\overline{\text{9}}$

13. This professional brings letters and packages to your door.

$\overline{\text{24}}$ $\overline{\text{9}}$ $\overline{\text{6}}$ $\overline{\text{1}}$ $\overline{\text{5}}$ $\overline{\text{6}}$ $\overline{\text{16}}$

14. This midday meal falls between breakfast and dinner.

$\overline{\text{9}}$ $\overline{\text{18}}$ $\overline{\text{26}}$ $\overline{\text{14}}$ $\overline{\text{5}}$ $\overline{\text{6}}$ $\overline{\text{22}}$ $\overline{\text{16}}$

15. A very young dog is referred to as this.

$\overline{\text{24}}$ $\overline{\text{9}}$ $\overline{\text{24}}$ $\overline{\text{2}}$ $\overline{\text{16}}$ $\overline{\text{6}}$ $\overline{\text{6}}$ $\overline{\text{16}}$

Cryptogram

Use the number-to-letter correspondence from the riddles to fill in the hidden message. When you are done, translate the Spanish message into English. What does it say?

14 U	27		26 O	16 i	13	15 S	10	26 O	16		5	27
5	10 S	17 P	9	7	16	18 l		13	15 i	24 C	5	
:		5	27		28	16	24	9 O				
	24 C	5	6 r	6 r	9	13	9	,		27	16 O	
5	27	1 t	6 r	9	27		26	16	10	24 C	9	10 S

Translation:

_____ _____ _____ _____ _____ _____ _____

_____ _____ _____ , _____

_____ _____ _____ .

Answer Key

Using Your Dictionary

a–c. Answers will vary

1. sonar, b
2. anillo, c
3. pista, e

4. tono, f
5. ring, d
6. círculo, a

Identifying Headwords

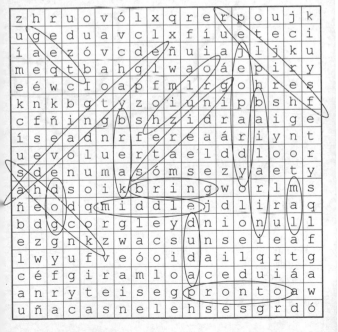

Alphabetization

algo, aquí, así, bastante, boleta, calle, ciudad, corazón, cuchillo,
despacio, disfraz, dulce, entender, escuela, fecha, flor, gritar, hasta,
hoy, jamás, lavaplatos, lente, llover, mágico, mañana, marrón, más,
miedo, miel, nadie, nos, otro, pie, piel, repente, silla, sueño, tiempo,
universo, vida, zapato

<u>M</u> E <u>X</u> I K <u>O</u>

Spelling

1. esfera
2. divisa
3. mentir
4. viuda
5. apagado

6. peor
7. manteca
8. jardín
9. corona

¡<u>E</u> S <u>T</u> <u>U</u> <u>P</u> E <u>N</u> <u>D</u> <u>O</u>!

Entries in Context

Word Families

1. ligero
2. mermelada
3. fósfero
4. patear
5. timbrazo

¡<u>G</u> <u>E</u> <u>S</u> <u>T</u> <u>O</u>!

Regional Variation

L. Am. carro	CSur majada	Mex tuna	C. Am. pelazón	L. Am. abarrotes
C. Am. afanar	L. Am. papa	Mex rebasar	CSur terno	S. Am. abalear
Rpl choclo	S. Am. ñapa	L. Am. corotos	C. Am. chichera	S. Am. chompa
L. Am. chicha	S. Am. frutilla	Pe huachafo	L. Am. egreso	Esp okupa
Mex plática	Mex vecindad	Mex hilachos	Rpl mañero	L. Am. guanaco

Latin America

Running Heads

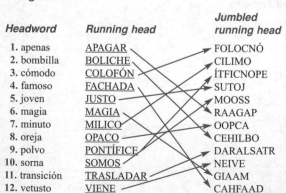

Headword	Running head	Jumbled running head
1. apenas	APAGAR	FOLOCNÓ
2. bombilla	BOLICHE	CILIMO
3. cómodo	COLOFÓN	ÍTFICNOPE
4. famoso	FACHADA	SUTOJ
5. joven	JUSTO	MOOSS
6. magia	MAGIA	RAAGAP
7. minuto	MILICO	OOPCA
8. oreja	OPACO	CEHILBO
9. polvo	PONTÍFICE	DARALSATR
10. sorna	SOMOS	NEIVE
11. transición	TRASLADAR	GIAAM
12. vetusto	VIENE	CAHFAAD

Parts of Speech

cocina	**correcto**	de	escapar
beber	a	espartano	**donación**
inferior	huelga	**montar**	para
en	jugar	lotería	móvil

él	la	**batir**	charla	entre	dócil
ascensor	en	antiguo	los	ella	**educar**
cierto	**descansar**	con	ellos	**cultura**	un
una	**nosotros**	cola	leer	**exclusivo**	sin
a	ejemplo	**las**	marinero	mantener	**Usted**
ejercer	diferente	**yo**	de	el	familia

Gender

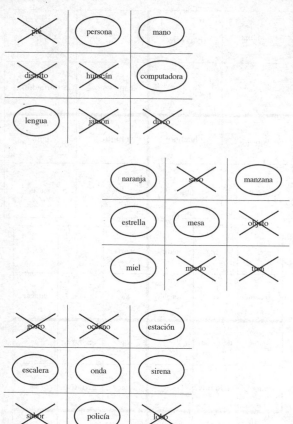

~~pie~~	persona	mano
disfruto	~~huracán~~	computadora
lengua	~~jabón~~	~~disco~~

naranja	~~saco~~	manzana
estrella	mesa	~~objeto~~
miel	~~miedo~~	~~tren~~

~~gorro~~	~~océano~~	estación
escalera	onda	sirena
~~sabor~~	policía	~~lobo~~

Feminine wins the most matches.

Adjectives

1. un examen **difícil**
2. una mujer **alta**
3. un mensaje **importante**
4. la escuela **secundaria**
5. los carros **rojos**
6. un picnic **inolvidable**
7. una chica **bonita**
8. una canción **romántica**
9. la **primera** vez
10. dos monumentos **peruanos**
11. una mochila **pesada**

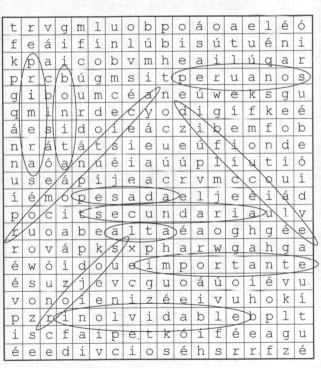

Verbs

Top puzzle

1. C
2. SON
3. B
4. LEO
5. DESCANSO
6.
7. DU...
8. TIENE
9. VAS
10. G
11. VAMOS
12. C
13. MIRAN
14. PIERDO
15. HACE
16. QUIERES
17. BUSCAN
18. ESTÁ

Down: COMPRENDEMOS, GANA, CAES, BAILAN, ALCANZA, DURAR, VIAJAMOS

Bottom puzzle

1. VOLVER
2. DAR
3. LLEGAR
4. GUSTAR
5. VENIR
6. HABLAR
7. GANAR
8. PREPARA
9. SUBE
10. HACER
11. CAER
12. TOMAR
13. ESCONDER
14. MORIR
15. DECIR
16. CUMPLIR
17. MORIR
18. COMPARTIR
19. PARECER

Down: COMER

Riddles

1. invierno
2. traje de baño
3. paraguas
4. fácil
5. cuatro
6. hospital
7. bicicleta
8. ballena
9. abuela
10. mes
11. cinturón de seguridad
12. manzana
13. cartero
14. almuerzo
15. cachorro

Cryptogram

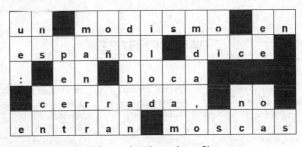

u	n		m	o	d	i	s	m	o		e	n
e	s	p	a	ñ	o	l		d	i	c	e	
:		e	n		b	o	c	a				
	c	e	r	r	a	d	a	,			n	o
e	n	t	r	a	n		m	o	s	c	a	s

A Spanish proverb says: into a closed mouth, no flies enter.

BASIC SPANISH PHRASES & GRAMMAR

Pronunciation

In this section we have used a simplified phonetic system to represent the sounds of Spanish. Simply read the pronunciation as if it were English.

Stress

The acute accent (´) is used in Spanish to indicate a syllable is stressed, e.g. **río** (reeo). Since some words have more than one meaning, the accent mark is also used to distinguish between them, e.g.: **él** (*he*) and **el** (*the*); **sí** (*yes*) and **si** (*if*).

BASIC PHRASES

Essential

Good afternoon!	¡Buenas tardes!	bweh-nahs tahrdehs
Good evening!	¡Buenas noches!	bweh-nahs nochehs
Goodbye!	¡Adiós!	ah-deeyos
..., please!	..., por favor.	por fahbor
Thank you!	¡Gracias!	grah-seeyahs
Yes.	Sí.	see
No.	No.	no
Sorry!	¡Lo siento!	lo seeyehn-to
Where are the restrooms?	¿Dónde están los baños?	dondeh ehstahn los bahnyos
When?	¿Cuándo?	kwahn-doh
What?	¿Qué?	keh
Where?	¿Dónde?	dondeh
Here.	Aquí.	ahkee
There.	Allí.	ahyee
On the right.	A la derecha.	ah lah dehrehchah
On the left.	A la izquierda.	ah lah eeskeeyehr-dah
Do you have ...?	¿Tiene ...?	teeyeh-neh
I'd like ...	Quisiera ...	keeseeyeh-rah
How much is that?	¿Cuánto cuesta?	kwahn-to kwehs-tah

| Where is ...? | ¿Dónde está ...? | dondeh ehstah |
| Where can I get ...? | ¿Dónde puedo encontrar ...? | dondeh pweh-doh ehnkontrahr |

Communication Difficulties

Do you speak English?	¿Habla inglés?	ah-blah een-glehs
Does anyone here speak English?	¿Hay alguien aquí que hable inglés?	eye ahl-geeyehn ah-keeh keh ah-bleh een-glehs
Did you understand that?	¿Ha entendido?	ah ehntehn-dee-doh
I understand.	Entiendo.	ehntiehn-doh
I didn't understand that.	No lo he entendido.	no lo eh ehntehn-dee-doh
Could you speak a bit more slowly, please?	¿Podría hablar un poco más despacio, por favor?	podree-ah ah-blahr oon poko mahs despah-seeyo por fahbor
Could you please repeat that?	¿Podría repetirlo, por favor?	podree-ah rehpeh-teer-lo por fahbor
What does ... mean?	¿Qué significa ...?	keh seegnee-fee-kah
Could you write it down for me, please?	¿Podría escribírmelo, por favor?	podree-ah ehskree-beer-mehlo por fahbor

Greetings

Good morning!	¡Buenos días!	bwehnos dee-ahs
Good afternoon!	¡Buenas tardes!	bwehnahs tahrdehs
Good evening/night!	¡Buenas noches!	bwehnahs nocheh
Hello!	¡Hola!	Olah
How are you?	¿Cómo está?	komo ehstah
How are things?	¿Qué tal?	keh tahl
Fine, thanks. And you?	Bien, gracias. ¿Y usted?	beeyehn grah-seeyahs ee oostehd
I'm afraid I have to go now.	Lo siento, pero me tengo que ir.	lo seeyehn-toh pehro meh tehngo keh eer
Goodbye!	¡Adiós!	ah-deeyos
See you soon / tomorrow!	¡Hasta pronto / mañana!	ahstah pronto / mah-nyah-nah

| It was nice meeting you. | Me alegro de haberle conocido. | meh ahleh-gro deh ah-behrleh kono-see-doh |
| Have a good trip! | ¡Buen viaje! | bwehn beeyah-kheh |

Meeting People

What's your name?	¿Cómo se llama / te llamas?	komo seh yahmah / teh yahmahs
My name is …	Me llamo …	meh yahmo
Where are you from?	¿De dónde es / eres?	deh dohndeh ehs / ehrehs
I'm from …	Soy de …	soy deh
– the US. –	los Estados Unidos.	los ehstah-dos oonee-dos
– Canada.	Canadá.	kah-nahdah
– the UK. –	Gran Bretaña.	grahn brehtah-nyah

Expressing Likes and Dislikes

Very good!	¡Muy bien!	mwee beeyehn
I'm very happy.	Estoy muy contento (m)/contenta (f).	ehs-toy mwee kon-tehnto/kon-tehn-tah
I like that.	Me gusta.	meh goos-tah
What a shame!	¡Qué pena!	keh pehnah
I'd rather …	Preferiría …	prehfehree-reeah
I don't like it.	No me gusta.	no meh goos-tah
I'd rather not.	No me apetece.	no meh ahpehteh-seh
Certainly not.	¡De ninguna manera!	deh neengoo-nah mahneh-rah

Expressing Requests and Thanks

Thank you very much.	Muchas gracias.	moochahs grah-seeyahs
Thanks, you too.	Gracias, igualmente.	grah-seeyahs eeg-wahl-mehnteh
May I?	¿Puedo?	pwehdoh

Please, ...	**Por favor ...**	por fahbor
No, thank you.	**No, gracias.**	no grah-seeyahs
Could you help me?	**¿Podría ayudarme?**	podree-ah ahy-oodahr-meh
That's very nice of you.	**Muy amable de su parte.**	mwee ahmah-bleh deh soo pahrteh
Thank you very much for all your trouble / help.	**Le agradezco las molestias / la ayuda.**	leh ahgrah-dehsko lahs molehs-teeyahs / lah ahyoodah
You're welcome.	**De nada.**	deh nahdah

Apologies

Sorry!	**¡Perdón!**	pehrdon
Excuse me!	**¡Perdone!**	pehr-doneh
I'm sorry about that.	**Lo siento.**	lo seeyehn-toh
Don't worry about it!	**¡No importa!**	no importah
How embarrassing!	**Esto me resulta muy desagradable.**	ehsto meh reh-sooltah mwee deh-sahgrah-dahbleh
It was a misunderstanding.	**Ha sido un malentendido.**	ah seedo oon mahlehn-tehndee-doh

GRAMMAR

Regular Verbs and Their Tenses

There are three verb types which follow a regular pattern, their infinitives ending in **-ar**, **-er**, and **-ir**, e.g. *to speak* **hablar**, *to eat* **comer**, *to live* **vivir**. Here are the most commonly used forms. The **vosotros** forms are only used in Spain. In Latin America **ustedes** is used to address more than one person formally or informally.

	Present	*Past*	*Future*
yo *I*	hablo	hablé	hablaré
tú *you (informal)*	hablas	hablaste	hablarás

él/ella/Ud. he/she/ you (form.)	habla	habló	hablará
nosotros we	hablamos	hablamos	hablaremos
vosotros you (pl. inform.) [Spain]	habláis	hablasteis	hablaréis
ellos/ellas/Uds. they/you (form.)	hablan	hablaron	hablarán

yo I	como	comí	comeré
tú you (inform.)	comes	comiste	comerás
él/ella/Ud. he/she/ you (form.)	come	comió	comerá
nosotros we	comemos	comimos	comeremos
vosotros you (pl. inform.) [Spain]	coméis	comisteis	comeréis
ellos/ellas/Uds. they/you (form.)	comen	comieron	comerán

yo I	vivo	viví	viviré
tú you (inform.)	vives	viviste	vivirás
él/ella/Ud. he/she/ you (form.)	vive	vivió	vivirá
nosotros we	vivimos	vivimos	viviremos
vosotros you (pl. inform.) [Spain]	vivís	vivisteis	viviréis
ellos/ellas/Uds. they/you (form.)	viven	vivieron	vivirán

Very often, people omit the pronoun, using only the verb form.

Examples: Vivo en Madrid. *I live in Madrid.*
¿Habla español? *Do you speak Spanish?*

There are many irregular verbs whose forms differ considerably.

To be – ser and estar

Spanish has two verbs for *to be*, **ser** and **estar**. Their usage is complex. Here are some general guidelines:

Ser is used to identify people or objects, to describe their basic and natural characteristics, also to tell time and dates.

Examples:	¡Es caro! *That is expensive!*
	Somos médicos. *We're doctors.*
	Son las dos. *It's 2 o'clock.*

Estar is used when the state of a person or object is changeable and to indicate locations.

Examples:	Estoy cansado. *I'm tired.*
	¿Dónde estuvo? *Where was he?*
	Estarán en Roma. *They'll be in Rome.*

	Present	**Past**	**Future**
yo	soy/estoy	fui/estuve	seré/estaré
tú	eres/estás	fuiste/estuviste	serás/estarás
él/ella/Ud.	es/está	fue/estuvo	será/estará
nosotros	somos/estamos	fuimos/estuvimos	seremos/estaremos
vosotros *[Spain]*	sois/estáis	fuisteis/estuvisteis	seréis/estaréis
ellos/ellas/Uds.	son/están	fueron/estuvieron	serán/estarán

Nouns and Articles

Generally nouns ending in **-o** are masculine, and those ending in **-a** are feminine. Their definite articles—meaning *the*—are **el** (m) and **la** (f). In the plural, the article is **los** (m) and **las** (f). Plural nouns end in **-s**, or **-es** when the singular form ends with a consonant.

Examples: Singular **el tren** *the train* Plural **los trenes** *the trains*
la mesa *the table* **las mesas** *the tables*

The definite articles also change according to gender: **un** (m), **una** (f), **unos** (m/pl), **unas** (f/pl).

Examples: Singular **un libro** *a book* Plural **unos libros** *books*
una casa *a house* **unas casas** *houses*

Possessive articles relate to the gender of the noun that follows:

Examples:	¿Dónde está su billete? *Where is your ticket?*
	Vuestro tren sale a las 8. *Your train leaves at 8.*
	Busco mis maletas. *I'm looking for my suitcases.*

	Singular	**Plural**
my	mi	mis
your (inform.)	tu	tus
his/her/its/your (form.)	su	sus
our	nuestro/a	nuestros/as
your (pl. inform.)[Spain]	vuestro/a	vuestros/as
their/your (pl. form.)	su	sus

Word Order

The conjugated verb comes after the subject.

Examples: Yo trabajo en Madrid. *I work in Madrid.*

Questions are formed by reversing the order of subject and verb, changing the intonation of the affirmative sentence, or using key question words like *when? ¿cuándo?*.

Examples: ¿Tiene Ud. mapas? *Do you have maps?*
¿Cuándo cerrará el banco? *When will the bank close?*

Negations

Negative sentences are formed by adding **no** (*not*) to that part of the sentence which is to be negated.

Examples: No fumamos. *We don't smoke.*
No es nuevo. *It's not new.*
El autobús no llegó. *The bus didn't arrive.*
¿Por qué no escuchas? *Why don't you listen?*

Imperatives (Command Form)

Imperative sentences are formed by using the stem of the verb with the appropriate ending.

Examples:

tú *you (inform.)*	**¡Habla!** *Speak!*	[no hables]
Ud. *you (form.)*	**¡Hable!** *Speak!*	
nosotros *we*	**¡Hablemos!** *Let's speak!*	
vosotros *you (inform. pl.)* [Spain]	**¡Hablad!** *Speak!*	[no habléis]
Uds. *you (form. pl.)*	**¡Hablen!** *Speak!*	

Comparative and Superlative

Comparative and superlative are formed by adding **más** (*more*), **lo más** (*the most*), **menos** (*less*) or **lo menos** (*the least*) before the adjective or noun.

Adjective	*Comparative*	*Superlative*
grande *big, large*	**más grande** *bigger*	**lo más grande** *the biggest*
costoso *expensive*	**menos costoso** *less expensive*	**lo menos costoso** *the least expensive*

Examples: **Estas postales son las más baratas.** *These postcards are the cheapest.*
Pepe tiene menos dinero que Juan. *Pepe has less money than Juan.*

Possessive Pronouns

Pronouns serve as substitutes and relate to the gender.

	Singular	*Plural*
mine	**mío/a**	**míos/as**
yours (inform. sing.)	**tuyo/a**	**tuyos/as**
yours (form.)	**suyo/a**	**suyos/as**
his/her/its	**suyo/a**	**suyos/as**
ours	**nuestro/a**	**nuestros/as**
yours (pl. inform.) [Spain]	**vuestro/a**	**vuestros/as**
theirs	**suyo/a**	**suyos/as**

Examples: Sus hijos y los míos. *Your children and mine.*
¿Es tuyo este café? *Is this coffee yours?*

Adjectives

Adjectives describe nouns. They agree with the noun in gender and number. Masculine forms end in -o, feminine forms in -a. In general, adjectives come after the noun. The feminine form is generally the same if the masculine form ends in -e or with a consonant.

Examples: Tenemos un coche viejo. *We have an old car.*
Mi jefa es simpática. *My boss is nice.*
El mar/La flor es azul. *The ocean / flower is blue.*

Most adjectives form their plurals the same way as nouns:

Examples: una casa roja *a red house*
unas casas rojas *red houses*

Adverbs and Adverbial Expressions

Adverbs describe verbs. They are formed by adding **-mente** to the feminine form of the adjective if it differs from the masculine. Otherwise add -mente to the masculine form.

Examples: María conduce lentamente. *Maria drives very slowly.*
Roberto conduce rápidamente. *Robert drives fast.*
Ud. habla español bien. *You speak Spanish well.*

Some common adverbial time expressions:

actualmente *presently*
todavía *still*
todavía no *not yet*
ya no *not anymore*

Part 2

English-Spanish Dictionary

A

a [ə] *stressed* [eɪ] *art* un(a); *$50 a ride* 50 dólares por viaje

a·back [ə'bæk] *adv*: **taken aback** desconcertado (**by** por)

a·ban·don [ə'bændən] *v/t* abandonar

a·bashed [ə'bæʃt] *adj* avergonzado

a·bate [ə'beɪt] *v/i of storm, flood* amainar

ab·at·toir ['æbətwɑːr] matadero *m*

ab·bey ['æbɪ] abadía *f*

ab·bre·vi·ate [ə'briːvɪeɪt] *v/t* abreviar

ab·bre·vi·a·tion [əbriːvɪ'eɪʃn] abreviatura *f*

ab·di·cate ['æbdɪkeɪt] *v/i* abdicar

ab·di·ca·tion [æbdɪ'keɪʃn] abdicación *f*

ab·do·men ['æbdəmən] abdomen *m*

ab·dom·i·nal [æb'dɑːmɪnl] *adj* abdominal

ab·duct [əb'dʌkt] *v/t* raptar, secuestrar

ab·duc·tion [əb'dʌkʃn] rapto *m*, secuestro *m*

◆ **a·bide by** [ə'baɪd] *v/t* atenerse a

a·bil·i·ty [ə'bɪlətɪ] capacidad *f*, habilidad *f*

a·blaze [ə'bleɪz] *adj* en llamas

a·ble ['eɪbl] *adj (skillful)* capaz, hábil; *be able to* poder; *I wasn't able to see / hear* no conseguí *or* pude ver / escuchar

a·ble-bod·ied [eɪbl'bɑːdiːd] *adj* sano

ab·nor·mal [æb'nɔːrml] *adj* anormal

ab·nor·mal·ly [æb'nɔːrməlɪ] *adv* anormalmente; *behave* de manera anormal

a·board [ə'bɔːrd] **1** *prep* a bordo de **2** *adv* a bordo; *be aboard* estar a bordo; *go aboard* subir a bordo

a·bol·ish [ə'bɑːlɪʃ] *v/t* abolir

a·bo·li·tion [æbə'lɪʃn] abolición *f*

a·bort [ə'bɔːrt] *v/t mission, launch* suspender, cancelar; COMPUT cancelar

a·bor·tion [ə'bɔːrʃn] aborto *m* *(provocado)*; *have an abortion* abortar

a·bor·tive [ə'bɔːrtɪv] *adj* fallido

a·bout [ə'baʊt] **1** *prep (concerning)* acerca de, sobre; *what's it about? of book, movie* ¿de qué trata? **2** *adv (roughly)* más o menos; *be about to ...* *(be going to)* estar a punto de ...; *be about (somewhere near)* estar por ahí; *there are a lot of people about* hay un montón de gente por ahí

a·bove [ə'bʌv] **1** *prep* por encima de; *500 m above sea level* 500 m sobre el nivel del mar; *above all* por encima de todo, sobre todo **2** *adv*: *on the floor above* en el piso de arriba

a·bove-men·tioned [əbʌv'menʃnd] *adj* arriba mencionado

a·bra·sion [ə'breɪʒn] abrasión *f*

a·bra·sive [ə'breɪsɪv] *adj personality* abrasivo

a·breast [ə'brest] *adv* de frente, en fondo; *keep abreast of* mantenerse al tanto de

a·bridge [ə'brɪdʒ] *v/t* abreviar, condensar

a·broad [ə'brɔːd] *adv live* en el extranjero; *go* al extranjero

a·brupt [ə'brʌpt] *adj departure* brusco, repentino; *manner* brusco, rudo

a·brupt·ly [ə'brʌptlɪ] *adv (suddenly)* repentinamente; *(curtly)* bruscamente

ab·scess ['æbsɪs] absceso *m*

ab·sence ['æbsəns] *of person* ausencia *f*; *(lack)* falta *f*

ab·sent ['æbsənt] *adj* ausente

ab·sen·tee [æbsən'tiː] *n* ausente *m/f*

ab·sen·tee·ism [æbsən'tiːɪzm] absentismo *m*

ab·sent-mind·ed [æbsənt'maɪndɪd] *adj* despistado, distraído

ab·sent-mind·ed·ly [æbsənt'maɪndɪdlɪ] *adv* distraídamente

ab·so·lute ['æbsəluːt] *adj power* absoluto; *idiot* completo; *mess* total

ab·so·lute·ly ['æbsəluːtlɪ] *adv (completely)* absolutamente, completamente; *absolutely not!* ¡en absoluto!; *do you agree? - absolutely!* ¿estás de acuerdo? - ¡completamente!

ab·so·lu·tion [æbsə'luːʃn] REL absolución *f*

ab·solve [əb'zɑːlv] *v/t* absolver

ab·sorb [əb'sɔːrb] *v/t* absorber; *absorbed in ...* absorto en ...

ab·sorb·en·cy [əb'sɔːrbənsɪ] absorbencia *f*

ab·sorb·ent [əb'sɔːrbənt] *adj* absorbente

ab·sorb·ent 'cot·ton algodón *m* hidrófilo

ab·sorb·ing [əb'sɔːrbɪŋ] *adj* absorbente

ab·stain [əb'steɪn] *v/i from voting* abstenerse

ab·sten·tion [əb'stenʃn] *in voting* abstención *f*

ab·stract ['æbstrækt] *adj* abstracto

ab·struse [əb'struːs] *adj* abstruso

ab·surd [əb'sɜːrd] *adj* absurdo

ab·surd·i·ty [əb'sɜːrdətɪ] lo absurdo

a·bun·dance [ə'bʌndəns] abundancia *f*

a·bun·dant [ə'bʌndənt] *adj* abundante

a·buse¹ [ə'bjuːs] *n (insults)* insultos *mpl*; *of thing* maltrato *m*; *he shouted abuse at me* me insultó; *(child) abuse physical* malos tratos *mpl* a menores; *sexual* agresión f sexual a menores

a·buse² [əˈbjuːz] v/t (*physically*) abusar de; (*verbally*) insultar

a·bu·sive [əˈbjuːsɪv] adj language insultante, injurioso; *become abusive* ponerse a insultar

a·bys·mal [əˈbɪʒml] adj F (*very bad*) desastroso F

a·byss [əˈbɪs] abismo m

AC [ˈeɪsiː] abbr (= *alternating current*) CA (= corriente f alterna)

ac·a·dem·ic [ækəˈdemɪk] 1 n académico(-a) m(f), profesor(a) m(f) 2 adj académico

a·cad·e·my [əˈkædəmɪ] academia f

ac·cede [əkˈsiːd] v/i accede; *accede to* acceder a

ac·cel·e·rate [əkˈseləreɪt] v/t & v/i acelerar

ac·cel·e·ra·tion [əkseləˈreɪʃn] aceleración f

ac·cel·e·ra·tor [əkˈseləreɪtər] of car acelerador m

ac·cent [ˈæksənt] when speaking acento m; (*emphasis*) énfasis m

ac·cen·tu·ate [əkˈsentʊeɪt] v/t acentuar

ac·cept [əkˈsept] v/t & v/i aceptar

ac·cep·ta·ble [əkˈseptəbl] adj aceptable

ac·cep·tance [əkˈseptəns] aceptación f

ac·cess [ˈækses] 1 n acceso m; *have access to* computer tener acceso a; child tener derecho a visitar 2 v/t also COMPUT acceder a

'ac·cess code COMPUT código m de acceso

ac·ces·si·ble [əkˈsesəbl] adj accesible

ac·ces·sion [əkˈseʃn] acceso m

ac·ces·so·ry [əkˈsesərɪ] for wearing accesorio m, complemento m; LAW cómplice m/f

'ac·cess road carretera f de acceso

'ac·cess time COMPUT tiempo m de acceso

ac·ci·dent [ˈæksɪdənt] accidente m; *by accident* por casualidad

ac·ci·den·tal [æksɪˈdentl] adj accidental

ac·ci·den·tal·ly [æksɪˈdentlɪ] adv sin querer

ac·claim [əˈkleɪm] 1 n alabanza f, aclamación f; *meet with acclaim* ser alabado or aclamado 2 v/t alabar, aclamar

ac·cla·ma·tion [ækləˈmeɪʃn] aclamación f

ac·cli·mate, ac·cli·ma·tize [əˈklaɪmət, əˈklaɪmətaɪz] v/t aclimatarse

ac·com·mo·date [əˈkuːmədeɪt] v/t alojar; requirements satisfacer, hacer frente a

ac·com·mo·da·tions [əkuːməˈdeɪʃnz] npl alojamiento m

ac·com·pa·ni·ment [əˈkʌmpənɪmənt] MUS acompañamiento m

ac·com·pa·nist [əˈkʌmpənɪst] MUS acompañante m/f

ac·com·pa·ny [əˈkʌmpənɪ] v/t (pret & pp *accompanied*) also MUS acompañar

ac·com·plice [əˈkʌmplɪs] cómplice m/f

ac·com·plish [əˈkʌmplɪʃ] v/t task realizar; goal conseguir, lograr

ac·com·plished [əˈkʌmplɪʃt] adj consumado

ac·com·plish·ment [əˈkʌmplɪʃmənt] of a task realización f; (*talent*) habilidad f; (*achievement*) logro m

accord [əˈkɔːrd] acuerdo m; *of one's own accord* de motu propio

ac·cord·ance [əˈkɔːrdəns]: *in accordance with* de acuerdo con

ac·cord·ing [əˈkɔːrdɪŋ] adv: *according to* según

ac·cord·ing·ly [əˈkɔːrdɪŋlɪ] adv (*consequently*) por consiguiente; (*appropriately*) como corresponde

ac·cor·di·on [əˈkɔːrdɪən] acordeón m

ac·cor·di·on·ist [əˈkɔːrdɪənɪst] acordeonista m/f

ac·count [əˈkaʊnt] financial cuenta f; (*report, description*) relato m, descripción f; *give an account of* relatar, describir; *on no account* de ninguna manera, bajo ningún concepto; *on account of* a causa de; *take sth into account, take account of sth* tener algo en cuenta, tener en cuenta algo

♦ account for v/t (*explain*) explicar; (*make up, constitute*) suponer, constituir

ac·count·abil·i·ty [əkaʊntəˈbɪlətɪ] responsabilidad f

ac·coun·ta·ble [əˈkaʊntəbl] adj responsable (*to* ante); *be held accountable* ser considerado responsable

ac·coun·tant [əˈkaʊntənt] contable m/f, L.Am. contador(a) m(f)

ac'count hold·er titular m/f de una cuenta

ac'count num·ber número m de cuenta

ac·counts [əˈkaʊnts] npl contabilidad f

ac·cu·mu·late [əˈkjuːmjʊleɪt] 1 v/t acumular 2 v/i acumularse

ac·cu·mu·la·tion [əkjuːmjʊˈleɪʃn] acumulación f

ac·cu·ra·cy [ˈækjʊrəsɪ] precisión f

ac·cu·rate [ˈækjʊrət] adj preciso

ac·cu·rate·ly [ˈækjʊrətlɪ] adv con precisión

ac·cu·sa·tion [ækjuːˈzeɪʃn] acusación f

ac·cuse [əˈkjuːz] v/t: *accuse s.o. of sth* acusar a alguien de algo; *be accused of* LAW ser acusado de

ac·cused [əˈkjuːzd] n LAW acusado(-a) m(f)

ac·cus·ing [əˈkjuːzɪŋ] *adj* acusador

ac·cus·ing·ly [əˈkjuːzɪŋlɪ] *adv* say in tono acusador; *he looked at me accusingly* me lanzó una mirada acusadora

ac·cus·tom [əˈkʌstəm] *v/t* acostumbrar; *get accustomed to* acostumbrarse a; *be accustomed to* estar acostumbrado a

ace [eɪs] *in cards* as *m*; (*in tennis: shot*) ace *m*

ache [eɪk] **1** *n* dolor *m* **2** *v/i* doler

a·chieve [əˈtʃiːv] *v/t* conseguir, lograr

a·chieve·ment [əˈtʃiːvmənt] *of ambition* consecución *f*, logro *m*; (*thing achieved*) logro *m*

ac·id [ˈæsɪd] *n* ácido *m*

a·cid·i·ty [əˈsɪdɪtɪ] acidez *f*; *fig* sarcasmo *m*

ac·id 'rain lluvia *f* ácida

'ac·id test *fig* prueba *f* de fuego

ac·knowl·edge [əkˈnɒlɪdʒ] *v/t* reconocer; *acknowledge receipt of a letter* acusar recibo de una carta

ac·knowl·edg(e)·ment [əkˈnɒlɪdʒmənt] reconocimiento *m*; *of a letter* acuse *m* de recibo

ac·ne [ˈækni] MED acné *m*, acne *m*

a·corn [ˈeɪkɔːrn] BOT bellota *f*

a·cous·tics [əˈkuːstɪks] acústica *f*

ac·quaint [əˈkweɪnt] *v/t fml*: *be acquainted with* conocer

ac·quaint·ance [əˈkweɪntəns] *person* conocido(-a) *m(f)*

ac·qui·esce [ækwɪˈes] *v/i fml* acceder

ac·qui·es·cence [ækwɪˈesns] *fml* aquiescencia *f*

ac·quire [əˈkwaɪr] *v/t* adquirir

ac·qui·si·tion [ækwɪˈzɪʃn] adquisición *f*

ac·quis·i·tive [æˈkwɪzətɪv] *adj* consumista

ac·quit [əˈkwɪt] *v/t* LAW absolver

ac·quit·tal [əˈkwɪtl] LAW absolución *f*

a·cre [ˈeɪkər] acre *m* (*4.047m2*)

a·cre·age [ˈeɪkrɪdʒ] superficie *f* en acres

ac·ri·mo·ni·ous [ækrɪˈmoʊnɪəs] *adj* áspero, agrio

ac·ro·bat [ˈækrəbæt] acróbata *m/f*

ac·ro·bat·ic [ækrəˈbætɪk] *adj* acrobático

ac·ro·bat·ics [ækrəˈbætɪks] *npl* acrobacias *fpl*

ac·ro·nym [ˈækrənɪm] acrónimo *m*

a·cross [əˈkrɔːs] **1** *prep* al otro lado de; *she lives across the street* vive al otro lado de la calle; *sail across the Atlantic* cruzar el Atlántico navegando **2** *adv* de un lado a otro; *it's too far to swim across* está demasiado lejos como para cruzar a nado; *once you're across* cuando hayas llegado al otro lado; *10 m across* 10 m de ancho

a·cryl·ic [əˈkrɪlɪk] *adj* acrílico

act [ækt] **1** *v/i* THEA actuar; (*pretend*) hacer teatro; *act as* actuar *or* hacer de **2** *n* (*deed*), *of play* acto *m*; *in vaudeville* número *m*; (*law*) ley *f*; *it's just an act* (*pretense*) es puro teatro; *act of God* caso *m* fortuito

act·ing [ˈæktɪŋ] **1** *n* in a play interpretación *f*; *as profession* teatro *m* **2** *adj* (*temporary*) en funciones

ac·tion [ˈækʃn] acción *f*; *out of action machine* sin funcionar; *person* fuera de combate; *take action* actuar; *bring an action against* LAW demandar a

ac·tion 're·play TV repetición *f* (de la jugada)

ac·tive [ˈæktɪv] *adj* also GRAM activo; *party member* en activo

ac·tiv·ist [ˈæktɪvɪst] POL activista *m/f*

ac·tiv·i·ty [ækˈtɪvətɪ] actividad *f*

ac·tor [ˈæktər] actor *m*

ac·tress [ˈæktrɪs] actriz *f*

ac·tu·al [ˈæktʃʊəl] *adj* verdadero, real

ac·tu·al·ly [ˈæktʃʊəlɪ] *adv* (*in fact, to tell the truth*) en realidad; *did you actually see her?* ¿de verdad llegaste a verla?; *he actually did it!* ¡aunque parezca mentira lo hizo!; *actually, I do know him* (*stressing converse*) pues sí, de hecho lo conozco; *actually, it's not finished yet* el caso es que todavía no está terminado

ac·u·punc·ture [ˈækjəpʌŋktʃər] acupuntura *f*

a·cute [əˈkjuːt] *adj pain* agudo; *sense* muy fino

a·cute·ly [əˈkjuːtlɪ] *adv* (*extremely*) extremadamente; *acutely aware* plenamente consciente

ad [æd] → **advertisement**

ad·a·mant [ˈædəmənt] *adj* firme

ad·a·mant·ly [ˈædəməntlɪ] *adv* firmemente

Ad·am's ap·ple [ædəmzˈæpəl] nuez *f*

a·dapt [əˈdæpt] **1** *v/t* adaptar **2** *v/i of person* adaptarse

a·dapt·a·bil·i·ty [ədæptəˈbɪlətɪ] adaptabilidad *f*

a·dapt·a·ble [əˈdæptəbl] *adj* adaptable

a·dap·ta·tion [ædæpˈteɪʃn] *of play etc* adaptación *f*

a·dapt·er [əˈdæptər] *electrical* adaptador *m*

add [æd] **1** *v/t* añadir; MATH sumar **2** *v/i of person* sumar

◆ **add on** *v/t 15% etc* sumar

◆ **add up 1** *v/t* sumar **2** *v/i fig* cuadrar

ad·der [ˈædər] víbora *f*

ad·dict [ˈædɪkt] adicto(-a) *m(f)*; *drug addict* drogadicto(-a) *m(f)*

ad·dic·ted [ə'dıktıd] *adj* adicto; *be addicted to* ser adicto a

ad·dic·tion [ə'dıkʃn] adicción *f*

ad·dic·tive [ə'dıktıv] *adj* adictivo

ad·di·tion [ə'dıʃn] MATH suma *f; to list, company etc* incorporación *f; of new drive etc* instalación *f; in addition* además; *in addition to* además de

ad·di·tion·al [ə'dıʃnl] *adj* adicional

ad·di·tive ['ædıtıv] aditivo *m*

add-on ['ædɒn] extra *m*, accesorio *m*

ad·dress [ə'dres] **1** *n* dirección *f; form of address* tratamiento *m* **2** *v/t letter* dirigir; *audience* dirigirse a; *how do you address the judge?* ¿qué tratamiento se le da al juez?

ad'dress book agenda *f* de direcciones

ad·dress·ee [ædre'si:] destinatario(-a) *m(f)*

ad·ept ['ædept] *adj* experto; *be adept at* ser un experto en

ad·e·quate ['ædıkwət] *adj* suficiente; *(satisfactory)* aceptable

ad·e·quate·ly ['ædıkwətlı] *adv* suficientemente; *(satisfactorily)* aceptablemente

ad·here [əd'hır] *v/i* adherirse

♦ **adhere to** *v/t surface* adherirse a; *rules* cumplir

ad·he·sive [əd'hi:sıv] *n* adhesivo *m*

ad·he·sive 'plas·ter esparadrapo *m*

ad·he·sive 'tape cinta *f* adhesiva

ad·ja·cent [ə'dʒeısnt] *adj* adyacente

ad·jec·tive ['ædʒıktıv] adjetivo *m*

ad·join [ə'dʒɔın] *v/t* lindar con

ad·join·ing [ə'dʒɔınıŋ] *adj* contiguo

ad·journ [ə'dʒɜːn] *v/i of court, meeting* aplazar

ad·journ·ment [ə'dʒɜːnmənt] aplazamiento *m*

ad·just [ə'dʒʌst] *v/t* ajustar, regular

ad·just·a·ble [ə'dʒʌstəbl] *adj* ajustable, regulable

ad·just·ment [ə'dʒʌstmənt] ajuste *m; psychological* adaptación *f*

ad lib [æd'lıb] **1** *adj* improvisado **2** *adv* improvisadamente **3** *v/i (pret & pp adbed)* improvisar

ad·min·is·ter [əd'mınıstər] *v/t* administrar

ad·min·is·tra·tion [ədmını'streıʃn] administración *f*

ad·min·is·tra·tive [ədmını'strətıv] *adj* administrativo

ad·min·is·tra·tor [əd'mınıstreıtər] administrador(a) *m(f)*

ad·mi·ra·ble ['ædmərəbl] *adj* admirable

ad·mi·ra·bly ['ædmərəblı] *adv* admirablemente

ad·mi·ral ['ædmərəl] almirante *m*

ad·mi·ra·tion [ædmə'reıʃn] admiración *f*

ad·mire [əd'maır] *v/t* admirar

ad·mir·er [əd'maırər] admirador(a) *m(f)*

ad·mir·ing [əd'maırıŋ] *adj* de admiración

ad·mir·ing·ly [əd'maırıŋlı] *adv* con admiración

ad·mis·si·ble [əd'mısəbl] *adj* admisible

ad·mis·sion [əd'mıʃn] *(confession)* confesión *f; admission free* entrada gratis

ad·mit [əd'mıt] *v/t (pret & pp admitted) to a place* dejar entrar; *to school, organization* admitir; *to hospital* ingresar; *(confess)* confesar; *(accept)* admitir

ad·mit·tance [əd'mıtəns] admisión *f; no admittance* prohibido el paso

ad·mit·ted·ly [əd'mıtedlı] *adv: he didn't use those exact words, admittedly* es verdad que no utilizó exactamente esas palabras

ad·mon·ish [əd'mɑːnıʃ] *v/t fml* reprender

a·do [ə'du:]: *without further ado* sin más dilación

ad·o·les·cence [ædə'lesns] adolescencia *f*

ad·o·les·cent [ædə'lesnt] **1** *n* adolescente *m/f* **2** *adj* de adolescente

a·dopt [ə'dɑːpt] *v/t child, plan* adoptar

a·dop·tion [ə'dɑːpʃn] *of child* adopción *f*

a·dop·tive 'par·ents [ədɑː'ptıv] *npl* padres *mpl* adoptivos

a·dor·a·ble [ə'dɔːrəbl] *adj* encantador

ad·o·ra·tion [ædə'reıʃn] adoración *f*

a·dore [ə'dɔːr] *v/t* adorar; *I adore chocolate* me encanta el chocolate

a·dor·ing [ə'dɔːrıŋ] *adj expression* lleno de adoración; *his adoring fans* sus entregados fans

ad·ren·al·in [ə'drenəlın] adrenalina *f*

a·drift [ə'drıft] *adj* a la deriva; *fig* perdido

ad·u·la·tion [ædʊ'leıʃn] adulación *f*

ad·ult ['ædʌlt] **1** *n* adulto(-a) *m(f)* **2** *adj* adulto

ad·ult ed·u'ca·tion educación *f* para adultos

a·dul·ter·ous [ə'dʌltərəs] *adj relationship* adúltero

a·dul·ter·y [ə'dʌltərı] adulterio *m*

'a·dult film *euph* película *f* para adultos

ad·vance [əd'væns] **1** *n* money adelanto *m; in science, MIL* avance *m; in advance* con antelación; *get money* por adelantado; *48 hours in advance* con 48 horas de antelación; *make advances (progress)* avanzar, progresar; *sexually* insinuarse **2** *v/i MIL* avanzar; *(make progress)* avanzar, progresar **3** *v/t theory* presentar; *sum of money* adelantar; *human knowledge, a cause* hacer avanzar

ad·vance 'book·ing reserva *f* (anticipa-

da)
ad·vanced [əd'vænst] adj country, level, learner avanzado
ad·vance 'no·tice aviso m previo
ad·vance 'pay·ment pago m por adelantado
ad·van·tage [əd'væntɪdʒ] ventaja f; **there's no advantage to be gained** no se gana nada; **it's to your advantage** te conviene; **take advantage of** aprovecharse de
ad·van·ta·geous [ædvən'teɪdʒəs] adj ventajoso
ad·vent ['ædvent] fig llegada f
'ad·vent cal·en·dar calendario m de Adviento
ad·ven·ture [əd'ventʃər] aventura f
ad·ven·tur·ous [əd'ventʃərəs] adj person aventurero; investment arriesgado
ad·verb ['ædvɜːrb] adverbio m
ad·ver·sa·ry ['ædvərseri] adversario(-a) m(f)
ad·verse ['ædvɜːrs] adj adverso
ad·vert ['ædvɜːrt] → **advertisement**
ad·ver·tise ['ædvərtaɪz] 1 v/t anunciar 2 v/i anunciarse, poner un anuncio
ad·ver·tise·ment [ædvər'taɪsmənt] anuncio m
ad·ver·tis·er ['ædvərtaɪzər] anunciante m/f
ad·ver·tis·ing ['ædvərtaɪzɪŋ] publicidad f
'ad·ver·tis·ing a·gen·cy agencia f de publicidad
'ad·ver·tis·ing budg·et presupuesto m para publicidad
'ad·ver·tis·ing cam·paign campaña f publicitaria
'ad·ver·tis·ing rev·e·nue ingresos mpl por publicidad
ad·vice [əd'vaɪs] consejo m; **he gave me some advice** me dio un consejo; **take s.o.'s advice** seguir el consejo de alguien
ad·vis·a·ble [əd'vaɪzəbl] adj aconsejable
ad·vise [əd'vaɪz] v/t person, caution aconsejar; government asesorar; **I advise you to leave** te aconsejo que te vayas
ad·vis·er [əd'vaɪzər] asesor(a) m(f)
ad·vo·cate ['ædvəkeɪt] v/t abogar por
aer·i·al ['erɪəl] n antena f
aer·i·al 'pho·to·graph fotografía f aérea
aer·o·bics [e'roubɪks] nsg aerobic m
aer·o·dy·nam·ic [eroudaɪ'næmɪk] adj aerodinámico
aer·o·nau·ti·cal [erou'nɒːtɪkl] adj aeronáutico
aer·o·plane ['eroupleɪn] Br avión m
aer·o·sol ['erəsɑːl] aerosol m
aer·o·space in·dus·try ['erəspeɪs] industria f aeroespacial

aes·thet·ic etc Br → **esthetic** etc
af·fa·ble ['æfəbl] adj afable
af·fair [ə'fer] (matter, business) asunto m; (love affair) aventura f, lío m; **foreign affairs** asuntos mpl exteriores, **have an affair with** tener una aventura or lío con
af·fect [ə'fekt] v/t also MED afectar
af·fec·tion [ə'fekʃn] afecto m, cariño
af·fec·tion·ate [ə'fekʃnət] adj afectuoso, cariñoso
af·fec·tion·ate·ly [ə'fekʃnətlɪ] adv con afecto, cariñosamente
af·fin·i·ty [ə'fɪnətɪ] afinidad f
af·fir·ma·tive [ə'fɜːrmətɪv] adj afirmativo; **answer in the affirmative** responder afirmativamente
af·flu·ence ['æfluəns] prosperidad f, riqueza f
af·flu·ent ['æfluənt] adj próspero, acomodado; **affluent society** sociedad f opulenta
af·ford [ə'fɔːrd] v/t permitirse; **be able to afford sth** financially poder permitirse algo; **I can't afford the time** no tengo tiempo; **it's a risk we can't afford to take** es un riesgo que no podemos permitirnos tomar
af·ford·a·ble [ə'fɔːrdəbl] adj asequible
a·float [ə'flout] adj boat a flote; **keep the company afloat** mantener la compañía a flote
a·fraid [ə'freɪd] adj: **be afraid** tener miedo; **be afraid of** tener miedo de; **I'm afraid of cats** tengo miedo a los gatos; **he's afraid of the dark** le da miedo la oscuridad; **I'm afraid of annoying him** me da miedo enfadarle; **I'm afraid expressing regret** me temo; **he's very ill, I'm afraid** me temo que está muy enfermo; **I'm afraid so** (me) temo que sí; **I'm afraid not** (me) temo que no
a·fresh [ə'freʃ] adv de nuevo
Af·ri·ca ['æfrɪkə] África
Af·ri·can ['æfrɪkən] 1 adj africano 2 n africano(-a) m(f)
af·ter ['æftər] 1 prep después de; **after all** después de todo; **after that** después de eso; **it's ten after two** son las dos y diez 2 adv después; **the day after** el día siguiente
af·ter·math ['æftərmæθ] time periodo m posterior (of a); state of affairs repercusiones fpl
af·ter·noon [æftər'nuːn] tarde f; **in the afternoon** por la tarde; **this afternoon** esta tarde; **good afternoon** buenas tardes
'af·ter sales serv·ice servicio m posventa
'af·ter·shave loción f para después del afeitado, after shave m

'af·ter·taste regusto *m*

af·ter·ward ['æftərwərd] *adv* después

a·gain [ə'geɪn] *adv* otra vez; *I never saw him again* no lo volví a ver

a·gainst [ə'genst] *prep Lean* contra; *the USA against Brazil* SP Estados Unidos contra *Brasil*; *I'm against the idea* estoy en contra de la idea; *what do you have against her?* ¿que tienes en contra de ella?; *against the law* ilegal

age [eɪdʒ] **1** *n of person, object* edad *f*; *(era)* era *f*; *at the age of ten* a los diez años; *under age* menor de edad; *she's five years of age* tiene cinco años; *I've been waiting for ages* llevo siglos esperando F; *I haven't seen him for ages* hace siglos que no lo veo F **2** *v/i* envejecer

aged¹ [eɪdʒd] *adj: aged 16* con 16 años de edad

a·ged² ['eɪdʒɪd] **1** *adj: her aged parents* sus ancianos padres **2** *n: the aged* los ancianos

'age group grupo *m* de edades

'age lim·it límite *m* de edad

a·gen·cy ['eɪdʒənsɪ] agencia *f*

a·gen·da [ə'dʒendə] orden *m* del día; *on the agenda* en el orden del día

a·gent ['eɪdʒənt] agente *m/f*, representante *m/f*

ag·gra·vate ['ægrəveɪt] *v/t* agravar; *(annoy)* molestar

ag·gre·gate ['ægrɪgət] *n* SP: *win on aggregate* ganar en el total de la eliminatoria

ag·gres·sion [ə'greʃn] agresividad *f*

ag·gres·sive [ə'gresɪv] *adj* agresivo; *(dynamic)* agresivo, enérgico

ag·gres·sive·ly [ə'gresɪvlɪ] *adv* agresivamente

a·ghast [ə'gæst] *adj* horrorizado

ag·ile ['ædʒəl] *adj* ágil

a·gil·i·ty [ə'dʒɪlətɪ] agilidad *f*

ag·i·tate ['ædʒɪteɪt] *v/i: agitate for* hacer campaña a favor de

ag·i·tat·ed ['ædʒɪteɪtɪd] *adj* agitado

ag·i·ta·tion [ædʒɪ'teɪʃn] agitación *f*

ag·i·ta·tor [ædʒɪ'teɪtər] agitador(a) *m(f)*

AGM [eɪdʒiː'em] *abbr* (= *annual general meeting*) junta *f* general annual

ag·nos·tic [æg'nɑːstɪk] *n* agnóstico(-a) *m(f)*

a·go [ə'gou] *adv: 2 days ago* hace dos días; *long ago* hace mucho tiempo; *how long ago?* ¿hace cuánto tiempo?; *how long ago did he leave?* ¿hace cuánto se marchó?

a·gog [ə'gɑːg] *adj: be agog at sth* estar emocionado con algo

ag·o·nize ['ægənaɪz] *v/i* atormentarse

(*over* por), angustiarse (*over* por)

ag·o·niz·ing ['ægənaɪzɪŋ] *adj pain* atroz; *wait* angustioso

ag·o·ny ['ægənɪ] agonía *f*

a·gree [ə'griː] **1** *v/i* estar de acuerdo; *of figures* coincidir; *(reach agreement)* ponerse de acuerdo; *I agree* estoy de acuerdo; *it doesn't agree with me* of food no me sienta bien **2** *v/t price* acordar; *agree that sth should be done* acordar que hay que hacer algo

a·gree·a·ble [ə'griːəbl] *adj* (*pleasant*) agradable; *be agreeable fml* (*in agreement*) estar de acuerdo

a·gree·ment [ə'griːmənt] (*consent, contract*) acuerdo *m*; *reach agreement on* llegar a un acuerdo sobre

ag·ri·cul·tur·al [ægrɪ'kʌltʃərəl] *adj* agrícola

ag·ri·cul·ture ['ægrɪkʌltʃər] agricultura *f*

a·head [ə'hed] *adv position* delante; *movement* adelante; *in race* por delante, en cabeza; *be ahead of* estar por delante de; *plan / think ahead* planear con antelación / pensar con anticipación

aid [eɪd] **1** *n* ayuda *f*; *come to s.o.'s aid* acudir a ayudar a alguien **2** *v/t* ayudar

aide [eɪd] asistente *m/f*

Aids [eɪdz] sida *m*

ail·ing ['eɪlɪŋ] *adj economy* débil, frágil

ail·ment ['eɪlmənt] achaque *m*

aim [eɪm] **1** *n in shooting* puntería *f*; (*objective*) objetivo *m* **2** *v/i in shooting* apuntar; *aim at doing sth, aim to do sth* tener como intención hacer algo **3** *v/t remark* dirigir; *he aimed the gun at me* me apuntó con la pistola; *be aimed at of remark etc* estar dirigido a; *of gun* estar apuntando a

aim·less ['eɪmlɪs] *adj* sin objetivos

air [er] **1** *n* aire *m*; *by air travel* en avión; *send mail* por correo aéreo; *in the open air* al libre; *on the air* RAD, TV en el aire **2** *v/t room* airear; *fig: views* airear, ventilar

'air·bag airbag *m*, bolsa *f* de aire

'air·base base *f* aérea

'air-con·di·tioned *adj* con aire acondicionado, climatizado

'air-con·di·tion·ing aire *m* acondicionado

'air·craft avión *m*, aeronave *f*

'air·craft car·ri·er portaaviones *m inv*

'air fare (precio *m* del) *Span* billete *m or L.Am.* boleto *m* de avión

'air·field aeródromo *m*, campo *m* de aviación

'air force fuerza *f* aérea

'air host·ess azafata *f*, *L.Am.* aeromoza *f*

'air let·ter aerograma *m*

'air·lift 1 *n* puente *m* aéreo 2 *v/t* transportar mediante puente aéreo

'air·line línea *f* aérea

'air·lin·er avión *m* de pasajeros

'air·mail: **by airmail** por correo aéreo

'air·plane avión *m*

'air·pock·et bolsa *f* de aire

'air pol·lu·tion contaminación *f* del aire

'air·port aeropuerto *m*

'air·sick: **get airsick** marearse (*en avión*)

'air·space espacio *m* aéreo

'air ter·mi·nal terminal *f* aérea

'air·tight *adj* container hermético

'air traf·fic tráfico *m* aéreo

'air-traf·fic con·trol control *m* del tráfico aéreo

'air-traf·fic con·trol·ler controlador(a) *m(f)* del tráfico aéreo

air·y ['eri] *adj* room aireado; *attitude* despreocupado, ligero

aisle [ail] pasillo *m*

'aisle seat asiento *m* de pasillo

a·jar [ə'dʒɑːr] *adj*: **be ajar** estar entreabierto

a·lac·ri·ty [ə'lækrəti] presteza *f*

a·larm [ə'lɑːrm] 1 *n* alarma *f*; **raise the alarm** dar la alarma 2 *v/t* alarmar

a'larm clock reloj *m* despertador

a·larm·ing [ə'lɑːrmɪŋ] *adj* alarmante

a·larm·ing·ly [ə'lɑːrmɪŋlɪ] *adv* de forma alarmante

al·bum ['ælbəm] *for photographs, (record)* álbum *m*

al·co·hol ['ælkəhɒl] alcohol *m*

al·co·hol·ic [ælkə'hɒlɪk] 1 *n* alcohólico(-a) *m(f)* 2 *adj* alcohólico

a·lert [ə'lɜːrt] 1 *n* signal alerta *f*; **be on the alert** estar alerta 2 *v/t* alertar 3 *adj* alerta

al·ge·bra ['ældʒɪbrə] álgebra *f*

a·li·bi ['ælɪbaɪ] coartada *f*

a·li·en ['eɪlɪən] 1 *n* (*foreigner*) extranjero(-a) *m(f)*; *from space* extraterrestre *m/f* 2 *adj* extraño; **be alien to s.o.** ser ajeno a alguien

a·li·en·ate ['eɪlɪəneɪt] *v/t* alienar, provocar el distanciamiento de

a·light [ə'laɪt] *adj* en llamas

a·lign [ə'laɪn] *v/t* alinear

a·like [ə'laɪk] 1 *adj*: **be alike** parecerse 2 *adv* igual; **old and young alike** viejos y jóvenes sin distinción

al·i·mo·ny ['ælɪmənɪ] pensión *f* alimenticia

a·live [ə'laɪv] *adj*: **be alive** estar vivo

all [ɒːl] 1 *adj* todo(s) 2 *pron* todo; **all of us / them** todos nosotros / ellos; **he ate all of it** se lo comió todo; **that's all, thanks** eso es todo, gracias; **for all I care** para lo que me importa; **for all I know**

por lo que sé; **all at once** (*suddenly*) de repente; (*at the same time*) a la vez; **all but** (*except*) todos menos; (*nearly*) casi; **all the better** mucho mejor; **all the time** desde el principio; **they're not at all alike** no se parecen en nada; **not at all!** ¡en absoluto!; **two all** SP empate a dos; **all right → alright**

al·lay [ə'leɪ] *v/t* apaciguar

al·le·ga·tion [ælɪ'geɪʃn] acusación *f*

al·lege [ə'ledʒ] *v/t* alegar

al·leged [ə'ledʒd] *adj* presunto

al·leg·ed·ly [ə'ledʒɪdlɪ] *adv* presuntamente, supuestamente

al·le·giance [ə'liːdʒəns] lealtad *f*

al·ler·gic [ə'lɜːrdʒɪk] *adj* alérgico; **be allergic to** ser alérgico a

al·ler·gy ['ælərdʒɪ] alergia *f*

al·le·vi·ate [ə'liːvɪeɪt] *v/t* aliviar

al·ley ['ælɪ] callejón *m*

al·li·ance [ə'laɪəns] alianza *f*

al·lo·cate ['æləkeɪt] *v/t* asignar

al·lo·ca·tion [ælə'keɪʃn] asignación *f*

al·lot [ə'lɒt] *v/t* (*pret & pp* **allotted**) asignar

al·low [ə'laʊ] *v/t* (*permit*) permitir; (*calculate for*) calcular; **they don't allow smoking** no está permitido fumar, está prohibido fumar; **it's not allowed** no está permitido; **he allowed us to leave** nos permitió salir

◆ **allow for** *v/t* tener en cuenta

al·low·ance [ə'laʊəns] (*money*) asignación *f*; (*pocket money*) paga *f*; **make allowances** *for weather etc* tener en cuenta; *for person* disculpar

al·loy ['ælɔɪ] aleación *f*

'all-pur·pose *adj* multiuso

'all-round *adj* completo

'all-time: **be at an all-time low** haber alcanzado un mínimo histórico

◆ al·lude to [ə'luːd] *v/t* aludir a

al·lur·ing [ə'lʊrɪŋ] *adj* atractivo, seductor

all-wheel 'drive *adj* con tracción a las cuatro ruedas

al·ly ['ælaɪ] *n* aliado(-a) *m(f)*

Al·might·y [ɒːl'maɪtɪ]: **the Almighty** el Todopoderoso

al·mond ['ɑːmənd] almendra *f*

al·most ['ɒːlmoʊst] *adv* casi

a·lone [ə'loʊn] *adj* solo

a·long [ə'lɒːŋ] 1 *prep* (*situated beside*) a lo largo de; **the shop is halfway along Baker Street** la tienda está a mitad de Baker Street; **walk along this path** sigue por esta calle 2 *adv*: **would you like to come along?** ¿te gustaría venir con nosotros?; **he always brings the dog along** siempre trae al perro; **along with** junto con; **all**

along (all the time) todo el tiempo, desde el principio

a·long·side [əlɒŋ'saɪd] prep (in co-operation with) junto a; (parallel to) al lado de

a·loof [ə'luːf] adj distante, reservado

a·loud [ə'laʊd] adv en voz alta

al·pha·bet ['ælfəbet] alfabeto m

al·pha·bet·i·cal [ælfə'betɪkl] adj alfabético

al·read·y [ɒːl'redɪ] adv ya

al·right [ɒːlraɪt] adj (not hurt, in working order) bien; **is it alright to leave now?** (permitted) ¿puedo irme ahora?; **is it alright to take these out of the country?** ¿se pueden sacar éstos del país?; **is it alright with you if I ...?** ¿te importa si ...?; **alright, you can have one!** de acuerdo, ¡puedes tomar uno!; **alright, I heard you!** vale, ¡te he oído!; **everything is alright now between them** vuelven a estar bien; **that's alright** (don't mention it) de nada; (I don't mind) no importa

al·so ['ɒːlsəʊ] adv también

al·tar ['ɒːltər] altar m

al·ter ['ɒːltər] v/t alterar

al·ter·a·tion [ɒːltə'reɪʃn] alteración f

al·ter·nate 1 v/i ['ɒːltərneɪt] alternar 2 adj ['ɒːltərnət] alterno

al·ter·nat·ing cur·rent ['ɒːltərneɪtɪŋ] corriente f alterna

al·ter·na·tive [ɒːlt'ɜːrnətɪv] 1 n alternativa f 2 adj alternativo

al·ter·na·tive·ly [ɒːlt'ɜːrnətɪvlɪ] adv si no

al·though [ɒːl'ðəʊ] conj aunque, si bien

al·ti·tude ['æltɪtuːd] of plane, city altitud f; of mountain altura f

al·to·geth·er [ɒːltə'geðər] adv (completely) completamente; (in all) en total

al·tru·ism ['æltruːɪzm] altruismo m

al·tru·is·tic [æltruː'ɪstɪk] adj altruista

a·lu·min·i·um [æljʊ'mɪnɪəm] Br, **a·lu·mi·num** [ə'luːmənəm] aluminio m

al·ways ['ɒːlweɪz] adv siempre

a. m. ['eɪem] abbr (= ante meridiem) a. m.; **at 11 a.m** a las 11 de la mañana

a·mal·gam·ate [ə'mælgəmeɪt] v/i of companies fusionarse

a·mass [ə'mæs] v/t acumular

am·a·teur ['æmətʃər] n unskilled aficionado(-a) m(f); sp amateur m/f

am·a·teur·ish ['æməʃʊrɪʃ] adj pej chapucero

a·maze [ə'meɪz] v/t asombrar

a·mazed [ə'meɪzd] adj asombrado; **we were amazed to hear ...** nos asombró oír ...

a·maze·ment [ə'meɪzmənt] asombro m

a·maz·ing [ə'meɪzɪŋ] adj (surprising)

asombroso; F (very good) alucinante F

a·maz·ing·ly [ə'meɪzɪŋlɪ] adv increíblemente

Am·a·zon ['æməzɒn] n: **the Amazon** el Amazonas

Am·a·zo·ni·an [æmə'zəʊnɪən] adj amazónico

am·bas·sa·dor [æm'bæsədər] embajador(a) m(f)

am·ber ['æmbər] adj ámbar; **at amber** en ámbar(f)

am·bi·dex·trous [æmbɪ'dekstrəs] adj ambidiestro

am·bi·ence ['æmbɪəns] ambiente m

am·bi·gu·i·ty [æmbɪ'gjuːətɪ] ambigüedad f

am·big·u·ous [æm'bɪgjʊəs] adj ambiguo

am·bi·tion [æm'bɪʃn] also pej ambición f

am·bi·tious [æm'bɪʃəs] adj ambicioso

am·biv·a·lent [æm'bɪvələnt] adj ambivalente

am·ble ['æmbl] v/i deambular

am·bu·lance ['æmbjʊləns] ambulancia f

am·bush ['æmbʊʃ] 1 n emboscada f 2 v/t tender una emboscada a

a·mend [ə'mend] v/t enmendar

a·mend·ment [ə'mendmənt] enmienda f

a·mends [ə'mendz] npl: **make amends for** compensar

a·men·i·ties [ə'miːnɪtɪz] npl servicios mpl

A·mer·i·ca [ə'merɪkə] continent América; USA Estados m pl Unidos

A·mer·i·can [ə'merɪkən] 1 n North American estadounidense m/f 2 adj North American estadounidense

A'mer·i·can plan pensión f completa

a·mi·a·ble ['eɪmɪəbl] adj afable, amable

a·mi·ca·ble ['æmɪkəbl] adj amistoso

a·mi·ca·bly ['æmɪkəblɪ] adv amistosamente

am·mu·ni·tion [æmjʊ'nɪʃn] munición f; fig argumentos mpl

am·ne·sia [æm'niːzɪə] amnesia f

am·nes·ty ['æmnəstɪ] amnistía f

a·mong(st) [ə'mʌŋ(st)] prep entre

a·mor·al [eɪ'mɒːrəl] adj amoral

a·mount [ə'maʊnt] cantidad f; (sum of money) cantidad f, suma f

◆ **amount to** v/t ascender a; **his contribution didn't amount to much** su contribución no fue gran cosa

am·phib·i·an [æm'fɪbɪən] anfibio m

am·phib·i·ous [æm'fɪbɪəs] adj animal, vehicle anfibio

am·phi·the·a·ter, Br **am·phi·the·a·tre** ['æmfɪθɪətər] anfiteatro m

am·ple ['æmpl] adj abundante; **$4 will be ample** 4 dólares serán más que sufi-

answer for

cientes

am·pli·fi·er ['æmplɪfaɪr] amplificador m

am·pli·fy ['æmplɪfaɪ] v/t (pret & pp **amplified**) sound amplificar

am·pu·tate ['æmpjʊteɪt] v/t amputar

am·pu·ta·tion [æmpjʊ'teɪʃn] amputación f

a·muse [ə'mjuːz] v/t (make laugh etc) divertir; (entertain) entretener

a·muse·ment [ə'mjuːzmənt] (merriment) diversión f; (entertainment) entretenimiento m; **amusements** (games) juegos mpl, **what do you do for amusement?** ¿qué haces para entretenerte?; **to our great amusement** para nuestro regocijo

a·muse·ment ar·cade [ɑːr'keɪd] salón m de juegos recreativos

a·muse·ment park parque m de atracciones

a·mus·ing [ə'mjuːzɪŋ] adj divertido

an·a·bol·ic ster·oid [ænə'bɑːlɪk] esteroide m anabolizante

a·nae·mi·a etc Br → **anemia** etc

an·aes·thet·ic etc Br → **anesthetic** etc

an·a·log ['ænəlɑːɡ] adj COMPUT analógico

a·nal·o·gy [ə'nælədʒɪ] analogía f

a·nal·y·sis [ə'næləsɪs] (pl **analyses** [ə'næləsiːz]) análisis m inv; (psychoanalysis) psicoanálisis m inv

an·a·lyst ['ænəlɪst] analista m/f; PSYCH psicoanalista m/f

an·a·lyt·i·cal [ænə'lɪtɪkl] adj analítico

an·a·lyze ['ænəlaɪz] v/t analizar; (psychoanalyze) psicoanalizar

an·arch·y ['ænərkɪ] anarquía f

a·nat·o·my [ə'nætəmɪ] anatomía f

an·ces·tor ['ænsestər] antepasado(-a) m(f)

an·chor ['æŋkər] 1 n NAUT ancla f; TV presentador(a) m(f) 2 v/i NAUT anclar

an·cient ['eɪnʃənt] adj antiguo

an·cil·lar·y [æn'sɪlərɪ] adj staff auxiliar

and [ænd] stressed [ænd] conj y

An·de·an ['ændɪən] adj andino

An·des ['ændiːz] npl: **the Andes** los Andes

an·ec·dote ['ænɪkdoʊt] anécdota f

a·ne·mia [ə'niːmɪə] anemia f

a·ne·mic [ə'niːmɪk] adj anémico

an·es·thet·ic [ænəs'θetɪk] n anestesia f

an·es·the·tist [ə'niːsθətɪst] anestesista m/f

an·gel ['eɪndʒl] REL ángel m; fig ángel m, cielo m

an·ger ['æŋɡər] 1 n enfado m, enojo m 2 v/t enfadar, enojar

an·gi·na [æn'dʒaɪnə] angina f (de pecho)

an·gle ['æŋɡl] n ángulo m

An·glo-Sax·on [æŋɡloʊ'sæksn] 1 adj an-

glosajón 2 n person anglosajón(-ona) m(f)

an·gry ['æŋɡrɪ] adj enfadado, enojado; **be angry with s.o.** estar enfadado o enojado con alguien

an·guish ['æŋɡwɪʃ] angustia f

an·gu·lar ['æŋɡjʊlər] adj anguloso

an·i·mal ['ænɪml] animal m

an·i·mated ['ænɪmeɪtɪd] adj animado

an·i·ma·ted car·toon dibujos mpl animados

an·i·ma·tion [ænɪ'meɪʃn] (liveliness), of cartoon animación f

an·i·mos·i·ty [ænɪ'mɑːsətɪ] animosidad f

an·kle ['æŋkl] tobillo m

an·nex ['æneks] 1 n building edificio m anexo 2 v/t state anexionar

an·nexe ['æneks] n Br edificio m anexo

an·ni·hi·late [ə'naɪəleɪt] v/t aniquilar

an·ni·hi·la·tion [ənaɪə'leɪʃn] aniquilación f

an·ni·ver·sa·ry [ænɪ'vɜːrsərɪ] (wedding anniversary) aniversario m

an·no·tate ['ænəteɪt] v/t report anotar

an·nounce [ə'naʊns] v/t anunciar

an·nounce·ment [ə'naʊnsmənt] anuncio m

an·nounc·er [ə'naʊnsər] TV, RAD presentador(a) m(f)

an·noy [ə'nɔɪ] v/t molestar, irritar; **be annoyed** estar molesto o irritado

an·noy·ance [ə'nɔɪəns] (anger) irritación f; (nuisance) molestia f

an·noy·ing [ə'nɔɪɪŋ] adj molesto, irritante

an·nu·al ['ænjʊəl] adj anual

an·nu·al gen·er·al 'meet·ing junta f general anual

an·nu·i·ty [ə'nuːətɪ] anualidad f

an·nul [ə'nʌl] v/t (pret & pp **annulled**) marriage anular

an·nul·ment [ə'nʌlmənt] anulación f

a·non·y·mous [ə'nɑːnɪməs] adj anónimo

an·o·rak ['ænəræk] Br anorak m

an·o·rex·i·a [ænə'reksɪə] anorexia f

an·o·rex·ic [ænə'reksɪk] adj anoréxico

an·oth·er [ə'nʌðər] 1 adj otro 2 pron otro(-a) m(f); **they helped one another** se ayudaron (el uno al otro); **do they know one another?** ¿se conocen?

ans·wer ['ænsər] 1 n to letter, person, question respuesta f, contestación f; to problem solución f 2 v/t letter, person, question responder, contestar; **answer the door** abrir la puerta; **answer the telephone** responder o Span coger al teléfono

◆ answer back v/t & v/i contestar, replicar

◆ answer for v/t responder de

an·swer·ing ma·chine ['ænsərɪŋ] TELEC contestador *m* (automático)

ans·wer·phone ['ænsərfoun] TELEC contestador *m* (automático)

ant [ænt] hormiga *f*

an·tag·o·nism [æn'tægənɪzm] antagonismo *m*

an·tag·o·nis·tic [æntægə'nɪstɪk] *adj* hostil

an·tag·o·nize [æn'tægənaɪz] *v/t* antagonizar, enfadar

Ant·arc·tic [ænt'ɑ:rktɪk] *n*: **the Antarctic** el Antártico

an·te·na·tal [æntɪ'neɪtl] *adj* prenatal

an·ten·na [æn'tenə] *of insect, for* TV antena *f*

an·thol·o·gy [æn'θɑ:lədʒɪ] antología *f*

an·thro·pol·o·gy [ænθrə'pɑ:lədʒɪ] antropología *f*

an·ti·bi·ot·ic [æntɪbaɪ'ɑ:tɪk] *n* antibiótico *m*

an·ti·bod·y ['æntɪbɑ:dɪ] anticuerpo *m*

an·tic·i·pate [æn'tɪsɪpeɪt] *v/t* esperar, prever

an·tic·i·pa·tion [æntɪsɪ'peɪʃn] expectativa *f*, previsión *f*

an·ti·clock·wise ['æntɪklɑ:kwaɪz] *adv* Br en dirección contraria a las agujas del reloj

an·tics ['æntɪks] *npl* payasadas *fpl*

an·ti·dote ['æntɪdout] antídoto *m*

an·ti·freeze ['æntɪfri:z] anticongelante *m*

an·tip·a·thy [æn'tɪpəθɪ] antipatía *f*

an·ti·quat·ed ['æntɪkweɪtɪd] *adj* anticuado

an·tique [æn'ti:k] *n* antigüedad *f*

an'tique dealer anticuario(-a) *m(f)*

an·tiq·ui·ty [æn'tɪkwətɪ] antigüedad *f*

an·ti·sep·tic [æntɪ'septɪk] **1** *adj* antiséptico **2** *n* antiséptico *m*

an·ti·so·cial [æntɪ'souʃl] *adj* antisocial, poco sociable

an·ti·vi·rus pro·gram [æntɪ'vaɪrəs] COMPUT (programa *m*) antivirus *m inv*

anx·i·e·ty [æŋ'zaɪətɪ] ansiedad *f*

anx·ious ['æŋkʃəs] *adj* preocupado; (*eager*) ansioso; **be anxious for** *for news etc* esperar ansiosamente

an·y ['enɪ] **1** *adj*: **are there any diskettes / glasses?** ¿hay disquetes / vasos?; **is there any bread / improvement?** ¿hay algo de pan / alguna mejora?; **there aren't any diskettes / glasses** no hay disquetes / vasos; **there isn't any bread / improvement** no hay pan / ninguna mejora; **have you any idea at all?** ¿tienes alguna idea al all? **any one of them could win** cualquiera de ellos podría ganar **2** *pron* alguno(-a); **do you**

have any? ¿tienes alguno(s)?; **there aren't any left** no queda ninguno; **there isn't any left** no queda; **any of them could be guilty** cualquiera de ellos podría ser culpable **3** *adv*: **is that any better / easier?** ¿es mejor / más fácil así?; **I don't like it any more** ya no me gusta

an·y·bod·y ['enɪbɑ:dɪ] *pron* alguien; **there wasn't anybody there** no había nadie allí

an·y·how ['enɪhaʊ] *adv* en todo caso, de todos modos; **if I can help you anyhow, please let me know** si puedo ayudarte de alguna manera, por favor dímelo

an·y·one ['enɪwʌn] → **anybody**

an·y·thing ['enɪθɪŋ] *pron* algo; *with negatives* nada; **I didn't hear anything** no oí nada; **anything but** todo menos; **anything else?** ¿algo más?

an·y·way ['enɪweɪ] → **anyhow**

an·y·where ['enɪwer] *adv* en alguna parte; **is Peter anywhere around?** ¿está Peter por ahí?; **he never goes anywhere** nunca va a ninguna parte; **I can't find it anywhere** no lo encuentro por ninguna parte

a·part [ə'pɑ:rt] *adv* aparte; **the two cities are 250 miles apart** las dos ciudades están a 250 millas la una de la otra; **live apart** *of people* vivir separado; **apart from** aparte de

a·part·ment [ə'pɑ:rtmənt] apartamento *m*, *Span* piso *m*, *Am* departamento *m*

a'part·ment block bloque *m* de apartamentos *or* Span pisos

ap·a·thet·ic [æpə'θetɪk] *adj* apático

ap·a·thy ['æpəθɪ] apatía *f*

ape [eɪp] simio *m*

a·pe·ri·tif [ə'perɪti:f] aperitivo *m*

a·per·ture ['æpərʧər] PHOT apertura *f*

a·piece [ə'pi:s] *adv* cada uno

a·pol·o·get·ic [əpɑ:lə'dʒetɪk] *adj letter* de disculpa; **he was very apologetic about ...** pedía constantes disculpas por ...

a·pol·o·gize [ə'pɑ:lədʒaɪz] *v/i* disculparse, pedir perdón

a·pol·o·gy [ə'pɑ:lədʒɪ] disculpa *f*

a·pos·tle [ə'pɑ:sl] REL apóstol *m*

a·pos·tro·phe [ə'pɑ:strəfɪ] GRAM apóstrofo *m*

ap·pall [ə'pɒl] *v/t* horrorizar, espantar

ap·pal·ling [ə'pɒlɪŋ] *adj* horroroso

ap·pa·ra·tus [æpə'reɪtəs] aparatos *mpl*

ap·par·ent [ə'pærənt] *adj* aparente, evidente; **become apparent that ...** hacerse evidente que ...

ap·par·ent·ly [ə'pærəntlɪ] *adv* al parecer, por lo visto

ap·pa·ri·tion [æpə'rɪʃn] (*ghost*) aparición

f

ap·peal [ə'piːl] **1** *n* (*charm*) atractivo *m*; *for funds etc* llamamiento *m*; LAW apelación *f* **2** *v/i* LAW apelar
◆ **appeal to** *v/t* (*be attractive to*) atraer a
◆ **appeal for** *v/t* solicitar
ap·peal·ing [ə'piːlɪŋ] *adj idea, offer* atractivo; *glance* suplicante
ap·pear [ə'pɪr] *v/i* aparecer; *in court* comparecer; (*look, seem*) parecer; *it appears that* ... parece que ...
ap·pear·ance [ə'pɪrəns] aparición *f*; *in court* comparecencia *f*; (*look*) apariencia *f*, aspecto *m*; *put in an appearance* hacer acto de presencia
ap·pease [ə'piːz] *v/t* apaciguar
ap·pen·di·ci·tis [əpendɪ'saɪtɪs] apendicitis *m*
ap·pen·dix [ə'pendɪks] MED, *of book etc* apéndice *m*
ap·pe·tite ['æpɪtaɪt] *also fig* apetito *m*
ap·pe·tiz·er ['æpɪtaɪzər] aperitivo *m*
ap·pe·tiz·ing ['æpɪtaɪzɪŋ] *adj* apetitoso
ap·plaud [ə'plɔːd] **1** *v/i* aplaudir **2** *v/t also fig* aplaudir
ap·plause [ə'plɔːz] aplauso *m*
ap·ple ['æpl] manzana *f*
ap·ple 'pie tarta *f* de manzana
ap·ple 'sauce compota *f* de manzana
ap·pli·ance [ə'plaɪəns] aparato *m*; *household* electrodoméstico *m*
ap·plic·a·ble [ə'plɪkəbl] *adj* aplicable; *it's not applicable to foreigners* no se aplica a extranjeros
ap·pli·cant ['æplɪkənt] solicitante *m/f*
ap·pli·ca·tion [æplɪ'keɪʃn] *for job, passport etc* solicitud *f*; *for university* solicitud *f* (de admisión)
ap·pli·ca·tion form *for passport* impreso *m* de solicitud; *for university* impreso *m* de solicitud de admisión
ap·ply [ə'plaɪ] **1** *v/t* (*pret & pp applied*) *rules, solution, ointment* aplicar **2** *v/i* (*pret & pp applied*) *of rule, law* aplicarse
◆ **apply for** *v/t job, passport* solicitar; *university* solicitar el ingreso en
◆ **apply to** *v/t* (*contact*) dirigirse a; (*affect*) aplicarse a
ap·point [ə'pɔɪnt] *v/t to position* nombrar, designar
ap·point·ment [ə'pɔɪntmənt] *to position* nombramiento *m*, designación *f*; *meeting* cita *f*; *make an appointment with the doctor* pedir hora con el doctor
ap·point·ments di·a·ry agenda *f* de citas
ap·prais·al [ə'preɪz(ə)l] evaluación *f*
ap·pre·ci·a·ble [ə'priːʃəbl] *adj* apreciable
ap·pre·ci·ate [ə'priːʃieɪt] **1** *v/t* (*value*) apreciar; (*be grateful for*) agradecer;

(*acknowledge*) ser consciente de; *thanks, I appreciate it* te lo agradezco **2** *v/i* FIN revalorizarse
ap·pre·ci·a·tion [əpriːʃɪ'eɪʃn] *of kindness etc* agradecimiento *m*; *of music etc* aprecio *m*
ap·pre·ci·a·tive [ə'priːʃətɪv] *adj* agradecido
ap·pre·hen·sive [æprɪ'hensɪv] *adj* aprensivo, temeroso
ap·pren·tice [ə'prentɪs] aprendiz(a) *m(f)*
ap·proach [ə'proʊtʃ] **1** *n* aproximación *f*; (*proposal*) propuesta *f*; *to problem* enfoque *m* **2** *v/t* (*get near to*) aproximarse a; (*contact*) ponerse en contacto con; *problem* enfocar
ap·proach·a·ble [ə'proʊtʃəbl] *adj person* accesible
ap·pro·pri·ate[1] [ə'proʊprɪət] *adj* apropiado, adecuado
ap·pro·pri·ate[2] [ə'proʊprieɪt] *v/t* apropiarse de; (*euph: steal*) apropiarse de
ap·prov·al [ə'pruːvl] aprobación *f*
ap·prove [ə'pruːv] **1** *v/i*: *my parents don't approve* a mis padres no les parece bien **2** *v/t* aprobar
◆ **approve of** *v/t* aprobar; *her parents don't approve of me* no les gusto a sus padres
ap·prox·i·mate [ə'prɑːksɪmət] *adj* aproximado
ap·prox·i·mate·ly [ə'prɑːksɪmətlɪ] *adv* aproximadamente
ap·prox·i·ma·tion [əprɑːksɪ'meɪʃn] aproximación *f*
APR [eɪpiː'ɑː] *abbr* (= *annual percentage rate*) TAE *f* (= tasa *f* anual equivalente)
a·pri·cot ['æprɪkɑːt] albaricoque *m*, *L.Am.* damasco *m*
A·pril ['eɪprəl] abril *m*
apt [æpt] *adj remark* oportuno; *be apt to* ... ser propenso a ...
ap·ti·tude ['æptɪtuːd] aptitud *f*; *he has a natural aptitude for* ... tiene aptitudes naturales para ...
'ap·ti·tude test prueba *f* de aptitud
aq·ua·lung ['ækwəlʌŋ] escafandra *f* autónoma
a·quar·i·um [ə'kwerɪəm] acuario *m*
A·quar·i·us [ə'kwerɪəs] ASTR Acuario *m/f inv*
a·quat·ic [ə'kwætɪk] *adj* acuático
Ar·ab ['ærəb] **1** *adj* árabe **2** *n* árabe *m/f*
Ar·a·bic ['ærəbɪk] **1** *adj* árabe **2** *n* árabe *m*
ar·a·ble ['ærəbl] *adj* arable, cultivable
ar·bi·tra·ry ['ɑːrbɪtrerɪ] *adj* arbitrario
ar·bi·trate ['ɑːrbɪtreɪt] *v/i* arbitrar
ar·bi·tra·tion [ɑːrbɪ'treɪʃn] arbitraje *m*

ar·bi·tra·tor ['ɑːrbɪ'treɪtər] árbitro(-a) *m(f)*

arch [ɑːrtʃ] *n* arco *m*

ar·chae·ol·o·gy *etc Br* → **archeology** *etc*

ar·cha·ic [ɑːr'keɪɪk] *adj* arcaico

ar·che·o·log·i·cal [ɑːrkɪə'lɑːdʒɪkl] *adj* arqueológico

ar·che·ol·o·gist [ɑːrkɪ'ɑːlədʒɪst] arqueólogo(-a) *m(f)*

ar·che·ol·o·gy [ɑːrkɪ'ɑːlədʒɪ] arqueología *f*

ar·cher ['ɑːrtʃər] arquero(-a) *m(f)*

ar·chi·tect ['ɑːrkɪtekt] arquitecto(-a) *m(f)*

ar·chi·tec·tur·al [ɑːrkɪ'tektʃərəl] *adj* arquitectónico

ar·chi·tec·ture ['ɑːrkɪtektʃər] arquitectura *f*

ar·chives ['ɑːrkaɪvz] *npl* archivos *mpl*

arch·way ['ɑːrtʃweɪ] arco *m*

Arc·tic ['ɑːrktɪk] *n*: **the Arctic** el Ártico

ar·dent ['ɑːrdənt] *adj* ardiente, ferviente

ar·du·ous ['ɑːrdjʊəs] *adj* arduo

ar·e·a ['erɪə] área *f*, zona *f*; *of activity, study etc* área *f*, ámbito *m*

'ar·e·a code TELEC prefijo *m*

a·re·na [ə'riːnə] SP estadio *m*

Ar·gen·ti·na [ɑːrdʒən'tiːnə] Argentina

Ar·gen·tin·i·an [ɑːrdʒən'tɪnɪən] **1** *adj* argentino **2** *n* argentino(-a) *m(f)*

ar·gu·a·bly ['ɑːrgjʊəblɪ] *adv* posiblemente

ar·gue ['ɑːrgjuː] **1** *v/i* (*quarrel*) discutir; (*reason*) argumentar **2** *v/t*: **argue that ...** argumentar que ...

ar·gu·ment ['ɑːrgjʊmənt] (*quarrel*) discusión *m*; (*reasoning*) argumento *m*

ar·gu·men·ta·tive [ɑːrgjʊ'mentətɪv] *adj* discutidor

a·ri·a ['ɑːrɪə] MUS aria *f*

ar·id ['ærɪd] *adj* land árido

Ar·i·es ['eriːz] ASTR Aries *m/f inv*

a·rise [ə'raɪz] *v/i* (*pret* **arose**, *pp* **arisen**) *of situation, problem* surgir

a·ris·en [ə'rɪzn] *pp* → **arise**

ar·is·toc·ra·cy [ærɪ'stɑːkrəsɪ] aristocracia *f*

ar·is·to·crat [ə'rɪstəkræt] aristócrata *m/f*

ar·is·to·crat·ic [ærɪstə'krætɪk] *adj* aristocrático

a·rith·me·tic [ə'rɪθmətɪk] aritmética *f*

arm[1] [ɑːrm] *n of person, chair* brazo *m*

arm[2] [ɑːrm] *v/t* armar

ar·ma·ments ['ɑːrməmənts] *npl* armamento *m*

arm·chair ['ɑːrmtʃer] sillón *m*

armed [ɑːrmd] *adj* armado

armed 'forc·es *npl* fuerzas *fpl* armadas

armed 'rob·ber·y atraco *m* a mano armada

ar·mor, *Br* **ar·mour** ['ɑːrmər] armadura *f*

ar·mored 've·hi·cle, *Br* **ar·moured 've·hi·cle** ['ɑːrmərd] vehículo *m* blindado

arm·pit ['ɑːrmpɪt] sobaco *m*

arms [ɑːrmz] *npl* (*weapons*) armas *fpl*

ar·my ['ɑːrmɪ] ejército *m*

a·ro·ma [ə'roʊmə] aroma *m*

a·rose [ə'roʊz] *pret* → **arise**

a·round [ə'raʊnd] **1** *prep* (*enclosing*) alrededor de; **it's around the corner** está a la vuelta de la esquina **2** *adv* (*in the area*) por ahí; (*encircling*) alrededor; (*roughly*) alrededor de, aproximadamente; (*with expressions of time*) en torno a; **he lives around here** vive por aquí; **walk around** pasear; **she has been around** (*has traveled, is experienced*) tiene mucho mundo; **he's still around** F (*alive*) todavía está rondando por ahí F

a·rouse [ə'raʊz] *v/t* despertar; *sexually* excitar

ar·range [ə'reɪndʒ] *v/t* (*put in order*) ordenar; *furniture* ordenar, disponer; *flowers, music* arreglar; *meeting, party etc* organizar; *time and place* acordar; **I've arranged to meet her** he quedado con ella

◆ **arrange for** *v/t*: **I arranged for Jack to collect it** quedé para que Jack lo recogiera

ar·range·ment [ə'reɪndʒmənt] (*plan*) plan *m*, preparativo *m*; (*agreement*) acuerdo *m*; (*layout: of furniture etc*) orden *m*, disposición *f*; *of flowers, music* arreglo *m*; **I've made arrangements for the neighbors to water my plants** he quedado con los vecinos para que rieguen mis plantas

ar·rears [ə'rɪərz] *npl* atrasos *mpl*; **be in arrears** *of person* ir atrasado

ar·rest [ə'rest] **1** *n* detención *f*, arresto *m*; **be under arrest** estar detenido *or* arrestado **2** *v/t* detener, arrestar

ar·riv·al [ə'raɪvl] llegada *f*; **on your arrival** al llegar; **arrivals** *at airport* llegadas *fsg*

ar·rive [ə'raɪv] *v/i* llegar

◆ **arrive at** *v/t place, decision etc* llegar a

ar·ro·gance ['ærəgəns] arrogancia *f*

ar·ro·gant ['ærəgənt] *adj* arrogante

ar·ro·gant·ly ['ærəgəntlɪ] *adv* con arrogancia

ar·row ['æroʊ] flecha *f*

arse [ɑːrs] *Br* P culo *m* P

ar·se·nic ['ɑːrsənɪk] arsénico *m*

ar·son ['ɑːrsn] incendio *m* provocado

ar·son·ist ['ɑːrsənɪst] pirómano(-a) *m(f)*

art [ɑːrt] arte *m*; **the arts** las artes

ar·te·ry ['ɑːrtərɪ] MED arteria *f*

'art gal·ler·y *public* museo *m*; *private* galería *f* de arte

ar·thri·tis [ɑːr'θraɪtɪs] artritis *f*

ar·ti·choke ['ɑːrtɪtʃoʊk] alcachofa *f*, *L.Am.* alcaucil *m*

ar·ti·cle ['ɑːrtɪkl] artículo *m*

ar·tic·u·late [ɑːr'tɪkjʊlət] *adj person* elocuente

ar·ti·fi·cial [ɑːrtɪ'fɪʃl] *adj* artificial

ar·ti·fi·cial in'tel·li·gence inteligencia *f* artificial

ar·til·le·ry [ɑːr'tɪləry] artillería *f*

ar·ti·san ['ɑːrtɪzæn] artesano(-a) *m(f)*

ar·tist ['ɑːrtɪst] *(painter, artistic person)* artista *m/f*

ar·tis·tic [ɑːr'tɪstɪk] *adj* artístico

'arts de·gree licenciatura *f* en letras

as [æz] **1** *conj (while, when)* cuando; *(because, like)* como; *as if* como si; *as usual* como de costumbre; *as necessary* como sea necesario **2** *adv* como; *as high / pretty as …* tan alto / guapa como …; *as much as that?* ¿tanto? **3** *prep* como; *work as a team* trabajar en equipo; *as a child / schoolgirl* cuando era un niño / una colegiala; *work as a teacher / translator* trabajar como profesor / traductor; *as for* por lo que respecta a; *as Hamlet* en el papel del Hamlet

asap ['eɪzæp] *abbr* (= *as soon as possible*) cuanto antes

as·bes·tos [æz'bestɑːs] amianto *m*, asbesto *m*

As·cen·sion [ə'senʃn] RPL Ascensión *f*

ash [æʃ] ceniza *f*; *ashes of person* cenizas *fpl*

a·shamed [ə'ʃeɪmd] *adj* avergonzado, *L.Am.* apenado; *be ashamed of* estar avergonzado *or L.Am.* apenado de; *you should be ashamed of yourself* debería darte vergüenza *or L.Am.* pena; *It's nothing to be ashamed of* no tienes por qué avergonzarte *or L.Am.* apenarte

'ash bin, 'ash can cubo *m* de la basura

a·shore [ə'ʃɔːr] *adv* en tierra; *go ashore* desembarcar

ash·tray ['æʃtreɪ] cenicero *m*

A·sia ['eɪʃə] Asia

A·sian ['eɪʃən] **1** *adj* asiático **2** *n* asiático(-a) *m(f)*

a·side [ə'saɪd] *adv* a un lado; *move aside please* apártense, por favor; *he took me aside* me llevó aparte; *aside from* aparte de

ask [æsk] **1** *v/t person, question* preguntar; *question* hacer; *(invite)* invitar; *favor* pedir; *can I ask you something?* ¿puedo hacerte una pregunta?; *ask s.o. for sth* pedir algo a alguien; *he asked me*

---

to leave me pidió que me fuera; *ask s.o. about sth* preguntar por algo a alguien **2** *v/i*: *all you need to do is ask* no tienes más que pedirlo

◆ ask after *v/t person* preguntar por

◆ ask for *v/t* pedir; *person* preguntar por

◆ ask out *v/t for a drink, night out* invitar a salir

ask·ing price ['æskɪŋ] precio *m* de salida

a·sleep [ə'sliːp] *adj* dormido; *be (fast) asleep* estar (profundamente) dormido; *fall asleep* dormirse, quedarse dormido

as·par·a·gus [ə'spærəgəs] espárragos *mpl*

as·pect ['æspekt] aspecto *m*

as·phalt ['æsfælt] *n* asfalto *m*

as·phyx·i·ate [əs'fɪksɪeɪt] *v/t* asfixiar

as·phyx·i·a·tion [əsfɪksɪ'eɪʃn] asfixia *f*

as·pi·ra·tion [æspə'reɪʃn] aspiración *f*

as·pi·rin ['æsprɪn] aspirina *f*

ass¹ [æs] *(idiot)* burro(-a) *m(f)*

ass² [æs] P *(backside)* culo P; *(sex)* sexo *m*

as·sai·lant [ə'seɪlənt] asaltante *m/f*

as·sas·sin [ə'sæsɪn] asesino(-a) *m(f)*

as·sas·sin·ate [ə'sæsɪneɪt] *v/t* asesinar

as·sas·sin·a·tion [əsæsɪ'neɪʃn] asesinato *m*

as·sault [ə'sɔːlt] **1** *n* agresión *f*; *(attack)* ataque *m* **2** *v/t* atacar, agredir

as·sem·ble [ə'sembl] **1** *v/t parts* montar **2** *v/i of people* reunirse

as·sem·bly [ə'sembli] *of parts* montaje *m*; POL asamblea *f*

as'sem·bly line cadena *f* de montaje

as'sem·bly plant planta *f* de montaje

as·sent [ə'sent] *v/i* asentir, dar el consentimiento

as·sert [ə'sɜːrt] *v/t* afirmar, hacer valer; *assert o.s.* mostrarse firme

as·ser·tive [ə'sɜːrtɪv] *adj person* seguro y firme

as·sess [ə'ses] *v/t situation* evaluar; *value* valorar

as·sess·ment [ə'sesmənt] evaluación *f*

as·set ['æset] FIN activo *m*; *fig* ventaja *f*; *she's an asset to the company* es un gran valor para la compañía

ass·hole ['æshoʊl] V ojete *m* V; *(idiot)* Span gilipollas *m/f inv* V, *L.Am.* pendejo(-a) *m(f)* V

as·sign [ə'saɪn] *v/t person, thing* asignar

as·sign·ment [ə'saɪnmənt] *(task, study)* trabajo *m*

as·sim·i·late [ə'sɪmɪleɪt] *v/t information* asimilar; *person into group* integrar

as·sist [ə'sɪst] *v/t* ayudar

as·sist·ance [ə'sɪstəns] ayuda *f*, asistencia *f*

as·sis·tant [ə'sɪstənt] ayudante *m/f*; Br in

store dependiente(-a) *m(f)*

as·sis·tant di'rec·tor director(a) *m(f)* adjunto

as·sis·tant 'man·ag·er *of business* subdirector(a) *m(f)*; *of hotel, restaurant, store* subdirector(a) *m(f)*, subgerente *m/f*

as·so·ci·ate **1** *v/t* [ə'souʃieit] asociar; *he has long been associated with the Royal Ballet* ha estado vinculado al Royal Ballet durante mucho tiempo **2** *v/i* [ə'souʃieit]: *associate with* relacionarse con **3** *n* [ə'souʃiət] colega *m/f*

as·so·ci·ate pro'fes·sor profesor(a) *m(f)* adjunto(a)

as·so·ci·a·tion [əsousi'eiʃn] asociación *f*; *in association with* conjuntamente con

as·sort·ed [ə'sɔːrtɪd] *adj* surtido, diverso

as·sort·ment [ə'sɔːrtmənt] *of food* surtido *m*; *of people* diversidad *f*

as·sume [ə'suːm] *v/t* (*suppose*) suponer

as·sump·tion [ə'sʌmpʃn] suposición *f*

as·sur·ance [ə'ʃurəns] garantía *f*; (*confidence*) seguridad *f*

as·sure [ə'ʃur] *v/t* (*reassure*) asegurar

as·sured [ə'ʃurd] *adj* (*confident*) seguro

as·ter·isk ['æstərɪsk] asterisco *m*

asth·ma ['æsmə] asma *f*

asth·mat·ic [æs'mætɪk] *adj* asmático

as·ton·ish [ə'stɑːnɪʃ] *v/t* asombrar, sorprender; *be astonished* estar asombrado *or* sorprendido

as·ton·ish·ing [ə'stɑːnɪʃɪŋ] *adj* asombroso, sorprendente

as·ton·ish·ing·ly [ə'stɑːnɪʃɪŋlɪ] *adv* asombrosamente

as·ton·ish·ment [ə'stɑːnɪʃmənt] asombro *m*, sorpresa *f*

as·tound [ə'staund] *v/t* pasmar

as·tound·ing [ə'staundɪŋ] *adj* pasmoso

a·stray [ə'streɪ] *adv*: *go astray* extraviarse; *morally* descarriarse

a·stride [ə'straɪd] **1** *adv* a horcajadas **2** *prep* a horcajadas sobre

as·trol·o·ger [ə'strɑːlədʒər] astrólogo(-a) *m(f)*

as·trol·o·gy [ə'strɑːlədʒɪ] astrología *f*

as·tro·naut ['æstrənɔːt] astronauta *m/f*

as·tron·o·mer [ə'strɑːnəmər] astrónomo(-a) *m(f)*

as·tro·nom·i·cal [æstrə'nɑːmɪkl] *adj price etc* astronómico

as·tron·o·my [ə'strɑːnəmɪ] astronomía *f*

a·stute [ə'stuːt] *adj* astuto, sagaz

a·sy·lum [ə'saɪləm] (*mental asylum*) manicomio *m*; *political* asilo *m*

at [ət] *stressed* [æt] *prep with places* en; *at Joe's house* en casa de Joe; *bar* en el bar de Joe; *at the door* a la puerta; *at 10 dollars* a 10 dólares; *at the age of 18* a los 18

años; *at 5 o'clock* a las 5; *at 150 km/h* a 150 km./h.; *be good / bad at sth* ser bueno / malo haciendo algo

ate [eit] *pret* → *eat*

a·the·ism ['eɪθɪɪzm] ateísmo *m*

a·the·ist ['eɪθɪɪst] ateo(-a) *m(f)*

ath·lete ['æθliːt] atleta *m/f*

ath·let·ic [æθ'letɪk] *adj* atlético

ath·let·ics [æθ'letɪks] atletismo *m*

At·lan·tic [ət'læntɪk] *n*: *the Atlantic* el Atlántico

at·las ['ætləs] atlas *m inv*

ATM [eɪtɪː'em] *abbr* (= *automatic teller machine*) cajero *m* automático

at·mos·phere ['ætməsfɪr] *of earth* atmósfera *f*; (*ambiance*) ambiente *m*

at·mos·pher·ic pol'lu·tion [ætməs'ferɪk] contaminación *f* atmosférica

at·om ['ætəm] átomo *m*

'at·om bomb bomba *f* atómica

a·tom·ic [ə'tɑːmɪk] *adj* atómico

a·tom·ic 'en·er·gy energía *f* atómica *or* nuclear

a·tom·ic 'waste desechos *mpl* radiactivos

a·tom·iz·er ['ætəmaɪzər] atomizador *m*

a·tone [ə'toun] *v/i*: *atone for* expiar

a·troc·i·ty [ə'trɑːsəti] atrocidad *f*

at·tach [ə'tætʃ] *v/t* sujetar, fijar; *importance* atribuir; *be attached to* (*fond of*) tener cariño a

at·tach·ment [ə'tætʃmənt] (*fondness*) cariño *m* (*to* por)

at·tack [ə'tæk] **1** *n* ataque *m* **2** *v/t* atacar

at·tempt [ə'tempt] **1** *n* intento *m*; *an attempt on the world record* un intento de batir el récord del mundo **2** *v/t* intentar

at·tend [ə'tend] *v/t* acudir a

◆ **attend to** *v/t* ocuparse de; *customer* atender

at·tend·ance [ə'tendəns] asistencia *f*

at·tend·ant [ə'tendənt] *in museum etc* vigilante *m/f*

at·ten·tion [ə'tenʃn] atención *f*; *bring sth to s.o.'s attention* informar a alguien de algo; *your attention please* atención, por favor; *pay attention* prestar atención

at·ten·tive [ə'tentɪv] *adj listener* atento

at·tic ['ætɪk] ático *m*

at·ti·tude ['ætɪtuːd] actitud *f*

attn *abbr* (= *for the attention of*) atn (= a la atención de)

at·tor·ney [ə'tɜːrnɪ] abogado(-a) *m(f)*; *power of attorney* poder *m* (notarial)

at·tract [ə'trækt] *v/t* atraer; *attract attention* llamar la atención; *attract s.o.'s attention* atraer la atención de alguien; *be*

attracted to s.o. sentirse atraído por alguien

at·trac·tion [əˈtrækʃn] atracción f, atractivo m; *romantic* atracción f

at·trac·tive [əˈtræktɪv] adj atractivo

at·trib·ute¹ [əˈtrɪbjuːt] v/t atribuir; **attribute sth to ...** atribuir algo a ...

at·trib·ute² [ˈætrɪbjuːt] n atributo m

au·ber·gine [ˈoʊbərʒiːn] Br berenjena f

auc·tion [ˈɔːkʃn] **1** n subasta f, L.Am. remate m **2** v/t subastar, L.Am. rematar

◆ **auction off** v/t subastar, L.Am. rematar

auc·tio·neer [ɔːkʃəˈnɪr] subastador(a) m(f), L.Am. rematador(a) m(f)

au·da·cious [ɔːˈdeɪʃəs] adj plan audaz

au·dac·i·ty [ɔːˈdæsətɪ] audacia f

au·di·ble [ˈɔːdəbl] adj audible

au·di·ence [ˈɔːdɪəns] in theater, at show público m, espectadores mpl; TV audiencia f

au·di·o [ˈɔːdɪoʊ] adj de audio

au·di·o·vi·su·al [ɔːdɪoʊˈvɪʒʊəl] adj audiovisual

au·dit [ˈɔːdɪt] **1** n auditoría f **2** v/t auditar; *course* asistir de oyente a

au·di·tion [ɔːˈdɪʃn] **1** n audición f **2** v/i hacer una prueba

au·di·tor [ˈɔːdɪtər] auditor(a) m(f)

au·di·to·ri·um [ɔːdɪˈtɔːrɪəm] of theater etc auditorio m

Au·gust [ˈɔːɡəst] agosto m

aunt [ænt] tía f

au pair [oʊˈper] au pair m/f

au·ra [ˈɔːrə] aura f

aus·pic·es [ˈɔːspɪsɪz] npl auspicios mpl; **under the auspices of** bajo los auspicios de

aus·pi·cious [ɔːˈspɪʃəs] adj propicio

aus·tere [ɔːˈstɪr] adj *interior* austero

aus·ter·i·ty [ɔːsˈterətɪ] *economic* austeridad f

Aus·tra·li·a [ɔːˈstreɪlɪə] Australia f

Aus·tra·li·an [ɔːˈstreɪlɪən] **1** adj australiano **2** n australiano(-a) m(f)

Aus·tri·a [ˈɔːstrɪə] Austria f

Aus·tri·an [ˈɔːstrɪən] **1** adj austriaco **2** n austriaco(-a) m(f)

au·then·tic [ɔːˈθentɪk] adj auténtico

au·then·tic·i·ty [ɔːθenˈtɪsətɪ] autenticidad f

au·thor [ˈɔːθər] of story, novel escritor(a) m(f); of text autor(a) m(f)

au·thor·i·tar·i·an [əθɔːrɪˈterɪən] adj autoritario

au·thor·i·ta·tive [əˈθɔːrɪtətɪv] adj autorizado

au·thor·i·ty [əˈθɔːrətɪ] autoridad f; (*permission*) autorización f; **be an authority on** ser una autoridad en; **the authorities** las autoridades

au·thor·i·za·tion [ɔːθərɪˈzeɪʃn] autorización f

au·thor·ize [ˈɔːθəraɪz] v/t autorizar; **be authorized to ...** estar autorizado para ...

au·tis·tic [ɔːˈtɪstɪk] adj autista

au·to·bi·og·ra·phy [ɔːtəbaɪˈɑːɡrəfɪ] autobiografía f

au·to·crat·ic [ɔːtəˈkrætɪk] adj autocrático

au·to·graph [ˈɔːtəɡræf] autógrafo m

au·to·mate [ˈɔːtəmeɪt] v/t automatizar

au·to·mat·ic [ɔːtəˈmætɪk] **1** adj automático **2** n car (coche m) automático m; gun pistola f automática; *washing machine* lavadora f automática

au·to·mat·i·cal·ly [ɔːtəˈmætɪklɪ] adv automáticamente

au·to·ma·tion [ɔːtəˈmeɪʃn] automatización f

au·ton·o·mous [ɔːˈtɑːnəməs] adj autónomo

au·ton·o·my [ɔːˈtɑːnəmɪ] autonomía f

au·to·pi·lot [ˈɔːtoʊpaɪlət] piloto m automático

au·top·sy [ˈɔːtɑːpsɪ] autopsia f

au·tumn [ˈɔːtəm] Br otoño m

aux·il·ia·ry [ɔːɡˈzɪljərɪ] adj auxiliar

a·vail [əˈveɪl] **1** n: **to no avail** en vano **2** v/t: **avail o.s. of** aprovechar

a·vai·la·ble [əˈveɪləbl] adj disponible

av·a·lanche [ˈævəlænʃ] avalancha f, alud m

av·a·rice [ˈævərɪs] avaricia f

av·e·nue [ˈævənuː] avenida f; fig camino m

av·e·rage [ˈævərɪdʒ] **1** adj medio; (*of mediocre quality*) regular **2** n promedio m, media f; **above** / **below average** por encima / por debajo del promedio; **on average** como promedio, de media **3** v/t: **I average six hours of sleep a night** duermo seis horas cada noche como promedio or de media

◆ **average out** v/t calcular el promedio or la media de

◆ **average out at** v/t salir a

a·verse [əˈvɜːrs] adj: **not be averse to** no ser reacio a

a·ver·sion [əˈvɜːrʃn] aversión f; **have an aversion to** tener aversión a

a·vert [əˈvɜːrt] v/t one's eyes apartar; crisis evitar

a·vi·a·tion [eɪvɪˈeɪʃn] aviación f

av·id [ˈævɪd] adj ávido

av·o·ca·do [ɑːvəˈkɑːdou] aguacate *m*, *S. Am.* palta *f*

a·void [əˈvɔid] *v/t* evitar; **you've been avoiding me** has estado huyendo de mí

a·void·a·ble [əˈvɔidəbl] *adj* evitable

a·wait [əˈweit] *v/t* aguardar, esperar

a·wake [əˈweik] *adj* despierto; **it kept me awake** no me dejó dormir

a·ward [əˈwɔːrd] **1** *n* (*prize*) premio *m* **2** *v/t* prize, *damages* conceder

a·ware [əˈwer] *adj*: **be aware of sth** ser consciente de algo; **become aware of sth** darse cuenta de algo

a·ware·ness [əˈwernis] conciencia *f*

a·way [əˈwei] *adv*: **look away** mirar hacia otra parte; **I'll be away until …** traveling voy a estar fuera hasta …; **sick** no voy a ir hasta …; **it's 2 miles away** está a 2 millas;

Christmas is still six weeks away todavía quedan seis semanas para Navidad; **take sth away from s.o.** quitar algo a alguien; **put sth away** guardar algo

a·way match sp partido *m* fuera de casa

awe·some [ˈɒːsəm] *adj* F (*terrific*) alucinante F

aw·ful [ˈɒːfəl] *adj* horrible, espantoso; **I feel awful** me siento fatal

aw·ful·ly [ˈɒːfəli] *adv* F (*very*) tremendamente; **awfully bad** malísimo

awk·ward [ˈɒːkwərd] *adj* (*clumsy*) torpe; (*difficult*) difícil; (*embarrassing*) embarazoso; **feel awkward** sentirse incómodo

awn·ing [ˈɒːniŋ] toldo *m*

ax, *Br* **axe** [æks] **1** *n* hacha *f* **2** *v/t project etc* suprimir; *budget, job* recortar

ax·le [ˈæksl] eje *m*

B

BA [biːˈei] *abbr* (= **Bachelor of Arts**) Licenciatura *f* en Filosofía y Letras

ba·by [ˈbeibi] *n* bebé *m*

ba·by boom explosión *f* demográfica

ba·by car·riage [ˈkærɪdʒ] cochecito *m* de bebé

ba·by·ish [ˈbeibiiʃ] *adj* infantil

ba·by·sit *v/i* (*pret & pp* **baby-sat**) hacer de *Span* canguro or *L.Am.* babysitter

ba·by·sit·ter [ˈsitər] *Span* canguro *m/f*, *L.Am.* babysitter *m/f*

bach·e·lor [ˈbætʃələr] soltero *m*

back [bæk] **1** *n of person, clothes* espalda *f*; *of car, bus, house* parte *f* trasera or de atrás; *of paper, book* dorso *m*; *of drawer* fondo *m*; *of chair* respaldo *m*; sp defensa *m/f*; **in back** *in store* en la trastienda; **in the back** (**of the car**) atrás (del coche); **at the back of the bus** en la parte trasera or de atrás del autobús; **back to front** del revés; **at the back of beyond** en el quinto pino **2** *adj* trasero; **back road** carretera *f* secundaria **3** *adv* atrás; **please stand back** póngase más para atrás **2 meters back from the edge** a 2 metros del borde; **back in 1935** allá por el año 1935; **give sth back to s.o.** devolver algo a alguien; **she'll be back tomorrow** volverá mañana; **when are you coming back?** ¿cuándo volverás?; **take sth back to the store** because unsatisfactory

devolver alguien a la tienda; **they wrote / phoned back** contestaron a la carta/a la llamada; **he hit me back** me devolvió el golpe **4** *v/t* (*support*) apoyar, respaldar; *horse* apostar por **5** *v/i* **he backed into the garage** entró en el garaje marcha atrás

◆ **back away** *v/i* alejarse (hacia atrás)

◆ **back down** *v/i* echarse atrás

◆ **back off** *v/i* echarse atrás

◆ **back onto** *v/t* dar por la parte de atrás a

◆ **back out** *v/i of commitment* echarse atrás

◆ **back up 1** *v/t* (*support*) respaldar; *file* hacer una copia de seguridad de; **traffic was backed up all the way to …** el atasco llegaba hasta … **2** *v/i in car* dar marcha atrás; *of drains* atascarse

back·ache dolor *m* de espalda

back·bit·ing cotilleo *m*, chismorreo *m*

back·bone ANAT columna *f* vertebral, espina *f* dorsal; (*fig: courage*) agallas *fpl*; (*fig: mainstay*) columna *f* vertebral

back·break·ing *adj* extenuante, deslomador

back burn·er: put sth on the back burner aparcar algo

back·date *v/t*: **a salary increase backdated to 1st January** una subida salarial con efecto retroactivo a partir del 1 de enero '**back·door** puerta *f* trasera

back·er ['bækər]: *the backers of the movie financially* las personas que financiaron la película

back'fire *v/i fig: it backfired on us* nos salió el tiro por la culata

'**back·ground** *n* fondo *m*; *of person* origen *m*, historia *f* personal; *of situation* contexto *m*; *she prefers to stay in the background* prefiere permanecer en un segundo plano

'**back·hand** *n in tennis* revés *m*

back·ing ['bækɪŋ] *n* (*support*) apoyo *m*, respaldo *m*; MUS acompañamiento *m*

'**back·ing group** MUS grupo *m* de acompañamiento

'**back·lash** reacción *f* violenta

'**back·log** acumulación *f*

'**back·pack 1** mochila *f* **2** *v/i* viajar con la mochila a cuestas

'**back·pack·er** mochilero(-a) *m(f)*

'**back·pack·ing** viajes *mpl* con la mochila a cuestas

'**back·ped·al** *v/i fig* echarse atrás, dar marcha atrás

'**back seat** *of car* asiento *m* trasero *or* de atrás

back-seat 'driv·er: *he's a terrible back-seat driver* va siempre incordiando al conductor con sus comentarios

'**back·space (key)** (tecla *f* de) retroceso *m*

'**back·stairs** *npl* escalera *f* de servicio

'**back street** callejuela *f*

'**back streets** *npl* callejuelas *fpl*; *poorer, dirtier part of a city* zonas *fpl* deprimidas

'**back·stroke** SP espalda *f*

'**back·track** *v/i* volver atrás, retroceder

'**back·up** (*support*) apoyo *m*, respaldo *m*; *for police* refuerzos *mpl*; COMPUT copia *f* de seguridad; *take a backup* COMPUT haz una copia de seguridad

'**back·up disk** COMPUT disquete *m* con la copia de seguridad

back·ward ['bækwərd] **1** *adj child* retrasado; *society* atrasado; *glance* hacia atrás **2** *adv* hacia atrás

'**back·yard** jardín *m* trasero; *in s.o.'s backyard fig* en la misma puerta de alguien

ba·con ['beɪkən] tocino *m*, *Span* bacon *m*

bac·te·ri·a [bæk'tɪrɪə] *npl* bacterias *fpl*

bad [bæd] *adj* malo; *before singular masculine noun* mal; *cold, headache etc* fuerte; *mistake, accident* grave; *I've had a bad day* he tenido un mal día; *smoking is bad for you* fumar es malo; *it's not bad* no está mal; *that's really too bad* (*shame*) es una verdadera pena; *feel bad about* (*guilty*) sentirse mal por; *I'm*

bad at math se me dan mal las matemáticas; *Friday's bad, how about Thursday?* el viernes me viene mal, ¿qué tal el jueves?

bad 'debt deuda *f* incobrable

badge [bædʒ] insignia *f*, chapa *f*; *of policeman* placa *f*

bad·ger ['bædʒər] *v/t* acosar, importunar

bad 'lan·guage palabrotas *fpl*

bad·ly ['bædlɪ] *adv injured* gravemente; *damaged* seriamente; *work* mal; *I did really badly in the exam* el examen me salió fatal; *he hasn't done badly in life, business etc* no le ha ido mal; *you're badly in need of a haircut* necesitas urgentemente un corte de pelo; *he is badly off poor* anda mal de dinero

bad-man·nered [bæd'mænərd] *adj*: *be bad-mannered* tener malos modales

bad·min·ton ['bædmɪntən] bádminton *m*

bad-tem·pered [bæd'tempərd] *adj* malhumorado

baf·fle ['bæfl] *v/t* confundir, desconcertar; *be baffled* estar confundido *or* desconcertado; *I'm baffled why she left* no consigo entender por qué se fue

baf·fling ['bæflɪŋ] *adj mystery, software* desconcertante, incomprensible

bag [bæg] bolsa *f*; *for school* cartera *f*; (*purse*) bolso *m*, *S. Am.* cartera *f*, *Mex* bolsa *f*

bag·gage ['bægɪdʒ] equipaje *m*

'**bag·gage car** RAIL vagón *m* de equipajes

'**bag·gage check** consigna *f*

'**bag·gage re·claim** ['riːkleɪm] recogida *f* de equipajes

bag·gy ['bægɪ] *adj* ancho, holgado

'**bag·pipes** *npl* gaita *f*

bail [beɪl] *n* LAW libertad *f* bajo fianza; (*money*) fianza *f*; *on bail* bajo fianza

♦ **bail out 1** *v/t* LAW pagar la fianza de **2** *v/i of airplane* tirarse en paracaídas

bait [beɪt] *n* cebo *m*

bake [beɪk] *v/t* hornear, cocer al horno

baked 'beans [beɪkt] *npl* alubias con salsa de tomate

baked po'ta·to *Span* patata *f* or *L.Am.* papa *f* asada (*con piel*)

bak·er ['beɪkər] panadero(-a) *m(f)*

bak·er·y ['beɪkərɪ] panadería *f*

bak·ing pow·der ['beɪkɪŋ] levadura *f*

bal·ance ['bæləns] **1** *n* equilibrio *m*; (*remainder*) resto *m*; *of bank account* saldo *m* **2** *v/t* poner en equilibrio; *balance the books* cuadrar las cuentas **3** *v/i* mantenerse en equilibrio; *of accounts* cuadrar

bal·anced ['bælənst] *adj* (*fair*) objetivo; *diet, personality* equilibrado

bal·ance of 'pay·ments balanza *f* de pa-

gos
bal·ance of 'trade balanza f comercial
'bal·ance sheet balance m
bal·co·ny ['bælkənɪ] of house balcón m; in theater anfiteatro m
bald [bɔːld] adj calvo; **he's going bald** se está quedando calvo; **bald spot** calva f
bald·ing ['bɔːldɪŋ] adj medio calvo
Bal·kan ['bɔːlkən] adj balcánico
Bal·kans ['bɔːlkənz] npl: **the Balkans** los Balcanes
ball [bɔːl] tennis-ball size pelota f; football size balón m, pelota f; billiard-ball size bola f; **on the ball** despierto; **play ball** fig cooperar; **the ball's in his court** le toca actuar a él, la pelota está en su tejado
bal·lad ['bæləd] balada f
ball 'bear·ing rodamiento m de bolas
bal·le·ri·na [bælə'riːnə] bailarina f
bal·let [bæ'leɪ] ballet m
'bal·let danc·er bailarín (-ina) m(f)
'ball game (baseball game) partido m de béisbol; **that's a different ball game** F esa es otra cuestión F
bal·lis·tic mis·sile [bə'lɪstɪk] misil m balístico
bal·loon [bə'luːn] globo m
bal·loon·ist [bə'luːnɪst] piloto m de globo aerostático
bal·lot ['bælət] **1** n voto m **2** v/t members consultar por votación
'bal·lot box urna f
'bal·lot pa·per papeleta f
'ball·park (baseball) campo m de béisbol; **you're in the right ballpark** F no vas descaminado
'ball·park fig·ure F cifra f aproximada
'ball·point (pen) bolígrafo m, Mex pluma f, Rpl birome m
balls [bɔːlz] npl V huevos mpl V; (courage) huevos mpl V; (nonsense) tonterías fpl, paridas fpl F
bam·boo [bæm'buː] n bambú m
ban [bæn] **1** n prohibición f **2** v/t (pret & pp **banned**) prohibir; **ban s.o. from doing sth** prohibir a alguien que haga algo
ba·nal [bə'næl] adj banal
ba·na·na [bə'nænə] plátano m, Rpl banana f
band [bænd] banda f; pop grupo m
ban·dage ['bændɪdʒ] **1** n vendaje m **2** v/t vendar
'Band-Aid® Span tirita f, L.Am. curita f
B&B [biːn'biː] abbr (= **bed and breakfast**) hostal m familiar
ban·dit ['bændɪt] bandido m
'band·wag·on: **jump on the bandwagon**

subirse al carro
ban·dy ['bændɪ] adj legs arqueado
bang [bæŋ] **1** n noise estruendo m, estrépito m; (blow) golpe m; **the door closed with a bang** la puerta se cerró de un portazo **2** v/t door cerrar de un portazo; (hit) golpear; **bang o.s. on the head** golpearse la cabeza **3** v/i of door dar golpes; **the door banged shut** la puerta se cerró de un portazo
ban·gle ['bæŋgl] brazalete m, pulsera f
bangs [bæŋz] flequillo m
ban·is·ters ['bænɪstərz] npl barandilla f
ban·jo ['bændʒoʊ] banjo m
bank¹ [bæŋk] of river orilla f
bank² [bæŋk] **1** n FIN banco m **2** v/i: **I bank with ...** mi banco es el ... **3** v/t money ingresar, depositar
◆ **bank on** v/t contar con; **don't bank on it** no cuentes con ello
'bank ac·count cuenta f (bancaria)
'bank bal·ance saldo m bancario
'bank bill billete m
bank·er ['bæŋkər] banquero m
'bank·er's card tarjeta f bancaria
bank·ing ['bæŋkɪŋ] banca f
'bank loan préstamo m bancario
'bank man·ag·er director(a) m(f) de banco
'bank rate tipo m de interés bancario
'bank·roll v/t financiar
bank·rupt ['bæŋkrʌpt] **1** adj en bancarrota or quiebra; **go bankrupt** quebrar, ir a la quiebra; of person arruinarse **2** v/t llevar a la quiebra
bank·rupt·cy ['bæŋkrʌpsɪ] of person, company quiebra f, bancarrota f
'bank state·ment extracto m bancario
ban·ner ['bænər] pancarta f
banns [bænz] npl amonestaciones fpl
ban·quet ['bæŋkwɪt] n banquete m
ban·ter ['bæntər] n bromas fpl
bap·tism ['bæptɪzm] bautismo m
bap·tize [bæp'taɪz] v/t bautizar
bar¹ [bɑːr] n of iron barra f; of chocolate tableta f; for drinks bar m; (counter) barra f; **a bar of soap** una pastilla de jabón; **be behind bars** (in prison) estar entre barrotes
bar² [bɑːr] v/t (pret & pp **barred**) from premises prohibir la entrada a; **bar s.o. from doing sth** prohibir a alguien que haga algo
bar³ [bɑːr] prep (except) excepto
bar·bar·i·an [bɑːr'beriən] bárbaro(-a) m(f)
bar·bar·ic [bɑːr'bærɪk] adj brutal, inhumano
bar·be·cue ['bɑːrbɪkjuː] **1** n barbacoa f **2**

v/t cocinar en la barbacoa

barbed 'wire [bɑːbd] alambre *f* de espino

bar·ber ['bɑːrbər] barbero *m*

bar·bi·tu·rate [bɑːr'bɪtjərət] barbitúrico *m*

'bar code código *m* de barras

bare [ber] *adj* (*naked*) desnudo; (*empty: room*) vacío; *mountainside* pelado, raso; *floor* descubierto; **in one's bare feet** descalzo

'bare·foot *adj* descalzo

bare·head·ed [ber'hedɪd] *adj* sin sombrero

'bare·ly ['berlɪ] *adv* apenas; **he's barely five** acaba de cumplir cinco años

bar·gain ['bɑːrgɪn] **1** *n* (*deal*) trato *m*; (*good buy*) ganga *f*; **into the bargain** además **2** *v/i* regatear, negociar

◆ **bargain for** *v/t* (*expect*) imaginarse, esperar

barge [bɑːrdʒ] *n* NAUT barcaza *f*

◆ **barge into** *v/t person* tropezarse con; *room* irrumpir en

bar·i·tone ['bærɪtoun] *n* barítono *m*

bark[1] [bɑːrk] **1** *n of dog* ladrido *m* **2** *v/i* ladrar

bark[2] [bɑːrk] *of tree* corteza *f*

bar·ley ['bɑːrlɪ] cebada *f*

'bar·maid *Br* camarera *f*, *L.Am.* mesera *f*, *Rpl* moza *f*

'bar·man camarero *m*, *L.Am.* mesero *m*, *Rpl* mozo *m*

barn [bɑːrn] granero *m*

ba·rom·e·ter [bə'rɑːmɪtər] *also fig* barómetro *m*

Ba·roque [bə'rɑːk] *adj* barroco

bar·racks ['bærəks] *npl* MIL cuartel *m*

bar·rage [bə'rɑːʒ] MIL barrera *f* (de fuego); *fig* aluvión *m*

bar·rel ['bærəl] (*container*) tonel *m*, barril *m*

bar·ren ['bærən] *adj land* yermo, árido

bar·ri·cade [bærɪ'keɪd] *n* barricada *f*

bar·ri·er ['bærɪər] *also fig* barrera *f*; **language barrier** barrera *f* lingüística

bar·ring ['bɑːrɪŋ] *prep* salvo, excepto; **barring accidents** salvo imprevistos

bar·ris·ter ['bærɪstər] *Br* abogado(-a) *m(f)* (*que aparece en tribunales*)

bar·row ['bærou] carretilla *f*

'bar ten·der camarero(-a) *m(f)*, *L.Am.* mesero(-a) *m(f)*, *Rpl* mozo(-a) *m(f)*

bar·ter ['bɑːrtər] **1** *n* trueque *m* **2** *v/t* cambiar, trocar (**for** por)

base [beɪs] **1** *n bottom, center base f; base camp* campamento *m* base **2** *v/t* basar (**on** en); **be based in** *of soldier* estar destinado en; *of company* tener su sede en

'base·ball *ball* pelota *f* de béisbol; *game*

béisbol *m*

'base·ball bat bate *m* de béisbol

'base·ball cap gorra *f* de béisbol

'base·ball play·er jugador(a) *m(f)* de béisbol, *L.Am.* pelotero(-a) *m(f)*

'base·board rodapié *m*

base·less ['beɪslɪs] *adj* infundado

base·ment ['beɪsmənt] *of house, store* sótano *m*

'base rate FIN tipo *m* de interés básico

bash [bæʃ] **1** *n* F porrazo *m* F **2** *v/t* F dar un porrazo a F

ba·sic ['beɪsɪk] *adj* (*rudimentary*) básico; *room* modesto, sencillo; *language skills* elemental; (*fundamental*) fundamental; **basic salary** sueldo *m* base

ba·sic·al·ly ['beɪsɪklɪ] *adv* básicamente

ba·sics ['beɪsɪks] *npl*: **the basics** lo básico, los fundamentos; **get down to basics** centrarse en lo esencial

bas·il ['bæzɪl] albahaca *f*

ba·sil·i·ca [bə'zɪlɪkə] basílica *f*

ba·sin ['beɪsn] *for washing* barreño *m*; *in bathroom* lavabo *m*

ba·sis ['beɪsɪs] (*pl bases* ['beɪsiːz]) base *f*; **on the basis of what you've told me** de acuerdo con lo que me has dicho

bask [bæsk] *v/i* tomar el sol

bas·ket ['bæskɪt] cesta *f*; *in basketball* canasta *f*

bas·ket·ball *game* baloncesto *m*, *L.Am.* básquetbol *m*; *ball* balón *m* o pelota *f* de baloncesto; **basketball player** baloncestista *m/f*, *L.Am.* basquebolista *m/f*

Basque [bæsk] **1** *adj* vasco **2** *n person* vasco(-a) *m(f)*; *language* vasco *m*

bass [beɪs] **1** *n part, singer* bajo *m*; *instrument* contrabajo *m* **2** *adj* bajo

bas·tard ['bæstərd] ilegítimo(-a) *m(f)*, bastardo(-a) *m(f)*; P cabrón(-ona) *m(f)* P; **poor bastard** pobre desgraciado; **stupid bastard** desgraciado

bat[1] [bæt] **1** *n for baseball* bate *m*; *for table tennis* pala *f* **2** *v/i* (*pret & pp batted*) *in baseball* batear

bat[2] [bæt] *v/t* (*pret & pp batted*): **he didn't bat an eyelid** no se inmutó

bat[3] [bæt] (*animal*) murciélago *m*

batch [bætʃ] *n of students* tanda *f*; *of data* conjunto *m*; *of bread* hornada *f*; *of products* lote *m*

ba·ted ['beɪtɪd] *adj*: **with bated breath** con la respiración contenida

bath [bæθ] baño *m*; **have a bath, take a bath** darse *or* tomar un baño

bathe [beɪð] *v/i* (*swim, have a bath*) bañarse

bath·ing cost·ume, bathing suit ['beɪðɪŋ] bañador *m*, traje *m* de baño

'**bath mat** alfombra f de baño
'**bath·robe** albornoz m
'**bath·room** for bath, washing hands, cuarto m de baño; (toilet) servicio m, L.Am. baño m
'**bath tow·el** toalla f de baño
'**bath·tub** bañera f
bat·on [bə'tɑ:n] of conductor batuta f
bat·tal·i·on [bə'tælɪən] MIL batallón m
bat·ter ['bætər] n masa f; in baseball bateador(a) m(f)
bat·tered ['bætərd] adj maltratado
bat·ter·y ['bætərɪ] in watch, flashlight pila f; in computer, car batería f
'**bat·ter·y charg·er** ['tʃɑ:rdʒər] cargador m de pilas / baterías
bat·ter·y-op·er·at·ed [bætərɪ'ɑ:pəreɪtɪd] adj que funciona con pilas
bat·tle ['bætl] 1 n also fig batalla f 2 v/i against illness etc luchar
'**bat·tle·field**, '**bat·tle·ground** campo m de batalla
'**bat·tle·ship** acorazado m
bawd·y ['bɔ:dɪ] adj picante, subido de tono
bawl [bɔ:l] v/i (shout) gritar, vociferar; (weep) berrear
◆ **bawl out** v/t F echar la bronca a F
bay [beɪ] (inlet) bahía f
bay·o·net ['beɪənət] n bayoneta f
bay 'win·dow ventana f en saliente
BC [bi:'si:] abbr (= before Christ) a.C. (= antes de Cristo)
be [bi:] ◇ v/i (pret was / were, pp been) permanent characteristics, profession, nationality ser; position, temporary condition estar; was she there? ¿estaba allí?; it's me soy yo; how much is / are ...? ¿cuánto es / son ...?; there is, there are hay; be careful ten cuidado; don't be sad no estés triste
◇ has the mailman been? ¿ha venido el cartero?; I've never been to Japan no he estado en Japón; I've been here for hours he estado aquí horas
◇ tags: that's right, isn't it? eso es, ¿no?; she's Chinese, isn't she? es china, ¿verdad?
◇ v/aux: I am thinking estoy pensando; he was running corría; you're being stupid estás siendo un estúpido
◇ obligation: you are to do what I tell you harás lo que yo te diga; I was to help him escape se suponía que le iba a ayudar a escaparse; you are not to tell anyone no debes decírselo a nadie
◇ passive: he was arrested fue detenido, lo detuvieron; they have been sold se han vendido

◆ **be in for** v/t: he's in for a big disappointment se va a llevar una gran desilusión
beach [bi:tʃ] n playa f
'**beach ball** pelota f de playa
'**beach·wear** ropa f playera
beads [bi:dz] npl cuentas fpl
beak [bi:k] pico m
'**be-all**: the be-all and end-all lo más importante del mundo
beam [bi:m] 1 n in ceiling etc viga f 2 v/i (smile) sonreír de oreja a oreja 3 v/t (transmit) emitir
bean [bi:n] judía f, alubia f, L.Am. frijol m, S. Am. poroto m; green beans judías fpl verdes, Mex ejotes mpl, S. Am. porotos mpl verdes; coffee beans granos mpl de café; be full of beans F estar lleno de vitalidad
'**bean·bag** cojín relleno de bolitas
bear[1] [ber] animal oso(-a) m(f)
bear[2] [ber] 1 v/t (pret bore, pp borne) weight resistir; costs correr con; (tolerate) aguantar, soportar; child dar a luz; she bore him six children le dio seis hijos 2 v/i (pret bore, pp borne): bring pressure to bear on ejercer presión sobre
◆ **bear out** v/t (confirm) confirmar
bear·a·ble ['berəbl] adj soportable
beard [bɪrd] barba f
beard·ed ['bɪrdɪd] adj con barba
bear·ing ['berɪŋ] in machine rodamiento m, cojinete m; that has no bearing on the case eso no tiene nada que ver con el caso
'**bear mar·ket** FIN mercado m a la baja
beast [bi:st] animal bestia f; person bestia m/f
beat [bi:t] 1 n of heart latido m; of music ritmo m 2 v/i (pret beat, pp beaten) of heart latir; of rain golpear; beat about the bush andarse por las ramas 3 v/t (pret beat, pp beaten) in competition derrotar, ganar a; (hit) pegar a; (pound) golpear; beat it! F ¡lárgate! F; it beats me no logro entender
◆ **beat up** v/t dar una paliza a
beat·en ['bi:tən] 1 adj: off the beaten track retirado 2 pp → beat
beat·ing ['bi:tɪŋ] (physical) paliza f
beat-up adj F destartalado F
beau·ti·cian [bju:'tɪʃn] esteticista m/f
beau·ti·ful ['bju:təfəl] adj woman, house, day, story, movie bonito, precioso, L.Am. lindo; smell, taste, meal delicioso, L.Am. rico; vacation estupendo; thanks, that's just beautiful! ¡muchísimas gracias, está maravilloso!
beau·ti·ful·ly ['bju:tɪfəlɪ] adv cooked, do-

ne perfectamente, maravillosamente

beaut·y ['bjuːtɪ] *of woman, sunset* belleza f

'beaut·y par·lor ['pɑːrlər] salón m de belleza

◆ **bea·ver away** v/i F trabajar como un burro F

be·came [bɪ'keɪm] pret → **become**

be·cause [bɪ'kɑːz] conj porque; *because it was too expensive* porque era demasiado caro; *because of* debido a, a causa de; *because of you, we can't go* gracias a ti, no podemos ir

beck·on ['bekn] v/i hacer señas

be·come [bɪ'kʌm] v/i (pret *became*, pp *become*) hacerse, volverse; *It became clear that ...* quedó claro que ...; *he became a priest* se hizo sacerdote; *she's becoming very forgetful* cada vez es más olvidadiza, *what's become of her?* ¿qué fue de ella?

be·com·ing [bɪ'kʌmɪŋ] adj favorecedor, apropiado

bed [bed] n cama f; *of flowers* macizo; *of sea* fondo m; *of river* cauce m, lecho m; *go to bed* ir a la cama; *he's still in bed* aún está en la cama; *go to bed with s.o.* irse a la cama or acostarse con alguien

'bed·clothes npl ropa f de cama

bed·ding ['bedɪ] ropa f de cama

bed·lam ['bedləm] F locura f, jaleo m

bed·rid·den ['bedrɪdən] adj: *be bedridden* estar postrado en cama

'bed·room dormitorio m, L.Am. cuarto m

'bed·side: *be at the bedside of* estar junto a la cama de

'bed·spread colcha f

'bed·time hora f de irse a la cama

bee [biː] abeja f

beech [biːtʃ] haya f

beef [biːf] 1 n carne f de vaca or vacuna; (*complaint*) queja f 2 v/i F (*complain*) quejarse

◆ **beef up** v/t reforzar, fortalecer

'beef·bur·ger hamburguesa f

'bee·hive colmena f

'bee·line: *make a beeline for* ir directamente a

been [bɪn] pp → **be**

beep [biːp] 1 n pitido m 2 v/i pitar 3 v/t (*call on pager*) llamar con el buscapersonas

beep·er ['biːpər] buscapersonas m inv, Span busca m

beer [bɪr] cerveza f

beet [biːt] remolacha f

bee·tle ['biːtl] escarabajo m

be·fore [bɪ'fɔːr] 1 prep (*time*) antes de; (*space, order*) antes de, delante de 2 adv antes; *I've seen this movie before* ya he visto esta película; *have you been to Japan before?* ¿habías estado antes or ya en Japón?; *the week / day before* la semana / el día anterior 3 conj antes de que

be·fore·hand adv de antemano

be·friend [bɪ'frend] v/t hacerse amigo de

beg [beg] 1 v/i (pret & pp *begged*) mendigar, pedir 2 v/t (pret & pp *begged*): *beg s.o. to sth* rogar or suplicar a alguien que haga algo

began [bɪ'gæn] pret → **begin**

beg·gar ['begər] n mendigo(-a) m(f)

be·gin [bɪ'gɪn] 1 v/i (pret *began*, pp *begun*) empezar, comenzar; *to begin with* (*at first*) en un primer momento, al principio; (*in the first place*) para empezar 2 v/t (pret *began*, pp *begun*) empezar, comenzar; *begin to do sth, begin doing sth* empezar or comenzar a hacer algo

be·gin·ner [bɪ'gɪnər] principiante m/f

be·gin·ning [bɪ'gɪnɪŋ] principio m, comienzo m; (*origin*) origen m

be·grudge [bɪ'grʌdʒ] v/t (*envy*) envidiar; (*give reluctantly*) dar a regañadientes

be·gun [bɪ'gʌn] pp → **begin**

be·half [bɪ'hɑːf]: *on behalf of, in behalf of* en nombre de; *on my / his behalf* en nombre mío / suyo

be·have [bɪ'heɪv] v/i comportarse, portarse; *be·have (o.s.)* comportarse or portarse bien; *behave (yourself)!* ¡pórtate bien!

be·hav·ior [bɪ'heɪvjər] comportamiento m, conducta f

be·hind [bɪ'haɪnd] 1 prep *in position, order* detrás de; *in progress* por detrás de; *be behind ...* (*responsible for*) estar detrás de ...; (*support*) respaldar ... 2 adv (*at the back*) detrás; *be behind in match* ir perdiendo; *be behind with sth* estar atrasado con algo; *leave sth behind* dejarse algo

beige [beɪʒ] adj beige, Span bcis

be·ing ['biːɪŋ] *existence, creature* ser m

be·lat·ed [bɪ'leɪtɪd] adj tardío

belch [beltʃ] 1 n eructo m 2 v/i eructar

Bel·gian ['beldʒən] 1 adj belga 2 n belga m/f

Bel·gium ['beldʒəm] Bélgica

be·lief [bɪ'liːf] creencia f; *it's my belief that* creo que ...

be·lieve [bɪ'liːv] v/t creer

◆ **believe in** v/t creer en

be·liev·er [bɪ'liːvər] REL creyente m/f; fig partidario(a) m(f) (*in* de)

be·lit·tle [bɪ'lɪtl] v/t menospreciar

Be·lize [be'liːz] n Belice

bell [bel] *of bike, door, school* timbre *m*; *of church* campana *f*

'bell·hop botones *m inv*

bel·lig·er·ent [bɪ'lɪdʒərənt] *adj* beligerante

bel·low ['beloʊ] **1** *n* bramido *m* **2** *v/i* bramar

bel·ly ['belɪ] *of person* estómago *m*, barriga *f*; *(fat stomach)* barriga *f*, tripa *f*; *of animal* panza *f*

'bel·ly·ache *v/i* F refunfuñar

be·long [bɪ'lɒŋ] *v/i*: **where does this belong?** ¿dónde va esto?; **I don't belong here** no encajo aquí

♦ **belong to** *v/t of object, money* pertenecer a; *club* pertenecer a, ser socio de

be·long·ings [bɪ'lɒŋɪŋz] *npl* pertenencias *fpl*

be·loved [bɪ'lʌvd] *adj* querido

be·low [bɪ'loʊ] **1** *prep* debajo de; *in amount, rate, level* por debajo de **2** *adv* abajo; *in text* más abajo; *see below* véase más abajo; *10 degrees below* 10 grados bajo cero

belt [belt] *n* cinturón *m*; *tighten one's belt fig* apretarse el cinturón

bench *seat* banco *m*; *(workbench)* mesa *f* de trabajo

'bench·mark punto *m* de referencia

bend [bend] **1** *n* curva *f* **2** *v/t (pret & pp bent)* doblar **3** *v/i (pret & pp bent)* torcer, girar; *of person* flexionarse

♦ **bend down** *v/i* agacharse

bend·er ['bendər] F parranda *f* F

be·neath [bɪ'niːθ] **1** *prep* debajo de; *she thinks a job like that is beneath her* cree que un trabajo como ése le supondría rebajarse **2** *adv* debajo

ben·e·fac·tor ['benɪfæktər] benefactor(a) *m(f)*

ben·e·fi·cial [benɪ'fɪʃl] *adj* beneficioso

ben·e·fi·ci·a·ry [benɪ'fɪʃərɪ] beneficiario(-a) *m(f)*

ben·e·fit ['benɪfɪt] **1** *n* beneficio *m*, ventaja *f* **2** *v/t* beneficiar **3** *v/i* beneficiarse

be·nev·o·lence [bɪ'nevələns] benevolencia *f*

be·nev·o·lent [bɪ'nevələnt] *adj* benevolente

be·nign [bɪ'naɪn] *adj* agradable; MED benigno

bent [bent] *pret & pp* → **bend**

be·queath [bɪ'kwiːð] *v/t also fig* legar

be·quest [bɪ'kwest] legado *m*

be·reaved [bɪ'riːvd] **1** *adj*: *the bereaved parents* los padres del difunto **2** *n*: *the bereaved* los familiares del difunto

be·ret ['beraɪ] boina *f*

ber·ry ['berɪ] baya *f*

ber·serk [bər'sɜːrk] *adv*: *go berserk* F volverse loco

berth [bɜːrθ] *on ship* litera *f*; *on train* camarote *m*; *for ship* amarradero *m*; *give s.o. a wide berth* evitar a alguien

be·seech [bɪ'siːtʃ] *v/t*: *beseech s.o. to do sth* suplicar a alguien que haga algo

be·side [bɪ'saɪd] *prep* al lado de, junto a; *be beside o.s.* estar fuera de sí; *that's beside the point* eso no tiene nada que ver

be·sides [bɪ'saɪdz] **1** *adv* además **2** *prep (apart from)* aparte de

be·siege [bɪ'siːdʒ] *v/t fig* asediar, cercar

best [best] **1** *adj* mejor **2** *adv* mejor; *which did you like best?* ¿cuál te gustó más?; *it would be best if ...* sería mejor si ...; *I like her best* ella es la que más me gusta **3** *n*: *do one's best* hacer todo lo posible; *I did my best to convince her* hice todo lo posible por convencerla; *the best person, thing* el / la mejor; *we insist on the best* insistimos en lo mejor; *we'll just have to make the best of it* tendremos que arreglárnoslas; *all the best!* ¡buena suerte!, ¡que te vaya bien!

best be'fore date fecha *f* de caducidad

best 'man *at wedding* padrino *m*

'best-sell·er éxito *m* de ventas, best-seller *m*

bet [bet] **1** *n* apuesta *f*; *place a bet* hacer una apuesta **2** *v/i also fig* apostar; *I bet he doesn't come* apuesto a que no viene; *you bet!* ¡ya lo creo!

be·tray [bɪ'treɪ] *v/t* traicionar; *husband, wife* engañar

be·tray·al [bɪ'treɪəl] traición *f*; *of husband, wife* engaño *m*

bet·ter ['betər] **1** *adj* mejor; *get better* in skills, health mejorar; *he's better in health* está mejor **2** *adv* mejor; *you'd better ask permission* sería mejor que pidieras permiso; *I'd really better not* mejor no; *all the better for us* tanto mejor para nosotros; *I like her better* me gusta más ella

bet·ter 'off *adj (wealthier)* más rico

be·tween [bɪ'twiːn] *prep* entre; *between you and me* entre tú y yo

bev·er·age ['bevərɪdʒ] *fml* bebida *f*

be·ware [bɪ'wer] *v/t*: *beware of* tener cuidado con

be·wil·der [bɪ'wɪldər] *v/t* desconcertar

be·wil·der·ment [bɪ'wɪldərmənt] desconcierto *m*

be·yond [bɪ'jɒnd] **1** *prep in space* más allá de; *she has changed beyond recognition* ha cambiado tanto que es difícil reconocerla; **it's beyond me** (*don't understand*) no logro entender; (*can't do it*) me es imposible **2** *adv* más allá

bi·as ['baɪəs] *n against* prejuicio *m*; *in favor of* favoritismo *m*

bi·as(s)ed ['baɪəst] *adj* parcial

bib [bɪb] *for baby* babero *m*

Bi·ble ['baɪbl] Biblia *f*

bib·li·cal ['bɪblɪkl] *adj* bíblico

bib·li·og·ra·phy [bɪblɪ'ɑːgrəfɪ] bibliografía *f*

bi·car·bon·ate of so·da [baɪ'kɑːrbəneɪt] bicarbonato *m* sódico

bi·cen·ten·ni·al [baɪsen'tenɪəl] bicentenario *m*

bi·ceps ['baɪseps] *npl* bíceps *mpl*

bick·er ['bɪkər] *v/i* reñir, discutir

bi·cy·cle ['baɪsɪkl] bicicleta *f*

bid [bɪd] **1** *n at auction* puja *f*; (*attempt*) intento *m* **2** *v/i* (*pret & pp* **bid**) *at auction* pujar

bid·der ['bɪdər] postor(a) *m(f)*; **the highest bidder** el mejor postor

bi·en·ni·al [baɪ'enɪəl] *adj* bienal

bi·fo·cals [baɪ'foʊkəlz] *npl* gafas *fpl* or *L.Am.* lentes *mpl* bifocales

big [bɪg] **1** *adj* grande; *before singular nouns* gran; *my big brother / sister* mi hermano / hermana mayor, **big name** nombre *m* importante **2** *adv*: *talk big* alardear, fanfarronear

big·a·mist ['bɪgəmɪst] bígamo(-a) *m(f)*

big·a·mous ['bɪgəməs] *adj* bígamo

big·a·my ['bɪgəmɪ] bigamia *f*

big·head 'big-head *F* creído(-a) *m(f) F*

big·head·ed [bɪg'hedɪd] *adj* F creído F

big·ot ['bɪgət] fanático(-a) *m(f)*, intolerante *m/f*

bike [baɪk] **1** *n* F bici *f F*; *motorbike* moto *f* F **2** *v/i* ir en bici

bik·er ['baɪkər] motero(-a) *m(f)*

bi·ki·ni [bɪ'kiːnɪ] biquini *m*

bi·lat·er·al [baɪ'lætərəl] *adj* bilateral

bi·lin·gual [baɪ'lɪŋgwəl] *adj* bilingüe

bill [bɪl] **1** *n for gas, electricity* factura *f*, recibo *m*; *Br in hotel, restaurant* cuenta *f*; (*money*) billete *m*; POL proyecto *m* de ley; (*poster*) cartel *m* **2** *v/t* (*invoice*) enviar la factura a

'**bill·board** valla *f* publicitaria

'**bill·fold** cartera *f*, billetera *f*

bil·li·ards ['bɪljərdz] *nsg* billar *m*

bil·li·on ['bɪljən] mil millones *mpl*, millardo *m*

bill of ex·change FIN letra *f* de cambio

bill of 'sale escritura *f* de compraventa

bin [bɪn] *n* cubo *m*

bi·na·ry ['baɪnərɪ] *adj* binario

bind [baɪnd] *v/t* (*pret & pp* **bound**) (*con-*

bind·ing ['baɪndɪŋ] **1** *adj agreement, promise* vinculante **2** *n of book* tapa *f*

bi·noc·u·lars [bɪ'nɑːkjʊlərz] *npl* prismáticos *mpl*

bi·o·chem·ist [baɪoʊ'kemɪst] bioquímico(-a) *m(f)*

bi·o·chem·is·try [baɪoʊ'kemɪstrɪ] bioquímica *f*

bi·o·de·gra·da·ble [baɪoʊdɪ'greɪdəbl] *adj* biodegradable

bi·og·ra·pher [baɪ'ɑːgrəfər] biógrafo(-a) *m(f)*

bi·og·ra·phy [baɪ'ɑːgrəfɪ] biografía *f*

bi·o·log·i·cal [baɪoʊ'lɑːdʒɪkl] *adj* biológico; *biological parents* padres *mpl* biológicos; *biological detergent* detergente *m* biológico

bi·ol·o·gist [baɪ'ɑːlədʒɪst] biólogo(-a) *m(f)*

bi·ol·o·gy [baɪ'ɑːlədʒɪ] biología *f*

bi·o·tech·nol·o·gy [baɪoʊtek'nɑːlədʒɪ] biotecnología *f*

bird [bɜːrd] ave *f*, pájaro *m*

'**bird·cage** jaula *f* para pájaros

bird of 'prey ave *f* rapaz

bird sanc·tu·a·ry reserva *f* de aves

bird's eye 'view vista *f* panorámica; *get a bird's eye view of sth* ver algo a vista de pájaro

bi·ro® ['baɪroʊ] *Br* bolígrafo *m*, *Mex* pluma *f*, *Rpl* birome *m*

birth [bɜːrθ] *also fig* nacimiento *m*; (*labor*) parto *m*; *give birth to child* dar a luz; *of animal* parir; *date of birth* fecha *f* de nacimiento; *the land of my birth* mi tierra natal

'**birth cer·tif·i·cate** partida *f* de nacimiento

'**birth con·trol** control *m* de natalidad

'**birth·day** cumpleaños *m inv*; *happy birthday!* ¡feliz cumpleaños!

'**birth·day cake** tarta *f* de cumpleaños

'**birth·mark** marca *f* de nacimiento, antojo *m*

'**birth·place** lugar *m* de nacimiento

'**birth·rate** tasa *f* de natalidad

bis·cuit ['bɪskɪt] bollo *m*, panecillo *m*; *Br* galleta *f*

bi·sex·u·al ['baɪsekʃʊəl] **1** *adj* bisexual **2** *n* bisexual *m/f*

bish·op ['bɪʃəp] obispo *m*

bit [bɪt] *n* (*piece*) trozo *m*; (*part*) parte *f*; *of puzzle* pieza *f*; COMPUT bit *m*; *a bit* (*a little*) un poco; *let's sit down for a bit* sentémonos un rato; *you haven't chan*... *a bit* no has cambiado nada; *a bit* ... *little*) un poco de; *a bit of news* un... ticia; *a bit of advice* un consejo...

bit poco a poco; *I'll be there in a bit* estaré allí dentro de un rato

bit² [bɪt] *pret* → **bite**

bitch [bɪtʃ] **1** *n dog* perra *f*; F *woman* zorra *f* F **2** *v/i* F (*complain*) quejarse

bitch·y ['bɪtʃɪ] *adj* F *person* malicioso; *remark* a mala leche F

bite [baɪt] **1** *n of dog* mordisco *m*; *of spider, mosquito* picadura *f*; *of snake* mordedura *f*, picadura *f*; *of food* bocado *m*; *let's have a bite (to eat)* vamos a comer algo **2** *v/t* (*pret* **bit**, *pp* **bitten**) *of dog* morder; *of mosquito, flea picar*; *of snake* picar, morder; *bite one's nails* morderse las uñas **3** *v/i* (*pret* **bit**, *pp* **bitten**) *of dog* morder; *of mosquito, flea* picar, morder, picar; *of fish* picar

bit·ten ['bɪtn] *pp* → **bite**

bit·ter ['bɪtər] *adj taste* amargo; *person* resentido; *weather* helador; *argument* agrio

bit·ter·ly ['bɪtərlɪ] *adv resent* amargamente; *it's bitterly cold* hace un frío helador

bi·zarre [bɪ'zɑːr] *adj* extraño, peculiar

blab [blæb] *v/i* (*pret & pp* **blabbed**) F irse de la lengua F

blab·ber·mouth ['blæbərmaʊθ] F bocazas *m/f inv* F

black [blæk] **1** *adj* negro; *coffee* solo; *tea* sin leche; *fig* negro, aciago **2** *n* (*color*) negro *m*; (*person*) negro(-a) *m(f)*; *be in the black* FIN no estar en números rojos; *in black and white* en blanco y negro; *in writing* por escrito

♦ **black out** *v/i* perder el conocimiento

'**black·ber·ry** mora *f*

'**black·bird** mirlo *m*

'**black·board** pizarra *f*, encerado *m*

black 'box caja *f* negra

black 'cof·fee café *m* solo

black e'con·o·my economía *f* sumergida

black·en ['blækn] *v/t fig: person's name* manchar

black 'eye ojo *m* morado

'**black·head** espinilla *f*, punto *m* negro

'**black 'ice** *Br* placas *fpl* de hielo

'**black·list 1** *n* lista *f* negra **2** *v/t* poner en la lista negra

'**black·mail 1** *n* chantaje *m*; *emotional blackmail* chantaje *m* emocional **2** *v/t* chantajear

'**black·mail·er** chantajista *m/f*

ack 'mar·ket mercado *m* negro

ck·ness ['blæknɪs] oscuridad *f*

k·out ELEC apagón *m*; MED desmayo

ave a blackout desmayarse

smith herrero *m*

blad·der ['blædər] vejiga *f*

blade [bleɪd] *of knife, sword* hoja *f*; *of propeller* pala *f*; *of grass* brizna *f*

blame [bleɪm] **1** *n* culpa *f*; *I got the blame for it* me echaron la culpa **2** *v/t* culpar; *blame s.o. for sth* culpar a alguien de algo

bland [blænd] *adj smile* insulso; *food* insípido, soso

blank [blæŋk] **1** *adj* (*not written on*) en blanco; *tape* virgen; *look* inexpresivo **2** *n* (*empty space*) espacio *m* en blanco; *my mind's a blank* tengo la mente en blanco

blank 'check, *Br* **blank 'cheque** cheque *m* en blanco

blan·ket ['blæŋkɪt] *n* manta *f*, *L.Am.* frazada *f*; *a blanket of snow* un manto de nieve

blare [bler] *v/i* retumbar

♦ **blare out 1** *v/i* retumbar **2** *v/t* emitir a todo volumen

blas·pheme [blæs'fiːm] *v/i* blasfemar

blas·phe·my ['blæsfəmɪ] blasfemia *f*

blast [blæst] **1** *n* (*explosion*) explosión *f*; (*gust*) ráfaga *f* **2** *v/t tunnel* abrir (con explosivos); *rock* volar; *blast!* F ¡mecachis! F

♦ **blast off** *v/i of rocket* despegar

'**blast fur·nace** alto horno *m*

'**blast-off** despegue *m*

bla·tant ['bleɪtənt] *adj* descarado

blaze [bleɪz] **1** *n of fire* incendio *m*; *a blaze of color* una explosión de color **2** *v/i of fire* arder

♦ **blaze away** *v/i with gun* disparar sin parar

blaz·er ['bleɪzər] americana *f*

bleach [bliːtʃ] **1** *n for clothes* lejía *f*; *for hair* decolorante *m* **2** *v/t hair* aclarar, desteñir

bleak [bliːk] *adj countryside* inhóspito; *weather* desapacible; *future* desolador

blear·y-eyed ['blɪrɪaɪd] *adj* con ojos de sueño

bleat [bliːt] *v/i of sheep* balar

bled [bled] *pret & pp* → **bleed**

bleed [bliːd] **1** *v/i* (*pret & pp* **bled**) sangrar; *he's bleeding internally* tiene una hemorragia interna; *bleed to death* desangrarse **2** *v/t* (*pret & pp* **bled**) *fig* sangrar

bleed·ing ['bliːdɪŋ] *n* hemorragia *f*

bleep [bliːp] **1** *n* pitido *m* **2** *v/i* pitar **3** *v/t* (*call on pager*) llamar con el buscapersonas

bleep·er ['bliːpər] buscapersonas *m inv*, *Span* busca *m*

blem·ish ['blemɪʃ] **1** *n* imperfección *f* **2** *v/t*

reputation manchar
blend [blend] **1** *n of coffee etc* mezcla *f*; *fig* combinación *f* **2** *v/t* mezclar
◆ **blend in 1** *v/i of person in environment* pasar desapercibido; *of animal with surroundings* confundirse; *of furniture etc* combinar **2** *v/t in cooking* añadir
blend·er ['blendər] *machine* licuadora *f*
bless [bles] *v/t* bendecir; (**God**) **bless you!** ¡que Dios te bendiga!; *in response to sneeze* ¡Jesús!; **be blessed with** tener la suerte de
bless·ing ['blesɪŋ] *also fig* bendición *f*
blew [blu:] *pret* → **blow²**
blind [blaɪnd] **1** *adj* ciego; *corner* sin visibilidad; **be blind to sth** *fig* no ver algo **2** *npl:* **the blind** los ciegos, los invidentes **3** *v/t of sun* cegar; **she was blinded in an accident** se quedó ciega a raíz de un accidente; **love blinded her to his faults** el amor le impedía ver sus defectos
blind 'al·ley callejón *m* sin salida
blind 'date cita *f* a ciegas
'blind·fold 1 *n* venda *f* **2** *v/t* vendar los ojos a **3** *adv* con los ojos cerrados
blind·ing ['blaɪndɪŋ] *adj light* cegador; *headache* terrible
blind·ly ['blaɪndlɪ] *adv* a ciegas; *fig* ciegamente
'blind spot *in road* punto *m* sin visibilidad; *in driving mirror* ángulo *m* muerto; (*ability that is lacking*) punto *m* flaco
blink [blɪŋk] *v/i* parpadear
blink·ered ['blɪŋkərd] *adj fig* cerrado
blip [blɪp] *on radar screen* señal *f*, luz *f*; **it's just a blip** *fig* es algo momentáneo
bliss [blɪs] felicidad *f*; **it was bliss** fue fantástico
blis·ter ['blɪstər] **1** *n* ampolla *f* **2** *v/i* ampollarse; *of paint* hacer burbujas
bliz·zard ['blɪzərd] ventisca *f*
bloat·ed ['bloʊtɪd] *adj* hinchado
blob [blɑ:b] *of liquid* goterón *m*
bloc [blɑ:k] POL bloque *m*
block [blɑ:k] **1** *n* bloque *m*; *buildings* manzana *f*, *L.Am.* cuadra *f*; *of shares* paquete *m*; (*blockage*) bloqueo *m* **2** *v/t* bloquear; *sink* atascar
◆ **block in** *v/t with vehicle* bloquear el paso a
◆ **block out** *v/t light* impedir el paso de
◆ **block up** *v/t sink etc* atascar
block·ade [blɑ:'keɪd] **1** *n* bloqueo *m* **2** *v/t* bloquear
block·age ['blɑ:kɪdʒ] obstrucción *f*
block·bust·er ['blɑ:kbʌstər] gran éxito *m*
block 'let·ters *npl* letras *fpl* mayúsculas
blond [blɑ:nd] *adj* rubio
blonde [blɑ:nd] *n woman* rubia *f*

blood [blʌd] sangre *f*; **in cold blood** a sangre fría
'blood al·co·hol lev·el nivel *m* de alcohol en sangre
'blood bank banco *m* de sangre
'blood bath baño *m* de sangre
'blood do·nor donante *m/f* de sangre
'blood group grupo *m* sanguíneo
blood·less ['blʌdlɪs] *adj coup* incruento, pacífico
'blood poi·son·ing septicemia *f*
'blood pres·sure tensión *f* (arterial), presión *f* sanguínea
'blood re·la·tion: she's not a blood relation of mine no nos unen lazos de sangre
'blood sam·ple muestra *f* de sangre
'blood·shed derramamiento *m* de sangre
'blood·shot *adj* enrojecido
'blood·stain mancha *f* de sangre
'blood·stain·ed *adj* ensangrentado, manchado de sangre
'blood·stream flujo *m* sanguíneo
'blood test análisis *m inv* de sangre
'blood·thirst·y *adj* sanguinario; *movie* macabro
'blood trans·fu·sion transfusión *f* sanguínea
'blood ves·sel vaso *m* sanguíneo
blood·y ['blʌdɪ] *adj hands etc* ensangrentado; *battle* sangriento, *Br* F maldito F, *Span* puñetero F; **bloody hell!** ¡jostras! F
bloom [blu:m] **1** *n flor f*; **in bloom** en flor **2** *v/i also fig* florecer
blos·som ['blɑ:səm] **1** *n* flores *fpl* **2** *v/i also fig* florecer
blot [blɑ:t] **1** *n* mancha *f*, borrón *m*; **be a blot on the landscape** estropear el paisaje **2** *v/t* (*pret & pp blotted*) (*dry*) secar
◆ **blot out** *v/t* borrar; *sun, view* ocultar
blotch [blɑ:tʃ] *on skin* erupción *f*, mancha *f*
blotch·y ['blɑ:tʃɪ] *adj:* **blotchy skin** piel con erupciones
blouse [blaʊz] blusa *f*
blow¹ [bloʊ] *n* golpe *m*
blow² [bloʊ] **1** *v/t* (*pret blew, pp blown*) *smoke* exhalar; *whistle* tocar; F (*spend*) fundir F; *opportunity* perder, desaprovechar; **blow one's nose** sonarse (la nariz) **2** *v/i* (*pret blew, pp blown*) *of wind, person* soplar; *of whistle* sonar; *of fuse* fundirse; *of tire* reventarse
◆ **blow off 1** *v/t* llevarse **2** *v/i* salir volando
◆ **blow out 1** *v/t candle* apagar **2** *v/i of candle* apagarse
◆ **blow over 1** *v/t* derribar, hacer caer **2** *v/i* caerse, derrumbarse; *of storm* amainar; *of argument* calmarse
◆ **blow up 1** *v/t with explosives* volar; *ba-*

lloon hinchar; *photograph* ampliar **2** v/i explotar; F (*become angry*) ponerse furioso

'**blow-dry** v/t (*pret & pp* **blow-dried**) secar (*con secador*)

'**blow-job** V mamada *f* V

'**blow-out** *of tire* reventón *m*; F (*big meal*) comilona *f* F

'**blow-up** *of photo* ampliación *f*

blown [bloun] *pp* → **blow²**

blue [bluː] **1** *adj* azul; F *movie* porno *inv* F **2** *n* azul *m*

'**blue·ber·ry** arándano *m*

blue 'chip *adj* puntero, de primera fila

blue-'col·lar work·er trabajador(a) *m(f)* manual

'**blue·print** plano *m*; (*fig: plan*) proyecto *m*, plan *m*

blues [bluːz] *npl* MUS blues *m inv*; **have the blues** estar deprimido

'**blues sing·er** cantante *m/f* de blues

bluff [blʌf] **1** *n* (*deception*) farol *m* **2** v/i *of* de farol

blun·der ['blʌndər] **1** *n* error *m* de bulto, metedura *f* de pata **2** v/i cometer un error de bulto, meter la pata

blunt [blʌnt] *adj pencil* sin punta; *knife* desafilado; *person* franco

blunt·ly ['blʌntlɪ] *adv speak* francamente

blur [blɜːr] **1** *n* imagen *f* desenfocada; **everything is a blur** todo está desenfocado **2** v/t (*pret & pp* **blurred**) desdibujar

blurb [blɜːrb] *on book* nota *f* promocional

◆ **blurt out** [blɜːrt] v/t soltar

blush [blʌʃ] **1** *n* rubor *m*, sonrojo *m* **2** v/i ruborizarse, sonrojarse

blush·er ['blʌʃər] *cosmetic* colorete *m*

blus·ter ['blʌstər] v/i protestar encolerizadamente

blus·ter·y ['blʌstərɪ] *adj* tempestuoso

BO [biːˈou] *abbr* (= **body odor**) olor *m* corporal

board [bɔːrd] **1** *n* tablón *m*, tabla *f*; *for game* tablero *m*; *for notices* tablón *m*; **board (of directors)** consejo *m* de administración; **on board** *on plane, boat, train* a bordo; **take on board** *comments etc* aceptar, tener en cuenta; (*fully realize truth of*) asumir; **across the board** de forma general **2** v/t *airplane etc* embarcar; *train* subir a **3** v/i *of passengers* embarcar; **board with** *as lodger* hospedarse con

◆ **board up** v/t cubrir con tablas

board·er ['bɔːrdər] huésped *m/f*

'**board game** juego *m* de mesa

'**board·ing card** tarjeta *f* de embarque

'**board·ing house** hostal *m*, pensión *f*

'**board·ing pass** tarjeta *f* de embarque

'**board·ing school** internado *m*

'**board meet·ing** reunión *m* del consejo de administración

'**board room** sala *f* de reuniones *or* juntas

'**board·walk** paseo *m* marítimo con tablas

boast [boust] **1** *n* presunción *f*, jactancia *f* **2** v/i presumir, alardear (**about** de)

boat [bout] barco *m*; *for leisure* barca *f*; **go by boat** ir en barco

bob¹ [bɑːb] *haircut* corte *m* a lo chico

bob² [bɑːb] v/i (*pret & pp* **bobbed**) *of boat etc* mecerse

◆ **bob up** v/i aparecer

'**bob·sleigh**, '**bob·sled** bobsleigh *m*

bod·ice ['bɑːdɪs] cuerpo *m*

bod·i·ly ['bɑːdɪlɪ] **1** *adj* corporal; *needs* físico; *function* fisiológico **2** *adv eject* en volandas

bod·y ['bɑːdɪ] cuerpo *m*; *dead* cadáver *m*; **body of water** masa *f* de agua

'**bod·y·guard** guardaespaldas *m/f inv*

'**body lan·guage** lenguaje *m* corporal

'**body o·dor** olor *m* corporal

'**bod·y pierc·ing** piercing *m*, perforaciones *fpl* corporales

'**bod·y·shop** MOT taller *m* de carrocería

'**body stock·ing** malla *f*

'**body suit** body *m* '**body·work** MOT carrocería *f*

bog·gle ['bɑːgl] v/i: **the mind boggles!** ¡no quiero ni pensarlo!

bo·gus ['bougəs] *adj* falso

boil¹ [bɔɪl] *n* (*swelling*) forúnculo *m*

boil² [bɔɪl] **1** v/t *liquid* hervir; *egg, vegetables* cocer **2** v/i hervir

◆ **boil down to** v/t reducirse a

◆ **boil over** v/i *of milk etc* salirse

boil·er ['bɔɪlər] caldera *f*

'**boil·ing point** ['bɔɪlɪŋ] *of liquid* punto *m* de ebullición; **reach boiling point** *fig* perder la paciencia

bois·ter·ous ['bɔɪstərəs] *adj* escandaloso

bold [bould] **1** *adj* valiente, audaz; *text* en negrita **2** *n* (*print*) negrita *f*; **in bold** en negrita

Bo·liv·i·a [bəˈlɪvɪə] *n* Bolivia

Bo·liv·i·an [bəˈlɪvɪən] **1** *adj* boliviano **2** *n* boliviano(-a) *m(f)*

bol·ster ['boulstər] v/t *confidence* reforzar

bolt [boult] **1** *n on door* cerrojo *m*, pestillo *m*; *with nut* perno *m*; *of lightning* rayo *m*; **like a bolt from the blue** de forma inesperada **2** *adv*: **bolt upright** erguido **3** v/t (*fix with bolts*) sujetar con pernos; *close* cerrar con cerrojo *or* pestillo **4** v/i (*run off*) fugarse, escaparse

bomb [bɑːm] **1** *n* bomba *f* **2** v/t MIL bombardear; *of terrorist* poner una bomba en

bom·bard [bɑːmˈbɑːrd] *v/t (attack)* bombardear; *bombard s.o. with questions* bombardear alguien con preguntas

'**bomb attack** atentado *m* con bomba

bomb·er [ˈbɑːmər] *airplane* bombardero *m; terrorist* terrorista *m/f (que pone bombas)*

'**bomb·er jack·et** cazadora *f* de aviador

'**bomb-proof** *adj* a prueba de bombas

'**bomb scare** amenaza *f* de bomba

'**bomb·shell** *(fig: news)* bomba *f*

bond [bɑːnd] **1** *n (tie)* unión *f;* FIN bono *m* **2** *v/i* of glue adherirse

bone [boʊn] **1** *n* hueso *m; of fish* espina *f* **2** *v/t meat* deshuesar; *fish* quitar las espinas a

bon·fire [ˈbɑːnfaɪr] hoguera *f*

bon·net [ˈbɑːnɪt] of car capó *m*

bo·nus [ˈboʊnəs] *money* plus *m*, bonificación *f; (something extra)* ventaja *f* adicional; *a Christmas bonus* un plus por Navidad

boo [buː] **1** *n* abucheo *m* **2** *v/t & v/i* abuchear

boob [buːb] *n* P *(breast)* teta *f* P

boo-boo [ˈbuːbuː] *n* F metedura *f* de pata

book [bʊk] **1** *n* libro *m; of matches* caja *f (de solapa)* **2** *v/t (reserve)* reservar; of policeman multar **3** *v/i (reserve)* reservar, hacer una reserva

'**book·case** estantería *f*, librería *f*

booked up [bʊktˈʌp] *adj* lleno, completo; *person* ocupado

book·ie [ˈbʊkɪ] F corredor(a) *m(f)* de apuestas

book·ing [ˈbʊkɪŋ] *(reservation)* reserva *f*

'**book·ing clerk** taquillero(-a) *m(f)*

'**book·keep·er** tenedor(a) *m(f)* de libros

'**book·keep·ing** contabilidad *f*

book·let [ˈbʊklɪt] folleto *m*

'**book·mak·er** corredor(a) *m(f)* de apuestas

books [bʊks] *npl (accounts)* contabilidad *f; do the books* llevar la contabilidad; *cook the books* falsificar las cuentas

'**book·sell·er** librero(-a) *m(f)*

'**book·shelf** estante *m*

'**book·store** librería *f*

'**book·stall** puesto *m* de venta de libros

'**book to·ken** vale *m* para comprar libros

boom[1] [buːm] **1** *n* boom *m* **2** *v/i of business* desarrollarse, experimentar un boom

boom[2] [buːm] *n noise* estruendo *m*

boon·ies [ˈbuːnɪz] *npl* F: *they live out in the boonies* viven en el quinto pino F

boor [bʊr] basto *m*, grosero *m*

boor·ish [ˈbʊrɪʃ] *adj* basto, grosero

boost [buːst] **1** *n to sales, economy* impul-

so *m; your confidence needs a boost* necesitas algo que te dé más confianza **2** *v/t production, prices* estimular; *morale* levantar

boot [buːt] *n* bota *f; Br of car* maletero *m*, *C.Am., Mex* cajuela *f*, *Rpl* baúl *m*

◆ **boot out** *v/t* F echar

◆ **boot up** *v/t & v/i* COMPUT arrancar

booth [buːð] *at market, fair* cabina *f; (in restaurant)* mesa rodeada por bancos fijos

booze [buːz] *n* F bebida *f*, *Span* priva *f* F

bor·der [ˈbɔːrdər] **1** *n between countries* frontera *f; (edge)* borde *m; on clothing* ribete *m* **2** *v/t country* limitar con; *river* bordear

◆ **border on** limitar con; *(be almost)* rayar en

'**bor·der·line** *adj*: *a borderline case* un caso dudoso

bore[1] [bɔːr] **1** *v/t hole* taladrar; *bore a hole in sth* taladrar algo

bore[2] [bɔːr] **1** *n (person)* pesado(-a) *m(f)*, pelma *m/f inv* F; *it's such a bore* ¡qué pesadez *or Span* lata! **2** *v/t* aburrir

bore[3] [bɔːr] *pret* → *bear*[2]

bored [bɔːrd] *adj* aburrido; *I'm bored* me aburro, estoy aburrido

bore·dom [ˈbɔːrdəm] aburrimiento *m*

bor·ing [ˈbɔːrɪŋ] *adj* aburrido; *be boring* ser aburrido

born [bɔːrn] *adj*: *be born* nacer; *where were you born?* ¿dónde naciste?; *be a born teacher* haber nacido para ser profesor

borne [bɔːrn] *pp* → *bear*[2]

bor·row [ˈbɑːroʊ] *v/t* tomar prestado

bos·om [ˈbʊzm] *of woman* pecho *m*

boss [bɑːs] *n* jefe(-a) *m(f)*

◆ **boss about** *v/t* dar órdenes a

boss·y [ˈbɑːsɪ] *adj* mandón

bo·tan·i·cal [bəˈtænɪkl] *adj* botánico

bo·tan·ic·(al) gar·dens *npl* jardín *m* botánico

bot·a·nist [ˈbɑːtənɪst] botánico(-a) *m(f)*

bot·a·ny [ˈbɑːtənɪ] botánica *f*

botch [bɑːtʃ] *v/t* arruinar, estropear

both [boʊθ] **1** *adj & pron* ambos, los dos; *I know both (of the) brothers* conozco a ambos hermanos, conozco a los dos hermanos; *both of them* ambos, los dos **2** *adv*: *both my mother and I* tanto mi madre como yo; *he's both handsome and intelligent* es guapo y además inteligente; *is it business or pleasure? - both* ¿es de negocios o de placer? - las dos cosas

both·er [ˈbɑːðər] **1** *n* molestias *fpl; it's no bother* no es ninguna molestia **2** *v/t (dis-*

B

turb) molestar; (*worry*) preocupar **3** *v/i* preocuparse; **don't bother!** (*you needn't do it*) ¡no te preocupes!; **you needn't have bothered** no deberías haberte molestado

bot·tle ['bɑːtl] **1** *n* botella *f*; *for baby* biberón *m* **2** *v/t* embotellar

◆ **bottle up** *v/t feelings* reprimir, contener

'**bot·tle bank** contenedor *m* de vidrio

bot·tled wa·ter ['bɑːtld] agua *f* embotellada

'**bot·tle·neck** *n in road* embotellamiento *m*, atasco *m*; *in production* cuello *m* de botella

'**bot·tle-o·pen·er** abrebotellas *m inv*

bot·tom ['bɑːtəm] **1** *adj* inferior, de abajo **2** *n of drawer, case, pan* fondo *m*; *of hill, page* pie *m*; *of pile* parte *f* inferior; (*underside*) parte *f* de abajo; *of street* final *m*; *of garden* fondo *m*; (*buttocks*) trasero *m*; **at the bottom of the screen** en la parte inferior de la pantalla

◆ **bottom out** *v/i* tocar fondo

bot·tom 'line (*fig: financial outcome*) saldo *m* final; (*real issue*) realidad *f*

bought [bɔːt] *pret & pp* → **buy**

boul·der ['bouldər] roca *f* redondeada

bounce [bauns] **1** *v/t ball* botar **2** *v/i of ball* botar, rebotar; *on sofa etc* saltar; *of rain* rebotar; *of check* ser rechazado

bounc·er ['baunsər] portero *m*, gorila *m*

bounc·y ['baunsɪ] *adj ball* que bota bien; *cushion, chair* mullido

bound[1] [baund] *adj:* **be bound to do sth** (*obliged to*) estar obligado a a hacer algo; **she's bound to call an election soon** (*sure to*) seguro que convoca elecciones pronto

bound[2] [baund] *adj:* **be bound for** *of ship* llevar destino a

bound[3] [baund] **1** *n* (*jump*) salto *m* **2** *v/i* saltar

bound[4] [baund] *pret & pp* → **bind**

bound·a·ry ['baundərɪ] límite *m*; *between countries* frontera *f*

bound·less ['baundlɪs] *adj* ilimitado, infinito

bou·quet [buːˈkeɪ] (*flowers*) ramo *m*

bour·bon ['bɜːrbən] bourbon *m*

bout [baut] MED ataque *m*; *in boxing* combate *m*

bou·tique [buːˈtiːk] boutique *f*

bow[1] [bau] **1** *n as greeting* reverencia *f* **2** *v/i* saludar con la cabeza **3** *v/t head* inclinar

bow[2] [bou] (*knot*) lazo *m*; MUS, *for archery* arco *m*

bow[3] [bau] *of ship* proa *f*

bow·els ['bauəlz] *npl* entrañas *fpl*

bowl[1] [boul] *for rice, cereals etc* cuenco *m*; *for soup* plato *m* sopero; *for salad* ensaladera *f*; *for washing* barreño *m*, palangana *f*

bowl[2] [boul] **1** *n* (*ball*) bola *f* **2** *v/i in bowling* lanzar la bola

◆ **bowl over** *v/t* (*fig: astonish*) impresionar, maravillar

bowl·ing ['boulɪŋ] bolos *mpl*

'**bowl·ing al·ley** bolera *f*

'**bow tie** [bou] pajarita *f*

box[1] [bɑːks] *n container* caja *f*; *on form* casilla *f*

box[2] [bɑːks] *v/i* boxear

box·er ['bɑːksər] boxeador(a) *m(f)*

'**box·er shorts** *npl* calzoncillos *mpl*, boxers *mpl*

box·ing ['bɑːksɪŋ] boxeo *m*

'**box·ing glove** guante *m* de boxeo

'**box·ing match** combate *m* de boxeo

'**box·ing ring** cuadrilátero *m*, ring *m*

'**box num·ber** *at post office* apartado *m* de correos

'**box of·fice** taquilla *f*, *L.Am.* boletería *f*

boy [bɔɪ] niño *m*, chico *m*; (*son*) hijo *m*

boy·cott ['bɔɪkɑːt] **1** *n* boicot *m* **2** *v/t* boicotear

'**boy·friend** novio *m*

boy·ish ['bɔɪɪʃ] *adj* varonil

boy scout boy scout *m*

bra [brɑː] *Br* sujetador *m*, sostén *m*

brace [breɪs] *on teeth* aparato *m*

brace·let ['breɪslɪt] pulsera *f*

brack·et ['brækɪt] *for shelf* escuadra *f*; (*square*) **bracket** *in text* corchete *m*

brag [bræɡ] *v/i* (*pret & pp* **bragged**) presumir, fanfarronear

braid [breɪd] *n in hair* trenza *f*; *trimming* trenzado *m*

braille [breɪl] braille *m*

brain [breɪn] *n* cerebro *m*; **use your brain** utiliza la cabeza

'**brain dead** MED clínicamente muerto

'**brain·less** ['breɪnlɪs] *adj* F estúpido

brains [breɪnz] *npl* (*intelligence*) inteligencia *f*; **the brains of the operation** el cerebro de la operación

'**brain·storm** idea *f* genial

brain·storm·ing ['breɪnstɔːrmɪŋ] tormenta *f* de ideas

'**brain sur·geon** neurocirujano(-a) *m(f)*

'**brain sur·ger·y** neurocirugía *f*

'**brain tu·mor** tumor *m* cerebral

'**brain·wash** *v/t* lavar el cerebro

'**brain·wave** (*brilliant idea*) idea *f* genial

brain·y ['breɪnɪ] *adj* F: **be brainy** tener mucho coco F, ser una lumbrera

brake [breɪk] **1** *n* freno *m*; **act as a brake on** frenar **2** *v/i* frenar 'brake flu·id MOT líquido *m* de frenos

'brake light MOT luz *f* de frenado

'brake ped·al MOT pedal *m* del freno

branch [brɑːntʃ] *n* of tree rama *f*; of bank, company sucursal *f*

◆ **branch off** *v/i* of road bifurcarse

◆ **branch out** *v/i* diversificarse; **they've branched out into furniture** han empezado a trabajar también con muebles

brand [brænd] **1** *n* marca *f* **2** *v/t*: **be branded a liar** ser tildado de mentiroso

brand 'im·age imagen *f* de marca

bran·dish ['brændɪʃ] *v/t* blandir

brand 'lead·er marca *f* líder del mercado

brand 'loy·al·ty lealtad *f* a una marca

'brand name nombre *m* comercial

brand-'new *adj* nuevo, flamante

bran·dy ['brændɪ] brandy *m*, coñac *m*

brass [brɑːs] *alloy* latón *m*; **the brass** MUS los metales

brass 'band banda *f* de música

bras·sière [brəˈzɪr] sujetador *m*, sostén *m*

brat [bræt] *pej* niñato(-a) *m(f)*

bra·va·do [brəˈvɑːdou] bravuconería *f*

brave [breɪv] *adj* valiente, valeroso

brave·ly ['breɪvlɪ] *adv* valientemente, valerosamente

brav·er·y ['breɪvərɪ] valentía *f*, valor *m*

brawl [brɔːl] **1** *n* pelea *f* **2** *v/i* pelearse

brawn·y ['brɔːnɪ] *adj* fuerte, musculoso

Bra·zil [brəˈzɪl] Brasil

Bra·zil·ian [brəˈzɪljən] **1** *adj* brasileño **2** *n* brasileño(-a) *m(f)*

breach [briːtʃ] *n* (*violation*) infracción *f*, incumplimiento *m*; *in party* ruptura *f*

breach of 'con·tract LAW incumplimiento *m* de contrato

bread [bred] *n* pan *m*

'bread·crumbs *npl for cooking* pan *m* rallado; *for birds* migas *fpl*

'bread knife cuchillo *m* del pan

breadth [bredθ] *of road* ancho *m*; *of knowledge* amplitud *f*

'bread·win·ner: **be the breadwinner** ser el que gana el pan

break [breɪk] **1** *n in bone etc* fractura *f*, rotura *f*; (*rest*) descanso *m*; *in relationship* separación *f* temporal; **give s.o. a break** F (*opportunity*) ofrecer una oportunidad a alguien; **take a break** descansar; **without a break** *work, travel* sin descanso **2** *v/t* (*pret* **broke**, *pp* **broken**) *machine, device* romper, estropear; *stick* romper, partir; *arm, leg* fracturar, romper; *glass, egg* romper; *rules, law* violar, incumplir; *promise* romper; *news* dar; *record* batir **3** *v/i* (*pret* **broke**, *pp* **broken**) *of machine, device* romperse, estropearse; *of glass, egg* romperse; *of stick* partirse, rom-

perse; *of news* saltar; *of storm* estallar, comenzar; *of boy's voice* cambiar

◆ **break away** *v/i* (*escape*) escaparse; *from family* separarse; *from organization* escindirse; *from tradition* romper (**from** con)

◆ **break down 1** *v/i of vehicle* averiarse, estropearse; *of machine* estropearse; *of talks* romperse; *in tears* romper a llorar; *mentally* venirse abajo **2** *v/t door* derribar; *figures* detallar, desglosar

◆ **break even** *v/i* COM cubrir gastos

◆ **break in** *v/i* (*interrupt*) interrumpir; *of burglar* entrar

◆ **break off 1** *v/t martir; relationship* romper; **they've broken it off** han roto **2** *v/i* (*stop talking*) interrumpirse

◆ **break out** *v/i* (*start up*) comenzar; *of fighting* estallar; *of disease* desatarse; *of prisoners* escaparse, darse a la fuga; **he broke out in a rash** le salió un sarpullido

◆ **break up 1** *v/t into component parts* descomponer; *fight* poner fin a **2** *v/i of ice* romperse; *of couple* terminar, separarse; *of band* separarse; *of meeting* terminar

break·a·ble ['breɪkəbl] *adj* rompible, frágil

break·age ['breɪkɪdʒ] rotura *f*

'break·down *of vehicle, machine* avería *f*; *of talks* ruptura *f*; (*nervous breakdown*) crisis *f* inv nerviosa; *of figures* desglose *m*

break-'e·ven point punto *m* de equilibrio

break·fast ['brekfəst] *n* desayuno *m*; **have breakfast** desayunar

'break·fast tel·e·vi·sion televisión *f* matinal

'break-in entrada *f* (*mediante la fuerza*); *robbery* robo *m*; **we've had a break-in** han entrado a robar

'break·through *of plan, negotiations* paso *m* adelante; *of science, technology* avance *m*

'break-up *of marriage, partnership* ruptura *f*, separación *f*

breast [brest] *of woman* pecho *m*

'breast-feed *v/t* (*pret & pp* **breastfed**) amamantar

'breast·stroke braza *f*

breath [breθ] respiración *f*; **get your breath back** recobrar el aliento; **be out of breath** estar sin respiración; **take a deep breath** respira hondo

Breath·a·lyz·er® ['breθəlaɪzər] alcoholímetro *m*

breathe [briːð] **1** *v/i* respirar **2** *v/t* (*inhale*) aspirar, respirar; (*exhale*) exhalar, espirar

◆ **breathe in** *v/t & v/i* aspirar, inspirar

◆ **breathe out** *v/i* espirar

breath·ing ['briːðɪŋ] *n* respiración *f*

breath·less ['breθlɪs] adj: **arrive breathless** llegar sin respiración, llegar jadeando

breath·less·ness ['breθlɪsnɪs] dificultad f para respirar

breath·tak·ing ['breθteɪkɪŋ] adj impresionante, sorprendente

bred [bred] pret & pp → **breed**

breed [bri:d] **1** n raza f **2** v/t (pret & pp **bred**) criar; plants cultivar; fig causar, generar **3** v/i (pret & pp **bred**) of animals reproducirse

breed·er ['bri:dər] of animals criador(a) m(f); of plants cultivador(a) m(f)

breed·ing ['bri:dɪŋ] of animals cría f; of plants cultivo m; of person educación f

breed·ing ground fig caldo m de cultivo

breeze [bri:z] brisa f

breez·i·ly ['bri:zɪlɪ] adv fig jovialmente, tranquilamente

breez·y ['bri:zɪ] adj ventoso; fig jovial, tranquilo

brew [bru:] **1** v/t beer elaborar; tea preparar, hacer **2** v/i of storm avecinarse; of trouble fraguarse

brew·er ['bru:ər] fabricante m/f de cerveza

brew·er·y ['bru:ərɪ] fábrica f de cerveza

bribe [braɪb] **1** n soborno m, Mex mordida f, S. Am. coima f **2** v/t sobornar

brib·er·y ['braɪbərɪ] soborno m, Mex mordida f, S. Am. coima f

brick [brɪk] ladrillo m

'**brick·lay·er** albañil m/f

brid·al suite ['braɪdl] suite f nupcial

bride [braɪd] novia f (en boda)

'**bride·groom** novio m (en boda)

'**brides·maid** dama f de honor

bridge¹ [brɪdʒ] **1** n also NAUT puente m; of nose caballete m **2** v/t gap superar, salvar

bridge² [brɪdʒ] card game bridge m

bri·dle ['braɪdl] brida f

brief¹ [bri:f] adj breve, corto

brief² [bri:f] **1** n (mission) misión f **2** v/t: **brief s.o. on sth** informar a alguien de algo

'**brief·case** maletín m

brief·ing ['bri:fɪŋ] reunión f informativa

brief·ly ['bri:flɪ] adv (for a short period of time) brevemente; (in a few words) en pocas palabras; (to sum up) en resumen

briefs [bri:fs] npl for women bragas fpl; for men calzoncillos mpl

bright [braɪt] adj color vivo; smile radiante; future brillante, prometedor; (sunny) soleado, luminoso; (intelligent) inteligente

◆ **bright·en up** ['braɪtn] **1** v/t alegrar **2** v/i of weather aclararse; of face, person alegrarse, animarse

bright·ly ['braɪtlɪ] adv shine intensamente, fuerte; smile alegremente

bright·ness ['braɪtnɪs] of light brillo m; of weather luminosidad f; of smile alegría f; (intelligence) inteligencia f

bril·liance ['brɪljəns] of person genialidad f; of color resplandor m

bril·liant ['brɪljənt] adj sunshine etc resplandeciente, radiante; (very good) genial; (very intelligent) brillante

brim [brɪm] of container borde m; of hat ala f

brim·ful ['brɪmfəl] adj rebosante

bring [brɪŋ] v/t (pret & pp brought) traer; **bring it here, will you** tráelo aquí, por favor; **can I bring a friend?** ¿puedo traer a un amigo?, puedo venir con un amigo?

◆ **bring about** v/t ocasionar; **bring about peace** traer la paz

◆ **bring around** v/t from a faint hacer volver en sí; (persuade) convencer, persuadir

◆ **bring back** v/t (return) devolver; (re-introduce) reinstaurar; memories traer

◆ **bring down** v/t fence, tree tirar, echar abajo; government derrocar; bird, airplane derribar; rates, inflation, price reducir

◆ **bring in** v/t interest, income generar; legislation introducir; verdict pronunciar

◆ **bring on** v/t illness provocar

◆ **bring out** v/t book, video, new product sacar

◆ **bring to** v/t from a faint hacer volver en sí

◆ **bring up** v/t child criar, educar; subject mencionar, sacar a colación; (vomit) vomitar

brink [brɪŋk] borde m; **be on the brink of sth** fig estar a punto de hacer algo

brisk [brɪsk] adj person, voice enérgico; walk rápido; trade animado

bris·tle ['brɪsl] v/i: **the streets are bristling with policemen** las calles están atestadas de policías

brist·les ['brɪslz] npl on chin pelos mpl; of brush cerdas fpl

Brit [brɪt] F británico(-a) m(f)

Brit·ain ['brɪtn] Gran Bretaña

Brit·ish ['brɪtɪʃ] **1** adj británico **2** n: **the British** los británicos

Brit·on ['brɪtn] británico(-a) m(f)

brit·tle ['brɪtl] adj frágil, quebradizo

broach [brəʊtʃ] v/t subject sacar a colación

broad [brɔ:d] **1** adj ancho; smile amplio; (general) general; **in broad daylight** a plena luz del día; **in broad terms** en líneas generales **2** n F (woman) tía f F

'**broad·cast 1** n emisión f; **a live broad-**

cast una retransmisión en directo **2** v/t emitir, retransmitir

'**broad·cast·er** presentador(a) m(f)

'**broad·cast·ing** televisión f

broad·en ['brɔːdn] **1** v/i ensancharse, ampliarse **2** v/t ensanchar; **broaden one's horizons** ampliar los horizontes

'**broad·jump** salto m de longitud

broad·ly ['brɔːdlɪ] adv en general; **broadly speaking** en términos generales

broad·mind·ed [brɔːd'maɪndɪd] adj tolerante, abierto

broad·mind·ed·ness [brɔːd'maɪndɪdnɪs] mentalidad f abierta

broc·co·li ['brɑːkəlɪ] brécol m, brócoli m

bro·chure ['brouʃər] folleto m

broil [brɔɪl] v/t asar a la parrilla

broil·er ['brɔɪlər] on stove parrilla f; chicken pollo m (para asar)

broke [brouk] **1** adj F: **be broke** temporarily estar sin blanca F; long term estar arruinado; **go broke** (go bankrupt) arruinarse **2** pret → **break**

bro·ken ['broukn] **1** adj roto; home deshecho; **they talk in broken English** chapurrean el inglés **2** pp → **break**

bro·ken-heart·ed [broukn'hɑːrtɪd] adj desconsolado, destrozado

bro·ker ['broukər] corredor(a) m(f), agente m/f

bron·chi·tis [brɑːŋ'kaɪtɪs] bronquitis f

bronze [brɑːnz] n bronce m

brooch [broutʃ] broche m

brood [bruːd] v/i of person darle vueltas a las cosas; **brood about sth** darle vueltas a algo

broom [bruːm] escoba f

broth [brɑːθ] soup sopa f; stock caldo m

broth·el ['brɑːθl] burdel m

broth·er ['brʌðər] hermano m

'**broth·er-in-law** (pl **brothers-in-law**) cuñado m

broth·er·ly ['brʌðərlɪ] adj fraternal

brought [brɔːt] pret & pp → **bring**

brow [brau] (forehead) frente f; of hill cima f

brown [braun] **1** n marrón m, L.Am. color m café **2** adj marrón; eyes, hair castaño; (tanned) moreno **3** v/t in cooking dorar **4** v/i in cooking dorarse

'**brown-bag** v/t (pret & pp **brown-bagged**) F: **brownbag it** llevar la comida al trabajo

Brown·ie ['braunɪ] escultista f

'**Brown·ie points** npl tantos mpl; **earn Brownie points** anotarse tantos

brown·ie ['braunɪ] (cake) pastel m de chocolate y nueces

'**brown-nose** v/t P lamer el culo a P

brown 'pa·per papel m de estraza

brown pa·per 'bag bolsa f de cartón

brown 'sug·ar azúcar m or f moreno(-a)

browse [brauz] v/i in store echar una ojeada; **browse through a book** hojear un libro

brows·er ['brauzər] COMPUT navegador m

bruise [bruːz] **1** n magulladura f, cardenal f; on fruit maca f **2** v/t arm, fruit magullar; (emotionally) herir **3** v/i of person hacerse cardenales; of fruit macarse

bruis·ing ['bruːzɪŋ] adj fig doloroso

brunch [brʌntʃ] combinación de desayuno y almuerzo

bru·nette [bruː'net] n morena f

brunt [brʌnt]: **this area bore the brunt of the flooding** esta zona fue la más castigada por la inundación; **we bore the brunt of the layoffs** fuimos los más perjudicados por los despidos

brush [brʌʃ] **1** n cepillo m; conflict roce m **2** v/t cepillar; (touch lightly) rozar; (move away) quitar

◆ **brush against** v/t rozar

◆ **brush aside** v/t hacer caso omiso a, no hacer caso a

◆ **brush off** v/t sacudir; criticism no hacer caso a

◆ **brush up** v/t repasar

'**brush·work** PAINT pincelada f

brusque [brusk] adj brusco

Brus·sels ['brʌslz] Bruselas

Brus·sels sprouts npl coles fpl de Bruselas

bru·tal ['bruːtl] adj brutal

bru·tal·i·ty [bruː'tælətɪ] brutalidad f

bru·tal·ly ['bruːtəlɪ] adv brutalmente; **be brutally frank** ser de una sinceridad aplastante

brute [bruːt] bestia m/f

brute 'force fuerza f bruta

bub·ble ['bʌbl] n burbuja f

'**bub·ble bath** baño m de espuma

'**bub·ble gum** chicle m

'**bub·ble wrap** n plástico m para embalar (con burbujas)

bub·bly ['bʌblɪ] n F (champagne) champán m

buck¹ [bʌk] n F (dollar) dólar m

buck² [bʌk] v/i of horse corcovear

buck³ [bʌk] n: **pass the buck** escurrir el bulto

buck·et ['bʌkɪt] n cubo m

buck·le¹ ['bʌkl] **1** n hebilla f **2** v/t belt abrochar

buck·le² ['bʌkl] v/i of wood, metal combarse

◆ **buckle down** v/i ponerse a trabajar

bud [bʌd] *n* BOT capullo *m*, brote *m*

bud-dy ['bʌdɪ] F amigo(-a) *m(f)*, *Span* colega *m/f* F; *form of address Span* colega *m/f* F, *L.Am.* compadre *m/f* F

budge [bʌdʒ] **1** *v/t* mover; *(make reconsider)* hacer cambiar de opinión F **2** *v/i* moverse; *(change one's mind)* cambiar de opinión

bud-ger-i-gar ['bʌdʒərɪgɑːr] periquito *m*

bud-get ['bʌdʒɪt] **1** *n* presupuesto *m*; *be on a budget* tener un presupuesto limitado **2** *v/i* administrarse

◆ **budget for** *v/t* contemplar en el presupuesto

bud-gie ['bʌdʒɪ] F periquito *m*

buff[1] [bʌf] *adj color* marrón claro

buff[2] [bʌf] *n* aficionado(-a) *m(f)*; *a movie buff* un cinéfilo

buf-fa-lo ['bʌfələʊ] búfalo *m*

buff-er ['bʌfər] RAIL tope *m*; COMPUT búfer *m*; *fig* barrera *f*

buf-fet[1] ['bʊfeɪ] *n (meal)* bufé *m*

buf-fet[2] ['bʌfɪt] *v/t of wind* sacudir

bug [bʌg] **1** *n insect* bicho *m*; *virus* virus *m inv*; *(spying device)* micrófono *m* oculto; COMPUT error *m* **2** *v/t (pret & pp bugged) room* colocar un micrófono en; F *(annoy)* fastidiar F, jorobar F

bug-gy ['bʌgɪ] *for baby* silla *f* de paseo

bu-gle ['bjuːgl] corneta *f*, clarín *m*

build [bɪld] **1** *n of person* constitución *f*, complexión *f* **2** *v/t (pret & pp built)* construir, edificar

◆ **build up 1** *v/t strength* aumentar; *relationship* fortalecer; *collection* acumular **2** *v/i of dirt* acumularse; *of pressure, excitement* aumentar

build-er ['bɪldər] albañil *m/f*; *company* constructora *f*

build-ing ['bɪldɪŋ] edificio *m*; *activity* construcción *f*

build-ing blocks *npl for child* piezas *fpl* de construcción

build-ing site obra *f*

build-ing so-ci-e-ty *Br* caja *f* de ahorros

build-ing trade industria *f* de la construcción

build-up *(accumulation)* acumulación *f*; *after all the build-up publicity* después de tantas expectativas

built [bɪlt] *pret & pp* → **build**

built-in ['bɪltɪn] *adj cupboard* empotrado; *flash* incorporado

built-up 'ar-e-a zona *f* urbanizada

bulb [bʌlb] BOT bulbo *m*; *(light bulb)* bombilla *f*, *L.Am.* foco *m*

bulge [bʌldʒ] **1** *n* bulto *m*, abultamiento *m* **2** *v/i of eyes* salirse de las órbitas; *of wall* abombarse

bu-lim-i-a [bʊ'lɪmɪə] bulimia *f*

bulk [bʌlk]: *the bulk of* el grueso *or* la mayor parte de; *in bulk* a granel

bulk-y ['bʌlkɪ] *adj* voluminoso

bull [bʊl] *animal* toro *m*

bull-doze ['bʊldəʊz] *v/t (demolish)* demoler, derribar; *bulldoze s.o. into sth fig* obligar a alguien a hacer algo

bull-doz-er ['bʊldəʊzər] bulldozer *m*

bul-let ['bʊlɪt] bala *f*

bul-le-tin ['bʊlɪtɪn] boletín *m*

'bul-le-tin board *on wall* tablón *m* de anuncios; COMPUT tablón *m* de anuncios, BBS *f*

'bul-let-proof *adj* antibalas *inv*

'bull fight corrida *f* de toros

'bull fight-er torero(-a) *m(f)*

'bull fight-ing tauromaquia *f*, los toros

'bull mar-ket FIN mercado *m* al alza

'bull ring plaza *f* de toros

'bull's-eye diana *f*, blanco *m*; *hit the bull's-eye* dar en el blanco

'bull-shit 1 *n* V *Span* gilipollez *f* V, *L.Am.* pendejada *f* V **2** *v/i (pret & pp bullshitted)* V decir *Span* gilipolleces V *or L.Am.* pendejadas V

bul-ly ['bʊlɪ] **1** *n* matón(-ona) *m(f)*; *child* abusón(-ona) *m(f)* **2** *v/t (pret & pp bullied)* intimidar

bul-ly-ing ['bʊlɪɪŋ] *n* intimidación *f*

bum [bʌm] **1** *n* F *(tramp)* vagabundo(-a) *m(f)*; *(worthless person)* inútil *m/f* **2** *adj* F *(useless)* inútil **3** *v/t (pret & pp bummed)* F *cigarette etc* gorronear

◆ **bum around**, **bum about** *v/i* F *(travel)* vagabundear *(in por)*; *(be lazy)* vaguear

bum-ble-bee ['bʌmblbiː] abejorro *m*

bump [bʌmp] **1** *n (swelling)* chichón *m*; *on road* bache *m*; *get a bump on the head* darse un golpe en la cabeza **2** *v/t* golpear

◆ **bump into** *v/t table* chocar con; *(meet)* encontrarse con

◆ **bump off** *v/t* F *(murder)* cargarse a F

◆ **bump up** *v/t* F *(prices)* aumentar

bump-er ['bʌmpər] **1** *n* MOT parachoques *m inv*; *the traffic was bumper to bumper* el tráfico estaba colapsado **2** *adj (extremely good)* excepcional, extraordinario

'bump-start *v/t car* arrancar un coche empujándolo; *fig: economy* reanimar

bump-y ['bʌmpɪ] *adj* con baches; *flight* movido

bun [bʌn] *hairstyle* moño *m*; *for eating* bollo *m*

bunch [bʌntʃ] *of people* grupo *m*; *of keys* manojo *m*; *of flowers* ramo *m*; *of grapes* racimo *m*; *thanks a bunch ironic* no sabes lo que te lo agradezco

bun·dle ['bʌndl] *of clothes* fardo *m*; *of wood* haz *m*
◆ **bundle up** *v/t* liar; (*dress warmly*) abrigar

bung [bʌŋ] *v/t Br* F echar

bun·gee jump·ing ['bʌndʒɪdʒʌmpɪŋ] puenting *m*

bun·gle ['bʌŋgl] *v/t* echar a perder

bunk [bʌŋk] litera *f*

bunk beds *npl* literas *fpl*

buoy [bɔɪ] *n* NAUT boya *f*

buoy·ant ['bɔɪənt] *adj* animado, optimista; *economy* boyante

bur·den ['bɜːrdn] **1** *n also fig* carga *f* **2** *v/t*: **burden s.o. with sth** *fig* cargar a alguien con algo

bu·reau ['bjʊroʊ] (*chest of drawers*) cómoda *f*; (*office*) departamento *m*, oficina *f*; **a translation bureau** una agencia de traducción

bu·reauc·ra·cy [bjʊ'rɑːkrəsɪ] burocracia *f*

bu·reau·crat ['bjʊrəkræt] burócrata *m/f*

bu·reau·crat·ic [bjʊrə'krætɪk] *adj* burocrático

burg·er ['bɜːrgər] hamburguesa *f*

bur·glar ['bɜːrglər] ladrón(-ona) *m(f)*

'bur·glar a·larm alarma *f* antirrobo

bur·glar·ize ['bɜːrgləraɪz] *v/t* robar

bur·glar·y ['bɜːrglərɪ] robo *m*

bur·gle ['bɜːgl] *v/t Br* robar

bur·i·al ['berɪəl] entierro *m*

bur·ly ['bɜːrlɪ] *adj* corpulento, fornido

burn [bɜːrn] **1** *n* quemadura *f* **2** *v/t* (*pret & pp burnt*) quemar; **be burned to death** morir abrasado **3** *v/i* (*pret & pp burnt*) *of wood, meat, in sun* quemarse
◆ **burn down 1** *v/t* incendiar **2** *v/i* incendiarse
◆ **burn out** *v/t*: **burn o.s. out** quemarse; **a burned-out car** un coche carbonizado

'burn·out F (*exhaustion*) agotamiento *m*

burnt [bɜːrnt] *pret & pp* → **burn**

burp [bɜːrp] **1** *n* eructo *m* **2** *v/i* eructar **3** *v/t baby* hacer eructar a

burst [bɜːrst] **1** *n in water pipe* rotura *f*; *of gunfire* ráfaga *f*; **in a burst of energy** en un arrebato de energía **2** *adj tire* reventado **3** *v/t* (*pret & pp burst*) *balloon* reventar **4** *v/i* (*pret & pp burst*) *of balloon, tire* reventar; **burst into a room** irrumpir en una habitación; **burst into tears** echarse a llorar; **burst out laughing** echarse a reír

bur·y ['berɪ] *v/t* (*pret & pp buried*) enterrar; **be buried under** (*covered by*) estar sepultado por; **bury o.s. in work** meterse de lleno en el trabajo

bus [bʌs] **1** *n local* autobús *m*, *Mex* ca-

mión *m*, *Arg* colectivo *m*, *C.Am.* guagua *f*; *long distance* autobús *m*, *Span* autocar *m*; **school bus** autobús *m* escolar **2** *v/t* (*pret & pp bussed*) llevar en autobús

'bus·boy ayudante *m* de camarero

'bus driv·er conductor(a) *m(f)* de autobús

bush [bʊʃ] *plant* arbusto *m*; *type of countryside* monte *m*

bushed [bʊʃt] *adj* (*tired*) molido F

bush·y ['bʊʃɪ] *adj beard* espeso

busi·ness ['bɪznɪs] negocios *mpl*; (*company*) empresa *f*; (*sector*) sector *m*; (*affair, matter*) asunto *m*; *as subject of study* empresariales *fpl*; **on business** de negocios; **that's none of your business!** ¡no es asunto tuyo!; **mind your own business!** ¡no te metas en lo que no te importa!

'busi·ness card tarjeta *f* de visita

'busi·ness class clase *f* ejecutiva

'busi·ness hours *npl* horario *m* de oficina

busi·ness·like ['bɪznɪslaɪk] *adj* eficiente

'busi·ness lunch almuerzo *m* de negocios

'busi·ness·man hombre *m* de negocios, ejecutivo *m*

'busi·ness meet·ing reunión *f* de negocios

'busi·ness school escuela *f* de negocios

'busi·ness stud·ies *nsg course* empresariales *mpl*

'busi·ness trip viaje *m* de negocios

'busi·ness·wom·an mujer *f* de negocios, ejecutiva *f*

'bus lane carril *m* bus

'bus shel·ter marquesina *f*

'bus sta·tion estación *f* de autobuses

'bus stop parada *f* de autobús

'bus tick·et billete *m* or *L.Am.* boleto *m* de autobús

bust[1] [bʌst] *n of woman* busto *m*

bust[2] [bʌst] **1** *adj* F (*broken*) escacharrado F: **go bust** quebrar **2** *v/t* F escacharrar F
◆ **bus·tle about** ['bʌsl] *v/i* trajinar

'bust-up F corte *m* F

bust·y ['bʌstɪ] *adj* pechugona

bus·y ['bɪzɪ] **1** *adj also* TELEC ocupado; *full of people* abarrotado; *of restaurant etc: making money* ajetreado; **the line was busy** estaba ocupado, *Span* comunicaba; **she leads a very busy life** lleva una vida muy ajetreada; **be busy doing sth** estar ocupado or atareado haciendo algo **2** *v/t* (*pret & pp busied*): **busy o.s. with** entretenerse con algo

'bus·y·bod·y metomentodo *m/f*, entrometido(-a) *m(f)*

'bus·y sig·nal señal *f* de ocupado *or* Span comunicando

but [bʌt] *unstressed* [bət] **1** *conj* pero; *it's not me but my father you want* no me quieres a mí sino a mi padre; *but then* (*again*) pero **2** *prep*: *all but him* todos excepto él; *the last but one* el penúltimo; *the next but one* el próximo no, el otro; *the next page but one* la página siguiente a la próxima; *but for you* si no hubiera sido por ti; *nothing but the best* sólo lo mejor

butch·er ['butʃər] carnicero(-a) *m(f)*; *murderer* asesino(-a) *m(f)*

butt [bʌt] **1** *n of cigarette* colilla *f*; *of joke* blanco *m*; F (*buttocks*) trasero *m* F **2** *v/t* dar un cabezazo a; *of goat, bull* embestir

◆ **butt in** *v/i* inmiscuirse, entrometerse

but·ter ['bʌtər] **1** *n* mantequilla *f* **2** *v/t* untar de mantequilla

◆ **butter up** *v/t* F hacer la pelota a F

'but·ter·fly *insect* mariposa *f*

but·tocks ['bʌtəks] *npl* nalgas *fpl*

but·ton ['bʌtn] **1** *n on shirt, machine* botón *m*; (*badge*) chapa *f* **2** *v/t* abotonar

◆ **button up** *v/t* abotonar

'but·ton·hole 1 *n in suit* ojal *m* **2** *v/t* acorralar

but·tress ['bʌtrəs] contrafuerte *m*

bux·om ['bʌksəm] *adj* de amplios senos

buy [baɪ] **1** *n* compra *f*, adquisición *f* **2** *v/t* (*pret & pp* **bought**) comprar; *can I buy you a drink?* ¿quieres tomar algo?; *$5 doesn't buy much* con 5 dólares no se puede hacer gran cosa

◆ **buy off** *v/t* (*bribe*) sobornar

◆ **buy out** COM comprar la parte de

◆ **buy up** *v/t* acaparar

buy·er [baɪr] comprador(a) *m(f)*

buzz [bʌz] **1** *n* zumbido *m*; *she gets a real buzz out of it* F (*thrill*) le vuelve loca, le entusiasma *f* **2** *v/i of insect* zumbar; *with buzzer* llamar por el interfono **3** *v/t with buzzer* llamar por el interfono

◆ **buzz off** *v/i* F largarse F, Span pirarse F

buz·zard ['bʌzərd] ratonero *m*

buzz·er ['bʌzər] timbre *m*

'buzz·word palabra *f* de moda

by [baɪ] **1** *prep to show agent* por; (*near, next to*) al lado de, junto a; (*no later than*) no más tarde de; *mode of transport* en; *she rushed by me* pasó rápidamente por mi lado; *as we drove by the church* cuando pasábamos por la iglesia; *side by side* uno junto al otro; *by day / night* de día / noche; *by bus / train* en autobús / tren; *by the dozen* por docenas; *by the hour / ton* por hora / por tonelada; *by my watch* en mi reloj; *by nature* por naturaleza; *a play by ...* una obra de ...; *by o.s. without company* solo; *I did it by myself* lo hice yo solito; *by a couple of minutes* por un par de minutos; *by 4 measurement* 2 por 4; *by this time tomorrow* mañana a esta hora; *by this time next year* el año que viene por estas fechas; *go by, pass by* pasar **2** *adv*: *by and by* (*soon*) dentro de poco

bye(-bye) [baɪ] adiós

by·gones ['baɪgɑːnz]: *let bygones be bygones* lo pasado, pasado está

'by·pass 1 *n road* circunvalación *f*; MED bypass *m* **2** *v/t* sortear

'by·prod·uct subproducto *m*

by·stand·er ['baɪstændər] transeúnte *m/f*

byte [baɪt] byte *m*

'by·word: *be a byword for* ser sinónimo de

C

cab [kæb] (*taxi*) taxi *m*; *of truck* cabina *f*; *cab driver* taxista *m/f*

cab·a·ret ['kæbəreɪ] cabaret *m*

cab·bage ['kæbɪdʒ] col *f*, repollo *m*

cab·in ['kæbɪn] *of plane* cabina *f*; *of ship* camarote *m*

'cab·in at·tend·ant auxiliar *m/f* de vuelo

'cab·in crew personal *m* de a bordo

cab·i·net ['kæbɪnɪt] armario *m*; POL gabi-

nete *m*; *drinks cabinet* mueble *m* bar; *medicine cabinet* botiquín *m*; *display cabinet* vitrina *f*

'cab·i·net mak·er ebanista *m/f*

ca·ble ['keɪbl] cable *m*; *cable (TV)* televisión *f* por cable

'ca·ble car teleférico *m*

'ca·ble tel·e·vi·sion televisión *f* por cable

'cab rank, 'cab stand parada *f* de taxis

cac·tus ['kæktəs] cactus *m inv*

ca·dav·er [kə'dævər] cadáver *m*

CAD [kæd] *abbr* (= *computer assisted design*) CAD *m* (= diseño asistido por *Span* ordenador *or L.Am.* computadora)

cad·die ['kædɪ] 1 *n in golf* caddie *m/f* 2 *v/i* hacer de caddie

ca·det [kə'det] cadete *m*

cadge [kædʒ] *v/t* F: *cadge sth from s.o.* gorronear algo a alguien

Cae·sar·e·an *Br* → *Cesarean*

ca·fé ['kæfeɪ] café *m*, cafetería *f*

caf·e·te·ri·a [kæfɪ'tɪrɪə] cafetería *f*, cantina *f*

caf·feine ['kæfiːn] cafeína *f*

cage [keɪdʒ] jaula *f*

ca·gey ['keɪdʒɪ] *adj* cauteloso, reservado; *he's cagey about how old he is* es muy reservado con respecto a su edad

ca·jole [kə'dʒoʊl] *v/t* engatusar, persuadir

cake [keɪk] 1 *n big* tarta *f*; *small* pastel *m*; *be a piece of cake* F estar chupado F 2 *v/i* endurecerse

ca·lam·i·ty [kə'læmətɪ] calamidad *f*

cal·ci·um ['kælsɪəm] calcio *m*

cal·cu·late ['kælkjʊleɪt] *v/t* calcular

cal·cu·lat·ing ['kælkjʊleɪtɪŋ] *adj* calculador

cal·cu·la·tion [kælkjʊ'leɪʃn] cálculo *m*

cal·cu·la·tor ['kælkjʊleɪtər] calculadora *f*

cal·en·dar ['kælɪndər] calendario *m*

calf[1] [kæf] (*pl calves* [kævz]) (*young cow*) ternero(-a) *m(f)*, becerro(-a) *m(f)*

calf[2] [kæf] (*pl calves* [kævz]) *of leg* pantorrilla *f*

'calf·skin *n* piel *f* de becerro

cal·i·ber, *Br* cal·i·bre ['kælɪbər] *of gun* calibre *m*; *a man of his calibre* un hombre de su calibre

Cal·i·for·ni·an [kælɪ'fɔːnɪən] 1 *adj* californiano 2 *n* californiano(-a) *m(f)*

call [kɔːl] 1 *n* llamada *f*; (*demand*) llamamiento *m*; *there's a call for you* tienes una llamada, te llaman; *I'll give you a call tomorrow* te llamaré mañana; *make a call* hacer una llamada; *a call for help* una llamada de socorro; *be on call* estar de guardia 2 *v/t also* TELEC llamar; *meeting* convocar; *he called him a liar* le llamó mentiroso; *what have they called the baby?* ¿qué nombre le han puesto al bebé?; *but we call him Tom* pero le llamamos Tom; *call s.o. names* insultar a alguien; *I called his name* lo llamé 3 *v/i also* TELEC llamar; (*visit*) pasarse; *can I tell him who's calling?* ¿quién le llama?; *call for help* pedir ayuda a gritos

◆ *call at v/t* (*stop at*) pasarse por; *of train* hacer parada en

◆ *call back 1 v/t* (*phone again*) volver a llamar; (*return call*) devolver la llamada; (*summon*) hacer volver 2 *v/i on phone* volver a llamar; (*make another visit*) volver a pasar

◆ *call for v/t* (*collect*) pasar a recoger; (*demand*) pedir, exigir; (*require*) requerir

◆ *call in 1 v/t* (*summon*) llamar 2 *v/i* (*phone*) llamar; *he called in sick* llamó para decir que estaba enfermo

◆ *call off v/t* (*cancel*) cancelar; *strike* desconvocar

◆ *call on v/t* (*urge*) instar; (*visit*) visitar

◆ *call out v/t* (*shout*) gritar; (*summon*) llamar

◆ *call up v/t* (*on phone*) llamar; COMPUT abrir, visualizar

'call cen·ter centro *m* de atención telefónica

call·er ['kɔːlər] *on phone* persona *f* que llama; (*visitor*) visitante *m/f*

'call girl prostituta *f* (*que concierta sus citas por teléfono*)

cal·lous ['kæləs] *adj* cruel, desalmado

cal·lous·ly ['kæləslɪ] *adv* cruelmente

cal·lous·ness ['kæləsnɪs] crueldad *f*

calm [kɑːm] 1 *adj sea* tranquilo; *weather* apacible; *person* tranquilo, sosegado; *please keep calm* por favor mantengan la calma 2 *n* calma *f*; *call for calm* pedir calma

◆ *calm down 1 v/t* calmar, tranquilizar 2 *v/i of sea, weather* calmarse; *of person* calmarse, tranquilizarse

calm·ly ['kɑːmlɪ] *adv* con calma, tranquilamente

cal·o·rie ['kælərɪ] caloría *f*

cam·cor·der ['kæmkɔːrdər] videocámara *f*

came [keɪm] *pret* → *come*

cam·e·ra ['kæmərə] cámara *f*

'cam·e·ra·man *n* cámara *m*, camarógrafo *m*

cam·i·sole ['kæmɪsoʊl] camisola *f*

cam·ou·flage ['kæməflɑːʒ] 1 *n* camuflaje *m* 2 *v/t* camuflar

camp [kæmp] 1 *n* campamento *m*; *make camp* acampar; *refugee camp* campo *m* de refugiados 2 *v/i* acampar

cam·paign [kæm'peɪn] 1 *n* campaña *f* 2 *v/i* hacer campaña (*for* a favor de)

cam·paign·er [kæm'peɪnər] defensor(a) *m(f)* (*for* de); *a campaigner against racism* una persona que hace campaña contra el racismo

camp·er ['kæmpər] *person* campista *m/f*; *vehicle* autocaravana *f* camp·ing ['kæmpɪŋ] acampada f; *on campsite* camping m; **go camping** ir de acampada *or* camping

'camp·site camping m

cam·pus ['kæmpəs] campus m

can¹ [kæn] *unstressed* [kən] v/aux (*pret* **could**) ◇ (*ability*) poder; **can you swim?** ¿sabes nadar?; **can you hear me?** ¿me oyes?; **I can't see** no veo; **can you speak French?** ¿hablas francés?; **can he call me back?** ¿me podría devolver la llamada?; **as fast / well as you can** tan rápido / bien como puedas; **I can't go any further - you can and you will!** no puedo más - ¡ya lo creo que puedes!
◇ (*permission*) poder; **can I help you?** ¿te puedo ayudar?; **can you help me?** ¿me puedes ayudar?; **can I have a beer / coffee?** ¿me pones una cerveza / un café?; **that can't be right** debe haber un error

can² [kæn] **1** n *for drinks etc* lata f **2** v/t (*pret & pp* **canned**) enlatar

Can·a·da ['kænədə] Canadá

Ca·na·di·an [kə'neɪdɪən] **1** adj canadiense **2** n canadiense m/f

ca·nal [kə'næl] *waterway* canal m

ca·nar·y [kə'nerɪ] canario m

can·cel ['kænsl] v/t cancelar

can·cel·la·tion [kænsə'leɪʃn] cancelación f

can·cel·la·tion fee tarifa f de cancelación de reserva

can·cer ['kænsər] cáncer m

Can·cer ['kænsər] ASTR Cáncer m/f inv

can·cer·ous ['kænsərəs] adj canceroso

c & f abbr (= **cost and freight**) C&F (= costo y flete)

can·did ['kændɪd] adj sincero, franco

can·di·da·cy ['kændɪdəsɪ] candidatura f

can·di·date ['kændɪdət] *for position* candidato(-a) m(f); *in exam* candidato(-a) m(f), examinando(-a) m(f)

can·did·ly ['kændɪdlɪ] adv sinceramente, francamente

can·died ['kændɪd] adj confitado

can·dle ['kændl] vela f

'can·dle·stick candelero m; *short* palmatoria f

can·dor, *Br* can·dour ['kændər] sinceridad f, franqueza f

can·dy ['kændɪ] (*sweet*) caramelo m; (*sweets*) dulces mpl; **a box of candy** una caja de caramelos *or* dulces

cane [keɪn] caña f; *for walking* bastón m

can·is·ter ['kænɪstər] bote m

can·na·bis ['kænəbɪs] cannabis m, hachís m

canned [kænd] adj *fruit, tomatoes* enlatado, en lata; (*recorded*) grabado

can·ni·bal·ize ['kænɪbəlaɪz] v/t canibalizar

can·not ['kænɑːt] → **can¹**

can·ny ['kænɪ] adj (*clever*) astuto

ca·noe [kə'nuː] canoa f, piragua f

'can o·pen·er abrelatas m inv

can't [kænt] → **can¹**

can·tan·ker·ous [kæn'tæŋkərəs] adj arisco, cascarrabias

can·teen [kæn'tiːn] *in plant* cantina f, cafetería f

can·vas ['kænvəs] *for painting* lienzo m; *material* lona f

can·vass ['kænvəs] **1** v/t (*seek opinion of*) preguntar **2** v/i POL hacer campaña (**for** in favor de)

can·yon ['kænjən] cañón m

cap [kæp] n *hat* gorro m; *with peak* gorra f; *of bottle, jar* tapón m; *of pen, of lens* tapa f

ca·pa·bil·i·ty [keɪpə'bɪlətɪ] capacidad f; **it's beyond my capabilities** no entra dentro de mis posibilidades

ca·pa·ble ['keɪpəbl] adj (*efficient*) capaz, competente; **be capable of** ser capaz de

ca·pac·i·ty [kə'pæsətɪ] capacidad f; *of car engine* cilindrada f; **a capacity crowd** un lleno absoluto; **the job is well within your capacity** el trabajo está dentro de tus posibilidades; **in my capacity as ...** en mi calidad de ...

cap·i·tal ['kæpɪtl] n *of country* capital f; (*capital letter*) mayúscula f; *money* capital m

cap·i·tal ex'pend·i·ture inversión f en activo fijo

cap·i·tal 'gains tax impuesto m sobre las plusvalías

cap·i·tal 'growth crecimiento m del capital

cap·i·tal·ism ['kæpɪtəlɪzm] capitalismo m

'cap·i·tal·ist ['kæpɪtəlɪst] **1** adj capitalista **2** n capitalista m/f

◆ cap·i·tal·ize on ['kæpɪtəlaɪz] v/t aprovecharse de

cap·i·tal 'let·ter letra f mayúscula

cap·i·tal 'pun·ish·ment pena f capital, pena f de muerte

ca·pit·u·late [kə'pɪtjuleɪt] v/i capitular

ca·pit·u·la·tion [kæpɪtju'leɪʃn] capitulación f

Cap·ri·corn ['kæprɪkɔːrn] ASTR Capricornio m/f inv

cap·size [kæp'saɪz] **1** v/i volcar **2** v/t hacer volcar

cap·sule ['kæpsul] *of medicine* cápsula f; (*space capsule*) cápsula f espacial

cap·tain ['kæptɪn] n of ship, team, MIL capitán(-ana) m(f); of aircraft comandante m/f

cap·tion ['kæpʃn] n pie m de foto

cap·ti·vate ['kæptɪveɪt] v/t cautivar, fascinar

cap·tive ['kæptɪv] **1** adj prisionero **2** n prisionero(-a) m(f)

cap·tive 'mar·ket mercado m cautivo

cap·tiv·i·ty [kæp'tɪvətɪ] cautividad f

cap·ture ['kæptʃər] **1** n of city toma f; of criminal, animal captura f **2** v/t person, animal capturar; city, building tomar; market share ganar; (portray) captar

car [kɑːr] coche m, L.Am. carro m, Rpl auto m; of train vagón m; **by car** en coche

ca·rafe [kə'ræf] garrafa f, jarra f

car·at ['kærət] quilate m

car·bo·hy·drate [kɑːrbou'haɪdreɪt] carbohidrato m

'car bomb coche m bomba

car·bon mon·ox·ide [kɑːrbənmən'ɑːksaɪd] monóxido m de carbono

car·bu·ret·er, car·bu·ret·or [kɑːrbu're-tər] carburador m

car·cass ['kɑːrkəs] cadáver m

car·cin·o·gen [kɑːr'sɪnədʒen] agente m cancerígeno or carcinógeno

car·cin·o·gen·ic [kɑːrsɪnə'dʒenɪk] adj cancerígeno, carcinógeno

card [kɑːrd] to mark occasion, COMPUT, business tarjeta f; (postcard) (tarjeta f) postal f; (playing card) carta f, naipe m; game of cards partida f de cartas

'card·board cartón m

card·board 'box caja f de cartón

car·di·ac ['kɑːrdɪæk] adj cardíaco

car·di·ac ar'rest paro m cardíaco

car·di·gan ['kɑːrdɪɡən] cárdigan m

car·di·nal ['kɑːrdɪnl] n REL cardenal m

'card in·dex fichero m

'card key llave f tarjeta

'card phone tarjeta f telefónica

care [ker] **1** n cuidado m; (medical care) asistencia f médica; (worry) preocupación f; **care of → c/o**; **take care** (be cautious) tener cuidado; **take care (of yourself)!** (goodbye) ¡cuídate!; **take care of** dog, tool, house, garden cuidar; baby cuidar (de); (deal with) ocuparse de; **I'll take care of the bill** yo pago la cuenta; **(handle) with care!** on label frágil **2** v/i preocuparse; **I don't care!** ¡me da igual!; **I couldn't care less** ¡me importa un pimiento!; **if you really cared ...** si de verdad te importara ...
◆ **care about** v/t preocuparse por
◆ **care for** v/t (look after: person) cuidar (de); (look after: plant) cuidar; **he**

doesn't care for me the way he used to ya no le gusto como antes; *would you care for a drink?* ¿le apetece tomar algo?

ca·reer [kə'rɪr] carrera f; *career prospects* perspectivas fpl profesionales

ca'reers of·fi·cer asesor(a) m(f) de orientación profesional

'care·free adj despreocupado

care·ful ['kerfəl] adj (cautious, thorough) cuidadoso; *be careful* ten cuidado; *(be) careful!* ¡(ten) cuidado!

care·ful·ly ['kerfəlɪ] adv (with caution) con cuidado; worded etc cuidadosamente

care·less ['kerlɪs] adj descuidado; *you are so careless!* ¡qué descuidado eres!

care·less·ly ['kerlɪslɪ] adv descuidadamente

car·er ['kerər] persona que cuida de un familiar o enfermo

ca·ress [kə'res] **1** n caricia f **2** v/t acariciar

care·tak·er ['kerteɪkər] conserje m

'care·worn adj agobiado

'car fer·ry ferry m, transbordador m

car·go ['kɑːrɡou] cargamento m

'car hire alquiler m de coches or automóviles

'car hire com·pa·ny empresa f de alquiler de coches or automóviles

car·i·ca·ture ['kærɪkətʃər] n caricatura f

car·ing ['kerɪŋ] adj person afectuoso, bondadoso; society solidario

'car me·chan·ic mecánico(-a) m(f) de coches or automóviles

car·nage ['kɑːrnɪdʒ] matanza f, carnicería f

car·na·tion [kɑːr'neɪʃn] clavel m

car·ni·val ['kɑːrnɪvl] feria f

car·ol ['kærəl] n villancico m

car·ou·sel [kærə'sel] at airport cinta f transportadora de equipajes; for slide projector carro m; (merry-go-round) tiovivo m

'car park Br estacionamiento m, Span aparcamiento m

car·pen·ter ['kɑːrpɪntər] carpintero(-a) m(f)

car·pet ['kɑːrpɪt] alfombra f

'car phone teléfono m de coche

'car·pool n acuerdo para compartir el vehículo entre varias personas que trabajan en el mismo sitio

'car port estacionamiento m con techo

'car ra·di·o autorradio m

car·ri·er ['kærɪər] company transportista m; airline línea f aérea; of disease portador(a) m(f)

car·rot ['kærət] zanahoria f

car·ry ['kærɪ] **1** v/t (pret & pp carried) of

person llevar; *disease* ser portador de; *of ship, plane, bus etc* transportar; *proposal* aprobar; **be carrying a child** *of pregnant woman* estar embarazada; **get carried away** dejarse llevar por la emoción, emocionarse **2** *v/i* (*pret & pp* **carried**) *of sound* oírse

◆ **carry on 1** *v/i* (*continue*) seguir, continuar; (*make a fuss*) organizar un escándalo; (*have an affair*) tener un lío **2** *v/t* (*conduct*) mantener; *business* efectuar

◆ **carry out** *survey etc* llevar a cabo

'car seat *for child* asiento *m* para niño

cart [kɑːrt] carro *m*

car·tel [kɑːr'tel] cartel *m*

car·ton ['kɑːrtn] *for storage, transport* caja *f* de cartón; *for milk etc* cartón *m*, tetrabrik *m* ®; *of cigarettes* cartón *m*

car·toon [kɑːr'tuːn] *in newspaper, magazine* tira *f* cómica; *on TV, movie* dibujos *mpl* animados

car·toon·ist [kɑːr'tuːnɪst] dibujante *m/f* de chistes

car·tridge ['kɑːrtrɪdʒ] *for gun* cartucho *m*

carve [kɑːrv] *v/t meat* trinchar; *wood* tallar

carv·ing ['kɑːrvɪŋ] *figure* talla *f*

'car wash lavado *m* de automóviles

case[1] [keɪs] *container* funda *f*; *of scotch, wine* caja *f*; (*suitcase*) maleta *f*

case[2] [keɪs] *n instance, criminal*, MED caso *m*; LAW causa *f*; **I think there's a case for dismissing him** creo que hay razones fundadas para despedirlo; **the case for the prosecution** (los argumentos jurídicos de) la acusación; **make a case for sth** defender algo; **in case ...** por si ...; **in case of emergency** en caso de emergencia; **in any case** en cualquier caso; **in that case** en ese caso

'case his·to·ry MED historial *m* médico

'case·load número *m* de casos

cash [kæʃ] **1** *n* (dinero *m* en) efectivo *m*; **I'm a bit short of cash** no tengo mucho dinero; **cash down** al contado; **pay (in) cash** pagar en efectivo; **cash on delivery** → **COD 2** *v/t check* hacer efectivo

◆ **cash in on** *v/t* sacar provecho de

'cash cow fuente *f* de ingresos

'cash desk caja *f*

cash 'dis·count descuento *m* por pago al contado

'cash di·spens·er *Br* cajero *m* automático

'cash flow flujo *m* de caja, cash-flow *m*; **cash flow problems** problemas *fpl* de liquidez

cash·ier [kæ'ʃɪr] *n in store etc* cajero(-a) *m(f)*

cash·mere ['kæʃmɪr] *adj* cachemir *m*

'cash·point cajero *m* automático

'cash re·gis·ter caja *f* registradora

ca·si·no [kə'siːnou] casino *m*

cas·ket ['kæskɪt] (*coffin*) ataúd *m*

cas·se·role ['kæsəroul] *n meal* guiso *m*; *container* cacerola *f*, cazuela *f*

cas·sette [kə'set] cinta *f*, casete *f*

cas'sette play·er, **cas'sette re·cord·er** casete *m*

cast [kæst] **1** *n of play* reparto *m*; (*mold*) molde *m* **2** *v/t* (*pret & pp* **cast**) *doubt, suspicion* proyectar; *metal* fundir; *play* seleccionar el reparto de; **they cast Alan as ...** le dieron a Alan el papel de ...

◆ **cast off** *v/i of ship* soltar amarras

caste [kæst] casta *f*

cast·er ['kæstər] *on chair etc* ruedecita *f*

Cas·til·ian [kæs'tɪlɪən] **1** *adj* castellano **2** *n person* castellano(-a) *m(f)*; *language* castellano

cast 'i·ron *n* hierro *m* fundido

cast-'i·ron *adj* de hierro fundido

cas·tle ['kæsl] castillo *m*

'cast-or ['kæstər] → **caster**

cas·trate [kæ'streɪt] *v/t* castrar

cas·tra·tion [kæ'streɪʃn] castración *f*

cas·u·al ['kæʒuəl] *adj* (*chance*) casual; (*offhand*) despreocupado; (*not formal*) informal; (*not permanent*) temporal; **it was just a casual remark** no era más que un comentario hecho de pasada; **he was very casual about the whole thing** parecía no darle mucha importancia al asunto; **casual sex** relaciones *fpl* sexuales (con parejas) ocasionales

cas·u·al·ly ['kæʒuəlɪ] *adv dressed* de manera informal; *say* a la ligera

cas·u·al·ty ['kæʒuəltɪ] víctima *f*

'cas·u·al wear ropa *f* informal

cat [kæt] gato *m*

Cat·a·lan ['kætələn] **1** *adj* catalán **2** *n person* catalán(-ana) *m(f)*; *language* catalán *m*

cat·a·log, *Br* **cat·a·logue** ['kætəlɑːg] *n* catálogo *m*

cat·a·lyst ['kætəlɪst] catalizador *m*

cat·a·lyt·ic con·vert·er [kætə'lɪtɪk] catalizador *m*

cat·a·pult ['kætəpʌlt] **1** *v/t fig to fame, stardom* catapultar, lanzar **2** *n toy* tirachinas *m inv*

cat·a·ract ['kætərækt] MED catarata *f*

ca·tas·tro·phe [kə'tæstrəfi] catástrofe *f*

cat·a·stroph·ic [kætə'strɑːfɪk] *adj* catastrófico

catch [kætʃ] **1** *n parada f* (*sin que la pelota toque el suelo*); *of fish* captura *f*, pesca *f*; (*locking device*) cierre *m*; (*problem*) pega f; **there has to be a catch** tiene que haber una trampa **2** v/t (pret & pp **caught**) ball agarrar, Span coger; animal atrapar; escaped prisoner capturar; (get on: bus, train) tomar, Span coger; (not miss: bus, train) alcanzar, Span coger; fish pescar; in order to speak to alcanzar, pillar; (hear) oír; illness agarrar, Span coger; **catch (a) cold** agarrar or Span coger un resfriado, resfriarse; **catch s.o.'s eye** of person, object llamar la atención de alguien; **catch sight of, catch a glimpse of** ver; **catch s.o. doing sth** atrapar or Span coger a alguien haciendo algo

◆ **catch on** v/i (become popular) cuajar, ponerse de moda; (understand) darse cuenta

◆ **catch up** v/i: **catch up with s.o.** alcanzar a alguien; **he's having to work hard to catch up** tiene que trabajar muy duro para ponerse al día

◆ **catch up on** v/t: **catch up on one's sleep** recuperar sueño; **there's a lot of work to catch up on** hay mucho trabajo atrasado

catch-22 [kætʃtwentɪ'tuː]: **it's a catch-22 situation** es como la pescadilla que se muerde la cola

catch·er ['kætʃər] in baseball cátcher m, catcher m

catch·ing ['kætʃɪŋ] adj also fig contagioso

catch·y ['kætʃɪ] adj tune pegadizo

cat·e·gor·ic [kætə'gɒrɪk] adj categórico

cat·e·gor·i·cal·ly [kætə'gɒrɪklɪ] adv categóricamente

cat·e·go·ry ['kætəgɒrɪ] categoría f

◆ **ca·ter for** ['keɪtər] v/t (meet the needs of) cubrir las necesidades de; (provide food for) organizar la comida para

ca·ter·er ['keɪtərər] hostelero(-a) m(f)

ca·ter·pil·lar ['kætərpɪlər] oruga f

ca·the·dral [kə'θiːdrl] catedral f

Cath·o·lic ['kæθəlɪk] **1** adj católico **2** n católico(-a) m(f)

Ca·thol·i·cism [kə'θɑːlɪsɪzm] catolicismo m

'cat·nap 1 n cabezada f **2** v/i (pret & pp **catnapped**) echarse una cabezada f

cat's eyes on road captafaros mpl (en el centro de la calzada)

cat·sup ['kætsʌp] ketchup m, catchup m

cat·tle ['kætl] npl ganado m

cat·ty ['kætɪ] adj malintencionado

'cat·walk pasarela f

caught [kɒːt] pret & pp → **catch**

cau·li·flow·er ['kɒːlɪflaʊər] coliflor f

cause [kɒːz] **1** n causa f; (grounds) motivo m, razón f **2** v/t causar, provocar

caus·tic ['kɒːstɪk] adj fig cáustico

cau·tion ['kɒːʃn] **1** n (carefulness) precaución f, prudencia f; **caution is advised** se recomienda prudencia **2** v/t (warn) prevenir (**against** contra)

cau·tious ['kɒːʃəs] adj cauto, prudente

cau·tious·ly ['kɒːʃəslɪ] adv cautelosamente, con prudencia

cav·al·ry ['kævəlrɪ] caballería f

cave [keɪv] cueva f

◆ **cave in** v/i of roof hundirse

cav·i·ar ['kævɪɑːr] caviar m

cav·i·ty ['kævətɪ] caries f inv

cc¹ [siː'siː] **1** abbr (= **carbon copy**) copia f **2** v/t memo enviar una copia de; person enviar una copia a

cc² [siː'siː] abbr (= **cubic centimeters**) cc (centímetros mpl cúbicos); MOT cilindrada f

CD [siː'diː] abbr (= **compact disc**) CD m (= disco m compacto)

CD play·er (reproductor m de) CD m

CD-ROM [siːdiː'rɑːm] CD-ROM m

CD-ROM drive lector m de CD-ROM

cease [siːs] **1** v/i cesar **2** v/t suspender; **cease doing sth** dejar de hacer algo

'cease-fire alto m el fuego

ceil·ing ['siːlɪŋ] of room techo m; (limit) tope m, límite m

cel·e·brate ['selɪbreɪt] **1** v/i: **let's celebrate with a bottle of champagne** celebrémoslo con una botella de champán **2** v/t celebrar, festejar; (observe) celebrar

cel·e·brat·ed ['selɪbreɪtɪd] adj célebre; **be celebrated for** ser célebre por

cel·e·bra·tion [selɪ'breɪʃn] celebración f

ce·leb·ri·ty [sɪ'lebrətɪ] celebridad f

cel·e·ry ['selərɪ] apio m

cel·i·ba·cy ['selɪbəsɪ] celibato m

cel·i·bate ['selɪbət] adj célibe

cell [sel] for prisoner, in spreadsheet celda f; BIO célula f

cel·lar ['selər] of house sótano m; for wine bodega f

cel·list ['tʃelɪst] violonchelista m/f

cel·lo ['tʃelou] violonchelo m

cel·lo·phane ['seləfeɪn] celofán m

'cell phone, cel·lu·lar phone ['seljələr] (teléfono m) móvil m, L.Am. (teléfono m) celular m

cel·lu·lite ['seljuːlaɪt] celulitis f

ce·ment [sɪ'ment] **1** n cemento m **2** v/t colocar con cemento; friendship consolidar

cem·e·tery ['semətrɪ] cementerio m

cen·sor ['sensər] v/t censor(a) m(f)

cen·sus ['sensəs] censo m

cent [sent] céntimo m

cen·te·na·ry [sen'tiːnərɪ] centenario m

cen·ter ['sentər] **1** n centro m; **in the cen-**

C

ter of en el centro de **2** *v/t* centrar

◆ **center on** *v/t* centrarse en

cen·ter of 'grav·i·ty centro *m* de gravedad

cen·ti·grade ['sentɪɡreɪd] *adj* centígrado; *10 degrees centigrade* 10 grados centígrados

cen·ti·me·ter, *Br* **cen·ti·me·tre** ['sentɪmiːtər] centímetro *m*

cen·tral ['sentrəl] *adj* central; *location, apartment* céntrico; *central Chicago* el centro de Chicago; *be central to sth* ser el eje de algo

Cen·tral A'mer·i·ca *n* Centroamérica, América Central

Cen·tral A'mer·i·can 1 *adj* centroamericano, de (la) América Central **2** *n* centroamericano(-a) *m(f)*

cen·tral 'heat·ing calefacción *f* central

cen·tral·ize ['sentrəlaɪz] *v/t* centralizar

cen·tral 'lock·ing MOT cierre *m* centralizado

cen·tral 'pro·ces·sing u·nit unidad *f* central de proceso

cen·tre *Br* → **center**

cen·tu·ry ['sentʃərɪ] siglo *m*

CEO [siːiː'oʊ] *abbr* (= *Chief Executive Officer*) consejero(-a) *m(f)* delegado

ce·ram·ic [sɪ'ræmɪk] *adj* de cerámica

ce·ram·ics [sɪ'ræmɪks] (*pl: objects*) objetos *mpl* de cerámica; (*sing: art*) cerámica *f*

ce·re·al ['sɪrɪəl] (*grain*) cereal *m*; (*breakfast cereal*) cereales *mpl*

cer·e·mo·ni·al [serɪ'moʊnɪəl] **1** *adj* ceremonial **2** *n* ceremonial *m*

cer·e·mo·ny ['serɪmənɪ] (*event, ritual*) ceremonia *f*

cer·tain ['sɜːrtn] *adj* (*sure*) seguro; (*particular*) cierto; *I'm certain* estoy seguro; *it's certain that ...* es seguro que ...; *a certain Mr S.* un cierto Sr. S.; *make certain* asegurarse; *know / say for certain* saber / decir con certeza

cer·tain·ly ['sɜːrtnlɪ] *adv* (*definitely*) claramente; (*of course*) por supuesto; *certainly not!* ¡por supuesto que no!

cer·tain·ty ['sɜːrtntɪ] (*confidence*) certeza *f*, certidumbre *f*; (*inevitability*) seguridad *f*; *it's a certainty* es seguro; *he's a certainty for the gold medal* va a ganar seguro la medalla de oro

cer·tif·i·cate [sər'tɪfɪkət] (*qualification*) título *m*; (*official paper*) certificado *m*

cer·ti·fied pub·lic ac·count·ant ['sɜːrtɪfaɪd] censor(a) *m(f)* jurado de cuentas

cer·ti·fy [sər'tɪfaɪ] *v/t* (*pret & pp certified*) certificar

Ce·sar·e·an [sɪ'zerɪən] *n* cesárea *f*

ces·sa·tion [se'seɪʃn] cese *m*

c/f *abbr* (= *cost and freight*) CF (= costo y

flete)

CFC [siːef'siː] *abbr* (= *chlorofluorocarbon*) CFC *m* (= clorofluorocarbono *m*)

chain [tʃeɪn] **1** *n also of hotels etc* cadena *f* **2** *v/t* encadenar: *chain sth / s.o. to sth* encadenar algo/a alguien a algo

chain re'ac·tion reacción *f* en cadena

'chain-smoke *v/i* fumar un cigarrillo tras otro, fumar como un carretero

'chain-smok·er persona que fuma un cigarrillo tras otro

'chain store *store* tienda *f* (de una cadena); *company* cadena *f* de tiendas

chair [tʃer] **1** *n* silla *f*; (*armchair*) sillón *m*; *at university* cátedra *f*; *the chair* (*electric chair*) la silla eléctrica; *go to the chair* ser ejecutado en la silla eléctrica; *take the chair* ocupar la presidencia **2** *v/t meeting* presidir

'chair lift telesilla *f*

'chair·man presidente *m*

chair·man·ship ['tʃermənʃɪp] presidencia *f*

'chair·per·son presidente(-a) *m(f)*

'chair·wom·an presidenta *f*

cha·let ['ʃæleɪ] chalet *m*, chalé *m*

chal·ice ['tʃælɪs] REL cáliz *m*

chalk [tʃɔːk] *for writing* tiza *f*; *in soil* creta *f*

chal·lenge ['tʃælɪndʒ] **1** *n* (*difficulty*) desafío *m*, reto *m*; *in race, competition* ataque *m* **2** *v/t* desafiar, retar; (*call into question*) cuestionar

chal·len·ger ['tʃælɪndʒər] aspirante *m/f*

chal·len·ging ['tʃælɪndʒɪŋ] *adj job, undertaking* estimulante

cham·ber·maid ['tʃeɪmbərmeɪd] camarera *f* de hotel

'cham·ber mu·sic música *f* de cámara

Cham·ber of 'Com·merce Cámara *f* de Comercio

cha·mois (leath·er) ['ʃæmɪ] ante *m*

cham·pagne [ʃæm'peɪn] champán *m*

cham·pi·on ['tʃæmpɪən] **1** *n* SP campeón(-ona) *m(f)*; *of cause* abanderado (-a) *m(f)* **2** *v/t* (*cause*) abanderar

cham·pi·on·ship ['tʃæmpɪənʃɪp] campeonato *m*

chance [tʃæns] (*possibility*) posibilidad *f*; (*opportunity*) oportunidad *f*; (*risk*) riesgo *m*; (*luck*) casualidad *f*, suerte *f*; *there's not much chance of that happening* no es probable que ocurra; *leave nothing to chance* no dejar nada a la improvisación; *by chance* por casualidad; *take a chance* correr el riesgo; *I'm not taking any chances* no voy a correr ningún riesgo

Chan·cel·lor ['tʃænsələr] *in Germany* canciller *m*; **Chancellor (of the Exchequer)** in *Britain* Ministro(-a) *m(f)* de Hacienda

chan·de·lier [ʃændə'lɪr] araña *f* (de luces)

change [ʧeɪndʒ] **1** *n* cambio *m*; (*small coins*) suelto *m*; *from purchase* cambio *m*, *Span* vuelta *f*, *L.Am.* vuelto *m*; **a change is as good as a rest** a veces cambiar es lo mejor; **that makes a nice change** eso es una novedad bienvenida; **for a change** para variar; **a change of clothes** una muda **2** *v/t* cambiar; **change trains** hacer transbordo; **change one's clothes** cambiarse de ropa **3** *v/i* cambiar; (*put on different clothes*) cambiarse; (*take different train/bus*) hacer transbordo; **the lights changed to green** el semáforo se puso verde

change·a·ble ['ʧeɪndʒəbl] *adj* variable, cambiante

'change·o·ver transición *f* (**to** a); *in relay race* relevo *m*

chang·ing room ['ʧeɪndʒɪŋ] SP vestuario *m*; *in shop* probador *m*

chan·nel ['ʧænl] *on* TV, *at sea* canal *m*

chant [ʧænt] **1** *n* REL canto *m*; *of fans* cántico *m*; *of demonstrators* consigna *f* **2** *v/i* gritar **3** *v/t* corear

cha·os ['keɪɑːs] caos *m*; **It was chaos at the airport** la situación en el aeropuerto era caótica

cha·ot·ic [keɪ'ɑːtɪk] *adj* caótico

chap [ʧæp] *n Br* F tipo *m* F, *Span* tío *m* F

chap·el ['ʧæpl] capilla *f*

chapped [ʧæpt] *adj lips* cortado; *hands* agrietado

chap·ter ['ʧæptər] *of book* capítulo *m*; *of organization* sección *f*

char·ac·ter ['kærəktər] *nature, personality, in printing* carácter *m*; *person, in book, play* personaje *m*; **he's a real character** es todo un personaje

char·ac·ter·is·tic [kærəktə'rɪstɪk] **1** *n* característica *f* **2** *adj* característico

char·ac·ter·is·ti·cal·ly [kærəktə'rɪstɪklɪ] *adv* de modo característico; **he was characteristically rude** fue grosero como de costumbre

char·ac·ter·ize ['kærɪktəraɪz] *v/t (be typical of)* caracterizar; (*describe*) describir, clasificar

cha·rade [ʃə'rɑːd] *fig* farsa *f*

char·broiled ['ʧɑːrbrɔɪld] *adj* a la brasa

char·coal ['ʧɑːrkoʊl] *for barbecue* carbón *m vegetal*; *for drawing* carboncillo *m*

charge [ʧɑːrdʒ] **1** *n* (*fee*) tarifa *f*; LAW cargo *m*, acusación *f*; **free of charge** gratis; **bank charges** comisiones *fpl* bancarias; **will that be cash or charge?** ¿pagará en efectivo o con tarjeta?; **be in charge** es-

tar a cargo; **take charge** hacerse cargo **2** *v/t sum of money* cobrar; (*put on account*) pagar con tarjeta; LAW acusar (**with** de); *battery* cargar; **please charge it to my account** cárguelo a mi cuenta **3** *v/i* (*attack*) cargar

'charge ac·count cuenta *f* de crédito

'charge card tarjeta *f* de compra

cha·ris·ma [kə'rɪzmə] carisma *m*

char·is·mat·ic [kærɪz'mætɪk] *adj* carismático

char·i·ta·ble ['ʧærɪtəbl] *adj institution, donation* de caridad; *person* caritativo

char·i·ty ['ʧærətɪ] *assistance* caridad *f*; *organization* entidad *f* benéfica

char·la·tan ['ʃɑːrlətən] charlatán(-ana) *m(f)*

charm [ʧɑːrm] **1** *n* (*appealing quality*) encanto *m*; *on bracelet etc* colgante *m* **2** *v/t* (*delight*) encantar

charm·ing ['ʧɑːrmɪŋ] *adj* encantador

charred [ʧɑːrd] *adj* carbonizado

chart [ʧɑːrt] (*diagram*) gráfico *m*; (*map*) carta *f* de navegación; **the charts** MUS las listas de éxitos

'char·ter flight vuelo *m* chárter

chase [ʧeɪs] **1** *n* persecución *f* **2** *v/t* perseguir

◆ **chase away** *v/t* ahuyentar

chas·sis ['ʃæsɪ] *of car* chasis *m inv*

chat [ʧæt] **1** *n* charla *f*, *Mex* plática *f* **2** *v/i* (*pret & pp* **chatted**) charlar, *Mex* platicar

'chat show tertulia *f* televisiva

'chat show host presentador(a) *m(f)* de tertulia televisiva

chat·ter ['ʧætər] **1** *n* cháchara *f* **2** *v/i talk* parlotear; *of teeth* castañetear

'chat·ter·box charlatán(-ana) *m(f)*

chat·ty ['ʧætɪ] *adj person* hablador

chauf·feur ['ʃoʊfər] *n* chófer *m*, *L.Am.* chofer *m*

'chauf·feur-driv·en *adj* con chófer *or L.Am.* chofer

chau·vin·ist ['ʃoʊvɪnɪst] *n* (*male chauvinist*) machista *m*

chau·vin·is·tic [ʃoʊvɪ'nɪstɪk] *adj* chovinista; (*sexist*) machista

cheap [ʧiːp] *adj* (*inexpensive*) barato; (*nasty*) chabacano; (*mean*) tacaño

cheat [ʧiːt] **1** *n* (*person*) tramposo(-a) *m(f)* **2** *v/t* engañar; **cheat s.o. out of sth** estafar algo a alguien **3** *v/i* in exam copiar; *in cards etc* hacer trampa; **cheat on one's wife** engañar a la esposa

check¹ [ʧek] **1** *adj shirt* a cuadros **2** *n* cuadro *m*

check² [ʧek] FIN cheque *m*; *in restaurant etc* cuenta *f*; **the check please** la cuenta, por favor check³ [tʃek] **1** *n to verify sth* comprobación *f*; **keep in check, hold in check** mantener bajo control; **keep a check on** llevar el control de **2** *v/t* (*verify*) comprobar; *machinery* inspeccionar; (*restrain, stop*) contener, controlar; *with a checkmark* poner un tic en; *coat* dejar en el guardarropa; *package* dejar en consigna **3** *v/i* comprobar; **check for** comprobar

◆ check in *v/i at airport* facturar; *at hotel* registrarse

◆ check off *v/t* marcar (*como comprobada*)

◆ check on *v/t* vigilar

◆ check out **1** *v/i of hotel* dejar el hotel **2** *v/t* (*look into*) investigar; *club, restaurant etc* probar

◆ check up on *v/t* hacer averiguaciones sobre, investigar

◆ check with *v/t of person* hablar con; (*tally: of information*) concordar con

'check·book talonario *m* de cheques, *L.Am.* chequera *f*

checked [tʃekt] *adj material* a cuadros

check·er·board ['tʃekərbɔːrd] tablero *m* de ajedrez

check·ered ['tʃekərd] *adj pattern* a cuadros; *career* accidentado

check·ers ['tʃekərz] *nsg* damas *fpl*

'check-in (coun·ter) mostrador *m* de facturación

check·ing ac·count ['tʃekɪŋ] cuenta *f* corriente

'check-in time hora *f* de facturación

'check·list lista *f* de verificación

'check mark tic *m*

'check·mate *n* jaque *m* mate

'check·out caja *f*

'check·out time *from hotel* hora *f* de salida

'check·point control *m*

'check·room *for coats* guardarropa *m*; *for baggage* consigna *f*

'check·up *medical* chequeo *m* (médico), revisión *f* (médica); *dental* revisión *f* (en el dentista)

cheek [tʃiːk] ANAT mejilla *f*

'cheek·bone pómulo *m*

cheer [tʃɪr] **1** *n* ovación *f*; **cheers!** *toast* ¡salud!; **the cheers of the fans** los vítores de los aficionados **2** *v/t* ovacionar, vitorear **3** *v/t* lanzar vítores

◆ cheer on *v/t* animar

◆ cheer up **1** *v/i* animarse; **cheer up!** ¡anímate! **2** *v/t* animar

cheer·ful ['tʃɪrfəl] *adj* alegre, contento

cheer·ing ['tʃɪrɪŋ] *n* vítores *mpl*

cheer·i·o [tʃɪrɪ'oʊ] *Br* F ¡chao! F

'cheer·lead·er animadora *f*

cheese [tʃiːz] queso *m*

'cheese·burg·er hamburguesa *f* de queso

'cheese·cake tarta *f* de queso

chef [ʃef] chef *m*, jefe *m* de cocina

chem·i·cal ['kemɪkl] **1** *adj* químico **2** *n* producto *m* químico

chem·i·cal 'war·fare guerra *f* química

chem·ist ['kemɪst] *in laboratory* químico(-a) *m(f)*; *Br dispensing* farmacéutico(-a) *m(f)*

chem·is·try ['kemɪstrɪ] química *f*; *fig* sintonía *f*, química *f*

chem·o·ther·a·py [kiːmoʊ'θerəpɪ] quimioterapia *f*

cheque [tʃek] *Br* → **check²**

cher·ish ['tʃerɪʃ] *v/t photo etc* apreciar mucho, tener mucho cariño a; *person* querer mucho; *hope* albergar

cher·ry ['tʃerɪ] *fruit* cereza *f*; *tree* cerezo *m*

cher·ub ['tʃerəb] *in painting, sculpture* querubín *m*

chess [tʃes] ajedrez *m*

'chess·board tablero *m* de ajedrez

'chess·man, 'chess·piece pieza *f* de ajedrez

chest [tʃest] *of person* pecho *m*; *box* cofre *m*; **get sth off one's chest** desahogarse

chest·nut ['tʃesnʌt] castaña *f*; *tree* castaño *m*

chest of 'draw·ers cómoda *f*

chew [tʃuː] *v/t* mascar, masticar; *of dog, rats* mordisquear

◆ chew out *v/t* F echar una bronca a F

chew·ing gum ['tʃuːɪŋ] chicle *m*

chic [ʃiːk] *adj* chic, elegante

chick [tʃɪk] *young chicken* pollito *m*; *young bird* polluelo *m*; F *girl* nena *f* F

chick·en ['tʃɪkɪn] **1** *n* gallina *f*; *food* pollo *m*; F (*coward*) gallina *f* F **2** *adj* F (*cowardly*) cobarde; **be chicken** ser un(a) gallina F

◆ chicken out *v/i* F acobardarse

'chick·en·feed F calderilla *f*

chief [tʃiːf] **1** *n* jefe(-a) *m(f)* **2** *adj* principal

chief ex·ec·u·tive 'of·fi·cer consejero(-a) *m(f)* delegado

chief·ly ['tʃiːflɪ] *adv* principalmente

chil·blain ['tʃɪlbleɪn] sabañón *m*

child [tʃaɪld] (*pl children* ['tʃɪldrən]) niño(-a) *m(f)*; *son* hijo *m*; *daughter* hija *f*; *pej* niño(-a) *m(f)*, crío(-a) *m(f)*

'child a·buse malos tratos *mpl* a menores

'child·birth parto *m*

child·hood ['tʃaɪldhʊd] infancia *f*

child·ish ['tʃaɪldɪʃ] *adj pej* infantil

child·ish·ness ['tʃaɪldɪʃnɪs] *pej* infantilismo *m*

child·ish·ly ['tʃaɪldɪʃlɪ] *adv pej* de manera infantil

child·less ['tʃaɪldlɪs] *adj* sin hijos

child·like ['tʃaɪldlaɪk] *adj* infantil

'**child·mind·er** niñero(-a) *m(f)*

'**child·ren** ['tʃɪldrən] *pl* → **child**

Chil·e ['tʃɪlɪ] *n* Chile

Chil·e·an ['tʃɪlɪən] **1** *adj* chileno **2** *n* chileno(-a) *m(f)*

chill [tʃɪl] **1** *n illness* resfriado *m*; **there's a chill in the air** hace bastante fresco **2** *v/t wine* poner a enfriar

◆ **chill out** *v/i* P tranquilizarse

chil·(l)i (pep·per) ['tʃɪlɪ] chile *m*, *Span* guindilla *f*

chill·y ['tʃɪlɪ] *adj weather, welcome* fresco; *I'm feeling a bit chilly* tengo fresco

chime [tʃaɪm] *v/i* campanada *f*

chim·ney ['tʃɪmnɪ] chimenea *f*

chim·pan·zee [tʃɪm'pænziː] chimpancé *m*

chin [tʃɪn] barbilla *f*

Chi·na ['tʃaɪnə] China

chi·na ['tʃaɪnə] porcelana *f*

Chi·nese [tʃar'niːz] **1** *adj* chino **2** *n (language)* chino *m*; *(person)* chino(-a) *m(f)*

chink [tʃɪŋk] *gap* resquicio *m*; *sound* tintineo *m*

chip [tʃɪp] **1** *n of wood* viruta *f*; *of stone* lasca *f*; *damage* mella *f*; *in gambling ficha f*; *chips* patatas *fpl* fritas **2** *v/t (pret & pp chipped) (damage)* mellar

◆ **chip in** *v/i (interrupt)* interrumpir; *with money* poner dinero

chip·munk ['tʃɪpmʌŋk] ardilla *f* listada

chi·ro·prac·tor ['kaɪroupræktər] quiropráctico(-a) *m(f)*

chirp [tʃɜːrp] *v/i* piar

chis·el ['tʃɪzl] *n for stone* cincel *m*; *for wood* formón *m*

chit·chat ['tʃɪtʃæt] charla *f*

chiv·al·rous ['ʃɪvlrəs] *adj* caballeroso

chive [tʃaɪv] cebollino *m*

chlo·rine ['klɔːriːn] cloro *m*

chlo·ro·form ['klɔːrəfɔːrm] *n* cloroformo *m*

choc·a·hol·ic [tʃɑːkə'hɑːlɪk] *n* F adicto(-a) al chocolate

chock-a-block [tʃɑːkə'blɑːk] *adj* F abarrotado F

chock-full [tʃɑːk'ful] *adj* F de bote en bote F

choc·o·late ['tʃɑːkələt] chocolate *m*; *a box of chocolates* una caja de bombones; *hot chocolate* chocolate *m* caliente

'**choc·o·late cake** pastel *m* de chocolate

choice [tʃɔɪs] **1** *n* elección *f*; *(selection)* selección *f*; *you have a choice of rice or potatoes* puedes elegir entre arroz y pa-

tatas; *the choice is yours* tú eliges; *I had no choice* no tuve alternativa **2** *adj (top quality)* selecto

choir [kwaɪr] coro *m*

'**choir-boy** niño *m* de coro

choke [tʃouk] **1** *n* MOT estárter *m* **2** *v/i* ahogarse; *choke on sth* atragantarse con algo **3** *v/t* estrangular; *screams* ahogar

cho·les·te·rol [kə'lestəroul] colesterol *m*

choose [tʃuːz] *v/t & v/i (pret chose, pp chosen)* elegir, escoger

choos·ey ['tʃuːzɪ] *adj* F exigente

chop [tʃɑːp] **1** *n* meat chuleta *f*; *with one chop of the ax* con un hachazo **2** *v/t (pret & pp chopped) wood* cortar; *meat* trocear; *vegetables* picar

◆ **chop down** *v/t tree* talar

chop·per ['tʃɑːpər] F *(helicopter)* helicóptero *m*

'**chop·sticks** palillos *mpl* (chinos)

cho·ral ['kɔːrəl] *adj* coral

chord [kɔːrd] MUS acorde *m*

chore [tʃɔːr] tarea *f*

chor·e·o·graph ['kɔːrɪəgræf] *v/t* coreografiar

chor·e·og·ra·pher [kɔːrɪ'ɑːgrəfər] coreógrafo(-a) *m(f)*

chor·e·og·ra·phy [kɔːrɪ'ɑːgrəfɪ] coreografía *f*

cho·rus ['kɔːrəs] *singers* coro *m*; *of song* estribillo *m*

chose [tʃouz] *pret* → **choose**

cho·sen ['tʃouzn] *pp* → **choose**

Christ [kraɪst] Cristo; *Christ!* ¡Dios mío!

chris·ten ['krɪsn] *v/t* bautizar

chris·ten·ing ['krɪsnɪŋ] bautizo *m*

Chris·tian ['krɪstʃən] **1** *n* cristiano(-a) *m(f)* **2** *adj* cristiano

Chris·ti·an·i·ty [krɪstɪ'ænətɪ] cristianismo *m*

'**Chris·tian name** nombre *m* de pila

Christ·mas ['krɪsməs] Navidad(es) *f(pl)*; *at Christmas* en Navidad(es); *Merry Christmas!* ¡Feliz Navidad!

'**Christ·mas card** crisma *m inv*, tarjeta *f* de Navidad

Christ·mas 'Day día *f* de Navidad

Christ·mas 'Eve Nochebuena *f*

'**Christ·mas present** regalo *m* de Navidad

'**Christ·mas tree** árbol *m* de Navidad

chrome, chro·mi·um [kroum, 'kroumɪəm] cromo *m*

chro·mo·some ['krouməsoum] cromosoma *m*

chron·ic ['krɑːnɪk] *adj* crónico

chron·o·log·i·cal [krɑːnə'lɑːdʒɪkl] *adj* cronológico; *in chronological order* en orden cronológico

chrys·an·the·mum [krɪ'sænθəməm] crisantemo *m*

chub·by ['tʃʌbɪ] *adj* rechoncho

chuck [tʃʌk] *v/t* F tirar

◆ **chuck out** *v/t* F *object* tirar; *person* echar

chuck·le ['tʃʌkl] **1** *n* risita *f* **2** *v/i* reírse por lo bajo

chum [tʃʌm] amigo(-a) *m(f)*

chum·my ['tʃʌmɪ] *adj* F: **be chummy with** ser amiguete de F

chunk [tʃʌŋk] trozo *m*

chunk·y ['tʃʌŋkɪ] *adj sweater* grueso; *person, build* cuadrado, fornido

church [tʃɜːrtʃ] iglesia *f*

church 'hall *sala parroquial empleada para diferentes actividades*

church 'serv·ice oficio *m* religioso

'church·yard cementerio *m* (al lado de iglesia)

churl·ish ['tʃɜːrlɪʃ] *adj* maleducado, grosero

chute [ʃuːt] rampa *f*; *for garbage* colector *m* de basura

CIA [siːaɪ'eɪ] *abbr* (= **Central Intelligence Agency**) CIA *f* (= Agencia *f* Central de Inteligencia)

ci·der ['saɪdər] sidra *f*

CIF [siːaɪ'ef] *abbr* (= **cost, insurance, freight**) CIF (= costo, seguro y flete)

ci·gar [sɪ'gɑːr] (cigarro *m*) puro *m*

cig·a·rette, cig·a·ret [sɪgə'ret] cigarrillo *m*

cig·a'rette end colilla *f*

cig·a'rette light·er encendedor *m*, mechero *m*

cig·a'rette pa·per papel *m* de fumar

cin·e·ma ['sɪnɪmə] cine *m*

cin·na·mon ['sɪnəmən] canela *f*

cir·cle ['sɜːrkl] **1** *n* círculo *m*; **sit in a circle** sentarse en círculo **2** *v/t* (*draw circle around*) poner un círculo alrededor de; **his name was circled in red** su nombre tenía un círculo rojo alrededor **3** *v/i of plane, bird* volar en círculo

cir·cuit ['sɜːrkɪt] circuito *m*; (*lap*) vuelta *f*

'cir·cuit board COMPUT placa *f* or tarjeta *f* de circuitos

'cir·cuit break·er ELEC cortacircuitos *m inv*

'cir·cuit train·ing SP: **do circuit training** hacer circuitos de entrenamiento

cir·cu·lar ['sɜːrkjʊlər] **1** *n giving information* circular *f* **2** *adj* circular

cir·cu·late ['sɜːrkjʊleɪt] **1** *v/i* circular **2** *v/t memo* hacer circular

cir·cu·la·tion [sɜːrkjʊ'leɪʃn] circulación *f*; *of newspaper, magazine* tirada *f*

cir·cum·fer·ence [sər'kʌmfərəns] circunferencia *f*

cir·cum·stanc·es ['sɜːrkəmstənsɪs] *npl* circunstancias *fpl*; *financial* situación *f* económica; **under no circumstances** en ningún caso, de ninguna manera; **under the circumstances** dadas las circunstancias

cir·cus ['sɜːrkəs] circo *m*

cir·rho·sis (of the liv·er) [sɪ'rousɪs] cirrosis *f* (hepática)

cis·tern ['sɪstɜːrn] cisterna *f*

cite [saɪt] *v/t* citar

cit·i·zen ['sɪtɪzn] ciudadano(-a) *m(f)*

cit·i·zen·ship ['sɪtɪznʃɪp] ciudadanía *f*

cit·rus ['sɪtrəs] *adj* cítrico; **citrus fruit** cítrico *m*

cit·y ['sɪtɪ] ciudad *f*

city 'cen·ter centro *m* de la ciudad

city 'hall ayuntamiento *m*

civ·ic ['sɪvɪk] *adj* cívico

civ·il ['sɪvl] *adj* civil; (*polite*) cortés

civ·il en·gi·neer ingeniero(-a) *m(f)* civil

ci·vil·i·an [sɪ'vɪljən] **1** *n* civil *m/f* **2** *adj clothes* de civil

ci·vil·i·ty [sɪ'vɪlɪtɪ] cortesía *f*

civ·i·li·za·tion [sɪvəlaɪ'zeɪʃn] civilización *f*

civ·i·lize ['sɪvəlaɪz] *v/t person* civilizar

civ·il 'rights *npl* derechos *mpl* civiles

civ·il 'ser·vant funcionario(-a) *m(f)*

civ·il 'ser·vice administración *f* pública

civ·il 'war guerra *f* civil

claim [kleɪm] **1** *n* (*request*) reclamación *f* (*for* de); (*right*) derecho *m*; (*assertion*) afirmación *f* **2** *v/t* (*ask for as a right*) reclamar; (*assert*) afirmar; *lost property* reclamar; **they have claimed responsibility for the attack** se han atribuido la responsabilidad del ataque

claim·ant ['kleɪmənt] reclamante *m/f*

clair·voy·ant [kler'vɔɪənt] *n* clarividente *m/f*, vidente *m/f*

clam [klæm] almeja *f*

◆ **clam up** *v/i* (*pret & pp clammed*) F cerrarse, callarse

clam·ber ['klæmbər] *v/i* trepar (*over* por)

clam·my ['klæmɪ] *adj* húmedo

clam·or, *Br* **clam·our** ['klæmər] *noise* griterío *m*; *outcry* clamor *m*

◆ **clamor for** *v/t justice* clamar por; *ice cream* pedir a gritos

clamp [klæmp] **1** *n fastener* abrazadera *f*, mordaza *f* **2** *v/t fasten* sujetar con abrazadera; *car* poner un cepo a

◆ **clamp down** *v/i* actuar contundentemente

◆ **clamp down on** *v/t* actuar contundentemente contra

clan [klæn] clan *m*

clan·des·tine [klæn'destɪn] *adj* clandestino

clang [klæŋ] **1** n sonido m metálico **2** v/i resonar; *the metal door clanged shut* la puerta metálica se cerró con gran estrépito

clap [klæp] v/t & v/i (pret & pp *clapped*) (*applaud*) aplaudir

clar-et ['klærɪt] wine burdeos m inv

clar-i-fi-ca-tion [klærɪfɪ'keɪʃn] aclaración f

clar-i-fy ['klærɪfaɪ] v/t (pret & pp *clarified*) aclarar

clar-i-net [klærɪ'net] clarinete m

clar-i-ty ['klærətɪ] claridad f

clash [klæʃ] **1** n choque m, enfrentamiento m; *of personalities* choque m **2** v/i chocar, enfrentarse; *of colors* desentonar; *of events* coincidir

clasp [klæsp] **1** n broche m, cierre m **2** v/t in hand estrechar; *he clasped the precious documents to him* agarró firmemente los valiosos documentos

class [klæs] **1** n lesson, students clase f; *social class* clase f social **2** v/t clasificar (*as* como)

clas-sic ['klæsɪk] **1** adj clásico **2** n clásico m

clas-si-cal ['klæsɪkl] adj music clásico

clas-si-fi-ca-tion [klæsɪfɪ'keɪʃn] clasificación f

clas-si-fied ['klæsɪfaɪd] adj information reservado

'clas-si-fied ad(ver-tise-ment) anuncio m por palabras

clas-si-fy ['klæsɪfaɪ] v/t (pret & pp *classified*) clasificar

'class-mate compañero(-a) m(f) de clase

'class-room clase f, aula f

'class war-fare lucha f de clases

class-y ['klæsɪ] adj F con clase

clat-ter ['klætər] **1** n estrépito m **2** v/i hacer ruido

clause [klɔːz] in agreement cláusula f; GRAM cláusula f, oración f

claus-tro-pho-bi-a [klɔːstrə'foʊbɪə] claustrofobia f

claw [klɔː] **1** n also fig garra f; of lobster pinza f **2** v/t (scratch) arañar

clay [kleɪ] arcilla f

clean [kliːn] **1** adj limpio **2** adv F (completely) completamente **3** v/t limpiar; *clean one's teeth* limpiarse los dientes; *I must have my coat cleaned* tengo que llevar el abrigo a la tintorería

◆ **clean out** v/t room, closet limpiar por completo; fig desplumar

◆ **clean up 1** v/t also fig limpiar; papers recoger **2** v/i limpiar; (wash) lavarse; on stock market etc ganar mucho dinero

clean-er ['kliːnər] person limpiador(a) m(f); (dry) *cleaner* tintorería f

clean-ing wom-an ['kliːnɪŋ] señora f de la limpieza

cleanse [klenz] v/t skin limpiar

cleans-er ['klenzər] for skin loción f limpiadora

cleans-ing cream ['klenzɪŋ] crema f limpiadora

clear [klɪr] **1** adj claro; weather, sky despejado; water transparente; conscience limpio; *I'm not clear about it* no lo tengo claro; *I didn't make myself clear* no me expliqué claramente **2** adv *stand clear of the doors* apartarse de las puertas; *steer clear of* evitar **3** v/t roads etc despejar; (acquit) absolver; (authorize) autorizar; (earn) ganar, sacar; *the guards cleared everybody out of the room* los guardias sacaron a todo el mundo de la habitación; *you're cleared for takeoff* tiene autorización or permiso para despegar; *clear one's throat* carraspear **4** v/i of sky, mist despejarse; of face alegrarse

◆ **clear away** v/t quitar

◆ **clear off** v/i F largarse F

◆ **clear out 1** v/t closet ordenar, limpiar **2** v/i marcharse

◆ **clear up 1** v/i of weather despejarse; of illness, rash desaparecer **2** v/t (tidy) ordenar; mystery, problem aclarar

clear-ance ['klɪrəns] space espacio m; (authorization) autorización f

clear-ance sale liquidación f

clear-ing ['klɪrɪŋ] claro m

clear-ly ['klɪrlɪ] adv claramente, *she is clearly upset* está claro que está disgustada

cleav-age ['kliːvɪdʒ] escote m

cleav-er ['kliːvər] cuchillo m de carnicero

clem-en-cy ['klemənsɪ] clemencia f

clench [klentʃ] v/t teeth, fist apretar

cler-gy ['klɜːrdʒɪ] clero m

cler-gy-man ['klɜːrdʒɪmæn] clérigo m

clerk [klɜːrk] administrative oficinista m/f; in store dependiente(-a) m/f

clev-er ['klevər] adj person, animal listo; idea, gadget ingenioso

clev-er-ly ['klevərlɪ] adv designed ingeniosamente

cli-ché ['kliːʃeɪ] tópico m, cliché m

cli-chéd ['kliːʃeɪd] adj estereotipado

click [klɪk] **1** n COMPUT clic m **2** v/i hacer clic

◆ **click on** v/t COMPUT hacer clic en

cli-ent ['klaɪənt] cliente m/f

cli-en-tele [kliːən'tel] clientela f

cli-mate ['klaɪmət] also fig clima m

'cli·mate change cambio m climático
cli·mat·ic [klaɪˈmætɪk] adj climático
cli·max ['klaɪmæks] n clímax m, punto m
culminante
climb [klaɪm] 1 n up mountain ascensión
f, escalada f 2 v/t hill, ladder subir; mountain subir, escalar; tree trepar a 3 v/i subir
(into a); up mountain subir, escalar; of
inflation etc subir
◆ climb down v/i from ladder etc bajar
climb·er ['klaɪmər] person escalador(a)
m(f), alpinista m/f, L.Am. andinista m/f
climb·ing ['klaɪmɪŋ] escalada f, alpinismo
m, L.Am. andinismo m
climb·ing wall rocódromo m
clinch [klɪntʃ] v/t deal cerrar; that clinches it ¡ahora sí que está claro!
cling [klɪŋ] v/i (pret & pp clung) of clothes pegarse al cuerpo
◆ cling to v/t person, idea aferrarse a
'cling·film plástico m transparente (para
alimentos)
cling·y ['klɪŋɪ] adj child, boyfriend pegajoso
clin·ic ['klɪnɪk] clínica f
clin·i·cal ['klɪnɪkl] adj clínico
clink [klɪŋk] 1 n noise tintineo m 2 v/i tintinear
clip¹ [klɪp] 1 n fastener clip m 2 v/t (pret &
pp clipped): clip sth to sth sujetar algo a
algo
clip² [klɪp] 1 n extract fragmento m 2 v/t
(pret & pp clipped) nails, grass cortar;
hedge podar
clip·pers ['klɪpərz] npl for hair maquinilla
f; for nails cortaúñas m inv; for gardening
tijeras fpl de podar
clip·ping ['klɪpɪŋ] from newspaper recorte m
clique [kliːk] camarilla f
cloak n capa f
'cloak·room Br guardarropa m
clock [klɑːk] reloj m
'clock ra·di·o radio m despertador
'clock·wise adv en el sentido de las agujas
del reloj
'clock·work: it went like clockwork salió
a la perfección
◆ clog up [klɑːg] 1 v/i (pret & pp
clogged) bloquearse 2 v/t (pret & pp
clogged) bloquear
clone [kloʊn] 1 n clon m 2 v/t clonar
close¹ [kloʊs] 1 adj family cercano; friend
íntimo; bear a close resemblance to
parecerse mucho a; the closest town
la ciudad más cercana; be close to
s.o. emotionally estar muy unido a alguien 2 adv cerca; close to the school
cerca del colegio; close at hand a mano;

close by cerca
close² [kloʊz] 1 v/t cerrar 2 v/i of door,
shop cerrar; of eyes cerrarse
◆ close down v/t & v/i cerrar
◆ close in v/i of fog acercarse encima; of
troops aproximarse, acercarse
◆ close up 1 v/t building cerrar 2 v/i (move closer) juntarse
closed [kloʊzd] adj store, eyes cerrado
closed-cir·cuit 'tel·e·vi·sion circuito m
cerrado de televisión
'close-knit adj muy unido
close·ly ['kloʊslɪ] adv listen, watch atentamente; cooperate de cerca
clos·et ['klɑːzɪt] armario m
close-up ['kloʊsʌp] primer plano m
clos·ing date ['kloʊzɪŋ] fecha f límite
'clos·ing time hora f de cierre
clo·sure ['kloʊʒər] cierre m
clot [klɑːt] 1 n of blood coágulo m 2 v/i
(pret & pp clotted) of blood coagularse
cloth [klɑːθ] (fabric) tela f, tejido m; for
cleaning trapo m
clothes [kloʊðz] npl ropa f
'clothes brush cepillo m para la ropa
'clothes hang·er percha f
'clothes·horse tendedero m plegable
'clothes-line cuerda f de tender la ropa
'clothes peg, 'clothes·pin pinza f (de la
ropa)
cloth·ing ['kloʊðɪŋ] ropa f
cloud [klaʊd] n nube f; a cloud of dust
una nube de polvo
◆ cloud over v/i of sky nublarse
'cloud·burst chaparrón m
cloud·less ['klaʊdlɪs] adj sky despejado
cloud·y ['klaʊdɪ] adj nublado
clout [klaʊt] (fig: influence) influencia f
clove of 'gar·lic [kloʊv] diente m de ajo
clown [klaʊn] also fig payaso m
club [klʌb] n weapon palo m, garrote m; in
golf palo m; organization club m; clubs
in cards tréboles
clue [kluː] pista f; I haven't a clue F (don't
know) no tengo idea F; he hasn't a clue
F (is useless) no tiene ni idea F
clued-up [kluːdˈʌp] adj F puesto F; be
clued-up on sth F estar puesto sobre algo
F
clump [klʌmp] n of earth terrón m; of flowers etc grupo m
clum·si·ness ['klʌmzɪnɪs] torpeza f
clum·sy ['klʌmzɪ] adj person torpe
clung [klʌŋ] pret & pp → cling
clus·ter ['klʌstər] 1 n grupo m 2 v/i of
people apiñarse; of houses agruparse
clutch [klʌtʃ] 1 n MOT embrague m 2 v/t
agarrar
◆ clutch at v/t: clutch at sth agarrarse a

algo
clut·ter ['klʌtər] **1** *n* desorden *m*; *all the clutter on my desk* la cantidad de cosas que hay encima de mi mesa **2** *v/t* (*also*: *clutter up*) abarrotar

Co. *abbr* (= *Company*) Cía. (= *Compañía f*)

c/o *abbr* (= *care of*) en el domicilio de

coach [koʊtʃ] **1** *n* (*trainer*) entrenador(a) *m(f)*; *of singer, actor* profesor(a) *m(f)*; *on train* vagón *m*; *Br* (*bus*) autobús *m* **2** *v/t footballer* entrenar; *singer* preparar

coach·ing ['koʊtʃɪŋ] entrenamiento *m*

co·ag·u·late [koʊ'ægjuleɪt] *v/i of blood* coagularse

coal [koʊl] carbón *m*

co·a·li·tion [koʊə'lɪʃn] coalición *f*

'coal·mine mina *f* de carbón

coarse [kɔːrs] *adj* áspero; *hair* basto; (*vulgar*) basto, grosero

coarse·ly ['kɔːrslɪ] *adv* (*vulgarly*) de manera grosera; *coarsely ground coffee* café molido grueso

coast [koʊst] *n* costa *f*; *at the coast* en la costa

coast·al ['koʊstl] *adj* costero

coast·er ['koʊstər] posavasos *m inv*

'coast·guard *organization* servicio *m* de guardacostas; *person* guardacostas *m/f inv*

'coast·line litoral *m*, costa *f*

coat [koʊt] **1** *n* chaqueta *f*, *L.Am.* saco *m*; (*overcoat*) abrigo *m*; *of animal* pelaje *m*; *of paint etc* capa *f*, mano *f* **2** *v/t* (*cover*) cubrir (*with* de)

'coat·hang·er percha *f*

'coat·ing ['koʊtɪŋ] capa *f*

co·au·thor ['koʊ:θər] **1** *n* coautor(a) *m(f)* **2** *v/t*: *co-author a book* escribir un libro conjuntamente

coax [koʊks] *v/t* persuadir; *coax sth out of s.o.* sonsacar algo a alguien

cob·bled ['kɑ:bld] *adj* adoquinado

cob·ble·stone ['kɑ:blstoʊn] adoquín *m*

cob·web ['kɑ:bweb] telaraña *f*

co·caine [kə'keɪn] cocaína *f*

cock [kɑ:k] *n* (*chicken*) gallo *m*; (*any male bird*) macho *m*

cock·eyed [kɑ:k'aɪd] *adj* F *idea etc* ridículo

'cock·pit *of plane* cabina *f*

cock·roach ['kɑ:kroʊtʃ] cucaracha *f*

'cock·tail cóctel *m* (*bebida*)

'cock·tail par·ty cóctel *m* (*fiesta*)

'cock·tail shak·er coctelera *f*

cock·y ['kɑ:kɪ] *adj* F creído, chulo

co·coa ['koʊkoʊ] *drink* cacao *m*

co·co·nut ['koʊkənʌt] coco *m*

'co·co·nut palm cocotero *m*

COD [si:oʊ'di:] *abbr* (= *collect on delivery*) entrega *f* contra reembolso

cod·dle ['kɑ:dl] *v/t sick person* cuidar; *pej*: *child* mimar

code [koʊd] *n* código *m*; *in code* cifrado

co·ed·u·ca·tion·al [koʊedʊ'keɪʃnl] *adj* mixto

co·erce [koʊ'ɜːrs] *v/t* coaccionar

co·ex·ist [koʊɪg'zɪst] *v/i* coexistir

co·ex·ist·ence [koʊɪg'zɪstəns] coexistencia *f*

cof·fee ['kɑ:fɪ] café *m*; *a cup of coffee* un café

'cof·fee bean grano *m* de café

'cof·fee break pausa *f* para el café

'cof·fee cup taza *f* de café

'cof·fee grind·er ['graɪndər] molinillo *m* de café

'cof·fee mak·er cafetera *f* (*para preparar*)

'cof·fee pot cafetera *f* (*para servir*)

'cof·fee shop café *m*, cafetería *f*

'cof·fee ta·ble mesa *f* de centro

cof·fin ['kɑ:fɪn] féretro *m*, ataúd *m*

cog [kɑ:g] diente *m*

co·gnac ['kɑ:njæk] coñac *m*

'cog·wheel rueda *f* dentada

co·hab·it [koʊ'hæbɪt] *v/i* cohabitar

co·her·ent [koʊ'hɪrənt] *adj* coherente

coil [kɔɪl] **1** *n of rope* rollo *m*; *of smoke* espiral *f*; *of snake* anillo *m* **2** *v/t*: *coil (up)* enrollar

coin [kɔɪn] *n* moneda *f*

co·in·cide [koʊɪn'saɪd] *v/i* coincidir

co·in·ci·dence [koʊ'ɪnsɪdəns] coincidencia *f*

coke [koʊk] P (*cocaine*) coca *f*

Coke® [koʊk] Coca Cola® *f*

cold [koʊld] **1** *adj also fig* frío; *I'm* (*feeling*) *cold* tengo frío; *it's cold of weather* hace frío; *in cold blood* a sangre fría; *get cold feet* F ponerse nervioso **2** *n* frío *m*; MED resfriado *m*; *I have a cold* estoy resfriado, tengo un resfriado

cold-blood·ed [koʊld'blʌdɪd] *adj* de sangre fría; *fig*: *murder* a sangre fría

cold call·ing ['kɔːlɪŋ] COM visitas o llamadas comerciales hechas sin cita previa

'cold cuts *npl* fiambres *mpl*

cold·ly ['koʊldlɪ] *adv* fríamente, con frialdad

cold·ness ['koʊldnɪs] frialdad *f*

'cold sore calentura *f*

cole·slaw ['koʊlslɔ:] ensalada de col, cebolla, zanahoria y mayonesa

col·ic ['kɑ:lɪk] cólico *m*

col·lab·o·rate [kə'læbəreɪt] *v/i* colaborar (*on* en)

col·lab·o·ra·tion [kəlæbə'reɪʃn] colaboración *f*

col·lab·o·ra·tor [kə'læbəreɪtər] colabora-
dor(a) *m(f)*; *with enemy* colaboracionis-
ta *m/f*

col·lapse [kə'læps] *v/i of roof, building*
hundirse, desplomarse; *of person* desplomarse

col·lap·si·ble [kə'læpsəbl] *adj* plegable

col·lar ['kɑːlər] cuello *m*; *for dog* collar *m*

'col·lar·bone clavícula *f*

col·league ['kɑːliːg] colega *m/f*

col·lect [kə'lekt] 1 *v/t* recoger; *as hobby*
coleccionar 2 *v/i* (*gather together*) reunirse 3 *adv:* *call collect* llamar a cobro
revertido

col·lect call llamada *f* a cobro revertido

col·lect·ed [kə'lektɪd] *adj works, poems
etc* completo; *person* sereno

col·lec·tion [kə'lekʃn] colección *f*; *in
church* colecta *f*

col·lec·tive [kə'lektɪv] *adj* colectivo

col·lec·tive 'bar·gain·ing negociación *f*
colectiva

col·lec·tor [kə'lektər] coleccionista *m/f*

col·lege ['kɑːlɪdʒ] universidad *f*

col·lide [kə'laɪd] *v/i* chocar, colisionar
(*with* con *or* contra)

col·li·sion [kə'lɪʒn] choque *m*, colisión *f*

col·lo·qui·al [kə'loʊkwɪəl] *adj* coloquial

Co·lom·bi·a [kə'lʌmbɪə] Colombia *f*

Co·lom·bi·an [kə'lʌmbɪən] 1 *adj* colombiano 2 *n* colombiano(-a) *m(f)*

co·lon ['koʊlən] *punctuation*) dos puntos
mpl; ANAT colon *m*

colo·nel ['kɜːrnl] coronel *m*

co·lo·ni·al [kə'loʊnɪəl] *adj* colonial

co·lo·nize [kə'lɑːnaɪz] *v/t country* colonizar

co·lo·ny ['kɑːlənɪ] colonia *f*

col·or ['kʌlər] 1 *n* color *m*; *in color movie
etc* en color; *colors* MIL bandera *f* 2 *v/t*
one's hair teñir 3 *v/i* (*blush*) ruborizarse

'col·or·blind *adj* daltónico

col·ored ['kʌlərd] *adj person* de color

'col·or fast *adj* que no se destiñe

col·or·ful ['kʌlərfəl] *adj* lleno de colores;
account colorido

col·or·ing ['kʌlərɪŋ] color *m*

'col·or pho·to·graph fotografía *f* en color

'col·or scheme combinación *f* de colores

'col·or TV televisión *f* en color

co·los·sal [kə'lɑːsl] *adj* colosal

col·our *etc Br →* **color** *etc*

colt [koʊlt] potro *m*

Co·lum·bus [kə'lʌmbəs] Colón *m*

col·umn ['kɑːləm] *architectural, of text*
columna *f*

col·umn·ist ['kɑːləmɪst] columnista *m/f*

co·ma ['koʊmə] coma *m*; *be in a coma*
estar en coma

comb [koʊm] 1 *n* peine *m* 2 *v/t hair, area*
peinar; *comb one's hair* peinarse

com·bat ['kɑːmbæt] 1 *n* combate *m* 2 *v/t*
combatir

com·bi·na·tion [kɑːmbɪ'neɪʃn] combinación *f*

com·bine [kəm'baɪn] 1 *v/t* combinar; *ingredients* mezclar 2 *v/i* combinarse

com·bine har·vest·er [kɑːmbaɪn'hɑːrvɪs-
tər] cosechadora *f*

com·bus·ti·ble [kəm'bʌstɪbl] *adj* combustible

com·bus·tion [kəm'bʌstʃn] combustión *f*

come [kʌm] *v/i* (*pret came*, *pp come*) *toward speaker* venir; *toward listener* ir; *of
train, bus* llegar, venir; *don't come too
close* no te acerques demasiado; *you'll
come to like it* llegará a gustarte; *how
come?* F ¿y eso?; *how come you've
stopped going to the club?* ¿cómo es
que has dejado de ir al club?

◆ **come about** *v/i* (*happen*) pasar, suceder

◆ **come across 1** *v/t* (*find*) encontrar 2
v/i: his humor comes across as ... su
humor da la impresión de ser ...; *she
comes across as ...* da la impresión
de ser ...

◆ **come along** *v/i* (*come too*) venir; (*turn
up*) aparecer; (*progress*) marchar; *why
don't you come along?* ¿por qué no
te vienes con nosotros?

◆ **come apart** *v/i* desmontarse; (*break*)
romperse

◆ **come around** *v/i to s.o.'s home* venir,
pasarse; (*regain consciousness*) volver
en sí

◆ **come away** *v/i* (*leave*) salir; *of button
etc* caerse

◆ **come back** *v/i* volver; *it came back to
me* lo recordé

◆ **come by 1** *v/i* pasarse 2 *v/t* (*acquire*)
conseguir; *how did you come by that
bruise?* ¿cómo te has dado ese golpe?

◆ **come down 1** *v/i* bajar; *of rain, snow*
caer 2 *v/t: he came down the stairs* bajó
las escaleras

◆ **come for** *v/t* (*attack*) atacar; (*collect
thing*) venir a por; (*collect person*) venir
a buscar a

◆ **come forward** *v/i* (*present o.s.*) presentarse

◆ **come from** *v/t* (*travel from*) venir de;
(*originate from*) ser de

◆ **come in** *v/i* entrar; *of train* llegar; *of tide* subir; *come in!* ¡entre!, ¡adelante!

◆ **come in for** *v/t* recibir; *come in for criticism* recibir críticas

◆ **come in on** *v/t: come in on a deal* par-

ticipar en un negocio
◆ **come off** v/i *of handle etc* soltarse, caerse; *of paint etc* quitarse
◆ **come on** v/i (*progress*) marchar, progresar; **come on!** ¡vamos!; **oh come on, you're exaggerating** ¡vamos, hombre!, estás exagerando
◆ **come out** v/i salir; *of book* publicarse; *of stain* irse, quitarse; *of gay* declararse homosexual públicamente
◆ **come to 1** v/t *place* llegar a; *of hair, dress, water* llegar hasta; **that comes to $70** eso suma 70 dólares **2** v/i (*regain consciousness*) volver en sí
◆ **come up** v/i subir; **something has come up** ha surgido algo
◆ **come up with** v/t *solution* encontrar; **John came up with a great idea** a John se le ocurrió una idea estupenda
'**come·back** regreso *m*; **make a comeback** regresar
co·me·di·an [kə'miːdiən] humorista *m/f*; *pej* payaso(-a) *m(f)*
'**come·down** gran decepción *f*
com·e·dy ['kɑːmədɪ] comedia *f*
com·et ['kɑːmɪt] cometa *m*
come·up·pance [kʌm'ʌpəns] *n* F: **he'll get his comeuppance** tendrá su merecido
com·fort ['kʌmfərt] **1** *n* comodidad *f*, confort *m*; (*consolation*) consuelo *m* **2** v/t consolar
com·for·ta·ble ['kʌmfərtəbl] *adj chair* cómodo; *house, room* cómodo, confortable; **be comfortable** *of person* estar cómodo; *financially* estar en una situación holgada
com·ic ['kɑːmɪk] **1** *n to read* cómic *m*; (*comedian*) cómico(-a) *m(f)* **2** *adj* cómico
com·i·cal ['kɑːmɪkl] *adj* cómico
'**com·ic book** cómic *m*
'**com·ics** ['kɑːmɪks] *npl* tiras *fpl* cómicas
'**com·ic strip** tira *f* cómica
com·ma ['kɑːmə] coma *f*
com·mand [kə'mænd] **1** *n* orden *f* **2** v/t ordenar, mandar
com·man·deer [kəmən'dɪr] v/t requisar
com·mand·er [kə'mændər] comandante *m/f*
com·mand·er·in·'chief comandante *m/f* en jefe
com·mand·ing of·fi·cer [kə'mændɪŋ] oficial *m/f* al mando
com·mand·ment [kə'mændmənt] mandamiento *m*: **the Ten Commandments** REL los Diez Mandamientos
com·mem·o·rate [kə'meməreɪt] v/t conmemorar
com·mem·o·ra·tion [kəmemə'reɪʃn]: **in**

commemoration of en conmemoración de
com·mence [kə'mens] v/t & v/i comenzar
com·mend [kə'mend] v/t encomiar, elogiar
com·mend·a·ble [kə'mendəbl] *adj* encomiable
com·men·da·tion [kəmen'deɪʃn] *for bravery* mención *f*
com·men·su·rate [kə'menʃərət] *adj*: **commensurate with** acorde con
com·ment ['kɑːment] **1** *n* comentario *m*; **no comment!** ¡sin comentarios! **2** v/i hacer comentarios (**on** sobre)
com·men·ta·ry ['kɑːmənterɪ] comentarios *mpl*
com·men·tate ['kɑːmənteɪt] v/i hacer de comentarista
com·men·ta·tor ['kɑːmənteɪtər] comentarista *m/f*
com·merce ['kɑːmɜːrs] comercio *m*
com·mer·cial [kə'mɜːrʃl] **1** *adj* comercial **2** *n* (*advert*) anuncio *m* (publicitario)
com·mer·cial 'break pausa *f* publicitaria
com·mer·cial·ize [kə'mɜːrʃlaɪz] v/t *Christmas* comercializar
com·mer·cial 'trav·el·er viajante *m/f* de comercio
com·mis·e·rate [kə'mɪzəreɪt] v/i: **she commiserated with me on my failure to get the job** me dijo cuánto sentía que no hubiera conseguido el trabajo
com·mis·sion [kə'mɪʃn] **1** *n* (*payment, committee*) comisión *f*; (*job*) encargo *m* **2** v/t: **she has been commissioned ...** se le ha encargado ...
com·mit [kə'mɪt] v/t (*pret & pp committed*) *crime* cometer; *money* comprometer; **commit o.s.** comprometerse
com·mit·ment [kə'mɪtmənt] compromiso *m* (**to** con); **he's afraid of commitment** tiene miedo de comprometerse
com·mit·tee [kə'mɪtɪ] comité *m*
com·mod·i·ty [kə'mɑːdətɪ] *raw material* producto *m* básico, *product* bien *m* de consumo
com·mon ['kɑːmən] *adj* común; **in common** al igual (**with** que); **have sth in common with s.o.** tener algo en común con alguien
com·mon·er ['kɑːmənər] plebeyo(-a) *m(f)*
com·mon 'law wife esposa *f* de hecho
com·mon·ly ['kɑːmənlɪ] *adv* comúnmente
Com·mon 'Mar·ket Mercado *m* Común
'**com·mon·place** *adj* común
Com·mons ['kɑːmənz] *npl*: **the Commons** *in Britain* la Cámara de los Co-

munes

com·mon 'sense sentido *m* común

com·mo·tion [kə'məʊʃn] alboroto *m*

com·mu·nal [kə'mjuːnl] *adj* comunal

com·mu·nal·ly [kə'mjuːnəlɪ] *adv* en comunidad

com·mu·ni·cate [kə'mjuːnɪkeɪt] **1** *v/i* comunicarse **2** *v/t* comunicar

com·mu·ni·ca·tion [kəmjuːnɪ'keɪʃn] comunicación *f*

com·mu·ni·ca·tions *npl* comunicaciones *fpl*

com·mu·ni·ca·tions sat·el·lite satélite *m* de telecomunicaciones

com·mu·ni·ca·tive [kə'mjuːnɪkətɪv] *adj person* comunicativo

Com·mu·nion [kə'mjuːnjən] REL comunión *f*

com·mu·ni·qué [kə'mjuːnɪkeɪ] comunicado *m*

Com·mu·nism ['kɑːmjʊnɪzəm] comunismo *m*

Com·mu·nist ['kɑːmjʊnɪst] **1** *adj* comunista **2** *n* comunista *m/f*

com·mu·ni·ty [kə'mjuːnɪtɪ] comunidad *f*

com'mu·ni·ty cen·ter centro *m* comunitario

com'mu·ni·ty serv·ice servicios *mpl* a la comunidad (como pena)

com·mute [kə'mjuːt] **1** *v/i* viajar al trabajo; *commute to work* viajar al trabajo **2** *v/t* LAW conmutar

com·mut·er [kə'mjuːtər] *persona que viaja al trabajo*

com'mut·er traf·fic *tráfico generado por los que se desplazan al trabajo*

com'mut·er train *tren de cercanías que utilizan los que se desplazan al trabajo*

com·pact **1** *adj* [kəm'pækt] compacto **2** *n* ['kɑːmpækt] MOT utilitario *m*

com·pact 'disc (disco *m*) compacto *m*

com·pan·ion [kəm'pænjən] compañero(-a) *m(f)*

com·pan·ion·ship [kəm'pænjənʃɪp] compañía *f*

com·pa·ny ['kʌmpənɪ] COM empresa *f*, compañía *f*; (*companionship, guests*) compañía *f*; *keep s.o. company* hacer compañía a alguien

com·pa·ny 'car coche *m* de empresa

com·pa·ny 'law derecho *m* de sociedades

com·pa·ra·ble ['kɑːmpərəbl] *adj* comparable

com·par·a·tive [kəm'pærətɪv] **1** *adj* (*relative*) relativo; *study* comparado; *comparative form* GRAM comparativo *m* **2** *n* GRAM comparativo *m*

com·par·a·tive·ly [kəm'pærətɪvlɪ] *adv* relativamente

com·pare [kəm'per] **1** *v/t* comparar; *compared with ...* comparado con ...; *you can't compare them* no se pueden comparar **2** *v/i* compararse

com·pa·ri·son [kəm'pærɪsn] comparación *f*; *there's no comparison* no hay punto de comparación

com·part·ment [kəm'pɑːrtmənt] compartimento *m*

com·pass ['kʌmpəs] brújula *f*; (*a pair of*) *compasses* GEOM un compás

com·pas·sion [kəm'pæʃn] compasión *f*

com·pas·sion·ate [kəm'pæʃənət] *adj* compasivo

com·pas·sion·ate 'leave *permiso laboral por muerte o enfermedad grave de un familiar*

com·pat·i·bil·i·ty [kəmpætə'bɪlɪtɪ] compatibilidad *f*

com·pat·i·ble [kəm'pætəbl] *adj* compatible; *we're not compatible* no somos compatibles

com·pel [kəm'pel] *v/t* (*pret & pp compelled*) obligar

com·pel·ling [kəm'pelɪŋ] *adj argument* poderoso; *movie, book* fascinante

com·pen·sate ['kɑːmpənseɪt] **1** *v/t with money* compensar **2** *v/i compensate for* compensar

com·pen·sa·tion [kɑːmpən'seɪʃn] (*money*) indemnización *f*; (*reward, comfort*) compensación *f*

com·pete [kəm'piːt] *v/i* competir (*for* por)

com·pe·tence ['kɑːmpɪtəns] competencia *f*

com·pe·tent ['kɑːmpɪtənt] *adj* competente; *I'm not competent to judge* no estoy capacitado para juzgar

com·pe·tent·ly ['kɑːmpɪtəntlɪ] *adv* competentemente

com·pe·ti·tion [kɑːmpə'tɪʃn] (*contest*) concurso *f*; SP competición *f*; (*competitors*) competencia *f*; *the government wants to encourage competition* el gobierno quiere fomentar la competencia

com·pet·i·tive [kəm'petətɪv] *adj* competitivo

com·pet·i·tive·ly [kəm'petətɪvlɪ] *adv* competitivamente; *competitively priced* con un precio muy competitivo

com·pet·i·tive·ness [kəm'petɪtɪvnɪs] COM competitividad *f*; *of person* espíritu *m* competitivo

com·pet·i·tor [kəm'petɪtər] *in contest* concursante *m/f*; SP competidor(a) *m(f)*, contrincante *m/f*; COM competidor(a) *m(f)*

com·pile [kəm'paɪl] *v/t* compilar

comrade

com·pla·cen·cy [kəm'pleɪsənsɪ] complacencia *f*

com·pla·cent [kəm'pleɪsənt] *adj* complaciente

com·plain [kəm'pleɪn] *v/i* quejarse, protestar; *to shop, manager* quejarse; *complain of* MED estar aquejado de

com·plaint [kəm'pleɪnt] queja *f*, protesta *f*; MED dolencia *f*

com·ple·ment ['kɑ:mplɪmənt] *v/t* complementar; *they complement each other* se complementan

com·ple·men·ta·ry [kɑ:mplɪ'mentərɪ] *adj* complementario; *the two are complementary* los dos se complementan

com·plete [kəm'pli:t] **1** *adj* (*total*) absoluto, total; (*full*) completo; (*finished*) finalizado, terminado; *I made a complete fool of myself* quedé como un verdadero tonto **2** *v/t task, building etc* finalizar, terminar; *course* completar; *form* rellenar

com·plete·ly [kəm'pli:tlɪ] *adv* completamente

com·ple·tion [kəm'pli:ʃn] finalización *f*, terminación *f*

com·plex ['kɑ:mpleks] **1** *adj* complejo **2** *n also* PSYCH complejo *m*

com·plex·ion [kəm'plekʃn] facial tez *f*

com·plex·i·ty [kəm'pleksɪtɪ] complejidad *f*

com·pli·ance [kəm'plaɪəns] cumplimiento (*with* de)

com·pli·cate ['kɑ:mplɪkeɪt] *v/t* complicar

com·pli·cat·ed ['kɑ:mplɪkeɪtɪd] *adj* complicado

com·pli·ca·tion [kɑ:mplɪ'keɪʃn] complicación *f*; *complications* MED complicaciones *fpl*

com·pli·ment ['kɑ:mplɪmənt] **1** *n* cumplido *m* **2** *v/t* hacer un cumplido a (**on** por)

com·pli·men·ta·ry [kɑ:mplɪ'mentərɪ] *adj* elogioso; (*free*) de regalo, gratis

'com·pli·ments slip nota *f* de cortesía

com·ply [kəm'plaɪ] *v/i* (*pret & pp complied*) cumplir; *comply with* cumplir

com·po·nent [kəm'pəʊnənt] pieza *f*, componente *m*

com·pose [kəm'pəʊz] *v/t also* MUS componer; *be composed of* estar compuesto de; *compose o.s.* serenarse

com·posed [kəm'pəʊzd] *adj* (*calm*) sereno

com·pos·er [kəm'pəʊzər] MUS compositor(a) *m(f)*

com·po·si·tion [kɑ:mpə'zɪʃn] *also* MUS composición *f*; (*essay*) redacción *f*

com·po·sure [kəm'pəʊʒər] compostura *f*

com·pound ['kɑ:mpaʊnd] *n* CHEM compuesto *m*

com·pound 'in·ter·est interés *m* compuesto *or* combinado

com·pre·hend [kɑ:mprɪ'hend] *v/t* (*understand*) comprender

com·pre·hen·sion [kɑ:mprɪ'henʃn] comprensión *f*

com·pre·hen·sive [kɑ:mprɪ'hensɪv] *adj* detallado

com·pre·hen·sive in·sur·ance seguro *m* a todo riesgo

com·pre·hen·sive·ly [kɑ:mprɪ'hensɪvlɪ] *adv* detalladamente

com·press **1** *n* ['kɑ:mprɛs] MED compresa *f* **2** *v/t* [kəm'pres] *air, gas* comprimir; *information* condensar

com·prise [kəm'praɪz] *v/t* comprender; *be comprised of* constar de

com·pro·mise ['kɑ:mprəmaɪz] **1** *n* solución *f* negociada; *I've had to make compromises all my life* toda mi vida he tenido que hacer concesiones **2** *v/i* transigir, efectuar concesiones **3** *v/t principles* traicionar; (*jeopardize*) poner en peligro; *compromise o.s.* ponerse en un compromiso

com·pul·sion [kəm'pʌlʃn] PSYCH compulsión *f*

com·pul·sive [kəm'pʌlsɪv] *adj behavior* compulsivo; *reading* absorbente

com·pul·so·ry [kəm'pʌlsərɪ] *adj* obligatorio

com·put·er [kəm'pju:tər] *Span* ordenador *m*, *L.Am.* computadora *f*; *have sth on computer* tener algo en el *Span* ordenador *or L.Am.* computadora

com·put·er-aid·ed de'sign [kəmpju:tər'eɪdɪd] diseño *m* asistido por *Span* ordenador *or L.Am.* computadora

com·put·er-aid·ed man·u'fac·ture fabricación *f* asistida por *Span* ordenador *or L.Am.* computadora

com·put·er-con'trolled *adj* controlado por *Span* ordenador *or L.Am.* computadora

com'put·er game juego *m* de *Span* ordenador *or L.Am.* computadora

com·put·er·ize [kəm'pju:təraɪz] *v/t* informatizar, *L.Am.* computarizar

com·put·er 'lit·er·ate *adj* con conocimientos de informática *or L.Am.* computación

com·put·er 'sci·ence informática *f*, *L.Am.* computación *f*

com·put·er 'sci·en·tist informático(-a) *m(f)*

com·put·ing [kəm'pju:tɪŋ] *n* informática *f*, *L.Am.* computación *f*

com·rade ['kɑ:mreɪd] (*friend*) compañero(-a) *m(f)*; POL camarada *m/f*

com·rade·ship ['kɑːmreɪdʃɪp] camaradería f

con [kɑːn] **1** n F timo m F **2** v/t (pret & pp **conned**) F timar F

con·ceal [kənˈsiːl] v/t ocultar

con·ceal·ment [kənˈsiːlmənt] ocultación f

con·cede [kənˈsiːd] v/t (admit) admitir, reconocer; goal encajar

con·ceit [kənˈsiːt] engreimiento m, presunción f

con·ceit·ed [kənˈsiːtɪd] adj engreido, presuntuoso

con·cei·va·ble [kənˈsiːvəbl] adj concebible

con·ceive [kənˈsiːv] v/i of woman concebir; *conceive of* (imagine) imaginar; *I can't conceive of that happening* no puedo imaginar que eso vaya a pasar

con·cen·trate ['kɑːnsəntreɪt] **1** v/i concentrarse **2** v/t one's attention, energies concentrar

con·cen·trat·ed ['kɑːnsəntreɪtɪd] adj juice etc concentrado

con·cen·tra·tion [kɑːnsənˈtreɪʃn] concentración f

con·cept ['kɑːnsept] concepto m

con·cep·tion [kənˈsepʃn] of child concepción f

con·cern [kənˈsɜːrn] **1** n (anxiety, care) preocupación f; (business) asunto m; (company) empresa f; *it's none of your concern* no es asunto tuyo; *cause concern* preocupar, inquietar **2** v/t (involve) concernir, incumbir; (worry) preocupar, inquietar; *concern o.s. with* preocuparse de

con·cerned [kənˈsɜːrnd] adj (anxious) preocupado, inquieto (about por); (caring) preocupado (about por); (involved) en cuestión; *as far as I'm concerned* por lo que a mí respecta

con·cern·ing [kənˈsɜːrnɪŋ] prep en relación con, sobre

con·cert ['kɑːnsərt] concierto m

con·cert·ed [kənˈsɜːrtɪd] adj (joint) concertado, conjunto

'con·cert·mas·ter primer violín m/f

con·cer·to [kənˈtʃertəʊ] concierto m

con·ces·sion [kənˈseʃn] (compromise) concesión f

con·cil·i·a·to·ry [kənsɪlɪˈeɪtərɪ] adj conciliador

con·cise [kənˈsaɪs] adj conciso

con·clude [kənˈkluːd] v/t & v/i (deduce, end) concluir (from de)

con·clu·sion [kənˈkluːʒn] (deduction) conclusión f; (end) conclusión f; *in conclusion* en conclusión

con·clu·sive [kənˈkluːsɪv] adj concluyente

con·coct [kənˈkɑːkt] v/t meal, drink preparar; excuse, story urdir

con·coc·tion [kənˈkɑːkʃn] food mejunje m; drink brebaje m, pócima f

con·crete ['kɑːŋkriːt] **1** adj concreto; *concrete jungle* jungla f de asfalto **2** n hormigón m, L.Am. concreto m

con·cur [kənˈkɜːr] v/i (pret & pp **concurred**) coincidir

con·cus·sion [kənˈkʌʃn] conmoción f cerebral

con·demn [kənˈdem] v/t condenar; building declarar en ruina; *condemn s.o. to a life of poverty* condenar a alguien a vivir en la miseria

con·dem·na·tion [kɑːndəmˈneɪʃn] of action condena f

con·den·sa·tion [kɑːndenˈseɪʃn] on walls, windows condensación f

con·dense [kənˈdens] **1** v/t (make shorter) condensar **2** v/i of steam condensarse

con·densed 'milk [kənˈdenst] leche f condensada

con·de·scend [kɑːndɪˈsend] v/i: *he condescended to speak to me* se dignó a hablarme

con·de·scend·ing [kɑːndɪˈsendɪŋ] adj (patronizing) condescendiente

con·di·tion [kənˈdɪʃn] **1** n (state) condiciones fpl; of health estado m; illness enfermedad f; (requirement, term) condición f; conditions (circumstances) condiciones fpl; *on condition that ...* a condición de que ...; *you're in no condition to drive* no estás en condiciones de conducir **2** v/t PSYCH condicionar

con·di·tion·al [kənˈdɪʃnl] **1** adj acceptance condicional **2** n GRAM condicional m

con·di·tion·er [kənˈdɪʃnər] for hair suavizante m, acondicionador m; for fabric suavizante m

con·di·tion·ing [kənˈdɪʃnɪŋ] PSYCH condicionamiento m

con·do ['kɑːndəʊ] F apartment apartamento m, Span piso m; building bloque de apartamentos

con·do·lenc·es [kənˈdəʊlənsɪz] npl condolencias fpl

con·dom ['kɑːndəm] condón m, preservativo m

con·do·min·i·um [kɑːndəˈmɪnɪəm] → *condo*

con·done [kənˈdəʊn] v/t actions justificar

con·du·cive [kənˈduːsɪv] adj: *conducive to* propicio para

con·duct 1 n ['kɑːndʌkt] (behavior) conducta f **2** v/t [kənˈdʌkt] (carry out) realizar, hacer; ELEC conducir; MUS dirigir; **conduct o.s.** comportarse

con·duct·ed 'tour [kən'dʌktɪd] visita f guiada

con·duc·tor [kən'dʌktər] MUS director(a) m(f) de orquesta; *on train* revisor(-a) m(f); PHYS conductor m

cone [kəʊn] GEOM, *on highway* cono m; *for ice cream* cucurucho m; *of pine tree* piña f

con·fec·tion·er [kən'fekʃənər] pastelero(-a) m(f)

con·fec·tion·er's sug·ar azúcar m or f glas

con·fec·tion·e·ry [kən'fekʃənrɪ] *(candy)* dulces mpl

con·fed·e·ra·tion [kənfedə'reɪʃn] confederación f

con·fer [kən'fɜːr] **1** v/t *(pret & pp **conferred**)*: **confer sth on s.o.** *(bestow)* conferir *or* otorgar algo a alguien **2** v/i *(pret & pp **conferred**)* *(discuss)* deliberar

con·fer·ence ['kɑːnfərəns] congreso m; *discussion* conferencia f

'con·fe·rence room sala f de conferencias

con·fess [kən'fes] **1** v/t confesar; **I confess I don't know** confieso que no lo sé **2** v/i confesar; REL confesarse; **confess to a weakness for sth** confesar una debilidad por algo

con·fes·sion [kən'feʃn] confesión f; **I've a confession to make** tengo algo que confesar

con·fes·sion·al [kən'feʃnl] REL confesionario m

con·fes·sor [kən'fesər] REL confesor m

con·fide [kən'faɪd] **1** v/t confiar **2** v/i: **confide in s.o.** confiarse a alguien

con·fi·dence ['kɑːnfɪdəns] confianza f; *(secret)* confidencia f; **in confidence** en confianza, confidencialmente

con·fi·dent ['kɑːnfɪdənt] adj *(self-assured)* seguro de sí mismo; *(convinced)* seguro

con·fi·den·tial [kɑːnfɪ'denʃl] adj confidencial, secreto

con·fi·den·tial·ly [kɑːnfɪ'denʃlɪ] adv confidencialmente

con·fi·dent·ly ['kɑːnfɪdəntlɪ] adv con seguridad

con·fine [kən'faɪn] v/t *(imprison)* confinar, recluir; *(restrict)* limitar; **be confined to one's bed** tener que guardar cama

con·fined [kən'faɪnd] adj *space* limitado

con·fine·ment [kən'faɪnmənt] *(imprisonment)* reclusión f; MED parto m

con·firm [kən'fɜːrm] v/t confirmar

con·fir·ma·tion [kɑːnfər'meɪʃn] confir-

mación f

con·firmed [kən'fɜːrmd] adj *(inveterate)* empedernido; **I'm a confirmed believer in ...** creo firmemente en ...

con·fis·cate ['kɑːnfɪskeɪt] v/t confiscar

con·flict 1 n [ˈkɑːnflɪkt] conflicto m **2** v/i [kən'flɪkt] *(clash)* chocar; **conflicting loyalties** lealtades fpl encontradas

con·form [kən'fɔːrm] v/i ser conformista; **conform to** *to standards etc* ajustarse a

con·form·ist [kən'fɔːrmɪst] n conformista m/f

con·front [kən'frʌnt] v/t *(face)* hacer frente a, enfrentarse; *(tackle)* hacer frente a

con·fron·ta·tion [kɑːnfrən'teɪʃn] confrontación f, enfrentamiento m

con·fuse [kən'fjuːz] v/t confundir; **confuse s.o. with s.o.** confundir a alguien con alguien

con·fused [kən'fjuːzd] adj *person* confundido; *situation, piece of writing* confuso

con·fus·ing [kən'fjuːzɪŋ] adj confuso

con·fu·sion [kən'fjuːʒn] *(muddle, chaos)* confusión f

con·geal [kən'dʒiːl] v/i *of blood* coagularse; *of fat* solidificarse

con·gen·ial [kən'dʒiːnɪəl] adj *person* simpático, agradable; *occasion, place* agradable

con·gen·i·tal [kən'dʒenɪtl] adj MED congénito

con·gest·ed [kən'dʒestɪd] adj *roads* congestionados

con·ges·tion [kən'dʒestʃn] *also* MED congestión f; **traffic congestion** congestión f circulatoria

con·grat·u·late [kən'græfʊleɪt] v/t felicitar

con·grat·u·la·tions [kəngræfʊ'leɪʃnz] npl felicitaciones fpl; **congratulations on ...** felicidades por ...; **let me offer my congratulations** permita que le dé la enhorabuena

con·grat·u·la·to·ry [kəngræfʊ'leɪtərɪ] adj de felicitación

con·gre·gate ['kɑːngrɪgeɪt] v/i *(gather)* congregarse

con·gre·ga·tion [kɑːngrɪ'geɪʃn] REL congregación f

con·gress ['kɑːngres] *(conference)* congreso m; **Congress** US Congreso m

Con·gres·sion·al [kən'greʃnl] adj del Congreso

Con·gress·man ['kɑːngresmən] congresista m

Con·gress·wo·man ['kɑːngreswʊmən] congresista f

co·ni·fer ['kɑːnɪfər] conífera *f*
con·jec·ture [kən'dʒektʃər] *n* (*speculation*) conjetura *f*
con·ju·gate ['kɑːndʒʊgeɪt] *v/t* GRAM conjugar
con·junc·tion [kən'dʒʌŋkʃn] GRAM conjunción *f*; *in conjunction with* junto con
con·junc·ti·vi·tis [kəndʒʌŋktɪ'vaɪtɪs] conjuntivitis *f*
◆ **con·jure up** ['kʌndʒər] *v/t* (*produce*) hacer aparecer; (*evoke*) evocar
con·jur·er, **con·jur·or** ['kʌndʒərər] (*magician*) prestidigitador(a) *m(f)*
con·jur·ing tricks ['kʌndʒərɪŋ] *npl* juegos *mpl* de manos
con man ['kɑːnmæn] F timador *m* F
con·nect [kə'nekt] *v/t* conectar; (*link*) relacionar, vincular; *to power supply* enchufar
con·nect·ed [kə'nektɪd] *adj*: *be well-connected* estar bien relacionado; *be connected with* estar relacionado con
con·nect·ing flight [kə'nektɪŋ] vuelo *m* de conexión
con·nec·tion [kə'nekʃn] conexión *f*; *when traveling* conexión *f*, enlace; (*personal contact*) contacto *m*; *in connection with* en relación con
con·nois·seur [kɑːnə'sɜːr] entendido(-a) *m(f)*
con·quer ['kɑːŋkər] *v/t* conquistar; *fig*: *fear etc* vencer
con·quer·or ['kɑːŋkərər] conquistador(a) *m(f)*
con·quest ['kɑːŋkwest] *of territory* conquista *f*
con·science ['kɑːnʃəns] conciencia *f*; *a guilty conscience* un sentimiento de culpa; *it was on my conscience* me remordía la conciencia
con·sci·en·tious [kɑːnʃɪ'enʃəs] *adj* concienzudo
con·sci·en·tious·ness [kɑːnʃɪ'enʃəsnəs] aplicación *f*
con·sci·en·tious ob·ject·or objetor(a) *m(f)* de conciencia
con·scious ['kɑːnʃəs] *adj* consciente; *be conscious of* ser consciente de
con·scious·ly ['kɑːnʃəslɪ] *adv* conscientemente
con·scious·ness ['kɑːnʃəsnɪs] (*awareness*) conciencia *f*; MED con(s)ciencia *f*; *lose / regain consciousness* quedar inconsciente / volver en sí
con·sec·u·tive [kən'sekjʊtɪv] *adj* consecutivo
con·sen·sus [kən'sensəs] consenso *m*
con·sent [kən'sent] **1** *n* consentimiento *m* **2** *v/i* consentir (*to* en)

con·se·quence ['kɑːnsɪkwəns] (*result*) consecuencia *f*; *as a consequence of* como consecuencia de
con·se·quent·ly ['kɑːnsɪkwəntlɪ] *adv* (*therefore*) por consiguiente
con·ser·va·tion [kɑːnsər'veɪʃn] (*preservation*) conservación *f*, protección *f*
con·ser·va·tion·ist [kɑːnsər'veɪʃnɪst] ecologista *m/f*
con·ser·va·tive [kən'sɜːrvətɪv] **1** *adj* (*conventional*) conservador; *estimate* prudente **2** *n Br* POL **Conservative** Conservador(a) *m(f)*
con·ser·va·to·ry [kən'sɜːrvətɔːrɪ] MUS conservatorio *m*
con·serve 1 *n* ['kɑːnsɜːrv] (*jam*) compota *f* **2** *v/t* [kən'sɜːrv] conservar
con·sid·er [kən'sɪdər] *v/t* (*regard*) considerar; (*show regard for*) mostrar consideración por; (*think about*) considerar; *it is considered to be ...* se considera que es ...
con·sid·e·ra·ble [kən'sɪdrəbl] *adj* considerable
con·sid·e·ra·bly [kən'sɪdrəblɪ] *adv* considerablemente
con·sid·er·ate [kən'sɪdərət] *adj* considerado
con·sid·er·ate·ly [kən'sɪdərətlɪ] *adv* con consideración
con·sid·e·ra·tion [kənsɪdə'reɪʃn] (*thoughtfulness, concern*) consideración *f*; (*factor*) factor *m*; *take sth into consideration* tomar algo en consideración; *after much consideration* tras muchas deliberaciones; *your proposal is under consideration* su propuesta está siendo estudiada
con·sign·ment [kən'saɪnmənt] COM envío *m*
◆ **con·sist of** [kən'sɪst] *v/t* consistir en
con·sis·ten·cy [kən'sɪstənsɪ] (*texture*) consistencia *f*; (*unchangingness*) coherencia *f*, consecuencia *f*; *of player* regularidad *f*, constancia *f*
con·sis·tent [kən'sɪstənt] *adj person* coherente, consecuente; *improvement, change* constante
con·sis·tent·ly [kən'sɪstəntlɪ] *adv perform* con regularidad *or* constancia; *improve* continuamente; *he's consistently late* llega tarde sistemáticamente
con·so·la·tion [kɑːnsə'leɪʃn] consuelo *m*; *if it's any consolation* si te sirve de consuelo
con·sole [kən'soʊl] *v/t* consolar
con·sol·i·date [kən'sɑːlɪdeɪt] *v/t* consolidar
con·so·nant ['kɑːnsənənt] *n* GRAM conso-

nante *f*

con·sor·ti·um [kən'sɔːrtɪəm] consorcio *m*

con·spic·u·ous [kən'spɪkjuəs] *adj* llamativo; *he felt very conspicuous* sentía que estaba llamando la atención

con·spir·a·cy [kən'spɪrəsɪ] conspiración *f*

con·spir·a·tor [kən'spɪrətər] conspirador(a) *m(f)*

con·spire [kən'spaɪr] *v/i* conspirar

con·stant ['kɑːnstənt] *adj (continuous)* constante

con·stant·ly ['kɑːnstəntlɪ] *adv* constantemente

con·ster·na·tion [kɑːnstər'neɪʃn] consternación *f*

con·sti·pat·ed ['kɑːnstɪpeɪtɪd] *adj* estreñido

con·sti·pa·tion [kɑːnstɪ'peɪʃn] estreñimiento *m*

con·sti·tu·ent [kən'stɪtjuənt] *n (component)* elemento *m* constitutivo, componente *m*

con·sti·tute ['kɑːnstɪtuːt] *v/t* constituir

con·sti·tu·tion [kɑːnstɪ'tuːʃn] constitución *f*

con·sti·tu·tion·al [kɑːnstɪ'tuːʃənl] *adj* POL constitucional

con·straint [kən'streɪnt] *(restriction)* restricción *f*, límite *m*

con·struct [kən'strʌkt] *v/t building etc* construir

con·struc·tion [kən'strʌkʃn] construcción *f*; *under construction* en construcción

con·struc·tion in·dus·try sector *m* de la construcción

con·struc·tion site obra *f*

con·struc·tion work·er obrero(-a) *m(f)* de la construcción

con·struc·tive [kən'strʌktɪv] *adj* constructivo

con·sul ['kɑːnsl] cónsul *m/f*

con·su·late ['kɑːnsʊlət] consulado *m*

con·sult [kən'sʌlt] *v/t (seek the advice of)* consultar

con·sul·tan·cy [kən'sʌltənsɪ] *company* consultoría *f*, asesoría *f*; *(advice)* asesoramiento *m*

con·sul·tant [kən'sʌltənt] *n (adviser)* asesor(a) *m(f)*, consultor(a) *m(f)*

con·sul·ta·tion [kɑːnsl'teɪʃn] consulta *f*; *have a consultation with* consultar con

con·sume [kən'suːm] *v/t* consumir

con·sum·er [kən'suːmər] *(purchaser)* consumidor(a) *m(f)*

con·sum·er 'con·fi·dence confianza *f* de los consumidores

con·sum·er goods *npl* bienes *mpl* de

consumo

con·sum·er so·ci·e·ty sociedad *f* de consumo

con·sump·tion [kən'sʌmpʃn] consumo *m*

con·tact ['kɑːntækt] **1** *n* contacto; *keep in contact with s.o.* mantenerse en contacto con alguien; *come into contact with s.o.* entrar en contacto con alguien **2** *v/t* contactar con, ponerse en contacto con

'con·tact lens lentes *fpl* de contacto, *Span* lentillas *fpl*

'con·tact num·ber número *m* de contacto

con·ta·gious [kən'teɪdʒəs] *adj also fig* contagioso

con·tain [kən'teɪn] *v/t (hold, hold back)* contener; *contain o.s.* contenerse

con·tain·er [kən'teɪnər] *(recipient)* recipiente *m*; COM contenedor *m*

con·tain·er ship buque *m* de transporte de contenedores

con·tam·i·nate [kən'tæmɪneɪt] *v/t* contaminar

con·tam·i·na·tion [kəntæmɪ'neɪʃn] contaminación *f*

con·tem·plate ['kɑːntəmpleɪt] *v/t* contemplar

con·tem·po·ra·ry [kən'tempərerɪ] **1** *adj* contemporáneo **2** *n* contemporáneo(-a) *m(f)*

con·tempt [kən'tempt] desprecio *m*, desdén *m*; *be beneath contempt* ser despreciable

con·tempt·i·ble [kən'temptəbl] *adj* despreciable

con·temp·tu·ous [kən'temptʃuəs] *adj* despectivo

con·tend [kən'tend] *v/i: contend for ...* competir por ...; *contend with* enfrentarse a

con·tend·er [kən'tendər] SP, POL contendiente *m/f*; *against champion* aspirante *m/f*

con·tent[1] ['kɑːntent] *n* contenido *m*

con·tent[2] [kən'tent] **1** *adj* satisfecho; *I'm quite content to sit here* me contento con sentarme aquí **2** *v/t*: *content o.s. with* contentarse con

con·tent·ed [kən'tentɪd] *adj* satisfecho

con·ten·tion [kən'tenʃn] *(assertion)* argumento *m*; *be in contention for* tener posibilidades de ganar

con·ten·tious [kən'tenʃəs] *adj* polémico

con·tent·ment [kən'tentmənt] satisfacción *f*

con·tents ['kɑːntents] *npl of house, letter, bag etc* contenido *m*; *list: in book* tabla *f* de contenidos

con·test[1] ['kɑːntest] *n (competition)* concurso *m*; *(struggle, for power)* lucha *f*

con·test² [kən'test] *v/t leadership etc* presentarse como candidato a; *decision, will* impugnar

con·tes·tant [kən'testənt] concursante *m/f*; *in competition* competidor(a) *m(f)*

con·text ['kɑːntekst] contexto *m*; **look at sth in context / out of context** examinar algo en contexto / fuera de contexto

con·ti·nent ['kɑːntɪnənt] *n* continente *m*

con·ti·nen·tal [kɑːntɪ'nentl] *adj* continental

con·tin·gen·cy [kən'tɪndʒənsɪ] contingencia *f*, eventualidad *f*

con·tin·u·al [kən'tɪnjuəl] *adj* continuo

con·tin·u·al·ly [kən'tɪnjuəlɪ] *adv* continuamente

con·tin·u·a·tion [kəntɪnjuˈeɪʃn] continuación *f*

con·tin·ue [kən'tɪnjuː] **1** *v/t* continuar; *to be continued* continuará; *he continued to drink* continuó bebiendo **2** *v/i* continuar

con·ti·nu·i·ty [kɑːntɪ'njuːətɪ] continuidad *f*

con·tin·u·ous [kən'tɪnjuəs] *adj* continuo

con·tin·u·ous·ly [kən'tɪnjuəslɪ] *adv* continuamente, ininterrumpidamente

con·tort [kən'tɔːrt] *v/t face* contraer; *body* contorsionar

con·tour ['kɑːntʊr] contorno *m*

con·tra·cep·tion [kɑːntrə'sepʃn] anticoncepción *f*

con·tra·cep·tive [kɑːntrə'septɪv] *n (device, pill)* anticonceptivo *m*

con·tract¹ ['kɑːntrækt] *n* contrato *m*

con·tract² [kən'trækt] **1** *v/i (shrink)* contraerse **2** *v/t illness* contraer

con·trac·tor [kən'træktər] contratista *m/f*; *building contractor* constructora *f*

con·trac·tu·al [kən'træktuəl] *adj* contractual

con·tra·dict [kɑːntrə'dɪkt] *v/t statement* desmentir; *person* contradecir

con·tra·dic·tion [kɑːntrə'dɪkʃn] contradicción *f*

con·tra·dic·to·ry [kɑːntrə'dɪktərɪ] *adj account* contradictorio

con·trap·tion [kən'træpʃn] F artilugio *m* F

con·tra·ry¹ ['kɑːntrərɪ] **1** *adj* contrario; *contrary to* al contrario de **2** *n: on the contrary* al contrario

con·tra·ry² [kən'trerɪ] *adj (perverse)* difícil

con·trast 1 *n* ['kɑːntræst] contraste *m*; *by contrast* por contraste **2** *v/t & v/i* [kən'træst] contrastar

con·trast·ing [kən'træstɪŋ] *adj* opuesto

con·tra·vene [kɑːntrə'viːn] *v/t* contravenir

con·trib·ute [kən'trɪbjuːt] **1** *v/i* contribuir (*to* a) **2** *v/t money, time, suggestion* contribuir con, aportar

con·tri·bu·tion [kɑːntrɪ'bjuːʃn] *money* contribución *f*; *to political party, church* donación *f*; *of time, effort, to debate* contribución *f*, aportación *f*; *to magazine* colaboración *f*

con·trib·u·tor [kən'trɪbjutər] *of money* donante *m/f*; *to magazine* colaborador(a) *m(f)*

con·trol [kən'troul] **1** *n* control *m*; *take / lose control of* tomar / perder el control de; *lose control of o.s.* perder el control; *circumstances beyond our control* circunstancias ajenas a nuestra voluntad; *be in control of* controlar; *we're in control of the situation* tenemos la situación controlada *or* bajo control; *get out of control* descontrolarse; *under control* bajo control; *controls of aircraft, vehicle* controles *mpl*; *(restrictions)* controles *mpl* **2** *v/t (pret & pp controlled) (govern)* controlar, dominar; *(restrict, regulate)* controlar; *control o.s.* controlarse

con·trol cen·ter, *Br* **con·trol cen·tre** centro *m* de control

con·trol freak F persona obsesionada con controlar todo

con·trol·ling 'in·ter·est [kən'troulɪŋ] FIN participación *f* mayoritaria, interés *m* mayoritario

con·trol pan·el panel *m* de control

con·trol tow·er torre *f* de control

con·tro·ver·sial [kɑːntrə'vɜːrʃl] *adj* polémico, controvertido

con·tro·ver·sy ['kɑːntrəvɜːrsɪ] polémica *f*, controversia *f*

con·vene [kən'viːn] *v/t* convocar

con·ve·ni·ence [kən'viːnɪəns] conveniencia *f*; *at your / my convenience* a su / mi conveniencia; *all (modern) conveniences* todas las comodidades

con·ve·ni·ence food comida *f* preparada

con·ve·ni·ence store tienda *f* de barrio

con·ve·ni·ent [kən'viːnɪənt] *adj location, device* conveniente; *time, arrangement* oportuno; *it's very convenient living so near the office* vivir cerca de la oficina es muy cómodo; *the apartment is convenient for the station* el apartamento está muy cerca de la estación; *I'm afraid Monday isn't convenient* me temo que el lunes no me va bien

con·ve·ni·ent·ly [kənˈviːnɪəntlɪ] adv convenientemente; ***conveniently located for theaters*** situado cerca de los teatros

con·vent [ˈkɑːnvənt] convento m

con·ven·tion [kənˈvenʃn] (tradition) convención f; (conference) congreso m

con·ven·tion·al [kənˈvenʃnl] adj convencional

con'ven·tion cen·ter palacio m de congresos

con·ven·tion·eer [kənˈvenʃnɪr] congresista m/f

◆ **con·verge on** [kənˈvɜːrdʒ] v/t converger en

con·ver·sant [kənˈvɜːrsənt] adj: ***be conversant with*** estar familiarizado con

con·ver·sa·tion [kɑːnvərˈseɪʃn] conversación f; ***make conversation*** conversar; ***have a conversation*** mantener una conversación

con·ver·sa·tion·al [kɑːnvərˈseɪʃnl] adj coloquial

con·verse [ˈkɑːnvɜːrs] n (opposite): ***the converse*** lo opuesto

con·verse·ly [kənˈvɜːrslɪ] adv por el contrario

con·ver·sion [kənˈvɜːrʃn] conversión f

con'ver·sion ta·ble tabla f de conversión

con·vert [ˈkɑːnvɜːrt] 1 n converso(-a) m(f) (***to*** a) 2 v/t [kənˈvɜːrt] convertir

con·ver·ti·ble [kənˈvɜːrtəbl] n car descapotable m

con·vey [kənˈveɪ] v/t (transmit) transmitir; (carry) transportar

con·vey·or belt [kənˈveɪər] cinta f transportadora

con·vict 1 n [ˈkɑːnvɪkt] convicto(-a) m(f) 2 v/t [kənˈvɪkt] LAW: ***convict s.o. of sth*** declarar a alguien culpable de algo

con·vic·tion [kənˈvɪkʃn] LAW condena f; (belief) convicción f

con·vince [kənˈvɪns] v/t convencer: ***I'm convinced he's lying*** estoy convencido de que miente

con·vinc·ing [kənˈvɪnsɪŋ] adj convincente

con·viv·i·al [kənˈvɪvɪəl] adj (friendly) agradable

con·voy [ˈkɑːnvɔɪ] of ships, vehicles convoy m

con·vul·sion [kənˈvʌlʃn] MED convulsión f

cook [kʊk] 1 n cocinero(-a) m(f); ***I'm a good cook*** soy un buen cocinero, cocino bien 2 v/t cocinar; ***a cooked meal*** una comida caliente; ***cook the books*** F falsificar las cuentas 3 v/i cocinar

'cook·book libro m de cocina

cook·e·ry [ˈkʊkərɪ] cocina f

cook·ie [ˈkʊkɪ] galleta f

cook·ing [ˈkʊkɪŋ] food cocina f

cool [kuːl] 1 n: ***keep one's cool*** F mantener la calma; ***lose one's cool*** F perder la calma 2 adj weather, breeze fresco; drink frío; (calm) tranquilo, sereno; (unfriendly) frío 3 v/i of food, interest enfriarse; of tempers calmarse 4 v/t: ***cool it*** F cálmate

◆ **cool down 1** v/i enfriarse; of weather refrescar; fig: of tempers calmarse, tranquilizarse 2 v/t food enfriar; fig calmar, tranquilizar

cool·ing-'off pe·ri·od fase f de reflexión

co·op·e·rate [kouˈɑːpəreɪt] v/i cooperar

co·op·e·ra·tion [kouɑːpəˈreɪʃn] cooperación f

co·op·e·ra·tive [kouˈɑːpərətɪv] 1 n COM cooperativa f 2 adj COM conjunto; (helpful) cooperativo

co·or·di·nate [kouˈɔːrdɪneɪt] v/t activities coordinar

co·or·di·na·tion [kouɔːrdɪˈneɪʃn] coordinación f

cop [kɑːp] n F poli m/f F

cope [koʊp] v/i arreglárselas; ***cope with*** poder con

cop·i·er [ˈkɑːpɪər] machine fotocopiadora f

co·pi·lot [ˈkoʊpaɪlət] copiloto m/f

co·pi·ous [ˈkoʊpɪəs] adj copioso

cop·per [ˈkɑːpər] n metal cobre m

cop·y [ˈkɑːpɪ] 1 n copia f; of book ejemplar m; of record, CD copia f; (written material) texto m; ***make a copy of a file*** COMPUT hacer una copia de un archivo 2 v/t (pret & pp **copied**) copiar

'cop·y cat F copión (-ona) m(f) F, copiota m/f F

'cop·y·cat crime delito inspirado en otro

'cop·y·right n copyright m, derechos mpl de reproducción

'cop·y·writ·er in advertising creativo(-a) m(f) (de publicidad)

cor·al [ˈkɑːrəl] coral m

cord [kɔːrd] (string) cuerda f, cordel m; (cable) cable m

cor·di·al [ˈkɔːrdʒəl] adj cordial

cord·less 'phone [ˈkɔːrdlɪs] teléfono m inalámbrico

cor·don [ˈkɔːrdn] cordón m

◆ **cordon off** v/t acordonar

cords [kɔːrdz] npl pants pantalones mpl de pana

cor·du·roy [ˈkɔːrdərɔɪ] pana f

core [kɔːr] 1 n of fruit corazón m; of problem meollo m; of organization, party núcleo m 2 v/t fruit sacar el corazón a

3 adj issue, meaning central

co·ri·an·der ['kɑːriændər] cilantro m

cork [kɔːrk] in bottle (tapón m de) corcho m; material corcho m

'cork-screw n sacacorchos m inv

corn [kɔːrn] grain maíz m

cor·ner ['kɔːrnər] **1** n of page, street esquina f; of room rincón m; (bend: on road) curva f; in soccer córner m, saque m de esquina; **in the corner** en el rincón; **I'll meet you on the corner** te veré en la esquina **2** v/t person arrinconar; **corner a market** monopolizar un mercado **3** v/i of driver, car girar

'cor·ner kick in soccer saque m de esquina, córner m

'corn-flakes npl copos mpl de maíz

'corn-starch harina f de maíz

corn·y ['kɔːrni] adj F (sentimental) cursi F; joke manido

cor·o·na·ry ['kɑːrəneri] **1** adj coronario **2** n infarto m de miocardio

cor·o·ner ['kɔːrənər] oficial encargado de investigar muertes sospechosas

cor·po·ral ['kɔːrpərəl] n cabo m/f

cor·po·ral 'pun·ish·ment castigo m corporal

cor·po·rate ['kɔːrpərət] adj com corporativo, de empresa; **corporate image** imagen f corporativa; **corporate loyalty** lealtad f a la empresa

cor·po·ra·tion [kɔːrpə'reɪʃn] (business) sociedad f anónima

corps [kɔːr] nsg cuerpo m

corpse [kɔːrps] cadáver m

cor·pu·lent ['kɔːrpjulənt] adj corpulento

cor·pus·cle ['kɔːrpʌsl] corpúsculo m

cor·ral [kəˈræl] n corral m

cor·rect [kəˈrekt] **1** adj correcto; time exacto; **you are correct** tiene razón **2** v/t corregir

cor·rec·tion [kəˈrekʃn] corrección f

cor·rect·ly [kəˈrektli] adv correctamente

cor·re·spond [kɑːrɪˈspɑːnd] v/i (match) corresponderse; **correspond to** corresponder a; **correspond with** corresponderse con; (write letters) mantener correspondencia con

cor·re·spon·dence [kɑːrɪˈspɑːndəns] (matching) correspondencia f, relación f; (letters) correspondencia f

cor·re·spon·dent [kɑːrɪˈspɑːndənt] (letter writer) correspondiente m/f; (reporter) corresponsal m/f

cor·re·spon·ding [kɑːrɪˈspɑːndɪŋ] adj (equivalent) correspondiente

cor·ri·dor ['kɔːrɪdər] in building pasillo m

cor·rob·o·rate [kəˈrɑːbəreɪt] v/t corroborar

cor·rode [kəˈroʊd] **1** v/t corroer **2** v/i corroerse

cor·ro·sion [kəˈroʊʒn] corrosión f

cor·ru·gat·ed 'card·board ['kɑːrəgeɪtɪd] cartón m ondulado

cor·ru·gat·ed 'i·ron chapa f ondulada

cor·rupt [kəˈrʌpt] **1** adj corrupto; COMPUT corrompido **2** v/t corromper; (bribe) sobornar

cor·rup·tion [kəˈrʌpʃn] corrupción f

cos·met·ic [kɑːzˈmetɪk] adj cosmético; fig superficial

cos·met·ics [kɑːzˈmetɪks] npl cosméticos mpl

cos·met·ic 'sur·geon especialista m/f en cirugía estética

cos·met·ic 'sur·ger·y cirugía f estética

cos·mo·naut ['kɑːzmənɔːt] cosmonauta m/f

cos·mo·pol·i·tan [kɑːzməˈpɑːlɪtən] adj city cosmopolita

cost¹ [kɑːst] **1** n also fig costo m, Span coste m; **at all costs** cueste lo que cueste; **I've learnt to my cost** por desgracia he aprendido **2** v/t (pret & pp cost) money, time costar; **how much does it cost?** ¿cuánto cuesta?; **it cost me my health** me costó mi salud

cost² [kɑːst] v/t (pret & pp costed) FIN proposal, project estimar el costo de

cost and 'freight com costo or Span coste y flete

Cos·ta Ri·ca ['kɑːstəˈriːkə] n Costa Rica

Cos·ta Ri·can ['kɑːstəˈriːkən] **1** adj costarricense **2** n costarricense m/f

'cost-con·scious adj consciente del costo or Span coste

'cost-ef·fec·tive adj rentable

cost, in·sur·ance, freight com costo or Span coste, seguro y flete

cost·ly ['kɑːstli] adj mistake caro

cost of 'liv·ing costo m or Span coste m de la vida

cost 'price precio m de costo or Span coste

cos·tume ['kɑːstuːm] for actor traje m

cos·tume 'jew·el·lery Br, **costume 'jew·el·ry** bisutería f

'cos·y Br → **cozy**

cot [kɑːt] (camp-bed) catre m

cot·tage ['kɑːtɪdʒ] casa f de campo, casita f

cot·tage 'cheese queso m fresco

cot·ton ['kɑːtn] **1** n algodón m **2** adj de algodón

♦ **cotton on** v/i F darse cuenta

♦ **cotton on to** v/t F darse cuenta de

♦ **cotton to** v/t F: **I never cottoned to her** nunca me cayó bien

cot·ton 'can·dy algodón *m* dulce

cot·ton 'wool *Br* algodón *m* (hidrófilo)

couch [kaʊtʃ] *n* sofá *m*

'couch po·ta·to F teleadicto(-a) *m(f)* F

cou·chette [kuːˈʃet] litera *f*

cough [kɑːf] 1 *n* tos *f*; *to get attention* carraspeo *m* 2 *v/i* toser; *to get attention* carraspear

♦ cough up *v/t blood etc* toser; F *money* soltar, *Span* apoquinar F 2 *v/i* F *(pay)* soltar dinero, *Span* apoquinar F

'cough med·i·cine, 'cough syr·up jarabe *m* para la tos

could [kʊd] 1 *v/aux: could I have my key?* ¿me podría dar la llave?; *could you help me?* ¿me podrías ayudar?; *this could be our bus* puede que éste sea nuestro autobús; *you could be right* puede que tengas razón; *I couldn't say for sure* no sabría decirlo con seguridad; *he could have got lost* a lo mejor se ha perdido; *you could have warned me!* ¡me podías haber avisado! 2 *pret* → *can¹*

coun·cil ['kaʊnsl] *n (assembly)* consejo *m*

'coun·cil·man concejal *m*

coun·cil·or ['kaʊnsələr] concejal(a) *m(f)*

coun·sel ['kaʊnsl] 1 *n (advice)* consejo *m*; *(lawyer)* abogado(-a) *m(f)* 2 *v/t course of action* aconsejar; *person* ofrecer apoyo psicológico

coun·sel·ing, *Br* coun·sel·ling ['kaʊnslɪŋ] apoyo *m* psicológico

coun·sel·or *Br*, coun·sel·or ['kaʊnslər] *(adviser)* consejero(-a) *m(f)*; *of student* orientador(a) *m(f)*; LAW abogado(-a) *m(f)*

count¹ [kaʊnt] 1 *n (number arrived at)* cuenta *f*; *(action of counting)* recuento *m*; *in baseball, boxing* cuenta *f*; *what is your count?* ¿cuántos has contado?; *keep count of* llevar la cuenta de; *lose count of* perder la cuenta de; *at the last count* en el último recuento 2 *v/i to have etc* contar; *(be important)* contar; *(qualify)* contar, valer 3 *v/t* contar

♦ count on *v/t* contar con

count² [kaʊnt] *nobleman* conde *m*

'count·down cuenta *f* atrás

coun·te·nance ['kaʊntənəns] *v/t* tolerar

coun·ter¹ ['kaʊntər] *n in shop* mostrador *m*; *in café* barra *f*; *in game* ficha *f*

coun·ter² ['kaʊntər] 1 *v/t* contrarrestar 2 *v/i (retaliate)* responder

coun·ter³ ['kaʊntər] *adv: run counter to* estar en contra de

'coun·ter·act *v/t* contrarrestar

coun·ter·at'tack 1 *n* contraataque *m* 2 *v/i* contraatacar

'coun·ter·bal·ance 1 *n* contrapeso *m* 2 *v/t* contrarrestar, contrapesar

coun·ter'clock·wise *adv* en sentido contrario al de las agujas del reloj

coun·ter·es·pi·o·nage contraespionaje *m*

coun·ter·feit ['kaʊntərfɪt] 1 *v/t* falsificar 2 *adj* falso

'coun·ter·part *(person)* homólogo(-a) *m(f)*

coun·ter·pro'duc·tive *adj* contraproducente

'coun·ter·sign *v/t* refrendar

coun·tess ['kaʊntɪs] condesa *f*

count·less ['kaʊntlɪs] *adj* incontables

coun·try ['kaʊntrɪ] *n (nation)* país *m*; *as opposed to town* campo *m*; *in the country* en el campo

coun·try and 'west·ern MUS música *f* country

'coun·try·man *(fellow countryman)* compatriota *m*

'coun·try·side campo *m*

coun·ty ['kaʊntɪ] condado *m*

coup [kuː] POL golpe *m* (de Estado); *fig* golpe *m* de efecto

cou·ple ['kʌpl] *n* pareja *f*; *just a couple* un par; *a couple of* un par de

cou·pon ['kuːpɑːn] cupón *m*

cour·age ['kʌrɪdʒ] valor *m*, coraje *m*

cou·ra·geous [kəˈreɪdʒəs] *adj* valiente

cou·ra·geous·ly [kəˈreɪdʒəslɪ] *adv* valientemente

cou·ri·er ['kʊrɪr] *(messenger)* mensajero(-a) *m(f)*; *with tourist party* guía *m/f*

course [kɔːrs] *n (series of lessons)* curso *m*; *(part of meal)* plato *m*; *of ship, plane* rumbo *m*; *for horse race* circuito *m*; *for golf* campo *m*; *for skiing, marathon* recorrido *m*; *change course of ship, plane* cambiar de rumbo; *of course (certainly)* claro, por supuesto; *(naturally)* por supuesto; *of course not* claro que no; *course of action* táctica *f*; *course of treatment* tratamiento *m*; *in the course of ...* durante ...

court [kɔːrt] *n* LAW tribunal *m*; *(courthouse)* palacio *m* de justicia; SP pista *f*, cancha *f*; *take s.o. to court* llevar a alguien a juicio

'court case proceso *m*, causa *f*

cour·te·ous ['kɜːrtɪəs] *adj* cortés

cour·te·sy ['kɜːrtəsɪ] cortesía *f*

'court·house palacio *m* de justicia

court 'mar·tial 1 *n* consejo *m* de guerra 2 *v/t* formar un consejo de guerra a

'court or·der orden *f* judicial

'court·room sala *f* de juicios

'court·yard patio *m*

cous·in ['kʌzn] primo(-a) *m(f)*

cove [kouv] (*small bay*) cala f
pequeño

cov·er ['kʌvər] **1** n *protective* funda f; *of book, magazine* portada f; (*shelter*) protección f; (*insurance*) cobertura f; *covers for bed* manta f y sábanas fpl; *we took cover from the rain* nos pusimos a cubierto de la lluvia **2** v/t cubrir
◆ *cover up* **1** v/t cubrir; *scandal* encubrir **2** v/i disimular; *cover up for s.o.* encubrir a alguien

cov·er·age ['kʌvərɪdʒ] *by media* cobertura f informativa

cov·er·ing let·ter ['kʌvrɪŋ] carta f

cov·ert [kou'vɜːrt] adj encubierto

'cov·er·up encubrimiento m

cow [kau] vaca f

cow·ard ['kauərd] cobarde m/f

cow·ard·ice ['kauərdɪs] cobardía f

cow·ard·ly ['kauərdlɪ] adj cobarde

'cow·boy vaquero m

cow·er ['kauər] v/i agacharse, amilanarse

co·work·er ['kouwɜːrkər] compañero(a) m(f) de trabajo

coy [kɔɪ] adj (*evasive*) evasivo; (*flirtatious*) coqueto

co·zy ['kouzɪ] adj *room* acogedor; *job* cómodo

CPU [siːpiː'juː] abbr (= *central processing unit*) CPU f (= unidad f central de proceso)

crab [kræb] n cangrejo m

crack [kræk] **1** n grieta f; *in cup, glass* raja f; (*joke*) chiste m (malo) **2** v/t *cup, glass* rajar; *nut* cascar; *code* descifrar; F (*solve*) resolver; *crack a joke* contar un chiste **3** v/i rajarse; *get cracking* F poner manos a la obra F
◆ *crack down on* v/t castigar severamente
◆ *crack up* v/i (*have breakdown*) sufrir una crisis nerviosa; F (*laugh*) desternillarse

'crack·brained adj F chiflado F

'crack·down medidas fpl severas

cracked [krækt] adj *cup, glass* rajado; F (*crazy*) chiflado F

crack·er ['krækər] *to eat* galleta f salada

crack·le ['krækl] v/i *of fire* crepitar

cra·dle ['kreɪdl] n *for baby* cuna f

craft[1] [kræft] NAUT embarcación f

craft[2] [kræft] (*skill*) arte m; (*trade*) oficio m

crafts·man ['kræftsmən] artesano m

craft·y ['kræftɪ] adj astuto

crag [kræg] *rock* peñasco m, risco m

cram [kræm] v/t embutir

cramp [kræmp] n calambre m; *stomach cramp* retorcijón m

cramped [kræmpt] adj *room, apartment*

cramps [kræmps] npl calambre m; *stomach cramps* retorcijón m

cran·ber·ry ['krænberɪ] arándano m agrio

crane [kreɪn] **1** n *machine* grúa f **2** v/t: *crane one's neck* estirar el cuello

crank [kræŋk] n *person* maniático(-a) m(f), persona f rara

'crank·shaft cigüeñal m

crank·y ['kræŋkɪ] adj (*bad-tempered*) gruñón

crash [kræʃ] **1** n *noise* estruendo m, estrépito m; *accident* accidente m; COM *quiebra f*, crac m; COMPUT bloqueo m; *a crash of thunder* un trueno **2** v/i *of car, airplane* estrellarse (*into* con or contra); *of thunder* sonar; COM *of market* hundirse, desplomarse; COMPUT bloquearse, colgarse; F (*sleep*) dormir, Span sobar F; *the waves crashed onto the shore* las olas chocaban contra la orilla; *the vase crashed to the ground* el jarrón se cayó con estruendo **3** v/t *car* estrellar
◆ *crash out* v/i F (*fall asleep*) dormirse, Span quedarse sobado

'crash bar·ri·er quitamiedos m inv

'crash course curso m intensivo

'crash di·et dieta f drástica

'crash hel·met casco m protector

'crash-land v/i realizar un aterrizaje forzoso

'crash 'land·ing aterrizaje m forzoso

crate [kreɪt] (*packing case*) caja f

cra·ter ['kreɪtər] *of volcano* cráter m

crave [kreɪv] v/t ansiar

crav·ing ['kreɪvɪŋ] ansia f, deseo m; *of pregnant woman* antojo m; *I have a craving for ...* me apetece muchísimo ...

crawl [krɒːl] **1** n *in swimming* crol m; *at a crawl* (*very slowly*) muy lentamente **2** v/i *on floor* arrastrarse; *of baby* andar a gatas; (*move slowly*) avanzar lentamente
◆ *crawl with* v/t estar abarrotado de

cray·fish ['kreɪfɪʃ] *freshwater* cangrejo m de río; *saltwater* langosta f

cray·on ['kreɪɑːn] n lápiz m de color

craze [kreɪz] locura f (*for* de); *the latest craze* la última locura or moda

cra·zy ['kreɪzɪ] adj loco; *be crazy about* estar loco por

creak [kriːk] **1** n *of hinge, door* chirrido m; *of floor* crujido m **2** v/i *of hinge, door* chirriar; *of floor, shoes* crujir

creak·y ['kriːkɪ] adj *hinge, door* que chirria; *floor, shoes* que cruje

cream [kriːm] **1** n *for skin* crema f; *for coffee, cake* nata f; (*color*) crema m **2** adj crema

cream 'cheese queso m blanco para un-

tar
cream·er ['kriːmər] (*pitcher*) jarra *f* para la nata; *for coffee* leche *f* en polvo
cream·y ['kriːmɪ] *adj with lots of cream* cremoso
crease [kriːs] **1** *n accidental* arruga *f*; *deliberate* raya *f* **2** *v/t accidentally* arrugar
cre·ate [krɪ'eɪt] *v/t & v/i* crear
cre·a·tion [krɪ'eɪʃn] creación *f*
cre·a·tive [krɪ'eɪtɪv] *adj* creativo
cre·a·tor [krɪ'eɪtər] creador(a) *m(f)*; (*founder*) fundador(a) *m(f)*; **the Creator** REL el Creador
crea·ture ['kriːtʃər] *animal, person* criatura *f*
crèche [kreʃ] *for children* guardería *f* (infantil); REL nacimiento *m*, belén *m*
cred·i·bil·i·ty [kredɪ'bɪlɪtɪ] credibilidad *f*
cred·i·ble ['kredəbl] *adj* creíble
cred·it ['kredɪt] **1** *n* FIN crédito *m*; (*honor*) crédito *m*, reconocimiento *m*; **be in credit** tener un saldo positivo; **get the credit for sth** recibir reconocimiento por algo **2** *v/t* (*believe*) creer; **would you credit it!** ¡te lo puedes creer!; **credit an amount to an account** abonar una cantidad en una cuenta
cred·i·ta·ble ['kredɪtəbl] *adj* estimable, honorable
'**cred·it card** tarjeta *f* de crédito
'**cred·it lim·it** límite *m* de crédito
'**cred·i·tor** ['kredɪtər] acreedor(a) *m(f)*
'**cred·it·wor·thy** *adj* solvente
cred·u·lous ['kredjʊləs] *adj* crédulo
creed [kriːd] (*beliefs*) credo *m*
creek [kriːk] (*stream*) arroyo *m*
creep [kriːp] **1** *n pej* asqueroso(-a) *m(f)* **2** *v/i* (*pret & pp* **crept**) moverse sigilosamente
creep·er ['kriːpər] BOT enredadera *f*
creeps [kriːps] *npl* F: **the house / he gives me the creeps** la casa / él me pone la piel de gallina F
creep·y ['kriːpɪ] *adj* F espeluznante F
cre·mate ['kriːmeɪt] *v/t* incinerar
cre·ma·tion [krɪ'meɪʃn] incineración *f*
cre·ma·to·ri·um [kremə'tɔːrɪəm] crematorio *m*
crept [krept] *pret & pp* → **creep**
cres·cent ['kresənt] *n shape* medialuna *f*; **crescent moon** cuarto *m* creciente
crest [krest] *of hill* cima *f*; *of bird* cresta *f*
crest·fal·len *adj* abatido
crev·ice ['krevɪs] grieta *f*
crew [kruː] *n of ship, airplane* tripulación *f*; *of repairmen etc* equipo *m*; (*crowd, group*) grupo *m*, pandilla *f*
'**crew cut** rapado *m*
'**crew neck** cuello *m* redondo

crib [krɪb] *n for baby* cuna *f*
crick [krɪk]: **have a crick in the neck** tener tortícolis
crick·et ['krɪkɪt] *insect* grillo *m*
crime [kraɪm] (*offense*) delito *m*; *serious, also fig* crimen *m*
crim·i·nal ['krɪmɪnl] **1** *n* delincuente *m/f*, criminal *m/f* **2** *adj* (*relating to crime*) criminal; (LAW: *not civil*) penal; (*shameful*) vergonzoso; *act* delictivo; **it's criminal** (*shameful*) es un crimen
crim·son ['krɪmzn] *adj* carmesí
cringe [krɪndʒ] *v/i with embarrassment* sentir vergüenza ajena
crip·ple ['krɪpl] **1** *n* (*disabled person*) inválido(-a) *m(f)* **2** *v/t person* dejar inválido; *fig: country, industry* paralizar
cri·sis ['kraɪsɪs] (*pl* **crises** ['kraɪsiːz]) crisis *f inv*
crisp [krɪsp] *adj weather, air* fresco; *lettuce, apple, bacon* crujiente; *new shirt, bills* flamante
cri·te·ri·on [kraɪ'tɪrɪən] (*standard*) criterio *m*
crit·ic ['krɪtɪk] crítico(-a) *m(f)*
crit·i·cal ['krɪtɪkl] *adj* (*making criticisms, serious*) crítico; *moment etc* decisivo
crit·i·cal·ly ['krɪtɪklɪ] *adv speak etc* en tono de crítica; **critically ill** en estado crítico
crit·i·cism ['krɪtɪsɪzm] crítica *f*
crit·i·cize ['krɪtɪsaɪz] *v/t* criticar
croak [krouk] **1** *n of frog* croar *m* **2** *v/i of frog* croar
cro·chet ['krouʃeɪ] **1** *n* ganchillo *m* **2** *v/t* hacer a ganchillo
crock·e·ry ['krɑːkərɪ] vajilla *f*
croc·o·dile ['krɑːkədaɪl] cocodrilo *m*
cro·cus ['kroukəs] azafrán *m*
cro·ny ['krounɪ] F amiguete *m* F
crook [krʊk] *n* ladrón (-ona) *m(f)*; *dishonest trader* granuja *m/f*
crook·ed ['krʊkɪd] *adj* (*not straight*) torcido; (*dishonest*) deshonesto
crop [krɑːp] **1** *n also fig* cosecha *f*; *plant grown* cultivo *m* **2** *v/t* (*pret & pp* **cropped**) *hair* cortar; *photo* recortar
◆ **crop up** *v/i* salir
cross [krɑːs] **1** *adj* (*angry*) enfadado, enojado **2** *n* cruz *f* **3** *v/t* (*go across*) cruzar; **cross o.s.** REL santiguarse; **cross one's legs** cruzar las piernas; **keep one's fingers crossed** cruzar los dedos; **it never crossed my mind** no se me ocurrió **4** *v/i* (*go across*) cruzar; *of lines* cruzarse, cortarse
◆ **cross off, cross out** *v/t* tachar
'**cross·bar** *of goal* larguero *m*; *of bicycle* barra *f*; *in high jump* listón *m*

'cross·check 1 n comprobación f 2 v/t comprobar

cross·coun·try ('ski·ing) esquí m de fondo

crossed 'check, Br crossed 'cheque [krɑːst] cheque m cruzado

cross-ex·am·i·na·tion LAW interrogatorio m

cross-ex'am·ine v/t LAW interrogar

cross-'eyed adj bizco

cross·ing ['krɑːsɪŋ] NAUT travesía f

'cross·roads nsg also fig encrucijada f

'cross-sec·tion of people muestra f representativa

'cross·walk paso m de peatones

'cross·word (puz·zle) crucigrama m

crotch [krɑːtʃ] of person, pants entrepierna f

crouch [kraʊtʃ] v/i agacharse

crow [kroʊ] n bird corneja f; as the crow flies en línea recta

'crow·bar palanca f

crowd [kraʊd] n multitud f, muchedumbre f; at sports event público m

crowd·ed ['kraʊdɪd] adj abarrotado (with de)

crown [kraʊn] 1 n on head, tooth corona f 2 v/t tooth poner una corona a

cru·cial ['kruːʃl] adj crucial

cru·ci·fix ['kruːsɪfɪks] crucifijo m

cru·ci·fix·ion [kruːsɪ'fɪkʃn] crucifixión f

cru·ci·fy ['kruːsɪfaɪ] v/t (pret & pp crucified) also fig crucificar

crude [kruːd] 1 adj (vulgar) grosero; (unsophisticated) primitivo 2 n: crude (oil) crudo m

crude·ly ['kruːdlɪ] adv speak groseramente; made de manera primitiva

cru·el ['kruːəl] adj cruel (to con)

cru·el·ty ['kruːəltɪ] crueldad f (to con)

cruise [kruːz] 1 n crucero m; go on a cruise ir de crucero 2 v/i of people hacer un crucero; of car ir a velocidad de crucero; of plane volar

'cruise lin·er transatlántico m

cruis·ing speed ['kruːzɪŋ] of vehicle velocidad f de crucero; fig: of project etc ritmo m normal

crumb [krʌm] miga f

crum·ble ['krʌmbl] 1 v/t desmigajar 2 v/i of bread desmigajarse; of stonework desmenuzarse; fig: of opposition etc desmoronarse

crum·bly ['krʌmblɪ] adj cookie que se desmigaja; stonework que se desmenuza

crum·ple ['krʌmpl] 1 v/t (crease) arrugar 2 v/i (collapse) desplomarse

crunch [krʌntʃ] 1 n: when it comes to the crunch a la hora de la verdad 2 v/i of snow, gravel crujir

cru·sade [kruː'seɪd] n also fig cruzada f

crush [krʌʃ] 1 n (crowd) muchedumbre f; have a crush on estar loco por 2 v/t aplastar; (crease) arrugar; they were crushed to death murieron aplastados 3 v/i (crease) arrugarse

crust [krʌst] on bread corteza f

crust·y ['krʌstɪ] adj bread crujiente

crutch [krʌtʃ] for injured person muleta f

cry [kraɪ] 1 n (call) grito m; have a cry llorar 2 v/t (pret & pp cried) (call) gritar 3 v/i (pret & pp cried) (weep) llorar

◆ cry out v/t & v/i gritar

◆ cry out for v/t (need) pedir a gritos

cryp·tic ['krɪptɪk] adj críptico

crys·tal ['krɪstl] cristal m

crys·tal·lize ['krɪstəlaɪz] 1 v/t cristalizar 2 v/i cristalizarse

cub [kʌb] cachorro m; of bear osezno m

Cu·ba ['kjuːbə] Cuba

Cu·ban ['kjuːbən] 1 adj cubano 2 n cubano(-a) m(f)

cube [kjuːb] shape cubo m

cu·bic ['kjuːbɪk] adj cúbico

cu·bic ca'pac·i·ty TECH cilindrada f

cu·bi·cle ['kjuːbɪkl] (changing room) cubículo m

cu·cum·ber ['kjuːkʌmbər] pepino m

cud·dle ['kʌdl] 1 n abrazo 2 v/t abrazar

cud·dly ['kʌdlɪ] adj kitten etc tierno

cue [kjuː] n for actor etc pie m, entrada f; for pool taco m

cuff [kʌf] 1 n of shirt puño m; of pants vuelta f; (blow) cachete m; off the cuff improvisado 2 v/t (hit) dar un cachete a

'cuff link gemelo m

cul-de-sac ['kʌldəsæk] callejón m sin salida

cu·li·nar·y ['kʌlɪnərɪ] adj culinario

cul·mi·nate ['kʌlmɪneɪt] v/i culminar (in en)

cul·mi·na·tion [kʌlmɪ'neɪʃn] culminación f

cul·prit ['kʌlprɪt] culpable m/f

cult [kʌlt] (sect) secta f

cul·ti·vate ['kʌltɪveɪt] v/t also fig cultivar

cul·ti·vat·ed ['kʌltɪveɪtɪd] adj person culto

cul·ti·va·tion [kʌltɪ'veɪʃn] of land cultivo m

cul·tur·al ['kʌltʃərəl] adj cultural

cul·ture ['kʌltʃər] artistic cultura f

cul·tured ['kʌltʃərd] adj (cultivated) culto

'cul·ture shock choque m cultural

cum·ber·some ['kʌmbərsəm] adj engorroso

cu·mu·la·tive ['kjuːmjʊlətɪv] adj acumulativo

cun·ning ['kʌnɪŋ] **1** n astucia f **2** adj astuto

cup [kʌp] n taza f; trophy copa f

cup·board ['kʌbərd] armario m

'cup fi·nal final f de (la) copa

cu·po·la ['kju:pələ] cúpula f

cu·ra·ble ['kjʊrəbl] adj curable

cu·ra·tor [kjʊ'reɪtər] conservador(a) m(f)

curb [kɜːrb] **1** n of street bordillo m; on powers etc freno m **2** v/t frenar

cur·dle ['kɜːrdl] v/i of milk cortarse

cure [kjʊr] **1** n MED cura f **2** v/t MED, meat curar

cur·few ['kɜːrfjuː] toque m de queda

cu·ri·os·i·ty [kjʊrɪ'ɑːsətɪ] (inquisitiveness) curiosidad f

cu·ri·ous ['kjʊrɪəs] adj (inquisitive, strange) curioso

cu·ri·ous·ly ['kjʊrɪəslɪ] adv (inquisitively) con curiosidad; (strangely) curiosamente; **curiously enough** curiosamente

curl [kɜːrl] **1** n in hair rizo m; of smoke voluta f **2** v/t hair rizar; (wind) enroscar **3** v/i of hair rizarse; of leaf, paper etc ondularse

◆ curl up v/i acurrucarse

curl·y ['kɜːrlɪ] adj hair rizado; tail enroscado

cur·rant ['kʌrənt] (dried fruit) pasa f de Corinto

cur·ren·cy ['kʌrənsɪ] money moneda f; **foreign currency** divisas fpl

cur·rent ['kʌrənt] **1** n in sea, ELEC corriente f **2** adj (present) actual

cur·rent af·fairs, cur·rent e·vents npl la actualidad

cur·rent af·fairs pro·gram programa m de actualidad

'cur·rent ac·count Br cuenta f corriente

cur·rent·ly ['kʌrəntlɪ] adv actualmente

cur·ric·u·lum [kə'rɪkjʊləm] plan m de estudios

cur·ric·u·lum vi·tae ['viːtaɪ] Br currículum m vitae

cur·ry ['kʌrɪ] curry m

curse [kɜːrs] **1** n (spell) maldición f; (swearword) palabrota f **2** v/t maldecir; (swear at) insultar **3** v/i (swear) decir palabrotas

cur·sor ['kɜːrsər] COMPUT cursor m

cur·so·ry ['kɜːrsərɪ] adj rápido, superficial

curt [kɜːrt] adj brusco, seco

cur·tail [kɜːr'teɪl] v/t acortar

cur·tain ['kɜːrtn] cortina f; THEA telón m

curve [kɜːrv] **1** n curva f **2** v/i (bend) curvarse

cush·ion ['kʊʃn] **1** n for couch etc cojín m **2** v/t blow, fall amortiguar

cus·tard ['kʌstərd] natillas fpl

cus·to·dy ['kʌstədɪ] of children custodia f; **in custody** LAW detenido

cus·tom ['kʌstəm] (tradition) costumbre f; COM clientela f; **it's the custom in France** es costumbre en Francia; **as was his custom** como era costumbre en él; **thank you for your custom** at shop gracias por comprar aquí

cus·tom·a·ry ['kʌstəmərɪ] adj acostumbrado, de costumbre; **it is customary to ...** es costumbre ...

cus·tom-'built adj hecho de encargo

cus·tom-'made adj hecho de encargo

cus·tom·er ['kʌstəmər] cliente(-a) m(f)

cus·tom·er re'la·tions npl relaciones fpl con los clientes

cus·tom·er 'serv·ice atención f al cliente

cus·toms ['kʌstəmz] npl aduana f

'cus·toms clear·ance despacho m de aduanas

'cus·toms in·spec·tion inspección f aduanera

'cus·toms of·fi·cer funcionario(-a) m(f) de aduanas

cut [kʌt] **1** n with knife etc, of garment corte m; (reduction) recorte (**in** de); **my hair needs a cut** necesito un corte de pelo **2** v/t (pret & pp **cut**) cortar; (reduce) recortar; hours acortar; **get one's hair cut** cortarse el pelo; **I've cut my finger** me he cortado el dedo

◆ cut back **1** v/i in costs recortar gastos **2** v/t staff numbers recortar

◆ cut down **1** v/t tree talar, cortar **2** v/i in expenses gastar menos; in smoking / drinking fumar / beber menos

◆ cut down on v/t: **cut down on the cigarettes** fumar menos; **cut down on chocolate** comer menos chocolate

◆ cut off v/t with knife, scissors etc cortar; (isolate) aislar; **I was cut off** se me ha cortado la comunicación

◆ cut out v/t with scissors recortar; (eliminate) eliminar; **cut that out!** F ¡ya está bien! F; **be cut out for sth** estar hecho para algo

◆ cut up v/t meat etc trocear

'cut·back recorte m

cute [kjuːt] adj (pretty) guapo, lindo; (sexually attractive) atractivo; (smart, clever) listo; **it looks really cute on you** eso te queda muy mono

cu·ti·cle ['kjuːtɪkl] cutícula f

'cut-off date fecha f límite

cut-'price adj goods rebajado; store de productos rebajados

'cut-throat adj competition despiadado

cut·ting ['kʌtɪŋ] **1** n from newspaper etc

recorte m **2** *adj remark* hiriente
cy·ber·space ['saɪbərspeɪs] ciberespacio m
cy·cle ['saɪkl] **1** n (*bicycle*) bicicleta f; (*series of events*) ciclo m **2** v/i ir en bicicleta
'**cy·cle path** vía f para bicicletas; *part of roadway* carril m bici
cy·cling ['saɪklɪŋ] ciclismo m
cy·clist ['saɪklɪst] ciclista m/f
cyl·in·der ['sɪlɪndər] cilindro m
cy·lin·dri·cal [sɪ'lɪndrɪkl] *adj* cilíndrico
cyn·ic ['sɪnɪk] escéptico(-a) m(f), suspi-

caz m/f
cyn·i·cal ['sɪnɪkl] *adj* escéptico, suspicaz
cyn·i·cal·ly ['sɪnɪklɪ] *adv smile, remark* con escepticismo *or* suspicacia
cyn·i·cism ['sɪnɪsɪzm] escepticismo m, suspicacia f
cy·press ['saɪprəs] ciprés m
cyst [sɪst] quiste m
Czech [tʃek] **1** *adj* checo; *the Czech Republic* la República Checa **2** n *person* checo(-a) m(f); *language* checo m

D

DA *abbr* (= *district attorney*) fiscal m/f (del distrito)
dab [dæb] **1** n *small amount* pizca f **2** v/t (*pret & pp dabbed*) (*remove*) quitar; (*apply*) poner
◆ **dab·ble in** v/t ser aficionado a
dad [dæd] *talking to him* papá m; *talking about him* padre m
dad·dy ['dædɪ] *talking to him* papi m; *talking about him* padre m
daf·fo·dil ['dæfədɪl] narciso m
dag·ger ['dægər] daga f
dai·ly ['deɪlɪ] **1** n (*paper*) diario m **2** *adj* diario
dain·ty ['deɪntɪ] *adj* grácil, delicado
dair·y ['derɪ] *on farm* vaquería f
'**dair·y prod·ucts** npl productos m lácteos
dais ['deɪɪs] tarima f
dai·sy ['deɪzɪ] margarita f
dam [dæm] **1** n *for water* presa f **2** v/t (*pret & pp dammed*) *river* embalsar
dam·age ['dæmɪdʒ] **1** n daños mpl; *fig: to reputation etc* daño m **2** v/t *also fig* dañar; *you're damaging your health* estás perjudicando tu salud
dam·ages ['dæmɪdʒɪz] npl LAW daños mpl y perjuicios
dam·ag·ing ['dæmɪdʒɪŋ] *adj* perjudicial
dame [deɪm] F (*woman*) mujer f, Span tía f F
damn [dæm] **1** *interj* F ¡mecachis! F **2** n F: *I don't give a damn!* ¡me importa un pimiento! F **3** *adj* F maldito F **4** *adv* F muy; *a damn stupid thing* una tontería monumental **5** v/t (*condemn*) condenar; *damn it!* F ¡maldita sea! F; *I'm damned if ...* F ya

lo creo que ... F
damned [dæmd] → *damn adj, adv*
damn·ing ['dæmɪŋ] *adj evidence* condenatorio; *report* crítico
damp [dæmp] *adj* húmedo
damp·en ['dæmpən] v/t humedecer
dance [dæns] **1** n baile m **2** v/i bailar; *would you like to dance?* ¿le gustaría bailar?
danc·er ['dænsər] bailarín (-ina) m(f)
danc·ing ['dænsɪŋ] baile m
dan·de·lion ['dændɪlaɪən] diente m de león
dan·druff ['dændrʌf] caspa f
dan·druff sham'poo champú m anticaspa
Dane [deɪn] danés(-esa) m(f)
dan·ger ['deɪndʒər] peligro m; *be in danger* estar en peligro; *out of danger* of patient estar fuera de peligro; *be in no danger* no estar en peligro
dan·ger·ous ['deɪndʒərəs] *adj* peligroso
dan·ger·ous 'driv·ing conducción f peligrosa
dan·ger·ous·ly ['deɪndʒərəslɪ] *adv drive* peligrosamente; *dangerously ill* gravemente enfermo
dan·gle ['dæŋgl] **1** v/t balancear **2** v/i colgar
Da·nish ['deɪnɪʃ] **1** *adj* danés **2** n *language* danés m
'**Da·nish (pas·try)** pastel m de hojaldre (*dulce*)
dare [der] **1** v/i atreverse; *dare to do sth* atreverse a hacer algo; *how dare you!* ¡cómo te atreves! **2** v/t: *dare s.o. to do sth* desafiar a alguien para que haga algo
dare·dev·il ['derdevɪl] temerario(-a) m(f)

dar·ing ['deərɪŋ] *adj* atrevido
dark [dɑːrk] **1** *n* oscuridad *f*; *in the dark* en la oscuridad; *after dark* después de anochecer; *keep s.o. in the dark about sth fig* no revelar algo a alguien **2** *adj* oscuro; *hair* oscuro, moreno; *dark green / blue* verde / azul oscuro
dark·en ['dɑːrkn] *v/i of sky* oscurecerse
dark 'glass·es *npl* gafas *fpl* oscuras, *L.Am.* lentes *fpl* oscuras
dark·ness ['dɑːrknɪs] oscuridad *f*; *in darkness* a oscuras
'dark·room PHOT cuarto *m* oscuro
dar·ling ['dɑːrlɪŋ] **1** *n* cielo *m*; *yes my darling* sí cariño **2** *adj* encantador; *darling Ann, how are you?* querida Ann, ¿cómo estás?
darn¹ [dɑːrn] **1** *n* (*mend*) zurcido *m* **2** *v/t* (*mend*) zurcir
darn², darned [dɑːrn, dɑːrnd] → *damn adj, adv*
dart [dɑːrt] **1** *n for throwing* dardo *m* **2** *v/i* lanzarse, precipitarse
darts [dɑːrts] *nsg* dardos *mpl*
'dart(s)·board diana *f*
dash [dæʃ] **1** *n punctuation* raya *f*; (*small amount*) chorrito *m*; (MOT: *dashboard*) salpicadero *m*; *make a dash for* correr hacia **2** *v/i* correr; *I must dash* tengo que darme prisa; *he dashed downstairs* bajó las escaleras corriendo **3** *v/t hopes* frustrar, truncar
♦ **dash off 1** *v/i* irse **2** *v/t* (*write quickly*) escribir rápidamente
'dash·board salpicadero *m*
da·ta ['deɪtə] datos *mpl*
'da·ta·base base *f* de datos
da·ta 'cap·ture captura *f* de datos
da·ta 'pro·cess·ing proceso *m or* tratamiento *m* de datos
da·ta pro'tec·tion protección *f* de datos
da·ta 'stor·age almacenamiento *m* de datos
date¹ [deɪt] *fruit* dátil *m*
date² [deɪt] **1** *n* fecha *f*; (*meeting*) cita *f*; (*person*) pareja *f*; *what's the date today?* ¿qué fecha es hoy?, ¿a qué fecha estamos?; *out of date clothes* pasado de moda; *passport* caducado; *up to date* al día **2** *v/t letter, check* fechar; (*go out with*) salir con; *that dates you* (*shows your age*) eso demuestra lo viejo que eres
dat·ed ['deɪtɪd] *adj* anticuado
daub [dɔːb] *v/t* embadurnar
daugh·ter ['dɔːtər] hija *f*
'daugh·ter-in-law (*pl* **daughters-in-law**) nuera *f*
daunt [dɔːnt] *v/t* acobardar, desalentar
daw·dle ['dɔːdl] *v/i* perder el tiempo

dawn [dɔːn] **1** *n* amanecer *m*, alba *f*; *fig: of new age* albores *mpl* **2** *v/i* amanecer; *it dawned on me that ...* me di cuenta de que ...
day [deɪ] día *m*; *what day is it today?* ¿qué día es hoy?, ¿a qué día estamos?; *day off* día *m* de vacaciones; *by day* durante el día; *day by day* día tras día; *the day after* el día siguiente; *the day after tomorrow* pasado mañana; *the day before* el día anterior; *the day before yesterday* anteayer; *day in day out* un día sí y otro también; *in those days* en aquellos tiempos; *one day* un día; *the other day* (*recently*) el otro día; *let's call it a day!* ¡dejémoslo!
'day·break amanecer *m*, alba *f*
'day care servicio *m* de guardería
'day·dream 1 *n* fantasía *f* **2** *v/i* soñar despierto
'day·dream·er soñador(a) *m(f)*
'day·light luz *f* del día
'day·light 'sav·ing time horario *m* de verano
'day·time: in the daytime durante el día
'day trip excursión *m* en el día
daze [deɪz] *n: in a daze* aturdido
dazed [deɪzd] *adj* aturdido
daz·zle ['dæzl] *v/t also fig* deslumbrar
DC [diː'siː] *abbr* (= *direct current*) corriente *f* continua; (= *District of Columbia*) Distrito *m* de Columbia
dead [ded] **1** *adj person, plant* muerto; *battery* agotado; *light bulb* fundido; F *place* muerto; *the phone is dead* no hay línea **2** *adv* F (*very*) tela de F, la mar de F; *dead beat, dead tired* hecho polvo; *that's dead right* tienes toda la razón del mundo **3** *n: the dead* (*dead people*) los muertos; *in the dead of night* a altas horas de la madrugada
dead·en ['dedn] *v/t pain, sound* amortiguar
dead 'end (*street*) callejón *m* sin salida
dead-'end job trabajo *m* sin salidas
dead 'heat empate *m*
'dead·line fecha *f* tope; *for newspaper, magazine* hora *f* de cierre; *meet a deadline* cumplir un plazo
'dead·lock in talks punto *m* muerto
dead·ly ['dedlɪ] *adj* (*fatal*) mortal; F (*boring*) mortal F
deaf [def] *adj* sordo
deaf-and-'dumb *adj* sordomudo
deaf·en ['defn] *v/t* ensordecer
deaf·en·ing ['defnɪŋ] *adj* ensordecedor
deaf·ness ['defnɪs] sordera *f*
deal [diːl] **1** *n* acuerdo *m*; *I thought we had a deal?* creía que habíamos hecho

un trato; **it's a deal!** ¡trato hecho!; **a good deal** (bargain) una ocasión; **a good deal** (a lot) mucho; **a great deal of** (lots) mucho(s) **2** v/t (pret & pp **dealt**) cards repartir; **deal a blow to** asestar un golpe a

◆ **deal in** v/t (trade in) comerciar con; **deal in drugs** traficar con drogas

◆ **deal out** v/t cards repartir

◆ **deal with** v/t (handle) tratar; situation hacer frente a; customer, applications encargarse de; (do business with) hacer negocios con

deal·er ['di:lər] (merchant) comerciante m/f; (drug dealer) traficante m/f

deal·ing ['di:lɪŋ] (drug dealing) tráfico m

deal·ings ['di:lɪŋz] npl (business) tratos mpl

dealt [delt] pret & pp → **deal**

dean [di:n] of college decano(-a) m(f)

dear [dɪr] adj querido; (expensive) caro; **Dear Sir** Muy Sr. Mío; **Dear Richard / Margaret** Querido Richard / Querida Margaret; **(oh) dear!, dear me!** ¡oh, cielos!

dear·ly ['dɪrlɪ] adv love muchísimo

death [deθ] muerte f

'death cer·tif·i·cate certificado m de defunción

'death pen·al·ty pena f de muerte

'death toll saldo m de víctimas mortales

de·ba·ta·ble [dɪ'beɪtəbl] adj discutible

de·bate [dɪ'beɪt] **1** n also POL debate m **2** v/i debatir; **I debated with myself whether to go** me debatía entre ir o no ir **3** v/t debatir

de·bauch·er·y [dɪ'bɔːtʃərɪ] libertinaje m

deb·it ['debɪt] **1** n cargo m **2** v/t account cargar en; amount cargar

'deb·it card tarjeta f de débito

de·bris ['debriː] of building escombros mpl; of airplane, car restos mpl

debt [det] deuda f; **be in debt** financially estar endeudado

debt·or ['detər] deudor(-a) m(f)

de·bug [diː'bʌɡ] v/t (pret & pp **debugged**) room limpiar de micrófonos; COMPUT depurar

dé·but ['deɪbjuː] n debut m

dec·ade [dekeɪd] década f

dec·a·dence ['dekədəns] decadencia f

dec·a·dent ['dekədənt] adj decadente

de·caf·fein·at·ed [dɪ'kæfɪneɪtɪd] adj descafeinado

de·cant·er [dɪ'kæntər] licorera f

de·cap·i·tate [dɪ'kæpɪteɪt] v/t decapitar

de·cay [dɪ'keɪ] **1** n of wood, plant putrefacción f; of civilization declive m; in teeth caries f inv **2** v/i of wood, plant pu-

drirse; of civilization decaer; of teeth cariarse

de·ceased [dɪ'siːst]: **the deceased** el difunto / la difunta

de·ceit [dɪ'siːt] engaño m, mentira f

de·ceit·ful [dɪ'siːtfʊl] adj mentiroso

de·ceive [dɪ'siːv] v/t engañar

De·cem·ber [dɪ'sembər] diciembre m

de·cen·cy ['diːsənsɪ] decencia f; **he had the decency to ...** tuvo la delicadeza de ...

de·cent ['diːsənt] adj decente; (adequately dressed) presentable

de·cen·tral·ize [diː'sentrəlaɪz] v/t descentralizar

de·cep·tion [dɪ'sepʃn] engaño m

de·cep·tive [dɪ'septɪv] adj engañoso

de·cep·tive·ly [dɪ'septɪvlɪ] adv: **it looks deceptively simple** parece muy fácil

dec·i·bel ['desɪbel] decibelio m

de·cide [dɪ'saɪd] **1** v/t decidir **2** v/i decidir; **you decide** decide tú; **it's so hard to decide** es tan difícil decidirse

de·cid·ed [dɪ'saɪdɪd] adj (definite) tajante

de·cid·er [dɪ'saɪdər]: **this match will be the decider** este partido será el que decida

de·cid·u·ous [dɪ'sɪdʊəs] adj de hoja caduca

dec·i·mal ['desɪml] n decimal m

dec·i·mal 'point coma f (decimal)

dec·i·mate ['desɪmeɪt] v/t diezmar

de·ci·pher [dɪ'saɪfər] v/t descifrar

de·ci·sion [dɪ'sɪʒn] decisión f; **come to a decision** llegar a una decisión

de·ci·sion-mak·er: **who's the decision-maker here?** ¿quién toma aquí las decisiones?

de·ci·sive [dɪ'saɪsɪv] adj decidido; (crucial) decisivo

deck [dek] of ship cubierta f; of cards baraja f

'deck-chair tumbona f

dec·la·ra·tion [deklə'reɪʃn] (statement) declaración f

de·clare [dɪ'kler] v/t (state) declarar

de·cline [dɪ'klaɪn] **1** n (fall) descenso m; in standards caída f; in health empeoramiento m **2** v/t invitation declinar; **decline to comment** declinar hacer declaraciones **3** v/i (refuse) rehusar; (decrease) declinar; of health empeorar

de·clutch [diː'klʌtʃ] v/i desembragar

de·code [diː'koʊd] v/t descodificar

de·com·pose [diːkəm'poʊz] v/i descomponerse

dé·cor ['deɪkɔːr] decoración f

dec·o·rate ['dekəreɪt] v/t with paint pintar; with paper empapelar; (adorn) decorar; *soldier* condecorar

dec·o·ra·tion [dekə'reɪʃn] *paint* pintado *m*; *paper* empapelado *m*; *(ornament)* decoración *f*

dec·o·ra·tive ['dekərətɪv] *adj* decorativo

dec·o·ra·tor ['dekəreɪtər] *(interior decorator)* decorador(a) *m(f)*; *with paint* pintor(a) *m(f)*; *with wallpaper* empapelador(a) *m(f)*

de·co·rum [dɪ'kɔːrəm] decoro *m*

de·coy ['diːkɔɪ] *n* señuelo *m*

de·crease **1** *n* ['diːkriːs] disminución *f*, reducción *f* (*in* de) **2** *v/t* [dɪ'kriːs] disminuir, reducir **3** *v/i* [dɪ'kriːs] disminuir, reducirse

de·crep·it [dɪ'krepɪt] *adj car, coat, shoes* destartalado; *person* decrépito

ded·i·cate ['dedɪkeɪt] *v/t book etc* dedicar; *dedicate o.s. to* dedicarse a

ded·i·cat·ed ['dedɪkeɪtɪd] *adj* dedicado

ded·i·ca·tion [dedɪ'keɪʃn] *in book* dedicatoria *f*; *to cause, work* dedicación *f*

de·duce [dɪ'djuːs] *v/t* deducir

de·duct [dɪ'dʌkt] *v/t* descontar; *deduct sth from sth* descontar alguien de alguien

de·duc·tion [dɪ'dʌkʃn] *from salary*, *(conclusion)* deducción *f*

dee·jay ['diːdʒeɪ] F *disk jockey* *m/f*, *Span* pincha *m/f*

deed [diːd] *n (act)* acción *f*, obra *f*; LAW escritura *f*

deem [diːm] *v/t* estimar

deep [diːp] *adj* profundo; *color* intenso; *be in deep trouble* estar metido en serios apuros

deep·en ['diːpn] **1** *v/t* profundizar **2** *v/i* hacerse más profundo; *of crisis, mystery* agudizarse

'deep freeze *n* congelador *m*

'deep-froz·en food comida *f* congelada

'deep-fry *v/t (pret & pp deep-fried)* freír (en mucho aceite)

deep 'fry·er freidora *f*

deer [dɪr] *n (pl deer)* ciervo *m*

de·face [dɪ'feɪs] *v/t* desfigurar, dañar

def·a·ma·tion [defə'meɪʃn] difamación *f*

de·fam·a·to·ry [dɪ'fæmətərɪ] *adj* difamatorio

de·fault [dɪ'fɔːlt] *adj* COMPUT por defecto

de·feat [dɪ'fiːt] **1** *n* derrota *f* **2** *v/t* derrotar; *of task, problem* derrotar, vencer

de·feat·ist [dɪ'fiːtɪst] *adj attitude* derrotista

de·fect ['diːfekt] *n* defecto *m*

de·fec·tive [dɪ'fektɪv] *adj* defectuoso

de·fence *etc* Br → *defense etc*

de·fend [dɪ'fend] *v/t* defender

de·fend·ant [dɪ'fendənt] acusado(-a)

m(f); *in civil case* demandado(-a) *m(f)*

de·fense [dɪ'fens] defensa *f*; *come to s.o.'s defense* salir en defensa de alguien

de'fense budg·et POL presupuesto *m* de defensa

de'fense law·yer abogado(-a) *m(f)* defensor(a)

de·fense·less [dɪ'fenslɪs] *adj* indefenso

de'fense play·er SP defensa *m/f*

De'fense Sec·re·ta·ry POL ministro(-a) *m(f)* de Defensa; *in USA* secretario *m* de Defensa

de'fense wit·ness LAW testigo *m/f* de la defensa

de·fen·sive [dɪ'fensɪv] **1** *n*: *on the defensive* a la defensiva; *go on the defensive* ponerse a la defensiva **2** *adj weaponry* defensivo; *stop being so defensive!* ¡no hace falta que te pongas tan a la defensiva!

de·fen·sive·ly [dɪ'fensɪvlɪ] *adv* a la defensiva

de·fer [dɪ'fɜːr] *v/t (pret & pp deferred)* *(postpone)* aplazar, diferir

def·er·ence ['defərəns] deferencia *f*

def·er·en·tial [defə'renʃl] *adj* deferente

de·fi·ance [dɪ'faɪəns] desafío *m*; *in defiance of* desafiando

de·fi·ant [dɪ'faɪənt] *adj* desafiante

de·fi·cien·cy [dɪ'fɪʃənsɪ] *(lack)* deficiencia *f*, carencia *f*

de·fi·cient [dɪ'fɪʃənt] *adj* deficiente, carente; *be deficient in ...* carecer de ...

def·i·cit ['defɪsɪt] déficit *m*

de·fine [dɪ'faɪn] *v/t word, objective* definir

def·i·nite ['defɪnɪt] *adj date, time, answer* definitivo; *improvement* claro; *(certain)* seguro; *are you definite about that?* ¿estás seguro de eso?; *nothing definite has been arranged* no se ha acordado nada de forma definitiva

def·i·nite 'ar·ti·cle GRAM artículo *m* determinado *or* definido

def·i·nite·ly ['defɪnɪtlɪ] *adv* con certeza, sin lugar a dudas

def·i·ni·tion [defɪ'nɪʃn] definición *f*

de·fin·i·tive [dɪ'fɪnətɪv] *adj* definitivo

de·flect [dɪ'flekt] *v/t* desviar; *criticism* distraer; *be deflected from* desviarse de

de·for·est·a·tion [diːfɒrɪs'teɪʃn] deforestación *f*

de·form [dɪ'fɔːrm] *v/t* deformar

de·for·mi·ty [dɪ'fɔːrmɪtɪ] deformidad *f*

de·fraud [dɪ'frɔːd] *v/t* defraudar

de·frost [diː'frɒst] *v/t food, fridge* descongelar

deft [deft] *adj* hábil, diestro

de·fuse [diː'fjuːz] *v/t bomb* desactivar; *si-*

tuation calmar

de·fy [dɪˈfaɪ] *v/t (pret & pp defied)* desafiar

de·gen·e·rate [dɪˈdʒenəreɪt] *v/i* degenerar; **degenerate into** degenerar en

de·grade [dɪˈgreɪd] *v/t* degradar

de·grad·ing [dɪˈgreɪdɪŋ] *adj position, work* degradante

de·gree [dɪˈgriː] *from university* título *m; of temperature, angle, latitude* grado *m;* **there is a degree of truth in that** hay algo de verdad en eso; *a degree of compassion* algo de compasión; *by degrees* gradualmente; *get one's degree* graduarse, *L.Am.* egresar

de·hy·drat·ed [diːhaɪˈdreɪtɪd] *adj* deshidratado

de·ice [diːˈaɪs] *v/t* deshelar

de·ic·er [diːˈaɪsər] *spray* descongelador *m,* descongelante *m*

deign [deɪn] *v/i:* **deign to** dignarse a

de·i·ty [ˈdiːɪtɪ] deidad *f*

de·ject·ed [dɪˈdʒektɪd] *adj* abatido, desanimado

de·lay [dɪˈleɪ] **1** *n* retraso *m* **2** *v/t* retrasar; *be delayed* llevar retraso **3** *v/i* retrasarse

del·e·gate [ˈdelɪgət] **1** *n* delegado(-a) *m(f)* **2** [ˈdelɪgeɪt] *v/t task* delegar; *person* delegar en

del·e·ga·tion [delɪˈgeɪʃn] delegación *f*

de·lete [dɪˈliːt] *v/t* borrar; *(cross out)* tachar; *delete where not applicable* táchese donde no corresponda

de·le·tion [dɪˈliːʃn] *act* borrado *m; that deleted* supresión *f*

del·i [ˈdelɪ] → *delicatessen*

de·lib·e·rate 1 *adj* [dɪˈlɪbərət] deliberado, intencionado **2** *v/i* [dɪˈlɪbəreɪt] deliberar

de·lib·e·rate·ly [dɪˈlɪbərətlɪ] *adv* deliberadamente, a propósito

del·i·ca·cy [ˈdelɪkəsɪ] delicadeza *f; of health* fragilidad *f; food* exquisitez *f,* manjar *m*

del·i·cate [ˈdelɪkət] *adj fabric, problem* delicado; *health* frágil

del·i·ca·tes·sen [delɪkəˈtesn] tienda *f* de productos alimenticios de calidad

de·li·cious [dɪˈlɪʃəs] *adj* delicioso

de·light [dɪˈlaɪt] *n* placer *m*

de·light·ed [dɪˈlaɪtɪd] *adj* encantado; *I'd be delighted to come* me encantaría venir

de·light·ful [dɪˈlaɪtfəl] *adj* encantador

de·lim·it [diːˈlɪmɪt] *v/t* delimitar

de·lin·quen·cy [dɪˈlɪŋkwənsɪ] delincuencia *f*

de·lin·quent [dɪˈlɪŋkwənt] *n* delincuente *m/f*

de·lir·i·ous [dɪˈlɪrɪəs] *adj* MED delirante;

(ecstatic) entusiasmado; *she's delirious about the new job* está como loca con el nuevo trabajo

de·liv·er [dɪˈlɪvər] *v/t* entregar, repartir; *message* dar; *baby* dar a luz; *speech* pronunciar

de·liv·er·y [dɪˈlɪvərɪ] *of goods, mail* entrega *f,* reparto *m; of baby* parto *m*

de·liv·er·y charge gastos *mpl* de envío

de·liv·er·y date fecha *f* de entrega

de·liv·er·y man repartidor *m*

de·liv·er·y note nota *f* de entrega

de·liv·er·y serv·ice servicio *m* de reparto

de·liv·er·y van furgoneta *f* de reparto

de·lude [dɪˈluːd] *v/t* engañar; *you're deluding yourself* te estás engañando a ti mismo

de·luge [ˈdeljuːdʒ] **1** *n* diluvio *m; fig* avalancha *f* **2** *v/t* fig inundar (*with* de)

de·lu·sion [dɪˈluːʒn] engaño *m; you're under a delusion if you think ...* te engañas si piensas que ...

de luxe [dəˈlʊks] *adj* de lujo

♦ **delve into** [delv] *v/t* rebuscar en

de·mand [dɪˈmænd] **1** *n* exigencia *f; by union* reivindicación *f;* COM demanda *f; in demand* solicitado **2** *v/t* exigir; *(require)* requirir

de·mand·ing [dɪˈmændɪŋ] *adj job* que exige mucho; *person* exigente

de·mean·ing [dɪˈmiːnɪŋ] *adj* degradante

de·ment·ed [dɪˈmentɪd] *adj* demente

de·mise [dɪˈmaɪz] fallecimiento *m; fig* desaparición *f*

dem·i·tasse [ˈdemɪtæs] taza *f* de café

dem·o [ˈdemoʊ] *protest* manifestación *f; of video etc* maqueta *f*

de·moc·ra·cy [dɪˈmɑːkrəsɪ] democracia *f*

dem·o·crat [ˈdeməkræt] demócrata *m/f;* **Democrat** POL Demócrata *m/f*

dem·o·crat·ic [deməˈkrætɪk] *adj* democrático

dem·o·crat·ic·al·ly [deməˈkrætɪklɪ] *adv* democráticamente

'dem·o disk disco *m* de demostración

de·mo·graph·ic [deməˈɡræfɪk] *adj* demográfico

de·mol·ish [dɪˈmɑːlɪʃ] *v/t building* demoler; *argument* destruir, echar por tierra

dem·o·li·tion [deməˈlɪʃn] *of building* demolición *f; of argument* destrucción *f*

de·mon [ˈdiːmən] demonio *m*

dem·on·strate [ˈdemənstreɪt] **1** *v/t* demostrar **2** *v/i politically* manifestarse

dem·on·stra·tion [demənˈstreɪʃn] demostración *f; protest* manifestación *f*

de·mon·stra·tive [dɪˈmɑːnstrətɪv] *adj person* extrovertido, efusivo; GRAM demostrativo

de·mon·stra·tor ['demənstreɪtər] *protester* manifestante *m/f*

de·mor·al·ized [dɪ'mɔːrəlaɪzd] *adj* desmoralizado

de·mor·al·iz·ing [dɪ'mɔːrəlaɪzɪŋ] *adj* desmoralizador

de·mote [diː'məʊt] *v/t* degradar

de·mure [dɪ'mjʊər] *adj* solemne, recatado

den [den] *(study)* estudio *m*

de·ni·al [dɪ'naɪəl] *of rumor, accusation* negación *f*; *of request* denegación *f*

den·im ['denɪm] tela *f* vaquera

den·ims ['denɪmz] *npl (jeans)* vaqueros *mpl*

Den·mark ['denmɑːrk] Dinamarca *f*

de·nom·i·na·tion [dɪnɑːmɪ'neɪʃn] *of money* valor *m*; *religious* confesión *f*

de·nounce [dɪ'naʊns] *v/t* denunciar

dense [dens] *adj smoke, fog* denso; *foliage* espeso; *crowd* compacto; F *(stupid)* corto

dense·ly ['densli] *adv:* **densely populated** densamente poblado

den·si·ty ['densɪtɪ] *of population* densidad *f*

dent [dent] **1** *n* abolladura *f* **2** *v/t* abollar

den·tal ['dentl] *adj* dental; **dental surgeon** odontólogo(-a) *m(f)*

dent·ed ['dentɪd] *adj* abollado

den·tist ['dentɪst] dentista *m/f*

den·tist·ry ['dentɪstrɪ] odontología *f*

den·tures ['dentʃərz] *npl* dentadura *f* postiza

de·ny [dɪ'naɪ] *v/t (pret & pp denied) charge, rumor* negar; *right, request* denegar

de·o·do·rant [diː'əʊdərənt] desodorante *m*

de·part [dɪ'pɑːrt] *v/i* salir; **depart from** *(deviate from)* desviarse de

de·part·ment [dɪ'pɑːrtmənt] departamento *m*; *of government* ministerio *m*

De·part·ment of 'De·fense Ministerio *m* de Defensa

De·part·ment of the In·te·ri·or Ministerio *m* del Interior

De·part·ment of 'State Ministerio *m* de Asuntos Exteriores

de'part·ment store grandes almacenes *mpl*

de·par·ture [dɪ'pɑːrtʃər] salida *f*; *of person from job* marcha *f*; *(deviation)* desviación *f*; **a new departure** *for government, organization* una innovación; *for company* un cambio; *for actor, artist, writer* una nueva experiencia

de'par·ture lounge sala *f* de embarque

de'par·ture time hora *f* de salida

de·pend [dɪ'pend] *v/i* depender; **that depends** depende; **it depends on the**

weather depende del tiempo; **I depend on you** dependo de ti

de·pen·da·ble [dɪ'pendəbl] *adj* fiable

de·pen·dant [dɪ'pendənt] → **dependent**

de·pen·dence, de·pen·den·cy [dɪ'pendəns, dɪ'pendənsɪ] dependencia *f*

de·pen·dent [dɪ'pendənt] **1** *n* persona a cargo de otra; **how many dependents do you have?** ¿cuántas personas tiene a su cargo? **2** *adj* dependiente **(on** de)

de·pict [dɪ'pɪkt] *v/t* describir

de·plete [dɪ'pliːt] *v/t* agotar, mermar

de·plor·a·ble [dɪ'plɔːrəbl] *adj* deplorable

de·plore [dɪ'plɔːr] *v/t* deplorar

de·ploy [dɪ'plɔɪ] *v/t (use)* utilizar; *(position)* desplegar

de·pop·u·la·tion [diːpɑːpjə'leɪʃn] despoblación *f*

de·port [dɪ'pɔːrt] *v/t* deportar

de·por·ta·tion [diːpɔːr'teɪʃn] deportación *f*

de·por·ta·tion or·der orden *f* de deportación

de·pose [dɪ'pəʊz] *v/t* deponer

de·pos·it [dɪ'pɑːzɪt] **1** *n in bank, of oil* depósito *m*; *of coal* yacimiento *m*; *on purchase* señal *f*, depósito *m* **2** *v/t money* depositar, *Span* ingresar; *(put down)* deponer

de'pos·it ac·count *Br* cuenta *f* de ahorro *or* de depósito

dep·o·si·tion [diːpəʊ'zɪʃn] LAW declaración *f*

de·pot ['diːpəʊ] *(train station)* estación *f* de tren; *(bus station)* estación *f* de autobuses; *for storage* depósito *m*

de·praved [dɪ'preɪvd] *adj* depravado

de·pre·ci·ate [dɪ'priːʃɪeɪt] *v/i* FIN depreciarse

de·pre·ci·a·tion [dɪpriːʃɪ'eɪʃn] FIN depreciación *f*

de·press [dɪ'pres] *v/t person* deprimir

de·pressed [dɪ'prest] *adj person* deprimido

de·press·ing [dɪ'presɪŋ] *adj* deprimente

de·pres·sion [dɪ'preʃn] MED, *economic* depresión *f*; *meteorological* borrasca *f*

dep·ri·va·tion [deprɪ'veɪʃn] privación *f*

de·prive [dɪ'praɪv] *v/t* privar; **deprive s.o. of sth** privar a alguien de algo

de·prived [dɪ'praɪvd] *adj* desfavorecido

depth [depθ] profundidad *f*; *of color* intensidad *f*; *in depth (thoroughly)* en profundidad; **in the depths of winter** en pleno invierno; **be out of one's depth** *in water* no tocar el fondo; *fig: in discussion etc* saber muy poco

dep·u·ta·tion [depjʊ'teɪʃn] delegación *f*

◆ **dep·u·tize for** [dep'jʊtaɪz] *v/t* sustituir

dep·u·ty ['depjʊtɪ] segundo(-a) *m(f)*

'dep·u·ty lead·er vicelíder *m/f*

de·rail [dɪ'reɪl] *v/t* hacer descarrilar; **be derailed** of train descarrilar

de·ranged [dɪ'reɪndʒd] *adj* perturbado, trastornado

de·reg·u·late [dɪ'regjʊleɪt] *v/t* liberalizar, desregular

de·reg·u·la·tion [dɪregjʊ'leɪʃn] liberalización *f*, desregulación *f*

der·e·lict ['derəlɪkt] *adj* en ruinas

de·ride [dɪ'raɪd] *v/t* ridiculizar, mofarse de

de·ri·sion [dɪ'rɪʒn] burla *f*, mofa *f*

de·ri·sive [dɪ'raɪsɪv] *adj* burlón

de·ri·sive·ly [dɪ'raɪsɪvlɪ] *adv* burlonamente

de·ri·so·ry [dɪ'raɪsərɪ] *adj amount, salary* irrisorio

de·riv·a·tive [dɪ'rɪvətɪv] *adj (not original)* poco original

de·rive [dɪ'raɪv] *v/t* obtener, encontrar; **be derived from** of word derivar(se) de

der·ma·tol·o·gist [dɜːrmə'tɑːlədʒɪst] dermatólogo(-a) *m(f)*

de·rog·a·to·ry [dɪ'rɑːgətɔːrɪ] *adj* despectivo

de·scend [dɪ'send] **1** *v/t* descender por; **be descended from** descender de **2** *v/i* descender; *of mood, darkness* caer

de·scen·dant [dɪ'sendənt] descendiente *m/f*

de·scent [dɪ'sent] descenso *m*; *(ancestry)* ascendencia *f*; *of Chinese descent* de ascendencia china

de·scribe [dɪ'skraɪb] *v/t* describir; **describe sth as sth** definir a algo como algo

de·scrip·tion [dɪ'skrɪpʃn] descripción *f*

des·e·crate ['desɪkreɪt] *v/t* profanar

des·e·cra·tion [desɪ'kreɪʃn] profanación *f*

de·seg·re·gate [diː'segrəgeɪt] *v/t* acabar con la segregación racial en

des·ert¹ ['dezərt] *n also fig* desierto *m*

des·ert² [dɪ'zɜːrt] **1** *v/t (abandon)* abandonar **2** *v/i of soldier* desertar

des·ert·ed [dɪ'zɜːrtɪd] *adj* desierto

de·sert·er [dɪ'zɜːrtər] MIL desertor(a) *m(f)*

de·ser·ti·fi·ca·tion [dɪzɜːrtɪfɪ'keɪʃn] desertización *f*

de·ser·tion [dɪ'zɜːrʃn] *(abandonment)* abandono *m*; MIL deserción *f*

des·ert 'is·land isla *f* desierta

de·serve [dɪ'zɜːrv] *v/t* merecer

de·sign [dɪ'zaɪn] **1** *n* diseño *m*; *(pattern)* motivo *m* **2** *v/t* diseñar; *not designed for heavy use* no está diseñado para ser utilizado constantemente

des·ig·nate ['dezɪgneɪt] *v/t person* designar; *area* declarar

de·sign·er [dɪ'zaɪnər] diseñador(a) *m(f)*

de·sign·er clothes *npl* ropa *f* de diseño

de·sign fault defecto *m* de diseño

de·sign school escuela *f* de diseño

de·sir·a·ble [dɪ'zaɪrəbl] *adj* deseable; *house* apetecible, atractivo

de·sire [dɪ'zaɪr] *n* deseo *m*; *I have no desire to see him* no me apetece verle

desk [desk] *in classroom* pupitre *m*; *in home, office* mesa *f*; *in hotel* recepción *f*

'desk clerk recepcionista *m/f*

'desk di·a·ry agenda *f*

'desk·top *also on screen* escritorio *m*; *computer* Span ordenador *m* de escritorio, *L.Am.* computadora *f* de escritorio

desk·top 'pub·lish·ing autoedición *f*

des·o·late ['desələt] *adj place* desolado

de·spair [dɪ'sper] **1** *n* desesperación *f*; *in despair* desesperado **2** *v/i* desesperarse; *I despair of finding something to wear* he perdido la esperanza de encontrar algo para ponerme

des·per·ate ['despərət] *adj* desesperado; *be desperate* estar desesperado; *be desperate for a drink / cigarette* necesitar una bebida / un cigarrillo desesperadamente

des·per·a·tion [despə'reɪʃn] desesperación *f*; *an act of desperation* un acto desesperado

des·pic·a·ble [dɪs'pɪkəbl] *adj* despreciable

de·spise [dɪ'spaɪz] *v/t* despreciar

de·spite [dɪ'spaɪt] *prep* a pesar de

de·spon·dent [dɪ'spɑːndənt] *adj* abatido, desanimado

des·pot ['despɑːt] déspota *m/f*

des·sert [dɪ'zɜːrt] postre *m*

des·ti·na·tion [destɪ'neɪʃn] destino *m*

des·tined ['destɪnd] *adj*: *be destined for* fig estar destinado a

des·ti·ny ['destɪnɪ] destino *m*

des·ti·tute ['destɪtuːt] *adj* indigente; *be destitute* estar en la miseria

de·stroy [dɪ'strɔɪ] *v/t* destruir

de·stroy·er [dɪ'strɔɪr] NAUT destructor *m*

de·struc·tion [dɪ'strʌkʃn] destrucción *f*

de·struc·tive [dɪ'strʌktɪv] *adj* destructivo; *child* revoltoso

de·tach [dɪ'tætʃ] *v/t* separar, soltar

de·tach·a·ble [dɪ'tætʃəbl] *adj* desmontable, separable

de·tached [dɪ'tætʃt] *adj (objective)* distanciado

de·tach·ment [dɪ'tætʃmənt] *(objectivity)* distancia *f*

de·tail ['diːteɪl] *n* detalle *m*; *in detail* en detalle

de·tailed ['diːteɪld] *adj* detallado

de·tain [dɪ'teɪn] v/t (*hold back*) entretener; *as prisoner* detener

de·tain·ee [di:teɪn'i:] detenido(-a) *m(f)*

de·tect [dɪ'tekt] v/t percibir; *of device* detectar

de·tec·tion [dɪ'tekʃn] *of criminal, crime* descubrimiento *m*; *of smoke etc* detección *f*

de·tec·tive [dɪ'tektɪv] detective *m/f*

de·tec·tive nov·el novela *f* policiaca *or* de detectives

de·tec·tor [dɪ'tektər] detector *m*

dé·tente [deɪtɑːnt] POL distensión *f*

de·ten·tion [dɪ'tenʃn] (*imprisonment*) detención *f*

de·ter [dɪ'tɜːr] v/t (*pret & pp* **deterred**) disuadir; *deter s.o. from doing sth* disuadir a alguien de hacer algo

de·ter·gent [dɪ'tɜːrdʒənt] detergente *m*

de·te·ri·o·rate [dɪ'tɪriəreɪt] v/i deteriorarse; *of weather* empeorar

de·te·ri·o·ra·tion [dɪtɪriə'reɪʃn] deterioro *m*; *of weather* empeoramiento *m*

de·ter·mi·na·tion [dɪtɜːrmɪ'neɪʃn] (*resolution*) determinación *f*

de·ter·mine [dɪ'tɜːrmɪn] v/t (*establish*) determinar

de·ter·mined [dɪ'tɜːrmɪnd] adj resuelto, decidido; *I'm determined to succeed* estoy decidido a triunfar

de·ter·rent [dɪ'terənt] *n* elemento *m* disuasorio; *act as a deterrent* actuar como elemento disuasorio; *nuclear deterrent* disuasión *f* nuclear

de·test [dɪ'test] v/t detestar

de·test·a·ble [dɪ'testəbl] adj detestable

de·to·nate ['detəneɪt] 1 v/t hacer detonar *or* explotar 2 v/i detonar, explotar

de·to·na·tion [detə'neɪʃn] detonación *f*, explosión *f*

de·tour ['diːtʊr] *n* rodeo *m*; (*diversion*) desvío *m*; *make a detour* dar un rodeo

♦ de·tract from [dɪ'trækt] v/t *achievement* quitar méritos a; *beauty* quitar atractivo a; *the bad weather didn't detract from their enjoyment* el mal tiempo no impidió que disfrutaran

de·tri·ment ['detrɪmənt]: *to the detriment of* en detrimento de

de·tri·men·tal [detrɪ'mentl] adj perjudicial (*to* para)

deuce [duːs] *in tennis* deuce *m*

de·val·u·a·tion [diːvæljuˈeɪʃn] *of currency* devaluación *f*

de·val·ue [diːˈvæljuː] v/t *currency* devaluar

dev·a·state ['devəsteɪt] v/t *crops, countryside, city* devastar; *fig: person* asolar

dev·a·stat·ing ['devəsteɪtɪŋ] adj devastador

de·vel·op [dɪ'veləp] 1 v/t *film* revelar; *land, site* urbanizar; *activity, business* desarrollar; (*originate*) desarrollar; (*improve on*) perfeccionar; *illness, cold* contraer 2 v/i (*grow*) desarrollarse; *develop into* convertirse en

de·vel·op·er [dɪ'veləpər] *of property* promotor(a) *m(f)* inmobiliario(-a)

de·vel·op·ing 'coun·try [dɪ'veləpɪŋ] país *m* en vías de desarrollo

de·vel·op·ment [dɪ'veləpmənt] *of film* revelado *m*; *of land, site* urbanización *f*; *of business, country* desarrollo *m*; (*event*) acontecimiento *m*; (*origination*) desarrollo *m*; (*improving*) perfeccionamiento *m*

de·vice [dɪ'vaɪs] *tool* aparato *m*, dispositivo *m*

dev·il ['devl] *also fig* diablo *m*, demonio *m*

de·vi·ous ['diːviəs] adj (*sly*) retorcido

de·vise [dɪ'vaɪz] v/t idear

de·void [dɪ'vɔɪd] adj: *be devoid of* estar desprovisto de

dev·o·lu·tion [diːvə'luːʃn] POL traspaso *m* de competencias

de·vote [dɪ'vəʊt] v/t dedicar (*to* a)

de·vot·ed [dɪ'vəʊtɪd] adj *son etc* afectuoso; *be devoted to s.o.* tener mucho cariño a alguien

dev·o·tee [dɪvəʊ'tiː] entusiasta *m/f*

de·vo·tion [dɪ'vəʊʃn] devoción *f*

de·vour [dɪ'vaʊər] v/t *food, book* devorar

de·vout [dɪ'vaʊt] adj devoto

dew [duː] rocío *m*

dex·ter·i·ty [dek'sterətɪ] destreza *f*

di·a·be·tes [daɪə'biːtiːz] *nsg* diabetes *f*

di·a·bet·ic [daɪə'betɪk] 1 *n* diabético(-a) *m(f)* 2 adj diabético; *foods* para diabéticos

di·ag·nose ['daɪəgnəʊz] v/t diagnosticar; *she has been diagnosed as having cancer* se le ha diagnosticado un cáncer

di·ag·no·sis [daɪəg'nəʊsɪs] (*pl* **diagnoses** [daɪəg'nəʊsiːz]) diagnóstico *m*

di·ag·o·nal [daɪ'ægənl] adj diagonal

di·ag·o·nal·ly [daɪ'ægənlɪ] adv diagonalmente, en diagonal

di·a·gram ['daɪəgræm] diagrama *m*

di·al ['daɪl] 1 *n of clock* esfera *f*; *of instrument* cuadrante *m*; TELEC disco *m* 2 v/t & v/i (*pret & pp* **dialed**, Br **dialled**) TELEC marcar

di·a·lect ['daɪəlekt] dialecto *m*

di·al·ling tone Br → **dial tone**

di·a·log, Br di·a·logue ['daɪəlɒg] diálogo *m*

di·a·log box COMPUT ventana *f* de diálogo

'di·al tone tono *m* de marcar

di·am·e·ter ['daɪæmɪtər] diámetro *m*; *a circle 6 cms in diameter* un círculo de 6 cms. de diámetro

di·a·met·ri·cal·ly [daɪə'metrɪkəlɪ] *adv*: *diametrically opposed* diametralmente opuesto

di·a·mond ['daɪmənd] *also in cards* diamante *m*; *shape* rombo *m*

di·a·per ['daɪpər] pañal *m*

di·a·phragm ['daɪəfræm] ANAT, *contraceptive* diafragma *m*

di·ar·rhe·a, *Br* **di·ar·rhoe·a** [daɪə'riːə] diarrea *f*

di·a·ry ['daɪrɪ] *for thoughts* diario *m*; *for appointments* agenda *f*

dice [daɪs] **1** *n* dado *m*; *pl* dados *mpl* **2** *v/t food* cortar en dados

di·chot·o·my [daɪ'kɑːtəmɪ] dicotomía *f*

dic·tate [dɪk'teɪt] *v/t* dictar

dic·ta·tion [dɪk'teɪʃn] dictado *m*

dic·ta·tor [dɪk'teɪtər] POL dictador(a) *m(f)*

dic·ta·to·ri·al [dɪktə'tɔːrɪəl] *adj* dictatorial

dic·ta·tor·ship [dɪk'teɪtərʃɪp] dictadura *f*

dic·tion·a·ry ['dɪkʃənerɪ] diccionario *m*

did [dɪd] *pret* → *do*

die [daɪ] *v/i* morir; *die of cancer / Aids* morir de cáncer / sida; *I'm dying to know / leave* me muero de ganas de saber / marchar

◆ **die away** *v/i of noise* desaparecer

◆ **die down** *v/i of noise* irse apagando; *of storm* amainar; *of fire* irse extinguiendo; *of excitement* calmarse

◆ **die out** *v/i of custom, species* desaparecer

die·sel ['diːzl] *fuel* gasoil *m*, gasóleo *m*

di·et ['daɪət] **1** *n (regular food)* dieta *f*; *for losing weight, for health reasons* dieta *f*, régimen *m* **2** *v/i to lose weight* hacer dieta *or* régimen

di·e·ti·tian [daɪə'tɪʃn] experto(-a) *m(f)* en dietética

dif·fer ['dɪfər] *v/i (be different)* ser distinto; *(disagree)* discrepar; *the male differs from the female in ...* el macho se diferencia de la hembra por ...

dif·fe·rence ['dɪfrəns] diferencia *f*; *(disagreement)* diferencia *f*, discrepancia *f*; *it doesn't make any difference (doesn't change anything)* no cambia nada; *(doesn't matter)* da lo mismo

dif·fe·rent ['dɪfrənt] *adj* diferente, distinto *(from, than de)*

dif·fe·ren·ti·ate [dɪfə'renʃɪeɪt] *v/i* diferenciar, distinguir *(between entre)*; *differentiate between treat differently* establecer diferencias entre

dif·fe·rent·ly ['dɪfrəntlɪ] *adv* de manera diferente

dif·fi·cult ['dɪfɪkəlt] *adj* difícil

dif·fi·cul·ty ['dɪfɪkəltɪ] dificultad *f*; *with difficulty* con dificultades

dif·fi·dence ['dɪfɪdəns] retraimiento *m*

dif·fi·dent ['dɪfɪdənt] *adj* retraído

dig [dɪg] *v/t & v/i (pret & pp dug)* cavar

◆ **dig out** *v/t (find)* encontrar

◆ **dig up** *v/t* levantar, cavar; *information* desenterrar

di·gest [daɪ'dʒest] *v/t also fig* digerir

di·gest·i·ble [daɪ'dʒestəbl] *adj food* digerible

di·ges·tion [daɪ'dʒestʃn] digestión *f*

di·ges·tive [daɪ'dʒestɪv] *adj* digestivo

dig·ger ['dɪgər] *machine* excavadora *f*

di·git ['dɪdʒɪt] número *m*; dígito *m*; *a 4 digit number* un número de 4 dígitos

di·gi·tal ['dɪdʒɪtl] *adj* digital

dig·ni·fied ['dɪgnɪfaɪd] *adj* digno

dig·ni·ta·ry ['dɪgnɪterɪ] dignatario(-a) *m(f)*

dig·ni·ty ['dɪgnɪtɪ] dignidad *f*

di·gress [daɪ'gres] *v/i* divagar, apartarse del tema

di·gres·sion [daɪ'greʃn] digresión *f*

dike [daɪk] *wall* dique *m*

di·lap·i·dat·ed [dɪ'læpɪdeɪtɪd] *adj* destartalado

di·late [daɪ'leɪt] *v/i of pupils* dilatarse

di·lem·ma [dɪ'lemə] dilema *m*; *be in a dilemma* estar en un dilema

dil·et·tante [dɪle'tæntɪ] diletante *m/f*

dil·i·gent ['dɪlɪdʒənt] *adj* diligente

di·lute [daɪ'luːt] *v/t* diluir

dim [dɪm] **1** *adj room* oscuro; *light* tenue; *outline* borroso, confuso; *(stupid)* tonto; *prospects* remoto **2** *v/t (pret & pp dimmed)*: atenuar; *dim the headlights* poner las luces cortas **3** *v/i (pret & pp dimmed) of lights* atenuarse

dime [daɪm] moneda de diez centavos

di·men·sion [daɪ'menʃn] *(measurement)* dimensión *f*

di·min·ish [dɪ'mɪnɪʃ] *v/t & v/i* disminuir

di·min·u·tive [dɪ'mɪnʊtɪv] **1** *n* diminutivo *m* **2** *adj* diminuto

dim·ple ['dɪmpl] hoyuelo *m*

din [dɪn] *n* estruendo *m*

dine [daɪn] *v/i fml* cenar

din·er ['daɪnər] *person* comensal *m/f*; *restaurant* restaurante *m* barato

din·ghy ['dɪŋgɪ] *(small yacht)* bote *m* de vela; *(rubber boat)* lancha *f* neumática

din·gy ['dɪndʒɪ] *adj* sórdido; *(dirty)* sucio

din·ing car ['daɪnɪŋ] RAIL vagón *m* restaurante, coche *m* comedor

'din·ing room comedor *m*

'din·ing ta·ble mesa *f* de comedor

din·ner ['dɪnər] *in the evening* cena *f*; *at midday* comida *f*; (*formal gathering*) cena *f* de gala

'din·ner guest invitado(-a) *m(f)* a cenar

'din·ner jack·et esmoquin *m*

'din·ner par·ty cena *f*

'din·ner serv·ice vajilla *f*

di·no·saur ['daɪnəsɔːr] dinosaurio *m*

dip [dɪp] **1** *n* (*swim*) baño *m*, zambullida *f*; *for food* salsa *f*; (*slope*) inclinación *f*, pendiente *f*; (*depression*) hondonada *f* **2** *v/t* (*pret & pp* **dipped**) meter; ***dip the headlights*** poner las luces cortas **3** *v/i* (*pret & pp* **dipped**) *of road* bajar

di·plo·ma [dɪ'ploumə] diploma *m*

di·plo·ma·cy [dɪ'plouməsɪ] *also fig* diplomacia *f*

di·plo·mat ['dɪpləmæt] diplomático(-a) *m(f)*

di·plo·mat·ic [dɪplə'mætɪk] *adj also fig* diplomático

dip·lo·mat·i·cal·ly [dɪplə'mætɪklɪ] *adv* de forma diplomática

dip·lo·mat·ic im'mu·ni·ty inmunidad *f* diplomática

dire [daɪr] *adj* terrible; ***be in dire need of*** necesitar acuciantemente

di·rect [daɪ'rekt] **1** *adj* directo **2** *v/t play, movie, attention* dirigir; ***can you direct me to the museum?*** ¿me podría indicar cómo se va al museo?

di·rect 'cur·rent ELEC corriente *f* continua

di·rec·tion [dɪ'rekʃn] dirección *f*; ***directions*** *to a place* indicaciones *fpl*; (*instructions*) instrucciones *fpl*; *for medicine* posología *f*; ***let's ask for directions*** preguntemos cómo se va; ***directions for use*** modo *m* de empleo

di·rec·tion 'in·di·ca·tor MOT intermitente *m*

di·rec·tive [dɪ'rektɪv] directiva *f*

di·rect·ly [dɪ'rektlɪ] **1** *adv* (*straight*) directamente; (*soon*) pronto; (*immediately*) ahora mismo **2** *conj* en cuanto

di·rec·tor [dɪ'rektər] director(a) *m(f)*

di·rec·to·ry [dɪ'rektərɪ] directorio *m*; TELEC guía *f* telefónica

dirt [dɜːrt] suciedad *f*

'dirt cheap *adj* F tirado F

dirt·y ['dɜːrtɪ] **1** *adj* sucio; (*pornographic*) pornográfico, obsceno **2** *v/t* (*pret & pp* **dirtied**) ensuciar

dirt·y 'trick jugarreta *f*; ***play a dirty trick on s.o.*** hacer una jugarreta a alguien

dis·a·bil·i·ty [dɪsə'bɪlətɪ] discapacidad *f*, minusvalía *f*

dis·a·bled [dɪs'eɪbld] **1** *n*: ***the disabled*** los discapacitados *mpl* **2** *adj* discapacita-do

dis·ad·van·tage [dɪsəd'væntɪdʒ] (*drawback*) desventaja *f*; ***be at a disadvantage*** estar en desventaja

dis·ad·van·taged [dɪsəd'væntɪdʒd] *adj* desfavorecido

dis·ad·van·ta·geous [dɪsædvæn'teɪdʒəs] *adj* desventajoso, desfavorable

dis·a·gree [dɪsə'griː] *v/i of person* no estar de acuerdo, discrepar; ***let's agree to disagree*** aceptemos que no nos vamos a poner de acuerdo

◆ **disagree with** *v/t of person* no estar de acuerdo con, discrepar con; *of food* sentar mal; ***lobster disagrees with me*** la langosta me sienta mal

dis·a·gree·a·ble [dɪsə'griːəbl] *adj* desagradable

dis·a·gree·ment [dɪsə'griːmənt] desacuerdo *m*; (*argument*) discusión *f*

dis·ap·pear [dɪsə'pɪr] *v/i* desaparecer

dis·ap·pear·ance [dɪsə'pɪrəns] desaparición *f*

dis·ap·point [dɪsə'pɔɪnt] *v/t* desilusionar, decepcionar

dis·ap·point·ed [dɪsə'pɔɪntɪd] *adj* desilusionado, decepcionado

dis·ap·point·ing [dɪsə'pɔɪntɪŋ] *adj* decepcionante

dis·ap·point·ment [dɪsə'pɔɪntmənt] desilusión *f*, decepción *f*

dis·ap·prov·al [dɪsə'pruːvl] desaprobación *f*

dis·ap·prove [dɪsə'pruːv] *v/i* desaprobar, estar en contra; ***disapprove of*** desaprobar, estar en contra de

dis·ap·prov·ing [dɪsə'pruːvɪŋ] *adj* desaprobatorio, de desaprobación

dis·ap·prov·ing·ly [dɪsə'pruːvɪŋlɪ] *adv* con desaprobación

dis·arm [dɪs'ɑːrm] **1** *v/t* desarmar **2** *v/i* desarmarse

dis·ar·ma·ment [dɪs'ɑːrməmənt] desarme *m*

dis·arm·ing [dɪs'ɑːrmɪŋ] *adj* cautivador

dis·as·ter [dɪ'zæstər] desastre *m*

di·sas·ter ar·e·a zona *f* catastrófica; (*fig: person*) desastre *m*

di·sas·trous [dɪ'zæstrəs] *adj* desastroso

dis·band [dɪs'bænd] **1** *v/t* disolver **2** *v/i* disolverse

dis·be·lief [dɪsbə'liːf] incredulidad *f*; ***in disbelief*** con incredulidad

disc [dɪsk] (*CD*) compact *m* (disc)

dis·card [dɪs'kɑːrd] *v/t* desechar; *boyfriend* deshacerse de

di·scern [dɪ'sɜːrn] *v/t* distinguir, percibir

di·scern·i·ble [dɪ'sɜːrnəbl] *adj* perceptible

D

di·scern·ing [dɪ'sɜːnɪŋ] adj entendido, exigente

dis·charge 1 n ['dɪstʃɑːrdʒ] from hospital alta f; from army licencia f 2 v/t [dɪs-'tʃɑːrdʒ] from hospital dar el alta a; from army licenciar; from job despedir

di·sci·ple [dɪ'saɪpl] religious discípulo m

dis·ci·pli·nar·y [dɪsɪ'plɪnərɪ] adj disciplinario

dis·ci·pline ['dɪsɪplɪn] 1 n disciplina f 2 v/t child, dog castigar; employee sancionar

'disc jock·ey disc jockey m/f, Span pinchadiscos m/f inv

dis·claim [dɪs'kleɪm] v/t negar

dis·close [dɪs'kloʊs] v/t revelar

dis·clo·sure [dɪs'kloʊʒər] revelación f

dis·co ['dɪskoʊ] discoteca f

dis·col·or, Br dis·col·our [dɪs'kʌlər] v/i decolorar

dis·com·fort [dɪs'kʌmfərt] (pain) molestia f; (embarrassment) incomodidad f

dis·con·cert [dɪskən'sɜːrt] v/t desconcertar

dis·con·cert·ed [dɪskən'sɜːrtɪd] adj desconcertado

dis·con·nect [dɪskə'nekt] v/t desconectar

dis·con·so·late [dɪs'kɑːnsələt] adj desconsolado

dis·con·tent [dɪskən'tent] descontento m

dis·con·tent·ed [dɪskən'tentɪd] adj descontento

dis·con·tin·ue [dɪskən'tɪnjuː] v/t product dejar de producir; bus, train service suspender; magazine dejar de publicar

dis·cord ['dɪskɔːrd] MUS discordancia f; in relations discordia f

dis·co·theque ['dɪskətek] discoteca f

dis·count 1 n ['dɪskaʊnt] descuento m 2 v/t [dɪs'kaʊnt] goods descontar; theory descartar

dis·cour·age [dɪs'kʌrɪdʒ] v/t (dissuade) disuadir (from de); (dishearten) desanimar, desalentar

dis·cour·age·ment [dɪs'kʌrɪdʒmənt] disuasión f; (being disheartened) desánimo m, desaliento m

dis·cov·er [dɪ'skʌvər] v/t descubrir

dis·cov·er·er [dɪ'skʌvərər] descubridor(a) m(f)

dis·cov·er·y [dɪ'skʌvərɪ] descubrimiento m

dis·cred·it [dɪs'kredɪt] v/t desacreditar

dis·creet [dɪ'skriːt] adj discreto

dis·creet·ly [dɪ'skriːtlɪ] adv discretamente

dis·crep·an·cy [dɪ'skrepənsɪ] discrepancia f

dis·cre·tion [dɪ'skreʃn] discreción f; at your discretion a discreción; use your discretion usa tu criterio

di·scrim·i·nate [dɪ'skrɪmɪneɪt] v/i discriminar (against contra); discriminate between (distinguish) distinguir entre

di·scrim·i·nat·ing [dɪ'skrɪmɪneɪtɪŋ] adj entendido, exigente

di·scrim·i·na·tion [dɪ'skrɪmɪneɪʃn] sexual, racial etc discriminación f

dis·cus ['dɪskəs] SP object disco m; event lanzamiento m de disco

di·scuss [dɪ'skʌs] v/t discutir; of article analizar

dis·cus·sion [dɪ'skʌʃn] discusión f

'dis·cus throw·er lanzador(a) m(f) de disco

dis·dain [dɪs'deɪn] n desdén m

dis·ease [dɪ'ziːz] enfermedad f

dis·em·bark [dɪsəm'bɑːrk] v/i desembarcar

dis·en·chant·ed [dɪsən'tʃæntɪd] adj: disenchanted with desencantado con

dis·en·gage [dɪsən'geɪdʒ] v/t soltar

dis·en·tan·gle [dɪsən'tæŋgl] v/t desenredar

dis·fig·ure [dɪs'fɪgər] v/t desfigurar

dis·grace [dɪs'greɪs] 1 n vergüenza f; it's a disgrace! ¡qué vergüenza!; in disgrace desacreditado 2 v/t deshonrar

dis·grace·ful [dɪs'greɪsfəl] adj behavior, situation vergonzoso, lamentable

dis·grun·tled [dɪs'grʌntld] adj descontento

dis·guise [dɪs'gaɪz] 1 n disfraz m; in disguise disfrazado 2 v/t voice, handwriting cambiar; fear, anxiety disfrazar; disguise o.s. as disfrazarse de; he was disguised as iba disfrazado de

dis·gust [dɪs'gʌst] 1 n asco m, repugnancia f; in disgust asqueado 2 v/t dar asco, repugnar; I'm disgusted by ... me da asco or me repuga ...

dis·gust·ing [dɪs'gʌstɪŋ] adj habit, smell, food asqueroso, repugnante; it is disgusting that ... da asco que ..., es repugnante que ...

dish [dɪʃ] (part of meal, container) plato m

'dish·cloth paño m de cocina

dis·heart·ened [dɪs'hɑːrtnd] adj desalentado, descorazonado

dis·heart·en·ing [dɪs'hɑːrtnɪŋ] adj descorazonador

di·shev·eled [dɪ'ʃevld] adj hair, clothes desaliñado; person despeinado

dis·hon·est [dɪs'ɑːnɪst] adj deshonesto

dis·hon·es·ty [dɪs'ɑːnɪstɪ] deshonestidad f

dis·hon·or [dɪs'ɑːnər] n deshonra f; bring dishonor on deshonrar a

dis·hon·o·ra·ble [dɪsˈɑːnərəbl] *adj* deshonroso

dis·hon·our *etc Br* → **dishonor** *etc*

dish·wash·er *person* lavaplatos *m/f inv*; *machine* lavavajillas *m inv*, lavaplatos *m inv*

dish·wash·ing liq·uid lavavajillas *m inv*

dish·wa·ter agua *f* de lavar los platos

dis·il·lu·sion [dɪsɪˈluːʒn] *v/t* desilusionar

dis·il·lu·sion·ment [dɪsɪˈluːʒnmənt] desilusión *f*

dis·in·clined [dɪsɪnˈklaɪnd] *adj*: **she was disinclined to believe him** no estaba inclinada a creerle

dis·in·fect [dɪsɪnˈfekt] *v/t* desinfectar

dis·in·fec·tant [dɪsɪnˈfektənt] desinfectante *m*

dis·in·her·it [dɪsɪnˈherɪt] *v/t* desheredar

dis·in·te·grate [dɪsˈɪntɪɡreɪt] *v/i* desintegrarse; *of marriage* deshacerse

dis·in·terest·ed [dɪsˈɪntrestɪd] *adj (unbiased)* desinteresado

dis·joint·ed [dɪsˈdʒɔɪntɪd] *adj* deshilvanado

disk [dɪsk] *also* COMPUT disco *m*; **on disk** en disco

disk drive COMPUT unidad *f* de disco

disk·ette [dɪsˈket] disquete *m*

dis·like [dɪsˈlaɪk] **1** *n* antipatía *f* **2** *v/t* **she dislikes being kept waiting** no le gusta que la hagan esperar; **I dislike him** no me gusta

dis·lo·cate [ˈdɪsləkeɪt] *v/t shoulder* dislocar

dis·lodge [dɪsˈlɑːdʒ] *v/t* desplazar, mover de su sitio

dis·loy·al [dɪsˈlɔɪəl] *adj* desleal

dis·loy·al·ty [dɪsˈlɔɪəltɪ] deslealtad *f*

dis·mal [ˈdɪzməl] *adj weather* horroroso, espantoso; *news, prospect* negro; *person (sad)* triste; *person (negative)* negativo; *failure* estrepitoso

dis·man·tle [dɪsˈmæntl] *v/t* desmantelar

dis·may [dɪsˈmeɪ] **1** *n (alarm)* consternación *f*; *(disappointment)* desánimo *m* **2** *v/t* consternar

dis·miss [dɪsˈmɪs] *v/t employee* despedir; *suggestion* rechazar; *idea, possibility* descartar

dis·miss·al [dɪsˈmɪsl] *of employee* despido *m*

dis·mount [dɪsˈmaunt] *v/i* desmontar

dis·o·be·di·ence [dɪsəˈbiːdɪəns] desobediencia *f*

dis·o·be·di·ent [dɪsəˈbiːdɪənt] *adj* desobediente

dis·o·bey [dɪsəˈbeɪ] *v/t* desobedecer

dis·or·der [dɪsˈɔːrdər] *(untidiness)* desorden *m*; *(unrest)* desórdenes *mpl*; MED dolencia *f*

dis·or·der·ly [dɪsˈɔːrdərlɪ] *adj room, desk* desordenado; *mob* alborotado

dis·or·gan·ized [dɪsˈɔːrɡənaɪzd] *adj* desorganizado

dis·o·ri·ent·ed [dɪsˈɔːrɪəntɪd] *adj* desorientado

dis·own [dɪsˈoun] *v/t* repudiar, renegar de

di·spar·ag·ing [dɪˈspærɪdʒɪŋ] *adj* despreciativo

di·spar·i·ty [dɪˈspærətɪ] disparidad *f*

dis·pas·sion·ate [dɪˈspæʃənət] *adj (objective)* desapasionado

di·spatch [dɪˈspætʃ] *v/t (send)* enviar

di·spen·sa·ry [dɪˈspensərɪ] *in pharmacy* dispensario *m*

◆ **di·spense with** [dɪˈspens] *v/t* prescindir de

di·sperse [dɪˈspɜːrs] **1** *v/t* dispersar **2** *v/i of crowd* dispersarse; *of mist* disiparse

di·spir·it·ed [dɪˈspɪrɪtɪd] *adj* desalentado, abatido

dis·place [dɪsˈpleɪs] *v/t (supplant)* sustituir

di·splay [dɪˈspleɪ] **1** *n* muestra *f*; *in store window* objetos *mpl* expuestos; COMPUT pantalla *f*; **be on display** estar expuesto **2** *v/t emotion* mostrar; *at exhibition, for sale* exponer; COMPUT visualizar

di·splay cab·i·net *in museum, shop* vitrina *f*

di·splease [dɪsˈpliːz] *v/t* desagradar, disgustar

dis·plea·sure [dɪsˈpleʒər] desagrado *m*, disgusto *m*

dis·po·sa·ble [dɪˈspouzəbl] *adj* desechable; **disposable income** ingreso(s) *m(pl)* disponible(s)

dis·pos·al [dɪˈspouzl] eliminación *f*; **I am at your disposal** estoy a su disposición; **put sth at s.o.'s disposal** poner algo a disposición de alguien

◆ **dis·pose of** [dɪˈspouz] *v/t (get rid of)* deshacerse de

dis·posed [dɪˈspouzd] *adj*: **be disposed to do sth (willing)** estar dispuesto a hacer algo; **be well disposed towards** estar bien dispuesto hacia

dis·po·si·tion [dɪspəˈzɪʃn] *(nature)* carácter *m*

dis·pro·por·tion·ate [dɪsprəˈpɔːrʃənət] *adj* desproporcionado

dis·prove [dɪsˈpruːv] *v/t* refutar

di·spute [dɪˈspjuːt] **1** *n* disputa *f*; *industrial conflicto m* laboral **2** *v/t* discutir; *(fight over)* disputarse; **I don't dispute that** eso no lo discuto

dis·qual·i·fi·ca·tion [dɪskwɑːlɪfɪˈkeɪʃn] descalificación *f*

dis·qual·i·fy [dɪs'kwɑːlɪfaɪ] *v/t* (*pret & pp* **disqualified**) descalificar

dis·re·gard [dɪsrə'gɑːrd] **1** *n* indiferencia *f* **2** *v/t* no tener en cuenta

dis·re·pair [dɪsrə'per]: *in a state of disrepair* deteriorado

dis·rep·u·ta·ble [dɪs'repjʊtəbl] *adj* poco respetable; *area* de mala reputación

dis·re·spect [dɪsrə'spekt] falta *f* de respeto

dis·re·spect·ful [dɪsrə'spektfəl] *adj* irrespetuoso

dis·rupt [dɪs'rʌpt] *v/t train service* trastornar, alterar; *meeting, class* interrumpir

dis·rup·tion [dɪs'rʌpʃn] *of train service* alteración *f*; *of meeting, class* interrupción *f*

dis·rup·tive [dɪs'rʌptɪv] *adj* perjudicial; *he's very disruptive in class* causa muchos problemas en clase

dis·sat·is·fac·tion [dɪssætɪs'fækʃn] insatisfacción *f*

dis·sat·is·fied [dɪs'sætɪsfaɪd] *adj* insatisfecho

dis·sen·sion [dɪ'senʃn] disensión *f*

dis·sent [dɪ'sent] **1** *n* discrepancia *f* **2** *v/i*: *dissent from* disentir de

dis·si·dent [dɪsɪdənt] *n* disidente *m/f*

dis·sim·i·lar [dɪs'sɪmɪlər] *adj* distinto

dis·so·ci·ate [dɪ'soʊʃɪeɪt] *v/t* disociar; *dissociate o.s. from* disociarse de

dis·so·lute ['dɪsəluːt] *adj* disoluto

dis·so·lu·tion ['dɪsəluːʃn] POL disolución *f*

dis·solve [dɪ'zɑːlv] **1** *v/t substance* disolver **2** *v/i of substance* disolverse

dis·suade [dɪ'sweɪd] *v/t* disuadir; *dissuade s.o. from doing sth* disuadir a alguien de hacer algo

dis·tance ['dɪstəns] **1** *n* distancia *f*; *in the distance* en la lejanía **2** *v/t* distanciar; *distance o.s. from* distanciarse de

dis·tant ['dɪstənt] *adj place, time, relative* distante, lejano; (*fig: aloof*) distante

dis·taste [dɪs'teɪst] desagrado *m*

dis·taste·ful [dɪs'teɪstfəl] *adj* desagradable

dis·till·er·y [dɪs'tɪlərɪ] destilería *f*

dis·tinct [dɪ'stɪŋkt] *adj* (*clear*) claro; (*different*) distinto; *as distinct from* a diferencia de

dis·tinc·tion [dɪ'stɪŋkʃn] (*differentiation*) distinción *f*; *hotel / product of distinction* un hotel / producto destacado

dis·tinc·tive [dɪ'stɪŋktɪv] *adj* característico

dis·tinct·ly [dɪ'stɪŋktlɪ] *adv* claramente, con claridad; (*decidedly*) verdaderamente

dis·tin·guish [dɪ'stɪŋgwɪʃ] *v/t* distinguir; *distinguish between X and Y* distinguir entre X e Y

dis·tin·guished [dɪ'stɪŋgwɪʃt] *adj* distinguido

dis·tort [dɪ'stɔːrt] *v/t* distorsionar

dis·tract [dɪ'strækt] *v/t* distraer

dis·trac·tion [dɪ'strækʃn] distracción *f*; *drive s.o. to distraction* sacar a alguien de quicio

dis·traught [dɪ'strɔːt] *adj* angustiado, consternado

dis·tress [dɪ'stres] **1** *n* sufrimiento *m*; *in distress of ship, aircraft* en peligro **2** *v/t* (*upset*) angustiar

dis·tress·ing [dɪ'stresɪŋ] *adj* angustiante

dis·tress sig·nal señal *m* de socorro

dis·trib·ute [dɪ'strɪbjuːt] *v/t* distribuir, repartir; COM distribuir

dis·tri·bu·tion [dɪstrɪ'bjuːʃn] distribución *f*

dis·tri·bu·tion ar·range·ment COM acuerdo *m* de distribución

dis·trib·u·tor [dɪs'trɪbjuːtər] COM distribuidor(a) *m(f)*

dis·trict ['dɪstrɪkt] (*area*) zona *f*; (*neighborhood*) barrio *m*

dis·trict at·tor·ney fiscal *m/f* del distrito

dis·trust [dɪs'trʌst] **1** *n* desconfianza *f* **2** *v/t* desconfiar de

dis·turb [dɪ'stɜːrb] *v/t* (*interrupt*) molestar; (*upset*) preocupar; *do not disturb* no molestar

dis·turb·ance [dɪ'stɜːrbəns] (*interruption*) molestia *f*; *disturbances* (*civil unrest*) disturbios *mpl*

dis·turbed [dɪ'stɜːrbd] *adj* (*concerned, worried*) preocupado, inquieto; *mentally* perturbado

dis·turb·ing [dɪ'stɜːrbɪŋ] *adj* (*worrying*) inquietante; *you may find some scenes disturbing* algunas de las escenas pueden herir la sensibilidad del espectador

dis·used [dɪs'juːzd] *adj* abandonado

ditch [dɪtʃ] **1** *n* zanja *f* **2** *v/t* F (*get rid of*) deshacerse de; *boyfriend* plantar F; *plan* abandonar

dith·er ['dɪðər] *v/i* vacilar

dive [daɪv] **1** *n* salto *m* de cabeza; *underwater* inmersión *f*; *of plane* descenso *m* en picado; F *bar etc* antro *m* F; *take a dive* F *of dollar etc* desplomarse **2** *v/i* (*pret also dove*) tirarse de cabeza; *underwater* bucear; *of plane* descender en picado

div·er ['daɪvər] *off board* saltador(a) *m(f)* de trampolín; *underwater* buceador(a) *m(f)*

di·verge [daɪ'vɜːrdʒ] *v/i* bifurcarse

di·verse [daɪ'vɜːrs] *adj* diverso

di·ver·si·fi·ca·tion [daɪvɜːrsɪfɪ'keɪʃn]
COM diversificación f

di·ver·si·fy [daɪ'vɜːrsɪfaɪ] v/i (pret & pp
diversified) COM diversificarse

di·ver·sion [daɪ'vɜːrʃn] for traffic desvío
f; to distract attention distracción f

di·ver·si·ty [daɪ'vɜːrsətɪ] diversidad f

di·vert [daɪ'vɜːrt] v/t traffic, attention desviar

di·vest [daɪ'vest] v/t: **divest s.o. of sth**
despojar a alguien de algo

di·vide [dɪ'vaɪd] v/t also fig dividir; **divide
16 by 4** dividir 16 entre 4

div·i·dend ['dɪvɪdend] FIN dividendo m;
pay dividends fig resultar beneficioso

di·vine [dɪ'vaɪn] adj also F divino

div·ing ['daɪvɪŋ] from board salto m de
trampolín; (scuba diving) buceo m, submarinismo m

'div·ing board trampolín m

di·vis·i·ble [dɪ'vɪzəbl] adj divisible

di·vi·sion [dɪ'vɪʒn] división f

di·vorce [dɪ'vɔːrs] **1** n divorcio m; **get a
divorce** divorciarse **2** v/t divorciarse
de; **get divorced** divorciarse **3** v/i divorciarse

di·vorced [dɪ'vɔːrst] adj divorciado

di·vor·cee [dɪvɔːr'siː] divorciado(-a)
m(f)

di·vulge [daɪ'vʌldʒ] v/t divulgar, dar a
conocer

DIY [diːaɪ'waɪ] abbr (= **do it yourself**) bricolaje m

DI'Y store tienda f de bricolaje

diz·zi·ness ['dɪzɪnɪs] mareo m

diz·zy ['dɪzɪ] adj mareado; **feel dizzy** estar mareado

DJ ['diːdʒeɪ] abbr (= **disc jockey**) disc
jockey m/f, Span pinchadiscos m/f inv;
(= **dinner jacket**) esmoquin m

DNA [diːen'eɪ] abbr (= **deoxyribonucleic
acid**) AND m (= ácido m desoxirribonucleico)

do [duː] **1** v/t (pret **did**, pp **done**) hacer;
100 mph etc ir a; **do one's hair** peinarse;
what are you doing tonight? ¿qué vas a
hacer esta noche?; **I don't know what to
do** no sé qué hacer; **do it right now!** hazlo ahora mismo; **have one's hair done**
arreglarse el pelo **2** v/i (pret **did**, pp **done**) (be suitable, enough): **that'll do nicely** eso bastará; **that will do!** ¡ya vale!;
do well of business ir bien; **he's doing
well** le van bien las cosas; **well done!**
(congratulations!) ¡bien hecho!; **how
do you do?** encantado de conocerle **3**
v/aux: **do you know him?** ¿lo conoces?;
I don't know no sé; **do be quick** date prisa, por favor; **do you like Des Moines?** -

yes I do ¿te gusta Des Moines? - sí; **he
works hard, doesn't he?** trabaja mucho, ¿verdad?; **don't you believe me?**
¿no me crees?; **you do believe me, don't
you?** me crees, ¿verdad?; **you don't
know the answer, do you? - no I don't**
no sabes la respuesta, ¿no es así? - no, no
la sé

◆ **do away with** v/t (abolish) abolir
◆ **do in** v/t F (exhaust) machacar F; **I'm done in** estoy hecho polvo F
◆ **do out of** v/t: **do s.o. out of sth** timar
alguien a algo F
◆ **do up** v/t (renovate) renovar; buttons,
coat abrocharse; laces atarse
◆ **do with** v/t: **I could do with ...** no me
vendría mal ...; **he won't have anything
to do with it** (won't get involved) no
quiere saber nada de ello
◆ **do without 1** v/i: **you'll have to do without** te las tendrás que arreglar **2** v/t pasar sin

do·cile ['dousal] adj dócil

dock[1] [dɑːk] **1** n NAUT muelle m **2** v/i of
ship atracar; of spaceship acoplarse

dock[2] [dɑːk] n LAW banquillo m (de los
acusados)

'dock·yard Br astillero m

doc·tor ['dɑːktər] n MED médico m; form
of address doctor m

doc·tor·ate ['dɑːktərət] doctorado m

doc·trine ['dɑːktrɪn] doctrina f

doc·u·dra·ma ['dɑːkjudrɑːmə] docudra-
ma m

doc·u·ment ['dɑːkjumənt] n documento
m

doc·u·men·ta·ry [dɑːkju'mentərɪ] n program documental m

doc·u·men·ta·tion [dɑːkjumen'teɪʃn]
documentación f

dodge [dɑːdʒ] v/t blow, person esquivar;
issue, question eludir

doe [dou] deer cierva f

dog [dɔːg] **1** n perro(-a) m(f) **2** v/t (pret &
pp **dogged**) of bad luck perseguir

'dog catch·er perrero(-a) m(f)

'dog-eared ['dɔːgɪrd] adj book sobado,
con las esquinas dobladas

dog·ged ['dɔːgɪd] adj tenaz

dog·gie ['dɔːgɪ] in children's language
perrito m

'dog·gy bag ['dɔːgɪbæg] bolsa para las sobras de la comida

'dog·house: be in the doghouse F haber
caído en desgracia

dog·ma ['dɔːgmə] dogma m

dog·mat·ic [dɔːg'mætɪk] adj dogmático

do-good·er ['duːgudər] pej buen(a) sa-
maritano(-a) m(f)

'**dog tag** MIL chapa *f* de identificación
'**dog-tired** *adj* F hecho polvo F
do-it-your-self [du:ɪtjər'self] bricolaje *m*
dol-drums ['dould rəmz]: *be in the doldrums of economy* estar en un bache; *doldrums of person* estar deprimido
◆ **dole out** *v/t* repartir
doll [dɑːl] *toy* muñeca *f*; F *woman* muñeca *f* F
◆ **doll up** *v/t*: *get dolled up* emperifollarse
dol-lar ['dɑːlər] dólar *m*
dol-lop ['dɑːləp] *n* F cucharada *f*
dol-phin ['dɑːlfɪn] delfín *m*
dome [doʊm] *of building* cúpula *f*
do-mes-tic [də'mestɪk] **1** *adj chores* doméstico, del hogar; *news, policy* nacional **2** *n* empleado(-a) *m(f)* del hogar
do-mes-tic 'an-i-mal animal *m* doméstico
do-mes-ti-cate [də'mestɪkeɪt] *v/t animal* domesticar; *be domesticated of person* estar domesticado
do-mes-tic flight vuelo *m* nacional
dom-i-nant ['dɑːmɪnənt] *adj* dominante
dom-i-nate ['dɑːmɪneɪt] *v/t* dominar
dom-i-na-tion [dɑːmɪ'neɪʃn] dominación *f*
dom-i-neer-ing [dɑːmɪ'nɪrɪŋ] *adj* dominante
dom-i-no ['dɑːmɪnoʊ] ficha *f* de dominó; *play dominoes* jugar al dominó
do-nate [doʊ'neɪt] *v/t* donar
do-na-tion [doʊ'neɪʃn] donación *f*, donativo *m*; MED donación *f*
done [dʌn] *pp* → **do**
don-key ['dɑːŋkɪ] burro *m*
do-nor ['doʊnər] *of money*, MED donante *m/f*
do-nut ['doʊnʌt] dónut *m*
doo-dle ['duːdl] *v/i* garabatear
doom [duːm] *n* (*fate*) destino *m*; (*ruin*) fatalidad *f*
doomed [duːmd] *adj project* condenado al fracaso; *we are doomed* (*bound to fail*) estamos condenados al fracaso; (*going to die*) vamos a morir
door [dɔːr] puerta *f*; *there's someone at the door* hay alguien en la puerta
'**door-bell** timbre *m*
'**door-knob** pomo *m*
'**door-man** portero *m*
'**door-mat** felpudo *m*
'**door-step** umbral *m*
'**door-way** puerta *f*
dope [doʊp] **1** *n* (*drugs*) droga *f*; F (*idiot*) lelo(-a) *m(f)*; F (*information*) información *f* **2** *v/t* drogar
dor-mant ['dɔːrmənt] *adj plant* aletargado; *volcano* inactivo

dor-mi-to-ry ['dɔːrmɪtɔːrɪ] dormitorio *m* (*colectivo*); (*hall of residence*) residencia *f* de estudiantes
dos-age ['doʊsɪdʒ] dosis *f inv*
dose [doʊs] *n* dosis *f inv*
dot [dɑːt] *n punto m*; *on the dot* (*exactly*) en punto
◆ **dote on** [doʊt] *v/t* adorar a
dot.com (**com-pa-ny**) [dɑːt'kɑːm] empresa *f* punto.com
dot-ing ['doʊtɪŋ] *adj*: *my doting aunt* mi tía, que tanto me adora
dot-ted line ['dɑːtɪd] línea *f* de puntos
doub-le ['dʌbl] **1** *n person* doble *m/f*; *room* habitación *f* doble **2** *adj* doble; *inflation is now in double figures* la inflación ha superado ya el 10% **3** *adv*: *they offered me double what the others did* me ofrecieron el doble que la otra gente **4** *v/t* doblar, duplicar **5** *v/i* doblarse, duplicarse; *it doubles as ...* hace también de ...
◆ **double back** *v/i* (*go back*) volver sobre sus pasos
◆ **double up** *v/i in pain* doblarse; (*share*) compartir habitación
doub-le-'bass contrabajo *m*
doub-le 'bed cama *f* de matrimonio
doub-le-breast-ed [dʌbl'brestɪd] *adj* cruzado
doub-le'check *v/t & v/i* volver a comprobar
doub-le 'chin papada *f*
doub-le'cross *v/t* engañar, traicionar
doub-le 'glaz-ing doble acristalamiento *m*
doub-le'park *v/i* aparcar en doble fila
'**doub-le-quick** *adj*: *in double-quick time* muy rápidamente
'**doub-le room** habitación *f* doble
doub-les ['dʌblz] *in tennis* dobles *mpl*
doubt [daʊt] **1** *n* duda *f*; (*uncertainty*) dudas *fpl*; *be in doubt* ser incierto; *not be in doubt* estar claro; *no doubt* (*probably*) sin duda **2** *v/t* dudar; *we never doubted you* nunca dudamos de ti
doubt-ful ['daʊtfəl] *adj remark, look* dubitativo; *be doubtful of person* tener dudas; *it is doubtful whether ...* es dudoso que ...
doubt-ful-ly ['daʊtfəlɪ] *adv* lleno de dudas
doubt-less ['daʊtlɪs] *adj* sin duda, indudablemente
dough [doʊ] *masa f*; F (*money*) *Span* pasta *f* F, *L.Am.* plata *f* F
dough-nut ['doʊnʌt] dónut *m*
dove¹ [dʌv] *also fig* paloma *f*
dove² [doʊv] *pret* → **dive**

dow·dy ['daʊdɪ] adj poco elegante

Dow Jones Av·er·age [daʊdʒoʊnz'ævə-rɪdʒ] índice m Dow Jones

down[1] [daʊn] n (feathers) plumón m

down[2] [daʊn] **1** adv (downward) (hacia) abajo; *pull the blind down* baja la persiana; *put it down on the table* ponlo en la mesa; *when the leaves come down* cuando se caen las hojas; *cut down a tree* cortar un árbol; *she was down on her knees* estaba arrodillada; *the plane was shot down* el avión fue abatido; *down there* allá abajo; *fall down* caerse; *die down* amainar; *$200 down (as deposit)* una entrada de 200 dólares; *down south* hacia el sur; *be down of price, rate* haber bajado; *of numbers, amount* haber descendido; (not working) no funcionar; F (depressed) estar deprimido or con la depre F **2** prep: *run down the stairs* bajar las escaleras corriendo; *the lava rolled down the hill* la lava descendía por la colina; *walk down the street* andar por la calle; *down the corridor* por el pasillo **3** v/t (swallow) tragar; (destroy) derribar

'down-and-out n vagabundo(-a) m(f)

'down·cast adj (dejected) deprimido

'down·fall caída f; *of person* perdición f

'down·grade v/t degradar; *the hurricane has been downgraded to a storm* el huracán ha sido reducido a la categoría de tormenta

down·heart·ed [daʊn'hɑːrtɪd] adj abatido

down·hill adv cuesta abajo; *go downhill fig* ir cuesta abajo

'down·hill ski·ing descenso m

'down·load v/t COMPUT descargar, bajar

'down·mar·ket adj barato

'down pay·ment entrada f; *make a down payment on sth* pagar la entrada de algo

'down·play v/t quitar importancia a

'down·pour chaparrón m, aguacero m

'down·right 1 adj lie evidente; *idiot* completo **2** adv dangerous extremadamente; *stupid* completamente

'down·side (disadvantage) desventaja f, inconveniente m

'down·size 1 v/t car reducir el tamaño de; *company* reajustar la plantilla de **2** v/i of *company* reajustar la plantilla

'down·stairs 1 adj del piso de abajo; *my downstairs neighbors* los vecinos de abajo **2** adv: *the kitchen is downstairs* la cocina está en el piso de abajo; *I ran downstairs* bajé corriendo

down-to-'earth adj approach, person práctico, realista

'down·town 1 n centro m **2** adj del centro **2** adv: *I'm going downtown* voy al centro; *he lives downtown* vive en el centro

'down·turn in economy bajón m

'down·ward ['daʊnwərd] **1** adj descendente **2** adv a la baja

doze [doʊz] **1** n cabezada f, sueño m **2** v/i echar una cabezada

◆ **doze off** v/i quedarse dormido

doz·en ['dʌzn] docena f; *dozens of* F montonadas de F

drab [dræb] adj gris

draft [dræft] **1** n of air corriente f; of document borrador m; MIL reclutamiento m; (beer), *beer on draft* cerveza f de barril **2** v/t document redactar un borrador de; MIL reclutar

'draft dodg·er recluta(-a) m(f)

draft·ee [dræft'iː] recluta m/f

drafts·man ['dræftsmən] delineante m/f

draft·y ['dræftɪ] adj: *it's drafty here* hace mucha corriente aquí

drag [dræg] **1** n: *it's a drag having to ...* F es un latazo tener que ... F; *he's a drag* F es un peñazo F; *the main drag* F la calle principal; *in drag* vestido de mujer **2** v/t (pret & pp *dragged*) (pull) arrastrar; (search) dragar **3** v/i (pret & pp *dragged*) *of time* pasar despacio; *of show, movie* ser pesado; *drag s.o. into sth* (involve) meter a alguien en algo; *drag sth out of s.o.* (get information from) arrancar algo de alguien

◆ **drag away** v/t: *drag o.s. away from the TV* despegarse de la TV

◆ **drag in** v/t into conversation introducir

◆ **drag on** v/i (last long time) alargarse

◆ **drag out** v/t (prolong) alargar

◆ **drag up** v/t F (mention) sacar a relucir

drag·on ['drægn] dragón m; fig ogro m

drain [dreɪn] **1** n pipe sumidero m, desagüe m; *under street* alcantarilla f; *a drain on resources* una sangría en los recursos **2** v/t water, vegetables escurrir; *land* drenar; *glass, tank, oil* vaciar; *person* agotar **3** v/i of dishes escurrir

◆ **drain away** v/i of liquid irse

◆ **drain off** v/t water escurrir

drain·age ['dreɪnɪdʒ] (drains) desagües mpl; *of water from soil* drenaje m

'drain·pipe tubo m de desagüe

dra·ma ['drɑːmə] (art form) drama m, teatro m; (excitement) dramatismo m; (play: on TV) drama m, obra f de teatro

dra·mat·ic [drə'mætɪk] adj dramático; *scenery* espectacular

dra·mat·i·cal·ly [drə'mætɪklɪ] adv say con dramatismo, de manera dramática; *decline, rise, change etc* espectacularmente

dram·a·tist ['dræmətɪst] dramaturgo(-a) m(f)

dram·a·ti·za·tion [dræmətaɪ'zeɪʃn] (play) dramatización f

dram·a·tize ['dræmətaɪz] v/t also fig dramatizar

drank [dræŋk] pret → **drink**

drape [dreɪp] v/t cloth cubrir; **draped in** (covered with) cubierto con

drap·er·y ['dreɪpərɪ] ropajes mpl

drapes [dreɪps] npl cortinas fpl

dras·tic ['dræstɪk] adj drástico

draught Br → **draft**

draw [drɔː] 1 n in match, competition empate m; in lottery sorteo m; (attraction) atracción f 2 v/t (pret **drew**, pp **drawn**) picture, map dibujar; cart tirar de; curtain correr; in lottery sortear; gun, knife sacar; (attract) atraer; (lead) llevar; from bank account sacar, retirar 3 v/i (pret **drew**, pp **drawn**) dibujar; in match, competition empatar; **draw near** acercarse

◆ **draw back 1** v/i (recoil) echarse atrás 2 v/t (pull back) retirar

◆ **draw on 1** v/i (approach) aproximarse 2 v/t (make use of) utilizar

◆ **draw out** v/t wallet, money from bank sacar

◆ **draw up 1** v/t document redactar; chair acercar 2 v/i of vehicle detenerse

'**draw·back** desventaja f, inconveniente m

draw·er¹ [drɔːr] of desk etc cajón m

draw·er² [drɔːr]: **she's a good drawer** dibuja muy bien

draw·ing [drɔːɪŋ] dibujo m

'**draw·ing board** tablero m de dibujo; **go back to the drawing board** fig volver a empezar otra vez

'**draw·ing pin** Br chincheta f

drawl [drɔːl] n acento m arrastrado

drawn [drɔːn] pp → **draw**

dread [dred] v/t tener pavor a; **I dread him ever finding out** me da pavor pensar que lo pueda llegar a descubrir; **I dread going to the dentist** me da pánico ir al dentista

dread·ful ['dredfəl] adj horrible, espantoso; **it's a dreadful pity you won't be there** es una auténtica pena que no vayas a estar ahí

dread·ful·ly ['dredfəlɪ] adv F (extremely) terriblemente, espantosamente F; behave fatal

dream [driːm] 1 n sueño m 2 adj: **win your dream house!** ¡gane la casa de sus sueños! 3 v/t soñar; (daydream) soñar (despierto) 4 v/i soñar; (daydream) soñar (despierto); **I dreamt about you last night** anoche soñé contigo

◆ **dream up** v/t inventar

dream·er ['driːmər] (daydreamer) soñador(a) m(f)

dream·y ['driːmɪ] adj voice, look soñador

drear·y ['drɪrɪ] adj triste, deprimente

dredge [dredʒ] v/t harbor, canal dragar

◆ **dredge up** v/t fig sacar a relucir

dregs [dregz] npl of coffee posos mpl; **the dregs of society** la escoria de la sociedad

drench [drentʃ] v/t empapar; **get drenched** empaparse

dress [dres] 1 n for woman vestido m; (clothing) traje m; **he has no dress sense** no sabe vestir(se); **the company has a dress code** la compañía tiene unas normas sobre la ropa que deben llevar los empleados 2 v/t person vestir; wound vendar; **get dressed** vestirse 3 v/i (get dressed) vestirse; well, in black etc vestir(se) (**in** de)

◆ **dress up** v/i arreglarse, vestirse elegante; (wear a disguise) disfrazarse (**as** de)

'**dress cir·cle** piso m principal

dress·er ['dresər] (dressing table) tocador f; in kitchen aparador m

dress·ing ['dresɪŋ] for salad aliño m, Span arreglo m; for wound vendaje m

dress·ing 'down regaño m; **give s.o. a dressing down** regañar a alguien

'**dress·ing room** in theater camerino m

'**dress·ing ta·ble** tocador f

'**dress·mak·er** modisto(-a) m(f)

'**dress re·hears·al** ensayo m general

dress·y ['dresɪ] adj F elegante

drew [druː] pret → **draw**

drib·ble ['drɪbl] v/i of person, baby babear; of water gotear; sp driblar

dried [draɪd] adj fruit etc seco

dri·er [draɪr] → **dryer**

drift [drɪft] 1 n of snow ventisquero m 2 v/i of snow amontonarse; of ship ir a la deriva; (go off course) desviarse del rumbo; of person vagar

◆ **drift apart** v/i of couple distanciarse

drift·er ['drɪftər] vagabundo(-a) m(f)

drill [drɪl] 1 n tool taladro m; exercise simulacro m; MIL instrucción f 2 v/t hole taladrar, perforar 3 v/i for oil hacer perforaciones; MIL entrenarse

'**dril·ling rig** ['drɪlɪŋrɪg] (platform) plataforma f petrolífera

dri·ly ['draɪlɪ] adv remark secamente, lacónicamente

drink [drɪŋk] 1 n bebida f; **a drink of ...** vaso de ...; **go for a drink** ir a tomar algo 2 v/t (pret **drank**, pp **drunk**) beber 3 v/i (pret **drank**, pp **drunk**) beber, L.Am.

tomar; *I don't drink* no bebo

◆ **drink up 1** *v/i* (*finish drink*) acabarse la bebida **2** *v/t* (*drink completely*) beberse todo

drink·a·ble ['drɪŋkəbl] *adj* potable

drink 'driv·ing conducción *f* bajo los efectos del alcohol

drink·er ['drɪŋkər] bebedor(a) *m(f)*

drink·ing ['drɪŋkɪŋ]: *I'm worried about his drinking* me preocupa que beba tanto; *a drinking problem* un problema con la bebida

'drink·ing wa·ter agua *f* potable

'drinks ma·chine máquina *f* expendedora de bebidas

drip [drɪp] **1** *n* gota *f*; MED gotero *m*, suero *m* **2** *v/i* (*pret & pp* **dripped**) gotear

'drip-dry *adj* que no necesita planchado

drip·ping ['drɪpɪŋ] *adv.* **dripping wet** empapado

drive [draɪv] **1** *n outing* vuelta *f*, paseo *m* (en coche); (*energy*) energía *f*; COMPUT unidad *f*; (*campaign*) campaña *f*; *it's a short drive from the station* está a poca distancia en coche de la estación; *with left/right-hand drive* MOT con el volante a la izquierda/a la derecha **2** *v/t* (*pret* **drove**, *pp* **driven**) *vehicle* conducir, *L.Am.* manejar, (*own*) tener; (*take in car*) llevar (en coche); TECH impulsar; *that noise/he is driving me mad* ese ruido/él me está volviendo loco **3** *v/i* (*pret* **drove**, *pp* **driven**) conducir, *L.Am.* manejar; *don't drink and drive* si bebes, no conduzcas; *I drive to work* voy al trabajo en coche

◆ **drive at** *v/t*: *what are you driving at?* ¿qué insinuas?

◆ **drive away 1** *v/t* llevarse en un coche; (*chase off*) ahuyentar **2** *v/i* marcharse

◆ **drive in** *v/t* nail remachar

◆ **drive off** → **drive away**

'drive-in *n* (*movie theater*) autocine *m*

driv·el ['drɪvl] *n* tonterías *fpl*

driv·en ['drɪvn] *pp* → **drive**

driv·er ['draɪvər] conductor(a) *m(f)*; *Br of train* maquinista *m/f*; COMPUT controlador *m*

'driv·er's li·cense carné *m* de conducir

drive-thru ['draɪvθru:] *restaurante/banco etc* en el que se atiende al cliente sin que salga del coche

'drive·way camino *m* de entrada

driv·ing ['draɪvɪŋ] **1** *n* conducción *f*; *his driving is appalling* conduce *or L.Am.* maneja fatal **2** *adj rain* torrencial

'driv·ing in·struct·or profesor(a) *m(f)* de autoescuela

'driv·ing les·son clase *f* de conducir

'driv·ing li·cence *Br* carné *m* de conducir

'driv·ing school autoescuela *f*

'driv·ing test examen *m* de conducir *or L.Am.* manejar

driz·zle ['drɪzl] **1** *n* llovizna *f* **2** *v/i* lloviznar

drone [droʊn] *n noise* zumbido *m*

droop [dru:p] *v/i of plant* marchitarse; *her shoulders drooped* se encorvó

drop [drɑːp] **1** *n* gota *f*; *in price, temperature* caída *f*; *could I have a drop more milk, please?* ¿me podría poner un poquitín más de leche, por favor? **2** *v/t* (*pret & pp* **dropped**) *object* dejar caer; *person from car* dejar; *person from team* excluir; (*stop seeing*) abandonar; *charges, demand etc* retirar; (*give up*) dejar; *drop a line* to mandar unas líneas a **3** *v/i* (*pret & pp* **dropped**) caer, caerse; (*decline*) caer; *of wind* amainar

◆ **drop in** *v/i* (*visit*) pasar a visitar

◆ **drop off 1** *v/t person* dejar; (*deliver*) llevar **2** *v/i* (*fall asleep*) dormirse; (*decline*) disminuir

◆ **drop out** *v/i* (*withdraw*) retirarse; *drop out of school* abandonar el colegio

'drop-out (*from school*) alumno que ha abandonado los estudios; *from society* marginado(-a) *m(f)*

drops [drɑːps] *npl for eyes* gotas *fpl*

drought [draʊt] sequía *f*

drove [droʊv] *pret* → **drive**

drown [draʊn] **1** *v/i* ahogarse **2** *v/t person, sound* ahogar; *be drowned* ahogarse

drow·sy ['draʊzɪ] *adj* soñoliento(-a)

drudg·e·ry ['drʌdʒərɪ]: *the job is sheer drudgery* el trabajo es terriblemente pesado

drug [drʌg] **1** *n* MED, *illegal* droga *f*; *be on drugs* drogarse **2** *v/t* (*pret & pp* **drugged**) drogar

'drug ad·dict drogadicto(-a) *m(f)*

'drug deal·er traficante *m/f* de (drogas)

drug·gist ['drʌgɪst] farmacéutico(-a) *m(f)*

'drug·store *tienda en la que se venden medicinas, cosméticos, periódicos y que a veces tiene un bar*

'drug traf·fick·ing tráfico *m* de drogas

drum [drʌm] *n* MUS tambor *m*; *container* barril *m*

◆ **drum into** *v/t* (*pret & pp* **drummed**): *drum sth into s.o.* meter algo en la cabeza de alguien

◆ **drum up** *v/t*: *drum up support* buscar apoyos

drum·mer ['drʌmər] tambor *m*, tamborilero(-a) *m(f)*

'drum·stick MUS baqueta *f*; *of poultry*

muslo *m*

drunk [drʌŋk] **1** *n* borracho(-a) *m(f)* **2** *adj* borracho; **get drunk** emborracharse **3** *pp* → **drink**

drunk·en [drʌŋkn] *voices, laughter* borracho; *party* con mucho alcohol

dry [draɪ] **1** *adj* seco; *where alcohol is banned* donde está prohibido el consumo de alcohol **2** *v/t & v/i* (*pret & pp* **dried**) secar

◆ **dry out** *v/i* secarse; *of alcoholic* desintoxicarse

◆ **dry up** *v/i of river* secarse; F (*be quiet*) cerrar el pico F

'**dry-clean** *v/t* limpiar en seco

'**dry clean·er** tintorería *f*

'**dry-clean·ing** (*clothes*): **would you pick up my drycleaning for me?** ¿te importaría recogerme la ropa de la tintorería?

dry·er [draɪr] *machine* secadora *f*

DTP [diːtiːpiː] *abbr* (= *desk-top publishing*) autoedición *f*

du·al [duːəl] *adj* doble

dub [dʌb] *v/t* (*pret & pp* **dubbed**) *movie* doblar

du·bi·ous [duːbɪəs] *adj* dudoso; (*having doubts*) inseguro; **I'm still dubious about the idea** todavía tengo mis dudas sobre la idea

duch·ess [dʌtʃɪs] duquesa *f*

duck [dʌk] **1** *n* pato *m*, pata *f* **2** *v/i* agacharse **3** *v/t one's head* agachar; *question* eludir

dud [dʌd] *n* F (*false bill*) billete *m* falso

due [duː] *adj* (*proper*) debido; **the money due me** el dinero que se me debe; **payment is now due** el pago se debe hacer efectivo ahora; **is there a train due soon?** ¿va a pasar un tren pronto?; **when is the baby due?** ¿cuando está previsto que nazca el bebé?; **he's due to meet him next month** tiene previsto reunirse con él el próximo mes; **due to** (*because of*) debido a; **be due to** (*be caused by*) ser debido a; **in due course** en su debido momento

dues [duːz] *npl* cuota *f*

du·et [duːet] MUS dúo *m*

dug [dʌg] *pret & pp* → **dig**

duke [duːk] duque *m*

dull [dʌl] *adj weather* gris; *sound, pain* sordo; (*boring*) aburrido, soso

du·ly [duːlɪ] *adv* (*as expected*) tal y como se esperaba; (*properly*) debidamente

dumb [dʌm] *adj* (*mute*) mudo; F (*stupid*) estúpido; **a pretty dumb thing to do** una tontería

dumb·found·ed [dʌmfaʊndɪd] *adj* boquiabierto

dum·my [dʌmɪ] *for clothes* maniquí *m*

dump [dʌmp] **1** *n* *for garbage* vertedero *m*, basurero *m*; (*unpleasant place*) lugar *m* de mala muerte **2** *v/t* (*deposit*) dejar; (*dispose of*) deshacerse de; *toxic waste, nuclear waste* verter

dump·ling [dʌmplɪŋ] *bola de masa dulce o salada*

dune [duːn] duna *f*

dung [dʌŋ] estiércol *m*

dun·ga·rees [dʌŋgəriːz] *npl* pantalones *mpl* de trabajo

dunk [dʌŋk] *v/t in coffee etc* mojar

du·o [duːoʊ] MUS dúo *m*

du·plex (**a·part·ment**) [duːpleks] dúplex *m*

du·pli·cate 1 *n* [duːplɪkət] duplicado *m*; **in duplicate** por duplicado **2** *v/t* [duːplɪkeɪt] (*copy*) duplicar, hacer un duplicado de; (*repeat*) repetir

du·pli·cate 'key llave *f* duplicada

du·ra·ble [duːrəbl] *adj material* duradero, durable; *relationship* duradero

du·ra·tion [duːreɪʃn] duración *f*; **for the duration of her visit** mientras dure su visita

du·ress [duːres]: **under duress** bajo coacción

dur·ing [dʊrɪŋ] *prep* durante

dusk [dʌsk] crepúsculo *m*, anochecer *m*

dust [dʌst] **1** *n* polvo *m* **2** *v/t* quitar el polvo a; **dust sth with sth** (*sprinkle*) espolvorear algo con algo

'**dust cov·er** *for book* sobrecubierta *f*

dust·er [dʌstər] (*cloth*) trapo *m* del polvo

'**dust jack·et** *of book* sobrecubierta *f*

'**dust·pan** recogedor *m*

dust·y [dʌstɪ] *adj* polvoriento

Dutch [dʌtʃ] **1** *adj* holandés; **go Dutch** F pagar a escote F **2** *n* (*language*) neerlandés *m*; **the Dutch** los holandeses

du·ty [duːtɪ] deber *m*; (*task*) obligación *f*, tarea *f*; *on goods* impuesto *m*; **be on duty** estar de servicio; **be off duty** estar fuera de servicio

du·ty-'free 1 *adj* libre de impuestos **2** *n* productos *mpl* libres de impuestos

du·ty-'free shop tienda *f* libre de impuestos

dwarf [dwɔːrf] **1** *n* enano *m* **2** *v/t* empequeñecer

◆ **dwell on** [dwel] *v/t*: **dwell on the past** pensar en el pasado; **don't dwell on what he said** no des demasiada importancia a lo que ha dicho

dwin·dle [dwɪndl] *v/i* disminuir, menguar

dye [daɪ] **1** *n* tinte *m* **2** *v/t* teñir

dy·ing [daɪɪŋ] *adj person* moribundo; *industry, tradition* en vías de desaparición

dy·nam·ic [daɪnæmɪk] *adj person* dinámico

dy·na·mism ['daɪnəmɪzm] dinamismo *m*
dy·na·mite ['daɪnəmaɪt] *n* dinamita *f*
dy·na·mo ['daɪnəmoʊ] TECH dinamo *f*, dínamo *f*

dy·nas·ty ['daɪnəstɪ] dinastía *f*
dys·lex·i·a [dɪs'leksɪə] dislexia *f*
dys·lex·ic [dɪs'leksɪk] **1** *adj* disléxico **2** *n* disléxico(-a) *m(f)*

E

each [iːtʃ] **1** *adj* cada **2** *adv*: *he gave us one each* nos dio uno a cada uno; *they're $1.50 each* valen 1.50 dólares cada uno **3** *pron* cada uno; *each other* el uno al otro; *we love each other* nos queremos

ea·ger ['iːgər] *adj* ansioso; *she's always eager to help* siempre está deseando ayudar

ea·ger·ly ['iːgərlɪ] *adv* ansiosamente

ea·ger·ness ['iːgərnɪs] entusiasmo *m*

ea·gle ['iːgl] águila *f*

ea·gle-eyed [iːgl'aɪd] *adj* con vista de lince

ear[1] [ɪr] *of person, animal* oreja *f*; *sense* oído *m*

ear[2] [ɪr] *of corn* espiga *f*

'ear·ache dolor *m* de oídos

'ear·drum tímpano *m*

'ear·lobe lóbulo *m*

ear·ly ['ɜːrlɪ] **1** *adj (not late)* temprano; *(ahead of time)* anticipado; *(farther back in time)* primero; *(in the near future)* pronto; *music* antiguo; *let's have an early supper* cenemos temprano; *in early October* a principios de octubre; *in the early hours of the morning* a primeras horas de la madrugada; *an early Picasso* un Picasso de su primera época; *I'm an early riser* soy madrugador **2** *adv (not late)* pronto, temprano; *(ahead of time)* antes de tiempo; *it's too early to say* es demasiado pronto como para poder decir nada; *earlier than* antes que

'ear·ly bird madrugador(a) *m(f)*

ear·mark ['ɪrmɑːrk] *v/t* destinar; *earmark sth for sth* destinar algo a algo

earn [ɜːrn] *v/t salary* ganar; *interest* devengar; *holiday, drink etc* ganarse; *earn one's living* ganarse la vida

ear·nest ['ɜːrnɪst] *adj* serio; *in earnest* en serio

earn·ings ['ɜːrnɪŋz] *npl* ganancias *fpl*

'ear·phones *npl* auriculares *fpl*

'ear-pierc·ing *adj* estrepitoso

'ear·ring pendiente *m*

'ear·shot: *within earshot* al alcance del oído; *out of earshot* fuera del alcance del oído

earth [ɜːrθ] *(soil)* tierra *f*; *(world, planet)* Tierra *f*; *where on earth ...?* F ¿dónde diablos ...? F

earth·en·ware ['ɜːrθnwer] *n* loza *mpl*

earth·ly ['ɜːrθlɪ] *adj* terrenal; *it's no earthly use* F no sirve para nada

earth·quake ['ɜːrθkweɪk] terremoto *m*

earth-shat·ter·ing ['ɜːrθʃætərɪŋ] *adj* extraordinario

ease [iːz] **1** *n* facilidad *f*; *be at (one's) ease, feel at ease* sentirse cómodo; *feel ill at ease* sentirse incómodo **2** *v/t (relieve)* aliviar **3** *v/i of pain* disminuir
◆ **ease off 1** *v/t (remove)* quitar con cuidado **2** *v/i of pain* disminuir; *of rain* amainar

ea·sel ['iːzl] caballete *m*

eas·i·ly ['iːzəlɪ] *adv (with ease)* fácilmente; *(by far)* con diferencia

east [iːst] **1** *n* este *m* **2** *adj* oriental, este; *wind* del este **3** *adv travel* hacia el este

Eas·ter ['iːstər] Pascua *f*; *period* Semana *f* Santa

Eas·ter 'Day Domingo *m* de Resurrección

'Eas·ter egg huevo *m* de pascua

eas·ter·ly ['iːstərlɪ] *adj* del este

Eas·ter 'Mon·day Lunes *m* Santo

Eas·ter 'Sun·day Domingo *m* de Resurrección

east·ern ['iːstərn] *adj* del este; *(oriental)* oriental

east·ern·er ['iːstərnər] *habitante de la costa oeste estadounidense*

east·ward ['iːstwərd] *adv* hacia el este

eas·y ['iːzɪ] *adj* fácil; *(relaxed)* tranquilo; *take things easy (slow down)* tomarse las cosas con tranquilidad; *take it easy!*

(calm down) ¡tranquilízate!

'eas·y chair sillón *m*

eas·y-go·ing ['i:zɪgouɪŋ] *adj* tratable

eat [i:t] *v/t & v/i (pret **ate**, pp **eaten**)* comer

◆ **eat out** *v/i* comer fuera

◆ **eat up** *v/t* comerse; *fig: use up* acabar con

eat·a·ble ['i:təbl] *adj* comestible

eat·en ['i:tn] *pp* → **eat**

eau de Co·logne [oudəkə'loun] agua *f* de colonia

eaves [i:vz] *npl* alero *m*

eaves·drop ['i:vzdrɑ:p] *v/i (pret & pp **eavesdropped**)* escuchar a escondidas *(on s.o.* alguien)

ebb [eb] *v/i of tide* bajar

◆ **ebb away** *v/i fig of courage, strength* desvanecerse

ec·cen·tric [ɪk'sentrɪk] **1** *adj* excéntrico **2** *n* excéntrico(-a) *m(f)*

ec·cen·tric·i·ty [ɪksen'trɪsɪtɪ] excentricidad *f*

ech·o ['ekou] **1** *n* eco *m* **2** *v/i* resonar **3** *v/t words* repetir; *views* mostrar acuerdo con

e·clipse [ɪ'klɪps] **1** *n* eclipse *m* **2** *v/t fig* eclipsar

e·co·lo·gi·cal [i:kə'lɑ:dʒɪkl] *adj* ecológico

e·co·lo·gi·cal·ly [i:kə'lɑ:dʒɪklɪ] *adv* ecológicamente

e·co·lo·gi·cal·ly 'friend·ly *adj* ecológico

e·col·o·gist [i:'kɑ:lədʒɪst] ecologista *m/f*

e·col·o·gy [i:'kɑ:lədʒɪ] ecología *f*

ec·o·nom·ic [i:kə'nɑ:mɪk] *adj* económico

ec·o·nom·i·cal [i:kə'nɑ:mɪkl] *adj (cheap)* económico; *(thrifty)* cuidadoso

ec·o·nom·i·cal·ly [i:kə'nɑ:mɪklɪ] *adv (in terms of economics)* económicamente; *(thriftily)* de manera económica

ec·o·nom·ics [i:kə'nɑ:mɪks] *nsg (science)* economía *f*; *(npl: financial aspects)* aspecto *m* económico

e·con·o·mist [ɪ'kɑ:nəmɪst] economista *m/f*

e·con·o·mize [ɪ'kɑ:nəmaɪz] *v/i* economizar, ahorrar

◆ **economize on** *v/t* economizar, ahorrar

e·con·o·my [ɪ'kɑ:nəmɪ] *of a country* economía *f*; *(saving)* ahorro *m*

e'con·o·my class clase *f* turista

e'con·o·my drive intento *m* de ahorrar

e'con·o·my size tamaño *m* económico

e·co·sys·tem ['i:kousɪstm] ecosistema *m*

e·co·tour·ism ['i:koutʊrɪzm] ecoturismo *m*

ec·sta·sy ['ekstəsɪ] éxtasis *m*

ec·sta·tic [ɪk'stætɪk] *adj* muy emocionado, extasiado

Ec·ua·dor ['ekwədɔ:r] *n* Ecuador

Ec·ua·dore·an [ekwə'dɔ:rən] **1** *adj* ecuatoriano **2** *n* ecuatoriano(-a) *m(f)*

ec·ze·ma ['eksmə] eczema *f*

edge [edʒ] **1** *n of knife* filo *m*; *of table, seat, road, cliff* borde *m*; *in voice* irritación *f*; **on edge** tenso **2** *v/t* ribetear **3** *v/i (move slowly)* acercarse despacio

edge·wise ['edʒwaɪz] *adv* de lado; **I couldn't get a word in edgewise** no me dejó decir una palabra

edg·y ['edʒɪ] *adj* tenso

ed·i·ble ['edɪbl] *adj* comestible

ed·it ['edɪt] *v/t text* corregir; *book* editar; *newspaper* dirigir; *TV program, movie* montar

e·di·tion [ɪ'dɪʃn] edición *f*

ed·i·tor ['edɪtər] *of text, book* editor(a) *m(f)*; *of newspaper* director(a) *m(f)*; *of TV program, movie* montador(a) *m(f)*; **sports / political editor** redactor(a) *m(f)* de deportes / política

ed·i·to·ri·al [edɪ'tɔ:rɪəl] **1** *adj* editorial **2** *n in newspaper* editorial *m*

EDP [i:di:'pi:] *abbr (= **electronic data processing**)* procesamiento *m* electrónico de datos

ed·u·cate ['edʒəkeɪt] *v/t child* educar; *consumers* concienciar

ed·u·cat·ed ['edʒəkeɪtɪd] *adj person* culto

ed·u·ca·tion [edʒə'keɪʃn] educación *f*; **the education system** el sistema educativo

ed·u·ca·tion·al [edʒə'keɪʃnl] *adj* educativo; *(informative)* instructivo

eel [i:l] anguila *f*

ee·rie ['ɪrɪ] *adj* escalofriante

ef·fect [ɪ'fekt] efecto *m*; **take effect** *of medicine, drug* hacer efecto; **come into effect** *of law* entrar en vigor

ef·fec·tive [ɪ'fektɪv] *adj (efficient)* efectivo; *(striking)* impresionante; **effective May 1** a partir del 1 de mayo

ef·fem·i·nate [ɪ'femɪnət] *adj* afeminado

ef·fer·ves·cent [efər'vesnt] *adj* efervescente; *personality* chispeante

ef·fi·cien·cy [ɪ'fɪʃənsɪ] *of person* eficiencia *f*; *of machine* rendimiento *f*; *of system* eficacia *f*

ef·fi·cient [ɪ'fɪʃənt] *adj person* eficiente; *machine* de buen rendimiento; *method* eficaz

ef·fi·cient·ly [ɪ'fɪʃəntlɪ] *adv* eficientemente

ef·flu·ent ['efluənt] aguas *fpl* residuales

ef·fort ['efərt] *(struggle, attempt)* esfuerzo *m*; **make an effort to do sth** hacer un esfuerzo por hacer algo

ef·fort·less ['efərtləs] *adj* fácil

ef·fron·te·ry [ɪ'frʌntərɪ] desvergüenza *f*

ef·fu·sive [ɪ'fjuːsɪv] adj efusivo

e.g. [iː'dʒiː] p. ej.

e·gal·i·tar·i·an [ɪgælɪ'terɪən] adj igualitario

egg [eg] huevo m; of woman óvulo m

♦ egg on v/t incitar

'egg·cup huevera f

'egg·head F cerebrito(-a) m(f) F

'egg·plant berenjena f

'egg·shell cáscara f de huevo

'egg tim·er reloj m de arena

e·go ['iːgou] PSYCH ego m; (self-esteem) amor m propio

e·go·cen·tric [iːgou'sentrɪk] adj egocéntrico

e·go·ism ['iːgouɪzm] egoismo m

e·go·ist ['iːgouɪst] egoísta m/f

E·gypt ['iːdʒɪpt] Egipto

E·gyp·tian [ɪ'dʒɪpʃn] 1 adj egipcio 2 n egipcio(-a) m(f)

ei·der·down ['aɪdərdaun] quilt edredón m

eight [eɪt] ocho

eigh·teen [eɪ'tiːn] dieciocho

eigh·teenth [eɪ'tiːnθ] n & adj decimoctavo

eighth [eɪtθ] n & adj octavo

eigh·ti·eth ['eɪtɪθ] n & adj octogésimo

eigh·ty ['eɪtɪ] ochenta

ei·ther ['aɪðər] 1 adj cualquiera de los dos; with negative constructions ninguno de los dos; (both) cada, ambos; he wouldn't accept either of the proposals no quería aceptar ninguna de las dos propuestas 2 pron cualquiera de los dos; with negative constructions ninguno de los dos 3 adv tampoco; I won't go either yo tampoco iré 4 conj: either ... or choice o ... o; with negative constructions ni ... ni

e·ject [ɪ'dʒekt] 1 v/t expulsar 2 v/i from plane eyectarse

♦ eke out [iːk] v/t (make last) hacer durar

el [el] → elevated railroad

e·lab·o·rate 1 adj [ɪ'læbərət] elaborado 2 v/t [ɪ'læbəreɪt] elaborar 3 v/i [ɪ'læbəreɪt] dar detalles

e·lab·o·rate·ly [ɪ'læbərətlɪ] adv elaboradamente

e·lapse [ɪ'læps] v/i pasar

e·las·tic [ɪ'læstɪk] 1 adj elástico 2 n elástico m

e·las·ti·cat·ed [ɪ'læstɪkeɪtɪd] adj elástico

e·las·tic·i·ty [ɪæs'tɪsətɪ] elasticidad f

e·las·ti·cized [ɪ'læstɪsaɪzd] adj elástico

e·lat·ed [ɪ'leɪtɪd] adj eufórico

e·la·tion [ɪ'leɪʃn] euforia f

el·bow ['elbou] 1 n codo m 2 v/t dar un codazo a; elbow out of the way apartar a codazos

el·der ['eldər] 1 adj mayor 2 n mayor m/f;

she's two years my elder es dos años mayor que yo

el·der·ly ['eldərlɪ] 1 adj mayor 2 n: the elderly las personas mayores

el·dest ['eldəst] 1 adj mayor 2 n mayor m/f; the eldest el mayor

e·lect [ɪ'lekt] v/t elegir; elect to do sth decidir hacer algo

e·lect·ed [ɪ'lektɪd] adj elegido

e·lec·tion [ɪ'lekʃn] elección f; call an election convocar elecciones

e'lec·tion cam·paign campaña f electoral

e'lec·tion day día m de las elecciones

e·lec·tive [ɪ'lektɪv] adj opcional; subject optativo

e·lec·tor [ɪ'lektər] elector(a) m(f), votante m/f

e·lec·to·ral sys·tem [ɪ'lektərəl] sistema m electoral

e·lec·to·rate [ɪ'lektərət] electorado m

e·lec·tric [ɪ'lektrɪk] adj eléctrico; fig atmosphere electrizado

e·lec·tri·cal [ɪ'lektrɪkl] adj eléctrico

e·lec·tri·cal en·gi·neer ingeniero(-a) m(f) electrónico

e·lec·tri·cal en·gi·neer·ing ingeniería f electrónica

e·lec·tric 'blan·ket manta f or L.Am. cobija f eléctrica

e·lec·tric 'chair silla f eléctrica

e·lec·tri·cian [ɪlek'trɪʃn] electricista m/f

e·lec·tri·ci·ty [ɪlek'trɪsətɪ] electricidad f

e·lec·tric 'ra·zor maquinilla f eléctrica

e·lec·tric 'shock descarga f eléctrica

e·lec·tri·fy [ɪ'lektrɪfaɪ] v/t (pret & pp electrified) electrificar; fig electrizar

e·lec·tro·cute [ɪ'lektrəkjuːt] v/t electrocutar

e·lec·trode [ɪ'lektroud] electrodo m

e·lec·tron [ɪ'lektrɑːn] electrón m

e·lec·tron·ic [ɪlek'trɑːnɪk] adj electrónico

e·lec·tron·ic da·ta 'pro·ces·sing procesamiento m electrónico de datos

e·lec·tron·ic 'mail correo m electrónico

e·lec·tron·ics [ɪlek'trɑːnɪks] electrónica f

el·e·gance ['elɪgəns] elegancia f

el·e·gant ['elɪgənt] adj elegante

el·e·gant·ly ['elɪgəntlɪ] adv elegantemente

el·e·ment ['elɪmənt] also CHEM elemento m

el·e·men·ta·ry [elɪ'mentərɪ] adj (rudimentary) elemental

el·e·men·ta·ry school escuela f primaria

el·e·men·ta·ry teach·er maestro(-a) m(f)

el·e·phant ['elɪfənt] elefante m

el·e·vate ['elɪveɪt] v/t elevar

el·e·vat·ed 'rail·road ['elɪveɪtɪd] ferrocarril m elevado

el·e·va·tion [elɪ'veɪʃn] (*altitude*) altura *f*

el·e·va·tor ['elɪveɪtər] ascensor *m*

el·e·ven [ɪ'levn] once

el·e·venth [ɪ'levnθ] *n* & *adj* undécimo; *at the eleventh hour* justo en el último minuto

el·i·gi·ble ['elɪdʒəbl] *adj* que reúne los requisitos; *eligible to vote* con derecho al voto; *be eligible to do sth* tener derecho a hacer algo

el·i·gi·ble 'bach·e·lor buen partido *m*

e·lim·i·nate [ɪ'lɪmɪneɪt] *v/t* eliminar; *poverty* acabar con; (*rule out*) descartar

e·lim·i·na·tion [ɪ'lɪmɪneɪʃn] eliminación *f*

e·lite [eɪ'liːt] **1** *n* élite *f* **2** *adj* de élite

elk [elk] ciervo *m* canadiense

e·lipse [ɪ'lɪps] elipse *f*

elm [elm] olmo *m*

e·lope [ɪ'loʊp] *v/i* fugarse con un amante

el·o·quence ['eləkwəns] elocuencia *f*

el·o·quent ['eləkwənt] *adj* elocuente

el·o·quent·ly ['eləkwəntlɪ] *adv* elocuentemente

El Sal·va·dor [el'sælvədɔːr] *n* El Salvador

else [els] *adv*: *anything else?* ¿algo más?; *if you've got nothing else to do* si no tienes nada más que hacer; *no one else* nadie más; *everyone else is going* todos (los demás) van, va todo el mundo; *who else was there?* ¿quién más estaba allí?; *someone else* otra persona; *something else* algo más; *let's go somewhere else* vamos a otro sitio; *or else* si no

else·where ['elswer] *adv* en otro sitio

e·lude [ɪ'luːd] *v/t* (*escape from*) escapar de; (*avoid*) evitar; *the name eludes me* no recuerdo el nombre

e·lu·sive [ɪ'luːsɪv] *adj* evasivo

e·ma·ci·at·ed [ɪ'meɪsɪeɪtɪd] *adj* demacrado

e-mail ['iːmeɪl] **1** *n* correo *m* electrónico **2** *v/t person* mandar un correo electrónico a

'e-mail ad·dress dirección *f* de correo electrónico, dirección *f* electrónica

e·man·ci·pat·ed [ɪ'mænsɪpeɪtɪd] *adj* emancipado

e·man·ci·pa·tion [ɪmænsɪ'peɪʃn] emancipación *f*

em·balm [ɪm'baːm] *v/t* embalsamar

em·bank·ment [ɪm'bæŋkmənt] *of river* dique *m*; RAIL terraplén *m*

em·bar·go [em'baːrgoʊ] embargo *m*

em·bark [ɪm'baːrk] *v/i* embarcar

◆ embark on *v/t* embarcarse en

em·bar·rass [ɪm'bærəs] *v/t* avergonzar; *he embarrassed me in front of everyone* me hizo pasar vergüenza delante de todos

em·bar·rassed [ɪm'bærəst] *adj* avergonzado; *I was embarrassed to ask* me daba vergüenza preguntar

em·bar·rass·ing [ɪm'bærəsɪŋ] *adj* embarazoso

em·bar·rass·ment [ɪm'bærəsmənt] embarazo *m*, apuro *m*

em·bas·sy ['embəsɪ] embajada *f*

em·bel·lish [ɪm'belɪʃ] *v/t* adornar; *story* exagerar

em·bers ['embərz] *npl* ascuas *fpl*

em·bez·zle [ɪm'bezl] *v/t* malversar

em·bez·zle·ment [ɪm'bezlmənt] malversación *f*

em·bez·zler [ɪm'bezlər] malversador(a) *m(f)*

em·bit·ter [ɪm'bɪtər] *v/t* amargar

em·blem ['embləm] emblema *m*

em·bod·i·ment [ɪm'baːdɪmənt] personificación *f*

em·bod·y [ɪm'baːdɪ] *v/t* (*pret* & *pp* **embodied**) personificar

em·bo·lism ['embəlɪzm] embolia *f*

em·boss [ɪm'baːs] *v/t metal* repujar; *paper* grabar en relieve

em·brace [ɪm'breɪs] **1** *n* abrazo *m* **2** *v/t* (*hug*) abrazar; (*take in*) abarcar **3** *v/i of two people* abrazarse

em·broi·der [ɪm'brɔɪdər] *v/t* bordar; *fig* adornar

em·broi·der·y [ɪm'brɔɪdərɪ] bordado *m*

em·bry·o ['embrɪoʊ] embrión *m*

em·bry·on·ic [embrɪ'aːnɪk] *adj fig* embrionario

em·e·rald ['emərəld] esmeralda *f*

e·merge [ɪ'mɜːrdʒ] *v/i* (*appear*) emerger, salir; *of truth* aflorar; *it has emerged that* se ha descubierto que

e·mer·gen·cy [ɪ'mɜːrdʒənsɪ] emergencia *f*; *in an emergency* en caso de emergencia

emer·gen·cy 'ex·it salida *f* de emergencia

e'mer·gen·cy land·ing aterrizaje *m* forzoso

e'mer·gen·cy serv·ices *npl* servicios *mpl* de urgencia

em·er·y board ['emərɪ] lima *f* de uñas

em·i·grant ['emɪgrənt] emigrante *m/f*

em·i·grate ['emɪgreɪt] *v/i* emigrar

em·i·gra·tion [emɪ'greɪʃn] emigración *f*

Em·i·nence ['emɪnəns] REL: *His Eminence* Su Eminencia

em·i·nent ['emɪnənt] *adj* eminente

em·i·nent·ly ['emɪnəntlɪ] *adv* sumamente

e·mis·sion [ɪ'mɪʃn] *of gases* emisión *f*

e·mit [ɪ'mɪt] *v/t* (*pret* & *pp* **emitted**) emitir; *heat*, *odor* desprender

e·mo·tion [ɪ'moʊʃn] emoción *f*

e·mo·tion·al [ɪ'mouʃənl] *adj problems, development* sentimental; *(full of emotion)* emotivo

em·pa·thize ['empəθaɪz] *v/i:* **empathize with** identificarse con

em·pe·ror ['empərər] emperador *m*

em·pha·sis ['emfəsɪs] *in word* acento *m; fig* énfasis *m*

em·pha·size ['emfəsaɪz] *v/t syllable* acentuar; *fig* hacer hincapié en

em·phat·ic [ɪm'fætɪk] *adj* enfático

em·pire ['empaɪr] imperio *m*

em·ploy [em'plɔɪ] *v/t* emplear; **he's employed as a ...** trabaja de ...

em·ploy·ee [emplɔɪ'iː] empleado(-a) *m(f)*

em·ploy·er [em'plɔɪər] empresario(-a) *m(f)*

em·ploy·ment [em'plɔɪmənt] empleo *m; (work)* trabajo *m;* **be looking for employment** buscar trabajo

em·ploy·ment a·gen·cy agencia *f* de colocaciones

em·press ['emprɪs] emperatriz *f*

emp·ti·ness ['emptɪnɪs] vacío *m*

emp·ty ['emptɪ] **1** *adj* vacío; *promise* vana **2** *v/t (pret & pp* **emptied)** *drawer, pockets* vaciar; *glass, bottle* acabar **3** *v/i (pret & pp* **emptied)** *of room, street* vaciarse

em·u·late ['emjuleɪt] *v/t* emular

e·mul·sion [ɪ'mʌlʃn] *paint* emulsión *f*

en·a·ble [ɪ'neɪbl] *v/t* permitir; **enable s.o. to do sth** permitir a alguien hacer algo

en·act [ɪ'nækt] *v/t law* promulgar; THEA representar

e·nam·el [ɪ'næml] *n* esmalte *m*

enc *abbr (= enclosure(s))* documento(s) *m(pl)* adjunto(s)

en·chant [ɪn'tʃænt] *v/t (delight)* encantar

en·chant·ing [ɪn'tʃæntɪŋ] *adj* encantador

en·cir·cle [ɪn'sɜːrkl] *v/t* rodear

encl *abbr (= en·clo·sure(s))* documento(s) *m(pl)* adjunto(s)

en·close [ɪn'kloʊz] *v/t Br in letter* adjuntar; *area* rodear; **please find enclosed ...** remito adjunto ...

en·clo·sure [ɪn'kloʊʒər] *with letter* documento *m* adjunto

en·core ['ɑːŋkɔːr] bis *m*

en·coun·ter [ɪn'kaʊntər] **1** *n* encuentro *m* **2** *v/t person* encontrarse con; *problem, resistance* tropezar con

en·cour·age [ɪn'kʌrɪdʒ] *v/t* animar; *violence* fomentar

en·cour·age·ment [ɪn'kʌrɪdʒmənt] ánimo *m*

en·cour·ag·ing [ɪn'kʌrɪdʒɪŋ] *adj* alentador

◆ en·croach on [ɪn'kroʊtʃ] *v/t land* inva-

dir; *rights* usurpar; *time* quitar

en·cy·clo·pe·di·a [ɪnsaɪklə'piːdɪə] enciclopedia *f*

end [end] **1** *n of journey, month* final *m; (extremity)* extremo *m; (bottom)* fondo *m; (conclusion, purpose)* fin *m;* **at the other end of town** al otro lado de la ciudad; *in the end* al final; *for hours on end* durante horas y horas; *stand sth on end* poner de pie algo; *at the end of July* a finales de julio; *in the end* al final; *put an end to* poner fin a **2** *v/t* terminar, finalizar **3** *v/i* terminar

◆ end up *v/i* acabar

en·dan·ger [ɪn'deɪndʒər] *v/t* poner en peligro

en·dan·gered spe·cies especie *f* en peligro de extinción

en·dear·ing [ɪn'dɪrɪŋ] *adj* simpático

en·deav·or [ɪn'devər] **1** *n* esfuerzo *m* **2** *v/t* procurar

en·dem·ic [ɪn'demɪk] *adj* endémico

end·ing ['endɪŋ] final *m;* GRAM terminación *f*

end·less ['endlɪs] *adj* interminable

en·dorse [ɪn'dɔːrs] *v/t check* endosar; *candidacy* apoyar; *product* representar

en·dorse·ment [ɪn'dɔːrsmənt] *of check* endoso *m; of candidacy* apoyo *m; of product* representación *f*

end 'prod·uct producto *m* final

end re'sult resultado *m* final

en·dur·ance [ɪn'dʊrəns] resistencia *f*

en·dure [ɪn'dʊər] **1** *v/t* resistir **2** *v/i (last)* durar

en·dur·ing [ɪn'dʊrɪŋ] *adj* duradero

end-'us·er usuario(-a) *m(f)* final

en·e·my ['enəmɪ] enemigo(-a) *m(f)*

en·er·get·ic [enər'dʒetɪk] *adj* enérgico

en·er·get·ic·al·ly [enər'dʒetɪklɪ] *adv* enérgicamente

en·er·gy ['enərdʒɪ] energía *f*

'en·er·gy-sav·ing *adj device* que ahorra energía

'en·er·gy sup·ply suministro *m* de energía

en·force [ɪn'fɔːrs] *v/t* hacer cumplir

en·gage [ɪn'geɪdʒ] **1** *v/t (hire)* contratar **2** *v/i* TECH engranar

◆ engage in *v/t* dedicarse a

en·gaged [ɪn'geɪdʒd] *adj to be married* prometido; *get engaged* prometerse

en·gaged tone *Br* TELEC señal *f* de ocupado *or Span* comunicando

en·gage·ment [ɪn'geɪdʒmənt] *(appointment, to be married)* compromiso *m;* MIL combate *m*

en·gage·ment ring anillo *m* de compromiso

en·gag·ing [ɪnˈgeɪdʒɪŋ] adj smile, person atractivo

en·gine [ˈendʒɪn] motor m

en·gi·neer [endʒɪˈnɪr] 1 n ingeniero(-a) m(f); NAUT, RAIL maquinista m/f 2 v/t fig: meeting etc tramar

en·gi·neer·ing [endʒɪˈnɪrɪŋ] ingeniería f

Eng·land [ˈɪŋglənd] Inglaterra

Eng·lish [ˈɪŋglɪʃ] 1 adj inglés(-esa) 2 n language inglés m; the English los ingleses

Eng·lish ˈChan·nel Canal m de la Mancha

ˈEng·lish·man inglés m

ˈEng·lish·wom·an inglesa f

en·grave [ɪnˈgreɪv] v/t grabar

en·grav·ing [ɪnˈgreɪvɪŋ] grabado m

en·grossed [ɪnˈgroust] adj absorto (in en)

en·gulf [ɪnˈgʌlf] v/t devorar

en·hance [ɪnˈhæns] v/t realzar

e·nig·ma [ɪˈnɪgmə] enigma m

e·nig·mat·ic [enɪgˈmætɪk] adj enigmático

en·joy [ɪnˈdʒɔɪ] v/t disfrutar; enjoy o.s. divertirse; enjoy (your meal)! ¡que aproveche!

en·joy·a·ble [ɪnˈdʒɔɪəbl] adj agradable

en·joy·ment [ɪnˈdʒɔɪmənt] diversión f

en·large [ɪnˈlɑːrdʒ] v/t ampliar

en·large·ment [ɪnˈlɑːrdʒmənt] ampliación f

en·light·en [ɪnˈlaɪtn] v/t educar

en·list [ɪnˈlɪst] v/i MIL alistarse 2 v/t: I enlisted his help conseguí que me ayudara

en·liv·en [ɪnˈlaɪvn] v/t animar

en·mi·ty [ˈenmətɪ] enemistad f

e·nor·mi·ty [ɪˈnɔːrmətɪ] magnitud f

e·nor·mous [ɪˈnɔːrməs] adj enorme; satisfaction, patience inmenso

e·nor·mous·ly [ɪˈnɔːrməslɪ] adv enormemente

e·nough [ɪˈnʌf] 1 adj pron suficiente, bastante; will $50 be enough? ¿llegará con 50 dólares?; I've had enough! ¡estoy harto!; that's enough, calm down! ¡ya basta, tranquilízate! 2 adv suficientemente, bastante; the bag isn't big enough la bolsa no es lo suficientemente or bastante grande; strangely enough curiosamente

en·quire [ɪnˈkwaɪr] → inquire

en·raged [ɪnˈreɪdʒd] adj enfurecido

en·rich [ɪnˈrɪtʃ] v/t enriquecer

en·roll [ɪnˈroul] v/i matricularse

en·roll·ment [ɪnˈroulmənt] matrícula f

en·sue [ɪnˈsuː] v/i suceder se

en suite [ˈɑːnswiːt] adj: en suite bathroom baño m privado

en·sure [ɪnˈʃʊər] v/t asegurar

en·tail [ɪnˈteɪl] v/t conllevar

en·tan·gle [ɪnˈtæŋgl] v/t in rope enredar; become entangled in enredarse en; become entangled with in love affair liarse con

en·ter [ˈentər] 1 v/t room, house entrar en; competition participar en; person, horse in race inscribir; (write down) escribir; COMPUT introducir 2 v/i entrar; THEA entrar en escena; in competition inscribirse 3 n COMPUT intro m

en·ter·prise [ˈentərpraɪz] (initiative) iniciativa f; (venture) empresa f

en·ter·pris·ing [ˈentərpraɪzɪŋ] adj con iniciativa

en·ter·tain [entərˈteɪn] 1 v/t (amuse) entretener; (consider: idea) considerar 2 v/i (have guests): we entertain a lot recibimos a mucha gente

en·ter·tain·er [entərˈteɪnər] artista m/f

en·ter·tain·ing [entərˈteɪnɪŋ] adj entretenido

en·ter·tain·ment [entərˈteɪnmənt] entretenimiento m

en·thrall [ɪnˈθrɔːl] v/t cautivar

en·thu·si·asm [ɪnˈθuːzɪæzm] entusiasmo m

en·thu·si·ast [ɪnˈθuːzɪæst] entusiasta m/f

en·thu·si·as·tic [ɪnθuːzɪˈæstɪk] adj entusiasta; be enthusiastic about sth estar entusiasmado con algo

en·thu·si·as·ti·cal·ly [ɪnθuːzɪˈæstɪklɪ] adv con entusiasmo

en·tice [ɪnˈtaɪs] v/t atraer

en·tire [ɪnˈtaɪr] adj entero; the entire school is going va a ir todo el colegio

en·tire·ly [ɪnˈtaɪrlɪ] adv completamente

en·ti·tle [ɪnˈtaɪtld] v/t: entitle s.o. to sth dar derecho a alguien a algo; be entitled to tener derecho a

en·ti·tled [ɪnˈtaɪtld] adj book titulado

en·trance [ˈentrəns] entrada f; THEA entrada f en escena

en·tranced [ɪnˈtrænst] adj encantado

ˈen·trance ex·am(·i·na·tion) examen m de acceso

ˈen·trance fee (cuota f de) entrada f

en·trant [ˈentrənt] participante m/f

en·treat [ɪnˈtriːt] v/t suplicar; entreat s.o. to do sth suplicar a alguien que haga algo

en·trenched [ɪnˈtrentʃt] adj attitudes arraigado

en·tre·pre·neur [ɑːntrəprəˈnɜːr] empresario(-a) m(f)

en·tre·pre·neur·i·al [ɑːntrəprəˈnɜːrɪəl] adj empresarial

en·trust [ɪnˈtrʌst] v/t confiar; entrust s.o.

with sth, entrust sth to s.o. confiar algo a alguien

en·try ['entrı] entrada *f; for competition* inscripción *f; in diary etc* entrada *f; no entry* prohibida la entrada; *the winning entry was painted by ...* el cuadro ganador fue pintado por ...

'en·try form impreso *m* de inscripción

'en·try·phone portero *m* automático

'en·try vi·sa visado *m*

e·nu·me·rate ['ɪnuːməreɪt] *v/t* enumerar

en·vel·op [ɪn'veləp] *v/t* cubrir

en·ve·lope ['envələʊp] sobre *m*

en·vi·a·ble ['envɪəbl] *adj* envidiable

en·vi·ous ['envɪəs] *adj* envidioso; *be envious of s.o.* tener envidia de alguien

en·vi·ron·ment [ɪn'vaɪrənmənt] *(nature)* medio *m* ambiente; *(surroundings)* entorno *m*, ambiente *m*

en·vi·ron·men·tal [ɪnvaɪrən'mentl] *adj* medioambiental

en·vi·ron·men·tal·ist [ɪnvaɪrən'mmentəlist] ecologista *m/f*

en·vi·ron·men·tal·ly 'friend·ly [ɪnvaɪrən'məntəlɪ] *adj* ecológico, que no daña el medio ambiente

en·vi·ron·men·tal pol'lu·tion contaminación *f* medioambiental

en·vi·ron·men·tal pro'tec·tion protección *f* medioambiental

en·vi·rons [ɪn'vaɪrənz] *npl* alrededores *mpl*

en·vis·age [ɪn'vɪzɪdʒ] *v/t* imaginar

en·voy ['envɔɪ] enviado(-a) *m(f)*

en·vy ['envɪ] **1** *n* envidia *f; be the envy of* ser la envidia de **2** *v/t (pret & pp envied)* envidiar; *envy s.o. sth* envidiar a alguien algo

e·phem·er·al [ɪ'femərəl] *adj* efímero

ep·ic ['epɪk] **1** *n* epopeya *f* **2** *adj journey* épico; *a task of epic proportions* una tarea monumental

ep·i·cen·ter ['epɪsentr] epicentro *m*

ep·i·dem·ic [epɪ'demɪk] epidemia *f*

ep·i·lep·sy ['epɪlepsɪ] epilepsia *f*

ep·i·lep·tic [epɪ'leptɪk] epiléptico(-a) *m(f)*

ep·i·lep·tic 'fit ataque *m* epiléptico

ep·i·log, *Br* **ep·i·logue** ['epɪlɑːg] epílogo *m*

ep·i·sode ['epɪsoʊd] *of story, soap opera* episodio *m*, capítulo *m; (happening)* episodio *m; let's forget the whole episode* olvidemos lo sucedido

ep·i·taph ['epɪtæf] epitafio *m*

e·poch ['iːpɑːk] época *f*

e·poch-mak·ing ['iːpɑːkmeɪkɪŋ] *adj* que hace época

e·qual [iːkwl] **1** *adj* igual; *equal amounts*

of milk and water la misma cantidad de leche y de agua; *equal opportunities* igualdad *f* de oportunidades; *be equal to a task* estar capacitado para **2** *n* igual *m/f* **3** *v/t (pret & pp equaled, Br equalled) (with numbers)* equivaler; *(be as good as)* igualar; *four times twelve equals 48* cuatro por doce, (igual a) cuarenta y ocho

e·qual·i·ty [ɪ'kwɑːlətɪ] igualdad *f*

e·qual·ize ['iːkwəlaɪz] **1** *v/t* igualar **2** *v/i Br SP* empatar

e·qual·iz·er ['iːkwəlaɪzər] *Br SP* gol *m* del empate

e·qual·ly ['iːkwəlɪ] *adv* igualmente; *share, divide* en partes iguales; *equally, ...* igualmente, ...

e·qual 'rights *npl* igualdad *f* de derechos

e·quate [ɪ'kweɪt] *v/t* equiparar; *equate sth with sth* equiparar algo con algo

e·qua·tion [ɪ'kweɪʒn] MATH ecuación *f*

e·qua·tor [ɪ'kweɪtər] ecuador *m*

e·qui·lib·ri·um [iːkwɪ'lɪbrɪəm] equilibrio *m*

e·qui·nox ['iːkwɪnɑːks] equinoccio *m*

e·quip [ɪ'kwɪp] *v/t (pret & pp equipped)* equipar; *he's not equipped to handle it fig* no está preparado para llevarlo

e·quip·ment [ɪ'kwɪpmənt] equipo *m*

eq·ui·ty ['ekwətɪ] FIN acciones *fpl* ordinarias

e·quiv·a·lent [ɪ'kwɪvələnt] **1** *adj* equivalente; *be equivalent to* equivaler a **2** *n* equivalente *m*

e·ra ['ɪrə] era *f*

e·rad·i·cate [ɪ'rædɪkeɪt] *v/t* erradicar

e·rase [ɪ'reɪz] *v/t* borrar

e·ras·er [ɪ'reɪzər] *for pencil* goma *f* (de borrar); *for chalk* borrador *m*

e·rect [ɪ'rekt] **1** *adj* erguido **2** *v/t* levantar, erigir

e·rec·tion [ɪ'rekʃn] *of building etc* construcción *f; of penis* erección *f*

er·go·nom·ic [ɜːrgoʊ'nɑːmɪk] *adj furniture* ergonómico

e·rode [ɪ'roʊd] *v/t also fig* erosionar

e·ro·sion [ɪ'roʊʒn] *also fig* erosión *f*

e·rot·ic [ɪ'rɑːtɪk] *adj* erótico

e·rot·i·cism [ɪ'rɑːtɪsɪzm] erotismo *m*

er·rand ['erənd] recado *m; run errands* hacer recados

er·rat·ic [ɪ'rætɪk] *adj* irregular; *course* errático

er·ror ['erər] error *m*

'er·ror mes·sage COMPUT mensaje *m* de error

e·rupt [ɪ'rʌpt] *v/i of volcano* entrar en erupción; *of violence* brotar; *of person* explotar e·rup·tion [ɪˈrʌpʃn] *of volcano* erupción *f*; *of violence* brote *f*

es·ca·late [ˈeskəleɪt] *v/i* intensificarse

es·ca·la·tion [eskəˈleɪʃn] intensificación *f*

es·ca·la·tor [ˈeskəleɪtər] escalera *f* mecánica

es·cape [ɪˈskeɪp] 1 *n of prisoner, animal* fuga *f*; *of gas* escape *m*, fuga *f*; *have a narrow escape* escaparse por los pelos 2 *v/i of prisoner, animal, gas* escaparse 3 *v/t: the word escapes me* no consigo recordar la palabra

es·cape chute AVIA tobogán *m* de emergencia

es·cort 1 [ˈeskɔːrt] acompañante *m/f*; *guard* escolta *m/f*; *under escort* escoltado 2 *v/t* [ɪˈskɔːrt] escoltar; *socially* acompañar

es·pe·cial [ɪˈspeʃl] → *special*

es·pe·cial·ly [ɪˈspeʃlɪ] *adv* especialmente

es·pi·o·nage [ˈespɪənɑːʒ] espionaje *m*

es·pres·so (cof·fee) [esˈpresoʊ] café *m* exprés

es·say [ˈeseɪ] *n creative* redacción *f*; *factual* trabajo *m*

es·sen·tial [ɪˈsenʃl] *adj* esencial; *the essential thing is …* lo esencial es …

es·sen·tial·ly [ɪˈsenʃlɪ] *adv* esencialmente; fundamentalmente

es·tab·lish [ɪˈstæblɪʃ] *v/t company* fundar; *(create, determine)* establecer; *establish o.s. as* establecerse como

es·tab·lish·ment [ɪˈstæblɪʃmənt] *firm, shop etc* establecimiento *m*; *the Establishment* el orden establecido

es·tate [ɪˈsteɪt] *(area of land)* finca *f*; *(possessions of dead person)* patrimonio *m*

es·tate a·gen·cy *Br* agencia *f* inmobiliaria

es·thet·ic [ɪsˈθetɪk] *adj* estético

es·ti·mate [ˈestɪmət] 1 *n* estimación *f*; *for job* presupuesto *m* 2 *v/t* estimar; *estimated time of arrival* hora *f* estimada de llegada

es·ti·ma·tion [estɪˈmeɪʃn] estima *f*; *he has gone up / down in my estimation* le tengo en más / menos estima; *in my estimation (opinion)* a mi parecer

es·tranged [ɪsˈtreɪndʒd] *adj wife, husband* separado

es·tu·a·ry [ˈestʃəwerɪ] estuario *m*

ETA [iːtiːˈeɪ] *abbr* (= *estimated time of arrival*) hora *f* estimada de llegada

etc [etˈsetrə] *abbr* (= *et cetera*) etc (= etcétera)

etch·ing [ˈetʃɪŋ] aguafuerte *m*

e·ter·nal [ɪˈtɜːrnl] *adj* eterno

e·ter·ni·ty [ɪˈtɜːrnətɪ] eternidad *f*

eth·i·cal [ˈeθɪkl] *adj* ético

eth·ics [ˈeθɪks] ética *f*; *code of ethics* código *m* ético

eth·nic [ˈeθnɪk] *adj* étnico

eth·nic ˈgroup grupo *m* étnico

eth·nic mi·ˈnor·i·ty minoría *f* étnica

EU [iːˈjuː] *abbr* (= *European Union*) UE *f* (=Unión *f* Europea)

eu·phe·mism [ˈjuːfəmɪzm] eufemismo *m*

eu·pho·ri·a [juːˈfɔːrɪə] euforia *f*

eu·ro [ˈjʊroʊ] euro *m*

Eu·rope [ˈjʊrəp] Europa

Eu·ro·pe·an [jʊrəˈpɪən] 1 *adj* europeo 2 *n* europeo(-a) *m(f)*

Eu·ro·pe·an Com·ˈmis·sion Comisión *f* Europea

Eu·ro·pe·an ˈPar·lia·ment Parlamento *m* Europeo

Eu·ro·pe·an plan media pensión *f*

Eu·ro·pe·an ˈUn·ion Unión *f* Europea

eu·tha·na·si·a [juːθəˈneɪzɪə] eutanasia *f*

e·vac·u·ate [ɪˈvækjueɪt] *v/t* evacuar

e·vade [ɪˈveɪd] *v/t* evadir

e·val·u·ate [ɪˈvæljueɪt] *v/t* evaluar

e·val·u·a·tion [ɪvæljuˈeɪʃn] evaluación *f*

e·van·gel·ist [ɪˈvændʒəlɪst] evangelista *m/f*

e·vap·o·rate [ɪˈvæpəreɪt] *v/i of water* evaporarse; *of confidence* desvanecerse

e·vap·o·ra·tion [ɪvæpəˈreɪʃn] *of water* evaporación *f*

e·va·sion [ɪˈveɪʒn] evasión *f*

e·va·sive [ɪˈveɪsɪv] *adj* evasivo

eve [iːv] víspera *f*

e·ven [ˈiːvn] 1 *adj (regular)* regular; *(level)* llano; *number* par; *distribution* igualado; *I'll get even with him* me las pagará 2 *adv incluso*; *even bigger / better* incluso *or* aún mayor / mejor; *not even* ni siquiera; *even so* aun así; *even if* aunque; *even if he begged me* aunque me lo suplicara 3 *v/t: even the score* empatar, igualar el marcador

eve·ning [ˈiːvnɪŋ] tarde *f*; *after dark* noche *f*; *in the evening* por la tarde / noche; *this evening* esta tarde / noche; *yesterday evening* anoche *f*; *good evening* buenas *fpl* noches

ˈeve·ning class clase *f* nocturna

ˈeve·ning dress *for woman* traje *f* de noche; *for man* traje *f* de etiqueta

eve·ning ˈpa·per periódico *m* de la tarde *or* vespertino

e·ven·ly [ˈiːvnlɪ] *adv (regularly)* regularmente

e·vent [ɪˈvent] acontecimiento *m*; SP prueba *f*; *at all events* en cualquier caso

e·vent·ful [ɪˈventfəl] *adj* agitado, lleno de incidentes

e·ven·tu·al [ɪ'ventʃʊəl] *adj* final

e·ven·tu·al·ly [ɪ'ventʃʊəlɪ] *adv* finalmente

ev·er ['evər] *adv*: **if I ever hear you ...** como te oiga ...; **have you ever been to Japan?** ¿has estado alguna vez en Japón?; **for ever** siempre; **ever since** desde entonces; **ever since she found out about it** desde que se enteró de ello; **ever since I've known him** desde lo que conozco

ev·er·green ['evərgri:n] *n* árbol *m* de hoja perenne

ev·er·last·ing [evər'læstɪŋ] *adj* love eterno

ev·ery ['evrɪ] *adj* cada; **I see him every day** le veo todos los días; **you have every reason to ...** tienes toda la razón para ...; **one in every ten** uno de cada diez; **every other day** cada dos días; **every now and then** de vez en cuando

ev·ery·bod·y ['evrɪbɑːdɪ] → **everyone**

ev·ery·day ['evrɪdeɪ] *adj* cotidiano

ev·ery·one ['evrɪwʌn] *pron* todo el mundo

ev·ery·thing ['evrɪθɪŋ] *pron* todo

ev·ery·where ['evrɪweɪr] *adv* en *or* por todos sitios; (*wherever*) dondequiera que

e·vict [ɪ'vɪkt] *v/t* desahuciar

ev·i·dence ['evɪdəns] *also* LAW prueba(s) *f(pl)*; **give evidence** prestar declaración

ev·i·dent ['evɪdənt] *adj* evidente

ev·i·dent·ly ['evɪdəntlɪ] *adv* (*clearly*) evidentemente; (*apparently*) aparentemente, al parecer

e·vil ['iːvl] 1 *adj* malo 2 *n* mal *m*

e·voke [ɪ'vəʊk] *v/t* image evocar

ev·o·lu·tion [iːvə'luːʃn] evolución *f*

e·volve [ɪ'vɑːlv] *v/i* evolucionar

ewe [juː] oveja *f*

ex- [eks] *pref* ex-

ex [eks] F (*former wife, husband*) ex *m/f* F

ex·act [ɪg'zækt] *adj* exacto

ex·act·ing [ɪg'zæktɪŋ] *adj* exigente; task duro

ex·act·ly [ɪg'zæktlɪ] *adv* exactamente; **exactly!** ¡exactamente!

ex·ag·ge·rate [ɪg'zædʒəreɪt] *v/t & v/i* exagerar

ex·ag·ge·ra·tion [ɪgzædʒə'reɪʃn] exageración *f*

ex·am [ɪg'zæm] examen *m*; **take an exam** hacer un examen; **pass / fail an exam** aprobar/ suspender un examen

ex·am·i·na·tion [ɪgzæmɪ'neɪʃn] examen *m*; *of patient* reconocimiento *m*

ex·am·ine [ɪg'zæmɪn] *v/t* examinar; *patient* reconocer

ex·am·in·er [ɪg'zæmɪnər] EDU examinador(a) *m(f)*

ex·am·ple [ɪg'zæmpl] ejemplo *m*; **for example** por ejemplo; **set a good / bad example** dar buen/ mal ejemplo

ex·as·pe·rat·ed [ɪg'zæspəreɪtɪd] *adj* exasperado

ex·as·pe·rat·ing [ɪg'zæspəreɪtɪŋ] *adj* exasperante

ex·ca·vate ['ekskəveɪt] *v/t* excavar

ex·ca·va·tion [ekskə'veɪʃn] excavación *f*

ex·ca·va·tor ['ekskəveɪtər] excavadora *f*

ex·ceed [ɪk'siːd] *v/t* (*be more than*) exceder; (*go beyond*) sobrepasar

ex·ceed·ing·ly [ɪk'siːdɪŋlɪ] *adj* sumamente

ex·cel [ɪk'sel] 1 *v/i* (*pret & pp excelled*) sobresalir (*at* en) 2 *v/t* (*pret & pp excelled*): **excel o.s.** superarse a sí mismo

ex·cel·lence ['eksələns] excelencia *f*

ex·cel·lent ['eksələnt] *adj* excelente

ex·cept [ɪk'sept] *prep* excepto; **except for** a excepción de; **except that** sólo que

ex·cep·tion [ɪk'sepʃn] excepción *f*; **with the exception of** a excepción de; **take exception to** molestarse por

ex·cep·tion·al [ɪk'sepʃnl] *adj* excepcional

ex·cep·tion·al·ly [ɪk'sepʃnlɪ] *adv* (*extremely*) excepcionalmente

ex·cerpt ['eksɜːrpt] extracto *m*

ex·cess [ɪk'ses] 1 *n* exceso *m*; **eat / drink to excess** comer/ beber en exceso; **in excess of** superior a 2 *adj* excedente

ex·cess 'bag·gage exceso *m* de equipaje

ex·cess 'fare suplemento *m*

ex·ces·sive [ɪk'sesɪv] *adj* excesivo

ex·change [ɪks'tʃeɪndʒ] 1 *n* intercambio *m*; **in exchange** a cambio (**for** de) 2 *v/t* cambiar

ex'change rate FIN tipo *m* de cambio

ex·ci·ta·ble [ɪk'saɪtəbl] *adj* excitable

ex·cite [ɪk'saɪt] *v/t* (*make enthusiastic*) entusiasmar

ex·cit·ed [ɪk'saɪtɪd] *adj* emocionado, excitado; *sexually* excitado; **get excited** emocionarse; **get excited about** emocionarse *or* excitarse con

ex·cite·ment [ɪk'saɪtmənt] emoción *f*, excitación *f*

ex·cit·ing [ɪk'saɪtɪŋ] *adj* emocionante, excitante

ex·claim [ɪk'skleɪm] *v/t* exclamar

ex·cla·ma·tion [eksklə'meɪʃn] exclamación *f*

ex·cla'ma·tion point signo *m* de admiración

ex·clude [ɪk'skluːd] *v/t* excluir; *possibility* descartar

ex·clud·ing [ɪk'skluːdɪŋ] *prep* excluyendo

ex·clu·sive [ɪk'skluːsɪv] *adj* exclusivo

ex·com·mu·ni·cate [ekskə'mjuːnɪkeɪt]

v/t REL excomulgar
ex·cru·ci·a·ting [ɪkˈskruːʃɪeɪtɪŋ] *adj* pain terrible
ex·cur·sion [ɪkˈskɜːrʃn] excursión *f*
ex·cuse 1 *n* [ɪkˈskjuːs] excusa *f* 2 *v/t* [ɪkˈskjuːz] (*forgive*) excusar, perdonar; (*allow to leave*) disculpar; **excuse s.o. from sth** dispensar a alguien de algo; **excuse me to get past, interrupting** perdone, disculpe; **to get attention** perdone, oiga
e·x·e·cute [ˈeksɪkjuːt] *v/t criminal, plan* ejecutar
ex·e·cu·tion [eksɪˈkjuːʃn] *of criminal, plan* ejecución *f*
ex·e·cu·tion·er [eksɪˈkjuːʃnər] verdugo *m*
ex·ec·u·tive [ɪgˈzekjutɪv] ejecutivo(-a) *m(f)*
ex·ec·u·tive ˈbrief·case maletín *m* de ejecutivo
ex·ec·u·tive ˈwash·room baño *m* para ejecutivos
ex·em·pla·ry [ɪgˈzemplərɪ] *adj* ejemplar
ex·empt [ɪgˈzempt] *adj* exento; **be exempt from** estar exento de
ex·er·cise [ˈeksərsaɪz] 1 *n* ejercicio *m*; **take exercise** hacer ejercicio 2 *v/t muscle* ejercitar; *dog* pasear; *caution* proceder con; **exercise restraint** controlarse 3 *v/i* hacer ejercicio
ˈex·er·cise bike bicicleta *f* estática
ˈex·er·cise book EDU cuaderno de ejercicios
ex·ert [ɪgˈzɜːrt] *v/t authority* ejercer; **exert o.s.** esforzarse
ex·er·tion [ɪgˈzɜːrʃn] esfuerzo *m*
ex·hale [eksˈheɪl] *v/t* exhalar
ex·haust [ɪgˈzɒːst] 1 *n fumes* gases *mpl* de la combustión; *pipe* tubo *m* de escape 2 *v/t* (*tire*) cansar; (*use up*) agotar
ex·haust·ed [ɪgˈzɒːstɪd] *adj* (*tired*) agotado
exˈhaust fumes *npl* gases *mpl* de la combustión
exˈhaust·ing [ɪgˈzɒːstɪŋ] *adj* agotador
exˈhaus·tion [ɪgˈzɒːstʃn] agotamiento *m*
exˈhaus·tive [ɪgˈzɒːstɪv] *adj* exhaustivo
exˈhaust pipe tubo *m* de escape
ex·hib·it [ɪgˈzɪbɪt] 1 *n in exhibition* objeto *m* expuesto 2 *v/t of gallery* exhibir; *of artist* exponer; (*give evidence of*) mostrar
ex·hi·bi·tion [eksɪˈbɪʃn] exposición *f*; *of bad behavior, skill* exhibición *f*
ex·hi·bi·tion·ist [eksɪˈbɪʃnɪst] exhibicionista *m/f*
ex·hil·a·ra·ting [ɪgˈzɪləreɪtɪŋ] *adj* estimulante
ex·ile [ˈeksaɪl] 1 *n* exilio *m*; *person* exilia-

do(-a) *m(f)* 2 *v/t* exiliar
ex·ist [ɪgˈzɪst] *v/i* existir; **exist on** subsistir a base de
ex·ist·ence [ɪgˈzɪstəns] existencia *f*; **be in existence** existir; **come into existence** crearse, nacer
ex·ist·ing [ɪgˈzɪstɪŋ] *adj* existente
ex·it [ˈeksɪt] 1 *n* salida *f*; THEA salida *f*, mutis *m* 2 *v/i* COMPUT salir
ex·on·e·rate [ɪgˈzɑːnəreɪt] *v/t* exonerar de
ex·or·bi·tant [ɪgˈzɔːrbɪtənt] *adj* exorbitante
ex·ot·ic [ɪgˈzɑːtɪk] *adj* exótico
ex·pand [ɪkˈspænd] 1 *v/t* expandir 2 *v/i of metal* dilatarse
♦ ex·pand on *v/t* desarrollar
ex·panse [ɪkˈspæns] extensión *f*
ex·pan·sion [ɪkˈspænʃn] expansión *f*; *of metal* dilatación *f*
ex·pat·ri·ate [eksˈpætrɪət] 1 *adj* expatriado 2 *n* expatriado(-a) *m(f)*
ex·pect [ɪkˈspekt] 1 *v/t* esperar; (*suppose*) suponer, imaginar(se); (*demand*) exigir 2 *v/i*: **be expecting** (*be pregnant*) estar en estado; **I expect so** eso espero, creo que sí
ex·pec·tant [ɪkˈspektənt] *adj crowd* expectante
ex·pec·tant ˈmoth·er futura madre *f*
ex·pec·ta·tion [ekspekˈteɪʃn] expectativa *f*; **live up to people's expectations of you** (*demands*) estar a la altura de lo que se espera de uno
ex·pe·di·ent [ɪkˈspiːdɪənt] *adj* oportuno, conveniente
ex·pe·di·tion [ekspɪˈdɪʃn] expedición *f*
ex·pel [ɪkˈspel] *v/t* (*pret & pp* **expelled**) *person* expulsar
ex·pend [ɪkˈspend] *v/t energy* gastar
ex·pend·a·ble [ɪkˈspendəbl] *adj person* prescindible
ex·pen·di·ture [ɪkˈspendɪtʃər] gasto *m*
ex·pense [ɪkˈspens] gasto *m*; **at great expense** gastando mucho dinero; **at the company's expense** a cargo de la empresa; **a joke at my expense** una broma a costa mía; **at the expense of his health** a costa de su salud
exˈpense ac·count cuenta *f* de gastos
ex·pen·ses [ɪkˈspensɪz] *npl* gastos *mpl*
ex·pen·sive [ɪkˈspensɪv] *adj* caro
ex·pe·ri·ence [ɪkˈspɪrɪəns] 1 *n* experiencia *f* 2 *v/t* experimentar
ex·pe·ri·enced [ɪkˈspɪrɪənst] *adj* experimentado
ex·per·i·ment [ɪkˈsperɪmənt] 1 *n* experimento *m* 2 *v/i* experimentar; **experiment on animals** experimentar con; **experiment with** (*try out*) probar

ex·per·i·men·tal [ɪksperɪˈmentl] *adj* experimental

ex·pert [ˈekspɜːrt] **1** *adj* experto **2** *n* experto(-a) *m(f)*

ex·pert ad·vice la opinión de un experto

ex·pert·ise [ekspɜːrˈtiːz] destreza *f*, pericia *f*

ex·pire [ɪkˈspaɪr] *v/i* caducar

ex·pi·ry [ɪkˈspaɪrɪ] *of lease, contract* vencimiento *m*; *of passport* caducidad *f*

ex·pi·ry date *of food, passport* fecha *f* de caducidad; *be past its expiry date* haber caducado

ex·plain [ɪkˈspleɪn] **1** *v/t* explicar **2** *v/i* explicarse

ex·pla·na·tion [ekspləˈneɪʃn] explicación *f*

ex·plan·a·to·ry [ɪkˈsplænətɔːrɪ] *adj* explicativo

ex·plic·it [ɪkˈsplɪsɪt] *adj instructions* explícito

ex·plic·it·ly [ɪkˈsplɪsɪtlɪ] *adv state* explícitamente; *forbid* terminantemente

ex·plode [ɪkˈspləʊd] **1** *v/i of bomb* explotar **2** *v/t bomb* hacer explotar

ex·ploit[1] [ˈeksplɔɪt] *n* hazaña *f*

ex·ploit[2] [ɪkˈsplɔɪt] *v/t person, resources* explotar

ex·ploi·ta·tion [eksplɔɪˈteɪʃn] *of person* explotación *f*

ex·plo·ra·tion [ekspləˈreɪʃn] exploración *f*

ex·plor·a·to·ry [ɪkˈsplɒrətɔːrɪ] *adj surgery* exploratorio

ex·plore [ɪkˈsplɔːr] *v/t country etc* explorar; *possibility* estudiar

ex·plor·er [ɪkˈsplɔːrər] explorador(a) *m(f)*

ex·plo·sion [ɪkˈspləʊʒn] *of bomb, in population* explosión *f*

ex·plo·sive [ɪkˈspləʊsɪv] *n* explosivo *m*

ex·port [ˈekspɔːrt] **1** *n action* exportación *f*; *item* producto *m* de exportación; ***ports*** *npl* exportaciones *fpl* **2** *v/t also* COMPUT exportar

'ex·port cam·paign campaña *f* de exportación

ex·port·er [ˈekspɔːrtər] exportador(a) *m(f)*

ex·pose [ɪkˈspəʊz] *v/t (uncover)* exponer; *scandal* sacar a la luz; *he's been exposed as a liar* ha quedado como un mentiroso; *expose sth to sth* exponer algo a algo

ex·po·sure [ɪkˈspəʊʒər] exposición *f*; PHOT foto(grafía) *f*

ex·press [ɪkˈspres] **1** *adj (fast)* rápido; *(explicit)* expreso **2** *n train* expreso *m*; *bus* autobús *m* directo **3** *v/t* expresar; *ex-*

press o.s. well / clearly expresarse bien / con claridad

ex·press el·e·va·tor ascensor rápido que sólo para en algunos pisos

ex·pres·sion [ɪkˈspreʃn] *voiced* muestra *f*; *phrase, on face* expresión *f*; *read with expression* leer con sentimiento

ex·pres·sive [ɪkˈspresɪv] *adj* expresivo

ex·press·ly [ɪkˈspreslɪ] *adv state* expresamente; *forbid* terminantemente

ex·press·way [ɪkˈspresweɪ] autopista *f*

ex·pul·sion [ɪkˈspʌlʃn] *from school, of diplomat* expulsión *f*

ex·qui·site [ekˈskwɪzɪt] *adj (beautiful)* exquisito

ex·tend [ɪkˈstend] **1** *v/t house, investigation* ampliar; *(make wider)* ensanchar; *(make bigger)* agrandar; *runway, path* alargar; *contract, visa* prorrogar; *thanks, congratulations* extender **2** *v/i of garden etc* llegar

ex·ten·sion [ɪkˈstenʃn] *to house* ampliación *f*; *of contract, visa* prórroga *f*; TELEC extensión *f*

ex·ten·sion ca·ble cable *m* de extensión

ex·ten·sive [ɪkˈstensɪv] *adj damage* cuantioso; *knowledge* considerable; *search* extenso, amplio

ex·tent [ɪkˈstent] alcance *m*; *to such an extent that* hasta el punto de que; *to a certain extent* hasta cierto punto

ex·ten·u·at·ing cir·cum·stances [ɪkˈstenʊeɪtɪŋ] *npl* circunstancias *fpl* atenuantes

ex·te·ri·or [ɪkˈstɪrɪər] **1** *adj* exterior **2** *n* exterior *m*

ex·ter·mi·nate [ɪkˈstɜːrmɪneɪt] *v/t* exterminar

ex·ter·nal [ɪkˈstɜːrnl] *adj (outside)* exterior, externo

ex·tinct [ɪkˈstɪŋkt] *adj species* extinguido

ex·tinc·tion [ɪkˈstɪŋkʃn] *of species* extinción *f*

ex·tin·guish [ɪkˈstɪŋgwɪʃ] *v/t fire* extinguir, apagar; *cigarette* apagar

ex·tin·guish·er [ɪkˈstɪŋgwɪʃər] extintor *m*

extort [ɪkˈstɔːrt] *v/t* obtener mediante extorsión; *extort money from* extorsionar a

ex·tor·tion [ɪkˈstɔːrʃn] extorsión *f*

ex·tor·tion·ate [ɪkˈstɔːrʃənət] *adj prices* desorbitado

ex·tra [ˈekstrə] **1** *n* extra *m*; *in movie* extra *m/f* **2** *adj* extra; *meals are extra* las comidas se pagan aparte; *that's $1 extra* cuesta 1 dólar más **3** *adv* super; *extra strong* extrafuerte; *extra special* muy especial

ex·tra 'charge recargo *m*
ex·tract¹ ['ekstrækt] *n* extracto *m*
ex·tract² [ɪk'strækt] *v/t* sacar; *coal, oil, tooth* extraer; *information* sonsacar
ex·trac·tion [ɪk'strækʃn] *of oil, coal, tooth* extracción *f*
ex·tra·dite ['ekstrədaɪt] *v/t* extraditar
ex·tra·di·tion [ekstrə'dɪʃn] extradición *f*
ex·tra·di·tion trea·ty tratado *m* de extradición
ex·tra·mar·i·tal [ekstrə'mærɪtl] *adj* extramarital
ex·tra·or·di·nar·i·ly [ekstrɔːrdɪn'erɪlɪ] *adv* extraordinariamente
ex·tra·or·di·na·ry [ɪk'strɔːrdɪnerɪ] *adj* extraordinario
ex·trav·a·gance [ɪk'strævəgəns] *with money* despilfarro *m; of claim etc* extravagancia *f*
ex·trav·a·gant [ɪk'strævəgənt] *adj with money* despilfarrador; *claim* extravagante
ex·treme [ɪk'striːm] **1** *n* extremo *m* **2** *adj* extremo; *views* extremista
ex·treme·ly [ɪk'striːmlɪ] *adv* extremada-

mente, sumamente
ex·trem·ist [ɪk'striːmɪst] extremista *m/f*
ex·tri·cate ['ekstrɪkeɪt] *v/t* liberar
ex·tro·vert ['ekstrəvɜːrt] **1** *adj* extrovertido **2** *n* extrovertido(-a) *m(f)*
ex·u·be·rant [ɪg'zuːbərənt] *adj* exuberante
ex·ult [ɪg'zʌlt] *v/i* exultar
eye [aɪ] **1** *n of person, needle* ojo *m;* ***keep an eye on*** *(look after)* estar pendiente de; *(monitor)* estar pendiente de, vigilar **2** *v/t* mirar
'eye·ball globo *m* ocular
'eye·brow ceja *f*
'eye-catch·ing *adj* llamativo
'eye·glass·es *npl* gafas *fpl, L.Am.* anteojos *mpl, L.Am.* lentes *mpl*
'eye·lash pestaña *f*
'eye·lid párpado *m*
'eye·lin·er lápiz *m* de ojos
'eye·sha·dow sombra *f* de ojos
'eye·sight vista *f*
'eye·sore engendro *m*, monstruosidad *f*
'eye strain vista *f* cansada
'eye·wit·ness testigo *m/f* ocular

F

F *abbr* (= ***Fahrenheit***) F
fab·ric ['fæbrɪk] *(material)* tejido *m*
fab·u·lous ['fæbjʊləs] *adj* fabuloso, estupendo
fab·u·lous·ly ['fæbjʊləslɪ] *adv rich* tremendamente; *beautiful* increíblemente
fa·çade [fə'sɑːd] *of building, person* fachada *f*
face [feɪs] **1** *n* cara *f;* ***face to face*** cara a cara; ***lose face*** padecer una *humillación* **2** *v/t (be opposite)* estar enfrente de; *(confront)* enfrentarse a
♦ **face up to** *v/t* hacer frente a
'face·cloth toallita *f*
'face·lift lifting *m*, estiramiento *m* de piel
'face pack mascarilla *f (facial)*
face 'val·ue: ***take sth at face value*** tomarse algo literalmente
fa·cial ['feɪʃl] *n* limpieza *f* de cutis
fa·cil·i·tate [fə'sɪlɪteɪt] *v/t* facilitar
fa·cil·i·ties [fə'sɪlətɪz] *npl* instalaciones *fpl*
fact [fækt] hecho *m;* ***in fact, as a matter of fact*** de hecho

fac·tion ['fækʃn] facción *f*
fac·tor ['fæktər] factor *m*
fac·to·ry ['fæktərɪ] fábrica *f*
fac·ul·ty ['fækəltɪ] *(hearing etc), at university* facultad *f*
fad [fæd] moda *f*
fade [feɪd] *v/i of colors* desteñirse, perder color; *of memories* desvanecerse
fad·ed ['feɪdɪd] *adj color, jeans* desteñido, descolorido
fag¹ [fæg] F *(homosexual)* maricón *m* F
fag² [fæg] *Br* F *(cigarette)* pitillo *m* F
Fahr·en·heit ['færənhaɪt] *adj* Fahrenheit
fail [feɪl] **1** *v/i* fracasar; *of plan* fracasar, fallar **2** *n:* ***without fail*** sin falta
fail·ing ['feɪlɪŋ] *n* fallo *m*
fail·ure ['feɪljər] fracaso *m; in exam* suspenso *m;* ***I feel such a failure*** me siento un fracasado
faint [feɪnt] **1** *adj line, smile* tenue; *smell, noise* casi imperceptible **2** *v/i* desmayarse
faint·ly ['feɪntlɪ] *adv smile, smell* levemente
fair¹ [fer] *n* COM feria *f*

fair² [fer] *adj* hair rubio; *complexion* claro; *(just)* justo

fair·ly ['ferlɪ] *adv* treat justamente, con justicia; *(quite)* bastante

fair·ness ['fernɪs] *of treatment* imparcialidad *f*

fai·ry ['ferɪ] hada *f*

'fai·ry tale cuento *m* de hadas

faith [feɪθ] fe *f*, confianza *f*; REL fe *f*

faith·ful ['feɪθfəl] *adj* fiel; **be faithful to one's partner** ser fiel a la pareja

faith·ful·ly ['feɪθfəlɪ] *adv* religiosamente

Falk·lan Is·lands ['fɔːlklənd] *npl*: **the Falkland Islands** las Islas Malvinas

fake [feɪk] **1** *n* falsificación *f* **2** *adj* falso **3** *v/t (forge)* falsificar; *(feign)* fingir

fall¹ [fɔːl] *n season* otoño *m*

fall² [fɔːl] **1** *v/i (pret fell, pp fallen) of person* caerse; *of government, prices, temperature, night* caer; **it falls on a Tuesday** cae en martes; **fall ill** enfermar, caer enfermo; **I fell off the wall** me caí del muro **2** *n* caída *f*

◆ **fall back on** *v/t* recurrir a

◆ **fall behind** *v/i with work, studies* retrasarse

◆ **fall down** *v/i* caerse

◆ **fall for** *v/t person* enamorarse de; *(be deceived by)* dejarse engañar por; **I'm amazed you fell for it** me sorprende mucho que picaras

◆ **fall out** *v/i of hair* caerse; *(argue)* pelearse

◆ **fall over** *v/i* caerse

◆ **fall through** *v/i of plans* venirse abajo

tal·len ['fɔːlən] *pp* → **fall²**

fal·li·ble ['fæləbl] *adj* falible

'fall-out lluvia *f* radiactiva

false [fɔːls] *adj* falso

false a'larm falsa alarma *f*

false·ly ['fɔːlslɪ] *adv*: **be falsely accused of sth** ser acusado falsamente de algo

false 'start *in race* salida *f* nula

false 'teeth *npl* dentadura *f* postiza

tal·si·fy ['fɔːlsɪfaɪ] *v/t (pret & pp falsified)* falsificar

fame [feɪm] fama *f*

fa·mil·i·ar [fə'mɪljər] *adj* familiar; **get familiar** *(intimate)* tomarse demasiadas confianzas; **be familiar with sth** estar familiarizado con algo; **that looks familiar** eso me resulta familiar; **that sounds familiar** me suena

fa·mil·i·ar·i·ty [fəmɪlɪ'ærɪtɪ] *with subject etc* familiaridad *f*

fa·mil·i·ar·ize [fə'mɪljəraɪz] *v/t*: **familiarize o.s. with ...** familiarizarse con ...

fam·i·ly ['fæmɪlɪ] familia *f*

fam·i·ly 'doc·tor médico *m/f* de familia

'fam·i·ly name apellido *m*

fam·i·ly 'plan·ning planificación *f* familiar

fam·i·ly 'plan·ning clin·ic clínica *f* de planificación familiar

fam·i·ly 'tree árbol *m* genealógico

fam·ine ['fæmɪn] hambruna *f*

fam·ished ['fæmɪʃt] *adj* F: **I'm famished** estoy muerto de hambre F

fa·mous ['feɪməs] *adj* famoso; **be famous for ...** ser famoso por ...

fan¹ [fæn] *n (supporter)* seguidor(a) *m(f)*; *of singer, band* admirador(a) *m(f)*, fan *m/f*

fan² [fæn] **1** *n electric* ventilador *m*; *handheld* abanico *m* **2** *v/t (pret & pp fanned)* abanicar; **fan o.s.** abanicarse

fa·nat·ic [fə'nætɪk] *n* fanático(-a) *m(f)*

fa·nat·i·cal [fə'nætɪkl] *adj* fanático

fa·nat·i·cism [fə'nætɪsɪzm] fanatismo *m*

'fan belt MOT correa *f* del ventilador

'fan club club *m* de fans

fan·cy ['fænsɪ] **1** *adj (luxurious)* de lujo; *(complicated)* sofisticado **2** *n*: **as the fancy takes you** como te apetezca; **take a fancy to s.o.** encapricharse de alguien **3** *v/t (pret & pp fancied)*: **do you fancy an ice cream?** ¿te apetece un helado?

fan·cy 'dress disfraz *m*

fan·cy-'dress par·ty fiesta *f* de disfraces

fang [fæŋ] colmillo *m*

'fan mail cartas *fpl* de los fans

fan·ta·size ['fæntəsaɪz] *v/i* fantasear *(about* sobre)

fan·tas·tic [fæn'tæstɪk] *adj (very good)* fantástico, excelente; *(very big)* inmenso

fan·tas·tic·al·ly [fæn'tæstɪklɪ] *adv (extremely)* sumamente, increíblemente

fan·ta·sy ['fæntəsɪ] fantasía *f*

far [fɑːr] *adv* lejos; *(much)* mucho; **far bigger / faster** mucho más grande / rápido; **far away** lejos; **how far is it to ...?** ¿a cuánto está ...?; **as far as the corner / hotel** hasta la esquina / el hotel; **as far as I can see** lo que yo veo yo; **as far as I know** que yo sepa; **you've gone too far in behavior** te has pasado; **so far so good** por ahora muy bien

farce [fɑːrs] farsa *f*

fare [fer] *n price* tarifa *f*; *actual money* dinero *m*

Far 'East Lejano Oriente *m*

fare·well [fer'wel] *n* despedida *f*

fare'well par·ty fiesta *f* de despedida

far-fetched [fɑːr'fetʃt] *adj* inverosímil, exagerado

farm [fɑːrm] *n* granja *f*

farm·er ['fɑːrmər] granjero(-a) *m(f)*

'farm·house granja *f*, alquería *f*

farm·ing ['fɑːrmɪŋ] n agricultura f

'**farm·work·er** trabajador(a) m(f) del campo

'**farm·yard** corral m

far-'off adj lejano

far-sight·ed [fɑːr'saɪtɪd] adj previsor; optically hipermétrope

fart [fɑːrt] **1** n F pedo m F **2** v/i F tirarse un pedo F

far·ther ['fɑːðər] adv más lejos; **farther away** más allá, más lejos

far·thest ['fɑːrðəst] adv travel etc más lejos

fas·ci·nate ['fæsɪneɪt] v/t fascinar; **be fascinated by ...** estar fascinado por ...

fas·ci·nat·ing ['fæsɪneɪtɪŋ] adj fascinante

fas·ci·na·tion [fæsɪ'neɪʃn] fascinación f

fas·cism ['fæʃɪzm] fascismo m

fas·cist ['fæʃɪst] **1** n fascista m/f **2** adj fascista

fash·ion ['fæʃn] n moda f; (manner) modo m, manera f; **in fashion** de moda; **out of fashion** pasado de moda

fash·ion·a·ble ['fæʃnəbl] adj de moda

fash·ion·a·bly ['fæʃnəblɪ] adv dressed a la moda

'**fash·ion-con·scious** adj que sigue la moda

'**fash·ion de·sign·er** modisto(-a) m(f)

'**fash·ion mag·a·zine** revista f de moda

'**fash·ion show** desfile f de moda, pase m de modelos

fast[1] [fæst] **1** adj rápido; **be fast** of clock ir adelantado **2** adv rápido; **stuck fast** atascado; **fast asleep** profundamente dormido

fast[2] [fæst] n not eating ayuno m

fas·ten ['fæsn] v/t window, lid cerrar (poniendo el cierre); dress abrochar; **fasten onto sth** asegurar algo a algo **2** v/i of dress etc abrocharse

fas·ten·er ['fæsnər] for dress, lid cierre f

fast 'food comida f rápida

'**fast-food 'res·tau·rant** restaurante f de comida rápida

fast 'for·ward **1** n on video etc avance m rápido **2** v/i avanzar

'**fast lane** on road carril f rápido; **in the fast lane** fig: of life con un tren de vida acelerado

'**fast train** (tren m) rápido m

fat [fæt] **1** adj gordo **2** n on meat, for baking grasa f

fa·tal ['feɪtl] adj illness mortal; error fatal

fa·tal·i·ty [fə'tælətɪ] víctima f mortal

fa·tal·ly ['feɪtəlɪ] adv mortalmente; **fatally injured** herido mortalmente

fate [feɪt] destino m

fat·ed ['feɪtɪd] adj: **be fated to do sth** es-

tar predestinado a hacer algo

'**fat-free** adj sin grasas

fa·ther ['fɑːðər] n padre m; **Father Martin** REL el Padre Martin

Fa·ther 'Christ·mas Br Papá m Noel

'**fa·ther·hood** ['fɑːðərhʊd] paternidad f

'**fa·ther-in-law** (pl **fathers-in-law**) suegro m

fa·ther·ly ['fɑːðəlɪ] adj paternal

fath·om ['fæðəm] n NAUT braza f

♦ **fathom out** v/t fig entender

fa·tigue [fə'tiːg] n cansancio m, fatiga f

fat·so ['fætsəʊ] F gordinflón (-ona) m(f) F

fat·ten ['fætn] v/t animal engordar

fat·ty ['fætɪ] **1** adj graso **2** n F (person) gordinflón (-ona) m(f) F

fau·cet ['fɒːsɪt] Span grifo m, L.Am. llave f

fault [fɒːlt] n (defect) fallo m; **it's your/ my fault** es culpa tuya / mía; **find fault with ...** encontrar defectos a ...

fault·less ['fɒːltlɪs] adj impecable

fault·y ['fɒːltɪ] adj goods defectuoso

fa·vor ['feɪvər] **1** n favor m; **do s.o. a favor** hacer un favor a alguien; **do me a favor!** (don't be stupid) ¡haz el favor!; **in favor of ...** a favor de ...; **be in favor of ...** estar a favor de ... **2** v/t (prefer) preferir

fa·vo·ra·ble ['feɪvərəbl] adj reply etc favorable

fa·vo·rite ['feɪvərɪt] **1** n favorito(-a) m(f); food comida f favorita **2** adj favorito

fa·vor·it·ism ['feɪvrɪtɪzm] favoritismo m

fa·vour etc Br → **favor** etc

fax [fæks] **1** n fax m; **send sth by fax** enviar algo por fax **2** v/t enviar por fax: **fax sth to s.o.** enviar algo por fax a alguien

FBI [efbiː'aɪ] abbr (= **Federal Bureau of Investigation**) FBI m

fear [fɪr] **1** n miedo m, temor m **2** v/t temer, tener miedo a

fear·less ['fɪrlɪs] adj valiente, audaz

fear·less·ly ['fɪrlɪslɪ] adv sin miedo

fea·si·bil·i·ty stud·y [fiːzə'bɪlətɪ] estudio m de viabilidad

fea·si·ble ['fiːzəbl] adj factible, viable

feast [fiːst] n banquete m, festín m

feat [fiːt] n hazaña f, proeza f

feath·er ['feðər] pluma f

fea·ture ['fiːtʃər] **1** n on face rasgo m, facción f; of city, building, plan, style característica f; article in paper reportaje m; movie largometraje f; **make a feature of ...** destacar ... **2** v/t **a movie featuring ...** una película en la que aparece ...

'**fea·ture film** largometraje m

Feb·ru·a·ry ['februerɪ] febrero m

fed [fed] pret & pp → **feed**

fed·e·ral ['fedərəl] *adj* federal

fed·e·ra·tion [fedə'reɪʃn] federación *f*

fed up *adj* F harto, hasta las narices F; *be fed up with ...* estar harto *or* hasta las narices de ...

fee [fiː] *of lawyer, doctor, consultant* honorarios *mpl*; *for entrance* entrada *f*; *for membership* cuota *f*

fee·ble ['fiːbl] *adj person, laugh* débil; *attempt* flojo; *excuse* harto

feed [fiːd] *v/t (pret & pp fed)* alimentar, dar de comer a

'feed·back *n* reacción *m*; *we'll give you some feedback as soon as possible* le daremos nuestra opinión *or* nuestras reacciones lo antes posible

feel [fiːl] **1** *v/t (pret & pp felt) (touch)* tocar; *(sense)* sentir; *(think)* creer, pensar; *you can feel the difference* se nota la diferencia **2** *v/i (pret & pp felt)*: *it feels like silk/cotton* tiene la textura de la seda / algodón; *your hand feels hot* tienes la mano caliente; *I feel hungry* tengo hambre; *I feel tired* estoy cansado; *how are you feeling today?* ¿cómo te encuentras hoy?; *how does it feel to be rich?* ¿qué se siente siendo rico?; *do you feel like a drink/meal?* ¿te apetece una bebida / comida?; *I feel like going/staying* me apetece ir / quedarme; *I don't feel like it* no me apetece
♦ **feel up to** *v/t* sentirse con fuerzas para

feel·er ['fiːlər] *of insect* antena *f*

'feel-good fac·tor sensación *f* positiva

feel·ing ['fiːlɪŋ] *n* sentimiento *m*; *(sensation)* sensación *f*; *what are your feelings about it?* ¿qué piensas sobre ello?; *I have mixed feelings about him* me inspira sentimientos contradictorios; *I have this feeling that ...* tengo el presentimiento de que ...

feet [fiːt] *pl* → **foot**

fe·line ['fiːlaɪn] *adj* felino

fell [fel] *pret* → **fall²**

fel·low ['feloʊ] *n (man)* tipo *m*

fel·low 'cit·i·zen conciudadano(-a) *m(f)*

fel·low 'coun·try·man compatriota *m/f*

fel·low 'man prójimo *m*

fel·on·y ['feləni] delito *m* grave

felt [felt] **1** *n* fieltro *m* **2** *pret & pp* → **feel**

felt 'tip, felt-tip 'pen rotulador *m*

fe·male ['fiːmeɪl] **1** *adj animal, plant* hembra; *relating to people* femenino **2** *n of animals, plants* hembra *f*; *person* mujer *f*

fem·i·nine ['femɪnɪn] **1** *adj also* GRAM femenino **2** *n* GRAM femenino *m*

fem·i·nism ['femɪnɪzm] feminismo *m*

fem·i·nist ['femɪnɪst] **1** *n* feminista *m/f* **2** *adj* feminista

fence [fens] *n around garden etc* cerca *f*, valla *f*; F *criminal* perista *m/f*; *sit on the fence* nadar entre dos aguas
♦ **fence in** *v/t land* cercar, vallar

fenc·ing ['fensɪŋ] SP esgrima *f*

fend [fend] *v/i*: *fend for o.s.* valerse por sí mismo

fend·er ['fendər] MOT aleta *f*

fer·ment¹ [fə'ment] *v/i of liquid* fermentar

fer·ment² ['fɜːrment] *n (unrest)* agitación *f*

fer·men·ta·tion [fɜːrmen'teɪʃn] fermentación *f*

fern [fɜːrn] helecho *m*

fe·ro·cious [fə'roʊʃəs] *adj* feroz

fer·ry ['feri] *n* ferry *m*, transbordador *m*

fer·tile ['fɜːrtaɪl] *adj* fértil

fer·til·i·ty [fɜːr'tɪlətɪ] fertilidad *f*

fer·til·i·ty drug medicamento *m* para el tratamiento de la infertilidad

fer·ti·lize ['fɜːrtəlaɪz] *v/t* fertilizar

fer·ti·liz·er ['fɜːrtəlaɪzər] *for soil* fertilizante *m*

fer·vent ['fɜːrvənt] *adj* admirer ferviente

fer·vent·ly ['fɜːrvəntlɪ] *adv* fervientemente

fes·ter ['festər] *v/i of wound* enconarse

fes·ti·val ['festɪvl] festival *m*

fes·tive ['festɪv] *adj* festivo; *the festive season* la época navideña, las Navidades

fes·tiv·i·ties [fe'stɪvətɪz] *npl* celebraciones *fpl*

fe·tal ['fiːtl] *adj* fetal

fetch [fetʃ] *v/t person* recoger; *thing* traer, ir a buscar; *price* alcanzar

fe·tus ['fiːtəs] feto *m*

feud [fjuːd] **1** *n* enemistad *f* **2** *v/i* estar enemistado

fe·ver ['fiːvər] fiebre *f*

fe·ver·ish ['fiːvərɪʃ] *adj* con fiebre; *fig: excitement* febril

few [fjuː] **1** *adj (not many)* pocos; *a few things* unos pocos; *quite a few, a good few (a lot)* bastantes **2** *pron (not many)* pocos(-as); *a few (some)* unos pocos, *quite a few, a good few (a lot)* bastantes; *few of them could speak English* de ellos muy pocos hablaban inglés

few·er ['fjuːər] *adj* menos; *fewer than ...* menos que ...; *with numbers* menos de ...

fi·an·cé [fɪ'ɑːnseɪ] prometido *m*, novio *m*

fi·an·cée [fɪ'ɑːnseɪ] prometida *f*, novia *f*

fi·as·co [fɪ'æskoʊ] fiasco *m*

fib [fɪb] *n* F bola *f* F

fi·ber ['faɪbər] *n* fibra *f*

'fi·ber·glass *n* fibra *f* de vidrio

fi·ber 'op·tic *adj* de fibra óptica

fi·ber 'op·tics fibra *f* óptica

fi·bre *Br* → fiber

fick·le ['fɪkl] *adj* inconstante, mudable

fic·tion ['fɪkʃn] *n* (*novels*) literatura *f* de ficción; (*made-up story*) ficción *f*

fic·tion·al ['fɪkʃnl] *adj* de ficción

fic·ti·tious [fɪk'tɪʃəs] *adj* ficticio

fid·dle ['fɪdl] **1** *n* (*violin*) violín *m*; **it's a fiddle** F (*cheat*) es un amaño **2** *v/i:* **fiddle around with** enredar con; **fiddle around with** enredar con **3** *v/t accounts, result* amañar

◆ **fiddle around** enredar con

fi·del·i·ty [fɪ'delətɪ] fidelidad *f*

fidg·et ['fɪdʒɪt] *v/i* moverse; **stop fidgeting!** ¡estate quieto!

fidg·et·y ['fɪdʒɪtɪ] *adj* inquieto

field [fiːld] *also of research etc* campo *m*; *for sports* campo *m*, *L.Am.* cancha *f*; (*competitors in race*) participantes *mpl*; **that's not my field** no es mi campo

field·er ['fiːldər] *in baseball* fildeador(-a) *m(f)*

'field e·vents *npl* pruebas *fpl* de salto y lanzamiento

fierce [fɪrs] *adj animal* feroz; *wind, storm* violento

fierce·ly ['fɪrslɪ] *adv* ferozmente

fi·er·y ['faɪrɪ] *adj* fogoso, ardiente

fif·teen [fɪf'tiːn] quince

fif·teenth [fɪf'tiːnθ] *n* & *adj* decimoquinto

fifth [fɪfθ] *n* & *adj* quinto

fif·ti·eth ['fɪftɪɪθ] *n* & *adj* quincuagésimo

fif·ty ['fɪftɪ] cincuenta

fif·ty-'fif·ty *adv* a medias

fig [fɪg] higo *m*

fight [faɪt] **1** *n* lucha *f*, pelea *f*; (*argument*) pelea *f*; *fig: for survival, championship etc* lucha *f*; *in boxing* combate *m*; **have a fight** (*argue*) pelearse **2** *v/t* (*pret & pp* **fought**) *enemy, person* luchar contra, pelear contra; *in boxing* pelear contra; *disease, injustice* luchar contra, combatir **3** *v/i* (*pret & pp* **fought**) luchar, pelear; (*argue*) pelearse

◆ **fight for** *v/t one's rights, a cause* luchar por

fight·er ['faɪtər] combatiente *m/f*; *airplane* caza *m*; (*boxer*) púgil *m*; **she's a fighter** tiene espíritu combativo

fight·ing ['faɪtɪŋ] *n physical, verbal* peleas *fpl*, MIL luchas *fpl*, combates *mpl*

fig·u·ra·tive ['fɪgjərətɪv] *adj* figurado

fig·ure ['fɪgər] **1** *n* figura *f*; (*digit*) cifra *f* **2** *v/t* F (*think*) imaginarse, pensar

◆ **figure on** *v/t* F (*plan*) pensar

◆ **figure out** *v/t* (*understand*) entender; *calculation* resolver

'fig·ure skat·er patinador(a) *m(f)* artístico(-a)

'fig·ure skat·ing patinaje *m* artístico

file¹ [faɪl] **1** *n of documents* expediente *m*; COMPUT archivo *m*, fichero *m* **2** *v/t documents* archivar

◆ **file away** *v/t documents* archivar

file² [faɪl] *n for wood, fingernails* lima *f*

'file cab·i·net archivador *m*

'file man·ag·er COMPUT administrador *m* de archivos

fi·li·al ['fɪljəl] *adj* filial

fill [fɪl] **1** *v/t* llenar; *tooth* empastar, *L.Am.* emplomar **2** *n:* **eat one's fill** hincharse

◆ **fill in** *v/t form, hole* rellenar; **fill s.o. in** poner a alguien al tanto

◆ **fill in for** *v/t* sustituir a

◆ **fill out 1** *v/t form* rellenar **2** *v/i* (*get fatter*) engordar

◆ **fill up 1** *v/t* llenar (hasta arriba) **2** *v/i of stadium, theater* llenarse

fill·ing ['fɪlɪŋ] **1** *n in sandwich* relleno *m*; *in tooth* empaste *m*, *L.Am.* emplomadura *f* **2** *adj:* **be filling** *of food* llenar mucho

'fill·ing sta·tion estación *f* de servicio, gasolinera *f*

film [fɪlm] **1** *n for camera* carrete *m*; (*movie*) película *f* **2** *v/t person, event* filmar

'film-mak·er cineasta *m/f*

'film star estrella *f* de cine

fil·ter ['fɪltər] **1** *n* filtro *m* **2** *v/t coffee, liquid* filtrar

◆ **filter through** *v/i of news reports* filtrarse

'fil·ter pa·per papel *m* de filtro

'fil·ter tip (*cigarette*) cigarrillo *m* con filtro

filth [fɪlθ] suciedad *f*, mugre *f*

filth·y ['fɪlθɪ] *adj* sucio, mugriento; *language etc* obsceno

fin [fɪn] *of fish* aleta *f*

fi·nal ['faɪnl] **1** *adj* (*last*) último; *decision* final, definitivo **2** *n* SP final *f*

fi·na·le [fɪ'næli] final *m*

fi·nal·ist ['faɪnəlɪst] finalista *m/f*

fi·nal·ize ['faɪnəlaɪz] *v/t plans, design* ultimar

fi·nal·ly ['faɪnəlɪ] *adv* finalmente, por último; (*at last*) finalmente, por fin

fi·nance ['faɪnæns] **1** *n* finanzas *fpl* **2** *v/t* financiar

fi·nanc·es ['faɪnænsɪz] *npl* finanzas *fpl*

fi·nan·cial [faɪ'nænʃl] *adj* financiero

fi·nan·cial·ly [faɪ'nænʃəlɪ] *adv* económicamente

fi·nan·cial 'year *Br* ejercicio *m* económico

fi·nan·cier [faɪ'nænsɪr] financiero(-a) *m(f)*

find [faɪnd] *v/t* (*pret & pp* **found**) encon-

trar, hallar; *if you find it too hot /cold* si
te parece demasiado frío / caliente; *find
s.o. innocent /guilty* LAW declarar a alguien inocente / culpable; *I find it strange that ...* me sorprende que ...; *how did
you find the hotel?* ¿qué te pareció el
hotel?
◆ **find out 1** *v/t* descubrir, averiguar **2** *v/i*
(*discover*) descubrir; *can you try to find
out?* ¿podrías enterarte?
find·ings ['faɪndɪŋz] *npl of report* conclusiones *fpl*
fine[1] [faɪn] *adj day, weather* bueno; *wine,
performance, city* excelente; *distinction,
line* fino; *how's that?* - *that's fine*
¿qué tal está? - bien; *that's fine by me*
por mí no hay ningún problema; *how
are you? - fine* ¿cómo estás? - bien
fine[2] [faɪn] **1** *n* multa *f* **2** *v/t* multar, poner
una multa a
fine-'tooth comb: *go through sth with a
fine-tooth comb* revisar algo minuciosamente
fine-'tune *v/t engine, fig* afinar, hacer los
últimos ajustes a
fin·ger ['fɪŋgər] **1** *n* dedo *m* **2** *v/t* tocar
'fin·ger·nail *n* uña *f*
'fin·ger·print 1 *n* huella *f* digital *or* dactilar **2** *v/t* tomar las huellas digitales *or*
dactilares a
'fin·ger·tip *n* punta *f* del dedo; *have sth at
one's fingertips* saberse algo al dedillo
fin·i·cky ['fɪnɪkɪ] *adj person* quisquilloso;
design enrevesado
fin·ish ['fɪnɪʃ] **1** *v/t* acabar, terminar; *finish doing sth* acabar *or* terminar de
hacer algo **2** *v/i* acabar, terminar **3** *n of
product* acabado *m*; *of race* final *f*
◆ **finish off** *v/t* acabar, terminar
◆ **finish up** *v/t food* acabar, terminar; *he
finished up liking it* acabó gustándole
◆ **finish with** *v/t boyfriend etc* cortar con
'fin·ish·ing line ['fɪnɪʃɪŋ] línea *f* de meta
Fin·land ['fɪnlənd] Finlandia
Finn [fɪn] finlandés (-esa) *m(f)*
Finn·ish ['fɪnɪʃ] **1** *adj* finlandés **2** *n language* finés *m*
fir [fɜːr] abeto *m*
fire [faɪr] **1** *n* fuego *m*; *electric, gas* estufa *f*;
(*blaze*) incendio *m*; (*bonfire, campfire
etc*) hoguera *f*; *be on fire* estar ardiendo;
catch fire prender; *set sth on fire, set
fire to sth* prender fuego a algo **2** *v/i*
(*shoot*) disparar (*on /at* sobre/a) **3** *v/t* F
(*dismiss*) despedir
'fire a·larm alarma *f* contra incendios
'fire·arm arma *f* de fuego
'fire·crack·er petardo *m*
'fire de·part·ment (cuerpo *m* de) bomberos *mpl*
'fire door puerta *f* contra incendios
'fire drill simulacro *m* de incendio; *Br* **'fire
en·gine** coche *m* de bomberos
'fire es·cape salida *f* de incendios
'fire ex·tin·guish·er extintor *m*
'fire fight·er bombero (-a) *m(f)*
'fire·guard pantalla *f*, parachispas *m inv*;
Br **'fire·man** bombero *m*
'fire·place chimenea *f*, hogar *m*
'fire sta·tion parque *m* de bomberos
'fire truck coche *m* de bomberos
'fire·wood leña *f*
'fire·works *npl* fuegos *mpl* artificiales
firm[1] [fɜːrm] *adj* firme; *a firm deal* un
acuerdo en firme
firm[2] [fɜːrm] *n* COM empresa *f*
first [fɜːrst] **1** *adj* primero; *who's first
please?* ¿quién es el primero, por favor?
2 *n* primero(-a) *m(f)* **3** *adv* primero; *first
of all* (*for one reason*) en primer lugar; *at
first* al principio
first 'aid primeros *mpl* auxilios
first-'aid box, first-'aid kit botiquín *m* de
primeros auxilios
'first·born *adj* primogénito
'first class 1 *adj ticket, seat* de primera
(clase); (*very good*) excelente **2** *adv travel*
en primera (clase)
first 'floor planta *f* baja, *Br* primer piso *m*
first'hand *adj* de primera mano
First 'La·dy of US primera dama *f*
first·ly ['fɜːrstlɪ] *adv* en primer lugar
first 'name nombre *m* (de pila)
first 'night estreno *m*
first of'fend·er delincuente *m/f* sin antecedentes
first of'fense primer delito *m*
first-'rate *adj* excelente
fis·cal ['fɪskl] *adj* fiscal
fis·cal 'year año *m* fiscal
fish [fɪʃ] **1** *n* (*pl fish*) *n* pez *m*; *to eat* pescado *m*; *drink like a fish* F beber como un
cosaco F; *feel like a fish out of water*
sentirse fuera de lugar **2** *v/i* pescar
'fish·bone espina *f* (de pescado)
fish·er·man ['fɪʃərmən] pescador *m*
fish·ing ['fɪʃɪŋ] pesca *f*
'fish·ing boat (barco *m*) pesquero *m*
'fish·ing line sedal *m*
'fish·ing rod caña *f* de pescar
'fish stick palito *m* de pescado
fish·y ['fɪʃɪ] *adj* F (*suspicious*) sospechoso
fit[1] [fɪt] *n* MED ataque *m*; *a fit of rage / jealousy* un arrebato de cólera / un ataque
de celos
fit[2] [fɪt] *adj physically* en forma; *morally*
adecuado; *he's not fit to be President*

no está en condiciones ser Presidente; **keep fit** mantenerse en forma

fit³ [fɪt] **1** v/t (attach) colocar; **these pants don't fit me any more** estos pantalones ya no me entran; **it fits you perfectly** te queda perfectamente **2** v/i (pret & pp **fitted**) of clothes quedar bien; of piece of furniture etc caber **3** n: **it's a good fit** of jacket etc queda bien; of piece of furniture cabe bien; **it's a tight fit** no hay mucho espacio

◆ **fit in 1** v/i of person in group encajar; **it fits in with our plans** encaja con nuestros planes **2** v/t: **fit s.o. in** into schedule etc hacer un hueco a alguien

fit·ful ['fɪtfəl] adj sleep intermitente
fit·ness ['fɪtnɪs] physical buena forma f
'fit·ness cen·ter, Br **'fit·ness cen·tre** gimnasio m
fit·ted 'kitch·en ['fɪtɪd] cocina f a medida
fit·ted 'sheet sábana f ajustable
fit·ter ['fɪtər] n técnico(-a) m(f)
fit·ting ['fɪtɪŋ] adj apropiado
fit·tings ['fɪtɪŋz] npl equipamiento m
five [faɪv] cinco
fix [fɪks] **1** n (solution) solución f; **be in a fix** F estar en un lío F **2** v/t (attach) fijar; (repair) arreglar, reparar; (arrange: meeting etc) organizar; lunch preparar; dishonestly: match etc amañar; **fix sth onto sth** fijar algo a algo; **I'll fix you a drink** te prepararé una bebida

◆ **fix up** v/t meeting organizar; **it's all fixed up** está todo organizado

fixed [fɪkst] adj lista
fix·ings ['fɪksɪŋz] npl guarnición f
fix·ture ['fɪkstʃər] (in room) parte fija del mobiliario o la decoración de una habitación

◆ **fiz·zle out** ['fɪzl] v/i F quedarse en nada
fiz·zy ['fɪzɪ] adj drink con gas
flab [flæb] on body grasa f
flab·ber·gast ['flæbərgæst] v/t F: **be flabbergasted** quedarse estupefacto or Span alucinado F
flab·by ['flæbɪ] adj muscles etc fofo
flag¹ [flæg] n bandera f
flag² [flæg] v/i (pret & pp **flagged**) (tire) desfallecer
'flag·pole asta f (de bandera)
fla·grant ['fleɪgrənt] adj flagrante
'flag·ship fig estandarte m
'flag·staff asta f (de bandera)
'flag·stone losa f
flair [fler] n (talent) don m; **have a natural flair for** tener dotes para
flake [fleɪk] n of snow copo m; of skin escama f; of plaster desconchón m

◆ **flake off** v/i of skin descamarse; of plas-

ter, paint desconcharse

flak·y ['fleɪkɪ] adj skin con escamas; paint desconchado
flak·y 'pas·try hojaldre m
flam·boy·ant [flæm'bɔɪənt] adj personality extravagante
flam·boy·ant·ly [flæm'bɔɪəntlɪ] adv dressed extravagantemente
flame [fleɪm] n llama f; **go up in flames** ser pasto de las llamas
fla·men·co [flə'meŋkou] flamenco m
fla·men·co danc·er bailaor(a) m(f)
flam·ma·ble ['flæməbəl] adj inflamable
flan [flæn] tarta f
flank [flæŋk] **1** n of horse etc costado m; MIL flanco m **2** v/t flanquear; **be flanked by** estar flanqueado por
flap [flæp] **1** n of envelope, pocket solapa f; of table hoja f; **be in a flap** F estar histérico F **2** v/t (pret & pp **flapped**) wings batir **3** v/i (pret & pp **flapped**) of flag etc ondear
flare [fler] **1** n (distress signal) bengala f; in dress vuelo m **2** v/t: **flare one's nostrils** hinchar las narices resoplando

◆ **flare up** v/i of violence estallar; of illness, rash exacerbarse, empeorar; of fire llamear; (get very angry) estallar
flash [flæʃ] **1** n of light destello m; PHOT flash m; **in a flash** F en un abrir y cerrar de ojos; **have a flash of inspiration** tener una inspiración repentina; **a flash of lightning** un relámpago **2** v/i of light destellar **3** v/t **flash one's headlights** echar las luces
'flash·back in movie flash-back m, escena f retrospectiva
flash·er ['flæʃər] MOT intermitente m
'flash·light linterna f; PHOT flash m
flash·y ['flæʃɪ] adj pej ostentoso, chillón
flask [flæsk] (hip flask) petaca f
flat¹ [flæt] **1** adj surface, land llano, plano; beer sin gas; battery descargado; tire desinflado; shoes bajo; MUS bemol; **and that's flat** F y sanseacabó F **2** adv MUS demasiado bajo; **flat out** work, run, drive a tope; **the factory is producing flat out** la fábrica está al máximo de su capacidad productiva **3** n Br (flat tire) pinchazo m
flat² [flæt] n Br apartamento m, Span piso m
flat-chest·ed [flæt'tʃestɪd] adj plana de pecho
flat·ly ['flætlɪ] adv refuse, deny rotundamente
'flat rate tarifa f única
flat·ten ['flætn] v/t land, road allanar, aplanar; by bombing, demolition arrasar
flat·ter ['flætər] v/t halagar, adular

flat·ter·er ['flætərər] adulador(a) m(f)

flat·ter·ing ['flætərɪŋ] adj comments halagador; color, clothes favorecedor

flat·ter·y ['flætərɪ] halagos mpl, adulación f

flat·u·lence ['flætjʊləns] flatulencia f

'flat·ware (cutlery) cubertería f

flaunt [flɔːnt] v/t hacer ostentación de, alardear de

flau·tist ['flɔːtɪst] flautista m/f

fla·vor ['fleɪvər] 1 n sabor m 2 v/t food condimentar

fla·vor·ing ['fleɪvərɪŋ] n aromatizante m

fla·vour etc Br → flavor etc

flaw [flɔː] n defecto m, fallo m

flaw·less ['flɔːlɪs] adj impecable

flea [fliː] n pulga f

fleck [flek] mota f

fled [fled] pret & pp → flee

flee [fliː] v/i (pret & pp fled) escapar, huir

fleece [fliːs] v/t F desplumar F

fleet [fliːt] n NAUT, of vehicles flota f

fleet·ing ['fliːtɪŋ] adj visit etc fugaz; catch a fleeting glimpse of vislumbrar fugazmente a

flesh [fleʃ] n carne f; of fruit pulpa f; meet / see s.o. in the flesh conocer / ver a alguien en persona

flex [fleks] v/t muscles flexionar

flex·i·bil·i·ty [fleksə'bɪlətɪ] flexibilidad f

flex·i·ble ['fleksəbl] adj flexible; I'm quite flexible about arrangements, timing soy bastante flexible

'flex·time ['flekstaɪm] horario m flexible

flew [fluː] pret → fly³

flick [flɪk] v/t tail sacudir; he flicked a fly off his hand espantó una mosca que tenía en la mano; she flicked her hair out of her eyes se apartó el pelo de los ojos

◆ flick through v/t book, magazine hojear

flick·er ['flɪkər] v/i of light, screen parpadear

fli·er [flaɪr] (circular) folleto m

flies [flaɪz] npl Br on pants bragueta f

flight [flaɪt] n in airplane vuelo m, (fleeing) huida f; not capable of flight incapaz de volar; flight (of stairs) tramo m (de escaleras)

'flight at·tend·ant auxiliar m/f de vuelo

'flight crew tripulación f

'flight deck AVIA cabina f del piloto

'flight num·ber número m de vuelo

'flight path ruta f de vuelo

'flight re·cord·er caja f negra

'flight time departure hora f del vuelo; duration duración f del vuelo

'flight·y ['flaɪtɪ] adj inconstante

flim·sy ['flɪmzɪ] adj structure, furniture

endeble; dress, material débil; excuse pobre

flinch [flɪntʃ] v/i encogerse

fling [flɪŋ] 1 v/t (pret & pp flung) arrojar, lanzar; fling o.s. into a chair dejarse caer en una silla 2 n F (affair) aventura f

◆ flip over [flɪp] v/i volcar

◆ flip through v/t (pret & pp flipped) magazine hojear

flip·per ['flɪpər] for swimming aleta f

flirt [flɜːrt] 1 v/i flirtear, coquetear 2 n ligón (-ona) m(f)

flir·ta·tious [flɜːr'teɪʃəs] adj coqueto

float [floʊt] v/i also FIN flotar

float·ing vot·er ['floʊtɪŋ] votante m/f indeciso(-a)

flock [flɑːk] 1 n of sheep rebaño m 2 v/i acudir en masa

flog [flɑːg] v/t (pret & pp flogged) (whip) azotar

flood [flʌd] 1 n inundación f 2 v/t of river inundar

◆ flood in v/i llegar en grandes cantidades

flood·ing ['flʌdɪŋ] inundaciones fpl

'flood·light n foco m

flood·lit ['flʌdlɪt] adj match con luz artificial

'flood wa·ters npl crecida f

floor [flɔːr] n suelo m; (story) piso m

'floor·board n tabla f del suelo

'floor cloth trapo m del suelo

'floor lamp lámpara f de pie

flop [flɑːp] 1 v/i (pret & pp flopped) dejarse caer; F (fail) pinchar F 2 n F (failure) pinchazo m F

flop·py ['flɑːpɪ] adj ears caído; hat blando; (weak) flojo

flop·py ('disk') disquete m

flor·ist ['flɔːrɪst] florista m/f

floss [flɑːs] 1 n for teeth hilo m dental 2 v/t: floss one's teeth limpiarse los dientes con hilo dental

flour [flaʊr] harina f

flour·ish ['flʌrɪʃ] v/i of plant crecer rápidamente; of business, civilization florecer, prosperar

flour·ish·ing ['flʌrɪʃɪŋ] adj business, trade floreciente, próspero

flow [floʊ] 1 v/i fluir 2 n flujo m

'flow·chart diagrama m de flujo

flow·er ['flaʊr] 1 n flor f 2 v/i florecer

'flow·er·bed parterre m

'flow·er·pot tiesto m, maceta f

'flow·er show exposición f floral

flow·er·y ['flaʊrɪ] adj pattern floreado; style of writing florido

flown [floʊn] pp → fly³

flu [fluː] gripe f

fluc·tu·ate ['flʌktjʊeɪt] *v/i* fluctuar

fluc·tu·a·tion [flʌktjʊ'eɪʃn] fluctuación *f*

flu·en·cy ['fluːənsɪ] *in a language* fluidez *f*

flu·ent ['fluːənt] *adj:* **he speaks fluent Spanish** habla español con soltura

flu·ent·ly ['fluːəntlɪ] *adv speak, write* con soltura

fluff [flʌf] *material* pelusa *f*

fluff·y ['flʌfɪ] *adj* esponjoso; **fluffy toy** juguete *m* de peluche

fluid ['fluːɪd] *n* fluido *m*

flung [flʌŋ] *pret & pp* → **fling**

flunk [flʌŋk] *v/t* F *subject* suspender, *Span* catear F

flu·o·res·cent [fluˈresnt] *adj light* fluorescente

flur·ry ['flʌrɪ] *of snow* torbellino *m*

flush [flʌʃ] **1** *v/t:* **flush the toilet** tirar de la cadena; **flush sth down the toilet** tirar algo por el retrete **2** *v/i (go red in the face)* ruborizarse; **the toilet won't flush** la cisterna no funciona **3** *adj (level):* **be flush with ...** estar a la misma altura que (...

◆ **flush away** *v/t:* **flush sth away** down toilet tirar algo por el retrete

◆ **flush out** *v/t rebels etc* hacer salir

flus·ter ['flʌstər] *v/t:* **get flustered** ponerse nervioso

flute [fluːt] MUS flauta *f*; *glass* copa *f* de champán

flut·ist ['fluːtɪst] flautista *m/f*

flut·ter ['flʌtər] *v/i of bird, wings* aletear; *of flag* ondear; *of heart* latir con fuerza

fly¹ [flaɪ] *n insect* mosca *f*

fly² [flaɪ] *n on pants* bragueta *f*

fly³ [flaɪ] **1** *v/i (pret flew, pp flown) of bird, airplane* volar; *in airplane* volar, ir en avión; *of flag* ondear; **fly into a rage** enfurecerse; **she flew out of the room** salió a toda prisa de la habitación **2** *v/t (pret flew, pp flown) airplane* pilotar; *airline* volar con; *(transport by air)* enviar por avión

◆ **fly away** *v/i of bird* salir volando; *of airplane* alejarse

◆ **fly back** *v/i (travel back)* volver en avión

◆ **fly in 1** *v/i of airplane, passengers* llegar en avión **2** *v/t supplies etc* transportar en avión

◆ **fly off** *v/i of hat etc* salir volando

◆ **fly out** *v/i* irse (en avión); **when do you fly out?** ¿cuándo os vais?

◆ **fly past** *v/i in formation* pasar volando en formación; *of time* volar

fly·ing ['flaɪɪŋ] *n* volar *m*

fly·ing 'sau·cer platillo *m* volante

foam [foʊm] *n on liquid* espuma *f*

foam 'rub·ber gomaespuma *f*

FOB [efoʊ'biː] *abbr (= free on board)* franco a bordo

fo·cus ['foʊkəs] **1** *n of attention,* PHOT foco *m*; **be in focus / out of focus** PHOT estar enfocado / desenfocado **2** *v/t:* **focus one's attention on** concentrar la atención en **3** *v/i* enfocar

◆ **focus on** *v/t problem, issue* concentrarse en; PHOT enfocar

fod·der ['fɑːdər] forraje *m*

fog [fɑːg] niebla *f*

◆ **fog up** *v/i (pret & pp fogged)* empañarse

'fog·bound *adj* paralizado por la niebla

fog·gy ['fɑːgɪ] *adj* neblinoso, con niebla; **it's foggy** hay niebla; **I haven't the foggiest idea** no tengo la más remota idea

foil¹ [fɔɪl] *n* papel *m* de aluminio

foil² [fɔɪl] *v/t (thwart)* frustrar

fold¹ [foʊld] **1** *v/t paper etc* doblar; **fold one's arms** cruzarse de brazos **2** *v/i of business* quebrar **3** *n in cloth etc* pliegue *m*

◆ **fold up 1** *v/t* plegar **2** *v/i of chair, table* plegarse

fold² [foʊld] *n for sheep etc* redil *m*

fold·er ['foʊldər] *for documents,* COMPUT carpeta *f*

fold·ing ['foʊldɪŋ] *adj* plegable; **folding chair** silla *f* plegable

fo·li·age ['foʊlɪɪdʒ] follaje *m*

folk [foʊk] *(people)* gente *f*; **my folks** *(family)* mi familia; **evening folks** F buenas noches, gente F

'folk dance baile *m* popular

'folk mu·sic música *f* folk *or* popular

'folk sing·er cantante *m/f* de folk

'folk song canción *m/f* folk *or* popular

fol·low ['fɑːloʊ] **1** *v/t seguir; (understand)* entender; **follow me** sígueme **2** *v/i logically* deducirse; **it follows from this that ...** de esto se deduce que...; **you go first and I'll follow** tú ve primero que yo te sigo; **the requirements are as follows** los requisitos son los siguientes

◆ **follow up** *v/t letter, inquiry* hacer el seguimiento de

fol·low·er ['fɑːloʊər] seguidor(a) *m(f)*

fol·low·ing ['fɑːloʊɪŋ] **1** *adj siguiente* **2** *n people* seguidores(-as) *mpl (fpl)*; **the following** lo siguiente

'fol·low-up meet·ing reunión *m* de seguimiento

'fol·low-up vis·it *to doctor etc* visita *f* de seguimiento

fol·ly ['fɑːlɪ] *(madness)* locura *f*

fond [fɑːnd] *adj (loving)* cariñoso; *memory* entrañable; **he's fond of travel /**

music le gusta viajar / la música; **I'm very fond of him** le tengo mucho cariño
fon·dle ['fɑːndl] *v/t* acariciar
fond·ness ['fɑːndnɪs] *for s.o.* cariño *m* (**for** por); *for wine, food* afición *f* (**for** por)
font [fɑːnt] *for printing* tipo *m*; *in church* pila *f* bautismal
food [fuːd] comida *f*
'food chain cadena *f* alimentaria
food·ie ['fuːdɪ] F gourmet *m/f*
'food mix·er robot *m* de cocina
food poi·son·ing ['fuːdpɔɪznɪŋ] intoxicación *f* alimentaria
fool [fuːl] **1** *n* tonto(-a) *m(f)*, idiota *m/f*; **you stupid fool!** ¡estúpido!; **make a fool of o.s.** ponerse en ridículo **2** *v/t* engañar
◆ **fool about, fool around** *v/i* hacer el tonto; *sexually* tener un lío
◆ **fool around with** *v/t* knife, drill etc enredar con algo; *sexually* tener un lío con ...
'fool·har·dy *adj* temerario
fool·ish ['fuːlɪʃ] *adj* tonto
fool·ish·ly ['fuːlɪʃlɪ] *adv*: **I foolishly ...** cometí la tontería de ...
'fool·proof *adj* infalible
foot [fut] (*pl* **feet** [fiːt]) *also measurement* pie *m*; *of animal* pata *f*; **on foot** a pie, caminando, andando; **I've been on my feet all day** llevo todo el día de pie; **be back on one's feet** estar recuperado; **at the foot of the page / hill** al pie de la página / de la colina; **put one's foot in it** F meter la pata F
'foot·age [fʊtɪdʒ] secuencias *fpl*, imágenes *fpl*
'foot·ball *Br* (*soccer*) fútbol *m*; *American style* fútbol *m* americano; *ball* balón *m* or pelota *f* (de fútbol)
'foot·ball play·er *American style* jugador(a) *m(f)* de fútbol americano; *Br in soccer* jugador(a) *m(f)* de fútbol, futbolista *m/f*
'foot·bridge puente *m* peatonal
foot·er ['futər] *in document* pie *m* de página
foot·hills ['futhɪlz] *npl* estribaciones *fpl*
'foot·hold *n in climbing* punto *m* de apoyo; **gain a foothold** *fig* introducirse
foot·ing ['futɪŋ] (*basis*): **put the business back on a secure footing** volver a afianzar la empresa; **lose one's footing** perder el equilibrio; **be on the same/a different footing** estar / no estar en igualdad de condiciones; **be on a friendly footing with ...** tener relaciones de amistad con ...
foot·lights ['futlaɪts] *npl* candilejas *fpl*
'foot·mark pisada *f*

'foot·note nota *f* a pie de página
'foot·path sendero *m*
'foot·print pisada *f*
'foot·step paso *m*; **follow in s.o.'s footsteps** seguir los pasos de alguien
'foot·stool escabel *m*
'foot·wear calzado *m*
for [fər, fɔːr] *prep* ◇ *purpose, destination etc* para; **a train for ...** un tren para or hacia ...; **clothes for children** ropa para niños; **it's too big / small for you** te queda demasiado grande / pequeño; **here's a letter for you** hay una carta para ti; **this is for you** esto es para ti; **what's for lunch?** ¿qué hay para comer?; **the steak is for me** el filete es para mí; **what is this for?** ¿para qué sirve esto?; **what for?** ¿para qué?
◇ *time* durante; **for three days / two hours** durante tres días / dos horas; **it lasts for two hours** dura dos horas; **please get it done for Monday** por favor tenlo listo (para) el lunes
◇ *distance*: **I walked for a mile** caminé una milla; **it stretches for 100 miles** se extiende 100 millas
◇ (*in favor of*): **I am for the idea** estoy a favor de la idea
◇ (*instead of, in behalf of*): **let me do that for you** déjame que te lo haga; **we are agents for ...** somos representantes de ...
◇ (*in exchange for*) por; **I bought it for $25** lo compré por 25 dólares; **how much did you sell it for?** ¿por cuánto lo vendiste?
for·bade [fər'bæd] *pret* → **forbid**
for·bid [fər'bɪd] *v/t* (*pret* **forbade**, *pp* **forbidden**) prohibir; **forbid s.o. to do sth** prohibir a alguien hacer algo
for·bid·den [fər'bɪdn] **1** *adj* prohibido; **smoking / parking forbidden** prohibido fumar / aparcar **2** *pp* → **forbid**
for·bid·ding [fər'bɪdɪŋ] *adj person, tone, look* amenazador; *rockface* imponente; *prospect* intimidador
force [fɔːrs] **1** *n* fuerza *f*; **come into force** *of law etc* entrar en vigor; **the forces** MIL las fuerzas **2** *v/t door, lock* forzar; **force s.o. to do sth** forzar a alguien a hacer algo; **force sth open** forzar algo
◆ **force back** *v/t tears* contener
forced [fɔːrst] *adj* forzado
forced 'land·ing aterrizaje *m* forzoso
force·ful ['fɔːrsfəl] *adj argument* poderoso; *speaker* vigoroso; *character* enérgico
force·ful·ly ['fɔːrsfəlɪ] *adv* de manera convincente
for·ceps ['fɔːrseps] *npl* MED fórceps *m inv*

for·ci·ble ['fɔːrsəbl] *adj* entry por la fuerza

for·ci·bly ['fɔːrsəbli] *adv* por la fuerza

ford [fɔːrd] *n* vado *m*

fore [fɔːr] *n*: **come to the fore** salir a la palestra

'fore·arm antebrazo *m*

fore·bears ['fɔːrberz] *npl* antepasados *mpl*

fore·bod·ing [fɔːr'boʊdɪŋ] premonición *f*

'fore·cast 1 *n* pronóstico *m*; *of weather* pronóstico *m* (del tiempo) **2** *v/t* (*pret & pp* **forecast**) pronosticar

'fore·court (*of garage*) explanada en la parte de delante

fore·fa·thers ['fɔːrfɑːðərz] *npl* ancestros *mpl*

'fore·fin·ger (dedo *m*) índice *m*

'fore·front: **be in the forefront of** estar a la vanguardia de

'fore·gone *adj*: **that's a foregone conclusion** eso ya se sabe de antemano

'fore·ground primer plano *m*

'fore·hand *in tennis* derecha *f*

'fore·head frente *f*

for·eign ['fɑːrən] *adj* extranjero; *a foreign holiday* unas vacaciones en el extranjero

for·eign af'fairs *npl* asuntos *mpl* exteriores

for·eign 'aid ayuda *f* al exterior

for·eign 'bod·y cuerpo *m* extraño

for·eign 'cur·ren·cy divisa *f* extranjera

for·eign·er ['fɑːrənər] extranjero(-a) *m(f)*

for·eign ex'change divisas *fpl*

for·eign 'lan·guage idioma *m* extranjero

'For·eign Of·fice *in UK* Ministerio *m* de Asuntos Exteriores

for·eign 'pol·i·cy política *f* exterior

For·eign 'Sec·re·ta·ry *in UK* Ministro(-a) *m(f)* de Asuntos Exteriores

'fore·man capataz *m*

'fore·most *adv* principal; *what was foremost in my mind was the worry that ...* mi principal preocupación era que ...

fo·ren·sic 'med·i·cine [fə'rensɪk] medicina *f* forense

fo·ren·sic 'sci·en·tist forense *m/f*

'fore·run·ner predecesor(a) *m(f)*

fore·see *v/t* (*pret* **foresaw**, *pp* **foreseen**) prever

fore·see·a·ble [fər'siːəbl] *adj* previsible; *in the foreseeable future* en un futuro próximo

fore·seen *pp* → **foresee**

'fore·sight previsión *f*

for·est ['fɑːrɪst] bosque *m*

for·est·ry ['fɑːrɪstrɪ] silvicultura

'fore·taste anticipo *m*

fore·tell *v/t* (*pret & pp* **foretold**) predecir

for·ev·er [fə'revər] *adv* siempre; *it is forever raining here* aquí llueve constantemente; *I will remember this day forever* no me olvidaré nunca de ese día

fore·word ['fɔːrwɜːrd] prólogo *m*

for·feit ['fɔːrfɪt] *v/t* (*lose*) perder; (*give up*) renunciar a

for·gave [fər'ɡeɪv] *pret* → **forgive**

forge [fɔːrdʒ] *v/t* falsificar

♦ **forge ahead** *v/i* progresar rápidamente

forg·er ['fɔːrdʒər] falsificador(a) *m(f)*

forg·er·y ['fɔːrdʒərɪ] falsificación *f*

for·get [fər'ɡet] *v/t* (*pret* **forgot**, *pp* **forgotten**) olvidar; *I forgot his name* se me olvidó su nombre; *forget to do sth* olvidarse de hacer algo

for·get·ful [fər'ɡetfəl] *adj* olvidadizo

for'get-me-not *n* nomeolvides *m inv*

for·give [fər'ɡɪv] *v/t & v/i* (*pret* **forgave**, *pp* **forgiven**) perdonar

for·giv·en [fər'ɡɪvn] *pp* → **forgive**

for·give·ness [fər'ɡɪvnɪs] perdón *m*

for·got [fər'ɡɑːt] *pret* → **forget**

for·got·ten [fər'ɡɑːtn] *pp* → **forget**

fork [fɔːrk] *n for eating* tenedor *m*; *for garden* horca *f*; *in road* bifurcación *f*

♦ **fork out** *v/t & v/i* F (*pay*) apoquinar F

forked *adj tongue* bífido; *stick* bifurcado

fork·lift 'truck carretilla *f* elevadora

form [fɔːrm] **1** *n shape* forma *f*; (*document*) formulario *m*, impreso *m*; *be on / off form* estar / no estar en forma **2** *v/t in clay etc* moldear; *friendship* establecer; *opinion* formarse; *past tense etc* formar; (*constitute*) formar, constituir **3** *v/i* (*take shape, develop*) formarse

form·al ['fɔːrml] *adj* formal; *recognition etc* oficial; *dress* de etiqueta

for·mal·i·ty [fər'mælətɪ] formalidad *f*; *it's just a formality* sólo es una formalidad; *the formalities* las formalidades

for·mal·ly ['fɔːrməlɪ] *adv speak, behave* formalmente; *accepted, recognized* oficialmente

for·mat ['fɔːrmæt] **1** *v/t* (*pret & pp* **formatted**) *diskette, document* formatear **2** *n of paper, program etc* formato *m*

for·ma·tion [fɔːr'meɪʃn] formación *f*; *formation flying* vuelo *m* en formación

for·ma·tive ['fɔːrmətɪv] *adj* formativo; *in his formative years* en sus años de formación

for·mer ['fɔːrmər] *adj* antiguo; *the former* el primero; *the former arrangement* la situación de antes

for·mer·ly ['fɔːrmərlɪ] *adv* antiguamente

for·mi·da·ble ['fɔːrmɪdəbl] *adj* persona-

fraud

lity formidable; *opponent, task* terrible

for·mu·la ['fɔːrmjʊlə] MATH, CHEM, *fig* fórmula *f*

for·mu·late ['fɔːrmjʊleɪt] *v/t (express)* formular

for·ni·cate ['fɔːrnɪkeɪt] *v/i fml* fornicar

for·ni·ca·tion [fɔːrnɪˈkeɪʃn] *fml* fornicación *f*

fort [fɔːrt] MIL fuerte *m*

forth [fɔːrθ] *adv:* **back and forth** de un lado para otro; *and so forth* y así sucesivamente; *from that day forth* desde ese día en adelante

forth·com·ing ['fɔːrθkʌmɪŋ] *adj (future)* próximo; *personality* comunicativo

'forth·right *adj* directo

for·ti·eth ['fɔːrtɪɪθ] *n & adj* cuadragésimo

fort·night ['fɔːrtnaɪt] *Br* quincena *f*

for·tress ['fɔːrtrɪs] MIL fortaleza *f*

for·tu·nate ['fɔːrtʃnət] *adj* afortunado

for·tu·nate·ly ['fɔːrtʃnətlɪ] *adv* afortunadamente

for·tune ['fɔːrtʃən] *(fate, money)* fortuna *f*; *(luck)* fortuna *f*, suerte *f*; *tell s.o.'s fortune* decir a alguien la buenaventura

'for·tune-tell·er adivino(-a) *m(f)*

for·ty ['fɔːrtɪ] cuarenta; *have forty winks* F echarse una siestecilla F

fo·rum ['fɔːrəm] *fig* foro *m*

for·ward ['fɔːrwərd] **1** *adv* hacia delante **2** *adj pej: person* atrevido **3** *n* SP delantero(-a) *m(f)* **4** *v/t letter* reexpedir

'for·ward·ing ad·dress ['fɔːrwərdɪŋ] *dirección a la que reexpedir correspondencia*

'for·ward·ing a·gent COM transitario(-a) *m(f)*

'for·ward-look·ing *adj* con visión de futuro, moderno

fos·sil ['fɑːsɪl] fósil *m*

fos·sil·ized ['fɑːsəlaɪzd] *adj* fosilizado

fos·ter ['fɑːstər] *v/t child* acoger, adoptar *(temporalmente); attitude, belief* fomentar

'fos·ter child niño(-a) *m(f)* en régimen de acogida

'fos·ter home hogar *m* de acogida

'fos·ter par·ents *npl* familia *f* de acogida

fought [fɔːt] *pret & pp* → **fight**

foul [faʊl] **1** *n* SP falta *f* **2** *adj smell, taste* asqueroso; *weather* terrible **3** *v/t* SP hacer (una) falta a

found¹ [faʊnd] *v/t school etc* fundar

found² [faʊnd] *pret & pp* → **find**

foun·da·tion [faʊnˈdeɪʃn] *of theory etc* fundamento *m*; *(organization)* fundación *f*

foun·da·tions [faʊnˈdeɪʃnz] *npl of building* cimientos *mpl*

found·er ['faʊndər] *n* fundador(a) *m(f)*

found·ing ['faʊndɪŋ] *n* fundación *f*

foun·dry ['faʊndrɪ] fundición *f*

foun·tain ['faʊntɪn] fuente *f*

'foun·tain pen pluma *f* (estilográfica)

four [fɔːr] cuatro; *on all fours* a gatas, a cuatro patas

four-let·ter 'word palabrota *f*

four-post·er ('bed) cama *f* de dosel

'four-star *adj hotel etc* de cuatro estrellas

four·teen [fɔːrˈtiːn] catorce

four·teenth [fɔːrˈtiːnθ] *n & adj* decimocuarto

fourth [fɔːrθ] *n & adj* cuarto

four-wheel 'drive MOT vehículo *m* con tracción a las cuatro ruedas; *type of drive* tracción *f* a las cuatro ruedas

fowl [faʊl] ave *f* de corral

fox [fɑːks] **1** *n* zorro **m 2** *v/t (puzzle)* dejar perplejo

toy·er ['fɔɪər] vestíbulo *m*

frac·tion ['frækʃn] fracción *f*; MATH fracción *f*, quebrado *m*

frac·tion·al·ly ['frækʃnəlɪ] *adv* ligeramente

frac·ture ['fræktʃər] **1** *n* fractura *f* **2** *v/t* fracturar; *he fractured his arm* se fracturó el brazo

fra·gile ['frædʒəl] *adj* frágil

frag·ment ['frægmənt] *n* fragmento *m*

frag·men·ta·ry [fræɡˈmentərɪ] *adj* fragmentario

fra·grance ['freɪgrəns] fragancia *f*

fra·grant ['freɪgrənt] *adj* fragante

frail [freɪl] *adj* frágil, delicado

frame [freɪm] **1** *n of picture, window* marco *m; of eyeglasses* montura *f; of bicycle* cuadro *m; frame of mind* estado *m* de ánimo **2** *v/t picture* enmarcar; F *person* tender una trampa a

'frame-up F trampa *f*

'frame·work estructura *f; for agreement* marco *m*

France [fræns] Francia *f*

fran·chise ['fræntʃaɪz] *n for business* franquicia *f*

frank [fræŋk] *adj* franco

frank·furt·er ['fræŋkfɜːrtər] salchicha *f* de Fráncfort

frank·ly ['fræŋklɪ] *adv* francamente; *frankly, it's not worth it* francamente *or* la verdad, no vale la pena

frank·ness ['fræŋknɪs] franqueza *f*

fran·tic ['fræntɪk] *adj* frenético

fran·ti·cal·ly ['fræntɪklɪ] *adv* frenéticamente

fra·ter·nal [frəˈtɜːrnl] *adj* fraternal

fraud [frɔːd] fraude *m; person* impostor(a) *m(f)*

fraud·u·lent ['frɔːdjʊlənt] *adj* fraudulento

fraud·u·lent·ly ['frɔːdjʊləntlɪ] *adv* fraudulentamente

frayed [freɪd] *adj cuffs* deshilachado

freak [friːk] 1 *n unusual event* fenómeno *m* anormal; *two-headed person, animal etc* monstruo *m*, monstruosidad *f*; *strange person* bicho *m* raro F; *movie / jazz freak* F un fanático del cine / jazz F 2 *adj wind, storm etc* anormal

freck·le ['frekl] peca *f*

free [friː] 1 *adj* libre; *no cost* gratis, gratuito; *are you free this afternoon?* ¿estás libre esta tarde?; *free and easy* relajado; *for free* travel, get sth gratis 2 *v/t prisoners* liberar

free·bie ['friːbɪ] F regalo *m*; *as a freebie* de regalo

free·dom ['friːdəm] libertad *f*

free·dom of 'speech libertad *f* de expresión

free·dom of the 'press libertad *f* de prensa

free 'en·ter·prise empresa *f* libre

free 'kick *in soccer* falta *f*, golpe *m* franco

free·lance ['friːlæns] 1 *adj* autónomo, free-lance 2 *adv: work freelance* trabajar como autónomo *or* free-lance

free·lanc·er ['friːlænsər] autónomo(-a) *m(f)*, free-lance *m(f)*

free·load·er ['friːloʊdər] F gorrón (-ona) *m(f)*

free·ly ['friːlɪ] *adv admit* libremente

free mar·ket e'con·o·my economía *f* de libre mercado

free-range 'chick·en pollo *m* de corral

free-range 'eggs *npl* huevos *mpl* de corral

free 'sam·ple muestra *f* gratuita

free 'speech libertad *f* de expresión

'free·way autopista *f*

free·wheel *v/i on bicycle* ir sin pedalear

free 'will libre albedrío *m*; *he did it of his own free will* lo hizo por propia iniciativa

freeze [friːz] 1 *v/t* (*pret froze, pp frozen*) *food, wages, video* congelar; *river* congelar, helar 2 *v/i* (*pret froze, pp frozen*) *of water* congelarse, helarse

◆ **freeze over** *v/i of river* helarse

'freeze-dried liofilizado

freez·er ['friːzər] congelador *m*

freez·ing ['friːzɪŋ] 1 *adj* muy frío; *it's freezing (cold)* *of weather* hace mucho frío; *of water* está muy frío; *I'm freezing (cold)* tengo mucho frío 2 *n: 10 below freezing* diez grados bajo cero

'freez·ing com·part·ment congelador *m*

'freez·ing point punto *m* de congelación

freight [freɪt] *n* transporte; *costs* flete *m*

'freight car *on train* vagón *m* de mercancías

freight·er ['freɪtər] *ship* carguero *m*; *airplane* avión *m* de carga

'freight train tren *m* de mercancías

French [frentʃ] 1 *adj* francés; *language* francés *m*; *the French* los franceses

French 'bread pan *m* de barra

French 'doors *npl* puerta *f* cristalera

'French fries *npl Span* patatas *fpl or L.Am.* papas *fpl* fritas

'French·man francés *m*

'French·wom·an francesa *f*

fren·zied ['frenzɪd] *adj attack, activity* frenético; *mob* desenfrenado

fren·zy ['frenzɪ] frenesí *m*; *whip s.o. into a frenzy* poner a alguien frenético

fre·quen·cy ['friːkwənsɪ] *also* RAD frecuencia *f*

fre·quent¹ ['friːkwənt] *adj* frecuente; *how frequent are the trains?* ¿con qué frecuencia pasan trenes?

fre·quent² [frɪ'kwent] *v/t bar* frecuentar

fre·quent·ly ['friːkwəntlɪ] *adv* con frecuencia

fres·co ['freskoʊ] fresco *m*

fresh [freʃ] *adj* fresco; *start* nuevo; *don't you get fresh with your mother!* ¡no seas descarado con tu madre!

fresh air aire *m* fresco

fresh·en ['freʃn] *v/i of wind* refrescar

◆ **freshen up** 1 *v/i* refrescarse 2 *v/t room, paintwork* renovar, revivir

fresh·ly ['freʃlɪ] *adv* recién

'fresh·man estudiante *m/f* de primer año

fresh·ness ['freʃnɪs] frescura *f*

'fresh·wa·ter *adj* de agua dulce

fret [fret] *v/i* (*pret & pp fretted*) ponerse nervioso, inquietarse

Freud·i·an ['frɔɪdɪən] *adj* freudiano

fric·tion ['frɪkʃn] PHYS rozamiento *m*; *between people* fricción *f*

'fric·tion tape cinta *f* aislante

Fri·day ['fraɪdeɪ] viernes *m inv*

fridge [frɪdʒ] nevera *f*, frigorífico *m*

fried [fraɪd] huevo *m* frito

fried po'ta·toes *npl Span* patatas *fpl or L.Am.* papas *fpl* fritas

friend [frend] amigo(-a) *m(f)*; *make friends* *of one person* hacer amigos; *of two people* hacer amigos; *make friends with s.o.* hacerse amigo de alguien

friend·li·ness ['frendlɪnɪs] simpatía *f*

friend·ly ['frendlɪ] *adj atmosphere* agradable; *person* agradable, simpático; *(easy to use)* fácil de usar; *argument, match, re-*

fucking

lations amistoso; *be friendly with s.o.*
(*be friends*) ser amigo de alguien
'friend·ship ['frendʃɪp] amistad *f*
fries [fraɪz] *npl Span* patatas *fpl* or *L.Am.*
papas *fpl* fritas
fright [fraɪt] susto *m*; *give s.o. a fright* dar
un susto a alguien, asustar a alguien;
scream with fright gritar asustado
fright·en ['fraɪtn] *v/t* asustar; *be frightened* estar asustado, tener miedo; *don't
be frightened* no te asustes, no tengas
miedo; *be frightened of* tener miedo de
♦ **frighten away** *v/t* ahuyentar, espantar
fright·en·ing ['fraɪtnɪŋ] *adj noise, person,
prospect* aterrador, espantoso
frig·id ['frɪdʒɪd] *adj sexually* frígido
frill [frɪl] *on dress etc* volante *m*; (*fancy extra*) extra *m*
frill·y ['frɪlɪ] *adj* de volantes
fringe [frɪndʒ] *on dress, curtains etc* flecos
mpl; *Br in hair* flequillo *m*; (*edge*) margen *m*
fringe ben·e·fits *npl* ventajas *fpl* adicio-
nales
frisk [frɪsk] *v/t* cachear
frisk·y ['frɪskɪ] *adj puppy etc* juguetón
♦ **fritter away** ['frɪtər] *v/t time* desperdiciar; *fortune* despilfarrar
fri·vol·i·ty [frɪ'vɒlətɪ] frivolidad *f*
friv·o·lous ['frɪvələs] *adj* frívolo
frizz·y ['frɪzɪ] *adj hair* crespo
frog [frɒg] rana *f*
'frog·man hombre *m* rana
from [frɒm] *prep* ◇ *in time* desde; *from
9 to 5 (o'clock)* de 9 a 5; *from the 18th
century* desde el siglo XVIII; *from today on* a partir de hoy; *from next Tuesday* a partir del próximo martes
◇ *in space* de, desde; *from here to there* de or desde aquí hasta allí; *we drove here from Paris* vinimos en coche desde
París
◇ *origin* de; *a letter from Jo* una carta
de Jo; *a gift from the management* un
regalo de la dirección; *It doesn't say
who it's from* no dice de quién es; *I
am from New Jersey* soy de Nueva Jersey; *made from bananas* hecho con
plátanos
◇ (*because of*): *tired from the journey*
cansado del viaje; *it's from overeating*
es por comer demasiado
front [frʌnt] **1** *n of building, book* portada
f; (*cover organization*) tapadera *f*; MIL, *of
weather* frente *m*; *in front* delante; *in a
race* en cabeza; *the car in front* el coche
de delante; *in front of* delante de; *at the
front of* en la parte de delante de **2** *adj
wheel, seat* delantero **3** *v/t* TV *program*

presentar
front 'cov·er portada *f*
front 'door puerta *f* principal
front 'en·trance entrada *f* principal
fron·tier ['frʌntɪr] frontera *f*; *fig: of knowledge, science* límite *m*
front 'line MIL línea *f* del frente
front 'page *of newspaper* portada *f*, primera *f* plana
front page 'news *nsg* noticia *f* de portada
or de primera plana
front 'row primera fila *f*
front seat 'pas·sen·ger *in car* pasaje-
ro(-a) *m(f)* de delante
front-wheel 'drive tracción *f* delantera
frost [frɒst] *n* escarcha *f*; *there was a
frost last night* anoche cayó una helada
'frost·bite congelación *f*
'frost·bit·ten *adj* congelado
frost·ed glass ['frɒstɪd] vidrio *m* esmerilado
'frost·ing ['frɒstɪŋ] *on cake* glaseado *m*
frost·y ['frɒstɪ] *adj weather* gélido; *fig:
welcome* glacial
froth [frɒθ] *n* espuma *f*
froth·y ['frɒθɪ] *adj cream etc* espumoso
frown [fraʊn] **1** *n*: *what's that frown for?*
¿por qué frunces el ceño? **2** *v/i* fruncir el
ceño
froze [frəʊz] *pret* → **freeze**
fro·zen ['frəʊzn] **1** *adj ground, food* congelado; *wastes* helado; *I'm frozen* estoy
helado or congelado F **2** *pp* → **freeze**
fro·zen 'food comida *f* congelada
fruit [fruːt] fruta *f*
'fruit cake bizcocho *m* de frutas
fruit·ful ['fruːtfəl] *adj discussions etc* fructífero
fruit juice *Span* zumo *m* or *L.Am.* jugo *m*
de fruta
fruit 'sal·ad macedonia *f*
frus·trate [frʌ'streɪt] *v/t person, plans*
frustrar
frus·trat·ed [frʌ'streɪtɪd] *adj* frustrado
frus·trat·ing [frʌ'streɪtɪŋ] *adj* frustrante
frus·tra·tion [frʌ'streɪʃn] frustración *f*;
sexual frustration frustración *f* sexual;
the frustrations of modern life las frus-
traciones de la vida moderna
fry [fraɪ] *v/t* (*pret & pp* **fried**) freír
'fry·pan sartén *f*
fuck [fʌk] *v/t* V *Span* follar con V, *L.Am.*
coger V; *fuck!* ¡joder! V; *fuck him!* ¡que
se joda! V
♦ **fuck off** *v/i* V: *fuck off!* ¡vete a la mierda! V
fuck·ing ['fʌkɪŋ] **1** *adj* V puto V **2** *adv* V:
it's fucking crazy es un estupidez
¡coño!; *it was fucking brilliant!* ¡estuvo

de puta madre! V

fu·el ['fjʊəl] **1** n combustible m **2** v/t fig avivar

fu·gi·tive ['fjuːdʒətɪv] n fugitivo(-a) m(f)

ful·fil Br, **ful·fill** [fʊl'fɪl] v/t dream cumplir, realizar; task realizar; contract cumplir; *feel fulfilled in job, life* sentirse realizado

ful·fill·ing [fʊl'fɪlɪŋ] adj: *I have a fulfilling job* mi trabajo me llena

ful·fil·ment Br, **ful·fill·ment** [fʊl'fɪlmənt] of contract cumplimiento m; moral, spiritual satisfacción f

full [fʊl] adj lleno; account, schedule completo; life pleno; *full of water etc* lleno de; *full up* hotel etc, with food lleno; *pay in full* pagar al contado

full 'board Br pensión f completa

'full-grown adj completamente desarrollado

'full-length adj dress de cuerpo entero; *full-length movie* largometraje m

full 'moon luna f llena

full 'stop Br punto m

full 'time 1 adj worker, job a tiempo completo **2** adv work a tiempo completo

ful·ly ['fʊlɪ] adv completamente; describe en detalle

fum·ble ['fʌmbl] v/t ball dejar caer
◆ **fumble about** v/i rebuscar

fume [fjuːm] v/i: *be fuming* F with anger echar humo F

fumes [fjuːmz] npl humos mpl

fun [fʌn] diversión f; *it was great fun* fue muy divertido; *bye, have fun!* ¡adiós, que lo paséis bien!; *for fun* para divertirse; *make fun of* burlarse de

func·tion ['fʌŋkʃn] **1** n (purpose) función f; (reception etc) acto m **2** v/i funcionar; *function as* hacer de

func·tion·al ['fʌŋkʃnl] adj funcional

fund [fʌnd] **1** n fondo m **2** v/t project etc financiar

fun·da·men·tal [fʌndə'mentl] adj fundamental; (crucial) esencial

fun·da·men·tal·ist [fʌndə'mentlɪst] n fundamentalista m/f

fun·da·men·tal·ly [fʌndə'mentlɪ] adv fundamentalmente

fund·ing ['fʌndɪŋ] (money) fondos mpl, financiación f

fu·ne·ral ['fjuːnərəl] funeral m

'fu·ne·ral di·rec·tor encargado(-a) m(f) de una funeraria

'fu·ne·ral home funeraria f

fun·gus ['fʌŋgəs] hongos mpl

fu·nic·u·lar ('rail·way) [fjuː'nɪkjʊlər] funicular m

fun·nel ['fʌnl] n of ship chimenea f

fun·nies ['fʌnɪz] npl F sección de humor

fun·ni·ly ['fʌnɪlɪ] adv (oddly) de modo extraño; (comically) de forma divertida; *funnily enough* curiosamente

fun·ny ['fʌnɪ] adj (comical) divertido, gracioso; (odd) curioso, raro; *that's not funny* eso no tiene gracia

'fun·ny bone hueso m de la risa

fur [fɜːr] piel f

fu·ri·ous ['fjʊrɪəs] adj (angry) furioso; (intense) furioso, feroz; effort febril; *at a furious pace* a un ritmo vertiginoso

fur·nace ['fɜːrnɪs] horno m

fur·nish ['fɜːrnɪʃ] v/t room amueblar; (supply) suministrar

fur·ni·ture ['fɜːrnɪtʃər] mobiliario m, muebles mpl; *a piece of furniture* un mueble

fur·ry ['fɜːrɪ] adj animal peludo

fur·ther ['fɜːrðər] **1** adj (additional) adicional; (more distant) más lejano; *there's been a further development* ha pasado algo nuevo; *until further notice* hasta nuevo aviso; *have you anything further to say?* ¿tiene algo más que añadir? **2** adv walk, drive más lejos; *further, I want to say ...* además, quiero decir ...; *two miles further (on)* dos millas más adelante **3** v/t cause etc promover

fur·ther'more adv es más

fur·thest ['fɜːrðɪst] **1** adj: *the furthest point north* el punto más al norte; *the furthest stars* las estrellas más lejanas **2** adv más lejos; *this is the furthest north I've ever been* nunca había estado tan al norte

fur·tive ['fɜːrtɪv] adj glance furtivo

fur·tive·ly ['fɜːrtɪvlɪ] adv furtivamente

fu·ry ['fjʊrɪ] (anger) furia f, ira f

fuse [fjuːz] **1** n ELEC fusible m **2** v/i ELEC fundirse; *the lights have fused* se han fundido los plomos **3** v/t ELEC fundir

'fuse·box caja f de fusibles

fu·se·lage ['fjuːzəlɑːʒ] fuselaje m

'fuse wire fusible m (hilo)

fu·sion ['fjuːʒn] fusión f

fuss [fʌs] n escándalo m; *make a fuss* (complain) armar un escándalo; (behave in exaggerated way) armar un escándalo; *make a fuss of* (be very attentive to) deshacerse en atenciones con

fuss·y ['fʌsɪ] adj person quisquilloso; design etc recargado; *be a fussy eater* ser un quisquilloso a la hora de comer

fu·tile ['fjuːtl] adj inútil, vano

fu·til·i·ty [fjuː'tɪlətɪ] inutilidad f

fu·ture ['fjuːtʃər] **1** n also GRAM futuro m; *in future* en el futuro **2** adj futuro

fu·tures ['fjuːtʃərz] npl FIN futuros mpl

'fu·tures mar·ket FIN mercado m de futuros

fu·tur·is·tic [fjuːˈʃəˈrɪstɪk] adj design futurista

fuze [fjuːz] → **fuse**

fuzz·y [ˈfʌzɪ] adj hair crespo; (out of focus) borroso

G

gab [gæb] n: **have the gift of the gab** F tener labia F

gab·ble [ˈgæbl] v/i farfullar

◆ **gad about** [gæd] v/i (pret & pp **gadded**) pendonear

gad·get [ˈgædʒɪt] artilugio m, chisme m

gaffe [gæf] metedura f de pata

gag [gæg] **1** n over mouth mordaza f; (joke) chiste m **2** v/t (pret & pp **gagged**) also fig amordazar

gain [geɪn] v/t (acquire) ganar; victory obtener; **gain speed** cobrar velocidad; **gain 10 pounds** engordar 10 libras

ga·la [ˈgælə] gala f

gal·ax·y [ˈgæləksɪ] AST galaxia f

gale [geɪl] vendaval m

gal·lant [ˈgælənt] adj galante

gall blad·der [ˈgɔːlblædər] vesícula f biliar

gal·le·ry [ˈgælərɪ] for art museo m; in theater galería f

gal·ley [ˈgælɪ] on ship cocina f

◆ **gal·li·vant around** [ˈgælɪvænt] v/i pendonear

gal·lon [ˈgælən] galón m (en EE.UU. 3,785 litros, en GB 4,546); **gallons of tea** F toneladas de té F

gal·lop [ˈgæləp] v/i galopar

gal·lows [ˈgæloʊz] npl horca f

gall·stone [ˈgɔːlstoʊn] cálculo m biliar

ga·lore [gəˈlɔːr] adj: **apples / novels galore** manzanas / novelas a montones

gal·va·nize [ˈgælvənaɪz] v/t TECH galvanizar; **galvanize s.o. into activity** hacer que alguien se vuelva más activo

gam·ble [ˈgæmbl] v/i jugar

gam·bler [ˈgæmblər] jugador(a) m(f)

gam·bling [ˈgæmblɪŋ] n juego m

game [geɪm] n (sport) partido m; children's juego m; in tennis juego m

'game re·serve coto m de caza

gang [gæŋ] of friends cuadrilla f, pandilla f; of criminals banda f

◆ **gang up on** v/t compincharse contra

'gang rape **1** n violación f colectiva **2** v/t violar colectivamente

gan·grene [ˈgæŋgriːn] MED gangrena f

gang·ster [ˈgæŋstər] gángster m

'gang war·fare lucha f entre bandas

'gang·way pasarela f

gaol [dʒeɪl] → **jail**

gap [gæp] in wall hueco m; for parking, in figures espacio m; in time intervalo m; in conversation interrupción f; between two people's characters diferencia f

gape [geɪp] v/i of person mirar boquiabierto

◆ **gape at** v/t mirar boquiabierto a

gap·ing [ˈgeɪpɪŋ] adj hole enorme

gar·age [gəˈrɑːʒ] n for parking garaje m; for gas gasolinera f; for repairs taller m

gar·bage [ˈgɑːrbɪdʒ] basura f; (fig: nonsense) tonterías fpl

'gar·bage bag bolsa f de la basura

'gar·bage can cubo m de la basura

'gar·bage truck camión m de la basura

gar·bled [ˈgɑːrbld] adj message confuso

gar·den [ˈgɑːrdn] jardín m

'gar·den cen·ter, Br 'gar·den cen·tre vivero m, centro m de jardinería

gar·den·er [ˈgɑːrdnər] aficionado(-a) m(f) a la jardinería; professional jardinero(-a) m(f)

gar·den·ing [ˈgɑːrdnɪŋ] jardinería f

gar·gle [ˈgɑːrgl] v/i hacer gárgaras

gar·goyle [ˈgɑːrgɔɪl] ARCHI gárgola f

gar·ish [ˈgerɪʃ] adj color chillón; design estridente

gar·land [ˈgɑːrlənd] n guirnalda f

gar·lic [ˈgɑːrlɪk] ajo m

gar·lic 'bread pan m con ajo

gar·ment [ˈgɑːrmənt] prenda f (de vestir)

gar·nish [ˈgɑːrnɪʃ] v/t guarnecer (**with** con)

gar·ret [ˈgærɪt] buhardilla f

gar·ri·son [ˈgærɪsn] n place plaza f; troops guarnición f

gar·ter [ˈgɑːrtər] liga f

gas [gæs] n gas m; (gasoline) gasolina f, Rpl nafta f

gash [gæʃ] n corte m profundo

gas·ket ['gæskɪt] junta f

gas·o·line ['gæsəliːn] gasolina f, Rpl nafta f

gasp [gæsp] 1 n grito m apagado 2 v/i lanzar un grito apagado; **gasp for breath** luchar por respirar

'gas ped·al acelerador m

'gas pipe·line gasoducto m

'gas pump surtidor m (de gasolina)

'gas stove cocina f de gas 'gas sta·tion gasolinera f, S. Am. bomba f

gas·tric ['gæstrɪk] adj MED gástrico

gas·tric 'flu MED gripe f gastrointestinal

gas·tric 'juic·es npl jugos mpl gástricos

gas·tric 'ul·cer MED úlcera f gástrica

gate [geɪt] of house, at airport puerta f; made of iron verja f

'gate·crash v/t: gatecrash a party colarse en una fiesta

'gate·way also fig entrada f

gath·er ['gæðər] 1 v/t facts, information reunir; am I to gather that ...? ¿debo entender que ...?; **gather speed** ganar velocidad 2 v/i of crowd reunirse

◆ gather up v/t possessions recoger

gath·er·ing ['gæðərɪŋ] n (group of people) grupo m de personas

gau·dy ['gɒːdɪ] adj chillón, llamativo

gauge [geɪdʒ] 1 n indicador m 2 v/t pressure medir, calcular; opinion estimar, evaluar

gaunt [gɒːnt] adj demacrado

gauze [gɒːz] gasa f

gave [geɪv] pret → give

gaw·ky ['gɒːkɪ] adj desgarbado

gawp [gɒːp] v/i F mirar boquiabierto; don't just stand there gawping! ¡no te quedes ahí boquiabierto!

gay [geɪ] 1 n (homosexual) homosexual m, gay m 2 adj homosexual, gay

gaze [geɪz] 1 n mirada f 2 v/i mirar fijamente

◆ gaze at v/t mirar fijamente

GB [dʒiːˈbiː] abbr (= Great Britain) GB (= Gran Bretaña)

GDP [dʒiːdiːˈpiː] abbr (= gross domestic product) PIB m (= producto m interior bruto)

gear [gɪr] n equipment equipo m; in vehicles marcha f

'gear·box MOT caja f de cambios

'gear le·ver, 'gear shift MOT palanca f de cambios

geese [giːs] pl → goose

gel [dʒel] for hair gomina f; for shower gel m

gel·a·tine ['dʒelətiːn] gelatina f

gel·ig·nite ['dʒelɪgnaɪt] gelignita f

gem [dʒem] gema f; (fig: book etc) joya f; (person) cielo m

Gem·i·ni ['dʒemɪnaɪ] ASTR Géminis m/f inv

gen·der ['dʒendər] género m

gene [dʒiːn] gen m; it's in his genes lo lleva en los genes

gen·e·ral ['dʒenrəl] 1 n MIL general m; in general en general, por lo general 2 adj general

gen·e·ral e'lec·tion elecciones fpl generales

gen·er·al·i·za·tion [dʒenrəlaɪˈzeɪʃn] generalización f; that's a generalization eso es generalizar

gen·er·al·ize ['dʒenrəlaɪz] v/i generalizar

gen·er·al·ly ['dʒenrəlɪ] adv generalmente, por lo general; **generally speaking** en términos generales

gen·e·ral prac·ti·tion·er médico(-a) m(f) de cabecera or de familia

gen·e·rate ['dʒenəreɪt] v/t generar; a feeling provocar

gen·e·ra·tion [dʒenəˈreɪʃn] generación f

gen·e·ra·tion gap conflicto m generacional

gen·e·ra·tor ['dʒenəreɪtər] generador m

ge·ner·ic drug [dʒəˈnerɪk] MED medicamento m genérico

gen·e·ros·i·ty [dʒenəˈrɑːsətɪ] generosidad f

gen·e·rous ['dʒenərəs] adj generoso

ge·net·ic [dʒɪˈnetɪk] adj genético

ge·net·i·cal·ly [dʒɪˈnetɪklɪ] adv genéticamente; **genetically modified** crops transgénico; be genetically modified estar modificado genéticamente

ge·net·ic 'code código m genético

ge·net·ic en·gi·neer·ing ingeniería f genética

ge·net·ic 'fin·ger·print identificación f genética

ge·net·i·cist [dʒɪˈnetɪsɪst] genetista m/f, especialista m/f en genética

ge·net·ics [dʒɪˈnetɪks] genética f

ge·ni·al ['dʒiːnjəl] adj afable, cordial

gen·i·tals ['dʒenɪtlz] npl genitales mpl

ge·ni·us ['dʒiːnjəs] genio m

gen·o·cide ['dʒenəsaɪd] genocidio m

gen·tle ['dʒentl] adj person tierno, delicado; touch, detergent suave; breeze suave, ligero; slope poco inclinado; **be gentle with it, it's fragile** ten mucho cuidado con él, es frágil

gen·tle·man ['dʒentlmən] caballero m; he's a real gentleman es todo un caballero

gen·tle·ness ['dʒentlnɪs] of person ternura f, delicadeza; of touch, detergent, breeze suavidad f; *of slope* poca inclinación f

gen·tly ['dʒentlɪ] *adv* con delicadeza, poco a poco; *a breeze blew gently* sopla una ligera *or* suave brisa

gents [dʒents] *nsg Br* toilet servicio *m* de caballeros

gen·u·ine ['dʒenʊɪn] *adj antique* genuino, auténtico; (*sincere*) sincero

gen·u·ine·ly ['dʒenʊɪnlɪ] *adv* realmente, de verdad

ge·o·graph·i·cal [dʒɪə'græfɪkl] *adj* features geográfico

ge·og·ra·phy [dʒɪ'ɑːgrəfɪ] geografía f

ge·o·log·i·cal [dʒɪə'lɑːdʒɪkl] *adj* geológico

ge·ol·o·gist [dʒɪ'ɑːlədʒɪst] geólogo(-a) *m(f)*

ge·ol·o·gy [dʒɪ'ɑːlədʒɪ] geología f

ge·o·met·ric, ge·o·met·ri·cal [dʒɪə'metrɪk(l)] *adj* geométrico

ge·om·e·try [dʒɪ'ɑːmətrɪ] geometría f

ge·ra·ni·um [dʒə'reɪnɪəm] geranio m

ger·i·at·ric [dʒerɪ'ætrɪk] 1 *adj* geriátrico 2 *n* anciano(-a) *m(f)*

germ [dʒɜːrm] *also fig* germen m

Ger·man ['dʒɜːrmən] 1 *adj* alemán 2 *n* *person* alemán (-ana) *m(f)*; *language* alemán m

Ger·man 'mea·sles *nsg* rubeola f

Ger·man 'shep·herd pastor *m* alemán

Germany ['dʒɜːrmənɪ] Alemania

ger·mi·nato ['dʒɜːrmɪneɪt] *v/i* of seed germinar

germ 'war·fare guerra f bacteriológica

ges·tic·u·late [dʒe'stɪkjʊleɪt] *v/i* gesticular

ges·ture ['dʒestʃər] *n also fig* gesto m

get [get] *v/t* (*pret got, pp got, gotten*) (*obtain*) conseguir; (*fetch*) traer; (*receive: letter, knowledge, respect*) recibir; (*catch: bus, train etc*) tomar, *Span* coger; (*arrive*) llegar; (*understand*) entender; *you can get them at the corner shop* los puedes comprar en la tienda de la esquina; *can I get you something to drink?* ¿quieres tomar algo?; *get tired* cansarse; *get drunk* emborracharse; *I'm getting old* me estoy haciendo mayor; *get the TV fixed* hacer que arreglen la televisión; *get s.o. to do sth* hacer que alguien haga algo; *get to do sth* (*have opportunity*) llegar a hacer algo; *get one's hair cut* cortarse el pelo; *get sth ready* preparar algo; *get going* (*leave*) marcharse, irse; *have got* tener; *he's got a lot of money* tiene mucho dinero; *I have got to study / see him* tengo que estudiar / verlo; *I don't want to, but I've got to* no

quiero, pero tengo que hacerlo; *get to know* llegar a conocer

◆ get about *v/i* (*travel*) viajar; (*be mobile*) desplazarse

◆ get along *v/i* (*come to party etc*) ir; *with s.o.* llevarse bien; *how are you getting along at school?* ¿cómo te van las cosas en el colegio?; *the patient is getting along nicely* el paciente está progresando satisfactoriamente

◆ get at *v/t* (*criticize*) meterse con; (*imply, mean*) querer decir

◆ get away 1 *v/i* (*leave*) marcharse, irse 2 *v/t*: *get sth away from s.o.* quitar algo a alguien

◆ get away with *v/t* salir impune de; *get away with it* salirse con la suya; *she lets him get away with anything* le permite todo; *I'll let you get away with it this time* por esta vez te perdonaré

◆ get back 1 *v/i* (*return*) volver; *I'll get back to you on that tomorrow* te responderé a eso mañana 2 *v/t* (*obtain again*) recuperar

◆ get by *v/i* (*pass*) pasar; *financially* arreglárselas

◆ get down 1 *v/i from ladder etc* bajarse (*from* de); (*duck etc*) agacharse 2 *v/t* (*depress*) desanimar, deprimir

◆ get down to *v/t* (*start: work*) ponerse a; *get down to the facts* ir a los hechos

◆ get in 1 *v/i* (*arrive*) llegar; *to car* subir(se), meterse; *how did they get in? of thieves, mice etc* ¿cómo entraron? 2 *v/t to suitcase etc* meter

◆ get into *v/t house* entrar en, meterse en; *car* subir(se) a, meterse en; *computer system* introducirse en

◆ get off 1 *v/i from bus etc* bajarse; (*finish work*) salir; (*not be punished*) librarse 2 *v/t* (*remove*) quitar; *clothes, hat, footgear* quitarse; *get off my bike!* ¡bájate de mi bici!; *get off the grass!* ¡no pises la hierba!

◆ get off with *v/t*: *get off with a small fine* tener que pagar sólo una pequeña multa

◆ get on 1 *v/i to bike, bus, train* montarse, subirse; (*be friendly*) llevarse bien; (*advance: of time*) hacerse tarde; (*become old*) hacerse mayor; (*make progress*) progresar; *how are you getting on with the new subjects?* ¿cómo te va con las nuevas asignaturas?; *it's getting on* getting late se está haciendo tarde; *he's getting on* se está haciendo mayor; *he's getting on for 50* está a punto de cumplir 50 2 *v/t*: *get on the bus / one's bike* montarse en el autobús / la bici; *get one's shoes on* ponerse los zapatos; **I can't get these pants on** estos pantalones no me entran

♦ **get out 1** v/i of car, prison etc salir; **get out!** ¡vete!, ¡fuera de aquí!; **let's get out of here** ¡salgamos de aquí!; **I don't get out much these days** últimamente no salgo mucho **2** v/t nail, something jammed sacar, extraer; stain quitar; gun, pen sacar

♦ **get over** v/t fence etc franquear; disappointment superar; lover etc olvidar

♦ **get over with** v/t terminar con; **let's get it over with** quitémonoslo de encima

♦ **get through** v/i on telephone conectarse; **obviously I'm just not getting through** está claro que no me estoy haciendo entender; **get through to s.o.** (make self understood) comunicarse con alguien

♦ **get up 1** v/i levantarse **2** v/t (climb) subir

'get·a·way from robbery fuga f, huida f
'get·a·way car coche m utilizado en la fuga
'get-to·geth·er reunión f
ghast·ly ['gæstlɪ] adj terrible
gher·kin ['gɜːrkɪn] pepinillo m
ghet·to ['getou] gueto m
ghost [goust] fantasma m
ghost·ly ['goustlɪ] adj fantasmal
'ghost town ciudad f fantasma
ghoul [guːl] macabro(-a) m(f), morboso(-a) m(f)
ghoul·ish ['guːlɪʃ] adj macabro, morboso
gi·ant ['dʒaɪənt] 1 n gigante m 2 adj gigantesco, gigante
gib·ber·ish ['dʒɪbərɪʃ] F memeces fpl F, majaderías fpl F
gibe [dʒaɪb] n pulla f
gib·lets ['dʒɪblɪts] npl menudillos mpl
gid·di·ness ['gɪdɪnɪs] mareo m
gid·dy ['gɪdɪ] adj mareado; **feel giddy** estar mareado
gift [gɪft] regalo m
gift cer·ti·fi·cate vale m de regalo
gift·ed ['gɪftɪd] adj con talento
'gift-wrap 1 n papel m de regalo 2 v/t (pret & pp giftwrapped) envolver para regalo
gig [gɪg] F concierto m, actuación f
gi·ga·byte ['gɪgəbaɪt] COMPUT gigabyte m
gi·gan·tic [dʒaɪ'gæntɪk] adj gigantesco
gig·gle ['gɪgl] 1 v/i soltar risitas 2 n risita f
gig·gly ['gɪglɪ] adj que suelta risitas
gill [gɪl] of fish branquia f
gilt [gɪlt] n dorado m; **gilts** FIN valores mpl del Estado
gim·mick ['gɪmɪk] truco m, reclamo m
gim·mick·y ['gɪmɪkɪ] adj superficial, artificioso

gin [dʒɪn] ginebra f; **gin and tonic** gin-tonic m
gin·ger ['dʒɪndʒər] 1 n spice jengibre m 2 adj cat color fuego; **he has ginger hair** es pelirrojo
gin·ger beer refresco con sabor a jengibre
'gin·ger·bread pan m de jengibre
gin·ger·ly ['dʒɪndʒərlɪ] adv cuidadosamente, delicadamente
gip·sy ['dʒɪpsɪ] gitano(-a) m(f)
gi·raffe [dʒɪ'ræf] jirafa f
gir·der ['gɜːrdər] n viga f
girl [gɜːrl] chica f; **young girl** niña f, chica f
'girl·friend of boy novia f; of girl amiga f
girl·ie mag·a·zine ['gɜːrlɪ] revista f porno
girl·ish ['gɜːrlɪʃ] adj de niñas
girl 'scout escultista f, scout f
gist [dʒɪst] esencia f
give [gɪv] v/t (pret **gave**, pp **given**) dar; as present regalar; (supply: electricity etc) proporcionar; talk, lecture dar, pronunciar; cry, groan soltar; **give her my love** dale recuerdos (de mi parte); **give s.o. a present** hacer un regalo a alguien
♦ **give away** v/t as present regalar; (betray) traicionar; **give o.s. away** descubrirse, traicionarse
♦ **give back** v/t devolver
♦ **give in 1** v/i (surrender) rendirse **2** v/t (hand in) entregar
♦ **give off** v/t smell, fumes emitir, despedir
♦ **give onto** v/t (open onto) dar a
♦ **give out 1** v/t leaflets etc repartir **2** v/i of supplies, strength agotarse
♦ **give up 1** v/t smoking etc dejar de; **give o.s. up to the police** entregarse a la policía **2** v/i (stop making effort) rendirse; **I find it hard to give up** me cuesta mucho dejarlo
♦ **give way** v/i of bridge etc hundirse
give-and-'take toma f y daca
giv·en ['gɪvn] pp → **give**
'giv·en name nombre m de pila
gla·ci·er ['gleɪʃər] glaciar m
glad [glæd] adj contento, alegre; **I was glad to see you** me alegré de verte
glad·ly ['glædlɪ] adv con mucho gusto
glam·or ['glæmər] atractivo m, glamour m
glam·or·ize ['glæməraɪz] v/t hacer atractivo, ensalzar
glam·or·ous ['glæmərəs] adj atractivo, glamoroso
glam·our Br → **glamor**
glance [glæns] 1 n ojeada f, vistazo 2 v/i echar una ojeada or vistazo
♦ **glance at** v/t echar una ojeada or vista-

zo a

gland [glænd] glándula *f*

glan·du·lar 'fe·ver ['glændʒələr] mononucleosis *f inv* infecciosa

glare [gler] **1** *n of sun, headlights* resplandor *m* **2** *v/i of headlights* resplandecer

◆ **glare at** *v/t* mirar con furia a

glar·ing ['glerɪŋ] *adj mistake* garrafal

glar·ing·ly ['glerɪŋlɪ] *adv*: **it's glaringly obvious** está clarísimo

glass [glæs] *material* vidrio *m*; *for drink* vaso *m*

glass 'case vitrina *f*

glass·es *npl* gafas *fpl*, *L.Am.* lentes *mpl*, *L.Am.* anteojos *mpl*

'glass·house invernadero *m*

glaze [gleɪz] *n* vidriado *m*

◆ **glaze over** *v/i of eyes* vidriarse

glazed [gleɪzd] *adj expression* vidrioso

gla·zi·er ['gleɪzɪr] cristalero(-a) *m(f)*, vidriero(-a) *m(f)*

glaz·ing ['gleɪzɪŋ] cristales *mpl*, vidrios *mpl*

gleam [gliːm] **1** *n* resplandor *m*, brillo *m* **2** *v/i* resplandecer, brillar

glee [gliː] júbilo *m*, regocijo *m*

glee·ful ['gliːfəl] *adj* jubiloso

glib [glɪb] *adj* fácil

glib·ly ['glɪblɪ] *adv* con labia

glide [glaɪd] *v/i of bird, plane* planear; *of piece of furniture* deslizarse

glid·er ['glaɪdər] planeador *m*

glid·ing ['glaɪdɪŋ] *n sport* vuelo *m* sin motor

glim·mer ['glɪmər] **1** *n of light* brillo *m* tenue; **glimmer of hope** rayo *m* de esperanza **2** *v/i* brillar tenuemente

glimpse [glɪmps] **1** *n* vistazo *m*; **catch a glimpse of** vislumbrar **2** *v/t* vislumbrar

glint [glɪnt] **1** *n* destello *m*; *in eyes* centelleo *m* **2** *v/i of light* destellar; *of eyes* centellear

glis·ten ['glɪsn] *v/i* relucir, centellear

glit·ter ['glɪtər] *v/i* resplandecer, destellar

glit·ter·ati *npl* famosos *mpl*

gloat [gloʊt] *v/i* regodearse

◆ **gloat over** *v/t* regodearse de

glo·bal ['gloʊbl] *adj* global

glo·bal e'con·o·my economía *f* global

glo·bal 'mar·ket mercado *m* global

glo·bal 'war·ming calentamiento *m* global

globe [gloʊb] *(the earth)* globo *m*; *(model of earth)* globo *m* terráqueo

gloom [gluːm] *(darkness)* tinieblas *fpl*, oscuridad *f*; *mood* abatimiento *m*, melancolía *f*

gloom·i·ly ['gluːmɪlɪ] *adv* con abatimiento, melancólicamente

gloom·y ['gluːmɪ] *adj room* tenebroso, oscuro; *mood, person* abatido, melancólico

glo·ri·ous ['glɔːrɪəs] *adj weather, day* espléndido, maravilloso; *victory* glorioso

glo·ry ['glɔːrɪ] *n* gloria *f*

gloss [glɑːs] *n (shine)* lustre *m*, brillo *m*; *(general explanation)* glosa *f*

◆ **gloss over** *v/t* pasar por alto

glos·sa·ry ['glɑːsərɪ] glosario *m*

'gloss paint pintura *f* brillante

gloss·y ['glɑːsɪ] **1** *adj paper* cuché, satinado **2** *n magazine* revista *f* en color (en papel cuché *or* satinado)

glove [glʌv] guante *m*

'glove com·part·ment *in car* guantera *f*

'glove pup·pet marioneta *f* de guiñol (de guante)

glow [gloʊ] **1** *n of light, fire* resplandor *m*, brillo *m*; *in cheeks* rubor *m* **2** *v/i of light, fire* resplandecer, brillar; *of cheeks* ruborizarse

glow·er [glaʊr] *v/i* fruncir el ceño

glow·ing ['gloʊɪŋ] *adj description* entusiasta

glu·cose ['gluːkoʊs] glucosa *f*

glue [gluː] **1** *n* pegamento *m*, cola *f* **2** *v/t* pegar, encolar; **glue sth to sth** pegar *or* encolar algo a algo; **be glued to the radio / TV** F estar pegado a la radio / televisión F

glum [glʌm] *adj* sombrío, triste

glum·ly ['glʌmlɪ] *adv* con tristeza

glut [glʌt] *n* exceso *m*, superabundancia *f*

glut·ton ['glʌtn] glotón(-ona) *m(f)*

glut·ton·y ['glʌtnɪ] gula *f*, glotonería *f*

GMT [dʒiːemˈtiː] *abbr* (= **Greenwich Mean Time**) hora *f* del meridiano de Greenwich

gnarled [nɑːrld] *adj* nudoso

gnat [næt] *tipo de* mosquito

gnaw [nɒː] *v/t bone* roer

GNP [dʒiːenˈpiː] *abbr* (= **gross national product**) PNB *m* (= producto *m* nacional bruto)

go [goʊ] **1** *n (try)* intento *m*; **it's my go** me toca a mí; **have a go at sth** *(try)* intentar algo; *(complain about)* protestar contra algo; **on the go** en marcha; **in one go** *drink, write etc* de un tirón **2** *v/i (pret went, pp gone)* ir (**to** a); *(leave)* irse, marcharse; *(work, function)* funcionar; *(come out: of stain etc)* irse; *(cease: of pain etc)* pasarse; *(match: of colors etc)* ir bien, pegar; **go shopping / jogging** ir de compras/a hacer footing; **I must be going** me tengo que ir; **let's go!** ¡vamos!; **go for a walk** ir a pasear *or* a dar un paseo; **go to bed** ir(se) a la cama; **go to school** ir al colegio; **how's the work**

going? ¿cómo va el trabajo?; *they're going for $50* (*being sold at*) se venden por 50 dólares; *hamburger to go* hamburguesa para llevar; *be all gone* (*finished*) haberse acabado; *go green* ponerse verde; *be going to do sth* ir a hacer algo

◆ **go ahead** *v/i and do sth* seguir adelante; *can I? - sure, go ahead* ¿puedo? - por supuesto, adelante

◆ **go ahead with** *v/t plans etc* seguir adelante con

◆ **go along with** *v/t suggestion* aceptar

◆ **go at** *v/t* (*attack*) atacar

◆ **go away** *v/i of person* irse, marcharse; *of rain, pain, clouds* desaparecer

◆ **go back** *v/i* (*return*) volver; (*date back*) remontarse; *we go back a long way* nos conocemos desde hace tiempo; *go back to sleep* volver a dormirse

◆ **go by** *v/i of car, time* pasar

◆ **go down** *v/i* bajar; *of sun* ponerse; *of ship* hundirse; *go down well / badly of suggestion* sentar bien o / mal

◆ **go for** *v/t* (*attack*) atacar; *I don't much go for gin* no me va mucho la ginebra

◆ **go in** *v/i to room, house* entrar; *of sun* ocultarse; (*fit: of part etc*) ir, encajar

◆ **go in for** *v/t competition, race* tomar parte en; *I used to go in for badminton quite a lot* antes jugaba mucho al bádminton

◆ **go off** *v/i* (*leave*) marcharse; *of bomb* explotar, estallar; *of gun* dispararse; *of alarm* saltar; *of milk etc* echarse a perder **2** *v/t*: *I've gone off whisky* ya no me gusta el whisky

◆ **go on** *v/i* (*continue*) continuar; (*happen*) ocurrir, pasar; *go on, do it!* (*encouraging*) ¡venga, hazlo!; *what's going on?* ¿qué pasa?

◆ **go on at** *v/t* (*nag*) meterse con

◆ **go out** *v/i of person* salir; *of light, fire* apagarse

◆ **go out with** *v/t romantically* salir con

◆ **go over** *v/t* (*check*) examinar; (*do again*) repasar

◆ **go through** *v/t illness, hard times* atravesar; (*check*) revisar, examinar; (*read through*) estudiar

◆ **go under** *v/i* (*sink*) hundirse; *of company* ir a la quiebra

◆ **go up** *v/i* subir

◆ **go without 1** *v/t food etc* pasar sin **2** *v/i* pasar privaciones

goad [goud] *v/t* pinchar; *goad s.o. into doing sth* pinchar a alguien para que haga algo

'**go-a·head 1** *n* luz *f* verde; *when we get the go-ahead* cuando nos den la luz

verde **2** *adj* (*enterprising, dynamic*) dinámico

goal [goul] SP *target* portería *f*, *L.Am.* arco *m*; SP *point* gol *m*; (*objective*) objetivo *m*, meta *f*

'**goal·ie** ['gouli] F portero(-a) *m(f)*, *L.Am.* arquero(-a) *m(f)*

'**goal·keep·er** portero(-a) *m(f)*, guardameta *m/f*, *Am* arquero(-a) *m(f)*

'**goal kick** saque *m* de puerta

'**goal-mouth** portería *f*

'**goal-post** poste *m*

goat [gout] cabra *f*

gob·ble ['gɑ:bl] *v/t* engullir

◆ **gobble up** *v/t* engullir

gob·ble·dy·gook ['gɑ:bldɪgu:k] F jerigonza *f* F

go-be·tween intermediario(-a) *m(f)*

god [gɑ:d] dios *m*; *thank God!* ¡gracias a Dios!; *oh God!* ¡Dios mío!

'**god·child** ahijado(-a) *m(f)*

'**god·daugh·ter** ahijada *f*

'**god·dess** ['gɑ:dɪs] diosa *f*

'**god·fa·ther** *also in mafia* padrino *m*

god-for·sak·en ['gɑ:dfərseɪkən] *adj place* dejado de la mano de Dios

'**god·moth·er** madrina *f*

'**god·pa·rent** *man* padrino *m*; *woman* madrina *f*

'**god·send** regalo *m* del cielo

'**god·son** ahijado *m*

go·fer ['goufər] F recadero(-a) *m(f)*

gog·gles ['gɑ:glz] *npl* gafas *fpl*

go·ing ['gouɪŋ] *adj price etc* vigente; *going concern* empresa *f* en marcha

go·ings-on [gouɪŋz'ɑ:n] *npl* actividades *fpl*

gold [gould] **1** *n* oro *m* **2** *adj* de oro

gold·en ['gouldn] *adj sky, hair* dorado

gold·en 'hand·shake gratificación entregada tras la marcha de un directivo

gold·en 'wed·ding (an·ni·ver·sa·ry) bodas *fpl* de oro

'**gold·fish** pez *m* de colores

'**gold mine** *fig* mina *f* de oro

'**gold·smith** orfebre *m/f*

golf [gɑ:lf] golf *m*

'**golf ball** pelota *f* de golf

'**golf club** *organization* club *m* de golf; *stick* palo *m* de golf

'**golf course** campo *m* de golf

golf·er ['gɑ:lfər] golfista *m/f*

gone [gɑ:n] *pp* → **go**

gong [gɑ:ŋ] gong *m*

good [gud] *adj* bueno; *food* bueno, rico; *a good many* muchos; *he's good at chess* se le da muy bien el ajedrez; *be good for s.o.* ser bueno para alguien

good·bye [gud'baɪ] adiós *m*, despedida *f*;

say goodbye to s.o., wish s.o. goodbye decir adiós a alguien, despedirse de alguien

'**good-for-no-thing** *n* inútil *m/f*

Good 'Fri-day Viernes *m inv* Santo

good-hu-mored, *Br* **good-hu-moured** [gud'hju:mərd] *adj* jovial, afable

good-'look-ing [gud'lukɪŋ] *adj woman, man* guapo

good-na-tured [gud'neɪtʃərd] bondadoso

good-ness ['gudnɪs] *adj moral* bondad *f; of fruit etc* propiedades *fpl*, valor *m* nutritivo; *thank goodness!* ¡gracias a Dios!

goods [gudz] *npl* COM mercancías *fpl*, productos *mpl*

good'will buena voluntad *f*

good-y-good-y ['gudɪgudɪ] *n* F: *she's a real goody-goody* es demasiado buena-za F

goo-ey ['gu:ɪ] *adj* pegajoso

goof [gu:f] *v/i* F meter la pata F

goose [gu:s] *(pl geese* [gi:s]) ganso *m*, oca *f*

goose-ber-ry ['guzberɪ] grosella *f*

'**goose bumps** *npl* carne *f* de gallina

'**goose pim-ples** *npl* carne *f* de gallina

gorge [gɔːrdʒ] **1** *n* garganta *f*, desfiladero *m* **2** *v/r* *gorge o.s. on sth* comer algo hasta hartarse

gor-geous ['gɔːrdʒəs] *adj weather* maravilloso, *dress, hair* precioso; *woman, man* buenísimo; *smell* estupendo

go-ril-la [gə'rɪlə] gorila *m*

gosh [gɑːʃ] *int* ¡caramba!, ¡vaya!

go-'slow huelga *f* de celo

gos-pel ['gɑːspl] *in Bible* evangelio *m; it's the gospel truth* es la pura verdad

gos-sip ['gɑːsɪp] **1** *n* cotilleo *m; person* cotilla *m/f* **2** *v/i* cotillear

'**gos-sip col-umn** ecos *mpl* de sociedad

'**gos-sip col-um-nist** escritor(a) *m(f)* de los ecos de sociedad

gos-sip-y ['gɑːsɪpɪ] *adj letter* lleno de cotilleos

got [gɑːt] *pret & pp* → **get**

got-ten ['gɑːtn] *pp* → **get**

gour-met ['gurmeɪ] *n* gastrónomo(-a) *m(f)*, gourmet *m/f*

gov-ern ['gʌvərn] *v/t country* gobernar

gov-ern-ment ['gʌvərnmənt] gobierno *m*

gov-er-nor ['gʌvərnər] gobernador(a) *m(f)*

gown [gaun] *long dress* vestido *m; wedding dress* traje *m; of academic, judge* toga *f; of surgeon* bata *f*

grab [græb] *v/t (pret & pp grabbed)* agarrar; *food* tomar; *grab some sleep* dormir

grace [greɪs] *of dancer etc* gracia *f*, elegancia *f; say grace* bendecir la mesa

grace-ful ['greɪsfəl] *adj* elegante

grace-ful-ly ['greɪsfəlɪ] *adv move* con gracia *or* elegancia

gra-cious ['greɪʃəs] *adj person* amable; *style, living* elegante; *good gracious!* ¡Dios mío!

grade [greɪd] **1** *n quality* grado *m;* EDU curso *m; (mark)* nota *f* **2** *v/t* clasificar

'**grade cross-ing** paso *m* a nivel

'**grade school** escuela *f* primaria

gra-di-ent ['greɪdɪənt] pendiente *f*

grad-u-al ['grædʒʊəl] *adj* gradual

grad-u-al-ly ['grædʒʊəlɪ] *adv* gradualmente, poco a poco

grad-u-ate ['grædʒʊət] **1** *n* licenciado (-a) *m(f); from high school* bachiller *m/f* **2** *v/i from university* licenciarse, *L.Am.* egresarse; *from high school* sacar el bachillerato

grad-u-a-tion [grædʒʊ'eɪʃn] graduación *f*

graf-fi-ti [grə'fiːtɪ] graffiti *m*

graft [græft] **1** *n* BOT, MED injerto *m; corruption* corrupción *f* **2** *v/t* BOT, MED injertar

grain [greɪn] grano *m; in wood* veta *f; go against the grain* ir contra la naturaleza de alguien

gram [græm] gramo *m*

gram-mar ['græmər] gramática *f*

gram-mat-i-cal [grə'mætɪkl] *adj* gramatical

gram-mat-i-cal-ly *adv* gramaticalmente

grand [grænd] **1** *adj* grandioso; F *(very good)* estupendo, genial **2** *n* F *($1000)* mil dólares *mpl*

gran-dad ['grændæd] abuelito *m*

'**grand-child** nieto(-a) *m(f)*

'**grand-daugh-ter** nieta *f*

gran-deur ['grændʒər] grandiosidad *f*

'**grand-fa-ther** abuelo *m*

'**grand-fa-ther clock** reloj *m* de pie

gran-di-ose ['grændɪous] *adj* grandioso

grand 'jur-y jurado *m* de acusación, gran jurado

'**grand-ma** F abuelita *f*, yaya *f* F

'**grand-moth-er** abuela *f*

'**grand-pa** F abuelito *m*, yayo *m* F

'**grand-par-ents** *npl* abuelos *mpl*

grand pi'an-o piano *m* de cola

grand 'slam gran slam *m*

'**grand-son** nieto *m*

'**grand-stand** tribuna *f*

gran-ite ['grænɪt] granito *m*

gran-ny ['grænɪ] F abuelita *f*, yaya *f* F

grant [grænt] **1** *n money* subvención *f* **2** *v/t* conceder; *take sth for granted* dar algo por sentado; *take s.o. for granted* no

apreciar a alguien lo suficiente
gran·u·lat·ed sug·ar ['grænʊleɪtɪd] azúcar *m or f* granulado(-a)
gran·ule ['grænjuːl] gránulo *m*
grape [greɪp] uva *f*
'**grape·fruit** pomelo *m*, *L.Am.* toronja *f*
'**grape·fruit juice** *Span* zumo *m* de pomelo, *L.Am.* jugo *m* de toronja
'**grape·vine**: *I've heard on the grapevine
that …* me ha contado un pajarito que …
graph [græf] gráfico *m*, gráfica *f*
graph·ic ['græfɪk] **1** *adj* (*vivid*) gráfico **2** *n*
COMPUT gráfico *m*
graph·i·cal·ly ['græfɪklɪ] *adv describe*
gráficamente
graph·ic de·sign·er diseñador(a) *m(f)*
gráfico(-a)
◆ **grap·ple with** ['græpl] *v/t attacker*
forcejear con; *problem etc* enfrentarse a
grasp [græsp] **1** *n physical* asimiento *m*;
mental comprensión *m* **2** *v/t physically*
agarrar; (*understand*) comprender
grass [græs] *n* hierba *f*
'**grass·hop·per** saltamontes *m inv*
grass 'roots *npl* people bases *fpl*
grass 'wid·ow mujer cuyo marido está a
menudo ausente durante largos periodos
de tiempo
grass 'wid·ow·er hombre cuya mujer está
a menudo ausente durante largos periodos de tiempo
gras·sy ['græsɪ] *adj* lleno de hierba
grate¹ [greɪt] *n metal* parrilla *f*, reja *f*
grate² [greɪt] **1** *v/t in cooking* rallar **2** *v/i of
sound* rechinar
grate·ful ['greɪtfʊl] *adj* agradecido; *we
are grateful for your help* (le) agradece-
mos su ayuda; *I'm grateful to him* le estoy agradecido
grate·ful·ly ['greɪtfʊlɪ] *adv* con agradecimiento
grat·er ['greɪtər] rallador *m*
grat·i·fy ['grætɪfaɪ] *v/t (pret & pp grati-
fied)* satisfacer, complacer
grat·ing ['greɪtɪŋ] **1** *n* reja *f* **2** *adj sound,
voice* chirriante
grat·i·tude ['grætɪtuːd] gratitud *f*
gra·tu·i·tous [grə'tuːɪtəs] *adj* gratuito
gra·tu·i·ty [grə'tuːətɪ] propina *f*, gratificación *f*
grave¹ [greɪv] *n* tumba *f*, sepultura *f*
grave² [greɪv] *adj* grave
grav·el ['grævl] *n* gravilla *f*
'**grave·stone** lápida *f*
'**grave·yard** cementerio *m*
◆ **grav·i·tate toward** ['grævɪteɪt] *v/t*
verse atraído por
grav·i·ty ['grævətɪ] PHYS gravedad *f*
gra·vy ['greɪvɪ] jugo *m* (de la carne)

gray [greɪ] *adj* gris; *be going gray* enca-
necer
gray-haired [greɪ'herd] *adj* canoso
'**gray·hound** galgo *m*
graze¹ [greɪz] *v/i of cow etc* pastar, pacer
graze² [greɪz] **1** *v/t arm etc* rozar, arañar **2**
n rozadura *f*, arañazo *m*
grease [griːs] *n* grasa *f*
grease·proof 'pa·per papel *m* de cera *or*
parafinado
greas·y ['griːsɪ] *adj food, hands, plate* grasiento; *hair, skin* graso
great [greɪt] *adj* grande, *before singular
noun* gran; F (*very good*) estupendo, genial; *how was it? - great!* ¿cómo fue? -
¡estupendo *or* genial!; *great to see you
again!* ¡me alegro de volver a verte!
Great 'Brit·ain Gran Bretaña
great·'grand·child bisnieto(-a) *m(f)*
great·'grand·daugh·ter bisnieta *f*
great·'grand·fa·ther bisabuelo *m*
great·'grand·moth·er bisabuela *f*
great·'grand·par·ents *npl* bisabuelos
mpl
great·'grand·son bisnieto *m*
great·ly ['greɪtlɪ] *adv* muy
great·ness ['greɪtnɪs] grandeza *f*
Greece [griːs] Grecia
greed [griːd] *for money* codicia *f*; *for food*
gula *f*, glotonería *f*
greed·i·ly ['griːdɪlɪ] *adv* con codicia; *eat*
con gula *or* glotonería
greed·y ['griːdɪ] *adj for food* glotón; *for
money* codicioso
Greek [griːk] **1** *adj* griego **2** *n person* grie-
go(-a) *m(f)*; *language* griego *m*
green [griːn] *adj* verde; *environmentally*
ecologista, verde
green 'beans *npl* judías *fpl* verdes, *L.Am.*
porotos *mpl* verdes, *Mex* ejotes *mpl*
'**green belt** cinturón *m* verde
'**green card** (*work permit*) permiso *m* de
trabajo
'**green·field site** terreno *m* edificable en
el campo
'**green·horn** F novato(-a) *m(f)* F
'**green·house** invernadero *m*
'**green·house ef·fect** efecto *m* invernadero
'**green·house gas** gas *m* invernadero
greens [griːnz] *npl* verduras *fpl*
green 'thumb: *have a green thumb* tener
buena mano con la jardinería
greet [griːt] *v/t* saludar
greet·ing ['griːtɪŋ] saludo *m*
'**greet·ing card** tarjeta *f* de felicitación
gre·gar·i·ous [grɪ'gerɪəs] *adj person* sociable
gre·nade [grɪ'neɪd] granada *f*

grew [gru:] pret → grow

grey Br → gray

grid [grɪd] reja f, rejilla f

'grid·iron SP campo de fútbol americano

'grid·lock in traffic paralización m del tráfico

grief [gri:f] dolor m, aflicción f

grief-strick·en ['gri:fstrɪkn] adj afligido

griev·ance ['gri:vəns] queja f

grieve [gri:v] v/i sufrir; grieve for s.o. llorar por alguien

grill [grɪl] 1 n on window reja f 2 v/t (interrogate) interrogar

grille [grɪl] reja f

grim [grɪm] adj face severo; prospects desolador; surroundings lúgubre

gri·mace ['grɪməs] n gesto m, mueca f

grime [graɪm] mugre f

grim·ly ['grɪmlɪ] adv speak en tono grave

grim·y ['graɪmɪ] adj mugriento

grin [grɪn] 1 n sonrisa f (amplia) 2 v/i (pret & pp grinned) sonreír abiertamente

grind [graɪnd] v/t (pret & pp ground) coffee moler; meat picar; grind one's teeth hacer rechinar los dientes

grip [grɪp] 1 n: he lost his grip on the rope se le escapó la cuerda; be losing one's grip (losing one's skills) estar perdiendo el control 2 v/t (pret & pp gripped) agarrar

gripe [graɪp] 1 n F queja f 2 v/i F quejarse

grip·ping ['grɪpɪŋ] adj apasionante

gris·tle ['grɪsl] cartílago m

grit [grɪt] 1 n (dirt) arenilla f, for roads gravilla f 2 v/t (pret & pp gritted): grit one's teeth apretar los dientes

grit·ty ['grɪtɪ] adj F book, movie etc duro F, descarnado

groan [groʊn] 1 n gemido m 2 v/i gemir

gro·cer ['groʊsər] tendero(-a) m(f)

gro·cer·ies ['groʊsərɪz] npl comestibles mpl

gro·cer·y store ['groʊsərɪ] tienda f de comestibles or Mex abarrotes

grog·gy ['grɑ:gɪ] adj F grogui F

groin [grɔɪn] ANAT ingle f

groom [gru:m] 1 n for bride novio m; for horse mozo m de cuadra 2 v/t horse almohazar; (train, prepare) preparar; well groomed in appearance bien arreglado

groove [gru:v] ranura f

grope [groʊp] 1 v/i in the dark caminar a tientas 2 v/t sexually manosear
  ◆ grope for v/t door handle, the right word intentar encontrar

gross [groʊs] adj (coarse, vulgar) grosero; exaggeration tremendo; error craso; FIN bruto

gross do·mes·tic 'prod·uct producto m interior bruto

gross na·tion·al 'prod·uct producto m nacional bruto

ground¹ [graʊnd] 1 n suelo m, tierra f; (reason) motivo m; ELEC tierra f; on the ground en el suelo 2 v/t ELEC conectar a tierra

ground² [graʊnd] pret & pp → grind

'ground con·trol control m de tierra

'ground crew personal m de tierra

ground·ing ['graʊndɪŋ] in subject fundamento m; he's had a good grounding in electronics tiene buenos fundamentos de electrónica

ground·less ['graʊndlɪs] adj infundado

ground 'meat carne f picada

'ground·nut cacahuete m, L.Am. maní m, Mex cacahuate m

'ground plan plano m

'ground staff SP personal m de mantenimiento; at airport personal m de tierra

'ground·work trabajos mpl preliminares

group [gru:p] 1 n grupo m 2 v/t agrupar

group·ie ['gru:pɪ] F grupi f F

group 'ther·a·py terapia f de grupo

grouse [graʊs] 1 n F queja f 2 v/i F quejarse, refunfuñar

grov·el ['grɑ:vl] v/i fig arrastrarse

grow [groʊ] 1 v/i (pret grew, pp grown) crecer; of number, amount crecer, incrementarse; grow old / tired envejecer / cansarse 2 v/t (pret grew, pp grown) flowers cultivar
  ◆ grow up v/i of person, city crecer; grow up! ¡no seas crío!

growl [graʊl] 1 n gruñido m 2 v/i gruñir

grown [groʊn] pp → grow

grown-up ['groʊnʌp] 1 n adulto(-a) m(f) 2 adj maduro

growth [groʊθ] of person, economy crecimiento m; (increase) incremento m; MED bulto m

grub [grʌb] of insect larva f, gusano m

grub·by ['grʌbɪ] adj mugriento m

grudge [grʌdʒ] 1 n rencor m; bear s.o. a grudge guardar rencor a alguien 2 v/t: grudge s.o. sth feel envy envidiar algo a alguien

grudg·ing ['grʌdʒɪŋ] adj rencoroso

grudg·ing·ly ['grʌdʒɪŋlɪ] adv de mala gana

gru·el·ing, Br gru·el·ling ['gru:əlɪŋ] adj agotador

gruff [grʌf] adj seco, brusco

grum·ble ['grʌmbl] v/i murmurar, refunfuñar

grum·bler ['grʌmblər] quejica m/f

grump·y ['grʌmpɪ] adj cascarrabias

grunt [grʌnt] 1 n gruñido m 2 v/i gruñir

G

guar·an·tee [gærən'tiː] **1** *n* garantía *f*; **guarantee period** periodo *m* de garantía **2** *v/t* garantizar

guar·an·tor [gærən'tɔːr] garante *m/f*

guard [gɑːrd] **1** *n* (*security guard*) guardia *m/f*, guarda *m/f*; MIL guardia *f*; *in prison* guardián (-ana) *m(f)*; **be on one's guard against** estar en guardia contra **2** *v/t* guardar, proteger

◆ **guard against** *v/t* evitar

'guard dog perro *m* guardián

guard·ed ['gɑːrdɪd] *adj reply* cauteloso

guard·i·an ['gɑːrdɪən] LAW tutor(a) *m(f)*

guard·i·an 'an·gel ángel *m* de la guardia

Gua·te·ma·la [gwætə'mɑːlə] *n* Guatemala

Gua·te·ma·lan [gwætə'mɑːlən] **1** *adj* guatemalteco **2** *n* guatemalteco(-a) *m(f)*

guer·ril·la [gə'rɪlə] guerrillero(-a) *m(f)*

guer·ril·la 'war·fare guerra *f* de guerrillas

guess [ges] **1** *n* conjetura *f*, suposición *f* **2** *v/t the answer* adivinar; **I guess so** me imagino *or* supongo que sí; **I guess not** me imagino *or* supongo que no **3** *v/i* adivinar

'guess·work conjeturas *fpl*

guest [gest] invitado(-a) *m(f)*

'guest·house casa *f* de huéspedes

'guest·room habitación *f* para invitados

guf·faw [gʌ'fɔː] **1** *n* carcajada *f*, risotada *f* **2** *v/i* carcajearse

guid·ance ['gaɪdəns] orientación *f*, consejo *m*

guide [gaɪd] **1** *n person* guía *m/f*; *book* guía *f* **2** *v/t* guiar

'guide·book guía *f*

guid·ed mis·sile ['gaɪdɪd] misil *m* teledirigido

'guide dog *Br* perro *m* lazarillo

guid·ed 'tour visita *f* guiada

'guide·lines ['gaɪdlaɪnz] *npl* directrices *fpl*, normas *fpl* generales

guilt [gɪlt] culpa *f*, culpabilidad *f*; LAW culpabilidad *f*

guilt·y ['gɪltɪ] *adj also* LAW culpable; **be guilty of sth** ser culpable de algo; **have a guilty conscience** tener remordimientos de conciencia

guin·ea pig ['gɪnɪpɪg] conejillo *m* de Indias, cobaya *f*; *fig* conejillo *m* de Indias

guise [gaɪz] apariencia *f*; **under the guise of** bajo la apariencia de

gui·tar [gɪ'tɑːr] guitarra *f*

gui·tar case estuche *m* de guitarra

gui·tar·ist [gɪ'tɑːrɪst] guitarrista *m/f*

gui·tar play·er guitarrista *m/f*

gulf [gʌlf] golfo *m*; *fig* abismo *m*; **the Gulf** el Golfo

Gulf of 'Mex·i·co Golfo *m* de México

gull [gʌl] *bird* gaviota *f*

gul·let ['gʌlɪt] ANAT esófago *m*

gul·li·ble ['gʌlɪbl] *adj* crédulo, ingenuo

gulp [gʌlp] **1** *n of water etc* trago *m* **2** *v/i in surprise* tragar saliva

◆ **gulp down** *v/t drink* tragar; *food* engullir

gum[1] [gʌm] *in mouth* encía *f*

gum[2] [gʌm] *n* (*glue*) pegamento *m*, cola *f*; (*chewing gum*) chicle *m*

gump·tion ['gʌmpʃn] sentido *m* común

gun [gʌn] *pistol, revolver* pistola *f*; *rifle* rifle *m*; *cannon* cañón *m*

◆ **gun down** *v/t* (*pret & pp* **gunned**) matar a tiros

'gun·fire disparos *mpl*

'gun·man hombre *m* armado

'gun·point: at gunpoint a punta de pistola

'gun·shot disparo *m*, tiro *m*

'gun·shot wound herida *f* de bala

gur·gle ['gɜːrgl] *v/i of baby* gorjear; *of drain* gorgotear

gu·ru ['guru] *fig* gurú *m*

gush [gʌʃ] *v/i of liquid* manar, salir a chorros

gush·y ['gʌʃɪ] *adj* F (*enthusiastic*) efusivo, exagerado

gust [gʌst] ráfaga *f*

gus·to ['gʌstou] entusiasmo *m*; **with gusto** con entusiasmo

gust·y ['gʌstɪ] *adj weather* ventoso, con viento racheado; **gusty wind** viento *m* racheado

gut [gʌt] **1** *n* intestino *m*; F (*stomach*) tripa *f* F **2** *v/t* (*pret & pp* **gutted**) (*destroy*) destruir

guts [gʌts] *npl* F (*courage*) agallas *fpl* F

guts·y ['gʌtsɪ] *adj* F (*brave*) valiente, con muchas agallas F

gut·ter ['gʌtər] *on sidewalk* cuneta *f*; *on roof* canal *m*, canalón *m*

guy [gaɪ] F tipo *m*, *Span* tío *m* F; **hey, you guys** eh, gente

guz·zle ['gʌzl] *v/t* tragar, engullir

gym [dʒɪm] gimnasio *m*

gym·na·si·um [dʒɪm'neɪzɪəm] gimnasio *m*

gym·nast ['dʒɪmnæst] gimnasta *m/f*

gym·nas·tics [dʒɪm'næstɪks] gimnasia *f*

'gym shoes *npl* zapatilla *fpl* de gimnasia

gy·nae·col·o·gy *etc Br* → **gynecology** *etc*

gy·ne·col·o·gy [gaɪnɪ'kɑːlədʒɪ] ginecología *f*

gy·ne·col·o·gist [gaɪnɪ'kɑːlədʒɪst] ginecólogo(-a) *m(f)*

gyp·sy ['dʒɪpsɪ] gitano(-a) *m(f)*

G

H

hab·it ['hæbɪt] hábito m, costumbre m; **get into the habit of doing sth** adquirir el hábito de hacer algo
hab·it·a·ble ['hæbɪtəbl] adj habitable
hab·i·tat ['hæbɪtæt] hábitat m
ha·bit·u·al [hə'bɪtʊəl] adj habitual
hack [hæk] n poor writer gacetillero(-a) m(f)
hack·er ['hækər] COMPUT pirata m/f informático(-a)
hack·neyed ['hæknɪd] adj manido
had [hæd] pret & pp → **have**
had·dock ['hædək] eglefino m
hag·gard ['hægərd] adj demacrado
hag·gle ['hægl] v/i regatear; **haggle over sth** regatear algo
hail [heɪl] n granizo m
'hail·stone piedra f de granizo
'hail·storm granizada f
hair [her] pelo m, cabello m; single pelo m; (body hair) vello m; **have short / long hair** tener el pelo corto / largo
'hair·brush cepillo m
'hair·cut corte m de pelo; **have a haircut** cortarse el pelo
'hair·do F peinado m
'hair·dress·er peluquero(-a) m(f); **at the hairdresser** en la peluquería
'hair·dri·er, 'hair·dry·er secador m (de pelo)
hair·less ['herlɪs] adj sin pelo
'hair·pin horquilla f
'hair·pin 'bend curva f muy cerrada
hair-rais·ing ['herreɪzɪŋ] adj espeluznante
hair re·mov·er [herɪ'muːvər] depilatorio m
'hair's breadth fig: **by a hair's breadth** por un pelo
'hair-split·ting ['hersplɪtɪŋ] n sutilezas fpl
'hair spray laca f
'hair·style peinado m
'hair·styl·ist estilista m/f, peluquero(-a) m(f)
hair·y ['herɪ] adj arm, animal peludo; F (frightening) espeluznante
half [hæf] **1** n (pl **halves** [hævz]) mitad f; **half past ten** las diez y media; **half after ten** las diez y media; **half an hour** media hora; **half a pound** media libra; **go halves with s.o. on sth** ir a medias con alguien en algo **2** adj medio; **at half price** a mitad de precio **3** adv a medias; **half finished** a medio acabar
half 'board Br media pensión f

half-heart·ed [hæf'hɑːrtɪd] adj desganado
half 'time **1** n SP descanso m **2** adj: **half time job** trabajo m a tiempo parcial; **half time score** marcador m en el descanso
half'way **1** adj stage, point intermedio **2** adv a mitad de camino
hall [hɔːl] large room sala f; (hallway in house) vestíbulo m
Hal·low·e'en [hæloʊ'wiːn] víspera de Todos los Santos
halo ['heɪloʊ] halo m
halt [hɔːlt] **1** v/i detenerse **2** v/t detener **3** n alto m; **come to a halt** detenerse
halve [hæv] v/t input, costs, effort reducir a la mitad; apple partir por la mitad
ham [hæm] jamón m
ham·burg·er ['hæmbɜːrgər] hamburguesa f
ham·mer ['hæmər] **1** n martillo m **2** v/i: **hammer at the door** golpear la puerta
ham·mock ['hæmək] hamaca f
ham·per¹ ['hæmpər] n for food cesta f
ham·per² v/t (obstruct) estorbar, obstaculizar
ham·ster ['hæmstər] hámster m
hand [hænd] n mano m; of clock manecilla f; (worker) brazo m; **at hand, to hand** a mano; **at first hand** de primera mano, directamente; **by hand** a mano; **on the one hand ..., on the other hand** por una parte ..., por otra parte; **the work is in hand** el trabajo se está llevando a cabo; **on your right hand** a mano derecha; **hands off!** ¡fuera las manos!; **hands up!** ¡arriba las manos!; **change hands** cambiar de manos; **give s.o. a hand** echar una mano a alguien
◆ **hand down** v/t transmitir
◆ **hand in** v/t entregar
◆ **hand on** v/t pasar
◆ **hand out** v/t repartir
◆ **hand over** v/t entregar
'hand·bag Br bolso m, L.Am. cartera f
'hand·book manual m
'hand·cuff v/t esposar
hand·cuffs ['hæn(d)kʌfs] npl esposas fpl
hand·i·cap ['hændɪkæp] n desventaja f
hand·i·capped ['hændɪkæpt] adj physically minusválido, disminuido; **handicapped by lack of funds** en desventaja por carecer de fondos
hand·i·craft ['hændɪkræft] artesanía f
hand·i·work ['hændɪwɜːrk] manuali-

dades *fpl*

hand·ker·chief ['hæŋkərʧıf] pañuelo *m*

han·dle ['hændl] **1** *n of door* manilla *f; of suitcase* asa *f; of pan, knife* mango *m* **2** *v/t goods,* difficult person manejar; *case,* deal llevar, encargarse de; *let me handle this* deja que me ocupe yo de esto

han·dle·bars ['hændlbɑːrz] *npl* manillar *m, L.Am.* manubrio *m*

'**hand lug·gage** equipaje *m* de mano

'hand·made [hæn(d)'meıd] *adj* hecho a mano

'**hand·rail** barandilla *f*

'**hand·shake** apretón *m* de manos

hands-off [hændz'ɑːf] *adj* no intervencionista

hand·some ['hænsəm] *adj* guapo, atractivo

hands-on [hændz'ɑːn] *adj* práctico; *he has a hands-on style of management* le gusta implicarse en todos los aspectos de la gestión

'**hand·writ·ing** caligrafía *f*

hand·writ·ten ['hændrıtn] *adj* escrito a mano

hand·y ['hændı] *adj tool, device* práctico; *it's handy for the shops* está muy cerca de las tiendas; *it might come in handy* nos puede venir muy bien

hang [hæŋ] **1** *v/t* (*pret & pp* **hung**) picture colgar; *person* colgar, ahorcar (*pret & pp* **hanged**) **2** *v/i* (*pret & pp* **hung**) colgar; *of dress, hair* caer, colgar; *v: get the hang of sth* F agarrarle el tranquilo a algo F

◆ **hang about** *v/i:* **he's always hanging about on the street corner** siempre está rondando por la esquina; *hang about a minute!* F ¡un momento!

◆ **hang on** *v/i* (*wait*) esperar

◆ **hang on to** *v/t* (*keep*) conservar; *do you mind if I hang on to it for a while?* ¿te importa si me lo quedo durante un tiempo?

◆ **hang up** *v/i* TELEC colgar

han·gar ['hæŋər] hangar *m*

hang·er ['hæŋər] *for clothes* percha *f*

hang glid·er ['hæŋglaıdər] *person* piloto *m* de ala delta; *device* ala *f* delta

hang glid·ing ['hæŋglaıdıŋ] ala *f* delta

'**hang·o·ver** resaca *f*

◆ **han·ker after** ['hæŋkər] *v/t* anhelar

han·kie ['hæŋkı] F pañuelo *m*

hap·haz·ard [hæp'hæzərd] *adj* descuidado

hap·pen ['hæpn] *v/i* ocurrir, pasar, suceder; *if you happen to see him* si por casualidad lo vieras; *what has happened to you?* ¿qué te ha pasado?

◆ **happen across** *v/t* encontrar por casualidad

hap·pen·ing ['hæpnıŋ] suceso *m*

hap·pi·ly ['hæpılı] *adv* alegremente; (*luckily*) afortunadamente

hap·pi·ness ['hæpınıs] felicidad *f*

hap·py ['hæpı] *adj* feliz, contento; *coincidence* afortunado

hap·py-go-luck·y *adj* despreocupado

'**hap·py hour** franja horaria en la que las bebidas son más baratas en los bares

har·ass [hə'ræs] *v/t* acosar; *enemy* asediar, hostigar

har·assed [hər'æst] *adj* agobiado

har·ass·ment [hə'ræsmənt] acoso *m; sexual harassment* acoso *m* sexual

har·bor, *Br* **har·bour** ['hɑːrbər] **1** *n* puerto *m* **2** *v/t criminal* proteger; *grudge* albergar

hard [hɑːrd] *adj* duro; (*difficult*) difícil; *facts, evidence* real; *hard of hearing* duro de oído

'**hard·back** *n* libro *m* de tapas duras

hard-boiled [hɑːrd'bɔıld] *adj egg* duro

'**hard cop·y** copia *f* impresa

'**hard core** *n* (*pornography*) porno *m* duro

hard 'cur·ren·cy divisa *f* fuerte

hard 'disk disco *m* duro

hard·en ['hɑːrdn] **1** *v/t* endurecer **2** *v/i of glue, attitude* endurecerse

'**hard hat** casco *m;* (*construction worker*) obrero(-a) *m(f)* (de la construcción)

hard-head·ed [hɑːrd'hedıd] *adj* pragmático

hard-heart·ed [hɑːrd'hɑːrtıd] *adj* insensible

hard 'line línea *f* dura; *take a hard line on* adoptar una línea dura en cuanto a

hard'lin·er partidario(-a) *m(f)* de la línea dura

hard·ly ['hɑːrdlı] *adv* apenas; *did you agree? – hardly!* ¿estuviste de acuerdo? – ¡en absoluto!

hard·ness ['hɑːrdnıs] dureza *f;* (*difficulty*) dificultad *f*

hard'sell venta *f* agresiva

hard·ship ['hɑːrdʃıp] penuria *f*, privación *f*

hard 'up *adj: be hard up* andar mal de dinero

'**hard·ware** ferretería *f;* COMPUT hardware *m*

'**hard·ware store** ferretería *f*

hard-work·ing [hɑːrd'wɜːrkıŋ] *adj* trabajador

har·dy ['hɑːrdı] *adj* resistente

hare [her] liebre *f*

hare-brained ['herbreınd] *adj* alocado

harm [hɑːrm] **1** *n* daño *m; it wouldn't do*

any harm to buy two por comprar dos
no pasa nada **2** v/t hacer daño a, dañar
harm·ful ['hɑːrmfəl] *adj* dañino, perjudicial
harm·less ['hɑːrmlɪs] *adj* inofensivo; *fun*
inocente
har·mo·ni·ous [hɑːr'moʊnɪəs] *adj* armonioso
har·mo·nize ['hɑːrmənaɪz] v/i armonizar
har·mo·ny ['hɑːrmənɪ] MUS, *fig* armonía *f*
harp [hɑːrp] *n* arpa *f*
◆ **harp on about** v/t F dar la lata con F
har·poon [hɑːr'puːn] *n* arpón *m*
harsh [hɑːʃ] *adj criticism, words* duro,
severo; *color* chillón; *light* potente
harsh·ly ['hɑːrʃlɪ] *adv* con dureza *or* severidad
har·vest ['hɑːrvɪst] *n* cosecha *f*
hash [hæʃ] F: **make a hash of** fastidiar
hash browns *npl Span* patatas *fpl or*
L.Am. papas *fpl* fritas
hash·ish ['hæʃiːʃ] *n* hachís *m*
'hash mark almohadilla *f, el signo* '#'
haste [heɪst] *n* prisa *f*
has·ten ['heɪsn] v/i: **hasten to do sth**
apresurarse en hacer algo
hast·i·ly ['heɪstɪlɪ] *adv* precipitadamente
hast·y ['heɪstɪ] *adj* precipitado
hat [hæt] *n* sombrero *m*
hatch [hætʃ] *n for serving food* trampilla *f*;
on ship escotilla *f*
◆ **hatch out** v/i *of eggs* romperse; *of*
chicks salir del cascarón
hatch·et ['hætʃɪt] *n* hacha *f*; **bury the hat-**
chet enterrar el hacha de guerra
hate [heɪt] **1** *n* odio *m* **2** v/t odiar
ha·tred ['heɪtrɪd] *n* odio *m*
haugh·ty ['hɔːtɪ] *adj* altanero
haul [hɔːl] **1** *n of fish* captura *f*; *of robbery*
botín *m* **2** v/t *(pull)* arrastrar
haul·age ['hɔːlɪdʒ] *n* transporte *m*
'haul·age com·pa·ny empresa *f* de trans-
portes
haul·i·er ['hɔːlɪr] *n* transportista *m*
haunch [hɔːntʃ] *of person* trasero *m*; *of*
animal pierna *f*
haunt [hɔːnt] **1** v/t: **this place is haunted**
en este lugar hay fantasmas **2** *n* lugar *m*
favorito
haunt·ing ['hɔːntɪŋ] *adj tune* fascinante
Ha·van·a [hə'vænə] *n* La Habana *f*
have [hæv] **1** v/t *(pret & pp had)* *(own)*
tener ◇ *breakfast, lunch* tomar
◇ *I don't have a TV* no tengo televisión;
can I have a coffee? ¿me da un café?;
can I have more time? ¿me puede dar
más tiempo?; **do you have ...?** ¿tiene
...?
◇ *must*: **have (got) to** tener que

◇ *causative*: **I'll have it faxed to you** te
lo mandaré por fax; **I'll have have it re-**
paired haré que lo arreglen; **I had my**
hair cut me corté el pelo
◇ v/aux: **I have eaten** he comido; **have**
you seen her? ¿la has visto?
◆ **have back** v/t: **when can I have it**
back? ¿cuándo me lo devolverá?
◆ **have on** v/t *(wear)* llevar puesto; **do**
you have anything on tonight? *(have*
planned) ¿tenéis algo planeado para esta
noche?
ha·ven ['heɪvn] *fig* refugio *m*
hav·oc ['hævək] estragos *mpl*; **play havoc**
with hacer estragos en
hawk [hɔːk] *also fig* halcón *m*
hay [heɪ] *n* heno *m*
'hay fe·ver fiebre *f* del heno
haz·ard ['hæzərd] *n* riesgo *m*, peligro *m*
'haz·ard lights *npl* MOT luces *fpl* de emergencia
haz·ard·ous ['hæzərdəs] *adj* peligroso,
arriesgado; **hazardous waste** residuos
mpl peligrosos
haze [heɪz] *n* neblina *f*
ha·zel ['heɪzl] *n tree* avellano *m*
'ha·zel·nut avellana *f*
haz·y ['heɪzɪ] *adj image, memories* confuso, vago; **I'm a bit hazy about it** no lo tengo muy claro
he [hiː] *pron* él; **he is French/a doctor** es
francés / médico; **you're funny, he's not**
tú tienes gracia, él no
head [hed] **1** *n* cabeza *f*; *(boss, leader)* je-
fe(-a) *m(f)*; *of school* director(a) *m(f)*;
on beer espuma *f*; *of nail, line* cabeza
f; **$15 a head** 15 dólares por cabeza;
heads or tails? ¿cara o cruz?; **at the he-**
ad of the list encabezando la lista; **head**
over heels *fall* rodando; *fall in love* locamente; **lose one's head** *(go crazy)* perder la cabeza **2** v/t *(lead)* estar a la cabeza
de; *ball* cabecear
◆ **head for** v/t dirigirse a *or* hacia
'head·ache dolor *m* de cabeza
'head·band cinta *f* para la cabeza
head·er ['hedər] *in soccer* cabezazo *m*; *in*
document encabezamiento *m*
'head·hunt v/t COM buscar, captar
'head·hunt·er COM cazatalentos *m/f inv*
head·ing ['hedɪŋ] *in list* encabezamiento
m
'head·lamp faro *m*
'head·light faro *m*
'head·line *n in newspaper* titular *m*; **make**
the headlines saltar a los titulares
'head·long *adv fall* de cabeza
'head·mas·ter director *m*
'head·mis·tress directora *f*

head 'of·fice *of company* central *f*

head-'on 1 *adv crash* de frente **2** *adj crash* frontal

'head·phones *npl* auriculares *mpl*

'head·quar·ters *npl of party, organization* sede *f; of army* cuartel *m* general

'head·rest reposacabezas *f inv*

'head·room *under bridge* gálibo *m; in car* espacio *m* vertical

'head·scarf pañuelo *m* (para la cabeza)

'head·strong *adj* cabezudo, testarudo

head 'teach·er director(a) *m(f)*

head 'wait·er maître *m*

'head·wind viento *m* contrario

head·y ['hedɪ] *adj drink, wine etc* que se sube a la cabeza

heal [hi:l] *v/t* curar

◆ **heal up** *v/i* curarse

health [helθ] salud *f; your health!* ¡a tu salud!

'health club gimnasio *m* (*con piscina, pista de tenis, sauna etc*)

'health food comida *f* integral

'health food store tienda *f* de comida integral

'health in·su·rance seguro *m* de enfermedad

'health re·sort centro *m* de reposo

health·y ['helθɪ] *adj person* sano; *food, lifestyle* saludable; *economy* saneado

heap [hi:p] *n* montón *m*

◆ **heap up** *v/t* amontonar

hear [hɪr] *v/t & v/i* (*pret & pp* **heard**) oír

◆ **hear about** *v/t: have you heard about Mike?* ¿te has enterado de lo de Mike?; *they're bound to hear about it sooner or later* se van a enterar tarde o temprano

◆ **hear from** *v/t* (*have news from*) tener noticias de

hear·ing ['hɪrɪŋ] oído *m;* LAW vista *f; his hearing is not so good now* ahora ya no oye tan bien; *she was within hearing / out of hearing* estaba / no estaba lo suficientemente cerca como para oírlo

'hear·ing aid audífono *m*

'hear·say rumores *mpl; by hearsay* de oídas

hearse [hɜːrs] coche *m* fúnebre

heart [hɑːrt] *also fig* corazón *m; of problem* meollo *m; know sth by heart* saber algo de memoria; *hearts in cards* corazones *mpl*

'heart at·tack infarto *m*

'heart·beat latido *m*

heart·break·ing ['hɑːrtbreɪkɪŋ] *adj* desgarrador

'heart·brok·en *adj* descorazonado

'heart·burn acidez *f* (de estómago)

'heart fail·ure paro *m* cardíaco

heart·felt ['hɑːrtfelt] *adj sympathy* sincero

hearth [hɑːrθ] chimenea *f*

heart·less ['hɑːrtlɪs] *adj* despiadado

heart-rend·ing ['hɑːrtrendɪŋ] *adj plea, sight* desgarrador

'heart throb *F* ídolo *m*

'heart trans·plant transplante *m* de corazón

heart·y ['hɑːrtɪ] *adj appetite* voraz; *meal* copioso; *person* cordial, campechano

heat [hi:t] *n* calor *m*

◆ **heat up** *v/t* calentar

heat·ed ['hi:tɪd] *adj swimming pool* climatizado; *discussion* acalorado

heat·er ['hi:tər] *in room* estufa *f; turn on the heater in car* enciende la calefacción

hea·then ['hi:ðn] *n* pagano(-a) *m(f)*

heath·er ['heðər] brezo *m*

heat·ing ['hi:tɪŋ] calefacción *f*

'heat·proof, 'heat·re·sis·tant *adj* resistente al calor

'heat·stroke insolación *f*

'heat·wave ola *f* de calor

heave [hi:v] *v/t* (*lift*) subir

heav·en ['hevn] cielo *m; good heavens!* ¡Dios mío!

heav·en·ly ['hevnlɪ] *adj* F divino F

heav·y ['hevɪ] *adj cold, rain, accent, loss* fuerte; *smoker, drinker* empedernido; *loss of life* grande; *bleeding* abundante; *there's heavy traffic* hay mucho tráfico

heav·y·'du·ty *adj* resistente

'heav·y·weight *adj* SP de los pesos pesados

heck·le ['hekl] *v/t* interrumpir (*molestando*)

hec·tic ['hektɪk] *adj* vertiginoso, frenético

hedge [hedʒ] *n* seto *m*

hedge·hog ['hedʒhɑːg] erizo *m*

hedge·row ['hedʒrou] seto *m*

heed [hi:d] *v/t: pay heed to …* hacer caso de …

heel [hi:l] *of foot* talón *m; of shoe* tacón *m*

'heel bar zapatería *f*

hef·ty ['heftɪ] *adj weight, suitcase* pesado; *person* robusto

height [haɪt] altura *f; at the height of the season* en plena temporada

height·en ['haɪtn] *v/t effect, tension* intensificar

heir [er] heredero *m*

heir·ess ['erɪs] heredera *f*

held [held] *pret & pp* → **hold**

hel·i·cop·ter ['helɪkɑːptər] helicóptero *m*

hell [hel] infierno *m; what the hell are you doing / do you want?* F ¿qué demonios estás haciendo / quieres? F: **go to hell!** F ¡vete a paseo! F; **a hell of a lot** F un montonazo F; **one hell of a nice guy** F un tipo muy simpático *or* Span legal F

hel·lo [hǝˈloʊ] hola; TELEC ¿sí?, *Span* ¿diga?, *Am* ¿aló?, *Rpl* ¿oigo?, *Mex* ¿bueno?; **say hello to s.o.** saludar a alguien

helm [helm] NAUT timón *m*

hel·met ['helmɪt] casco *m*

help [help] **1** *n* ayuda *f*; **help!** ¡socorro! **2** *v/t* ayudar; **just help yourself** *to food* toma lo que quieras; **I can't help it** no puedo evitarlo; **I couldn't help laughing** no pude evitar reírme

help·er ['helpǝr] ayudante *m/f*

help·ful ['helpfǝl] *adj advice* útil; *person* servicial

help·ing ['helpɪŋ] *of food* ración *f*

help·less ['helplɪs] *adj (unable to cope)* indefenso; *(powerless)* impotente

help·less·ly ['helplɪslɪ] *adv* impotentemente

help·less·ness ['helplɪsnɪs] impotencia *f*

'help screen COMPUT pantalla *f* de ayuda

hem [hem] *n of dress etc* dobladillo *m*

hem·i·sphere ['hemɪsfɪr] hemisferio *m*

'hem·line bajo *m*

hem·or·rhage ['hemǝrɪdʒ] **1** *n* hemorragia *f* **2** *v/i* sangrar

hen [hen] gallina *f*

hench·man ['henʧmǝn] *pej* sicario *m*

'hen par·ty despedida *f* de soltera

hen-pecked ['henpekt] *adj:* **henpecked husband** calzonazos *mpl*

hep·a·ti·tis [hepǝ'taɪtɪs] hepatitis *f*

her [hɜːr] **1** *adj* su; **her ticket** su entrada; **her books** sus libros **2** *pron direct object* la; *indirect object* le; *after prep* ella; **I know her** la conozco; **I gave her the keys** le di las llaves; **I sold it to her** se lo vendí; **this is for her** esto es para ella; **who do you mean? - her** ¿a quién te refieres? - a ella

herb [ɜːrb] hierba *f*

herb(al) 'tea ['ɜːrb(ǝl)] infusión *f*

herd [hɜːrd] *n* rebaño *m*; *of elephants* manada *f*

here [hɪr] *adv* aquí; **over here** aquí; **here's to you!** *as toast* ¡a tu salud!; **here you are** *giving sth* ¡aquí tienes!; **here we are!** *finding sth* ¡aquí está!

he·red·i·ta·ry [hǝˈredɪterɪ] *adj disease* hereditario

he·red·i·ty [hǝˈredɪtɪ] herencia *f*

her·i·tage ['herɪtɪdʒ] patrimonio *m*

her·mit ['hɜːrmɪt] ermitaño(-a) *m(f)*

her·ni·a ['hɜːrnɪǝ] MED hernia *f*

he·ro ['hɪroʊ] héroe *m*

he·ro·ic [hɪˈroʊɪk] *adj* heroico

he·ro·i·cal·ly [hɪˈroʊɪklɪ] *adv* heroicamente

her·o·in ['heroʊɪn] heroína *f*

'her·o·in ad·dict heroinómano(-a) *m(f)*

her·o·ine ['heroʊɪn] heroína *f*

her·o·ism ['heroʊɪzm] heroísmo *m*

her·on ['herǝn] garza *f*

her·pes ['hɜːrpiːz] MED herpes *m*

her·ring ['herɪŋ] arenque *m*

hers [hɜːrz] *pron* el suyo, la suya; **hers are red** los suyos son rojos; **that book is hers** ese libro es suyo; **a cousin of hers** un primo suyo

her·self [hɜːrˈself] *pron reflexive* se; *emphatic* ella misma; **she hurt herself** se hizo daño; **when she saw herself in the mirror** cuando se vio en el espejo; **he saw it herself** lo vio ella misma; **by herself** *(alone)* sola; *(without help)* ella sola, ella misma

hes·i·tant ['hezɪtǝnt] *adj* indeciso

hes·i·tant·ly ['hezɪtǝntlɪ] *adv* con indecisión

hes·i·tate ['hezɪteɪt] *v/i* dudar, vacilar

hes·i·ta·tion [hezɪ'teɪʃn] vacilación *f*

het·er·o·sex·u·al [hetǝroʊ'sekʃʊǝl] *adj* heterosexual

hey·day ['heɪdeɪ] apogeo *m*

hi [haɪ] *int* ¡hola!

hi·ber·nate ['haɪbǝrneɪt] *v/i* hibernar

hic·cup ['hɪkʌp] *n* hipo *m*; *(minor problem)* tropiezo *m*, traspié *m*; **have the hiccups** tener hipo

hick [hɪk] *pej* F palurdo(-a) *m(f)* F, pueblerino(-a) *m(f)* F

'hick town *pej* F ciudad *f* provinciana

hid [hɪd] *pret* → **hide¹**

hid·den ['hɪdn] **1** *adj meaning, treasure* oculto **2** *pp* → **hide¹**

hid·den a'gen·da *fig* objetivo *m* secreto

hide¹ [haɪd] **1** *v/t (pret hid, pp hidden)* esconder **2** *v/i (pret hid, pp hidden)* esconderse

hide² *n of animal* escondrijo *m*

hide-and-'seek escondite *m*

'hide·a·way escondite *m*

hid·e·ous ['hɪdɪǝs] *adj* espantoso, horrendo; *person* repugnante

hid·ing¹ ['haɪdɪŋ] *(beating)* paliza *f*

hid·ing² ['haɪdɪŋ]: **be in hiding** estar escondido; **go into hiding** esconderse

'hid·ing place escondite *m*

hi·er·ar·chy ['haɪrɑːrkɪ] jerarquía *f*

hi-fi ['haɪfaɪ] equipo *m* de alta fidelidad

high [haɪ] **1** *adj* alto; *wind* fuerte; *(on drugs)* colocado P; **have a very high opinion of** tener muy buena opinión de; **high in the sky** en lo alto; **it is high time you understood** ya va siendo hora de que entiendas **2** *n* MOT directa *f*; *in statistics* máximo *m*; EDU escuela *f* secundaria, *Span* instituto **3** *adv*: *that's as high as we can go* eso es lo máximo que podemos ofrecer

'high·brow *adj* intelectual
'high·chair trona *f*
high·'class *adj* de categoría
High 'Court Tribunal *m* Supremo
high 'div·ing salto *m* de trampolín
high·'fre·quen·cy *adj* de alta frecuencia
high·'grade *adj* de calidad superior
high-hand·ed [haɪ'hændɪd] *adj* despótico
high-'heeled [haɪ'hiːld] *adj* de tacón alto
'high jump salto *m* de altura
high·'lev·el *adj* de alto nivel
'high life buena vida *f*
'high·light 1 *n (main event)* momento *m* cumbre; *in hair* reflejo *m* **2** *v/t with pen* resaltar; COMPUT seleccionar, resaltar
'high·light·er *pen* fluorescente *m*
high·ly ['haɪlɪ] *adv* *desirable, likely* muy; *be highly paid* estar muy bien pagado; *think highly of s.o.* tener una buena opinión de alguien
high·ly 'strung *adj* muy nervioso
high per'form·ance *adj* *drill, battery* de alto rendimiento
high-pitched [haɪ'pɪtʃt] *adj* agudo
'high point *of life, career* punto *m* culminante
high-pow·ered [haɪ'paʊərd] *adj* *engine* potente; *intellectual* de alto(s) vuelo(s); *salesman* enérgico
high 'pres·sure 1 *n* *weather* altas presiones *fpl* **2** *adj* TECH a gran presión; *salesman* agresivo; *job, lifestyle* muy estresante
high 'priest sumo sacerdote *m*
'high school escuela *f* secundaria, *Span* instituto *m*
high so'ci·e·ty alta sociedad *f*
high-speed 'train tren *m* de alta velocidad
high 'tech 1 *n* alta *f* tecnología **2** *adj* de alta tecnología
high 'tide marea *f* alta
high 'wa·ter: *at high water* con la marea alta
'high·way autopista *f*
'high wire *in circus* cuerda *f* floja
hi·jack ['haɪdʒæk] **1** *v/t* *plane, bus* secuestrar **2** *n* *of plane, bus* secuestro *m*
hi·jack·er ['haɪdʒækər] *of plane, bus* secuestrador(a) *m(f)*
hike¹ [haɪk] **1** *n* caminata *f* **2** *v/i* caminar
hike² [haɪk] *n* *in prices* subida *f*
hik·er ['haɪkər] senderista *m/f*
hik·ing ['haɪkɪŋ] senderismo *m*

'hik·ing boots *npl* botas *fpl* de senderismo
hi·lar·i·ous [hɪ'leriəs] *adj* divertidísimo, graciosísimo
hill [hɪl] colina *f*; *(slope)* cuesta *f*
hill·bil·ly ['hɪlbɪlɪ] F rústico montañés
hill·side ['hɪlsaɪd] ladera *f*
hill·top ['hɪltɑːp] cumbre *f*
hill·y ['hɪlɪ] *adj* con colinas
hilt [hɪlt] puño *m*
him [hɪm] *pron* *direct object* lo; *indirect object* le; *after prep* él; *I know him* lo conozco; *I gave him the keys* le di las llaves; *I sold it to him* se lo vendí; *this is for him* esto es para él; *who do you mean? - him* ¿a quién te refieres? - a él
him·self [hɪm'self] *pron* *reflexive* se; *emphatic* él mismo; *he hurt himself* se hizo daño; *when he saw himself in the mirror* cuando se vio en el espejo; *he saw it himself* lo vio él mismo; *by himself* *(alone)* solo; *(without help)* él solo, él mismo
hind [haɪnd] *adj* trasero
hin·der ['hɪndər] *v/t* obstaculizar, entorpecer
hin·drance ['hɪndrəns] estorbo *m*, obstáculo *m*
hind·sight ['haɪndsaɪt]: *with hindsight* a posteriori
hinge [hɪndʒ] *n* bisagra *f*
◆ **hinge on** *v/t* depender de
hint [hɪnt] *n* *(clue)* pista *f*; *(piece of advice)* consejo *m*; *(implied suggestion)* indirecta *f*; *of red, sadness etc* rastro *m*
hip [hɪp] *n* cadera *f*
hip 'pock·et bolsillo *m* trasero
hip·po·pot·a·mus [hɪpə'pɑːtəməs] hipopótamo *m*
hire [haɪr] *v/t* alquilar
his [hɪz] **1** *adj* su; *his ticket* su entrada; *his books* sus libros **2** *pron* el suyo, la suya; *his are red* los suyos son rojos; *that ticket is his* esa entrada es suya; *a cousin of his* un primo suyo
His·pan·ic [hɪ'spænɪk] **1** *n* hispano(-a) *m(f)* **2** *adj* hispano, hispánico
hiss [hɪs] *v/i* *of snake, audience* silbar
his·to·ri·an [hɪ'stɔːriən] historiador(a) *m(f)*
his·tor·ic [hɪ'stɑːrɪk] *adj* histórico
his·tor·i·cal [hɪ'stɑːrɪkl] *adj* histórico
his·to·ry ['hɪstərɪ] historia *f*
hit [hɪt] **1** *v/t* *(pret & pp hit)* golpear; *(collide with)* chocar contra; *he was hit by a bullet* le alcanzó una bala; *it suddenly hit me* *(I realized)* de repente me di cuenta; *hit town* *(arrive)* llegar a la ciudad **2** *n* *(blow)* golpe *m*; MUS, *(success)*

éxito *m*

◆ **hit back** v/i *physically* devolver el golpe; *verbally, with actions* responder

◆ **hit on** v/t *idea* dar con

◆ **hit out at** v/t (*criticize*) atacar

hit-and-run *adj*: **hit-and-run accident** accidente en el que el vehículo causante se da a la fuga

hitch [hɪtʃ] **1** *n* (*problem*) contratiempo *m*; **without a hitch** sin ningún contratiempo **2** v/t enganchar; **hitch sth to sth** enganchar algo a algo; **hitch a ride** hacer autostop **3** v/i (*hitchhike*) hacer autostop

◆ **hitch up** v/t *wagon, trailer* enganchar

'**hitch-hike** v/i hacer autostop

'**hitch-hik-er** autoestopista *m/f*

'**hitch-hik-ing** autostop *m*

hi-'tech 1 *n* alta tecnología *f* **2** *adj* de alta tecnología

'**hit-list** lista *f* de blancos

'**hit-man** asesino *m* a sueldo

hit-or-'miss *adj* a la buena ventura

'**hit squad** grupo *m* de intervención especial

HIV [eɪtʃaɪˈviː] *abbr* (= *human immunodeficiency virus*) VIH *m* (= virus *m inv* de la inmunodeficiencia *humana*)

hive [haɪv] *n* (*for bees*) colmena *f*

◆ **hive off** v/t (COM: *separate off*) desprenderse de

HIV-'pos·i·tive *adj* seropositivo

hoard [hɔːrd] **1** *n* reserva *f* **2** v/t hacer acopio de; *money* acumular

hoard·er [ˈhɔːrdər] acaparador(a) *m(f)*

hoarse [hɔːrs] *adj* ronco

hoax [houks] *n* bulo *m*, engaño *m*; **bomb hoax** amenaza *f* falsa de bomba

hob [hɑːb] *on cooker* placa *f*

hob·ble [ˈhɑːbl] v/i cojear

hob·by [ˈhɑːbɪ] hobby *m*, afición *f*

ho·bo [ˈhoubou] F vagabundo(-a) *m(f)*

hock·ey [ˈhɑːkɪ] (*ice hockey*) hockey *m* sobre hielo

hog [hɑːg] *n* (*pig*) cerdo *m*, *L.Am.* chancho *m*

hoist [hɔɪst] **1** *n* montacargas *m inv*; *manual* elevador *m* **2** v/t (*lift*) levantar, subir; *flag* izar; **they hoisted the winner up onto their shoulders** subieron al ganador a hombros

ho·kum [ˈhoukəm] F (*nonsense*) tonterías *fpl*; (*sentimental stuff*) cursilería *f*

hold [hould] **1** v/t (*pret & pp held*) *in hand* llevar; (*support, keep in place*) sostener; *passport, license* tener; *prisoner, suspect* retener; (*contain*) contener; *job, post* ocupar; *course* mantener; **hold my hand** dame la mano; **hold one's breath** aguantar la respiración; **he can hold**

his drink sabe beber; **hold s.o. responsible** hacer a alguien responsable; **hold that ...** (*believe, maintain*) mantener que ...; **hold the line, please** TELEC espere, por favor **2** *n in ship, plane* bodega *f*; **take hold of sth** agarrar algo; **lose one's hold on sth** *on rope* soltar algo; *on reality* perder el contacto con algo

◆ **hold against** v/t: **hold sth against s.o.** tener algo contra alguien

◆ **hold back 1** v/t *crowds* contener; *facts, information* guardar **2** v/i (*not tell all*): **I'm sure he's holding back** estoy seguro de que no dice todo lo que sabe

◆ **hold on** v/i (*wait*) esperar; **now hold on a minute!** ¡un momento!

◆ **hold on to** v/t (*keep*) guardar; *belief* aferrarse a

◆ **hold out 1** v/t *hand* tender; *prospect* ofrecer **2** v/i *of supplies* durar; (*survive*) resistir, aguantar

◆ **hold up 1** v/t *hand* levantar; *bank etc* atracar; (*make late*) retrasar; **I was held up by the traffic** he llegado tarde por culpa del tráfico; **hold sth up as an example** poner a alguien como ejemplo

◆ **hold with** v/t (*approve of*): **I don't hold with that sort of behavior** no me parece bien ese tipo de comportamiento

'**hold-all** *Br* bolsa *f*

hold·er [ˈhouldər] (*container*) receptáculo *m*; *of passport, ticket etc* titular *m/f*; *of record* poseedor(a) *m(f)*

'**hold·ing com·pa·ny** holding *m*

'**hold·up** (*robbery*) atraco *m*; (*delay*) retraso *m*

hole [houl] *in sleeve, wood, bag* agujero *m*; *in ground* hoyo *m*

hol·i·day [ˈhɑːlədeɪ] *single day* día *m* de fiesta; *period* vacaciones *fpl*; **take a holiday** tomarse unas vacaciones

Hol·land [ˈhɑːlənd] Holanda

hol·low [ˈhɑːlou] *adj object* hueco; *cheeks* hundido; *promise* vacío

hol·ly [ˈhɑːlɪ] acebo *m*

hol·o·caust [ˈhɑːləkɔːst] holocausto *m*

hol·o·gram [ˈhɑːləgræm] holograma *m*

hol·ster [ˈhoulstər] pistolera *f*

ho·ly [ˈhoulɪ] *adj* santo

Ho·ly 'Spir·it Espíritu *m* Santo

'**Ho·ly Week** Semana *f* Santa

home [houm] **1** *n* casa *f*; (*native country*) tierra *f*; *for old people* residencia *f*; **New York is my home** Nueva York es mi hogar; **at home** (*in house*) en casa; (*in country*) en mi / su / nuestra tierra; **make yourself at home** ponte cómodo; **at home and abroad** en el país y en el extranjero; **at home** SP en casa; **work from ho-**

me trabajar desde casa **2** *adv* a casa; *go home* ir a casa; *to country* ir a mi / tu / su tierra; *to town, part of country* ir a mi / tu / su ciudad

'home ad·dress domicilio *m*

home 'bank·ing telebanca *f*, banca *f* electrónica

'home·com·ing vuelta *f* a casa

home com'put·er *Span* ordenador *m*, *L.Am.* computadora *f* doméstica

home·less ['houmlɪs] *adj* sin casa; *the homeless* los sin casa

'home·lov·ing *adj* hogareño

home·ly ['houmlɪ] *adj* (*homeloving*) hogareño; (*not good-looking*) feúcho

'home·made *adj* casero

'home match partido *m* en casa

home 'mov·ie película *f* casera

ho·me·op·a·thy [houmɪ'ɑ:pəθɪ] homeopatía *f*

'home page *web site* página *f* personal; *on web site* página *f* inicial

'home·sick *adj* nostálgico; *be homesick* tener morriña

'home town ciudad *f* natal

'home·ward ['houmwərd] *adv to own house* a casa; *to own country* a mi país

'home·work EDU deberes *mpl*

'home·work·ing COM teletrabajo *m*

hom·i·cide ['hɑ:mɪsaɪd] *crime* homicidio *m*; *police department* brigada *f* de homicidios

hom·o·graph ['hɑ:məgræf] homógrafo *m*

ho·mo·pho·bi·a [hɑ:mə'foubɪə] homofobia *f*

ho·mo·sex·u·al [hɑ:mə'sekʃʊəl] **1** *adj* homosexual **2** *n* homosexual *m/f*

Hon·du·ras [hɑːn'dʊrəs] *n* Honduras

Hon·du·ran [hɑːn'dʊrən] **1** *adj* hondureño **2** *n* hondureño(-a) *m(f)*

hon·est ['ɑ:nɪst] *adj* honrado

hon·est·ly ['ɑ:nɪstlɪ] *adv* honradamente; *honestly!* ¡desde luego!

hon·es·ty ['ɑ:nɪstɪ] honradez *f*

hon·ey ['hʌnɪ] miel *f*; F (*darling*) cariño *m*, vida *f* mía

'hon·ey·comb panal *m*

'hon·ey·moon n luna *f* de miel

honk [hɑ:ŋk] *v/t horn* tocar

hon·or ['ɑ:nər] **1** *n* honor *m* **2** *v/t* honrar

hon·or·a·ble ['ɑ:nrəbl] *adj* honorable

hon·our *etc Br* → **honor** *etc*

hood [hʊd] *over head* capucha *f*; *over cooker* campana *f* extractora; MOT capó *m*; F (*gangster*) matón(-ona) *m(f)*

hood·lum ['hu:dləm] matón(-ona) *m(f)*

hoof [hu:f] casco *m*

hook [hʊk] gancho *m*; *to hang clothes on* colgador *m*; *for fishing* anzuelo *m*; *off*

the hook TELEC descolgado

hooked [hʊkt] *adj* enganchado; *be hooked on sth on drugs, fig* estar enganchado a algo

hook·er ['hʊkər] F fulana *f* F

hook·ey ['hʊkɪ] F: *play hookey* hacer novillos, *Mex* irse de pinta, *S. Am.* hacerse la rabona

hoop [hu:p] aro *m*

hoot [hu:t] **1** *v/t horn* tocar **2** *v/i of car* dar bocinazos; *of owl* ulular

hoo·ver® ['hu:vər] **1** *n* aspirador *m*, aspiradora *f* **2** *v/t carpets, room* pasar el aspirador por, aspirar

hop¹ [hɑ:p] *n plant* lúpulo *m*

hop² [hɑ:p] *v/i* (*pret & pp hopped*) saltar

hope [houp] **1** *n* esperanza *f*; *there's no hope of that* no hay esperanza de eso **2** *v/i* esperar; *hope for sth* esperar algo; *we all hope for peace* todos ansiamos la paz **3** *v/t: I hope you like it* espero que te guste; *I hope so* eso espero; *I hope not* espero que no

hope·ful ['houpfəl] *adj* prometedor; *I'm hopeful that ...* espero que ...

hope·ful·ly ['houpfəlɪ] *adv say, wait* esperanzadamente; *hopefully he hasn't forgotten* esperemos que no se haya olvidado

hope·less ['houplɪs] *adj position, prospect* desesperado; (*useless: person*) inútil

ho·ri·zon [hə'raɪzn] horizonte *m*

hor·i·zon·tal [hɑ:rɪ'zɑ:ntl] *adj* horizontal

hor·mone ['hɔ:rmoun] hormona *f*

horn [hɔ:rn] *of animal* cuerno *m*; MOT bocina *f*, claxon *m*

hor·net ['hɔ:rnɪt] avispón *m*

horn-rimmed 'spec·ta·cles ['hɔ:rnrɪmd] *npl* gafas *fpl* de concha

horn·y ['hɔ:rnɪ] *adj F sexually* cachondo F

hor·o·scope ['hɑ:rəskoup] horóscopo *m*

hor·ri·ble ['hɑ:rɪbl] *adj* horrible; *person* muy antipático

hor·ri·fy ['hɑ:rɪfaɪ] *v/t* (*pret & pp horrified*) horrorizar; *I was horrified* me quedé horrorizado

hor·ri·fy·ing ['hɑ:rɪfaɪɪŋ] *adj* horroroso

hor·ror ['hɑ:rər] horror *m*

'hor·ror mov·ie película *f* de terror

hors d'oeu·vre [ɔ:r'dɜ:rv] entremés *m*

horse [hɔ:rs] caballo *m*

'horse·back: *on horseback* a caballo

horse 'chest·nut castaño *m* de Indias

'horse·pow·er caballo *m* (de vapor)

'horse race carrera *f* de caballos

'horse·shoe herradura *f*

hor·ti·cul·ture ['hɔːrtɪkʌltʃər] horticultura f

hose [həʊz] n manguera f

hos·pice ['hɑːspɪs] hospital m para enfermos terminales

hos·pi·ta·ble [hɑːˈspɪtəbl] adj hospitalario

hos·pi·tal ['hɑːspɪtl] hospital m; **go into the hospital** ir al hospital

hos·pi·tal·i·ty [hɑːspɪˈtælətɪ] hospitalidad f

host [həʊst] n at party, reception anfitrión m; of TV program presentador(a) m(f)

hos·tage ['hɑːstɪdʒ] rehén m; **take s.o. hostage** tomar a alguien como rehén

'hos·tage tak·er persona que toma rehenes

hos·tel ['hɑːstl] for students residencia f; (youth hostel) albergue m

hos·tess ['həʊstes] at party, reception anfitriona f; on airplane azafata f; in bar cabaretera f

hos·tile ['hɑːstl] adj hostil

hos·til·i·ty [hɑːˈstɪlətɪ] of attitude hostilidad f; **hostilities** hostilidades fpl

hot [hɑːt] adj weather caluroso; object, water, food caliente; (spicy) picante; **it's hot** of weather hace calor; **I'm hot** tengo calor; **she's pretty hot at math** F (good) es una fenómena con las matemáticas F

'hot dog perrito m caliente

ho·tel [həʊˈtel] hotel m

'hot·plate placa f

'hot spot military, political punto m caliente

hour [aʊr] hora f

hour·ly ['aʊrlɪ] adj: **at hourly intervals** a intervalos de una hora; **an hourly bus** un autobús que pasa cada hora

house [haʊs] n casa f; **at your house** en tu casa

'house·boat barco-vivienda f

'house·break·ing allanamiento m de morada

'house·hold hogar m

'house·hold 'name nombre m conocido

'house hus·band amo m de casa

'house·keep·er ama f de llaves

'house·keep·ing activity tareas fpl domésticas; money dinero m para gastos domésticos

House of Rep·re·sent·a·tives npl Cámara f de Representantes

house·warm·ing (par·ty) ['haʊswɔːrmɪŋ] fiesta f de estreno de una casa

'house·wife ama f de casa

'house·work tareas fpl domésticas

hous·ing ['haʊzɪŋ] vivienda f; TECH cubierta f

'hous·ing con·di·tions npl condiciones fpl de la vivienda

hov·el ['hɑːvl] chabola f

hov·er ['hɑːvər] v/i of bird cernerse; of helicopter permanecer inmóvil en el aire

'hov·er·craft aerodeslizador m, hovercraft m

how [haʊ] adv cómo; **how are you?** ¿cómo estás?; **how about ...?** ¿qué te parece ...?; **how about a drink?** ¿te apetece tomar algo?; **how much?** ¿cuánto?; **how much is it?** of cost ¿cuánto vale o cuesta?; **how many?** ¿cuántos?; **how often?** ¿con qué frecuencia?; **how funny / sad!** ¡qué divertido / triste!

how·ev·er adv sin embargo; **however big / rich / small they are** independientemente de lo grandes / ricos / pequeños que sean

howl [haʊl] v/i of dog aullido m; of person in pain alarido m; with laughter risotada f

howl·er ['haʊlər] (mistake) error m garrafal

hub [hʌb] of wheel cubo m

'hub·cap tapacubos m inv

♦ hud·dle together ['hʌdl] v/i apiñarse, acurrucarse

hue [hjuː] tonalidad f

huff [hʌf]: **be in a huff** estar enfurruñado

hug [hʌg] v/t (pret & pp hugged) abrazar

huge [hjuːdʒ] adj enorme

hull [hʌl] casco m

hul·la·ba·loo [hʌləbəˈluː] alboroto m

hum [hʌm] 1 v/t (pret & pp hummed) song, tune tararear 2 v/i (pret & pp hummed) of person tararear; of machine zumbar

hu·man ['hjuːmən] 1 n humano m 2 adj humano; **human error** error m or fallo m humano

hu·man 'be·ing ser humano m

hu·mane [hjuːˈmeɪn] adj humano

hu·man·i·tar·i·an [hjuːmænɪˈterɪən] adj humanitario

hu·man·i·ty [hjuːˈmænətɪ] humanidad f

hu·man 'race raza f humana

hu·man re'sources npl recursos mpl humanos

hum·ble ['hʌmbl] adj humilde

hum·drum ['hʌmdrʌm] adj monótono, anodino

hu·mid ['hjuːmɪd] adj húmedo

hu·mid·i·fi·er [hjuːˈmɪdɪfaɪr] humidificador m

hu·mid·i·ty [hjuːˈmɪdətɪ] humedad f

hu·mil·i·ate [hjuːˈmɪlɪeɪt] v/t humillar

hu·mil·i·at·ing [hjuːˈmɪlɪeɪtɪŋ] adj humillante

H

hu·mil·i·a·tion [hjuːmɪlɪˈeɪʃn] humillación f

hu·mil·i·ty [hjuːˈmɪlətɪ] humildad f

hu·mor [ˈhjuːmər] humor m; **sense of humor** sentido m del humor

hu·mor·ous [ˈhjuːmərəs] adj gracioso

hu·mour Br → **humor**

hump [hʌmp] **1** n of camel, person joroba f; on road bache m **2** v/t F (carry) acarrear

hunch [hʌntʃ] n (idea) presentimiento m, corazonada f

hun·dred [ˈhʌndrəd] cien m; **a hundred dollars** cien dólares; **hundreds of birds** cientos or centenares de aves; **a hundred and one** ciento uno; **two hundred** doscientos

hun·dredth [ˈhʌndrədθ] n & adj centésimo

'hun·dred·weight 43 kilogramos

hung [hʌŋ] pret & pp → **hang**

Hun·gar·i·an [hʌŋˈgeriən] **1** adj húngaro **2** n person húngaro(-a) m(f); language húngaro m

Hun·ga·ry [ˈhʌŋgəri] Hungría

hun·ger [ˈhʌŋgər] n hambre f

hung-'o·ver adj: **be hung-over** tener resaca

hun·gry [ˈhʌŋgrɪ] adj hambriento; **I'm hungry** tengo hambre

hunk [hʌŋk] n cacho m, pedazo m; F man cachas m inv F

hun·ky-dor·y [hʌŋkɪˈdɔːrɪ] adj F: **everything's hunky-dory** todo va de perlas

hunt [hʌnt] **1** n caza f, búsqueda f **2** v/t animal cazar

◆ **hunt for** v/t buscar

hunt·er [ˈhʌntər] cazador(a) m(f)

hunt·ing [ˈhʌntɪŋ] caza f

hur·dle [ˈhɜːrdl] SP valla f; (fig: obstacle) obstáculo m

hur·dler [ˈhɜːrdlər] SP vallista m/f

hur·dles npl SP vallas fpl

hurl [hɜːrl] v/t lanzar

hur·ray [huˈreɪ] int ¡hurra!

hur·ri·cane [ˈhʌrɪkən] huracán m

hur·ried [ˈhʌrɪd] adj apresurado

hur·ry [ˈhʌrɪ] **1** n prisa f; **be in a hurry** tener prisa **2** v/i (pret & pp **hurried**) darse prisa

◆ **hurry up 1** v/i darse prisa; **hurry up!** ¡date prisa! **2** v/t meter prisa a

hurt [hɜːrt] **1** v/i (pret & pp **hurt**) doler; **does it hurt?** ¿te duele? **2** v/t (pret & pp **hurt**) physically hacer daño a; emotionally herir; **I've hurt my hand** me he hecho daño en la mano; **did he hurt you?** ¿te hizo daño?

hus·band [ˈhʌzbənd] marido m

hush [hʌʃ] n silencio m; **hush!** ¡silencio!

◆ **hush up** v/t scandal etc acallar

husk [hʌsk] of peanuts etc cáscara f

hus·ky [ˈhʌskɪ] adj voice áspero

hus·tle [ˈhʌsl] **1** n agitación f; **hustle and bustle** ajetreo m **2** v/t person empujar

hut [hʌt] cabaña f, refugio m; workman's cobertizo m

hy·a·cinth [ˈhaɪəsɪnθ] jacinto m

hy·brid [ˈhaɪbrɪd] n híbrido m

hy·drant [ˈhaɪdrənt] boca f de riego or de incendios

hy·drau·lic [haɪˈdrɔːlɪk] adj hidráulico

hy·dro·e·lec·tric [haɪdrouɪˈlektrɪk] adj hidroeléctrico

'hy·dro·foil [ˈhaɪdrəfɔɪl] boat hidroplaneador m

hy·dro·gen [ˈhaɪdrədʒən] hidrógeno m

'hy·dro·gen bomb bomba f de hidrógeno

hy·giene [ˈhaɪdʒiːn] higiene f

hy·gien·ic [haɪˈdʒiːnɪk] adj higiénico

hymn [hɪm] himno m

hype [haɪp] n bombo m

hy·per·ac·tive [haɪpərˈæktɪv] adj hiperactivo

hy·per·sen·si·tive [haɪpərˈsensɪtɪv] adj hipersensible

hy·per·ten·sion [haɪpərˈtenʃn] hipertensión f

hy·per·text [ˈhaɪpərtekst] COMPUT hipertexto m

hy·phen [ˈhaɪfn] guión m

hyp·no·sis [hɪpˈnoʊsɪs] hipnosis f

hyp·no·ther·a·py [hɪpnoʊˈθerəpɪ] hipnoterapia f

hyp·no·tize [ˈhɪpnətaɪz] v/t hipnotizar

hy·po·chon·dri·ac [haɪpəˈkɑːndriæk] n hipocondríaco(-a) m(f)

hy·poc·ri·sy [hɪˈpɑːkrəsɪ] hipocresía f

hyp·o·crite [ˈhɪpəkrɪt] hipócrita m/f

hyp·o·crit·i·cal [hɪpəˈkrɪtɪkl] adj hipócrita

hy·po·ther·mi·a [haɪpoʊˈθɜːrmɪə] hipotermia f

hy·poth·e·sis [haɪˈpɑːθəsɪs] (pl **hypotheses** [haɪˈpɑːθəsiːz]) hipótesis f inv

hy·po·thet·i·cal [haɪpəˈθetɪkl] adj hipotético

hys·ter·ec·to·my [hɪstəˈrektəmɪ] histerectomía f

hys·te·ri·a [hɪˈstɪrɪə] histeria f

hys·ter·i·cal [hɪˈsterɪkl] adj person, laugh histérico; F (very funny) tronchante F; **become hysterical** ponerse histérico

hys·ter·ics [hɪˈsterɪks] npl ataque f de histeria; (laughter) ataque f de risa

I

I [aɪ] *pron* yo; ***I am English/a student*** soy inglés / estudiante; ***you're crazy, I'm not*** tú estás loco, yo no

ice [aɪs] *in drink, on road* hielo *m*; ***break the ice*** *fig* romper el hielo

♦ **ice up** *v/i of engine, wings* helarse

ice-berg ['aɪsbɜːrg] iceberg *m*

'ice-box nevera *f, Rpl* heladera *f*

'ice-break-er *ship* rompehielos *m inv*

'ice cream helado *m*

'ice cream par-lor heladería *f*

'ice cube cubito *m* de hielo

iced [aɪst] *adj drink* helado

iced 'cof-fee café *m* helado

'ice hock-ey hockey *m* sobre hielo

'ice rink pista *f* de hielo

'ice skate patín *m* de cuchilla

'ice skat-ing patinaje *m* sobre hielo

i-ci-cle ['aɪsɪkl] carámbano *m*

i-con ['aɪkɑːn] *also* COMPUT icono *m*

icy ['aɪsɪ] *adj road* con hielo; *surface* helado; *welcome* frío

ID [aɪ'diː] *abbr* (= *identity*) documentación *f*; ***have you got any ID on you?*** ¿lleva algún tipo de documentación?

idea [aɪ'diːə] idea *f*; ***good idea!*** ¡buena idea!; ***I have no idea*** no tengo ni idea; ***it's not a good idea to …*** no es buena idea …

i-deal [aɪ'diːəl] *adj* (*perfect*) ideal

i-deal-is-tic [aɪdiːə'lɪstɪk] *adj* idealista

i-deal-ly [aɪ'diːəlɪ] *adv*: ***ideally situated*** en una posición ideal; ***ideally, we would do it like this*** lo ideal sería que lo hiciéramos así

i-den-ti-cal [aɪ'dentɪkl] *adj* idéntico; ***identical twins*** gemelos(-as) *mpl (fpl)* idénticos(-as)

i-den-ti-fi-ca-tion [aɪdentɪfɪ'keɪʃn] identificación *f*; *papers etc* documentación *f*

i-den-ti-fy [aɪ'dentɪfaɪ] *v/t (pret & pp identified)* identificar

i-den-ti-ty [aɪ'dentətɪ] identidad *f*; ***identity card*** carné *m* de identidad

i-de-o-log-i-cal [aɪdɪə'lɑːdʒɪkl] *adj* ideológico

i-de-ol-o-gy [aɪdɪ'ɑːlədʒɪ] ideología *f*

id-i-om ['ɪdɪəm] (*saying*) modismo *m*

id-i-o-mat-ic [ɪdɪə'mætɪk] *adj natural* natural

id-i-o-syn-cra-sy [ɪdɪə'sɪŋkrəsɪ] peculiaridad *f*, rareza *f*

id-i-ot ['ɪdɪət] idiota *m/f*, estúpido(-a) *m/f*

id-i-ot-ic [ɪdɪ'ɑːtɪk] *adj* idiota, estúpido

i-dle ['aɪdl] **1** *adj not working* desocupado; (*lazy*) vago; *threat* vano; *machinery* inactivo; ***in an idle moment*** en un momento libre **2** *v/i of engine* funcionar al ralentí

♦ **idle away** *v/t the time etc* pasar ociosamente

i-dol ['aɪdl] ídolo *m*

i-dol-ize ['aɪdəlaɪz] *v/t* idolatrar

i-dyl-lic [ɪ'dɪlɪk] *adj* idílico

if [ɪf] *conj* si; ***if only I hadn't shouted at her*** ojalá no le hubiera gritado

ig-nite [ɪg'naɪt] *v/t* inflamar

ig-ni-tion [ɪg'nɪʃn] *in car* encendido *m*; ***ignition key*** llave *m* de contacto

ig-no-rance ['ɪgnərəns] ignorancia *f*

ig-no-rant ['ɪgnərənt] *adj* ignorante; (*rude*) maleducado; ***be ignorant of sth*** desconocer *or* ignorar algo

ig-nore [ɪg'nɔːr] *v/t* ignorar; COMPUT omitir

ill [ɪl] *adj* enfermo; ***fall ill, be taken ill*** caer enfermo; ***feel ill at ease*** no sentirse a gusto, sentirse incómodo

il-le-gal [ɪ'liːgl] *adj* ilegal

il-le-gi-ble [ɪ'ledʒəbl] *adj* ilegible

il-le-git-i-mate [ɪlɪ'dʒɪtɪmət] *adj child* ilegítimo

ill-fat-ed [ɪl'feɪtɪd] *adj* infortunado

il-li-cit [ɪ'lɪsɪt] *adj* ilícito

il-lit-e-rate [ɪ'lɪtərət] *adj* analfabeto

ill-man-nered [ɪl'mænərd] *adj* maleducado

ill-na-tured [ɪl'neɪtʃərd] *adj* malhumorado

ill-ness ['ɪlnɪs] enfermedad *f*

il-log-i-cal [ɪ'lɑːdʒɪkl] *adj* ilógico

ill-tem-pered [ɪl'tempərd] *adj* malhumorado

ill'treat *v/t* maltratar

il-lu-mi-nate [ɪ'luːmɪneɪt] *v/t building etc* iluminar

il-lu-mi-nat-ing [ɪ'luːmɪneɪtɪŋ] *adj remarks etc* iluminador, esclarecedor

il-lu-sion [ɪ'luːʒn] ilusión *f*

il-lus-trate ['ɪləstreɪt] *v/t* ilustrar

il-lus-tra-tion [ɪlə'streɪʃn] ilustración *f*

il-lus-tra-tor [ɪlə'streɪtər] ilustrador(a) *m(f)*

ill 'will rencor *m*

im-age ['ɪmɪdʒ] imagen *f*; ***he's the image of his father*** es la viva imagen de su padre

'im-age-con-scious *adj* preocupado por la imagen

i-ma-gi-na-ble [ɪ'mædʒɪnəbl] *adj* imaginable; *the biggest / smallest size ima-ginable* la talla más grande / más pequeña que se pueda imaginar

i·ma·gi·na·ry [ɪ'mædʒɪnərɪ] *adj* imaginario

i·ma·gi·na·tion [ɪmædʒɪ'neɪʃn] imaginación *f*; *it's all in your imagination* son imaginaciones tuyas

i·ma·gi·na·tive [ɪ'mædʒɪnətɪv] *adj* imaginativo

i·ma·gine [ɪ'mædʒɪn] *v/t* imaginar, imaginarse; *I can just imagine it* me lo imagino; *you're imagining things* son imaginaciones tuyas

im·be·cile ['ɪmbəsiːl] imbécil *m/f*

IMF [aɪem'ef] *abbr* (= *International Monetary Fund*) FMI *m* (= Fondo *m* Monetario Internacional)

im·i·tate ['ɪmɪteɪt] *v/t* imitar

im·i·ta·tion [ɪmɪ'teɪʃn] imitación *f*; *learn by imitation* aprender imitando

im·mac·u·late [ɪ'mækjʊlət] *adj* inmaculado

im·ma·te·ri·al [ɪmə'tɪrɪəl] *adj* (*not relevant*) irrelevante

im·ma·ture [ɪmə'tʃʊər] *adj* inmaduro

im·me·di·ate [ɪ'miːdɪət] *adj* inmediato; *the immediate family* los familiares más cercanos; *in the immediate neighborhood* en la vecindades

im·me·di·ate·ly [ɪ'miːdɪətlɪ] *adv* inmediatamente; *immediately after the bank / church* justo después del banco / la iglesia

im·mense [ɪ'mens] *adj* inmenso

im·merse [ɪ'mɜːrs] *v/t* sumergir; *immerse o.s. in* sumergirse en

im·mer·sion heat·er [ɪ'mɜːrʃn] calentador *m* de agua eléctrico

im·mi·grant ['ɪmɪɡrənt] *n* inmigrante *m/f*

im·mi·grate ['ɪmɪɡreɪt] *v/i* inmigrar

im·mi·gra·tion [ɪmɪ'ɡreɪʃn] inmigración *f*; *Immigration government department* (Departamento *m* de) Inmigración *f*

im·mi·nent ['ɪmɪnənt] *adj* inminente

im·mo·bi·lize [ɪ'moʊbɪlaɪz] *v/t factory* paralizar; *person, car* inmovilizar

im·mo·bi·liz·er [ɪ'moʊbɪlaɪzər] *on car* inmovilizador *m*

im·mod·er·ate [ɪ'mɑːdərət] *adj* desmedido, exagerado

im·mor·al [ɪ'mɔːrəl] *adj* inmoral

im·mor·al·i·ty [ɪmɔː'rælɪtɪ] inmoralidad *f*

im·mor·tal [ɪ'mɔːrtl] *adj* inmortal

im·mor·tal·i·ty [ɪmɔːr'tælɪtɪ] inmortalidad *f*

im·mune [ɪ'mjuːn] *adj to illness, infection* inmune; *from ruling, requirement* con inmunidad

im·mune sys·tem MED sistema *m* inmunológico

im·mu·ni·ty [ɪ'mjuːnətɪ] inmunidad *f*; *diplomatic immunity* inmunidad *f* diplomática

im·pact ['ɪmpækt] *n* impacto *m*; *the warning had no impact on him* el aviso no le hizo cambiar lo más mínimo

im·pair [ɪm'per] *v/t* dañar

im·paired [ɪm'perd] *adj*: *with impaired hearing / sight* con problemas auditivos / visuales

im·par·tial [ɪm'pɑːrʃl] *adj* imparcial

im·pass·a·ble [ɪm'pæsəbl] *adj road* intransitable

im·passe ['ɪmpæs] *in negotiations etc* punto *m* muerto

im·pas·sioned [ɪm'pæʃnd] *adj speech, plea* apasionado

im·pas·sive [ɪm'pæsɪv] *adj* impasible

im·pa·tience [ɪm'peɪʃəns] impaciencia *f*

im·pa·tient [ɪm'peɪʃənt] *adj* impaciente

im·pa·tient·ly [ɪm'peɪʃəntlɪ] *adv* impacientemente

im·peach [ɪm'piːtʃ] *v/t President* iniciar un proceso de destitución contra

im·pec·ca·ble [ɪm'pekəbl] *adj* impecable

im·pec·ca·bly [ɪm'pekəblɪ] *adv* impecablemente

im·pede [ɪm'piːd] *v/t* dificultar

im·ped·i·ment [ɪm'pedɪmənt] *in speech* defecto *m* del habla

im·pend·ing [ɪm'pendɪŋ] *adj* inminente

im·pen·e·tra·ble [ɪm'penɪtrəbl] *adj* impenetrable

im·per·a·tive [ɪm'perətɪv] **1** *adj* imprescindible **2** *n* GRAM imperativo *m*

im·per·cep·ti·ble [ɪmpər'septɪbl] *adj* imperceptible

im·per·fect [ɪm'pɜːrfekt] **1** *adj* imperfecto **2** *n* GRAM imperfecto *m*

im·pe·ri·al [ɪm'pɪrɪəl] *adj* imperial

im·per·son·al [ɪm'pɜːrsənl] *adj* impersonal

im·per·so·nate [ɪm'pɜːrsəneɪt] *v/t as a joke* imitar; *illegally* hacerse pasar por

im·per·ti·nence [ɪm'pɜːrtɪnəns] impertinencia *f*

im·per·ti·nent [ɪm'pɜːrtɪnənt] *adj* impertinente

im·per·tur·ba·ble [ɪmpər'tɜːrbəbl] *adj* imperturbable

im·per·vi·ous [ɪm'pɜːrvɪəs] *adj*: *impervious to* inmune a

im·pe·tu·ous [ɪm'petʃʊəs] *adj* impetuoso

im·pe·tus ['ɪmpɪtəs] *of campaign etc* ímpetu *m*

im·ple·ment **1** *n* ['ɪmplɪmənt] utensilio *m* **2** *v/t* ['ɪmplɪment] *measures etc* poner en práctica

im·pli·cate ['ɪmplɪkeɪt] *v/t* implicar; *implicate s.o. in sth* implicar a alguien en algo

im·pli·ca·tion [ɪmplɪ'keɪʃn] consecuencia *f*; *the implication is that …* implica que …

im·plic·it [ɪm'plɪsɪt] *adj* implícito; *trust* inquebrantable

im·plore [ɪm'plɔːr] *v/t* implorar

im·ply [ɪm'plaɪ] *v/i (pret & pp implied)* implicar; *are you implying I lied?* ¿insinúas que mentí?

im·po·lite [ɪmpə'laɪt] *adj* maleducado

im·port ['ɪmpɔːrt] **1** *n* importación *f* **2** *v/t* importar

im·por·tance [ɪm'pɔːrtəns] importancia *f*

im·por·tant [ɪm'pɔːrtənt] *adj* importante

im·por·ter [ɪm'pɔːrtər] importador(a) *m(f)*

im·pose [ɪm'pouz] *v/t tax* imponer; *impose o.s. on s.o.* molestar a alguien

im·pos·ing [ɪm'pouzɪŋ] *adj* imponente

im·pos·si·bil·i·ty [ɪmpɑːsɪ'bɪlɪti] imposibilidad *f*

im·pos·sible [ɪm'pɑːsɪbəl] *adj* imposible

im·pos·tor [ɪm'pɑːstər] impostor(a) *m(f)*

im·po·tence ['ɪmpətəns] impotencia *f*

im·po·tent ['ɪmpətənt] *adj* impotente

im·pov·er·ished [ɪm'pɑːvərɪʃt] *adj* empobrecido

im·prac·ti·cal [ɪm'præktɪkəl] *adj* poco práctico

im·press [ɪm'pres] *v/t* impresionar; *be impressed by s.o./sth* quedar impresionado por alguien / algo; *I'm not impressed* no me parece nada extraordinario

im·pres·sion [ɪm'preʃn] impresión *f*; (*impersonation*) imitación *f*; *make a good / bad impression on s.o.* causar a alguien buena / mala impresión; *I get the impression that …* me da la impresión de que …

im·pres·sion·a·ble [ɪm'preʃənəbl] *adj* influenciable

im·pres·sive [ɪm'presɪv] *adj* impresionante

im·print ['ɪmprɪnt] *n of credit card* impresión *f*

im·pris·on [ɪm'prɪzn] *v/t* encarcelar

im·pris·on·ment [ɪm'prɪznmənt] encarcelamiento *m*

im·prob·a·ble [ɪm'prɑːbəbəl] *adj* improbable

im·prop·er [ɪm'prɑːpər] *adj behavior* incorrecto

im·prove [ɪm'pruːv] *v/t & v/i* mejorar

im·prove·ment [ɪm'pruːvmənt] mejora *f*, mejoría *f*

im·pro·vise ['ɪmprəvaɪz] *v/i* improvisar

im·pu·dent ['ɪmpjudənt] *adj* insolente, desvergonzado

im·pulse ['ɪmpʌls] impulso *m*; *do sth on an impulse* hacer algo impulsivamente

'impulse buy compra *f* impulsiva

im·pul·sive [ɪm'pʌlsɪv] *adj* impulsivo

im·pu·ni·ty [ɪm'pjuːnəti] impunidad *f*; *with impunity* impunemente

im·pure [ɪm'pjʊr] *adj* impuro

in [ɪn] **1** *prep* ◇ en; *in Washington / Milan* en Washington / Milán; *in the street* en la calle; *in the box* en voz baja; *put it in your pocket* méteteloen el bolsillo; *wounded in the leg / arm* herido en la pierna / el brazo

◇ *in 1999* en 1999; *in two hours from now* dentro de dos horas

◇ (*over period of*) en; *in the morning* por la mañana; *in the summer* en verano; *in August* en agosto

◇ *in English / Spanish* en inglés / español; *in a loud voice* en voz alta; *in his style* en su estilo; *in yellow* de amarillo

◇ *in crossing the road* (*while*) al cruzar la calle; *in agreeing to this* (*by virtue of*) al expresar acuerdo con esto

◇ *in his novel* en su novela; *in Faulkner* en Faulkner

◇ *three in all* tres en total; *one in ten* uno de cada diez **2** *adv*: *is he in?* at home ¿está en casa?; *is the express in yet?* ¿ha llegado ya el expreso?; *when the diskette is in* cuando el disquete está dentro; *in here* aquí dentro **3** *adj* (*fashionable, popular*) de moda; *be in* estar de moda

in·a·bil·i·ty [ɪnə'bɪlɪti] incapacidad *f*

in·ac·ces·si·ble [ɪnək'sesɪbl] *adj* inaccesible

in·ac·cu·rate [ɪn'ækjurət] *adj* inexacto

in·ac·tive [ɪn'æktɪv] *adj* inactivo

in·ad·e·quate [ɪn'ædɪkwət] *adj* insuficiente

in·ad·vis·a·ble [ɪnəd'vaɪzəbl] *adj* poco aconsejable

in·an·i·mate [ɪn'ænɪmət] *adj* inanimado

in·ap·pro·pri·ate [ɪnə'prouprɪət] *adj* *remark, thing to do* inadecuado, improcedente; *choice* inapropiado

in·ar·tic·u·late [ɪnɑːr'tɪkjulət] *adj*: *be inarticulate* expresarse mal

in·au·di·ble [ɪn'ɔːdəbl] *adj* inaudible

in·au·gu·ral [ɪ'nɔːgjʊrəl] *adj speech* inaugural

in·au·gu·rate [ɪ'nɔːgjʊreɪt] *v/t* inaugurar

in·born ['ɪnbɔːrn] *adj* innato

in·breed·ing ['ɪnbriːdɪŋ] endogamia *f*

inc. *abbr* (= *incorporated*) S.A. (= sociedad *f* anónima)

in·cal·cu·la·ble [ɪnˈkælkjʊləbl] *adj damage* incalculable

in·ca·pa·ble [ɪnˈkeɪpəbl] *adj* incapaz; *be incapable of doing sth* ser incapaz de hacer algo

in·cen·di·a·ry de'vice [ɪnˈsendɪrɪ] artefacto *m* incendiario

in·cense¹ [ˈɪnsens] *n* incienso *m*

in·cense² [ɪnˈsens] *v/t* encolerizar

in·cen·tive [ɪnˈsentɪv] incentivo *m*

in·ces·sant [ɪnˈsesnt] *adj* incesante

in·ces·sant·ly [ɪnˈsesntlɪ] *adv* incesantemente

in·cest [ˈɪnsest] incesto *m*

inch [ɪntʃ] *n* pulgada *f*

in·ci·dent [ˈɪnsɪdənt] incidente *m*

in·ci·den·tal [ɪnsɪˈdentl] *adj* sin importancia; *incidental expenses* gastos *mpl* varios

in·ci·den·tal·ly [ɪnsɪˈdentlɪ] *adv* a propósito

in·cin·e·ra·tor [ɪnˈsɪnəreɪtər] incinerador *m*

in·ci·sion [ɪnˈsɪʒn] incisión *f*

in·ci·sive [ɪnˈsaɪsɪv] *adj* incisivo

in·cite [ɪnˈsaɪt] *v/t* incitar; *incite s.o. to do sth* incitar a alguien a que haga algo

in·clem·ent [ɪnˈklemənt] *adj* inclemente

in·cli·na·tion [ɪnklɪˈneɪʃn] (*tendency, liking*) inclinación *f*

in·cline [ɪnˈklaɪn] *v/t: be inclined to do sth* tender a hacer algo

in·close, in·clos·ure → **enclose, enclosure**

in·clude [ɪnˈkluːd] *v/t* incluir

in·clud·ing [ɪnˈkluːdɪŋ] *prep* incluyendo

in·clu·sive [ɪnˈkluːsɪv] **1** *adj price* total, global **2** *prep: inclusive of* incluyendo, incluido **3** *adv: from Monday to Thursday inclusive* de lunes al jueves, ambos inclusive; *it costs $ 1000 inclusive* cuesta 1000 dólares todo incluido

in·co·her·ent [ɪnˈkouˈhɪrənt] *adj* incoherente

in·come [ˈɪnkəm] ingresos *mpl*

'in·come tax impuesto *m* sobre la renta

in·com·ing [ˈɪnkʌmɪŋ] *adj tide* que sube; *incoming flight* vuelo *f* que llega; *incoming mail* correo *m* recibido; *incoming calls* llamadas *fpl* recibidas

in·com·pa·ra·ble [ɪnˈkɑːmpərəbl] *adj* incomparable

in·com·pat·i·bil·i·ty [ɪnkəmpætɪˈbɪlɪtɪ] incompatibilidad *f*

in·com·pat·i·ble [ɪnkəmˈpætɪbl] *adj* incompatible

in·com·pe·tence [ɪnˈkɑːmpɪtəns] incompetencia *f*

in·com·pe·tent [ɪnˈkɑːmpɪtənt] *adj* incompetente

in·com·plete [ɪnkəmˈpliːt] *adj* incompleto

in·com·pre·hen·si·ble [ɪnkɑːmprɪˈhensɪbl] *adj* incomprensible

in·con·cei·va·ble [ɪnkənˈsiːvəbl] *adj* inconcebible

in·con·clu·sive [ɪnkənˈkluːsɪv] *adj* no concluyente

in·con·gru·ous [ɪnˈkɑːŋgrʊəs] *adj* incongruente

in·con·sid·er·ate [ɪnkənˈsɪdərət] *adj* desconsiderado

in·con·sis·tent [ɪnkənˈsɪstənt] *adj argument, behavior* incoherente, inconsecuente; *player* irregular; *be inconsistent with sth* no ser consecuente con algo

in·con·so·la·ble [ɪnkənˈsoʊləbl] *adj* inconsolable, desconsolado

in·con·spic·u·ous [ɪnkənˈspɪkjʊəs] *adj* discreto

in·con·ve·ni·ence [ɪnkənˈviːnɪəns] *n* inconveniencia *f*

in·con·ve·ni·ent [ɪnkənˈviːnɪənt] *adj* inconveniente, inoportuno

in·cor·po·rate [ɪnˈkɔːrpəreɪt] *v/t* incorporar

in·cor·po·rat·ed [ɪnˈkɔːrpəreɪtɪd] *adj* COM: *ABC Incorporated* ABC, sociedad *f* anónima

in·cor·rect [ɪnkəˈrekt] *adj* incorrecto

in·cor·rect·ly [ɪnkəˈrektlɪ] *adv* incorrectamente

in·cor·ri·gi·ble [ɪnˈkɑːrɪdʒəbl] *adj* incorregible

in·crease 1 *v/t & v/i* [ɪnˈkriːs] aumentar **2** *n* [ˈɪnkriːs] aumento *m*

in·creas·ing [ɪnˈkriːsɪŋ] *adj* creciente

in·creas·ing·ly [ɪnˈkriːsɪŋlɪ] *adv* cada vez más; *we're getting increasingly concerned* cada vez estamos más preocupados

in·cred·i·ble [ɪnˈkredɪbl] *adj* (*amazing, very good*) increíble

in·crim·i·nate [ɪnˈkrɪmɪneɪt] *v/t* incriminar; *incriminate o.s.* incriminarse

in·cu·ba·tor [ˈɪŋkjʊbeɪtər] incubadora *f*

in·cur [ɪnˈkɜːr] *v/t* (*pret & pp incurred*) *costs* incurrir en; *debts* contraer; *s.o.'s anger* provocar

in·cu·ra·ble [ɪnˈkjʊrəbl] *adj* incurable

in·debt·ed [ɪnˈdetɪd] *adj: be indebted to s.o.* estar en deuda con alguien

in·de·cent [ɪnˈdiːsnt] *adj* indecente

in·de·ci·sive [ɪndɪˈsaɪsɪv] *adj* indeciso

in·de·ci·sive·ness [ɪndɪˈsaɪsɪvnɪs] indecisión *f*

in·deed [ɪnˈdiːd] *adv* (*in fact*) ciertamente,

efectivamente; *yes, agreeing* ciertamente, en efecto; *very much indeed*
muchísimo; *thank you very much indeed* muchísimas gracias

in·de·fi·na·ble [ɪndɪˈfaɪnəbl] *adj* indefini-
ble

in·def·i·nite [ɪnˈdefɪnɪt] *adj* indefinido;
indefinite article GRAM artículo *m* indefinido

in·def·i·nite·ly [ɪnˈdefɪnɪtlɪ] *adv* indefinidamente

in·del·i·cate [ɪnˈdelɪkət] *adj* poco delicado

in·dent 1 *n* [ˈɪndent] *in text* sangrado *m* **2**
v/t [ɪnˈdent] *line* sangrar

in·de·pen·dence [ɪndɪˈpendəns] independencia *f*

In·de·pen·dence Day Día *m* de la Independencia

in·de·pen·dent [ɪndɪˈpendənt] *adj* independiente

in·de·pen·dent·ly [ɪndɪˈpendəntlɪ] *adv*
deal with por separado; *independently
of* al margen de

in·de·scrib·a·ble [ɪndɪˈskraɪbəbl] *adj* indescriptible

in·de·scrib·a·bly [ɪndɪˈskraɪbəblɪ] *adv* in-
descriptiblemente

in·de·struc·ti·ble [ɪndɪˈstrʌktəbl] *adj* indestructible

in·de·ter·mi·nate [ɪndɪˈtɜːrmɪnət] *adj* indeterminado

in·dex [ˈɪndeks] *n for book* índice *m*

'in·dex card ficha *f*

'in·dex fin·ger (dedo *m*) índice *m*

in·dex-'linked *adj* indexado

In·di·a [ˈɪndɪə] (la) India

In·di·an [ˈɪndɪən] **1** *adj* indio **2** *n from India* indio(-a) *m(f)*, hindú *m/f; American*
indio(-a) *m(f)*

In·di·an 'sum·mer *in northern hemisphere* veranillo *m* de San Martín; *in southern
hemisphere* veranillo *m* de San Juan

in·di·cate [ˈɪndɪkeɪt] **1** *v/t* indicar **2** *v/i*
when driving poner el intermitente

in·di·ca·tion [ɪndɪˈkeɪʃn] indicio *m*

in·di·ca·tor [ˈɪndɪkeɪtər] *on car* intermitente *m*

in·dict [ɪnˈdaɪt] *v/t* acusar

in·dif·fer·ence [ɪnˈdɪfrəns] indiferencia *f*

in·dif·fer·ent [ɪnˈdɪfrənt] *adj* indiferente;
(mediocre) mediocre; *are you totally indifferent to the way I feel?* ¿no te importa lo más mínimo lo que sienta yo?

in·di·ges·ti·ble [ɪndɪˈdʒestɪbl] *adj* indigesto

in·di·ges·tion [ɪndɪˈdʒestʃn] indigestión *f*

in·dig·nant [ɪnˈdɪgnənt] *adj* indignado

in·dig·na·tion [ɪndɪgˈneɪʃn] indignación *f*

in·di·rect [ɪndɪˈrekt] *adj* indirecto

in·di·rect·ly [ɪndɪˈrektlɪ] *adv* indirecta-
mente

in·dis·creet [ɪndɪˈskriːt] *adj* indiscreto

in·dis·cre·tion [ɪndɪˈskreʃn] indiscreción
f

in·dis·crim·i·nate [ɪndɪˈskrɪmɪnət] *adj* indiscriminado

in·dis·pen·sa·ble [ɪndɪˈspensəbl] *adj* indispensable, imprescindible

in·dis·posed [ɪndɪˈspoʊzd] *adj (not well)*
indispuesto; *be indisposed* hallarse indispuesto

in·dis·pu·ta·ble [ɪndɪˈspjuːtəbl] *adj* indiscutible

in·dis·pu·ta·bly [ɪndɪˈspjuːtəblɪ] *adv* indiscutiblemente

in·dis·tinct [ɪndɪˈstɪŋkt] *adj* indistinto,
impreciso

in·dis·tin·guish·a·ble [ɪndɪˈstɪŋgwɪʃəbl]
adj indistinguible

in·di·vid·u·al [ɪndɪˈvɪdʒʊəl] **1** *n* individuo
m **2** *adj* individual

in·di·vid·u·a·list [ɪndɪˈvɪdʒʊəlɪst] *adj* individualista

in·di·vid·u·al·ly [ɪndɪˈvɪdʒʊəlɪ] *adv* indi-
vidualmente

in·di·vis·i·ble [ɪndɪˈvɪzɪbl] *adj* indivisible

in·doc·tri·nate [ɪnˈdɔːktrɪneɪt] *v/t* adoctrinar

in·do·lence [ˈɪndələns] indolencia *f*

in·do·lent [ˈɪndələnt] *adj* indolente

In·do·ne·sia [ɪndəˈniːʒə] Indonesia

In·do·ne·sian [ɪndəˈniːʒən] **1** *adj* indone-
sio **2** *n person* indonesio(-a) *m(f)*

in·door [ˈɪndɔːr] *adj activities* de interior;
sport de pista cubierta; *arena* cubierto;
athletics en pista cubierta

in·doors [ɪnˈdɔːrz] *adv* dentro

in·dorse → *endorse*

in·dulge [ɪnˈdʌldʒ] **1** *v/t o.s., one's tastes*
satisfacer **2** *v/i: indulge in a pleasure* entregarse a un placer; *if I might indulge in
a little joke* si se me permite contar un
chiste

in·dul·gent [ɪnˈdʌldʒənt] *adj* indulgente

in·dus·tri·al [ɪnˈdʌstrɪəl] *adj* industrial;
industrial action acciones *fpl* reivindi-
cativas

in·dus·tri·al dis·pute conflicto *m* laboral

in·dus·tri·al·ist [ɪnˈdʌstrɪəlɪst] industrial
m/f

in·dus·tri·al·ize [ɪnˈdʌstrɪəlaɪz] **1** *v/t* industrializar **2** *v/i* industrializarse

in·dus·tri·al 'waste residuos *mpl* industri-
ales

in·dus·tri·ous [ɪnˈdʌstrɪəs] *adj* trabajador, aplicado

in·dus·try [ˈɪndəstrɪ] industria *f*

in·ef·fec·tive [ɪnɪˈfektɪv] *adj* ineficaz
in·ef·fec·tu·al [ɪnɪˈfektʃʊəl] *adj person* inepto, incapaz
in·ef·fi·cient [ɪnɪˈfɪʃənt] *adj* ineficiente
in·el·i·gi·ble [ɪnˈelɪdʒɪbl] *adj:* **be ineligible** no reunir las condiciones
in·ept [ɪˈnept] *adj* inepto
in·e·qual·i·ty [ɪnɪˈkwɑːlɪti] desigualdad *f*
in·es·ca·pa·ble [ɪnɪˈskeɪpəbl] *adj* inevitable
in·es·ti·ma·ble [ɪnˈestɪməbl] *adj* inestimable
in·ev·i·ta·ble [ɪnˈevɪtəbl] *adj* inevitable
in·ev·i·ta·bly [ɪnˈevɪtəbli] *adv* inevitablemente
in·ex·cu·sa·ble [ɪnɪkˈskjuːzəbl] *adj* inexcusable, injustificable
in·ex·haus·ti·ble [ɪnɪgˈzɔːstəbl] *adj supply* inagotable
in·ex·pen·sive [ɪnɪkˈspensɪv] *adj* barato, económico
in·ex·pe·ri·enced [ɪnɪkˈspɪriənst] *adj* inexperto
in·ex·plic·a·ble [ɪnɪkˈsplɪkəbl] *adj* inexplicable
in·ex·pres·si·ble [ɪnɪkˈspresɪbl] *adj joy* indescriptible
in·fal·li·ble [ɪnˈfælɪbl] *adj* infalible
in·fa·mous [ˈɪnfəməs] *adj* infame
in·fan·cy [ˈɪnfənsi] infancia *f*
in·fant [ˈɪnfənt] bebé *m*
in·fan·tile [ˈɪnfəntaɪl] *adj pej* infantil, pueril
in·fan·try [ˈɪnfəntri] infantería *f*
in·fan·try 'sol·dier soldado *m/f* de infantería, infante *m/f*
'in·fant school colegio *m* de párvulos
in·fat·u·at·ed [ɪnˈfætʃʊeɪtɪd] *adj:* **be infatuated with s.o.** estar encaprichado de alguien
in·fect [ɪnˈfekt] *v/t* infectar; **he infected everyone with his cold** contagió el resfriado a todo el mundo; **become infected** *of wound* infectarse; *of person* contagiarse
in·fec·tion [ɪnˈfekʃn] infección *f*
in·fec·tious [ɪnˈfekʃəs] *adj disease* infeccioso; *laughter* contagioso
in·fer [ɪnˈfɜːr] *v/t* (*pret & pp* **inferred**) inferir, deducir (**from**)
in·fe·ri·or [ɪnˈfɪriər] *adj* inferior (**to** a)
in·fe·ri·or·i·ty [ɪnfɪriˈɑːrəti] *in quality* inferioridad *f*
in·fe·ri·or·i·ty com·plex complejo *m* de inferioridad
in·fer·tile [ɪnˈfɜːrtl] *adj woman, plant* estéril; *soil* estéril, yermo
in·fer·til·i·ty [ɪnfərˈtɪlɪti] esterilidad *f*
in·fi·del·i·ty [ɪnfɪˈdelɪti] infidelidad *f*

in·fil·trate [ˈɪnfɪltreɪt] *v/t* infiltrarse en
in·fi·nite [ˈɪnfɪnət] *adj* infinito
in·fin·i·tive [ɪnˈfɪnətɪv] infinitivo *m*
in·fin·i·ty [ɪnˈfɪnəti] infinidad *f*
in·firm [ɪnˈfɜːrm] *adj* enfermo, achacoso
in·fir·ma·ry [ɪnˈfɜːrməri] enfermería *f*
in·fir·mi·ty [ɪnˈfɜːrməti] debilidad *f*
in·flame [ɪnˈfleɪm] *v/t* despertar
in·flam·ma·ble [ɪnˈflæməbl] *adj* inflamable
in·flam·ma·tion [ɪnfləˈmeɪʃn] MED inflamación *f*
in·flat·a·ble [ɪnˈfleɪtəbl] *adj dinghy* hinchable, inflable
in·flate [ɪnˈfleɪt] *v/t tire, dinghy* hinchar, inflar; *economy* inflar
in·fla·tion [ɪnˈfleɪʃən] inflación *f*
in·fla·tion·a·ry [ɪnˈfleɪʃənəri] *adj* inflacionario, inflacionista
in·flec·tion [ɪnˈflekʃn] inflexión *f*
in·flex·i·ble [ɪnˈfleksɪbl] *adj* inflexible
in·flict [ɪnˈflɪkt] *v/t* infligir; **inflict sth on s.o.** infligir algo a alguien
'in-flight *adj:* **in-flight entertainment** entretenimiento *m* durante el vuelo
in·flu·ence [ˈɪnfluəns] **1** *n* influencia *f*; **be a good / bad influence on s.o.** tener una buena / mala influencia en alguien **2** *v/t* influir en, influenciar
in·flu·en·tial [ɪnfluˈenʃl] *adj* influyente
in·flu·en·za [ɪnfluˈenzə] gripe *f*
in·form [ɪnˈfɔːrm] **1** *v/t* informar; **inform s.o. about sth** informar a alguien de algo; **please keep me informed** por favor manténme informado **2** *v/i:* **inform on s.o.** delatar a alguien
in·for·mal [ɪnˈfɔːrml] *adj* informal
in·for·mal·i·ty [ɪnfɔːrˈmælɪti] informalidad *f*
in·form·ant [ɪnˈfɔːrmənt] confidente *m/f*
in·for·ma·tion [ɪnfərˈmeɪʃn] información *f*; **a piece of information** una información
in·for·ma·tion 'sci·ence informática *f*
in·for·ma·tion 'sci·en·tist informático(-a) *m(f)*
in·for·ma·tion tech'nol·o·gy tecnologías *fpl* de la información
in·for·ma·tive [ɪnˈfɔːrmətɪv] *adj* informativo; **you're not being very informative** no estás dando mucha información
in·form·er [ɪnˈfɔːrmər] confidente *m/f*
in·fra·red [ɪnfrəˈred] *adj* infrarrojo
in·fra·struc·ture [ˈɪnfrəstrʌktʃər] infraestructura *f*
in·fre·quent [ɪnˈfriːkwənt] *adj* poco frecuente
in·fu·ri·ate [ɪnˈfjʊrieɪt] *v/t* enfurecer, exasperar

in·fu·ri·at·ing [ɪnˈfjʊrɪeɪtɪŋ] adj exasperante

in·fuse [ɪnˈfjuːz] v/i of tea infundir

in·fu·sion [ɪnˈfjuːʒn] (herb tea) infusión f

in·ge·ni·ous [ɪnˈdʒiːnɪəs] adj ingenioso

in·ge·nu·i·ty [ɪndʒɪˈnuːətɪ] lo ingenioso

in·got [ˈɪŋɡət] lingote m

in·gra·ti·ate [ɪnˈɡreɪʃɪeɪt] v/t: **ingratiate o.s. with s.o.** congraciarse con alguien

in·grat·i·tude [ɪnˈɡrætɪtuːd] ingratitud f

in·gre·di·ent [ɪnˈɡriːdɪənt] also fig ingrediente m

in·hab·it [ɪnˈhæbɪt] v/t habitar

in·hab·it·a·ble [ɪnˈhæbɪtəbl] adj habitable

in·hab·i·tant [ɪnˈhæbɪtənt] habitante m/f

in·hale [ɪnˈheɪl] **1** v/t inhalar **2** v/i when smoking tragarse el humo

in·ha·ler [ɪnˈheɪlər] inhalador m

in·her·it [ɪnˈherɪt] v/t heredar

in·her·i·tance [ɪnˈherɪtəns] herencia f

in·hib·it [ɪnˈhɪbɪt] v/t growth impedir; conversation inhibir, cohibir

in·hib·it·ed [ɪnˈhɪbɪtɪd] adj inhibido, cohibido

in·hi·bi·tion [ɪnhɪˈbɪʃn] inhibición f

in·hos·pi·ta·ble [ɪnhɑːˈspɪtəbl] adj person inhospitalario; city, climate inhóspito

'in·house **1** adj facilities en el lugar de trabajo; **in-house team** equipo m en plantilla **2** adv work en la empresa

in·hu·man [ɪnˈhjuːmən] adj inhumano

i·ni·tial [ɪˈnɪʃl] **1** adj inicial **2** n inicial f **3** v/t (write initials on) poner las iniciales en

i·ni·tial·ly [ɪˈnɪʃlɪ] adv inicialmente, al principio

i·ni·ti·ate [ɪˈnɪʃɪeɪt] v/t iniciar

i·ni·ti·a·tion [ɪnɪʃɪˈeɪʃn] iniciación f, inicio m

i·ni·tia·tive [ɪˈnɪʃətɪv] iniciativa f; **do sth on one's own initiative** hacer algo por iniciativa propia

in·ject [ɪnˈdʒekt] v/t drug, fuel, capital inyectar

in·jec·tion [ɪnˈdʒekʃn] of drug, fuel, capital inyección f

'in·joke: **it's an in-joke** es un chiste que entendemos nosotros

in·jure [ˈɪndʒər] v/t lesionar; **he injured his leg** se lesionó la pierna

in·jured [ˈɪndʒərd] **1** adj leg lesionado; feelings herido **2** npl: **the injured** los heridos

in·ju·ry [ˈɪndʒərɪ] lesión f; wound herida f

'in·ju·ry time SP tiempo m de descuento

in·jus·tice [ɪnˈdʒʌstɪs] injusticia f

ink [ɪŋk] tinta f

'ink-jet ('prin·ter) impresora f de chorro de tinta

in·land [ˈɪnlənd] adj interior; mail nacional

in·laws [ˈɪnlɔːz] npl familia f política

in·lay [ˈɪnleɪ] n incrustación f

in·let [ˈɪnlet] of sea ensenada f; in machine entrada f

in·mate [ˈɪnmeɪt] of prison recluso(-a) m(f); of mental hospital paciente m/f

inn [ɪn] posada f, mesón m

in·nate [ɪˈneɪt] adj innato

in·ner [ˈɪnər] adj interior; **the inner ear** el oído interno

in·ner 'cit·y burrios degradados del centro de la ciudad; **inner city decay** degradación m del centro de la ciudad

in·ner·most adj feelings más íntimo; recess más recóndito

in·no·cence [ˈɪnəsəns] inocencia f

in·no·cent [ˈɪnəsənt] adj inocente

in·noc·u·ous [ɪˈnɑːkjuəs] adj innocuo

in·no·va·tion [ɪnəˈveɪʃn] innovación f

in·no·va·tive [ɪnəˈveɪtɪv] adj innovador

in·no·va·tor [ˈɪnəveɪtər] innovador(a) m(f)

in·nu·me·ra·ble [ɪˈnuːmərəbl] adj innumerable

i·noc·u·late [ɪˈnɑːkjuleɪt] v/t inocular

i·noc·u·la·tion [ɪˈnɑːkjuˈleɪʃn] inoculación f

in·of·fen·sive [ɪnəˈfensɪv] adj inofensivo

in·or·gan·ic [ɪnɔːrˈɡænɪk] adj inorgánico

'in-pa·tient paciente m/f interno(-a)

in·put [ˈɪnput] **1** n into project etc contribución f, aportación f; COMPUT entrada f **2** v/t (pret & pp **inputted** or **input**) into project contribuir, aportar; COMPUT introducir

in·quest [ˈɪnkwest] investigación f (**into** sobre)

in·quire [ɪnˈkwaɪr] v/i preguntar; **inquire into sth** investigar algo

in·quir·y [ɪnˈkwaɪrɪ] consulta f, pregunta f; into rail crash etc investigación f

in·quis·i·tive [ɪnˈkwɪzətɪv] adj curioso, inquisitivo

in·sane [ɪnˈseɪn] adj person loco, demente; idea descabellada

in·san·i·ta·ry [ɪnˈsænɪterɪ] adj antihigiénico

in·san·i·ty [ɪnˈsænɪtɪ] locura f, demencia f

in·sa·tia·ble [ɪnˈseɪʃəbl] adj insaciable

in·scrip·tion [ɪnˈskrɪpʃn] inscripción f

in·scru·ta·ble [ɪnˈskruːtəbl] adj inescrutable

in·sect [ˈɪnsekt] insecto m

in·sec·ti·cide [ɪnˈsektɪsaɪd] insecticida f

'in·sect re·pel·lent repelente m contra insectos

in·se·cure [ɪnsɪˈkjʊr] *adj* inseguro
in·se·cu·ri·ty [ɪnsɪˈkjʊrɪtɪ] inseguridad *f*
in·sen·si·tive [ɪnˈsensɪtɪv] *adj* insensible
in·sen·si·tiv·i·ty [ɪnsensɪˈtɪvɪtɪ] insensibilidad *f*
in·sep·a·ra·ble [ɪnˈseprəbl] *adj* inseparable
in·sert 1 *n* [ˈɪnsɜːrt] *in magazine etc* encarte *m* 2 *v/t* [ɪnˈsɜːrt] *coin, finger, diskette* introducir, meter; *extra text* insertar; *insert sth into sth* introducir *or* meter algo en algo
in·ser·tion [ɪnˈsɜːrʃn] *act* introducción *f*, inserción *f*; *of text* inserción *f*
in·side [ɪnˈsaɪd] **1** *n of house, box* interior *m*; *somebody on the inside* alguien de dentro; *inside out* del revés; *turn sth inside out* dar la vuelta a algo (*de dentro a fuera*); *know sth inside out* saberse algo al dedillo **2** *prep* dentro de; *inside the house* dentro de la casa; *inside of 2 hours* dentro de 2 horas **3** *adv stay, remain* dentro; *go, carry* adentro; *we went inside* entramos **4** *adj: inside information* información *f* confidencial; *inside lane* SP calle *f* de dentro; *on road* carril *m* de la derecha; *inside pocket* bolsillo *m* interior
in·sid·er [ɪnˈsaɪdər] persona con acceso a información confidencial
in·sid·er ˈdeal·ing FIN uso *m* de información privilegiada
in·sides [ɪnˈsaɪdz] *npl* tripas *mpl*
in·sid·i·ous [ɪnˈsɪdɪəs] *adj* insidioso
in·sight [ˈɪnsaɪt]: *this film offers an insight into local customs* esta película permite hacerse una idea de las costumbres locales; *full of insight* muy perspicaz
in·sig·nif·i·cant [ɪnsɪɡˈnɪfɪkənt] *adj* insignificante
in·sin·cere [ɪnsɪnˈsɪr] *adj* poco sincero, falso
in·sin·cer·i·ty [ɪnsɪnˈserɪtɪ] falta *f* de sinceridad
in·sin·u·ate [ɪnˈsɪnʊeɪt] *v/t* (*imply*) insinuar
in·sist [ɪnˈsɪst] *v/i* insistir; *please keep it, I insist* por favor, insisto en que te lo quedes
♦ **insist on** *v/t* insistir en
in·sis·tent [ɪnˈsɪstənt] *adj* insistente
in·so·lent [ˈɪnsələnt] *adj* insolente
in·sol·u·ble [ɪnˈsɑːljʊbl] *adj problem* irresoluble; *substance* insoluble
in·sol·vent [ɪnˈsɑːlvənt] *adj* insolvente
in·som·ni·a [ɪnˈsɑːmnɪə] insomnio *m*
in·spect [ɪnˈspekt] *v/t* inspeccionar
in·spec·tion [ɪnˈspekʃn] inspección *f*

in·spec·tor [ɪnˈspektər] *in factory, of police* inspector(a) *m(f)*; *on buses* revisor(a) *m(f)*
in·spi·ra·tion [ɪnspəˈreɪʃn] inspiración *f*
in·spire [ɪnˈspaɪr] *v/t respect etc* inspirar; *be inspired by s.o./sth* estar inspirado por alguien / algo
in·sta·bil·i·ty [ɪnstəˈbɪlɪtɪ] *of character, economy* inestabilidad *f*
in·stall [ɪnˈstɔːl] *v/t* instalar
in·stal·la·tion [ɪnstəˈleɪʃn] instalación *f*; *military installation* instalación *f* militar
in·stall·ment *Br*, **in·stall·ment** [ɪnˈstɔːlmənt] *of story, TV drama etc* episodio *m*; *payment* plazo *m*
in·stall·ment plan compra *f* a plazos
in·stance [ˈɪnstəns] (*example*) ejemplo *m*; *for instance* por ejemplo
in·stant [ˈɪnstənt] **1** *adj* instantáneo **2** *n* instante *m*; *in an instant* en un instante
in·stan·ta·ne·ous [ɪnstənˈteɪnɪəs] *adj* instantáneo
in·stant ˈcof·fee café *m* instantáneo
in·stant·ly [ˈɪnstəntlɪ] *adv* al instante
in·stead [ɪnˈsted] *adv*: *I'll take that one instead* me llevaré mejor ese otro; *would you like coffee instead?* ¿preferiría mejor café?; *I'll have coffee instead of tea* tomaré té en vez de café; *he went instead of me* fue en mi lugar
in·step [ˈɪnstep] empeine *m*
in·stinct [ˈɪnstɪŋkt] instinto *m*
in·stinc·tive [ɪnˈstɪŋktɪv] *adj* instintivo
in·sti·tute [ˈɪnstɪtuːt] **1** *n* instituto *m*; *for elderly* residencia *f* de ancianos; *for mentally ill* psiquiátrico *m* **2** *v/t new law* establecer; *inquiry* iniciar
in·sti·tu·tion [ɪnstɪˈtuːʃn] institución *f*; (*setting up*) iniciación *f*
in·struct [ɪnˈstrʌkt] *v/t* (*order*) dar instrucciones a; (*teach*) instruir; *instruct s.o. to do sth* (*order*) ordenar a alguien que haga algo
in·struc·tion [ɪnˈstrʌkʃn] instrucción *f*; *instructions for use* instrucciones *fpl* de uso
in·struc·tion man·u·al manual *m* de instrucciones
in·struc·tive [ɪnˈstrʌktɪv] *adj* instructivo
in·struc·tor [ɪnˈstrʌktər] instructor(a) *m(f)*
in·stru·ment [ˈɪnstrəmənt] MUS, *tool* instrumento *m*
in·sub·or·di·nate [ɪnsəˈbɔːrdɪnət] *adj* insubordinado
in·suf·fi·cient [ɪnsəˈfɪʃnt] *adj* insuficiente
in·su·late [ˈɪnsəleɪt] *v/t also* ELEC aislar
in·su·la·tion [ɪnsəˈleɪʃn] ELEC aislamiento *m*; *against cold* aislamiento *m* (térmico)

in·su·lin ['ɪnsəlɪn] insulina f

in·sult 1 n ['ɪnsʌlt] insulto m **2** v/t [ɪn'sʌlt] insultar

in·sur·ance [ɪn'ʃʊrəns] seguro m

in·sur·ance com·pa·ny compañía f de seguros, aseguradora f

in·sur·ance pol·i·cy póliza f de seguros

in·sur·ance pre·mi·um prima f (del seguro)

in·sure [ɪn'ʃʊr] v/t asegurar

in·sured [ɪn'ʃʊrd] **1** adj asegurado; **be insured** estar asegurado **2** n: **the insured** el asegurado, la asegurada

in·sur·moun·ta·ble [ɪnsər'maʊntəbl] adj insuperable

in·tact [ɪn'tækt] adj (not damaged) intacto

in·take ['ɪnteɪk] of college etc remesa f; **we have an annual intake of 300 students** cada año admitimos a 300 alumnos

in·te·grate ['ɪntɪgreɪt] v/t integrar (**into** en)

in·te·grat·ed 'cir·cuit ['ɪntɪgreɪtɪd] circuito m integrado

in·teg·ri·ty [ɪn'tegrɪtɪ] (honesty) integridad f, **a man of integrity** un hombre íntegro

in·tel·lect ['ɪntəlekt] intelecto m

in·tel·lec·tual [ɪntə'lektʃʊəl] **1** adj intelectual **2** n intelectual m/f

in·tel·li·gence [ɪn'telɪdʒəns] inteligencia f; (information) información f secreta

in·tel·li·gence of·fi·cer agente m/f del servicio de inteligencia

in·tel·li·gence ser·vice servicio m de inteligencia

in·tel·li·gent [ɪn'telɪdʒənt] adj inteligente

in·tel·li·gi·ble [ɪn'telɪdʒəbl] adj inteligible

in·tend [ɪn'tend] v/i: **intend to do sth** tener la intención de hacer algo; **that's not what I intended** esa no era mi intención

in·tense [ɪn'tens] adj sensation, pleasure, heat, pressure intenso; personality serio

in·ten·si·fy [ɪn'tensɪfaɪ] **1** v/t (pret & pp **intensified**) effect, pressure intensificar **2** v/i (pret & pp **intensified**) intensificarse

in·ten·si·ty [ɪn'tensətɪ] intensidad f

in·ten·sive [ɪn'tensɪv] adj study, training, treatment intensivo

in·ten·sive 'care (u·nit) MED (unidad f de) cuidados mpl intensivos

in·ten·sive 'course of language study curso m intensivo

in·tent [ɪn'tent] adj: **be intent on doing sth** (determined to do) estar decidido a hacer algo; (concentrating on) estar concentrado haciendo algo

in·ten·tion [ɪn'tenʃn] intención f; **I have no intention of ...** (refuse to) no tengo intención de ...

in·ten·tion·al [ɪn'tenʃənl] adj intencionado

in·ten·tion·al·ly [ɪn'tenʃnlɪ] adv a propósito, adrede

in·ter·ac·tion [ɪntər'ækʃn] interacción f

in·ter·ac·tive [ɪntər'æktɪv] adj interactivo

in·ter·cede [ɪntər'siːd] v/i interceder

in·ter·cept [ɪntər'sept] v/t interceptar

in·ter·change ['ɪntərtʃeɪndʒ] n of highways nudo m vial

in·ter·change·a·ble [ɪntər'tʃeɪndʒəbl] adj intercambiable

in·ter·com ['ɪntərkɑːm] in office, ship interfono m; for front door portero m automático

in·ter·course ['ɪntərkɔːrs] sexual coito m

in·ter·de·pend·ent [ɪntərdɪ'pendənt] adj interdependiente

in·ter·est ['ɪntrəst] **1** n also FIN interés m; **take an interest in sth** interesarse por algo **2** v/t interesar; **does that offer interest you?** ¿te interesa esa oferta?

in·ter·est·ed ['ɪntrəstɪd] adj interesado; **be interested in sth** estar interesado en algo; **thanks, but I'm not interested** gracias, pero no me interesa

in·terest-free 'loan préstamo m sin intereses

in·ter·est·ing ['ɪntrəstɪŋ] adj interesante

'in·terest rate tipo m de interés

in·ter·face ['ɪntərfeɪs] **1** n interface m, interfaz f **2** v/i relacionarse

in·ter·fere [ɪntər'fɪr] v/i interferir, entrometerse

♦ **interfere with** v/t afectar a; **the lock had been interfered with** alguien había manipulado la cerradura

in·ter·fer·ence [ɪntər'fɪrəns] intromisión f; on radio interferencia f

in·te·ri·or [ɪn'tɪrɪər] **1** adj interior **2** n interior m; **Department of the Interior** Ministerio m del Interior

in·te·ri·or 'dec·o·ra·tor interiorista m/f, decorador(a) m(f) de interiores

in·te·ri·or de'sign interiorismo m

in·te·ri·or de'sign·er interiorista m/f

in·ter·lude ['ɪntərluːd] at theater entreacto m, intermedio m; at concert intermedio m; (period) intervalo m

in·ter·mar·ry [ɪntər'mærɪ] v/i (pret & pp **intermarried**) casarse (con miembros de otra raza, religión o grupo); **the two tribes intermarried** los dos tribus se casaron entre sí

in·ter·me·di·ar·y [ɪntər'miːdɪərɪ] n intermediario

in·ter·me·di·ate [ɪntər'miːdɪət] *adj* intermedio *m*

in·ter·mis·sion [ɪntər'mɪʃn] *in theater* entreacto *m*, intermedio *m*; *in movie theater* intermedio *m*, descanso *m*

in·tern [ɪn'tɜːrn] *v/t* recluir

in·ter·nal [ɪn'tɜːrnl] *adj* interno

in·ter·nal com'bus·tion en·gine motor *m* de combustión interna

in·ter·nal·ly [ɪn'tɜːrnəli] *adv* internamente

In·ter·nal 'Rev·e·nue (Ser·vice) Hacienda *f*, *Span* Agencia *f* Tributaria

in·ter·na·tion·al [ɪntər'næʃnl] **1** *adj* internacional **2** *n match* partido *m* internacional; *player* internacional *m/f*

In·ter·na·tion·al Court of 'Jus·tice Tribunal *m* Internacional de Justicia

in·ter·na·tion·al·ly [ɪntər'næʃnəli] *adv* internacionalmente

In·ter·na·tion·al 'Mon·e·tar·y Fund Fondo *m* Monetario Internacional

In·ter·net ['ɪntərnet] Internet *f*; *on the Internet* en Internet

in·ter·nist [ɪn'tɜːrnɪst] internista *m/f*

in·ter·pret [ɪn'tɜːrprɪt] *v/t & v/i* interpretar

in·ter·pre·ta·tion [ɪntɜːrprɪ'teɪʃn] interpretación *f*

in·ter·pret·er [ɪn'tɜːrprɪtər] intérprete *m/f*

in·ter·re·lat·ed [ɪntərɪ'leɪtɪd] *adj facts* interrelacionados

in·ter·ro·gate [ɪn'terəgeɪt] *v/t* interrogar

in·ter·ro·ga·tion [ɪnterə'geɪʃn] interrogatorio *m*

in·ter·rog·a·tive [ɪntər'rɑːgətɪv] *n* GRAM (forma *f*) interrogativa *f*

in·ter·ro·ga·tor [ɪnterə'geɪtər] interrogador(a) *m(f)*

in·ter·rupt [ɪntər'rʌpt] **1** *v/t speaker* interrumpir **2** *v/i* interrumpir

in·ter·rup·tion [ɪntər'rʌpʃn] interrupción *f*

in·ter·sect [ɪntər'sekt] **1** *v/t* cruzar **2** *v/i* cruzarse

in·ter·sec·tion ['ɪntərsekʃn] (*crossroads*) intersección *f*

in·ter·state ['ɪntərsteɪt] *n* autopista *f* interestatal

in·ter·val ['ɪntərvl] intervalo *m*; *in theater* entreacto *m*, intermedio *m*; *at concert* intermedio *m*

in·ter·vene [ɪntər'viːn] *v/i of person, police etc* intervenir

in·ter·ven·tion [ɪntər'venʃn] intervención *f*

in·ter·view ['ɪntərvjuː] **1** *n* entrevista *f* **2** *v/t* entrevistar

in·ter·view·ee [ɪntərvjuː'iː] *on* TV entrevistado(-a) *m(f)*; *for job* candidato(-a) *m(f)*

in·ter·view·er ['ɪntərvjuːər] entrevistador(a) *m(f)*

in·tes·tine [ɪn'testɪn] intestino *m*

in·ti·ma·cy ['ɪntɪməsɪ] *of friendship* intimidad *f*; *sexual* relaciones *fpl* íntimas

in·ti·mate ['ɪntɪmət] *adj* íntimo

in·tim·i·date [ɪn'tɪmɪdeɪt] *v/t* intimidar

in·tim·i·da·tion [ɪntɪmɪ'deɪʃn] intimidación *f*

in·to ['ɪntuː] *prep* en; *he put it into his suitcase* lo puso en su maleta; *translate into English* traducir al inglés; *he's into classical music* F (*likes*) le gusta *or Span* le va mucho la música clásica; *he's into local politics* F (*is involved with*) está muy metido en el mundillo de la política local; *when you're into the job* cuando te hayas metido en el trabajo

in·tol·e·ra·ble [ɪn'tɑːlərəbl] *adj* intolerable

in·tol·e·rant [ɪn'tɑːlərənt] *adj* intolerante

in·tox·i·cat·ed [ɪn'tɑːksɪkeɪtɪd] *adj* ebrio, embriagado

in·tran·si·tive [ɪn'trænsɪtɪv] *adj* intransitivo

in·tra·ve·nous [ɪntrə'viːnəs] *adj* intravenoso

in·trep·id [ɪn'trepɪd] *adj* intrépido

in·tri·cate ['ɪntrɪkət] *adj* intrincado, complicado

in·trigue **1** *n* ['ɪntriːg] intriga *f* **2** *v/t* [ɪn'triːg] intrigar; *I would be intrigued to know ...* tendría curiosidad por saber ...

in·trigu·ing [ɪn'triːgɪŋ] *adj* intrigante

in·tro·duce [ɪntrə'duːs] *v/t* presentar; *new technique etc* introducir; *may I introduce ...?* permítame presentarle a ...; *he introduced me to his wife* me presentó a su esposa; *introduce s.o. to a new sport* iniciar a alguien en un deporte nuevo

in·tro·duc·tion [ɪntrə'dʌkʃn] *to person* presentación *f*; *to a new food, sport etc* iniciación *f*; *in book, of new techniques et* introducción *f*

in·tro·vert ['ɪntrəvɜːrt] *n* introvertido(-a) *m(f)*

in·trude [ɪn'truːd] *v/i* molestar

in·trud·er [ɪn'truːdər] intruso(-a) *m(f)*

in·tru·sion [ɪn'truːʒn] intromisión *f*

in·tu·i·tion [ɪntuː'ɪʃn] intuición *f*

in·vade [ɪn'veɪd] *v/t* invadir

in·val·id[1] [ɪn'vælɪd] *adj* nulo

in·va·lid[2] ['ɪnvəlɪd] *n* MED minusválido(-a) *m(f)*

in·val·i·date [ɪnˈvælɪdeɪt] v/t *claim, theory etc* invalidar

in·val·u·a·ble [ɪnˈvæljʊbl] *adj help, contributor* inestimable

in·var·i·a·bly [ɪnˈveɪrɪəblɪ] *adv (always)* invariablemente, siempre

in·va·sion [ɪnˈveɪʒn] invasión *f*

in·vent [ɪnˈvent] v/t inventar

in·ven·tion [ɪnˈvenʃn] *action* invención *f; thing invented* invento *m*

in·ven·tive [ɪnˈventɪv] *adj* inventivo, imaginativo

in·ven·tor [ɪnˈventər] inventor(a) *m(f)*

in·ven·to·ry [ˈɪnvəntɔːrɪ] inventario *m*

in·verse [ɪnˈvɜːrs] *adj order* inverso

in·vert [ɪnˈvɜːrt] v/t invertir

in·vert·ed ˈcom·mas [ɪnˈvɜːrtɪd] *npl* comillas *fpl*

in·ver·te·brate [ɪnˈvɜːrtɪbrət] *n* invertebrado *m*

in·vest [ɪnˈvest] **1** v/t invertir **2** v/i invertir (*in* en)

in·ves·ti·gate [ɪnˈvestɪgeɪt] v/t investigar

in·ves·ti·ga·tion [ɪnvestɪˈgeɪʃn] investigación *f*

in·ves·ti·ga·tive ˈjour·nal·ism [ɪnˈvestɪgətɪv] periodismo *m* de investigación

in·vest·ment [ɪnˈvestmənt] inversión *f*

inˈvest·ment bank banco *m* de inversiones

in·ves·tor [ɪnˈvestər] inversor(a) *m(f)*

in·vig·or·at·ing [ɪnˈvɪgəreɪtɪŋ] *adj climate* vigorizante

in·vin·ci·ble [ɪnˈvɪnsəbl] *adj* invencible

in·vis·i·ble [ɪnˈvɪzɪbl] *adj* invisible

in·vi·ta·tion [ɪnvɪˈteɪʃn] invitación *f*

in·vite [ɪnˈvaɪt] v/t invitar; *he invited me out for a meal* me invitó a comer

♦ invite in v/t: *invite s.o. in* invitar a alguien a que entre

in·voice [ˈɪnvɔɪs] **1** *n* factura *f* **2** v/t *customer* enviar la factura a

in·vol·un·ta·ry [ɪnˈvɑːləntərɪ] *adj* involuntario

in·volve [ɪnˈvɑːlv] v/t *hard work, expense* involucrar, entrañar; *it would involve emigrating* supondría emigrar; *this doesn't involve you* esto no tiene nada que ver contigo; *what does it involve?* ¿en qué consiste?; *get involved with sth* involucrarse *or* meterse en algo; *the police didn't want to get involved* la policía no quería intervenir; *get involved with s.o. emotionally, romantically* tener una relación sentimental con alguien

in·volved [ɪnˈvɑːlvd] *adj (complex)* complicado

in·volve·ment [ɪnˈvɑːlvmənt] *in a project,*

crime etc participación *f*, intervención *f*

in·vul·ne·ra·ble [ɪnˈvʌlnərəbl] *adj* invulnerable

in·ward [ˈɪnwərd] **1** *adj feeling, smile* interior **2** *adv* hacia dentro

in·ward·ly [ˈɪnwərdlɪ] *adv* por dentro

i·o·dine [ˈaɪoʊdiːn] yodo *m*

IOU [aɪoʊˈjuː] *abbr* (= *I owe you*) pagaré *m*

IQ [aɪˈkjuː] *abbr* (= *intelligence quotient*) cociente *m* intelectual

I·ran [ɪˈrɑːn] Irán

I·ra·ni·an [ɪˈreɪnɪən] **1** *adj* iraní **2** *n* iraní *m/f*

I·raq [ɪˈræk] Iraq, Irak

I·ra·qi [ɪˈrækɪ] **1** *adj* iraquí **2** *n* iraquí *m/f*

Ire·land [ˈaɪrlənd] Irlanda

i·ris [ˈaɪrɪs] *of eye* iris *m inv; flower* lirio *m*

I·rish [ˈaɪrɪʃ] *adj* irlandés

ˈI·rish·man irlandés *m*

ˈI·rish·wom·an irlandesa *f*

i·ron [ˈaɪərn] **1** *n substance* hierro *m; for clothes* plancha *f* **2** v/t *shirts etc* planchar

i·ron·ic(al) [aɪˈrɑːnɪk(l)] *adj* irónico

i·ron·ing [ˈaɪərnɪŋ] planchado *m; do the ironing* planchar

ˈi·ron·ing board tabla *f* de planchar

ˈi·ron·works fundición *f*

i·ron·y [ˈaɪrənɪ] ironía *f; the irony of it all is that ...* lo irónico del tema es que ...

ir·ra·tion·al [ɪˈræʃənl] *adj* irracional

ir·rec·on·ci·la·ble [ɪrekənˈsaɪləbl] *adj* irreconciliable

ir·re·cov·e·ra·ble [ɪrɪˈkʌvərəbl] *adj* irrecuperable

ir·re·gu·lar [ɪˈregjʊlər] *adj* irregular

ir·rel·e·vant [ɪˈreləvənt] *adj* irrelevante

ir·rep·a·ra·ble [ɪˈrepərəbl] *adj* irreparable

ir·re·place·a·ble [ɪrɪˈpleɪsəbl] *adj object, person* irreemplazable

ir·re·pres·si·ble [ɪrɪˈpresəbl] *adj sense of humor* incontenible; *person* irreprimible

ir·re·proa·cha·ble [ɪrɪˈproʊtʃəbl] *adj* irreprochable

ir·re·sis·ti·ble [ɪrɪˈzɪstəbl] *adj* irresistible

ir·re·spec·tive [ɪrɪˈspektɪv] *adv: irrespective of* independientemente de

ir·re·spon·si·ble [ɪrɪˈspɑːnsəbl] *adj* irresponsable

ir·re·trie·va·ble [ɪrɪˈtriːvəbl] *adj* irrecuperable

ir·rev·e·rent [ɪˈrevərənt] *adj* irreverente

ir·re·vo·ca·ble [ɪˈrevəkəbl] *adj* irrevocable

ir·ri·gate [ˈɪrɪgeɪt] v/t regar

ir·ri·ga·tion [ɪrɪˈgeɪʃn] riego *m*

ir·ri·ga·tion ca·nal acequia *f*

ir·ri·ta·ble [ˈɪrɪtəbl] *adj* irritable

ir·ri·tate [ˈɪrɪteɪt] v/t irritar

ir·ri·tat·ing ['ɪrɪteɪtɪŋ] adj irritante
ir·ri·ta·tion [ɪrɪ'teɪʃn] irritación f
Is·lam ['ɪzlɑːm] (el) Islam
Is·lam·ic [ɪz'læmɪk] adj islámico
is·land ['aɪlənd] isla f; **(traffic) island** isleta f
is·land·er ['aɪləndər] isleño(-a) m(f)
is·o·late ['aɪsəleɪt] v/t aislar
is·o·lat·ed ['aɪsəleɪtɪd] adj aislado
is·o·la·tion [aɪsə'leɪʃn] of a region aislamiento m; **in isolation** aisladamente
i·so'la·tion ward pabellón m de enfermedades infecciosas
ISP [aɪes'piː] abbr (= **Internet service provider**) proveedor m de (acceso a) Internet
Is·rael ['ɪzreɪl] Israel
Is·rae·li [ɪz'reɪlɪ] **1** adj israelí **2** n person israelí m/f
is·sue ['ɪʃuː] **1** n (matter) tema m, asunto m; of magazine número m; **the point at issue** el tema que se debate; **take issue with s.o./sth** discrepar de algo / alguien **2** v/t coins emitir; passports, visa expedir; warning dar; **issue s.o. with sth** entregar algo a alguien
IT [aɪ'tiː] abbr (= **information technology**) tecnologías fpl de la información; **IT department** departamento de informática

it [ɪt] pron as object lo m, la f; **what color is it? - it is red** ¿de qué color es? - es rojo; **it's raining** llueve; **it's me / him** soy yo / es él; **it's Charlie here** TELEC soy Charlie; **it's your turn** te toca; **that's it!** (that's right) ¡eso es!; (finished) ¡ya está!
I·tal·i·an [ɪ'tæljən] **1** adj italiano **2** n person italiano(-a) m(f); language italiano m
I·ta·ly ['ɪtəlɪ] Italia
itch [ɪtʃ] **1** n picor m **2** v/i picar
i·tem ['aɪtəm] in list, accounts, (article) artículo m; on agenda punto m; of news noticia f
i·tem·ize ['aɪtəmaɪz] v/t invoice detallar
i·tin·e·ra·ry [aɪ'tɪnərerɪ] itinerario m
its [ɪts] poss adj su; **where is its box?** ¿dónde está su caja?; **the dog has hurt its leg** el perro se ha hecho daño en la pata
it's [ɪts] → **it is, it has**
it·self [ɪt'self] pron reflexive se; **the dog hurt itself** el perro se hizo daño; **the hotel itself is fine** el hotel en sí (mismo) está bien; **by itself** (alone) aislado, solo; (automatically) solo
i·vo·ry ['aɪvərɪ] marfil m
i·vy ['aɪvɪ] hiedra f

J

jab [dʒæb] v/t (pret & pp **jabbed**) clavar; **he jabbed his elbow into my ribs** me clavó el codo en las costillas
jab·ber ['dʒæbər] v/i parlotear
jack [dʒæk] мот gato m; in cards jota f
♦ **jack up** v/t мот levantar con el gato
jack·et ['dʒækɪt] (coat) chaqueta f; of book sobrecubierta f
jack·et po'ta·to Span patata f or L.Am. papa f asada (con piel)
'jack·knife **1** n navaja f **2** v/i derrapar (por la parte del remolque)
'jack·pot gordo m; **he hit the jackpot** le tocó el gordo
ja·cuz·zi [dʒə'kuːzɪ] jacuzzi m
jade [dʒeɪd] n jade m
jad·ed ['dʒeɪdɪd] adj harto; appetite hastiado
jag·ged ['dʒægɪd] adj accidentado

jag·u·ar ['dʒægʊər] jaguar m
jail [dʒeɪl] n cárcel f; **he's in jail** está en la cárcel
jam¹ [dʒæm] n for bread mermelada f
jam² [dʒæm] **1** n мот atasco m; F (difficulty) aprieto m; **be in a jam** estar en un aprieto **2** v/t (pret & pp **jammed**) (ram) meter, embutir; (cause to stick) atascar; broadcast provocar interferencias en; **be jammed** of roads estar colapsado; of door, window estar atascado; **jam on the brakes** dar un frenazo **3** v/i (pret & pp **jammed**) (stick) atascarse; **all ten of us managed to jam into the car** nos las arreglamos para meternos los diez en el coche
jam-'packed adj F abarrotado (**with** de)
jan·i·tor ['dʒænɪtər] portero(-a) m(f)
Jan·u·a·ry ['dʒænʊerɪ] enero m

Ja·pan [dʒə'pæn] Japón

Jap·a·nese [dʒæpə'niːz] **1** *adj* japonés **2** *n person* japonés(-esa) *m(f)*; *language* japonés *m*; *the Japanese* los japoneses

jar¹ [dʒɑːr] *n container* tarro *m*

jar² [dʒɑːr] *v/i (pret & pp jarred) of noise* rechinar; *jar on* rechinar en

jar·gon [dʒɑːrgən] jerga *f*

jaun·dice [dʒɒːndɪs] *n* ictericia *f*

jaun·diced [dʒɒːndɪst] *adj fig* resentido

jaunt [dʒɒːnt] *n* excursión *f*; *go on a jaunt* ir de excursión

jaun·ty [dʒɒːntɪ] *adj* desenfadado

jav·e·lin [dʒævlɪn] *(spear)* jabalina *f*; *event* (lanzamiento *m* de) jabalina *f*

jaw [dʒɒː] *n* mandíbula *f*

jay·walk·er [dʒeɪwɒːkər] peatón(-ona) *m(f)* imprudente

jay·walk·ing cruzar la calle de manera imprudente

jazz [dʒæz] *n* jazz *m*

◆ **jazz up** *v/t* F animar

jeal·ous [dʒeləs] *adj* celoso; *be jealous of in love* tener celos de; *of riches etc* tener envidia de

jeal·ous·ly [dʒeləslɪ] *adv* celosamente; *relating to possessions* con envidia

jeal·ous·y [dʒeləsɪ] celos *mpl*; *of possessions* envidia *f*

jeans [dʒiːnz] *npl* vaqueros *mpl*, jeans *mpl*

jeep [dʒiːp] jeep *m*

jeer [dʒɪr] **1** *n* abucheo *m* **2** *v/i* abuchear; *jeer at* burlarse de

Jel·lo® [dʒelou] gelatina *f*

jel·ly [dʒelɪ] mermelada *f*

jel·ly bean gominola *f*

jel·ly·fish *(sweater)* medusa *f*

jeop·ar·dize [dʒepərdaɪz] *v/t* poner en peligro

jeop·ar·dy [dʒepərdɪ]: *be in jeopardy* estar en peligro

jerk¹ [dʒɜːrk] **1** *n* sacudida *f* **2** *v/t* dar un tirón a

jerk² [dʒɜːrk] *n* F imbécil *m/f*, *Span* gilipollas *m/f inv* F

jerk·y [dʒɜːrkɪ] *adj movement* brusco

jer·sey [dʒɜːrzɪ] *(sweater)* suéter *m*, *Span* jersey *m*

jest [dʒest] **1** *n* broma *f*; *in jest* en broma **2** *v/i* bromear

Je·sus [dʒiːzəs] Jesús

jet¹ [dʒet] **1** *n of water* chorro *m*; *(nozzle)* boquilla *f*; *(airplane)* reactor *m*, avión *m* a reacción **2** *v/i (pret & pp jetted) travel* viajar en avión

jet-'black *adj* azabache

jet en·gine reactor *m*

jet lag desfase *m* horario, jet lag *m*

jet·ti·son [dʒetɪsn] *v/t also fig* tirar por la borda

jet·ty [dʒetɪ] malecón *m*

Jew [dʒuː] judío(-a) *m(f)*

jew·el [dʒuːəl] joya *f*, alhaja *f*; *fig: person* joya *f*

jew·el·er, *Br* **jew·el·ler** [dʒuːlər] joyero(-a) *m(f)*

jew·el·ry, *Br* **jew·el·ry** [dʒuːlrɪ] joyas *fpl*, alhajas *fpl*

Jew·ish [dʒuːɪʃ] *adj* judío

jif·fy [dʒɪfɪ] F: *in a jiffy* en un periquete F

jig·saw (puzzle) [dʒɪgsɔː] rompecabezas *m inv*, puzzle *m*

jilt [dʒɪlt] *v/t* dejar plantado

jin·gle [dʒɪŋgl] **1** *n (song)* melodía *f* publicitaria **2** *v/i of keys, coins* tintinear

jinx [dʒɪŋks] *n* gafe *m*; *there's a jinx on this project* este proyecto está gafado

jit·ters [dʒɪtərz] *npl* F: *I got the jitters* me entró el pánico *or Span* canguelo F

jit·ter·y [dʒɪtərɪ] *adj* F nervioso

job [dʒɑːb] *(employment)* trabajo *m*, empleo *m*; *(task)* tarea *f*, trabajo *m*; *it's not my job to answer the phone* no me corresponde a mí contestar el teléfono; *I've got a few jobs to do around the house* tengo que hacer unas cuantas cosas en la casa; *out of a job* sin trabajo *or* empleo; *it's a good job you warned me* menos mal que me avisaste; *you'll have a job (it'll be difficult)* te va a costar Dios y ayuda

job de·scrip·tion (descripción *f* de las) responsabilidades *fpl* del puesto

job hunt *v/i*: *be job hunting* buscar trabajo

job·less [dʒɑːblɪs] *adj* desempleado, *Span* parado

job sat·is·fac·tion satisfacción *f* con el trabajo

jock·ey [dʒɑːkɪ] *n* jockey *m/f*

jog [dʒɑːg] **1** *n*: *go for a jog* ir a hacer jogging *or* footing **2** *v/i (pret & pp jogged) as exercise* hacer jogging *or* footing **3** *v/t (pret & pp jogged) jog s.o.'s memory* refrescar la memoria de alguien; *somebody jogged my elbow* alguien me dio en el codo

◆ **jog along** *v/i* F ir tirando P

jog·ger [dʒɑːgər] *person* persona *f* que hace jogging *or* footing; *shoe* zapatilla *f* de jogging *or* footing

jog·ging [dʒɑːgɪŋ] jogging *m*, footing *m*; *go jogging* ir a hacer jogging *or* footing

jog·ging suit chándal *m*

john [dʒɑːn] P *(toilet)* baño *m*, váter *m*

join [dʒɔɪn] **1** *n* juntura *f* **2** *v/i of roads, rivers* juntarse; *(become a member)* ha-

J

cerse socio **3** v/t (connect) unir; person unirse a; club hacerse socio de; (go to work for) entrar en; of road desembocar en; **I'll join you at the theater** me reuniré contigo en el teatro

◆ **join in** v/i participar
◆ **join up** v/i MIL alistarse

join·er ['dʒɔɪnər] carpintero(-a) m(f)

joint [dʒɔɪnt] **1** n ANAT articulación f; in woodwork junta f; of meat pieza f; F (place) garito m F; of cannabis porro m F, canuto m F **2** adj (shared) conjunto

joint ac·count cuenta f conjunta

joint 'ven·ture empresa f conjunta

joke [dʒəʊk] **1** n story chiste m; (practical joke) broma f; **play a joke on** gastar una broma a; **it's no joke** no tiene ninguna gracia f v/i bromear

jok·er ['dʒəʊkər] person bromista m/f; F pej payaso(-a) m(f); in cards comodín m

jok·ing ['dʒəʊkɪŋ]: **joking apart** bromas aparte

jok·ing·ly ['dʒəʊkɪŋlɪ] adv en broma

jol·ly ['dʒɑːlɪ] adj alegre

jolt [dʒəʊlt] **1** n (jerk) sacudida f **2** v/t (push) **somebody jolted my elbow** alguien me dio en el codo

jos·tle ['dʒɑːsl] v/t empujar

◆ **jot down** [dʒɑːt] v/t (pret & pp **jotted**) apuntar, anotar

jour·nal ['dʒɜːrnl] (magazine) revista f; (diary) diario m

jour·nal·ism ['dʒɜːrnəlɪzm] periodismo m

jour·nal·ist ['dʒɜːrnəlɪst] periodista m/f

jour·ney ['dʒɜːrnɪ] n viaje m

jo·vi·al ['dʒəʊvɪəl] adj jovial

joy [dʒɔɪ] alegría f, gozo m

'joy·stick COMPUT joystick m

ju·bi·lant ['dʒuːbɪlənt] adj jubiloso

ju·bi·la·tion [dʒuːbɪ'leɪʃn] júbilo m

judge [dʒʌdʒ] **1** n LAW juez m/f, jueza f; in competition juez m/f, miembro m del jurado **2** v/t juzgar; (estimate) calcular **3** v/i juzgar; **judge for yourself** júzgalo por ti mismo

judg·ment ['dʒʌdʒmənt] LAW fallo m; (opinion) juicio m; **an error of judgment** una equivocación; **he showed good judgment** mostró tener criterio; **against my better judgment** a pesar de no estar convencido; **the Last Judgment** REL el Juicio Final

'Judg(e)·ment Day Día m del Juicio Final

ju·di·cial [dʒuː'dɪʃl] adj judicial

ju·di·cious [dʒuː'dɪʃəs] adj juicioso

ju·do ['dʒuːdəʊ] judo m

jug·gle [dʒʌgl] v/t also fig hacer malabarismos con

jug·gler ['dʒʌglər] malabarista m/f

juice [dʒuːs] n Span zumo m, L.Am. jugo m

juic·y ['dʒuːsɪ] adj jugoso; news, gossip jugoso, sabroso

juke·box ['dʒuːkbɑːks] máquina f de discos

Ju·ly [dʒʊ'laɪ] julio m

jum·ble ['dʒʌmbl] n revoltijo m

◆ **jumble up** v/t revolver

jum·bo (jet) ['dʒʌmbəʊ] jumbo m

'jum·bo(-sized) adj gigante

jump [dʒʌmp] **1** n salto m; (increase) incremento m, subida f; **give a jump** of surprise dar un salto **2** v/i saltar; (increase) dispararse; **you made me jump!** ¡me diste un susto!; **jump to one's feet** ponerse de pie de un salto; **jump to conclusions** sacar conclusiones precipitadas **3** v/t fence etc saltar; F (attack) asaltar; **jump the lights** saltarse el semáforo, pasarse un semáforo en rojo

◆ **jump at** v/t opportunity no dejar escapar

jump·er[1] ['dʒʌmpər] dress pichi m

jump·er[2] ['dʒʌmpər] SP saltador(a) m(f); horse caballo m de saltos

jump·y ['dʒʌmpɪ] adj nervioso; **get jumpy** ponerse nervioso

junc·tion ['dʒʌŋkʃn] of roads cruce m

junc·ture ['dʒʌŋktʃər] fml: **at this juncture** en esta coyuntura

June [dʒuːn] junio m

jun·gle ['dʒʌŋgl] selva f, jungla f

ju·ni·or ['dʒuːnjər] **1** adj subordinate de rango inferior; younger más joven **2** n in rank subalterno(-a) m(f); **she is ten years my junior** es diez años menor que yo

ju·ni·or 'high escuela f secundaria (para alumnos de entre 12 y 14 años)

junk [dʒʌŋk] n trastos mpl

'junk food comida f basura

junk·ie ['dʒʌŋkɪ] F drogata m/f F

'junk mail propaganda f postal

'junk shop cacharrería f

'junk·yard depósito m de chatarra

ju·ris·dic·tion [dʒʊrɪs'dɪkʃn] LAW jurisdicción f

ju·ror ['dʒʊrər] miembro m del jurado

ju·ry ['dʒʊrɪ] jurado m

just [dʒʌst] **1** adj law, cause justo **2** adv (barely) justo; (exactly) justo, justamente; (only) sólo, solamente; **have just done sth** acabar de hacer algo; **I've just seen her** la acabo de ver; **just about** (almost) casi; **I was just about to leave when ...** estaba a punto de salir cuando ...; **just like that** (abruptly) de repente;

just now (*at the moment*) ahora mismo; *I saw her just now* (*a few moments ago*) la acabo de ver; *just you wait!* ¡ya verás!; *just be quiet!* ¡cállate de una vez!

jus·tice ['dʒʌstɪs] justicia *f*

jus·ti·fi·a·ble [dʒʌstɪ'faɪəbl] *adj* justificable

jus·ti·fi·a·bly [dʒʌstɪ'faɪəblɪ] *adv* justificadamente

jus·ti·fi·ca·tion [dʒʌstɪfɪ'keɪʃn] justificación *f*; *there's no justification for behavior like that* ese comportamiento es injustificable *or* no tiene justificación

jus·ti·fy ['dʒʌstɪfaɪ] *v/t* (*pret & pp justified*) *also text* justificar

just·ly ['dʒʌstlɪ] *adv* (*fairly*) con justicia; (*rightly*) con razón

◆ **jut out** [dʒʌt] *v/i* (*pret & pp jutted*) sobresalir

ju·ve·nile ['dʒuːvənl] **1** *adj crime* juvenil; *court* de menores; *pej* infantil **2** *n fml* menor *m/f*

ju·ve·nile de·lin·quen·cy delincuencia *f* juvenil

ju·ve·nile de·lin·quent delincuente *m/f* juvenil

K

k [keɪ] *abbr* (= *kilobyte*) k (= kilobyte *m*); (= *thousand*) mil

kan·ga·roo [kæŋgə'ruː] canguro *m*

ka·ra·te [kə'rɑːtɪ] kárate *m*

ka·ra·te chop *n* golpe *m* de kárate

ke·bab [kɪ'bæb] pincho *m*, brocheta *f*

keel [kiːl] NAUT quilla *f*

◆ **keel over** *v/i of structure* desplomarse; *of person* desmayarse

keen [kiːn] *adj* entusiasta, interesado; *interest* gran; *competition* reñido; *she's keen to learn* tiene mucho interés en aprender; *he's keen on football* / *her* le gusta el fútbol / ella; *I'm not keen on the idea* no me entusiasma la idea; *be keen to do sth* estar muy interesado en hacer algo

keep [kiːp] **1** *n* (*maintenance*) manutención *f*; *for keeps* F para siempre **2** *v/t* (*pret & pp kept*) guardar; (*not lose*) conservar; (*detain*) entretener; *family* mantener; *animals* tener, criar; *you can keep it* (*it's for you*) te lo puedes quedar; *keep trying!* ¡sigue intentándolo!; *don't keep interrupting!* ¡deja de interrumpirme!; *keep a promise* cumplir una promesa; *keep s.o. company* hacer compañía a alguien; *keep s.o. waiting* hacer esperar a alguien; *he can't keep anything to himself* no sabe guardar un secreto; *I kept the news of the accident to myself* no dije nada sobre el accidente; *keep sth from s.o.* ocultar algo a alguien; *we kept the news from him* no le contamos la noticia **3** *v/i* (*pret & pp kept*) *of food, milk* aguantar, conser-

varse; *keep calm!* ¡tranquilízate!; *keep quiet!* ¡cállate!

◆ **keep away 1** *v/i*: *keep away from that building* no te acerques a ese edificio **2** *v/t*: *keep the children away from the stove* no dejes que los niños se acerquen a la cocina

◆ **keep back** *v/t* (*hold in check*) contener; *information* ocultar

◆ **keep down** *v/t voice* bajar; *costs, inflation etc* reducir; *food* retener; *keep your voices down in the library* hablen en voz baja en la biblioteca; *tell the kids to keep the noise down* diles a los niños que no hagan tanto ruido; *I can't keep anything down* devuelvo todo lo que como

◆ **keep in** *v/t in school* castigar (*a quedarse en clase*); *the hospital's keeping her in* la tienen en observación

◆ **keep off 1** *v/t* (*avoid*) evitar; *keep off the grass!* ¡prohibido pisar el césped! **2** *v/i*: *If the rain keeps off* si no llueve

◆ **keep on 1** *v/i* continuar; *if you keep on interrupting me* si no dejas de interrumpirme; *keep on trying* sigue intentándolo **2** *v/t: the company kept them on* la empresa los mantuvo en el puesto; *keep your coat on!* *item of clothing* ¡no te quites el abrigo!

◆ **keep on at** *v/t* (*nag*): *my parents keep on at me to get a job* mis padres no dejan de decirme que busque un trabajo

◆ **keep out 1** *v/t: it keeps the cold out* protege del frío; *they must be kept out* no pueden entrar **2** *v/i: I told you**

to keep out! *of a place* ¡te dije que no entraras!; *I would keep out of it if I were you* yo en tu lugar no me metería; *keep out as sign* prohibida la entrada, prohibido el paso

◆ **keep to** *v/t path* seguir; *rules* cumplir, respetar

◆ **keep up 1** *v/i when walking, running etc* seguir *or* mantener el ritmo (**with** de); *keep up with s.o.* (*stay in touch with*) mantener contacto con alguien **2** *v/t pace* seguir, mantener; *payments* estar al corriente de; *bridge, plane* sujetar

keep·ing ['ki:piŋ] *n*: *be in keeping with decor* combinar con; *in keeping with promises* de acuerdo con

'**keep·sake** recuerdo *m*

keg [keg] barril *m*

ken·nel ['kenl] *n* caseta *f* del perro

ken·nels ['kenlz] *npl* residencia *f* canina

kept [kept] *pret & pp* → **keep**

ker·nel ['kɜːrnl] almendra *f*

ker·o·sene ['kerəsiːn] queroseno *m*

ketch·up ['ketʃʌp] ketchup *m*

ket·tle ['ketl] hervidor *m*

key [kiː] **1** *n to door, drawer* llave *f*; *on keyboard, piano* tecla *f*; *of piece of music* clave *f*; *on map* leyenda *f* **2** *adj* (*vital*) clave, crucial **3** *v/t & v/i* COMPUT teclear

◆ **key in** *v/t data* introducir, teclear

'**key·board** COMPUT, MUS teclado *m*

key·board·er COMPUT operador(a) *m(f)*, *persona que introduce datos en el ordenador*

'**key·card** tarjeta *f* (de hotel)

keyed-up [kiːd'ʌp] *adj* nervioso

'**key·hole** ojo *m* de la cerradura

'**key·note** '**speech** discurso *m* central

'**key·ring** llavero *m*

kha·ki ['kæki] *adj* caqui

kick [kik] **1** *n* patada *f*; *he got a kick out of watching them suffer* disfrutó viéndoles sufrir; (*just*) *for kicks* F por diversión **2** *v/t* dar una patada a; F *habit* dejar; *I kicked him in the shins* le di una patada en la espinilla **3** *v/i of person* patalear; *of horse, mule* cocear

◆ **kick around** *v/t ball* dar patadas a; F (*discuss*) comentar

◆ **kick in** *v/t* P *money* apoquinar F

◆ **kick off** *v/i* comenzar, sacar de centro; F (*start*) empezar

◆ **kick out** *v/t of bar, company* echar; *of country, organization* expulsar

◆ **kick up** *v/t: kick up a fuss* montar un numerito

'**kick·back** F (*bribe*) soborno *m*

'**kick·off** SP saque *m*

kid [kid] **1** *n* F (*child*) crío *m* F, niño *m*;

when I was a kid cuando era pequeño; *kid brother* hermano *m* pequeño; *kid sister* hermana *f* pequeña **2** *v/t* (*pret & pp kidded*) F tomar el pelo a F **3** *v/i* (*pret & pp kidded*) F bromear; *I was only kidding* estaba bromeando

kid·der ['kidər] F vacilón *m* F

kid 'gloves: handle s.o. with kid gloves tratar a alguien con guante de seda

kid·nap ['kidnæp] *v/t* (*pret & pp kidnapped*) secuestrar

kid·nap·(p)er ['kidnæpər] secuestrador *m*

'**kid·nap·(p)ing** ['kidnæpiŋ] secuestro *m*

kid·ney ['kidni] ANAT riñón *m*; *in cooking* riñones *mpl*

'**kid·ney bean** alubia *f* roja de riñón

'**kid·ney ma·chine** MED riñón *m* artificial, máquina *f* de diálisis

kill [kil] *v/t* matar; *the drought killed all the plants* las plantas murieron como resultado de la sequía; *I had six hours to kill* tenía seis horas sin nada que hacer; *be killed in an accident* morirse en un accidente; *kill o.s.* suicidarse; *kill o.s. laughing* F morirse de risa F

kil·ler ['kilər] (*murderer*) asesino *m*; *be a killer of disease* ser mortal

kil·ling ['kiliŋ] *n* asesinato *m*; *make a killing* F (*lots of money*) forrarse F

kil·ling·ly ['kiliŋli] *adv* F: *killingly funny* para morirse de risa

kiln [kiln] horno *m*

ki·lo ['kiːlou] kilo *m*

'**ki·lo·byte** ['kiloubait] COMPUT kilobyte *m*

ki·lo·gram ['kiləgræm] kilogramo *m*

ki·lo·me·ter, *Br* **ki·lo·me·tre** [kɪ'lɑːmɪtər] kilómetro *m*

kind¹ [kaind] *adj* agradable, amable

kind² [kaind] *n* (*sort*) tipo *m*; (*make, brand*) marca *f*; *all kinds of people* toda clase de personas; *I did nothing of the kind!* ¡no hice nada parecido!; *kind of ... sad, lonely, etc* un poco ...; *that's very kind of you* gracias por tu amabilidad

kin·der·gar·ten ['kindərgɑːrtn] guardería *f*, jardín *m* de infancia

kind-heart·ed [kaind'hɑːrtid] *adj* agradable, amable

kind·ly ['kaindli] **1** *adj* amable, agradable **2** *adv* con amabilidad; *kindly don't interrupt* por favor, no me interrumpa; *kindly lower your voice* ¿le importaría hablar más bajo?

kind·ness ['kaindnis] amabilidad *f*

king [kiŋ] rey *m*

king·dom ['kiŋdəm] reino *m*

'**king-size(d)** *adj* F *cigarettes* extralargo; *king-size(d) bed* cama *f* de matrimonio grande

kink [kɪŋk] *n* in hose etc doblez *f*

kink·y ['kɪŋkɪ] *adj* F vicioso

kiosk ['kiːɒsk] quiosco *m*

kiss [kɪs] **1** *n* beso *m* **2** *v/t* besar **3** *v/i* besarse

kiss of 'life boca *m* a boca, respiración *f* artificial; *give s.o. the kiss of life* hacer a alguien el boca a boca

kit [kɪt] (*equipment*) equipo *m*; *first aid kit* botiquín *m*; *tool kit* caja *f* de herramientas

kitch·en ['kɪtʃɪn] cocina *f*

kitch·en·ette [kɪtʃɪ'net] cocina pequeña

kitch·en 'sink: you've got everything but the kitchen sink F llevas la casa a cuestas F

kite [kaɪt] cometa *f*

kit·ten ['kɪtn] gatito *m*

kit·ty ['kɪtɪ] *money* fondo *m*

klutz [klʌts] F (*clumsy person*) manazas *m*

knack [næk] habilidad *f*; *he has a knack of upsetting people* tiene la habilidad de disgustar a la gente; *I soon got the knack of the new machine* le pillé el truco a la nueva máquina rápidamente

knead [niːd] *v/t dough* amasar

knee [niː] *n* rodilla *f*

'knee·cap *n* rótula *f*

kneel [niːl] *v/i* (*pret & pp knelt*) arrodillarse

'knee-length *adj* hasta la rodilla

knelt [nelt] *pret & pp* → *kneel*

knew [nuː] *pret* → *know*

knick-knacks ['nɪknæks] *npl* F baratijas *fpl*

knife [naɪf] **1** *n* (*pl knives* [naɪvz]) *for food* cuchillo *m*; *carried outside* navaja *f* **2** *v/t* acuchillar, apuñalar

knight [naɪt] *n* caballero *m*

knit [nɪt] **1** *v/t* (*pret & pp knitted*) tejer **2** *v/i* (*pret & pp knitted*) tricotar

◆ **knit together** *v/i of broken bone* soldarse

knit·ting ['nɪtɪŋ] punto *m*

'knit·ting nee·dle aguja *f* para hacer punto

'knit·wear prendas *fpl* de punto

knob [nɒb] *on door* pomo *m*; *on drawer* tirador *m*; *of butter* nuez *f*, trocito *m*

knock [nɒk] **1** *n on door* golpe *m*; (*blow*) golpe *m*; *there was a knock on the door* llamaron a la puerta **2** *v/t* (*hit*) golpear; F (*criticize*) criticar, meterse con F; *he was knocked to the ground* le tiraron al su-

elo **3** *v/i on the door* llamar

◆ **knock around 1** *v/t* F (*beat*) pegar a **2** *v/i* F (*travel*) viajar

◆ **knock down** *v/t of car* atropellar; *building* tirar; *object* tirar al suelo; F (*reduce the price of*) rebajar

◆ **knock off 1** *v/t* P (*steal*) mangar P **2** *v/i* F (*stop work for the day*) acabar, *Span* plegar F

◆ **knock out** *v/t* (*make unconscious*) dejar K.O.; *of medicine* dejar para el arrastre F; *power lines etc* destruir; (*eliminate*) eliminar

◆ **knock over** *v/t* tirar; *of car* atropellar

'knock·down *adj: at a knockdown price* tirado

knock-kneed [nɑːk'niːd] *adj* patizambo

knock-out *n in boxing* K.O. *m*

knot [nɑːt] **1** *n* nudo *m* **2** *v/t* (*pret & pp knotted*) anudar

'knot·ty ['nɑːtɪ] *adj problem* complicado

know [noʊ] **1** *v/t* (*pret knew*, *pp known*) *fact, language, how to do sth* saber; *person, place* conocer; (*recognize*) reconocer; *will you let him know that …?* ¿puedes decirle que …? **2** *v/i* (*pret knew*, *pp known*) saber; *I don't know* no (lo) sé; *yes, I know* sí, lo sé **3** *n: people in the know* los enterados

'know-how pericia *f*

know·ing ['noʊɪŋ] *adj* cómplice

know·ing·ly ['noʊɪŋlɪ] *adv* (*wittingly*) deliberadamente; *smile etc* con complicidad

'know-it-all F sabiondo F

knowl·edge ['nɑːlɪdʒ] conocimiento *m*; *to the best of my knowledge* por lo que sé; *have a good knowledge of …* tener buenos conocimientos de …

knowl·edge·a·ble ['nɑːlɪdʒəbl] *adj: she's very knowledgeable about music* sabe mucho de música

known [noʊn] *pp* → *know*

knuck·le ['nʌkl] nudillo *m*

◆ **knuckle down** *v/i* F aplicarse F

◆ **knuckle under** *v/i* F pasar por el aro F

KO [keɪ'oʊ] (*knockout*) K.O.

Ko·ran [kəˈræn] Corán *m*

Ko·re·a [kəˈriːə] Corea

Ko·re·an [kəˈriːən] **1** *adj* coreano **2** *n* coreano(a) *m(f)*; *language* coreano *m*

ko·sher ['koʊʃər] *adj* REL kosher; F legal F

kow·tow ['kaʊtaʊ] *v/i* F reverenciar

ku·dos ['kjuːdɑːs] reconocimiento *m*, prestigio *m*

L

lab [læb] laboratorio *m*

la·bel ['leɪbl] 1 *n* etiqueta *f* 2 *v/t baggage* etiquetar

la·bor ['leɪbər] *n* (*work*) trabajo *m*; *in pregnancy* parto *m*; **be in labor** estar de parto

la·bor·a·to·ry ['læbrətɔːrɪ] laboratorio *m*

la·bor·a·to·ry tech'ni·cian técnico(-a) *m(f)* de laboratorio

la·bo·ri·ous [lə'bɔːrɪəs] *adj* laborioso

la·bored ['leɪbərd] *adj style, speech* elaborado

la·bor·er ['leɪbərər] obrero(-a) *m(f)*

'la·bor u·ni·on sindicato *m*

'la·bor ward MED sala *f* de partos

la·bour *etc Br* → **labor** *etc*

lace [leɪs] *n material* encaje *m*; *for shoe* cordón *m*

◆ lace up *v/t shoes* atar

lack [læk] 1 *n* falta *f*, carencia *f* 2 *v/t* carecer de; **he lacks confidence** le falta confianza 3 *v/i*: **be lacking** faltar

lac·quer ['lækər] *n for hair* laca *f*

lad [læd] muchacho *m*, chico *m*

lad·der ['lædər] *n* escalera *f* (de mano)

la·den ['leɪdn] *adj* cargado (**with** de)

la·dies room ['leɪdiːz] servicio *m* de señoras

la·dle ['leɪdl] *n* cucharón *m*, cazo *m*

la·dy ['leɪdɪ] señora *f*

'la·dy·bug mariquita *f*

'la·dy·like *adj* femenino

lag [læg] *v/t* (*pret & pp lagged*) *pipes* revestir con aislante

◆ lag behind *v/i* quedarse atrás

la·ger ['lɑːgər] cerveza *f* rubia

laid [leɪd] *pret & pp* → **lay¹**

laid-back [leɪd'bæk] *adj* tranquilo, despreocupado

lain [leɪn] *pp* → **lie²**

lake [leɪk] lago *m*

lamb [læm] *animal, meat* cordero *m*

lame [leɪm] *adj person* cojo; *excuse* pobre

la·ment [lə'ment] 1 *n* lamento *m* 2 *v/t* lamentar

lam·en·ta·ble ['læməntəbl] *adj* lamentable

lam·i·nat·ed ['læmɪneɪtɪd] *adj surface* laminado; *paper* plastificado

lam·i·nat·ed 'glass cristal *m* laminado

lamp [læmp] lámpara *f*

'lamp·post farola *f*

'lamp·shade pantalla *f* (de lámpara)

land [lænd] 1 *n* tierra *f*; **by land** por tierra; **on land** en tierra; **work on the land** *as farmer* trabajar la tierra 2 *of airplane* aterrizar; *job* conseguir 3 *v/i of airplane* aterrizar; *of capsule on the moon* alunizar; *of ball, sth thrown* caer; *it landed right on top of his head* le cayó justo en la cabeza

land·ing ['lændɪŋ] *n of airplane* aterrizaje *m*; *on moon* alunizaje *m*; *of staircase* rellano *m*

'land·ing field pista *f* de aterrizaje

'land·ing gear tren *m* de aterrizaje

'land·ing strip pista *f* de aterrizaje

'land·la·dy *of bar* patrona *f*; *of hostel etc* dueña *f*; *of rented room* casera *f*

'land·lord *of bar* patrón *m*; *of hostel etc* dueño *m*; *of rented room* casero *m*

'land·mark punto *m* de referencia; *fig* hito *m*

'land own·er terrateniente *m/f*

land·scape ['lændskeɪp] 1 *n* (*also painting*) paisaje *m* 2 *adv print* en formato apaisado

'land·slide corrimiento *m* de tierras

'land·slide 'vic·to·ry victoria *f* arrolladora

lane [leɪn] *in country* camino *m*, vereda *f*; (*alley*) callejón *m*; MOT carril *m*

lan·guage ['læŋgwɪdʒ] lenguaje *m*; *of nation* idioma *f*, lengua *f*

'lan·guage lab laboratorio *m* de idiomas

lank [læŋk] *adj hair* lacio

lank·y ['læŋkɪ] *adj person* larguirucho

lan·tern ['læntərn] farol *m*

lap¹ [læp] *n of track* vuelta *f*

lap² [læp] *n of water* chapoteo *m*

◆ lap up *v/t* (*pret & pp lapped*) *drink, milk* beber a lengüetadas; *flattery* deleitarse con

lap³ [læp] *n of person* regazo *m*

la·pel [lə'pel] solapa *f*

lapse [læps] 1 *n* (*mistake, slip*) desliz *m*; *of time* lapso *m*; *a lapse of attention* un momento de distracción; *a lapse of memory* un olvido 2 *v/i of membership* vencer; *lapse into silence / despair* sumirse en el silencio / la desesperación; *she lapsed into English* empezó a hablar en inglés

lap·top ['læptɑːp] COMPUT ordenador *m* portátil, *L.Am.* computadora *f* portátil

lar·ce·ny ['lɑːrsənɪ] latrocinio *m*

lard [lɑːrd] manteca *f* de cerdo

lar·der ['lɑːrdər] despensa *f*

large [lɑːrdʒ] *adj* grande; *be at large of criminal, wild animal* andar suelto

large·ly ['lɑːrdʒli] *adv* (*mainly*) en gran parte, principalmente

lark [lɑːrk] *bird* alondra *f*

lar·va ['lɑːrvə] larva *f*

lar·yn·gi·tis [lærɪn'dʒaɪtɪs] laringitis *f*

lar·ynx ['lærɪŋks] laringe *f*

la·ser ['leɪzər] láser *m*

la·ser beam rayo *m* láser

la·ser print·er impresora *f* láser

lash[1] [læʃ] *v/t with whip* azotar

◆ **lash down** *v/t with rope* amarrar

◆ **lash out** *v/i with fists, words* atacar (**at** a), arremeter (**at** contra)

lash[2] [læʃ] *n (eyelash)* pestaña *f*

lass [læs] muchacha *f*, chica *f*

last[1] [læst] **1** *adj in series* último; (*preceding*) anterior; *last Friday* el viernes pasado; *last but one* penúltimo; *last night* anoche; *last but not least* por último, pero no por ello menos importante **2** *adv* **at last** por fin, al fin

last[2] [læst] *v/i* durar

last·ing ['læstɪŋ] *adj* duradero

last·ly ['læstlɪ] *adv* por último, finalmente

latch [lætʃ] *n* pestillo *m*

late [leɪt] **1** *adj*: *the bus is late again* el autobús vuelve a llegar tarde; *it's late* es tarde; *it's getting late* se está haciendo tarde; *of late* últimamente, recientemente; *the late 19th/20th century* la última parte del siglo XIX / XX; *in the late 19th/20th century* a finales del siglo XIX / XX **2** *adv arrive, leave* tarde

late·ly ['leɪtlɪ] *adv* últimamente, recientemente

lat·er ['leɪtər] *adv* más tarde; *see you later!* ¡hasta luego!; *later on* más tarde

lat·est ['leɪtɪst] *adj news, girlfriend* último

lathe [leɪð] *n* torno *m*

la·ther ['lɑːðər] *n from soap* espuma *f*; *in a lather* (*sweaty*) empapado de sudor

Lat·in ['lætɪn] **1** *adj* latino **2** *n* latín *m*

Lat·in A·mer·i·ca Latinoamérica, América Latina

La·tin A·mer·i·can 1 *n* latinoamericano(-a) *m(f)* **2** *adj* latinoamericano

La·ti·no [læ'tiːnou] **1** *adj* latino **2** *n* latino(-a)

lat·i·tude ['lætɪtuːd] *geographical* latitud *f*; (*freedom to act*) libertad *f*

lat·ter ['lætər] **1** *adj* último **2** *n*: *Mr Brown and Mr White, of whom the latter was ...* el Señor Brown y el Señor White, de quien el segundo *or* este último era ...

laugh [læf] **1** *n* risa *f*; *it was a laugh* F fue genial **2** *v/i* reírse

◆ **laugh at** *v/t* reírse de

laugh·ing stock: *make o.s. a laughing stock* ponerse en ridículo; *become a laughing stock* ser el hazmerreír

laugh·ter ['læftər] risas *fpl*

launch [lɔːntʃ] **1** *n small boat* lancha *f*; *of ship* botadura *f*; *of rocket, new product* lanzamiento *m* **2** *v/t rocket, new product* lanzar; *ship* botar

launch cer·e·mo·ny ceremonia *f* de lanzamiento

launch·(ing) pad plataforma *f* de lanzamiento

laun·der ['lɔːndər] *v/t clothes* lavar (y planchar); *money* blanquear

laun·dro·mat ['lɔːndrəmæt] lavandería *f*

laun·dry ['lɔːndrɪ] *place* lavandería *f*; *dirty clothes* ropa *f* sucia; *clean clothes* ropa *f* lavada; *do the laundry* lavar la ropa, *Span* hacer la colada

lau·rel ['lɔːrəl] laurel *m*

lav·a·to·ry ['lævətɔːrɪ] *place* cuarto *m* de baño, lavabo *m*; *equipment* retrete *m*

lav·en·der ['lævəndər] espliego *m*, lavanda *f*

lav·ish ['lævɪʃ] *adj* espléndido

law [lɔː] ley *f*; *subject* derecho *m*; *be against the law* estar prohibido, ser ilegal

law-a·bid·ing ['lɔːabaɪdɪŋ] *adj* respetuoso con la ley

law court juzgado *m*

law·ful ['lɔːfəl] *adj* legal; *wife* legítimo

law·less ['lɔːlɪs] *adj* sin ley

lawn [lɔːn] césped *m*

lawn mow·er cortacésped *m*

law·suit pleito *m*

law·yer ['lɔːjər] abogado(-a) *m(f)*

lax [læks] *adj* poco estricto

lax·a·tive ['læksətɪv] *n* laxante *m*

lay[1] [leɪ] *v/t (pret & pp laid) (put down)* dejar, poner; *eggs* poner; V *sexually* tirarse a V

lay[2] [leɪ] *pret → lie*[2]

◆ **lay into** *v/t (attack)* arremeter contra

◆ **lay off** *v/t workers* despedir

◆ **lay on** *v/t (provide)* organizar

◆ **lay out** *v/t objects* colocar, disponer; *page* diseñar, maquetar

lay·a·bout F gandul(a) *m(f)* F

lay-by *on road* área *f* de descanso

lay·er ['leɪər] estrato *m*; *of soil, paint* capa *f*

lay·man laico *m*

lay-off despido *m*

◆ **laze around** [leɪz] *v/i* holgazanear

la·zy ['leɪzɪ] *adj person* holgazán, perezoso; *day* ocioso

lb *abbr* (= *pound*) libra *f* (de peso)

LCD [elsiː'diː] *abbr* (= *liquid crystal dis-*

play) LCD, pantalla *f* de cristal líquido

lead¹ [liːd] **1** *v/t* (*pret & pp* **led**) *procession, race* ir al frente de; *company, team* dirigir; (*guide, take*) conducir **2** *v/i* (*pret & pp* **led**) *in race, competition* ir en cabeza; (*provide leadership*) tener el mando; *a street leading off the square* una calle que sale de la plaza; *where is this leading?* ¿adónde nos lleva esto? **3** *n in race* ventaja *f*; *be in the lead* estar en cabeza; *take the lead* ponerse en cabeza; *lose the lead* perder la cabeza

♦ **lead on** *v/t* (*go in front*) ir delante

♦ **lead up to** *v/t* preceder a; *I wonder what she's leading up to* me pregunto a dónde quiere ir a parar

lead² [liːd] *for dog* correa *f*

lead³ [led] *substance* plomo *m*

lead·ed [ledɪd] *adj gas* con plomo

lead·er [ˈliːdər] líder *m*

lead·er·ship [ˈliːdərʃɪp] *of party etc* liderazgo *m*; *under his leadership* bajo su liderazgo

ˈlead·er·ship con·test pugna *f* por el liderazgo

lead-free [ˈledfriː] *adj gas* sin plomo

lead·ing [ˈliːdɪŋ] *adj runner* en cabeza; *company, product* puntero

ˈlead·ing-edge *adj company* en la vanguardia; *technology* de vanguardia

leaf [liːf] (*pl* **leaves** [liːvz]) hoja *f*

♦ **leaf through** *v/t* hojear

leaf·let [ˈliːflət] folleto *m*

league [liːg] liga *f*

leak [liːk] **1** *n in roof* gotera *f*; *in pipe* agujero *m*; *of air, gas* fuga *f*, escape *m*; *of information* filtración *f* **2** *v/i of boat* hacer agua; *of pipe* tener un agujero; *of liquid, gas* fugarse, escaparse

♦ **leak out** *v/i of air, gas* fugarse, escaparse; *of news* filtrarse

leak·y [ˈliːkɪ] *adj pipe* con agujeros; *boat* que hace agua

lean¹ [liːn] **1** *v/i* (*be at an angle*) estar inclinado; *lean against sth* apoyarse en algo **2** *v/t* apoyar; *lean sth against sth* apoyar algo contra algo

lean² [liːn] *adj meat* magro; *style, prose* pobre, escueto

leap [liːp] **1** *n* salto *m*; *a great leap forward* un gran salto adelante **2** *v/i* (*pret & pp* **leaped** *or* **leapt**) saltar; *he leapt over the fence* saltó la valla; *they leapt into the river* se tiraron al río

leapt [lept] *pret & pp* → **leap**

ˈleap year año *m* bisiesto

learn [lɜːrn] **1** *v/t* aprender; (*hear*) enterarse de; *learn how to do sth* aprender a hacer algo **2** *v/i* aprender

learn·er [ˈlɜːrnər] estudiante *m/f*

ˈlearn·er driv·er conductor(a) *m(f)* en prácticas

learn·ing [ˈlɜːrnɪŋ] *n* (*knowledge*) conocimientos *mpl*; *act* aprendizaje *m*

ˈlearn·ing curve curva *f* de aprendizaje; *be on the learning curve* tener que aprender cosas nuevas

lease [liːs] **1** *n* (*contrato m de*) arrendamiento *m* **2** *v/t apartment, equipment* arrendar

♦ **lease out** *v/t apartment, equipment* arrendar

lease 'pur·chase arrendamiento *m* con opción de compra

leash [liːʃ] *for dog* correa *f*

least [liːst] **1** *adj* (*slightest*) menor; *the least amount, money, baggage* menos; *there's not the least reason to …* no hay la más mínima razón para que … **2** *adv* menos **3** *n* lo menos; *he drank the least* fue el que menos bebió; *not in the least surprised* en absoluto sorprendido; *at least* por lo menos

leath·er [ˈleðər] **1** *n* piel *f*, cuero **2** *adj* de piel, de cuero

leave [liːv] **1** *n* (*vacation*) permiso *m*; *on leave* de permiso **2** *v/t* (*pret & pp* **left**) *city, place* marcharse de, irse de; *person, food, memory*, (*forget*) dejar; *let's leave things as they are* dejemos las cosas tal y como están; *how did you leave things with him?* ¿cómo quedaron las cosas con él?; *leave s.o./sth alone* (*not touch, not interfere with*) dejar a alguien / algo en paz; *be left* quedar; *there is nothing left* no queda nada; *I only have one left* sólo me queda uno **3** *v/i* (*pret & pp* **left**) *of person* marcharse, irse; *of plane, train, bus* salir

♦ **leave behind** *v/t intentionally* dejar; (*forget*) olvidarse

♦ **leave on** *v/t hat, coat* dejar puesto; TV, *computer* dejar encendido

♦ **leave out** *v/t word, figure* omitir; (*not put away*) no guardar; *leave me out of this* a mí no me metas en esto

ˈleav·ing par·ty fiesta *f* de despedida

lec·ture [ˈlektʃər] **1** *n* clase *f*; *to general public* conferencia *f* **2** *v/i at university* dar clases (*in* en); *to general public* dar una conferencia

ˈlec·ture hall sala *f* de conferencias

lec·tur·er [ˈlektʃərər] profesor(a) *m(f)*

LED [eliːˈdiː] *abbr* (= **light-emitting diode**) LED *m* (= diodo *m* emisor de luz)

led [led] *pret & pp* → **lead¹**

ledge [ledʒ] *of window* alféizar *f*; *on rock face* saliente *m*

level

ledg·er ['ledʒər] COM libro *m* mayor

leek [liːk] puerro *m*

leer [lɪr] *n sexual* mirada *f* impúdica; *evil mirada f maligna*

left [left] **1** *adj* izquierdo **2** *n also* POL izquierda *f*; **on the left** a la izquierda; **on the left of sth** a la izquierda de algo; **to the left** *turn, look* a la izquierda **3** *adv turn, look* a la izquierda

left² [left] *pret & pp* → **leave**

'left-hand *adj* de la izquierda; **on your left-hand side** a tu izquierda; **bend** a la izquierda

'left-hand 'drive: **this car is left-hand drive** este coche tiene el volante a la izquierda

'left-'handed *adj* zurdo

left 'lug·gage (of·fice) *Br* consigna *f*

'left-overs *npl food* sobras *fpl*

'left-wing *adj* POL izquierdista, de izquierdas

leg [leg] *of person* pierna *f*; *of animal* pata *f*; **pull s.o.'s leg** tomar el pelo a alguien

leg·a·cy ['legəsɪ] legado *m*

le·gal ['liːgl] *adj* legal

le·gal ad'vis·er asesor(a) *m(f)* jurídico(-a)

le·gal·i·ty [lɪ'gælɪtɪ] legalidad *f*

le·gal·ize ['liːgəlaɪz] *v/t* legalizar

leg·end ['ledʒənd] leyenda *f*

leg·en·da·ry ['ledʒəndrɪ] *adj* legendario

le·gi·ble ['ledʒəbl] *adj* legible

le·gis·late ['ledʒɪsleɪt] *v/i* legislar

le·gis·la·tion [ledʒɪs'leɪʃn] legislación *f*

le·gis·la·tive ['ledʒɪslətɪv] *adj* legislativo

le·gis·la·ture ['ledʒɪsləʃər] POL legislativo *m*

le·git·i·mate [lɪ'dʒɪtɪmət] *adj* legítimo

'leg room espacio *m* para las piernas

lei·sure ['liːʒər] ocio *m*; **I look forward to having more leisure** estoy deseando tener más tiempo libre; **do it at your leisure** tómate tu tiempo para hacerlo

'lei·sure cen·ter, *Br* 'lei·sure cen·tre centro *m* recreativo

lei·sure·ly ['liːʒəlɪ] *adj pace, lifestyle* tranquilo, relajado

'lei·sure time tiempo *m* libre

le·mon ['lemən] limón *m*

le·mon·ade [lemə'neɪd] limonada *f*

'le·mon juice zumo *m* de limón, *L.Am.* jugo de limón

'le·mon 'tea té *m* con limón

lend [lend] *v/t (pret & pp* **lent**) prestar

length [leŋθ] longitud *f*; *(piece: of material etc)* pedazo *m*; **at length** *describe, explain* detalladamente; *(finally)* finalmente

length·en ['leŋθən] *v/t* alargar

length·y ['leŋθɪ] *adj speech, stay* largo

le·ni·ent ['liːnɪənt] *adj* indulgente, poco severo

lens [lenz] *of camera* objetivo *m*, lente *f*; *of eyeglasses* cristal *m*; *of eye* cristalino *m*; *(contact lens)* lente *m* de contacto, *Span* lentilla *f*

'lens cov·er *of camera* tapa *f* del objetivo

Lent [lent] REL Cuaresma *f*

lent [lent] *pret & pp* → **lend**

len·til ['lentl] lenteja *f*

len·til 'soup sopa *f* de lentejas

Leo ['liːoʊ] Lco ASTR *m/f inv*

leop·ard ['lepərd] leopardo *m*

le·o·tard ['liːoʊtɑːrd] malla *f*

les·bi·an ['lezbɪən] **1** *n* lesbiana *f* **2** *adj* lésbico, lesbiano

less [les] *adv* menos; *eat / talk less* comer / hablar menos; *less interesting / serious* menos interesante / serio; *it costs less* cuesta menos; *less than $200* menos de 200 dólares

les·sen ['lesn] **1** *v/t* disminuir **2** *v/i* reducirse, disminuir

les·son ['lesn] lección *f*

let [let] *v/t (pret & pp* **let***) (allow)* dejar, permitir; *let s.o. do sth* dejar a alguien hacer algo; *let me go!* ¡déjame!; *let him come in!* ¡déjale entrar!; *let's go / stay* vamos / quedémonos; *let's not argue* no discutamos; *let alone* mucho menos; *let go of sth of rope, handle* soltar algo; *let go of me!* ¡suéltame!

◆ **let down** *v/t hair* soltarse; *blinds* bajar; *(disappoint)* decepcionar, defraudar; *dress, pants* alargar

◆ **let in** *v/t to house* dejar pasar

◆ **let off** *v/t (not punish)* perdonar; *from car* dejar; *the court let him off with a small fine* el tribunal sólo le impuso una pequeña multa

◆ **let out** *v/t of room, building* alquilar, *Mex* rentar; *jacket etc* agrandar; *groan, yell* soltar

◆ **let up** *v/i (stop)* amainar

le·thal ['liːθl] *adj* letal

le·thar·gic [lɪ'θɑːrdʒɪk] *adj* aletargado, apático

le·thar·gy ['leθərdʒɪ] sopor *m*, apatía *f*

let·ter ['letər] *of alphabet* letra *f*; *in mail* carta *f*

'let·ter·box buzón *m*

'let·ter·head *(heading)* membrete *m*; *(headed paper)* papel *m* con membrete

'let·ter of cred·it COM carta *f* de crédito

let·tuce ['letɪs] lechuga *f*

'let·up: *without a letup* sin interrupción

leu·ke·mia [luːˈkiːmɪə] leucemia *f*

lev·el ['levl] **1** *adj field, surface* nivelado,

llano; *in competition, scores* igualado; **draw level with s.o.** *in race* ponerse a la altura de alguien **2** *n on scale, in hierarchy, (amount)* nivel *m*; **on the level** F *(honest)* honrado

lev·el-head·ed [levl'hedɪd] *adj* ecuánime, sensato

le·ver ['liːvər] **1** *n* palanca *f* **2** *v/t*: **lever sth open** abrir algo haciendo palanca

lev·er·age ['liːvrɪdʒ] apalancamiento *m*; *(influence)* influencia *f*

lev·y ['levɪ] *v/t (pret & pp levied) taxes* imponer

lewd [luːd] *adj* obsceno

li·a·bil·i·ty [laɪə'bɪlətɪ] *(responsibility)* responsabilidad *f*; *(likeliness)* propensión *f* **(to** a)

li·a·ble ['laɪəbl] *adj (responsible)* responsable **(for** de); **be liable to** *(likely)* ser propenso a

◆ **li·ai·se with** [lɪ'eɪz] *v/t* actuar de enlace con

li·ai·son [lɪ'eɪzɑːn] *(contacts)* contacto *m*, enlace *m*

li·ar [laɪr] mentiroso(-a) *m(f)*

li·bel ['laɪbl] **1** *n* calumnia *f*, difamación *f* **2** *v/t* calumniar, difamar

lib·e·ral ['lɪbərəl] *adj (broad-minded)*, POL liberal; *(generous: portion etc)* abundante

lib·e·rate ['lɪbəreɪt] *v/t* liberar

lib·e·rat·ed ['lɪbəreɪtɪd] *adj* liberado

lib·e·ra·tion [lɪbə'reɪʃn] liberación *f*

lib·er·ty ['lɪbərtɪ] libertad *f*; **at liberty** *of prisoner etc* en libertad; **be at liberty to do sth** tener libertad para hacer algo

Li·bra ['liːbrə] ASTR Libra *m/f inv*

li·brar·i·an [laɪ'brerɪən] bibliotecario(-a) *m(f)*

li·bra·ry ['laɪbrerɪ] biblioteca *f*

Lib·y·a ['lɪbɪə] Libia

Lib·y·an ['lɪbɪən] **1** *adj* libio **2** *n* libio(-a) *m(f)*

lice [laɪs] *pl* → **louse**

li·cence *Br* → **license 1** *n*

li·cense ['laɪsns] **1** *n* permiso *m*, licencia *f* **2** *v/t* autorizar; **be licensed** tener permiso *or* licencia

'li·cense num·ber (número *m* de) matrícula *f*

'li·cense plate *of car* (placa *f* de) matrícula *f*

lick [lɪk] **1** *n* lamedura *f* **2** *v/t* lamer; **lick one's lips** relamerse

lick·ing ['lɪkɪŋ] F *(defeat)*: **we got a licking** nos dieron una paliza F

li·co·rice ['lɪkərɪs] regaliz *m*

lid [lɪd] *(top)* tapa *f*

lie[1] [laɪ] **1** *n* mentira *f* **2** *v/i* mentir

lie[2] [laɪ] *v/i (pret lay, pp lain) of person* estar tumbado; *of object* estar; *(be situated)* estar, encontrarse; **lie on your stomach** túmbate boca abajo

◆ **lie down** *v/i* tumbarse

'lie-in: **have a lie-in** quedarse un rato más en la cama

lieu [luː]: **in lieu of** en lugar de

lieu·ten·ant [luː'tenənt] teniente *m/f*

life [laɪf] *(pl lives* [laɪvz]*)* vida *f*; *of machine* vida *f*, duración *f*; **all her life** toda su vida; **that's life!** ¡así es la vida!

'life belt salvavidas *m inv*

'life-boat *from ship* bote *m* salvavidas; *from land* lancha *f* de salvamento

'life ex·pect·an·cy esperanza *f* de vida

'life·guard socorrista *m/f*

'life his·to·ry historia *f* de la vida

life im·pris·on·ment cadena *f* perpetua

'life jack·et chaleco *m* salvavidas

life·less ['laɪflɪs] *adj* sin vida

life·like ['laɪflaɪk] *adj* realista

'life·long de toda la vida

'life pre·serv·er salvavidas *m inv*

'life-sav·ing *adj medical equipment, drug* que salva vidas

'life-sized *adj* de tamaño natural

'life-threat·en·ing *adj* que puede ser mortal

'life·time vida *f*; **in my lifetime** durante mi vida

lift [lɪft] **1** *v/t* levantar **2** *v/i of fog* disiparse **3** *n (Br: elevator)* ascensor *m*; **give s.o. a lift** llevar a alguien (en coche)

◆ **lift off** *v/i of rocket* despegar

'lift-off *of rocket* despegue *m*

lig·a·ment ['lɪgəmənt] ligamento *m*

light[1] [laɪt] **1** *n* luz *f*; **in the light of** a la luz de; **have you got a light?** ¿tienes fuego? **2** *v/t (pret & pp lighted or lit) fire, cigarette* encender; *(illuminate)* iluminar **3** *adj color, sky* claro; *room* luminoso

light[2] [laɪt] **1** *adj (not heavy)* ligero **2** *adv*: **travel light** viajar ligero de equipaje

◆ **light up 1** *v/t (illuminate)* iluminar **2** *v/i (start to smoke)* encender un cigarrillo

'light bulb bombilla *f*

light·en[1] ['laɪtn] *v/t color* aclarar

light·en[2] ['laɪtn] *v/t load* aligerar

◆ **lighten up** *v/i of person* alegrarse; **come on, lighten up** venga, no te tomes las cosas tan en serio

light·er ['laɪtər] *for cigarettes* encendedor *m*, Span mechero *m*

light-head·ed [laɪt'hedɪd] *(dizzy)* mareado

light-'heart·ed [laɪt'hɑːrtɪd] *adj* alegre

'light·house faro *m*

light·ing ['laɪtɪŋ] iluminación *f*

light·ly ['laɪtlɪ] *adv touch* ligeramente; *get off lightly* salir bien parado

light·ness¹ ['laɪtnɪs] *of room, color* claridad *f*

light·ness² ['laɪtnɪs] *in weight* ligereza *f*

light·ning ['laɪtnɪŋ] un relámpago; *they were struck by lightning* les cayó un rayo

'light·ning con·duc·tor pararrayos *m inv*

'light pen lápiz *m* óptico

'light·weight *n in boxing* peso *m* ligero

'light year año *m* luz

like¹ [laɪk] **1** *prep* como; *be like s.o.* como alguien; *what is she like?* ¿cómo es?; *it's not like him* (*not his character*) no es su estilo **2** *conj* F (*as*) como; *like I said* como dije

like² [laɪk] *v/t*: *I like it / her* me gusta; *I would like ...* querría ...; *I would like to ...* me gustaría ...; *would you like ...?* ¿querrías ...?; *would you like to ...?* ¿querrías ...?; *she likes to swim* le gusta nadar; *if you like* si quieres

like·a·ble ['laɪkəbl] *adj* simpático

like·li·hood ['laɪklɪhʊd] probabilidad *f*; *in all likelihood* con toda probabilidad

like·ly ['laɪklɪ] *adj* (*probable*) probable; *not likely!* ¡ni hablar!

like·ness ['laɪknɪs] (*resemblance*) parecido *m*

'like·wise ['laɪkwaɪz] *adv* igualmente; *pleased to meet you - likewise!* encantado de conocerle - ¡lo mismo digo!

lik·ing ['laɪkɪŋ] afición *f* (*for* a); *to your liking* a su gusto; *take a liking to s.o.* tomar cariño a alguien

li·lac ['laɪlək] *flower* lila *f*; *color* lila *m*

li·ly ['lɪlɪ] lirio *m*

li·ly of the 'val·ley lirio *m* de los valles

limb [lɪm] miembro *m*

lime¹ [laɪm] *fruit, tree* lima *f*

lime² [laɪm] *substance* cal *f*

lime'green *adj* verde lima

'lime·light *be in the limelight* estar en el candelero

lim·it ['lɪmɪt] **1** *n* límite *m*; *within limits* dentro de un límite; *be off limits of place* ser zona prohibida; *that's the limit!* F ¡es el colmo! F **2** *v/t* limitar

lim·i·ta·tion [lɪmɪ'teɪʃn] limitación *f*

lim·it·ed 'com·pa·ny sociedad *f* limitada

li·mo ['lɪmoʊ] F limusina *f*

lim·ou·sine ['lɪməziːn] limusina *f*

limp¹ [lɪmp] *adj* flojo

limp² [lɪmp] *n*: *he has a limp* cojea

line¹ [laɪn] *of text, on road, TELEC* línea *f*; *of trees* fila *f*, hilera *f*; *of people* fila *f*, cola *f*; *of business* especialidad *f*; *what line are you in?* ¿a qué te dedicas?; *the line is busy* está ocupado, *Span* está comunicando; *hold the line* no cuelgue; *draw the line at sth* no estar dispuesto a hacer algo; *line of inquiry* línea *f* de investigación; *line of reasoning* argumentación *f*; *stand in line* hacer cola; *in line with ...* (*conforming with*) en las mismas líneas que

line² [laɪn] *v/t* forrar

◆ **line up** *v/i* hacer cola

lin·e·ar ['lɪnɪər] *adj* lineal

lin·en ['lɪnɪn] *material* lino *m*; (*sheets etc*) ropa *f* blanca

lin·er ['laɪnər] *ship* transatlántico *m*

lines·man ['laɪnzmən] SP juez *m* de línea, linier *m*

lin·ger ['lɪŋgər] *v/i of person* entretenerse; *of pain* persistir

lin·ge·rie ['lænʒərɪ] lencería *f*

lin·guist ['lɪŋgwɪst] lingüista *m/f*; *she's a good linguist* se le dan bien los idiomas

lin·guis·tic [lɪŋ'gwɪstɪk] *adj* lingüístico

lin·ing ['laɪnɪŋ] *of clothes* forro *m*; *of brakes, pipe* revestimiento *m*

link [lɪŋk] **1** *n* (*connection*) conexión *f*; *between countries* vínculo *m*; *in chain* eslabón *m* **2** *v/t* conectar

◆ **link up** *v/i* encontrarse; TV conectar

li·on ['laɪən] león *m*

lip [lɪp] labio *m*

'lip·read *v/i* (*pret & pp* **lipread** [red]) leer los labios

'lip·stick barra *f* de labios

li·queur [lɪ'kjʊr] licor *m*

liq·uid ['lɪkwɪd] **1** *n* líquido *m* **2** *adj* líquido

liq·ui·date ['lɪkwɪdeɪt] *v/t assets* liquidar; F (*kill*) cepillarse a F

liq·ui·da·tion [lɪkwɪ'deɪʃn] liquidación *f*; *go into liquidation* ir a la quiebra

liq·ui·di·ty [lɪ'kwɪdɪtɪ] FIN liquidez *f*

liq·uid·ize ['lɪkwɪdaɪz] *v/t* licuar

liq·uid·iz·er ['lɪkwɪdaɪzər] licuadora *f*

liq·uor ['lɪkər] bebida *f* alcohólica

'liq·uor store tienda *f* de bebidas alcohólicas

lisp [lɪsp] **1** *n* ceceo *m* **2** *v/i* cecear

list [lɪst] **1** *n* lista *f* **2** *v/t* enumerar; COMPUT listar

lis·ten ['lɪsn] *v/i* escuchar; *I tried to persuade him, but he wouldn't listen* intenté convencerle, pero no me hizo ningún caso

◆ **listen in** *v/i* escuchar

◆ **listen to** *v/t radio, person* escuchar

lis·ten·er ['lɪsnər] *to radio* oyente *m/f*; *he's a good listener* sabe escuchar

list·ings mag·a·zine ['lɪstɪŋz] guía *f* de espectáculos

list·less ['lɪstlɪs] adj apático, lánguido
lit [lɪt] pret & pp → **light¹**
li·ter ['liːtər] litro m
lit·er·al ['lɪtərəl] adj literal
lit·er·al·ly ['lɪtərəlɪ] adv literalmente
lit·er·a·ry ['lɪtərerɪ] adj literario
lit·er·ate ['lɪtərət] adj culto; **be literate** saber leer y escribir
lit·er·a·ture ['lɪtrətʃər] literatura f; *about a product* folletos *mpl*, prospectos *mpl*
li·tre Br → **liter**
lit·ter ['lɪtər] basura f; *of animal* camada f
'lit·ter bas·ket papelera f
'lit·ter bin cubo m de la basura
lit·tle ['lɪtl] **1** adj pequeño; **the little ones** los pequeños **2** *n* poco *m*; **the little I know** lo poco que sé; **a little** un poco; **a little bread / wine** un poco de pan / vino; **a little is better than nothing** más vale poco que nada **3** adv: poco; **little by little** poco a poco; **a little better / bigger** un poco mejor / más grande; **a little before 6** un poco antes de las 6
live¹ [lɪv] *v/i* vivir
♦ live on **1** *v/t rice, bread* sobrevivir a base de **2** *v/i (continue living)* sobrevivir, vivir
♦ live up: *live it up* pasarlo bien
♦ live up to *v/t* responder a
♦ live with *v/t* cargar con
live² [laɪv] adj *broadcast* en directo; *ammunition* real; *wire* con corriente
live·li·hood ['laɪvlɪhʊd] vida f, sustento m; *earn one's livelihood* ganarse la vida
live·li·ness ['laɪvlɪnɪs] *of person, music* vivacidad f; *of debate* lo animado
live·ly ['laɪvlɪ] adj animado
liv·er ['lɪvər] MED, *food* hígado m
live·stock ['laɪvstɑːk] ganado m
liv·id ['lɪvɪd] adj *(angry)* enfurecido, furioso
liv·ing ['lɪvɪŋ] **1** adj vivo **2** vida f; *what do you do for a living?* ¿en qué trabajas?; *earn one's living* ganarse la vida; *standard of living* estándar m de vida
'liv·ing room sala f de estar, salón m
liz·ard ['lɪzərd] lagarto m
load [loʊd] **1** *n also* ELEC carga f; *loads of F* montones de F **2** *v/t car, truck, gun* cargar; *camera* poner el carrete a; COMPUT: *software* cargar (en memoria); *load sth onto sth* cargar algo en algo
load·ed ['loʊdɪd] adj F *(very rich)* forrado F; *(drunk)* como una cuba
loaf [loʊf] *n (pl loaves* [loʊvz]*)* pan m; *a loaf of bread* una barra de pan, un pan
♦ loaf about *v/i* F holgazanear F
loaf·er ['loʊfər] *shoe* mocasín m
loan [loʊn] **1** *n* préstamo m; *on loan* prestado **2** *v/t* prestar; *loan s.o. sth* prestar

algo a alguien
loathe [loʊð] *v/t* detestar, aborrecer
loath·ing ['loʊðɪŋ] odio m, aborrecimiento m
lob·by ['lɑːbɪ] *n in hotel, theater* vestíbulo m; POL lobby m, grupo m de presión
lobe [loʊb] *of ear* lóbulo m
lob·ster ['lɑːbstər] langosta f
lo·cal ['loʊkl] **1** adj local; *the local people* la gente del lugar; *I'm not local* no soy de aquí **2** *n: the locals* los del lugar; *are you a local?* ¿eres de aquí?
'lo·cal call TELEC llamada f local
lo·cal e'lec·tions *npl* elecciones *fpl* municipales
local 'gov·ern·ment administración f municipal
lo·cal·i·ty [loʊ'kælətɪ] localidad f
lo·cal·ly ['loʊkəlɪ] adv *live, work* cerca, en la zona; *it's well known locally* es muy conocido en la zona; *they are grown locally* son cultivados en la región
lo·cal 'pro·duce productos *mpl* del lugar
'lo·cal time hora f local
lo·cate [loʊ'keɪt] *v/t new factory etc* emplazar, ubicar; *(identify position of)* situar; *be located* encontrarse
lo·ca·tion [loʊ'keɪʃn] *(siting)* emplazamiento m; *(identifying position of)* localización f; *on location movie* en exteriores
lock¹ [lɑːk] *of hair* mechón m
lock² [lɑːk] **1** *n on door* cerradura f **2** *v/t door* cerrar (con llave)
♦ lock away *v/t* guardar bajo llave
♦ lock in *v/t person* encerrar; *I locked myself in* me quedé encerrado
♦ lock out *v/t of house* dejar fuera
♦ lock up *v/t in prison* encerrar
lock·er ['lɑːkər] taquilla f
'lock·er room vestuario m
lock·et ['lɑːkɪt] guardapelo m
lock·smith ['lɑːksmɪθ] cerrajero(-a) m(f)
lo·cust ['loʊkəst] langosta f
lodge [lɑːdʒ] **1** *v/t complaint* presentar **2** *v/i of bullet* alojarse
lodg·er ['lɑːdʒər] huésped m/f
loft [lɑːft] buhardilla f, desván m
loft·y ['lɑːftɪ] adj *heights, ideals* elevado
log [lɑːg] *n wood* tronco m; *written record* registro m
♦ log off *v/i (pret & pp logged)* salir
♦ log on *v/i* entrar
♦ log on to *v/t* entrar a
'log·book *captain's* cuaderno m de bitácora; *driver's* documentación f del vehículo
log 'cab·in cabaña f
log·ger·heads ['lɑːgərhedz]: *be at log-*

gerheads estar enfrentado

lo·gic ['lɑːdʒɪk] lógica f

lo·gic·al ['lɑːdʒɪkl] adj lógico

lo·gic·al·ly ['lɑːdʒɪklɪ] adv lógicamente

lo·gis·tics [lə'dʒɪstɪks] logística f

lo·go ['lougou] logotipo m

loi·ter ['lɔɪtər] v/i holgazanear

lol·li·pop ['lɑːlɪpɑːp] piruleta f

Lon·don ['lʌndən] Londres

lone·li·ness ['lounlɪnɪs] of person, place soledad f

lone·ly ['lounlɪ] adj person solo; place solitario

lon·er ['lounər] solitario(-a) m(f)

long[1] [lɔːŋ] **1** adj largo; it's a long way hay un largo camino; it's two feet long mide dos pies de largo; the movie is three hours long la película dura tres horas **2** adv mucho tiempo; don't be long no tardes mucho; 5 weeks is too long 5 semanas son mucho tiempo; will it take long? ¿llevará mucho tiempo?; that was long ago eso fue hace mucho tiempo; long before then mucho antes; before long al poco tiempo; we can't wait any longer no podemos esperar más tiempo; she no longer works here ya no trabaja aquí; so long as (provided) siempre que; so long! ¡hasta la vista!

long[2] [lɔːŋ] v/i: long for sth home echar en falta algo; change anhelar or desear algo; be longing to do sth anhelar or desear hacer algo

long-'dis·tance adj race de fondo; flight de larga distancia; a long-distance phone-call una llamada de larga distancia, una conferencia interurbana

lon·gev·i·ty [lɑːn'dʒevɪtɪ] longevidad f

long·ing ['lɔːŋɪŋ] n anhelo m, deseo m

lon·gi·tude ['lɑːŋgɪtuːd] longitud f

'long jump Br salto m de longitud

'long-range missile de largo alcance; forecast a largo plazo

long-sight·ed [lɔːŋ'saɪtɪd] adj hipermétrope

long-sleeved [lɔːŋ'sliːvd] adj de manga larga

'long-stand·ing adj antiguo

'long-term adj a largo plazo

'long wave RAD onda f larga

'long-wind·ed [lɔːŋ'wɪndɪd] adj prolijo

look [luk] **1** n (appearance) aspecto m; (glance) mirada f; give s.o./sth a look mirar a alguien / mirar algo; have a look at sth (examine) echar un vistazo a algo; can I have a look? ¿puedo echarle un vistazo?; can I have a look around? in shop etc ¿puedo echar un vistazo?; looks (beauty) atractivo m, guapura f **2**

v/i mirar; (search) buscar; (seem) parecer; you look tired / different pareces cansado / diferente; he looks about 25 aparenta 25 años; how do things look to you? ¿qué te parece cómo están las cosas?; that looks good tiene buena pinta

◆ **look after** v/t children cuidar (de); property, interests proteger

◆ **look ahead** v/i fig mirar hacia el futuro

◆ **look around 1** v/i mirar **2** v/t museum, city dar una vuelta por

◆ **look at** v/t mirar; (examine) estudiar; (consider) considerar; it depends how you look at it depende de cómo lo mires

◆ **look back** v/i mirar atrás

◆ **look down on** v/t mirar por encima del hombro a

◆ **look for** v/t buscar

◆ **look forward to** v/t estar deseando; I'm looking forward to the vacation tengo muchas ganas de empezar las vacaciones

◆ **look in on** v/t (visit) hacer una visita a

◆ **look into** v/t (investigate) investigar

◆ **look on 1** v/i (watch) quedarse mirando **2** v/t: look on s.o./sth as (consider) considerar a alguien / algo como

◆ **look onto** v/t garden, street dar a

◆ **look out** v/i through, from window etc mirar; (pay attention) tener cuidado; look out! ¡cuidado!

◆ **look out for** v/t buscar; (be on guard against) tener cuidado con

◆ **look out of** v/t window mirar por

◆ **look over** v/t translation revisar, repasar; house inspeccionar

◆ **look round** v/t museum, city dar una vuelta por

◆ **look through** v/t magazine, notes echar un vistazo a, hojear

◆ **look to** v/t (rely on): we look to you for help acudimos a usted en busca de ayuda

◆ **look up 1** v/i from paper etc levantar la mirada; (improve) mejorar; things are looking up las cosas están mejorando **2** v/t word, phone number buscar; (visit) visitar

◆ **look up to** v/t (respect) admirar

'look·out person centinela m, vigía m; be on the lookout for estar buscando

◆ **loom up** [luːm] v/i aparecer (out of de entre)

loon·y ['luːnɪ] **1** n F chalado(-a) m(f) F **2** adj F chalado F

loop [luːp] n bucle m

'loop·hole in law etc resquicio m or vacío m legal

loose [luːs] adj connection, button suelto; clothes suelto, holgado; morals disoluto, relajado; *wording* impreciso; **loose change** suelto *m*, *L.Am.* sencillo *m*; **loose ends** *of problem, discussion* cabos *mpl* sueltos

loose·ly ['luːslɪ] *adv* worded vagamente

loos·en ['luːsn] *v/t* collar, knot aflojar

loot [luːt] **1** *n* botín *m* **2** *v/i* saquear

loot·er ['luːtər] saqueador(a) *m(f)*

◆ **lop off** [lɑːp] *v/t* (*pret & pp* **lopped**) branch cortar; podar

lop·sid·ed [lɑːp'saɪdɪd] *adj* torcido; *balance of committee* desigual

Lord [lɔːrd] (*God*) Señor *m*

Lord's 'Prayer padrenuestro *m*

lor·ry ['lɔːrɪ] *Br* camión *m*

lose [luːz] **1** *v/t* (*pret & pp* **lost**) object, match perder **2** *v/i* (*pret & pp* **lost**) SP perder; *of clock* retrasarse; *I'm late* me he perdido; **get lost!** F ¡vete a paseo!

◆ **lose out** *v/i* salir perdiendo

los·er ['luːzər] perdedor(-a) *m(f)*; F *in life* fracasado(-a) *m(f)*

loss [lɑːs] pérdida *f*; **make a loss** tener pérdidas; *I'm at a loss what to say* no sé qué decir

lost [lɑːst] **1** *adj* perdido **2** *pret & pp* → **lose**

lost-and-'found, *Br* **lost 'prop·er·ty** (**office**) oficina *f* de objetos perdidos

lot [lɑːt]: **the lot** todo; **a lot (of), lots (of)** mucho, muchos; **a lot of books, lots of books** muchos libros; **a lot of butter, lots of butter** mucha mantequilla; **a lot better/easier** mucho mejor/más fácil

lo·tion ['loʊʃn] loción *f*

lot·te·ry ['lɑːtərɪ] lotería *f*

loud [laʊd] *adj* voice, noise fuerte; *music* fuerte, alto; *color* chillón

loud'speak·er altavoz *m*, *L.Am.* altoparlante *m*

lounge [laʊndʒ] *in house* salón *m*

◆ **lounge about** *v/i* holgazanear

'lounge suit traje *m* de calle

louse [laʊs] (*pl* **lice** [laɪs]) piojo *m*

lous·y ['laʊzɪ] *adj* F asqueroso F; *I feel lousy* me siento de pena F

lout [laʊt] gamberro *m*

lov·a·ble ['lʌvəbl] *adj* adorable, encantador

love [lʌv] **1** *n* amor *m*; *in tennis* nada *f*; *be in love* estar enamorado (**with** de); *I'm in love with you* estoy enamorado de ti; *fall in love* enamorarse (**with** de); *make love* hacer el amor; *make love to ...* hacer el amor con; *yes, my love* sí, amor *m*; **2** *v/t person, country, wine* amar; *she loves to watch tennis* le encanta ver tenis

'love af·fair aventura *f* amorosa

'love·life vida *f* amorosa

'love let·ter carta *f* de amor

love·ly ['lʌvlɪ] *adj* face, hair, color, tune precioso, lindo; *person, character* encantador; *holiday, weather, meal* estupendo; *we had a lovely time* no lo pasamos de maravilla

lov·er ['lʌvər] amante *m/f*

lov·ing ['lʌvɪŋ] *adj* cariñoso

lov·ing·ly ['lʌvɪŋlɪ] *adv* con cariño

low [loʊ] **1** *adj* bridge, salary, price, voice, quality bajo; *be feeling low* estar deprimido; *we're low on gas/tea* nos queda poca gasolina/té **2** *n in weather* zona *f* de bajas presiones, borrasca *f*; *in sales, statistics* mínimo *m*

low·brow ['loʊbraʊ] *adj* poco intelectual, popular

low·'cal·o·rie *adj* bajo en calorías

'low-cut *adj* dress escotado

low·er ['loʊər] *v/t* to the ground, hemline, price bajar; *flag* arriar; *pressure* reducir

'low-fat *adj* de bajo contenido graso

'low-key *adj* discreto, mesurado

'low·lands *npl* tierras *fpl* bajas

low·'pres·sure ar·e·a zona *f* de bajas presiones, borrasca *f*

'low sea·son temporada *f* baja

'low tide marea *f* baja

loy·al ['lɔɪəl] *adj* leal, fiel (**to** a)

loy·al·ly ['lɔɪəlɪ] *adv* lealmente, fielmente

loy·al·ty ['lɔɪəltɪ] lealtad *f* (**to** a)

loz·enge ['lɑːzɪndʒ] *shape* rombo *m*; *tablet* pastilla *f*

Ltd *abbr* (= **limited**) S.L. (= sociedad *f* limitada)

lu·bri·cant ['luːbrɪkənt] lubricante *m*

lu·bri·cate ['luːbrɪkeɪt] *v/t* lubricar

lu·bri·ca·tion [luːbrɪ'keɪʃn] lubricación *f*

lu·cid ['luːsɪd] *adj* (*clear, sane*) lúcido

luck [lʌk] suerte *f*; *bad luck* mala suerte; *hard luck!* ¡mala suerte!; *good luck!* ¡buena suerte!

◆ **luck out** *v/i* F tener mucha suerte

luck·i·ly ['lʌkɪlɪ] *adv* afortunadamente, por suerte

luck·y ['lʌkɪ] *adj* person, coincidence afortunado; *day, number* de la suerte; *you were lucky* tuviste suerte; *she's lucky to be alive* tiene suerte de estar con vida; *that's lucky!* ¡qué suerte!

lu·cra·tive ['luːkrətɪv] *adj* lucrativo

lu·di·crous ['luːdɪkrəs] *adj* ridículo

lug [lʌg] *v/t* (*pret & pp* **lugged**) arrastrar

lug·gage ['lʌgɪdʒ] equipaje *m*

luke·warm ['luːkwɔːrm] *adj* water tibio, templado; *reception* indiferente

lull [lʌl] **1** *n in storm, fighting* tregua *f*; *in conversation* pausa *f* **2** *v/t*: *lull s.o. into a*

false sense of security dar a alguien una falsa sensación de seguridad

lul·la·by ['lʌləbaɪ] canción *f* de cuna, nana *f*

lum·ba·go [lʌmˈbeɪgou] lumbago *m*

lum·ber ['lʌmbər] *n* (*timber*) madera *f*

lu·mi·nous ['luːmɪnəs] *adj* luminoso

lump [lʌmp] *n of sugar, earth* terrón *m*; (*swelling*) bulto *m*

◆ **lump together** *v/t* agrupar

lump 'sum pago *m* único

lump·y ['lʌmpɪ] *adj liquid, sauce* grumoso; *mattress* lleno de bultos

lu·na·cy ['luːnəsɪ] locura *f*

lu·nar ['luːnər] *adj* lunar

lu·na·tic ['luːnətɪk] *n* lunático(-a) *m(f)*, loco(-a) *m(f)*

lunch [lʌntʃ] *n* almuerzo *m*, comida *f*; ***have lunch*** almorzar, comer

'lunch box fiambrera *f*

'lunch break pausa *f* para el almuerzo

'lunch hour hora *f* del almuerzo

'lunch·time hora *f* del almuerzo

lung [lʌŋ] pulmón *m*

'lung can·cer cáncer *m* de pulmón

◆ **lunge at** [lʌndʒ] *v/t* arremeter contra

lurch [lɜːrtʃ] *v/i of drunk* tambalearse; *of ship* dar sacudidas

lure [lʊr] **1** *n* atractivo *m* **2** *v/t* atraer

lu·rid ['lʊrɪd] *adj color* chillón; *details* espeluznante

lurk [lɜːrk] *v/i of person* estar oculto, estar al acecho

lus·cious ['lʌʃəs] *adj fruit, dessert* jugoso, exquisito; F *woman, man* cautivador

lush [lʌʃ] *adj vegetation* exuberante

lust [lʌst] *n* lujuria *f*

lux·u·ri·ous [lʌgˈʒʊrɪəs] *adj* lujoso

lux·u·ri·ous·ly [lʌgˈʒʊrɪəslɪ] *adv* lujosamente

lux·u·ry ['lʌkʃərɪ] **1** *n* lujo *m* **2** *adj* de lujo

lymph gland ['lɪmfglænd] ganglio *m* linfático

lynch [lɪntʃ] *v/t* linchar

lyr·i·cist ['lɪrɪsɪst] letrista *m/f*

lyr·ics ['lɪrɪks] *npl* letra *f*

M

M [em] *abbr* (= **medium**) M (= talla *f* media)

MA [em'eɪ] *abbr* (= **Master of Arts**) Máster *m* en Humanidades

ma'am [mæm] señora *f*

mac [mæk] F (*mackintosh*) impermeable *m*

ma·chine [məˈʃiːn] **1** *n* máquina *f* **2** *v/t with sewing machine* coser a máquina; TECH trabajar a máquina

ma'chine gun *n* ametralladora *f*

ma·chine-'read·a·ble *adj* legible por *Span* el ordenador *or L.Am.* la computadora

ma·chin·e·ry [məˈʃiːnərɪ] (*machines*) maquinaria *f*

ma·chine trans'la·tion traducción *f* automática

ma·chis·mo [məˈkɪzmou] machismo *m*

mach·o ['mætʃou] *adj* macho

mack·in·tosh ['mækɪntɑːʃ] impermeable *m*

mac·ro ['mækrou] COMPUT macro *m*

mad [mæd] *adj* (*insane*) loco; F (*angry*) enfadado; *a mad idea* una idea disparatada; *be mad about* F estar loco por; *drive*

s.o. mad volver loco a alguien; *go mad* (*become insane*) volverse loco; F (*with enthusiasm*) volverse loco F; *like mad* F *run, work* como un loco F; *Pa got real mad when I told him* papá se puso hecho una furia cuando se lo conté

mad·den ['mædən] *v/t* (*infuriate*) sacar de quicio

mad·den·ing ['mædnɪŋ] *adj* exasperante

made [meɪd] *pret & pp →* **make**

'mad·house *fig* casa *f* de locos

mad·ly ['mædlɪ] *adv* como loco; *madly in love* locamente enamorado

'mad·man loco *m*

mad·ness ['mædnɪs] locura *f*

Ma·don·na [məˈdɑːnə] madona *f*

Ma·fi·a ['mɑːfɪə]: *the Mafia* la mafia

mag·a·zine [mægəˈziːn] (*printed*) revista *f*

mag·got ['mægət] gusano *m*

Ma·gi ['meɪdʒaɪ] REL: *the Magi* los Reyes Magos

ma·gic ['mædʒɪk] **1** *n* magia *f*; *as if by magic, like magic* como por arte de magia **2** *adj* mágico; *there's nothing magic about it* no tiene nada de mágico

mag·i·cal ['mædʒɪkl] *adj* mágico

ma·gi·cian [mə'dʒɪʃn] *performer* mago(-a) *m(f)*

ma·gic 'spell hechizo *m*

ma·gic 'trick truco *m* de magia

ma·gic 'wand varita *f* mágica

mag·nan·i·mous [mæg'nænɪməs] *adj* magnánimo

mag·net ['mægnɪt] imán *m*

mag·net·ic [mæg'netɪk] *adj* magnético; *fig: personality* cautivador

mag·net·ic 'stripe banda *f* magnética

mag·net·ism ['mægnɪtɪzm] *of person* magnetismo *m*

mag·nif·i·cence [mæg'nɪfɪsəns] magnificencia *f*

mag·nif·i·cent [mæg'nɪfɪsənt] *adj* magnífico

mag·ni·fy ['mægnɪfaɪ] *v/t* (*pret & pp* **magnified**) aumentar; *difficulties* magnificar

mag·ni·fy·ing glass lupa *f*

mag·ni·tude ['mægnɪtuːd] magnitud *f*

ma·hog·a·ny [mə'hɑːɡənɪ] caoba *f*

maid [meɪd] (*servant*) criada *f*; *in hotel* camarera *f*

'maid·en name ['meɪdn] apellido *m* de soltera

maid·en 'voy·age viaje *m* inaugural

mail [meɪl] **1** *n* correo *m*; *put sth in the mail* echar algo al correo **2** *v/t letter* enviar (por correo)

'mail·box *also* COMPUT buzón *m*

'mail·ing list lista *f* de direcciones

'mail·man cartero *m*

'mail·or·der cat·a·log, *Br* **mail·'or·der cat·a·logue** catálogo *m* de venta por correo

mail·or·der firm empresa *f* de venta por correo

'mail·shot mailing *m*

maim [meɪm] *v/t* mutilar

main [meɪn] *adj* principal; *she's alive, that's the main thing* está viva, que es lo principal

'main course plato *m* principal

main 'en·trance entrada *f* principal

'main·frame *Span* ordenador *m* central, *L.Am.* computadora *f* central

'main·land tierra *f* firme; *on the mainland* en el continente

main·ly ['meɪnlɪ] *adv* principalmente

main 'road carretera *f* general

'main street calle *f* principal

main·tain [meɪn'teɪn] *v/t* mantener

main·te·nance ['meɪntənəns] mantenimiento *m*; *pay maintenance* pagar una pensión alimenticia

'main·te·nance costs *npl* gastos *mpl* de mantenimiento

'main·te·nance staff personal *m* de mantenimiento

ma·jes·tic [mə'dʒestɪk] *adj* majestuoso

ma·jes·ty ['mædʒestɪ] majestuosidad *f*; *Her Majesty* Su Majestad

ma·jor ['meɪdʒər] **1** *adj* (*significant*) importante, principal; *in C major* MUS en C mayor **2** *n* MIL comandante *m*

◆ **major in** *v/t* especializarse en

ma·jor·i·ty [mə'dʒɑːrətɪ] *also* POL mayoría *f*; *be in the majority* ser mayoría

make [meɪk] **1** *n* (*brand*) marca *f* **2** *v/t* (*pret & pp* **made**) hacer; *cars* fabricar, producir; *movie* rodar; *speech* pronunciar; (*earn*) ganar; MATH hacer; *two and two make four* dos y dos son cuatro; *make s.o. do sth* (*force to*) obligar a alguien a hacer algo; (*cause to*) hacer que alguien haga algo; *you can't make me do it!* ¡no puedes obligarme a hacerlo!; *make s.o. happy / angry* hacer feliz/enfadar a alguien; *make a decision* tomar una decisión; *make a telephone call* hacer una llamada telefónica; *made in Japan* hecho en Japón; *make it* (*catch bus, train*) llegar a tiempo; (*come*) ir; (*succeed*) tener éxito; (*survive*) sobrevivir; *what time do you make it?* ¿qué hora llevas?; *make believe* imaginarse; *make do with* conformarse con; *what do you make of it?* ¿qué piensas?

◆ **make for** *v/t* (*go toward*) dirigirse hacia

◆ **make off** *v/i* escaparse

◆ **make off with** *v/t* (*steal*) llevarse

◆ **make out** *v/t list* hacer, elaborar; *check* extender; (*see*) distinguir; (*imply*) pretender

◆ **make over** ceder

◆ **make up 1** *v/i of woman, actor* maquillarse; *after quarrel* reconciliarse **2** *v/t story, excuse* inventar; *face* maquillar; (*constitute*) suponer, formar; *be made up of* estar compuesto de; *make up one's mind* decidirse; *make it up after quarrel* reconciliarse

◆ **make up for** *v/t* compensar por

'make-be·lieve *n* ficción *f*, fantasía *f*

mak·er ['meɪkər] (*manufacturer*) fabricante *m*

make·shift ['meɪkʃɪft] *adj* improvisado

make·up ['meɪkʌp] (*cosmetics*) maquillaje *m*

'make-up bag bolsa *f* del maquillaje

mal·ad·just·ed [mælə'dʒʌstɪd] *adj* inadaptado

male [meɪl] **1** *adj* (*masculine*) masculino; *animal, bird, fish* macho; *male bosses* los jefes varones; *a male teacher* un profesor **2** *n man* hombre *m*, varón *m*; *ani-*

mal, bird, fish macho m

male 'chau·vin·ism machismo m

male chau·vin·ist 'pig machista m

male 'nurse enfermero m

ma·lev·o·lent [mə'levələnt] adj malévolo

mal·func·tion [mæl'fʌŋkʃn] 1 n un fallo m (in de) 2 v/i fallar

mal·ice ['mælɪs] malicia f

ma·li·cious [mə'lɪʃəs] adj malicioso

ma·lig·nant [mə'lɪgnənt] adj tumor maligno

mall [mɔːl] (shopping mall) centro m comercial

mal·nu·tri·tion [mælnuːˈtrɪʃn] desnutrición f

mal·treat [mælˈtriːt] v/t maltratar

mal·treat·ment [mælˈtriːtmənt] maltrato m

mam·mal ['mæml] mamífero m

mam·moth ['mæməθ] adj (enormous) gigantesco

man [mæn] 1 n (pl men [men]) hombre m; (humanity) el hombre; in checkers ficha f 2 v/t (pret & pp manned) telephones, front desk atender; spacecraft tripular

man·age ['mænɪdʒ] 1 v/t business dirigir; money gestionar; suitcase poder con; manage to ... conseguir ... 2 v/i (cope) arreglárselas

man·age·a·ble ['mænɪdʒəbl] adj (easy to handle) manejable; (feasible) factible

man·age·ment ['mænɪdʒmənt] (managing) gestión f, administración f; (managers) dirección f; under his management bajo su gestión

man·age·ment 'buy-out compra de una empresa por sus directivos

man·age·ment con'sult·ant consultor(a) m(f) en administración de empresas

'man·age·ment stud·ies estudios mpl de administración de empresas

'man·age·ment team equipo m directivo

man·ag·er ['mænɪdʒər] of hotel, company director(a) m(f); of shop, restaurant encargado(a) m(f)

man·a·ge·ri·al [mænɪˈdʒɪrɪəl] adj de gestión; a managerial post un puesto directivo

man·ag·ing di'rec·tor director(a) m(f) gerente

man·da·rin (or·ange) [mændərɪn/'ɔːrɪndʒ] mandarina f

man·date ['mændeɪt] (authority) mandato m; (task) tarea f

man·da·to·ry ['mændətɔːrɪ] adj obligatorio

mane [meɪn] of horse crines fpl

ma·neu·ver [mə'nuːvər] 1 n maniobra f 2 v/t maniobrar; she maneuvered him in-

to giving her the assignment consiguió convencerle para que le diera el trabajo

man·gle ['mæŋgl] v/t (crush) destrozar

man·han·dle ['mænhændl] v/t mover a la fuerza

man·hood ['mænhʊd] (maturity) madurez f; (virility) virilidad f

'man-hour hora-hombre f

'man·hunt persecución f

ma·ni·a ['meɪnɪə] (craze) pasión f

ma·ni·ac ['meɪnɪæk] F chiflado(-a) m(f) F

man·i·cure ['mænɪkjʊr] manicura f

man·i·fest ['mænɪfest] 1 adj manifiesto 2 v/t manifestar; manifest itself manifestarse

ma·nip·u·late [mə'nɪpjəleɪt] v/t person, bones manipular

ma·nip·u·la·tion [mənɪpjə'leɪʃn] of person, bones manipulación f

ma·nip·u·la·tive [mə'nɪpjələtɪv] adj manipulador

man'kind la humanidad

man·ly ['mænlɪ] adj (brave) de hombres, (strong) varonil

'man-made adj fibers, materials sintético, crater, structure artificial

man·ner ['mænər] of doing sth manera f, modo m; (attitude) actitud f

man·ners ['mænərz] npl modales mpl; good / bad manners buena / mala educación; have no manners ser un maleducado

ma·noeu·vre Br → maneuver

'man·pow·er (workers) mano f de obra; for other tasks recursos mpl humanos

man·sion ['mænʃn] mansión f

'man·slaugh·ter Br homicidio m sin premeditación

man·tel·piece ['mæntlpiːs] repisa f de chimenea

man·u·al ['mænjʊəl] 1 adj manual 2 n manual m

man·u·al·ly ['mænjʊəlɪ] adv a mano

man·u·fac·ture [mænjʊ'fæktʃər] 1 n fabricación f 2 v/t equipment fabricar

man·u·fac·tur·er [mænjʊ'fæktʃərər] fabricante m

man·u·fac·tur·ing [mænjʊ'fæktʃərɪŋ] adj industry manufacturero

ma·nure [mə'nʊr] estiércol m

man·u·script ['mænjʊskrɪpt] manuscrito m

man·y ['menɪ] 1 adj muchos; take as many apples as you like toma todas las manzanas que quieras; many times muchas veces; not many people / taxis no mucha gente / muchos taxis; too many problems / beers demasiados problemas / demasiadas cervezas 2 pron muchos; **a great many, a good many** muchos; **how many do you need?** ¿cuántos necesitas?; **as many as 200 are still missing** hay hasta 200 desaparecidos

'**man-year** año-hombre *m*

map [mæp] mapa *m*

◆ **map out** *v/t* (*pret & pp **mapped***) proyectar

ma·ple ['meɪpl] arce *m*

mar [mɑːr] *v/t* (*pret & pp **marred***) empañar

mar·a·thon ['mærəθɑːn] *race* maratón *m or f*

mar·ble ['mɑːrbl] *material* mármol *m*

March [mɑːrtʃ] marzo *m*

march [mɑːrtʃ] **1** *n* marcha *f* **2** *v/i* marchar

march·er ['mɑːrtʃər] manifestante *mf*

mare [mer] yegua *f*

mar·ga·rine [mɑːrdʒə'riːn] margarina *f*

mar·gin ['mɑːrdʒɪn] *also* COM margen *m*; **by a narrow margin** por un estrecho margen

mar·gin·al ['mɑːrdʒɪnl] *adj* (*slight*) marginal

mar·gin·al·ly ['mɑːrdʒɪnlɪ] *adv* (*slightly*) ligeramente

mar·i·hua·na, mar·i·jua·na [mærɪ'hwɑːnə] marihuana *f*

ma·ri·na [mə'riːnə] puerto *m* deportivo

mar·i·nade [mærɪ'neɪd] *n* adobo *m*

mar·i·nate ['mærɪneɪt] *v/t* adobar, marinar

ma·rine [mə'riːn] **1** *adj* marino **2** *n* MIL marine *m/f*, infante *m/f* de marina

mar·i·tal ['mærɪtl] *adj* marital

mar·i·tal 'sta·tus estado *m* civil

mar·i·time ['mærɪtaɪm] *adj* marítimo

mar·jo·ram ['mɑːrdʒərəm] mejorana *f*

mark¹ [mɑːrk] FIN marco *m*

mark² [mɑːrk] **1** *n* señal *f*, marca *f*; (*stain*) marca *f*, mancha *f*; (*sign, token*) signo *m*, señal *f*; (*trace*) señal *f*; EDU nota *f*; **leave one's mark** dejar huella **2** *v/t* (*stain*) manchar; EDU calificar; (*indicate, commemorate*) marcar **3** *v/i* of fabric mancharse

◆ **mark down** *v/t* goods rebajar

◆ **mark out** *v/t* with a line etc marcar; (*fig: set apart*) distinguir

◆ **mark up** *v/t* price subir; goods subir de precio

marked [mɑːrkt] *adj* (*definite*) marcado, notable

mark·er ['mɑːrkər] (*highlighter*) rotulador *m*

mar·ket ['mɑːrkɪt] **1** *n* mercado *m*; (*stock market*) bolsa *f*; **on the market** en el mercado **2** *v/t* comercializar

mar·ket·a·ble ['mɑːrkɪtəbl] *adj* comercializable

mar·ket e'con·o·my economía *f* de mercado

'**mar·ket for·ces** *npl* fuerzas *fpl* del mercado

'**mar·ket·ing** ['mɑːrkɪtɪŋ] marketing *m*

'**mar·ket·ing cam·paign** campaña *f* de marketing

'**mar·ket·ing de·part·ment** departamento *m* de marketing

'**mar·ket·ing mix** marketing mix *m*, *el producto, el precio, la distribución y la promoción*

'**mar·ket·ing strat·e·gy** estrategia *f* de marketing

mar·ket 'lead·er líder *m* del mercado

'**mar·ket·place** in town plaza *f* del mercado; for commodities mercado *m*

mar·ket re'search investigación *m* de mercado

mar·ket 'share cuota *f* de mercado

mark·up ['mɑːrkʌp] margen *m*

mar·ma·lade ['mɑːrməleɪd] mermelada *f* de naranja

mar·quee [mɑːr'kiː] carpa *f*

mar·riage ['mærɪdʒ] matrimonio *m*; event boda *f*

'**mar·riage cer·tif·i·cate** certificado *m* de matrimonio

mar·riage 'guid·ance coun·se·lor consejero(-a) *m(f)* matrimonial

mar·ried ['mærɪd] *adj* casado; **be married to ...** estar casado con ...

mar·ried 'life vida *f* matrimonial

mar·ry ['mærɪ] *v/t* (*pret & pp **married***) casarse con; of priest casar; **get married** casarse

marsh [mɑːrʃ] pantano *m*, ciénaga *f*

mar·shal ['mɑːrʃl] *n* in police jefe(-a) *m(f)* de policía; in security service miembro *m* del servicio de seguridad

marsh·mal·low [mɑːrʃ'mæloʊ] dulce de consistencia blanda

marsh·y ['mɑːrʃɪ] *adj* pantanoso

mar·tial arts [mɑːrʃl'ɑːrts] *npl* artes *fpl* marciales

mar·tial 'law ley *f* marcial

mar·tyr ['mɑːrtər] mártir *m/f*

mar·tyred ['mɑːrtərd] *adj* fig de mártir

mar·vel ['mɑːrvl] maravilla *f*

◆ **marvel at** *v/t* maravillarse de

mar·ve·lous, Br **mar·vel·lous** ['mɑːrvələs] *adj* maravilloso

Marx·ism ['mɑːrksɪzm] marxismo *m*

Marx·ist ['mɑːrksɪst] **1** *adj* marxista **2** *n* marxista *m/f*

mar·zi·pan ['mɑːrzɪpæn] mazapán *m*

mas·ca·ra [mæ'skærə] rímel *m*

mas·cot ['mæskət] mascota *f*

mas·cu·line ['mæskjʊlɪn] *adj* masculino

mas·cu·lin·i·ty [mæskjʊ'lɪnɪtɪ] (*virility*) masculinidad *f*

mash [mæʃ] *v/t* hacer puré de, majar

mashed po·ta·toes [mæʃt] *npl* puré m de patatas f, *L.Am.* majado

mask [mæsk] **1** *n* máscara f; *to cover mouth, nose* mascarilla f **2** *v/t feelings* enmascarar

'mask·ing tape cinta *f* adhesiva de pintor

mas·och·ism ['mæsəkɪzm] masoquismo *m*

mas·och·ist ['mæsəkɪst] masoquista *m/f*

ma·son ['meɪsn] cantero *m*

ma·son·ry ['meɪsnrɪ] albañilería *f*

mas·que·rade [mæskə'reɪd] **1** *n fig* mascarada f **2** *v/i*: *masquerade as* hacerse pasar por

mass¹ [mæs] **1** *n* (*great amount*) gran cantidad f; (*body*) masa f; *the masses* las masas; *masses of* F un montón de F **2** *v/i* concentrarse

mass² [mæs] REL misa *f*

mas·sa·cre ['mæsəkər] **1** *n* masacre f, matanza f; F *in sport* paliza f **2** *v/t* masacrar; F *in sport* dar una paliza a

mas·sage ['mæsɑːʒ] **1** *n* masaje m **2** *v/t* dar un masaje en; *figures* maquillar

'mas·sage par·lor, *Br* 'mas·sage parlour salón *m* de masajes

mas·seur [mæ'sɜːr] masajista *m*

mas·seuse [mæ'sɜːz] masajista *f*

mas·sive ['mæsɪv] *adj* enorme; *heart attack* muy grave

mass 'me·di·a *npl* medios *mpl* de comunicación

mass-pro'duce *v/t* fabricar en serie

mass pro'duc·tion fabricación *f* en serie

mast [mæst] *of ship* mástil m; *for radio signal* torre *f*

mas·ter ['mæstər] **1** *n of dog* dueño m, amo m; *of ship* patrón m; *be a master of* ser un maestro de **2** *v/t skill, language, situation* dominar

'mas·ter bed·room dormitorio *m* principal

'mas·ter key llave *f* maestra

mas·ter·ly ['mæstəlɪ] *adj* magistral

'mas·ter·mind **1** *n* cerebro m **2** *v/t* dirigir, organizar

Mas·ter of 'Arts Máster *m* en Humanidades

mas·ter of 'cer·e·mo·nies maestro *m* de ceremonias

'mas·ter·piece obra *f* maestra

'mas·ter's (de·gree) máster *m*

mas·ter·y ['mæstərɪ] dominio *m*

mas·tur·bate ['mæstərbeɪt] *v/i* masturbarse

mat [mæt] *for floor* estera f; *for table* salvamanteles *m inv*

match¹ [mætʃ] *for cigarette* cerilla f, fósforo *m*

match² [mætʃ] **1** *n* SP partido m; *in chess* partida f; *be no match for s.o.* no estar a la altura de alguien; *meet one's match* encontrar la horma de su zapato **2** *v/t* (*be the same as*) coincidir con; (*be in harmony with*) hacer juego con; (*equal*) igualar **3** *v/i of colors, patterns* hacer juego

'match·box caja *f* de cerillas

match·ing ['mætʃɪŋ] *adj* a juego

'match stick cerilla f, fósforo *m*

mate [meɪt] **1** *n of animal* pareja f; NAUT oficial m/f **2** *v/i* aparearse; *these birds mate for life* estas aves viven con la misma pareja toda la vida

ma·te·ri·al [mə'tɪrɪəl] **1** *n* (*fabric*) tejido m; (*substance*) material m; *materials* materiales *mpl* **2** *adj* material

ma·te·ri·al·ism [mə'tɪrɪəlɪzm] materialismo *m*

ma·te·ri·al·ist [mətɪrɪə'lɪst] materialista *m/f*

ma·te·ri·al·is·tic [mətɪrɪə'lɪstɪk] *adj* materialista

ma·te·ri·al·ize [mə'tɪrɪəlaɪz] *v/i* (*appear*) aparecer; (*come into existence*) hacerse realidad

ma·ter·nal [mə'tɜːrnl] *adj* maternal; *my maternal grandfather* mi abuelo materno

ma·ter·ni·ty [mə'tɜːrnətɪ] maternidad *f*

ma·ter·ni·ty dress vestido *m* premamá

ma·ter·ni·ty leave baja *m* por maternidad

ma·ter·ni·ty ward pabellón *m* de maternidad

math [mæθ] matemáticas *fpl*

math·e·mat·i·cal [mæθə'mætɪkl] *adj* matemático

math·e·ma·ti·cian [mæθəmə'tɪʃn] matemático(-a) *m(f)*

math·e·mat·ics [mæθ'mætɪks] matemáticas *fpl*

maths *Br* → math

mat·i·née ['mætɪneɪ] sesión *f* de tarde

ma·tri·arch ['meɪtrɪɑːrk] matriarca *f*

mat·ri·mo·ny ['mætrəmoʊnɪ] matrimonio *m*

matt [mæt] *adj* mate

mat·ter ['mætər] **1** *n* (*affair*) asunto m; PHYS materia f; *you're only making matters worse* sólo estás empeorando las cosas; *as a matter of course* automáticamente; *as a matter of fact* de hecho; *what's the matter?* ¿qué pasa?; *no matter what she says* diga lo que diga **2** *v/i* importar; *it doesn't matter* no importa

mat·ter-of-'fact *adj* tranquilo

mat·tress ['mætrɪs] colchón *m*

ma·ture [məˈtʃʊr] 1 *adj* maduro 2 *v/i of person* madurar; *of insurance policy etc* vencer

ma·tu·ri·ty [məˈtʃʊrətɪ] madurez *f*

maul [mɔːl] *v/t of lion, tiger* atacar; *of critics* destrozar

max·i·mize ['mæksɪmaɪz] *v/t* maximizar

max·i·mum ['mæksɪməm] 1 *adj* máximo; *it will cost $500 maximum* costará 500 dólares como máximo 2 *n* máximo *m*

May [meɪ] mayo *m*

may [meɪ] *v/aux ◇ possibility*: *it may rain* puede que llueva; *you may be right* puede que tengas razón; *it may not happen* puede que no ocurra

◆

◇ *permission* poder; *may I help / smoke?* ¿puedo ayudar / fumar?

may·be ['meɪbiː] *adv* quizás, tal vez

'May Day el Primero de Mayo

may·o, may·on·naise ['meɪoʊ, meɪə-ˈneɪz] mayonesa *f*

may·or [mer] alcalde *m*

maze [meɪz] laberinto *m*

MB *abbr* (= *megabyte*) MB (= megabyte *m*)

MBA [embiː'eɪ] *abbr* (= *Master of Business Administration*) MBA *m* (= Máster *m* en Administración de Empresas)

MBO [embiː'oʊ] *abbr* (= *management buyout*) compra de una empresa por sus directivos

MC [em'siː] *abbr* (= *master of ceremonies*) maestro *m* de ceremonias

MD [em'diː] *abbr* (= *Doctor of Medicine*) Doctor(a) *m(f)* en Medicina; (= *managing director*) director(a) *m(f)* gerente

me [miː] *pron direct & indirect object* me; *after prep* mí; *he knows me* me conoce; *he gave me the keys* me dio las llaves; *he sold it to me* me lo vendió; *this is for me* esto es para mí; *who do you mean? - me?* ¿a quién te refieres? - ¿a mí?; *with me* conmigo; *it's me* soy yo; *taller than me* más alto que yo

mead·ow ['medoʊ] prado *m*

mea·ger, *Br* mea·gre ['miːgər] *adj* escaso, exiguo

meal [miːl] comida *f*; *enjoy your meal* ¡que aproveche!

'meal·time hora *f* de comer

mean¹ [miːn] *adj with money* tacaño; (*nasty*) malo, cruel; *that was a mean thing to say* ha estado fatal que dijeras eso

mean² [miːn] 1 *v/t* (*pret & pp meant*) (*intend to say*) querer decir; (*signify*) querer decir, significar; *you weren't meant to hear that* no era mi intención que oyeras eso; *mean to do sth* tener la intención de hacer algo; *be meant for* ser para; *of remark* ir dirigido a; *doesn't it mean anything to you?* (*doesn't it matter?*) ¿no te importa para nada? 2 *v/i* (*pret & pp meant*): *mean well* tener buena intención

mean·ing ['miːnɪŋ] *of word* significado *m*

mean·ing·ful ['miːnɪŋfʊl] *adj* (*comprehensible*) con sentido; (*constructive*), *glance* significativo

mean·ing·less ['miːnɪŋlɪs] *adj* sin sentido

means [miːnz] *npl financial* medios *mpl*; (*nsg: way*) medio *m*; *a means of transport* un medio de transporte; *by all means* (*certainly*) por supuesto; *by all means check my figures* comprueba mis cifras, faltaría más; *by no means rich / poor* ni mucho menos rico / pobre; *by means of* mediante

meant [ment] *pret & pp →* *mean²*

mean·time ['miːntaɪm] 1 *adv* mientras tanto 2 *n*: *in the meantime* mientras tanto

mean·while ['miːnwaɪl] 1 *adv* mientras tanto 2 *n*: *in the meanwhile* mientras tanto

mea·sles ['miːzlz] *nsg* sarampión *m*

mea·sure ['meʒər] 1 *n* (*step*) medida *f*; *we've had a measure of success* (*certain amount*) hemos tenido cierto éxito 2 *v/t* medir 3 *v/i* medir

◆ *measure out v/t area, drink, medicine* medir; *sugar, flour, ingredients* pesar

◆ *measure up v/i* estar a la altura (*to* de)

mea·sure·ment ['meʒərmənt] medida *f*; *system of measurement* sistema *m* de medidas

meas·ur·ing jug ['meʒərɪŋ] jarra *m* graduada

'mea·sur·ing tape cinta *f* métrica

meat [miːt] carne *f*

'meat·ball albóndiga *f*

'meat·loaf masa de carne cocinada en forma de barra de pan que se come fría

me·chan·ic [mɪ'kænɪk] mecánico(-a) *m(f)*

me·chan·i·cal [mɪ'kænɪkl] *adj also fig* mecánico

me·chan·i·cal en·gi·neer ingeniero(-a) *m(f)* industrial

me·chan·i·cal en·gi·neer·ing ingeniería *f* industrial

me·chan·i·cal·ly [mɪ'kænɪklɪ] *adv also fig* mecánicamente

memorial

mech·a·nism ['mekənızm] mecanismo *m*

mech·a·nize ['mekənaız] *v/t* mecanizar

med·al ['medl] medalla *f*

med·a·list, *Br* med·al·list ['medəlıst] medallista *m/f*

med·dle ['medl] *v/i* entrometerse; **don't meddle with the TV** no enredes con la televisión

me·di·a ['mi:dıə] *npl:* **the media** los medios de comunicación

'me·di·a cov·er·age cobertura *f* informativa

'me·di·a e·vent acontecimiento *m* informativo

me·di·a 'hype revuelo *m* informativo

'me·di·a stud·ies ciencias *fpl* de la información

me·di·an strip [mi:dıən'strıp] mediana *f*

me·di·ate ['mi:dıeıt] *v/i* mediar

me·di·a·tion [mi:dı'eıʃn] mediación *f*

me·di·a·tor ['mi:dıeıtər] mediador(a) *m(f)*

med·i·cal ['medıkl] **1** *adj* médico **2** *n* reconocimiento *m* médico

'med·i·cal cer·tif·i·cate certificado *m* médico

'med·i·cal ex·am·i·na·tion reconocimiento *m* médico

'med·i·cal his·to·ry historial *m* médico

'med·i·cal pro·fes·sion profesión *f* médica; *(doctors)* médicos *mpl*

'med·i·cal re·cord ficha *m* médica

Med·i·care ['medıker] seguro de enfermedad para los ancianos en Estados Unidos

med·i·cat·ed ['medıkeıtıd] *adj* medicinal

med·i·ca·tion [medı'keıʃn] medicamento *m*, medicina *f*; **are you on any medication?** ¿está tomando algún medicamento?

me·di·ci·nal [mı'dısınl] *adj* medicinal

medi·cine ['medsən] *science* medicina *f*; *(medication)* medicina *f*, medicamento *m*

'med·i·cine cab·i·net botiquín *m*

med·i·e·val [medı'i:vl] *adj* medieval

me·di·o·ore [mi:dı'oukər] *adj* mediocre

me·di·oc·ri·ty [mi:dı'ɑ:krətı] *of work etc*, *person* mediocridad *f*

med·i·tate ['medıteıt] *v/i* meditar

med·i·ta·tion [medı'teıʃn] meditación *f*

Med·i·ter·ra·ne·an [medıtə'reınıən] **1** *adj* mediterráneo **2** *n:* **the Mediterranean** el Mediterráneo

me·di·um ['mi:dıəm] **1** *adj (average)* medio; *steak* a punto **2** *n size* talla *f* media; *(means)* medio *m*; *(spiritualist)* médium *m/f*

me·di·um-sized ['mi:dıəmsaızd] *adj* de tamaño medio

me·di·um 'term: *in the medium term* a medio plazo

'me·di·um wave RAD onda *f* media

med·ley ['medlı] *(assortment)* mezcla *f*

meek [mi:k] *adj* manso, dócil

meet [mi:t] **1** *v/t (pret & pp* **met)** *by appointment* encontrarse con, reunirse con; *by chance, of eyes* encontrarse con; *(get to know)* conocer; *(collect)* ir a buscar; *in competition* enfrentarse con; *(satisfy)* satisfacer; **meet a deadline** cumplir un plazo **2** *v/i (pret & pp* **met)** encontrarse; *in competition* enfrentarse; *of committee etc* reunirse; **have you two met?** ¿os conocíais? **3** *n SP* reunión *f*

meet·ing ['mi:tıŋ] *by chance* encuentro *m*; *of committee, in business* reunión *f*; **he's in a meeting** está reunido

'meet·ing place lugar *m* de encuentro

meg·a·byte ['megəbaıt] COMPUT megabyte *m*

mel·an·chol·y ['melənkəlı] *adj* melancólico

mel·low ['melou] **1** *adj* suave **2** *v/i of person* suavizarse, sosegarse

me·lo·di·ous [mı'loudıəs] *adj* melodioso

mel·o·dra·mat·ic [melədrə'mætık] *adj* melodramático

mel·o·dy ['melədı] melodía *f*

mel·on ['melən] melón *m*

melt [melt] **1** *v/i* fundirse, derretirse **2** *v/t* fundir, derretir

◆ melt away *v/i fig* desvanecerse

◆ melt down *v/t metal* fundir

melt·ing pot ['meltıŋpɑ:t] *fig* crisol *m*

mem·ber ['membər] miembro *m*

Mem·ber of 'Con·gress diputado(-a) *m(f)*

Mem·ber of 'Par·lia·ment *Br* diputado(-a) *m(f)*

mem·ber·ship ['membərʃıp] afiliación *f*; *(number of members)* número *m* de miembros; **he applied for membership of the club** solicitó ser admitido en el club

'mem·ber·ship card tarjeta *f* de socio

mem·brane ['membreın] membrana *f*

me·men·to [me'mentou] recuerdo *m*

mem·o ['memou] nota *f*

mem·oirs ['memwɑ:rz] *npl* memorias *fpl*

'mem·o pad bloc *m* de notas

mem·o·ra·ble ['memərəbl] *adj* memorable

me·mo·ri·al [mı'mɔ:rıəl] **1** *adj* conmemorativo **2** *n* monumento *m* conmemorativo

M

Me·mo·ri·al Day Día *f* de los Caídos

mem·o·rize ['memoraiz] *v/t* memorizar

mem·o·ry ['memori] *(recollection)* recuerdo *m*; *(power of recollection)*, COMPUT memoria *f*; **I have no memory of the accident** no recuerdo el accidente; **have a good / bad memory** tener buena / mala memoria; **in memory of** en memoria de

men [men] *pl* → **man**

men·ace ['menis] **1** *n (threat)* amenaza *f; person* peligro *m* **2** *v/t* amenazar

men·ac·ing ['menisiŋ] amenazador

mend [mend] **1** *v/t* reparar; *clothes* coser, remendar; *shoes* remendar **2** *n*: **be on the mend** *after illness* estar recuperándose

me·ni·al ['miːniəl] *adj* ingrato, penoso

men·in·gi·tis [menin'dʒaitis] meningitis *f*

men·o·pause ['menəpɔːz] menopausia *f*

'men's room servicio *m* de caballeros

men·stru·ate ['menstrueit] *v/i* menstruar

men·stru·a·tion [menstru'eiʃn] menstruación *f*

men·tal ['mentl] *adj* mental; F *(crazy)* chiflado F, pirado F

men·tal a'rith·me·tic cálculo *m* mental

men·tal 'cru·el·ty crueldad *f* mental

'men·tal hos·pi·tal hospital *m* psiquiátrico

men·tal 'ill·ness enfermedad *f* mental

men·tal·i·ty [men'tæləti] mentalidad *f*

men·tal·ly ['mentəli] *adv (inwardly)* mentalmente

men·tal·ly 'hand·i·capped *adj* con minusvalía psíquica

men·tal·ly 'ill *adj*: **be mentally ill** sufrir una enfermedad mental

men·tion ['menʃn] **1** *n* mención *f*; **she made no mention of it** no lo mencionó **2** *v/t* mencionar; **don't mention it** *(you're welcome)* no hay de qué

men·tor ['mentɔːr] mentor(a) *m(f)*

men·u ['menjuː] *for food*, COMPUT menú *m*

mer·ce·na·ry ['mɜːrsɪnəri] **1** *adj* mercenario **2** *n* MIL mercenario(-a) *m(f)*

mer·chan·dise ['mɜːrtʃəndaiz] mercancías *fpl, L.Am.* mercadería *f*

mer·chant ['mɜːrtʃənt] comerciante *m/f*

mer·chant 'bank *Br* banco *m* mercantil

mer·ci·ful ['mɜːrsɪfəl] *adj* compasivo, piadoso

mer·ci·ful·ly ['mɜːrsɪfəli] *adv (thankfully)* afortunadamente

mer·ci·less ['mɜːrsɪlɪs] *adj* despiadado

mer·cu·ry ['mɜːrkjuri] mercurio *m*

mer·cy ['mɜːrsi] clemencia *f*, compasión *f*; **be at s.o.'s mercy** estar a merced de alguien

mere [mir] *adj* mero, simple

mere·ly ['mirli] *adv* meramente, simplemente

merge [mɜːrdʒ] *v/i of two lines etc* juntarse, unirse; *of companies* fusionarse

merg·er ['mɜːrdʒər] COM fusión *f*

mer·it ['merit] **1** *n (worth)* mérito *m*; *(advantage)* ventaja *f*; **she got the job on merit** consiguió el trabajo por méritos propios **2** *v/t* merecer

mer·ry ['meri] *adj* alegre; **Merry Christmas!** ¡Feliz Navidad!

'mer·ry-go-round tiovivo *m*

mesh [meʃ] malla *f*

mess [mes] *(untidiness)* desorden *m*; *(trouble)* lío *m*; **I'm in a bit of a mess** estoy metido en un lío; **be a mess** *of room, desk* estar desordenado; *of hair* estar revuelto; *of situation, s.o.'s life* ser un desastre

◆ **mess about, mess around 1** *v/i* enredar **2** *v/t person* jugar con

◆ **mess around with** *v/t* enredar con; *s.o.'s wife* tener un lío con

◆ **mess up** *v/t room, papers* desordenar; *task* convertir en una chapuza; *plans, marriage* estropear, arruinar

mes·sage ['mesidʒ] *also of movie etc* mensaje *m*

mes·sen·ger ['mesindʒər] *(courier)* mensajero(-a) *m(f)*

mess·y ['mesi] *adj room, person* desordenado; *job* sucio; *divorce, situation* desagradable

met [met] *pret & pp* → **meet**

me·tab·o·lism [mə'tæbəlizm] metabolismo *m*

met·al ['metl] **1** *adj* metálico **2** *n* metal *m*

me·tal·lic [mi'tælik] *adj* metálico

met·a·phor ['metəfər] metáfora *f*

me·te·or ['miːtiɔːr] meteoro *m*

me·te·or·ic [miːti'ɑːrik] *adj fig* meteórico

me·te·or·ite ['miːtiərait] meteorito *m*

me·te·or·o·log·i·cal [miːtiərə'lɑːdʒikl] *adj* meteorológico

me·te·or·ol·o·gist [miːtiə'rɑːlədʒist] meteorólogo(-a) *m(f)*

me·te·or·ol·o·gy [miːtiə'rɑːlədʒi] meteorología *f*

me·ter[1] ['miːtər] *for gas, electricity* contador *m*; *(parking meter)* parquímetro *m*

me·ter[2] ['miːtər] *unit of length* metro *m*

'me·ter read·ing lectura *f* del contador

meth·od ['meθəd] método *m*

me·thod·i·cal [mi'θɑːdikl] *adj* metódico

me·thod·i·cal·ly [mi'θɑːdikli] *adv* metódicamente

me·tic·u·lous [mə'tikjuləs] *adj* meticuloso, minucioso

me·tre *Br* → **meter**[2]

met·ric ['metrɪk] *adj* métrico

me·trop·o·lis [mɪ'trɒpəlɪs] metrópolis *f*

met·ro·pol·i·tan [metrə'pɒlɪtən] *adj* metropolitano

mew [mjuː] → **miaow**

Mex·i·can ['meksɪkən] **1** *adj* mexicano, mejicano **2** *n* mexicano(-a) *m(f)*, mejicano(-a) *m(f)*

Mex·i·co ['meksɪkəʊ] México, Méjico

Mex·i·co 'Cit·y *n* Ciudad *f* de México, *Mex* México, *Mex* el Distrito Federal, *Mex* el D.F.

mez·za·nine (floor) ['mezəniːn] entresuelo *m*

mi·aow [mɪaʊ] **1** *n* maullido *m* **2** *v/i* maullar

mice [maɪs] *pl* → **mouse**

mick·ey mouse [mɪkɪ'maʊs] *adj P course, qualification* de tres al cuarto P

mi·cro·bi·ol·o·gy [maɪkrəʊbaɪ'ɒlədʒɪ] microbiología *f*

'mi·cro·chip microchip *m*

'mi·cro·cli·mate microclima *m*

mi·cro·cosm ['maɪkrəʊkɒzm] microcosmos *m inv*

'mi·cro·e·lec·tron·ics microelectrónica *f*

'mi·cro·film microfilm *m*

'mi·cro·or·gan·ism microorganismo *m*

'mi·cro·phone micrófono *m*

'mi·cro·pro·ces·sor microprocesador *m*

'mi·cro·scope microscopio *m*

mi·cro·scop·ic [maɪkrə'skɒpɪk] *adj* microscópico

'mi·cro·wave oven microondas *m inv*

mid·air [mɪd'er]: **in midair** en pleno vuelo

mid·day [mɪd'deɪ] mediodía *m*

mid·dle ['mɪdl] **1** *adj* del medio; **the middle child of five** el tercero de cinco hermanos **2** *n* medio *m*; **it's the middle of the night!** ¡estamos en plena noche!; **in the middle of** *floor, room* en medio de; *of period of time* a mitad *or* mediados de; **in the middle of winter** en pleno invierno; **be in the middle of doing sth** estar ocupado haciendo algo

'mid·dle-aged *adj* de mediana edad

'Mid·dle Ages *npl* Edad *f* Media

mid·dle 'class *adj* de clase media; **the middle class(es)** la clase media, las clases medias

Mid·dle 'East Oriente *m* Medio

'mid·dle·man intermediario *m*

mid·dle 'man·age·ment mandos *mpl* intermedios

mid·dle 'name segundo nombre *m*

'mid·dle·weight *boxer* peso *m* medio

mid·dling ['mɪdlɪŋ] *adj* regular

mid·field·er [mɪd'fiːldər] centrocampista *m/f*

midge [mɪdʒ] mosquito *m* (pequeño)

midg·et ['mɪdʒɪt] *adj* en miniatura

'mid·night ['mɪdnaɪt] medianoche *f*; **at midnight** a medianoche

'mid·sum·mer pleno verano *m*

'mid·way *adv*: **we'll stop for lunch midway** pararemos para comer a mitad de camino; **midway through the meeting** a mitad de la reunión

'mid·week *adv* a mitad de semana

'Mid·west Medio Oeste *m* (de Estados Unidos)

'mid·wife comadrona *f*

'mid·win·ter pleno invierno *m*

might[1] [maɪt] *v/aux* poder, ser posible que; **I might be late** puede *or* es posible que llegue tarde; **it might rain** puede *or* es posible que llueva; **it might never happen** puede *or* es posible que no ocurra nunca; **he might have left** a lo mejor se ha ido; **you might have told me!** ¡me lo podías haber dicho!

might[2] [maɪt] (*power*) poder *m*, fuerza *f*

might·y ['maɪtɪ] **1** *adj* poderoso **2** *adv* F (*extremely*) muy, cantidad de F

mi·graine ['miːɡreɪn] migraña *f*

mi·grant work·er ['maɪɡrənt] trabajador(a) *m(f)* itinerante

mi·grate [maɪ'ɡreɪt] *v/i* emigrar

mi·gra·tion [maɪ'ɡreɪʃn] emigración *f*

mike [maɪk] F micro *m* F

mild [maɪld] *adj weather, climate* apacible; *cheese, voice* suave; *curry* no muy picante; *person* afable, apacible

mil·dew ['mɪlduː] moho *m*

mild·ly ['maɪldlɪ] *adv say sth* con suavidad; *spicy* ligeramente; **to put it mildly** por no decir algo peor

mild·ness ['maɪldnɪs] *of weather, voice* suavidad *f*; *of person* afabilidad *f*

mile [maɪl] milla *f*; **be miles better / easier** F ser mil veces mejor / más fácil F

mile·age ['maɪlɪdʒ] millas *fpl* recorridas; **unlimited mileage** kilometraje *m* ilimitado

'mile·stone *fig* hito *m*

mil·i·tant ['mɪlɪtənt] **1** *adj* militante **2** *n* militante *m/f*

mil·i·ta·ry ['mɪlɪterɪ] **1** *adj* militar **2** *n*: **the military** el ejército, las fuerzas armadas

mil·i·ta·ry a'cad·e·my academia *f* militar

mil·i·ta·ry po'lice policía *f* militar

mil·i·tar·y 'serv·ice servicio *m* militar

mi·li·tia [mɪ'lɪʃə] milicia *f*

milk [mɪlk] **1** *n* leche *f* **2** *v/t* ordeñar

milk 'choc·o·late chocolate *m* con leche

'milk jug jarra *f* de leche

milk of mag'ne·sia leche *f* de magnesia

'milk·shake batido *m*

M

milky   452

'milk·y ['mɪlkɪ] adj with lots of milk con
mucha leche; made with milk con leche

Milk·y 'Way Vía f Láctea

mill [mɪl] for grain molino m; for textiles
fábrica f de tejidos

◆ mill about, mill around v/i pulular

mil·len·ni·um [mɪ'lenɪəm] milenio m

mil·li·gram, Br mil·li·gramme ['mɪlɪ-
græm] miligramo m

mil·li·me·ter, Br mil·li·me·tre ['mɪlɪmiː-
tər] milímetro m

mil·lion ['mɪljən] millón m

mil·lion·aire [mɪljə'ner] millonario(-a)
m(f)

mime [maɪm] v/t representar con gestos

mim·ic ['mɪmɪk] 1 n imitador(a) m(f) 2 v/t
(pret & pp mimicked) imitar

mince [mɪns] v/t picar

'mince·meat carne f picada

mince 'pie empanada de carne picada

mind [maɪnd] 1 n mente f; it's uppermost
in my mind es lo que más me preocupa;
it's all in your mind son imaginaciones
tuyas; be out of one's mind haber perdido el juicio; bear, keep sth in mind recordar; I've a good mind to ... estoy con-
siderando seriamente ...; change one's
mind cambiar de opinión; it didn't enter
my mind no se me ocurrió; give s.o. a
piece of one's mind cantarle a alguien
las cuarenta; make up one's mind decidirse; have something on one's mind
tener algo en la cabeza; keep one's
mind on sth concentrarse en algo 2 v/t
(look after) cuidar (de); (heed) prestar
atención a; I don't want what we do no
me importa lo que hagamos; do
you mind if I smoke?, do you mind
my smoking? ¿le importa que fume?;
would you mind opening the window?
¿le importaría abrir la ventana?; mind
the step! ¡cuidado con el escalón!; mind
your own business! ¡métete en tus
asuntos! 3 v/i: mind! ¡ten cuidado!; never mind! ¡no importa!; I don't mind
no me importa, me da igual

mind-bog·gling ['maɪndbɔːglɪŋ] adj increíble

mind·less ['maɪndlɪs] adj violence gratuito

mine¹ [maɪn] pron el mío, la mía; mine
are red los míos son rojos; that book
is mine eso libro es mío; a cousin of mine un primo mío

mine² [maɪn] 1 n for coal etc mina f 2 v/i:
mine for extraer

mine³ [maɪn] 1 n (explosive) mina f 2 v/t
minar

'mine·field MIL campo m de minas; fig

campo m minado

min·er ['maɪnər] minero(-a) m(f)

min·e·ral ['mɪnərəl] n mineral m

'min·e·ral wa·ter agua f mineral

'mine·sweep·er NAUT dragaminas m inv

min·gle ['mɪŋgl] v/i of sounds, smells mezclarse; at party alternar

min·i ['mɪnɪ] skirt minifalda f

min·i·a·ture ['mɪnɪtʃər] adj en miniatura

'min·i·bus microbús m

min·i·mal ['mɪnɪməl] adj mínimo

min·i·mal·ism ['mɪnɪməlɪzm] minimalis-
mo m

min·i·mize ['mɪnɪmaɪz] v/t risk, delay
minimizar, reducir al mínimo; (down-
play) minimizar, quitar importancia a

min·i·mum ['mɪnɪməm] 1 adj mínimo 2 n
mínimo m

min·i·mum 'wage salario m mínimo

min·ing ['maɪnɪŋ] minería f

'min·i·se·ries TV miniserie f

'min·i·skirt minifalda f

min·is·ter ['mɪnɪstər] POL ministro(-a)
m(f); REL ministro(-a) m(f), pastor(a)
m(f)

min·is·te·ri·al [mɪnɪ'stɪrɪəl] adj ministerial

min·is·try ['mɪnɪstrɪ] POL ministerio m

mink [mɪŋk] animal, fur visón m; coat
abrigo m de visón

mi·nor ['maɪnər] 1 adj problem, setback
menor, pequeño; operation, argument
de poca importancia; aches and pains
leve; in D minor MUS en D menor 2 n
LAW menor m/f de edad

mi·nor·i·ty [maɪ'nɑːrətɪ] minoría f; be in
the minority ser minoría

mint [mɪnt] n herb menta f; chocolate pastilla f de chocolate con sabor a menta;
hard candy caramelo m de menta

mi·nus ['maɪnəs] 1 n (minus sign) (signo
m de) menos m 2 prep menos; tempera-
tures of minus 18 temperaturas de 18
grados bajo cero

mi·nus·cule ['mɪnəskjuːl] adj minúsculo

min·ute¹ ['mɪnɪt] of time minuto m; in a
minute (soon) en un momento; just a
minute un momento

min·ute² [maɪ'njuːt] adj (tiny) diminuto,
minúsculo; (detailed) minucioso; in minute detail minuciosamente

'mi·nute hand ['mɪnɪt] minutero m

mi·nute·ly [maɪ'njuːtlɪ] adv in detail minuciosamente; (very slightly) mínima-
mente

min·utes ['mɪnɪts] npl of meeting acta(s)
f(pl)

mir·a·cle ['mɪrəkl] milagro m

mi·rac·u·lous [mɪ'rækjuləs] adj milagro-

M

so
mi·rac·u·lous·ly [mɪ'rækjʊləslɪ] *adv* milagrosamente

mi·rage ['mɪrɑ:ʒ] espejismo *m*

mir·ror ['mɪrər] **1** *n* espejo *m*; MOT (espejo *m*) retrovisor *m* **2** *v/t* reflejar

mis·an·thro·pist [mɪ'zænθrəpɪst] misántropo(-a) *m(f)*

mis·ap·pre·hen·sion [mɪsæprɪ'henʃn]: *be under a misapprehension* estar equivocado

mis·be·have [mɪsbə'heɪv] *v/i* portarse mal

mis·be·hav·ior, *Br* **mis·be·hav·iour** [mɪsbə'heɪvɪər] mal comportamiento *m*

mis·cal·cu·late [mɪs'kælkjʊleɪt] *v/t & v/i* calcular mal

mis·cal·cu·la·tion [mɪs'kælkjʊleɪʃn] error *m* de cálculo

mis·car·riage ['mɪskærɪdʒ] MED aborto *m* (espontáneo); *miscarriage of justice* error *m* judicial

mis·car·ry ['mɪskærɪ] *v/i* (*pret & pp mis-carried*) *of plan* fracasar

mis·cel·la·ne·ous [mɪsə'leɪnɪəs] *adj* diverso; *put it in the file marked "miscellaneous"* ponlo en la carpeta de "varios"

mis·chief ['mɪstʃɪf] (*naughtiness*) travesura *f*, trastada *f*

mis·chie·vous ['mɪstʃɪvəs] *adj* (*naughty*) travieso; (*malicious*) malicioso

mis·con·cep·tion [mɪskən'sepʃn] idea *f* equivocada

mis·con·duct [mɪs'kɑ:ndʌkt] mala conducta *f*

mis·con·strue [mɪskən'stru:] *v/t* malinterpretar

mis·de·mea·nor, *Br* **mis·de·mea·nour** [mɪsdə'mi:nər] falta *f*, delito *m* menor

mi·ser ['maɪzər] avaro(-a) *m(f)*

mis·e·ra·ble ['mɪzrəbl] *adj* (*unhappy*) triste, infeliz; *weather, performance* horroroso

mi·ser·ly ['maɪzərlɪ] *adj* person avaro; *a miserly $150* 150 míseros dólares

mis·e·ry ['mɪzərɪ] (*unhappiness*) tristeza *f*, infelicidad *f*; (*wretchedness*) miseria *f*

mis·fire [mɪs'faɪr] *v/i* of *joke, scheme* salir mal

mis·fit ['mɪsfɪt] *in society* inadaptado(-a) *m(f)*

mis·for·tune [mɪs'fɔ:rtʃən] desgracia *f*

mis·giv·ings [mɪs'gɪvɪŋz] *npl* recelo *m*, duda *f*

mis·guid·ed [mɪs'gaɪdɪd] *adj* person equivocado; *attempt, plan* desacertado

mis·han·dle [mɪs'hændl] *v/t* situation llevar mal

mis·hap ['mɪshæp] contratiempo *m*

mis·in·form [mɪsɪn'fɔ:rm] *v/t* informar mal

mis·in·ter·pret [mɪsɪn'tɜ:rprɪt] *v/t* malinterpretar

mis·in·ter·pre·ta·tion [mɪsɪntɜ:rprɪ'teɪʃn] mala interpretación *f*

mis·judge [mɪs'dʒʌdʒ] *v/t* person, situation juzgar mal

mis·lay [mɪs'leɪ] *v/t* (*pret & pp mislaid*) perder

mis·lead [mɪs'li:d] *v/t* (*pret & pp misled*) engañar

mis·lead·ing [mɪs'li:dɪŋ] *adj* engañoso

mis·man·age [mɪs'mænɪdʒ] *v/t* gestionar mal

mis·man·age·ment [mɪs'mænɪdʒmənt] mala gestión *f*

mis·match ['mɪsmætʃ]: *there's a mismatch between the two sets of figures* los dos grupos de cifras no se corresponden

mis·placed ['mɪspleɪst] *adj loyalty* inmerecido; *enthusiasm* inoportuno

mis·print ['mɪsprɪnt] errata *f*

mis·pro·nounce [mɪsprə'naʊns] *v/t* pronunciar mal

mis·pro·nun·ci·a·tion [mɪsprənʌnsɪ'eɪʃn] pronunciación *f* incorrecta

mis·read [mɪs'ri:d] *v/t* (*pret & pp mis-read* [red]) *word, figures* leer mal; *situation* malinterpretar

mis·rep·re·sent [mɪsreprɪ'zent] *v/t* deformar, tergiversar

miss¹ [mɪs]: *Miss Smith* la señorita Smith; *miss!* ¡señorita!

miss² [mɪs] **1** *n* sE fallo *m*; *give sth a miss* meeting, party etc no ir a algo **2** *v/t* target no dar en; *emotionally* echar de menos; *bus, train, airplane* perder; (*not notice*) pasar por alto; (*not be present at*) perderse; *I ducked and he missed me* me agaché y no me dio; *you just missed her* (*she's just left*) se acaba de marchar; *we must have missed the turnoff* nos hemos debido pasar el desvío; *you don't miss much!* ¡no se te escapa una!; *miss a class* faltar a una clase **3** *v/i* fallar

mis·shap·en [mɪs'ʃeɪpən] *adj* deforme

mis·sile ['mɪsəl] *arma f* arrojadiza; *weapon* misil *m*

miss·ing ['mɪsɪŋ] *adj* desaparecido; *be missing* of *person, plane* haber desaparecido; *the missing money* el dinero que falta

mis·sion ['mɪʃn] *task* misión *f*; *people* delegación *f*

mis·sion·a·ry ['mɪʃənrɪ] REL misionero(-a) *m(f)*

M

mis·spell [mɪsˈspel] *v/t* escribir incorrectamente

mist [mɪst] neblina *f*

◆ **mist over** *v/i of eyes* empañarse

◆ **mist up** *v/i of mirror, window* empañarse

mis·take [mɪˈsteɪk] **1** *n* error *m*, equivocación *f*; *make a mistake* cometer un error *or* una equivocación, equivocarse; *by mistake* por error *or* equivocación **2** *v/t* (*pret* **mistook**, *pp* **mistaken**) confundir; *mistake X for Y* confundir X con Y

mis·tak·en [mɪˈsteɪkən] *adj* erróneo, equivocado; *be mistaken* estar equivocado **2** *pp* → **mistake**

mis·ter [ˈmɪstər] → **Mr**

mis·took [mɪˈstʊk] *pret* → **mistake**

mis·tress [ˈmɪstrɪs] *lover* amante *f*, querida *f*; *of servant* ama *f*; *of dog* dueña *f*, ama *f*

mis·trust [mɪsˈtrʌst] **1** *n* desconfianza *f* (*of* en) **2** *v/t* desconfiar de

mist·y [ˈmɪstɪ] *adj weather* neblinoso; *eyes* empañado; *color* borroso

mis·un·der·stand [mɪsʌndərˈstænd] *v/t* (*pret & pp* **misunderstood**) entender mal

mis·un·der·stand·ing [mɪsʌndərˈstændɪŋ] (*mistake*) malentendido *m*; (*argument*) desacuerdo *m*

mis·use 1 *n* [mɪsˈjuːs] uso *m* indebido **2** *v/t* [mɪsˈjuːz] usar indebidamente

miti·gat·ing cir·cum·stances [ˈmɪtɪgeɪtɪŋ] *npl* circunstancias *fpl* atenuantes

mitt [mɪt] *in baseball* guante *m* de béisbol

mit·ten [ˈmɪtən] mitón *f*

mix [mɪks] **1** *n* (*mixture*) mezcla *f*; *cooking: ready to use* preparado *m* **2** *v/t* mezclar; *mix the flour in well* mezclar la harina bien; *cement* preparar **3** *v/i socially* relacionarse

◆ **mix up** *v/t* (*confuse*) confundir (*with* con); (*put in wrong order*) revolver, desordenar; *be mixed up emotionally* tener problemas emocionales; *of figures* estar confundido; *of papers* estar revuelto *or* desordenado; *be mixed up in* estar metido en; *get mixed up with* verse liado con

◆ **mix with** *v/t* (*associate with*) relacionarse con

mixed [mɪkst] *adj feelings* contradictorio; *reactions, reviews* variado

mixed 'mar·riage matrimonio *m* mixto

mix·er [ˈmɪksər] *for food* batidora *f*; *drink* refresco *m* (*para mezclar con bebida alcohólica*); *she's a good mixer* es muy sociable

mix·ture [ˈmɪkstʃər] mezcla *f*; *medicine*

preparado *m*

mix-up [ˈmɪksʌp] confusión *f*

moan [moʊn] **1** *n of pain* gemido *m* **2** *v/i in pain* gemir

mob [mɑːb] **1** *n* muchedumbre *f* **2** *v/t* (*pret & pp* **mobbed**) asediar, acosar

mo·bile [ˈmoʊbəl] **1** *adj person* con movilidad; (*that can be moved*) móvil; *she's a lot less mobile now* ahora tiene mucha menos movilidad **2** *n* móvil *m*

mo·bile 'home casa *f* caravana

mo·bile 'phone *Br* teléfono *m* móvil

mo·bil·i·ty [məˈbɪlətɪ] movilidad *f*

mob·ster [ˈmɑːbstər] gángster *m*

mock [mɑːk] **1** *adj* fingido, simulado; *mock-Tudor houses* casas de estilo Tudor simulado; *mock exams / elections* exámenes *mpl*/elecciones *fpl* de prueba **2** *v/t* burlarse de

mock·er·y [ˈmɑːkərɪ] (*derision*) burlas *fpl*; (*travesty*) farsa *f*

mock-up [ˈmɑːkʌp] (*model*) maqueta *f*, modelo *m*

mode [moʊd] (*form*), COMPUT modo *m*; *mode of transportation* medio *m* de transporte

mod·el [ˈmɑːdl] **1** *adj employee, husband* modélico, modelo; *model boat / plane* maqueta *f* de un barco / avión **2** *n miniature* maqueta *f*, modelo *m*; (*pattern*) modelo *m*; (*fashion model*) modelo *m/f*; *male model* modelo *m* **3** *v/t*: *model clothes* trabajar de modelo; *she models swimsuits* trabaja de modelo de bañadores **4** *v/i for designer* trabajar de modelo; *for artist, photographer* posar

mo·dem [ˈmoʊdem] módem *m*

mod·e·rate 1 *adj* [ˈmɑːdərət] moderado **2** *n* [ˈmɑːdərət] POL moderado(-a) *m(f)* **3** *v/t* [ˈmɑːdəreɪt] moderar

mod·e·rate·ly [ˈmɑːdərətlɪ] *adv* medianamente, razonablemente

mod·e·ra·tion [mɑːdəˈreɪʃn] (*restraint*) moderación *f*; *in moderation* con moderación

mod·ern [ˈmɑːdn] *adj* moderno; *in the modern world* en el mundo contemporáneo

mod·ern·i·za·tion [mɑːdənaɪˈzeɪʃn] modernización *f*

mod·ern·ize [ˈmɑːdənaɪz] **1** *v/t* modernizar **2** *v/i of business, country* modernizarse

mod·ern 'lan·guages *npl* lenguas *fpl* modernas

mod·est [ˈmɑːdɪst] *adj* modesto

mod·es·ty [ˈmɑːdɪstɪ] modestia *f*

mod·i·fi·ca·tion [mɑːdɪfɪˈkeɪʃn] modificación *f*

mod·i·fy ['mɑ:dɪfaɪ] *v/t* (*pret & pp modified*) modificar

mod·u·lar ['mɑ:dʊlər] *adj furniture* por módulos

mod·ule ['mɑ:duːl] módulo *m*

moist [mɔɪst] *adj* húmedo

moist·en ['mɔɪsn] *v/t* humedecer

mois·ture ['mɔɪstʃər] humedad *f*

mois·tur·iz·er ['mɔɪstʃəraɪzər] *for skin* crema *f* hidratante

mo·lar ['moʊlər] muela *f*, molar *m*

mo·las·ses [mə'læsɪz] *npl* melaza *f*

mold[1] [moʊld] *on food* moho *m*

mold[2] [moʊld] **1** *n* molde *m* **2** *v/t clay, character* moldear

mold·y ['moʊldɪ] *adj food* mohoso

mole [moʊl] *on skin* lunar *m*

mo·lec·u·lar [mə'lekjʊlər] *adj* molecular

mol·e·cule ['mɑ:lɪkjuːl] molécula *f*

mo·lest [mə'lest] *v/t child, woman* abusar sexualmente de

mol·ly·cod·dle ['mɑ:lɪkɑ:dl] *v/t* F mimar, consentir

mol·ten ['moʊltən] *adj* fundido

mom [mɑ:m] F mamá *f*

mo·ment ['moʊmənt] momento *m*; *at the moment* en estos momentos, ahora mismo; *for the moment* por el momento, por ahora

mo·men·tar·i·ly [moʊmən'terɪlɪ] *adv* (*for a moment*) momentáneamente; (*in a moment*) de un momento a otro

mo·men·ta·ry ['moʊməntrɪ] *adj* momentáneo

mo·men·tous [mə'mentəs] *adj* trascendental, muy importante

mo·men·tum [mə'mentəm] cobrar / perder impulso

mon·arch ['mɑ:nərk] monarca *m/f*

mon·ar·chy ['mɑ:nərkɪ] monarquía *f*

mon·as·tery ['mɑ:nəsterɪ] monasterio *m*

mo·nas·tic [mə'næstɪk] *adj* monástico

Mon·day ['mʌndeɪ] lunes *m inv*

mon·e·ta·ry ['mɑ:nɪterɪ] *adj* monetario

mon·ey ['mʌnɪ] dinero *m*; *he's making a lot of money* está ganando mucho dinero

'mon·ey belt faltriquera *f*

'mon·ey-lend·er prestamista *m/f*

'mon·ey mar·ket mercado *m* monetario

'mon·ey or·der giro *m* postal

mon·grel ['mʌŋɡrəl] perro *m* cruzado

mon·i·tor ['mɑ:nɪtər] **1** *n* COMPUT monitor *m* **2** *v/t* controlar

monk [mʌŋk] monje *m*

mon·key ['mʌŋkɪ] mono *m*; F *child* diablillo *m* F

◆ **monkey about with** *v/t* F enredar con

'mon·key wrench llave *f* inglesa

mon·o·gram ['mɑ:nəgræm] monograma *m*

mon·o·grammed ['mɑ:nəgræmd] con monograma

mon·o·log, *Br* **mon·o·logue** ['mɑ:nəlɑ:g] monólogo *m*

mo·nop·o·lize [mə'nɑ:pəlaɪz] *v/t* monopolizar

mo·nop·o·ly [mə'nɑ:pəlɪ] monopolio *m*

mo·not·o·nous [mə'nɑ:tənəs] *adj* monótono

mo·not·o·ny [mə'nɑ:tənɪ] monotonía *f*

mon·soon [mɑ:n'suːn] monzón *m*

mon·ster ['mɑ:nstər] *n* monstruo *m*

mon·stros·i·ty [mɑ:n'strɑ:sətɪ] monstruosidad *f*

mon·strous ['mɑ:nstrəs] *adj* (*frightening, huge*) monstruoso; (*shocking*) escandaloso

month [mʌnθ] mes *m*; *how much do you pay a month?* ¿cuánto pagas al mes?

month·ly ['mʌnθlɪ] **1** *adj* mensual **2** *adv* mensualmente **3** *n magazine* revista *f* mensual

mon·u·ment ['mɑ:nʊmənt] monumento *m*

mon·u·ment·al [mɑ:nʊ'mentl] *adj fig* monumental

mood [muːd] (*frame of mind*) humor *m*; (*bad mood*) mal humor *m*; *of meeting, country* atmósfera *f*; *be in a good / bad mood* estar de buen / mal humor; *I'm in the mood for a pizza* me apetece una pizza

mood·y ['muːdɪ] *adj* temperamental; (*bad-tempered*) malhumorado

moon [muːn] *n* luna *f*

'moon·light 1 *n* luz *f* de luna **2** *v/i* F estar pluriempleado irregularmente; *he's moonlighting as a barman* tiene un segundo empleo de camarero

'moon·lit *adj* iluminado por la luna

moor [mʊr] *v/t boat* atracar

moor·ing ['mʊrɪŋ] atracadero *m*

moose [muːs] alce *m* americano

mop [mɑ:p] **1** *n for floor* fregona *f*; *for dishes* estropajo *m* (*con mango*) **2** *v/t* (*pret & pp mopped*) *floor* fregar; *eyes, face* limpiar

◆ **mop up** *v/t* limpiar; MIL acabar con

mope [moʊp] *v/i* estar abatido

mor·al ['mɔ:rəl] **1** *adj* moral; *person, behavior* moralista **2** *n of story* moraleja *f*; *morals* moral *f*, moralidad *f*

mo·rale [mə'ræl] moral *f*

mo·ral·i·ty [mə'rælətɪ] moralidad *f*

mor·bid ['mɔ:rbɪd] *adj* morboso

more [mɔ:r] **1** *adj* más; *there are no more eggs* no quedan huevos; *some more*

M

tea? ¿más té?; **more and more stu-dents / time** cada vez más estudiantes / tiempo **2** *adv* más; **more important** más importante; **more often** más a menudo; **more and more** cada vez más; **more or less** más o menos; **once more** una vez más; **he paid more than \$100 for it** pagó más de 100 dólares por él; **he earns more than I do** gana más que yo; **I don't live there any more** ya no vivo allí **3** *pron* más; **do you want some more?** ¿quieres más?; **a little more** un poco más

more·o·ver [mɔːˈrouvər] *adv* además, lo que es más

morgue [mɔːrg] depósito *m* de cadáveres

morn·ing [ˈmɔːrnɪŋ] mañana *f*; **in the morning** por la mañana; **this morning** esta mañana; **tomorrow morning** mañana por la mañana; **good morning** buenos días

morn·ing 'sick·ness náuseas *fpl* matutinas (*típicas del embarazo*)

mo·ron [ˈmɔːrɑːn] F imbécil *m/f* F, subnormal *m/f* F

mo·rose [məˈrous] *adj* hosco, malhumorado

mor·phine [ˈmɔːrfiːn] morfina *f*

mor·sel [ˈmɔːrsl] pedacito *m*

mor·tal [ˈmɔːrtl] **1** *adj* mortal **2** *n* mortal *m/f*

mor·tal·i·ty [mɔːrˈtælətɪ] mortalidad *f*

mor·tar[1] [ˈmɔːrtər] MIL mortero *m*

mor·tar[2] [ˈmɔːrtər] (*cement*) mortero *m*, argamasa *f*

mort·gage [ˈmɔːrgɪdʒ] **1** *n* hipoteca *f*, préstamo *m* hipotecario **2** *v/t* hipotecar

mor·ti·cian [mɔːrˈtɪʃn] encargado(-a) *m(f)* de una funeraria

mor·tu·a·ry [ˈmɔːrtuerɪ] depósito *m* de cadáveres

mo·sa·ic [mouˈzeɪɪk] mosaico *m*

Mos·cow [ˈmɑːskau] Moscú

Mos·lem [ˈmuzlɪm] **1** *adj* musulmán **2** *n* musulmán(-ana) *m(f)*

mosque [mɑːsk] mezquita *f*

mos·qui·to [mɑːsˈkiːtou] mosquito *m*

moss [mɑːs] musgo *m*

moss·y [ˈmɑːsɪ] *adj* cubierto de musgo

most [moust] **1** *adj* la mayoría de **2** *adv* (*very*) muy, sumamente; **the most beautiful / interesting** el más hermoso / interesante; **that's the one I like most** ése es el que más me gusta; **most of all** sobre todo **3** *pron* la mayoría de; **I've read most of her novels** he leído la mayoría de sus novelas; **at (the) most** como mucho; **make the most of** aprovechar al máximo

most·ly [ˈmoustlɪ] *adv* principalmente, sobre todo

mo·tel [mouˈtel] motel *m*

moth [mɑːθ] mariposa *f* nocturna; (*clothes moth*) polilla *f*

'moth·ball bola *f* de naftalina

moth·er [ˈmʌðər] **1** *n* madre *f* **2** *v/t* mimar

'moth·er·board COMPUT placa *f* madre

'moth·er·hood maternidad *f*

Moth·er·ing 'Sun·day → **Mother's Day**

'moth·er-in-law (*pl* **mothers-in-law**) suegra *f*

moth·er·ly [ˈmʌðərlɪ] *adj* maternal

moth·er-of-'pearl nácar *m*

'Moth·er's Day Día *f* de la Madre

'moth·er tongue lengua *f* materna

mo·tif [mouˈtiːf] motivo *m*

mo·tion [ˈmouʃn] **1** *n* (*movement*) movimiento *m*; (*proposal*) moción *f*; **put, set things in motion** poner las cosas en marcha **2** *v/t*: **he motioned me forward** me indicó con un gesto que avanzara

mo·tion·less [ˈmouʃnlɪs] *adj* inmóvil

mo·ti·vate [ˈmoutɪveɪt] *v/t person* motivar

mo·ti·va·tion [moutɪˈveɪʃn] motivación *f*

mo·tive [ˈmoutɪv] motivo *m*

mo·tor [ˈmoutər] motor *m*

'mo·tor·bike moto *f*

'mo·tor·boat lancha *f* motora

'mo·tor·cade [ˈmoutəkeɪd] caravana *f*, desfile *m* de coches

'mo·tor·cy·cle motocicleta *f*

'mo·tor·cy·clist motociclista *m/f*

'mo·tor home autocaravana *f*

'mo·tor·ist [ˈmoutərɪst] conductor(a) *m(f)*, automovilista *m/f*

'mo·tor me·chan·ic mecánico(-a) *m(f)* (de automóviles)

'mo·tor rac·ing carreras *fpl* de coches

'mo·tor·scoot·er vespa®*f*

'mo·tor ve·hi·cle vehículo *m* de motor

'mo·tor·way *Br* autopista *f*

mot·to [ˈmɑːtou] lema *f*

mould *etc Br* → **mold[2]** *etc*

mound [maund] montículo *m*

mount [maunt] **1** *n* (*mountain*) monte *m*; (*horse*) montura *f*; **Mount McKinley** el Monte McKinley **2** *v/t steps* subir; *horse, bicycle, campaign, photo* montar en; *campaign, photo* montar **3** *v/i* aumentar, crecer

◆ **mount up** *v/i* acumularse

moun·tain [ˈmauntɪn] montaña *f*

'moun·tain bike bicicleta *f* de montaña

moun·tain·eer [mauntɪˈnɪr] montañero(-a) *m(f)*, alpinista *m/f*, *L.Am.* andinista *m/f*

moun·tain·eer·ing [maontɪˈnɪrɪŋ] montañismo *m*, alpinismo *m*, *L.Am.* andinismo *m*

moun·tain·ous ['maʊntɪnəs] *adj* montañoso

mount·ed po'lice ['maʊntɪd] policía *f* montada

mourn [mɔːrn] **1** *v/t* llorar **2** *v/i*: *mourn for s.o.* llorar la muerte de alguien

mourn·er ['mɔːrnər] doliente *m/f*

mourn·ful ['mɔːrnfəl] *adj voice, face* triste

mourn·ing ['mɔːrnɪŋ] luto *m*, duelo *m*; *be in mourning* estar de luto; *wear mourning* vestir de luto

mouse [maʊs] (*pl* **mice** [maɪs]) *also* COMPUT ratón *m*

'**mouse mat** COMPUT alfombrilla *f*

mous·tache → **mustache**

mouth [maʊθ] *of person* boca *f*; *of river* desembocadura *f*

mouth·ful ['maʊθfʊl] *of food* bocado *m*; *of drink* trago *m*

'**mouth·or·gan** armónica *f*

'**mouth·piece** *of instrument* boquilla *f*; (*spokesperson*) portavoz *m/f*

'**mouth·wash** enjuague *m* bucal, elixir *m* bucal

'**mouth·wa·ter·ing** *adj* apetitoso

move [muːv] **1** *n in chess, checkers* movimiento *m*; (*step, action*) paso *m*; (*change of house*) mudanza *f*; *make the first move* dar el primer paso; *get a move on!* F ¡espabílate! F; *don't make a move!* ¡ni te muevas! **2** *v/t object* mover; (*transfer*) trasladar; *emotionally* conmover; *move those papers out of your way* aparta esos papeles; *move house* mudarse de casa **3** *v/i* moverse; (*transfer*) trasladarse

◆ **move around** *v/i in room* andar; *from place to place* trasladarse, mudarse

◆ **move away** *v/i* alejarse, apartarse; (*move house*) mudarse

◆ **move in** *v/i to house, neighborhood* mudarse; *to office* trasladarse

◆ **move on** *v/i to another town* mudarse; *to another job* cambiarse; *to another subject* pasar a hablar de

◆ **move out** *v/i of house* mudarse; *of area* marcharse

◆ **move up** *v/i in league* ascender, subir; (*make room*) correrse

move·ment ['muːvmənt] *also organization*, MUS movimiento *m*

mov·ers ['muːvərz] *npl firm* empresa *f* de mudanzas; (*men*) empleados *mpl* de una empresa de mudanzas

mov·ie ['muːvɪ] película *f*; *go to a movie, the movies* ir al cine

mov·ie·go·er ['muːvɪgoʊər] aficionado(a) *m/f* al cine

'**mov·ie thea·ter** cine *m*, sala *f* de cine

mov·ing ['muːvɪŋ] *adj which can move*

movible; *emotionally* conmovedor

mow [moʊ] *v/t grass* cortar

◆ **mow down** *v/t* segar la vida de

mow·er ['moʊər] cortacésped *m*

MP [em'piː] *abbr* (= *Member of Parliament*) *Br* diputado(-a) *m(f)*; *abbr* (= *Military Policeman*) policía *m* militar

mph [empiː'eɪtʃ] *abbr* (= *miles per hour*) millas *fpl* por hora

Mr ['mɪstər] Sr.

Mrs ['mɪsɪz] Sra.

Ms [mɪz] Sra. (*casda o no casada*)

Mt *abbr* (= *Mount*) Monte *m*

much [mʌtʃ] **1** *adj* mucho; *so much money* tanto dinero; *as much ... as ...* tanto ... como **2** *adv* mucho; *I don't like him much* no me gusta mucho; *he's much more intelligent than ...* es mucho más inteligente que ...; *the house is much too large for one person* la casa es demasiado grande para una sola persona; *very much* mucho; *thank you very much* muchas gracias; *I love you very much* te quiero muchísimo; *too much* demasiado; *as much as ...* tanto ... como; *it may cost as much as half a million dollars* puede que haya malversado hasta medio millón de dólares; *I thought as much* eso es lo que pensaba **3** *pron* mucho; *what did she say? - nothing much* ¿qué dijo? - no demasiado

muck [mʌk] (*dirt*) suciedad *f*

mu·cus ['mjuːkəs] mocos *mpl*, mucosidad *f*

mud [mʌd] barro *m*

mud·dle ['mʌdl] **1** *n* lío *m* **2** *v/t person* liar; *you've got the story all muddled* te has hecho un lío con la *historia*

◆ **muddle up** *v/t* desordenar; (*confuse*) liar

mud·dy ['mʌdɪ] *adj* embarrado

mues·li ['mjuːzlɪ] muesli *m*

muf·fin ['mʌfɪn] magdalena *f*

muf·fle ['mʌfl] *v/t* ahogar, amortiguar

◆ **muffle up** *v/i* abrigarse

muf·fler ['mʌflər] MOT silenciador *m*

mug¹ [mʌg] *for tea, coffee* taza *f*; F (*face*) jeta F, *Span* careto *m* F

mug² [mʌg] *v/t* (*pret & pp* **mugged**) (*attack*) atracar

mug·ger ['mʌgər] atracador(a) *m(f)*

mug·ging ['mʌgɪŋ] atraco *m*

mug·gy ['mʌgɪ] *adj* bochornoso

mule [mjuːl] *animal* mulo/-a *m(f)*; (*slipper*) pantufla *f*

◆ **mull over** [mʌl] *v/t* reflexionar sobre

mul·ti·lat·er·al [mʌltɪ'lætərəl] *adj* POL multilateral

M

mul·ti·lin·gual [mʌltɪˈlɪŋgwəl] *adj* multilingüe

mul·ti·me·di·a [mʌltɪˈmiːdɪə] **1** *n* multimedia *f* **2** *adj* multimedia

mul·ti·na·tion·al [mʌltɪˈnæʃnl] **1** *adj* multinacional **2** *n* COM multinacional *f*

mul·ti·ple [ˈmʌltɪpl] *adj* múltiple

mul·ti·ple 'choice ques·tion pregunta *f* tipo test

mul·ti·ple scle·ro·sis [sklɪˈrəʊsɪs] esclerosis *f* múltiple

mul·ti·pli·ca·tion [mʌltɪplɪˈkeɪʃn] multiplicación *f*

mul·ti·ply [ˈmʌltɪplaɪ] **1** *v/t* (*pret & pp **multiplied***) multiplicar **2** *v/i* (*pret & pp **multiplied***) multiplicarse

mum·my [ˈmʌmɪ] *Br* mamá *f*

mum·ble [ˈmʌmbl] **1** *n* murmullo *m* **2** *v/t* farfullar **3** *v/i* hablar entre dientes

mumps [mʌmps] *nsg* paperas *fpl*

munch [mʌntʃ] **1** *v/t* mascar **2** *v/i* mascar

mu·ni·ci·pal [mjuːˈnɪsɪpl] *adj* municipal

mu·ral [ˈmjʊərəl] mural *m*

mur·der [ˈmɜːrdər] **1** *n* asesinato *m* **2** *v/t person* asesinar, matar; *song* destrozar

mur·der·er [ˈmɜːrdərər] asesino(-a) *m(f)*

mur·der·ous [ˈmɜːrdrəs] *adj rage, look* asesino

murk·y [ˈmɜːrkɪ] *adj water* turbio, oscuro; *fig* turbio

mur·mur [ˈmɜːrmər] **1** *n* murmullo *m* **2** *v/t* murmurar

mus·cle [ˈmʌsl] músculo *m*

mus·cu·lar [ˈmʌskjʊlər] *adj pain, strain* muscular; *person* musculoso

muse [mjuːz] *v/i* meditar, reflexionar

mu·se·um [mjuːˈzɪəm] museo *m*

mush·room [ˈmʌʃrʊm] **1** *n* seta *f*, hongo *m*; (*button mushroom*) champiñón *m* **2** *v/i* crecer rápidamente

mu·sic [ˈmjuːzɪk] música *f*; *in written form* partitura *f*

mu·sic·al [ˈmjuːzɪkl] **1** *adj* musical; *person* con talento para la música **2** *n* musical *m*

'mu·sic(·al) box caja *f* de música

mu·sic·al 'in·stru·ment instrumento *m* musical

mu·si·cian [mjuːˈzɪʃn] músico(-a) *m(f)*

mus·sel [ˈmʌsl] mejillón *m*

must [mʌst] *v/aux* ◇ *necessity* tener que, deber; *I must be on time* tengo que *or* debo llegar a la hora; *do you have to leave now? yes, I must* ¿tienes que marcharte ahora? - sí, debo marcharme; *I mustn't be late* no tengo que llegar tarde, no debo llegar tarde
◇ *probability* deber de; *it must be about 6 o'clock* deben de ser las seis; *they must have arrived by now* ya deben de haber llegado

mus·tache [məˈstæʃ] bigote *m*

mus·tard [ˈmʌstərd] mostaza *f*

must·y [ˈmʌstɪ] *adj room* que huele a humedad; *smell* a humedad

mute [mjuːt] *adj animal* mudo

mut·ed [ˈmjuːtɪd] *adj color* apagado; *criticism* débil

mu·ti·late [ˈmjuːtɪleɪt] *v/t* mutilar

mu·ti·ny [ˈmjuːtɪnɪ] **1** *n* motín *m* **2** *v/i* (*pret & pp **mutinied***) amotinarse

mut·ter [ˈmʌtər] *v/t & v/i* murmurar

mut·ton [ˈmʌtn] carnero *m*

mu·tu·al [ˈmjuːtʃʊəl] *adj* mutuo

muz·zle [ˈmʌzl] **1** *n of animal* hocico *m*; *for dog* bozal *m* **2** *v/t* poner un bozal a; *muzzle the press* amordazar a la prensa

my [maɪ] *adj* mi; *my house* mi casa; *my parents* mis padres

my·op·ic [maɪˈɒpɪk] *adj* miope

my·self [maɪˈself] *pron reflexive* me; *emphatic* yo mismo(-a); *when I saw myself in the mirror* cuando me vi en el espejo; *I saw it myself* lo vi yo mismo; *by myself* (*alone*) solo; (*without help*) yo solo, yo mismo

mys·te·ri·ous [mɪˈstɪrɪəs] *adj* misterioso

mys·te·ri·ous·ly [mɪˈstɪrɪəslɪ] *adv* misteriosamente

mys·te·ry [ˈmɪstərɪ] misterio *m*; *mystery (story)* relato *m* de misterio

mys·ti·fy [ˈmɪstɪfaɪ] *v/t* (*pret & pp **mystified***) dejar perplejo

myth [mɪθ] *also fig* mito *m*

myth·i·cal [ˈmɪθɪkl] *adj* mítico

my·thol·o·gy [mɪˈθɑːlədʒɪ] mitología *f*

N

nab [næb] *v/t (pret & pp **nabbed**)* F *(take for o.s.)* pescar F, agarrar

nag [næg] **1** *v/i (pret & pp **nagged**) of person* dar la lata **2** *v/t (pret & pp **nagged**)*: **nag s.o. to do sth** dar la lata a alguien para que haga algo

nag·ging ['nægɪŋ] *adj person* quejica; *doubt* persistente; *pain* continuo

nail [neɪl] *for wood* clavo *m*; *on finger, toe* uña *f*

'**nail clip·pers** *npl* cortaúñas *m inv*

'**nail file** lima *f* de uñas

'**nail pol·ish** esmalte *m* de uñas

'**nail pol·ish re·mov·er** quitaesmaltes *m inv*

'**nail scis·sors** *npl* tijeras *fpl* de manicura

'**nail var·nish** esmalte *m* de uñas

na·ïve [naɪˈiːv] *adj* ingenuo

naked ['neɪkɪd] *adj* desnudo; **to the naked eye** a simple vista

name [neɪm] **1** *n* nombre *m*; **what's your name?** ¿cómo te llamas?; **call s.o. names** insultar a alguien; **make a name for o.s.** hacerse un nombre **2** *v/t*: **they named him Ben** le llamaron Ben

◆ **name for** *v/t*: **name s.o. for s.o.** poner a alguien el nombre de alguien

name·ly ['neɪmlɪ] *adv* a saber

'**name·sake** tocayo(-a) *m(f)*; homónimo(-a) *m(f)*

'**name·tag** *on clothing etc* etiqueta *f*

nan·ny ['nænɪ] *n* niñera *f*

nap [næp] *n* cabezada *f*; **have a nap** echar una cabezada

nape [neɪp]: **nape of the neck** nuca *f*

nap·kin ['næpkɪn] *(table napkin)* servilleta *f*; *(sanitary napkin)* compresa *f*

nar·cot·ic [nɑːrˈkɑːtɪk] *n* narcótico *m*, estupefaciente *m*

nar·cot·ics a·gent agente *m/f* de la brigada de estupefacientes

nar·rate [nəˈreɪt] *v/t* narrar

nar·ra·tion [nəˈreɪʃn] *(telling)* narración *f*

nar·ra·tive ['nærətɪv] **1** *n (story)* narración *f* **2** *adj poem, style* narrativo

nar·ra·tor [nəˈreɪtər] narrador(a) *m(f)*

nar·row ['næroʊ] *adj street, bed, victory* estrecho; *views, mind* cerrado

nar·row·ly ['næroʊlɪ] *adv win* por poco; **narrowly escape sth** escapar por poco de algo

nar·row-mind·ed [næroʊˈmaɪndɪd] *adj* cerrado

na·sal ['neɪzl] *adj voice* nasal

nas·ty ['næstɪ] *adj person, smell* desagradable, asqueroso; *thing to say* malintencionado; *weather* horrible; *cut, wound* feo; *disease* serio

na·tion ['neɪʃn] nación *f*

na·tion·al ['næʃənl] **1** *adj* nacional **2** *n* ciudadano(-a) *m(f)*

na·tion·al 'an·them himno *m* nacional

na·tion·al 'debt deuda *f* pública

na·tion·al·ism ['næʃənəlɪzm] nacionalismo *m*

na·tion·al·i·ty [næʃəˈnælətɪ] nacionalidad *f*

na·tion·al·ize ['næʃənəlaɪz] *v/t industry etc* nacionalizar

na·tion·al 'park parque *m* nacional

na·tive ['neɪtɪv] **1** *adj* nativo; *native language* lengua *f* materna **2** *n* nativo(-a) *m(f)*, natural *m/f*; *tribesman* nativo(-a) *m(f)*, indígena *m/f*; *he's a native of New York* es natural de Nueva York

na·tive 'coun·try país *m* natal

na·tive 'speak·er hablante *m/f* nativo(-a)

NATO ['neɪtoʊ] *abbr (= North Atlantic Treaty Organization)* OTAN *f* (= Organización *f* del Tratado del Atlántico Norte)

nat·u·ral ['nætʃrəl] *adj* natural; *a natural blonde* una rubia natural

nat·u·ral 'gas gas *m* natural

nat·u·ral·ist ['nætʃrəlɪst] naturalista *m/f*

nat·u·ral·ize ['nætʃrəlaɪz] *v/t*: *become naturalized* naturalizarse, nacionalizarse

nat·u·ral·ly ['nætʃərəlɪ] *adv (of course)* naturalmente; *behave, speak con naturalidad; (by nature)* por naturaleza

nat·u·ral 'sci·ence ciencias *fpl* naturales

nat·u·ral 'sci·en·tist experto(-a) *m(f)* en ciencias naturales

na·ture ['neɪtʃər] naturaleza *f*

na·ture re'serve reserva *f* natural

naugh·ty ['nɔːtɪ] *adj* travieso, malo; *photograph, word etc* picante

nau·se·a ['nɔːzɪə] náusea *f*

nau·se·ate ['nɔːzɪeɪt] *v/t (fig: disgust)* dar náuseas a

nau·se·at·ing ['nɔːzɪeɪtɪŋ] *adj smell, taste* nauseabundo; *person* repugnante

nau·seous ['nɔːʃəs] *adj* nauseabundo; *feel nauseous* sentir náuseas

nau·ti·cal ['nɔːtɪkl] *adj* náutico

'**nau·ti·cal mile** milla *f* náutica

na·val ['neɪvl] *adj* naval

'**na·val base** base *f* naval

na·vel ['neɪvl] ombligo m

nav·i·ga·ble ['nævɪgəbl] adj river navegable

nav·i·gate ['nævɪgeɪt] v/i in ship, airplane, COMPUT navegar; in car hacer de copiloto

nav·i·ga·tion [nævɪ'geɪʃn] navegación f; in car direcciones fpl

nav·i·ga·tor ['nævɪgeɪtər] on ship oficial m de derrota; in airplane navegante m/f; in car copiloto m/f

na·vy ['neɪvɪ] armada f, marina f (de guerra)

na·vy 'blue 1 n azul m marino 2 adj azul marino

near [nɪr] 1 adv cerca; come a bit nearer acércate un poco más 2 prep cerca de; near the bank cerca del banco; do you go near the bank? ¿pasa cerca del banco? 3 adj cercano, próximo; the nearest bus stop la parada de autobús más cercana or próxima; in the near future en un futuro próximo

near·by [nɪr'baɪ] adv live cerca

near·ly ['nɪrlɪ] adv casi

near-sight·ed [nɪr'saɪtɪd] adj miope

neat [niːt] adj ordenado; whisky solo, seco; solution ingenioso; F (terrific) genial F, estupendo F

ne·ces·sar·i·ly ['nesəserəlɪ] adv necesariamente

ne·ces·sa·ry ['nesəserɪ] adj necesario, preciso; it is necessary to ... es necesario ..., hay que ...

ne·ces·si·tate [nɪ'sesɪteɪt] v/t exigir, hacer necesario

ne·ces·si·ty [nɪ'sesɪtɪ] (being necessary) necesidad f; (something necessary) necesidad f, requisito m imprescindible

neck [nek] cuello m

neck·lace ['neklɪs] collar m

'neck·line of dress escote m

'neck·tie corbata f

née [neɪ] adj de soltera

need [niːd] 1 n necesidad f; if need be si fuera necesario; in need necesitado; be in need of sth necesitar algo; there's no need to be rude / upset no hace falta ser grosero /que te enfades 2 v/t necesitar; you'll need to buy one tendrás que comprar uno; you don't need to wait no hace falta que esperes; I need to talk to you tengo que or necesito hablar contigo; need I say more? ¿hace falta que añada algo?

nee·dle ['niːdl] for sewing, injection, on dial aguja f

'nee·dle·work costura f

need·y ['niːdɪ] adj necesitado

neg·a·tive ['negətɪv] adj negativo; answer in the negative dar una respuesta negativa

ne·glect [nɪ'glekt] 1 n abandono m, descuido m 2 v/t garden, one's health descuidar, desatender; neglect to do sth no hacer algo

ne·glect·ed [nɪ'glektɪd] adj gardens abandonado, descuidado; author olvidado; feel neglected sentirse abandonado

neg·li·gence ['neglɪdʒəns] negligencia f

neg·li·gent ['neglɪdʒənt] adj negligente

neg·li·gi·ble ['neglɪdʒəbl] adj quantity, amount insignificante

ne·go·ti·a·ble [nɪ'goʊʃəbl] adj salary, contract negociable

ne·go·ti·ate [nɪ'goʊʃɪeɪt] 1 v/i negociar 2 v/t deal, settlement negociar; obstacles franquear, salvar; bend in road tomar

ne·go·ti·a·tion [nɪgoʊʃɪ'eɪʃn] negociación f; be under negotiation estar siendo negociado

ne·go·ti·a·tor [nɪ'goʊʃɪeɪtər] negociador(a) m(f)

Ne·gro ['niːgroʊ] negro(-a) m(f)

neigh [neɪ] v/i relinchar

neigh·bor ['neɪbər] vecino(-a) m(f)

neigh·bor·hood ['neɪbərhʊd] in town vecindario m, barrio m; in the neighborhood of ... fig alrededor de ...

neigh·bor·ing ['neɪbərɪŋ] adj house, state vecino, colindante

neigh·bor·ly ['neɪbərlɪ] adj amable

neigh·bour etc Br → neighbor etc

nei·ther ['niːðər] 1 adj ninguno; neither applicant was any good ninguno de los candidatos era bueno 2 pron ninguno(-a) m(f) 3 adv: neither ... nor ... ni ... ni 4 conj: neither do I yo tampoco; neither can I yo tampoco

ne·on light ['niːɑːn] luz f de neón

neph·ew ['nefjuː] sobrino m

nerd [nɜːrd] F petardo(-a) m(f)

nerve [nɜːrv] nervio m; (courage) valor m; (impudence) descaro m; it's bad for my nerves me pone de los nervios; get on s.o.'s nerves sacar de quicio a alguien

nerve-rack·ing ['nɜːrvrækɪŋ] adj angustioso, exasperante

ner·vous ['nɜːrvəs] adj person nervioso, inquieto; twitch nervioso; I'm nervous about meeting them la reunión con ellos me pone muy nervioso

ner·vous 'break·down crisis f inv nerviosa

ner·vous 'en·er·gy energía f

ner·vous·ness ['nɜːrvəsnɪs] nerviosismo m

ner·vous 'wreck manojo m de nervios

nerv·y ['nɜːrvɪ] adj (fresh) descarado

nest [nest] n nido m

nes·tle ['nesl] v/i acomodarse

net¹ [net] for fishing, tennis red f

net² [net] adj price, weight neto

net 'cur·tain visillo m

net 'pro·fit beneficio m neto

net·tle ['netl] ortiga f

'net·work of contacts, cells, COMPUT red f

neu·rol·o·gist [nʊəˈrɑːlədʒɪst] neurólogo(-a) m(f)

neu·ro·sis [nʊˈroʊsɪs] neurosis f inv

neu·rot·ic [nʊˈrɑːtɪk] adj neurótico

neu·ter ['nuːtər] v/t animal castrar

neu·tral ['nuːtrl] 1 adj country neutral; color neutro 2 n gear punto m muerto; in neutral en punto muerto

neu·tral·i·ty [nʊˈtrælətɪ] neutralidad f

neu·tral·ize ['nuːtrəlaɪz] v/t neutralizar

nev·er ['nevər] adv nunca; you're never going to believe this no te vas a creer esto; you never promised, did you? no llegaste a prometer, ¿verdad?

nev·er-'end·ing adj interminable

nev·er·the·less [nevərðəˈles] adv sin embargo, no obstante

new [nuː] adj nuevo; this system is still new to me todavía no me he hecho con este sistema; I'm new to the job soy nuevo en el trabajo; that's nothing new no es nada nuevo

'new·born adj recién nacido

new·com·er ['nuːkʌmər] recién llegado(-a) m(f)

new·ly ['nuːlɪ] adv (recently) recientemente, recién

new·ly weds [wedz] npl recién casados mpl

new 'moon luna f nueva

news [nuːz] nsg noticias fpl; on TV noticias fpl, telediario m; on radio noticias fpl; that's news to me no sabía eso

'news·a·gen·cy agencia f de noticias

'news·a·gent quiosquero(-a) m(f)

'news·cast TV noticias fpl, telediario m; on radio noticias fpl

'news·cast·er TV presentador(a) m(f) de informativos

'news flash flash m informativo, noticia f de última hora

'news·pa·per periódico m

'news·read·er TV etc presentador(a) m(f) de informativos

'news re·port reportaje m

'news·stand quiosco m

'news·ven·dor vendedor(a) m(f) de periódicos

'New Year año m nuevo; Happy New Year! ¡Feliz Año Nuevo!

New Year's 'Day Día m de Año Nuevo

New Year's 'Eve Nochevieja f

New York [jɔːrk] 1 adj neoyorquino 2 n: New York (City) Nueva York

New York·er ['jɔːrkər] n neoyorquino(-a) m(f)

New Zea·land ['ziːlənd] Nueva Zelanda

New Zea·land·er ['ziːləndər] neozelandés(-esa) m(f), neocelandés(-esa) m(f)

next [nekst] 1 adj in time próximo, siguiente; in space siguiente, de al lado; the next week la próxima semana, la semana que viene; the next week he came back again volvió a la semana siguiente; who's next? ¿quién es el siguiente? 2 adv luego, después; next, we're going to study ... a continuación, vamos a estudiar ...; next to (beside) al lado de; (in comparison with) en comparación con

next 'door 1 adj neighbor de al lado 2 adv live al lado

next of 'kin pariente m más cercano

nib·ble ['nɪbl] v/t mordisquear

Nic·a·ra·gua [nɪkəˈrɑːgwə] Nicaragua

Nic·a·ra·guan [nɪkəˈrɑːgwən] 1 adj nicaragüense 2 n nicaragüense m/f

nice [naɪs] adj trip, house, hair bonito, L.Am. lindo; person agradable, simpático; weather bueno, agradable; meal, food bueno, rico; be nice to your sister! ¡trata bien a tu hermana!; that's very nice of you es muy amable de tu parte

nice·ly ['naɪslɪ] adv written, presented bien; (pleasantly) amablemente

nice·ties ['naɪsɪtɪz] npl refinamientos fpl; social niceties cumplidos mpl

niche [niːʃ] in market hueco m, nicho m; (special position) hueco m

nick [nɪk] n (cut) muesca f, mella f; in the nick of time justo a tiempo

nick·el ['nɪkl] níquel m; (coin) moneda de cinco centavos

'nick·name n apodo m, mote m

niece [niːs] sobrina f

nig·gard·ly ['nɪgərdlɪ] adj amount, person mísero

night [naɪt] noche f; tomorrow night mañana por la noche; 11 o'clock at night las 11 de la noche; travel by night viajar de noche; during the night por la noche; stay the night quedarse a dormir; a room for 2 nights una habitación para 2 noches; work nights trabajar de noche; good night buenas noches; in the middle of the night en mitad de la noche

'night·cap drink copa f (tomada antes de ir a dormir)

'night·club club m nocturno, discoteca f

N

'night·dress camisón m
'night·fall: *at nightfall* al anochecer
'night flight vuelo m nocturno
'night-gown camisón m
night·ie ['naɪtɪ] camisón m
nigh·tin·gale ['naɪtɪŋgeɪl] ruiseñor m
'night·life vida f nocturna
night·ly ['naɪtlɪ] 1 *adj: a nightly event* algo que sucede todas las noches 2 *adv* todas las noches
'night·mare *also fig* pesadilla f
'night por·ter portero m de noche
'night school escuela f nocturna
'night shift turno m de noche
'night·shirt camisa f de dormir
'night-spot local m nocturno
'night·time: *at nighttime, in the nighttime* por la noche
nil [nɪl] *Br* cero
nim·ble ['nɪmbl] *adj* ágil
nine [naɪn] nueve
nine·teen [naɪn'ti:n] diecinueve
nine·teenth [naɪn'ti:nθ] n & *adj* decimonoveno
nine·ti·eth ['naɪntɪɪθ] n & *adj* nonagésimo
nine·ty ['naɪntɪ] noventa
ninth [naɪnθ] n & *adj* noveno
nip [nɪp] n (*pinch*) pellizco m; (*bite*) mordisco m
nip·ple ['nɪpl] pezón m
ni·tro·gen ['naɪtrədʒn] nitrógeno m
no [nou] 1 *adv* no 2 *adj: there's no coffee / tea left* no queda café / té; *I have no family / money* no tengo familia / dinero; *I'm no linguist / expert* no soy un lingüista / experto; *no smoking / parking* prohibido fumar / aparcar
no·bil·i·ty [nou'bɪlətɪ] nobleza f
no·ble ['noubl] *adj* noble
no·bod·y ['noubədɪ] *pron* nadie; *nobody knows* nadie lo sabe; *there was nobody at home* no había nadie en casa
nod [nɑːd] 1 n movimiento m de la cabeza 2 *v/i* (*pret & pp nodded*) asentir con la cabeza
◆ nod off *v/i* (*fall asleep*) quedarse dormido
no-hop·er [nou'houpər] F inútil m/f F
noise [nɔɪz] ruido m
nois·y ['nɔɪzɪ] *adj* ruidoso
nom·i·nal ['nɑːmɪnl] *adj amount* simbólico
nom·i·nate ['nɑːmɪneɪt] *v/t* (*appoint*) nombrar; *nominate s.o. for a post* (*propose*) proponer a alguien para un puesto
nom·i·na·tion [nɑːmɪ'neɪʃn] (*appointment*) nombramiento m; (*proposal*) nominación f; *who was your nomination?* ¿a quién propusiste?

nom·i·nee [nɑːmɪ'niː] candidato(-a) m(f)
non ... [nɑːn] no ...
non·al·co·hol·ic *adj* sin alcohol
non·a·ligned *adj* no alineado
non·cha·lant ['nɑːnʃələnt] *adj* despreocupado
non·com·mis·sioned 'of·fi·cer suboficial m/f
non·com'mit·tal *adj* person, response evasivo
non·de·script ['nɑːndɪskrɪpt] *adj* anodino
none [nʌn] *pron: none of the students* ninguno de los estudiantes; *none of the water* nada del agua; *there are none left* no queda ninguno; *there is none left* no queda nada
non·en·ti·ty nulidad f
none·the·less [nʌnðə'les] *adv* sin embargo, no obstante
non·ex'ist·ent *adj* inexistente
non'fic·tion no ficción f
non·(in)'flam·ma·ble *adj* incombustible, no inflamable
non·in·ter'fer·ence, non·in·ter'ven·tion no intervención f
non-'i·ron *adj shirt* que no necesita plancha
'no-no: *that's a no-no* F de eso nada
no-'non·sense *adj approach* directo
non'pay·ment impago m
non·pol'lut·ing *adj* que no contamina
non·res·i·dent n no residente m/f
non·re·turn·a·ble [nɑːnrɪ'tɜːrnəbl] *adj* no retornable
non·sense ['nɑːnsns] disparate m, tontería f; *don't talk nonsense* no digas disparates *or* tonterías; *nonsense, it's easy!* tonterías, ¡es fácil!
non'skid *adj tires* antideslizante
non'slip *adj surface* antideslizante
non'smok·er *person* no fumador(a) m(f)
non'stand·ard *adj* no estándar
non'stick *adj pans* antiadherente
non'stop 1 *adj flight, train* directo, sin escalas; *chatter* ininterrumpido 2 *adv fly, travel* directamente; *chatter, argue* sin parar
non'swim·mer: *be a nonswimmer* no saber nadar
non'u·nion *adj* no sindicado
non'vi·o·lence no violencia f
non'vi·o·lent *adj* no violento
noo·dles ['nuːdlz] *npl* tallarines *mpl* (chinos)
nook [nʊk] rincón m
noon [nuːn] mediodía m; *at noon* al mediodía
noose [nuːs] lazo m corredizo

nor [nɔːr] *conj* ni; **nor do I** yo tampoco, ni yo

norm [nɔːrm] norma *f*

nor·mal ['nɔːrml] *adj* normal

nor·mal·i·ty [nɔːr'mælətɪ] normalidad *f*

nor·mal·ize ['nɔːrməlaɪz] *v/t relationships* normalizar

nor·mal·ly ['nɔːrməlɪ] *adv* (*usually*) normalmente; (*in a normal way*) normalmente, con normalidad

north [nɔːθ] **1** *n* norte *m*; **to the north of** al norte de **2** *adj* norte **3** *adv travel* al norte; **north of** al norte de

North Am·er·i·ca América del Norte, Norteamérica

North Am·er·i·can **1** *n* norteamericano(-a) *m(f)* **2** *adj* norteamericano

north·east [nɔːθ'iːst] *n* noreste, noreste *m*

nor·ther·ly ['nɔːrðəlɪ] *adj* norte, del norte

nor·thern ['nɔːrðən] norteño, del norte

nor·thern·er ['nɔːrðənər] norteño(-a) *m(f)*

North Ko·re·a Corea del Norte

North Ko·re·an **1** *adj* norcoreano **2** *n* norcoreano(-a) *m(f)*

North Pole Polo *m* Norte

north·ward ['nɔːrðwərd] *adv travel* hacia el norte

north·west [nɔːrð'west] *n* noroeste *m*

Nor·way ['nɔːweɪ] Noruega

Nor·we·gian [nɔːr'wiːdʒn] **1** *adj* noruego **2** *n person* noruego(-a) *m(f)*; *language* noruego *m*

nose [nəuz] nariz *m*; *of animal* hocico *m*; **it was right under my nose!** ¡lo tenía delante de mis narices!

♦ nose about *v/i* F husmear

'nose·bleed: **have a nosebleed** sangrar por la nariz

nos·tal·gia [nɑːˈstældʒɪə] nostalgia *f*

nos·tal·gic [nɑːˈstældʒɪk] *adj* nostálgico

nos·tril ['nɑːstrəl] ventana *f* de la nariz

nos·y ['nəuzɪ] *adj* F entrometido

not [nɑːt] *adv* no; **not this one, that one** éste no, ése; **not now** ahora no; **not there** no allí; **not like that** así no; **not before Tuesday / next week** no antes del martes / de la próxima semana; **not for me, thanks** para mí no, gracias; **not a lot** no mucho; **it's not ready / allowed** no está listo / permitido; **I don't know** no lo sé; **I am not American** no soy americano; **he didn't help** no ayudó

no·ta·ble ['nəutəbl] *adj* notable

no·ta·ry ['nəutərɪ] notario(-a) *m(f)*

notch [nɑːtʃ] muesca *f*, mella *f*

note [nəut] *n written*, MUS nota *f*; **take notes** tomar notas; **take note of sth** prestar atención a algo

♦ note down *v/t* anotar

'note·book cuaderno *m*, libreta *f*; COMPUT *Span* ordenador *m* portátil, *L.Am.* computadora *f* portátil

not·ed ['nəutɪd] *adj* destacado

'note·pad bloc *m* de notas

'note·pa·per papel *m* de carta

noth·ing ['nʌθɪŋ] nada; **nothing but** sólo; **nothing much** no mucho; **for nothing** (*for free*) gratis; (*for no reason*) por nada; **I'd like nothing better** me encantaría

no·tice ['nəutɪs] **1** *n on bulletin board*, *in street* cartel *m*, letrero *m*; (*advance warning*) aviso *m*; *in newspaper* anuncio *m*; **at short notice** con poca antelación; **until further notice** hasta nuevo aviso; **give s.o. his / her notice** to quit job despedir a alguien; *to leave house* comunicar a alguien que tiene que abandonar la casa; **hand in one's notice** to employer presentar la dimisión; **four weeks' notice** cuatro semanas de preaviso; **take notice of sth** observar algo, prestar atención a algo; **take no notice of s.o. / sth** no hacer caso de alguien / algo **2** *v/t* notar, fijarse en

no·tice·a·ble ['nəutɪsəbl] *adj* apreciable, evidente

no·ti·fy ['nəutɪfaɪ] *v/t* (*pret & pp notified*) notificar, informar

no·tion ['nəuʃn] noción *f*, idea *f*

no·tions ['nəusnz] *npl* artículos *mpl* de costura

no·to·ri·ous [nəuˈtɔːrɪəs] *adj* de mala fama

nou·gat ['nuːgət] *especie de turrón*

nought [nɔːt] cero *m*

noun [naun] nombre *m*, sustantivo *m*

nour·ish·ing ['nʌrɪʃɪŋ] *adj* nutritivo

nour·ish·ment ['nʌrɪʃmənt] alimento *m*, alimentación *f*

nov·el ['nɑːvl] *n* novela *f*

nov·el·ist ['nɑːvlɪst] novelista *m/f*

nov·el·ty ['nɑːvltɪ] (*being new*) lo novedoso; (*something new*) novedad *f*

No·vem·ber [nəuˈvembər] noviembre *m*

nov·ice ['nɑːvɪs] principiante *m/f*

now [nau] *adv* ahora; **now and again**, **now and then** de vez en cuando; **by now** ya; **from now on** de ahora en adelante; **right now** ahora mismo; **just now** (*at this moment*) en este momento; (*a little while ago*) hace un momento; **now, now!** ¡vamos!, ¡venga!; **now, where did I put it?** ¿y ahora dónde lo he puesto?

now·a·days ['nauədeɪz] *adv* hoy en día

no·where ['nəuwer] *adv* en ningún lugar;

N

it's nowhere near finished no está acabado ni mucho menos; **he was nowhere to be seen** no se le veía en ninguna parte

noz·zle ['nɑːzl] boquilla f

nu·cle·ar ['nuːklɪər] adj nuclear

nu·cle·ar 'en·er·gy energía f nuclear

nu·cle·ar 'fis·sion fisión f nuclear

'nu·cle·ar-free adj desnuclearizado

nu·cle·ar 'phys·ics física f nuclear

nu·cle·ar 'pow·er energía f nuclear; POL potencia f nuclear

nu·cle·ar 'pow·er sta·tion central f nuclear

nu·cle·ar re'ac·tor reactor m nuclear

nu·cle·ar 'waste residuos mpl nucleares

nu·cle·ar 'weap·on arma f nuclear

nude [nuːd] **1** adj desnudo **2** n painting desnudo m; **in the nude** desnudo

nudge [nʌdʒ] v/t dar un toque con el codo a

nud·ist ['nuːdɪst] n nudista m/f

nui·sance ['nuːsns] incordio m, molestia f; **make a nuisance of o.s.** dar la lata; **what a nuisance!** ¡qué incordio!

nuke [nuːk] v/t F atacar con armas nucleares

null and 'void [nʌl] adj nulo y sin efecto

numb [nʌm] adj entumecido; emotionally insensible

num·ber ['nʌmbər] **1** n número m; **a number of people** un cierto número de personas **2** v/t (put a number on) numerar

numeral ['nuːmərəl] número m

nu·me·rate ['nuːmərət] adj que sabe sumar y restar

nu·me·rous ['nuːmərəs] adj numeroso

nun [nʌn] monja f

nurse [nɜːrs] enfermero(-a) m(f)

nur·se·ry ['nɜːrsərɪ] guardería f; for plants vivero m

'nur·se·ry rhyme canción f infantil

'nur·se·ry school parvulario m, jardín m de infancia

'nur·se·ry school teach·er profesor(a) m(f) de parvulario

nurs·ing ['nɜːrsɪŋ] enfermería f

'nurs·ing home for old people residencia f

nut [nʌt] nuez f; for bolt tuerca f; **nuts** (testicles) pelotas fpl F

'nut·crack·ers npl cascanueces m inv

nu·tri·ent ['nuːtrɪənt] n nutriente m

nu·tri·tion [nuː'trɪʃn] nutrición f

nu·tri·tious [nuː'trɪʃəs] adj nutritivo

nuts [nʌts] adj F (crazy) chalado F, pirado F; **be nuts about s.o.** estar coladito por alguien F

'nut·shell: in a nutshell en una palabra

nut·ty ['nʌtɪ] adj taste a nuez; F (crazy) chalado F, pirado F

ny·lon ['naɪlɑːn] **1** n nylon m **2** adj de nylon

O

oak [oʊk] tree, wood roble m

oar [ɔːr] remo m

o·a·sis [oʊ'eɪsɪs] (pl **oases** [oʊ'eɪsiːz]) also fig oasis m inv

oath [oʊθ] LAW, (swearword) juramento m; **on oath** bajo juramento

'oat·meal harina f de avena

oats [oʊts] npl copos mpl de avena

o·be·di·ence [oʊ'biːdɪəns] obediencia f

o·be·di·ent [oʊ'biːdɪənt] adj obediente

o·be·di·ent·ly [oʊ'biːdɪəntlɪ] adv obedientemente

o·bese [oʊ'biːs] adj obeso

o·bes·i·ty [oʊ'biːsɪtɪ] obesidad f

o·bey [oʊ'beɪ] v/t obedecer

o·bit·u·a·ry [ə'bɪtʊerɪ] n necrología f, obituario m

ob·ject¹ ['ɑːbdʒɪkt] n (thing) objeto m;

(aim) objetivo m; GRAM objeto m

ob·ject² [əb'dʒekt] v/i oponerse

◆ **object to** v/t oponerse a

ob·jec·tion [əb'dʒekʃn] objeción f

ob·jec·tio·na·ble [əb'dʒekʃnəbl] adj (unpleasant) desagradable

ob·jec·tive [əb'dʒektɪv] **1** adj objetivo **2** n objetivo m

ob·jec·tive·ly [əb'dʒektɪvlɪ] adv objetivamente

ob·jec·tiv·i·ty [əb'dʒektɪvətɪ] objetividad f

ob·li·ga·tion [ɑːblɪ'geɪʃn] obligación f; **be under an obligation to s.o.** tener una obligación para con alguien

ob·lig·a·to·ry [ə'blɪgətɔːrɪ] adj obligatorio

o·blige [ə'blaɪdʒ] v/t obligar; **much o-**

bliged! muy agradecido

o·blig·ing [əˈblaɪdʒɪŋ] *adj* atento, servicial

o·blique [əˈbliːk] **1** *adj reference* indirecto **2** *n in punctuation* barra *f* inclinada

o·blit·er·ate [əˈblɪtəreɪt] *v/t city* destruir, arrasar; *memory* borrar

o·bliv·i·on [əˈblɪvɪən] olvido *m*; *fall into oblivion* caer en el olvido

o·bliv·i·ous [əˈblɪvɪəs] *adj.* **be oblivious of sth** no ser consciente de algo

ob·long [ˈɑːblɒŋ] *adj* rectangular

ob·nox·ious [əbˈnɑːkʃəs] *adj person* detestable, odioso; *smell* repugnante

ob·scene [ɑːbˈsiːn] *adj* obsceno; *salary, poverty* escandaloso

ob·scen·i·ty [əbˈsenətɪ] obscenidad *f*

ob·scure [əbˈskjʊr] *adj* oscuro

ob·scu·ri·ty [əbˈskjʊrətɪ] oscuridad *f*

ob·ser·vance [əbˈzɜːrvns] *of festival* práctica *f*

ob·ser·vant [əbˈzɜːrvnt] *adj* observador

ob·ser·va·tion [ɑːbzəˈveɪʃn] *of nature, stars* observación *f*; *(comment)* observación *f*, comentario *m*

ob·ser·va·to·ry [əbˈzɜːrvətɔːrɪ] observatorio *m*

ob·serve [əbˈzɜːrv] *v/t* observar

ob·serv·er [əbˈzɜːrvər] observador(a) *m(f)*

ob·sess [ɑːbˈses] *v/t* obsesionar; *be obsessed by / with* estar obsesionado con / por

ob·ses·sion [ɑːbˈseʃn] obsesión *f*

ob·ses·sive [ɑːbˈsesɪv] *adj* obsesivo

ob·so·lete [ˈɑːbsəliːt] *adj* obsoleto

ob·sta·cle [ˈɑːbstəkl] obstáculo *m*

ob·ste·tri·cian [ɑːbstəˈtrɪʃn] obstetra *m/f*, tocólogo(-a) *m(f)*

ob·stet·rics [ɑːbˈstetrɪks] obstetricia *f*, tocología *f*

ob·sti·na·cy [ˈɑːbstɪnəsɪ] obstinación *f*

ob·sti·nate [ˈɑːbstɪnət] *adj* obstinado

ob·sti·nate·ly [ˈɑːbstɪnətlɪ] *adv* obstinadamente

ob·struct [əbˈstrʌkt] *v/t road* obstruir; *investigation, police* obstaculizar

ob·struc·tion [əbˈstrʌkʃn] *on road etc* obstrucción *f*

ob·struc·tive [əbˈstrʌktɪv] *adj behavior, tactics* obstruccionista

ob·tain [əbˈteɪn] *v/t* obtener, lograr

ob·tain·a·ble [əbˈteɪnəbl] *adj products* disponible

ob·tru·sive [əbˈtruːsɪv] *adj* molesto; *the plastic chairs are rather obtrusive* las sillas de plástico desentonan por completo

ob·tuse [əbˈtuːs] *adj fig* duro de mollera

ob·vi·ous [ˈɑːbvɪəs] *adj* obvio, evidente

ob·vi·ous·ly [ˈɑːbvɪəslɪ] *adv* obviamente; *obviously!* ¡por supuesto!

oc·ca·sion [əˈkeɪʒn] ocasión *f*

oc·ca·sion·al [əˈkeɪʒənl] *adj* ocasional, esporádico; *I like the occasional whisky* me gusta tomarme un whisky de vez en cuando

oc·ca·sion·al·ly [əˈkeɪʒnlɪ] *adv* ocasionalmente, de vez en cuando

oc·cult [əˈkʌlt] **1** *adj* oculto **2** *n*: *the occult* lo oculto

oc·cu·pant [ˈɑːkjupənt] ocupante *m/f*

oc·cu·pa·tion [ɑːkjuˈpeɪʃn] ocupación *f*

oc·cu·pa·tion·al 'ther·a·pist [ɑːkjuˈpeɪʃnl] terapeuta *m/f* ocupacional

oc·cu·pa·tion·al 'ther·a·py terapia *f* ocupacional

oc·cu·py [ˈɑːkjupaɪ] *v/t (pret & pp occupied)* ocupar

oc·cur [əˈkɜːr] *v/i (pret & pp occurred)* ocurrir, suceder; *it occurred to me that ...* se me ocurrió que ...

oc·cur·rence [əˈkʌrəns] acontecimiento *m*

o·cean [ˈoʊʃn] océano *m*

o·ce·a·nog·ra·phy [oʊʃnˈɑːgrəfɪ] oceanografía *f*

o'clock [əˈklɑːk]: *at five / six o'clock* a las cinco / seis

Oc·to·ber [ɑːkˈtoʊbər] octubre *m*

oc·to·pus [ˈɑːktəpəs] pulpo *m*

OD [oʊˈdiː] *v/i* **F OD on** *drug* tomar una sobredosis de

odd [ɑːd] *adj (strange)* raro, extraño; *(not even)* impar; *the odd one out* el bicho raro; *50 odd* cerca de 50

'odd·ball F bicho *m* raro F

odds [ɑːdz] *npl*: *be at odds with sth / s.o.* no concordar con algo / estar peleado con alguien; *the odds are 10 to one* las apuestas están en 10 a 1; *the odds are that ...* lo más probable es que ...; *against all the odds* contra lo que se esperaba

odds and 'ends *npl objects* cacharros *mpl*; *things to do* cosillas *fpl*

'odds-on *adj* favorito indiscutible

o·di·ous [ˈoʊdɪəs] *adj* odioso

o·dom·e·ter [oʊˈdɑːmətər] cuentakilómetros *m inv*

o·dor, *Br* **o·dour** [ˈoʊdər] olor *m*

of [ɑːv], [əv] *prep possession* de; *the name of the street / hotel* el nombre de la calle / del hotel; *the color of the car* el color del coche; *the works of Dickens* las obras de Dickens; *five / ten minutes of twelve* las doce menos cinco / diez; *die of cancer* morir de cáncer; *love of*

money / adventure amor por el dinero / la aventura; **of the three this is ...** de los tres éste es ...

off [ɑːf] **1** prep: **off the main road** (away from) apartado de la carretera principal; (leading off) saliendo de la carretera principal; **$20 off the price** una rebaja en el precio de 20 dólares; **he's off his food** no come nada, está desganado **2** adv: **be off** of light, TV, machine estar apagado; of brake, lid, top no estar puesto; not at work faltar; on vacation estar de vacaciones; (canceled) estar cancelado; **we're off tomorrow** (leaving) nos vamos mañana; **I'm off to New York** me voy a Nueva York; **with his pants / hat off** sin los pantalones / el sombrero; **take a day off** tomarse un día de fiesta or un día libre; **it's 3 miles off** está a tres millas de distancia; **it's a long way off** in distance está muy lejos; in future todavía queda mucho tiempo; **he got into his car and drove off** se subió al coche y se marchó; **off and on** de vez en cuando **3** adj: **the off switch** el interruptor de apagado

of·fence Br → offense

of·fend [əˈfend] v/t (insult) ofender

of·fend·er [əˈfendər] LAW delincuente m/f; **offenders will be prosecuted** se procesará a los infractores

of·fense [əˈfens] LAW delito m; **take offense at sth** ofenderse por algo

of·fen·sive [əˈfensɪv] **1** adj behavior, remark ofensivo; smell repugnante **2** n (MIL: attack) ofensiva f; **go on(to) the offensive** pasar a la ofensiva

of·fer [ˈɑːfər] **1** n oferta f **2** v/t ofrecer; **offer s.o. sth** ofrecer algo a alguien

off·hand adj attitude brusco

of·fice [ˈɑːfɪs] building oficina f; room oficina f, despacho m; position cargo m

'of·fice block bloque m de oficinas

'of·fice hours npl horas fpl de oficina

of·fi·cer [ˈɑːfɪsər] MIL oficial m/f; in police agente m/f

of·fi·cial [əˈfɪʃl] **1** adj oficial **2** n funcionario(-a) m(f)

of·fi·cial·ly [əˈfɪʃlɪ] adv oficialmente

of·fi·ci·ate [əˈfɪʃɪeɪt] v/i: **with X officiating** con X celebrando la ceremonia

of·fi·cious [əˈfɪʃəs] adj entrometido

'off·line adv work fuera de línea; **be offline** of printer etc estar desconectado; **go offline** desconectarse

'off·peak adj rates, vacation fuera de las horas punta; **offpeak electricity** electricidad f en horas valle or fuera de las horas punta

'off·sea·son **1** adj rates, vacation de tem-

porada baja **2** n temporada f baja

'off·set v/t (pret & pp offset) losses, disadvantage compensar

'off·shore adj drilling rig cercano a la costa; investment en el exterior

'off·side **1** adj wheel etc del lado del conductor **2** adv SP fuera de juego

'off·spring of person vástagos mpl, hijos mpl; of animal crías fpl

off-the-'rec·ord adj confidencial

'off·white adj blancuzco

of·ten [ˈɑːfn] adv a menudo, frecuentemente m

oil [ɔɪl] **1** n for machine, food, skin aceite m; petroleum petróleo m **2** v/t hinges, bearings engrasar

'oil change cambio m del aceite

'oil com·pa·ny compañía f petrolera

'oil·field yacimiento m petrolífero

'oil-fired adj central heating de gasóleo or fuel

'oil paint·ing óleo m

'oil-pro·duc·ing coun·try país m productor de petróleo

'oil re·fin·e·ry refinería f de petróleo

'oil rig plataforma f petrolífera

'oil·skins npl ropa f impermeable

'oil slick marea f negra

'oil tank·er petrolero m

'oil well pozo m petrolífero

oil·y [ˈɔɪlɪ] adj grasiento

oint·ment [ˈɔɪntmənt] ungüento m, pomada f

ok [ouˈkeɪ] adj, adv F **can I? - ok** ¿puedo? - de acuerdo or Span vale; **is it ok with you if ...?** ¿te parecería bien si ...?; **does that look ok?** ¿queda bien?; **that's ok by me** por mí, ningún problema; **are you ok?** (well, not hurt) ¿estás bien?; **are you ok for Friday?** ¿te va bien el viernes?; **he's ok** (is a good guy) es buena persona; **is this bus ok for ...?** ¿este autobús va a ...?

old [ould] adj viejo; (previous) anterior, antiguo; **an old man / woman** un anciano / una anciana, un viejo / una vieja; **how old are you / is he?** ¿cuántos años tienes / tiene?; **he's getting old** está haciéndose mayor

old age vejez f

old-'fash·ioned adj clothes, style, ideas anticuado, pasado de moda, word anticuado

ol·ive [ˈɑːlɪv] aceituna f, oliva f

'ol·ive oil aceite m de oliva

O·lym·pic 'Games [əˈlɪmpɪk] npl Juegos mpl Olímpicos

om·e·let, Br om·e·lette [ˈɑːmlɪt] tortilla f (francesa)

om·i·nous ['ɑ:mɪnəs] *adj* siniestro

o·mis·sion [ou'mɪʃn] omisión *f*

o·mit [ə'mɪt] *v/t* (*pret & pp **omitted***) omitir; ***omit to do sth*** no hacer algo

om·nip·o·tent [ɑ:m'nɪpətənt] *adj* omnipotente

om·nis·ci·ent [ɑ:m'nɪsɪənt] *adj* omnisciente

on [ɑ:n] **1** *prep* en; ***on the table / wall*** en la mesa / la pared; ***on the bus / train*** en el autobús / el tren; ***on TV / the radio*** en la televisión / la radio; ***on Sunday*** el domingo; ***on the 1st of ...*** el uno de ...; ***this is on me*** (*I'm paying*) invito yo; ***have you any money on you?*** ¿llevas dinero encima?; ***on his arrival / departure*** cuando llegue / se marche; ***on hearing this*** al escuchar esto **2** *adv*: ***be on*** of light, TV, *computer etc* estar encendido *or* L.Am. prendido, *of brake, lid, top* estar puesto; *of meeting etc*: *be scheduled to happen*; ***it's on at 5 am*** *of* TV *program* lo dan *or* Span ponen a las cinco; ***what's on tonight?*** *on* TV *etc* ¿qué dan *or* Span ponen esta noche?; (*what's planned?*) ¿qué planes hay para esta noche?; ***with his hat on*** con el sombrero puesto; ***you're on*** (*I accept your offer etc*) trato hecho; ***that's not on*** (*not allowed, not fair*) eso no se hace; ***on you go*** (*go ahead*) adelante; ***walk / talk on*** seguir caminando / hablando; ***and so on*** etcétera; ***on and on*** *talk etc* sin parar **3** *adj*: ***the on switch*** el interruptor de encendido

once [wʌns] **1** *adv* (*one time, formerly*) una vez; ***once again, once more*** una vez más; ***at once*** (*immediately*) de inmediato, inmediatamente; ***all at once*** (*suddenly*) de repente; (*all*) al mismo tiempo; ***once upon a time there was ...*** érase una vez ...; ***once in a while*** de vez en cuando; ***once and for all*** de una vez por todas; ***for once*** por una vez **2** *conj* una vez que; ***once you have finished*** una vez que hayas acabado

one [wʌn] **1** *number* uno *m* **2** *adj* un(a); ***one day*** un día **3** *pron* uno(-a); ***which one?*** ¿cuál?; ***one by one*** *enter, deal with* uno por uno; ***we help one another*** nos ayudamos mutuamente; ***what can one say / do?*** ¿qué puede uno decir / hacer?; ***the little ones*** los pequeños; ***I for one*** yo personalmente

one-'off *n* (*unique event, person*) hecho *m* aislado; (*exception*) excepción *f*

one-par·ent 'fam·i·ly familia *f* monoparental

one'self *pron* uno(-a) mismo(-a) *m*(*f*); ***do***

sth by oneself hacer algo sin ayuda; ***look after oneself*** cuidarse; ***be by oneself*** estar solo

one-sid·ed [wʌn'saɪdɪd] *adj* *discussion, fight* desigual

one-track 'mind *hum*: ***have a one-track mind*** ser un obseso

'one-way street calle *f* de sentido único

'one-way tick·et billete *m* de ida

on·ion ['ʌnjən] cebolla *f*

'on-line *adv* en línea; ***go on-line to*** conectarse a

'on-line serv·ice COMPUT servicio *m* en línea

on·look·er ['ɑ:nlʊkər] espectador(a) *m*(*f*), curioso(-a) *m*(*f*)

on·ly ['ounlɪ] **1** *adv* sólo, solamente; ***he was here only yesterday*** estuvo aquí ayer mismo; ***not only ... but also ...*** no sólo *or* solamente ... sino también ...; ***only just*** por poco **2** *adj* único; ***only son*** hijo único

'on·set comienzo *m*

'on·side *adv* SP en posición reglamentaria

on-the-job 'train·ing formación *f* continua

on·to ['ɑ:ntu:] *prep*: ***put sth onto sth*** poner algo encima de algo

on·ward ['ɑ:nwərd] *adv* hacia adelante; ***from ... onward*** de ... en adelante

ooze [u:z] **1** *v/i* of liquid, mud rezumar **2** *v/t* rezumar; ***he oozes charm*** rezuma *or* rebosa encanto

OPEC ['oupek] *abbr* (= ***Organization of Petroleum Exporting Countries***) OPEP *f* (= Organización *f* de Países Exportadores de Petróleo)

o·paque [ou'peɪk] *adj* glass opaco

o·pen ['oupən] **1** *adj* (*also honest*) abierto; ***in the open air*** al aire libre **2** *v/t* abrir **3** *v/i* of door, shop abrir; of flower abrirse

♦ **open up** *v/i* of person abrirse

o·pen-'air *adj* meeting, concert al aire libre; pool descubierto

'o·pen day jornada *f* de puertas abiertas

o·pen-'end·ed *adj* contract etc abierto

o·pen·ing ['oupənɪŋ] in wall etc abertura *f*; (*beginning*) of film, novel etc) comienzo *m*; (*job*) puesto *m* vacante

'o·pen·ing hours *npl* horario *m* de apertura

o·pen·ly ['oupənlɪ] *adv* (*honestly, frankly*) abiertamente

o·pen-mind·ed [oupən'maɪndɪd] *adj* de mentalidad abierta

o·pen 'plan of·fice oficina *f* de planta abierta

'o·pen tick·et billete *m* abierto

op·e·ra ['ɑ:pərə] ópera *f*

O

'op·e·ra glass·es npl gemelos mpl, prismáticos mpl

'op·e·ra house (teatro m de la) ópera f

'op·e·ra sing·er cantante m/f de ópera

op·e·rate ['ɑːpəreɪt] **1** v/i of company operar, actuar; of airline, bus service, MED operar; of machine funcionar (**on** con) **2** v/t machine manejar

◆ **operate on** v/t MED operar; **they operated on his leg** le operaron de la pierna

'op·e·rat·ing in·struc·tions npl instrucciones fpl de funcionamiento

'op·e·rat·ing room MED quirófano m

'op·e·rat·ing sys·tem COMPUT sistema m operativo

op·e·ra·tion [ɑːpə'reɪʃn] MED operación f; of machine manejo m; **operations** of company operaciones fpl; **have an operation** MED ser operado

op·e·ra·tor ['ɑːpəreɪtər] TELEC operador(a) m(f); of machine operario(-a) m(f); (tour operator) operador m turístico

oph·thal·mol·o·gist [ɑːfθæl'mɑːlədʒɪst] oftalmólogo(-a) m(f)

o·pin·ion [ə'pɪnjən] opinión f; **in my opinion** en mi opinión

o'pin·ion poll encuesta f de opinión

op·po·nent [ə'pəʊnənt] oponente m/f, adversario(-a) m(f)

op·por·tune ['ɑːpərtuːn] adj fml oportuno

op·por·tun·ist [ɑːpər'tuːnɪst] oportunista m/f

op·por·tu·ni·ty [ɑːpər'tuːnətɪ] oportunidad f

op·pose [ə'pəʊz] v/t oponerse a; **be opposed to ...** estar en contra de ...; **John, as opposed to George ...** John, al contrario que George ...

op·po·site ['ɑːpəzɪt] **1** adj contrario; views, characters, meaning opuesto; **the opposite side of town / end of the road** el otro lado de la ciudad / el otro extremo de la calle; **the opposite sex** el sexo opuesto **2** n: **the opposite of** lo contrario de

op·po·site 'num·ber homólogo(-a) m(f)

op·po·si·tion [ɑːpə'zɪʃn] to plan, POL oposición f; **meet with opposition** encontrar oposición

op·press [ə'pres] v/t the people oprimir

op·pres·sive [ə'presɪv] adj rule, dictator opresor; weather agobiante

opt [ɑːpt] v/t: **opt to do sth** optar por hacer algo

op·ti·cal il·lu·sion ['ɑːptɪkl] ilusión f óptica

op·ti·cian [ɑːp'tɪʃn] óptico(-a) m(f)

op·ti·mism ['ɑːptɪmɪzm] optimismo m

op·ti·mist ['ɑːptɪmɪst] optimista m/f

op·ti·mis·tic [ɑːptɪ'mɪstɪk] adj optimista

op·ti·mist·ic·ally [ɑːptɪ'mɪstɪklɪ] adv con optimismo

op·ti·mum ['ɑːptɪməm] **1** adj óptimo **2** n: **the optimum** lo ideal

op·tion ['ɑːpʃn] opción f

op·tion·al ['ɑːpʃnl] adj optativo

op·tion·al 'ex·tras npl accesorios mpl opcionales

or [ɔːr] conj o; before a word beginning with the letter o u ; **or else!** ¡más vale que no llegues tarde, ¡de lo contrario!

o·ral ['ɔːrəl] adj exam, sex oral; hygiene bucal

or·ange ['ɔːrɪndʒ] **1** adj color naranja **2** n fruit naranja f; color naranja m

'or·ange juice Span zumo m or L.Am. jugo de naranja

or·ange 'squash naranjada f

or·a·tor ['ɔːrətər] orador(a) m(f)

or·bit ['ɔːrbɪt] **1** n of earth órbita f; **send sth into orbit** poner algo en órbita **2** v/t the earth girar alrededor de

or·chard ['ɔːrtʃərd] huerta f (de frutales)

or·ches·tra ['ɔːrkɪstrə] orquesta f

or·chid ['ɔːrkɪd] orquídea f

or·dain [ɔːr'deɪn] v/t ordenar

or·deal [ɔːr'diːl] calvario m, experiencia f penosa

or·der ['ɔːrdər] **1** n (command) orden f; (sequence, being well arranged) orden m; for goods pedido m; **take s.o.'s order** in restaurant preguntar a alguien lo que va a tomar; **in order to** para; **out of order** (not functioning) estropeado; (not in sequence) desordenado **2** v/t (put in sequence, proper layout) ordenar; goods pedir, encargar; meal pedir; **order s.o. to do sth** ordenar a alguien hacer algo or que haga algo **3** v/i in restaurant pedir

or·der·ly ['ɔːrdəlɪ] **1** adj lifestyle ordenado, metódico **2** n in hospital celador(a) m(f)

or·di·nal num·ber ['ɔːrdɪnl] (número m) ordinal m

or·di·nar·i·ly [ɔːrdɪ'nerɪlɪ] adv (as a rule) normalmente

or·di·nary ['ɔːrdɪnerɪ] adj común, normal

ore [ɔːr] mineral, mena f

or·gan ['ɔːrgən] ANAT, MUS órgano m

or·gan·ic [ɔːr'gænɪk] adj food ecológico, biológico; fertilizer orgánico

or·gan·i·cal·ly [ɔːr'gænɪklɪ] adv grown ecológicamente, biológicamente

or·gan·ism ['ɔːrgənɪzm] organismo m

or·gan·i·za·tion [ɔːrgənaɪ'zeɪʃn] organización f

or·gan·ize ['ɔːrgənaiz] v/t organizar

or·gan·ized 'crime crimen m organizado

or·gan·iz·er ['ɔːrgənaizər] person organizador(a) m(f)

or·gasm ['ɔːrgæzml] orgasmo m

O·ri·ent ['ɔːriənt] Oriente

O·ri·en·tal [ɔːri'entl] 1 adj oriental 2 n oriental m/f

o·ri·en·tate ['ɔːriənteit] v/t (direct) orientar; **orientate o.s.** (get bearings) orientarse

or·i·gin ['ɑːridʒin] origen m; **idea / person of Chinese origin** una idea / una persona de origen chino

o·rig·i·nal [ə'ridʒənl] 1 adj (not copied, first) original 2 n painting etc original m

o·rig·i·nal·i·ty [əridʒən'ælətɪ] originalidad f

o·rig·i·nal·ly [ə'ridʒənəlɪ] adv originalmente; (at first) originalmente, en un principio

o·rig·i·nate [ə'ridʒineit] 1 v/t scheme, idea crear 2 v/i of idea, belief originarse, of family proceder

o·rig·i·na·tor [ə'ridʒineitər] of scheme etc creador(a) m(f); **he's not an originator** no es un creador nato

or·na·ment ['ɔːrnəmənt] adorno m

or·na·men·tal [ɔːrnə'mentl] adj ornamental

or·nate [ɔːr'neit] adj style, architecture recargado

or·phan ['ɔːrfn] n huérfano(-a) m(f)

or·phan·age ['ɔːrfənidʒ] orfanato m

or·tho·dox ['ɔːrθədɑːks] adj REL, fig ortodoxo

or·tho·pe·dic [ɔːrθə'piːdɪk] adj ortopédico

os·ten·si·bly [ɑː'stensəblɪ] adv aparentemente

os·ten·ta·tion [ɑːsten'teiʃn] ostentación f

os·ten·ta·tious [ɑːsten'teiʃəs] adj ostentoso

os·ten·ta·tious·ly [ɑːsten'teiʃəslɪ] adv de forma ostentosa

os·tra·cize ['ɑːstrəsaiz] v/t condenar al ostracismo

oth·er ['ʌðər] 1 adj otro; **other people might not agree** puede que otros no estén de acuerdo; **the other day** (recently) el otro día; **every other day / person** cada dos días / personas 2 n: **the other** el otro; **the others** los otros

oth·er·wise ['ʌðərwaiz] adv de lo contrario, si no; (differently) de manera diferente

ot·ter ['ɑːtər] nutria f

ought [ɔːt] v/aux: **I/you ought to know** debo / debes saberlo; **he / they ought**

to know debe / deben saberlo; **you ought to have done it** deberías haberlo hecho

ounce [auns] onza f

our [aur] adj nuestro m, nuestra f; **our brother** nuestro hermano; **our books** nuestros libros

ours [aurz] pron el nuestro, la nuestra; **ours are red** los nuestros son rojos; **that book is ours** ese libro es nuestro; **a friend of ours** un amigo nuestro

our·selves [aur'selvz] pron reflexive nos; emphatic nosotros mismos mpl, nosotras mismas fpl; **we hurt ourselves** nos hicimos daño; **when we saw ourselves in the mirror** cuando nos vimos en el espejo; **we saw it ourselves** lo vimos nosotros mismos; **by ourselves** (alone) solos; (without help) nosotros solos, nosotros mismos

oust [aust] v/t from office derrocar

out [aut] adv: **be out** of light, fire estar apagado; of flower estar en flor; (not at home, not in building), of sun haber salido; of calculations estar equivocado; (be published) haber sido publicado; (no longer in competition) estar eliminado; (no longer in fashion) estar pasado de moda; **the secret is out** el secreto ha sido revelado; **out here in Dallas** aquí en Dallas; **he's out in the garden** está en el jardín; (get) **out!** ¡vete!; (get) **out of my room!** ¡fuera de mi habitación!; **that's out!** (out of the question) ¡eso es imposible!; **he's out to win** (fully intends to) va a por la victoria

out·board 'mo·tor motor m de fueraborda

'out·break of violence, war estallido m

'out·build·ing edificio m anexo

'out·burst emotional arrebato m, arranque m

'out·cast n paria m/f

'out·come resultado m

'out·cry protesta f

out·dat·ed adj anticuado

out·do v/t (pret **outdid**, pp **outdone**) superar

out·door adj toilet, activities, life al aire libre

out·doors adv fuera

out·er ['autər] adj wall etc exterior

out·er 'space espacio m exterior

'out·fit clothes traje m, conjunto m; (company, organization) grupo m

'out·go·ing adj flight saliente; personality extrovertido

out·grow v/t (pret **outgrew**, pp **outgrown**) old ideas dejar atrás

O

out·ing ['aʊtɪŋ] (*trip*) excursión *f*
out·last *v/t* durar más que
'out·let *of pipe* desagüe *m*; *for sales* punto *m* de venta
'out·line 1 *n of person, building etc* perfil *m*, contorno *m*; *of plan, novel* resumen *m* **2** *v/t plans etc* resumir
out·live *v/t* sobrevivir a
'out·look (*prospects*) perspectivas *fpl*
'out·ly·ing *adj areas* periférico
out·num·ber *v/t* superar en número
out of *prep* ◇ *motion* fuera de; *run out of the house* salir corriendo de la casa; *it fell out of the window* se cayó por la ventana
◇ *position*: *20 miles out of of Detroit* a 20 millas de Detroit
◇ *cause*: *out of jealousy / curiosity* por celos / curiosidad
◇ *without*: *we're out of gas / beer* no nos queda gasolina / cerveza
◇ *from a group* de cada; *5 out of 10* 5 de cada 10
out-of-'date *adj* anticuado, desfasado
out-of-the-'way *adj* apartado
'out·pa·tient paciente *m/f* externo(-a)
'out·pa·tients' (*clin·ic*) clínica *f* ambulatoria
'out·per·form *v/t* superar a
'out·put 1 *n of factory* producción *f*; COMPUT salida *f* **2** *v/t* (*pret & pp outputted or output*) (*produce*) producir
'out·rage 1 *n feeling* indignación *f*; *act* ultraje *m*, atrocidad *f* **2** *v/t* indignar, ultrajar; *I was outraged to hear ...* me indignó escuchar que ...
out·ra·geous [aʊt'reɪdʒəs] *adj acts* atroz; *prices* escandaloso
'out·right 1 *adj winner* absoluto **2** *adv* win completamente; *kill* en el acto
out·run *v/t* (*pret outran, pp outrun*) correr más que
'out·set principio *m*, comienzo *m*; *from the outset* desde el principio *or* comienzo
out·shine *v/t* (*pret & pp outshone*) eclipsar
'out·side 1 *adj surface, wall* exterior; *lane* de fuera **2** *adv sit, go* fuera **3** *prep* fuera de; (*apart from*) aparte de **4** *n of building, case etc* exterior *m*; *at the outside* a lo sumo
out·side 'broad·cast emisión *f* desde exteriores
out·sid·er [aʊt'saɪdər] *in life* forastero(-a) *m(f)*; *be an outsider in election, race* no ser uno de los favoritos
'out·size *adj clothing* de talla especial
'out·skirts *npl* afueras *fpl*

out·smart → **outwit**
out·stand·ing *adj success, quality* destacado, sobresaliente; *writer, athlete* excepcional; FIN: *invoice, sums* pendiente
out-stretched ['aʊtstretʃt] *adj hands* extendido
out·vote *v/t*: *be outvoted* perder la votación
out·ward ['aʊtwərd] *adj appearance* externo; *outward journey* viaje *m* de ida
out·ward·ly ['aʊtwərdlɪ] *adv* aparentemente
out·weigh *v/t* pesar más que
out·wit *v/t* (*pret & pp outwitted*) mostrarse más listo que
o·val ['oʊvl] *adj* oval, ovalado
o·va·ry ['oʊvərɪ] ovario *m*
o·va·tion [oʊ'veɪʃn] ovación *f*; *give s.o. a standing ovation* aplaudir a alguien de pie
ov·en ['ʌvn] horno *m*
'ov·en glove, 'ov·en mitt manopla *f* para el horno
'ov·en-proof *adj* refractario
'ov·en-read·y *adj* listo para el horno
o·ver ['oʊvər] **1** *prep* (*above*) sobre, encima de; (*across*) al otro lado de; (*more than*) más de; (*during*) durante; *she walked over the street* cruzó la calle; *travel all over Brazil* viajar por todo Brasil; *let's talk over a drink / meal* hablemos mientras tomamos una bebida / comemos; *we're over the worst* lo peor ya ha pasado; *over and above* además de **2** *adv*: *be over* (*finished*) haber acabado; *there were just 6 over* sólo quedaban seis; *over to you* (*your turn*) te toca a ti; *over in Japan* allá en Japón; *over here / there* por aquí / allá; *it hurts all over* me duele por todas partes; *painted white all over* pintado todo de blanco; *it's all over* se ha acabado; *over and over again* una y otra vez; *do sth over* (*again*) volver a hacer algo
o·ver·all ['oʊvərɔːl] **1** *adj length* total **2** *adv* (*in general*) en general; *it measures six feet overall* mide en total seis pies
o·ver·alls ['oʊvərɔːlz] *npl Span* mono *m*, *L.Am.* overol *m*
o·ver·awe *v/t* intimidar; *be overawed by s.o./sth* sentirse intimidado por alguien / algo
o·ver·bal·ance *v/i* perder el equilibrio
o·ver·bear·ing *adj* dominante, despótico
o·ver·board *adv* por la borda; *man overboard!* ¡hombre al agua!; *go overboard for s.o./sth* entusiasmarse muchísimo con alguien / algo
o·ver·cast *adj day* nublado; *sky* cubierto

o·ver·charge v/t *customer* cobrar de más a

'o·ver·coat abrigo m

o·ver·come v/t (pret **overcame**, pp **overcome**) *difficulties*, *shyness* superar, vencer; **be overcome by emotion** estar embargado por la emoción

o·ver·crowd·ed adj *train* atestado; *city* superpoblado

o·ver·do v/t (pret **overdid**, pp **overdone**) (*exaggerate*) exagerar; *in cooking* recocer, cocinar demasiado; **you're overdoing things** te estás excediendo

o·ver·done adj *meat* demasiado hecho

'o·ver·dose n sobredosis f inv

'o·ver·draft descubierto m; **have an overdraft** tener un descubierto

o·ver·draw v/t (pret **overdrew**, pp **overdrawn**) *account* dejar al descubierto; **be $800 overdrawn** tener un descubierto de 800 dólares

o·ver·dressed adj demasiado trajeado

'o·ver·drive MOT superdirecta f

o·ver·due adj: **his apology was long overdue** se debía haber disculpado hace tiempo; **an overdue alteration** un cambio que había que haber efectuado hace tiempo

o·ver·es·ti·mate v/t *abilities*, *value* sobreestimar

o·ver·ex·pose v/t *photograph* sobreexponer

'o·ver·flow¹ n *pipe* desagüe m, rebosadero m

o·ver·flow² v/i *of water* desbordarse

o·ver·grown adj *garden* abandonado, cubierto de vegetación; **he's an overgrown baby** es como un niño

o·ver·haul v/t *engine*, *plans* revisar

'o·ver·head 1 adj *lights*, *railway* elevado 2 n FIN gastos mpl generales

o·ver·hear v/t (pret & pp **overheard**) oír por casualidad

o·ver·heat·ed adj recalentado

o·ver·joyed [ouvər'dʒɔid] adj contentísimo, encantado

'o·ver·kill: **that's overkill** eso es exagerar

'o·ver·land 1 adj *route* terrestre 2 adv *travel* por tierra

o·ver·lap v/i (pret & pp **overlapped**) *of tiles etc* solaparse; *of periods of time* coincidir; *of theories* tener puntos en común

o·ver·leaf adv: **see overleaf** véase al dorso

o·ver·load v/t *vehicle*, ELEC sobrecargar

o·ver·look v/t *of tall building etc* dominar; (*not see*) pasar por alto

o·ver·ly ['ouvərli] adv excesivamente, demasiado

'o·ver·night adv *travel* por la noche; **stay overnight** quedarse a pasar la noche

o·ver·night 'bag bolso m de viaje

o·ver·paid adj: **be overpaid** cobrar demasiado

'o·ver·pass paso m elevado

o·ver·pop·u·lat·ed [ouvə'pɑ:pjʊleitid] adj superpoblado

o·ver·pow·er v/t *physically* dominar

o·ver·pow·er·ing [ouvə'pauriŋ] adj *smell* fortísimo; *sense of guilt* insoportable

o·ver·priced [ouvər'praist] adj demasiado caro

o·ver·rat·ed [ouvə'reitid] adj sobrevalorado

o·ver·re·act v/i reaccionar exageradamente

o·ver·ride v/t (pret **overrode**, pp **overridden**) anular

o·ver·rid·ing adj *concern* primordial

o·ver·rule v/t *decision* anular

o·ver·run v/t (pret **overran**, pp **overrun**) *country* invadir, *time* superar; **be overrun with** estar plagado de

o·ver·seas 1 adv *live*, *work* en el extranjero; **go** al extranjero 2 adj extranjero

o·ver·see v/t (pret **oversaw**, pp **overseen**) supervisar

o·ver·shad·ow v/t *fig* eclipsar

'o·ver·sight descuido m

o·ver·sim·pli·fi·ca·tion simplificación f excesiva

o·ver·sim·pli·fy v/t (pret & pp **oversimplified**) simplificar en exceso

o·ver·sleep v/i (pret & pp **overslept**) quedarse dormido

o·ver·state v/t exagerar

o·ver·state·ment exageración f

o·ver·step v/t (pret & pp **overstepped**) *fig* traspasar; **overstep the mark** propasarse, pasarse de la raya

o·ver·take v/t (pret **overtook**, pp **overtaken**) *in work*, *development* adelantarse a; *Br* MOT adelantar

o·ver·throw¹ v/t (pret **overthrew**, pp **overthrown**) derrocar

'o·ver·throw² n derrocamiento m

'o·ver·time 1 n SP: **in overtime** en la prórroga 2 adv: **work in overtime** hacer horas extras

o·ver·ture ['ouvərtʃur] MUS obertura f; **make overtures to** establecer contactos con

o·ver·turn 1 v/t *vehicle* volcar; *object* dar la vuelta a; *government* derribar 2 v/i *of vehicle* volcar

'o·ver·view visión f general

o·ver·weight adj con sobrepeso; **be overweight** estar demasiado gordo

O

o·ver·whelm [oʊvər'welm] v/t with work abrumar, inundar; with emotion abrumar; **be overwhelmed by** by response estar abrumado por

o·ver·whelm·ing [oʊvər'welmɪŋ] adj feeling abrumador; majority aplastante

o·ver·work 1 n exceso m de trabajo 2 v/i trabajar en exceso 3 v/t hacer trabajar en exceso

owe [oʊ] v/t deber; **owe s.o. $500** deber a alguien 500 dólares; **owe s.o. an apology** deber disculpas a alguien; **how much do I owe you?** ¿cuánto te debo?

ow·ing to ['oʊɪŋ] prep debido a

owl [aʊl] búho m

own¹ [oʊn] v/t poseer; **who owns the restaurant?** ¿de quién es el restaurante?, ¿quién es el propietario del restaurante?

own² [oʊn] **1** adj propio **2** pron: **a car / an apartment of my own** mi propio coche/apartamento; **on my / his own** yo / él solo

◆ **own up** v/i confesar

own·er ['oʊnər] dueño(-a) m(f), propietario(-a) m(f)

own·er·ship ['oʊnərʃɪp] propiedad f

ox [ɑːks] buey m

ox·ide ['ɑːksaɪd] óxido m

ox·y·gen ['ɑːksɪdʒən] oxígeno m

oy·ster ['ɔɪstər] ostra f

oz abbr (= **ounce(s)**) onza/s f(pl)

o·zone ['oʊzoʊn] ozono m

'o·zone lay·er capa f de ozono

P

PA [piː'eɪ] abbr (= **personal assistant**) secretario(-a) m(f) personal

pace [peɪs] **1** n (step) paso m; (speed) ritmo m **2** v/i: **pace up and down** pasear de un lado a otro

'pace·mak·er MED marcapasos m inv; SP liebre f

Pa·cif·ic [pə'sɪfɪk]: **the Pacific (Ocean)** el (Océano) Pacífico

pac·i·fi·er ['pæsɪfaɪər] chupete m

pac·i·fism ['pæsɪfɪzm] pacifismo m

pac·i·fist ['pæsɪfɪst] n pacifista m/f

pac·i·fy ['pæsɪfaɪ] v/t (pret & pp **pacified**) tranquilizar; country pacificar

pack [pæk] **1** n (backpack) mochila f; of cereal, food, cigarettes paquete m; of cards baraja f **2** v/t item of clothing etc meter en la maleta; goods empaquetar; groceries meter en una bolsa; **pack one's bag / suitcase** hacer la bolsa / la maleta **3** v/i hacer la maleta

pack·age ['pækɪdʒ] **1** n paquete m; **employment package** of offers etc condiciones fpl de empleo **2** v/t in packs embalar; idea, project presentar

'pack·age deal for holiday paquete m

'pack·age tour viaje m organizado

pack·ag·ing ['pækɪdʒɪŋ] of product embalaje m; of idea, project presentación f; **it's all packaging** fig es sólo imagen

pack·ed [pækt] adj (crowded) abarrotado

pack·et ['pækɪt] paquete m

pact [pækt] pacto m

pad¹ [pæd] **1** n for protection almohadilla f; for absorbing liquid compresa f; for writing bloc m **2** v/t (pret & pp **padded**) with material acolchar; speech, report meter paja en

pad² v/i (move quietly) caminar silenciosamente

pad·ded shoulders ['pædɪd] hombreras fpl

pad·ding ['pædɪŋ] material relleno m; in speech etc paja f

pad·dle ['pædl] **1** n for canoe canalete m, remo m **2** v/i in canoe remar; in water chapotear

pad·dling pool ['pædlɪŋ] piscina f para niños

pad·dock ['pædək] potrero m

pad·lock ['pædlɑːk] **1** n candado m **2** v/t gate cerrar con candado; **I padlocked my bike to the railings** até mi bicicleta a la verja con candado

page¹ [peɪdʒ] n of book etc página f; **page number** número m de página

page² [peɪdʒ] v/t (call) llamar; by PA llamar por megafonía; by beeper llamar por el buscapersonas or Span busca

pag·er ['peɪdʒər] buscapersonas m inv, Span busca m

paid [peɪd] pret & pp → **pay**

paid em'ploy·ment empleo m remunerado

pail [peɪl] cubo *m*
pain [peɪn] dolor *m*; **be in pain** sentir dolor; **take pains to ...** tomarse muchas molestias por ...; **a pain in the neck** F una lata F, un tostón F
pain·ful ['peɪnfəl] *adj* dolorido; *blow, condition, subject* doloroso; (*laborious*) difícil; *my arm is still very painful* me sigue doliendo mucho el brazo
pain·ful·ly ['peɪnfəlɪ] *adv* (*extremely, acutely*) extremadamente
pain·kill·er ['peɪnkɪlər] analgésico *m*
pain·less ['peɪnlɪs] *adj* indoloro; **be completely painless** doler nada
pains·tak·ing ['peɪnzteɪkɪŋ] *adj* meticuloso
paint [peɪnt] **1** *n* pintura *f* **2** *v/t* pintar
paint·brush ['peɪntbrʌʃ] *large* brocha *f*; *small* pincel *m*
paint·er ['peɪntər] *decorator* pintor(a) *m(f)* (de brocha gorda); *artist* pintor(a) *m(f)*
paint·ing ['peɪntɪŋ] *activity* pintura *f*, *picture* cuadro *m*
paint·work ['peɪntwɜːrk] pintura *f*
pair [per] *of shoes, gloves, objects* par *m*; *of people, animals* pareja *f*
pa·ja·ma ['jæk·et camisa *f* de pijama
pa·ja·ma ['pants pantalón *m* de pijama
pa·ja·mas [pəˈdʒɑːməz] *npl* pijama *m*
Pa·ki·stan [pɑːkɪˈstɑːn] Paquistán, Pakistán
Pa·ki·sta·ni [pɑːkɪˈstɑːnɪ] **1** *n* paquistaní *m/f*, pakistaní *m/f* **2** *adj* paquistaní, pakistaní
pal [pæl] F (*friend*) amigo(-a) *m(f)*; *Span* colega *m/f* F; **hey pal, got a light?** oye amigo *or Span* tío, ¿tienes fuego?
pal·ace ['pælɪs] palacio *m*
pal·ate ['pælət] paladar *m*
pa·la·tial [pəˈleɪʃl] *adj* palaciego
pale [peɪl] *adj person* pálido; **she went pale** palideció; **pale pink / blue** rosa / azul claro
Pal·es·tine ['pæləstaɪn] Palestina
Pal·es·tin·i·an [pæləˈstɪnɪən] **1** *n* palestino(-a) *m(f)* **2** *adj* palestino
pal·let ['pælɪt] palé *m*
pal·lor ['pælər] palidez *f*
palm [pɑːm] *of hand* palma *f*; *tree* palmera *f*
pal·pi·ta·tions [pælpɪˈteɪʃnz] *npl* MED palpitaciones *fpl*
pal·try ['pɔːltrɪ] *adj* miserable
pam·per ['pæmpər] *v/t* mimar
pam·phlet ['pæmflɪt] *for information* folleto *m*; *political* panfleto *m*
pan [pæn] *for cooking* cacerola *f*; *for frying* sartén *f* **2** *v/t* (*pret & pp panned*) F

(*criticize*) poner por los suelos F
◆ **pan out** *v/i* (*develop*) salir
Pan·a·ma ['pænəmɑː] *n* Panamá
Pan·a·ma Ca·nal *n: the Panama Canal* el Canal de Panamá
Pan·a·ma 'Cit·y *n* Ciudad *f* de Panamá
Pan·a·ma·ni·an [pænəˈmeɪnɪən] **1** *adj* panameño **2** *n* panameño(-a) *m(f)*
pan·cake ['pænkeɪk] crepe *m*, *L.Am.* panqueque *m*
pan·da ['pændə] (oso *m*) panda *m*
pan·de·mo·ni·um [pændɪˈmoʊnɪəm] pandemónium *m*, pandemonio *m*
◆ **pan·der to** ['pændər] *v/t* complacer
pane [peɪn] *of glass* hoja *f*
pan·el ['pænl] *n* panel *m*; *people* grupo *m*, panel *m*
pan·el·ing ['pænəlɪŋ] paneles *mpl*; *of ceiling* artesonado *m*
pang [pæŋ]: *pangs of hunger* retortijones *mpl*; *pangs of remorse* remordimientos *mpl*
'pan·han·dle *v/i* ⊢ mendigar
pan·ic ['pænɪk] **1** *n* pánico *m* **2** *v/i* (*pret & pp panicked*) ser presa del pánico; **don't panic** ¡que no cunda el pánico!
'pan·ic buy·ing FIN compra *f* provocada por el pánico
'pan·ic sel·ling FIN venta *f* provocada por el pánico
'pan·ic-strick·en presa del pánico
pan·o·ra·ma [pænəˈrɑːmə] panorama *m*
pa·no·ram·ic [pænəˈræmɪk] *adj view* panorámico
pan·sy ['pænzɪ] *flower* pensamiento *m*
pant [pænt] *v/i* jadear
pan·ties ['pæntɪz] *npl Span* bragas *fpl*, *L.Am.* calzones *mpl*
pantihose → **pantyhose**
pants [pænts] *npl* pantalones *mpl*
pan·ty·hose ['pæntɪhoʊz] medias *fpl*, pantis *mpl*
pa·pal ['peɪpəl] *adj* papal
pa·per ['peɪpər] **1** *n* papel *m*; (*newspaper*) periódico *m*; *academic* estudio *m*; *at conference* ponencia *f*; (*examination paper*) examen *m*; *papers* (*documents*) documentos *mpl*; *of vehicle* (*identity papers*) papeles *mpl*, documentación *f*; *a piece of paper* un trozo de papel **2** *adj* de papel **3** *v/t room, walls* empapelar
'paperback libro *m* en rústica
paper 'bag bolsa *f* de papel
'paper boy repartidor *m* de periódicos
'paper clip clip *m*
'paper cup vaso *m* de papel
'paperwork papeleo *m*
par [pɑːr] *in golf* par *m*; **be on a par with** ser comparable a; **feel below par** sen-

tirse en baja forma

par·a·chute ['pærəʃuːt] **1** n paracaídas m inv **2** v/i saltar en paracaídas **3** v/t troops, supplies lanzar en paracaídas

par·a·chut·ist ['pærəʃuːtɪst] paracaidista m/f

pa·rade [pə'reɪd] **1** n procession desfile m **2** v/i (walk about) pasearse **3** v/t knowledge, new car hacer ostentación de

par·a·dise ['pærədaɪs] paraíso m

par·a·dox ['pærədɑːks] paradoja f

par·a·dox·i·cal [pærə'dɑːksɪkl] adj paradójico

par·a·dox·i·cal·ly [pærə'dɑːksɪklɪ] adv paradójicamente

par·a·graph ['pærəgræf] párrafo m

Par·a·guay ['pærəgwaɪ] n Paraguay

Par·a·guay·an [pærə'gwaɪən] **1** adj paraguayo **2** n paraguayo(-a) m(f)

par·al·lel ['pærəlel] **1** n in geometry paralela f; GEOG paralelo m; fig paralelismo m; draw a parallel establecer un paralelismo; do two things in parallel hacer dos cosas al mismo tiempo **2** adj also fig paralelo **3** v/t (match) equipararse a

pa·ral·y·sis [pə'ræləsɪs] parálisis f

par·a·lyze ['pærəlaɪz] v/t also fig paralizar

par·a·med·ic [pærə'medɪk] n auxiliar m/f sanitario(a)

pa·ram·e·ter [pə'ræmɪtər] parámetro m

par·a·mil·i·tar·y [pærə'mɪlɪterɪ] **1** adj paramilitar **2** n paramilitar m/f

par·a·mount ['pærəmaʊnt] adj supremo, extremo; be paramount ser de importancia capital

par·a·noi·a [pærə'nɔɪə] paranoia f

par·a·noid ['pærənɔɪd] adj paranoico

par·a·pher·na·li·a [pærəfər'neɪlɪə] parafernalia f

par·a·phrase ['pærəfreɪz] v/t parafrasear

par·a·pleg·ic [pærə'pliːdʒɪk] n parapléjico(-a) m(f)

par·a·site ['pærəsaɪt] also fig parásito m

par·a·sol ['pærəsɑːl] sombrilla f

par·a·troop·er ['pærətruːpər] paracaidista m/f (militar)

par·cel ['pɑːrsl] n paquete m

♦ **parcel up** v/t empaquetar

parch [pɑːrtʃ] v/t secar; be parched F of person estar muerto de sed F

par·don ['pɑːrdn] **1** n LAW indulto m; I beg your pardon? (what did you say?) ¿cómo ha dicho?; I beg your pardon (I'm sorry) discúlpeme **2** v/t perdonar; LAW indultar; pardon me? ¿perdón?; pardon me? ¿qué?

pare [per] v/t (peel) pelar

par·ent ['perənt] father padre m; mother madre f; my parents mis padres

pa·ren·tal [pə'rentl] adj de los padres

'par·ent com·pa·ny empresa f matriz

par·ent-'teach·er as·so·ci·a·tion asociación f de padres y profesores

pa·ren·the·sis [pə'renθəsɪs] (pl parentheses [pə'renθəsiːz]) paréntesis m inv

par·ish ['pærɪʃ] parroquia f

park¹ [pɑːrk] n parque m

park² v/t & v/i MOT estacionar, Span aparcar

par·ka ['pɑːrkə] parka f

park·ing ['pɑːrkɪŋ] MOT estacionamiento m, Span aparcamiento m; no parking prohibido aparcar

'park·ing disc disco m (de aparcamiento)

'park·ing ga·rage párking m, Span aparcamiento m

'park·ing lot estacionamiento m, Span aparcamiento m (al aire libre)

'park·ing me·ter parquímetro m

'park·ing place (plaza f de) estacionamiento or Span aparcamiento, sitio m para estacionar or Span aparcar

'park·ing tick·et multa f de estacionamiento

par·lia·ment ['pɑːrləmənt] parlamento m

par·lia·men·ta·ry [pɑːrlə'mentərɪ] adj parlamentario

pa·role [pə'roʊl] **1** n libertad f condicional; be on parole estar en libertad condicional **2** v/t poner en libertad condicional; be paroled salir en libertad condicional

par·rot ['pærət] loro m

pars·ley ['pɑːrslɪ] perejil m

part [pɑːrt] **1** n (portion, area) parte f; (episode) parte f, episodio m; of machine pieza f (de repuesto); in play, film papel m; in hair raya f; take part in tomar parte en **2** adv (partly) en parte; part American part Spanish medio americano medio español; part fact, part fiction con una parte de realidad y una parte de ficción **3** v/i separarse **4** v/t: part one's hair hacerse la raya

♦ **part with** v/t desprenderse de

'part ex·change: take sth in part exchange llevarse algo como parte del pago

par·tial ['pɑːrʃl] adj (incomplete) parcial; be partial to tener debilidad por

par·tial·ly ['pɑːrʃəlɪ] adv parcialmente

par·ti·ci·pant [pɑːr'tɪsɪpənt] participante m/f

par·ti·ci·pate [pɑːr'tɪsɪpeɪt] v/i participar

par·ti·ci·pa·tion [pɑːrtɪsɪ'peɪʃn] participación f

par·ti·cle ['pɑːrtɪkl] PHYS partícula f; (small amount) pizca f

par·tic·u·lar [pərˈtɪkjələr] *adj* (*specific*) particular, concreto; (*demanding*) exigente; *about friends, employees* selectivo; *pej* especial, quisquilloso; *you know how particular she is* ya sabes lo especial que es; *this particular morning* precisamente esta mañana; *in particular* en particular; *it's a particular favorite of mine* es uno de mis preferidos

par·tic·u·lar·ly [pərˈtɪkjələrlɪ] *adv* particularmente, especialmente

par·ti·tion [pɑːrˈtɪʃn] **1** *n* (*screen*) tabique *m*; *of country* partición *f*, división *f* **2** *v/t country* dividir

◆ **partition off** *v/t* dividir con tabiques

part·ly [ˈpɑːrtlɪ] *adv* en parte

part·ner [ˈpɑːrtnər] COM socio(-a) *m(f)*; *in relationship* compañero(-a) *m(f)*; *in tennis, dancing* pareja *f*

part·ner·ship [ˈpɑːrtnərʃɪp] COM sociedad *f*; *in particular activity* colaboración *f*

part of 'speech parte *f* de la oración

'part own·er copropietario(-a) *m(f)*

'part-time 1 *adj* a tiempo parcial **2** *adv work* a tiempo parcial

part-'tim·er: *be a part-timer* trabajar a tiempo parcial

par·ty [ˈpɑːrtɪ] **1** *n* (*celebration*) fiesta *f*; POL partido *m*; (*group of people*) grupo *m*; *be a party to* tomar parte en **2** *v/i* (*pret & pp partied*) F salir de marcha F

pass [pæs] **1** *n for entry*, SP pase *m*; *in mountains* desfiladero *m*; *make a pass at* tirarle los tejos a **2** *v/t* (*hand*) pasar; (*go past*) pasar por delante de; (*overtake*) adelantar; (*go beyond*) sobrepasar; (*approve*) aprobar; *pass an exam* aprobar un examen; *pass sentence* LAW dictar sentencia; *pass the time* pasar el tiempo **3** *v/i of time* pasar; *in exam* aprobar; (*go away*) pasarse

◆ **pass around** *v/t* repartir

◆ **pass away** *v/i euph* fallecer, pasar a mejor vida

◆ **pass by 1** *v/t* (*go past*) pasar por **2** *v/i* (*go past*) pasarse

◆ **pass on 1** *v/t information, book* pasar; *pass on the savings to …* *of supermarket etc* revertir el ahorro en … **2** *v/i* (*euph: die*) fallecer, pasar a mejor vida

◆ **pass out** *v/i* (*faint*) desmayarse

◆ **pass through** *v/t town* pasar por

◆ **pass up** *v/t opportunity* dejar pasar

pass·a·ble [ˈpæsəbl] *adj road* transitable; (*acceptable*) aceptable

pas·sage [ˈpæsɪdʒ] (*corridor*) pasillo *m*; *from poem, book* pasaje *m*; *of time* paso *m*

pas·sage·way [ˈpæsɪdʒweɪ] pasillo *m*

pas·sen·ger [ˈpæsɪndʒər] pasajero(-a) *m(f)*

'pas·sen·ger seat asiento *m* de pasajero

pas·ser-by [pæsərˈbaɪ] (*pl **passers-by***) transeúnte *m/f*

pas·sion [ˈpæʃn] pasión *f*; *a crime of passion* un crimen pasional

pas·sion·ate [ˈpæʃənət] *adj lover* apasionado; (*fervent*) fervoroso

pas·sive [ˈpæsɪv] **1** *adj* pasivo **2** *n* GRAM (*voz f*) pasiva *f*; *in the passive* en pasiva

'pass mark EDU nota *f* mínima para aprobar

Pass·o·ver [ˈpæsoʊvər] REL Pascua *f* de los hebreos

pass·port [ˈpæspɔːrt] pasaporte *m*

'pass·port control control *m* de pasaportes

pass·word [ˈpæswɜːrd] contraseña *f*

past [pæst] **1** *adj* (*former*) pasado; *his past life* su pasado; *the past few days* los últimos días; *that's all past now* todo eso es agua pasada **2** *n pasado; in the past* antiguamente **3** *prep in position* después de; *it's half past two* son las dos y media; *it's past seven o'clock* pasan de las siete; *it's past your bedtime* hace rato que tenías que haberte ido a la cama **4** *adv*: *run / walk past* pasar

pas·ta [ˈpæstə] pasta *f*

paste [peɪst] **1** *n* (*adhesive*) cola *f* **2** *v/t* (*stick*) pegar

pas·tel [ˈpæstl] **1** *n color* pastel *m* **2** *adj* pastel

pas·time [ˈpæstaɪm] pasatiempo *m*

past par·ti·ci·ple GRAM participio *m* pasado

pas·tra·mi [pæˈstrɑːmɪ] pastrami *m*, *carne de vaca ahumada con especias*

pas·try [ˈpeɪstrɪ] *for pie* masa *f*; *small cake* pastel *m*

'past tense GRAM (*tiempo m*) pasado *m*

pas·ty [ˈpeɪstɪ] *adj complexion* pálido

pat [pæt] **1** *n* palmadita *f*; *give s.o. a pat on the back fig* dar una palmadita a alguien en la espalda **2** *v/t* (*pret & pp patted*) dar palmaditas a

patch [pætʃ] **1** *n on clothing* parche *m*; (*area*) mancha *f*; *a bad patch* (*period of time*) un mal momento, una mala racha; *patches of fog* zonas de niebla; *not be a patch on fig* no tener ni punto de comparación con **2** *v/t clothing* remendar

◆ **patch up** *v/t* (*repair temporarily*) hacer un remiendo a, arreglar a medias; *quarrel* solucionar

patch·work [ˈpætʃwɜːrk] **1** *n needlework* labor *f* de retazo **2** *adj* hecho de remiendos

P

patch·y ['pætʃɪ] *quality* desigual; *work, performance* irregular

pâ·té [pɑːˈteɪ] *paté m*

pa·tent ['peɪtnt] **1** *adj* patente, evidente **2** *n for invention* patente *f* **3** *v/t invention* patentar

pa·tent 'leath·er charol *m*

pa·tent·ly ['peɪtntlɪ] *(clearly)* evidentemente, claramente

pa·ter·nal [pəˈtɜːrnl] *relative* paterno; *pride, love* paternal

pa·ter·nal·ism [pəˈtɜːrnlɪzm] paternalismo *m*

pa·ter·nal·is·tic [pətɜːrnlˈɪstɪk] *adj* paternalista

pa·ter·ni·ty [pəˈtɜːrnɪtɪ] paternidad *f*

path [pæθ] *also fig* camino *m*

pa·thet·ic [pəˈθetɪk] *invoking pity* patético; F *(very bad)* lamentable F

path·o·log·i·cal [pæθəˈlɑːdʒɪkl] *adj* patológico

pa·thol·o·gy [pəˈθɑːlədʒɪ] patología *f*

pa·thol·o·gist [pəˈθɑːlədʒɪst] patólogo(-a) *m(f)*

pa·tience ['peɪʃns] paciencia *f*

pa·tient ['peɪʃnt] **1** *n* paciente *m/f* **2** *adj* paciente; *just be patient!* ¡ten paciencia!

pa·tient·ly ['peɪʃntlɪ] *adv* pacientemente

pat·i·o ['pætɪoʊ] patio *m*

pat·ri·ot ['peɪtrɪət] patriota *m/f*

pat·ri·ot·ic [peɪtrɪˈɑːtɪk] *adj* patriótico

pat·ri·ot·ism ['peɪtrɪətɪzm] patriotismo *m*

pa·trol [pəˈtroʊl] **1** *n* patrulla *f*; *be on patrol* estar de patrulla **2** *v/t (pret & pp patrolled) streets, border* patrullar

pa·trol car coche *m* patrulla

pa·trol·man policía *m*, patrullero *m*

pa·trol wag·on furgón *m* policial

pa·tron ['peɪtrən] *of store, movie theater* cliente *m/f*; *of artist, charity etc* patrocinador(a) *m(f)*

pa·tron·ize ['pætrənaɪz] *v/t store* ser cliente de; *person* tratar con condescendencia *or* como a un niño

pa·tron·iz·ing ['pætrənaɪzɪŋ] condescendiente

pa·tron 'saint santo(-a) *m(f)* patrón(-ona), patrón(-ona) *m(f)*

pat·ter ['pætər] **1** *n of rain etc* repiqueteo *m*; F *(of salesman)* parloteo *m* F **2** *v/i* repiquetear

pat·tern ['pætərn] *n on wallpaper, fabric* estampado *m*; *for knitting, sewing* diseño *m*; *(model)* modelo *m*; *in behavior, events* pauta *f*

pat·terned ['pætərnd] *adj* estampado

paunch [pɔːntʃ] barriga *f*

pause [pɔːz] **1** *n* pausa *f* **2** *v/i* parar; *when speaking* hacer una pausa **3** *v/t tape* poner en pausa

pave [peɪv] *with concrete* pavimentar; *with slabs* adoquinar; *pave the way for fig* preparar el terreno para

pave·ment ['peɪvmənt] *(Am: roadway)* calzada *f*; *(Br: sidewalk)* acera *f*

pav·ing stone ['peɪvɪŋ] losa *f*

paw [pɔː] **1** *n of animal* pata *f*; F *(hand)* pezuña *f* F **2** *v/t* F sobar F

pawn[1] [pɔːn] *n in chess* peón *m*; *fig* títere *m*

pawn[2] [pɔːn] *v/t* empeñar

'pawn·bro·ker prestamista *m/f*

'pawn·shop casa *f* de empeños

pay [peɪ] **1** *n* paga *f*, sueldo *m*; *in the pay of* a sueldo de **2** *v/t (pret & pp paid) employee, sum, bill* pagar; *pay attention* prestar atención; *pay s.o. a compliment* hacer un cumplido a alguien **3** *v/i (pret & pp paid)* pagar; *(be profitable)* ser rentable; *it doesn't pay to ...* no conviene ...; *pay for purchase* pagar; *you'll pay for this! fig* ¡me las pagarás!

◆ **pay back** *v/t person* devolver el dinero a *; loan* devolver

◆ **pay in** *v/t to bank* ingresar

◆ **pay off 1** *v/t debt* liquidar; *(bribe)* sobornar **2** *v/i (be profitable)* valer la pena

◆ **pay up** *v/i* pagar

pay·a·ble ['peɪəbl] *adj* pagadero

'pay check cheque *m* del sueldo

'pay·day día *m* de paga

pay·ee [peɪˈiː] beneficiario(-a) *m(f)*

'pay en·ve·lope sobre *m* con la paga

pay·er ['peɪər] pagador(a) *m(f)*; *they are good payers* pagan puntualmente

pay·ment ['peɪmənt] pago *m*

'pay phone teléfono *m* público

'pay·roll ['peɪroʊl] *money* salarios *mpl*; *employees* nómina *f*; *be on the payroll* estar en nómina

'pay-slip ['peɪslɪp] nómina *f (papel)*

PC [piːˈsiː] *abbr* (= *personal computer*) PC *m*, *Span* ordenador *m* or *L.Am.* computadora personal; (= *politically correct*) políticamente correcto

pea [piː] *Span* guisante *m*, *L.Am.* arveja *f*, *Mex* chícharo *m*

peace [piːs] paz *f*; *(quietness)* tranquilidad

peace·a·ble ['piːsəbl] *adj person* pacífico

'Peace Corps organización gubernamental estadounidense de ayuda al desarrollo

peace·ful ['piːsfəl] *adj* tranquilo; *demonstration* pacífico

peace·ful·ly ['piːsfəlɪ] *adv* pacíficamente

peach [piːtʃ] *fruit* melocotón *m*, *L.Am.* durazno *m*; *tree* melocotonero *m*, *L.Am.* duraznero *m* pea·cock ['piːkɑːk] pavo *m* real

peak [piːk] **1** *n of mountain* cima *f*; *mountain* pico *m*; *fig* clímax *m* **2** *v/i* alcanzar el máximo

'peak time *npl* horas *fpl* punta

pea·nut ['piːnʌt] cacahuete *m*, *L.Am.* maní *m*, *Mex* cacahuate *m*; **get paid pea·nuts** F cobrar una miseria F; **that's pea·nuts to him** F eso es calderilla para él F

pea·nut 'but·ter crema *f* de cacahuete

pear [per] pera *f*

pearl [pɜːrl] perla *f*

peas·ant ['peznt] campesino(-a) *m(f)*

peb·ble ['pebl] guijarro *m*

pe·can [pɪ'kən] pacana *f*

peck [pek] **1** *n bite* picotazo *m*; *kiss* besito *m* **2** *v/it bite* picotear; *kiss* dar un besito a

pe·cu·li·ar [pɪ'kjuːljər] *adj (strange)* raro; **peculiar to** *(special)* característico de

pe·cu·li·ar·i·ty [pɪkjuːlɪ'ærətɪ] *(strangeness)* rareza *f*; *(special feature)* peculiaridad *f*, característica *f*

ped·al ['pedl] **1** *n of bike* pedal *m* **2** *v/i (turn pedals)* pedalear; *(cycle)* recorrer en bicicleta

pe·dan·tic [pɪ'dæntɪk] *adj* puntilloso

ped·dle ['pedl] *v/t drugs* traficar *or* trapichear con

ped·es·tal ['pedəstl] *for statue* pedestal *m*

pe·des·tri·an [pɪ'destrɪən] *n* peatón(-ona) *m(f)*

pe·des·tri·an 'cros·sing paso *m* de peatones

pe·di·at·ric [piːdɪ'ætrɪk] *adj* pediátrico

pe·di·a·tri·cian [piːdɪə'trɪʃn] pediatra *m/f*

pe·di·at·rics [piːdɪ'ætrɪks] pediatría *f*

ped·i·cure ['pedɪkjʊr] pedicura *f*

ped·i·gree ['pedɪɡriː] **1** *n of animal* pedigrí; *of person* linaje *m* **2** *adj* con pedigrí

pee [piː] *v/i* F hacer pis F, mear F

peek [piːk] **1** *n* ojeada *f*, vistazo *m* **2** *v/i* echar una ojeada *or* vistazo

peel [piːl] **1** *n* piel *f* **2** *v/t fruit, vegetables* pelar **3** *v/i of nose, shoulders* pelarse; *of paint* levantarse

◆ peel off **1** *v/t wrapper etc* quitar; *jacket etc* quitarse **2** *v/i of wrapper* quitarse

peep [piːp] → **peek**

peep·hole ['piːphoʊl] mirilla *f*

peer¹ [pɪr] *(equal)* igual *m*

peer² [pɪr] *v/i* mirar; **peer through the mist** buscar con la mirada entre la niebla; **peer at** forzar la mirada para ver

peeved [piːvd] F mosqueado F

peg [peɡ] *n for hat, coat* percha *f*; *for tent* clavija *f*; **off the peg** de confección

pe·jo·ra·tive [pɪ'dʒɑːrətɪv] *adj* peyorativo

pel·let ['pelɪt] pelotita *f*; *(bullet)* perdigón *m*

pelt [pelt] **1** *v/t*: **pelt s.o. with sth** tirar algo a alguien **2** *v/i*: **they pelted along the road** F fueron a toda mecha por la carretera F; **it's pelting down** F está diluviando F

pel·vis ['pelvɪs] pelvis *f*

pen¹ [pen] *n (ballpoint pen)* bolígrafo *m*; *(fountain pen)* pluma *f* (estilográfica)

pen² [pen] *(enclosure)* corral *m*

pen³ [pen] → **penitentiary**

pe·nal·ize ['piːnəlaɪz] *v/t* penalizar

pen·al·ty ['penltɪ] sanción *f*; *SP* penalti *m*; **take the penalty** *in soccer* lanzar el penalti

'pen·al·ty ar·e·a *SP* área *f* de castigo

'pen·al·ty clause *LAW* cláusula *f* de penalización

'pen·al·ty kick (lanzamiento *m* de) penalti *m*

'pen·al·ty 'shoot-out tanda *f* de penaltis

'pen·al·ty spot punto *m* de penalti

pen·cil ['pensɪl] lápiz *m*

pen·cil sharp·en·er sacapuntas *m inv*

pen·dant ['pendənt] *(necklace)* colgante *m*

pend·ing ['pendɪŋ] **1** *prep* en espera de **2** *adj* pendiente; **be pending** *awaiting a decision* estar pendiente; *about to happen* ser inminente

pen·e·trate ['penɪtreɪt] *v/t (pierce)* penetrar; *market* penetrar en

pen·e·trat·ing ['penɪtreɪtɪŋ] *adj stare, scream* penetrante; *analysis* exhaustivo

pen·e·tra·tion [penɪ'treɪʃn] penetración *f*; *of defences* incursión *f*; *of market* entrada *f*

'pen friend amigo(-a) *m(f)* por correspondencia

pen·guin ['peŋɡwɪn] pingüino *m*

pen·i·cil·lin [penɪ'sɪlɪn] penicilina *f*

pe·nin·su·la [pə'nɪnsʊlə] península *f*

pe·nis ['piːnɪs] pene *m*

pen·i·tence ['penɪtəns] *(remorse)* arrepentimiento *m*

pen·i·tent ['penɪtənt] *adj* arrepentido

pen·i·ten·ti·a·ry [penɪ'tenʃərɪ] prisión *f*, cárcel *f*

pen·knife ['pennaɪf] navaja *f*

'pen name seudónimo *m*

pen·nant ['penənt] banderín *f*

pen·ni·less ['penɪlɪs] *adj* sin un centavo

pen·ny ['penɪ] penique *m*

'pen pal amigo(-a) *m(f)* por correspondencia

pen·sion ['penʃn] pensión *f*

◆ pension off *v/t* jubilar

'pen·sion fund fondo *m* de pensiones

'pen·sion scheme plan *m* de jubilación

pen·sive ['pensɪv] *adj* pensativo

Pen·ta·gon ['pentəgɑːn]: *the Pentagon* el Pentágono

pen·tath·lon [pen'tæθlən] pentatlón m

Pen·te·cost ['pentɪkɑːst] Pentecostés m

pent·house ['penthaʊs] ático m (de lujo)

pent-up ['pentʌp] adj reprimido

pe·nul·ti·mate [pe'nʌltɪmət] adj penúltimo

peo·ple ['piːpl] npl gente f; (*individuals*) personas fpl; (*nsg: race, tribe*) pueblo m; *the people* (*citizens*) el pueblo, los ciudadanos; *the Spanish people* los españoles; *a lot of people think …* muchos piensan que …; *people say …* se dice que …, dicen que …

pep·per ['pepər] *spice* pimienta f; *vegetable* pimiento m

pep·per·mint *sweet* caramelo m de menta

pep talk ['peptɔːk]: *give a pep talk* decir unas palabras de aliento

per [pɜːr] prep por; *per annum* al año, por año

per·ceive [pər'siːv] v/t *with senses* percibir; (*view, interpret*) interpretar

per·cent [pər'sent] adv por ciento

per·cen·tage [pər'sentɪdʒ] porcentaje m, tanto m por ciento

per·cep·ti·ble [pər'septəbl] adj perceptible

per·cep·ti·bly [pər'septəblɪ] adv visiblemente

per·cep·tion [pər'sepʃn] *through senses* percepción f; *of situation* apreciación f; (*insight*) perspicacia f

per·cep·tive [pər'septɪv] adj perceptivo

perch [pɜːrtʃ] **1** n *for bird* percha f **2** v/i *of bird* posarse; *of person* sentarse

per·co·late ['pɜːrkəleɪt] v/i *of coffee* filtrarse

per·co·la·tor ['pɜːrkəleɪtər] cafetera f de filtro

per·cus·sion [pər'kʌʃn] percusión f

per·cus·sion in·stru·ment instrumento m de percusión

pe·ren·ni·al [pə'renɪəl] n BOT árbol m de hoja perenne

per·fect 1 n ['pɜːrfɪkt] GRAM pretérito m perfecto **2** adj perfecto **3** v/t [pər'fekt] perfeccionar

per·fec·tion [pər'fekʃn] perfección f; *do sth to perfection* hacer algo a la perfección

per·fec·tion·ist [pər'fekʃnɪst] perfeccionista m/f

per·fect·ly ['pɜːrfɪktlɪ] perfectamente; (*totally*) completamente

per·fo·rat·ed ['pɜːrfəreɪtɪd] adj *line* perforado

per·fo·ra·tions [pɜːrfə'reɪʃnz] npl perforaciones fpl

per·form [pər'fɔːrm] **1** v/t (*carry out*) realizar, llevar a cabo; *of actors, musician etc* interpretar, representar **2** v/i *of actor, musician, dancer* actuar; *of machine* funcionar

per·form·ance [pər'fɔːrməns] *by actor, musician etc* actuación f, interpretación f; *of play* representación f; *of employee* rendimiento m; *of official, company, in sport* actuación f; *of machine* rendimiento m

per'form·ance car coche m de gran rendimiento

per·form·er [pər'fɔːrmər] intérprete m/f

per·fume ['pɜːrfjuːm] perfume m

per·func·to·ry [pər'fʌŋktərɪ] adj superficial

per·haps [pər'hæps] adv quizá(s), tal vez; *perhaps it's not too late* puede que no sea demasiado tarde

per·il ['perəl] peligro m

per·il·ous ['perələs] adj peligroso

pe·rim·e·ter [pə'rɪmɪtər] perímetro m

pe·rim·e·ter fence cerca f

pe·ri·od ['pɪrɪəd] periodo m, período m; (*menstruation*) periodo, regla f; *punctuation mark* punto m; *I don't want to, period!* F ¡no me da la gana y punto! F

pe·ri·od·ic [pɪrɪ'ɑːdɪk] adj periódico

pe·ri·od·i·cal [pɪrɪ'ɑːdɪkl] n publicación f periódica

pe·ri·od·i·cal·ly [pɪrɪ'ɑːdɪklɪ] adv periódicamente, con periodicidad

pe·riph·e·ral [pə'rɪfərəl] **1** adj (*not crucial*) secundario **2** n COMPUT periférico m

pe·riph·e·ry [pə'rɪfərɪ] periferia f

per·ish ['perɪʃ] v/i *of rubber* estropearse, picarse; *of person* perecer

per·ish·a·ble ['perɪʃəbl] adj *food* perecedero

per·jure ['pɜːrdʒər] v/t: *perjure o.s.* perjurar

per·ju·ry ['pɜːrdʒərɪ] perjurio m

perk [pɜːrk] n *of job* ventaja f

♦ **perk up 1** v/t animar **2** v/i animarse

perk·y ['pɜːrkɪ] (*cheerful*) animado

perm [pɜːrm] **1** n permanente f **2** v/t hacer la permanente; *she had her hair permed* se hizo la permanente

per·ma·nent ['pɜːrmənənt] adj permanente

per·ma·nent·ly ['pɜːrmənəntlɪ] adv permanentemente

per·me·a·ble ['pɜːrmɪəbl] adj permeable

per·me·ate ['pɜːrmɪeɪt] v/t impregnar

per·mis·si·ble [pər'mɪsəbl] adj permisible

per·mis·sion [pər'mɪʃn] permiso m; *ask*

s.o.'s permission to ... pedir permiso a alguien para ...

per·mis·sive [pər'mɪsɪv] *adj* permisivo

per·mit ['pɜːrmɪt] **1** *n* licencia *f* **2** *v/t* (*pret & pp* **permitted**) [pər'mɪt] permitir; *permit s.o. to do sth* permitir a alguien que haga algo

per·pen·dic·u·lar [pɜːrpən'dɪkjʊlər] *adj* perpendicular

per·pet·u·al *adj* perpetuo; *interruptions* continuo

per·pet·u·al·ly [pər'petʊəlɪ] *adv* constantemente

per·pet·u·ate [pər'petʃʊeɪt] *v/t* perpetuar

per·plex [pər'pleks] *v/t* dejar perplejo

per·plexed [pər'plekst] *adj* perplejo

per·plex·i·ty [pər'pleksɪtɪ] perplejidad *f*

per·se·cute ['pɜːrsɪkjuːt] *v/t* perseguir; (*hound*) acosar

per·se·cu·tion [pɜːrsɪ'kjuːʃn] persecución *f*; (*harassment*) acoso *m*

per·se·cu·tor [pɜːrsɪ'kjuːtər] perseguidor(a) *m(f)*

per·se·ver·ance [pɜːrsɪ'vɪrəns] perseverancia *f*

per·se·vere [pɜːrsɪ'vɪr] *v/i* perseverar

per·sist [pər'sɪst] *v/i* persistir; *persist in* persistir en

per·sis·tence [pər'sɪstəns] (*perseverance*) perseverancia *f*; (*continuation*) persistencia *f*

per·sis·tent [pər'sɪstənt] *adj person, questions* perseverante; *rain, unemployment etc* persistente

per·sis·tent·ly [pər'sɪstəntlɪ] *adv* (*continually*) constantemente

per·son ['pɜːrsn] persona *f*; *in person* en persona

per·son·al ['pɜːrsənl] *adj* (*private*) personal; *life* privado; *don't make personal remarks* no hagas comentarios personales

per·son·al as·sis·tant secretario(-a) *m(f)* personal

'per·son·al col·umn sección *f* de anuncios personales

per·son·al com·put·er *Span* ordenador *m* personal, *L.Am.* computadora *f* personal

per·son·al 'hy·giene higiene *f* personal

per·son·al·i·ty [pɜːrsə'nælətɪ] personalidad *f*; (*celebrity*) personalidad *f*, personaje *m*

per·son·al·ly ['pɜːrsənəlɪ] *adv* (*for my part*) personalmente; (*in person*) en persona; *don't take it personally* no te lo tomes como algo personal

per·son·al 'or·gan·iz·er organizador *m* personal

per·son·al 'pro·noun pronombre *m* personal

per·son·al 'ster·e·o walkman *m* ®

per·son·i·fy [pɜːr'sɒnɪfaɪ] *v/t* (*pret & pp* **personified**) *of person* personificar

per·son·nel [pɜːrsə'nel] *employees, department* personal *m*

per·son'nel man·a·ger director(a) *m(f)* de personal

per·spec·tive [pər'spektɪv] PAINT perspectiva *f*; *get sth into perspective* poner algo en perspectiva

per·spi·ra·tion [pɜːrspɪ'reɪʃn] sudor *m*, transpiración *f*

per·spire [pər'spaɪr] *v/i* sudar, transpirar

per·suade [pər'sweɪd] *v/t person* persuadir; *persuade s.o. to do sth* persuadir a alguien para que haga algo

per·sua·sion [pər'sweɪʒn] persuasión *f*

per·sua·sive [pər'sweɪsɪv] persuasivo

per·ti·nent ['pɜːrtɪnənt] *adj fml* pertinente

per·turb [pər'tɜːrb] *v/t* perturbar

per·turb·ing [pər'tɜːrbɪŋ] *adj* perturbador

Pe·ru [pə'ruː] *n* Perú

pe·ruse [pə'ruːz] *v/t fml* leer atentamente

Pe·ru·vi·an [pə'ruːvɪən] **1** *adj* peruano **2** *n* peruano(-a) *m(f)*

per·va·sive [pər'veɪsɪv] *adj influence, ideas* dominante

per·verse [pər'vɜːrs] *adj* (*awkward*) terco; *just to be perverse* sólo para llevar la contraria

per·ver·sion [pər'vɜːrʃn] *sexual* perversión *f*

per·vert ['pɜːrvɜːrt] *n sexual* pervertido(-a) *m(f)*

pes·si·mism ['pesɪmɪzm] pesimismo *m*

pes·si·mist ['pesɪmɪst] pesimista *m/f*

pes·si·mist·ic [pesɪ'mɪstɪk] *adj* pesimista

pest [pest] plaga *f*; F *person* tostón *m* F

pes·ter ['pestər] *v/t* acosar; *pester s.o. to do sth* molestar *or* dar la lata a alguien para que haga algo

pes·ti·cide ['pestɪsaɪd] pesticida *f*

pet [pet] **1** *n animal* animal *m* doméstico *or* de compañía; (*favorite*) preferido(-a) *m(f)* **2** *adj* preferido, favorito **3** *v/t* (*pret & pp* **petted**) *animal* acariciar **4** *v/i* (*pret & pp* **petted**) *of couple* magrearse F

pet·al ['petl] pétalo *m*

◆ **pe·ter out** ['piːtər] *v/i of rain* amainar; *of rebellion* irse extinguiendo; *of path* ir desapareciendo

pe·tite [pə'tiːt] *adj* chiquito(-a); *size* menudo

pe·ti·tion [pə'tɪʃn] *n* petición *f*

'pet name nombre *m* cariñoso

pet·ri·fied ['petrɪfaɪd] *adj person* petrifi-

P

cado; *scream, voice* aterrorizado

pet·ri·fy ['petrɪfaɪ] *v/t (pret & pp **petri-fied**)* dejar petrificado

pet·ro·chem·i·cal [petrou'kemɪkl] *adj* petroquímico

pet·rol ['petrl] *Br* gasolina *f, Arg* nafta *f*

pe·tro·le·um [pɪ'trouliəm] petróleo *m*

pet·ting ['petɪŋ] magreo *m* F

pet·ty ['petɪ] *adj person, behavior* mezquino; *details, problem* sin importancia

pet·ty 'cash dinero *m* para gastos menores

pet·u·lant ['petʃələnt] *adj* caprichoso

pew [pju:] banco *m (de iglesia)*

pew·ter ['pju:tər] peltre *m*

phar·ma·ceu·ti·cal [fɑːrmə'su:tɪkl] *adj* farmacéutico

phar·ma·ceu·ti·cals [fɑːmə'su:tɪklz] *npl* fármacos *mpl*

phar·ma·cist ['fɑːrməsɪst] *in store* farmacéutico(-a) *m(f)*

phar·ma·cy ['fɑːrməsɪ] *store* farmacia *f*

phase [feɪz] fase *f; **go through a difficult phase** atravesar una mala etapa

◆ **phase in** *v/t* introducir gradualmente

◆ **phase out** *v/t* eliminar gradualmente

PhD [pi:eɪtʃ'di:] *abbr (= **Doctor of Philosophy**)* Doctorado *m*

phe·nom·e·nal [fɪ'nɑːmɪnl] *adj* fenomenal

phe·nom·e·nal·ly [fɪ'nɑːmɪnlɪ] *adv* extraordinariamente; *stupid* increíblemente

phe·nom·e·non [fɪ'nɑːmɪnɑn] fenómeno *m*

phil·an·throp·ic [fɪlən'θrɑːpɪk] *adj* filantrópico

phi·lan·thro·pist [fɪ'lænθrəpɪst] filántropo(-a) *m(f)*

phi·lan·thro·py [fɪ'lænθrəpɪ] filantropía *f*

Phil·ip·pines ['fɪlɪpi:nz] *npl: **the Philippines** las Filipinas

phil·is·tine ['fɪlɪstaɪn] *n* filisteo(-a) *m(f)*

phi·los·o·pher [fɪ'lɑːsəfər] filósofo(-a) *m(f)*

phil·o·soph·i·cal [fɪlə'sɑːfɪkl] *adj* filosófico

phi·los·o·phy [fɪ'lɑːsəfɪ] filosofía *f*

pho·bi·a ['foubiə] fobia *f*

phone [foun] **1** *n* teléfono *m; **be on the phone** *have a phone* tener teléfono; *be talking* estar hablando por teléfono **2** *v/t* llamar (por teléfono) a **3** *v/i* llamar (por teléfono)

'phone book guía *f (de teléfonos)*

'phone booth cabina *f (de teléfono)*

'phone call llamada *f (telefónica)*

'phone card *Br* tarjeta *f* telefónica

'phone num·ber número *m* de teléfono

pho·net·ics [fə'netɪks] fonética *f*

pho·n(e)y ['founɪ] *adj* F falso

pho·to ['foutou] *n* foto *f*

'pho·to al·bum álbum *m* de fotos

'pho·to·cop·i·er fotocopiadora *f*

'pho·to·cop·y 1 *n* fotocopia *f* **2** *v/t (pret & pp **photocopied**)* fotocopiar

pho·to·gen·ic [foutou'dʒenɪk] *adj* fotogénico

pho·to·graph ['foutəgræf] **1** *n* fotografía *f* **2** *v/t* fotografiar

pho·tog·ra·pher [fə'tɑːgrəfər] fotógrafo(-a) *m(f)*

pho·tog·ra·phy [fə'tɑːgrəfɪ] fotografía *f*

phrase [freɪz] **1** *n* frase *f* **2** *v/t* expresar

'phrase·book guía *f* de conversación

phys·i·cal ['fɪzɪkl] **1** *adj* físico **2** *n* MED reconocimiento *m* médico

phys·i·cal 'hand·i·cap minusvalía *f* física

phys·i·cal·ly ['fɪzɪklɪ] *adv* físicamente

phys·i·cal·ly 'hand·i·capped disminuido(-a) *m(f)* físico

phy·si·cian [fɪ'zɪʃn] médico(-a) *m(f)*

phys·i·cist ['fɪzɪsɪst] físico(-a) *m(f)*

phys·ics ['fɪzɪks] física *f*

phys·i·o·ther·a·pist [fɪzɪou'θerəpɪst] fisioterapeuta *m/f*

phys·i·o·ther·a·py [fɪzɪou'θerəpɪ] fisioterapia *f*

phy·sique [fɪ'zi:k] físico *m*

pi·a·nist ['pɪənɪst] pianista *m/f*

pi·an·o [pɪ'ænou] piano *m*

pick [pɪk] **1** *n: **take your pick** elige el que prefieras **2** *v/t (choose)* escoger, elegir; *flowers, fruit* recoger; **pick one's nose** meterse el dedo en la nariz **3** *v/i: **pick and choose** ser muy exigente

◆ **pick at** *v/t: **pick at one's food** comer como un pajarito

◆ **pick on** *v/t (treat unfairly)* meterse con; *(select)* elegir

◆ **pick out** *v/t (identify)* identificar

◆ **pick up 1** *v/t object* recoger, *Span* coger; *habit* adquirir, *Span* coger; *illness* contraer, *Span* coger; *in car, from ground, from airport etc* recoger; *telephone* descolgar; *language, skill* aprender; *(buy)* comprar; *criminal* detener; **pick s.o. up** *sexually* ligar con alguien; **pick up the tab** F pagar **2** *v/i (improve)* mejorar

pick·et ['pɪkɪt] **1** *n of strikers* piquete *m* **2** *v/t* hacer piquete delante de

'pick·et fence valla *f* de estacas

'pick·et line piquete *m*

pick·le ['pɪkl] *v/t* encurtir; *fish* poner en escabeche; *meat* poner en adobo

pick·les ['pɪklz] *npl (dill pickles)* encurtidos *mpl*

'pick·pock·et carterista *m/f*

pick·up (truck) ['pɪkʌp] camioneta f

pick·y ['pɪkɪ] adj F tiquismiquis F

pic·nic ['pɪknɪk] n 2 v/i (pret & pp **picnicked**) ir de picnic

pic·ture ['pɪktʃər] 1 n (photo) fotografía f; (painting) cuadro m; (illustration) dibujo m; (movie) película f; on TV imagen f; **keep s.o. in the picture** mantener a alguien al día 2 v/t imaginar

'pic·ture book libro m ilustrado

pic·ture 'post·card postal f

pic·tur·esque [pɪktʃə'resk] adj pintoresco

pie [paɪ] pastel m

piece [piːs] (fragment) fragmento m; component, in board game pieza f; **a piece of pie / bread** un trozo de pastel / una rebanada de pan; **a piece of advice** un consejo; **go to pieces** derrumbarse; **take to pieces** desmontar

◆ piece together v/t broken plate recomponer; facts, evidence reconstruir

piece·meal ['piːsmiːl] adv poco a poco

piece·work ['piːswɜːrk] n trabajo m a destajo

pier [pɪr] at seaside malecón m

pierce [pɪrs] v/t (penetrate) perforar; ears agujerear

pierc·ing ['pɪrsɪŋ] adj scream desgarrador; gaze penetrante; wind cortante

pig [pɪg] also fig cerdo m; greedy glotón(-a) m(f)

pi·geon ['pɪdʒɪn] paloma f

'pi·geon·hole 1 n casillero m 2 v/t person encasillar; proposal archivar

pig·gy·bank ['pɪgɪbæŋk] hucha f

pig·head·ed [pɪg'hedɪd] adj F cabezota F

'pig·pen also fig pocilga f

'pig·skin piel f de cerdo

'pig·tail coleta f

pile [paɪl] montón m, also **a pile of work** F un montón de trabajo F

◆ pile up 1 v/i of work, bills acumularse 2 v/t amontonar

piles [paɪlz] nsg MED hemorroides fpl

pile-up ['paɪlʌp] MOT choque m múltiple

pil·fer·ing ['pɪlfərɪŋ] hurtos mpl

pil·grim ['pɪlgrɪm] peregrino(-a) m(f)

pil·grim·age ['pɪlgrɪmɪdʒ] peregrinación f

pill [pɪl] pastilla f; **be on the pill** tomar la píldora

pil·lar ['pɪlər] pilar m

pil·lion ['pɪljən] of motor bike asiento m trasero

pil·low ['pɪloʊ] n almohada f

'pil·low·case, 'pil·low·slip funda f de almohada

pi·lot ['paɪlət] 1 n of airplane piloto m/f; for ship práctico m 2 v/t airplane pilotar

'pi·lot scheme plan m piloto

pimp [pɪmp] n proxeneta m, Span chulo m F

pim·ple ['pɪmpl] grano m

pin [pɪn] 1 n for sewing alfiler m; in bowling bolo m; (badge) pin m; ELEC clavija f; **safety pin** imperdible m 2 v/t (pret & pp **pinned**) (hold down) mantener; (attach) sujetar

◆ pin down v/t: **pin s.o. down to a date** forzar a alguien a concretar una fecha

◆ pin up v/t notice sujetar con chinchetas

PIN [pɪn] PIN m personal identification number número m de identificación personal

pin·cers ['pɪnsərz] npl of crab pinzas fpl; tool tenazas fpl; **a pair of pincers** unas tenazas fpl

pinch [pɪntʃ] 1 n of salt, sugar etc pizca f; **at a pinch** si no queda otro remedio; **at a pinch** with numbers como máximo 2 v/t pellizcar 3 v/i of shoes apretar

pine[1] [paɪn] n tree pino m; wood (madera f de) pino m

pine[2] [paɪn] v/i: **pine for** echar de menos

pine·ap·ple ['paɪnæpl] piña f, L.Am. ananá(s) f

ping [pɪŋ] 1 n sonido m metálico 2 v/i hacer un sonido metálico

ping-pong ['pɪŋpɑːŋ] pimpón m, ping-pong m

pink [pɪŋk] adj rosa

pin·na·cle ['pɪnəkl] fig cima f

'pin·point determinar

pins and 'nee·dles hormigueo m

'pin·stripe adj a rayas

pint [paɪnt] pinta f, medida equivalente a 0,473 litros en Estados Unidos o a 0,568 litros en Gran Bretaña

'pin-up modelo m/f de revista

pi·o·neer [paɪə'nɪr] 1 n fig pionero(-a) m(f) 2 v/t ser pionero en

pi·o·neer·ing [paɪə'nɪrɪŋ] adj work pionero

pi·ous ['paɪəs] piadoso

pip [pɪp] n of fruit pepita f

pipe [paɪp] 1 n for smoking pipa f; for water, gas, sewage tubería f 2 v/t conducir por tuberías

◆ pipe down v/i F cerrar el pico F

piped mu·sic [paɪpt'mjuːzɪk] hilo m musical

pipe·line for oil oleoducto m; for gas gasoducto m; **in the pipeline** fig en trámite

pip·ing ho·t [paɪpɪŋ'hɑːt] adj muy caliente

pi·rate ['paɪrət] 1 n pirata m/f 2 v/t software piratear

Pis·ces ['paɪsiːz] ASTR Piscis m/f inv

piss [pɪs] 1 v/i P (urinate) mear P; **take the**

P

piss out of s.o. P cachondearse de alguien P **2** *n* P (*urine*) meada *f* P
◆ **piss off** *v/i* largarse F; **piss off!** P ¡vete al cuerno! P

pissed [pɪst] *adj* P (*annoyed*) cabreado P; *Br* P (*drunk*) borracho, pedo F

pis·tol ['pɪstl] pistola *f*

pis·ton ['pɪstən] pistón *m*

pit [pɪt] *n* (*hole*) hoyo *m*; (*coal mine*) mina *f*

pitch¹ [pɪtʃ] *n* MUS tono *m*

pitch² [pɪtʃ] **1** *v/i in baseball* lanzar la pelota **2** *v/t tent* montar; *ball* lanzar

'**pitch black** *adj* negro como el carbón

pitch·er¹ ['pɪtʃər] *baseball player* lanzador(a) *m(f)*, pítcher *m/f*

pitch·er² ['pɪtʃər] *container* jarra *f*

pit·e·ous ['pɪtɪəs] *adj* patético

pit·fall ['pɪtfɔːl] dificultad *f*

pith [pɪθ] *of citrus fruit* piel *f* blanca

pit·i·ful ['pɪtɪfəl] *adj sight* lamentable; *excuse, attempt* lamentable

pit·i·less ['pɪtɪləs] *adj* despiadado

pits [pɪts] *npl in motor racing* boxes *mpl*

'**pit stop** *in motor racing* parada *f* en boxes

pit·tance ['pɪtns] miseria *f*

pit·y ['pɪtɪ] **1** *n* pena *f*, lástima *f*; *it's a pity that* es una pena *or* lástima que; *what a pity!* ¡qué pena!; *take pity on* compadecerse de **2** *v/t* (*pret & pp pitied*) *person* compadecerse de

piv·ot ['pɪvət] *v/i* pivotar

piz·za ['piːtsə] pizza *f*

plac·ard ['plækɑːrd] pancarta *f*

place [pleɪs] **1** *n* sitio *m*; *in race, competition* puesto *m*; (*seat*) sitio *m*, asiento *m*; *I've lost my place in book* no sé por dónde iba; *at my / his place* en mi / su casa; *in place of* en lugar de; *feel out of place* sentirse fuera de lugar; *take place* tener lugar, llevarse a cabo; *in the first place* (*firstly*) en primer lugar; (*in the beginning*) en principio **2** *v/t* (*put*) poner, colocar; *I know you but I can't quite place you* te conozco pero no recuerdo de qué; *place an order* hacer un pedido

'**place mat** mantel *m* individual

plac·id ['plæsɪd] *adj* apacible

pla·gia·rism ['pleɪdʒərɪzm] plagio *m*

pla·gia·rize ['pleɪdʒəraɪz] *v/t* plagiar

plague [pleɪg] **1** *n* plaga *f* **2** *v/t* (*bother*) molestar

plain¹ [pleɪn] *n* llanura *f*

plain² [pleɪn] **1** *adj* (*clear, obvious*) claro; (*not fancy*) simple; (*not pretty*) feíllo; (*not patterned*) liso; (*blunt*) directo; *plain chocolate* chocolate amargo **2** *adv* verdaderamente; *it's plain crazy*

es una verdadera locura

'**plain-clothes**: *in plain-clothes* de paisano

plain·ly ['pleɪnlɪ] *adv* (*clearly*) evidentemente; (*bluntly*) directamente; (*simply*) con sencillez; *he's plainly upset* está claro que está enfadado

plain 'spo·ken *adj* directo

plain·tiff ['pleɪntɪf] demandante *m/f*

plain·tive ['pleɪntɪv] *adj* quejumbroso

plan [plæn] **1** *n* (*project, intention*) plan *m*; (*drawing*) plano *m*; *wedding plans* preparaciones *fpl* para la boda **2** *v/t* (*pret & pp planned*) (*prepare*) planear; (*design*) hacer los planos de; *plan to do sth, plan on doing sth* planear hacer algo **3** *v/i* (*pret & pp planned*) hacer planes

plane¹ [pleɪn] *n* (*airplane*) avión *m*

plane² [pleɪn] *tool* cepillo *m*

plan·et ['plænɪt] planeta *f*

plank [plæŋk] *of wood* tablón *m*; *fig: of policy* punto *m*

plan·ning ['plænɪŋ] planificación *f*; *at the planning stage* en fase de estudio

plant¹ [plænt] **1** *n* planta *f* **2** *v/t* plantar

plant² [plænt] *n* (*factory*) fábrica *f*, planta *f*; (*equipment*) maquinaria *f*

plan·ta·tion [plæn'teɪʃn] plantación *f*

plaque [plæk] *on wall, teeth* placa *f*

plas·ter ['plæstər] **1** *n on wall, ceiling* yeso *m* **2** *v/t wall, ceiling* enyesar; *be plastered with* estar recubierto de

plas·ter cast escayola *f*

plas·tic ['plæstɪk] **1** *n* plástico *m* **2** *adj* (*made of plastic*) de plástico

'**plas·tic 'bag** bolsa *f* de plástico

'**plas·tic (mon·ey)** plástico *m*, tarjetas *fpl* de pago

plas·tic 'sur·geon cirujano(-a) *m(f)* plástico(-a)

plas·tic 'sur·ge·ry cirugía *f* estética

plate [pleɪt] *n for food* plato *m*; (*sheet of metal*) chapa *f*; F PHOT placa *f*

pla·teau ['plætou] meseta *f*

plat·form ['plætfɔːrm] (*stage*) plataforma *f*; *of railroad station* andén *m*; *fig: political* programa *f*

plat·i·num ['plætɪnəm] **1** *n* platino *m* **2** *adj* de platino

plat·i·tude ['plætɪtuːd] tópico *m*

pla·ton·ic [plə'tɑːnɪk] *adj relationship* platónico

pla·toon [plə'tuːn] *of soldiers* sección *f*

plat·ter ['plætər] *for meat, fish* fuente *f*

plau·si·ble ['plɔːzəbl] *adj* plausible

play [pleɪ] **1** *n in theater, on* TV obra *f* (de teatro); *of children, in match,* TECH juego *m* **2** *v/i* jugar; *of musician* tocar **3** *v/t musical instrument* tocar; *piece of music in-*

plunge

terpretar, tocar; *game* jugar; *tennis, football* jugar a; *opponent* jugar contra; *(perform: Macbeth etc)* representar; *particular role* interpretar, hacer el papel de; **play a joke on** gastar una broma a
◆ **play around** v/i F *(be unfaithful)* acostarse con otras personas
◆ **play down** v/t quitar importancia a
◆ **play up** v/t *of machine* dar problemas; *of child* dar guerra
play·act ['pleɪækt] v/i *(pretend)* fingir
play·boy ['pleɪbɔɪ] playboy *m*
play·er ['pleɪr] sp jugador(a) *m(f)*; *(musician)* intérprete *m/f*; *(actor)* actor *m*, actriz *f*
play·ful ['pleɪfəl] adj *punch etc* de broma
play·ground ['pleɪgraʊnd] zona *f* de juegos
'**play·group** guardería *f*
play·ing card ['pleɪɪŋkɑːrd] carta *f*
play·ing field ['pleɪɪŋfiːld] campo *m* de deportes
play·mate ['pleɪmeɪt] compañero(-a) *m(f)* de juego
play·wright ['pleɪraɪt] autor(a) *m(f)*
pla·za ['plɑːzə] *for shopping* centro *m* comercial
plc [piːel'siː] abbr (= *Br public limited company*) S.A. *f* (= sociedad *f* anónima)
plea [pliː] *n* súplica *f*
plead [pliːd] v/i: **plead for mercy** pedir clemencia; **plead guilty / not guilty** declararse culpable / inocente; **she pleaded with me not to go** me suplicó que no fuera
pleas·ant ['pleznt] adj agradable
please [pliːz] **1** adv por favor; **more tea? - yes, please** ¿más té? - sí, por favor; **please do** claro que sí, por supuesto **2** v/t complacer; **please yourself!** ¡haz lo que quieras!
pleased [pliːzd] adj contento; *(satisfied)* satisfecho; **pleased to meet you** encantado de conocerle; **I'm very pleased to be here** estoy muy contento de estar aquí
pleas·ing ['pliːzɪŋ] adj agradable
pleas·ure ['pleʒər] *(happiness, satisfaction, delight)* satisfacción *f*; *as opposed to work* placer *m*; **it's a pleasure** *(you're welcome)* no hay de qué; **with pleasure** faltaría más
pleat [pliːt] *n in skirt* tabla *f*
pleat·ed skirt ['pliːtɪd] falda *f* de tablas
pledge [pledʒ] **1** *n (promise)* promesa *f*; *(guarantee)* compromiso *m*; *(money)* donación *f*; **Pledge of Allegiance** juramento de lealtad a la bandera estadounidense **2** v/t *(promise)* prometer; *(guarantee)* comprometerse; *money* donar

plen·ti·ful ['plentɪfəl] adj abundante
plen·ty ['plentɪ] *(abundance)* abundancia *f*; **plenty of books / food** muchos libros / mucha comida; **we've got plenty of room** tenemos espacio más que suficiente; **that's plenty** es suficiente; **there's plenty for everyone** hay (suficiente) para todos
pli·a·ble ['plaɪəbl] adj flexible
pli·ers ['plaɪərz] npl alicates *mpl*; **a pair of pliers** unos alicates
plight [plaɪt] situación *f* difícil
plod [plɑːd] v/i *(pret & pp plodded)* *(walk)* arrastrarse
◆ **plod on** v/i *with a job* avanzar laboriosamente
plod·der ['plɑːdər] *(at work, school)* persona no especialmente lista pero muy trabajadora
plot[1] [plɑːt] *n (land)* terreno *m*
plot[2] [plɑːt] **1** *n (conspiracy)* complot *m*; *of novel* argumento *m* **2** v/t *(pret & pp plotted)* tramar **3** v/i *(pret & pp plotted)* conspirar
plot·ter ['plɑːtər] conspirador(a) *m(f)*; COMPUT plóter *m*
plough *Br*, **plow** [plaʊ] **1** *n* arado *m* **2** v/t & v/i arar
◆ **plow back** v/t *profits* reinvertir
pluck [plʌk] v/t *eyebrows* depilar; *chicken* desplumar
◆ **pluck up** v/t: **pluck up courage to ...** reunir el valor para ...
plug [plʌg] **1** *n for sink, bath* tapón *m*; *electrical* enchufe *m*; *(spark plug)* bujía *f*; **give a book a plug** dar publicidad a un libro **2** v/t *(pret & pp plugged)* *hole* tapar; *new book etc* hacer publicidad de
◆ **plug away at** v/t F trabajar con esfuerzo en
◆ **plug in** v/t enchufar
plum [plʌm] **1** *n in fruit* ciruela *f*; *tree* ciruelo *m* **2** adj F: **plum job** un chollo de trabajo
plum·age ['pluːmɪdʒ] plumaje *m*
plumb [plʌm] adj vertical
◆ **plumb in** v/t *washing machine* conectar a la red del agua
plumb·er ['plʌmər] *Span* fontanero(-a) *m(f)*, *L.Am.* plomero(-a) *m(f)*
plumb·ing ['plʌmɪŋ] *(pipes)* tuberías *fpl*
plume [pluːm] *n (feather)* pluma *f*; *of smoke* nube *f*
plum·met ['plʌmɪt] v/i *of airplane, prices* caer en picado
plump [plʌmp] adj rellenito
◆ **plump for** v/t decidirse por
plunge [plʌndʒ] **1** *n* salto *m*; *in prices* caída *f*; **take the plunge** dar el paso **2** v/i precipitarse; *of prices* caer en picado **3**

P

v/t hundir; (*into water*) sumergir; ***the city
was plunged into darkness*** la ciudad
quedó inmersa en la oscuridad; ***the
news plunged him into despair*** la noticia lo hundió en la desesperación

plung·ing ['plʌndʒɪŋ] *adj* neckline escotado

plu·per·fect ['pluː'pɜːrfɪkt] *n* GRAM pluscuamperfecto *m*

plu·ral ['plʊərəl] **1** *n* plural *m* **2** *adj* plural

plus [plʌs] **1** *prep* más; ***I want John plus
two other volunteers …*** quiero a John y
a otros dos voluntarios **2** *adj* más de;
$500 plus más de 500 dólares **3** *n symbol*
signo *m* más; (*advantage*) ventaja *f* **4** *conj*
(*moreover, in addition*) además

plush [plʌʃ] *adj* lujoso

'plus sign signo *m* más

ply·wood ['plaɪwʊd] madera *f* contracha-
pada

PM [piː'em] *Br abbr* (= *Prime Minister*)
Primer(a) *m(f)* Ministro(-a)

p.m. [piː'em] *abbr* (= *post meridiem*)
p.m.; ***at 3 p.m*** a las 3 de la tarde; ***at 11
p.m*** a las 11 de la noche

pneu·mat·ic [nuː'mætɪk] *adj* neumático

pneu·mat·ic 'drill martillo *m* neumático

pneu·mo·ni·a [nuː'moʊnɪə] pulmonía *f*,
neumonía *f*

poach[1] [poʊtʃ] *v/t* (*cook*) hervir

poach[2] [poʊtʃ] *v/t & v/i* (*hunt*) cazar furtivamente; *fish* pescar furtivamente

poached egg [poʊtʃt'eg] huevo *m* escalfado

poach·er ['poʊtʃər] *of game* cazador(a)
m(f) furtivo(a); *of fish* pescador(a)
m(f) furtivo(a)

P.O. Box [piː'oʊbɑːks] apartado *m* de correos

pock·et[1] ['pɑːkɪt] **1** *n* bolsillo *m*; ***line one's
pockets*** llenarse los bolsillos; ***be $10
out of pocket*** salir perdiendo 10 dólares
2 *adj* radio, dictionary de bolsillo **3** *v/t*
meter en el bolsillo

'pock·et·book (*handbag*) bolso *m*; (*wallet*) cartera *f*; (*book*) libro *m* de bolsillo

pock·et 'cal·cu·la·tor calculadora *f* de
bolsillo

'pock·et·knife navaja *f*

po·di·um ['poʊdɪəm] podio *m*

po·em ['poʊɪm] poema *m*

po·et ['poʊɪt] poeta *m*; poeta *f*, poetisa *f*

po·et·ic [poʊ'etɪk] *adj* poético

po·et·ic 'jus·tice justicia *f* divina

po·et·ry ['poʊɪtrɪ] poesía *f*

poign·ant ['pɔɪnjənt] *adj* conmovedor

point [pɔɪnt] **1** *n of pencil, knife* punta *f*;
in competition, argument punto *m*; (*purpose*) objetivo *m*; (*moment*) momento *m*;

in decimals coma *f*; ***what's the point of
telling him?*** ¿qué se consigue diciéndo-
selo?; ***the point I'm trying to make …*** lo
que estoy intentando decir …; ***at one
point*** en un momento dado; ***that's beside the point*** eso no viene a cuento; ***be
on the point of*** estar a punto de; ***get
to the point*** ir al grano; ***the point is
…*** la cuestión es que …; ***there's no point
in waiting / trying*** no vale la pena esperar / intentarlo **2** *v/i* señalar con el dedo **3**
v/t: ***he pointed the gun at me*** me apuntó
con la pistola

◆ **point out** *v/t* sights indicar; advantages
etc destacar

◆ **point to** *v/t* with finger señalar con el
dedo; (*fig: indicate*) indicar

'point-blank 1 *adj* refusal, denial categórico; ***at point-blank range*** a quemarropa
2 *adv* refuse, deny categóricamente

point·ed ['pɔɪntɪd] *adj* remark mordaz

point·er ['pɔɪntər] *for teacher* puntero *m*;
(*hint*) consejo *m*; (*sign, indication*) indicador *m*

point·less ['pɔɪntləs] *adj* inútil; ***it's pointless trying*** no sirve de nada intentarlo

'point of sale *place* punto *m* de venta;
promotional material material *m* promocional

'point of view punto *m* de vista

poise [pɔɪz] confianza *f*

poised [pɔɪzd] *adj* person con aplomo

poi·son ['pɔɪzn] **1** *n* veneno *m* **2** *v/t* envenenar

poi·son·ous ['pɔɪznəs] *adj* venenoso

poke [poʊk] **1** *n* empujón *m* **2** *v/t* (*prod*)
empujar; (*stick*) clavar; ***he poked his
head out of the window*** asomó la cabeza por la ventana; ***poke fun at*** reírse de;
poke one's nose into F meter las narices
en F

◆ **poke around** *v/i* F husmear

pok·er ['poʊkər] *card game* póquer *m*

pok·y ['poʊkɪ] *adj* F (*cramped*) enano, minúsculo

Po·land ['poʊlənd] Polonia

po·lar ['poʊlər] *adj* polar

po·lar bear oso *m* polar *or* blanco

po·lar·ize ['poʊləraɪz] *v/t* polarizar

Pole [poʊl] polaco(-a) *m(f)*

pole[1] [poʊl] *for support* poste *m*; *for tent,
pushing things* palo *m*

pole[2] [poʊl] *of earth* polo *m*

'pole star estrella *f* polar

'pole-vault salto *m* con pértiga

'pole-vault·er saltador(a) *m(f)* de pértiga

po·lice [pə'liːs] *n* policía *f*

po·lice car coche *m* de policía

po·lice·man policía *m*

P

po'lice state estado *m* policial

po'lice sta·tion comisaría *f* (de policía)

po'lice·wo·man (mujer *f*) policía *f*

pol·i·cy¹ ['pɑːlɪsɪ] política *f*

pol·i·cy² ['pɑːlɪsɪ] (*insurance policy*) póliza *f*

po·li·o ['pouliou] polio *f*

Pol·ish ['poulɪʃ] 1 *adj* polaco 2 *n* polaco *m*

pol·ish ['pɑːlɪʃ] 1 *n* abrillantador *m*; (*nail polish*) esmalte *m* de uñas 2 *v/t* dar brillo a; *speech* pulir

◆ polish off *v/t food* acabar, comerse

◆ polish up *v/t skill* perfeccionar

pol·ished ['pɑːlɪʃt] *adj performance* brillante

po·lite [pə'laɪt] *adj* educado

po·lite·ly [pə'laɪtlɪ] *adv* educadamente

po·lite·ness [pə'laɪtnɪs] educación *f*

po·lit·i·cal [pə'lɪtɪkl] *adj* político

po·lit·i·cal·ly cor·rect [pə'lɪtɪklɪ kə'rekt] politicamente correcto

pol·i·ti·cian [pɑːlɪ'tɪʃn] político(-a) *m*(*f*)

pol·i·tics ['pɑːlətɪks] política *f*; **I'm not interested in politics** no me interesa la política; **what are his politics?** ¿cuáles son sus ideas políticas?

poll [poul] 1 *n* (*survey*) encuesta *f*, sondeo *m*; **the polls** (*election*) las elecciones; **go to the polls** (*vote*) acudir a las urnas 2 *v/t people* sondear; *votes* obtener

pol·len ['pɑːlən] polen *m*

'pol·len count concentración *f* de polen en el aire

'poll·ing booth ['poulɪŋ] cabina *f* electoral

'poll·ing day día *m* de las elecciones

poll·ster ['poulstər] encuestador(a) *m*(*f*)

pol·lu·tant [pə'luːtənt] contaminante *m*

pol·lute [pə'luːt] *v/t* contaminar

pol·lu·tion [pə'luːʃn] contaminación *f*

po·lo ['poulou] sp polen *m*

'po·lo neck *sweater* suéter *m* de cuello alto

'po·lo shirt polo *m*

pol·y·eth·yl·ene [pɑːlɪ'eθɪliːn] polietileno *m*

pol·y·es·ter [pɑːlɪ'estər] poliéster *m*

pol·y·sty·rene [pɑːlɪ'staɪriːn] poliestireno *m*

pol·y·un·sat·u·rat·ed [pɑːlɪʌn'sætʃəreɪtɪd] *adj* poliinsaturado

pom·pous ['pɑːmpəs] *adj* pomposo

pond [pɑːnd] estanque *m*

pon·der ['pɑːndər] *v/i* reflexionar

pon·tiff ['pɑːntɪf] pontífice *m*

po·ny ['pouni] poni *m*

'po·ny·tail coleta *f*

poo·dle ['puːdl] caniche *m*

pool¹ [puːl] 1 *n* (*swimming pool*) piscina *f*,

L.Am. pileta *f*, *Mex* alberca *f*; *of water, blood* charco *m*

pool² [puːl] *game* billar *m* americano

pool³ [puːl] 1 *n* (*common fund*) bote *m*, fondo *m* común 2 *v/t resources* juntar

'pool hall sala *f* de billares

'pool table mesa *f* de billar americano

poop·ed [puːpt] *adj* F hecho polvo F

poor [pur] 1 *adj* pobre; (*not good*) mediocre, malo; **be in poor health** estar enfermo; **poor old Tony!** ¡pobre(cito) Tony! 2 *n*: **the poor** los pobres

poor·ly ['purlɪ] 1 *adv* mal 2 *adj* (*unwell*): **feel poorly** encontrarse mal

pop¹ [pɑːp] 1 *n noise* pequeño *m* ruido 2 *v/i* (*pret & pp* **popped**) *of balloon etc* estallar 3 *v/t* (*pret & pp* **popped**) *cork* hacer saltar; *balloon* pinchar

pop² [pɑːp] 1 *n* MUS pop *m* 2 *adj* pop

pop³ [pɑːp] F (*father*) papá *m* F

pop⁴ [pɑːp] F (*put*) meter

◆ pop in *v/i* F (*make a brief visit*) pasar un momento

◆ pop out *v/i* F (*go out for a short time*) salir un momento

◆ pop up *v/i* F (*appear suddenly*) aparecer

'pop con·cert concierto *m* (de música) pop

pop·corn ['pɑːpkɔːrn] palomitas *fpl* de maíz

pope [poup] papa *m*

'pop group grupo *m* (de música) pop

pop·py ['pɑːpɪ] amapola *f*

Pop·sicle® ['pɑːpsɪkl] polo *m* (*helado*)

'pop song canción *f* pop

pop·u·lar ['pɑːpjulər] *adj* popular; **contrary to popular belief** contrariamente a lo que se piensa

pop·u·lar·i·ty [pɑːpju'lærətɪ] popularidad *f*

pop·u·late ['pɑːpjuleɪt] *v/t* poblar

pop·u·la·tion [pɑːpju'leɪʃn] población *f*

porce·lain ['pɔːrsəlɪn] 1 *n* porcelana *f* 2 *adj* de porcelana

porch [pɔːrtʃ] porche *m*

por·cu·pine ['pɔːrkjupaɪn] puercoespín *m*

pore [pɔːr] *of skin* poro *m*

◆ pore over *v/t* estudiar detenidamente

pork [pɔːrk] cerdo *m*

porn [pɔːrn] *n* F porno *m*

porn(o) [pɔːrn, 'pɔːrnou] *adj* F porno F

por·no·graph·ic [pɔːrnə'græfɪk] *adj* pornográfico

porn·og·ra·phy [pɔːr'nɑːgrəfɪ] pornografía *f*

po·rous ['pɔːrəs] *adj* poroso

port¹ [pɔːrt] *n town, area* puerto *m*

port² [pɔːrt] *adj* (*left-hand*) a babor

por·ta·ble ['pɔːrtəbl] **1** *adj* portátil **2** *n* COMPUT portátil *m*; TV televisión *f* portátil

por·ter ['pɔːrtər] mozo(-a) *m(f)*

port·hole ['pɔːrthoul] NAUT portilla *f*

por·tion ['pɔːrʃn] *n* parte *f*; *of food* ración *f*

por·trait ['pɔːrtreit] **1** *n* retrato *m* **2** *adv* *print* en formato vertical

por·tray [pɔːr'trei] *of artist, photographer* retratar; *of actor* interpretar; *of author* describir

por·tray·al [pɔːr'treiəl] *by actor* interpretación *f*, representación *f*; *by author* descripción *f*

Por·tu·gal ['pɔːrtʃugl] Portugal

Por·tu·guese [pɔːrtʃu'giːz] **1** *adj* portugués **2** *person* portugués(-esa) *m(f)*; *language* portugués *m*

pose [pouz] **1** *n (pretense)* pose *f*; *it's all a pose* no es más que una pose **2** *v/i for artist, photographer* posar; *pose as* hacerse pasar por **3** *v/t*: *pose a problem/a threat* representar un problema / una amenaza

posh [pɑːʃ] *adj Br* F elegante, *pej* pijo

po·si·tion [pə'zɪʃn] **1** *n* posición *f*; *(stance, point of view)* postura *f*; *(job)* puesto *m*, empleo *m*; *(status)* posición *f* (social) **2** *v/t* situar, colocar

pos·i·tive ['pɑːzətɪv] *adj* positivo; *be positive (sure)* estar seguro

pos·i·tive·ly ['pɑːzətɪvlɪ] *adv (decidedly)* verdaderamente, sin lugar a dudas; *(definitely)* claramente

pos·sess [pə'zes] *v/t* poseer

pos·ses·sion [pə'zeʃn] posesión *f*; *possessions* posesiones *fpl*

pos·ses·sive [pə'zesɪv] *adj person*, GRAM posesivo

pos·si·bil·i·ty [pɑːsə'bɪlətɪ] posibilidad *f*; *there is a possibility that ...* cabe la posibilidad de que ...

pos·si·ble ['pɑːsəbl] *adj* posible; *the shortest / quickest route possible* la ruta más corto / rápido posible; *the best possible ...* el mejor ...

possibly ['pɑːsəblɪ] *adv (perhaps)* puede ser, quizás; *that can't possibly be right* no puede ser cierto; *they're doing everything they possibly can* están haciendo todo lo que pueden; *could you possibly tell me ...?* ¿tendría la amabilidad de decirme ...?

post¹ [poust] **1** *n of wood, metal* poste *m* **2** *v/t notice* pegar; *on notice board* poner; *profits* presentar; *keep s.o. posted* mantener a alguien al corriente

post² [poust] **1** *n (place of duty)* puesto *m* **2** *v/t soldier, employee* destinar; *guards* apostar

post³ [poust] **1** *n Br (mail)* correo *m* **2** *v/t Br letter* echar al correo

post·age ['poustɪdʒ] franqueo *m*

'post·age stamp *fml* sello *m*, *L.Am.* estampilla *f*, *Mex* timbre *m*

post·al [poustl] *adj* postal

'post·card *(tarjeta f)* postal *f*

'post·code *Br* código *m* postal

'post·date *v/t* posfechar

post·er ['poustər] póster *m*, *L.Am.* afiche *m*

pos·te·ri·or [pɑː'stɪrɪər] *n (hum: buttocks)* trasero *m*

pos·ter·i·ty [pɑː'sterətɪ] posteridad *f*; *for posterity* para la posteridad

post·grad·u·ate ['poustɡrædʒuət] **1** *n* posgraduado(-a) *m(f)* **2** *adj* de posgrado

post·hu·mous ['pɑːstuməs] *adj* póstumo

post·hu·mous·ly ['pɑːstuməslɪ] *adv* póstumamente

post·ing ['poustɪŋ] *(assignment)* destino *m*

post·mark ['poustmɑːrk] matasellos *m inv*

post·mor·tem [poust'mɔːrtəm] autopsia *f*

'post of·fice oficina *f* de correos

post·pone [poust'poun] *v/t* posponer, aplazar

post·pone·ment [poust'pounmənt] aplazamiento *m*

pos·ture ['pɑːstʃər] postura *f*

'post-war *adj* de posguerra

pot¹ [pɑːt] *for cooking* olla *f*; *for coffee* cafetera *f*; *for tea* tetera *f*; *for plant* maceta *f*

pot² [pɑːt] F *(marijuana)* maría *f* F

po·ta·to [pə'teɪtou] *Span* patata *f*, *L.Am.* papa *f*

po·ta·to chips, *Br* **po·ta·to crisps** *npl Span* patatas *fpl* fritas, *L.Am.* papas *fpl* fritas

'pot·bel·ly ['pɑːtbelɪ] barriga *f*

po·tent ['poutənt] *adj* potente

po·ten·tial [pə'tenʃl] **1** *adj* potencial **2** *n* potencial *m*

po·ten·tial·ly [pə'tenʃəlɪ] *adv* potencialmente

pot·hole ['pɑːthoul] *in road* bache *m*

pot·ter ['pɑːtər] *n* alfarero(-a) *m(f)*

pot·ter·y ['pɑːtərɪ] *n* alfarería *f*

pot·ty ['pɑːtɪ] *n for baby* orinal *m*

pouch [pautʃ] *(bag)* bolsa *f*; *for tobacco* petaca *f*; *for amunition* cartuchera *f*; *for mail* saca *m*

poul·try ['poultrɪ] *birds* aves *fpl* de corral; *meat* carne *f* de ave

pounce [pauns] *v/i of animal* saltar; *fig* echarse encima

pound¹ [paʊnd] *n weight* libra *f (453,6 gr)*
pound² [paʊnd] *n for strays* perrera *f; for cars* depósito *m*
pound³ [paʊnd] *v/i of heart* palpitar con fuerza; **pound on** (*hammer on*) golpear en
pound 'ster·ling libra *f* esterlina
pour [pɔːr] **1** *v/t into a container* verter; *spill* derramar; **pour s.o. some coffee** servir café a alguien **2** *v/i*: **it's pouring (with rain)** está lloviendo a cántaros
◆ **pour out** *v/t liquid* servir; *troubles* contar
pout [paʊt] *v/i* hacer un mohín
pov·er·ty ['pɑːvərtɪ] pobreza *f*
pov·er·ty-strick·en ['pɑːvərtɪstrɪkn] depauperado
pow·der ['paʊdər] **1** *n* polvo *m; for face* polvos *m,* colorete *m* **2** *v/t face* empolvarse
pow·er ['paʊər] **1** *n* (*strength*) tuerza *f; of engine* potencia; (*authority*) poder *m;* (*energy*) energía *f;* (*electricity*) electricidad *f;* **in power** POL en el poder; **fall from power** POL perder el poder **2** *v/t:* **be powered by** estar impulsado por
'pow·er-as·sist·ed steering dirección *f* asistida
'pow·er cut apagón *m*
'pow·er fail·ure apagón *m*
pow·er·ful ['paʊərfəl] *adj* poderoso; *car* potente; *drug* fuerte
pow·er·less ['paʊərlɪs] *adj* impotente; **be powerless to ...** ser incapaz de ...
'pow·er line línea *f* de conducción eléctrica
'pow·er out·age apagón *m*
'pow·er sta·tion central *f* eléctrica
'pow·er steer·ing dirección *f* asistida
'pow·er u·nit fuente *f* de alimentación
PR [piːˈɑːr] *abbr* (= **public relations**) relaciones *fpl* públicas
prac·ti·cal ['præktɪkl] *adj* práctico; *layout* funcional
prac·ti·cal 'joke broma *f* (*que se gasta*)
prac·ti·cal·ly ['præktɪklɪ] *adv behave, think* de manera práctica; (*almost*) prácticamente, casi
prac·tice ['præktɪs] **1** *n* práctica *f;* (*rehearsal*) ensayo *m;* (*custom*) costumbre *f;* **in practice** (*in reality*) en la práctica; **be out of practice** estar desentrenado; **practice makes perfect** a base de práctica se aprende **2** *v/i* practicar; *of musician* ensayar; *of footballer* entrenarse **3** *v/t* practicar; *law, medicine* ejercer
prac·tise *Br →* **practice** *v/i & v/t*
prag·mat·ic [præɡˈmætɪk] *adj* pragmático
prag·ma·tism ['præɡmətɪzm] pragmatis-

mo *m*
prai·rie ['preri] pradera *f*
praise [preɪz] **1** *n* elogio *m,* alabanza *f* **2** *v/t* elogiar
'praise·wor·thy *adj* elogiable
prank [præŋk] *n* travesura *f*
prat·tle ['prætl] *v/i* F parlotear F
prawn [prɔːn] gamba *f*
pray [preɪ] *v/i* rezar
prayer [prer] oración *f*
preach [priːtʃ] **1** *v/i in church* predicar; (*moralize*) sermonear **2** *v/t sermon* predicar
preach·er ['priːtʃər] predicador(a) *m(f)*
pre·am·ble [priːˈæmbl] preámbulo *m*
pre·car·i·ous [prɪˈkeriəs] *adj* precario
pre·car·i·ous·ly [prɪˈkeriəslɪ] *adv* precariamente
pre·cau·tion [prɪˈkɒʃn] prccaución *f;* **as a precaution** como precaución
pre·cau·tion·a·ry [prɪˈkɒʃnrɪ] *adj measure* preventivo
pre·cede [prɪˈsiːd] *v/t in time* preceder; (*walk in front of*) ir delante de
pre·ce·dent ['presɪdənt] precedente *m*
pre·ce·ding [prɪˈsiːdɪŋ] *adj week, chapter* anterior
pre·cinct ['priːsɪŋkt] (*district*) distrito *m*
pre·cious ['preʃəs] *adj* preciado; *gem* precioso
pre·cip·i·tate [prɪˈsɪpɪteɪt] *v/t crisis* precipitar
pré·cis ['preɪsiː] *n* resumen *m*
pre·cise [prɪˈsaɪs] *adj* preciso
pre·cise·ly [prɪˈsaɪslɪ] *adv* exactamente
pre·ci·sion [prɪˈsɪʒn] precisión *f*
pre·co·cious [prɪˈkoʊʃəs] *adj child* precoz
pre·con·ceived ['priːkənsiːvd] *adj idea* preconcebido
pre·con·di·tion [priːkənˈdɪʃn] condición *f* prcvia
pred·a·tor ['predətər] *animal* depredador(a) *m(f)*
pred·a·to·ry ['predətɔːrɪ] *adj* depredador
pre·de·ces·sor ['priːdɪsesər] *in job* predecesor(a) *m(f); machine* modelo *m* anterior
pre·des·ti·na·tion [priːdestɪˈneɪʃn] predestinación *f*
pre·des·tined [priːˈdestɪnd] *adj:* **be predestined to** estar predestinado a
pre·dic·a·ment [prɪˈdɪkəmənt] apuro *m*
pre·dict [prɪˈdɪkt] *v/t* predecir, pronosticar
pre·dict·a·ble [prɪˈdɪktəbl] *adj* predecible
pre·dic·tion [prɪˈdɪkʃn] predicción *f,* pronóstico *m*
pre·dom·i·nant [prɪˈdɑːmɪnənt] *adj* pre-

dominante

pre·dom·i·nant·ly [prɪ'dɑ:mɪnəntlɪ] adv predominantemente

pre·dom·i·nate [prɪ'dɑ:mɪneɪt] v/i predominar

pre·fab·ri·cat·ed [pri:'fæbrɪkeɪtɪd] adj prefabricado

pref·ace ['prefɪs] n prólogo m, prefacio m

pre·fer [prɪ'fɜːr] v/t (pret & pp preferred) preferir; **prefer X to Y** preferir X a Y; **prefer to do** preferir hacer

pref·e·ra·ble ['prefərəbl] adj preferible; **anywhere is preferable to this** cualquier sitio es mejor que éste

pref·e·ra·bly ['prefərəblɪ] adv preferentemente

pref·e·rence ['prefərəns] preferencia f

pref·er·en·tial [prefə'renʃl] adj preferente

pre·fix ['pri:fɪks] prefijo m

preg·nan·cy ['pregnənsɪ] embarazo m

preg·nant ['pregnənt] adj woman embarazada; animal preñada

pre·heat ['pri:hi:t] v/t oven precalentar

pre·his·tor·ic [pri:hɪs'tɑːrɪk] adj prehistórico

pre·judge [pri:'dʒʌdʒ] v/t prejuzgar, juzgar de antemano

prej·u·dice ['predʒʊdɪs] 1 n prejuicio m 2 v/t person predisponer, influir; chances perjudicar

prej·u·diced ['predʒʊdɪst] adj parcial, predispuesto

pre·lim·i·na·ry [prɪ'lɪmɪnerɪ] adj preliminar

pre·mar·i·tal [pri:'mærɪtl] adj prematrimonial

pre·ma·ture ['pri:mətʊr] adj prematuro

pre·med·i·tat·ed [pri:'medɪteɪtɪd] adj premeditado

prem·i·er ['premɪr] n (Prime Minister) primer(a) ministro(-a) m(f)

prem·i·ère ['premɪr] n estreno m

prem·is·es ['premɪsɪz] npl local m

pre·mi·um ['pri:mɪəm] n in insurance prima f

pre·mo·ni·tion [premə'nɪʃn] premonición f, presentimiento m

pre·na·tal [pri:'neɪtl] adj prenatal

pre·oc·cu·pied [pri:'ɑːkjʊpaɪd] adj preocupado

prep·a·ra·tion [prepə'reɪʃn] preparación f; **in preparation for** como preparación a; **preparations** preparativos mpl

pre·pare [prɪ'per] 1 v/t preparar; **be prepared to do sth** (willing) estar dispuesto a hacer algo; **be prepared for sth** (be expecting, ready) estar preparado para algo 2 v/i prepararse

prep·o·si·tion [prepə'zɪʃn] preposición f

pre·pos·ter·ous [prɪ'pɑːstərəs] adj ridículo, absurdo

prep school ['prepskuːl] escuela f primaria privada

pre·req·ui·site [pri:'rekwɪzɪt] requisito m previo

pre·scribe [prɪ'skraɪb] v/t of doctor recetar

pre·scrip·tion [prɪ'skrɪpʃn] MED receta f

pres·ence ['prezns] presencia f; **in the presence of** en presencia de, delante de

pres·ence of 'mind presencia f de ánimo

pres·ent¹ ['preznt] 1 adj (current) actual; **be present** estar presente 2 n: **the present** also GRAM el presente; **at present** en este momento

pres·ent² ['preznt] n (gift) regalo m

pre·sent³ [prɪ'zent] v/t presentar; award entregar; program presentar; **present s.o. with sth, present sth to s.o.** entregar algo a alguien

pres·en·ta·tion [prezn'teɪʃn] to audience presentación f

pres·ent-day [preznt'deɪ] adj actual

pre·sent·er [prɪ'zentər] presentador(a) m(f)

pres·ent·ly ['prezntlɪ] adv (at the moment) actualmente; (soon) pronto

'pres·ent tense tiempo m presente

pres·er·va·tion [prezər'veɪʃn] conservación f; of standards, peace mantenimiento m

pre·ser·va·tive [prɪ'zɜːrvətɪv] n conservante m

pre·serve [prɪ'zɜːrv] 1 n (domain) dominio m 2 v/t standards, peace etc mantener; food, wood conservar

pre·side [prɪ'zaɪd] v/i at meeting presidir; **preside over** meeting presidir

pres·i·den·cy ['prezɪdənsɪ] presidencia f

pres·i·dent ['prezɪdənt] POL, of company presidente(-a) m(f)

pres·i·den·tial [prezɪ'denʃl] adj presidencial

press [pres] 1 n: **the press** la prensa 2 v/t button pulsar, presionar; (urge) presionar; (squeeze) apretar; clothes planchar 3 v/i: **press for** presionar para obtener

'press a·gen·cy agencia f de prensa

'press con·fer·ence rueda f or conferencia f de prensa

press·ing ['presɪŋ] adj urgente

pres·sure ['preʃər] 1 n presión f; **be under pressure** estar sometido a presión; **he is under pressure to resign** lo están presionando para que dimita 2 v/t presionar

pres·tige [pre'stiːʒ] prestigio m

pres·ti·gious [pre'stɪdʒəs] adj prestigioso

pre·su·ma·bly [prɪˈzuːməblɪ] *adv* presumiblemente, probablemente

pre·sume [prɪˈzuːm] suponer; **they were presumed dead** los dieron por muertos; **presume to do sth** *fml* tomarse la libertad de hacer algo

pre·sump·tion [prɪˈzʌmpʃn] *of innocence, guilt* presunción *f*

pre·sump·tu·ous [prɪˈzʌmptuəs] *adj* presuntuoso

pre·sup·pose [priːsəˈpoʊs] *v/t* presuponer

pre·tax [ˈpriːtæks] *adj* antes de impuestos

pre·tence *Br* → **pretense**

pre·tend [prɪˈtend] **1** *v/t* fingir, hacer como si; *claim* pretender; **pretend to be s.o.** hacerse pasar por alguien; **the children are pretending to be spacemen** los niños están jugando a que son astronautas **2** *v/i* fingir

pre·tense [prɪˈtens] farsa *f*

pre·ten·tious [prɪˈtenʃəs] *adj* pretencioso

pre·text [ˈpriːtekst] pretexto *m*

pret·ty [ˈprɪtɪ] **1** *adj village, house, fabric etc* bonito, lindo; *child, woman* guapo, lindo **2** *adv (quite)* bastante

pre·vail [prɪˈveɪl] *v/i (triumph)* prevalecer

pre·vail·ing [prɪˈveɪlɪŋ] *adj* predominante

pre·vent [prɪˈvent] *v/t* impedir, evitar; **prevent s.o. (from) doing sth** impedir que alguien haga algo

pre·ven·tion [prɪˈvenʃn] prevención *f*

pre·ven·tive [prɪˈventɪv] *adj* preventivo

pre·view [ˈpriːvjuː] **1** *n of movie, exhibition* preestreno *m* **2** *v/t* hacer la presentación previa de

pre·vi·ous [ˈpriːvɪəs] *adj* anterior, previo

pre·vi·ous·ly [ˈpriːvɪəslɪ] *adv* anteriormente, antes

pre·war [ˈpriːwɔːr] *adj* de preguerra, de antes de la guerra

prey [preɪ] *n* presa *f*; **prey to** presa de

♦ **prey on** *v/t* atacar; *fig: of con man etc* aprovecharse de

price [praɪs] **1** *n* precio *m* **2** *v/t* COM poner precio a

price·less [ˈpraɪslɪs] *adj* que no tiene precio

'price tag etiqueta *f* del precio

'price war guerra *f* de precios

price·y [ˈpraɪsɪ] *adj* F carillo F

prick¹ [prɪk] **1** *n pain* punzada *f* **2** *v/t (jab)* pinchar

prick² [prɪk] *n* V (*penis*) polla *f* V, carajo *m* V; V *person Span* gilipollas *m inv* V, *L.Am.* pendejo *m* V

♦ **prick up** *v/t*: **prick up one's ears** *of dog* aguzar las orejas; *of person* prestar atención

prick·le [ˈprɪkl] *on plant* espina *f*

prick·ly [ˈprɪklɪ] *adj beard, plant* que pincha; (*irritable*) irritable

pride [praɪd] **1** *n in person, achievement* orgullo *m*; (*self-respect*) amor *m* propio **2** *v/t*: **pride o.s. on** enorgullecerse de

priest [priːst] sacerdote *m*; (*parish priest*) cura *m*

pri·ma·ri·ly [praɪˈmerɪlɪ] *adv* principalmente

pri·ma·ry [ˈpraɪmərɪ] **1** *adj* principal **2** *n* POL elecciones *fpl* primarias

prime [praɪm] **1** *n*: **be in one's prime** estar en la flor de la vida **2** *adj example, reason* primordial; **of prime importance** de suprema importancia

prime 'min·is·ter primer(a) ministro(-a) *m(f)*

'prime time *n* TV horario *m* de mayor audiencia

prim·i·tive [ˈprɪmɪtɪv] *adj* primitivo

prince [prɪns] príncipe *m*

prin·cess [prɪnˈses] princesa *f*

prin·ci·pal [ˈprɪnsəpl] **1** *adj* principal **2** *n of school* director(a) *m(f)*; *of university* rector(a) *m(f)*

prin·ci·pal·ly [ˈprɪnsəplɪ] *adv* principalmente

prin·ci·ple [ˈprɪnsəpl] principio *m*; **on principle** por principios; **in principle** en principio

print [prɪnt] **1** *n in book, newspaper etc* letra *f*; (*photograph*) grabado *m*; **out of print** agotado **2** *v/t* imprimir; *use block capitals* escribir en mayúsculas

♦ **print out** *v/t* imprimir

print·ed mat·ter [ˈprɪntɪd] impresos *mpl*

print·er [ˈprɪntər] *person* impresor(a) *m(f)*; *machine* impresora *f*; *company* imprenta *f*

print·ing press [ˈprɪntɪŋpres] imprenta *f*

'print·out copia *f* impresa

pri·or [praɪr] **1** *adj* previo **2** *prep*: **prior to** antes de

pri·or·i·tize [praɪˈɔːrətaɪz] *v/t (put in order of priority)* ordenar atendiendo a las prioridades; (*give priority to*) dar prioridad a

pri·or·i·ty [praɪˈɔːrətɪ] prioridad *f*; **have priority** tener prioridad

pris·on [ˈprɪzn] prisión *f*, cárcel *f*

pris·on·er [ˈprɪznər] prisionero(-a) *m(f)*; **take s.o. prisoner** hacer prisionero a alguien

pris·on·er of 'war prisionero(-a) *m(f)* de guerra

priv·a·cy [ˈprɪvəsɪ] intimidad *f*

pri·vate [ˈpraɪvət] **1** *adj* privado **2** *n* MIL soldado *m/f* raso; **in private** en privado

P

pri·vate·ly ['praɪvətlɪ] *adv* (*in private*) en privado; *with one other* a solas; (*inwardly*) para sí; **privately owned** en manos privadas

'**pri·vate sec·tor** sector *m* privado

pri·va·tize ['praɪvətaɪz] *v/t Br* privatizar

priv·i·lege ['prɪvɪlɪdʒ] (*special treatment*) privilegio *m*; (*honor*) honor *m*

priv·i·leged ['prɪvɪlɪdʒd] *adj* privilegiado

prize [praɪz] **1** *n* premio *m* **2** *v/t* apreciar, valorar

prize·win·ner ['praɪzwɪnər] premiado(-a) *m(f)*

prize·win·ning ['praɪzwɪnɪŋ] *adj* premiado

pro[1] [prou] *n*: **the pros and cons** los pros y los contras

pro[2] [prou] → **professional**

pro[3] [prou]: **be pro ...** (*in favor of*) estar a favor de; **the pro Clinton Democrats** los demócratas partidarios de Clinton

prob·a·bil·i·ty [prɑːbə'bɪlətɪ] probabilidad *f*

prob·a·ble ['prɑːbəbl] *adj* probable

prob·a·bly ['prɑːbəblɪ] *adv* probablemente

pro·ba·tion [prə'beɪʃn] *in job* período *m* de prueba; LAW libertad *f* condicional; **be given probation** ser puesto en libertad condicional

pro·'ba·tion of·fi·cer oficial encargado de la vigilancia de los que están en libertad condicional

pro·'ba·tion pe·ri·od *in job* período *m* de prueba

probe [proub] **1** *n* (*investigation*) investigación *f*; *scientific* sonda *f* **2** *v/t* examinar; (*investigate*) investigar

prob·lem ['prɑːbləm] problema *f*; **no problem!** ¡claro!

pro·ce·dure [prə'siːdʒər] procedimiento *m*

pro·ceed [prə'siːd] *v/i* (*go: of people*) dirigirse; *of work etc* proseguir, avanzar; **proceed to do sth** pasar a hacer algo

pro·ceed·ings [prə'siːdɪŋz] *npl* (*events*) actos *mpl*

pro·ceeds ['prousiːdz] *npl* recaudación *f*

'**pro·cess** ['prɑːses] **1** *n* proceso *m*; **in the process** (*while doing it*) al hacerlo **2** *v/t food* tratar; *raw materials, data* procesar; *application* tramitar

pro·ces·sion [prə'seʃn] desfile *m*; *religious* procesión *f*

pro·claim [prə'kleɪm] *v/t* declarar, proclamar

prod [prɑːd] **1** *n* empujoncito *m* **2** *v/t* (*pret & pp* **prodded**) dar un empujoncito a; *with elbow* dar un codazo a

prod·i·gy ['prɑːdɪdʒɪ]: (*infant*) **prodigy** niño(-a) *m(f)* prodigio

prod·uce[1] ['prɑːduːs] *n* productos *mpl* del campo

pro·duce[2] [prə'duːs] *v/t* producir; (*manufacture*) fabricar; (*bring out*) sacar

pro·duc·er [prə'duːsər] productor(a) *m(f)*; (*manufacturer*) fabricante *m/f*

prod·uct ['prɑːdʌkt] producto *m*

pro·duc·tion [prə'dʌkʃn] producción *f*

pro·'duc·tion ca·pac·i·ty capacidad *f* de producción

pro·'duc·tion costs *npl* costos *mpl* de producción

pro·duc·tive [prə'dʌktɪv] *adj* productivo

pro·duc·tiv·i·ty [prɑːdʌk'tɪvətɪ] productividad *f*

pro·fane [prə'feɪn] *adj language* profano

pro·fess [prə'fes] *v/t* manifestar

pro·fes·sion [prə'feʃn] profesión *f*; **what's your profession?** ¿a qué se dedica?

pro·fes·sion·al [prə'feʃnl] **1** *adj* profesional; **turn professional** hacerse profesional **2** *n* profesional *m/f*

pro·fes·sion·al·ly [prə'feʃnlɪ] *adv play sport* profesionalmente; (*well, skillfully*) con profesionalidad

pro·fes·sor [prə'fesər] catedrático(-a) *m(f)*

pro·fi·cien·cy [prə'fɪʃnsɪ] competencia *f*

pro·fi·cient [prə'fɪʃnt] competente; (*skillful*) hábil

'**pro·file** ['proufaɪl] *of face* perfil *m*

prof·it ['prɑːfɪt] **1** *n* beneficio *m* **2** *v/i*: **profit by, profit from** beneficiarse de

prof·it·a·bil·i·ty [prɑːfɪtə'bɪlətɪ] rentabilidad *f*

prof·it·a·ble ['prɑːfɪtəbl] *adj* rentable

'**prof·it mar·gin** margen *m* de beneficios

pro·found [prə'faund] *adj* profundo

pro·found·ly [prə'faundlɪ] *adv* profundamente, enormemente; *thank, apologize* efusivamente

prog·no·sis [prɑːg'nousɪs] pronóstico *m*

pro·gram, *Br* **pro·gramme** ['prougræm] **1** *n* programa *m* **2** *v/t* (*pret & pp* **programmed**) COMPUT programar

pro·gram·mer ['prougræmər] COMPUT programador(a) *m(f)*

pro·gress 1 *n* [prɑːgres] progreso *m*; **make progress** hacer progresos; **in progress** en curso **2** *v/i* [prɑːgres] (*advance in time*) avanzar; (*move on*) pasar; (*make progress*) progresar; **how is the work progressing?** ¿cómo avanza el trabajo?

pro·gres·sive [prə'gresɪv] *adj* (*enlightened*) progresista; (*which progresses*) progresivo

pro·gres·sive·ly [prə'gresɪvlɪ] *adv* progresivamente

pro·hib·it [prə'hɪbɪt] *v/t* prohibir

pro·hi·bi·tion [prouhɪ'bɪʃn] prohibición *f*; ***during Prohibition*** durante la ley seca

pro·hi·bi·tive [prə'hɪbɪtɪv] *adj prices* prohibitivo

proj·ect¹ ['prɑːdʒekt] *n* (*plan, undertaking*) proyecto *m*; EDU trabajo *m*; *housing area* barriada *f* de viviendas sociales

pro·ject² [prə'dʒekt] **1** *v/t movie* proyectar; *figures, sales* calcular **2** *v/i* (*stick out*) sobresalir

pro·jec·tion [prə'dʒekʃn] (*forecast*) previsión *f*

pro·jec·tor [prə'dʒektər] *for slides* proyector *m*

pro·lif·ic [prə'lɪfɪk] *adj writer, artist* prolífico

pro·log, *Br* **pro·logue** ['proʊlɑːg] prólogo *m*

pro·long [prə'lɒːŋ] *v/t* prolongar

prom [prɑːm] (*school dance*) baile de fin de curso

prom·i·nent ['prɑːmɪnənt] *adj nose, chin* prominente; (*significant*) destacado

prom·is·cu·i·ty [prɑːmɪ'skjuːətɪ] promiscuidad *f*

pro·mis·cu·ous [prə'mɪskjʊəs] *adj* promiscuo

prom·ise ['prɑːmɪs] **1** *n* promesa *f* **2** *v/t* prometer; ***she promised to help*** prometió ayudar; ***promise sth to s.o.*** prometer algo a alguien **3** *v/i*: ***do you promise?*** ¿lo prometes?

prom·is·ing ['prɑːmɪsɪŋ] *adj* prometedor

pro·mote [prə'moʊt] *v/t employee* ascender; (*encourage, foster*) promover; COM promocionar

pro·mot·er [prə'moʊtər] *of sports event* promotor(a) *m(f)*

pro·mo·tion [prə'moʊʃn] *of employee* ascenso *m*; *of scheme, idea,* COM promoción *f*

prompt [prɑːmpt] **1** *adj* (*on time*) puntual; (*speedy*) rápido **2** *adv*: ***at two o'clock prompt*** a las dos en punto **3** *v/t* (*cause*) provocar; *actor* apuntar **4** *n* COMPUT mensaje *m*; ***go to the c prompt*** ir a c:\

prompt·ly ['prɑːmptlɪ] *adv* (*on time*) puntualmente; (*immediately*) inmediatamente

prone [proʊn] *adj*: ***be prone to*** ser propenso a

pro·noun ['proʊnaʊn] pronombre *m*

pro·nounce [prə'naʊns] *v/t word* pronunciar; (*declare*) declarar

pro·nounced [prə'naʊnst] *adj accent* marcado; *views* fuerte

pron·to ['prɑːntoʊ] *adv* F ya, en seguida

pro·nun·ci·a·tion [prənʌnsɪ'eɪʃn] pronunciación *f*

proof [pruːf] *n* prueba(s) *f(pl)*; *of book* prueba *f*

prop [prɑːp] **1** *v/t* (*pret & pp propped*) apoyar **2** *n* THEA accesorio *m*
◆ **prop up** *v/t* apoyar

prop·a·gan·da [prɑːpə'gændə] propaganda *f*

pro·pel [prə'pel] *v/t* (*pret & pp propelled*) propulsar

pro·pel·lant [prə'pelənt] *in aerosol* propelente *m*

pro·pel·ler [prə'pelər] *of boat* hélice *f*

prop·er ['prɑːpər] *adj* (*real*) de verdad; (*fitting*) adecuado; ***it's not proper*** no está bien; ***put it back in its proper place*** vuelve a ponerlo en su sitio

prop·er·ly ['prɑːpərlɪ] *adv* (*correctly*) bien; (*fittingly*) adecuadamente

prop·er·ty ['prɑːpərtɪ] propiedad *f*; (*land*) propiedad(es) *f(pl)*

prop·er·ty de·vel·op·er promotor(a) *m(f)* inmobiliario(a)

proph·e·cy ['prɑːfəsɪ] profecía *f*

proph·e·sy ['prɑːfəsaɪ] *v/t* (*pret & pp prophesied*) profetizar

pro·por·tion [prə'pɔːrʃn] proporción *f*; ***a large proportion of North Americans*** gran parte de los norteamericanos; ***proportions*** (*dimensions*) proporciones *fpl*

pro·por·tion·al [prə'pɔːrʃnl] *adj* proporcional

pro·por·tion·al rep·re·sen·ta·tion POL representación *f* proporcional

pro·pos·al [prə'poʊzl] (*suggestion*) propuesta *f*; *of marriage* proposición *f*

pro·pose [prə'poʊz] **1** *v/t* (*suggest*) sugerir, proponer; (*plan*) proponerse **2** *v/i* (*make offer of marriage*) pedir la mano

prop·o·si·tion [prɑːpə'zɪʃn] **1** *n* propuesta *f* **2** *v/t woman* hacer proposiciones a

pro·pri·e·tor [prə'praɪətər] propietario(-a) *m(f)*

pro·pri·e·tress [prə'praɪətrɪs] propietaria *f*

prose [proʊz] prosa *f*

pros·e·cute ['prɑːsɪkjuːt] *v/t* LAW procesar

pros·e·cu·tion [prɑːsɪ'kjuːʃn] LAW procesamiento *m*; *lawyers* acusación *f*; ***he's facing prosecution*** lo van a procesar

pros·e·cu·tor → **public prosecutor** fiscal *m/f*

pros·pect ['prɑːspekt] **1** *n* (*chance, likelihood*) probabilidad *f*; (*thought of something in the future*) perspectiva *f*; ***prospects*** perspectivas *fpl* (de futuro)

2 v/i: **prospect for** gold buscar

pro·spec·tive [prə'spektɪv] adj potencial

pros·per ['prɑːspər] v/i prosperar

pros·per·i·ty [prɑː'sperətɪ] prosperidad f

pros·per·ous ['prɑːspərəs] adj próspero

pros·ti·tute ['prɑːstɪtuːt] n prostituta f; **male prostitute** prostituto m

pros·ti·tu·tion [prɑːstɪ'tuːʃn] prostitución f

pros·trate ['prɑːstreɪt] adj postrado; **be prostrate with grief** postrado por el dolor

pro·tect [prə'tekt] v/t proteger

pro·tec·tion [prə'tekʃn] protección f

pro·tec·tion mon·ey dinero pagado a delincuentes a cambio de obtener protección; paid to terrorists impuesto m revolucionario

pro·tec·tive [prə'tektɪv] adj protector

pro·tec·tive 'cloth·ing ropa f protectora

pro·tec·tor [prə'tektər] protector(a) m(f)

pro·tein ['proutiːn] proteína f

pro·test ['proutest] protesta f **2** v/t [prə'test] protestar, quejarse de; (object to) protestar contra **3** v/i [prə'test] protestar

Prot·es·tant ['prɑːtɪstənt] **1** n protestante m/f **2** adj protestante

pro·test·er [prə'testər] manifestante m/f

pro·to·col ['proutəkɑːl] protocolo m

pro·to·type ['proutətaɪp] prototipo m

pro·tract·ed [prə'træktɪd] adj prolongado, largo

pro·trude [prə'truːd] v/i sobresalir

pro·trud·ing [prə'truːdɪŋ] adj saliente; ears, teeth prominente

proud [praud] adj orgulloso; **be proud of** estar orgulloso de

proud·ly ['praudlɪ] adv con orgullo, orgullosamente

prove [pruːv] v/t demostrar, probar

prov·erb ['prɑːvɜːrb] proverbio m, refrán m

pro·vide [prə'vaɪd] v/t proporcionar; **provide sth to s.o., provide s.o. with sth** proporcionar algo a alguien; **provided (that)** (on condition that) con la condición de que, siempre que

◆ **provide for** v/t family mantener; of law etc prever

prov·ince ['prɑːvɪns] provincia f

pro·vin·cial [prə'vɪnʃl] adj city provincial; pej: attitude de pueblo, provinciano

pro·vi·sion [prə'vɪʒn] (supply) suministro m; of law, contract disposición f

pro·vi·sion·al [prə'vɪʒnl] adj provisional

pro·vi·so [prə'vaɪzou] condición f

prov·o·ca·tion [prɑːvə'keɪʃn] provocación f

pro·voc·a·tive [prə'vɑːkətɪv] adj provocador; sexually provocativo

pro·voke [prə'vouk] v/t (cause, annoy) provocar

prow [prau] NAUT proa f

prow·ess ['prauɪs] proezas fpl

prowl [praul] v/i of tiger, burglar merodear

prowl·er ['praulər] merodeador(a) m(f)

prox·im·i·ty [prɑːk'sɪmətɪ] proximidad f

prox·y ['prɑːksɪ] (authority) poder m; person apoderado(-a) m(f)

prude [pruːd] mojigato(-a) m(f)

pru·dence ['pruːdns] prudencia f

pru·dent ['pruːdnt] adj prudente

prud·ish ['pruːdɪʃ] adj mojigato

prune¹ [pruːn] n ciruela f pasa

prune² [pruːn] v/t plant podar; fig reducir

pry [praɪ] v/i (pret & pp **pried**) entrometerse

◆ **pry into** v/t entrometerse en

PS ['piːes] abbr (= **postscript**) PD (= posdata f)

pseu·do·nym ['suːdənɪm] pseudónimo m

psy·chi·at·ric [saɪkɪ'ætrɪk] adj psiquiátrico

psy·chi·a·trist [saɪ'kaɪətrɪst] psiquiatra m/f

psy·chi·a·try [saɪ'kaɪətrɪ] psiquiatría f

psy·chic ['saɪkɪk] adj research paranormal; **I'm not psychic** no soy vidente

psy·cho·a·nal·y·sis [saɪkouən'æləsɪs] psicoanálisis m

psy·cho·an·a·lyst [saɪkou'ænəlɪst] psicoanalista m/f

psy·cho·an·a·lyze [saɪkou'ænəlaɪz] v/t psicoanalizar

psy·cho·log·i·cal [saɪkə'lɑːdʒɪkl] adj psicológico

psy·cho·log·i·cal·ly [saɪkə'lɑːdʒɪklɪ] adv psicológicamente

psy·chol·o·gist [saɪ'kɑːlədʒɪst] psicólogo(-a) m(f)

psy·chol·o·gy [saɪ'kɑːlədʒɪ] psicología f

psy·cho·path ['saɪkoupæθ] psicópata m/f

psy·cho·so·mat·ic [saɪkousə'mætɪk] adj psicosomático

PTO [piːtiː'ou] abbr (= **please turn over**) véase al dorso

pub [pʌb] Br bar m

pu·ber·ty ['pjuːbərtɪ] pubertad f

pu·bic hair ['pjuːbɪk] vello m púbico

pub·lic ['pʌblɪk] **1** adj público **2** n: **the public** el público; **in public** en público

pub·li·ca·tion [pʌblɪ'keɪʃn] publicación f

pub·lic 'hol·i·day día m festivo

pub·lic·i·ty [pʌb'lɪsətɪ] publicidad f

pub·li·cize ['pʌblɪsaɪz] v/t (make known) publicar, hacer público; COM dar publicidad a

pub·lic 'li·bra·ry biblioteca *f* pública

pub·lic·ly ['pʌblɪklɪ] *adv* públicamente

pub·lic 'pros·e·cu·tor fiscal *m/f*

pub·lic re'la·tions *npl* relaciones públicas *fpl*

'pub·lic school *Br* colegio *m* privado; *Am* colegio *m* público

'pub·lic sec·tor sector *m* público

pub·lish ['pʌblɪʃ] *v/t* publicar

pub·lish·er ['pʌblɪʃər] *person* editor(a) *m(f)*; *company* editorial *f*

pub·lish·ing ['pʌblɪʃɪŋ] industria *f* editorial

'pub·lish·ing com·pa·ny editorial *f*

pud·ding ['pudɪŋ] *Br dish* pudín *m*; *part of meal* postre *m*

pud·dle ['pʌdl] charco *m*

Puer·to Ri·can [pwertoʊ'riːkən] **1** *adj* portorriqueño, puertorriqueño **2** *n* portorriqueño(-a) *m(f)*, puertorriqueño(-a) *m(f)*

Puer·to Ri·co [pwertoʊ'riːkoʊ] *n* Puerto Rico

puff [pʌf] **1** *n of wind* racha *f*; *from cigarette* calada *f*; *of smoke* bocanada *f* **2** *v/i* (*pant*) resoplar; **puff on a cigarette** dar una calada a un cigarrillo

puff·y ['pʌfɪ] *adj eyes, face* hinchado

puke [pjuːk] **1** *n* P *substance* vomitona *f* P **2** *v/i* P echar la pota P

pull [pul] **1** *n on rope* tirón *m*; F (*appeal*) gancho *m* F; F (*influence*) enchufe *m* F **2** *v/t* (*drag*) arrastrar; (*tug*) tirar de; *tooth* sacar; **pull a muscle** sufrir un tirón en un músculo **3** *v/t* tirar

♦ **pull ahead** *v/i in race, competition* adelantarse

♦ **pull apart** *v/t* (*separate*) separar

♦ **pull away** *v/t* apartar

♦ **pull down** *v/t* (*lower*) bajar; (*demolish*) derribar

♦ **pull in** *v/i of bus, train* llegar

♦ **pull off** *v/t* quitar; *item of clothing* quitarse; F conseguir

♦ **pull out 1** *v/t* sacar; *troops* retirar, **2** *v/i of an agreement, of troops* retirarse; *of ship* salir

♦ **pull over** *v/i* parar en el arcén

♦ **pull through** *v/i from an illness* recuperarse

♦ **pull together 1** *v/i* (*cooperate*) cooperar **2** *v/t*: **pull o.s. together** tranquilizarse

♦ **pull up** *v/t* (*raise*) subir; *item of clothing* subirse; *plant, weeds* arrancar **2** *v/i of car* etc parar

pul·ley ['pulɪ] polea *f*

pull·o·ver ['puloʊvər] suéter *m*, *Span* jersey *m*

pulp [pʌlp] *of fruit* pulpa *f*; *for paper-making* pasta *f*

pul·pit ['pulpɪt] púlpito *m*

pul·sate [pʌl'seɪt] *v/i of heart, blood* palpitar; *of music* vibrar

pulse [pʌls] pulso *m*

pul·ver·ize ['pʌlvəraɪz] *v/t* pulverizar

pump [pʌmp] **1** *n* bomba *f*; (*gas pump*) surtidor *m* **2** *v/t* bombear

♦ **pump up** *v/t* inflar

pump·kin ['pʌmpkɪn] calabaza *f*

pun [pʌn] juego *m* de palabras

punch [pʌntʃ] **1** *n* (*blow*) puñetazo *m*; *implement* perforadora *f* **2** *v/t with fist* dar un puñetazo a; *hole, ticket* agujerear

'punch line *última frase de un chiste*

punc·tu·al ['pʌŋktʃʊəl] *adj* puntual

punc·tu·al·i·ty [pʌŋktʃʊ'ælətɪ] puntualidad *f*

punc·tu·al·ly ['pʌŋktʃʊəlɪ] *adv* puntualmente

punc·tu·ate ['pʌŋktʃʊeɪt] *v/t* puntuar

punc·tu·a·tion [pʌŋktʃʊ'eɪʃn] puntuación *f*

punc·tu'a·tion mark signo *m* de puntuación

punc·ture ['pʌŋktʃər] **1** *n* perforación *f* **2** *v/t* perforar

pun·gent ['pʌndʒənt] *adj* fuerte

pun·ish ['pʌnɪʃ] *v/t person* castigar

pun·ish·ing ['pʌnɪʃɪŋ] *adj schedule* exigente; *pace* fuerte

pun·ish·ment ['pʌnɪʃmənt] castigo *m*

punk (rock) ['pʌŋk(rɑːk)] MUS (música *f*) punk *m*

pu·ny ['pjuːnɪ] *adj person* enclenque

pup [pʌp] cachorro *m*

pu·pil¹ ['pjuːpl] *of eye* pupila *f*

pu·pil² ['pjuːpl] (*student*) alumno(-a) *m(f)*

pup·pet ['pʌpɪt] *also fig* marioneta *f*

'pup·pet gov·ern·ment gobierno *m* títere

pup·py ['pʌpɪ] cachorro *m*

pur·chase¹ ['pɜːrtʃəs] **1** *n* adquisición *f*, compra *f* **2** *v/t* adquirir, comprar

pur·chase² ['pɜːrtʃəs] (*grip*) agarre *m*

pur·chas·er ['pɜːrtʃəsər] comprador(a) *m(f)*

pure [pjʊr] *adj* puro; **pure new wool** pura lana *f* virgen

pure·ly ['pjʊrlɪ] *adv* puramente

pur·ga·to·ry ['pɜːrgətɔːrɪ] purgatorio *m*

purge [pɜːrdʒ] **1** *n of political party* purga *f* **2** *v/t* purgar

pu·ri·fy ['pjʊrɪfaɪ] *v/t* (*pret & pp purified*) *water* depurar

pu·ri·tan ['pjʊrɪtən] puritano(-a) *m(f)*

pu·ri·tan·i·cal [pjʊrɪ'tænɪkl] *adj* puritano

pu·ri·ty ['pjʊrɪtɪ] pureza *f*

pur·ple ['pɜːrpl] *adj* morado

Pur·ple 'Heart MIL *medalla concedida a los soldados heridos en combate*

pur·pose ['pɜːrpəs] (*aim, object*) propósito *m*, objeto *m*; **on purpose** a propósito; *what is the purpose of your visit?* ¿cuál es el objeto de su visita?

pur·pose·ful ['pɜːrpəsfəl] *adj* decidido

pur·pose·ly ['pɜːrpəslɪ] *adv* decididamente

purr [pɜːr] *v/i of cat* ronronear

purse [pɜːrs] *n* (*pocket book*) bolso *m*; Br: *for money* monedero *m*

pur·sue [pər'suː] *v/t person* perseguir; *career* ejercer; *course of action* proseguir

pur·su·er [pər'suːər] perseguidor(a) *m(f)*

pur·suit [pər'suːt] (*chase*) persecución *f*; *of happiness etc* búsqueda *f*; (*activity*) actividad *f*; *those in pursuit* los perseguidores

pus [pʌs] pus *m*

push [pʊʃ] **1** *n* (*shove*) empujón *m*; *at the push of a button* apretando un botón **2** *v/t* (*shove*) empujar; *button* apretar, pulsar; (*pressurize*) presionar; F *drugs* pasar F, mercadear con; *be pushed for cash* F estar pelado F, estar sin un centavo; *be pushed for time* F ir mal de tiempo F; *be pushing 40* F rondar los 40 **3** *v/i* empujar

◆ **push ahead** *v/i* seguir adelante

◆ **push along** *v/t cart etc* empujar

◆ **push away** *v/t* apartar

◆ **push off 1** *v/t lid* destapar; **2** *v/i* Br F (*leave*) largarse F

◆ **push on** *v/i* (*continue*) continuar

◆ **push up** *v/t prices* hacer subir

push·er ['pʊʃər] F *of drugs* camello *m* F

push-up ['pʊʃʌp] flexión *f* (de brazos)

push·y ['pʊʃɪ] *adj* F avasallador, agresivo

puss, pus·sy (cat) [pʊs, 'pʊsɪ (kæt)] F minino *m* F

◆ **pussy foot about** ['pʊsɪfʊt] *v/i* F andarse con rodeos

put [pʊt] *v/t* (*pret & pp put*) poner; *question* hacer; *put the cost at ...* estimar el costo en ...

◆ **put across** *v/t idea etc* hacer llegar

◆ **put aside** *v/t money* apartar, ahorrar; *work* dejar a un lado

◆ **put away** *v/t in closet etc* guardar; *in institution* encerrar; F (*consume*) consumir, cepillarse F; *money* apartar, ahorrar;

animal sacrificar

◆ **put back** *v/t* (*replace*) volver a poner

◆ **put by** *v/t money* apartar, ahorrar

◆ **put down** *v/t* dejar; *deposit* entregar; *rebellion* reprimir; (*belittle*) dejar en mal lugar; (*in writing*) poner por escrito; *put one's foot down in car* apretar el acelerador; (*be firm*) plantarse; *put sth down to sth* (*attribute*) atribuir algo a algo

◆ **put forward** *v/t idea etc* proponer, presentar

◆ **put in** *v/t* meter; *time* dedicar; *request, claim* presentar

◆ **put in for** *v/t* (*apply for*) solicitar

◆ **put off** *v/t light, radio, TV* apagar; (*postpone*) posponer, aplazar; (*deter*) desalentar; (*repel*) desagradar; *I was put off by the smell* el olor me quitó las ganas; *that put me off shellfish for life* me quitó las ganas de volver a comer marisco

◆ **put on** *v/t light, radio, TV* encender, *L.Am.* prender; *tape, music* poner; *jacket, shoes, eye glasses* ponerse; (*perform*) representar; (*assume*) fingir; *put on make-up* maquillarse; *put on the brake* frenar; *put on weight* engordar; *she's just putting it on* está fingiendo

◆ **put out** *v/t hand* extender; *fire, light* apagar

◆ **put through** *v/t: put s.o. through to s.o. on phone* poner a alguien con alguien

◆ **put together** *v/t* (*assemble, organize*) montar

◆ **put up** *v/t hand* levantar; *person* alojar; (*erect*) levantar; *prices* subir; *poster, notice* colocar; *money* aportar; *put your hands up!* ¡arriba las manos!; *put up for sale* poner en venta

◆ **put up with** *v/t* (*tolerate*) aguantar

putt [pʌt] *v/i* SP golpear con el putter

put·ty ['pʌtɪ] masilla *f*

puz·zle ['pʌzl] **1** *n* (*mystery*) enigma *m*; *game* pasatiempos *mpl*; (*jigsaw puzzle*) puzzle *m*; (*crossword puzzle*) crucigrama *m* **2** *v/t* desconcertar; *one thing puzzles me* hay algo que no acabo de entender

puz·zling ['pʌzlɪŋ] *adj* desconcertante

PVC [piːviː'siː] *abbr* (= *polyvinyl chloride*) PVC *m* (= cloruro *m* de polivinilo)

py·ja·mas Br → **pajamas**

py·lon ['paɪlən] torre *f* de alta tensión

Q

quack¹ [kwæk] **1** *n of duck* graznido *m* **2** *v/i* graznar

quack² [kwæk] *n* F (*bad doctor*) matasanos *m/f inv* F

quad·ran·gle ['kwɑːdræŋgl] *figure* cuadrángulo *m*; *courtyard* patio *m*

quad·ru·ped ['kwɑːdrʊped] cuadrúpedo *m*

quad·ru·ple ['kwɑːdrʊpl] *v/i* cuadruplicarse

quad·ru·plets ['kwɑːdrʊplɪts] *npl* cuatrillizos(-as) *mpl* (*fpl*)

quads [kwɑːdz] *npl* F cuatrillizos(-as) *mpl* f(*fpl*)

quag·mire ['kwɑːgmaɪr] *fig* atolladero *m*

quail [kweɪl] *v/i* temblar (**at** ante)

quaint [kweɪnt] *adj cottage* pintoresco; (*slightly eccentric: ideas etc*) extraño

quake [kweɪk] **1** *n* (*earthquake*) terremoto *m* **2** *v/i of earth, with fear* temblar

qual·i·fi·ca·tion [kwɑːlɪfɪ'keɪʃn] *from university etc* título *m*; **have the right qualifications for a job** estar bien cualificado para un trabajo

qual·i·fied ['kwɑːlɪfaɪd] *adj doctor, engineer, plumber etc* titulado; (*restricted*) limitado; *I am not qualified to judge* no estoy en condiciones de poder juzgar

qual·i·fy ['kwɑːlɪfaɪ] **1** *v/t* (*pret & pp qualified*) *of degree, course etc* habilitar; *remark etc* matizar **2** *v/i* (*pret & pp qualified*) (*get degree etc*) titularse, *L.Am.* egresar; *in competition* calificarse; *they qualified for the final* se clasificaron para la final; *that doesn't qualify as …* eso no cuenta como …

qual·i·ty ['kwɑːlɪtɪ] calidad *f*, (*characteristic*) cualidad *f*

qual·i·ty con·trol control *m* de calidad

qualm [kwɑːm]: *have no qualms about …* no tener reparos en …

quan·da·ry ['kwɑːndərɪ] dilema *m*

quan·ti·fy ['kwɑːntɪfaɪ] *v/t* (*pret & pp quantified*) cuantificar

quan·ti·ty ['kwɑːntɪtɪ] cantidad *f*

quan·tum 'phys·ics ['kwɑːntəm] física *f* cuántica

quar·an·tine ['kwɑːrəntiːn] cuarentena *f*

quar·rel ['kwɑːrəl] **1** *n* pelea *f* **2** *v/i* (*pret & pp quarrelled*, *Br* **quarrelled**) pelearse

quar·rel·some ['kwɑːrəlsʌm] *adj* peleón

quar·ry¹ ['kwɑːrɪ] *in hunt* presa *f*

quar·ry² ['kwɑːrɪ] *for mining* cantera *f*

quart [kwɔːrt] cuarto *m* de galón

quar·ter ['kwɔːrtər] cuarto *m*; *25 cents* cuarto *m* de dólar; *part of town* barrio *m*; *a quarter of an hour* un cuarto de hora; *a quarter of 5* las cinco menos cuarto; *a quarter after 5* las cinco y cuarto

'quar·ter·back SP quarterback *m*, *en fútbol americano, jugador que dirige el juego de ataque*

quar·ter-'fi·nal cuarto *m* de final

quar·ter-'fi·nal·ist cuartofinalista *m/f*

quar·ter·ly ['kwɔːrtəlɪ] **1** *adj* trimestral **2** *adv* trimestralmente

'quar·ter·note MUS negra *f*

quar·ters ['kwɔːrtəz] *npl* MIL alojamiento *m*

quar·tet [kwɔːr'tet] MUS cuarteto *m*

quartz [kwɔːrts] cuarzo *m*

quash [kwɑːʃ] *v/t rebellion* aplastar, sofocar; *court decision* revocar

qua·ver ['kweɪvər] **1** *n in voice* temblor *m* **2** *v/i of voice* temblar

quay [kiː] muelle *m*

'quay·side muelle *m*

quea·sy ['kwiːzɪ] *adj* mareado; *get queasy* marearse

queen [kwiːn] reina *f*

queen 'bee abeja *f* reina

queer [kwɪr] *adj* (*peculiar*) raro, extraño

queer·ly ['kwɪrlɪ] *adv* de manera extraña

quell [kwel] *v/t protest, crowd* acallar; *riot* aplastar, sofocar

quench [kwentʃ] *v/t thirst* saciar; *flames* apagar

que·ry ['kwɪrɪ] **1** *n* duda *f*, pregunta *f* **2** *v/t* (*pret & pp queried*) (*express doubt about*) cuestionar; (*check*) comprobar; *query sth with s.o.* preguntar algo a alguien

quest [kwest] busca *f*

ques·tion ['kwestʃn] **1** *n* pregunta *f*; (*matter*) cuestión *f*, asunto *m*; *in question* (*being talked about*) en cuestión; (*in doubt*) en duda; *it's a question of money / time* una cuestión de dinero / tiempo; *that's out of the question* eso es imposible **2** *v/t person* preguntar a; LAW interrogar; (*doubt*) cuestionar, poner en duda

ques·tion·a·ble ['kwestʃnəbl] *adj* cuestionable, dudoso

ques·tion·ing ['kwestʃnɪŋ] **1** *adj look, tone* inquisitivo **2** *n* interrogatorio *m*

'ques·tion mark signo *m* de interrogación

ques·tion·naire [kwestʃə'ner] cuestionario *m*

queue [kju:] *n Br* cola *f*

quib·ble ['kwɪbl] *v/i* discutir (*por algo insignificante*)

quick [kwɪk] *adj* rápido; *be quick!* ¡date prisa!; *let's have a quick drink* vamos a tomarnos algo rápidamente; *can I have a quick look?* ¿me dejas echarle un vistazo?; *that was quick!* ¡qué rápido!

quick·ie ['kwɪkɪ] *F*: *have a quickie* (*quick drink*) tomarse una copa rápida

quick·ly ['kwɪklɪ] *adv* rápidamente, rápido, deprisa

'quick·sand arenas *fpl* movedizas

'quick·sil·ver azogue *m*

quick·wit·ted [kwɪk'wɪtɪd] *adj* agudo

qui·et ['kwaɪət] *adj* tranquilo; *engine* silencioso; *keep quiet about sth* guardar silencio sobre algo; *quiet!* ¡silencio!

♦ **qui·et·en down** ['kwaɪətn] **1** *v/t children, class* tranquilizar, hacer callar **2** *v/i of children* tranquilizarse, callarse; *of political situation* calmarse

quiet·ly ['kwaɪətlɪ] *adv* (*not loudly*) silenciosamente; (*without fuss*) discretamente; (*peacefully*) tranquilamente; *speak quietly* hablar en voz baja

quiet·ness ['kwaɪətnɪs] *n of voice* suavidad *f*; *of night, street* silencio *m*, calma *f*

quilt [kwɪlt] *on bed* edredón *m*

quilt·ed ['kwɪltɪd] *adj* acolchado

quin·ine ['kwɪniːn] quinina *f*

quin·tet [kwɪn'tet] MUS quinteto *m*

quip [kwɪp] **1** *n joke* broma *f*; *remark* salida *f* **2** *v/i* (*pret & pp* **quipped**) bromear

quirk [kwɜːrk] peculiaridad *f*, rareza *f*

quirk·y ['kwɜːrkɪ] *adj* peculiar, raro

quit [kwɪt] **1** *v/t* (*pret & pp* **quit**) *job* dejar, abandonar; *quit doing sth* dejar de hacer algo *rápidamente*; *can I have a quick look?* dimitir; COMPUT salir; *get one's notice to quit from landlord* recibir la notificación de desalojo

quite [kwaɪt] *adv* (*fairly*) bastante; (*completely*) completamente; *not quite ready* no listo del todo; *I didn't quite understand* no entendí bien; *is that right? - not quite* ¿es verdad? - no exactamente; *quite!* ¡exactamente!; *quite a lot* bastante; *quite a few* bastantes; *it was quite a surprise/change* fue toda una sorpresa / un cambio

quits [kwɪts] *adj*: *be quits with s.o.* estar en paz con alguien

quit·ter ['kwɪtər] *F* persona que abandona *fácilmente*

quiv·er ['kwɪvər] *v/i* estremecerse

quiz [kwɪz] **1** *n* concurso *m* (*de preguntas y respuestas*) **2** *v/t* (*pret & pp* **quizzed**) interrogar (*about* sobre)

'quiz mas·ter presentador de un concurso de preguntas y respuestas

'quiz pro·gram, *Br* **'quiz pro·gramme** programa *m* concurso (*de preguntas y respuestas*)

quo·ta ['kwoʊtə] cuota *f*

quo·ta·tion [kwoʊ'teɪʃn] *from author* cita *f*; (*price*) presupuesto *m*

quo'ta·tion marks *npl* comillas *fpl*

quote [kwoʊt] **1** *n from author* cita *f*; (*price*) presupuesto *m*; (*quotation mark*) comilla *f*; *in quotes* entre comillas **2** *v/t text* citar; *price* dar **3** *v/i*: *quote from an author* citar de un autor

---

R

R

rab·bi ['ræbaɪ] rabino *m*

rab·bit ['ræbɪt] conejo *m*

rab·ble ['ræbl] chusma *f*, multitud *f*

rab·ble-rous·er ['ræblraʊzər] agitador(a) *m(f)*

ra·bies ['reɪbiːz] *nsg* rabia *f*

rac·coon [rə'kuːn] mapache *m*

race[1] [reɪs] *n of people* raza *f*

race[2] [reɪs] **1** *n* SP carrera *f*; *the races* horse races las carreras **2** *v/i* (*run fast*) correr; *he raced through his meal/work* acabó

su comida / trabajo a toda velocidad **3** *v/t* correr contra; *I'll race you* te echo una carrera

'race·course hipódromo *m*

'race·horse caballo *m* de carreras

'race riot disturbios *mpl* raciales

'race·track circuito *m*; *for horses* hipódromo *m*

ra·cial ['reɪʃl] *adj* racial; *racial equality* igualdad *f* racial

rac·ing ['reɪsɪŋ] carreras *fpl*

rac·ism ['reɪsɪzm] racismo *m*

ra·cist ['reɪsɪst] **1** *n* racista *m/f* **2** *adj* racista

rack [ræk] **1** *n* (*for bikes*) barras para aparcar bicicletas; *for bags on train* portaequipajes *m inv*; *for CDs* mueble *m* **2** *v/t*: **rack one's brains** devanarse los sesos

rack·et¹ ['rækɪt] SP raqueta *f*

rack·et² ['rækɪt] (*noise*) jaleo *m*; (*criminal activity*) negocio *m* sucio

ra·dar ['reɪdɑːr] radar *m*

'ra·dar screen pantalla *f* de radar

'ra·dar trap control *m* de velocidad por radar

ra·di·al 'tire, *Br* **ra·di·al 'tyre** ['reɪdɪəl] neumático *m* radial

ra·di·ance ['reɪdɪəns] esplendor *m*, brillantez *f*

ra·di·ant ['reɪdɪənt] *adj smile, appearance* resplandeciente, brillante

ra·di·ate ['reɪdɪeɪt] *v/i of heat, light* irradiar

ra·di·a·tion [reɪdɪ'eɪʃn] PHYS radiación *f*

ra·di·a·tor ['reɪdɪeɪtər] *in room, car* radiador *m*

rad·i·cal ['rædɪkl] **1** *adj* radical **2** *n* POL radical *m/f*

rad·i·cal·ism ['rædɪkəlɪzm] POL radicalismo *m*

rad·i·cal·ly ['rædɪklɪ] *adv* radicalmente

ra·di·o ['reɪdɪoʊ] radio *f*; **on the radio** en la radio; **by radio** por radio

ra·di·o·ac·tive [reɪdɪoʊ'æktɪv] *adj* radiactivo

ra·di·o·ac·tive 'waste residuos *mpl* radiactivos

ra·di·o·ac·tiv·i·ty [reɪdɪoʊæk'tɪvətɪ] radiactividad *f*

ra·di·o a'larm radio *f* despertador

ra·di·og·ra·pher [reɪdɪ'ɑːɡrəfər] técnico(-a) *m(f)* de rayos X

ra·di·og·ra·phy [reɪdɪ'ɑːɡrəfɪ] radiografía *f*

'ra·di·o sta·tion emisora *f* de radio

'ra·di·o tax·i radiotaxi *m*

ra·di·o·ther·a·py radioterapia *f*

rad·ish ['rædɪʃ] rábano *m*

ra·di·us ['reɪdɪəs] radio *m*

raf·fle ['ræfl] *n* rifa *f*

raft [ræft] balsa *f*

raf·ter ['ræftər] viga *f*

rag [ræɡ] *n for cleaning etc* trapo *m*; **in rags** con harapos

rage [reɪdʒ] **1** *n* ira *f*, cólera *f*; **be in a rage** estar encolerizado; **be all the rage** F estar arrasando F **2** *v/i of storm* bramar

rag·ged ['ræɡɪd] *adj* andrajoso

raid [reɪd] **1** *n by troops* incursión *f*; *by police* redada *f*; *by robbers* atraco *m*; FIN ataque *m*, incursión *f* **2** *v/t of troops* realizar una incursión en; *of police* realizar una redada en; *of robbers* atracar; *fridge, orchard* saquear

raid·er ['reɪdər] *on bank etc* atracador(a) *m(f)*

rail [reɪl] *n on track* riel *m*, carril *m*; (*handrail*) pasamanos *m inv*, baranda *f*; *for towel* barra *f*; **by rail** en tren

rail·ings ['reɪlɪŋz] *npl around park etc* verja *f*

rail·road ['reɪlroʊd] ferrocarril *m*

'rail·road sta·tion estación *f* de ferrocarril *or* de tren

rail·way ['reɪlweɪ] *Br* ferrocarril *m*

rain [reɪn] **1** *n* lluvia *f*; **in the rain** bajo la lluvia **2** *v/i* llover; **it's raining** llueve

'rain·bow arco *m* iris

'rain·check: **can I take a raincheck on that?** F ¿lo podríamos aplazar para algún otro momento?

'rain·coat impermeable *m*

'rain·drop gota *f* de lluvia

'rain·fall pluviosidad *f*, precipitaciones *fpl*

'rain for·est selva *f*

'rain·proof *adj fabric* impermeable

'rain·storm tormenta *f*, aguacero *m*

rain·y ['reɪnɪ] *adj* lluvioso; **it's rainy** llueve mucho

'rain·y sea·son estación *f* de las lluvias

raise [reɪz] **1** *n in salary* aumento *m* de sueldo **2** *v/t shelf etc* levantar; *offer* incrementar; *children* criar; *question* plantear; *money* reunir

rai·sin ['reɪzn] pasa *f*

rake [reɪk] *n for garden* rastrillo *m*

♦ **rake up** *v/t leaves* rastrillar; *fig* sacar a la luz

ral·ly ['rælɪ] *n* (*meeting, reunion*) concentración *f*; *political* mitin *m*; MOT rally *m*; *in tennis* peloteo *m*

♦ **rally round 1** *v/i* (*pret & pp* **rallied**) acudir a ayudar **2** *v/t* (*pret & pp* **rallied**): **rally round s.o.** acudir a ayudar a alguien

ram [ræm] **1** *n* carnero *m* **2** *v/t* (*pret & pp* **rammed**) *ship, car* embestir

RAM [ræm] COMPUT *abbr* (= **random access memory**) RAM *f* (= memoria *f* de acceso aleatorio)

ram·ble ['ræmbl] **1** *n walk* caminata *f*, excursión *f* **2** *v/i walk* caminar; *in speaking* divagar; (*talk incoherently*) hablar sin decir nada coherente

ram·bler ['ræmblər] *walker* senderista *m/f*, excursionista *m/f*

ram·bling ['ræmblɪŋ] **1** *n walking* senderismo *m*; *in speech* divagaciones *fpl* **2** *adj speech* inconexo

R

ramp [ræmp] rampa f; *for raising vehicle* elevador m

ram·page ['ræmpeɪdʒ] **1** v/i pasar arrasando con todo **2** n: *go on the rampage* pasar arrasando con todo

ram·pant ['ræmpənt] adj *inflation* galopante

ram·part ['ræmpɑːrt] muralla f

ram·shack·le ['ræmʃækl] adj destartalado, desvencijado

ran [ræn] pret → **run**

ranch [ræntʃ] rancho m

ranch·er ['ræntʃər] ranchero(-a) m(f)

ran·cid ['rænsɪd] adj rancio

ran·cor ['ræŋkər] rencor

R & D [ɑːrən'diː] abbr (= **research and development**) I+D f (= investigación f y desarrollo)

ran·dom ['rændəm] **1** adj al azar; *random sample* muestra f aleatoria **2** n: *at random* al azar

ran·dy ['rændɪ] adj Br F cachondo F; *it makes me randy* me pone cachondo

rang [ræŋ] pret → **ring²**

range [reɪndʒ] **1** n *of products* gama f; *of gun, airplane* alcance m; *of voice* registro m; *of mountains* cordillera f; *at close range* de cerca **2** v/i: *range from X to Y* ir desde X a Y

rang·er ['reɪndʒər] guardabosques m/f inv

rank [ræŋk] **1** n MIL, *in society* rango m; *the ranks* MIL la tropa **2** v/t clasificar

♦ **rank among** v/t figurar entre

ran·kle ['ræŋkl] v/i doler; *it still rankles (with him)* todavía le duele

ran·sack ['rænsæk] v/t saquear

ran·som ['rænsəm] n rescate m; *hold s.o. to ransom* pedir un rescate por alguien

'ran·som mon·ey (dinero m del) rescate m

rant [rænt] v/i: *rant and rave* despotricar

rap [ræp] **1** n *at door etc* golpe m; MUS rap m **2** v/t (pret & pp **rapped**) *table etc* golpear

♦ **rap at** v/t *window etc* golpear

rape¹ [reɪp] **1** n violación f **2** v/t violar

rape² [reɪp] n BOT colza f

'rape vic·tim víctima m/f de una violación

rap·id ['ræpɪd] adj rápido

ra·pid·i·ty [rə'pɪdətɪ] rapidez f

rap·id·ly ['ræpɪdlɪ] adv rápidamente

rap·ids ['ræpɪdz] npl rápidos mpl

rap·ist ['reɪpɪst] violador(a) m(f)

rap·port [ræ'pɔːr] relación f; *we've got a good rapport* nos entendemos muy bien

rap·ture ['ræptʃər]: *go into raptures over* extasiarse con

rap·tur·ous ['ræptʃərəs] adj clamoroso

rare [rer] adj raro; *steak* poco hecho

rare·ly ['rerlɪ] adv raramente, raras veces

rar·i·ty ['rerətɪ] rareza f

ras·cal ['ræskl] pícaro(-a) m(f)

rash¹ [ræʃ] n MED sarpullido m, erupción f cutánea

rash² [ræʃ] adj *action, behavior* precipitado

rash·ly ['ræʃlɪ] adv precipitadamente

rasp·ber·ry ['ræzberɪ] frambuesa f

rat [ræt] n rata f

rate [reɪt] **1** n *of exchange* tipo m; *of pay* tarifa f; (price) tarifa f, precio m; (speed) ritmo m; *rate of interest* FIN tipo m de interés; *at this rate* (at this speed) a este ritmo; (if we carry on like this) si seguimos así; *at any rate* (anyway) en todo caso; (at least) por lo menos **2** v/t: *rate s.o. as ...* considerar a alguien (como) ...; *rate s.o. highly* tener buena opinión de alguien

rath·er ['ræðər] adv bastante; *I would rather stay here* preferiría quedarme aquí; *or would you rather ...?* ¿o preferiría ...?

rat·i·fi·ca·tion [rætɪfɪ'keɪʃn] ratificación f

rat·i·fy ['rætɪfaɪ] v/t (pret & pp **ratified**) ratificar

rat·ings ['reɪtɪŋz] npl índice m de audiencia

ra·ti·o ['reɪʃɪoʊ] proporción f

ra·tion ['ræʃn] **1** n ración f **2** v/t *supplies* racionar

ra·tion·al ['ræʃnl] adj racional

ra·tion·al·i·ty [ræʃə'nælɪtɪ] racionalidad f

ra·tion·al·i·za·tion [ræʃənəlaɪ'zeɪʃn] racionalización f

ra·tion·al·ize ['ræʃənəlaɪz] **1** v/t racionalizar **2** v/i buscar una explicación racional

ra·tion·al·ly ['ræʃnlɪ] adv racionalmente

'rat race la vida frenética y competitiva

rat·tle ['rætl] **1** n *noise* traqueteo m, golpeteo m; *toy* sonajero m **2** v/t *chains etc* entrechocar **3** v/i *of chains etc* entrechocarse; *of crates* traquetear

♦ **rattle off** v/t *poem, list of names* decir rápidamente

♦ **rattle through** v/t hacer rápidamente

'rat·tle·snake serpiente f de cascabel

rau·cous ['rɔːkəs] adj *laughter, party* estridente

rav·age ['rævɪdʒ] **1** n: *the ravages of time* los estragos del tiempo **2** v/t arrasar; *ravaged by war* arrasado por la guerra

rave [reɪv] **1** v/i (talk deliriously) delirar; (talk wildly) desvariar; *rave about sth* (be very enthusiastic) estar muy entusiasmado con algo **2** n *party* fiesta f tecno

rave re·view crítica f muy entusiasta

ra·ven ['reɪvn] cuervo m

rav·e·nous ['rævənəs] *adj appetite* voraz;
 have a ravenous appetite tener un
 hambre canina

rav·e·nous·ly ['rævənəsli] *adv* con voraci-
dad

ra·vine [rə'viːn] barranco *m*

rav·ing ['reɪvɪŋ] *adv*: *raving mad* chalado

rav·ish·ing ['rævɪʃɪŋ] *adj* encantador,
cautivador

raw [rɔː] *adj meat, vegetable* crudo; *sugar*
sin refinar; *iron* sin tratar

raw ma'te·ri·als *npl* materias *fpl* primas

ray [reɪ] rayo *m*; *a ray of hope* un rayo de
esperanza

raze [reɪz] *v/t*: *raze to the ground* arrasar
or asolar por completo

ra·zor ['reɪzər] maquinilla *f* de afeitar

'ra·zor blade cuchilla *f* de afeitar

re [riː] *prep* COM con referencia a

reach [riːtʃ] **1** *n*: *within reach* al alcance;
 out of reach fuera del alcance **2** *v/t* llegar
a; *decision, agreement, conclusion* alcanzar, llegar a; *can you reach it?* ¿alcan-
zas?, ¿llegas?

◆ reach out *v/i* extender el brazo

re·act [rɪ'ækt] *v/i* reaccionar

re·ac·tion [rɪ'ækʃn] reacción *f*

re·ac·tion·ar·y [rɪ'ækʃnrɪ] **1** *n* POL reaccio-
nario(-a) *m(f)* **2** *adj* POL reaccionario

re·ac·tor [rɪ'æktər] *nuclear* reactor *m*

read [riːd] **1** *v/t* (*pret & pp* **read** [red]) *also*
 COMPUT leer **2** *v/i* (*pret & pp* **read** [red])
leer; *read to s.o.* leer a alguien

◆ read out *v/t* aloud leer en voz alta

◆ read up on *v/t* leer mucho sobre, estudiar

rea·da·ble ['riːdəbl] *adj handwriting* legible; *book* ameno

read·er ['riːdər] *person* lector(a) *m(f)*

read·i·ly ['redɪlɪ] *adv admit, agree* de buena gana

read·i·ness ['redɪnɪs]: *in a state of readi-
ness* preparado *or* para actuar; *their readi-
ness to help* la facilidad con la que ayudaron

read·ing ['riːdɪŋ] *activity* lectura *f*; *take a
reading from the meter* leer el contador

'read·ing mat·ter lectura *f*

re·ad·just [riːə'dʒʌst] **1** *v/t equipment,
controls* reajustar **2** *v/i to conditions* volver a adaptarse

read-'on·ly file COMPUT archivo *m* sólo de
lectura

read-'on·ly mem·o·ry COMPUT memoria *f*
sólo de lectura

read·y ['redɪ] *adj* (*prepared*) listo, preparado; (*willing*) dispuesto; *get* (*o.s.*) *ready*
prepararse; *get sth ready* preparar algo

read·y 'cash dinero *m* contante y sonante

read·y-made *adj stew etc* precocinado; *solution* ya hecho

read·y-to-wear *adj* de confección

real [riːl] *adj* real; *surprise, genius* auténtico; *he's a real idiot* es un auténtico idiota

'real es·tate bienes *mpl* inmuebles

'real es·tate a·gent agente *m/f* inmobi-
liario(-a)

re·al·ism ['rɪəlɪzəm] realismo *m*

re·a·list ['rɪəlɪst] realista *m/f*

re·a·lis·tic [rɪə'lɪstɪk] *adj* realista

re·a·lis·ti·cal·ly [rɪə'lɪstɪklɪ] *adv* realísti-
camente

re·al·i·ty [rɪ'ælətɪ] realidad *f*

re·a·li·za·tion [rɪələr'zeɪʃn]: *the realization dawned on me that ...* me di cuenta
de que ...

re·a·lize ['rɪəlaɪz] *v/t* darse cuenta de; FIN
(*yield*) producir; (*sell*) realizar, liquidar; *I
realize now that ...* ahora me doy cuenta
de que ...

real·ly ['rɪəlɪ] *adv in truth* de verdad; *big,
small* muy; *I am really really sorry* lo
siento en el alma; *really?* ¿de verdad?;
not really as reply la verdad es que no

real 'time *n* COMPUT tiempo *m* real

real-time *adj* COMPUT en tiempo real

re·al·tor ['riːltər] agente *m/f* inmobilia-
rio(-a)

re·al·ty ['riːltɪ] bienes *mpl* inmuebles

reap [riːp] *v/t* cosechar

re·ap·pear [riːə'pɪr] *v/i* reaparecer

reappearance [riːə'pɪrəns] reaparición *f*

rear [rɪr] **1** *n* parte *f* de atrás **2** *adj legs* de
atrás; *seats, wheels, lights* trasero

rear 'end **1** *n* F *of person* trasero *m* **2** *v/t*
MOT F dar un golpe por atrás a

rear 'light *of car* luz *f* trasera

re·arm [riː'ɑːrm] **1** *v/t* rearmar **2** *v/i* rear-
marse

'rear·most *adj* último

re·ar·range [riːə'reɪndʒ] *v/t flowers* volver
a colocar; *furniture* reordenar; *schedule,
meetings* cambiar

rear·view 'mir·ror espejo *m* retrovisor

rea·son ['riːzn] **1** *n faculty* razón *f*; (*cause*)
razón *f*, motivo *m*; *see* / *listen to reason*
atender a razones **2** *v/i*: *reason with s.o.*
razonar con alguien

rea·so·na·ble ['riːznəbl] *adj person* razonable; *a reasonable number of people* un buen número de personas

rea·son·a·bly ['riːznəblɪ] *adv act, behave*
razonablemente; (*quite*) bastante

rea·son·ing ['riːznɪŋ] razonamiento *m*

re·as·sure [riːə'ʃʊr] *v/t* tranquilizar; *she
reassured us of her continued support*
nos aseguró que continuábamos contan-

R

do con su apoyo

re·as·sur·ing [riːəˈʃʊrɪŋ] *adj* tranquilizador

re·bate [ˈriːbeɪt] *money back* reembolso *m*

reb·el[1] [ˈrebl] *n* rebelde *m/f*; **rebel troops** tropas *fpl* rebeldes

reb·el[2] [rɪˈbel] *v/i (pret & pp* **rebelled**) rebelarse

reb·el·lion [rɪˈbeljən] rebelión *f*

reb·el·lious [rɪˈbeljəs] *adj* rebelde

reb·el·lious·ly [rɪˈbeljəslɪ] *adv* con rebeldía

reb·el·lious·ness [rɪˈbeljəsnɪs] rebeldía *f*

re·bound [rɪˈbaʊnd] *v/i of ball etc* rebotar

re·buff [rɪˈbʌf] *n* desaire *m*, rechazo *m*

re·build [ˈriːbɪld] *v/t (pret & pp* **rebuilt**) reconstruir

re·buke [rɪˈbjuːk] *v/t* reprender

re·call [rɪˈkɔːl] *v/t goods* retirar del mercado; *(remember)* recordar

re·cap [ˈriːkæp] *v/i (pret & pp* **recapped**) recapitular

re·cap·ture [riːˈkæptʃər] *v/t* MIL reconquistar; *criminal* volver a detener

re·cede [rɪˈsiːd] *v/i of flood waters* retroceder

re·ced·ing [rɪˈsiːdɪŋ] *adj forehead, chin* hundido; **have a receding hairline** tener entradas

re·ceipt [rɪˈsiːt] *for purchase* recibo *m*; **acknowledge receipt of sth** acusar recibo de algo; **receipts** FIN ingresos *mpl*

re·ceive [rɪˈsiːv] *v/t* recibir

re·ceiv·er [rɪˈsiːvər] *of letter* destinatario(-a) *m(f)*; TELEC auricular *m; for radio* receptor *m; in tennis* jugador(a) *m(f)* al resto

re·ceiv·er·ship [rɪˈsiːvərʃɪp]: **be in receivership** estar en suspensión de pagos

re·cent [ˈriːsnt] *adj* reciente

re·cent·ly [ˈriːsntlɪ] *adv* recientemente

re·cep·tion [rɪˈsepʃn] recepción *f; (welcome)* recibimiento *m*

re'cep·tion desk recepción *f*

re·cep·tion·ist [rɪˈsepʃnɪst] recepcionista *m/f*

re·cep·tive [rɪˈseptɪv] *adj*: **be receptive to sth** ser receptivo a algo

re·cess [ˈriːses] *n in wall* hueco *m*; EDU recreo *m; of parliament* periodo *m* vacacional

re·ces·sion [rɪˈseʃn] *economic* recesión *f*

re·charge [riːˈtʃɑːrdʒ] *v/t battery* recargar

re·ci·pe [ˈresəpɪ] receta *f*

're·ci·pe book libro *m* de cocina, recetario *m*

re·cip·i·ent [rɪˈsɪpɪənt] *of parcel etc* destinatario(-a) *m(f); of payment* receptor(a) *m(f)*

re·cip·ro·cal [rɪˈsɪprəkl] *adj* recíproco

re·cit·al [rɪˈsaɪtl] MUS recital *m*

re·cite [rɪˈsaɪt] *v/t poem* recitar; *details, facts* enumerar

reck·less [ˈreklɪs] *adj* imprudente; *driving* temerario

reck·less·ly [ˈreklɪslɪ] *adv* con imprudencia; *drive* con temeridad

reck·on [ˈrekən] *v/i (think, consider)* estimar, considerar; **I reckon it won't happen** creo que no va a pasar

◆ **reckon on** *v/t* contar con

◆ **reckon with** *v/t*: **have s.o./sth to reckon with** tener que vérselas con alguien / algo

reck·on·ing [ˈrekənɪŋ] estimaciones *fpl*, cálculos *mpl*; **by my reckoning** según mis cálculos

re·claim [rɪˈkleɪm] *v/t land from sea* ganar, recuperar; *lost property, rights* reclamar

re·cline [rɪˈklaɪn] *v/i* reclinarse

re·clin·er [rɪˈklaɪnər] *chair* sillón *m* reclinable

re·cluse [rɪˈkluːs] solitario(-a) *m(f)*

rec·og·ni·tion [rekəɡˈnɪʃn] *of state, s.o.'s achievements* reconocimiento *m*; **in recognition of** en reconocimiento a; **be changed beyond recognition** estar irreconocible

rec·og·niz·a·ble [rekəɡˈnaɪzəbl] *adj* reconocible

rec·og·nize [ˈrekəɡnaɪz] *v/t* reconocer

re·coil [rɪˈkɔɪl] *v/i* echarse atrás, retroceder

rec·ol·lect [rekəˈlekt] *v/t* recordar

rec·ol·lec·tion [rekəˈlekʃn] recuerdo *m*; **I have no recollection of the accident** no me acuerdo del accidente

rec·om·mend [rekəˈmend] *v/t* recomendar

rec·om·men·da·tion [rekəmənˈdeɪʃn] recomendación *f*

rec·om·pense [ˈrekəmpens] *n* recompensa *f*

rec·on·cile [ˈrekənsaɪl] *v/t people* reconciliar; *differences, facts* conciliar; **reconcile o.s. to ...** hacerse a la idea de ...; **be reconciled** *of two people* haberse reconciliado

rec·on·cil·i·a·tion [rekənsɪlɪˈeɪʃn] *of people* reconciliación *f; of differences, facts* conciliación *f*

re·con·di·tion [riːkənˈdɪʃn] *v/t* reacondicionar

re·con·nais·sance [rɪˈkɑːnɪsns] MIL reconocimiento *m*

re·con·sid·er [riːkənˈsɪdər] **1** *v/t offer, one's position* reconsiderar **2** *v/i*: **won't**

you please reconsider? ¿por qué no lo reconsideras, por favor?

re·con·struct [ri:kən'strʌkt] *v/t* reconstruir

rec·ord¹ ['rekɔːrd] *n* MUS disco *m*; SP *etc* récord *m*; *written document etc* registro *m*, documento *m*; *in database* registro *m*; **records** archivos *mpl*; **say sth off the record** decir algo oficiosamente; **have a criminal record** tener antecedentes penales; **have a good record for sth** tener un buen *historial* en materia de algo

re·cord² [rɪ'kɔːrd] *v/t electronically* grabar; *in writing* anotar

'rec·ord-break·ing *adj* récord

re·cord·er [rɪ'kɔːrdər] MUS flauta *f* dulce

'rec·ord hold·er plusmarquista *m/f*

re·cord·ing [rɪ'kɔːrdɪŋ] grabación *f*

re'cord·ing stu·di·o estudio *m* de grabación

re'cord play·er tocadiscos *m inv*

re·count [rɪ'kaʊnt] *v/t (tell)* relatar

re-count ['riːkaʊnt] **1** *n of votes* segundo recuento *m* **2** *v/t (count again)* volver a contar

re·coup [rɪ'kuːp] *v/t financial losses* resarcirse de

re·cov·er [rɪ'kʌvər] **1** *v/t sth lost, stolen goods* recuperar; *composure* recobrar **2** *v/i from illness* recuperarse

re·cov·er·y [rɪ'kʌvərɪ] recuperación *f*; **he has made a good recovery** se ha recuperado muy bien

rec·re·a·tion [rekrɪ'eɪʃn] ocio *m*

rec·re·a·tion·al [rekrɪ'eɪʃnl] *adj done for pleasure* recreativo

re·cruit [rɪ'kruːt] **1** *n* MIL recluta *m/f*; *to company* nuevo(-a) trabajador(a) **2** *v/t new staff* contratar

re·cruit·ment [rɪ'kruːtmənt] MIL reclutamiento *m*; *to company* contratación *f*

re'cruit·ment drive MIL campaña *f* de reclutamiento; *to company* campaña *f* de contratación

rec·tan·gle ['rektæŋgl] rectángulo *m*

rec·tan·gu·lar [rek'tæŋgjʊlər] *adj* rectangular

rec·ti·fy ['rektɪfaɪ] *v/t (pret & pp* **rectified***)* rectificar

re·cu·pe·rate [rɪ'kuːpəreɪt] *v/i* recuperarse

re·cur [rɪ'kɜːr] *v/i (pret & pp* **recurred***) of error, event* repetirse; *of symptoms* reaparecer

re·cur·rent [rɪ'kʌrənt] *adj* recurrente

re·cy·cla·ble [riː'saɪkləbl] *adj* reciclable

re·cy·cle [riː'saɪkl] *v/t* reciclar

re·cy·cling [riː'saɪklɪŋ] reciclado *m*

red [red] *adj* rojo; **in the red** FIN en números rojos

Red 'Cross Cruz *f* Roja

red·den ['redn] *v/i (blush)* ponerse colorado

re·dec·o·rate [riː'dekəreɪt] *v/t with paint* volver a pintar; *with paper* volver a empapelar

re·deem [rɪ'diːm] *v/t debt* amortizar; REL redimir

re·deem·ing fea·ture [rɪ'diːmɪŋ]: **his one redeeming feature is that ...** lo único que lo salva es que ...

re·demp·tion [rɪ'dempʃn] REL redención *f*

re·de·vel·op [riːdɪ'veləp] *v/t part of town* reedificar

red-hand·ed [red'hændɪd] *adj:* **catch s.o. red-handed** coger a alguien con las manos en la masa

'red·head pelirrojo(-a) *m(f)*

red-'hot *adj* al rojo vivo

red-'let·ter day día *m* señalado

red 'light *at traffic light* semáforo *m* (en) rojo

red 'light dis·trict zona *f* de prostitución

red 'meat carne *f* roja

'red·neck F individuo racista y reaccionario, *normalmente de clase trabajadora*

re·dou·ble [riː'dʌbl] *v/t:* **redouble one's efforts** redoblar los esfuerzos

red 'pep·per *vegetable* pimiento *m* rojo

red 'tape F burocracia *f*, papeleo *m*

re·duce [rɪ'duːs] *v/t* reducir; *price* rebajar

re·duc·tion [rɪ'dʌkʃn] reducción *f*; *in price* rebaja *f*

re·dun·dant [rɪ'dʌndənt] *adj (unnecessary)* innecesario; **be made redundant** Br *at work* ser despedido

reed [riːd] BOT junco *m*

reef [riːf] *in sea* arrecife *m*

'reef knot nudo *m* de rizos

reek [riːk] *v/i* apestar **(of** a)

reel [riːl] *n of film* rollo *m*; *of thread* carrete *m*

◆ **reel off** *v/t* soltar

re-e'lect *v/t* reelegir

re-e'lec·tion reelección *f*

re-'en·try *of spacecraft* reentrada *f*

ref [ref] F árbitro(-a) *m(f)*

re·fer [rɪ'fɜːr] *v/t (pret & pp* **referred***):* **refer a decision / problem to s.o.** remitir una decisión / un problema a alguien

◆ **refer to** *v/t (allude to)* referirse a; *dictionary etc* consultar

ref·er·ee [refə'riː] SP árbitro(-a) *m(f)*; *(for job)* persona que pueda dar referencias

ref·er·ence ['refərəns] referencia *f*; **with reference to** con referencia a

'ref·er·ence book libro *m* de consulta

'reference li·bra·ry biblioteca f de consulta

'ref·er·ence num·ber número m de referencia

ref·er·en·dum [refə'rendəm] referéndum m

re·fill ['ri:fɪl] v/t tank, glass volver a llenar

re·fine [rɪ'faɪn] v/t oil, sugar refinar; technique perfeccionar

re·fined [rɪ'faɪnd] adj manners, language refinado

re·fine·ment [rɪ'faɪnmənt] to process, machine mejora f

re·fin·e·ry [rɪ'faɪnərɪ] refinería f

re·fla·tion [ri:fleɪʃn] reflación f

re·flect [rɪ'flekt] 1 v/t light reflejar; be reflected in reflejarse en 2 v/i (think) reflexionar

re·flec·tion [rɪ'flekʃn] in water, glass etc reflejo f; (consideration) reflexión f

re·flex ['ri:fleks] in body reflejo m

re·flex re'ac·tion acto m reflejo

re·form [rɪ'fɔ:rm] 1 n reforma f 2 v/t reformar

re·form·er [rɪ'fɔ:rmər] reformador(a) m(f)

re·frain[1] [rɪ'freɪn] v/i fml abstenerse; please refrain from smoking se ruega no fumar

re·frain[2] [rɪ'freɪn] n in song, poem estribillo m

re·fresh [rɪ'freʃ] v/t person refrescar; feel refreshed sentirse fresco

refresh·er course [rɪ'freʃər] curso m de actualización or reciclaje

re·fresh·ing [rɪ'freʃɪŋ] adj drink refrescante; experience reconfortante

re·fresh·ments [rɪ'freʃmənts] npl refrigerio m

re·frig·e·rate [rɪ'frɪdʒəreɪt] v/t refrigerar; keep refrigerated conservar refrigerado

re·frig·e·ra·tor [rɪ'frɪdʒəreɪtər] frigorífico m, refrigerador m

re·fu·el [ri:'fjuəl] 1 v/t airplane reabastecer de combustible a 2 v/i of airplane repostar

ref·uge ['refju:dʒ] refugio m; take refuge from storm etc refugiarse

ref·u·gee [refju'dʒi:] refugiado(-a) m(f)

ref·u'gee camp campo m de refugiados

re·fund ['ri:fʌnd] 1 n reembolso m; give s.o. a refund devolver el dinero a alguien 2 v/t [rɪ'fʌnd] reembolsar

re·fus·al [rɪ'fju:zl] negativa f

re·fuse[1] [rɪ'fju:z] 1 v/t negarse 2 v/t help, food rechazar; refuse s.o. sth negar algo a alguien; refuse to do sth negarse a hacer algo

ref·use[2] ['refju:s] (garbage) basura f

'ref·use col·lec·tion recogida f de basuras

'ref·use dump vertedero m

re·gain [rɪ'geɪn] v/t recuperar

re·gal ['ri:gl] adj regio

re·gard [rɪ'gɑ:rd] 1 n: have great regard for s.o. sentir gran estima por alguien; in this regard en este sentido; with regard to con respecto a; (kind) regards saludos; give my regards to Paula dale saludos or recuerdos a Paula de mi parte; with no regard for sin tener en cuenta 2 v/t: regard s.o./sth as sth considerar a alguien / algo como algo; I regard it as an honor para mí es un honor; as regards con respecto a

re·gard·ing [rɪ'gɑ:rdɪŋ] prep con respecto a

re·gard·less [rɪ'gɑ:rdlɪs] adv a pesar de todo; regardless of sin tener en cuenta

re·gime [reɪ'ʒi:m] (government) régimen m

re·gi·ment ['redʒɪmənt] n regimiento m

re·gion ['ri:dʒən] región f; in the region of del orden de

re·gion·al [ri:dʒənl] adj regional

re·gis·ter ['redʒɪstər] 1 n registro m; at school lista f 2 v/t birth, death registrar; vehicle matricular; letter certificar; emotion mostrar; send a letter registered enviar una carta por correo certificado 3 v/i at university, for a course matricularse; with police registrarse

re·gis·tered let·ter ['redʒɪstərd] carta f certificada

re·gis·tra·tion [redʒɪ'streɪʃn] registro m; at university, for course matriculación f

re·gis'tra·tion num·ber Br MOT (número m de) matrícula f

re·gret [rɪ'gret] 1 v/t (pret & pp regretted) lamentar, sentir 2 n arrepentimiento m, pesar m

re·gret·ful [rɪ'gretfəl] adj arrepentido

re·gret·ful·ly [rɪ'gretfəlɪ] adv lamentablemente

re·gret·ta·ble [rɪ'gretəbl] adj lamentable

re·gret·ta·bly [rɪ'gretəblɪ] adv lamentablemente

reg·u·lar ['regjʊlər] 1 adj regular; (normal, ordinary) normal 2 n at bar etc habitual m/f

reg·u·lar·i·ty [regjʊ'lærətɪ] regularidad f

reg·u·lar·ly ['regjʊlərlɪ] adv regularmente

reg·u·late ['regʊleɪt] v/t regular

reg·u·la·tion [regʊ'leɪʃn] (rule) regla f, norma f

re·hab ['ri:hæb] F rehabilitación f

re·ha·bil·i·tate [ri:hə'bɪlɪteɪt] v/t ex-criminal rehabilitar

re·hears·al [rɪ'hɜːrsl] ensayo *m*

re·hearse [rɪ'hɜːrs] *v/t & v/i* ensayar

reign [reɪn] **1** *n* reinado *m* **2** *v/i* reinar

re·im·burse [riːɪm'bɜːrs] *v/t* reembolsar

rein [reɪn] rienda *f*

re·in·car·na·tion [riːɪnkɑːr'neɪʃn] reencarnación *f*

re·in·force [riːɪn'fɔːrs] *v/t structure* reforzar; *beliefs* reafirmar

re·in·forced con·crete [riːɪn'fɔːrst] hormigón *m* armado

re·in·force·ments [riːɪn'fɔːrsmənts] *npl* MIL refuerzos *mpl*

re·in·state [riːɪn'steɪt] *v/t person in office* reincorporar; *paragraph in text* volver a colocar

re·it·er·ate [riː'ɪtəreɪt] *v/t fml* reiterar

re·ject [rɪ'dʒekt] *v/t* rechazar

re·jec·tion [rɪ'dʒekʃn] rechazo *m*; *he felt a sense of rejection* se sintió rechazado

re·lapse [ˈriːlæps] *n* MED recaída *f*; *have a relapse* sufrir una recaída

re·late [rɪ'leɪt] **1** *v/t story* relatar, narrar; *relate sth to sth connect* relacionar algo con algo **2** *v/i*: *relate to be connected with* estar relacionado con; *he doesn't relate to people* no se relaciona fácilmente con la gente

re·lat·ed [rɪ'leɪtɪd] *adj by family* emparentado; *events, ideas etc* relacionado; *are you two related?* ¿sois parientes?

re·la·tion [rɪ'leɪʃn] *in family* pariente *m/f*; *(connection)* relación *f*; *business / diplomatic relations* relaciones *fpl* comerciales / diplomáticas

re·la·tion·ship [rɪ'leɪʃnʃɪp] relación *f*

rel·a·tive ['relətɪv] **1** *n* pariente *m/f* **2** *adj* relativo; *X is relative to Y* X está relacionado con Y

rel·a·tive·ly ['relətɪvlɪ] *adv* relativamente

re·lax [rɪ'læks] **1** *v/i* relajarse; *relax!, don't get angry* ¡tranquilízate!, no te enfades **2** *v/t muscle, pace* relajar

re·lax·a·tion [riːlæk'seɪʃn] relajación *f*; *what do you do for relaxation?* ¿qué haces para relajarte?

re·laxed [rɪ'lækst] *adj* relajado

re·lax·ing [rɪ'læksɪŋ] *adj* relajante

re·lay [riː'leɪ] **1** *v/t message* pasar; *radio, TV signals* retransmitir **2** *n*: *relay (race)* carrera *f* de relevos

re·lease [rɪ'liːs] **1** *n from prison* liberación *f*, puesta *f* en libertad; *of CD etc* lanzamiento *m*; *CD, record* trabajo *m* **2** *v/t prisoner* liberar, poner en libertad; *parking brake* soltar; *information* hacer público

rel·e·gate ['relɪgeɪt] *v/t* relegar

re·lent [rɪ'lent] *v/i* ablandarse, ceder

re·lent·less [rɪ'lentlɪs] *adj (determined)*

re·lent·less·ly [rɪ'lentlɪslɪ] *adv* implacablemente; *rain* sin cesar

rel·e·vance ['relɪvəns] pertinencia *f*

rel·e·vant ['relɪvənt] *adj* pertinente

re·li·a·bil·i·ty [rɪlaɪə'bɪlətɪ] fiabilidad *f*

re·li·a·ble [rɪ'laɪəbl] *adj* fiable; *information* fiable, fidedigna

re·li·a·bly [rɪ'laɪəblɪ] *adv*: *I am reliably informed that* sé de buena fuente que

re·li·ance [rɪ'laɪəns] confianza *f*, dependencia *f*; *reliance on s.o./sth* confianza en alguien / algo, dependencia de alguien / algo

re·li·ant [rɪ'laɪənt] *adj*: *be reliant on* depender de

rel·ic ['relɪk] reliquia *f*

re·lief [rɪ'liːf] alivio *m*; *that's a relief* qué alivio; *in relief in art* en relieve

re·lieve [rɪ'liːv] *v/t pressure, pain* aliviar; *(take over from)* relevar; *be relieved at news etc* sentirse aliviado

re·li·gion [rɪ'lɪdʒən] religión *f*

re·li·gious [rɪ'lɪdʒəs] *adj* religioso

re·li·gious·ly [rɪ'lɪdʒəslɪ] *adv (conscientiously)* religiosamente

re·lin·quish [rɪ'lɪŋkwɪʃ] *v/t* renunciar a

rel·ish ['relɪʃ] **1** *n sauce* salsa *f*; *(enjoyment)* goce *m* **2** *v/t idea, prospect* gozar con; *I don't relish the idea* la idea no me entusiasma

re·live [riː'lɪv] *v/t the past, an event* revivir

re·lo·cate [riːlə'keɪt] *v/i of business, employee* trasladarse

re·lo·ca·tion [riːlə'keɪʃn] *of business, employee* traslado *m*

re·luc·tance [rɪ'lʌktəns] reticencia *f*

re·luc·tant [rɪ'lʌktənt] *adj* reticente, reacio; *be reluctant to do sth* ser reacio a hacer algo

re·luc·tant·ly [rɪ'lʌktəntlɪ] *adv* con reticencia

◆ **re·ly on** [rɪ'laɪ] *v/t (pret & pp relied)* depender de; *rely on s.o. to do sth* contar con alguien para hacer algo

re·main [rɪ'meɪn] *v/i (be left)* quedar; MATH restar; *(stay)* permanecer

re·main·der [rɪ'meɪndər] **1** *n also* MATH resto *m* **2** *v/t* vender como saldo

re·main·ing [rɪ'meɪnɪŋ] *adj* restante

re·mains [rɪ'meɪnz] *npl of body* restos *mpl (mortales)*

re·make ['riːmeɪk] *n of movie* nueva versión *f*

re·mand [rɪ'mænd] **1** *v/t*: *remand s.o. in custody* poner a alguien en prisión preventiva **2** *n*: *be on remand in prison* estar en prisión preventiva; *on bail* estar en libertad bajo fianza

R

re·mark [rɪ'mɑːrk] **1** *n* comentario *m*, observación *f* **2** *v/t* comentar, observar

re·mark·a·ble [rɪ'mɑːrkəbl] *adj* notable, extraordinario

re·mark·a·bly [rɪ'mɑːrkəblɪ] *adv* extraordinariamente

re·mar·ry [riː'mærɪ] *v/i* (*pret & pp* **remarried**) volver a casarse

rem·e·dy ['remədɪ] *n* MED, *fig* remedio *m*

re·mem·ber [rɪ'membər] **1** *v/t s.o., sth* recordar, acordarse de; *remember to lock the door* acuérdate de cerrar la puerta; *remember me to her* dale recuerdos de mi parte **2** *v/i* recordar, acordarse; *I don't remember* no recuerdo, no me acuerdo

re·mind [rɪ'maɪnd] *v/t*: *remind s.o. of sth* recordar algo a alguien; *remind s.o. of s.o.* recordar alguien a alguien; *you remind me of your father* me recuerdas a tu padre

re·mind·er [rɪ'maɪndər] recordatorio *m*; *for payment* recordatorio *m* de pago

rem·i·nisce [remɪ'nɪs] *v/i* contar recuerdos

rem·i·nis·cent [remɪ'nɪsənt] *adj*: *be reminiscent of sth* recordar a algo, tener reminiscencias de algo

re·miss [rɪ'mɪs] *adj fml* negligente, descuidado

re·mis·sion [rɪ'mɪʃn] remisión *f*; *go into remission* MED remitir

rem·nant ['remnənt] resto *m*

re·morse [rɪ'mɔːrs] remordimientos *mpl*

re·morse·less [rɪ'mɔːrslɪs] *adj person* despiadado; *pace, demands* implacable

re·mote [rɪ'moʊt] *adj village, possibility* remoto; *(aloof)* distante; *ancestor* lejano

re·mote 'ac·cess COMPUT acceso *m* remoto

re·mote con'trol control *m* remoto; *for TV* mando *m* a distancia

re·mote·ly [rɪ'moʊtlɪ] *adv related, connected* remotamente; *it's just remotely possible* es una posibilidad muy remota

re·mote·ness [rɪ'moʊtnəs]: *the remoteness of the house* la lejanía *or* lo aislado de la casa

re·mov·a·ble [rɪ'muːvəbl] *adj* de quita y pon

re·mov·al [rɪ'muːvl] eliminación *f*

re·move [rɪ'muːv] *v/t* eliminar; *top, lid* quitar; *coat etc* quitarse; *doubt, suspicion* despejar; *growth, organ* extirpar

re·mu·ner·a·tion [rɪmjuːnə'reɪʃn] remuneración *f*

re·mu·ner·a·tive [rɪ'mjuːnərətɪv] *adj* bien remunerado

re·name [riː'neɪm] *v/t* cambiar el nombre a

ren·der ['rendər] *v/t service* prestar; *render s.o. helpless / unconscious* dejar a alguien indefenso / inconsciente

ren·der·ing ['rendərɪŋ] *of piece of music* interpretación *f*

ren·dez·vous ['rɑːndeɪvuː] *romantic* cita *f*; MIL encuentro *m*

re·new [rɪ'nuː] *v/t contract, license* renovar; *discussions* reanudar; *feel renewed* sentirse como nuevo

re·new·al [rɪ'nuːəl] *of contract etc* renovación *f*; *of discussions* reanudación *f*

re·nounce [rɪ'naʊns] *v/t title, rights* renunciar a

ren·o·vate ['renəveɪt] *v/t* renovar

ren·o·va·tion [renə'veɪʃn] renovación *f*

re·nown [rɪ'naʊn] renombre *m*

re·nowned [rɪ'naʊnd] *adj* renombrado; *be renowned for sth* ser célebre por algo

rent [rent] **1** *n* alquiler *m*; *for rent* se alquila **2** *v/t apartment, car, equipment* alquilar, *Mex* rentar

rent·al ['rentl] *for apartment, for TV* alquiler *m*, *Mex* renta *f*

'rent·al a·gree·ment acuerdo *m* de alquiler

'rent·al car coche *m* de alquiler

'rent-'free *adv* sin pagar alquiler

re·o·pen [riː'oʊpn] **1** *v/t* reabrir; *negotiations* reanudar **2** *v/i of theater etc* volver a abrir

re·or·gan·i·za·tion [riːɔːrgənaɪ'zeɪʃn] reorganización *f*

re·or·gan·ize [riː'ɔːrgənaɪz] *v/t* reorganizar

rep [rep] COM representante *m/f*, comercial *m/f*

re·paint [riː'peɪnt] *v/t* repintar

re·pair [rɪ'per] **1** *v/t fence, TV* reparar; *shoes* arreglar **2** *n to fence, TV* reparación *f*; *of shoes* arreglo *m*; *in a good / bad state of repair* en buen / mal estado

re'pair·man técnico *m*

re·pa·tri·ate [riː'pætrɪeɪt] *v/t* repatriar

re·pa·tri·a·tion [riː'pætrɪeɪʃn] repatriación *f*

re·pay [riː'peɪ] *v/t* (*pret & pp* **repaid**) *money* devolver; *person* pagar

re·pay·ment [riː'peɪmənt] devolución *f*; *installment* plazo *m*

re·peal [rɪ'piːl] *v/t law* revocar

re·peat [rɪ'piːt] **1** *v/t* repetir; *am I repeating myself?* ¿me estoy repitiendo? **2** *n TV program etc* repetición *f*

re·peat 'busi·ness COM negocio *m* que se repite

re·peat·ed [rɪ'piːtɪd] *adj* repetido

re·peat·ed·ly [rɪ'piːtɪdlɪ] *adv* repetidamente, repetidas veces

re·peat 'or·der COM pedido *m* repetido

re·pel [rɪ'pel] *v/t (pret & pp repelled) invaders, attack* rechazar; *insects* repeler, ahuyentar; *(disgust)* repeler, repugnar

re·pel·lent [rɪ'pelənt] **1** *n (insect repellent)* repelente *m* **2** *adj* repelente, repugnante

re·pent [rɪ'pent] *v/i* arrepentirse

re·per·cus·sions [riːpər'kʌʃnz] *npl* repercusiones *fpl*

rep·er·toire ['repərtwɑːr] repertorio *m*

rep·e·ti·tion [repɪ'tɪʃn] repetición *f*

re·pet·i·tive [rɪ'petɪtɪv] *adj* repetitivo

re·place [rɪ'pleɪs] *v/t (put back)* volver a poner; *(take the place of)* reemplazar, sustituir

re·place·ment [rɪ'pleɪsmənt] *n person* sustituto(-a) *m(f); thing* recambio *m*, reemplazo *m*

re·place·ment 'part (pieza *f* de) recambio *m*

re·play ['riːpleɪ] **1** *n recording* repetición *f* (de la jugada); *match* repetición *f* (del partido) **2** *v/t match* repetir

rep·li·ca ['replɪkə] réplica *f*

re·ply [rɪ'plaɪ] **1** *n* respuesta *f*, contestación *f* **2** *v/t & v/i (pret & pp replied)* responder, contestar

re·port [rɪ'pɔːrt] **1** *n (account)* informe *m; by journalist* reportaje *m* **2** *v/t facts* informar; *to authorities* informar de, dar parte de; *report a person to the police* denunciar a alguien a la policía; *he is reported to be in Washington* se dice que está en Washington **3** *v/i of journalist* informar; *(present o.s.)* presentarse *(to* ante*)*

◆ report to *v/t in business* trabajar a las órdenes de

re'port card boletín *m* de evaluación

re·port·er [rɪ'pɔːrtər] reportero(-a) *m(f)*

re·pos·sess [riːpə'zes] *v/t* COM embargar

rep·re·hen·si·ble [reprɪ'hensəbl] *adj* recriminable

rep·re·sent [reprɪ'zent] *v/t* representar

rep·re·sen·ta·tive [reprɪ'zentətɪv] **1** *n* representante *m/f*; POL representante *m/f*, diputado(-a) *m(f)* **2** *adj (typical)* representativo

re·press [rɪ'pres] *v/t revolt* reprimir; *feelings, laughter* reprimir, controlar

re·pres·sion [rɪ'preʃn] POL represión *f*

re·pres·sive [rɪ'presɪv] *adj* POL represivo

re·prieve [rɪ'priːv] **1** *n* LAW indulto *m; fig* aplazamiento *m* **2** *v/t prisoner* indultar

rep·ri·mand ['reprɪmænd] *v/t* reprender

re·print ['riːprɪnt] **1** *n* reimpresión *f* **2** *v/t* reimprimir

re·pri·sal [rɪ'praɪzl] represalia *f; take reprisals* tomar represalias; *in reprisal for* en represalia por

re·proach [rɪ'proutʃ] **1** *n* reproche *m; be beyond reproach* ser irreprochable **2** *v/t: reproach s.o. for sth* reprochar algo a alguien

re·proach·ful [rɪ'proutʃfəl] *adj* de reproche

re·proach·ful·ly [rɪ'proutʃfəlɪ] *adv look* con una mirada de reproche; *say* con tono de reproche

re·pro·duce [riːprə'duːs] **1** *v/t atmosphere, mood* reproducir **2** *v/i* BIO reproducirse

re·pro·duc·tion [riːprə'dʌkʃn] reproducción *f*

re·pro·duc·tive [riːprə'dʌktɪv] *adj* reproductivo

rep·tile ['reptaɪl] reptil *m*

re·pub·lic [rɪ'pʌblɪk] república *f*

re·pub·li·can [rɪ'pʌblɪkən] **1** *n* republicano(-a) *m(f)* **2** *adj* republicano

re·pu·di·ate [rɪ'pjuːdɪeɪt] *v/t (deny)* rechazar

re·pul·sive [rɪ'pʌlsɪv] *adj* repulsivo

rep·u·ta·ble ['repjʊtəbl] *adj* reputado, acreditado

rep·u·ta·tion [repjʊ'teɪʃn] reputación *f; have a good/bad reputation* tener una buena / mala reputación

re·put·ed [rɪ'pjuːtɪd] *adj: be reputed to be* tener fama de ser

re·put·ed·ly [rɪ'pjuːtɪdlɪ] *adv* según se dice

re·quest [rɪ'kwest] **1** *n* petición *f*, solicitud *f; on request* por encargo **2** *v/t* pedir, solicitar

re·quiem ['rekwɪəm] MUS réquiem *m*

re·quire [rɪ'kwaɪr] *v/t (need)* requerir, necesitar; *it requires great care* se requiere mucho cuidado; *as required by law* como estipula la ley; *guests are required to …* se ruega a los invitados que …

re·quired [rɪ'kwaɪrd] *adj (necessary)* necesario

re·quire·ment [rɪ'kwaɪrmənt] *n (need)* necesidad *f; (condition)* requisito *m*

req·ui·si·tion [rekwɪ'zɪʃn] *v/t* requisar

re·route [riː'ruːt] *v/t plane etc* desviar

re·run ['riːrʌn] **1** *n of TV program* reposición *f* **2** *v/t (pret reran, pp rerun) tape* volver a poner

re·sched·ule [riː'ʃeduːl] *v/t* volver a programar

res·cue ['reskjuː] **1** *n* rescate *m; come to*

s.o.'s rescue acudir al rescate de alguien **2** v/t rescatar

'res·cue par·ty equipo m de rescate

re·search [rɪ'sɜːtʃ] n investigación f
◆ **research** into v/t investigar

re·search and de'vel·op·ment investigación f y desarrollo

re·search as·sist·ant ayudante m/f de investigación

re·search·er [rɪ'sɜːtʃər] investigador(a) m(f)

re·search proj·ect proyecto m de investigación

re·sem·blance [rɪ'zembləns] parecido m, semejanza f

re·sem·ble [rɪ'zembl] v/t parecerse a

re·sent [rɪ'zent] v/t estar molesto por

re·sent·ful [rɪ'zentfəl] adj resentido

re·sent·ful·ly [rɪ'zentfəlɪ] adv con resentimiento

re·sent·ment [rɪ'zentmənt] resentimiento m

res·er·va·tion [rezər'veɪʃn] reserva f; **I have a reservation** in hotel, restaurant tengo una reserva

re·serve [rɪ'zɜːrv] **1** n reserva f; SP reserva m/f; **reserves** FIN reservas fpl; **keep sth in reserve** tener algo en la reserva **2** v/t seat, table reservar; judgment reservarse

re·served [rɪ'zɜːrvd] adj table, manner reservado

res·er·voir ['rezərvwɑːr] for water embalse m, pantano m

re·shuf·fle ['riːʃʌfl] **1** n POL remodelación f **2** POL remodelar

re·side [rɪ'zaɪd] v/i fml residir

res·i·dence ['rezɪdəns] (fml: house etc) residencia f; (stay) estancia f

'res·i·dence per·mit permiso m de residencia

'res·i·dent ['rezɪdənt] **1** n residente m/f **2** adj (living in a building) residente

res·i·den·tial [rezɪ'denʃl] adj district residencial

res·i·due ['rezɪduː] residuo m

re·sign [rɪ'zaɪn] **1** v/t position dimitir de; **resign o.s. to** resignarse a **2** v/i from job dimitir

res·ig·na·tion [rezɪg'neɪʃn] from job dimisión f; (mental) resignación f

re·signed [rɪ'zaɪnd] adj resignado; **we have become resigned to the fact that** ... nos hemos resignado a aceptar que ...

re·sil·i·ent [rɪ'zɪliənt] adj personality fuerte; material resistente

res·in ['rezɪn] resina f

re·sist [rɪ'zɪst] **1** v/t resistir; new measures oponer resistencia a **2** v/i resistir

re·sist·ance [rɪ'zɪstəns] resistencia f

re·sis·tant [rɪ'zɪstənt] adj material resistente; **resistant to heat / rust** resistente al calor/a la oxidación

res·o·lute ['rezəluːt] adj resuelto

res·o·lu·tion [rezə'luːʃn] resolución f; made at New Year etc propósito m

re·solve [rɪ'zɑːlv] v/t problem, mystery resolver; **resolve to do sth** resolver hacer algo

re·sort [rɪ'zɔːrt] n place centro m turístico; **as a last resort** como último recurso
◆ **resort to** v/t violence, threats recurrir a
◆ **re·sound with** [rɪ'zaund] v/t resonar con

re·sound·ing [rɪ'zaundɪŋ] adj success, victory clamoroso

re·source [rɪ'sɔːrs] recurso m; **leave s.o. to his own resources** dejar que alguien se las arregle solo

re·source·ful [rɪ'sɔːrsfəl] adj person lleno de recursos; attitude, approach ingenioso

re·spect [rɪ'spekt] **1** n respeto m; **show respect to** mostrar respeto hacia; **with respect to** con respecto a; **in this / that respect** en cuanto a esto / eso; **in many respects** en muchos aspectos; **pay one's last respects to s.o.** decir el último adiós a alguien **2** v/t respetar

re·spect·a·bil·i·ty [rɪspektə'bɪlətɪ] respetabilidad f

re·spec·ta·ble [rɪ'spektəbl] adj respetable

re·spec·ta·bly [rɪ'spektəblɪ] adv respetablemente

re·spect·ful [rɪ'spektfəl] adj respetuoso

re·spect·ful·ly [rɪ'spektfəlɪ] adv respetuosamente, con respeto

re·spec·tive [rɪ'spektɪv] adj respectivo

re·spec·tive·ly [rɪ'spektɪvlɪ] adv respectivamente

res·pi·ra·tion [respɪ'reɪʃn] respiración f

res·pi·ra·tor [respɪ'reɪtər] MED respirador m

re·spite ['respaɪt] respiro m; **without respite** sin respiro

re·spond [rɪ'spɑːnd] v/i responder

re·sponse [rɪ'spɑːns] respuesta f

re·spon·si·bil·i·ty [rɪspɑːnsɪ'bɪlətɪ] responsabilidad f; **accept responsibility for** aceptar responsabilidad de; **a job with more responsibility** un trabajo con más responsabilidad

re·spon·si·ble [rɪ'spɑːnsəbl] adj responsable (for de); job de responsabilidad

re·spon·sive [rɪ'spɑːnsɪv] adj brakes que responde bien; **a responsive audience** una audiencia que muestra interés

rest¹ [rest] **1** n descanso m; **he needs a rest** necesita descansar; **set s.o.'s mind**

at rest tranquilizar a alguien **2** v/i descansar; **rest on** *of theory, box* apoyarse en; **it all rests with him** todo depende de él **3** v/t *(lean, balance)* apoyar

rest² [rest]: **the rest** el resto

res·tau·rant ['restrɑ:nt] restaurante *m*

'res·tau·rant car vagón *m or* coche *m* restaurante

'rest cure cura *f* de reposo *or* descanso

rest·ful ['restfʊl] *adj* tranquilo, relajante

'rest home residencia *f* de ancianos

rest·less ['restlɪs] *adj* inquieto; **have a restless night** pasar una mala noche

rest·less·ly ['restlɪslɪ] *adv* sin descanso

res·to·ra·tion [restə'reɪʃn] restauración *f*

re·store [rɪ'stɔ:r] v/t *building etc* restaurar; *(bring back)* devolver

re·strain [rɪ'streɪn] v/t contener; **restrain o.s.** contenerse

re·straint [rɪ'streɪnt] *(moderation)* moderación *f*, comedimiento *m*

re·strict [rɪ'strɪkt] v/t restringir, limitar; **I'll restrict myself to ...** me limitaré a ...

re·strict·ed [rɪ'strɪktɪd] *adj view* limitado

re·strict·ed 'ar·e·a MIL zona *f* de acceso restringido

re·stric·tion [rɪ'strɪkʃn] restricción *f*, limitación *f*; **place restrictions upon s.o.** imponer restricciones *or* limitaciones a alguien

'rest room *Am* aseo *m*, servicios *mpl*

re·sult [rɪ'zʌlt] *n* resultado *m*; **as a result of this** como resultado de esto

◆ **result from** v/t resultar de

◆ **result in** v/t tener como resultado

re·sume [rɪ'zju:m] **1** v/t reanudar **2** v/i continuar

ré·sum·é ['rezʊmeɪ] currículum *m* (vitae)

re·sump·tion [rɪ'zʌmpʃn] reanudación *f*

re·sur·face [ri:'sɜ:fɪs] **1** v/t *roads* volver a asfaltar **2** v/i *(reappear)* reaparecer

res·ur·rec·tion [rezə'rekʃn] REL resurrección *f*

re·sus·ci·tate [rɪ'sʌsɪteɪt] v/t resucitar, revivir

re·sus·ci·ta·tion [rɪsʌsɪ'teɪʃn] resucitación *f*

re·tail ['ri:teɪl] **1** *adv*: **sell sth retail** vender algo al por menor **2** v/i: **retail at ...** su precio de venta al público es de ...

re·tail·er ['ri:teɪlər] minorista *m/f*

're·tail out·let punto *m* de venta

're·tail price precio *m* de venta al público

re·tain [rɪ'teɪn] v/t conservar; *heat* retener

re·tain·er [rɪ'teɪnər] FIN anticipo *m*

re·tal·i·ate [rɪ'tælɪeɪt] v/i tomar represalias

re·tal·i·a·tion [rɪtælɪ'eɪʃn] represalias *fpl*; **in retaliation for** como represalia por

re·tard·ed [rɪ'tɑːrdɪd] *adj mentally* retrasado mental

re·think [ri:'θɪŋk] v/t *(pret & pp re·thought)* replantear

re·ti·cence ['retɪsns] reserva *f*

re·ti·cent ['retɪsnt] *adj* reservado

re·tire [rɪ'taɪr] v/i *from work* jubilarse

re·tired [rɪ'taɪrd] *adj* jubilado

re·tire·ment [rɪ'taɪrmənt] jubilación *f*

re'tire·ment age edad *f* de jubilación

re·tir·ing [rɪ'taɪrɪŋ] *adj* retraído, reservado

re·tort [rɪ'tɔ:rt] **1** *n* réplica *f* **2** v/t replicar

re·trace [rɪ'treɪs] v/t: **they retraced their footsteps** volvieron sobre sus pasos

re·tract [rɪ'trækt] v/t *claws* retraer; *undercarriage* replegar; *statement* retirar

re·train [ri:'treɪn] v/i reciclarse

re·treat [rɪ'tri:t] **1** v/i retirarse **2** *n* MIL retirada *f*; *place* retiro *m*

re·trieve [rɪ'tri:v] v/t recuperar

re·triev·er [rɪ'tri:vər] *dog* perro *m* cobrador

ret·ro·ac·tive [retrou'æktɪv] *adj law etc* retroactivo

ret·ro·ac·tive·ly [retrou'æktɪvlɪ] *adv* con retroactividad

ret·ro·grade ['retrəgreɪd] *adj move, decision* retrógrado

ret·ro·spect ['retrəspekt]: **in retrospect** en retrospectiva

ret·ro·spec·tive [retrə'spektɪv] *n* retrospectiva *f*

re·turn [rɪ'tɜ:rn] **1** *n to a place* vuelta *f*, regreso *m*; *(giving back)* devolución *f*; COMPUT retorno *m*; *in tennis* resto *m*; *(profit)* rendimiento *m*; *Br ticket* billete *m or* L.Am. boleto *m* de ida y vuelta; **by return (of post)** a vuelta de correo; **many happy returns (of the day)** feliz cumpleaños; **in return for** a cambio de **2** v/t devolver; *(put back)* volver a colocar **3** v/i *(go back, come back)* volver, regresar; *of good times, doubts etc* volver

re·turn 'flight vuelo *m* de vuelta

re·turn 'jour·ney viaje *m* de vuelta

re·u·ni·fi·ca·tion [ri:ju:nɪfɪ'keɪʃn] reunificación *f*

re·u·nion [ri:'ju:njən] reunión *f*

re·u·nite [ri:ju:'naɪt] v/t reunir

re·us·a·ble [ri:'ju:zəbl] *adj* reutilizable

re·use [ri:'ju:z] v/t reutilizar

rev [rev] *n* revolución *f*; **revs per minute** revoluciones por minuto

◆ **rev up** v/t *(pret & pp revved) engine* revolucionar

re·val·u·a·tion [ri:væljʊ'eɪʃn] revaluación *f*

re·veal [rɪ'vi:l] v/t *(make visible)* revelar;

R

(*make known*) revelar, desvelar

re·veal·ing [rɪˈviːlɪŋ] *adj remark* revelador; *dress* insinuante, atrevido

◆ **rev·el in** [ˈrevl] *v/t* (*pret & pp* **reveled**, *Br* **revelled**) deleitarse con

rev·e·la·tion [revəˈleɪʃn] revelación *f*

re·venge [rɪˈvendʒ] *n* venganza *f*; **take one's revenge** vengarse; **in revenge for** como venganza por

rev·e·nue [ˈrevənuː] *n* ingresos *mpl*

re·ver·be·rate [rɪˈvɜːrbəreɪt] *v/i of sound* reverberar

re·vere [rɪˈvɪr] *v/t* reverenciar

rev·e·rence [ˈrevərəns] reverencia *f*

Rev·e·rend [ˈrevərənd] REL Reverendo *m*

rev·e·rent [ˈrevərənt] *adj* reverente

re·verse [rɪˈvɜːrs] **1** *adj* sequence inverso; **in reverse order** en orden inverso **2** *n* (*back*) dorso *m*; MOT marcha *f* atrás; **the reverse** (*the opposite*) lo contrario **3** *v/t* sequence invertir; **reverse a vehicle** hacer marcha atrás con un vehículo **4** *v/i* MOT hacer marcha atrás

revert [rɪˈvɜːrt] *v/i*: **revert to** volver a

re·view [rɪˈvjuː] **1** *n of book, movie* reseña *f*, crítica *f*; *of troops* revista *f*; *of situation etc* revisión *f* **2** *v/t book, movie* reseñar, hacer una crítica de; *troops* pasar revista a; *situation* revisar; EDU repasar

re·view·er [rɪˈvjuːər] *of book, movie* crítico(-a) *m(f)*

re·vise [rɪˈvaɪz] *v/t opinion, text* revisar

re·vi·sion [rɪˈvɪʒn] *of opinion, text* revisión *f*

re·viv·al [rɪˈvaɪvl] *of custom, old style etc* resurgimiento *m*; *of patient* reanimación *f*

re·vive [rɪˈvaɪv] **1** *v/t custom, old style etc* hacer resurgir; *patient* reanimar **2** *v/i of business, exchange rate etc* reactivarse

re·voke [rɪˈvoʊk] *v/t law* derogar; *license* revocar

re·volt [rɪˈvoʊlt] **1** *n* rebelión *f* **2** *v/i* rebelarse

re·volt·ing [rɪˈvoʊltɪŋ] *adj* (*disgusting*) repugnante

rev·o·lu·tion [revəˈluːʃn] POL revolución *f*; (*turn*) vuelta *f*, revolución *f*

rev·o·lu·tion·ar·y [revəˈluːʃnərɪ] **1** *n* POL revolucionario(-a) *m(f)* **2** *adj* revolucionario

rev·o·lu·tion·ize [revəˈluːʃnaɪz] *v/t* revolucionar

re·volve [rɪˈvɑːlv] *v/i* girar (**around** en torno a)

re·volv·er [rɪˈvɑːlvər] revólver *m*

re·volv·ing 'door [rɪˈvɑːlvɪŋ] puerta *f* giratoria

re·vue [rɪˈvjuː] THEA revista *f*

re·vul·sion [rɪˈvʌlʃn] repugnancia *f*

re·ward [rɪˈwɔːrd] **1** *n* recompensa *f* **2** *v/t financially* recompensar

re·ward·ing [rɪˈwɔːrdɪŋ] *adj experience* gratificante

re·wind [riːˈwaɪnd] *v/t* (*pret & pp* **rewound**) *film, tape* rebobinar

re·write [riːˈraɪt] *v/t* (*pret* **rewrote**, *pp* **rewritten**) reescribir

rhe·to·ric [ˈretərɪk] retórica *f*

rhe·to·ri·cal 'ques·tion [rɪˈtɑːrɪkl] pregunta *f* retórica

rheu·ma·tism [ˈruːmətɪzm] reumatismo *m*

rhi·no·ce·ros [raɪˈnɑːsərəs] rinoceronte *m*

rhu·barb [ˈruːbɑːrb] ruibarbo *m*

rhyme [raɪm] **1** *n* rima *f* **2** *v/i* rimar

rhythm [ˈrɪðm] ritmo *m*

rib [rɪb] ANAT costilla *f*

rib·bon [ˈrɪbən] cinta *f*

rice [raɪs] arroz *m*

rich [rɪtʃ] **1** *adj* (*wealthy*) rico; *food* sabroso; **it's too rich** es muy pesado **2** *n*: **the rich** los ricos

rich·ly [ˈrɪtʃlɪ] *adv*: **be richly deserved** ser muy merecido

rick·et·y [ˈrɪkətɪ] *adj* desvencijado

ric·o·chet [ˈrɪkəʃeɪ] *v/i* rebotar

rid [rɪd]: **get rid of** deshacerse de

rid·dance [ˈrɪdns] F: **good riddance to her!** ¡espero no volver a verla nunca!

rid·den [ˈrɪdn] *pp* → **ride**

rid·dle [ˈrɪdl] **1** *n* acertijo *m* **2** *v/t*: **be riddled with** estar lleno de

ride [raɪd] **1** *n on horse, in vehicle* paseo *m*, vuelta *f*; (*journey*) viaje *m*; **do you want a ride into town?** ¿quieres que te lleve al centro? **2** *v/t* (*pret* **rode**, *pp* **ridden**) *horse* montar a; *bike* montar en **3** *v/i* (*pret* **rode**, *pp* **ridden**) *on horse* montar; **can you ride?** ¿sabes montar?; **those who were riding at the back of the bus** los que iban en la parte de atrás del autobús

rid·er [ˈraɪdər] *on horse* jinete *m*, amazona *f*; *on bicycle* ciclista *m/f*; *on motorbike* motorista *m/f*

ridge [rɪdʒ] *raised strip* borde *m*; *of mountain* cresta *f*; *of roof* caballete *m*

rid·i·cule [ˈrɪdɪkjuːl] **1** *n* burlas *fpl* **2** *v/t* ridiculizar, poner en ridículo

ri·dic·u·lous [rɪˈdɪkjʊləs] *adj* ridículo

ri·dic·u·lous·ly [rɪˈdɪkjʊləslɪ] *adv expensive, difficult* terriblemente; **it's ridiculously easy** es facilísimo

rid·ing [ˈraɪdɪŋ] *on horseback* equitación *f*

ri·fle [ˈraɪfl] *n* rifle *m*

rift [rɪft] *in earth* grieta *f*; *in party etc* escisión *f*

rig [rɪg] **1** *n* (*oil rig*) plataforma *f* petrolífera; (*truck*) camión *m* **2** *v/t* (*pret & pp* **rigged**) *elections* amañar

right [raɪt] **1** *adj* (*correct*) correcto; (*suitable*) adecuado, apropiado; (*not left*) derecho; **it's not right to treat people like that** no está bien tratar así a la gente; **it's the right thing to do** es lo que hay que hacer; **be right** *of answer* estar correcto; *of person* tener razón; *of clock* ir bien; **put things right** arreglar las cosas; **that's right!** ¡eso es!; **that's all right** *doesn't matter* no te preocupes; *when s.o. says thank you* de nada; *is quite good* está bastante bien; **I'm all right** *not hurt* estoy bien; *have got enough* no, gracias; **all right, that's enough!** ¡ahora sí que ya está bien! **2** *adv* (*directly*) justo; (*not left*) a la derecha; **he broke it right off** lo rompió por completo; **right back in 1982** allá en 1982; **right now** ahora mismo **3** *n* civil, *legal etc* derecho *m*; *not left*, POL derecha *f*; **on the right** *also* POL a la derecha; **turn to the right, take a right** gira a la derecha; **be in the right** tener razón; **know right from wrong** distinguir lo que está bien de lo que está mal

right-'an·gle ángulo *m* recto; **at right-angles to** en *or* formando ángulo recto con

right·ful ['raɪtfəl] *adj heir, owner etc* legítimo

'right-hand *adj*: **on the right-hand side** a mano derecha

right-hand 'drive *n* MOT vehículo *m* con el volante a la derecha

right-hand·ed [raɪt'hændɪd] *adj person* diestro

right-hand 'man mano *f* derecha

right of 'way *in traffic* preferencia *f*; *across land* derecho *m* de paso

right 'wing *n* POL la derecha *f*; SP la banda derecha

right-'wing *adj* POL de derechas

right-wing ex'trem·ism POL extremismo *m* de derechas

'right-wing·er POL derechista *m/f*

rig·id ['rɪdʒɪd] *adj* rígido

rig·or ['rɪgər] *of discipline* rigor *m*; **the rigors of the winter** los rigores del invierno

rig·or·ous ['rɪgərəs] *adj* riguroso

rig·or·ous·ly ['rɪgərəslɪ] *adv check, examine* rigurosamente

rig·our *Br* → **rigor**

rile [raɪl] *v/t* F fastidiar, *Span* mosquear F

rim [rɪm] *of wheel* llanta *f*; *of cup* borde *m*;

of eye glasses montura *f*

ring¹ [rɪŋ] *n* (*circle*) círculo *m*; *on finger* anillo *m*; *in boxing* cuadrilátero *m*, ring *m*; *at circus* pista *f*

ring² [rɪŋ] **1** *n of bell* timbrazo; *of voice* tono *m*; **give s.o. a ring** *Br* TELEC dar un telefonazo a alguien **2** *v/t* (*pret* **rang**, *pp* **rung**) *bell* hacer sonar **3** *v/i* (*pret* **rang**, *pp* **rung**) *of bell* sonar; **please ring for attention** toque el timbre para que lo atiendan

'ring-lead·er cabecilla *m/f*

'ring-pull anilla *f*

rink [rɪŋk] pista *f* de patinaje

rinse [rɪns] **1** *n for hair color* reflejo *m* **2** *v/t* aclarar

ri·ot ['raɪət] **1** *n* disturbio *m* **2** *v/i* causar disturbios

ri·ot·er ['raɪətər] alborotador(a) *m(f)*

'riot police policía *f* antidisturbios

rip [rɪp] **1** *n in cloth etc* rasgadura *f* **2** *v/t* (*pret & pp* **ripped**) *cloth etc* rasgar; **rip sth open** romper algo rasgándolo

◆ **rip off** *v/t* F *customers* robar F, clavar F; (*cheat*) timar

◆ **rip up** *v/t letter, sheet* hacer pedazos

ripe [raɪp] *adj fruit* maduro

rip·en ['raɪpn] *v/i of fruit* madurar

ripe·ness ['raɪpnəs] *of fruit* madurez *f*

'rip-off *n* F robo *m* F

rip·ple ['rɪpl] *on water* onda *f*

rise [raɪz] **1** *v/i* (*pret* **rose**, *pp* **risen**) *from chair etc* levantarse; *of sun* salir; *of rocket* ascender, subir; *of price, temperature, water* subir **2** *n in price, temperature* subida *f*, aumento *m*; *in water level* subida *f*; *in salary* aumento *m*; **give rise to** dar pie a

ris·en ['rɪzn] *pp* → **rise**

ris·er ['raɪzər]: **be an early riser** ser un madrugador; **be a late riser** levantarse tarde

risk [rɪsk] **1** *n* riesgo *m*, peligro *m*; **take a risk** arriesgarse **2** *v/t* arriesgar; **let's risk it** arriesguémonos

risk·y ['rɪskɪ] *adj* arriesgado

ris·qué [rɪ'skeɪ] *adj* subido de tono

rit·u·al ['rɪtʊəl] **1** *n* ritual *m* **2** *adj* ritual

ri·val ['raɪvl] **1** *n* rival *m/f* **2** *v/t* rivalizar con; **I can't rival that** no puedo rivalizar con eso

ri·val·ry ['raɪvlrɪ] rivalidad *f*

riv·er ['rɪvər] río *m*

'riv·er·bank ribera *f*

'riv·er·bed lecho *m*

Riv·er 'Plate *n*: **the River Plate** el Río de la Plata

'riv·er·side **1** *adj* a la orilla del río **2** *n* ribera *f*, orilla *f* del río

riv·et ['rɪvɪt] **1** n remache m **2** v/t remachar; **rivet sth to sth** unir algo a algo con remaches

riv·et·ing ['rɪvɪtɪŋ] adj fascinante

road [roʊd] in country carretera f; in city calle f; **it's just down the road** está muy cerca

'road·block control m de carretera

'road hog conductor(a) temerario(-a)

'road-hold·ing of vehicle adherencia f, agarre m

'road map mapa m de carreteras

road 'safe·ty seguridad f vial

'road·side: at the roadside al borde de la carretera

'road-sign señal f de tráfico

'road·way calzada f

'road·wor·thy adj en condiciones de circular

roam [roʊm] v/i vagar

roar [rɔːr] **1** n of traffic, engine estruendo m; of lion rugido m; of person grito m, bramido m **2** v/i of engine, lion rugir; of person gritar, bramar; **roar with laughter** reírse a carcajadas

roast [roʊst] **1** n of beef etc asado m **2** v/t asar **3** v/i of food asarse; **we're roasting** nos estamos asando

roast 'beef rosbif m

'roast·ing tin [roʊstɪŋ] fuente f para asar

roast 'pork cerdo m asado

rob [rɑːb] v/t (pret & pp **robbed**) person robar a; bank atracar, robar; **I've been robbed** me han robado

rob·ber ['rɑːbər] atracador(a) m(f)

rob·ber·y ['rɑːbərɪ] atraco m, robo m

robe [roʊb] of judge toga f; of priest sotana f; (bathrobe) bata f

rob·in ['rɑːbɪn] petirrojo m

ro·bot ['roʊbɑːt] robot m

ro·bust [roʊ'bʌst] adj person, structure robusto; material resistente; **be in robust health** tener una salud de hierro

rock [rɑːk] **1** n roca f; MUS rock m; **on the rocks** of drink con hielo; **their marriage is on the rocks** su matrimonio está en crisis **2** v/t baby acunar; cradle mecer; (surprise) sorprender, impactar **3** v/i on chair mecerse; of boat balancearse

'rock band grupo m de rock

rock 'bot·tom: reach rock bottom tocar fondo

'rock-bot·tom adj prices mínimo

'rock climb·er escalador(a) m(f)

'rock climb·ing escalada f (en roca)

rock·et ['rɑːkɪt] **1** n cohete m **2** v/i of prices etc dispararse

'rock·ing chair ['rɑːkɪŋ] mecedora f

'rock·ing horse caballito m de juguete

rock 'n roll [rɑːkn'roʊl] rock and roll m

'rock star estrella f del rock

rock·y ['rɑːkɪ] adj beach, path pedregoso

rod [rɑːd] vara f; for fishing caña f

rode [roʊd] pret → **ride**

ro·dent ['roʊdnt] roedor m

rogue [roʊg] granuja m/f, bribón(-ona) m(f)

role [roʊl] papel m

'role mod·el ejemplo m

roll [roʊl] **1** n (bread roll) panecillo m; of film rollo m; of thunder retumbo m; (list, register) lista f **2** v/i of ball etc rodar; of boat balancearse **3** v/t: **roll sth into a ball** hacer una bola con algo; **roll sth along the ground** hacer rodar algo por el suelo

◆ **roll over 1** v/i darse la vuelta **2** v/t person, object dar la vuelta a; (renew) renovar; (extend) refinanciar

◆ **roll up 1** v/t sleeves remangar **2** v/i F (arrive) llegar

'roll-call lista f

roll·er ['roʊlər] for hair rulo m

'roll·er blade® n patín m en línea

'roll·er blind persiana f

'roll·er coast·er ['roʊlərkoʊstər] montaña f rusa

'roll·er skate n patín m (de ruedas)

'roll·ing pin ['roʊlɪŋ] rodillo m de cocina

ROM [rɑːm] COMPUT abbr (= **read only memory**) ROM f (= memoria f de sólo lectura)

Ro·man ['roʊmən] **1** adj romano **2** n romano(-a) m(f)

Ro·man 'Cath·o·lic 1 n REL católico(-a) m(f) romano(-a) **2** adj católico romano

ro·mance [roʊ'mæns] (affair) aventura f (amorosa); novel novela f rosa; movie película f romántica

ro·man·tic [roʊ'mæntɪk] adj romántico

ro·man·ti·cal·ly [roʊ'mæntɪklɪ] adv: **be romantically involved with s.o.** tener un romance con alguien

roof [ruːf] techo m, tejado m; **have a roof over one's head** tener un techo donde dormir

'roof-rack MOT baca f

rook·ie ['rʊkɪ] F novato(-a) m(f)

room [ruːm] habitación f; (space) espacio m, sitio m; **there's no room for ...** no hay sitio para ..., no cabe ...

'room clerk recepcionista m/f

'room·mate sharing room compañero(-a) m(f) de habitación; sharing apartment compañero(-a) m(f) de apartamento

'room ser·vice servicio m de habitaciones

room 'tem·per·a·ture temperatura f ambiente

room·y ['ruːmɪ] adj house, car etc espacioso; *clothes* holgado

root [ruːt] *n* raíz *f*; **roots** *of person* raíces *fpl*

◆ **root for** *v/t* F apoyar

◆ **root out** *v/t (get rid of)* cortar de raíz; *(find)* encontrar

rope [roup] *n* cuerda *f*; *thick* soga *f*; **show s.o. the ropes** F poner a alguien al tanto

◆ **rope off** *v/t* acordonar

ro·sa·ry ['rouzəri] REL rosario *m*

rose¹ [rouz] BOT rosa *f*

rose² [rouz] *pret* → **rise**

rose·ma·ry ['rouzmeri] romero *m*

ros·trum ['rɑːstrəm] estrado *m*

ros·y ['rouzi] *adj cheeks* sonrosado; *future* de color de rosa

rot [rɑːt] **1** *n in wood* putrefacción *f* **2** *v/i (pret & pp* **rotted)** *of food, wood* pudrirse; *of teeth* cariarse

ro·ta ['routə] turnos *mpl*; *actual document* calendario *m* con los turnos

ro·tate [rou'teit] **1** *v/i of blades, earth* girar **2** *v/t* hacer girar; *crops* rotar

ro·ta·tion [rou'teiʃn] *around the sun etc* rotación *f*; **do sth in rotation** hacer algo por turnos rotatorios

rot·ten ['rɑːtn] *adj food, wood etc* podrido; *weather, luck* horrible; **that was a rotten trick** ¡qué mala idea!

rough [rʌf] **1** *adj surface, ground* accidentado; *hands, skin* áspero; *voice* ronco; *(violent)* bruto; *crossing* movido; *seas* bravo; *(approximate)* aproximado; **rough draft** borrador *m* **2** *adv*: **sleep rough** dormir a la intemperie **3** *n in golf* rough *m* **4** *v/t*: **rough it** apañárselas

◆ **rough up** *v/t* F dar una paliza a

rough·age ['rʌfidʒ] *in food* fibra *f*

rough·ly ['rʌfli] *adv (approximately)* aproximadamente; *(harshly)* brutalmente; **roughly speaking** aproximadamente

rou·lette [ruː'let] ruleta *f*

round [raund] **1** *adj* redondo; **in round figures** en números redondos **2** *n of mailman, doctor, drinks, competition* ronda *f*; *of toast* rebanada *f*; *in boxing match* round *m*, asalto *m* **3** *v/t corner* doblar **4** *adv, prep* → **around**

◆ **round off** *v/t edges* redondear; *meeting, night out* concluir

◆ **round up** *v/t figure* redondear (hacia la cifra más alta); *suspects, criminals* detener

round·a·bout ['raundəbaut] **1** *adj route, way of saying sth* indirecto **2** *n* Br *on road* rotonda *f*, Span glorieta *f*

'round-the-world *adj* alrededor del mundo

round 'trip viaje *m* de ida y vuelta

round trip 'tick·et billete *m* or *L.Am.* boleto *m* de ida y vuelta

'round-up *of cattle* rodeo *m*; *of suspects, criminals* redada *f*; *of news* resumen *m*

rouse [rauz] *v/t from sleep* despertar; *interest, emotions* excitar, provocar

rous·ing ['rauziŋ] *adj speech, finale* emocionante

route [ruːt] *n* ruta *f*, recorrido *m*

rou·tine [ruː'tiːn] **1** *adj* habitual **2** *n* rutina *f*; **as a matter of routine** como rutina

row¹ [rou] *n (line)* hilera *f*; **5 days in a row** 5 días seguidos

row² [rou] **1** *v/t boat* llevar remando **2** *v/i* remar

row³ [rau] *n (quarrel)* pelea *f*, discusión *f*; *(noise)* alboroto *m*

'row·boat ['roubout] bote *m* de remos

row·dy ['raudi] *adj* alborotador, Span follonero

roy·al ['rɔiəl] *adj* real

roy·al·ty ['rɔiəlti] *royal persons* realeza *f*; *on book, recording* derechos *mpl* de autor

rub [rʌb] *v/t (pret & pp* **rubbed)** frotar

◆ **rub down** *v/t to clean* lijar

◆ **rub in** *v/t cream, ointment* extender, frotar; **don't rub it in!** *fig* ¡no me lo restriegues por las narices!

◆ **rub off** **1** *v/t dirt* limpiar frotando; *paint etc* borrar **2** *v/i*: **it rubs off on you** se te contagia

rub·ber ['rʌbər] **1** *n material* goma *f*, caucho *m*; P *(condom)* goma *f* P **2** *adj* de goma *or* caucho

rub·ber 'band goma *f* elástica

rub·ber 'gloves *npl* guantes *mpl* de goma

rub·bish ['rʌbiʃ] *n* basura *f*; *poor quality* basura *f*, porquería *f*; *(nonsense)* tonterías *fpl*; **this radio is rubbish** esta radio es una basura *or* porquería; **don't talk rubbish!** ¡no digas tonterías!

rub·ble ['rʌbl] escombros *mpl*

ru·by ['ruːbi] *jewel* rubí *m*

ruck·sack ['rʌksæk] mochila *f*

rud·der ['rʌdər] timón *m*

rud·dy ['rʌdi] *adj complexion* rubicundo

rude [ruːd] *adj person, behavior* maleducado, grosero; *language* grosero; **it is rude to …** es de mala educación …; **I didn't mean to be rude** no pretendía faltar al respeto

rude·ly ['ruːdli] *adv (impolitely)* groseramente

rude·ness ['ruːdnis] mala *f* educación, grosería *f*

ru·di·men·ta·ry [ruːdi'mentəri] *adj* rudimentario

R

ru·di·ments ['ru:dɪmənts] *npl* rudimentos *mpl*

rue·ful ['ru:fəl] *adj* arrepentido, compungido

rue·ful·ly ['ru:fəlɪ] *adv* con arrepentimiento

ruf·fi·an ['rʌfɪən] rufián *m*

ruf·fle ['rʌfl] **1** *n on dress* volante *m* **2** *v/t hair* despeinar; *clothes* arrugar; *person* alterar, enfadar; **get ruffled** alterarse

rug [rʌg] alfombra *f*; (*blanket*) manta *f* (de viaje)

rug·by ['rʌgbɪ] rugby *m*

'rug·by match partido *m* de rugby

'rug·by play·er jugador(a) *m(f)* de rugby

rug·ged ['rʌgɪd] *adj scenery, cliffs* escabroso, accidentado; *face* de rasgos duros; *resistance* decidido

ru·in ['ru:ɪn] **1** *n* ruina *f*; **ruins** ruinas *fpl*; **in ruins** *city, building* en ruinas; *of plans, marriage* arruinado **2** *v/t* arruinar; **be ruined** *financially* estar arruinado *or* en la ruina

rule [ru:l] **1** *n of club, game* regla *f*, norma *f*; *of monarch* reinado *m*; *for measuring* regla *f*; **as a rule** por regla general **2** *v/t country* gobernar; **the judge ruled that ...** el juez dictaminó que ... **3** *v/i of monarch* reinar

♦ **rule out** *v/t* descartar

rul·er ['ru:lər] *for measuring* regla *f*; *of state* gobernante *m/f*

rul·ing ['ru:lɪŋ] **1** *n* fallo *m*, decisión *f* **2** *adj party* gobernante, en el poder

rum [rʌm] *n drink* ron *m*

rum·ble ['rʌmbl] *v/i of stomach* gruñir; *of train in tunnel* retumbar

♦ **rum·mage around** ['rʌmɪdʒ] *v/i* buscar revolviendo

'rum·mage sale rastrillo *m* benéfico

ru·mor ['ru:mər] **1** *n* rumor *m* **2** *v/t*: **it is rumored that ...** se rumorea que ...

rump [rʌmp] *of animal* cuartos *mpl* traseros

rum·ple ['rʌmpl] *v/t clothes, paper* arrugar

rump·'steak filete *m* de lomo

run [rʌn] **1** *n on foot* carrera *f*; *in car* viaje *m*; *in tights* carrera *f*; THEA: *of play* temporada *f*; **it has had a three year run** *of play* lleva tres años en cartel; **go for a run** ir a correr; **go for a run in the car** ir a dar una vuelta en el coche; **make a run for it** salir corriendo; **a criminal on the run** un criminal fugado; **in the short / long run** a corto / largo plazo; **a run on the dollar** un movimiento especulativo contra el dólar **2** *v/i* (*pret* **ran**, *pp* **run**) *of person, animal* correr; *of river* correr, discurrir; *of paint, make-up* correrse; *of play* estar

en cartel; *of engine, machine, software* funcionar; *in election* presentarse; **run for President** presentarse a las elecciones presidenciales; **the trains run every ten minutes** pasan trenes cada diez minutos; **it doesn't run on Saturdays** *of bus, train* no funciona los sábados; **don't leave the tap running** no dejes el grifo abierto; **his nose is running** le moquea la nariz; **her eyes are running** le lloran los ojos **3** *v/t* (*pret* **ran**, *pp* **run**) *race* correr; *business, hotel, project etc* dirigir; *software etc* (*start*) ejecutar; *car* tener; (*use*) usar; **can I run you to the station?** ¿te puedo llevar hasta la estación?; **he ran his eye down the page** echó una ojeada a la página

♦ **run across** *v/t* (*meet*) encontrarse con; (*find*) encontrar

♦ **run away** *v/i* salir corriendo, huir; *from home* escaparse

♦ **run down 1** *v/t* (*knock down*) atropellar; (*criticize*) criticar; *stocks* reducir **2** *v/i of battery* agotarse

♦ **run into** *v/t* (*meet*) encontrarse con; *difficulties* tropezar con

♦ **run off 1** *v/i* salir corriendo **2** *v/t* (*print off*) tirar

♦ **run out** *v/i of contract* vencer; *of supplies* agotarse; **time has run out** se ha acabado el tiempo

♦ **run out of** *v/t time, supplies* quedarse sin; **I ran out of gas** me quedé sin gasolina; **I'm running out of patience** se me está acabando la paciencia

♦ **run over 1** *v/t* (*knock down*) atropellar; **can we run over the details again?** ¿podríamos repasar los detalles otra vez? **2** *v/i of water etc* desbordarse

♦ **run through** *v/t* (*rehearse, go over*) repasar

♦ **run up** *v/t debts, large bill* acumular; *clothes* coser

run·a·way ['rʌnəweɪ] *n* persona que se ha fugado de casa

run·'down *adj person* débil, apagado; *part of town, building* ruinoso

rung[1] [rʌŋ] *of ladder* peldaño *m*

rung[2] [rʌŋ] *pp* → **ring**[2]

run·ner ['rʌnər] *athlete* corredor(a) *m(f)*

run·ner 'beans *npl* judías *fpl* verdes, *L.Am.* porotos *mpl* verdes, *Mex* ejotes *mpl*

run·ner-'up subcampeón(-ona) *m(f)*

run·ning ['rʌnɪŋ] **1** *n* SP el correr; (*jogging*) footing *m*; *of business* gestión *f* **2** *adj*: **for two days running** durante dos días seguidos

run·ning 'wa·ter agua *f* corriente

run·ny ['rʌnɪ] adj mixture fluido, líquido; nose que moquea

'run-up SP carrerilla f; in the run-up to en el periodo previo a

'run·way SP pista f de aterrizaje / despegue

rup·ture ['rʌptʃər] 1 n ruptura f 2 v/i of pipe etc romperse

ru·ral ['rʊrəl] adj rural

ruse [ruːz] artimaña f

rush [rʌʃ] 1 n prisa f; do sth in a rush hacer algo con prisas; be in a rush tener prisa; what's the big rush? ¿qué prisa tenemos? 2 v/t person meter prisa a; meal comer a toda prisa; rush s.o. to hospital llevar a alguien al hospital a toda prisa 3 v/i darse prisa

'rush hour hora f punta

Rus·sia ['rʌʃə] Rusia

Rus·sian ['rʌʃən] 1 adj ruso 2 n ruso(-a) m(f); language ruso m

rust [rʌst] 1 n óxido m 2 v/i oxidarse

rus·tle ['rʌsl] 1 n of silk, leaves susurro m 2 v/i of silk, leaves susurrar

'rust-proof adj inoxidable

rust re·mov·er ['rʌstrɪmuːvər] desoxidante m

rust·y ['rʌstɪ] adj oxidado; my French is pretty rusty tengo el francés muy abandonado; I'm a little rusty estoy un poco falto de forma

rut [rʌt] in road rodada f; be in a rut fig estar estancado

ruth·less ['ruːθlɪs] adj implacable, despiadado

ruth·less·ly ['ruːθlɪslɪ] adv sin compasión, despiadadamente

ruth·less·ness ['ruːθlɪsnɪs] falta f de compasión

rye [raɪ] centeno m

'rye bread pan m de centeno

S

sab·bat·i·cal [sə'bætɪkl] n year año m sabático; a 6 month sabbatical 6 meses de excedencia

sab·o·tage ['sæbətɑːʒ] 1 n sabotaje m 2 v/t sabotear

sab·o·teur [sæbə'tɜːr] saboteador(a) m(f)

sac·cha·rin ['sækərɪn] n sacarina f

sa·chet ['sæʃeɪ] of shampoo, cream etc sobrecito m

sack [sæk] 1 n bag saco m; for groceries bolsa f; he got the sack F lo echaron 2 v/t F echar

sa·cred ['seɪkrɪd] adj sagrado

sac·ri·fice ['sækrɪfaɪs] 1 n sacrificio m; make sacrifices fig hacer sacrificios 2 v/t sacrificar

sac·ri·lege ['sækrɪlɪdʒ] sacrilegio m

sad [sæd] adj person, face, song triste; state of affairs lamentable, desgraciado

sad·dle ['sædl] 1 n silla f de montar 2 v/t horse ensillar; saddle s.o. with sth fig endilgar algo a alguien

sa·dism ['seɪdɪzm] sadismo m

sa·dist ['seɪdɪst] sádico(-a) m(f)

sa·dis·tic [sə'dɪstɪk] adj sádico

sad·ly ['sædlɪ] adv look, say etc con tristeza; (regrettably) lamentablemente

sad·ness ['sædnɪs] tristeza f

safe [seɪf] 1 adj seguro; driver prudente; (not in danger) a salvo; is it safe to walk here? ¿se puede andar por aquí sin peligro? 2 n caja f fuerte

'safe·guard 1 n garantía f; as a safeguard against como garantía contra 2 v/t salvaguardar

safe·ly ['seɪflɪ] adv arrive sin percances; (successfully) sin problemas; drive prudentemente; assume con certeza

'safe keep·ing: give sth to s.o. for safe keeping dar algo a alguien para que lo custodie

safe·ty ['seɪftɪ] seguridad f

'safety belt cinturón m de seguridad

'safe·ty-con·scious adj: be safety-conscious tener en cuenta la seguridad

safe·ty 'first prevención f de accidentes

'safe·ty pin imperdible m

sag [sæg] 1 n in ceiling etc combadura f 2 v/i (pret & pp sagged) of ceiling combarse; of rope destensarse; of tempo disminuir

sa·ga ['sɑːgə] saga f

sage [seɪdʒ] n herb salvia f

Sa·git·tar·i·us [sædʒɪ'terɪəs] ASTR Sagitario m/f inv

said [sed] pret & pp → say

sail [seɪl] 1 n of boat vela f; trip viaje m (en

barco); **go for a sail** salir a navegar **2** *v/t yacht* manejar **3** *v/i* navegar; (*depart*) zarpar, hacerse a la mar

'**sail·board 1** *n* tabla *f* de windsurf **2** *v/i* hacer windsurf

'**sail·board·ing** windsurf *m*

'**sail·boat** barco *m* de vela, velero *m*

'**sail·ing** [seɪl] SP vela *f*

'**sail·ing ship** barco *m* de vela, velero *m*

'**sail·or** ['seɪlər] *in the navy* marino *m/f*; *in the merchant navy*, SP marinero(-a) *m(f)*; *I'm a good/bad sailor* no me mareo / me mareo con facilidad

saint [seɪnt] santo *m*

sake [seɪk]: *for my sake* por mí; *for the sake of peace* por la paz

sal·ad ['sæləd] ensalada *f*

sal·ad 'dress·ing aliño *m* or aderezo *m* para ensalada

sal·a·ry ['sælərɪ] sueldo *m*, salario *f*

'**sal·a·ry scale** escala *f* salarial

sale [seɪl] venta *f*; *reduced prices* rebajas *fpl*; *for sale sign* se vende; *is this for sale?* ¿está a la venta?; *be on sale* estar a la venta; *at reduced prices* estar de rebajas

sales [seɪlz] *npl department* ventas *fpl*

'**sales clerk** *in store* vendedor(a) *m(f)*, dependiente(-a) *m(f)*

'**sales fig·ures** *npl* cifras *fpl* de ventas

'**sales·man** vendedor *m*

'**sales 'man·ag·er** jefe(-a) *m(f)* de ventas

'**sales meet·ing** reunión *f* del departamento de ventas

'**sales·wo·man** vendedora *f*

sa·li·ent ['seɪlɪənt] *adj* sobresaliente, destacado

sa·li·va [sə'laɪvə] saliva *f*

sal·mon ['sæmən] (*pl salmon*) salmón *m*

sa·loon [sə'luːn] MOT turismo *m*; (*bar*) bar *m*

salt [sɒːlt] **1** *n* sal *f* **2** *v/t food* salar

'**salt·cel·lar** salero *m*

salt 'wa·ter agua *f* salada

'**salt-wa·ter fish** pez *m* de agua salada

salt·y ['sɒːltɪ] *adj* salado

sal·u·tar·y ['sæljʊtərɪ] *adj experience* beneficioso

sa·lute [sə'luːt] **1** *n* MIL saludo; *take the salute* presidir un desfile **2** *v/t* saludar; *fig (hail)* saludar **3** *v/i* MIL saludar

Sal·va·dor(e)·an [sælvə'dɔːrən] **1** *adj* salvadoreño **2** *n* salvadoreño(-a) *m(f)*

sal·vage ['sælvɪdʒ] *v/t from wreck* rescatar

sal·va·tion [sæl'veɪʃn] *also fig* salvación *f*

Sal·va·tion 'Ar·my Ejército *m* de Salvación

same [seɪm] **1** *adj* mismo **2** *pron: the same* lo mismo; *Happy New Year - the same to you* Feliz Año Nuevo - igualmente; *he's not the same any more* ya no es el mismo; *life isn't the same without you* la vida es distinta sin ti; *all the same* (*even so*) aun así; *men are all the same* todos los hombres son iguales; *it's all the same to me* me da lo mismo, me da igual **3** *adv*: *the same* igual

sam·ple ['sæmpl] *n* muestra *f*

sanc·ti·mo·ni·ous [sæŋktɪ'məʊnɪəs] *adj* mojigato

sanc·tion ['sæŋkʃn] **1** *n* (*approval*) consentimiento *m*, aprobación *f*; (*penalty*) sanción *f* **2** *v/t* (*approve*) sancionar

sanc·ti·ty ['sæŋktətɪ] carácter *m* sagrado

sanc·tu·a·ry ['sæŋktʃʊerɪ] santuario *m*

sand [sænd] **1** *n* arena *f* **2** *v/t with sandpaper* lijar

san·dal ['sændl] sandalia *f*

'**sand·bag** saco *m* de arena

'**sand·blast** *v/t* arenar

'**sand dune** duna *f*

sand·er ['sændər] *tool* lijadora *f*

'**sand·pa·per 1** *n* lija *f* **2** *v/t* lijar

'**sand·stone** arenisca *f*

'**sand·wich** ['sænwɪtʃ] **1** *n* Span bocadillo *m*, *L.Am.* sandwich *m* **2** *v/t*: *be sandwiched between two ...* estar encajonado entre dos ...

sand·y ['sændɪ] *adj soil* arenoso; *feet, towel etc* lleno de arena; *hair* rubio oscuro; *sandy beach* playa *f* de arena

sane [seɪn] *adj* cuerdo

sang [sæŋ] *pret* → **sing**

san·i·tar·i·um [sænɪ'terɪəm] sanatorio *m*

san·i·tar·y ['sænɪterɪ] *adj conditions* salubre, higiénico; *sanitary installations* instalaciones *fpl* sanitarias

'**san·i·tar·y nap·kin** compresa *f*

san·i·ta·tion [sænɪ'teɪʃn] (*sanitary installations*) instalaciones *fpl* sanitarias; (*removal of waste*) saneamiento *f*

san·i·ta·tion de·part·ment servicio *m* de limpieza

san·i·ty ['sænətɪ] razón *f*, juicio *m*

sank [sæŋk] *pret* → **sink**

San·ta Claus ['sæntəklɔːz] Papá Noel *m*, Santa Claus *m*

sap [sæp] **1** *n in tree* savia *f* **2** *v/t* (*pret & pp sapped*) *s.o.'s energy* consumir

sap·phire ['sæfaɪr] *n jewel* zafiro *m*

sar·casm [sɑː'kæzm] sarcasmo *m*

sar·cas·tic [sɑː'kæstɪk] *adj* sarcástico

sar·cas·ti·cal·ly [sɑː'kæstɪklɪ] *adv* sarcásticamente

sar·dine [sɑː'diːn] sardina *f*

sar·don·ic [sɑː'dɒnɪk] *adj* sardónico

sar·don·i·cal·ly [sɑː'dɒnɪklɪ] *adv* sardónicamente

sash [sæʃ] *on dress* faja *f; on uniform* fajín *m*

sat [sæt] *pret & pp* → **sit**

Sa·tan ['seɪtn] Satán, Satanás

satch·el ['sætʃl] *for schoolchild* cartera *f*

sat·el·lite ['sætəlaɪt] satélite *m*

'sat·el·lite dish antena *f* parabólica

sat·el·lite T·V televisión *f* por satélite

sat·in ['sætɪn] **1** *adj* satinado **2** *n* satín *m*

sat·ire ['sætaɪr] sátira *f*

sa·tir·i·cal [sə'tɪrɪkl] *adj* satírico

sat·i·rist ['sætərɪst] escritor(a) *m(f)* de sátiras

sat·i·rize ['sætəraɪz] *v/t* satirizar

sat·is·fac·tion [sætɪs'fækʃn] satisfacción *f; I get satisfaction out of my job* mi trabajo me produce satisfacción; *is that to your satisfaction madam?* *fml* ¿está al gusto de la señora?

sat·is·fac·to·ry [sætɪs'fæktərɪ] *adj* satisfactorio; (*just good enough*) suficiente

sat·is·fy ['sætɪsfaɪ] *v/t* (*pret & pp* **satisfied**) satisfacer; *conditions* cumplir; *I am satisfied* (*had enough to eat*) estoy lleno; *I am satisfied that …* (*convinced*) estoy convencido or satisfecho de que …; *I hope you're satisfied!* ¡estarás contento!

Sat·ur·day ['sætərdeɪ] sábado *m*

sauce [sɔːs] salsa *f*

'sauce·pan cacerola *f*

sau·cer ['sɔːsər] plato *m* (*de taza*)

sauc·y ['sɔːsɪ] *adj person, dress* descarado

Sa·u·di A·ra·bi·a [saʊdɪə'reɪbɪə] Arabia Saudí *or* Saudita

Sa·u·di A·ra·bi·an [saʊdɪə'reɪbɪən] **1** *adj* saudita, saudí **2** *n* saudita *m/f*, saudí *m/f*

sau·na ['sɔːnə] sauna *f*

saun·ter ['sɔːntər] *v/i* andar sin prisas

saus·age ['sɔɪsɪdʒ] salchicha *f*

sav·age ['sævɪdʒ] **1** *adj animal, attack* salvaje; *criticism* feroz **2** *n* salvaje *m/f*

sav·age·ry ['sævɪdʒrɪ] crueldad *f*

save [seɪv] **1** *v/t* (*rescue*) rescatar, salvar; *money, time, effort* ahorrar; (*collect*) guardar; COMPUT guardar; *goal* parar; REL salvar **2** *v/i* (*put money aside*) ahorrar; SP hacer una parada **3** *n* SP parada *f*

♦ **save up for** *v/t* ahorrar para

sav·er ['seɪvər] *person* ahorrador(a) *m(f)*

sav·ing ['seɪvɪŋ] *amount saved, activity* ahorro *m*

sav·ings ['seɪvɪŋz] *npl* ahorros *mpl*

'sav·ings ac·count cuenta *f* de ahorros

sav·ings and 'loan caja *f* de ahorros

'sav·ings bank caja *f* de ahorros

sa·vior, *Br* **sa·viour** ['seɪvjər] REL salva-

dor *m*

sa·vor ['seɪvər] *v/t* saborear

sa·vor·y ['seɪvərɪ] *adj not sweet* salado

sa·vour *etc Br* → **savor** *etc*

saw[1] [sɔː] **1** *n tool* serrucho *m*, sierra *f* **2** *v/t* aserrar

saw[2] [sɔː] *pret* → **see**

♦ **saw off** *v/t* cortar (con un serrucho)

'saw·dust serrín *m*, aserrín *m*

sax·o·phone ['sæksəfoʊn] saxofón *m*

say [seɪ] **1** *v/t* (*pret & pp* **said**) decir; *poem* recitar; *that is to say* es decir; *what do you say to that?* ¿qué opinas de eso?; *what does the note say?* ¿qué dice la nota?, ¿qué pone en la nota? **2** *n: have one's say* expresar una opinión

say·ing ['seɪɪŋ] dicho *m*

scab [skæb] *on skin* costra *f*

scaf·fold·ing ['skæfəldɪŋ] *on building* andamiaje *m*

scald [skɔːld] *v/t* escaldar

scale[1] [skeɪl] *on fish, reptile* escama *f*

scale[2] [skeɪl] **1** *n* (*size*) escala *f*, tamaño *m*; *on thermometer, map,* MUS escala *f*; *on a larger scale* a gran escala; *on a smaller scale* a pequeña escala **2** *v/t cliffs etc* escalar

♦ **scale down** *v/t* disminuir, reducir

scale 'draw·ing dibujo *m* a escala

scales [skeɪlz] *npl for weighing* báscula *f*, peso *m*

scal·lop ['skæləp] *n shellfish* vieira *f*

scalp [skælp] *n* cuero *m* cabelludo

scal·pel ['skælpl] bisturí *m*

scam [skæm] F chanchullo *m* F

scam·pi ['skæmpɪ] gambas *fpl* rebozadas

scan [skæn] **1** *v/t* (*pret & pp* **scanned**) *horizon* otear; *page* ojear; COMPUT escanear **2** *n of brain* escáner *m; of fetus* ecografía *f*

♦ **scan in** *v/t* COMPUT escanear

scan·dal ['skændl] escándalo *m*

scan·dal·ize ['skændəlaɪz] *v/t* escandalizar

scan·dal·ous ['skændələs] *adj affair, prices* escandaloso

Scan·di·na·vi·a [skændɪ'neɪvɪə] Escandinavia

scan·ner ['skænər] MED, COMPUT escáner *m; for foetus* ecógrafo *m*

scant [skænt] *adj* escaso

scant·i·ly ['skæntɪlɪ] *adv: be scantily clad* andar ligero de ropa

scant·y ['skæntɪ] *adj skirt* cortísimo; *bikini* mínimo

scape·goat ['skeɪpgoʊt] cabeza *f* de turco, chivo *m* expiatorio

scar [skɑːr] **1** *n* cicatriz *f* **2** *v/t* (*pret & pp*

S

scarred) cicatrizar

scarce [skers] *adj in short supply* escaso; **make o.s. scarce** desaparecer

scarce·ly ['skersli] *adv*: **he had scarcely said it when ...** apenas lo había dicho cuando ...; **there was scarcely anything left** no quedaba casi nada; **I scarcely know her** apenas la conozco

scar·ci·ty ['skersiti] escasez *f*

scare [sker] **1** *v/t* asustar, atemorizar; **be scared of** tener miedo de **2** *n (panic, alarm)* miedo *m*, temor *m*; **give s.o. a scare** dar a alguien un susto

◆ **scare away** *v/t* ahuyentar

'scare·crow espantapájaros *m inv*

scare·mon·ger ['skermʌŋgər] alarmista *m/f*

scarf [skɑːrf] *around neck, over head* pañuelo *m*; *woollen* bufanda *f*

scar·let ['skɑːrlət] *adj* escarlata

scar·let 'fe·ver escarlatina *f*

scar·y ['skeri] *adj sight* espeluznante; **scary music** música de miedo

scath·ing ['skeiðiŋ] *adj* feroz

scat·ter ['skætər] **1** *v/t leaflets* esparcir; *seeds* diseminar; **be scattered all over the room** estar esparcido por toda la habitación **2** *v/i of people* dispersarse

scat·ter·brained ['skætərbreind] *adj* despistado

scat·tered ['skætərd] *adj showers, family, villages* disperso

scav·enge ['skævindʒ] *v/i* rebuscar; **scavenge for sth** rebuscar en busca de algo

scav·en·ger ['skævindʒər] *animal, bird* carroñero *m*; *(person)* persona que busca comida entre la basura

sce·na·ri·o [si'nɑːriou] *n* situación *f*

scene [siːn] escena *f*; *of accident, crime etc* lugar *m*; *(argument)* escena *f*, número *m*; **make a scene** hacer una escena, montar un número; **scenes** THEA decorados *mpl*; **jazz / rock scene** mundo del jazz / rock; **behind the scenes** entre bastidores

sce·ne·ry ['siːnəri] THEA escenario *m*

scent [sent] *n* olor *m*; *(perfume)* perfume *m*, fragancia *f*

scep·tic *etc Br* ▶ **skeptic** *etc*

sched·ule ['ʃedjuːl] **1** *n of events, work* programa *m*; *of exams* calendario *m*; *for train, work, of lessons* horario *m*; **be on schedule** *of work* ir según lo previsto; *of train* ir a la hora prevista; **be behind schedule** *of work, train etc* ir con retraso **2** *v/t (put on schedule)* programar; **it's scheduled for completion next month** está previsto que se complete el próximo mes

sched·uled 'flight ['ʃedjuːld] vuelo *m* regular

scheme [skiːm] **1** *n (plan)* plan *m*, proyecto *m*; *(plot)* confabulación *f* **2** *v/i (plot)* confabularse

schem·ing ['skiːmiŋ] *adj* maquinador

schiz·o·phre·ni·a [skitsə'friːniə] esquizofrenia *f*

schiz·o·phren·ic [skitsə'frenik] **1** *n* esquizofrénico(-a) *m(f)* **2** *adj* esquizofrénico

schol·ar ['skɑːlər] erudito(-a) *m(f)*

schol·ar·ly ['skɑːlərli] *adj* erudito

schol·ar·ship ['skɑːlərʃip] *scholarly work* estudios *mpl*; *financial award* beca *f*

school [skuːl] escuela *f*, colegio *m*; *(university)* universidad *f*

'school bag *(satchel)* cartera *f*

'school·boy escolar *m*

'school·chil·dren *npl* escolares *mpl*

'school days *npl*; **do you remember your school days?** ¿te acuerdas de cuándo ibas al colegio?

'school·girl escolar *f*

'school·mate compañero *m* de colegio

'school·teach·er maestro(-a) *m(f)*, profesor(a) *m(f)*

sci·at·i·ca [sai'ætikə] ciática *f*

sci·ence ['saiəns] ciencia *f*

sci·ence 'fic·tion ciencia *f* ficción

sci·en·tif·ic [saiən'tifik] *adj* científico

sci·en·tist ['saiəntist] científico(-a) *m(f)*

scis·sors ['sizərz] *npl* tijeras *fpl*

scoff¹ [skɑːf] *v/t* F *(eat fast)* zamparse F

scoff² [skɑːf] *v/i (mock)* burlarse, mofarse

◆ **scoff at** *v/t* burlarse de, mofarse de

scold [skould] *v/t child, husband* regañar

scoop [skuːp] **1** *n implement* cuchara *f*; *for mud* pala *f*; *(story)* exclusiva *f* **2** *v/t*: **scoop sth into sth** recoger algo para meterlo en algo

◆ **scoop up** *v/t* recoger

scoot·er ['skuːtər] *with motor* escúter *m*; *child's* patinete *m*

scope [skoup] alcance *m*; *(freedom, opportunity)* oportunidad *f*; **he wants more scope to do his own thing** quiere más libertad para hacer lo que quiere

scorch [skɔːrtʃ] *v/t* quemar

scorch·ing ['skɔːrtʃiŋ] *adj* abrasador

score [skɔːr] **1** *n* SP resultado *m*; *in competition* puntuación *f*; *(written music)* partitura *f*; *of movie etc* banda *f* sonora, música *f*; **what's the score?** SP ¿cómo van?; **have a score to settle with s.o.** tener una cuenta pendiente con alguien; **keep (the) score** llevar el tanteo **2** *v/t goal* marcar; *point* anotar; *(cut: line)* marcar **3** v/i marcar; (keep the score) llevar al tanteo; *that's where he scores* ése es su punto fuerte

'score·board marcador m

scor·er ['skɔːrər] of goal goleador(a) m(f); of point anotador(a) m(f); (official score-keeper) encargado del marcador

scorn [skɔːrn] **1** n desprecio m; *pour scorn on sth* despreciar algo, menospreciar algo **2** v/t idea, suggestion despreciar

scorn·ful ['skɔːrnfəl] adj despreciativo

scorn·ful·ly ['skɔːrnfəlɪ] adv con desprecio

Scor·pi·o ['skɔːrpɪoʊ] ASTR Escorpio m/f inv

Scot [skɑːt] escocés(-esa) m(f)

Scotch [skɑːtʃ] (whisky) whisky m escocés

Scotch 'tape® celo m, L.Am. Durex® m

scot-'free adv: *get off scot-free* salir impune

Scot·land ['skɑːtlənd] Escocia

Scots·man ['skɑːtsmən] escocés m

Scots·wom·an ['skɑːtswʊmən] escocesa f

Scot·tish ['skɑːtɪʃ] adj escocés

scoun·drel ['skaʊndrəl] canalla m/f

scour¹ ['skaʊər] v/t (search) rastrear, peinar

scour² ['skaʊər] v/t pans fregar

scout [skaʊt] n (boy scout) boy-scout m

scowl [skaʊl] **1** n ceño m **2** v/i fruncir el ceño

scram [skræm] v/i (pret & pp *scrammed*) F largarse F; *scram!* ¡largo!

scram·ble ['skræmbl] **1** n (rush) prisa f **2** v/t message cifrar, codificar **3** v/i (climb) trepar; *he scrambled to his feet* se levantó de un salto

scram·bled 'eggs ['skræmbld] npl huevos mpl revueltos

scrap [skræp] **1** n metal chatarra f; (fight) pelea f; of food trocito m; of evidence indicio m; of common sense pizca f **2** v/t (pret & pp *scrapped*) plan, project abandonar; paragraph borrar

'scrap·book álbum m de recortes

scrape [skreɪp] **1** n on paintwork etc arañazo m **2** v/t paintwork rayar; *scrape a living* apañarse

♦ **scrape through** v/i in exam aprobar por los pelos

'scrap heap: *be good for the scrap heap* of person estar para el arrastre; of object estar para tirar

scrap 'met·al chatarra f

scrap 'pa·per papel m usado

scrap·py ['skræpɪ] adj work, writing desorganizado

scratch [skrætʃ] **1** n mark marca f; *have a scratch to stop itching* rascarse; *start from scratch* empezar desde cero; *your work isn't up to scratch* tu trabajo es insuficiente **2** v/t (mark: skin) arañar; (mark: paint) rayar; because of itch rascarse **3** v/i of cat etc arañar; because of itch rascarse

scrawl [skrɔːl] **1** n garabato m **2** v/t garabatear

scraw·ny ['skrɔːnɪ] adj escuálido

scream [skriːm] **1** n grito m; *screams of laughter* carcajadas fpl **2** v/i gritar

screech [skriːtʃ] **1** n of tires chirrido m; (scream) chillido m **2** v/i of tires chirriar; (scream) chillar

screen [skriːn] **1** n in room, hospital mampara f; protective cortina f; in movie theater pantalla f; COMPUT monitor m, pantalla f **2** v/t (protect, hide) ocultar; movie proyectar; for security reasons investigar

'screen·play guión m

'screen sav·er COMPUT salvapantallas m inv

'screen test for movie prueba f

screw [skruː] **1** n tornillo m; V (sex) polvo m V **2** v/t: *screw sth to sth* atornillar algo a algo; V (have sex with) echar un polvo con V; F (cheat) timar F

♦ **screw up 1** v/t eyes cerrar; piece of paper arrugar; F (make a mess of) fastidiar F **2** v/i F (make a bad mistake) meter la pata F

'screw·driv·er destornillador m

screwed 'up adj F psychologically acomplejado

'screw top on bottle tapón m de rosca

screw·y ['skruːɪ] adj chiflado F; idea, film descabellado F

scrib·ble ['skrɪbl] **1** n garabato m **2** v/t & v/i garabatear

scrimp [skrɪmp] v/i: *scrimp and scrape* pasar apuros, pasar estrecheces

script [skrɪpt] for movie, play guión m; form of writing caligrafía f

scrip·ture ['skrɪptʃər] escritura f; *the (Holy) Scriptures* las Sagradas Escrituras

'script·writ·er guionista m/f

scroll [skroʊl] n (manuscript) manuscrito m

♦ **scroll down** v/i COMPUT avanzar

♦ **scroll up** v/i COMPUT retroceder

scrounge [skraʊndʒ] v/t gorronear

scroung·er ['skraʊndʒər] gorrón(-ona) m(f)

scrub [skrʌb] v/t (pret & pp *scrubbed*) floors fregar; hands frotar

scrub·bing brush ['skrʌbɪŋ] for floor ce-

S

pillo m para fregar

scruff·y ['skrʌfɪ] adj andrajoso, desaliñado

scrum [skrʌm] in rugby melé f

◆ **scrunch up** [skrʌntʃ] v/t plastic cup etc
estrujar

scru·ples ['skruːplz] npl escrúpulos mpl

scru·pu·lous ['skruːpjələs] adj with moral principles escrupuloso; (thorough)
meticuloso; attention to detail minucioso

scru·pu·lous·ly ['skruːpjələslɪ] adv (me-
ticulously) minuciosamente

scru·ti·nize ['skruːtɪnaɪz] v/t (examine
closely) estudiar, examinar

scru·ti·ny ['skruːtɪnɪ] escrutinio m; **come
under scrutiny** ser objeto de investigación

scu·ba div·ing ['skuːbə] submarinismo m

scuf·fle ['skʌfl] n riña f

sculp·tor ['skʌlptər] escultor(a) m(f)

sculp·ture ['skʌlptʃər] escultura f

scum [skʌm] on liquid película f de suciedad; (pej: people) escoria f

sea [siː] n mar m; **by the sea** junto al mar

'sea·bed fondo m marino

'sea·bird ave f marina

sea·far·ing ['siːferɪŋ] adj nation marinero

'sea·food marisco m

'sea·front paseo m marítimo

sea·go·ing adj vessel de altura

'sea·gull gaviota f

seal[1] [siːl] n animal foca f

seal[2] [siːl] **1** n on document sello m; TECH
junta f, sello m **2** v/t container sellar

◆ **seal off** v/t area aislar

'sea lev·el: above sea level sobre el nivel
del mar; **below sea level** bajo el nivel
del mar

seam [siːm] n on garment costura f; of ore
filón m

'sea·man marinero m

seam·stress ['siːmstrɪs] modista f

'sea·port puerto m marítimo

'sea pow·er nation potencia f marítima

search [sɜːrtʃ] **1** n búsqueda f; **be in
search of** estar en busca de **2** v/t baggage, person registrar; **search a place for
s.o.** buscar a alguien en un lugar

◆ **search for** v/t buscar

search·ing ['sɜːrtʃɪŋ] adj look escrutador;
question difícil

'search·light reflector m

'search par·ty grupo m de rescate

'search war·rant orden f de registro

'sea·shore orilla f

'sea·sick adj mareado; **get seasick** marearse

'sea·side costa f, playa f; **seaside resort**
centro m de veraneo costero

sea·son ['siːzn] n (winter, spring etc) estación f; for tourism etc temporada f;
plums aren't in season at the moment
ahora no es temporada de ciruelas

sea·son·al ['siːznl] adj fruit, vegetables
del tiempo; employment temporal

sea·soned ['siːznd] adj wood seco; traveler, campaigner experimentado

sea·son·ing ['siːznɪŋ] condimento m

'sea·son tick·et abono m

seat [siːt] **1** n in room, bus, plane asiento;
in theater butaca f; of pants culera f;
please take a seat siéntese, tome asiento
2 v/t (have seating for): **the hall can seat
200 people** la sala tiene capacidad para
200 personas; **please remain seated** por
favor, permanezcan sentados

'seat belt cinturón m de seguridad

'sea ur·chin erizo m de mar

'sea·weed alga(s) f(pl)

se·clud·ed [sɪ'kluːdɪd] adj apartado

se·clu·sion [sɪ'kluːʒn] aislamiento m

sec·ond[1] ['sekənd] **1** n of time segundo m
2 adj segundo **3** adv come in en segundo
lugar **4** v/t motion apoyar

se·cond[2] [sɪ'kɑːnd] v/t: **be seconded to**
ser asignado a

sec·ond·a·ry ['sekənderɪ] adj secundario;
of secondary importance de menor importancia

sec·ond·a·ry ed·u·ca·tion educación f secundaria

sec·ond 'best adj: **be second best** ser el
segundo mejor; inferior ser un segun-
dón; **the second best runner in the
school** el segundo mejor corredor del
colegio

sec·ond 'big·gest adj: **it is the second
biggest company in the area** es la segunda empresa más grande de la zona

sec·ond 'class adj ticket de segunda clase

sec·ond 'floor tercer piso m, Br segundo
piso m

'sec·ond hand n on clock segundero m

sec·ond-'hand **1** adj de segunda mano **2**
adv buy de segunda mano

sec·ond·ly ['sekəndlɪ] adv en segundo lugar

sec·ond-'rate adj inferior

**sec·ond 'thoughts: I've had second
thoughts** he cambiado de idea

se·cre·cy ['siːkrəsɪ] secretismo m

se·cret ['siːkrət] **1** n secreto m; **in secret**
en secreto **2** adj secreto

se·cret 'a·gent agente m/f secreto

sec·re·tar·i·al [sekrə'terɪəl] adj tasks, job
de secretario

sec·re·tar·y ['sekrətərɪ] secretario(-a)
m(f); POL ministro(-a) m(f)

S

Sec·re·tar·y of 'State *in USA* Secretario(-a) *m(f)* de Estado

se·crete [sɪˈkriːt] *v/t (give off)* segregar; *(hide away)* esconder

se·cre·tion [sɪˈkriːʃn] secreción *f*

se·cre·tive [ˈsiːkrətɪv] *adj* reservado

se·cret·ly [ˈsiːkrətlɪ] *adv* en secreto

se·cret po'lice policía *f* secreta

se·cret 'ser·vice servicio *m* secreto

sect [sekt] secta *f*

sec·tion [ˈsekʃn] *of book, company, text* sección *f*; *of building* zona *f*; *of apple* parte *f*

sec·tor [ˈsektər] sector *m*

sec·u·lar [ˈsekjʊlər] *adj* laico

se·cure [sɪˈkjʊr] **1** *adj shelf etc* seguro; *job, contract* fijo **2** *v/t shelf etc* asegurar; *s.o.'s help* conseguir

se·cu·ri·ty [sɪˈkjʊrətɪ] seguridad *f*; *for investment* garantía *f*

se'cu·ri·ties mar·ket FIN mercado *m* de valores

se·cu·ri·ty a·lert alerta *f*

se·cu·ri·ty check control *m* de seguridad

se·cu·ri·ty-con·scious *adj* consciente de la seguridad

se·cu·ri·ty guard guardia *m/f* de seguridad

se·cu·ri·ty risk *person* peligro *m* (para la seguridad)

se·dan [sɪˈdæn] turismo *m*

se·date [sɪˈdeɪt] *v/t* sedar

se·da·tion [sɪˈdeɪʃn]: *be under sedation* estar sedado

sed·a·tive [ˈsedətɪv] *n* sedante *m*

sed·en·ta·ry [ˈsedəntərɪ] *adj job* sedentario

sed·i·ment [ˈsedɪmənt] sedimento *m*

se·duce [sɪˈduːs] *v/t* seducir

se·duc·tion [sɪˈdʌkʃn] seducción *f*

se·duc·tive [sɪˈdʌktɪv] *adj dress* seductor; *offer* tentador

see [siː] *v/t (pret saw, pp seen)* ver; *(understand)* entender, ver; *romantically* ver, salir con; *I see* ya veo; *can I see the manager?* ¿puedo ver al encargado?; *you should see a doctor* deberías ir a que te viera un médico; *see s.o. home* acompañar a alguien a casa; *see you!* F ¡hasta la vista!, ¡chao! F

◆ **see about** *v/t (look into)*: *I'll see about getting it repaired* me encargaré de que lo arreglen

◆ **see off** *v/t at airport etc* despedir; *(chase away)* espantar

◆ **see out** *v/t*: *see s.o. out* acompañar a alguien a la puerta

◆ **see to** *v/t*: *see to sth* ocuparse de algo; *see to it that sth gets done* asegurarse de que algo se haga

seed [siːd] semilla *f*; *in tennis* cabeza *f* de serie; *go to seed of person* descuidarse; *of district* empeorarse

seed·ling [ˈsiːdlɪŋ] planta *f* de semillero

seed·y [ˈsiːdɪ] *adj bar, district* de mala calaña

see·ing 'eye dog [ˈsiːɪŋ] perro *m* lazarillo

see·ing (that) [ˈsiːɪŋ] *conj* dado que, ya que

seek [siːk] *v/t (pret & pp sought)* buscar

seem [siːm] *v/i* parecer; *it seems that ...* parece que ...

seem·ing·ly [ˈsiːmɪŋlɪ] *adv* aparentemente

seen [siːn] *pp* → **see**

seep [siːp] *v/i of liquid* filtrarse

◆ **seep out** *v/i of liquid* filtrarse

see·saw [ˈsiːsɔː] *n* sube y baja *m*

seethe [siːð] *v/i*: *be seething with anger* estar a punto de estallar (de cólera)

seg·ment [ˈsegmənt] segmento *m*

seg·ment·ed [segˈmentɪd] *adj* segmentado, dividido

seg·re·gate [ˈsegrɪgeɪt] *v/t* segregar

seg·re·ga·tion [segrɪˈgeɪʃn] segregación *f*

seis·mol·o·gy [saɪzˈmɑːlədʒɪ] sismología *f*

seize [siːz] *v/t s.o., s.o.'s arm* agarrar; *opportunity* aprovechar; *of Customs, police etc* incautarse de

◆ **seize up** *v/i of engine* atascarse

sei·zure [ˈsiːʒər] MED ataque *m*; *of drugs etc* incautación *f*; *amount seized* alijo *m*

sel·dom [ˈseldəm] *adv* raramente, casi nunca

se·lect [sɪˈlekt] **1** *v/t* seleccionar **2** *adj (exclusive)* selecto

se·lec·tion [sɪˈlekʃn] selección *f*; *(choosing)* elección *f*

se'lec·tion pro·cess proceso *m* de selección

se·lec·tive [sɪˈlektɪv] *adj* selectivo

self [self] *(pl selves* [selvz]*)* ego *m*; *my other self* mi otro yo

self-ad·dressed 'en·ve·lope [selfəˈdrest]: *send us a self-addressed envelope* envíenos un sobre con sus datos

self-as'sur·ance confianza *f* en sí mismo

self-assured [selfəˈʃʊrd] *adj* seguro de sí mismo

self-ca·ter·ing a'part·ment [selfˈkeɪtərɪŋ] *Br* apartamento *m or Span* piso *m* sin servicio de comidas

self-'cen·tered, *Br* **self-'cen·tred** [self-

'sent[ə]rd] adj egoísta

self-'clean·ing adj oven con autolimpieza

self-con'fessed [selfkən'fest] adj: **he's a self-confessed megalomaniac** se confiesa megalómano

self-'con·fi·dence confianza f en sí mismo

self-'con·fi·dent adj seguro de sí mismo

self-'con·scious adj tímido

self-'con·scious·ness timidez f

self-con·tained [selfkən'teɪnd] adj *apartment* independiente

self con'trol autocontrol m

self-de'fence Br, self-de'fense autodefensa f; **in self-defence** en defensa propia

self-'dis·ci·pline autodisciplina f

self-'doubt inseguridad f

self-em·ployed [selfɪm'plɔɪd] adj autónomo

self-e'steem autoestima f

self-ex'pres·sion autoexpresión f

self-'ev·i·dent adj obvio

self-'gov·ern·ment autogobierno m

self-'in·terest interés m propio

self·ish ['selfɪʃ] adj egoísta

self·less ['selflɪs] adj desinteresado

self-made 'man [self'meɪd] hombre m hecho a sí mismo

self-'pit·y autocompasión f

self-'por·trait autorretrato m

self-pos·sessed [selfpə'zest] adj sereno

self-re'li·ant [selfrɪ'laɪənt] adj autosuficiente

self-re'spect amor m propio

self-right·eous [self'raɪtʃəs] adj pej santurrón, intolerante

self-sat·is·fied [self'sætɪzfaɪd] adj pej pagado de sí mismo

self-'ser·vice adj de autoservicio

self-ser·vice 'res·tau·rant (restaurante m) autoservicio m

self-taught [self'tɔːt] adj autodidacta

sell [sel] v/t & v/i (pret & pp **sold**) vender

◆ sell out v/i of product agotarse; **we've sold out** se nos ha(n) agotado

◆ sell out of v/t agotar las existencias de

◆ sell up v/i vender todo

'sell-by date fecha f límite de venta; **be past its sell-by date** haber pasado la fecha límite de venta

sell·er ['selər] vendedor(a) m(f)

sell·ing ['selɪŋ] n COM ventas fpl

'sell·ing point ventaja f

Sel·lo·tape® ['seləteɪp] Br celo m, L.Am. Durex® m

se·men ['siːmən] semen m

se·mes·ter [sɪ'mestər] semestre m

sem·i ['semi] n truck camión m semirremolque

'sem·i·cir·cle semicírculo m

sem·i·cir·cu·lar adj semicircular

semi·'co·lon punto m y coma

sem·i·con'duc·tor ELEC semiconductor m

semi'fi·nal semifinal f

semi'fi·nal·ist semifinalista m/f

sem·i·nar ['seminɑːr] seminario m

sem·i·'skilled adj semicualificado

sen·ate ['senət] senado m

sen·a·tor ['senətər] senador(a) m(f); **Senator George Schwarz** el Senador George Schwarz

send [send] v/t (pret & pp **sent**) enviar, mandar; **the doctor sent him to a specialist** el médico lo envió or mandó a un especialista; **send her my best wishes** dale recuerdos de mi parte

◆ send back v/t devolver

◆ send for v/t mandar buscar

◆ send in v/t troops, application enviar, mandar; *next interviewee* hacer pasar

◆ send off v/t *letter, fax etc* enviar, mandar

send·er ['sendər] of letter remitente m/f

se·nile ['siːnaɪl] adj senil

se·nil·i·ty [sɪ'nɪlətɪ] senilidad f

se·ni·or ['siːnjər] adj (older) mayor; in rank superior

se·ni·or 'cit·i·zen persona f de la tercera edad

se·ni·or·i·ty [siːnɪ'ɑːrətɪ] in job antigüedad f

sen·sa·tion [sen'seɪʃn] sensación f

sen·sa·tion·al [sen'seɪʃnl] adj news, discovery sensacional

sense [sens] 1 n (meaning, point, hearing etc) sentido m; (feeling) sentimiento m; (common sense) sentido m común, sensatez f; **in a sense** en cierto sentido; **talk sense, man!** ¡no digas tonterías!; **come to one's senses** entrar en razón; **it doesn't make sense** no tiene sentido; **there's no sense in waiting** no tiene sentido que esperemos 2 v/t s.o.'s presence sentir, notar; **I could sense that something was wrong** tenía la sensación de que no iba a bien

sense·less ['senslɪs] adj (pointless) absurdo

sen·si·ble ['sensəbl] adj sensato; clothes, shoes práctico, apropiado

sen·si·bly ['sensəblɪ] adv con sensatez; **she wasn't sensibly dressed** no llevaba ropa apropiada

sen·si·tive ['sensətɪv] adj skin, person sensible

sen·si·tiv·i·ty [sensə'tɪvətɪ] of skin, person sensibilidad f

sen·sor ['sensər] sensor m

sen·su·al ['senʃuəl] adj sensual

sen·su·al·i·ty [senʃu'ælətɪ] sensualidad f

sen·su·ous ['senʃuəs] adj sensual

sent [sent] pret & pp → **send**

sen·tence ['sentəns] 1 n GRAM oración f; LAW sentencia f 2 v/t LAW sentenciar, condenar

sen·ti·ment ['sentɪmənt] (sentimentality) sentimentalismo m; (opinion) opinión f

sen·ti·men·tal [sentɪ'mentl] adj sentimental

sen·ti·men·tal·i·ty [sentɪmen'tælətɪ] sentimentalismo m

sen·try ['sentrɪ] centinela m

sep·a·rate¹ ['sepərət] adj separado; **keep sth separate from sth** guardar algo separado de algo

separate² ['sepəreɪt] 1 v/t separar; **separate sth from sth** separar algo de algo 2 v/i of couple separarse

sep·a·rat·ed ['sepəreɪtɪd] adj couple separado

cop·a·rate·ly ['sepərətlɪ] adv puy, treat por separado

sep·a·ra·tion [sepə'reɪʃn] separación f

Sep·tem·ber [sep'tembər] septiembre m

sep·tic ['septɪk] adj séptico; **go septic** of wound infectarse

se·quel ['siːkwəl] continuación f

se·quence ['siːkwəns] n secuencia f; **in sequence** en orden; **out of sequence** en desorden; **the sequence of events** la secuencia de hechos

se·rene [sɪ'riːn] adj sereno

ser·geant ['sɑːrdʒənt] sargento m/f

se·ri·al ['sɪrɪəl] n on TV, radio serie f, serial m; in magazine novela f por entregas

se·ri·al·ize ['sɪrɪəlaɪz] v/t novel on TV emitir en forma de serie; in newspaper publicar por entregas

'se·ri·al kill·er asesino(-a) m(f) en serie

'se·ri·al num·ber of product número m de serie

'se·ri·al port COMPUT puerto m (en) serie

se·ries ['sɪriːz] nsg serie f

se·ri·ous ['sɪrɪəs] adj situation, damage, illness grave; (person: earnest) serio; company serio; **I'm serious** lo digo en serio; **we'd better take a serious look at it** deberíamos examinarlo seriamente

se·ri·ous·ly ['sɪrɪəslɪ] adv injured gravemente; **seriously intend to ...** tener intenciones firmes de ...; **seriously?** ¿en serio?; **take s.o. seriously** tomar a alguien en serio

se·ri·ous·ness ['sɪrɪəsnɪs] of person seriedad f; of situation seriedad f, gravedad f; of illness gravedad f

ser·mon ['sɜːrmən] sermón m

ser·vant ['sɜːrvənt] sirviente(-a) m(f)

serve [sɜːrv] 1 n in tennis servicio m, saque m 2 v/t food, meal servir; customer in shop atender; one's country, the people servir a; **it serves you right** ¡te lo mereces! 3 v/i servir; in tennis servir, sacar
◆ **serve up** v/t meal servir

serv·er ['sɜːrvər] in tennis jugador(a) m(f) al servicio; COMPUT servidor m

ser·vice ['sɜːrvɪs] 1 n to customers, community servicio m; for vehicle, machine revisión f; in tennis servicio m, saque m; **services** (service sector) el sector servicios; **the services** MIL las fuerzas armadas 2 v/t vehicle, machine revisar

'ser·vice ar·e·a área f de servicio

'ser·vice charge in restaurant servicio m (tarifa)

'ser·vice in·dus·try industria f de servicios

'ser·vice·man MIL militar m

'ser·vice pro·vid·er COMPUT proveedor m de servicios

'ser·vice sec·tor sector m servicios

'ser·vice sta·tion estación f de servicio

ser·vi·ette [sɜːrvi'et] servilleta f

ser·vile ['sɜːrvəl] adj pej servil

serv·ing ['sɜːrvɪŋ] n of food ración f

ses·sion ['seʃn] sesión f; with boss reunión f

set [set] 1 n of tools juego m; of books colección f; (group of people) grupo m; MATH conjunto m; (THEA: scenery) decorado m; where a movie is made plató m; in tennis set m; television set televisor m; **a set of dishes** una vajilla; **a set of glasses** una cristalería 2 v/t (pret & pp set) (place) colocar; movie, novel etc ambientar; date, time, limit fijar; mechanism, alarm poner; clock poner en hora; broken limb recomponer; jewel engastar; (typeset) componer; **set the table** poner la mesa 3 v/i (pret & pp set) of sun ponerse; of glue solidificarse 4 adj views, ideas fijo; (ready) preparado; **be dead set on sth** estar empeñado en hacer algo; **be very set in one's ways** ser de ideas fijas; **set meal** menú m (del día)
◆ **set apart** v/t distinguir
◆ **set aside** v/t material, food apartar; money ahorrar
◆ **set back** v/t in plans etc retrasar; **it set me back $400** me salió por 400 dólares
◆ **set off 1** v/i on journey salir 2 v/t explosion provocar; bomb hacer explotar; chain reaction desencadenar; alarm activar
◆ **set out 1** v/i on journey salir (**for** hacia) 2 v/t ideas, goods exponer; **set out to do**

S

sth (*intend*) tener la intención de hacer algo

◆ **set to** *v/i* (*start on a task*) empezar a trabajar

◆ **set up 1** *v/t new company* establecer; *equipment, machine* instalar; *market stall* montar; *meeting* organizar; F (*frame*) tender una trampa a **2** *v/i in business* emprender un negocio

'**set-back** contratiempo *m*

set·tee [se'ti:] (*couch, sofa*) sofá *m*

set·ting ['setɪŋ] *n of novel etc* escenario *m*; *of house* ubicación *f*

set·tle ['setl] **1** *v/i of bird, dust* posarse; *of building* hundirse; *to live* establecerse **2** *v/t dispute, uncertainty* resolver, solucionar; *debts* saldar; *nerves, stomach* calmar; *that settles it!* ¡está decidido!

◆ **settle down** *v/i* (*stop being noisy*) tranquilizarse; (*stop wild living*) sentar la cabeza; *in an area* establecerse

◆ **settle for** *v/t* (*take, accept*) conformarse con

◆ **settle up** *v/i* (*pay*) ajustar cuentas con

set·tled ['setld] *adj weather* estable

set·tle·ment ['setlmənt] *of claim* resolución *f*; *of debt* liquidación *f*; *of dispute* acuerdo *m*; (*payment*) suma *f*; *of building* hundimiento *m*

set·tler ['setlər] *in new country* colono *m*

'**set-up** (*structure*) estructura *f*; (*relationship*) relación *f*; F (*frameup*) trampa *f*

sev·en ['sevn] siete

sev·en·teen [sevn'ti:n] diecisiete

sev·en·teenth [sevn'ti:nθ] *n & adj* decimoséptimo

sev·enth ['sevnθ] *n & adj* séptimo

sev·en·ti·eth ['sevntɪθ] *n & adj* septuagésimo

sev·en·ty ['sevntɪ] setenta

sev·er ['sevər] *v/t* cortar; *relations* romper

sev·e·ral ['sevrəl] **1** *adj* varios **2** *pron* varios(-as) *mpl* (*fpl*)

se·vere [sɪ'vɪr] *adj illness* grave; *penalty, winter, weather* severo; *teacher* estricto

se·vere·ly [sɪ'vɪrlɪ] *adv punish, speak* con severidad; *injured, disrupted* gravemente

se·ver·i·ty [sɪ'verətɪ] severidad *f*; *of illness* gravedad *f*

Se·ville [sə'vɪl] *n* Sevilla

sew [soʊ] *v/t & v/i* (*pret sewed*, *pp sewn*) coser

◆ **sew on** *v/t button* coser

sew·age ['su:ɪdʒ] aguas *fpl* residuales

'**sew·age plant** planta *f* de tratamiento de aguas residuales, depuradora *f*

sew·er ['su:ər] alcantarilla *f*, cloaca *f*

sew·ing ['soʊɪŋ] *skill* costura *f*; *that being sewn* labor *f*

'**sew·ing ma·chine** máquina *f* de coser

sewn [soʊn] *pp* → **sew**

sex [seks] (*act, gender*) sexo *m*; *have sex with* tener relaciones sexuales con, acostarse con

sex·ist ['seksɪst] **1** *adj* sexista **2** *n* sexista *m/f*

sex·u·al ['sekʃʊəl] *adj* sexual

sex·u·al as'sault agresión *f* sexual

sex·u·al ha'rass·ment acoso *m* sexual

sex·u·al 'in·ter·course relaciones *fpl* sexuales

sex·u·al·i·ty [sekʃʊ'ælətɪ] sexualidad *f*

sex·u·al·ly ['sekʃʊlɪ] *adv* sexualmente; *sexually transmitted disease* enfermedad *f* de transmisión sexual

sex·y ['seksɪ] *adj* sexy *inv*

shab·bi·ly ['ʃæbɪlɪ] *adv dressed* con desaliño; *treat* muy mal, de manera muy injusta

shab·by ['ʃæbɪ] *adj coat etc* desgastado, raído; *treatment* malo, muy injusto

shack [ʃæk] choza *f*

shade [ʃeɪd] **1** *n for lamp* pantalla *f*; *of color* tonalidad *f*; *on window* persiana *f*; *in the shade* a la sombra **2** *v/t from sun, light* proteger de la luz

shad·ow ['ʃædoʊ] *n* sombra *f*

shad·y ['ʃeɪdɪ] *adj spot* umbrío; *character, dealings* sospechoso

shaft [ʃæft] TECH eje *m*, árbol *m*; *of mine* pozo *m*

shag·gy ['ʃægɪ] *adj hair, dog* greñudo

shake [ʃeɪk] **1** *n* sacudida *f*; *give sth a good shake* agitar algo bien **2** *v/t* (*pret shook*, *pp shaken*) agitar; *emotionally* conmocionar; *he shook his head* negó con la cabeza; *shake hands* estrechar *or* darse la mano; *shake hands with s.o.* estrechar *or* dar la mano a alguien **3** *v/i* (*pret shook*, *pp shaken*) *of voice, building, person* temblar

shak·en ['ʃeɪkən] **1** *adj emotionally* conmocionado **2** *pp* → **shake**

'**shake-up** reestructuración *f*

shak·y ['ʃeɪkɪ] *adj table etc* inestable; *after illness* débil; *after shock* conmocionado; *grasp of sth, grammar etc* flojo; *voice, hand* tembloroso

shall [ʃæl] *v/aux* ◇ *future*: *I shall do my best* haré todo lo que pueda; *I shan't see them* no los veré
◇ *suggesting*: *shall we go?* ¿nos vamos?

shal·low ['ʃæloʊ] *adj water* poco profundo; *person* superficial

sham·bles ['ʃæmblz] *nsg* caos *m*

shame [ʃeɪm] **1** *n* vergüenza *f*, Col, Mex, Ven pena *f*; *bring shame on* avergonzar *or* Col, Mex, Ven apenar a; **shame on you!** ¡debería darte vergüenza!; **what a shame!** ¡qué pena *or* lástima! **2** *v/t* avergonzar, Col, Mex, Ven apenar; **shame s.o. into doing sth** avergonzar a alguien para que haga algo

shame·ful ['ʃeɪmfǝl] *adj* vergonzoso

shame·ful·ly ['ʃeɪmfǝlɪ] *adv* vergonzosamente

shame·less ['ʃeɪmlɪs] *adj* desvergonzado

sham·poo [ʃæm'puː] **1** *n* champú *m* **2** *v/t customer* lavar la cabeza a; *hair* lavar

shan·ty town ['ʃæntɪ] Span barrio *m* de chabolas, *Am* barriada *f*

shape [ʃeɪp] **1** *n* forma *f* **2** *v/t clay* modelar; *person's life, character* determinar; *the future* dar forma a

shape·less ['ʃeɪplɪs] *adj dress etc* amorfo

shape·ly ['ʃeɪplɪ] *adv figure* esbelto

share [ʃer] **1** *n* parte *f*; FIN acción *f*; **I did my share of the work** hice la parte del trabajo que me correspondía **2** *v/t feelings, opinions* compartir **3** *v/i* compartir
♦ **share out** *v/t* repartir

'share·hold·er accionista *m/f*

shark [ʃɑːrk] *fish* tiburón *m*

sharp [ʃɑːrp] **1** *adj knife* afilado; *mind* vivo; *pain* agudo; *taste* ácido **2** *adv* MUS demasiado alto; **at 3 o'clock sharp** a las tres en punto

sharp·en ['ʃɑːrpn] *v/t knife* afilar; *pencil* sacar punta a; *skills* perfeccionar

sharp 'prac·tice triquiñuelas *fpl*, tejemanejes *mpl*

shat [ʃæt] *pret & pp* → **shit**

shat·ter ['ʃætǝr] **1** *v/t glass* hacer añicos; *illusions* destrozar **2** *v/i of glass* hacerse añicos

shat·tered ['ʃætǝrd] *adj* F *(exhausted)* destrozado F, hecho polvo F; *(very upset)* destrozado F

shat·ter·ing ['ʃætǝrɪŋ] *adj news, experience* demoledor, sorprendente

shave [ʃeɪv] **1** *v/t* afeitar **2** *v/i* afeitarse **3** *n* afeitado *m*; **have a shave** afeitarse; **that was a close shave** ¡le faltó un pelo!
♦ **shave off** *v/t beard* afeitar; *from piece of wood* rebajar

shav·en ['ʃeɪvn] *adj head* afeitado

shav·er ['ʃeɪvǝr] *electric* máquinilla *f* de afeitar (eléctrica)

shav·ing brush ['ʃeɪvɪŋ] brocha *f* de afeitar

'shav·ing soap jabón *m* de afeitar

shawl [ʃɔːl] chal *m*

she [ʃiː] *pron* ella; **she is German/a student** es alemana / estudiante; **you're funny, she's not** tú tienes gracia, ella no

shears [ʃɪrz] *npl for gardening* tijeras *fpl*

(de podar); *for sewing* tijeras *fpl* (*grandes*)

sheath [ʃiːθ] *n for knife* funda *f*; *contraceptive* condón *m*

shed[1] [ʃed] *v/t (pret & pp shed) blood, tears* derramar; *leaves* perder; **shed light on** *fig* arrojar luz sobre

shed[2] [ʃed] *n* cobertizo *m*

sheep [ʃiːp] (*pl sheep*) oveja *f*

'sheep·dog perro *m* pastor

sheep·herd·er ['ʃiːphɜːrdǝr] pastor *m*

sheep·ish ['ʃiːpɪʃ] *adj* avergonzado

'sheep·skin *adj lining* (de piel) de borrego

sheer [ʃɪr] *adj madness, luxury* puro, verdadero; *hell* verdadero; *drop, cliffs* escarpado

sheet [ʃiːt] *for bed* sábana *f*; *of paper* hoja *f*; *of metal* chapa *f*, plancha *f*; *of glass* hoja *f*, lámina *f*

shelf [ʃelf] (*pl shelves* [ʃelvz]) estante *m*; **shelves** estanterías *fpl*

shell [ʃel] **1** *n of mussel etc* concha *f*, *of egg* cáscara *f*; *of tortoise* caparazón *m*; MIL proyectil *m*; **come out of one's shell** *fig* salir del caparazón **2** *v/t peas* pelar; MIL bombardear (*con artillería*)

'shell·fire fuego *m* de artillería

'shell·fish marisco *m*

shel·ter ['ʃeltǝr] **1** *n* refugio *m*; *(bus shelter)* marquesina *f* **2** *v/i from rain, bombing etc* refugiarse **3** *v/t (protect)* proteger

shel·tered ['ʃeltǝrd] *adj place* resguardado; **lead a sheltered life** llevar una vida protegida

shelve [ʃelv] *v/t fig* posponer

shep·herd ['ʃepǝrd] *n* pastor *m*

sher·iff ['ʃerɪf] sheriff *m/f*

sher·ry ['ʃerɪ] jerez *m*

shield [ʃiːld] **1** *n* escudo *m*; *sports trophy* trofeo *m (en forma de escudo)*; TECH placa *f* protectora; *of policeman* placa *f* **2** *v/t (protect)* proteger

shift [ʃɪft] **1** *n* cambio *m*; *(period of work)* turno *m* **2** *v/t (move)* mover; *stains etc* eliminar **3** *v/i (move)* moverse; *(change)* trasladarse, desplazarse; *of wind* cambiar; **he was shifting!** F iba a toda mecha F

'shift key COMPUT tecla *f* de mayúsculas

'shift work trabajo *m* por turnos

'shift work·er trabajador(a) *m(f)* por turnos

shift·y ['ʃɪftɪ] *adj pej* sospechoso

shil·ly-shal·ly ['ʃɪlɪʃælɪ] *v/i (pret & pp shilly-shallied)* F titubear

shim·mer ['ʃɪmǝr] *v/i* brillar; *of roads in heat* reverberar

S

shin [ʃɪn] n espinilla f

shine [ʃaɪn] 1 v/i (pret & pp shone) brillar; fig: of student etc destacar (at en) 2 v/t (pret & pp shone): could you shine a light in here? ¿podrías alumbrar aquí? 3 n on shoes etc brillo m

shin·gle ['ʃɪŋgl] on beach guijarros mpl

shin·gles ['ʃɪŋglz] nsg MED herpes m

shin·y ['ʃaɪnɪ] adj surface brillante

ship [ʃɪp] 1 n barco m, buque m 2 v/t (pret & pp shipped) (send) enviar; by sea enviar por barco

ship·ment ['ʃɪpmənt] (consignment) envío m

'ship·own·er naviero(-a) m(f), armador(a) m(f)

ship·ping ['ʃɪpɪŋ] n (sea traffic) navíos mpl, buques mpl; (sending) envío m; (sending by sea) envío m por barco

'ship·ping com·pa·ny (compañía f) naviera f

ship·ping costs npl gastos mpl de envío

'ship·shape adj ordenado, organizado

'ship·wreck 1 n naufragio m 2 v/t: be shipwrecked naufragar

'ship·yard astillero m

shirk [ʃɜːrk] v/t eludir

shirk·er ['ʃɜːrkər] vago(-a) m(f)

shirt [ʃɜːrt] camisa f; in his shirt sleeves en mangas de camisa

shit [ʃɪt] 1 n P mierda f P; I need a shit tengo que cagar P 2 v/i (pret & pp shat) P cagar P 3 interj P mierda P

shit·ty ['ʃɪtɪ] adj F asqueroso F; I feel shitty me encuentro de pena F

shiv·er ['ʃɪvər] v/i tiritar

shock [ʃɑːk] 1 n shock m, impresión f; ELEC descarga f; be in shock MED estar en estado de shock 2 v/t impresionar, dejar boquiabierto; I was shocked by the news la noticia me impresionó or dejó boquiabierto; an artist who tries to shock his public un artista que intenta escandalizar a su público

'shock ab·sorb·er [əb'sɔːrbər] MOT amortiguador m

shock·ing ['ʃɑːkɪŋ] adj behavior, poverty impresionante, escandaloso; F prices escandaloso; F weather, spelling terrible

shock·ing·ly ['ʃɑːkɪŋlɪ] adv behave escandalosamente

shod·dy ['ʃɑːdɪ] adj goods de mala calidad; behavior vergonzoso

shoe [ʃuː] zapato m

'shoe·horn n calzador m

'shoe·lace cordón m

'shoe·mak·er zapatero(-a) m(f)

'shoe mender zapatero(-a) m(f) remendón(-ona)

'shoe·store zapatería f

'shoe·string: do sth on a shoestring hacer algo con cuatro duros

shone [ʃɑːn] pret & pp → shine

◆ shoo away [ʃuː] v/t children, chicken espantar

shook [ʃuːk] pret → shake

shoot [ʃuːt] 1 n BOT brote m 2 v/t (pret & pp shot) disparar; and kill matar de un tiro; movie rodar; shoot s.o. in the leg disparar a alguien en la pierna

◆ shoot down v/t airplane derribar; fig: suggestion echar por tierra

◆ shoot off v/i (rush off) irse deprisa

◆ shoot up v/i of prices dispararse; of children crecer mucho; of new suburbs, buildings aparecer de repente; F of drug addict chutarse F

shoot·ing 'star ['ʃuːtɪŋ] estrella f fugaz

shop [ʃɑːp] 1 n tienda f; talk shop hablar del trabajo 2 v/i (pret & pp shopped) comprar; go shopping ir de compras

'shop·keep·er ['ʃɑːkiːpər] tendero(-a) m(f)

'shop·lift·er ['ʃɑːplɪftər] ladrón(-ona) m(f) (en tienda)

'shop·lift·ing ['ʃɑːplɪftɪŋ] n hurtos mpl (en tiendas)

'shop·per ['ʃɑːpər] person comprador(a) m(f)

shop·ping ['ʃɑːpɪŋ] items compra f; I hate shopping odio hacer la compra; do one's shopping hacer la compra

'shop·ping bag bolsa f de la compra

'shop·ping cen·ter, Br 'shop·ping cen·-tre centro m comercial

'shop·ping list lista f de la compra

'shop·ping mall centro m comercial

shop 'stew·ard representante m/f sindical

shop 'win·dow escaparate m, L.Am. vidriera f, Mex aparador m

shore [ʃɔːr] orilla f; on shore (not at sea) en tierra

short [ʃɔːrt] 1 adj corto; in height bajo; it's just a short walk está a poca distancia a pie; we're short of fuel nos queda poco combustible; he's not short of ideas no le faltan ideas; time is short hay poco tiempo 2 adv: cut short vacation, meeting interrumpir; stop a person short hacer pararse a una persona; go short of pasar sin; in short en resumen

short·age ['ʃɔːrtɪdʒ] escasez f, falta f

short 'cir·cuit n cortocircuito m

short·com·ing ['ʃɔːrtkʌmɪŋ] defecto m

'short cut atajo m

short·en ['ʃɔːrtn] v/t dress, hair, vacation acortar; chapter, article abreviar; work *day* reducir

short·en·ing ['ʃɔ:rtnɪŋ] *n* grasa utilizada para hacer masa de pastelería

'**short·fall** déficit *m*

'**short·hand** *n* taquigrafía *f*

short·hand·ed [ʃɔ:rt'hændɪd] *adj* falto de personal

short-lived ['ʃɔ:rtlɪvd] *adj* efímero

short·ly ['ʃɔ:rtlɪ] *adv* (*soon*) pronto; **shortly before / after** justo antes / después

short·ness ['ʃɔ:rtnɪs] *of visit* brevedad *f*; *in height* baja *f* estatura

shorts [ʃɔ:rts] *npl* pantalones *mpl* cortos, shorts *mpl; underwear* calzoncillos *mpl*

short-sight·ed [ʃɔ:rt'saɪtɪd] *adj* miope; *fig* corto de miras

short-sleeved ['ʃɔ:rtsli:vd] *adj* de manga corta

short-staffed [ʃɔ:rt'stæft] *adj* falto de personal

short 'sto·ry relato *m* or cuento corto

short-tem·pered [ʃɔ:rt'tempərd] *adj* Irascible

'**short-term** *adj* a corto plazo

'**short time:** *be on short time of workers* trabajar a jornada reducida

'**short wave** onda *f* corta

shot[1] [ʃɑ:t] *from gun* disparo *m;* (*photograph*) fotografía *f; (injection)* inyección *f; be a good / poor shot* tirar bien / mal; *he accepted like a shot* aceptó al instante; *he ran off like a shot* se fue como una bala

shot[2] [ʃɑ:t] *pret & pp* → **shoot**

'**shot·gun** escopeta *f*

should [ʃʊd] *v/aux: what should I do?* ¿qué debería hacer?; *you shouldn't do that* no deberías hacer eso; *that should be long enough* debería ser lo suficientemente largo; *you should have heard him!* ¡tendrías que haberle oído!

shoul·der ['ʃoʊldər] *n* ANAT hombro *m*

'**shoul·der bag** bolso *m* (de bandolera)

'**shoul·der blade** omóplato *m,* omoplato

'**shoul·der strap** *of brassiere, dress* tirante *m; of bag* correa *f*

shout [ʃaʊt] **1** *n* grito *m* **2** *v/t & v/i* gritar

◆ **shout at** *v/t* gritar a

shout·ing ['ʃaʊtɪŋ] *n* griterío *m*

shove [ʃʌv] **1** *n* empujón *m* **2** *v/t & v/i* empujar

◆ **shove in** *v/i in line* meterse empujando

◆ **shove off** *v/i* F (*go away*) largarse F

shov·el ['ʃʌvl] **1** *n* pala *f* **2** *v/t: shovel snow off the path* retirar a paladas la nieve del camino

show [ʃoʊ] **1** *n* THEA espectáculo *m;* TV programa *m; of emotion* muestra *f; on*

show at exhibition expuesto, en exposición **2** *v/t (pret* **showed,** *pp* **shown)** *passport, ticket* enseñar, mostrar; *interest, emotion* mostrar; *at exhibition* exponer; *movie* proyectar; **show s.o. sth, show sth to s.o.** enseñar *or* mostrar algo a alguien **3** *v/i (pret* **showed,** *pp* **shown)** (*be visible*) verse; *what's showing at ...? of movie* qué ponen en el ...?

◆ **show around** *v/t* enseñar; *he showed us around* nos enseñó la casa / el edificio *etc*

◆ **show in** *v/t* hacer pasar a

◆ **show off 1** *v/t skills* mostrar **2** *v/i pej* presumir, alardear

◆ **show up 1** *v/t shortcomings etc* poner de manifiesto; *don't show me up in public* (*embarrass*) no me avergüences en público **2** *v/i (be visible)* verse; F (*arrive, turn up*) aparecer

'**show busi·ness** el mundo del espectáculo

'**show·case** *n* vitrina *f; fig* escaparate *m*

'**show·down** enfrentamiento *m*

show·er ['ʃaʊər] **1** *n of rain* chaparrón *m,* chubasco *m; to wash* ducha *f,* Mex regadera *f; (party)* fiesta *f* con motivo de un bautizo, una boda etc., en la que los invitados llevan obsequios; **take a shower** ducharse **2** *v/i* ducharse **3** *v/t: shower s.o. with compliments / praise* colmar a alguien de cumplidos / alabanzas

'**show·er cap** gorro *m* de baño

'**show·er cur·tain** cortina *f* de ducha

'**show·er·proof** *adj* impermeable

'**show·jump·ing** concurso *m* de saltos

shown [ʃoʊn] *pp* → **show**

'**show-off** *n pej* fanfarrón (-ona) *m(f)*

'**show·room** sala *f* de exposición *f; in showroom condition* como nuevo

show·y ['ʃoʊɪ] *adj jacket, behavior* llamativo

shrank [ʃræŋk] *pret* → **shrink**[1]

shred [ʃred] **1** *n of paper etc* trozo *m; of fabric* jirón *m; there isn't a shred of evidence* no hay prueba alguna **2** *v/t (pret & pp* **shredded)** *paper* hacer trizas; *in cooking* cortar en tiras

shred·der ['ʃredər] *for documents* trituradora *f* (de documentos)

shrewd [ʃru:d] *adj person* astuto; *judgment, investment* inteligente

shrewd·ness ['ʃru:dnɪs] *of person* astucia *f; of decision* inteligencia *f*

shriek [ʃri:k] **1** *n* alarido *m,* chillido *m* **2** *v/i* chillar

shrill [ʃrɪl] *adj* estridente, agudo

shrimp [ʃrɪmp] gamba *f; larger Span* langostino *m,* L.Am. camarón *m*

S

shrine [ʃraɪn] santuario *m*

shrink[1] [ʃrɪŋk] *v/i* (*pret* **shrank**, *pp* **shrunk**) *of material* encoger(se); *level of support etc* reducirse

shrink[2] [ʃrɪŋk] *n* F (*psychiatrist*) psiquiatra *m/f*

'shrink-wrap *v/t* (*pret & pp* **shrink-wrapped**) envolver en plástico adherente

'shrink-wrap·ping *material plástico adherente para envolver*

shriv·el [ʃrɪvl] *v/i of skin* arrugarse; *of leaves* marchitarse

Shrove 'Tues·day [ʃrouv] martes *m inv* de Carnaval

shrub [ʃrʌb] arbusto *m*

shrub·be·ry [ʃrʌbərɪ] arbustos *mpl*

shrug [ʃrʌg] **1** *n*: ... **with a shrug** ... dijo encogiendo los hombros **2** *v/i* (*pret & pp* **shrugged**) encoger los hombros **3** *v/t* (*pret & pp* **shrugged**): **shrug one's shoulders** encoger los hombros

shrunk [ʃrʌŋk] *pp* → **shrink**[1]

shud·der [ʃʌdər] **1** *n of fear, disgust* escalofrío *m*; *of earth, building* temblor *m* **2** *v/i with fear, disgust* estremecerse; *of earth, building* temblar; **I shudder to think** me estremezco de pensar

shuf·fle [ʃʌfl] **1** *v/t cards* barajar **2** *v/i in walking* arrastrar los pies

shun [ʃʌn] *v/t* (*pret & pp* **shunned**) rechazar

shut [ʃʌt] *v/t & v/i* (*pret & pp* **shut**) cerrar
◆ **shut down 1** *v/t business* cerrar; *computer* apagar **2** *v/i of business* cerrarse; *of computer* apagarse
◆ **shut off** *v/t* cortar
◆ **shut up** *v/i* F (*be quiet*) callarse; **shut up!** ¡cállate!

shut·ter [ʃʌtər] *on window* contraventana *f*; PHOT obturador *m*

'shut·ter speed PHOT tiempo *m* de exposición

shut·tle [ʃʌtl] *v/i*: **shuttle between** *of bus* conectar; *of airplane* hacer el puente aéreo entre

'shut·tle-bus *at airport* autobús *m* de conexión

'shut·tle·cock SP volante *m*

'shut·tle ser·vice servicio *m* de conexión

shy [ʃaɪ] *adj* tímido

shy·ness [ʃaɪnɪs] timidez *f*

Si·a·mese 'twins [saɪəˈmiːz] *npl* siameses *mpl* (*fpl*)

sick [sɪk] *adj* enfermo; *sense of humor* morboso, macabro; *society* enfermo; **be sick of** (*fed up with*) estar harto de

sick·en [ˈsɪkn] **1** *v/t* (*disgust*) poner enfermo **2** *v/i*: **be sickening for sth** estar incubando algo

sick·en·ing [ˈsɪknɪŋ] *adj stench* nauseabundo; *behavior, crime* repugnante

'sick leave baja *f* (por enfermedad); **be on sick leave** estar de baja

sick·ly [ˈsɪklɪ] *adj person* enfermizo; *color* pálido

sick·ness [ˈsɪknɪs] enfermedad *f*; (*vomiting*) vómitos *mpl*

side [saɪd] *n of box, house, field* lado *m*; *of mountain* ladera *f*; vertiente *f*; *of person* costado *m*; SP equipo *m*; **take sides** (*favor one side*) tomar partido (**with** por); **I'm on your side** estoy de parte tuya; **side by side** uno al lado del otro; **at the side of the road** al lado de la carretera; **on the big / small side** un poco grande / pequeño
◆ **side with** *v/t* tomar partido por

'side·board aparador *m*

'side·burns *npl* patillas *fpl*

'side dish plato *m* de acompañamiento

'side ef·fect efecto *m* secundario

'side·light MOT luz *f* de posición

'side·line 1 actividad *f* complementaria **2** *v/t*: **feel sidelined** sentirse marginado

'side·step *v/t* (*pret & pp* **sidestepped**) *fig* evadir

'side street bocacalle *f*

'side·track *v/t* distraer; **get sidetracked** distraerse

'side·walk acera *f*, *Rpl* vereda *f*, *Mex* banqueta *f*

side·walk 'ca·fé terraza *f*

side·ways [ˈsaɪdweɪz] *adv* de lado

siege [siːdʒ] sitio *m*; **lay siege to** sitiar

sieve [sɪv] *n* tamiz *m*

sift [sɪft] *v/t flour* tamizar; *data* examinar a fondo
◆ **sift through** *v/t details, data* pasar por el tamiz

sigh [saɪ] **1** *n* suspiro *m*; **heave a sigh of relief** suspirar de alivio **2** *v/i* suspirar

sight [saɪt] *n* vista *f*; (*power of seeing*) vista *f*, visión *f*; **sights** *of city* lugares *mpl* de interés; **he can't stand the sight of blood** no aguanta ver sangre; **I caught sight of him just as ...** lo vi justo cuando ...; **know by sight** conocer de vista; **within sight of** a la vista de; **as soon as the car was out of sight** en cuanto se dejó de ver el coche; **what a sight you look!** ¡qué pintas llevas!; **lose sight of** *objective* olvidarse de

sight·see·ing [ˈsaɪtsiːɪŋ] *n*: **we like sightseeing** nos gusta hacer turismo; **go sightseeing** hacer turismo

'sight·see·ing tour visita *f* turística

sight·seer [ˈsaɪtsiːər] turista *m/f*

sign [saɪn] **1** *n* señal *f*; *outside shop, on*

building cartel m, letrero m; **it's a sign of
the times** es un signo de los tiempos que
corren **2** v/t & v/i firmar
◆ **sign in** v/i registrarse
◆ **sign up** v/i (join the army) alistarse
sig·nal ['sɪɡnl] **1** n señal f; **send out all
the wrong signals** dar a una impresión
equivocada **2** v/i of driver poner el intermitente
sig·na·to·ry ['sɪɡnətɔːrɪ] n signatario(-a)
m(f), firmante m/f
sig·na·ture ['sɪɡnətʃər] n firma f
sig·na·ture 'tune sintonía f
sig·net ring ['sɪɡnɪt] sello m (anillo)
sig·nif·i·cance [sɪɡ'nɪfɪkəns] importancia f, relevancia f
sig·nif·i·cant [sɪɡ'nɪfɪkənt] adj event etc
importante, relevante; (quite large) considerable
sig·nif·i·cant·ly [sɪɡ'nɪfɪkəntlɪ] adv larger,
more expensive considerablemente
sig·ni·fy ['sɪɡnɪfaɪ] v/t (pret & pp **signi-
fied**) significar, suponer
'**sign lan·guage** lenguaje m por señas
'**sign·post** señal f
si·lence ['saɪləns] **1** n silencio m; **in silence** work, march en silencio; **silence!** ¡silencio! **2** v/t hacer callar
si·lenc·er ['saɪlənsər] on gun silenciador
m
si·lent ['saɪlənt] adj silencioso; movie mudo; **stay silent** (not comment) permanecer callado
sil·hou·ette [sɪluː'et] n silueta f
sil·i·con ['sɪlɪkən] silicio m
sil·i·con 'chip chip m de silicio
sil·i·cone ['sɪlɪkəʊn] silicona f
silk [sɪlk] **1** n seda f **2** adj shirt etc de seda
silk·y ['sɪlkɪ] adj hair, texture sedoso
sil·li·ness ['sɪlɪnɪs] tontería f, estupidez f
sil·ly ['sɪlɪ] adj tonto, estúpido
si·lo ['saɪləʊ] silo m
sil·ver ['sɪlvər] **1** n metal, medal plata f;
(silver objects) (objetos mpl de) plata f
2 adj ring de plata; hair canoso
sil·ver·plat·ed [sɪlvər'pleɪtɪd] adj plateado
sil·ver·ware ['sɪlvərwer] plata f
sil·ver 'wed·ding bodas fpl de plata
sim·i·lar ['sɪmɪlər] adj parecido, similar;
be similar to ser parecido a, parecerse a
sim·i·lar·i·ty [sɪmɪ'lærətɪ] parecido m,
similitud f
sim·i·lar·ly ['sɪmɪlərlɪ] adv de la misma
manera
sim·mer ['sɪmər] v/i in cooking cocer a
fuego lento; **be simmering (with rage)**
estar a punto de explotar
◆ **simmer down** v/i tranquilizarse

sim·ple ['sɪmpl] adj (easy, not fancy) sencillo; person simple
sim·ple-mind·ed [sɪmpl'maɪndɪd] adj pej
simplón
sim·plic·i·ty [sɪm'plɪsətɪ] of task, design
sencillez f, simplicidad f
sim·pli·fy ['sɪmplɪfaɪ] v/t (pret & pp **simplified**) simplificar
sim·plis·tic [sɪm'plɪstɪk] adj simplista
sim·ply ['sɪmplɪ] adv sencillamente; **it is
simply the best** es sin lugar a dudas el
mejor
sim·u·late ['sɪmjuleɪt] v/t simular
si·mul·ta·ne·ous [saɪml'teɪnɪəs] adj simultáneo
si·mul·ta·ne·ous·ly [saɪml'teɪnɪəslɪ] adv
simultáneamente
sin [sɪn] **1** n pecado m **2** v/i (pret & pp
sinned) pecar
since [sɪns] **1** prep desde; **since last
week** desde la semana pasada **2** adv
desde entonces; **I haven't seen him since** no lo he visto desde entonces **3** conj in
expressions of time desde que; (seeing
that) ya que, dado que; **since you left**
desde que te marchaste; **since I have
been living here** desde que vivo aquí;
since you don't like it ya que or dado
que no te gusta
sin·cere [sɪn'sɪr] adj sincero
sin·cere·ly [sɪn'sɪrlɪ] adv sinceramente; **I
sincerely hope he appreciates it** espero
de verdad que lo aprecie; **Yours sincerely** atentamente
sin·cer·i·ty [sɪn'serətɪ] sinceridad f
sin·ful ['sɪnfəl] adj person pecador; things
pecaminoso; **it is sinful to ...** es pecado
...
sing [sɪŋ] v/t & v/i (pret **sang**, pp **sung**)
cantar
singe [sɪndʒ] v/t chamuscar
sing·er ['sɪŋər] cantante m/f
sin·gle ['sɪŋɡl] **1** adj (sole) único, solo;
(not double) único; (not married) soltero
m; **there wasn't a single mistake** no
había ni un solo error; **in single file**
en fila india; **single currency** moneda
única **2** n MUS sencillo m; (single room)
habitación f individual; person solte-
ro(-a) m(f); Br ticket billete m or
L.Am. boleto m de ida; **holidays for singles** vacaciones para gente sin pareja;
singles in tennis individuales mpl
◆ **single out** v/t (choose) seleccionar;
(distinguish) distinguir
sin·gle-breast·ed [sɪŋɡl'brestɪd] adj recto, con una fila de botones
sin·gle-'hand·ed [sɪŋɡl'hændɪd] **1** adj en
solitario **2** adv en solitario

sin·gle-mind·ed [sɪŋgl'maɪndɪd] *adj* determinado, resuelto

Sin·gle 'Mar·ket Mercado *m* Único

sin·gle 'moth·er madre *f* soltera

sin·gle 'pa·rent padre *m*/madre *f* soltero(-a)

single pa·rent 'fam·i·ly familia *f* monoparental

sin·gle 'room habitación *f* individual

sin·gu·lar ['sɪŋgjʊlər] **1** *adj* GRAM singular **2** *n* GRAM singular *m*; *in the singular* en singular

sin·is·ter ['sɪnɪstər] *adj* siniestro; *sky* amenazador

sink [sɪŋk] **1** *n in kitchen* fregadero *m*; *in bathroom* lavabo *m* **2** *v/i (pret sank, pp sunk) of ship, object* hundirse; *of sun* ponerse; *of interest rates, pressure etc* descender, bajar; *he sank onto the bed* se tiró a la cama **3** *v/t (pret sank, pp sunk) ship* hundir; *funds* investir

♦ **sink in** *v/i of liquid* penetrar; *it still hasn't really sunk in of realization* todavía no lo he asumido

sin·ner ['sɪnər] pecador(a) *m(f)*

si·nus ['saɪnəs] seno *m (nasal)*

si·nus·i·tis [saɪnə'saɪtɪs] MED sinusitis *f*

sip [sɪp] **1** *n* sorbo *m* **2** *v/t (pret & pp sipped)* sorber

sir [sɜːr] señor *m*; *excuse me, sir* perdone, caballero

si·ren ['saɪrən] sirena *f*

sir·loin ['sɜːrlɔɪn] solomillo *m*

sis·ter ['sɪstər] hermana *f*

sis·ter-in-law (*pl sisters-in-law*) cuñada *f*

sit [sɪt] **1** *v/i (pret & pp sat)* estar sentado; *(sit down)* sentarse **2** *v/t (pret & pp sat) exam* presentarse a

♦ **sit down** *v/i* sentarse

♦ **sit up** *v/i in bed* incorporarse; *(straighten back)* sentarse derecho; *(wait up at night)* esperar levantado

sit·com ['sɪtkɑːm] telecomedia *f*, comedia *f* de situación

site [saɪt] **1** *n* emplazamiento *m*; *of battle* lugar *m* **2** *v/t new offices etc* situar

sit·ting ['sɪtɪŋ] *of committee, court, for artist* sesión *f*; *for meals* turno *m*

'sit·ting room sala *f* de estar, salón *m*

sit·u·at·ed ['sɪtʊeɪtɪd] *adj* situado

sit·u·a·tion [sɪtʊ'eɪʃn] situación *f*

six [sɪks] seis

six·teen [sɪks'tiːn] dieciséis

six·teenth [sɪks'tiːnθ] *n & adj* decimosexto

sixth [sɪksθ] *n & adj* sexto

six·ti·eth ['sɪkstɪɪθ] *n & adj* sexagésimo

six·ty ['sɪkstɪ] sesenta

size [saɪz] tamaño *m*; *of loan* importe *m*; *of jacket* talla *f*; *of shoes* número *m*

♦ **size up** *v/t* evaluar, examinar

size·a·ble ['saɪzəbl] *adj house, order* considerable; *meal* copioso

siz·zle ['sɪzl] *v/i* chisporrotear

skate [skeɪt] **1** *n* patín *m* **2** *v/i* patinar

skate·board ['skeɪtbɔːrd] *n* monopatín *m*

skate·board·er ['skeɪtbɔːrdər] *persona que patina en monopatín*

skate·board·ing ['skeɪtbɔːrdɪŋ] patinaje *m* en monopatín

skat·er ['skeɪtər] patinador(a) *m(f)*

skat·ing ['skeɪtɪŋ] *n* patinaje *m*

'skat·ing rink pista *f* de patinaje

skel·e·ton ['skelɪtn] esqueleto *m*

'skel·e·ton key llave *f* maestra

skep·tic ['skeptɪk] escéptico(-a) *m(f)*

skep·ti·cal ['skeptɪkl] *adj* escéptico

skep·ti·cism ['skeptɪsɪzm] escepticismo *m*

sketch [sketʃ] **1** *n* boceto *m*, esbozo *m*; THEA sketch *m* **2** *v/t* bosquejar

'sketch·book cuaderno *m* de dibujo

sketch·y ['sketʃɪ] *adj knowledge etc* básico, superficial

skew·er ['skjʊər] *n* brocheta *f*

ski [skiː] **1** *n* esquí *m* **2** *v/i* esquiar

'ski boots *npl* botas *fpl* de esquí

skid [skɪd] **1** *n of car* patinazo *m*; *of person* resbalón *m* **2** *v/i (pret & pp skidded) of car* patinar; *of person* resbalar

ski·er ['skiːər] esquiador(a) *m(f)*

ski·ing ['skiːɪŋ] esquí *m*

'ski in·struc·tor monitor(a) *m(f)* de esquí

skil·ful *etc Br → skillful etc*

'ski lift remonte *m*

skill [skɪl] destreza *f*, habilidad *f*

skilled [skɪld] *adj* capacitado, preparado

skilled 'work·er trabajador(a) *m(f)* cualificado

'skill·ful ['skɪlfəl] *adj* hábil, habilidoso

skill·ful·ly ['skɪlfəlɪ] *adv* con habilidad *or* destreza

skim [skɪm] *v/t (pret & pp skimmed) surface* rozar; *milk* desnatar, descremar

♦ **skim off** *v/t the best* escoger

♦ **skim through** *v/t text* leer por encima

skimmed 'milk [skɪmd] leche *f* desnatada *or* descremada

skimp·y ['skɪmpɪ] *adj account etc* superficial; *dress* cortísimo; *bikini* mínimo

skin [skɪn] **1** *n* piel *f* **2** *v/t (pret & pp skinned)* despellejar, desollar

'skin div·ing buceo *m* (*en bañador*)

skin·flint ['skɪnflɪnt] F agarrado(a) *m(f)* F, roñoso(-a) *m(f)*

'skin graft injerto *m* de piel

skin·ny ['skɪnɪ] *adj* escuálido

'skin-tight adj ajustado

skip [skɪp] 1 n (little jump) brinco m, saltito m 2 v/i (pret & pp **skipped**) brincar 3 v/t (pret & pp **skipped**) (omit) pasar por alto

'ski pole bastón m de esquí

skip-per ['skɪpər] NAUT patrón(-ona) m(f), capitán (-ana) m(f); of team capitán(-ana) m(f)

'ski re-sort estación f de esquí

skirt [skɜːrt] n falda f

'ski run pista f de esquí

'ski tow telesquí m

skull [skʌl] n cráneo m

skunk [skʌŋk] n mofeta f

sky [skaɪ] cielo m

'sky-light claraboya f

'sky-line horizonte m

'sky-scrap-er ['skaɪskreɪpər] rascacielos m inv

slab [slæb] of stone losa f; of cake etc trozo m grande

slack [slæk] adj rope flojo; work descuidado; period tranquilo; **discipline is very slack** no hay disciplina

slack-en ['slækn] v/t rope, pace aflojar; pace

♦ slacken off v/i of trading, pace disminuir

slacks [slæks] npl pantalones mpl

slain [sleɪn] pp → slay

slam [slæm] 1 v/t (pret & pp **slammed**) door cerrar de un golpe 2 v/i (pret & pp **slammed**) of door cerrarse de golpe

♦ slam down v/t estampar

slan-der ['slændər] 1 n difamación f 2 v/t difamar

slan-der-ous ['slændərəs] adj difamatorio

slang [slæŋ] argot m, jerga f; of a specific group jerga f

slant [slænt] 1 v/i inclinarse 2 n inclinación f; given to a story enfoque m

slant-ing ['slæntɪŋ] adj roof inclinado; eyes rasgado

slap [slæp] 1 n (blow) bofetada f, cachete m 2 v/t (pret & pp **slapped**) dar una bofetada or un cachete a; **slap s.o. in the face** dar una bofetada a alguien

'slap-dash adj chapucero

slash [slæʃ] 1 n (cut) corte m, raja f; in punctuation barra f 2 v/t skin etc cortar; prices, costs recortar drásticamente; **slash one's wrists** cortarse las venas

slate [sleɪt] n pizarra f

slaugh-ter ['slɔːtər] 1 n of animals sacrificio m; of people, troops matanza f 2 v/t animals sacrificar; people, troops masacrar

'slaugh-ter-house for animals matadero m

Slav [slɑːv] adj eslavo

slave [sleɪv] n esclavo(-a) m(f)

'slave-driv-er F negrero(-a) m(f) F

slay [sleɪ] v/t (pret slew, pp slain) asesinar

slay-ing ['sleɪɪŋ] (murder) asesinato m

sleaze [sliːz] POL corrupción f

slea-zy ['sliːzɪ] adj bar sórdido; person de mala calaña

sled, sledge [sled, sledʒ] n trineo m

'sledge ham-mer mazo m

sleep [sliːp] 1 n sueño m; **go to sleep** dormirse; **I need a good sleep** necesito dormir bien; **I couldn't get to sleep** no pude dormirme 2 v/i (pret & pp **slept**) dormir

♦ sleep in v/i (have a long lie) dormir hasta tarde

♦ sleep on v/t; **sleep on sth** decision consultar algo con la almohada

♦ sleep with v/t (have sex with) acostarse con

sleep-i-ly ['sliːpɪlɪ] adv: **say sth sleepily** decir algo medio dormido

'sleep-ing bag ['sliːpɪŋ] saco m de dormir

'sleep-ing car RAIL coche m cama

'sleep-ing pill somnífero m, pastilla f para dormir

sleep-less ['sliːplɪs] adj: **have a sleepless night** pasar la noche en blanco

'sleep-walk-er sonámbulo(-a) m(f)

'sleep-walk-ing sonambulismo m

sleep-y ['sliːpɪ] adj adormilado, somnoliento; town tranquilo; **I'm sleepy** tengo sueño

sleet [sliːt] n aguanieve f

sleeve [sliːv] of jacket etc manga f

sleeve-less ['sliːvlɪs] adj sin mangas

sleigh [sleɪ] n trineo m

sleight of 'hand [slaɪt] juegos mpl de manos

slen-der ['slendər] adj figure, arms esbelto; income, margin escaso; chance remoto

slept [slept] pret & pp → sleep

slew [sluː] pret → slay

slice [slaɪs] 1 n of bread rebanada f; of cake trozo m; of salami, cheese loncha f; fig: of profits etc parte f 2 v/t loaf etc cortar (en rebanadas)

sliced 'bread [slaɪst] pan m de molde en rebanadas; **the greatest thing since sliced bread** F lo mejor desde que se inventó la rueda F

slick [slɪk] 1 adj performance muy logrado; (pej: cunning) con mucha labia 2 n of oil marea f negra

slid [slɪd] pret & pp → slide

slide [slaɪd] 1 n for kids tobogán m; PHOT

diapositiva f 2 v/i (pret & pp **slid**) deslizarse; of exchange rate etc descender 3 v/t (pret & pp **slid**) deslizar

slid·ing 'door ['slaɪdɪŋ] puerta f corredera

slight [slaɪt] 1 adj person, figure menudo; (small) pequeño; accent ligero; **I have a slight headache** me duele un poco la cabeza; **no, not in the slightest** no, en absoluto

slight·ly ['slaɪtlɪ] adv un poco

slim [slɪm] 1 adj delgado; chance remoto 2 v/i (pret & pp **slimmed**): **I'm slimming** estoy a dieta

slime [slaɪm] (mud) lodo m; of slug etc baba f

slim·y ['slaɪmɪ] adj liquid viscoso; river bed lleno de lodo

sling [slɪŋ] 1 n for arm cabestrillo m 2 v/t (pret & pp **slung**) tirar

slip [slɪp] 1 n on ice etc resbalón m; (mistake) desliz m; **a slip of paper** un trozo de papel; **a slip of the tongue** un lapsus; **give s.o. the slip** dar esquinazo a alguien 2 v/i (pret & pp **slipped**) on ice etc resbalar; of quality etc empeorar; **he slipped out of the room** se fue de la habitación sigilosamente 3 v/t (pret & pp **slipped**) (put): **he slipped it into his briefcase** lo metió en su maletín sigilosamente; **it slipped my mind** se me olvidó

◆ **slip away** v/i of time pasar; of opportunity esfumarse; (die quietly) morir tranquilamente

◆ **slip off** v/t jacket etc quitarse

◆ **slip on** v/t jacket etc ponerse

◆ **slip out** v/i (go out) salir (sigilosamente)

◆ **slip up** v/i equivocarse

slipped 'disc [slɪpt] hernia f discal

slip·per ['slɪpər] zapatilla f (de estar por casa)

slip·per·y ['slɪpərɪ] adj surface, road resbaladizo; fish escurridizo

slip·shod ['slɪpʃɑːd] adj chapucero

'slip-up (mistake) error m

slit [slɪt] 1 n (tear) raja f; (hole) rendija f; in skirt corte m 2 v/t (pret & pp **slit**) abrir; **slit s.o.'s throat** degollar a alguien

slith·er ['slɪðər] v/i deslizarse

sliv·er ['slɪvər] trocito m; of wood, glass astilla f

slob [slɑːb] pej dejado(-a) m/f, guarro(-a) m/f

slob·ber ['slɑːbər] v/i babear

slog [slɑːɡ] n paliza f

slo·gan ['sloʊɡən] eslogan m

slop [slɑːp] v/t (pret & pp **slopped**) der-

ramar

slope [sloʊp] 1 n of roof, handwriting inclinación f; of mountain ladera f; **built on a slope** construir en una pendiente 2 v/i inclinarse; **the road slopes down to the sea** la carretera baja hasta el mar

slop·py ['slɑːpɪ] adj descuidado; too sentimental sensiblero

slot [slɑːt] 1 n ranura f; in schedule hueco m

◆ **slot in** 1 v/t (pret & pp **slotted**) introducir 2 v/i (pret & pp **slotted**) encajar

'slot ma·chine for cigarettes, food máquina f expendedora; for gambling máquina f tragaperras

slouch [slaʊtʃ] v/i: **don't slouch** ponte derecho

slov·en·ly ['slʌvnlɪ] adj descuidado

slow [sloʊ] adj lento; **be slow** of clock ir retrasado

◆ **slow down** 1 v/t work, progress restrasar; traffic, production ralentizar 2 v/i in walking, driving reducir la velocidad; of production etc relantizarse; **you need to slow down** in lifestyle tienes que tomarte las cosas con calma

'slow-down in production ralentización f

slow·ly ['sloʊlɪ] adv despacio, lentamente

slow 'mo·tion: in slow motion a cámara lenta

slow·ness ['sloʊnɪs] lentitud f

'slow·poke F tortuga f F

slug [slʌɡ] n animal babosa f

slug·gish ['slʌɡɪʃ] adj lento

slum [slʌm] n suburbio m, arrabal

slump [slʌmp] 1 n in trade desplome m 2 v/i economically desplomarse, hundirse; (collapse: of person) desplomarse

slung [slʌŋ] pret & pp → **sling**

slur [slɜːr] 1 n on s.o.'s character difamación f 2 v/t (pret & pp **slurred**) words arrastrar

slurred [slɜːrd] adj: **his speech was slurred** habló arrastrando las palabras

slurp [slɜːrp] v/t sorber

slush [slʌʃ] nieve f derretida; (pej: sentimental stuff) sensiblería f

'slush fund fondo m para corruptelas

slush·y ['slʌʃɪ] adj snow derretido; movie, novel sensiblero

slut [slʌt] pej fulana f

sly [slaɪ] adj ladino; **on the sly** a escondidas

smack [smæk] 1 n: **a smack on the bottom** un azote; **a smack in the face** una bofetada 2 v/t child pegar; bottom dar un azote en

small [smɔːl] adj pequeño, L.Am. chico

small 'change cambio m, suelto m,

L.Am. sencillo *m*

small 'hours *npl* madrugada *f*

small-pox ['smɔːlpɑːks] viruela *f*

'small print letra *f* pequeña

'small talk: make small talk hablar de banalidades *or* trivialidades

smart [smɑːrt] **1** *adj* (*elegant*) elegante; (*intelligent*) inteligente; *pace* rápido; **get smart with** hacerse el listillo con **2** *v/i* (*hurt*) escocer

'smart ass F sabelotodo *m/f* F

'smart card tarjeta *f* inteligente

◆ **smart-en up** *v/t: smart-en up* ['smɑːrtn] *v/t appearance* mejorar; *room* arreglar

smart-ly ['smɑːrtlɪ] *adv dressed* con elegancia

smash [smæʃ] **1** *n noise* estruendo *m*; (*car crash*) choque *m*; *in tennis* smash *m*, mate *m* **2** *v/t break* hacer pedazos *or* añicos; **he smashed the toys against the wall** estrelló los juguetes contra la pared; **he smashed his fist on the table** dio un puñetazo en la mesa; **smash oth to pieces** hacer algo añicos **3** *v/i break* romperse; **the driver smashed into ...** el conductor se estrelló contra ...

◆ **smash up** *v/t place* destrozar

smash 'hit F exitazo *m* F

smat-ter-ing ['smætərɪŋ] *of a language* nociones *fpl*

smear [smɪr] **1** *n of ink* borrón *m*; *of paint* mancha *f*; MED citología *f*; *on character* difamación *f* **2** *v/t character* difamar; **smear X over Y** untar *or* embadurnar Y de X

'smear cam-paign campaña *f* de difamación

smell [smel] **1** *n* olor *m*; **it has no smell** no huele a nada; **sense of smell** sentido *m* del olfato **2** *v/t* oler **3** *v/i unpleasantly* oler (mal); (*sniff*) olfatear; **you smell of beer** hueles a cerveza; **it smells good** huele bien

smell-y ['smelɪ] *adj* apestoso; **she had smelly feet** le olían los pies; **it's so smelly in here!** ¡qué mal huele aquí!

smile [smaɪl] **1** *n* sonrisa *f* **2** *v/i* sonreír

◆ **smile at** *v/t* sonreír a

smirk [smɜːrk] **1** *n* sonrisa *f* maligna **2** *v/i* sonreír malignamente

smog [smɑːg] niebla *f* tóxica

smoke [smoʊk] **1** *n* humo *m*; **have a smoke** fumarse un cigarrillo **2** *v/t cigarettes* fumar; *bacon* ahumar **3** *v/i of person* fumar

smok-er ['smoʊkər] *person* fumador(a) *m(a)*

smok-ing ['smoʊkɪŋ]: **smoking is bad for you** fumar es malo; **no smoking sign** prohibido fumar

'smok-ing com-part-ment RAIL compartimento *m* de fumadores

smok-y ['smoʊkɪ] *adj room, air* lleno de humo

smooth [smuːð] **1** *adj surface, skin* liso, suave; *sea* en calma; (*peaceful*) tranquilo; *ride, drive* sin vibraciones; *transition* sin problemas; *pej: person* meloso **2** *v/t hair* alisar

◆ **smooth down** *v/t with sandpaper etc* alisar

◆ **smooth out** *v/t paper, cloth* alisar

◆ **smooth over** *v/t: smooth things over* suavizar las cosas

smooth-ly ['smuːðlɪ] *adv without any problems* sin incidentes

smoth-er ['smʌðər] *v/t flames* apagar, sofocar; *person* asfixiar; **smother s.o. with kisses** comerse a alguien a besos; **he smothered the bread with jam** cubrió *or* embadurnó el pan de mermelada

smoul-der, *Br* **smoul-der** ['smoʊldər] *v/i of fire* arder (*los rescoldos*); *fig: with anger* arder de rabia; *fig: with desire* arder en deseos

smudge [smʌdʒ] **1** *n of paint* mancha *f*; *of ink* borrón *m* **2** *v/t ink* emborronar; *paint* difuminar

smug [smʌg] *adj* engreído

smug-gle ['smʌgl] *v/t* pasar de contrabando

smug-gler ['smʌglər] contrabandista *m/f*

smug-gling ['smʌglɪŋ] contrabando *m*

smug-ly ['smʌglɪ] *adv* con engreimiento *or* suficiencia

smut-ty ['smʌtɪ] *adj joke, sense of humor* obsceno

snack [snæk] *n* tentempié *m*, aperitivo *m*

'snack bar cafetería *f*

snag [snæg] *n* (*problem*) inconveniente *m*, pega *f*

snail [sneɪl] caracol *m*

snake [sneɪk] *n* serpiente *f*

snap [snæp] **1** *n* chasquido *m*; PHOT foto *f* **2** *v/t* (*pret & pp* **snapped**) *break* romper **3** *v/i* (*pret & pp* **snapped**) *break* romperse; (*none of your business, she snapped* no es asunto tuyo, saltó **4** *adj decision, judgment* rápido, súbito

◆ **snap up** *v/t bargains* llevarse

snap fast-en-er ['snæpfæsnər] automático *m*, corchete *m*

snap-py ['snæpɪ] *adj person, mood* irascible; *decision, response* rápido; (*elegant*) elegante

'snap-shot foto *f*

snarl [snɑːrl] **1** *n of dog* gruñido *m* **2** *v/i* gruñir

S

snatch [snætʃ] **1** v/t arrebatar; (*steal*) robar; (*kidnap*) secuestrar; **snatch sth from s.o.** arrebatar algo a alguien **2** v/i: *don't snatch* no lo agarres
◆ **snatch at** v/t intentar agarrar

snaz·zy ['snæzɪ] adj F vistoso, *Span* chulo F

sneak [sni:k] **1** n (*telltale*) chivato(-a) m(f) **2** v/t (*remove, steal*) llevarse; **sneak a glance at** mirar con disimulo a **3** v/i (*tell tales*) chivarse; **sneak into the room** entrar a la habitación a hurtadillas

sneak·ers ['sni:kərz] npl zapatillas fpl de deporte

sneak·ing ['sni:kɪŋ] adj: **have a sneaking suspicion that ...** sospechar que ...

sneak·y ['sni:kɪ] adj F (*crafty*) ladino, cuco F

sneer [snɪr] **1** n mueca f desdeñosa **2** v/i burlarse (*at* de)

sneeze [sni:z] **1** n estornudo m **2** v/i estornudar

snick·er ['snɪkər] **1** n risita f **2** v/i reírse (*en voz baja*)

sniff [snɪf] **1** v/i to clear nose sorberse los mocos; *of dog* olfatear **2** v/t (*smell*) oler; *of dog* olfatear

snip [snɪp] n F (*bargain*) ganga f

snip·er ['snaɪpər] francotirador(a) m(f)

sniv·el ['snɪvl] v/i gimotear

snob [snɑb] presuntuoso(-a) m(f)

snob·ber·y ['snɑbərɪ] presuntuosidad f

snob·bish ['snɑbɪʃ] adj presuntuoso

snoop [snu:p] n fisgón(-ona) m(f)
◆ **snoop around** v/i fisgonear

snoot·y ['snu:tɪ] adj presuntuoso

snooze [snu:z] **1** n cabezada f; **have a snooze** echar una cabezada **2** v/i echar una cabezada

snore [snɔ:r] v/i roncar

snor·ing ['snɔ:rɪŋ] n ronquidos mpl

snor·kel ['snɔ:rkl] n snorkel m, tubo m para buceo

snort [snɔ:rt] v/i of bull, person bufar, resoplar

snout [snaʊt] of pig, dog hocico m

snow [snoʊ] **1** n nieve f **2** v/i nevar
◆ **snow under** v/i: **be snowed under** estar desbordado

'**snow·ball** bola f de nieve

'**snow·bound** adj aislado por la nieve

'**snow chains** npl MOT cadenas fpl para la nieve

'**snow·drift** nevero m

'**snow·drop** campanilla f de invierno

'**snow·flake** copo m de nieve

'**snow·man** muñeco m de nieve

'**snow·plow** quitanieves m inv

'**snow·storm** tormenta f de nieve

snow·y ['snoʊɪ] adj weather de nieve; roads, hills nevado

snub [snʌb] **1** n desaire m **2** v/t (*pret & pp* **snubbed**) desairar

snub-nosed ['snʌbnoʊzd] adj con la nariz respingona

snug [snʌg] adj (*tight-fitting*) ajustado; *we are nice and snug in here* aquí se está muy a gusto
◆ **snug·gle down** ['snʌgl] v/i acurrucarse
◆ **snug·gle up to** v/t acurrucarse contra

so [soʊ] **1** adv tan; *it was so easy* fue tan fácil; *I'm so cold* tengo tanto frío; *that was so kind of you* fue muy amable de tu parte; *not so much* no tanto; *so much easier* mucho más fácil; *you shouldn't eat / drink so much* no deberías comer / beber tanto; *I miss you so* te echo tanto de menos; *so am / do I* yo también; *so is she / does she* ella también; *and so on* etcétera **2** pron: *I hope / think so* eso espero / creo; *you didn't tell me - I did so* no me lo dijiste - sí que lo hice; *50 or so* unos 50 **3** conj for that reason así que; *in order that* para que; *I got up late and so I missed the train* me levanté tarde y por eso perdí el tren; *so (that) I could come too* para que yo también pudiera venir; *so what?* F ¿y qué? F

soak [soʊk] v/t (*steep*) poner en remojo; of water, rain empapar
◆ **soak up** v/t liquid absorber; **soak up the sun** tostarse al sol

soaked [soʊkt] adj empapado; **be soaked to the skin** estar calado hasta los huesos

soak·ing (wet) ['soʊkɪŋ] adj empapado

so-and-so ['soʊənsoʊ] F (*unknown person*) fulanito m; (*euph: annoying person*) canalla m/f

soap [soʊp] for washing jabón m

'**soap (op·e·ra)** telenovela f

soap·y ['soʊpɪ] adj water jabonoso

soar [sɔ:r] v/i of rocket etc elevarse; of prices dispararse

sob [sɑb] **1** n sollozo m **2** v/i (*pret & pp* **sobbed**) sollozar

so·ber ['soʊbər] adj (*not drunk*) sobrio; (*serious*) serio
◆ **sober up** v/i: **he sobered up** se le pasó la borrachera

so-'called adj (*referred to as*) así llamado; (*incorrectly referred to as*) mal llamado

soc·cer ['sɑːkər] fútbol m

'**soc·cer hoo·li·gan** hincha m violento

so·cia·ble ['soʊʃəbl] adj sociable

so·cial ['soʊʃl] adj social

so·cial 'dem·o·crat socialdemócrata m/f

so·cial·ism ['souʃəlɪzm] socialismo *m*

so·cial·ist ['souʃəlɪst] **1** *adj* socialista **2** *n* socialista *m/f*

so·cial·ize ['souʃəlaɪz] *v/i* socializar (**with** con)

'**soc·ial life** vida *f* social

'so·cial 'sci·ence ciencia *f* social

'**so·cial work** trabajo *m* social

'**so·cial work·er** asistente(-a) *m(f)* social

so·ci·e·ty [sə'saɪətɪ] sociedad *f*

so·ci·ol·o·gist [sousɪ'ɑːlədʒɪst] sociólogo(-a) *m(f)*

so·ci·ol·o·gy [sousɪ'ɑːlədʒɪ] sociología *f*

sock[1] [sɑːk] *for wearing* calcetín *m*

sock[2] [sɑːk] **1** *n (punch)* puñetazo *m* **2** *v/t (punch)* dar un puñetazo a

sock·et ['sɑːkɪt] *for light bulb* casquillo *m; of arm* cavidad *f; of eye* cuenca *f; Br electric* enchufe *m*

so·da ['soudə] *(soda water)* soda *f; (ice--cream soda)* refresco *m* de soda con helado

sod·den ['sɑːdn] *adj* empapado

so·fa ['soufə] sofá *m*

'**so·fa-bed** sofá cama *m*

soft [sɑːft] *adj voice, light, color, skin* suave; *pillow, attitude* blando; **have a soft spot for** tener una debilidad por

'**soft drink** refresco *m*

'**soft drug** droga *f* blanda

soft·en ['sɑːfn] **1** *v/t position* ablandar; *impact, blow* amortiguar **2** *v/i of butter, ice cream* ablandarse, reblandecerse

soft·ly ['sɑːftlɪ] *adv* suavemente

soft 'toy peluche *m*

soft·ware ['sɑːftwer] software *m*

sog·gy ['sɑːgɪ] *adj* empapado

soil[1] [sɔɪl] **1** *n (earth)* tierra *f* **2** *v/t* ensuciar

soil[2] [sɔɪl] *v/t* ensuciar

so·lar 'en·er·gy ['soulər] energía *f* solar

'**so·lar pan·el** panel *m* solar

'**so·lar sys·tem** sistema *m* solar

sold [sould] *pret & pp* → **sell**

sol·dier ['souldʒər] soldado *m*

◆ **soldier on** *v/i* seguir adelante; **we'll have to soldier on without her** nos las tendremos que arreglar sin ella

sole[1] [soul] *n of foot* planta *f; of shoe* suela *f*

sole[2] [soul] *adj* único

sole·ly ['soullɪ] *adv* únicamente

sol·emn ['sɑːləm] *adj* solemne

so·lem·ni·ty [sə'lemnətɪ] solemnidad *f*

sol·emn·ly ['sɑːləmlɪ] *adv* solemnemente

so·lic·it [sə'lɪsɪt] *v/i of prostitute* abordar clientes

so·lic·i·tor [sə'lɪsɪtər] *Br* abogado(-a) *m(f) (que no aparece en tribunales)*

sol·id ['sɑːlɪd] *adj* sólido; *(without holes)* compacto; *gold, silver* macizo; **a solid hour** una hora seguida

sol·i·dar·i·ty [sɑːlɪ'dærətɪ] solidaridad *f*

so·lid·i·fy [sə'lɪdɪfaɪ] *v/i (pret & pp solidified)* solidificarse

sol·id·ly ['sɑːlɪdlɪ] *adv built* sólidamente; *in favor of sth* unánimente

so·lil·o·quy [sə'lɪləkwɪ] soliloquio *m*

sol·i·taire [sɑːlɪ'ter] *card game* solitario *m*

sol·i·ta·ry ['sɑːlɪterɪ] *adj life, activity* solitario; *(single)* único

sol·i·ta·ry con'fine·ment prisión *f* incomunicada

sol·i·tude ['sɑːlɪtuːd] soledad *f*

so·lo ['soulou] **1** *n MUS* solo *m* **2** *adj* en solitario

so·lo·ist ['soulouɪst] solista *m/f*

sol·u·ble ['sɑːljubl] *adj substance, problem* soluble

so·lu·tion [sə'luːʃn] solución *f* (**to** a); *(mixture)* solución *f*

solve [sɑːlv] *v/t problem* solucionar, resolver; *mystery* resolver; *crossword* resolver, sacar

sol·vent ['sɑːlvənt] *adj financially* solvente

som·ber, *Br* **som·bre** ['sɑːmbər] *adj (dark)* oscuro; *(serious)* sombrío

some [sʌm] **1** *adj: would you like some water / cookies?* ¿quieres agua / galletas?; **some countries** algunos países; *I gave him some money* le di (algo de) dinero; **some people say that ...** hay quien dice ... **2** *pron: some of the group* parte del grupo; **would you like some?** ¿quieres?; *milk? - no thanks, I've got some* ¿leche? - gracias, ya tengo **3** *adv (a bit):* **we'll have to wait some** tendremos que esperar algo *or* un poco

some·bod·y ['sʌmbədɪ] *pron* alguien

'**some·day** *adv* algún día

'**some·how** *adv (by one means or another)* de alguna manera; *(for some unknown reason)* por alguna razón; *I've never liked him somehow* por alguna razón u otra nunca me cayó bien

'**some·one** *pron* → **somebody**

'**some·place** *adv* → **somewhere**

som·er·sault ['sʌmərsɔːlt] **1** *n* salto mortal **2** *v/i* dar un salto mortal

'**some·thing** *pron* algo; **would you like something to drink / eat?** ¿te gustaría beber / comer algo?; *is something wrong?* ¿pasa algo?

'**some·time** *adv: let's have lunch sometime* quedemos para comer un día de éstos; *sometime last year* en algún momento del año pasado

'**some·times** ['sʌmtaɪmz] *adv* a veces

'**some·what** *adv* un tanto

'**some·where 1** *adv* en alguna parte *or* al-

S

gún lugar **2** *pron*: **let's go to somewhere quiet** vamos a algún sitio tranquilo; **I was looking for somewhere to park** buscaba un sitio donde aparcar

son [sʌn] hijo *m*

so·na·ta [sə'nɑːtə] MUS sonata *f*

song [sɒŋ] canción *f*

'song·bird pájaro *m* cantor

'song·writ·er cantautor(a) *m(f)*

'son-in-law (*pl* **sons-in-law**) yerno *m*

'son·net ['sɑːnɪt] soneto *m*

soon [suːn] *adv* pronto; **how soon can you be ready to leave?** ¿cuándo estarás listo para salir?; **he left soon after I arrived** se marchó al poco de llegar yo; **can't you get here any sooner?** ¿no podrías llegar antes?; **as soon as** tan pronto como; **as soon as possible** lo antes posible; **sooner or later** tarde o temprano; **the sooner the better** cuanto antes mejor

soot [sut] hollín *m*

soothe [suːð] *v/t* calmar

so·phis·ti·cat·ed [sə'fɪstɪkeɪtɪd] *adj* sofisticado

so·phis·ti·ca·tion [səfɪstɪ'keɪʃn] sofisticación *f*

soph·o·more ['sɑːfəmɔːr] estudiante *m/f* de segundo año

sop·py ['sɑːpɪ] *adj* F sensiblero

so·pra·no [sə'prænou] *n singer* soprano *m/f*; *voice voz f* de soprano

sor·did ['sɔːrdɪd] *adj affair, business* sórdido

sore [sɔːr] **1** *adj* (*painful*) dolorido; F (*angry*) enojado, *Span* mosqueado F; **is it sore?** ¿duele?; **I'm sore all over** me duele todo el cuerpo **2** *n* llaga *f*

sor·row ['sɑːrou] *n* pena *f*

sor·ry ['sɑːrɪ] *adj* (*sad: day, sight*) triste; (*I'm*) **sorry!** *apologizing* ¡lo siento!; **I'm sorry that I didn't tell you sooner** lamento no habértelo dicho antes; **I was so sorry to hear of her death** me dio mucha pena oír lo de su muerte; (*I'm*) **sorry but I can't help** lo siento pero no puedo ayudar; **I won't be sorry to leave** no me arrepentiré de irme de aquí; **I feel sorry for her** siento pena *or* lástima por ella; **be a sorry sight** ofrecer un espectáculo lamentable

sort [sɔːrt] **1** *n clase f, tipo m; **sort of** F un poco, algo; **is it finished? - sort of** F ¿está acabado? - más o menos **2** *v/t* ordenar, clasificar; COMPUT ordenar

◆ **sort out** *v/t papers* ordenar, clasificar; *problem* resolver, arreglar

SOS [esou'es] SOS *m*; *fig* llamada *f* de auxilio

so·'so *adv* F así así F

sought [sɔːt] *pret & pp* → **seek**

soul [soul] REL, *fig: of a nation etc* alma *f*; *character* personalidad *f*; **the poor soul** el pobrecillo

sound¹ [saund] **1** *adj* (*sensible*) sensato; (*healthy*) sano; *sleep* profundo **2** *adv*: **be sound asleep** estar profundamente dormido

sound² [saund] **1** *n* sonido *m*; (*noise*) ruido *m* **2** *v/t* (*pronounce*) pronunciar; MED auscultar; **sound one's horn** tocar la bocina **3** *v/i*: **that sounds interesting** parece interesante; **she sounded unhappy** parecía triste

◆ **sound out** *v/t* sondear; **I sounded her out about the idea** sondeé a ver qué le parecía la idea

'sound card COMPUT tarjeta *f* de sonido

'sound ef·fects *npl* efectos *mpl* sonoros

sound·ly ['saundlɪ] *adv sleep* profundamente; *beaten* rotundamente

'sound·proof *adj* insonorizado

'sound·track banda *f* sonora

soup [suːp] sopa *f*

'soup bowl cuenco *m*

souped-up [suːpt'ʌp] *adj* F trucado

'soup plate plato *m* sopero

'soup spoon cuchara *f* sopera

sour [saur] *adj apple, orange* ácido, agrio; *milk* cortado; *comment* agrio

source [sɔːrs] *n* fuente *f*; *of river* nacimiento *m*; (*person*) fuente *f*

'sour cream nata *f* agria

south [sauθ] **1** *adj* sur, del sur **2** *n* sur *m*; **to the south of** al sur de **3** *adv* al sur; **south of** al sur de

South 'Af·ri·ca Sudáfrica

South 'Af·ri·can 1 *adj* sudafricano **2** *n* sudafricano(-a) *m(f)*

South A'mer·i·ca Sudamérica, América del Sur

South A'mer·i·can 1 *adj* sudamericano **2** *n* sudamericano(-a) *m(f)*

south'east 1 *n* sudeste *m*, sureste *m* **2** *adj* sudeste, sureste **3** *adv* al sudeste *or* sureste; **southeast of** al sudeste de

south'·east·ern *adj* del sudeste

south·er·ly ['sʌðərlɪ] *adj wind* sur, del sur; *direction* sur

south·ern ['sʌðərn] *adj* sureño

south·ern·er ['sʌðərnər] sureño(-a) *m(f)*

south·ern·most ['sʌðərnmoust] *adj* más al sur

South 'Pole Polo *m* Sur

south·ward ['sauθwərd] *adv* hacia el sur

south·'west 1 *n* sudoeste *m*, suroeste *m* **2** *adj* sudoeste, suroeste **3** *adv* al sudoeste *or* suroeste; **southwest of** al sudoeste *or* suroeste de

south·west·ern *adj* del sudoeste *or* sur-oeste

sou·ve·nir [suːvəˈnɪr] recuerdo *m*

sove·reign [ˈsɑːvrɪn] *adj state* soberano

sove·reign·ty [ˈsɑːvrɪntɪ] *of state* sobera-nía *f*

So·vi·et [ˈsouviət] *adj* soviético

So·vi·et 'U·nion Unión *f* Soviética

sow[1] [sau] *n (female pig)* cerda *f*, puerca *f*

sow[2] [sou] *v/t (pret **sowed**, pp **sown**) seeds* sembrar

sown [soun] *pp → **sow**[2]*

'soy bean [sɔɪ] semilla *f* de soja

soy 'sauce salsa *f* de soja

space [speɪs] *n* espacio *m*

◆ **space out** *v/t* espaciar

'space-bar COMPUT barra *f* espaciadora

'space·craft nave *f* espacial

'space·ship nave *f* espacial

'space shut·tle transbordador *m* espacial

'space sta·tion estación *f* espacial

'space·suit traje *m* espacial

spa·cious [ˈspeɪʃəs] *adj* espacioso

spade [speɪd] *for digging* pala *f*; **spades** *in card game* picas *fpl*

'spade·work *fig* trabajo *m* preliminar

Spain [speɪn] España *f*

span [spæn] *v/t (pret & pp **spanned**)* abarcar; *of bridge* cruzar

Span·iard [ˈspænjərd] español(a) *m(f)*

Span·ish [ˈspænɪʃ] **1** *adj* español **2** *n language* español *m*; **the Spanish** los espa-ñoles

spank [spæŋk] *v/t* azotar

spank·ing [ˈspæŋkɪŋ] azotaina *f*

span·ner [ˈspænər] *Br* llave *f*

spare [sper] **1** *v/t:* **can you spare me $50?** ¿me podrías dejar 50 dólares?; **we can't spare a single employee** no podemos prescindir ni de un solo traba-jador; **can you spare the time?** ¿tienes tiempo?; **I have time to spare** me sobra el tiempo; **there were 5 to spare** sobra-ban cinco **2** *adj pair of glasses, set of keys* de repuesto; **do you have any spare cash?** ¿no te sobrará algo de dinero? **3** *n* recambio *m*, repuesto *m*

spare 'part pieza *f* de recambio *or* repues-to

spare 'ribs costillas *fpl* de cerdo

spare 'room habitación *f* de invitados

spare 'time tiempo *m* libre

spare 'tire, *Br* **spare 'tyre** MOT rueda *f* de recambio *or* repuesto

spar·ing [ˈsperɪŋ] *adj* moderado; **be spa-ring with** no derrochar

spa·ring·ly [ˈsperɪŋlɪ] *adv* con modera-

ción

spark [spɑːrk] *n* chispa *f*

spar·kle [ˈspɑːrkl] *v/i* destellar

spar·kling 'wine [ˈspɑːrklɪŋ] vino *m* espu-moso

'spark plug bujía *f*

spar·row [ˈspærou] gorrión *m*

sparse [spɑːrs] *adj vegetation* escaso

sparse·ly [ˈspɑːrslɪ] *adv:* **sparsely popu-lated** poco poblado

spar·tan [ˈspɑːrtn] *adj room* espartano

spas·mod·ic [spæzˈmɑːdɪk] *adj* intermi-tente

spat [spæt] *pret & pp → **spit***

spate [speɪt] *fig* oleada *f*

spa·tial [ˈspeɪʃl] *adj* espacial

spat·ter [ˈspætər] *v/t:* **the car spattered mud all over me** el coche me salpicó de barro

speak [spiːk] **1** *v/i (pret **spoke**, pp **spo-ken**)* hablar (**to** con); *(make a speech)* dar una charla; **we're not speaking (to each other)** *(we've quarreled)* no nos ha-blamos; **speaking** TELEC al habla **2** *v/t (pret **spoke**, pp **spoken**) foreign langua-ge* hablar; **she spoke her mind** dijo lo que pensaba

◆ **speak for** *v/t* hablar en nombre de

◆ **speak out** *v/i:* **speak out against in-justice** denunciar la injusticia

◆ **speak up** *v/i (speak louder)* hablar más alto

speak·er [ˈspiːkər] *at conference* confer-enciante *m/f*; *(orator)* orador(a) *m(f)*; *of sound system* altavoz *m*, *L.Am.* alto-parlante *m*; *of language* hablante *m/f*

spear [spɪr] lanza *f*

spear·mint [ˈspɪrmɪnt] hierbabuena *f*

spe·cial [ˈspeʃl] *adj* especial; **be on spe-cial** estar de oferta

spe·cial ef·fects *npl* efectos *mpl* espe-ciales

spe·cial·ist [ˈspeʃlɪst] especialista *m/f*

spe·cial·ize [ˈspeʃəlaɪz] *v/i* especializarse (**in** en)

spe·cial·ly [ˈspeʃlɪ] *adv → **especially***

spe·cial·i·ty [speʃɪˈælətɪ] *Br*, **spe·cial·ty** [ˈspeʃəltɪ] especialidad *f*

spe·cies [ˈspiːʃiːz] *nsg* especie *f*

spe·cif·ic [spəˈsɪfɪk] *adj* específico

spe·cif·i·cal·ly [spəˈsɪfɪklɪ] *adv* específi-camente

spec·i·fi·ca·tions [spesɪfɪˈkeɪʃnz] *npl of machine etc* especificaciones *fpl*

spe·ci·fy [ˈspesɪfaɪ] *v/t (pret & pp **speci-fied**)* especificar

spe·ci·men [ˈspesɪmən] muestra *f*

speck [spek] *of dust, soot* mota *f*

specs [speks] *npl* F *(spectacles)* gafas *fpl*,

L.Am. lentes *mpl*

spec·ta·cle ['spektəkl] (*impressive sight*) espectáculo *m*; (*a pair of*) **spectacles** unas gafas, *L.Am.* unos lentes

spec·tac·u·lar [spek'tækjulər] *adj* espectacular

spec·ta·tor [spek'teɪtər] espectador(a) *m(f)*

spec·ta·tor sport deporte *m* espectáculo

spec·trum ['spektrəm] *fig* espectro *m*

spec·u·late ['spekjuleɪt] *v/i also* FIN especular

spec·u·la·tion [spekju'leɪʃn] *also* FIN especulación *f*

spec·u·la·tor ['spekjuleɪtər] FIN especulador(a) *m(f)*

sped [sped] *pret & pp* → **speed**

speech [spiːtʃ] (*address*) discurso *m*; *in play* parlamento *m*; (*ability to speak*) habla *f*, dicción *f*; (*way of speaking*) forma *f* de hablar

speech de·fect defecto *m* del habla

speech·less ['spiːtʃlɪs] *adj with shock, surprise* sin habla; *I was left speechless* me quedé sin habla

speech ther·a·pist logopeda *m/f*

speech ther·a·py logopedia *f*

speech writ·er redactor(a) *m(f)* de discursos

speed [spiːd] **1** *n* velocidad *f*; (*promptness*) rapidez *f*; *at a speed of 150 mph* a una velocidad de 150 millas por hora **2** *v/i* (*pret & pp* **sped**) *run* correr; *drive too quickly* sobrepasar el límite de velocidad; *we were speeding along* íbamos a toda velocidad

◆ **speed by** *v/i* pasar a toda velocidad

◆ **speed up** **1** *v/i of car, driver* acelerar; *when working* apresurarse **2** *v/t process* acelerar

speed·boat motora *f*, planeadora *f*

speed bump resalto *m* (*para reducir la velocidad del tráfico*), *Arg* despertador *m*, *Mex* tope *m*

speed·i·ly ['spiːdɪlɪ] *adv* con rapidez

speed·ing ['spiːdɪŋ] *n: fined for speeding* multado por exceso de velocidad

speed·ing fine multa *f* por exceso de velocidad

speed lim·it *on roads* límite *m* de velocidad

speed·om·e·ter [spiː'dɑːmɪtər] velocímetro *m*

speed trap control *m* de velocidad por radar

speed·y ['spiːdɪ] *adj* rápido

spell¹ [spel] **1** *v/t word* deletrear *how do you spell ...?* ¿cómo se escribe ... ? **2** *v/i* deletrear

spell² [spel] *n* (*period of time*) periodo *m*, temporada; *I'll take a spell at the wheel* te relevaré un rato al volante

spell·bound *adj* hechizado

spell·check COMPUT: *do a spellcheck on* pasar el corrector ortográfico a

spell·check·er COMPUT corrector *m* ortográfico

spell·ing ['spelɪŋ] ortografía *f*

spend [spend] *v/t* (*pret & pp* **spent**) *money* gastar; *time* pasar

spend·thrift *n pej* derrochador(a) *m(f)*

spent [spent] *pret & pp* → **spend**

sperm [spɜːrm] espermatozoide *m*; (*semen*) esperma *f*

sperm bank banco *m* de esperma

sperm count recuento *m* espermático

sphere [sfɪr] *also fig* esfera *f*; *sphere of influence* ámbito *m* de influencia

spice [spaɪs] *n* (*seasoning*) especia *f*

spic·y ['spaɪsɪ] *adj food* con especias; (*hot*) picante

spi·der ['spaɪdər] araña *f*

spi·der·web telaraña *f*, tela *f* de araña

spike [spaɪk] *n* pincho *m*; *on running shoe* clavo *m*

spill [spɪl] **1** *v/t* derramar **2** *v/i* derramarse **3** *n* derrame *m*

spin¹ [spɪn] **1** *n* (*turn*) giro *m* **2** *v/t* (*pret & pp* **spun**) *of wheel* girar **3** *v/i* (*pret & pp* **spun**) *of wheel* girar, dar vueltas; *my head is spinning* me da vueltas la cabeza

spin² [spɪn] *v/t wool, cotton* hilar; *web* tejer

◆ **spin around** *v/i of person, car* darse la vuelta

◆ **spin out** *v/i* alargar

spin·ach ['spɪnɪdʒ] espinacas *fpl*

spi·nal ['spaɪnl] *adj* de la columna vertebral

spi·nal col·umn columna *f* vertebral

spi·nal cord médula *f* espinal

spin doc·tor F asesor encargado de dar la mejor prensa posible a un político o asunto

spin-dry *v/t* centrifugar

spin-'dry·er centrifugadora *f*

spine [spaɪn] *of person, animal* columna *f* vertebral; *of book* lomo *m*; *on plant, hedgehog* espina *f*

spine·less ['spaɪnlɪs] *adj* (*cowardly*) débil

spin·off producto *m* derivade

spin·ster ['spɪnstər] solterona *f*

spin·y ['spaɪnɪ] *adj* espinoso

spi·ral ['spaɪrəl] **1** *n* espiral **2** *v/i* (*rise quickly*) subir vertiginosamente

spi·ral 'stair·case escalera *f* de caracol

spire [spaɪr] aguja *f*

spir·it ['spɪrɪt] *n* espíritu *m*; (*courage*) valor *m*; *in a spirit of cooperation* con espíritu de cooperación

spir·it·ed ['spɪrɪtɪd] *adj* (*energetic*) enérgico

'**spir·it lev·el** *n* el nivel *m* de burbuja

'**spir·its**[1] ['spɪrɪts] *npl* (*alcohol*) licores *mpl*

spir·its[2] ['spɪrɪts] *npl* (*morale*) la moral; *be in good / poor spirits* tener la moral alta / baja

spir·i·tu·al ['spɪrɪtʃʊəl] *adj* espiritual

spir·it·u·al·ism ['spɪrɪtʃəlɪzm] espiritismo *m*

spir·it·u·al·ist ['spɪrɪtʃəlɪst] *n* espiritista *m/f*

spit [spɪt] *v/i* (*pret & pp* **spat**) *of person* escupir; *it's spitting with rain* está chispeando

◆ **spit out** *v/t food, liquid* escupir

spite [spaɪt] *n* rencor *m*; *in spite of* a pesar de

spite·ful ['spaɪtfəl] *adj* malo, malicioso

spite·ful·ly ['spaɪtfəlɪ] *adv* con maldad *or* malicia

spit·ting 'im·age ['spɪtɪŋ]: *be the spitting image of s.o.* ser el vivo retrato de alguien

splash [splæʃ] **1** *n small amount of liquid* chorrito *m*; *of color* mancha *f* **2** *v/t person* salpicar; *the car splashed mud all over me* el coche me salpicó de barro **3** *v/i* chapotear; *of water* salpicar

◆ **splash down** *v/i of spacecraft* amerizar

◆ **splash out** *v/i in spending* gastarse una fortuna

'**splash·down** amerizaje *m*

splen·did ['splendɪd] *adj* espléndido

splen·dor, *Br* **splen·dour** ['splendər] esplendor *m*

splint [splɪnt] *n* MED tablilla *f*

splin·ter ['splɪntər] **1** *n* astilla *f* **2** *v/i* astillarse

'**splin·ter group** grupo *m* escindido

split [splɪt] **1** *n damage* raja *f*; (*disagreement*) escisión *f*; (*division, share*) reparto *m* **2** *v/t* (*pret & pp* **split**) *damage* rajar; *logs* partir en dos; (*cause disagreement in*) escindir; (*share*) repartir **3** *v/i* (*pret & pp* **split**) (*tear*) rajarse; (*disagree*) escindirse

◆ **split up** *v/i of couple* separarse

split per·son·al·i·ty PSYCH doble personalidad *f*

split·ting ['splɪtɪŋ] *adj*: *splitting headache* dolor *m* de cabeza atroz

splut·ter ['splʌtər] *v/i* farfullar

spoil [spɔɪl] *v/t* estropear, arruinar

'**spoil·sport** F aguafiestas *m/f inv* F

spoilt [spɔɪlt] *adj child* consentido, mimado; *be spoilt for choice* tener mucho donde elegir

spoke[1] [spəʊk] *of wheel* radio *m*

spoke[2] [spəʊk] *pret* → **speak**

spo·ken ['spəʊkən] *pp* → **speak**

spokes·man ['spəʊksmən] portavoz *m*

spokes·per·son ['spəʊkspɜːrsən] portavoz *m/f*

spokes·wom·an ['spəʊkswʊmən] portavoz *f*

sponge [spʌndʒ] *n* esponja *f*

◆ **sponge off**, **sponge on** *v/t* F vivir a costa de

'**sponge cake** bizcocho *m*

spong·er ['spʌndʒər] F gorrón(-ona) *m(f)* F

spon·sor ['spɑːnsər] **1** *n* patrocinador *m* **2** *v/t* patrocinar

spon·sor·ship ['spɑːnsərʃɪp] patrocinio *m*

spon·ta·ne·ous [spɑːn'teɪnɪəs] *adj* espontáneo

spon·ta·ne·ous·ly [spɑːn'teɪnɪəslɪ] *adv* espontáneamente

spook·y ['spuːkɪ] *adj* F espeluznante, terrorífico

spool [spuːl] *n* carrete *m*

spoon [spuːn] *n* cuchara *f*

'**spoon-feed** *v/t* (*pret & pp* **spoonfed**) *fig* dar todo mascado a

spoon·ful ['spuːnfʊl] cucharada *f*

spo·rad·ic [spə'rædɪk] *adj* esporádico

sport [spɔːrt] *n* deporte *m*

sport·ing ['spɔːrtɪŋ] *adj* deportivo; *a sporting gesture* un gesto deportivo

'**sports car** [spɔːrts] (coche *m*) deportivo *m*

'**sports·coat** chaqueta *f* de sport

sports 'jour·nal·ist periodista *m/f* deportivo(-a)

'**sports med·i·cine** medicina *f* deportiva

'**sports news** *nsg* noticias *fpl* deportivas

'**sports page** página *f* de deportes

'**sports·wear** ropa *f* de sport

'**sports·wom·an** deportista *f*

sport·y ['spɔːrtɪ] *adj person* deportista; *clothes* deportivo

spot[1] [spɑːt] (*pimple etc*) grano *m*; (*part of pattern*) lunar *m*; *a spot of ...* (*a little*) algo de ..., un poco de ...

spot[2] [spɑːt] (*place*) lugar *m*, sitio *m*; *on the spot* (*in the place in question*) en el lugar; (*immediately*) en ese momento; *put s.o. on the spot* poner a alguien en un aprieto

spot[3] [spɑːt] *v/t* (*pret & pp* **spotted**) (*notice*) ver; (*identify*) ver, darse cuenta de

spot 'check *n* control *m* al azar; *carry out*

spot check checks llevar a cabo controles al azar

spot·less ['spɒːtlɪs] *adj* inmaculado, impecable

'**spot·light** 1 *n* foco *m*

spot·ted ['spɒːtɪd] *adj* fabric de lunares

spot·ty ['spɒːtɪ] *adj* with pimples con granos

spouse [spaʊs] *fml* cónyuge *m/f*

spout [spaʊt] 1 *n* pitorro *m* 2 *v/i* of liquid chorrear 3 *v/t* F soltar F

sprain [spreɪn] 1 *n* esguince *m* 2 *v/t* hacerse un esguince en

sprang [spræŋ] *pret* → **spring³**

sprawl [sprɔːl] *v/i* despatarrarse; *of city* expandirse; **send s.o. sprawling** *of punch* derribar de un golpe

sprawl·ing ['sprɔːlɪŋ] *adj* city, suburbs en expansión

spray [spreɪ] 1 *n* of sea water, from fountain rociada f; for hair spray *m*; container aerosol *m*, spray *m* 2 *v/t* rociar; **spray sth with sth** rociar algo de algo

'**spray·gun** pistola f pulverizadora

spread [spred] 1 *n* of disease, religion etc propagación f; F (big meal) comilona f F 2 *v/t* (pret & pp **spread**) (lay) extender; butter, jelly untar; news, rumor difundir; disease propagar; arms, legs extender 3 *v/i* (pret & pp **spread**) of disease, fire propagarse; of rumor, news difundirse; of butter extenderse, untarse

'**spread·sheet** COMPUT hoja f de cálculo

spree [spriː] F: **go (out) on a spree** ir de juerga; **go on a shopping spree** salir a comprar a lo loco

sprig [sprɪg] ramita f

spright·ly ['spraɪtlɪ] *adj* lleno de energía

spring¹ [sprɪŋ] *n* (season) primavera f

spring² [sprɪŋ] *n* (device) muelle *m*

spring³ [sprɪŋ] 1 *n* (jump) brinco *m*, salto *m*; (stream) manantial *m* 2 *v/i* (pret **sprang**, pp **sprung**) brincar, saltar; **spring from** proceder de; **he sprang to his feet** se levantó de un salto

'**spring·board** trampolín *m*

spring 'chick·en hum: **she's no spring chicken** no es ninguna niña

spring-'clean·ing limpieza f a fondo

'**spring·time** primavera f

spring·y ['sprɪŋɪ] *adj* mattress, ground mullido; walk ligero; piece of elastic elástico

sprin·kle ['sprɪŋkl] *v/t* espolvorear; **sprinkle sth with sth** espolvorear algo con algo

sprin·kler ['sprɪŋklər] for garden aspersor *m*; in ceiling rociador *m* contra incendios

sprint [sprɪnt] 1 *n* esprint *m*; SP carrera f de velocidad 2 *v/i* (run fast) correr a toda velocidad; of runner esprintar

sprint·er ['sprɪntər] SP esprínter *m/f*, velocista *m/f*

sprout [spraʊt] 1 *v/i* of seed brotar 2 *n*: (**Brussels**) **sprouts** coles fpl de Bruselas

spruce [spruːs] *adj* pulcro

sprung [sprʌŋ] *pp* → **spring³**

spry [spraɪ] *adj* lleno *m* de energía

spun [spʌn] *pret & pp* → **spin¹**

spur [spɜːr] *n* espuela f; fig incentivo; **on the spur of the moment** sin pararse a pensar

◆ **spur on** *v/t* (pret & pp **spurred**) (encourage) espolear

spurt [spɜːrt] 1 *n* in race arrancada f; **put on a spurt** acelerar 2 *v/i* of liquid chorrear

sput·ter ['spʌtər] *v/i* of engine chisporrotear

spy [spaɪ] 1 *n* espía *m/f* 2 *v/i* (pret & pp **spied**) espiar 3 *v/t* (pret & pp **spied**) (see) ver

◆ **spy on** *v/t* espiar

squab·ble ['skwɑːbl] 1 *n* riña f 2 *v/i* reñir

squal·id ['skwɑːlɪd] *adj* inmundo, miserable

squal·or ['skwɑːlər] inmundicia f

squan·der ['skwɑːndər] *v/t* money despilfarrar

square [skwer] 1 *adj* in shape cuadrado; **square miles** millas cuadradas f 2 *n* also MATH cuadrado *m*; in town plaza f; in board game casilla f; **we're back to square one** volvemos al punto de partida

◆ **square up** *v/i* hacer cuentas

square 'root raíz f cuadrada

squash¹ [skwɑːʃ] *n* vegetable calabacera f

squash² [skwɑːʃ] *n* game squash *m*

squash³ [skwɑːʃ] *v/t* (crush) aplastar

squat [skwɑːt] 1 *adj* person, build chaparro; figure, buildings bajo 2 *v/i* (pret & pp **squatted**) sit agacharse; **squat in a building** ocupar ilegalmente un edificio

squat·ter ['skwɑːtər] ocupante *m/f* ilegal, Span okupa *m/f* F

squeak [skwiːk] 1 *n* of mouse chillido *m*; of hinge chirrido *m* 2 *v/i* of mouse chillar; of hinge chirriar; of shoes crujir

squeak·y ['skwiːkɪ] *adj* hinge chirriante; shoes que crujen; voice chillón

'**squeak·y clean** *adj* F bien limpio

squeal [skwiːl] 1 *n* chillido; **there was a squeal of brakes** se oyó una frenada estruendosa 2 *v/i* chillar; of brakes armar un estruendo

squeam·ish ['skwiːmɪʃ] *adj* aprensivo

squeeze [skwiːz] 1 *n* of hand, shoulder

apretón m **2** v/t (press) apretar; (remove juice from) exprimir

◆ **squeeze in 1** v/i to a car etc meterse a duras penas **2** v/t hacer hueco para

◆ **squeeze up** v/i to make space apretarse

squid [skwɪd] calamar m

squint [skwɪnt] n: **she has a squint** es estrábica, tiene estrabismo

squirm [skwɜːrm] v/i retorcerse

squir·rel ['skwɪrl] n ardilla f

squirt [skwɜːrt] **1** v/t lanzar un chorro de **2** n F pej canijo(-a) m(f) F, mequetrefe m/f F

St abbr (= **saint**) Sto; Sta (= santo m; santa f); (= **street**) c/ (= calle f)

stab [stæb] **1** n F intento m; **have a stab at sth** intentar algo **2** v/t (pret & pp **stabbed**) person apuñalar

sta·bil·i·ty [stəˈbɪlətɪ] estabilidad f

sta·bil·ize ['steɪbɪlaɪz] **1** v/t prices, boat estabilizar **2** v/i of prices etc estabilizarse

sta·ble¹ ['steɪbl] n for horses establo m

sta·ble² ['steɪbl] adj estable; patient's condition estacionario

stack [stæk] **1** n (pile) pila f; (smokestack) chimenea f; **stacks of** F montones de F **2** v/t apilar

sta·di·um ['steɪdɪəm] estadio m

staff [stæf] npl (employees) personal m; (teachers) profesorado m; **staff are not allowed to …** los empleados no tienen permitido …

staf·fer ['stæfər] empleado(-a) m(f)

'**staff·room** in school sala f de profesores

stag [stæg] ciervo m

stage¹ [steɪdʒ] in life, project etc etapa f

stage² [steɪdʒ] **1** n THEA escenario m; **go on the stage** hacerse actor / actriz **2** v/t play escenificar, llevar a escena; demonstration llevar a cabo

'**stage door** entrada f de artistas

'**stage fright** miedo m escénico

'**stage hand** tramoyista m/f

stag·ger ['stægər] **1** v/i tambalearse **2** v/t (amaze) dejar anonadado; coffee breaks etc escalonar

stag·ger·ing ['stægərɪŋ] adj asombroso

stag·nant ['stægnənt] adj also fig estancado

stag·nate [stægˈneɪt] v/i fig estancarse

stag·na·tion [stægˈneɪʃn] estancamiento m

'**stag par·ty** despedida f de soltero

stain [steɪn] **1** n (dirty mark) mancha f; for wood tinte m **2** v/t (dirty) manchar; wood teñir **3** v/i of wine etc manchar, dejar mancha; of fabric mancharse

stained-glass 'win·dow [steɪnd] vidriera f

stain·less 'steel ['steɪnlɪs] n acero m inoxidable

'**stain re·mov·er** [rɪˈmuːvər] quitamanchas m inv

stair [ster] escalón m; **the stairs** la(s) escalera(s)

'**stair·case** escalera(s) f(/pl)

stake [steɪk] **1** n of wood estaca f; when gambling apuesta f; (investment) participación f; **be at stake** estar en juego **2** v/t tree arrodrigar; money apostar; reputation jugarse; person ayudar (económicamente)

stale [steɪl] adj bread rancio; air viciado; fig news viejo

'**stale·mate** in chess tablas fpl (por rey ahogado); fig punto m muerto

stalk¹ [stɔːk] of fruit, plant tallo m

stalk² [stɔːk] v/t (follow) acechar; person seguir

stalk·er ['stɔːkər] persona que sigue a otra obsesivamente

stall¹ [stɔːl] n at market puesto m; for cow, horse casilla f

stall² [stɔːl] **1** v/i of vehicle, engine calarse; of plane entrar en pérdida; (play for time) intentar ganar tiempo **2** v/t engine calar; person retener

stal·li·on ['stæljən] semental m

stalls [stɔːlz] npl patio m de butacas

stal·wart ['stɔːlwərt] adj support, supporter incondicional

stam·i·na ['stæmɪnə] resistencia f

stam·mer ['stæmər] **1** n tartamudeo m **2** v/i tartamudear

stamp¹ [stæmp] **1** n for letter sello m, L.Am. estampilla f, Mex timbre m; device tampón m; mark made with device sello m **2** v/t sellar; **stamped addressed envelope** sobre m franqueado con la dirección

stamp² [stæmp] v/t: **stamp one's feet** patear

◆ **stamp out** v/t (eradicate) terminar con

'**stamp col·lec·ting** filatelia f

'**stamp col·lec·tion** collección f de sellos or L.Am. estampillas or Mex timbres

'**stamp col·lec·tor** coleccionista m/f de sellos or L.Am. estampillas or Mex timbres

stam·pede [stæmˈpiːd] **1** n of cattle etc estampida f; of people desbandada f **2** v/i of cattle etc salir de estampida; of people salir en desbandada

stance [stæns] (position) postura f

stand [stænd] **1** n at exhibition puesto m, stand m; (witness stand) estrado m; (support, base) soporte m; **take the stand** LAW subir al estrado **2** v/i (pret & pp **stood**) of

building encontrarse, hallarse; *as opposed to sit* estar de pie; *(rise)* ponerse de pie; *did you notice two men standing near the window?* ¿viste a dos hombres al lado de la ventana?; *there was a large box standing in the middle of the floor* había una caja muy grande en mitad del suelo; *the house stands at the corner of ...* la casa se encuentra en la esquina de ...; *stand still* quedarse quieto; *where do you stand with Liz?* ¿cual es tu situación con Liz? 3 *v/t (pret & pp stood)* *(tolerate)* aguantar, soportar; *(put)* colocar; *you don't stand a chance* no tienes ninguna posibilidad; *stand s.o. a drink* invitar a alguien a una copa; *stand one's ground* mantenerse firme
◆ **stand back** *v/i* echarse atrás
◆ **stand by 1** *v/i (not take action)* quedarse sin hacer nada; *(be ready)* estar preparado 2 *v/t person* apoyar; *decision* atenerse a
◆ **stand down** *v/i (withdraw)* retirarse
◆ **stand for** *v/t (tolerate)* aguantar; *(represent)* significar
◆ **stand in for** *v/t* sustituir
◆ **stand out** *v/i* destacar
◆ **stand up 1** *v/i* levantarse 2 *v/t* F plantar F
◆ **stand up for** *v/t* defender; *stand up for yourself!* ¡defiéndete!
◆ **stand up to** *v/t* hacer frente a
stan-dard ['stændərd] 1 *adj (usual)* habitual 2 *n (level of excellence)* nivel *m;* TECH estándar *m; be up to standard* cumplir el nivel exigido; *not be up to standard* estar por debajo del nivel exigido; *my parents set very high standards* mis padres exigen mucho
stan-dard-ize ['stændərdaɪz] *v/t* normalizar
stan-dard of 'li-ving nivel *m* de vida
'**stand-by 1** *n ticket* billete *m* stand-by; *be on standby* estar en stand-by *or* en lista de espera 2 *adv fly* con un billete stand-by
'**stand-by pas-sen-ger** pasajero(-a) *m(f)* en stand-by *or* en lista de espera
stand-ing ['stændɪŋ] *n in society etc* posición *f; (repute)* reputación *f; a musician / politician of some standing* un reputado músico / político; *a relationship of long standing* una relación establecida hace mucho tiempo
'**stand-ing room:** *standing room only* no quedan asientos
'**stand-off-ish** [stænd'ɑ:fɪʃ] *adj* distante
'**stand-point** punto *m* de vista
'**stand-still:** *be at a standstill* estar para-

lizado; *bring to a standstill* paralizar
stank [stæŋk] *pret → stink*
stan-za ['stænzə] estrofa *f*
sta-ple¹ ['steɪpl] *n foodstuff* alimento *m* básico
sta-ple² ['steɪpl] 1 *n (fastener)* grapa *f* 2 *v/t* grapar
sta-ple 'di-et dieta *f* básica
sta-ple gun grapadora *f* industrial
sta-pler ['steɪplər] grapadora *f*
star [stɑ:r] 1 *n also person* estrella *f* 2 *v/t (pret & pp starred) of movie* estar protagonizado por 3 *v/i (pret & pp starred) in movie: Depardieu starred in ...* Depardieu protagonizó ...
'**star-board** *adj* de estribor
starch [stɑ:rtʃ] *in foodstuff* fécula *f*
stare [ster] 1 *n* mirada *f* fija 2 *v/i* mirar fijamente; *stare at* mirar fijamente
'**star-fish** estrella *f* de mar
stark [stɑ:rk] 1 *adj landscape* desolado; *reminder, picture etc* desolador; *in stark contrast to* en marcado contraste con 2 *adv: stark naked* completamente desnudo
star-ling ['stɑ:rlɪŋ] estornino *m*
star-ry ['stɑ:rɪ] *adj night* estrellado
star-ry-eyed [stɑ:rɪ'aɪd]] *adj person* cándido, ingenuo
Stars and 'Stripes la bandera estadounidense
start [stɑ:rt] 1 *n (beginning)* comienzo *m,* principio *m; of race* salida *f; get off to a good / bad start* empezar bien / mal; *from the start* desde el principio; *well, it's a start!* bueno, ¡algo es algo! 2 *v/i* empezar, comenzar; *of engine, car* arrancar; *starting from tomorrow* a partir de mañana 3 *v/t* empezar, comenzar; *engine, car* arrancar; *business* montar; *start to do sth, start doing sth* empezar *or* comenzar a hacer algo; *he started to cry* se puso a llorar
start-er ['stɑ:rtər] *(part of meal)* entrada *m,* entrante *m; of car* motor *m* de arranque
'**start-ing point** punto *m* de partida
'**start-ing sal-a-ry** sueldo *m* inicial
star-tle ['stɑ:rtl] *v/t* sobresaltar
start-ling ['stɑ:rtlɪŋ] *adj* sorprendente, asombroso
starv-a-tion [stɑ:r'veɪʃn] inanición *f,* hambre *f*
starve [stɑ:rv] *v/i* pasar hambre; *starve to death* morir de inanición *or* hambre; *I'm starving* F me muero de hambre F
state¹ [steɪt] 1 *n (condition, country)* estado *m; the States* (los) Estados Unidos 2 *adj capital etc* estatal, del estado; *ban-*

quet etc de estado

state² [steɪt] *v/t* declarar

'State De·part·ment Departamento *m* de Estado, *Ministerio de Asuntos Exteriores*

state·ment ['steɪtmənt] declaración *f*; (*bank statement*) extracto *m*

state of e'mer·gen·cy estado *m* de emergencia

state-of-the-'art *adj* modernísimo

states·man ['steɪtsmən] hombre *m* de estado

state 'troop·er policía *m/f* estatal

State 'vis·it visita *f* de estado

stat·ic (**e·lec·tric·i·ty**) ['stætɪk] electricidad *f* estática

sta·tion ['steɪʃn] **1** *n* RAIL estación *f*; RAD emisora *f*; TV canal *m* **2** *v/t guard etc* apostar; **be stationed in** *of soldier* estar destinado en

sta·tion·a·ry ['steɪʃənrɪ] *adj* parado

sta·tion·er ['steɪʃənər] papelería *f*

sta·tion·er·y ['steɪʃənrɪ] artículos *mpl* de papelería

sta·tion 'man·ag·er RAIL jefe *m* de estación

'sta·tion wag·on ranchera *f*

sta·tis·ti·cal [stə'tɪstɪkl] *adj* estadístico

sta·tis·ti·cal·ly [stə'tɪstɪklɪ] *adv* estadísticamente

sta·tis·ti·cian [stætɪs'tɪʃn] estadístico(-a) *m(f)*

sta·tis·tics [stə'tɪstɪks] (*nsg: science*) estadística *f*; (*npl: figures*) estadísticas *fpl*

stat·ue ['stætʃuː] estatua *f*

Stat·ue of 'Lib·er·ty Estatua *f* de la Libertad

sta·tus ['steɪtəs] categoría *f*, posición *f*; **women want equal status with men** las mujeres quieren igualdad con los hombres

'sta·tus bar COMPUT barra *f* de estado

'sta·tus sym·bol símbolo *m* de estatus

stat·ute ['stætʃuːt] estatuto *m*

staunch [stɔːntʃ] *adj supporter* incondicional; *friend* fiel

stay [steɪ] **1** *n* estancia *f*, *L.Am.* estadía *f* **2** *v/i in a place* quedarse; *in a condition* permanecer; **stay in a hotel** alojarse en un hotel; **stay right there!** ¡quédate ahí!; **stay put** no moverse

♦ **stay away** *v/i*: **tell the children to stay away** diles a los niños que no se acerquen

♦ **stay away from** *v/t* no acercarse a

♦ **stay behind** *v/i* quedarse

♦ **stay up** *v/i* (*not go to bed*) quedarse levantado

stead·i·ly ['stedɪlɪ] *adv improve etc* constantemente

stead·y ['stedɪ] **1** *adj* (*not shaking*) firme; (*continuous*) continuo; *beat* regular; *boyfriend* estable **2** *adv*: **they've been going steady for two years** llevan saliendo dos años; **steady on!** ¡un momento! **3** *v/t* (*pret & pp steadied*) afianzar; *voice* calmar

steak [steɪk] filete *m*

steal [stiːl] **1** *v/t* (*pret stole*, *pp stolen*) *money etc* robar **2** *v/i* (*pret stole*, *pp stolen*) (*be a thief*) robar; **he stole into the bedroom** entró furtivamente en la habitación

stealth bomb·er [stelθ] bombardero *m* invisible

stealth·y ['stelθɪ] *adj* sigiloso

steam [stiːm] **1** *n* vapor *m* **2** *v/t food* cocinar al vapor

♦ **steam up** *v/i of window* empañarse

steamed up [stiːmd'ʌp] *adj* F enojado, *Span* mosqueado F

steam·er ['stiːmər] *for cooking* olla *f* para cocinar al vapor

'steam i·ron plancha *f* de vapor

steel [stiːl] **1** *n* acero *m* **2** *adj* (*made of steel*) de acero

'steel·work·er trabajador(a) *m(f)* del acero

'steel·works acería *f*

steep¹ [stiːp] *adj hill etc* empinado; F: *prices* caro

steep² [stiːp] *v/t* (*soak*) poner en remojo

stee·ple ['stiːpl] torre *f*

'stee·ple·chase *in athletics* carrera *f* de obstáculos

steep·ly ['stiːplɪ] *adv*: **climb steeply** *of path* subir pronunciadamente; *of prices* dispararse

steer¹ [stɪr] *n animal* buey *m*

steer² [stɪr] *v/t car* conducir, *L.Am.* manejar; *boat* gobernar; *person* guiar; *conversation* llevar

steer·ing ['stɪrɪŋ] *n* MOT dirección *f*

'steer·ing wheel volante *m*, *S.Am.* timón *m*

stem¹ [stem] *n of plant* tallo *m*; *of glass* pie *m*; *of pipe* tubo *m*; *of word* raíz *f*

♦ **stem from** *v/t* (*pret & pp stemmed*) derivarse de

stem² [stem] *v/t* (*block*) contener

'stem·ware ['stemwer] cristalería *f*

stench [stentʃ] peste *f*, hedor *m*

sten·cil ['stensɪl] **1** *n* plantilla *f* **2** *v/t* (*pret & pp stenciled*, *Br stencilled*) *pattern* estarcir

step [step] **1** *n* (*pace*) paso *m*; (*stair*) escalón *m*; (*measure*) medida *f*; **step by step** paso a paso **2** *v/i* (*pret & pp stepped*): **step on sth** pisar algo; **step into a pud-**

dle pisar un charco; **I stepped back** di un paso atrás; **step forward** dar un paso adelante

◆ **step down** *v/i from post etc* dimitir
◆ **step up** *v/t (increase)* incrementar

'**step·broth·er** hermanastro *m*
'**step·daugh·ter** hijastra *f*
'**step·fa·ther** padrastro *m*
'**step·lad·der** escalera *f* de tijera
'**step·moth·er** madrastra *f*
step·ping stone ['stepɪŋ] pasadera *f*; *fig* trampolín *m*
'**step·sis·ter** hermanastra *f*
'**step·son** hijastro *m*
ster·e·o ['steriou] *n (sound system)* equipo *m* de música
ster·e·o·type ['steriəutaip] *n* estereotipo *m*
ster·ile ['sterəl] *adj* estéril
ster·il·ize ['sterəlaiz] *v/t woman* esterilizar; *equipment* esterilizar
ster·ling ['stɜːrlɪŋ] *n* FIN libra *f* esterlina
stern[1] [stɜːrn] *adj* severo
stern[2] [stɜːrn] *n* NAUT popa *f*
stern·ly ['stɜːrnlɪ] *adv* con severidad
ster·oids ['sterɔidz] *npl* esteroides *mpl*
steth·o·scope ['steθəskoup] fonendoscopio *m*, estetoscopio *m*
Stet·son® ['stetsn] sombrero *m* de vaquero
ste·ve·dore ['stiːvədɔːr] estibador(a) *m(f)*
stew [stuː] *n* guiso *m*
stew·ard ['stuːərd] *n on plane* auxiliar *m* de vuelo; *on ship* camarero *m*; *at demonstration, meeting* miembro *m* de la organización
stew·ard·ess [stuːər'des] *on plane* auxiliar *f* de vuelo; *on ship* camarera *f*
stewed [stuːd] *adj apples, plums* en compota
stick[1] [stik] *n* palo *m*; *of policeman* porra *f*; *(walking stick)* bastón *m*; **live out in the sticks** F vivir en el quinto pino F, vivir en el campo
stick[2] [stik] **1** *v/t (pret & pp **stuck**) with adhesive* pegar; F *(put)* meter **2** *v/i (pret & pp **stuck**) (jam)* atascarse; *(adhere)* pegarse

◆ **stick around** *v/i* F quedarse
◆ **stick by** *v/t* F apoyar, no abandonar
◆ **stick out** *v/i (protrude)* sobresalir; *(be noticeable)* destacar; **his ears stick out** tiene las orejas salidas
◆ **stick to** *v/t (adhere to)* pegarse a; F *(keep to)* seguir; F *(follow)* pegarse a F
◆ **stick together** *v/i* mantenerse unidos
◆ **stick up** *v/t poster, leaflet* pegar
◆ **stick up for** *v/t* F defender

stick·er ['stikər] pegatina *f*
'**stick-in-the-mud** F aburrido(-a) *m(f)* F, soso(-a) *m(f)*
stick·y ['stiki] *adj hands, surface* pegajoso; *label* adhesivo
stiff [stif] **1** *adj cardboard, manner* rígido; *brush, penalty, competition* duro; *muscle, body* agarrotado; *paste* consistente; *drink* cargado **2** *adv:* **be scared stiff** F estar muerto de miedo F; **be bored stiff** F aburrirse como una ostra F
stiff·en ['stifn] *v/i of person* agarrotarse
◆ **stiffen up** *v/i of muscle* agarrotarse
stiff·ly ['stifli] *adv* con rigidez; *fig* forzadamente
stiff·ness ['stifnəs] *of muscles* agarrotamiento *m*; *fig: of manner* rigidez *f*
sti·fle ['staifl] *v/t yawn, laugh* reprimir, contener; *criticism, debate* reprimir
sti·fling ['staiflɪŋ] *adj* sofocante; **it's stifling in here** hace un calor sofocante aquí dentro
stig·ma ['stigmə] estigma *m*
sti·let·tos [sti'letouz] *npl shoes* zapatos *mpl* de tacón de aguja
still[1] [stil] **1** *adj (not moving)* quieto; *with no wind* sin viento; **it was very still** no wind no soplaba nada de viento **2** *adv:* **keep still!** ¡estáte quieto!; **stand still!** ¡no te muevas!
still[2] [stil] *adv (yet)* todavía, aún; *(nevertheless)* de todas formas; **do you still want it?** ¿todavía *or* aún lo quieres?; **she still hasn't finished** todavía *or* aún no ha acabado; **I still don't understand** sigo sin entenderlo; **she might still come** puede que aún venga; **they are still my parents** siguen siendo mis padres; **still more** *(even more)* todavía más
'**still·born** *adj:* **be stillborn** nacer muerto
still life naturaleza *f* muerta, bodegón *m*
stilt·ed ['stiltid] *adj* forzado
stim·u·lant ['stimjulənt] estimulante *m*
stim·u·late ['stimjuleit] *v/t person* estimular; *growth, demand* estimular, provocar
stim·u·lat·ing ['stimjuleitiŋ] *adj* estimulante
stim·u·la·tion [stimju'leiʃn] estimulación *f*
stim·u·lus ['stimjuləs] *(incentive)* estímulo *m*
sting [stiŋ] **1** *n from bee, jellyfish* picadura *f* **2** *v/t (pret & pp **stung**) of bee, jellyfish* picar **3** *v/i (pret & pp **stung**) of eyes, scratch* escocer
sting·ing ['stiŋiŋ] *adj remark, criticism* punzante
sting·y ['stindʒi] *adj* F agarrado F, rácano

F

stink [stɪŋk] **1** n (bad smell) peste f, hedor m; F (fuss) escándalo F; **kick up a stink** F armar un escándalo F **2** v/i (pret **stank**, pp **stunk**) (smell bad) apestar; F (be very bad) dar asco

stint [stɪnt] n temporada f; **do a stint in the army** pasar una temporada en el ejército

◆ **stint on** v/t F racanear F

stip·u·late ['stɪpjʊleɪt] v/t estipular

stip·u·la·tion [stɪpjʊ'leɪʃn] estipulación f

stir [stɜːr] **1** n: **give the soup up a stir** darle vueltas a la sopa; **cause a stir** causar revuelo **2** v/t (pret & pp **stirred**) remover, dar vueltas a **3** v/i (pret & pp **stirred**) of sleeping person moverse

◆ **stir up** v/t crowd agitar; bad memories traer a la memoria

stir·'cra·zy adj F majareta F

'stir-fry v/t (pret & pp **stir-fried**) freír rápidamente y dando vueltas

'stir-ring ['stɜːrɪŋ] adj music, speech conmovedor

stir-rup ['stɪrəp] estribo m

stitch [stɪtʃ] **1** n in sewing puntada f; in knitting punto m; **stitches** MED puntos mpl; **be in stitches** laughing partirse de risa; **have a stitch** tener flato **2** v/t sew coser

◆ **stitch up** v/t wound coser, suturar

stitch·ing ['stɪtʃɪŋ] (stitches) cosido m

stock [stɑːk] **1** n (reserves) reservas fpl; COM of store existencias fpl; (animals) ganado m; FIN acciones mpl; for soup etc caldo m; **in stock** en existencias; **out of stock** agotado; **take stock** hacer balance **2** v/t COM (have) tener en existencias; COM (sell) vender

◆ **stock up on** v/t aprovisionarse de

'stock-breed·er ganadero(-a) m(f)

'stock-bro·ker corredor(a) m(f) de bolsa

'stock cube pastilla f de caldo concentrado

'stock ex·change bolsa f (de valores)

'stock-hold·er accionista m/f

stock·ing ['stɑːkɪŋ] media f

'stock·ist ['stɑːkɪst] distribuidor(a) m(f)

'stock mar·ket mercado m de valores

'stock·mar·ket crash crack m bursátil

'stock·pile 1 n of food, weapons reservas fpl **2** v/t acumular

'stock·room almacén m

stock·'still adv: **stand stock-still** quedarse inmóvil

'stock-tak·ing inventario m

'stock·y ['stɑːkɪ] adj bajo y robusto

stodg·y ['stɑːdʒɪ] adj food pesado

sto·i·cal ['stoʊɪkl] adj estoico

sto·i·cism ['stoʊɪsɪzm] estoicismo m

stole [stoʊl] pret → **steal**

stol·en ['stoʊlən] pp → **steal**

stom·ach ['stʌmək] **1** n estómago m, tripa f **2** v/t (tolerate) soportar

'stom·ach-ache dolor m de estómago

stone [stoʊn] n piedra f; in fruit hueso m

stoned [stoʊnd] adj F (on drugs) colocado F

stone-'deaf adj: **be stone-deaf** estar más sordo que una tapia

'stone·wall v/i F andarse con evasivas

ston·y ['stoʊnɪ] adj ground, path pedregoso

stood [stʊd] pret & pp → **stand**

stool [stuːl] (seat) taburete m

stoop[1] [stuːp] n: **have a stoop** estar encorvado **2** v/i (bend down) agacharse

stoop[2] [stuːp] n (porch) porche m

stop [stɑːp] **1** n for train, bus parada f; **come to a stop** detenerse; **put a stop to** poner fin a **2** v/t (pret & pp **stopped**) (put an end to) poner fin a; (prevent) impedir; (cease) parar; person in street parar; car, bus, train, etc: of driver detener; check bloquear; **stop doing sth** dejar de hacer algo; **it has stopped raining** ha parado or dejado de llover; **I stopped her from leaving** impedí que se fuera **3** v/i (pret & pp **stopped**) (come to a halt) pararse, detenerse; in a particular place: of bus, train parar

◆ **stop by** v/i (visit) pasarse

◆ **stop off** v/i hacer una parada

◆ **stop over** v/i hacer escala

◆ **stop up** v/t sink atascar

'stop-gap solución f intermedia

'stop-light (traffic light) semáforo m; (brake light) luz m de freno

'stop·o·ver n parada f; in air travel escala f

stop·per ['stɑːpər] for bath, bottle tapón m

stop·ping ['stɑːpɪŋ]: **no stopping** sign prohibido estacionar

'stop sign (señal f de) stop m

'stop·watch cronómetro m

stor·age ['stɔːrɪdʒ] almacenamiento m; **put sth in storage** almacenar algo; **be in storage** estar almacenado

'stor·age ca·pac·i·ty COMPUT capacidad f de almacenamiento

'stor·age space espacio m para guardar cosas

store [stɔːr] **1** n tienda f; (stock) reserva f; (storehouse) almacén m **2** v/t almacenar; COMPUT guardar

'store·front fachada f de tienda

'store·house almacén m

S

'store·keep·er tendero(-a) *m(f)*

'store·room almacén *m*

sto·rey *Br* → **story²**

stork [stɔːrk] cigüeña *f*

storm [stɔːrm] *n* tormenta *f*

'storm drain canal *m* de desagüe

'storm warn·ing aviso *m* de tormenta

storm 'win·dow contraventana *f*

storm·y ['stɔːrmɪ] *adj weather, relationship* tormentoso

sto·ry¹ ['stɔːrɪ] *(tale)* cuento *m*; *(account)* historia *f*; *(newspaper article)* artículo *m*; F *(lie)* cuento *m*

sto·ry² ['stɔːrɪ] *of building* piso *m*, planta *f*

stout [staʊt] *adj person* relleno, corpulento; *boots* resistente; *defender* valiente

stove [stoʊv] *for cooking* cocina *f*, Col, Mex, Ven estufa *f*; *for heating* estufa *f*

stow [stoʊ] *v/t* guardar

◆ stow away *v/i* viajar de polizón

'stow·a·way *n* polizón *m*

strag·gler ['stræɡlər] rezagado(-a) *m(f)*

straight [streɪt] **1** *adj line, back* recto; *hair* liso; *(honest, direct)* franco, *whisky* solo; *(tidy)* en orden; *(conservative)* serio; *(not homosexual)* heterosexual; *be a straight A student* sacar sobresaliente en todas las asignaturas; *keep a straight face* contener la risa **2** *adv (in a straight line)* recto; *(directly, immediately)* directamente; *(clearly)* con claridad; *stand up straight!* ¡ponte recto!; *look s.o. straight in the eye* mirar a los ojos de alguien; *go straight* F *of criminal* reformarse; *give it to me straight* F dímelo sin rodeos; *straight ahead* be situated todo derecho; *walk, drive* todo recto; *look straight ahead* mira hacia delante; *carry straight on* of driver etc seguir recto; *straight away, straight off* en seguida; *straight out* directamente; *straight up* without ice solo

straight·en ['streɪtn] *v/t* enderezar

◆ straighten out **1** *v/t situation* resolver; F *person* poner por el buen camino **2** *v/i of road* hacerse recto

◆ straighten up *v/i* ponerse derecho

straight'for·ward *adj (honest, direct)* franco; *(simple)* simple

strain¹ [streɪn] **1** *n on rope* tensión *f*; *on engine, heart* esfuerzo *m*; *on person* agobio *m* **2** *v/t fig: finances, budget* crear presión en; *strain one's back* hacerse daño en la espalda; *strain one's eyes* forzar la vista

strain² [streɪn] *v/t vegetables* escurrir; *oil, fat etc* colar

strain³ [streɪn] *n of virus* cepa *f*

strained [streɪnd] *adj relations* tirante

strain·er ['streɪnər] *for vegetables etc* colador *m*

strait [streɪt] estrecho *m*

strait-laced [streɪt'leɪst] *adj* mojigato

strand¹ [strænd] *n of wool, thread* hebra *f*; *a strand of hair* un pelo

strand² [strænd] *v/t* abandonar; *be stranded* quedarse atrapado *or* tirado

strange [streɪndʒ] *adj (odd, curious)* extraño, raro; *(unknown, foreign)* extraño

strange·ly ['streɪndʒlɪ] *adv (oddly)* de manera extraña; *strangely enough* aunque parezca extraño

strang·er ['streɪndʒər] *(person you don't know)* extraño(-a) *m(f)*, desconocido(-a) *m(f)*; *I'm a stranger here myself* yo tampoco soy de aquí

stran·gle ['stræŋɡl] *v/t person* estrangular

strap [stræp] *n of purse, watch* correa *f*; *of brassiere, dress* tirante *m*; *of shoe* tira *f*

◆ strap in *v/t (pret & pp strapped)* poner el cinturón de seguridad a

◆ strap on *v/t* ponerse

strap·less ['stræplɪs] *adj* sin tirantes

stra·te·gic [strə'tiːdʒɪk] *adj* estratégico

strat·e·gy ['strætədʒɪ] estrategia *f*

straw¹ [strɔː] *material* paja *f*; *that's the last straw!* ¡es la gota que colma el vaso!

straw² [strɔː] *for drink* pajita *f*

straw·ber·ry ['strɔːberɪ] *fruit* fresa *f*, S. Am. frutilla *f*

stray [streɪ] **1** *adj animal* callejero; *bullet* perdido **2** *n dog* perro *m* callejero; *cat* gato *m* callejero **3** *v/i of animal, child* extraviarse, perderse; *fig: of eyes, thoughts* desviarse

streak [striːk] **1** *n of dirt, paint* raya *f*; *in hair* mechón *m*; *fig: of nastiness etc* vena *f* **2** *v/i move quickly* pasar disparado

streak·y ['striːkɪ] *adj* veteado

stream [striːm] **1** *n* riachuelo *m*; *fig: of people, complaints* oleada *f*; *come on stream* entrar en funcionamiento **2** *v/i*: *there were tears streaming down my face* me bajaban ríos de lágrimas por la cara; *people streamed out of the building* la gente salía en masa

stream·er ['striːmər] serpentina *f*

'stream·line *v/t fig* racionalizar

'stream·lined *adj car, plane* aerodinámico; *fig: organization* racionalizado

street [striːt] calle *f*

'street·car tranvía *f*

'street·light farola *f*

'street peo·ple *npl* los sin techo

'street val·ue *of drugs* valor *m* en la calle

'street·walk·er F prostituta *f*

'street·wise *adj* espabilado

strength [streŋθ] fuerza *f*; *(fig: strong*

point) punto *m* fuerte; *of friendship etc* solidez *f*; *of emotion* intensidad *f*; *of currency* fortaleza *f*

strength·en ['streŋθn] **1** *v/t muscles, currency* fortalecer; *bridge* reforzar; *country, ties, relationship* consolidar **2** *v/i of bonds, ties* consolidarse; *of currency* fortalecerse

stren·u·ous ['strenjʊəs] *adj* agotador

stren·u·ous·ly ['strenjʊəslɪ] *adv* deny tajantemente

stress [stres] **1** *n (emphasis)* énfasis *m*; *(tension)* estrés *m*; *on syllable* acento *m*; **be under stress** estar estresado **2** *v/t (emphasize: syllable)* acentuar; *importance etc* hacer hincapié en; **I must stress that ...** quiero hacer hincapié en que ...

stressed 'out [strest] *adj* F estresado

stress·ful ['stresfəl] *adj* estresante

stretch [stretʃ] **1** *n of land, water* extensión *m*; *of road* tramo *m*; **at a stretch** *(non-stop)* de un tirón **2** *adj fabric* elástico **3** *v/t material, income* estirar; F *rules* ser flexible con; **he stretched out his hand** estiró la mano; **my job stretches me** mi trabajo me obliga a esforzarme **4** *v/i to relax muscles, reach* sth estirarse; *(spread)* extenderse; *of fabric* estirarse, dar de sí

stretch·er ['stretʃər] camilla *f*

strict [strɪkt] *adj* estricto

strict·ly ['strɪktlɪ] *adv* con rigor; **it is strictly forbidden** está terminantemente prohibido

strid·den ['strɪdn] *pp → **stride***

stride [straɪd] **1** *n* zancada *f*; **take sth in one's stride** tomarse algo con tranquilidad; **make great strides** *fig* avanzar a pasos agigantados **2** *v/i (pret strode, pp stridden)* caminar dando zancadas

stri·dent ['straɪdnt] *adj also fig* estridente

strike [straɪk] **1** *n of workers* huelga *f*; *in baseball* strike *m*; *of oil* descubrimiento *m*; **be on strike** estar en huelga; **go on strike** ir a la huelga **2** *v/i (pret & pp struck)* *of workers* hacer huelga; *(attack)* atacar; *of disaster* sobrevenir; *of clock* dar las horas; **the clock struck three** el reloj dio las tres **3** *v/t (pret & pp struck)* *(hit)* golpear; *fig: of disaster* sacudir; *match* encender; *oil* descubrir; **didn't it ever strike you that ...?** ¿no se te ocurrió que ...?; **she struck me as being ...** me dio la impresión de ser ...

◆ **strike out 1** *v/t* tachar; *in baseball* eliminar a, *L.Am.* ponchar **2** *v/i in baseball* quedar eliminado, *L.Am.* poncharse

'**strike·break·er** esquirol(a) *m(f)*

strik·er ['straɪkər] *(person on strike)* huelguista *m/f*; *in soccer* delantero(-a) *m(f)*

strik·ing ['straɪkɪŋ] *adj (marked)* sorprendente, llamativo; *(eye-catching)* deslumbrante

string [strɪŋ] *n also of violin, racket etc* cuerda *f*; **strings** *musicians* la sección de cuerda; **pull strings** mover hilos; **a string of** *(series)* una serie de

◆ **string along 1** *v/i (pret & pp strung)* F apuntarse F **2** *v/t (pret & pp strung)* F: **string s.o. along** dar falsas esperanzas a alguien

◆ **string up** *v/t* F colgar

stringed 'in·stru·ment [strɪŋd] instrumento *m* de cuerda

strin·gent ['strɪndʒənt] *adj* riguroso

'**string play·er** instrumentista *m/f* de cuerda

strip [strɪp] **1** *n of land* franja *f*; *of cloth* tira *f*; *(comic strip)* tira *f* cómica **2** *v/t (pret & pp stripped)* *(remove)* quitar; *(undress)* desnudar; **strip s.o. of sth** despojar a alguien de algo **3** *v/i (pret & pp stripped)* *(undress)* desnudarse; *of stripper* hacer striptease

'**strip club** club *m* de striptease

stripe [straɪp] raya *f*; *indicating rank* galón *m*

striped [straɪpt] *adj* a rayas

'**strip joint** F → **strip club**

strip·per ['strɪpər] artista *m/f* de striptease; **male stripper** artista *m* de striptease

'**strip show** espectáculo *m* de striptease

strip'tease striptease *m*

strive [straɪv] *v/i (pret strove, pp striven)* esforzarse; **strive to do sth** esforzarse por hacer algo; **strive for** luchar por

striv·en ['strɪvn] *pp → **strive***

strobe (**light**) [strəʊb] luz *f* estroboscópica

strode [strəʊd] *pret → **stride***

stroke [strəʊk] **1** *n* MED derrame *m* cerebral, *when writing* trazo *m*; *when painting* pincelada *f*; *(style of swimming)* estilo *m*; **stroke of luck** golpe de suerte; **she never does a stroke (of work)** no pega ni golpe **2** *v/t* acariciar

stroll [strəʊl] **1** *n* paseo *m* **2** *v/i* caminar

stroll·er ['strəʊlər] *for baby* silla *f* de paseo

strong [strɒŋ] *adj* fuerte; *structure* resistente; *candidate* claro, con muchos posibilidades; *support, supporter, views, objection* firme; *tea, coffee* cargado, fuerte

'**strong·hold** *fig* baluarte *m*

strong·ly ['strɒŋlɪ] *adv* fuertemente, rotundamente

strong-mind·ed [strɒːŋˈmaɪndɪd] *adj* decidido

'**strong point** (punto *m*) fuerte *m*

'**strong-room** cámara *f* acorazada

strong-willed [strɒːŋˈwɪld] *adj* tenaz

strove [stroʊv] *pret* → **strive**

struck [strʌk] *pret & pp* → **strike**

struc·tur·al [ˈstrʌktʃərl] *adj* estructural

struc·ture [ˈstrʌktʃər] **1** *n* (*something built*) construcción *f*; *of novel, society etc* estructura *f* **2** *v/t* estructurar

strug·gle [ˈstrʌɡl] **1** *n* lucha *f* **2** *v/i with a person* forcejear; (*have a hard time*) luchar; **they struggled for the gun** forcejearon por conseguir la pistola; **he was struggling with the door** tenía problemas para abrir la puerta; **struggle to do sth** luchar por hacer algo

strum [strʌm] *v/t* (*pret & pp* **strummed**) *guitar* rasguear

strung [strʌŋ] *pret & pp* → **string**

strut [strʌt] *v/i* (*pret & pp* **strutted**) pavonearse

stub [stʌb] **1** *n of cigarette* colilla *f*; *of check* matriz *f*; *of ticket* resguardo *m* **2** *v/t* (*pret & pp* **stubbed**): **stub one's toe** darse un golpe en el dedo (del pie)
◆ **stub out** *v/t* apagar (apretando)

stub·ble [ˈstʌbl] *on man's face* barba *f* incipiente

stub·born [ˈstʌbərn] *adj person* testarudo, terco; *defense, refusal, denial* tenaz, pertinaz

stub·by [ˈstʌbɪ] *adj* regordete

stuck [stʌk] **1** *pret & pp* → **stick**² **2** *adj* F: **be stuck on s.o.** estar colado por alguien F

stuck-'up *adj* F engreído

stu·dent [ˈstuːdnt] *at high school* alumno(-a) *m(f)*; *at college, university* estudiante *m/f*

stu·dent 'nurse estudiante *m/f* de enfermería

stu·dent 'teach·er profesor(a) *m(f)* en prácticas

stu·di·o [ˈstuːdɪoʊ] *of artist, sculptor* estudio *m*; (*film studio, TV studio*) estudio *m*, plató *m*

stu·di·ous [ˈstuːdɪəs] *adj* estudioso

stud·y [ˈstʌdɪ] **1** *n* estudio *m*; (*room*) (cuarto *m* de) estudio *m* **2** *v/t & v/i* (*pret & pp* **studied**) estudiar

stuff [stʌf] **1** *n* (*things*) cosas *fpl* **2** *v/t turkey* rellenar; **stuff sth into sth** meter algo dentro de algo

stuffed 'toy [stʌft] muñeco *m* de peluche

stuff·ing [ˈstʌfɪŋ] relleno *m*

stuff·y [ˈstʌfɪ] *adj room* cargado; *person*

anticuado, estirado

stum·ble [ˈstʌmbl] *v/i* tropezar
◆ **stumble across** *v/t* toparse con
◆ **stumble over** *v/t* tropezar con; *words* trastrabillarse con

stum·bling-block [ˈstʌmblɪŋ] escollo *m*

stump [stʌmp] **1** *n of tree* tocón *m* **2** *v/t of question, questioner* dejar perplejo
◆ **stump up** *v/t* F aflojar, *Span* apoquinar F

stun [stʌn] *v/t* (*pret & pp* **stunned**) *of blow* dejar sin sentido; *of news* dejar atónito or de piedra

stung [stʌŋ] *pret & pp* → **sting**

stunk [stʌŋk] *pp* → **stink**

stun·ning [ˈstʌnɪŋ] *adj* (*amazing*) increíble, sorprendente; (*very beautiful*) imponente

stunt [stʌnt] *n for publicity* truco *m*; *in movie* escena *f* peligrosa

'**stunt·man** *in movie* doble *m*, especialista *m*

stu·pe·fy [ˈstuːpɪfaɪ] *v/t* (*pret & pp* **stupefied**) dejar perplejo

stu·pen·dous [stuːˈpendəs] *adj* extraordinario

stu·pid [ˈstuːpɪd] *adj* estúpido; **what a stupid thing to say / do!** ¡qué estúpido!

stu·pid·i·ty [stuːˈpɪdətɪ] estupidez *f*

stu·por [ˈstuːpər] aturdimiento *m*

stur·dy [ˈstɜːrdɪ] *adj person* robusto; *table, plant* resistente

stut·ter [ˈstʌtər] *v/i* tartamudear

sty [staɪ] *for pig* pocilga *f*

style [staɪl] *n* estilo *m*; (*fashion*) moda *f*; **go out of style** pasarse de moda

styl·ish [ˈstaɪlɪʃ] *adj* elegante

styl·ist [ˈstaɪlɪst] (*hair stylist*) estilista *m/f*

sub·com·mit·tee [ˈsʌbkəmɪtɪ] subcomité *m*

sub·com·pact (**car**) [sʌbˈkɑːmpækt] *utilitario de pequeño tamaño*

sub·con·scious [sʌbˈkɑːnʃəs] *adj* subconsciente; **the subconscious** (**mind**) el subconsciente

sub·con·scious·ly [sʌbˈkɑːnʃəslɪ] *adv* inconscientemente

sub·con·tract [sʌbkənˈtrækt] *v/t* subcontratar

sub·con·trac·tor [sʌbkənˈtræktər] subcontratista *m/f*

sub·di·vide [sʌbdɪˈvaɪd] *v/t* subdividir

sub·due [səbˈduː] *v/t rebellion, mob* someter, contener

sub·dued [səbˈduːd] *adj* apagado

sub·head·ing [ˈsʌbhedɪŋ] subtítulo *m*

sub·hu·man [sʌbˈhjuːmən] *adj* inhumano

sub·ject 1 *n* [ˈsʌbdʒɪkt] (*topic*) tema *m*; (*branch of learning*) asignatura *f*, materia f; GRAM sujeto m; of monarch súbdito(-a) m(f); **change the subject** cambiar de tema 2 adj ['sʌbdʒɪkt]: **be subject to** have tendency to ser propenso a; be regulated by estar sujeto a; **subject to availability** of goods promoción válida hasta fin de existencias 3 v/t [səb'dʒekt] someter

sub·jec·tive [səb'dʒektɪv] adj subjetivo

sub·junc·tive [səb'dʒʌŋktɪv] n GRAM subjuntivo m

sub·let ['sʌblet] v/t (pret & pp **sublet**) realquilar

sub·ma·chine gun metralleta f

sub·ma·rine ['sʌbməriːn] submarino m

sub·merge [səb'mɜːrdʒ] 1 v/t sumergir 2 v/i of submarine sumergirse

sub·mis·sion [səb'mɪʃn] (surrender) sumisión f; to committee etc propuesta f

sub·mis·sive [səb'mɪsɪv] adj sumiso

sub·mit [səb'mɪt] 1 v/t (pret & pp **submitted**) plan, proposal presentar 2 v/i (pret & pp **submitted**) someterse

sub·or·di·nate [sə'bɔːrdɪneɪt] 1 adj employee, position subordinado 2 n subordinado(-a) m(f)

sub·poe·na [sə'piːnə] 1 n citación f 2 v/t person citar

◆ **sub·scribe to** [səb'skraɪb] v/t magazine etc suscribirse a; theory suscribir

sub·scrib·er [səb'skraɪbər] to magazine suscriptor(a) m(f)

sub·scrip·tion [səb'skrɪpʃn] suscripción f

sub·se·quent ['sʌbsɪkwənt] adj posterior

sub·se·quent·ly ['sʌbsɪkwəntlɪ] adv posteriormente

sub·side [səb'saɪd] v/i of flood waters bajar; of high winds amainar; of building hundirse; of fears, panic calmarse

sub·sid·i·a·ry [səb'sɪdɪerɪ] n filial f

sub·si·dize ['sʌbsɪdaɪz] v/t subvencionar

sub·si·dy ['sʌbsɪdɪ] subvención f

◆ **sub·sist on** v/t subsistir a base de

sub·sis·tence farm·er [səb'sɪstəns] agricultor(a) m(f) de subsistencia

sub·sis·tence lev·el nivel m mínimo de subsistencia

sub·stance ['sʌbstəns] (matter) sustancia f

sub·stan·dard [sʌb'stændərd] adj performance deficiente; shoes, clothes con tara

sub·stan·tial [səb'stænʃl] adj sustancial, considerable

sub·stan·tial·ly [səb'stænʃlɪ] adv (considerably) considerablemente; (in essence) sustancialmente, esencialmente

sub·stan·ti·ate [səb'stænʃɪeɪt] v/t probar

sub·stan·tive [səb'stæntɪv] adj significativo

sub·sti·tute ['sʌbstɪtuːt] 1 n for person sustituto(-a) m(f); for commodity sustituto m; SP suplente m/f 2 v/t sustituir, reemplazar; **substitute X for Y** sustituir Y por X 3 v/i: **substitute for s.o.** sustituir a alguien

sub·sti·tu·tion [sʌbstɪ'tuːʃn] (act) sustitución f; **make a substitution** SP hacer un cambio or sustitución

sub·ti·tle ['sʌbtaɪtl] n subtítulo m

sub·tle ['sʌtl] adj sutil

sub·tract [səb'trækt] v/t number restar

sub·urb ['sʌbɜːrb] zona f residencial de la periferia

sub·ur·ban [sə'bɜːrbən] adj housing de la periferia; attitudes, lifestyle aburguesado

sub·ver·sive [səb'vɜːrsɪv] 1 adj subversivo 2 n subversivo(-a) m(f)

sub·way ['sʌbweɪ] metro m

sub 'ze·ro adj bajo cero

suc·ceed [sək'siːd] 1 v/i (be successful) tener éxito; to throne suceder en el trono; **succeed in doing sth** conseguir hacer algo 2 v/t (come after) suceder

suc·ceed·ing [sək'siːdɪŋ] adj siguiente

suc·cess [sək'ses] éxito m; **be a success** of book, play, idea ser un éxito; of person tener éxito

suc·cess·ful [sək'sesfəl] adj person con éxito; **be successful in business** tener éxito en los negocios; **be successful in doing sth** lograr hacer algo

suc·cess·ful·ly [sək'sesfəlɪ] adv con éxito

suc·ces·sion [sək'seʃn] sucesión f; **three days in succession** tres días seguidos

suc·ces·sive [sək'sesɪv] adj sucesivo

suc·ces·sor [sək'sesər] sucesor(a) m(f)

suc·cinct [sək'sɪŋkt] adj sucinto

suc·cu·lent ['sʌkjulənt] adj meat, fruit suculento

suc·cumb [sə'kʌm] v/i (give in) sucumbir

such [sʌtʃ] 1 adj (of that kind) tal; **such men are dangerous** los hombres así son peligrosos; **I know of many such cases** conozco muchos casos así; **don't make such a fuss** no armes tanto alboroto; **I never thought it would be such a success** nunca imaginé que sería un éxito tal; **such as** como; **there is no such word as …** no existe la palabra … 2 adv tan; **as such** como tal

suck [sʌk] 1 v/t candy etc chupar; **suck one's thumb** chuparse el dedo 2 v/i P: **it sucks** (is awful) es una mierda P

◆ **suck up** 1 v/t absorber 2 v/i F: **suck up to s.o.** hacer la pelota a alguien

suck·er ['sʌkər] F (person) primo(-a) m/f F, ingenuo(-a) m/f; F (lollipop) piruleta f

S

suc·tion ['sʌkʃn] succión *f*

sud·den ['sʌdn] *adj* repentino; **all of a sudden** de repente

sud·den·ly ['sʌdnlɪ] *adv* de repente

suds [sʌdz] *npl* (*soap suds*) espuma *f*

sue [su:] *v/t* demandar

suede [sweɪd] *n* ante *m*

suf·fer ['sʌfər] 1 *v/i* (*be in great pain*) sufrir; (*deteriorate*) deteriorarse; **be suffering from** 2 *v/t loss, setback, heart attack* sufrir

suf·fer·ing ['sʌfərɪŋ] *n* sufrimiento *m*

suf·fi·cient [sə'fɪʃnt] *adj* suficiente

suf·fi·cient·ly [sə'fɪʃntlɪ] *adv* suficientemente

suf·fo·cate ['sʌfəkeɪt] 1 *v/i* asfixiarse 2 *v/t* asfixiar

suf·fo·ca·tion [sʌfə'keɪʃn] asfixia *f*

sug·ar ['ʃʊgər] 1 *n* azúcar *m or f*; **how many sugars?** ¿cuántas cucharadas de azúcar? 2 *v/t* echar azúcar a; **is it sugared?** ¿lleva azúcar?

'sug·ar bowl azucarero *m*

'sug·ar cane caña *f* de azúcar

sug·gest [sə'dʒest] *v/t* sugerir; **I suggest that we stop now** sugiero que paremos ahora

sug·ges·tion [sə'dʒestʃən] sugerencia *f*

su·i·cide ['su:ɪsaɪd] suicidio *m*; **commit suicide** suicidarse

suit [su:t] 1 *n* traje *m*; *in cards* palo *m* 2 *v/t of clothes, color* sentar bien a; **suit yourself!** F ¡haz lo que quieras!; **be suited for sth** estar hecho para algo

suit·a·ble ['su:təbl] *adj partner, words, clothing* apropiado, adecuado; *time* apropiado

suit·a·bly ['su:təblɪ] *adv* apropiadamente, adecuadamente

'suit·case maleta *f*, *L.Am.* valija *f*

suite [swi:t] *of rooms*, MUS suite *f*; *furniture* tresillo *m*

sul·fur ['sʌlfər] azufre *m*

sul·fur·ic ac·id [sʌl'fju:rɪk] ácido *m* sulfúrico

sulk [sʌlk] *v/i* enfurruñarse; **be sulking** estar enfurruñado

sulk·y ['sʌlkɪ] *adj* enfurruñado

sul·len ['sʌlən] *adj* malhumorado, huraño

sul·phur *etc Br* → **sulfur** *etc*

sul·try ['sʌltrɪ] *adj climate* sofocante, bochornoso; *sexually* sensual

sum [sʌm] (*total*) total *m*, suma *f*; (*amount*) cantidad *f*; *in arithmetic* suma *f*; **a large sum of money** una gran cantidad de dinero; **sum insured** suma *f* asegurada; **the sum total of his efforts** la suma de sus esfuerzos

◆ **sum up** 1 *v/t* (*pret & pp summed*)

(*summarize*) resumir; (*assess*) catalogar 2 *v/i* (*pret & pp summed*) LAW recapitular

sum·mar·ize ['sʌməraɪz] *v/t* resumir

sum·ma·ry ['sʌmərɪ] *n* resumen *m*

sum·mer ['sʌmər] verano *m*

sum·mit ['sʌmɪt] *of mountain* cumbre *f*, cima *f*; POL cumbre *f*

'sum·mit meet·ing → **summit**

sum·mon ['sʌmən] *v/t staff, ministers* llamar; *meeting* convocar

◆ **summon up** *v/t*: **he summoned up his strength** hizo acopio de fuerzas

sum·mons ['sʌmənz] *nsg* LAW citación *f*

sump [sʌmp] *for oil* cárter *m*

sun [sʌn] sol *m*; **in the sun** al sol; **out of the sun** a la sombra; **he has had too much sun** le ha dado demasiado el sol

'sun·bathe *v/i* tomar el sol

'sun·bed cama *f* de rayos UVA

'sun·block crema *f* solar de alta protección

'sun·burn quemadura *f* (del sol)

'sun·burnt *adj* quemado (por el sol)

Sun·day ['sʌndeɪ] domingo *m*

'sun·dial reloj *m* de sol

sun·dries ['sʌndrɪz] *npl* varios *mpl*

sung [sʌŋ] *pp* → **sing**

'sun·glass·es *npl* gafas *fpl or L.Am.* anteojos *mpl* de sol

sunk [sʌŋk] *pp* → **sink**

sunk·en ['sʌŋkn] *adj ship, cheeks* hundido

sun·ny ['sʌnɪ] *adj day* soleado; *disposition* radiante; **it is sunny** hace sol

'sun·rise amanecer *m*

'sun·set atardecer *m*, puesta *f* de sol

'sun·shade sombrilla *f*

'sun·shine sol *m*

'sun·stroke insolación *f*

'sun·tan bronceado *m*; **get a suntan** broncearse

su·per ['su:pər] 1 *adj* F genial F, estupendo F 2 *n* (*janitor*) portero(-a) *m(f)*

su·perb [su'pɜ:rb] *adj* excelente

su·per·fi·cial [su:pər'fɪʃl] *adj* superficial

su·per·flu·ous [su'pɜ:rfluəs] *adj* superfluo

su·per·hu·man *adj efforts* sobrehumano

su·per·in·tend·ent [su:pərɪn'tendənt] *of apartment block* portero(-a) *m(f)*; *Br of police* inspector(a) *m(f)* jefe

su·pe·ri·or [su'pɪrɪər] 1 *adj* (*better*) superior; *pej: attitude* arrogante 2 *n in organization* superior *m*

su·per·la·tive [su'pɜ:rlətɪv] 1 *adj* superb excelente 2 *n* GRAM superlativo *m*

'su·per·mar·ket supermercado *m*

su·per·nat·u·ral 1 *adj powers* sobrenatural **2** *n*: **the supernatural** lo sobrenatural

'su·per·pow·er POL superpotencia *f*

su·per·son·ic [suːpərˈsɑːnɪk] *adj flight, aircraft* supersónico

su·per·sti·tion [suːpərˈstɪʃn] superstición *f*

su·per·sti·tious [suːpərˈstɪʃəs] *adj person* supersticioso

su·per·vise [ˈsuːpərvaɪz] *v/t class* vigilar; *workers* supervisar; *activities* dirigir

su·per·vi·sor [ˈsuːpərvaɪzər] *at work* supervisor(a) *m(f)*

sup·per [ˈsʌpər] cena *f*, *L.Am.* comida *f*

sup·ple [ˈsʌpl] *adj person* ágil; *limbs, material* flexible

sup·ple·ment [ˈsʌplɪmənt] *(extra payment)* suplemento *m*

sup·pli·er [səˈplaɪər] COM proveedor *m*

sup·ply [səˈplaɪ] **1** *n* suministro *m*, abastecimiento *m*; **supply and demand** la oferta y la demanda; **supplies** *of food* provisiones *fpl*; **office supplies** material *f* de oficina **2** *v/t (pret & pp supplied) goods* suministrar; **supply s.o. with sth** suministrar algo a alguien; **be supplied with ...** venir con ...

sup·port [səˈpɔːrt] **1** *n for structure* soporte *m*; *(backing)* apoyo *m* **2** *v/t building, structure* soportar, sostener; *financially* mantener; *(back)* apoyar

sup·port·er [səˈpɔːrtər] partidario(-a) *m(f)*; *of football team etc* seguidor(a) *m(f)*

sup·port·ive [səˈpɔːrtɪv] *adj* comprensivo; **be supportive** apoyar *(toward, of a)*

sup·pose [səˈpouz] *v/t (imagine)* suponer; **I suppose so** supongo (que sí); **you are not supposed to ...** (*not allowed to)* no deberías ...; **it is supposed to be delivered today** *(be meant to)* se supone que lo van a entregar hoy; **it's supposed to be very beautiful** *is said to be* se supone que es hermosísima

sup·pos·ed·ly [səˈpouzɪdlɪ] *adv* supuestamente

sup·pos·i·to·ry [səˈpɑːzɪtɔːrɪ] MED supositorio *m*

sup·press [səˈpres] *v/t rebellion etc* reprimir, sofocar

sup·pres·sion [səˈpreʃn] represión *f*

su·prem·a·cy [suːˈpreməsɪ] supremacía *f*

su·preme [suːˈpriːm] *adj* supremo

sur·charge [ˈsɜːrtʃɑːrdʒ] *n* recargo *m*

sure [ʃʊr] **1** *adj* seguro; **I'm not sure** no estoy seguro; **be sure about sth** estar seguro de algo; **make sure that ...** asegurarse de que ... **2** *adv*: **sure enough** efectivamente; **it sure is hot today** F vaya calor que hace F; **sure!** F ¡claro!

sure·ly [ˈʃʊrlɪ] *adv (gladly)* claro que sí; **surely you don't mean that!** ¡ no lo dirás en serio!; **surely somebody knows** alguien tiene que saberlo

sure·ty [ˈʃʊrətɪ] *for loan* fianza *f*, depósito *m*

surf [sɜːrf] **1** *n on sea* surf *m* **2** *v/t*: **surf the Net** navegar por Internet

sur·face [ˈsɜːrfɪs] **1** *n of table, object, water* superficie *f*; **on the surface** *fig* a primera vista **2** *v/i of swimmer, submarine* salir a la superficie; *(appear)* aparecer

'sur·face mail correo *m* terrestre

'surf·board tabla *f* de surf

surf·er [ˈsɜːrfər] *on sea* surfista *m/f*

surf·ing [ˈsɜːrfɪŋ] surf *m*; **go surfing** ir a hacer surf

surge [sɜːrdʒ] *n in electric current* sobrecarga *f*; *in demand etc* incremento *m* repentino

◆ **surge forward** *v/i of crowd* avanzar atropelladamente

sur·geon [ˈsɜːrdʒən] cirujano(-a) *m(f)*

sur·ge·ry [ˈsɜːrdʒərɪ] cirugía *f*; **undergo surgery** ser intervenido quirúrgicamente

sur·gi·cal [ˈsɜːrdʒɪkl] *adj* quirúrgico

sur·gi·cal·ly [ˈsɜːrdʒɪklɪ] *adv* quirúrgicamente

sur·ly [ˈsɜːrlɪ] *adj* arisco, hosco

sur·mount [sərˈmaunt] *v/t difficulties* superar

sur·name [ˈsɜːrneɪm] apellido *m*

sur·pass [sərˈpæs] *v/t* superar

sur·plus [ˈsɜːrpləs] **1** *n* excedente *m* **2** *adj* excedente

sur·prise [sərˈpraɪz] **1** *n* sorpresa *f*; **it came as no surprise** no me sorprendió **2** *v/t* sorprender; **be / look surprised** estar / parecer sorprendido

sur·pris·ing [sərˈpraɪzɪŋ] *adj* sorprendente; **it's not surprising that ...** no me sorprende que ...

sur·pris·ing·ly [sərˈpraɪzɪŋlɪ] *adv* sorprendentemente

sur·ren·der [sərˈrendər] **1** *v/i of army* rendirse **2** *v/t (hand in: weapons etc)* entregar **3** *n* rendición *f*; *(handing in)* entrega *f*

sur·ro·gate 'moth·er [ˈsʌrəgət] madre *f* de alquiler

sur·round [səˈraund] **1** *v/t* rodear; **surrounded by** rodeado de *or* por **2** *n of picture etc* marco *m*

sur·round·ing [səˈraundɪŋ] *adj* circundante

sur·round·ings [səˈraundɪŋz] *npl of village* alrededores *mpl*; *(environment)* entorno *m*

sur·vey [ˈsɜːrveɪ] **1** *n* [ˈsɜːrveɪ] *of modern*

S

literature etc estudio *m*; *of building* tasación *f*, peritaje; *poll* encuesta *f* 2 *v/t* [sər-'veɪ] (*look at*) contemplar; *building* tasar, peritar

sur·vey·or [sɜːr'veɪr] tasador(a) *m(f)* or perito (-a) *m(f)* de la propiedad

sur·viv·al [sər'vaɪvl] supervivencia *f*

sur·vive [sər'vaɪv] 1 *v/i* sobrevivir; *how are you? - I'm surviving* ¿cómo estás? - voy tirando; *his two surviving daughters* las dos hijas que aún viven 2 *v/t accident, operation* sobrevivir a; (*outlive*) sobrevivir

sur·vi·vor [sər'vaɪvər] superviviente *m/f*; *he's a survivor fig* es incombustible

sus·cep·ti·ble [sə'septəbl] *adj emotionally* sensible, susceptible; *be susceptible to the cold/heat* ser sensible al frío / calor

sus·pect 1 *n* ['sʌspekt] sospechoso(-a) *m(f)* 2 *v/t* [sə'spekt] *person* sospechar de; (*suppose*) sospechar

sus·pect·ed [sə'spektɪd] *adj murderer* presunto; *cause, heart attack etc* supuesto

sus·pend [sə'spend] *v/t* (*hang*) colgar; *from office, duties* suspender

sus·pend·ers [sə'spendərz] *npl for pants* tirantes *mpl*, S. Am. suspensores *mpl*

sus·pense [sə'spens] *Span* suspense *m*, L.Am. suspenso *m*

sus·pen·sion [sə'spenʃn] MOT, *from duty* suspensión *f*

sus·pen·sion bridge puente *m* colgante

sus·pi·cion [sə'spɪʃn] sospecha *f*

sus·pi·cious [sə'spɪʃəs] *adj* (*causing suspicion*) sospechoso; (*feeling suspicion*) receloso, desconfiado; *be suspicious of* sospechar de

sus·pi·cious·ly [sə'spɪʃəslɪ] *adv behave* de manera sospechosa; *ask* con recelo or desconfianza

sus·tain [sə'steɪn] *v/t* sostener

sus·tain·a·ble [sə'steɪnəbl] *adj* sostenible

swab [swɑːb] *material* torunda *f*; *test* muestra *f*

swag·ger ['swægər] *n*: *walk with a swagger* caminar pavoneándose

swal·low¹ ['swɑːloʊ] 1 *v/t liquid, food* tragar, tragarse 2 *v/i* tragar

swal·low² ['swɑːloʊ] *n bird* golondrina *f*

swam [swæm] *pret* → *swim*

swamp [swɑːmp] 1 *n* pantano *m* 2 *v/t*: *be swamped with* estar inundado de

swamp·y ['swɑːmpɪ] *adj* pantanoso

swan [swɑːn] cisne *m*

swap [swɑːp] 1 *v/t* (*pret & pp swapped*) cambiar; *swap sth for sth* cambiar algo por algo 2 *v/i* (*pret & pp swapped*) hacer un cambio

swarm [swɔːrm] 1 *n of bees* enjambre *m* 2 *v/i*: *the town was swarming with ...* la ciudad estaba abarrotada de ...

swar·thy ['swɔːrðɪ] *adj face, complexion* moreno

swat [swɑːt] *v/t* (*pret & pp swatted*) *insect, fly* aplastar, matar

sway [sweɪ] 1 *n* (*influence, power*) dominio *m* 2 *v/i* tambalearse

swear [swer] *v/t* (*pret swore, pp sworn*) (*use swearword*) decir palabrotas or tacos; *swear at s.o.* insultar a alguien; *I swear* lo juro 2 *v/t* (*pret swore, pp sworn*) (*promise*), LAW jurar

◆ swear in *v/t witnesses etc* tomar juramento a

'swear·word palabrota *f*, taco *m*

sweat [swet] 1 *n* sudor *m*; *covered in sweat* empapado de sudor 2 *v/i* sudar

'sweat·band banda *f* (en la frente); *on wrist* muñequera *f*

sweat·er ['swetər] suéter *m*, Span jersey *m*

'sweat·shirt sudadera *f*

sweat·y ['swetɪ] *adj hands* sudoroso

Swede [swiːd] sueco(-a) *m(f)*

Swe·den ['swiːdn] Suecia

Swe·dish ['swiːdɪʃ] 1 *adj* sueco 2 *n* sueco *m*

sweep [swiːp] 1 *v/t* (*pret & pp swept*) *floor, leaves* barrer 2 *n* (*long curve*) curva *f*

◆ sweep up *v/t mess, crumbs* barrer

sweep·ing ['swiːpɪŋ] *adj statement* demasiado generalizado; *changes* radical

sweet [swiːt] *adj taste, tea* dulce; F (*kind*) amable; F (*cute*) mono

sweet and 'sour *adj* agridulce

'sweet·corn maíz *m*, S. Am. choclo *m*

sweet·en ['swiːtn] *v/t drink, food* endulzar

sweet·en·er ['swiːtnər] *for drink* edulcorante *m*

'sweet·heart novio(-a) *m(f)*

swell [swel] 1 *v/i of wound, limb* hincharse 2 *adj* F (*good*) genial F, fenomenal F 3 *n of the sea* oleaje *m*

swell·ing ['swelɪŋ] *n* MED hinchazón *f*

swel·ter·ing ['sweltərɪŋ] *adj heat, day* sofocante

swept [swept] *pret & pp* → *sweep*

swerve [swɜːrv] *v/i of driver, car* girar bruscamente, dar un volantazo

swift [swɪft] *adj* rápido

swim [swɪm] 1 *v/i* (*pret & pp swum*) nadar; *go swimming* ir a nadar; *my head is swimming* me da vueltas la cabeza 2 *n* baño *m*; *go for a swim* ir a darse un baño swim·mer ['swimər] nadador(a) m(f)

swim·ming ['swimiŋ] natación f

'swim·ming cos·tume traje m de baño, bañador m

'swim·ming pool piscina f, Mex alberca f, Rpl pileta f

swin·dle ['swindl] 1 n timo m, estafa f 2 v/t timar, estafar; **swindle s.o. out of sth** estafar algo a alguien

swine [swain] F (person) cerdo(-a) m(f)

swing [swiŋ] 1 n oscilación f; for child columpio m; **swing to the Democrats** giro favorable a los Demócratas 2 v/t (pret & pp **swung**) balancear; hips menear 3 v/i (pret & pp **swung**) balancearse; (turn) girar; of public opinion etc cambiar

swing·'door puerta f basculante or de vaivén

Swiss [swis] 1 adj suizo 2 n person suizo(-a) m(f); **the Swiss** los suizos

switch [switʃ] 1 n for light interruptor m; (change) cambio m 2 v/t (change) cambiar de 3 v/i (change) cambiar

◆ switch off v/t lights, engine, PC, TV apagar

◆ switch on v/t lights, engine, PC, TV encender, L.Am. prender

'switch·board centralita f, L.Am. conmutador

'switch·o·ver to new system cambio m (to a)

Swit·zer·land ['switsərlənd] Suiza

swiv·el ['swivl] v/i (pret & pp **swiveled**, Br **swivelled**) of chair, monitor girar

swol·len ['swoulən] adj hinchado

swoop [swu:p] v/i of bird volar en picado

◆ swoop down on v/t prey caer en picado sobre

◆ swoop on v/t of police etc hacer una redada contra

sword [sɔ:rd] espada f

'sword·fish pez f espada

swore [swɔ:r] pret → **swear**

sworn [swɔ:rn] pp → **swear**

swum [swʌm] pp → **swim**

swung [swʌŋ] pret & pp → **swing**

syc·a·more ['sikəmɔ:r] plátano m (árbol)

syl·la·ble ['siləbl] sílaba f

syl·la·bus ['siləbəs] plan m de estudios

sym·bol ['simbəl] símbolo m

sym·bol·ic [sim'bɑ:lik] adj simbólico

sym·bol·ism ['simbəlizm] simbolismo m

sym·bol·ist ['simbəlist] simbolista m/f

sym·bol·ize ['simbəlaiz] v/t simbolizar

sym·met·ri·c(al) [si'metrikl] adj simétrico

sym·me·try ['simətri] simetría f

sym·pa·thet·ic [simpə'θetik] adj (showing pity) compasivo; (understanding) comprensivo; **be sympathetic toward a person / an idea** simpatizar con una persona / idea

◆ sym·pa·thize with ['simpəθaiz] v/t person, views comprender

sym·pa·thiz·er ['simpəθaizər] POL simpatizante m/f

sym·pa·thy ['simpəθi] (pity) compasión f; (understanding) comprensión f; **don't expect any sympathy from me!** no esperes que te compadezca

sym·pho·ny ['simfəni] sinfonía f

'sym·pho·ny or·ches·tra orquesta f sinfónica

symp·tom ['simptəm] also fig síntoma f

symp·to·mat·ic [simptə'mætik] adj: **be symptomatic of** fig ser sintomático de

syn·chro·nize ['siŋkrənaiz] v/t sincronizar

syn·o·nym ['sinənim] sinónimo m

sy·non·y·mous [si'nɑ:niməs] adj sinónimo; **be synonymous with** fig ser sinónimo de

syn·tax ['sintæks] sintaxis f inv

syn·the·siz·er ['sinθəsaizər] MUS sintetizador m

syn·thet·ic [sin'θetik] adj sintético

syph·i·lis ['sifilis] sífilis f

Syr·i·a ['siriə] Siria

Syr·i·an ['siriən] 1 adj sirio 2 n sirio(-a) m(f)

sy·ringe [si'rindʒ] n jeringuilla f

syr·up ['sirəp] almíbar m

sys·tem ['sistəm] also COMPUT sistema f; **the braking system** el sistema de frenado; **the digestive system** el aparato digestivo

sys·te·mat·ic [sistə'mætik] adj sistemático

sys·tem·at·i·cal·ly [sistə'mætikli] adv sistemáticamente

sys·tems 'an·a·lyst ['sistəmz] COMPUT analista m/f de sistemas

S

T

tab [tæb] *n for pulling* lengüeta *f*; *in text* tabulador *m*; *bill* cuenta *f*; **pick up the tab** pagar (la cuenta)

ta·ble ['teɪbl] *n* mesa *f*; *of figures* cuadro *m*

'ta·ble·cloth mantel *m*

'table lamp lámpara *f* de mesa

table of 'con·tents índice *m* (de contenidos)

'ta·ble·spoon *object* cuchara *f* grande; *quantity* cucharada *f* grande

ta·blet ['tæblɪt] MED pastilla *f*

'ta·ble ten·nis tenis *m* de mesa

tab·loid ['tæblɔɪd] *n newspaper* periódico *m* sensacionalista *(de tamaño tabloide)*

ta·boo [təˈbuː] *adj* tabú *inv*

ta·cit ['tæsɪt] *adj* tácito

ta·ci·turn ['tæsɪtɜːrn] *adj* taciturno

tack [tæk] **1** *n* (*nail*) tachuela *f* **2** *v/t* (*sew*) hilvanar **3** *v/i of yacht* dar bordadas

tack·le ['tækl] **1** *n* (*equipment*) equipo *m*; SP entrada *f*; **fishing tackle** aparejos *mpl* de pesca **2** *v/t* SP entrar or a; *problem* abordar; *intruder* hacer frente a

tack·y ['tækɪ] *adj paint, glue* pegajoso; F (*cheap, poor quality*) chabacano, Span hortera F; *behavior* impresentable

tact [tækt] tacto *m*

tact·ful ['tæktfəl] *adj* diplomático

tact·ful·ly ['tæktfəlɪ] *adv* diplomáticamente

tac·ti·cal ['tæktɪkl] *adj* táctico

tac·tics ['tæktɪks] *npl* táctica *f*

tact·less ['tæktlɪs] *adj* indiscreto

tad·pole ['tædpoʊl] renacuajo *m*

tag [tæg] *n* (*label*) etiqueta *f*

◆ **tag along** *v/i* (*pret & pp* **tagged**) pegarse

tail [teɪl] *n of bird, fish* cola *f*; *of mammal* cola *f*, rabo *m*

'tail·back Br caravana *f*

'tail light luz *f* trasera

tai·lor ['teɪlər] *n* sastre *m*

tai·lor-made [teɪlərˈmeɪd] *adj suit, solution* hecho a medida

'tail·pipe *of car* tubo *m* de escape

'tail·wind viento *m* de cola

taint·ed ['teɪntɪd] *adj food* contaminado; *reputation* empañado

Tai·wan [taɪˈwɑːn] Taiwán

Tai·wan·ese [taɪwɑːˈniːz] **1** *adj* taiwanés **2** *n* taiwanés(-esa) *m(f)*; *dialect* taiwanés *m*

take [teɪk] *v/t* (*pret* **took**, *pp* **taken**) (*remove*) llevarse; *Span* coger; (*steal*) llevarse; (*transport, accompany*) llevar; (*accept: money, gift, credit cards*) aceptar; (*study: maths, French*) hacer, estudiar; (*photograph, photocopy*) hacer, sacar; *exam, degree* hacer; *shower* darse; *stroll* dar; *medicine, s.o.'s temperature, taxi* tomar; (*endure*) aguantar; **how long does it take?** ¿cuánto tiempo lleva?; **I'll take it** *when shopping* me lo llevo; **it takes a lot of courage** se necesita mucho valor

◆ **take after** *v/t* parecerse a

◆ **take apart** *v/t* (*dismantle*) desmontar; F (*criticize*) hacer pedazos; F (*reprimand*) echar una bronca a F; F *in physical fight* machacar F

◆ **take away** *v/t pain* hacer desaparecer; (*remove: object*) quitar; MATH restar; **take sth away from s.o.** quitar algo a alguien

◆ **take back** *v/t* (*return: object*) devolver; *person* llevar de vuelta; (*accept back: husband etc*) dejar volver; **that takes me back** *of music, thought etc* me trae recuerdos

◆ **take down** *v/t from shelf* bajar; *scaffolding* desmontar; *trousers* bajarse; (*write down*) anotar, apuntar

◆ **take in** *v/t* (*take indoors*) recoger; (*give accommodation to*) acoger; (*make narrower*) meter; (*deceive*) engañar; (*include*) incluir

◆ **take off 1** *v/t clothes, hat* quitarse; *10% etc* descontar; (*mimic*) imitar; (*cut off*) cortar; **take a day / week off** tomarse un día / una semana de vacaciones **2** *v/i of airplane* despegar, *L.Am.* decolar; (*become popular*) empezar a cuajar

◆ **take on** *v/t job* aceptar; *staff* contratar

◆ **take out** *v/t from bag, pocket* sacar; *tooth* sacar, extraer; *word from text* quitar, borrar; *money from bank* sacar; *insurance policy* suscribir; **he took her out to dinner** la llevó a cenar; **take the dog out** sacar al perro a pasear; **take the kids out to the park** llevar a los niños al parque; **don't take it out on me!** ¡no la pagues conmigo!

◆ **take over** *v/t company etc* absorber, adquirir; **tourists took over the town** los turistas invadieron la ciudad **2** *v/i of new management etc* asumir el cargo; *of new government* asumir el poder; (*do sth in s.o.'s place*) tomar el relevo

◆ **take to** *v/t* (*like*): **how did they take to**

the new idea? ¿qué les pareció la nueva idea?; **I immediately took to him** me cayó bien de inmediato; **he has taken to getting up early** le ha dado por levantarse temprano; **she took to drink** se dio a la bebida

◆ **take up** v/t carpet etc levantar; (carry up) subir; (shorten: dress etc) acortar; hobby empezar a hacer; subject empezar a estudiar; offer aceptar; new job comenzar; space, time ocupar; **I'll take you up on your offer** aceptaré tu oferta

'take-home pay salario m neto

'take-off of airplane despegue m, L.Am. decolaje m; (impersonation) imitación f

'take-o·ver com absorción f, adquisición f

'take-o·ver bid oferta f pública de adquisición, OPA f

tak·en ['teɪkn] pp → take

ta·kings ['teɪkɪŋz] npl recaudación f

tal·cum pow·der ['tælkəmpaʊdər] polvos mpl de talco

tale [teɪl] cuento m, historia f

tal·ent ['tælənt] talento m

tal·ent·ed ['tæləntɪd] adj con talento; **she's very talented** tiene mucho talento

'tal·ent scout cazatalentos m inv

talk [tɔːk] **1** v/i hablar; **can I talk to …?** ¿podría hablar con …?; **I'll talk to him about it** hablaré del tema con él **2** v/t English etc hablar; **talk business / politics** hablar de negocios / de política; **talk s.o. into sth** persuadir a alguien para que haga algo **3** n (conversation) charla f, C.Am., Mex plática f; (lecture) conferencia f, **give a talk on sth** dar una conferencia sobre algo; charla f; **talks** negociaciones fpl; **he's all talk** pej habla mucho y no hace nada

◆ **talk back** v/i responder, contestar

◆ **talk down to** v/t hablar con aires de superioridad a

◆ **talk over** v/t hablar de, discutir

talk·a·tive ['tɔːkətɪv] adj hablador

talk·ing-to ['tɔːkɪŋtu] sermón m, rapapolvo m; **give s.o. a good talking-to** echar a alguien un buen sermón or rapapolvo

'talk show programa m de entrevistas

tall [tɔːl] adj alto; **it is ten meters tall** mide diez metros de alto

tall 'or·der: **that's a tall order** eso es muy difícil

tall 'sto·ry cuento m chino

tal·ly ['tælɪ] **1** n cuenta f **2** v/i (pret & pp tallied) cuadrar, encajar

◆ **tally with** v/t cuadrar con, encajar con

tame [teɪm] adj animal manso, domesticado; joke etc soso

◆ **tam·per with** ['tæmpər] v/t lock intentar forzar; brakes tocar

tam·pon ['tæmpɑn] tampón m

tan [tæn] **1** n from sun bronceado m; **get a tan** ponerse moreno; (color) marrón m claro **2** v/i (pret & pp tanned) in sun broncearse **3** v/t (pret & pp tanned) leather curtir

tan·dem ['tændəm] (bike) tándem m

tan·gent ['tændʒənt] MATH tangente f

tan·ge·rine [tændʒə'riːn] mandarina f

tan·gi·ble ['tændʒɪbl] adj tangible

tan·gle ['tæŋgl] n lío m, maraña f

◆ **tangle up**: **get tangled up** of string etc quedarse enredado

tan·go ['tæŋgoʊ] n tango m

tank [tæŋk] for water depósito m, tanque m; for fish pecera f; MOT depósito m; MIL, for skin diver tanque m

tank·er ['tæŋkər] truck camión m cisterna; ship buque m cisterna; for oil petrolero m

'tank top camiseta f sin mangas

tanned [tænd] adj moreno, bronceado

Tan·noy® ['tænɔɪ] megafonía f

tan·ta·liz·ing ['tæntəlaɪzɪŋ] adj sugerente

tan·ta·mount ['tæntəmaʊnt] adj: **be tantamount to** equivaler a

tan·trum ['tæntrəm] rabieta f

tap [tæp] **1** n grifo m, L.Am. llave f **2** v/t (pret & pp tapped) (knock) dar un golpecito en; phone intervenir

◆ **tap into** v/t resources explotar

'tap dance n claqué m

tape [teɪp] **1** n cinta f **2** v/t conversation etc grabar; with sticky tape pegar con cinta adhesiva

'tape deck pletina f

'tape drive COMPUT unidad f de cinta

'tape meas·ure cinta f métrica

tap·er ['teɪpər] v/i estrecharse

◆ **taper off** v/i of production, figures disminuir

'tape re·cor·der magnetófon m, L.Am. grabador m

'tape re·cor·ding grabación f (magnetofónica)

ta·pes·try ['tæpɪstrɪ] cloth tapiz m; art tapicería f

'tape·worm tenia f, solitaria f

tar [tɑːr] n alquitrán m

tar·dy ['tɑːrdɪ] adj tardío

tar·get ['tɑːrgɪt] **1** n in shooting blanco m; for sales, production objetivo m **2** v/t market apuntar a

tar·get 'au·di·ence audiencia f a la que está orientado el programa

'tar·get date fecha f fijada

tar·get 'fig·ure cifra f objetivo

'tar·get group COM grupo *m* estratégico

'tar·get mar·ket mercado *m* objetivo

tar·iff ['tærɪf] (*price*) tarifa *f*; (*tax*) arancel *m*

tar·mac ['tɑːrmæk] *for road surface* asfalto *m*; *at airport* pista *f*

tar·nish ['tɑːrnɪʃ] *v/t metal* deslucir, deslustrar; *reputation* empañar

tar·pau·lin [tɑːr'pɔːlɪn] lona *f* (*impermeable*)

tart¹ [tɑːrt] *n* tarta *f*, pastel *m*

tart² [tɑːrt] *n* F *woman* fulana *f* F

tar·tan ['tɑːrtn] tartán *m*

task [tæsk] tarea *f*

'task force *for a special job* equipo *m* de trabajo; MIL destacamento

tas·sel ['tæsl] borla *f*

taste [teɪst] 1 *n* gusto *m*; *of food etc* sabor *m*; *he has no taste* tiene mal gusto 2 *v/t also fig* probar

taste·ful ['teɪstfəl] *adj* de buen gusto

taste·ful·ly ['teɪstfəlɪ] *adv* con buen gusto

taste·less ['teɪstlɪs] *adj food* insípido; *remark* de mal gusto

tast·ing ['teɪstɪŋ] *of wine* cata *f*, degustación *f*

tast·y ['teɪstɪ] *adj* sabroso, rico

tat·tered ['tætərd] *adj clothes* andrajoso; *book* destrozado

tat·ters ['tætərz]: *in tatters clothes* hecho jirones; *reputation, career* arruinado

tat·too [tə'tuː] *n* tatuaje *m*

tat·ty ['tætɪ] *adj* sobado, gastado

taught [tɔːt] *pret & pp → teach*

taunt [tɔːnt] 1 *n* pulla *f* 2 *v/t* mofarse de

Tau·rus ['tɔːrəs] ASTR Tauro *m/f inv*

taut [tɔːt] *adj* tenso

taw·dry ['tɔːdrɪ] *adj* barato, cursi

tax [tæks] 1 *n* impuesto *m*; *before / after tax* sin descontar / descontando impuestos 2 *v/t people* cobrar impuestos a; *product* gravar

tax·a·ble 'in·come ingresos *mpl* gravables

ta·x·a·tion [tæk'seɪʃn] (*act of taxing*) imposición *f* de impuestos; (*taxes*) fiscalidad *f*, impuestos *mpl*

'tax avoid·ance elusión *f* legal de impuestos

'tax brack·et banda *f* impositiva

'tax de·duct·i·ble *adj* desgravable

'tax eva·sion evasión *f* fiscal

'tax free *adj* libre de impuestos

'tax haven paraíso *m* fiscal

tax·i ['tæksɪ] *n* taxi *m*

'tax·i dri·ver taxista *m/f*

tax·ing ['tæksɪŋ] *adj* difícil, arduo

'tax in·spec·tor inspector(a) *m(f)* de Hacienda

'tax·i rank, tax·i stand parada *f* de taxis

'tax pay·er contribuyente *m/f*

'tax re·turn *form* declaración *f* de la renta

'tax year año *m* fiscal

TB [tiː'biː] *abbr* (= *tuberculosis*) tuberculosis *f*

tea [tiː] *drink* té *m*; *meal* merienda *f*

'tea·bag ['tiːbæg] bolsita *f* de té

teach [tiːtʃ] 1 *v/t* (*pret & pp taught*) *person, subject* enseñar; *teach s.o. to do sth* enseñar a alguien a hacer algo 2 *v/i* (*pret & pp taught*): *I taught at that school* di clases en ese colegio; *he always wanted to teach* siempre quiso ser profesor

tea·cher ['tiːtʃər] *at primary school* maestro(-a) *m(f)*; *at secondary school, university* profesor(a) *m(f)*

tea·cher 'train·ing formación *f* pedagógica, magisterio *m*

tea·ching ['tiːtʃɪŋ] *profession* enseñanza *f*, docencia *f*

'tea·ching aid material *m* didáctico

'tea cloth paño *m* de cocina

'tea·cup taza *f* de té

'tea drink·er bebedor(a) *m(f)* de té

teak [tiːk] teca *f*

'tea leaf hoja *f* de té

team [tiːm] equipo *m*

'team-mate compañero(-a) *m(f)* de equipo

team 'spir·it espíritu *m* de equipo

team·ster ['tiːmstər] camionero(-a) *m(f)*

'team·work trabajo *m* en equipo

'tea·pot tetera *f*

tear¹ [ter] 1 *n in cloth etc* desgarrón *m*, rotura *f* 2 *v/t* (*pret tore, pp torn*) *paper, cloth* rasgar; *be torn between two alternatives* debatirse entre dos alternativas 3 *v/i* (*pret tore, pp torn*) (*run fast, drive fast*) ir a toda velocidad

◆ tear down *v/t* poster arrancar; *building* derribar

◆ tear out *v/t* arrancar

◆ tear up *v/t paper* romper, rasgar; *agreement* romper

tear² [tɪr] *in eye* lágrima *f*; *burst into tears* echarse a llorar; *be in tears* estar llorando

tear·drop ['tɪrdrɑːp] lágrima *f*

tear·ful ['tɪrfəl] *adj* lloroso

'tear gas gas *m* lacrimógeno

tease [tiːz] *v/t person* tomar el pelo a, burlarse de; *animal* hacer rabiar

'tea serv·ice, 'tea set servicio *m* de té

'tea·spoon *object* cucharilla *f*; *quantity* cucharadita *f*

'tea strain·er colador *m* de té

teat [tiːt] teta *f*

'tea to·wel *Br* paño *m* de cocina

tech·ni·cal ['teknɪkl] *adj* técnico

tech·ni·cal·i·ty [teknɪ'kælətɪ] (*technical nature*) tecnicismo *m*; LAW detalle *m* técnico

tech·ni·cal·ly ['teknɪklɪ] *adv* técnicamente

tech·ni·cian [tek'nɪʃn] técnico(-a) *m(f)*

tech·nique [tek'niːk] técnica *f*

tech·no·log·i·cal [teknə'lɑːdʒɪkl] *adj* tecnológico

tech·no·lo·gy [tek'nɑːlədʒɪ] tecnología *f*

tech·no·phob·i·a [teknə'foubɪə] rechazo *m* de las nuevas tecnologías

ted·dy bear ['tedɪber] osito *m* de peluche

te·di·ous ['tiːdɪəs] *adj* tedioso

tee [tiː] *n* in golf tee *m*

teem [tiːm] *v/i:* *be teeming with rain* llover a cántaros; *be teeming with tourists / ants* estar abarrotado de turistas / lleno de hormigas

teen·age ['tiːneɪdʒ] *adj fashions* adolescente, juvenil; *teenage boy / girl* un adolescente / una adolescente

teen·ag·er ['tiːneɪdʒər] adolescente *m/f*

teens [tiːnz] *npl* adolescencia *f*; *be in one's teens* ser un adolescente; *reach one's teens* alcanzar la adolescencia

tee·ny ['tiːnɪ] *adj* F chiquitín F

teeth [tiːθ] *pl* → **tooth**

teethe [tiːð] *v/i* echar los dientes

'teeth·ing prob·lems *npl* problemas *fpl* iniciales

tee·to·tal [tiː'toutl] *adj person* abstemio

tee·to·tal·er [tiː'toutlər] abstemio(-a) *m(f)*

tel·e·com·mu·ni·ca·tions [telɪkəmjuːnɪ-'keɪʃnz] telecomunicaciones *fpl*

tel·e·gram ['telɪgræm] telegrama *m*

tel·e·graph pole ['telɪgræf] poste *m* telegráfico

tel·e·path·ic [telɪ'pæθɪk] *adj* telepático; *you must be telepathic!* ¡debes tener telepatía!

te·lep·a·thy [tɪ'lepəθɪ] telepatía *f*

tel·e·phone ['telɪfoun] **1** *n* teléfono *m*; *be on the telephone* (*be speaking*) estar hablando por teléfono; (*possess a phone*) tener teléfono **2** *v/t person* telefonear, llamar por teléfono a **3** *v/i* telefonear, llamar por teléfono

'tel·e·phone bill factura *f* del teléfono

'tel·e·phone book guía *f* telefónica, listín *m* telefónico

'tel·e·phone booth cabina *f* telefónica

'tel·e·phone call llamada *f* telefónica

'tel·e·phone con·ver·sa·tion conversación *f* por teléfono *or* telefónica

'tel·e·phone di·rec·to·ry guía *f* telefónica, listín *m* telefónico

'tel·e·phone ex·change central *f* telefónica, centralita *f*

'tel·e·phone mes·sage mensaje *m* telefónico

'tel·e·phone num·ber número *m* de teléfono

tel·e·pho·to lens [telɪ'foutoulenz] teleobjetivo *m*

tel·e·sales ['telɪseɪlz] televentas *fpl*

tel·e·scope ['telɪskoup] telescopio *n*

tel·e·thon ['telɪθɑːn] maratón *m* benéfico televisivo

tel·e·vise ['telɪvaɪz] *v/t* televisar

tel·e·vi·sion ['telɪvɪʒn] televisión *f*; *set* televisión *f*, televisor *m*; *on television* en *or* por (la) televisión; *watch television* ver la televisión

'tel·e·vi·sion au·di·ence audiencia *f* televisiva

'tel·e·vision pro·gram programa *m* televisivo

'tel·e·vision set televisión *f*, televisor *m*

'tel·e·vision stu·di·o estudio *m* de televisión

tell [tel] **1** *v/t* (*pret & pp* *told*) *story* contar; *lie* decir, contar; *I can't tell the difference* no veo la diferencia; *tell s.o. sth* decir algo a alguien; *don't tell Mom* no se lo digas a mamá; *could you tell me the way to …?* ¿me podría decir por dónde se va a …?; *tell s.o. to do sth* decir a alguien que haga algo; *you're telling me!* F ¡a mí me lo vas a contar! **2** *v/i* (*pret & pp* *told*) (*have effect*) hacerse notar; *the heat is telling on him* el calor está empezando a afectarle; *time will tell* el tiempo lo dirá

tell·er ['telər] cajero(-a) *m(f)*

tell·ing ['telɪŋ] *adj* contundente

tell·ing 'off regañina *f*

tell·tale ['telteɪl] **1** *adj signs* revelador **2** *n* chivato(-a) *m(f)*

temp [temp] **1** *n employee* trabajador(a) *m(f)* temporal **2** *v/i* hacer trabajo temporal

tem·per ['tempər] (*bad temper*) mal humor *m*; *be in a temper* estar de mal humor; *keep one's temper* mantener la calma; *lose one's temper* perder los estribos

tem·pe·ra·ment ['tempərəmənt] temperamento *m*

tem·pe·ra·men·tal [temprə'mentl] *adj* (*moody*) temperamental

tem·pe·rate ['tempərət] *adj* templado

tem·pe·ra·ture ['temprətʃər] temperatura *f*; (*fever*) fiebre *f*; *have a temperature* tener fiebre

tem·ple[1] ['templ] REL templo *m*

tem·ple² ['templ] ANAT sien f

tem·po ['tempou] tempo m

tem·po·rar·i·ly [tempə'rerılı] adv temporalmente

tem·po·ra·ry ['tempərerı] adj temporal

tempt [tempt] v/t tentar

temp·ta·tion [temp'teıʃn] tentación f

tempt·ing ['temptıŋ] adj tentador

ten [ten] diez

te·na·cious [tı'neıʃəs] adj tenaz

te·nac·i·ty [tı'næsıtı] tenacidad f

ten·ant ['tenənt] of building inquilino(-a) m(f); of farm, land arrendatario m

tend¹ [tend] v/t (look after) cuidar (de)

tend² [tend]: **tend to do sth** soler hacer algo; **tend toward sth** tender hacia algo

ten·den·cy ['tendənsı] tendencia f

ten·der¹ ['tendər] adj (sore) sensible, delicado; (affectionate) cariñoso, tierno; steak tierno

ten·der² ['tendər] n COM oferta f

ten·der·ness ['tendərnıs] (soreness) dolor m; of kiss etc cariño m, ternura f

ten·don ['tendən] tendón m

ten·nis ['tenıs] tenis m

'ten·nis ball pelota f de tenis

'ten·nis court pista f de tenis; cancha f de tenis

'ten·nis pla·yer tenista m/f

'ten·nis rack·et raqueta f de tenis

ten·or ['tenər] MUS tenor m

tense¹ [tens] n GRAM tiempo m

tense² [tens] adj muscle, moment tenso; voice, person tenso, nervioso

◆ **tense up** v/i ponerse tenso

ten·sion ['tenʃn] of rope tensión f; in atmosphere, voice tensión f, tirantez f; in film, novel tensión f

tent [tent] tienda f

ten·ta·cle ['tentəkl] tentáculo m

ten·ta·tive ['tentətıv] adj move, offer provisional

ten·ter·hooks ['tentərhʊks]: **be on tenterhooks** estar sobre ascuas

tenth [tenθ] 1 adj décimo 2 n décimo m, décima parte f; of second, degree décima f

tep·id ['tepıd] adj water, reaction tibio

term [tɜːrm] in office etc mandato m; EDU trimestre m; (condition) término m, condición f; (word) término m; **be on good / bad terms with s.o.** llevarse bien / mal con alguien; **in the long / short term** a largo / corto plazo; **come to terms with sth** llegar a aceptar algo

ter·mi·nal ['tɜːrmınl] 1 n at airport, for buses, for containers terminal f; ELEC, COMPUT terminal m; of battery polo m 2 adj illness terminal

ter·mi·nal·ly ['tɜːrmınəlı] adv: **terminally ill** en la fase terminal de una enfermedad

ter·mi·nate ['tɜːrmıneıt] 1 v/t contract rescindir; pregnancy interrumpir 2 v/i finalizar

ter·mi·na·tion [tɜːrmı'neıʃn] of contract rescisión f; of pregnancy interrupción f

ter·mi·nol·o·gy [tɜːrmı'nɑːlədʒı] terminología f

ter·mi·nus ['tɜːrmınəs] for buses final m de trayecto; for trains estación f terminal

ter·race ['terəs] terraza f

ter·ra cot·ta [terə'kɑːtə] adj de terracota

ter·rain [te'reın] terreno m

ter·res·tri·al [te'restrıəl] n terrestre m 2 adj television por vía terrestre

ter·ri·ble ['terəbl] adj terrible, horrible

ter·ri·bly ['terəblı] adv (very) tremendamente

ter·rif·ic [tə'rıfık] adj estupendo

ter·rif·i·cal·ly [tə'rıfıklı] adv (very) tremendamente

ter·ri·fy ['terıfaı] v/t (pret & pp **terrified**) aterrorizar; **be terrified** estar aterrorizado

ter·ri·fy·ing ['terıfaıŋ] adj aterrador

ter·ri·to·ri·al [terı'tɔːrıəl] adj territorial

ter·ri·to·ri·al 'wa·ters npl aguas fpl territoriales

ter·ri·to·ry ['terıtɔːrı] territorio m; fig ámbito m, territorio m

ter·ror ['terər] terror m

ter·ror·ism ['terərızm] terrorismo m

ter·ror·ist ['terərıst] terrorista m

'ter·ror·ist at·tack atentado m terrorista

'ter·ror·ist or·gan·i·za·tion organización f terrorista

ter·ror·ize ['terəraız] v/t aterrorizar

terse [tɜːrs] adj tajante, seco

test [test] 1 n prueba f; academic, for driving examen m 2 v/t probar, poner a prueba

tes·ta·ment ['testəmənt] to s.o.'s life etc testimonio m; **Old / New Testament** REL Viejo / Nuevo Testamento m

'test-drive v/t (pret **test-drove**, pp **test-driven**) car probar en carretera

tes·ti·cle ['testıkl] testículo m

tes·ti·fy ['testıfaı] v/i (pret & pp **testified**) LAW testificar, prestar declaración

tes·ti·mo·ni·al [testı'mounıəl] n referencias fpl

tes·ti·mo·ny ['testımənı] LAW testimonio m

'test tube tubo m de ensayo, probeta f

'test-tube ba·by niño(-a) m(f) probeta

tes·ty ['testı] adj irritable

te·ta·nus ['tetənəs] tétanos m

teth·er ['teðər] 1 v/t horse atar 2 n correa

f; **be at the end of one's tether** estar al a punto de perder la paciencia

text [tekst] texto *m*

'text·book libro *m* de texto

tex·tile ['tekstəl] textil

tex·ture ['tekstʃər] textura *f*

Thai [taɪ] **1** *adj* tailandés **2** *n person* tailandés(-esa) *m(f)*; *language* tailandés *m*

Thai·land ['taɪlænd] Tailandia

than [ðæn] *adv que*; *bigger / faster than me* más grande / más rápido que yo; *more than 50* más de 50

thank [θæŋk] *v/t* dar las gracias a; *thank you* gracias; *no thank you* no, gracias

thank·ful ['θæŋkfəl] *adj* agradecido; *we have to be thankful that ...* tenemos que dar gracias de que ...

thank·ful·ly ['θæŋkfəlɪ] *adv* (*luckily*) afortunadamente

thank·less *adj* task ingrato

thanks [θæŋks] *npl* gracias *fpl*; *thanks!* ¡gracias!; *thanks to* gracias a

Thanks·giv·ing (Day) [θæŋks'gɪvɪŋdeɪ] Día *m* de Acción de Gracias

that [ðæt] **1** *adj ese m, esa f; more remote* aquel *m*, aquella; *that one* ése **2** *pron* ése *m*, ésa; *more remote* aquél *m*, aquella *f*; *what is that?* ¿qué es eso?; *who is that?* ¿quién es ése?; *that's mine* ése es mío; *that's tea* es té; *that's very kind* qué amable; *I think that ...* creo que ...; *the person / car that you see* el coche / la persona que ves **3** *adv* (*so*) tan; *that big / expensive* tan grande / caro

thaw [θɔː] *v/i of snow* derretirse, fundirse; *of frozen food* descongelarse

the [ðə] el, la; *plural* los, las; *the sooner the better* cuanto antes, mejor

the·a·ter ['θɪətər] teatro *m*

'the·a·ter crit·ic crítico *m* teatral

the·a·tre *Br* → **theater**

the·at·ri·cal [θɪ'ætrɪkl] *also fig* teatral

theft [θeft] robo *m*

their [ðer] *adj* su; (*his or her*) su; *their brother* su hermano; *their books* sus libros

theirs [ðerz] *pron* el suyo, la suya; *theirs are red* los suyos son rojos; *that book is theirs* ese libro es suyo; *a friend of theirs* un amigo suyo

them [ðem] *pron direct object* los *mpl*, las *fpl; indirect object* les; *after prep* ellos *mpl*, ellas *fpl; I know them* los / las conozco; *I gave them the keys* les di las llaves; *I sold it to them* se lo vendí; *he lives with them* vive con ellos / ellas; *if a person asks for help, you should help them* him / her si una persona pide ayuda, hay que ayudarla

theme [θiːm] tema *m*

'theme park parque *m* temático

'theme song tema *m* musical

them·selves [ðem'selvz] *pron reflexive* se; *emphatic* ellos mismos *mpl*, ellas mismas *fpl; they hurt themselves* se hicieron daño; *when they saw themselves in the mirror* cuando se vieron en el espejo; *they saw it themselves* lo vieron ellos mismos; *by themselves* (*alone*) solos; (*without help*) ellos solos, ellos mismos

then [ðen] *adv* (*at that time*) entonces; (*after that*) luego, después; *deducing* entonces; *by then* para entonces

the·o·lo·gian [θɪə'loʊdʒɪən] teólogo *m*

the·ol·o·gy [θɪ'ɑːlədʒɪ] teología *f*

the·o·ret·i·cal [θɪə'retɪkl] *adj* teórico

the·o·ret·i·cal·ly [θɪə'retɪklɪ] *adv* en teoría

the·o·ry ['θɪrɪ] teoría *f*; *in theory* en teoría

ther·a·peu·tic [θerə'pjuːtɪk] *adj* terapéutico

ther·a·pist ['θerəpɪst] terapeuta *m/f*

ther·a·py ['θerəpɪ] terapia *f*

there [ðer] *adv* allí, ahí, allá; *over there* allí, ahí, allá; *down there* allí or ahí or allá abajo; *there is / are ...* hay ...; *there is / are not ...* no hay ...; *there you are giving sth* aquí tienes; *finding sth* aquí está; *completing sth* ya está; *there and back* ida y vuelta; *it's 5 miles there and back* entre ida y vuelta hay cinco millas; *there he is!* ¡ahí está!; *there, there!* ¡venga!

there·a·bouts [ðerə'baʊts] *adv* aproximadamente

there·fore [ðerfɔːr] *adv* por (lo) tanto

ther·mom·e·ter [θər'mɑːmɪtər] termómetro *m*

ther·mos flask ['θɜːrməs] termo *m*

ther·mo·stat ['θɜːrməstæt] termostato *m*

these [ðiːz] **1** *adj* estos(-as) **2** *pron* éstos *mpl*, éstas *fpl*

the·sis ['θiːsɪs] (*pl* **theses** ['θiːsiːz]) tesis *f inv*

they [ðeɪ] *pron* ellos *mpl*, ellas *fpl; they are Mexican* son mexicanos; *they're going, but we're not* ellos van, pero nosotros no; *if anyone looks at this, they will see that ...* si alguien mira esto, verá que ...; *they say that ...* dicen que ...; *they are going to change the law* van a cambiar la ley

thick [θɪk] *adj soup* espeso; *fog* denso; *wall, book* grueso; *hair* poblado; *crowd* compacto; F (*stupid*) corto; *it's 3 cm thick* tiene 3 cm de grosor

thick·en ['θɪkən] *v/t sauce* espesar

thick·set ['θɪkset] *adj* fornido

thick-skinned [θɪk'skɪnd] *adj fig* insensible

thief [θiːf] (*pl* **thieves** [θiːvz]) ladrón(-ona) *m(f)*

thigh [θaɪ] muslo *m*

thim·ble ['θɪmbl] dedal *m*

thin [θɪn] *adj person* delgado; *hair* ralo, escaso; *soup* claro; *coat, line* fino

thing [θɪŋ] cosa *f*; **things** (*belongings*) cosas *fpl*; **how are things?** ¿cómo te va?; **it's a good thing you told me** menos mal que me lo dijiste; **what a thing to do / say!** ¡qué barbaridad!

thing·um·a·jig ['θɪŋʌmədʒɪg] F *object* chisme *m*; *person* fulanito *m*

think [θɪŋk] *v/t & v/i* (*pret & pp* **thought**) pensar; **hold an opinion** pensar, creer; **I think so** creo que sí; **I don't think so** creo que no; **I think so too** pienso lo mismo; **what do you think?** ¿qué piensas o crees?; **what do you think of it?** ¿qué te parece?; **I can't think of anything more** no se me ocurre nada más; **think hard!** ¡piensa más!; **I'm thinking about emigrating** estoy pensando en emigrar

◆ **think over** *v/t* reflexionar sobre

◆ **think through** *v/t* pensar bien

◆ **think up** *v/t plan* idear

'think tank grupo *m* de expertos

thin-skinned [θɪn'skɪnd] *adj* sensible

third [θɜːrd] **1** *adj* tercero **2** *n* tercero(a) *m(f)*; *fraction* tercio *m*, tercera parte *f*

third·ly ['θɜːrdlɪ] *adv* en tercer lugar

third 'par·ty tercero *m*

third-par·ty in'sur·ance seguro *m* a terceros

third 'per·son GRAM tercera persona *f*

'third-rate *adj* de tercera, de pacotilla F

Third 'World Tercer Mundo *m*

thirst [θɜːrst] sed *f*

thirst·y ['θɜːrstɪ] *adj* sediento; **be thirsty** tener sed

thir·teen [θɜːr'tiːn] trece

thir·teenth [θɜːr'tiːnθ] *n & adj* decimotercero

thir·ti·eth ['θɜːrtɪθ] *n & adj* trigésimo

thir·ty ['θɜːrtɪ] treinta

this [ðɪs] **1** *adj* este *m*, esta *f*; **this one** éste **2** *pron* esto *m*, esta *f*; **this is good** esto es bueno; **this is ...** *introducing s.o.* éste / ésta es ...; TELEC soy ... **3** *adv*: **this big / high** así de grande / de alto

thorn [θɔːrn] espina *f*

thorn·y ['θɔːrnɪ] *adj also fig* espinoso

thor·ough ['θɜːroʊ] *adj search* minucioso; *knowledge* profundo; *person* concienzudo

thor·ough·bred ['θɜːroʊbred] *horse* pura-

sangre *m*

thor·ough·ly ['θɜːroʊlɪ] *adv* completamente; *clean up* a fondo; *search* minuciosamente; **I'm thoroughly ashamed** estoy avergonzadísimo

those [ðoʊz] **1** *adj* esos *mpl*, esas *fpl*; *more remote* aquellos *mpl*, aquellas *fpl* **2** *pron* ésos *mpl*, ésas *fpl*; aquéllos *mpl*, aquéllas *mpl*

though [ðoʊ] **1** *conj* (*although*) aunque; **as though** como si **2** *adv* sin embargo; **it's not finished though** pero no está acabado

thought¹ [θɔːt] *single* idea *f*; *collective* pensamiento *m*

thought² [θɔːt] *pret & pp* → **think**

thought·ful ['θɔːtfəl] *adj* pensativo; *book* serio; (*considerate*) atento

thought·less ['θɔːtlɪs] *adj* desconsiderado

thou·sand ['θaʊznd] mil *m*; **thousands of** miles de; **a thousand and ten** mil diez

thou·sandth ['θaʊzndθ] *n & adj* milésimo

thrash [θræʃ] *v/t* golpear, dar una paliza a; SP dar una paliza a

◆ **thrash about** *v/i with arms etc* revolverse

◆ **thrash out** *v/t solution* alcanzar

thrash·ing ['θræʃɪŋ] *also* SP paliza *f*

thread [θred] **1** *n* hilo *m*; *of screw* rosca *f* **2** *v/t needle* enhebrar; *beads* ensartar

thread·bare ['θredber] *adj* raído

threat [θret] amenaza *f*

threat·en ['θretn] *v/t* amenazar

threat·en·ing ['θretnɪŋ] *adj* amenazador

three [θriː] tres

three-'quart·ers tres cuartos *mpl*

thresh [θreʃ] *v/t corn* trillar

thresh·old ['θreʃhoʊld] *of house, new age* umbral *m*; **on the threshold of** en el umbral *or* en puertas del

threw [θruː] *pret* → **throw**

thrift [θrɪft] ahorro *m*

thrift·y ['θrɪftɪ] *adj* ahorrativo

thrill [θrɪl] **1** *n* emoción *f*, estremecimiento *m* **2** *v/t*: **be thrilled** estar entusiasmado

thrill·er ['θrɪlər] *movie* película *f* de *Span* suspense *or* L.Am. suspenso; *novel* novela *f* de *Span* suspense *or* L.Am. suspenso

thrill·ing ['θrɪlɪŋ] *adj* emocionante

thrive [θraɪv] *v/i of plant* medrar, crecer bien; *of business, economy* prosperar

throat [θroʊt] garganta *f*

'throat loz·enge pastilla *f* para la garganta

throb [θrɑːb] **1** *n of heart* latido *m*; *of music* zumbido *m* **2** *v/i* (*pret & pp* **throbbed**) *of heart* latir; *of music* zumbar

throm·bo·sis [θrɑːmˈboʊsɪs] trombosis *f*
throne [θroʊn] trono *m*
throng [θrɑːŋ] *n* muchedumbre *f*
throt·tle [ˈθrɑːtl] **1** *n on motorbike* acelerador *m*; *on boat* palanca *f* del gas; *on motorbike* mango *m* del gas **2** *v/t* (*strangle*) estrangular
◆ **throttle back** *v/i* desacelerar
through [θruː] **1** *prep* ◇ (*across*) a través de; *go through the city* atravesar la ciudad
◇ (*during*) durante; *through the winter / summer* durante el invierno / verano; *Monday through Friday* de lunes a viernes
◇ (*by means of*) a través de, por medio de; *arranged through him* acordado por él **2** *adv*: *wet through* completamente mojado; *watch a film through* ver una película de principio a fin; *read a book through* leerse un libro de principio a fin **3** *adj*: *be through* of couple haber terminado; (*have arrived*: of news etc) haber llegado; *you're through* TELEC ya puede hablar; *I'm through with ...* (*finished with*) he terminado con ...
'through flight vuelo *m* directo
through·out [θruːˈaʊt] **1** *prep* durante, a lo largo de **2** *adv* (*in all parts*) en su totalidad
'through train tren *m* directo
throw [θroʊ] **1** *v/t* (*pret* **threw**, *pp* **thrown**) tirar; *of horse* tirar, desmontar; (*disconcert*) desconcertar; *party* dar **2** *n* lanzamiento *m*; *it's your throw* se toca tirar
◆ **throw away** *v/t* tirar, *L.Am.* botar
◆ **throw off** *v/t jacket etc* quitarse rápidamente; *cold etc* deshacerse de
◆ **throw on** *v/t clothes* ponerse rápidamente
◆ **throw out** *v/t old things* tirar, *L.Am.* botar; *from bar, job, home* echar; *from country* expulsar; *plan* rechazar
◆ **throw up 1** *v/t ball* lanzar hacia arriba; *throw up one's hands* echarse las manos a la cabeza **2** *v/i* (*vomit*) vomitar
'throw·a·way *adj remark* insustancial, pasajero; (*disposable*) desechable
'throw-in SP saque *m* de banda
thrown [θroʊn] *pp* → **throw**
thru [θruː] → **through**
thrush [θrʌʃ] *bird* zorzal *m*
thrust [θrʌst] *v/t* (*pret & pp* **thrust**) (*push hard*) empujar; *knife* hundir; *thrust sth into s.o.'s hands* poner algo en las manos de alguien; *thrust one's way through the crowd* abrirse paso a empujones entre la multitud
thud [θʌd] *n* golpe *m* sordo

thug [θʌg] matón *m*
thumb [θʌm] **1** *n* pulgar *m* **2** *v/t*: *thumb a ride* hacer autostop
thumb·tack [ˈθʌmtæk] chincheta *f*
thump [θʌmp] **1** *n blow* porrazo *m*, golpe *m* sordo **2** *v/t person* dar un porrazo a; *thump one's fist on the table* pegar un puñetazo en la mesa **3** *v/i of heart* latir con fuerza; *thump on the door* aporrear la puerta
thun·der [ˈθʌndər] *n* truenos *mpl*
thun·der·ous [ˈθʌndərəs] *adj applause* tormenta *f*
thun·der·storm [ˈθʌndərstɔːrm] tormenta *f* (*con truenos*)
thun·der·struck *adj* atónito
thun·der·y [ˈθʌndərɪ] *adj weather* tormentoso
Thurs·day [ˈθɜːrzdeɪ] jueves *m inv*
thus [ðʌs] *adv* (*in this way*) así
thwart [θwɔːrt] *v/t person, plans* frustrar
thyme [taɪm] tomillo *m*
thy·roid gland [ˈθaɪrɔɪdglænd] (glándula *f*) tiroides *m inv*
tick [tɪk] **1** *n of clock* tictac *m*; *in text* señal *f* de visto bueno **2** *v/i of clock* hacer tictac
tick·et [ˈtɪkɪt] *for bus, train, lottery* billete *m*, *L.Am.* boleto *m*; *for airplane* billete *m*, *L.Am.* pasaje *m*; *for theater, concert, museum* entrada *f*, *L.Am.* boleto *m*; *for speeding etc* multa *f*
'tick·et col·lec·tor revisor(a) *m(f)*
'tick·et in·spec·tor revisor(a) *m(f)*
'tick·et ma·chine máquina *f* expendedora de billetes
'tick·et of·fice *at station* mostrador *m* de venta de billetes; THEA taquilla *f*, *L.Am.* boletería *f*
tick·ing [ˈtɪkɪŋ] *noise* tictac *m*
tick·le [ˈtɪkl] **1** *v/t person* hacer cosquillas a **2** *v/i of material* hacer cosquillas; *stop that, you're tickling!* ¡para ya, me haces cosquillas!
tick·lish [ˈtɪklɪʃ] *adj person* tener cosquillas
ti·dal wave [ˈtaɪdlweɪv] maremoto *m* (*ola*)
tide [taɪd] marea *f*; *high tide* marea alta; *low tide* marea baja; *the tide is in / out* la marea está alta / baja
◆ **tide over** *v/t*: *20 dollars will tide me over* 20 dólares me bastarán
ti·di·ness [ˈtaɪdɪnɪs] orden *m*
ti·dy [ˈtaɪdɪ] *adj* ordenado
◆ **tidy away** *v/t* (*pret & pp* **tidied**) guardar
◆ **tidy up 1** *v/t room, shelves* ordenar; *tidy o.s. up* arreglarse **2** *v/i* recoger
tie [taɪ] **1** *n* (*necktie*) corbata *f*; SP (*even result*) empate *m*; *he doesn't have any*

T

ties no está atado a nada **2** *v/t knot* hacer, atar; *hands* atar; *tie two ropes together* atar dos cuerdas **3** *v/i* SP empatar

◆ **tie down** *v/t also fig* atar

◆ **tie up** *v/t person, laces* atar; *boat* amarrar; *hair* recoger; *I'm tied up tomorrow* (*busy*) mañana estaré muy ocupado

tier [tɪr] *of hierarchy* nivel *m*; *in stadium* grada *f*

ti·ger ['taɪgər] tigre *m*

tight [taɪt] **1** *adj clothes* ajustado, estrecho; *security* estricto; (*hard to move*) apretado; (*properly shut*) cerrado; (*not leaving much time*) justo de tiempo; F (*drunk*) como una cuba F **2** *adv hold* fuerte; *shut* bien

tight·en ['taɪtn] *v/t screw* apretar; *control* endurecer; *security* intensificar; *tighten one's grip on sth* on rope etc asir algo con más fuerza; *on power etc* incrementar el control sobre algo

◆ **tighten up** *v/i in discipline, security* ser más estricto

tight-fist·ed [taɪt'fɪstɪd] *adj* agarrado

tight·ly ['taɪtlɪ] *adv* → **tight**

tight·rope ['taɪtroʊp] cuerda *f* floja

tights [taɪts] *npl Br* medias *fpl*, pantis *mpl*

tile [taɪl] *on floor* baldosa *f*; *on wall* azulejo *m*; *on roof* teja *f*

till[1] [tɪl] → **until**

till[2] [tɪl] *n* (*cash register*) caja *f* (registradora)

till[3] [tɪl] *v/t soil* labrar

tilt [tɪlt] **1** *v/t* inclinar **2** *v/i* inclinarse

tim·ber ['tɪmbər] madera *f* (de construcción)

time [taɪm] tiempo *m*; (*occasion*) vez *f*; *time is up* se acabó (el tiempo); *for the time being* por ahora, por el momento; *have a good time* pasarlo bien; *have a good time!* ¡que lo paséis bien!; *what's the time?, do you have the time?* ¿qué hora es?; *the first time* la primera vez; *four times* cuatro veces; *time and again* una y otra vez; *all the time* todo el rato; *two / three at a time* de dos en dos / de tres en tres; *at the same time* speak, reply etc a la vez; (*however*) al mismo tiempo; *in time* con tiempo; *on time* puntual; *in no time* en un santiamén

'time bomb bomba *f* de relojería

'time clock *in factory* reloj *m* registrador

'time-con·sum·ing *adj* que lleva mucho tiempo

'time dif·fer·ence diferencia *f* horaria

'time-lag intervalo *m*

'time lim·it plazo *m*

time·ly ['taɪmlɪ] *adj* oportuno

time out SP tiempo *m* muerto

tim·er ['taɪmər] *device* temporizador *m*; *person* cronometrador *m*

'time-sav·ing *n* ahorro *m* de tiempo

'time-scale *of project* plazo *m* (de tiempo)

'time switch temporizador *m*

'time-warp salto *m* en el tiempo

'time zone huso *m* horario

tim·id ['tɪmɪd] *adj* tímido

tim·ing ['taɪmɪŋ] *of dancer* sincronización *f*; *of actor* utilización *f* de las pausas y del ritmo; *the timing of the announcement was perfect* el anuncio due realizado en el momento perfecto

tin [tɪn] *metal* estaño *m*; *Br* (*can*) lata *f*

tin-foil ['tɪnfɔɪl] papel *m* de aluminio

tinge [tɪndʒ] *n of color, sadness* matiz *m*

tin·gle ['tɪŋgl] *n* hormigueo *m*

◆ **tin·ker with** ['tɪŋkər] *v/t* enredar con

tin·kle ['tɪŋkl] *n of bell* tintineo *m*

tin·sel ['tɪnsl] espumillón *m*

tint [tɪnt] **1** *n of color* matiz *m*; *in hair* tinte *m* **2** *v/t hair* teñir

tint·ed ['tɪntɪd] *glasses* con un tinte; *paper* coloreado

ti·ny ['taɪnɪ] *adj* diminuto, minúsculo

tip[1] [tɪp] *n of stick, finger* punta *f*; *of mountain* cumbre *f*; *of cigarette* filtro *m*

tip[2] [tɪp] **1** *n advice* consejo *m*; *money* propina *f* **2** *v/t* (*pret & pp* **tipped**) *waiter etc* dar propina a

◆ **tip off** *v/t* avisar

◆ **tip over** *v/t jug* volcar; *liquid* derramar; *he tipped water all over me* derramó agua encima mío

'tip-off soplo *m*

tipped [tɪpt] *adj cigarettes* con filtro

Tipp-Ex® *n* Tipp-Ex *m*

tip·py-toe ['tɪpɪtoʊ]: *on tippy-toe* de puntillas

tip·sy ['tɪpsɪ] *adj* achispado

tire[1] [taɪr] *n* neumático *m*, *L.Am.* llanta *f*

tire[2] [taɪr] **1** *v/t* cansar, fatigar **2** *v/i* cansarse, fatigarse; *he never tires of telling the story* nunca se cansa de contar la historia

tired [taɪrd] *adj* cansado, fatigado; *be tired of s.o./sth* estar cansado de algo / de alguien

tired·ness ['taɪrdnɪs] cansancio *m*, fatiga *f*

tire·less ['taɪrlɪs] *adj efforts* incansable, infatigable

tire·some ['taɪrsəm] *adj* (*annoying*) pesado

tir·ing ['taɪrɪŋ] *adj* agotador

tis·sue ['tɪʃuː] ANAT tejido *m*; (*handkerchief*) pañuelo *m* de papel, Kleenex® *m*

'tis·sue pa·per papel *m* de seda

tit[1] [tɪt] *bird* herrerillo *m*

tit² [tɪt]: *give s.o. tit for tat* pagar a alguien con la misma moneda

tit³ [tɪt] V *(breast)* teta f V

ti·tle ['taɪtl] *of novel, person etc* título m; LAW título m de propiedad

'ti·tle-hold·er SP campeón(-ona) m(f)

tit·ter ['tɪtər] v/i reírse tontamente

to [tuː] *unstressed* [tə] **1** prep a; *to Japan / Chicago* a Japón / Chicago; *let's go to my place* vamos a mi casa; *walk to the station* camina a la estación; *to the north / south of ...* al norte / sur de ...; *give sth to s.o.* dar algo a alguien; *from Monday to Wednesday* de lunes a miércoles; *from 10 to 15 people* de 10 a 15 personas **2** *with verbs: to speak, to shout* hablar, chillar; *learn to swim* aprender a nadar; *nice to eat* sabroso; *too heavy to carry* demasiado pesado para llevarlo; *to be honest with you ...* para ser sincero ... **3** adv: *to and fro* de un lado para otro

toad [toʊd] sapo m

toad·stool ['toʊdstuːl] seta f venenosa

toast [toʊst] **1** n pan m tostado; *drinking* brindis m inv; *propose a toast to s.o.* proponer un brindis en honor de alguien **2** v/t *drinking* brindar por

toast·er ['toʊstər] tostador(a) m(f)

to·bac·co [təˈbækoʊ] tabaco m

to·bog·gan [təˈbɑːɡən] n tobogán m

to·day [təˈdeɪ] hoy

tod·dle ['tɑːdl] v/i *of child* dar los primeros pasos

tod·dler ['tɑːdlər] niño m pequeño

to-do [təˈduː] F revuelo m

toe [toʊ] **1** n dedo m del pie; *of shoe* puntera f **2** v/t: *toe the line* acatar la disciplina

toe·nail ['toʊneɪl] uña f del pie

to·geth·er [təˈɡeðər] adv juntos(-as); *mix two drinks together* mezclar dos bebidas; *don't all talk together* no hablen todos a la vez

toil [tɔɪl] n esfuerzo m

toi·let ['tɔɪlɪt] *place* cuarto m de baño, servicio m; *equipment* retrete m; *go to the toilet* ir al baño

'toi·let pa·per papel m higiénico

toi·let·ries ['tɔɪlɪtrɪz] npl artículos mpl de tocador

'toi·let roll rollo m de papel higiénico

to·ken ['toʊkən] *(sign)* muestra f; *for gambling* ficha f; *(gift token)* vale m

told [toʊld] pret & pp → **tell**

tol·e·ra·ble ['tɑːlərəbl] adj *pain etc* soportable; *(quite good)* aceptable

tol·e·rance ['tɑːlərəns] tolerancia f

tol·e·rant ['tɑːlərənt] adj tolerante

tol·e·rate ['tɑːləreɪt] v/t *noise, person* tolerar; *I won't tolerate it!* ¡no lo toleraré!

toll¹ [toʊl] v/i *of bell* tañer

toll² [toʊl] n *(deaths)* mortandad f, número m de víctimas

toll³ [toʊl] n *for bridge, road* peaje m; TELEC tarifa f

'toll booth cabina f de peaje

'toll-free adj TELEC gratuito

'toll road carretera f de peaje

to·ma·to [təˈmeɪtoʊ] tomate m, Mex jitomate m

to·ma·to 'ketch·up ketchup m

to·ma·to 'sauce *for pasta etc* salsa f de tomate

tomb [tuːm] tumba f

tom·boy ['tɑːmbɔɪ] niña f poco femenina

tomb·stone ['tuːmstoʊn] lápida f

tom·cat ['tɑːmkæt] gato m

to·mor·row [təˈmɔːroʊ] mañana; *the day after tomorrow* pasado mañana; *tomorrow morning* mañana por la mañana

ton [tʌn] tonelada f (907 kg)

tone [toʊn] *of color, conversation* tono m; *of musical instrument* timbre m; *of neighborhood* nivel m; *tone of voice* tono m de voz

◆ **tone down** v/t *demands, criticism* bajar el tono de

ton·er ['toʊnər] tóner m

tongs [tɑːŋz] npl tenazas fpl; *for hair* tenacillas fpl de rizar

tongue [tʌŋ] n lengua f

ton·ic ['tɑːnɪk] MED tónico m

'ton·ic (wa·ter) agua f tónica f

to·night [təˈnaɪt] esta noche

ton·sil ['tɑːnsl] amígdala f

ton·sil·li·tis [tɑːnsəˈlaɪtɪs] amigdalitis f

too [tuː] adv *(also)* también; *(excessively)* demasiado; *me too* yo también; *too big / hot* demasiado grande / caliente; *too much rice* demasiado arroz; *eat too much* comer demasiado

took [tuːk] pret → **take**

tool [tuːl] herramienta f

toot [tuːt] v/t F tocar

tooth [tuːθ] (pl **teeth** [tiːθ]) diente m

'tooth·ache dolor m de muelas

'tooth·brush cepillo m de dientes

'tooth·less ['tuːθlɪs] adj desdentado

'tooth·paste pasta f de dientes, dentífrico m

'tooth·pick palillo m

top [tɑːp] **1** n *of mountain* cima f; *of tree* copa f; *of wall, screen, page* parte f superior; *(lid: of bottle etc)* tapón m; *of pen* capucha f; *clothing* camiseta f, top m; (MOT: *gear*) directa f; *on top of* encima de, sobre; *at the top of the page* en la

T

parte superior de la página; **at the top of the mountain** en la cumbre; **the top of the class / league** person, team ser el primero de la clase / de la liga; **get to the top** of company, mountain llegar a la cumbre; of mountain; **be over the top** (exaggerated) ser una exageración **2** v/t branches superior; floor de arriba, último; management, official alto; player mejor; speed, note máximo **3** v/t (pret & pp **topped**): **topped with ...** of cake etc con una capa de ... por encima

◆ **top up** v/t glass, tank llenar

top 'hat sombrero m de copa

top 'heav·y adj sobrecargado en la parte superior

top·ic ['tɑːpɪk] tema m

top·ic·al ['tɑːpɪkl] adj de actualidad

top·less ['tɑːplɪs] adj en topless

top·most ['tɑːpmoʊst] adj branches, floor superior

top·ping ['tɑːpɪŋ] on pizza ingrediente m

top·ple ['tɑːpl] **1** v/i derrumbarse **2** v/t government derrocar

top 'se·cret adj altamente confidencial

top·sy-tur·vy [tɑːpsɪ'tɜːrvɪ] adj (in disorder) desordenado; world al revés

torch [tɔːrtʃ] with flame antorcha f

tore [tɔːr] pret → **tear**[1]

tor·ment **1** n ['tɔːrment] tormento m **2** v/t [tɔːr'ment] person, animal atormentar; **tormented by doubt** atormentado por la duda

torn [tɔːrn] pp → **tear**[1]

tor·na·do [tɔːr'neɪdoʊ] tornado m

tor·pe·do [tɔːr'piːdoʊ] **1** n torpedo m also fig torpedear

tor·rent ['tɑːrənt] also fig torrente m; of lava colada f

tor·ren·tial [təˈrenʃl] adj rain torrencial

tor·toise ['tɔːrtəs] tortuga f

tor·ture ['tɔːrtʃər] **1** n tortura f **2** v/t torturar

toss [tɑːs] **1** v/t ball lanzar, echar; rider desmontar; salad remover; **toss a coin** echar a cara o cruz **2** v/i: **toss and turn** dar vueltas

to·tal ['toʊtl] **1** n total m **2** adj sum, amount total; disaster rotundo, completo; idiot de tomo y lomo; stranger completo **3** v/t F cargarse F; **the truck was totaled** el camión quedó destrozado

to·tal·i·tar·i·an [toʊtælɪ'terɪən] adj totalitario

to·tal·ly ['toʊtlɪ] adv totalmente

tote bag ['toʊtbæg] bolsa f grande

tot·ter ['tɑːtər] v/i of person tambalearse

touch [tʌtʃ] **1** n toque m; sense tacto m; **lose touch with s.o.** perder el contacto

con alguien; **keep in touch with s.o.** mantenerse en contacto con alguien; **we kept in touch** seguimos en contacto; **be out of touch** no estar al corriente; **the leader was out of touch with the people** el líder estaba desconectado de lo que pensaba la gente; **in touch** SP fuera **2** v/t tocar; emotionally conmover **3** v/i of two lines etc tocarse

◆ **touch down** v/i of airplane aterrizar; SP marca un ensayo

◆ **touch on** v/t (mention) tocar, mencionar

◆ **touch up** v/t photo retocar; sexually manosear

touch·down ['tʌtʃdaʊn] of airplane aterrizaje m; SP touchdown m, ensayo m

touch·ing ['tʌtʃɪŋ] adj conmovedor

touch·line ['tʌtʃlaɪn] SP línea f de banda

touch screen pantalla f táctil

touch·y ['tʌtʃɪ] adj person susceptible

tough [tʌf] adj person, meat, punishment duro; question, exam difícil; material resistente, fuerte

◆ **tough·en up** ['tʌfn] v/t person hacer más fuerte

'tough guy F tipo m duro F

tour [tʊr] **1** n of museum etc recorrido m; of area viaje m (of por); of band ecc gira f **2** v/t area recorrer **3** v/i of band etc estar de gira

'tour guide guía m/f turístico(-a)

tour·i·sm ['tʊrɪzm] turismo m

tour·i·st ['tʊrɪst] turista m/f

'tour·ist at·trac·tion atracción f turística

'tour·ist in·dus·try industria f turística

'tour·ist (in·for·ma·tion) of·fice oficina f de turismo

'tour·ist sea·son temporada f turística

tour·na·ment ['tɜːrnəmənt] torneo m

'tour op·er·a·tor operador m turístico

tous·led ['taʊzld] adj hair revuelto

tow [toʊ] **1** v/t car, boat remolcar **2** n: **give s.o. a tow** remolcar a alguien

◆ **tow away** v/t car llevarse

to·ward [tɔːrd] prep hacia; **we are working toward a solution** estamos intentando encontrar una solución

tow·el ['taʊəl] toalla f

tow·er ['taʊər] n torre f

◆ **tow·er over** v/t of building elevarse por encima de; of person ser mucho más alto que

town [taʊn] ciudad f

town 'cen·ter centro m de la ciudad / del pueblo

town 'coun·cil ayuntamiento m

town 'hall ayuntamiento m

'tow·rope cuerda f para remolcar

tox·ic ['tɑːksɪk] *adj* tóxico

tox·ic 'waste residuos *mpl* tóxicos

tox·in ['tɑːksɪn] BIO toxina *f*

toy [tɔɪ] juguete *m*

'toy store juguetería *f*, tienda *f* de juguetes

◆ **toy with** *v/t object* juguetear con; *idea* darle vueltas a

trace [treɪs] **1** *n of substance* resto *m* **2** *v/t (find)* localizar; *(follow: footsteps of)* seguir el rastro a; *(draw)* trazar

track [træk] *n (path)* senda *f*, camino; *for horses* hipódromo *m*; *for dogs* canódromo *m*; *for cars* circuito *m*; *for athletics* pista *f*; *on CD* canción *f*, corte *m*; RAIL vía *f*; **track 10** RAIL vía 10; **keep track of sth** llevar la cuenta de algo

'track down *v/t* localizar

'track·suit chándal *m*

trac·tor ['træktər] tractor *m*

trade [treɪd] **1** *n (commerce)* comercio *m*; *(profession, craft)* oficio *m* **2** *v/i (do business)* comerciar; **trade in sth** comerciar en algo **3** *v/t (exchange)* intercambiar; **trade sth for sth** intercambiar algo por algo

◆ **trade in** *v/t when buying* entregar como parte del pago

'trade fair feria *f* de muestras

'trade·mark marca *f* registrada

'trade mis·sion misión *f* comercial

trad·er ['treɪdər] comerciante *m*

trade 'se·cret secreto *m* de la casa, secreto *m* comercial

trades·man ['treɪdzmən] *(plumber etc)* electricista, fontanero / plomero *etc*

tra·di·tion [trə'dɪʃn] tradición *f*

tra·di·tion·al [trə'dɪʃnl] *adj* tradicional

tra·di·tion·al·ly [trə'dɪʃnlɪ] *adv* tradicionalmente

traf·fic ['træfɪk] *n on roads, in drugs* tráfico *m*

◆ **traffic in** *v/t (pret & pp **trafficked**) drugs* traficar con

'traf·fic cir·cle rotonda *f*, Span glorieta *f*

'traf·fic cop F poli *m* de tráfico F

'traf·fic is·land isleta *f*

'traf·fic jam atasco *m*

'traf·fic light semáforo *m*

'traf·fic po·lice policía *f* de tráfico

'traf·fic sign señal *f* de tráfico

tra·ge·dy ['trædʒədɪ] tragedia *f*

tra·gic ['trædʒɪk] *adj* trágico

trail [treɪl] **1** *n (path)* camino *m*, senda *f*; *of blood* rastro *m* **2** *v/t (follow)* seguir la pista de; *(tow)* arrastrar **3** *v/i (lag behind)* ir a la zaga

trail·er ['treɪlər] *pulled by vehicle* remolque *m*; *(mobile home)* caravana *f*; *of film*

avance *m*, tráiler *m*

train[1] [treɪn] *n* tren *m*; **go by train** ir en tren

train[2] [treɪn] **1** *v/t team, athlete* entrenar; *employee* formar; *dog* adiestrar **2** *v/i of team, athlete* entrenarse; *of teacher etc* formarse

train·ee [treɪ'niː] aprendiz(a) *m(f)*

train·er ['treɪnər] SP entrenador(a) *m(f)*; *of dog* adiestrador(a) *m(f)*

train·ers ['treɪnərz] *npl Br shoes* zapatillas *fpl* de deporte

train·ing ['treɪnɪŋ] *of new staff* formación *f*; SP entrenamiento *m*; **be in training** SP estar entrenándose; **be out of training** SP estar desentrenado

'train·ing course cursillo *m* de formación

'train·ing scheme plan *m* de formación

'train sta·tion estación *f* de tren

trait [treɪt] rasgo *m*

trai·tor ['treɪtər] traidor(a) *m(f)*

tramp [træmp] **1** *n (vagabond)* vagabundo(-a) *m(f)* **2** *v/i* caminar con pasos pesados

tram·ple ['træmpl] *v/t* pisotear; **be trampled to death** morir pisoteado; **be trampled underfoot** ser pisoteado

◆ **trample on** *v/t person, object* pisotear

tram·po·line ['træmpəlɪn] cama *f* elástica

trance [træns] trance *m*; **go into a trance** entrar en trance

tran·quil ['træŋkwɪl] *adj* tranquilo

tran·quil·i·ty [træŋ'kwɪlətɪ] tranquilidad *f*

tran·quil·iz·er ['træŋkwɪlaɪzər] tranquilizante *m*

trans·act [træn'zækt] *v/t deal* negociar

trans·ac·tion [træn'zækʃn] *action* transacción *f*; *deal* negociación *f*

trans·at·lan·tic [trænzət'læntɪk] *adj* transatlántico

tran·scen·den·tal [trænsen'dentl] *adj* trascendental

tran·script ['trænskrɪpt] transcripción *f*

trans·fer 1 *v/t* [træns'fɜːr] *(pret & pp **transferred**)* transferir **2** *v/i (pret & pp **transferred**) in traveling* hacer transbordo; *from one language to another* pasar **3** *n* ['trænsfɜːr] transferencia *f*; *in travel* transbordo *m*; *of money* transferencia *f*

trans·fer·a·ble [træns'fɜːrəbl] *adj ticket* transferible

'trans·fer fee *for football player* traspaso *m*

trans·form [træns'fɔːrm] *v/t* transformar

trans·form·a·tion [trænsfər'meɪʃn] transformación *f*

trans·form·er [træns'fɔːrmər] ELEC transformador *m*

trans·fu·sion [træns'fjuːʒn] transfusión *f*

T

tran·sis·tor [træn'zɪstər] transistor *m*; (*radio*) transistor *m*, radio *m* transistor

tran·sit ['trænzɪt]: *in transit* en tránsito

tran·si·tion [træn'sɪʒn] transición *f*

tran·si·tion·al [træn'sɪʒnl] *adj* de transición

'tran·sit lounge *at airport* sala *f* de tránsito

'trans·it pas·sen·ger pasajero *m* en tránsito

trans·late [træns'leɪt] *v/t* & *v/i* traducir

trans·la·tion [træns'leɪʃn] traducción *f*

trans·la·tor [træns'leɪtər] traductor(a) *m(f)*

trans·mis·sion [trænz'mɪʃn] *of news, program* emisión *f*; *of disease* transmisión *f*; MOT transmisión *f*

trans·mit [trænz'mɪt] *v/t* (*pret* & *pp* **transmitted**) *news, program* emitir; *disease* transmitir

trans·mit·ter [trænz'mɪtər] *for radio, TV* emisora *f*

trans·par·en·cy [træns'pærənsɪ] PHOT diapositiva *f*

trans·par·ent [træns'pærənt] *adj* transparente; (*obvious*) obvio

trans·plant 1 *v/t* [træns'plænt] MED transplantar **2** *n* ['trænsplænt] MED transplante *m*

trans·port 1 *v/t* [træns'pɔːrt] *goods, people* transportar **2** *n* ['trænspɔːrt] *of goods, people* transporte *m*

trans·por·ta·tion [trænspɔːr'teɪʃn] *of goods, people* transporte *m*; *means of transportation* medio *m* de transporte; *public transportation* transporte *m* público; *Department of Transportation* Ministerio *m* de Transporte

trans·ves·tite [træns'vestaɪt] travestí *m*, travestido *m*

trap [træp] **1** *n* trampa *f*; *set a trap for s.o.* tender una trampa a alguien **2** *v/t* (*pret* & *pp* **trapped**) atrapar; *be trapped by enemy, flames, landslide etc* quedar atrapado

'trap·door ['træpdɔːr] trampilla *f*

tra·peze [trə'piːz] trapecio *m*

trap·pings ['træpɪŋz] *npl of power* parafernalia *f*

trash [træʃ] *(garbage)* basura *f*; *(poor product)* bazofia *f*; *(despicable person)* escoria *f*

'trash·can ['træʃkæn] cubo *m* de la basura

trash·y ['træʃɪ] *adj goods, novel* barato

trau·mat·ic [trɒ'mætɪk] *adj* traumático

trau·ma·tize ['trɒmətaɪz] *v/t* traumatizar

trav·el ['trævl] **1** *n* viajes *mpl*; *do you like travel?* ¿te gusta viajar?; *on my travels* en mis viajes **2** *v/i* (*pret* & *pp* **traveled**, *Br* **travelled**) viajar **3** *v/t miles* viajar, recorrer

'trav·el a·gen·cy agencia *f* de viajes

'trav·el a·gent agente *m* de viajes

'trav·el bag bolsa *f* de viaje

trav·el·er, *Br* **trav·el·ler** ['trævələr] viajero(-a) *m(f)*

'trav·el·er's check, *Br* **'trav·el·ler's cheque** cheque *m* de viaje

'trav·el ex·pens·es *npl* gastos *mpl* de viaje

'trav·el in·sur·ance seguro *m* de asistencia en viaje

'trav·el pro·gram, *Br* **'trav·el pro·gramme** *on TV etc* programa *m* de viajes

'trav·el·sick *adj* mareado

trawl·er ['trɒːlər] (barco *m*) arrastrero *m*

tray [treɪ] bandeja *f*

treach·er·ous ['tretʃərəs] *adj* traicionero

treach·er·y ['tretʃərɪ] traición *f*

tread [tred] **1** *n* pasos *mpl*; *of staircase* huella *f* (del peldaño); *of tyre* dibujo *m* **2** *v/i* (*pret* **trod,** *pp* **trodden**) andar; *mind where you tread* cuida dónde pisas

♦ **tread on** *v/t s.o.'s foot* pisar

trea·son ['triːzn] traición *f*

trea·sure ['treʒər] **1** *n* tesoro *m*; *person* tesoro *m* **2** *v/t gift etc* apreciar mucho

trea·sur·er ['treʒərər] tesorero(-a) *m(f)*

Trea·sur·y De·part·ment ['treʒərɪ] Ministerio *m* de Hacienda

treat [triːt] **1** *n* placer *m*; *it was a real treat* fue un auténtico placer; *I have a treat for you* tengo una sorpresa agradable para ti; *it's my treat (I'm paying)* yo invito **2** *v/t* tratar; *treat s.o. to sth* invitar a alguien a algo

treat·ment ['triːtmənt] tratamiento *m*

treat·y ['triːtɪ] tratado *m*

tre·ble¹ ['trebl] *n* MUS soprano *m*

tre·ble² ['trebl] **1** *adv*: *treble the price* el triple del precio **2** *v/i* triplicarse

tree [triː] árbol *m*

trem·ble ['trembl] *v/i* temblar

tre·men·dous [trɪ'mendəs] *adj* (*very good*) estupendo; (*enormous*) enorme

tre·men·dous·ly [trɪ'mendəslɪ] *adv* (*very*) tremendamente; (*a lot*) enormemente

trem·or ['tremər] *of earth* temblor *m*

trench [trentʃ] trinchera *f*

trend [trend] tendencia *f*; (*fashion*) moda *f*

trend·y ['trendɪ] *adj* de moda; *views* moderno

tres·pass ['trespæs] *v/i* entrar sin autorización; *no trespassing* prohibido el paso

♦ **trespass on** *v/t s.o.'s land* entrar sin autorización en; *s.o.'s privacy* entrometerse en

tres·pass·er ['trespæsər] intruso(-a) *m(f)*

tri·al ['traɪəl] LAW juicio *m*; *of equipment* prueba *f*; *be on trial* LAW estar siendo juzgado; *have sth on trial equipment* tener algo a prueba

tri·al 'pe·ri·od periodo *m* de prueba

tri·an·gle ['traɪæŋgl] triángulo *m*

tri·an·gu·lar [traɪ'æŋgjʊlər] *adj* triangular

tribe [traɪb] tribu *f*

tri·bu·nal [traɪ'bjuːnl] tribunal *m*

tri·bu·ta·ry ['trɪbjʊtərɪ] *of river* afluente *m*

trick [trɪk] **1** *n* (*to deceive, knack*) truco *m*; *play a trick on s.o.* gastar una broma a alguien **2** *v/t* engañar; *trick s.o. into doing sth* engañar a alguien para que haga algo

trick·er·y ['trɪkərɪ] engaños *mpl*

trick·le ['trɪkl] **1** *n* hilo *m*, reguero *m*; *fig: of money* goteo *m* **2** *v/i* gotear, escurrir

trick·ster ['trɪkstər] embaucador(a) *m(f)*

trick·y ['trɪkɪ] *adj* (*difficult*) difícil

tri·cy·cle ['traɪsɪkl] triciclo *m*

tri·fle ['traɪfl] *n* (*triviality*) nadería *f*

tri·fling ['traɪflɪŋ] *adj* insignificante

trig·ger ['trɪgər] *n on gun* gatillo *m*; *on camcorder* disparador *m*

◆ **trigger off** *v/t* desencadenar

trim [trɪm] **1** *adj* (*neat*) muy cuidado; *figure* delgado **2** *v/t* (*pret & pp* **trimmed**) *hair, hedge* recortar; *budget, costs* recortar, reducir; (*decorate: dress*) adornar **3** *n* (*light cut*) recorte *m*; *just a trim, please to hairdresser* corte sólo las puntas, por favor; *in good trim* en buenas condiciones

trim·ming ['trɪmɪŋ] *on clothes* adorno *m*; *with all the trimmings dish* con la guarnición clásica; *car* con todos los extras

trin·ket ['trɪŋkɪt] baratija *f*

tri·o ['triːoʊ] MUS trío *m*

trip [trɪp] **1** *n* (*journey*) viaje *m* **2** *v/i* (*pret & pp* **tripped**) (*stumble*) tropezar **3** *v/t* (*pret & pp* **tripped**) (*make fall*) poner la zancadilla a

◆ **trip up** *v/t* (*make fall*) poner la zancadilla a; (*cause to go wrong*) confundir **2** *v/i* (*stumble*) tropezar; (*make a mistake*) equivocarse

tripe [traɪp] mondongo *m*, *Span* callos *mpl*

trip·le ['trɪpl] → **treble²**

trip·lets ['trɪplɪts] *npl* trillizos *mpl*

tri·pod ['traɪpɑːd] PHOT trípode *m*

trite [traɪt] *adj* manido

tri·umph ['traɪʌmf] *n* triunfo *m*

triv·i·al ['trɪvɪəl] *adj* trivial

triv·i·al·i·ty [trɪvɪ'ælətɪ] trivialidad *f*

trod [trɑːd] *pret* → **tread**

trod·den ['trɑːdn] *pp* → **tread**

trol·ley ['trɑːlɪ] (*streetcar*) tranvía *f*

trol·ley·bus ['trɑːlɪbʌs] trolebús *m*

trom·bone [trɑːm'boʊn] trombón *m*

troops [truːps] *npl* tropas *fpl*

tro·phy ['troʊfɪ] trofeo *m*

trop·ic ['trɑːpɪk] trópico *m*

trop·i·cal ['trɑːpɪkl] *adj* tropical

trop·ics ['trɑːpɪks] *npl* trópicos *mpl*

trot [trɑːt] *v/i* (*pret & pp* **trotted**) trotar

trou·ble ['trʌbl] **1** *n* (*difficulties*) problema *m*, problemas *mpl*; (*inconvenience*) molestia *f*; (*disturbance*) conflicto *m*, desorden *m*; *go to a lot of trouble to do sth* complicarse mucho la vida para hacer algo; *no trouble!* no es molestia; *get into trouble* meterse en líos **2** *v/t* (*worry*) preocupar, inquietar; (*bother, disturb*) molestar

trou·ble-free *adj* sin complicaciones

trou·ble-mak·er alborotador(a) *m(f)*

trou·ble-shoot·er (*mediator*) persona encargada de resolver problemas

trou·ble-shoot·ing resolución *f* de problemas

trou·ble·some ['trʌblsəm] *adj* problemático

trou·sers ['traʊzərz] *npl* pantalones *mpl*

trout [traʊt] (*pl* **trout**) trucha *f*

tru·ant ['truːənt]: *play truant* hacer novillos, *Mex* irse de pinta, *S. Am.* hacerse la rabona

truce [truːs] tregua *f*

truck [trʌk] camión *m*

truck driv·er camionero(-a) *m(f)*

truck farm huerta *f*

truck farm·er horticultor(a) *m(f)*

truck stop restaurante *m* de carretera

trudge [trʌdʒ] **1** *v/i* caminar fatigosamente **2** *n* caminata *f*

true [truː] *adj* verdadero, cierto; *friend, American* auténtico; *come true of hopes, dream* hacerse realidad

tru·ly ['truːlɪ] *adv* verdaderamente, realmente; *Yours truly* le saluda muy atentamente

trum·pet ['trʌmpɪt] trompeta *f*

trum·pet·er ['trʌmpɪtər] trompetista *m/f*

trunk [trʌŋk] *of tree, body* tronco *m*; *of elephant* trompa *f*; (*large case*) baúl *m*; *of car* maletero *m*, *C.Am.*, *Mex* cajuela *f*, *Rpl* baúl *m*

trunks [trʌŋks] *npl Br for swimming* bañador *m*

trust [trʌst] **1** *n* confianza *f*; FIN fondo *m* de inversión **2** *v/t* confiar en

trusted [trʌstɪd] *adj* de confianza

trust·ee [trʌsˈtiː] fideicomisario(-a) *m(f)*

trust·ful, trust·ing ['trʌstful, 'trʌstɪŋ] *adj* confiado

trust·wor·thy ['trʌstwɜːrðɪ] *adj* de confianza

truth [truːθ] verdad *f*

truth·ful ['truːθfəl] *adj person* sincero; *account* verdadero

try [traɪ] **1** *n* (*pret & pp* **tried**) probar; LAW juzgar; ***try to do sth*** intentar hacer algo, tratar de hacer algo **2** *v/i* (*pret & pp* **tried**): ***he didn't even try*** ni siquiera lo intentó; ***you must try harder*** debes esforzarte más **3** *n* intento *m*; ***can I have a try?*** *of food* ¿puedo probar?; *at doing sth* ¿puedo intentarlo?

◆ **try on** *v/t clothes* probar

◆ **try out** *v/t new machine, new method* probar

try·ing ['traɪɪŋ] *adj* (*annoying*) molesto, duro

T-shirt ['tiːʃɜːrt] camiseta *f*

tub [tʌb] (*bath*) bañera *f*, *L.Am.* tina *f*; *for liquid* cuba *f*; *for yoghurt, ice cream* envase *m*

tub·by ['tʌbɪ] *adj* rechoncho

tube [tuːb] tubo *m*

tube·less ['tuːblɪs] *adj tire* sin cámara de aire

tu·ber·cu·lo·sis [tuːbɜːrkjəˈloʊsɪs] tuberculosis *f*

tuck [tʌk] **1** *n in dress* pinza *f* **2** *v/t* (*put*) meter

◆ **tuck away** *v/t* (*put away*) guardar; F (*eat quickly*) zamparse F

◆ **tuck in** *v/t children* arropar; *sheets* remeter **2** *v/i* (*start eating*) ponerse a comer

◆ **tuck up** *v/t sleeves etc* remangar; ***tuck s.o. up in bed*** meter a alguien en la cama

Tues·day ['tuːzdeɪ] martes *m inv*

tuft [tʌft] *of hair* mechón *m*; *of grass* mata *f*

tug [tʌg] **1** *n* (*pull*) tirón *m*; NAUT remolcador *m* **2** *v/t* (*pret & pp* **tugged**) (*pull*) tirar de

tu·i·tion [tuːˈɪʃn] clases *fpl*

tu·lip ['tuːlɪp] tulipán *m*

tum·ble ['tʌmbl] *v/i* caer, caerse

tum·ble-down ['tʌmbldaʊn] *adj* destartalado

tum·ble-dry·er ['tʌmbldraɪr] secadora *f*

tum·bler ['tʌmblər] *for drink* vaso *m*; *in circus* acróbata *m/f*

tum·my ['tʌmɪ] F tripa *f* F, barriga *f* F

'tum·my ache dolor *m* de tripa *or* barriga

tu·mor ['tuːmər] tumor *m*

tu·mult ['tuːmʌlt] tumulto *m*

tu·mul·tu·ous [tuːˈmʌltʃʊəs] *adj* tumultuoso

tu·na ['tuːnə] atún *m*

tune [tuːn] **1** *n* melodía *f*; ***be in tune** of instrument* estar afinado; ***sing in tune*** cantar sin desafinar; ***be out of tune** of singer* desafinar; *of instrument* estar desafinado **2** *v/t instrument* afinar

◆ **tune in** *v/i* Radio, TV sintonizar

◆ **tune in to** *v/t* Radio, TV sintonizar (con)

◆ **tune up** *v/i of orchestra, players* afinar **2** *v/t engine* poner a punto

tune·ful ['tuːnfəl] *adj* melodioso

tun·er ['tuːnər] *hi-fi* sintonizador *m*

tune-up ['tuːnʌp] *of engine* puesta *f* a punto

tun·nel ['tʌnl] *n* túnel *m*

tur·bine ['tɜːrbaɪn] turbina *f*

tur·bu·lence ['tɜːrbjələns] *in air travel* turbulencia *f*

tur·bu·lent ['tɜːrbjələnt] *adj* turbulento

turf [tɜːrf] césped *m*; *piece* tepe *m*

Turk [tɜːrk] turco(-a) *m(f)*

Tur·key ['tɜːrkɪ] Turquía

tur·key ['tɜːrkɪ] pavo *m*

Turk·ish ['tɜːrkɪʃ] **1** *adj* turco **2** *n language* turco *m*

tur·moil ['tɜːrmɔɪl] desorden *m*, agitación *f*

turn [tɜːrn] **1** *n* (*rotation*) vuelta *f*; *in road* curva *f*; *junction* giro *m*; *in vaudeville* número *m*; ***take turns in doing sth*** turnarse para hacer algo; ***it's my turn*** me toca a mí; ***it's not your turn yet*** no te toca todavía; ***take a turn at the wheel*** turnarse para conducir *or L.Am.* manejar; ***do s.o. a good turn*** hacer un favor a alguien **2** *v/t wheel* girar; *corner* dar la vuelta a; ***turn one's back on s.o.*** dar la espalda a alguien **3** *v/i of driver, car, wheel* girar; *of person: turn around* volverse; ***turn left / right here*** gira aquí a la izquierda/a la derecha; ***it has turned sour / cold*** se ha cortado / enfriado; ***it turned blue*** se volvió *or* puso azul; ***he has turned 40*** ha cumplido cuarenta años

◆ **turn around 1** *v/t object* dar la vuelta a; *company* dar un vuelco a; (COM: *deal with*) procesar, preparar **2** *v/i or person* volverse, darse la vuelta; *of driver* dar la vuelta

◆ **turn away 1** *v/t* (*send away*) rechazar; ***the doorman turned us away*** el portero no nos dejó entrar **2** *v/i* (*walk away*) marcharse; (*look away*) desviar la mirada

◆ **turn back 1** *v/t edges, sheets* doblar **2** *v/i of walkers etc* volver; *in course of action* echarse atrás

◆ **turn down** *v/t offer, invitation* rechazar; *volume, TV, heating* bajar; *edge, collar* doblar

◆ **turn in 1** *v/i* (*go to bed*) irse a dormir **2** *v/t* *to police* entregar

◆ **turn off 1** *v/t* TV, *engine* apagar; *tap* cerrar; *heater* apagar; *it turns me off* F *sexually* me quita las ganas F **2** *v/i* *of car, driver* doblar

◆ **turn on 1** *v/t* TV, *engine, heating* encender, L.Am. prender; *tap* abrir; F *sexually* excitar F **2** *v/i* *of machine* encenderse, L.Am. prenderse

◆ **turn out 1** *v/t* *lights* apagar **2** *v/i*: *it turned out well* salió bien; *as it turned out* al final; *he turned out to be ...* resultó ser ...

◆ **turn over 1** *v/i* *in bed* darse la vuelta; *of vehicle* volcar, dar una vuelta de campana **2** *v/t* (*put upside down*) dar la vuelta a; *page* pasar; FIN facturar

◆ **turn up 1** *v/t* *collar* subirse; *volume, heating* subir **2** *v/i* (*arrive*) aparecer

turn·ing ['tɜːrnɪŋ] giro *m*

'turn·ing point punto *m* de inflexión

tur·nip ['tɜːrnɪp] nabo *m*

'turn·out *of people* asistencia *f*

'turn·o·ver *of* FIN facturación *f*; *staff turnover* rotación *f* de personal

'turn·pike autopista *f* de peaje

'turn sig·nal *on car* intermitente *m*

'turn·stile torniquete *m* (*de entrada*)

'turn·ta·ble *of record player* plato *m*,

tur·quoise ['tɜːrkwɔɪz] *adj* turquesa

tur·ret ['tʌrɪt] *of castle* torrecilla *f*; *of tank* torreta *f*

tur·tle ['tɜːrtl] tortuga *f* (*marina*)

tur·tle·neck 'sweat·er suéter *m* de cuello alto

tusk [tʌsk] colmillo *m*

tu·tor ['tuːtər] *at university* tutor *m*, (*private*) *tutor* profesor(a) *m(f)* particular

tu·xe·do [tʌk'siːdou] esmoquin *m*

TV [tiː'viː] televisión *f*; *on TV* en la televisión

T'V din·ner menú *m* precocinado

T'V guide guía *f* televisiva

T'V pro·gram programa *m* de televisión

twang [twæŋ] **1** *n in voice* entonación *f* nasal **2** *v/t* *guitar string* puntear

tweez·ers ['twiːzərz] *npl* pinzas *fpl*

twelfth [twelfθ] *n & adj* duodécimo

twelve [twelv] doce

twen·ti·eth ['twentɪɪθ] *n & adj* vigésimo

twen·ty ['twentɪ] veinte

twice [twaɪs] *adv* dos veces; *twice as* *much* el doble

twid·dle ['twɪdl] *v/t* dar vueltas a; *twiddle one's thumbs* holgazanear

twig [twɪg] *n* ramita *f*

twi·light ['twaɪlaɪt] crepúsculo *m*

twin [twɪn] gemelo *m*

'twin beds *npl* camas *fpl* gemelas

twinge [twɪndʒ] *of pain* punzada *f*

twin·kle ['twɪŋkl] *v/i of stars* parpadeo *m*; *of eyes* brillo *m*

twin 'room habitación *f* con camas gemelas

'twin town ciudad *f* hermana

twirl [twɜːrl] **1** *v/t* hacer girar **2** *n of cream etc* voluta *f*

twist [twɪst] **1** *v/t* retorcer; *twist one's ankle* torcerse el tobillo **2** *v/i of road, river* serpentear **3** *n in rope, road* vuelta *f*; *in plot, story* giro *m* inesperado

twist·y ['twɪstɪ] *adj road* serpenteante

twit [twɪt] F memo(-a) *m(f)* F

twitch [twɪtʃ] **1** *n nervous* tic *m* **2** *v/i* (*jerk*) moverse (ligeramente)

twit·ter ['twɪtər] *v/i of birds* gorjear

two [tuː] dos; *the two of them* los dos, ambos

two-faced ['tuːfeɪst] *adj* falso

'two-piece (*woman's suit*) traje *m*

two-stroke *adj engine* de dos tiempos

two-way 'traf·fic tráfico *m* en dos direcciones

ty·coon [taɪ'kuːn] magnate *m*

type [taɪp] **1** *n* (*sort*) tipo *m*, clase *f*; *what type of ...?* ¿qué tipo o clase de ...? **2** *v/i* (*use a keyboard*) escribir a máquina **3** *v/t with a typewriter* mecanografiar, escribir a máquina

type·writ·er ['taɪpraɪtər] máquina *f* de escribir

ty·phoid ['taɪfɔɪd] fiebre *f* tifoidea

ty·phoon [taɪ'fuːn] tifón *m*

ty·phus ['taɪfəs] tifus *m*

typ·i·cal ['tɪpɪkl] *adj* típico; *that's typical of you / him!* ¡típico tuyo / de él!

typ·i·cal·ly ['tɪpɪklɪ] *adv* típicamente; *typically American* típicamente americano

typ·ist ['taɪpɪst] mecanógrafo(-a) *m(f)*

ty·ran·ni·cal [tɪ'rænɪkl] *adj* tiránico

ty·ran·nize ['tɪrənaɪz] *v/t* tiranizar

ty·ran·ny ['tɪrənɪ] tiranía *f*

ty·rant ['taɪrənt] tirano(-a) *m(f)*

tyre *Br* → *tire¹*

U

ug·ly ['ʌglɪ] *adj* feo

UK [juː'keɪ] *abbr* (= **United Kingdom**) RU *m* (= Reino *m* Unido)

ul·cer ['ʌlsər] úlcera *f*; *in mouth* llaga *f*

ul·ti·mate ['ʌltɪmət] *adj* (*final*) final; (*basic*) esencial; *the ultimate car* (*best, definitive*) lo último en coches

ul·ti·mate·ly ['ʌltɪmətlɪ] *adv* (*in the end*) en última instancia

ul·ti·ma·tum [ʌltɪ'meɪtəm] ultimátum *m*

ul·tra·sound ['ʌltrəsaʊnd] MED ultrasonido *m*; (*scan*) ecografía *f*

ul·tra·vi·o·let [ʌltrə'vaɪələt] *adj* ultravioleta

um·bil·i·cal cord [ʌm'bɪlɪkl] cordón *m* umbilical

um·brel·la [ʌm'brelə] paraguas *m inv*

um·pire ['ʌmpaɪr] *n* árbitro *m*; *in tennis* juez *m/f* de silla

ump·teen [ʌmp'tiːn] *adj* F miles de F

UN [juː'en] *abbr* (= **United Nations**) ONU *f* (= Organización *f* de las Naciones Unidas)

un·a·ble [ʌn'eɪbl] *adj*: *be unable to do sth* (*not know how to*) no saber hacer algo; (*not be in a position to*) no poder hacer algo

un·ac·cept·a·ble [ʌnək'septəbl] *adj* inaceptable; *it is unacceptable that* es inaceptable que

un·ac·count·a·ble [ʌnə'kaʊntəbl] *adj* inexplicable

un·ac·cus·tomed [ʌnə'kʌstəmd] *adj*: *be unaccustomed to sth* no estar acostumbrado a algo

un·a·dul·ter·at·ed [ʌnə'dʌltəreɪtɪd] *adj* (*fig: absolute*) absoluto

un·A·mer·i·can [ʌnə'merɪkən] *adj* poco americano; *activities* antiamericano

u·nan·i·mous [juː'nænɪməs] *adj verdict* unánime; *be unanimous on* ser unánime respecto a

u·nan·i·mous·ly [juː'nænɪməslɪ] *adv* *vote, decide* unánimemente

un·ap·proach·a·ble [ʌnə'proʊtʃəbl] *adj person* inaccesible

un·armed [ʌn'ɑːrmd] *adj person* desarmado; *unarmed combat* combate *m* sin armas

un·as·sum·ing [ʌnə'suːmɪŋ] *adj* sin pretensiones

un·at·tached [ʌnə'tætʃt] *adj* (*without a partner*) sin compromiso, sin pareja

un·at·tend·ed [ʌnə'tendɪd] *adj* desatendi-

do; *leave sth unattended* dejar algo desatendido

un·au·thor·ized [ʌn'ɔːθəraɪzd] *adj* no autorizado

un·a·void·a·ble [ʌnə'vɔɪdəbl] *adj* inevitable

un·a·void·a·bly [ʌnə'vɔɪdəblɪ] *adv*: *unavoidably detained* entretenerse sin poder evitarlo

un·a·ware [ʌnə'wer] *adj*: *be unaware of* no ser consciente de

un·a·wares [ʌnə'werz] *adv* desprevenido; *catch s.o. unawares* agarrar *or Span* coger a alguien desprevenido

un·bal·anced [ʌn'bælənst] *adj also* PSYCH desequilibrado

un·bear·a·ble [ʌn'berəbl] *adj* insoportable

un·beat·a·ble [ʌn'biːtəbl] *adj team* invencible; *quality* insuperable

un·beat·en [ʌn'biːtn] *adj team* invicto

un·be·knownst: [ʌnbɪ'noʊnst] *adj*: *unbeknownst to her* sin que ella lo supiera

un·be·lie·va·ble [ʌnbɪ'liːvəbl] *adj also* F increíble; *he's unbelievable* F (*very good/bad*) es increíble

un·bi·as(s)ed [ʌn'baɪəst] *adj* imparcial

un·block [ʌn'blɑːk] *v/t pipe* desatascar

un·born [ʌn'bɔːrn] *adj* no nacido

un·break·a·ble [ʌn'breɪkəbl] *adj plates* irrompible; *world record* inalcanzable

un·but·ton [ʌn'bʌtn] *v/t* desabotonar

un·called-for [ʌn'kɔːldfɔːr] *adj*: *be uncalled-for* estar fuera de lugar

un·can·ny [ʌn'kænɪ] *adj resemblance* increíble, asombroso; *skill* inexplicable; (*worrying: feeling*) extraño, raro

un·ceas·ing [ʌn'siːsɪŋ] *adj* incesante

un·cer·tain [ʌn'sɜːrtn] *adj future, origins* incierto; *be uncertain about sth* no estar seguro de algo; *what will happen? - it's uncertain* ¿qué ocurrirá? - no se sabe

un·cer·tain·ty [ʌn'sɜːrtntɪ] incertidumbre *f*; *there is still uncertainty about his health* todavía hay incertidumbre en torno a su estado de salud

un·checked [ʌn'tʃekt] *adj*: *let sth go unchecked* no controlar algo

un·cle ['ʌŋkl] tío *m*

un·com·for·ta·ble [ʌn'kʌmftəbl] *adj chair, hotel* incómodo; *feel uncomfortable about sth about decision etc* sentirse incómodo con algo; *I feel uncomfortable with him* me siento incómodo con él

un·com·mon [ʌn'kɑːmən] *adj* poco corriente, raro; *it's not uncommon* no es raro *or* extraño

un·com·pro·mis·ing [ʌn'kɑːmprəmaɪzɪŋ] *adj* inflexible

un·con·cerned [ʌnkən'sɜːrnd] *adj* indiferente; *be unconcerned about s.o./sth* no preocuparse por alguien / algo

un·con·di·tion·al [ʌnkən'dɪʃnl] *adj* incondicional

un·con·scious [ʌn'kɑːnʃəs] *adj* MED, PSYCH inconsciente; *knock unconscious* dejar inconsciente; *be unconscious of sth (not aware)* no ser consciente de algo

un·con·trol·la·ble [ʌnkən'troʊləbl] *adj* anger, children incontrolable; desire incontrolable, irresistible

un·con·ven·tion·al [ʌnkən'venʃnl] *adj* poco convencional

un·co·op·er·a·tive [ʌnkoʊ'ɑːpərətɪv] *adj*: *be uncooperative* no estar dispuesto a colaborar

un·cork [ʌn'kɔːrk] *v/t bottle* descorchar

un·cov·er [ʌn'kʌvər] *v/t remove cover from* destapar; *plot, ancient remains* descubrir

un·dam·aged [ʌn'dæmɪdʒd] *adj* intacto

un·daunt·ed [ʌn'dɔːntɪd] *adj* impertérrito; *carry on undaunted* seguir impertérrito

un·de·cid·ed [ʌndɪ'saɪdɪd] *adj question* sin resolver; *be undecided about s.o./sth* estar indeciso sobre alguien / algo

un·de·ni·a·ble [ʌndɪ'naɪəbl] *adj* innegable

un·de·ni·a·bly [ʌndɪ'naɪəblɪ] *adv* innegablemente

un·der ['ʌndər] 1 *prep (beneath)* debajo de, bajo; *(less than)* menos de; *under the water* bajo el agua; *it is under review / investigation* está siendo revisado / investigado 2 *adv (anesthetized)* anestesiado

un·der·age *adj*: *underage drinking* el consumo de alcohol por menores de edad

un·der·arm *adv*: *throw a ball underarm* lanzar una pelota soltándola por debajo de la altura del hombro

un·der·car·riage tren *m* de aterrizaje

un·der·cov·er *adj agent* secreto

un·der·cut *v/t (pret & pp undercut)* COM vender más barato que

un·der·dog *n*: *support the underdog* apoyar al más débil

un·der·done *adj meat* poco hecho

un·der·es·ti·mate *v/t* subestimar

un·der·ex·posed *adj* PHOT subexpuesto

un·der·fed *adj* malnutrido

un·der·go *v/t (pret underwent, pp undergone)* surgery, treatment ser sometido a; experiences sufrir; *the hotel is undergoing refurbishment* se están efectuando renovaciones en el hotel

un·der·grad·u·ate *m/f* Br estudiante *m/f* universitario(-a) *(todavía no licenciado(a))*

un·der·ground 1 *adj passages etc* subterráneo; POL resistance, newpaper etc clandestino 2 *adv work* bajo tierra; *go underground* POL pasar a la clandestinidad

un·der·growth maleza *f*

un·der·hand *adj (devious)* poco honrado

un·der·lie *v/t (form basis of system)* sostentar

un·der·line *v/t text* subrayar

un·der·ly·ing *adj causes, problems* subyacente

un·der·mine *v/t s.o.'s position, theory* minar, socavar

un·der·neath [ʌndər'niːθ] 1 *prep* debajo de, bajo 2 *adv* debajo

un·der·pants *npl* calzoncillos *mpl*

un·der·pass *for pedestrians* paso *m* subterráneo

un·der·priv·i·leged [ʌndər'prɪvɪlɪdʒd] *adj* desfavorecido

un·der·rate *v/t* subestimar, infravalorar

un·der·shirt camiseta *f*

un·der·sized [ʌndər'saɪzd] *adj* demasiado pequeño

un·der·skirt enaguas *fpl*

un·der·staffed [ʌndər'stæft] *adj* sin suficiente personal

un·der·stand [ʌndər'stænd] 1 *v/t (pret & pp understood)* entender, comprender; language entender; *I understand that you ...* tengo entendido que ...; *they are understood to be in Canada* se cree que están en Canadá 2 *v/i (pret & pp understood)* entender, comprender

un·der·stand·a·ble [ʌndər'stændəbl] *adj* comprensible

un·der·stand·a·bly [ʌndər'stændəblɪ] *adv* comprensiblemente

un·der·stand·ing [ʌndər'stændɪŋ] 1 *adj person* comprensivo 2 *n of problem, situation* interpretación *f*; *(agreement)* acuerdo *m*; *on the understanding that ... (condition)* a condición de que ...

un·der·state·ment *n*: *that's an understatement* ¡y te quedas corto!

un·der·take *v/t (pret undertook, pp undertaken)* task emprender; *undertake to do sth (agree to)* encargarse de hacer algo

U

un·der·tak·er ['ʌndərˈteɪkər] Br encargado m de una funeraria

'un·der·tak·ing (enterprise) proyecto m, empresa f; **give an undertaking to do sth** comprometerse a hacer algo

un·der'val·ue v/t infravalorar

'un·der·wear ropa f interior

un·der'weight adj: **be underweight** pesar menos de lo normal

'un·der·world criminal hampa f; in mythology Hades m

un·der'write v/t (pret **underwrote**, pp **underwritten**) FIN asegurar, garantizar

un·de·served [ʌndɪˈzɜːrvd] adj inmerecido

un·de·sir·a·ble [ʌndɪˈzaɪrəbl] adj features, changes no deseado; person indeseable; **undesirable element** persona f problemática

un·dis·put·ed [ʌndɪˈspjuːtɪd] adj champion, leader indiscutible

un·do [ʌnˈduː] v/t (pret **undid**, pp **undone**) parcel, wrapping abrir; buttons, shirt desabrochar; shoelaces desatar; s.o. else's work deshacer

un·doubt·ed·ly [ʌnˈdaʊtɪdlɪ] adv indudablemente

un·dreamt-of [ʌnˈdremtəv] adj riches inimaginable

un·dress [ʌnˈdres] **1** v/t desvestir, desnudar; **get undressed** desvestirse, desnudarse **2** v/i desvestirse, desnudarse

un·due [ʌnˈduː] adj (excessive) excesivo

un·du·ly [ʌnˈduːlɪ] adv punished, blamed injustamente; (excessively) excesivamente

un·earth [ʌnˈɜːrθ] v/t descubrir; ancient remains desenterrar

un·earth·ly [ʌnˈɜːrθlɪ] adv: **at this unearthly hour** a esta hora intempestiva

un·eas·y [ʌnˈiːzɪ] adj relationship, peace tenso; **feel uneasy about** estar inquieto por

un·eat·a·ble [ʌnˈiːtəbl] adj incomible

un·e·co·nom·ic [ʌniːkəˈnɑːmɪk] adj antieconómico, no rentable

un·ed·u·cat·ed [ʌnˈedʒəkeɪtɪd] adj inculto, sin educación

un·em·ployed [ʌnɪmˈplɔɪd] adj desempleado, Span parado

un·em·ploy·ment [ʌnɪmˈplɔɪmənt] desempleo m, Span paro m

un·end·ing [ʌnˈendɪŋ] adj interminable

un·e·qual [ʌnˈiːkwəl] adj desigual; **be unequal to the task** no estar a la altura de lo que requiere el trabajo

un·er·ring [ʌnˈerɪŋ] adj judgment, instinct infalible

un·e·ven [ʌnˈiːvn] adj quality desigual;

surface, ground irregular

un·e·ven·ly [ʌnˈiːvnlɪ] adv distributed, applied de forma desigual; **be unevenly matched** of two contestants no estar en igualdad de condiciones

un·e·vent·ful [ʌnɪˈventfəl] adj day, journey sin incidentes

un·ex·pect·ed [ʌnɪkˈspektɪd] adj inesperado

un·ex·pect·ed·ly [ʌnɪkˈspektɪdlɪ] adv esperadamente, de forma inesperada

un·fair [ʌnˈfer] adj injusto; **that's unfair** eso no es justo

un·faith·ful [ʌnˈfeɪθfəl] adj husband, wife infiel; **be unfaithful to s.o.** ser infiel a alguien

un·fa·mil·i·ar [ʌnfəˈmɪljər] adj desconocido, extraño; **be unfamiliar with sth** desconocer algo

un·fas·ten [ʌnˈfæsn] v/t belt desabrochar

un·fa·vo·ra·ble, Br **un·fa·vou·ra·ble** [ʌnˈfeɪvərəbl] adj desfavorable

un·feel·ing [ʌnˈfiːlɪŋ] adj person insensible

un·fin·ished [ʌnˈfɪnɪʃt] adj inacabado; **leave sth unfinished** dejar algo sin acabar

un·fit [ʌnˈfɪt] adj: **be unfit** physically estar en baja forma; **be unfit to eat** no ser apto para el consumo; **be unfit to drink** no ser potable; **he's unfit to be a parent** no tiene lo que se necesita para ser padre

un·fix [ʌnˈfɪks] v/t part soltar, desmontar

un·flap·pa·ble [ʌnˈflæpəbl] adj F impasible

un·fold [ʌnˈfoʊld] **1** v/t sheets, letter desdoblar; one's arms descruzar **2** v/i of story etc desarrollarse; of view abrirse

un·fore·seen [ʌnfɔːrˈsiːn] adj imprevisto

un·for·get·ta·ble [ʌnfərˈgetəbl] adj inolvidable

un·for·giv·a·ble [ʌnfərˈgɪvəbl] adj imperdonable; **that was unforgivable of you** eso ha sido imperdonable

un·for·tu·nate [ʌnˈfɔːrtʃənət] adj people desafortunado; event desgraciado; choice of words desafortunado, desacertado; **that's unfortunate for you** has tenido muy mala suerte

un·for·tu·nate·ly [ʌnˈfɔːrtʃənətlɪ] adv desgraciadamente

un·found·ed [ʌnˈfaʊndɪd] adj infundado

un·friend·ly [ʌnˈfrendlɪ] adj person antipático; place desagradable; welcome hostil; software de difícil manejo

un·fur·nished [ʌnˈfɜːrnɪʃt] adj sin amueblar

un·god·ly [ʌnˈgɑːdlɪ] adj: **at this ungodly hour** a esta hora intempestiva

U

un·grate·ful [ʌnˈɡreɪtfəl] adj desagradecido

un·hap·pi·ness [ʌnˈhæpɪnɪs] infelicidad f

un·hap·py [ʌnˈhæpɪ] adj person, look infeliz; day triste; customer etc descontento

un·harmed [ʌnˈhɑːrmd] adj ileso; **be unharmed** salir ileso

un·health·y [ʌnˈhelθɪ] adj person enfermizo; conditions, food, economy poco saludable

un·heard-of [ʌnˈhɜːrdəv] adj inaudito

un·hurt [ʌnˈhɜːrt] adj: **be unhurt** salir ileso

un·hy·gi·en·ic [ʌnhaɪˈdʒiːnɪk] adj antihigiénico

u·ni·fi·ca·tion [juːnɪfɪˈkeɪʃn] unificación f

u·ni·form [ˈjuːnɪfɔːrm] 1 n uniforme m 2 adj uniforme

u·ni·fy [ˈjuːnɪfaɪ] v/t (pret & pp unified) unificar

u·ni·lat·er·al [juːnɪˈlætərəl] adj unilateral

un·i·ma·gi·na·ble [ʌnɪˈmædʒɪnəbl] adj inimaginable

un·i·ma·gi·na·tive [ʌnɪˈmædʒɪnətɪv] adj sin imaginación

un·im·por·tant [ʌnɪmˈpɔːrtənt] adj poco importante

un·in·hab·i·ta·ble [ʌnɪnˈhæbɪtəbl] adj inhabitable

un·in·hab·it·ed [ʌnɪnˈhæbɪtɪd] adj building deshabitado; region desierto

un·in·jured [ʌnˈɪndʒərd] adj: **be uninjured** salir ileso

un·in·tel·li·gi·ble [ʌnɪnˈtelɪdʒəbl] adj ininteligible

un·in·ten·tion·al [ʌnɪnˈtenʃnl] adj no intencionado; **sorry, that was unintentional** lo siento, ha sido sin querer

un·in·ten·tion·al·ly [ʌnɪnˈtenʃnlɪ] adv sin querer

un·in·te·rest·ing [ʌnˈɪntrɪstɪŋ] adj sin interés

un·in·ter·rupt·ed [ʌnɪntəˈrʌptɪd] adj sleep, two hours' work interrumpido

un·ion [ˈjuːnjən] POL unión f; (labor union) sindicato m

u·nique [juːˈniːk] adj único

u·nit [ˈjuːnɪt] unidad f; **unit of measurement** unidad f de medida; **power unit** fuente f de alimentación

u·nit ˈcost COM costo m or Span coste m unitario or por unidad

u·nite [juːˈnaɪt] 1 v/t unir 2 v/i unirse

u·nit·ed [juːˈnaɪtɪd] adj unido

U·nit·ed ˈKing·dom Reino m Unido

U·nit·ed ˈNa·tions Naciones fpl Unidas

U·nit·ed ˈStates (of A·mer·i·ca) Estados mpl Unidos (de América)

u·ni·ty [ˈjuːnətɪ] unidad f

u·ni·ver·sal [juːnɪˈvɜːrsl] adj universal

u·ni·ver·sal·ly [juːnɪˈvɜːrsəlɪ] adv universalmente

u·ni·verse [ˈjuːnɪvɜːrs] universo m

u·ni·ver·si·ty [juːnɪˈvɜːrsətɪ] 1 n universidad f; **he is at university** está en la universidad 2 adj universitario

un·just [ʌnˈdʒʌst] adj injusto

un·kempt [ʌnˈkempt] adj appearance descuidado; hair revuelto

un·kind [ʌnˈkaɪnd] adj desagradable, cruel

un·known [ʌnˈnoʊn] 1 adj desconocido 2 n: **a journey into the unknown** un viaje hacia lo desconocido

un·lead·ed [ʌnˈledɪd] adj sin plomo

un·less [ənˈles] conj a menos que, a no ser que; **don't say anything unless you're sure** no digas nada a menos que or a no ser que estés seguro

un·like [ʌnˈlaɪk] prep (not similar to) diferente de; **it's unlike him to drink so much** él no suele beber tanto; **that photograph is so unlike you** has salido completamente diferente en esa fotografía

un·like·ly [ʌnˈlaɪklɪ] adj (improbable) improbable; explanation inverosímil; **he is unlikely to win** es improbable or poco probable que gane

un·lim·it·ed [ʌnˈlɪmɪtɪd] adj ilimitado

un·list·ed [ʌnˈlɪstɪd] adj: **be unlisted** no aparecer en la guía telefónica

un·load [ʌnˈloʊd] v/t descargar

un·lock [ʌnˈlʊk] v/t abrir

un·luck·i·ly [ʌnˈlʌkɪlɪ] adv desgraciadamente, por desgracia

un·luck·y [ʌnˈlʌkɪ] adj day, choice aciago, funesto; person sin suerte; **that was so unlucky for you!** ¡qué mala suerte tuviste!

un·manned [ʌnˈmænd] adj spacecraft no tripulado

un·mar·ried [ʌnˈmærɪd] adj soltero

un·mis·ta·ka·ble [ʌnmɪˈsteɪkəbl] adj inconfundible

un·moved [ʌnˈmuːvd] adj: **he was unmoved by her tears** sus lágrimas no lo conmovieron

un·mu·si·cal [ʌnˈmjuːzɪkl] adj person sin talento musical; sounds estridente

un·nat·u·ral [ʌnˈnætʃrəl] adj anormal; **it's not unnatural to be annoyed** es normal estar enfadado

un·ne·ces·sa·ry [ʌnˈnesəserɪ] adj innecesario

un·nerv·ing [ʌnˈnɜːrvɪŋ] adj desconcertante

un·no·ticed [ʌnˈnoʊtɪst] adj: **it went un-**

U

noticed pasó desapercibido

un·ob·tain·a·ble [ʌnəb'teɪnəbl] *adj goods* no disponible; TELEC desconectado

un·ob·tru·sive [ʌnəb'truːsɪv] *adj* discreto

un·oc·cu·pied [ʌn'ɑːkjupaɪd] *adj building, house* desocupado; *post* vacante

un·of·fi·cial [ʌnə'fɪʃl] *adj* no oficial; *this is still unofficial but ...* esto todavía no es oficial, pero ...

un·of·fi·cial·ly [ʌnə'fɪʃlɪ] *adv* extraoficialmente

un·or·tho·dox [ʌn'ɔːrθədɑːks] *adj* poco ortodoxo

un·pack [ʌn'pæk] **1** *v/t* deshacer **2** *v/i* deshacer el equipaje

un·paid [ʌn'peɪd] *adj work* no remunerado

un·pleas·ant [ʌn'pleznt] *adj* desagradable; *he was very unpleasant to her* fue muy desagradable con ella

un·plug [ʌn'plʌg] *v/t (pret & pp **unplugged**)* TV, *computer* desenchufar

un·pop·u·lar [ʌn'pɑːpjələr] *adj* impopular

un·pre·ce·den·ted [ʌn'presɪdentɪd] *adj* sin precedentes; *it was unprecedented for a woman to ...* no tenía precedentes que una mujer ...

un·pre·dict·a·ble [ʌnprɪ'dɪktəbl] *adj person, weather* imprevisible, impredecible

un·pre·ten·tious [ʌnprɪ'tenʃəs] *adj person, style, hotel* modesto, sin pretensiones

un·prin·ci·pled [ʌn'prɪnsɪpld] *adj* sin principios

un·pro·duc·tive [ʌnprə'dʌktɪv] *adj meeting, discussion* infructuoso; *soil* improductivo

un·pro·fes·sion·al [ʌnprə'feʃnl] *adj* poco profesional

un·prof·i·ta·ble [ʌn'prɑːfɪtəbl] *adj* no rentable

un·pro·nounce·a·ble [ʌnprə'naʊnsəbl] *adj* impronunciable

un·pro·tect·ed [ʌnprə'tektɪd] *adj borders* desprotegido, sin protección; *unprotected sex* sexo *m* sin preservativos

un·pro·voked [ʌnprə'vəʊkt] *adj attack* no provocado

un·qual·i·fied [ʌn'kwɑːlɪfaɪd] *adj worker, doctor etc* sin titulación

un·ques·tio·na·bly [ʌn'kwestʃnəblɪ] *adv (without doubt)* indiscutiblemente

un·ques·tion·ing [ʌn'kwestʃnɪŋ] *adj attitude, loyalty* incondicional

un·rav·el [ʌn'rævl] *v/t (pret & pp **unraveled**, Br **unravelled**)* string, knitting* desenredar; *mystery, complexities* desentrañar

un·rea·da·ble [ʌn'riːdəbl] *adj book* ilegible

un·re·al [ʌn'rɪəl] *adj* irreal; *this is unreal!* F ¡esto es increíble! F

un·re·a·lis·tic [ʌnrɪə'lɪstɪk] *adj* poco realista

un·rea·so·na·ble [ʌn'riːznəbl] *adj person* poco razonable, irrazonable; *demand, expectation* excesivo, irrazonable; *you're being unreasonable* no estás siendo razonable

un·re·lat·ed [ʌnrɪ'leɪtɪd] *adj issues* no relacionado; *people* no emparentado

un·re·lent·ing [ʌnrɪ'lentɪŋ] *adj* implacable

un·re·li·a·ble [ʌnrɪ'laɪəbl] *adj car, machine* poco fiable; *person* informal

un·rest [ʌn'rest] *malestar m; (rioting)* disturbios *mpl*

un·re·strained [ʌnrɪ'streɪnd] *adj emotions* incontrolado

un·road·wor·thy [ʌn'roʊdwɜːrðɪ] *adj* que no está en condiciones de circular

un·roll [ʌn'roʊl] *v/t carpet, scroll* desenrollar

un·ru·ly [ʌn'ruːlɪ] *adj* revoltoso

un·safe [ʌn'seɪf] *adj* peligroso; *it's unsafe to drink / eat* no se puede beber / comer

un·san·i·tar·y [ʌn'sænɪterɪ] *adj conditions, drains* insalubre

un·sat·is·fac·to·ry [ʌnsætɪs'fæktərɪ] *adj* insatisfactorio

un·sa·vo·ry [ʌn'seɪvərɪ] *adj person, reputation* indeseable; *district* desagradable

un·scathed [ʌn'skeɪðd] *adj (not injured)* ileso; *(not damaged)* intacto

un·screw [ʌn'skruː] *v/t top* desenroscar; *shelves, hooks* desatornillar

un·scru·pu·lous [ʌn'skruːpjələs] *adj* sin escrúpulos

un·self·ish [ʌn'selfɪʃ] *adj* generoso

un·set·tled [ʌn'setld] *adj issue* sin decidir; *weather, stock market, lifestyle* inestable; *bills* sin pagar

un·shav·en [ʌn'ʃeɪvn] *adj* sin afeitar

un·sight·ly [ʌn'saɪtlɪ] *adj* horrible, feo

un·skilled [ʌn'skɪld] *adj* no cualificado

un·so·cia·ble [ʌn'soʊʃəbl] *adj* insociable

un·so·phis·ti·cat·ed [ʌnsə'fɪstɪkeɪtɪd] *adj person, beliefs* sencillo; *equipment* simple

un·sta·ble [ʌn'steɪbl] *adj* inestable

un·stead·y [ʌn'stedɪ] *adj hand* tembloroso; *ladder* inestable; *be unsteady on one's feet* tamblearse

un·stint·ing [ʌn'stɪntɪŋ] *adj* generoso; *be unstinting in one's efforts / generosity* no escatimar esfuerzos / generosidad

un·stuck [ʌnˈstʌk] *adj:* **come unstuck** F
of plan etc irse al garete F

un·suc·cess·ful [ʌnsəkˈsesfəl] *adj writer
etc* fracasado; *candidate* perdedor; *party,
attempt* fallido; **he tried but was unsuccessful** lo intentó sin éxito

un·suc·cess·ful·ly [ʌnsəkˈsesfəlɪ] *adv
try, apply* sin éxito

un·suit·a·ble [ʌnˈsuːtəbl] *adj partner,
film, clothing* inadecuado; *thing to say* inoportuno

un·sus·pect·ing [ʌnsəsˈpektɪŋ] *adj* confiado

un·swerv·ing [ʌnˈswɜːrvɪŋ] *adj loyalty,
devotion* inquebrantable

un·think·a·ble [ʌnˈθɪŋkəbl] *adj* impensa-
ble

un·ti·dy [ʌnˈtaɪdɪ] *adj room, desk* desordenado; *hair* revuelto

un·tie [ʌnˈtaɪ] *v/t knot, laces, prisoner* desatar

un·til [ənˈtɪl] **1** *prep* hasta; **from Monday
until Friday** desde el lunes hasta el
viernes; **I can wait until tomorrow** puedo esperar hasta mañana; **not until Friday** no antes del viernes; **it won't be finished until July** no estará acabado hasta julio **2** *conj* hasta que; **can you wait
until I'm ready?** ¿puedes esperar hasta
que esté listo?; **they won't do anything
until you say so** no harán nada hasta
que (no) se lo digas

un·time·ly [ʌnˈtaɪmlɪ] *adj death* prematuro

un·tir·ing [ʌnˈtaɪrɪŋ] *adj efforts* incansable

un·told [ʌnˈtoʊld] *adj suffering* indecible;
riches inconmensurable; *story* nunca
contado

un·trans·lat·a·ble [ʌntrænsˈleɪtəbl] *adj*
intraducible

un·true [ʌnˈtruː] *adj* falso

un·used¹ [ʌnˈjuːzd] *adj goods* sin usar

un·used² [ʌnˈjuːst] *adj:* **be unused to sth**
no estar acostumbrado a algo; **be unused to doing sth** no estar acostumbrado
a hacer algo

un·u·su·al [ʌnˈjuːʒl] *adj* poco corriente; **it
is unusual …** es raro *or* extraño …

un·u·su·al·ly [ʌnˈjuːʒəlɪ] *adv* inusitada-
mente; **the weather's unusually cold**
hace un frío inusual

un·veil [ʌnˈveɪl] *v/t memorial, statue etc*
desvelar

un·well [ʌnˈwel] *adj* indispuesto, malo; **be
unwell** sentirse indispuesto *or* mal

un·will·ing [ʌnˈwɪlɪŋ] *adj* poco dispuesto,
reacio; **be unwilling to do sth** no estar
dispuesto a hacer algo, ser reacio a hacer

algo

un·will·ing·ly [ʌnˈwɪlɪŋlɪ] *adv* de mala gana, a regañadientes

un·wind [ʌnˈwaɪnd] **1** *v/t (pret & pp unwound) tape* desenrollar **2** *v/i (pret &
pp unwound) of tape* desenrollarse; *of
story* irse desarrollando; F *(relax)* relajarse

un·wise [ʌnˈwaɪz] *adj* imprudente

un·wrap [ʌnˈræp] *v/t (pret & pp unwrap-
ped) gift* desenvolver

un·writ·ten [ʌnˈrɪtn] *adj law, rule* no escrito

un·zip [ʌnˈzɪp] *v/t (pret & pp unzipped)
dress etc* abrir la cremallera de; COMPUT
descomprimir

up [ʌp] **1** *adv position* arriba; *movement*
hacia arriba; **up in the sky / up on the
roof** (arriba) en el cielo / tejado; **up here / there** aquí / allí arriba; **be up** *(out of
bed)* estar levantado; *of sun* haber salido;
(be built) haber sido construido, estar
acabado; *of shelves* estar montado; *of
prices, temperature* haber subido; *(have
expired)* haberse acabado; **what's up?**
F ¿qué pasa?; **up to the year 1989** hasta
el año 1989; **he came up to me** se me
acercó; **what are you up to these days?**
¿qué es de tu vida?; **what are those kids
up to?** ¿qué están tramando esos niños?;
be up to something (bad) estar tramando algo; **I don't feel up to it** no me siento en condiciones de hacerlo; **it's up to you**
tú decides; **it is up to them to solve it**
(their duty) les corresponde a ellos resol-
verlo; **be up and about** *after illness* estar
recuperado **2** *prep:* **further up the mountain** más arriba de la montaña; **he climb-
ed up a tree** se subió a un árbol; **they ran
up the street** corrieron por la calle; **the
water goes up this pipe** el agua sube
por esta tubería; **we traveled up to
Chicago** subimos hasta Chicago **3** *n:*
ups and downs altibajos *mpl*

'up·bring·ing *n* educación *f*

'up·com·ing *adj (forthcoming)* próximo

up'date¹ *v/t file, records* actualizar; **update s.o. on sth** poner a alguien al corriente de algo

'up·date² *n* actualización *f*; **can you give
me an update on the situation?** ¿me
puedes poner al corriente de la situación?

up'grade *v/t computers etc* actualizar; *(replace with new versions)* modernizar;
product modernizar; **upgrade s.o. to
business class** cambiar a alguien a
clase ejecutiva

up·heav·al [ʌpˈhiːvl] *emotional* conmo-

U

ción *m*; *physical* trastorno *m*; *political, social* sacudida *f*

up·hill 1 *adv* [ʌp'hɪl] *walk* cuesta arriba **2** *adj* ['ʌphɪl] *struggle* arduo, difícil

up'hold *v/t* (*pret & pp* **upheld**) *traditions, rights* defender, conservar; (*vindicate*) confirmar

up·hol·ster·y [ʌp'houlstərɪ] (*coverings of chairs*) tapicería *f*; (*padding of chairs*) relleno *m*

'up·keep *of buildings, parks etc* mantenimiento *m*

'up·load *v/t* COMPUT cargar

up'mar·ket *adj restaurant, hotel* de categoría

up·on [ə'pɒn] *prep* → **on**

up·per ['ʌpər] *adj part of sth* superior; *stretches of a river* alto; *deck* superior, de arriba

up·per 'class *adj accent, family* de clase alta

up·per 'clas·ses *npl* clases *fpl* altas

'up·right 1 *adj citizen* honrado **2** *adv* sit derecho

'up·right (**'pi·an·o**) piano *m* vertical

'up·ris·ing levantamiento *m*

'up·roar (*loud noise*) alboroto *m*; (*protest*) tumulto *m*

up'set 1 *v/t* (*pret & pp* **upset**) *drink, glass* tirar; *emotionally* disgustar **2** *adj emotionally* disgustado; **get upset about sth** disgustarse por algo; **have an upset stomach** tener el estómago mal

up'set·ting *adj* triste

'up·shot (*result, outcome*) resultado *m*

up·side 'down *adv* boca abajo; **turn sth upside down** *box etc* poner algo al revés *or* boca abajo

up'stairs 1 *adv* arriba **2** *adj room* de arriba

'up·start advenedizo(-a) *m(f)*

up'stream *adv* río arriba

'up·take FIN respuesta *f* (**of** a); **be quick / slow on the uptake** F ser / no ser muy espabilado F

up'tight *adj* F (*nervous*) tenso; (*inhibited*) estrecho

up-to-'date *adj information* actualizado; *fashions* moderno

'up turn *in economy* mejora *f*

up·ward ['ʌpwərd] *adv fly, move* hacia arriba; **upward of 10,000** más de 10.000

u·ra·ni·um [jʊ'reɪnɪəm] uranio *m*

ur·ban ['ɜːrbən] *adj* urbano

ur·ban·i·za·tion [ɜːrbənaɪ'zeɪʃn] urbanización *f*

ur·chin ['ɜːrtʃɪn] golfillo(-a) *m(f)*

urge [ɜːrdʒ] **1** *n* impulso *m*; **I felt an urge to hit her** me entraron ganas de pegarle; **I**

have an urge to do something new siento la necesidad de hacer algo nuevo **2** *v/t*: **urge s.o. to do sth** rogar a alguien que haga algo

◆ **urge on** *v/t* (*encourage*) animar

ur·gen·cy ['ɜːrdʒənsɪ] *of situation* urgencia *f*

ur·gent ['ɜːrdʒənt] *adj job, letter* urgente; **be in urgent need of sth** necesitar algo urgentemente; **is it urgent?** ¿es urgente?

u·ri·nate ['jʊrəneɪt] *v/i* orinar

u·rine ['jʊrɪn] orina *f*

urn [ɜːrn] urna *f*

U·ru·guay ['jʊrəɡwaɪ] *n* Uruguay

U·ru·guay·an [jʊrə'ɡwaɪən] **1** *adj* uruguayo **2** *n* uruguayo(-a) *m(f)*

us [ʌs] *pron* nos; *after prep* nosotros(-as); **they love us** nos quieren; **she gave us the keys** nos dio las llaves; **he sold it to us** nos lo vendió; **that's for us** eso es para nosotros; **who's that? - it's us** ¿quién es? - ¡somos nosotros!

US [juː'es] *abbr* (= *United States*) EE.UU. *mpl* (= Estados *mpl* Unidos)

USA [juːes'eɪ] *abbr* (= *United States of America*) EE.UU. (= Estados Unidos)

us·a·ble ['juːzəbl] *adj* utilizable; **it's not usable** no se puede utilizar

us·age ['juːzɪdʒ] uso *m*

use 1 *v/t* [juːz] *tool, word* utilizar, usar; *skills, knowledge, car* usar; *a lot of gas* consumir; *pej: person* utilizar; **I could use a drink** F no me vendría mal una copa **2** *n* [juːs] uso *m*, utilización *f*; **be of great use to s.o.** ser de gran utilidad para alguien; **it's of no use to me** no me sirve; **is that of any use?** ¿eso sirve para algo?; **it's no use** no sirve de nada; **it's no use trying / waiting** no sirve de nada intentarlo / esperar

◆ **use up** *v/t* agotar

used¹ [juːzd] *adj car etc* de segunda mano

used² [juːst] *adj*: **be used to s.o./sth** estar acostumbrado a alguien / algo; **get used to s.o./sth** acostumbrarse a alguien / algo; **be used to doing sth** estar acostumbrado a hacer algo; **get used to doing sth** acostumbrarse a hacer algo

used³ [juːst]: **I used to like him** antes me gustaba; **they used to meet every Saturday** solían verse todos los sábados

use·ful ['juːsfəl] *adj* útil

use·ful·ness ['juːsfʊlnɪs] utilidad *f*

use·less ['juːslɪs] *adj inútil*; *machine, computer* inservible; **be useless** F *person* ser un inútil F; **it's useless trying** (*there's no point*) no vale la pena intentarlo

us·er ['juːzər] *of product* usuario
us·er-'friend·ly *adj software, device* de fácil manejo
ush·er ['ʌʃər] *n (at wedding)* persona que se encarga de indicar a los asistentes dónde se deben sentar
◆ **usher in** *v/t new era* anunciar
ush·er·ette [ʌʃəˈret] acomodadora *f*
u·su·al ['juːʒl] *adj* habitual, acostumbrado; *as usual* como de costumbre; *the usual, please* lo de siempre, por favor
u·su·al·ly ['juːʒlɪ] *adv* normalmente; *I usually start at 9* suelo empezar a las 9
u·ten·sil [juːˈtensl] utensilio *m*

u·te·rus ['juːtərəs] útero *m*
u·til·i·ty [juːˈtɪlətɪ] *(usefulness)* utilidad *f*; *public utilities* servicios *mpl* públicos
u·til·ize ['juːtɪlaɪz] *v/t* utilizar
ut·most ['ʌtmoust] **1** *adj* sumo **2** *n*: *do one's utmost* hacer todo lo posible
ut·ter ['ʌtər] **1** *adj* completo, total **2** *v/t sound* decir, pronunciar
ut·ter·ly ['ʌtərlɪ] *adv* completamente, totalmente
U-turn ['juːtɜːrn] cambio *m* de sentido; *do a U-turn fig: in policy etc* dar un giro de 180 grados

V

va·can·cy ['veɪkənsɪ] *at work* puesto *m* vacante
va·cant ['veɪkənt] *adj building* vacío; *position* vacante; *look, expression* vago, distraído
va·cant·ly ['veɪkəntlɪ] *adv* distraídamente
va·cate [veɪˈkeɪt] *v/t room* desalojar
va·ca·tion [veɪˈkeɪʃn] *n vacaciones fpl*; *be on vacation* estar de vacaciones; *go to … on vacation* ir de vacaciones a …
va·ca·tion·er [veɪˈkeɪʃənər] turista *m/f*; *summer* veraneante *m/f*
vac·cin·ate ['væksɪneɪt] *v/t* vacunar; *be vaccinated against …* estar vacunado contra …
vac·cin·a·tion [væksɪˈneɪʃn] *action* vacunación *f*; *(vaccine)* vacuna *f*
vac·cine ['væksiːn] vacuna *f*
vac·u·um ['vækjʊəm] **1** *n* PHYS, *fig* vacío *m* **2** *v/t floors* pasar el aspirador por, aspirar
'vac·u·um clean·er aspirador *m*, aspiradora *f*
'vac·u·um flask termo *m*
vac·u·um-'packed *adj* envasado al vacío
vag·a·bond ['væɡəbɑːnd] vagabundo(-a) *m(f)*
va·gi·na [vəˈdʒaɪnə] vagina *f*
va·gi·nal ['vædʒɪnl] *adj* vaginal
va·grant ['veɪɡrənt] vagabundo(-a) *m(f)*
vague [veɪɡ] *adj* vago; *he was very vague about it* no fue muy preciso
vague·ly ['veɪɡlɪ] *adv answer, (slightly)* vagamente; *possible* muy poco

vain [veɪn] **1** *adj person* vanidoso; *hope* vano **2** *n*: *in vain* en vano; *their efforts were in vain* sus esfuerzos fueron en vano
val·en·tine ['væləntaɪn] *card* tarjeta *f* del día de San Valentín; *Valentine's Day* día de San Valentín *or* de los enamorados
val·et 1 *n* ['væleɪ] *person* mozo *m* **2** *v/t* ['vælət] *car* lavar y limpiar
'val·et ser·vice *for clothes* servicio *m* de planchado; *for cars* servicio *m* de lavado y limpiado
val·iant ['væljənt] *adj* valiente, valeroso
val·iant·ly ['væljəntlɪ] *adv* valientemente, valerosamente
val·id ['vælɪd] *adj* válido
val·i·date ['vælɪdeɪt] *v/t with official stamp* sellar; *s.o.'s alibi* dar validez a
va·lid·i·ty [vəˈlɪdətɪ] validez *f*
val·ley ['vælɪ] valle *m*
val·u·a·ble ['væljʊbl] **1** *adj* valioso **2** *n*: *valuables* objetos *mpl* de valor
val·u·a·tion [væljʊˈeɪʃn] tasación *f*, valoración *f*
val·ue ['væljuː] **1** *n* valor *m*; *be good value* ofrecer buena relación calidad-precio; *get value for money* recibir una buena relación calidad-precio; *rise / fall in value* aumentar / disminuir de valor **2** *v/t s.o.'s friendship, one's freedom* valorar; *I value your advice* valoro tus consejos; *have an object valued* pedir la valoración *or* tasación de un objeto
valve [vælv] válvula *f*
van [væn] camioneta *f*, furgoneta *f*

V

van·dal ['vændl] vándalo *m*, gamberro(-a) *m(f)*

van·dal·ism ['vændəlɪzm] vandalismo *m*

van·dal·ize ['vændəlaɪz] *v/t* destrozar (*intencionadamente*)

van·guard ['vænguːrd] vanguardia *f*; *be in the vanguard of fig* estar a la vanguardia de

va·nil·la [vəˈnɪlə] **1** *n* vainilla *f* **2** *adj* de vainilla

van·ish ['vænɪʃ] *v/i* desaparecer

van·i·ty ['vænətɪ] *of person* vanidad *f*

'van·i·ty case neceser *m*

van·tage point ['væntɪdʒ] *on hill etc* posición *f* aventajada

va·por ['veɪpər] vapor *m*

va·por·ize ['veɪpəraɪz] *v/t of atomic bomb, explosion* vaporizar

'va·por trail *of airplane* estela *f*

va·pour *Br* → **vapor**

var·i·a·ble ['verɪəbl] **1** *adj* variable **2** *n* MATH, COMPUT variable *f*

var·i·ant ['verɪənt] *n* variante *f*

var·i·a·tion [verɪˈeɪʃn] variación *f*

var·i·cose vein ['værɪkəʊs] variz *f*

var·ied ['verɪd] *adj* variado

va·ri·e·ty [vəˈraɪətɪ] (*variedness, type*) variedad *f*; *a variety of things to do* (*range, mixture*) muchas cosas para hacer

var·i·ous ['verɪəs] *adj* (*several*) varios; (*different*) diversos

var·nish ['vuːrnɪʃ] **1** *n for wood* barniz *m*; *for fingernails* esmalte *m* **2** *v/t wood* barnizar; *fingernails* poner esmalte a, pintar

var·y ['verɪ] **1** *v/i* (*pret & pp varied*) variar; *it varies* depende **2** *v/t* (*pret & pp varied*) variar

vase [veɪz] jarrón *m*

vas·ec·to·my [vəˈsektəmɪ] vasectomía *f*

vast [væst] *adj desert, knowledge* vasto; *number, improvement* enorme

vast·ly ['væstlɪ] *adv* enormemente

VAT [viːeɪˈtiː, væt] *Br abbr* (= *value-added tax*) IVA *m* (= impuesto *m* sobre el valor añadido)

Vat·i·can ['vætɪkən]: *the Vatican* el Vaticano

vau·de·ville ['vɔːdvɪl] *adj* vodevil *m*

vault¹ [vɔːlt] *n in roof* bóveda *f*; *vaults* (*cellar*) sótano *m*; *of bank* cámara *f* acorazada

vault² [vɔːlt] **1** *n* SP salto *m* **2** *v/t beam etc* saltar

VCR [viːsiːˈɑːr] *abbr* (= *video cassette recorder*) aparato *m* de Span vídeo or L.Am. video

VDU [viːdiːˈjuː] *abbr* (= *visual display unit*) monitor *m*

veal [viːl] ternera *f*

veer [vɪr] *v/i* girar, torcer

ve·gan ['viːgn] **1** *n* vegetariano(-a) *m(f)* estricto (-a) (*que no come ningún producto de origen animal*) **2** *adj* vegetariano estricto

vege·ta·ble ['vedʒtəbl] hortaliza *f*; *vegetables* verduras *fpl*

ve·ge·tar·i·an [vedʒɪˈterɪən] **1** *n* vegetariano(-a) *m(f)* **2** *adj* vegetariano

ve·ge·tar·i·an·ism [vedʒɪˈterɪənɪzm] vegetarianismo *m*

veg·e·ta·tion [vedʒɪˈteɪʃn] vegetación *f*

ve·he·mence ['viːəməns] vehemencia *f*

ve·he·ment ['viːəmənt] *adj* vehemente

ve·he·ment·ly ['viːəməntlɪ] *adv* vehementemente

ve·hi·cle ['viːɪkl] *also fig* vehículo *m*

veil [veɪl] **1** *n* velo *m* **2** *v/t* cubrir con un velo

vein [veɪn] ANAT vena *f*; *in this vein fig* en este tono

Vel·cro® ['velkrəʊ] velcro *m*

ve·loc·i·ty [vɪˈlɑːsətɪ] velocidad *f*

vel·vet ['velvɪt] *n* terciopelo *m*

vel·vet·y ['velvɪtɪ] *adj* aterciopelado

ven·det·ta [venˈdetə] vendetta *f*

vend·ing ma·chine ['vendɪŋ] máquina *f* expendedora

vend·or ['vendər] LAW parte *f* vendedora

ve·neer [vəˈnɪr] *on wood* chapa *f*; *of politeness etc* apariencia *f*, fachada

ven·e·ra·ble ['venərəbl] *adj* venerable

ven·e·rate ['venəreɪt] *v/t* venerar

ven·e·ra·tion [venəˈreɪʃn] veneración *f*

ven·e·re·al dis·ease [vɪˈnɪrɪəl] enfermedad *f* venérea

ve·ne·tian 'blind persiana *f* veneciana

Ven·e·zue·la [venɪzˈweɪlə] *n* Venezuela

Ven·e·zue·lan [venɪzˈweɪlən] **1** *adj* venezolano **2** *n* venezolano(-a) *m(f)*

ven·geance ['vendʒəns] venganza *f*; *with a vengeance* con ganas

ven·i·son ['venɪsən] venado *m*

ven·om ['venəm] *also fig* veneno *m*

ven·om·ous ['venəməs] *adj snake* venenoso; *fig* envenenado

vent [vent] *n for air* respiradero *m*; *give vent to feelings* dar rienda suelta a

ven·ti·late ['ventɪleɪt] *v/t* ventilar

ven·ti·la·tion [ventɪˈleɪʃn] ventilación *f*

ven·ti·la·tion shaft pozo *m* de ventilación

ven·ti·la·tor ['ventɪleɪtər] ventilador *m*; MED respirador *m*

ven·tril·o·quist [venˈtrɪləkwɪst] ventrilocuo(-a) *m(f)*

ven·ture ['ventʃər] **1** *n* (*undertaking*) iniciativa *f* **2** COM empresa *f* **2** *v/i* aventurarse

ven·ue ['venjuː] *for meeting* lugar *m*; *for concert* local *m*, sala *f* ve·ran·da [vəˈrændə] porche m

verb [vɜːrb] verbo m

verb·al [ˈvɜːrbl] adj (spoken) verbal

verb·al·ly [ˈvɜːrbəlɪ] adv de palabra

ver·ba·tim [vɜːrˈbeɪtɪm] adv literalmente

ver·dict [ˈvɜːrdɪkt] LAW veredicto m;
  what's your verdict? ¿qué te parece?,
  ¿qué opinas?

verge [vɜːrdʒ] n of road arcén m; **be on
  the verge of ruin** estar al borde de; **tears**
  estar a punto de

◆ verge on v/t rayar en

ver·i·fi·ca·tion [verɪfɪˈkeɪʃn] (checking)
  verificación f; (confirmation) confirmación f

ver·i·fy [ˈverɪfaɪ] v/t (pret & pp verified)
  (check) verificar; (confirm) confirmar

ver·mi·cel·li [vɜːrmɪˈtʃelɪ] nsg fideos mpl

ver·min [ˈvɜːrmɪn] npl bichos mpl, alima-
  ñas fpl

ver·mouth [vɜːrˈmuːθ] vermut m

ver·nac·u·lar [vərˈnækjələr] n lenguaje m
  de la calle

ver·sa·tile [ˈvɜːrsətəl] adj polifacético,
  versátil

ver·sa·til·i·ty [vɜːrsəˈtɪlətɪ] polivalencia f,
  versatilidad f

verse [vɜːrs] verso m

versed [vɜːrst] adj: **be well versed in a
  subject** estar muy versado en una materia

ver·sion [ˈvɜːrʃn] versión f

ver·sus [ˈvɜːrsəs] prep SP, LAW contra

ver·te·bra [ˈvɜːrtɪbrə] vértebra f

ver·te·brate [ˈvɜːrtɪbreɪt] n vertebra-
  do(-a) m(f)

ver·ti·cal [ˈvɜːrtɪkl] adj vertical

ver·ti·go [ˈvɜːrtɪɡoʊ] vértigo m

ver·y [ˈverɪ] **1** adv muy; **was it cold? - not
  very** ¿hizo frío? - no mucho; **the very
  best** el mejor de todos **2** adj: **at that very
  moment** en ese mismo momento; **that's
  the very thing I need** (exact) eso es precisamente lo que necesito; **the very
  thought** (mere) sólo de pensar en; **right
  at the very top / bottom** arriba / al fondo
  del todo

ves·sel [ˈvesl] NAUT buque m

vest [vest] chaleco m

ves·tige [ˈvestɪdʒ] vestigio m; vestigio m
  de la calle

vet¹ [vet] n (veterinary surgeon) veterina-
  rio(-a) m(f)

vet² [vet] v/t (pret & pp vetted) applicants
  etc examinar, investigar

vet³ [vet] v/t MIL veterano(-a) m(f)

vet·e·ran [ˈvetərən] **1** n veterano(-a) m(f)
  2 adj veterano

vet·e·ri·nar·i·an [vetərəˈnerɪən] veteri-
  nario(-a) m(f)

ve·to [ˈviːtoʊ] **1** n veto m **2** v/t vetar

vex [veks] v/t (concern, worry) molestar,
  irritar

vexed [vekst] adj (worried) molesto, irritado; **the vexed question of** la polémica
  cuestión de

vi·a [ˈvaɪə] prep vía

vi·a·ble [ˈvaɪəbl] adj viable

vi·brate [vaɪˈbreɪt] v/i vibrar

vi·bra·tion [vaɪˈbreɪʃn] vibración f

vic·ar [ˈvɪkər] vicario m

vic·ar·age [ˈvɪkərɪdʒ] vicaría f

vice¹ [vaɪs] vicio m, **the problem of vice**
  el problema del vicio

vice²Br → vise

vice pres·i·dent vicepresidente(-a) m(f)

'vice squad brigada f antivicio

vi·ce ver·sa [vaɪs ˈvɜːrsə] adv viceversa

vi·cin·i·ty [vɪˈsɪnətɪ] zona f; **in the vicinity of ...** the church etc en las cercanías
  de ...; $500 etc rondando ...

vi·cious [ˈvɪʃəs] adj dog fiero; attack, temper, criticism feroz

vi·cious 'cir·cle círculo m vicioso

vi·cious·ly [ˈvɪʃəslɪ] adv con brutalidad

vic·tim [ˈvɪktɪm] víctima f

vic·tim·ize [ˈvɪktɪmaɪz] v/t tratar injustamente

vic·tor [ˈvɪktər] vencedor(a) m(f)

vic·to·ri·ous [vɪkˈtɔːrɪəs] adj victorioso

vic·to·ry [ˈvɪktərɪ] victoria f; **win a victory over ...** obtener una victoria sobre
  ...

vid·e·o [ˈvɪdɪoʊ] **1** n Span vídeo m, L.Am.
  video m; **have X on video** tener a X en
  Span vídeo or L.Am. video **2** v/t grabar
  en Span vídeo or L.Am. video

'vid·e·o cam·e·ra videocámara f

vid·e·o cas'sette videocasete m

'vid·e·o con·fer·ence TELEC videoconferencia f

'vid·e·o game videojuego m

'vid·e·o·phone videoteléfono m

'vid·e·o re·cord·er aparato m de Span
  vídeo or L.Am. video

'vid·e·o re·cord·ing grabación f en Span
  vídeo or L.Am. video

'vid·e·o·tape cinta f de Span vídeo or
  L.Am. video

vie [vaɪ] v/i competir

Vi·et·nam [vɪetˈnɑːm] Vietnam m

Vi·et·nam·ese [vɪetnəˈmiːz] **1** adj vietnamita **2** n vietnamita m/f; language vietnamita m

view [vjuː] **1** n vista f; of situation opinión
  f; **in view of** teniendo en cuenta; **be on
  view** of paintings estar expuesto al público; **with a view to** con vistas a **2** v/t
  events, situation ver, considerar; TV pro-

gram, house ver **3** v/i *(watch TV)* ver la televisión

view·er ['vjuːər] TV telespectador(a) *m(f)*

'**view·find·er** PHOT visor *m*

'**view·point** punto *m* de vista

vig·or ['vɪɡər] *(energy)* vigor *m*

vig·or·ous ['vɪɡərəs] *adj shake* vigoroso; *person* enérgico; *denial* rotundo

vig·or·ous·ly ['vɪɡərəslɪ] *adv shake* con vigor; *deny, defend* rotundamente

vig·our *Br* → **vigor**

vile [vaɪl] *adj smell* asqueroso; *thing to do* vil

vil·la ['vɪlə] chalet *m*; *in the country* villa *f*

vil·lage ['vɪlɪdʒ] pueblo *m*

vil·lag·er ['vɪlɪdʒər] aldeano(-a) *m(f)*

vil·lain ['vɪlən] malo(a) *m(f)*

vin·di·cate ['vɪndɪkeɪt] v/t *(show to be correct)* dar la razón a; *(show to be innocent)* vindicar; *I feel vindicated* los hechos me dan ahora la razón

vin·dic·tive [vɪn'dɪktɪv] *adj* vengativo

vin·dic·tive·ly [vɪn'dɪktɪvlɪ] *adv* vengativamente

vine [vaɪn] vid *f*

vin·e·gar ['vɪnɪɡər] vinagre *m*

vine·yard ['vɪnjɑːrd] viñedo *m*

vin·tage ['vɪntɪdʒ] **1** *n of wine* cosecha *f* **2** *adj (classic)* clásico *m*

vi·o·la [vɪ'oʊlə] MUS viola *f*

vi·o·late ['vaɪəleɪt] v/t violar

vi·o·la·tion [vaɪə'leɪʃn] violación *f*; *(traffic violation)* infracción *f*

vi·o·lence ['vaɪələns] violencia *f*; *outbreak of violence* estallido de violencia

vi·o·lent ['vaɪələnt] *adj* violento; *have a violent temper* tener muy mal genio

vi·o·lent·ly ['vaɪələntlɪ] *adv react* violentamente; *object* rotundamente; *fall violently in love with s.o.* enamorarse perdidamente de alguien

vi·o·let ['vaɪələt] *n color, plant* violeta *m*

vi·o·lin [vaɪə'lɪn] violín *m*

vi·o·lin·ist [vaɪə'lɪnɪst] violinista *m/f*

VIP [viːaɪ'piː] *abbr* (= *very important person*) VIP *m*

vi·per ['vaɪpər] *snake* víbora *f*

vi·ral ['vaɪrəl] *adj infection* vírico, viral

vir·gin ['vɜːrdʒɪn] virgen *m/f*

vir·gin·i·ty [vɜːr'dʒɪnətɪ] virginidad *f*; *lose one's virginity* perder la virginidad

Vir·go ['vɜːrɡoʊ] ASTR Virgo *m/f inv*

vir·ile ['vɪrəl] *adj man* viril; *prose* vigoroso

vi·ril·i·ty [vɪ'rɪlətɪ] virilidad *f*

vir·tu·al ['vɜːrtʃʊəl] *adj* virtual

vir·tu·al·ly ['vɜːrtʃʊəlɪ] *adv (almost)* virtualmente, casi

vir·tu·al re·al·i·ty realidad *f* virtual

vir·tue ['vɜːrtʃuː] virtud *f*; *in virtue of* en

virtud de

vir·tu·o·so [vɜːrtʃuː'oʊzoʊ] MUS virtuoso(-a) *m(f)*

vir·tu·ous ['vɜːrtʃʊəs] *adj* virtuoso

vir·u·lent ['vɪrʊlənt] *adj* virulento

vi·rus ['vaɪrəs] MED, COMPUT virus *m inv*

vi·sa ['viːzə] visa *f*, visado *m*

vise [vaɪs] torno *m* de banco

vis·i·bil·i·ty [vɪzə'bɪlətɪ] visibilidad *f*

vis·i·ble ['vɪzəbl] *adj object, difference* visible; *anger* evidente; *not visible to the naked eye* no ser visible a simple vista

vis·i·bly ['vɪzəblɪ] *adv different* visiblemente; *he was visibly moved* estaba visiblemente conmovido

vi·sion ['vɪʒn] *also* REL visión *f*

vis·it ['vɪzɪt] **1** *n* visita *f*; *pay a visit to the doctor / dentist* visitar al doctor / dentista; *pay s.o. a visit* hacer una visita a alguien **2** *v/t* visitar

vis·it·ing card ['vɪzɪtɪŋ] tarjeta *f* de visita

'**vis·it·ing hours** *npl at hospital* horas *fpl* de visita

vis·it·or ['vɪzɪtər] *(guest)* visita *f*; *(tourist)*, *to museum etc* visitante *m/f*

vi·sor ['vaɪzər] visera *f*

vis·u·al ['vɪʒʊəl] *adj* visual

vis·u·al 'aid medio *m* visuale

vis·u·al dis·play u·nit monitor *m*

vis·u·al·ize ['vɪʒʊəlaɪz] v/t visualizar; *(foresee)* prever

vis·u·al·ly ['vɪʒʊlɪ] *adv* visualmente

vis·u·al·ly im·paired *adj* con discapacidad visual

vi·tal ['vaɪtl] *adj (essential)* vital; *it is vital that …* es vital que …

vi·tal·i·ty [vaɪ'tælətɪ] *of person, city etc* vitalidad *f*

vi·tal·ly ['vaɪtəlɪ] *adv*: *vitally important* de importancia vital

vi·tal 'or·gans *npl* órganos *mpl* vitales

vi·tal sta·tis·tics *npl of woman* medidas *fpl*

vit·a·min ['vaɪtəmɪn] vitamina *f*

'**vit·a·min pill** pastilla *f* vitamínica

vit·ri·ol·ic [vɪtrɪ'ɑːlɪk] *adj* virulento

vi·va·cious [vɪ'veɪʃəs] *adj* vivaz

vi·vac·i·ty [vɪ'væsətɪ] vivacidad *f*

viv·id ['vɪvɪd] *adj color* vivo; *memory, imagination* vívido

viv·id·ly ['vɪvɪdlɪ] *adv (brightly)* vivamente; *(clearly)* vívidamente

V-neck ['viːnek] cuello *m* de pico

vo·cab·u·la·ry [voʊ'kæbjʊlərɪ] vocabulario *m*

vo·cal ['voʊkl] *adj to do with the voice* vocal; *expressing opinions* ruidoso; *a vocal opponent* un declarado adversario

'vo·cal cords *npl* cuerdas *fpl* vocales

'vo·cal group MUS grupo *m* vocal

vo·cal·ist ['vəʊkəlɪst] MUS vocalista *m/f*

vo·ca·tion [və'keɪʃn] (*calling*) vocación *f*; (*profession*) profesión *f*

vo·ca·tion·al [və'keɪʃnl] *adj guidance* profesional

vod·ka ['vɑːdkə] vodka *m*

vogue [vəʊg] moda *f*; **be in vogue** estar en boga

voice [vɔɪs] **1** *n* voz *f* **2** *v/t opinions* expresar

'voice mail correo *m* de voz

void [vɔɪd] **1** *n* vacío *m* **2** *adj*: **void of** carente de

vol·a·tile ['vɑːlətəl] *adj personality, moods* cambiante; *markets* inestable

vol·ca·no [vɑːl'keɪnəʊ] volcán *m*

vol·ley ['vɑːlɪ] *n of shots* ráfaga *f*; *in tennis* volea *f*

'vol·ley·ball voleibol *m*, balonvolea *m*

volt [vəʊlt] voltio *m*

volt·age ['vəʊltɪdʒ] voltaje *m*

vol·ume ['vɑːljəm] volumen *m*; *of container* capacidad *f*; *of book* volumen *m*, tomo *m*

'vol·ume con·trol control *m* del volumen

vol·un·tar·i·ly [vɑːlən'terɪlɪ] *adv* voluntariamente

vol·un·ta·ry ['vɑːlənterɪ] *adj* voluntario

vol·un·teer [vɑːlən'tɪr] **1** *n* voluntario(-a) *m(f)* **2** *v/i* ofrecerse voluntariamente

vo·lup·tu·ous [və'lʌpʧʊəs] *adj woman, figure* voluptuoso

vom·it ['vɑːmət] **1** *n* vómito *m* **2** *v/i* vomitar

◆ **vomit up** *v/t* vomitar

vo·ra·cious [və'reɪʃəs] *adj appetite* voraz

vo·ra·cious·ly [və'reɪʃəslɪ] *also fig* vorazmente

vote [vəʊt] **1** *n* voto *m*; **have the vote** (*be entitled to vote*) tener el derecho al voto **2** *v/i* POL votar; **vote for / against** votar a favor / en contra **3** *v/t*: **they voted him President** lo votaron presidente; **they voted to stay behind** votaron (a favor de) quedarse atrás

◆ **vote in** *v/t new member* elegir en votación

◆ **vote on** *v/t issue* someter a votación

◆ **vote out** *v/t of office* rechazar en votación

vot·er ['vəʊtər] POL votante *m/f*

vot·ing ['vəʊtɪŋ] POL votación *f*

'vot·ing booth cabina *f* electoral

◆ **vouch for** [vaʊʧ] *v/t truth of sth* dar te de; *person* responder por

vouch·er ['vaʊʧər] vale *m*

vow [vaʊ] **1** *n* voto *m* **2** *v/t*: **vow to do sth** prometer hacer algo

vow·el [vaʊl] vocal *f*

voy·age ['vɔɪɪdʒ] *n* viaje *m*

vul·gar ['vʌlgər] *adj person, language* vulgar, grosero

vul·ne·ra·ble ['vʌlnərəbl] *adj to attack, criticism* vulnerable

vul·ture ['vʌlʧər] buitre *m*

W

wad [wɑːd] *n of paper, absorbent cotton etc* bola *f*; **a wad of $100 bills** un fajo de billetes de 100 dólares

wad·dle ['wɑːdl] *v/i of duck* caminar; *of person* anadear

wade [weɪd] *v/i* caminar en el agua

◆ **wade through** *v/t book, documents* leerse

wa·fer ['weɪfər] *cookie* barquillo *m*; REL hostia *f*

'wa·fer-thin *adj* muy fino

waf·fle¹ ['wɑːfl] *n to eat* gofre *m*

waf·fle² ['wɑːfl] *v/i* andarse con rodeos

wag [wæg] **1** *v/t* (*pret & pp wagged*) *tail, finger* menear **2** *v/i* (*pret & pp wagged*)

of tail menearse

wage¹ [weɪdʒ] *v/t*: **wage war** hacer la guerra

wage² [weɪdʒ] *n* salario *m*, sueldo *m*; **wages** salario *m*, sueldo *m*

'wage earn·er asalariado(-a) *m(f)*

'wage freeze congelación *f* salarial

'wage ne·go·ti·a·tions *npl* negociación *f* salarial

'wage pack·et *fig* salario *m*, sueldo *m*

wag·gle ['wægl] *v/t hips* menear; *ears, loose screw etc* mover

wag·gon, *Br* **wag·on** ['wægən] RAIL vagón *m*; **be on the wagon** F haber dejado la bebida

wail [weɪl] **1** *n of person, baby* gemido *m*; *of siren* sonido *m*, aullido *m* **2** *v/i of person, baby* gemir; *of siren* sonar, aullar

waist [weɪst] cintura *f*

'waist·coat *Br* chaleco *m*

'waist·line cintura *f*

wait [weɪt] **1** *n* espera *f*; **I had a long wait for a train** esperé mucho rato el tren **2** *v/i* esperar; **have you been waiting long?** ¿llevan mucho rato esperando? **2** *v/t*: **don't wait supper for me** no me esperéis a cenar; **wait table** trabajar de camarero
◆ **wait for** *v/t* esperar; **wait for me!** ¡esperadme!
◆ **wait on** *v/t* (*serve*) servir; (*wait for*) esperar
◆ **wait up** *v/i* esperar levantado

wait·er ['weɪtər] camarero *m*

wait·ing ['weɪtɪŋ] *n* espera *f*; **no waiting** *sign* señal *f* de prohibido estacionar

'wait·ing list lista *f* de espera

'wait·ing room sala *f* de espera

wait·ress ['weɪtrɪs] camarera *f*

waive [weɪv] *v/t right* renunciar; *requirement* no aplicar

wake[1] [weɪk] **1** *v/i* (*pret* **woke**, *pp* **woken**) (*wake (up)*) despertarse **2** *v/t* (*pret* **woke**, *pp* **woken**): **wake (up)** despertar

wake[2] [weɪk] *n of ship* estela *f*; **in the wake of** fig tras; **missionaries followed in the wake of the explorers** a los exploradores siguieron los misioneros

'wake-up call: **could I have a wake-up call at 6.30?** ¿me podrían despertar a las 6.30?

Wales [weɪlz] *n* Gales

walk [wɔːk] **1** *n* paseo *m*; *longer* caminata *f*; (*path*) camino *m*; (*short* **walk to the office** hay una caminata / un paseo hasta la oficina; **go for a walk** salir a dar un paseo, salir de paseo; **it's a five-minute walk** está a cinco minutos a pie **2** *v/i* caminar, andar; **she walked over to the window** se acercó a la ventana; **I walked over to her place** fui a su casa **3** *v/t dog* sacar a pasear; **walk the streets** (*walk around*) caminar por las calles
◆ **walk out** *v/i of spouse* marcharse; *from theater etc* salir; (*go on strike*) declararse en huelga
◆ **walk out on** *v/t*: **walk out on s.o.** abandonar a alguien

walk·er ['wɔːkər] (*hiker*) excursionista *m/f*; *for baby, old person* andador *m*; **be a slow / fast walker** caminar *or* andar despacio / rápido

walk·ie-'talk·ie [wɔːkɪ'tɔːkɪ] walkie-talkie *m*

walk-in 'clos·et vestidor *m*, armario *m* empotrado

walk·ing ['wɔːkɪŋ] *n* (*hiking*) excursionismo *m*; **walking is one of the best forms of exercise** caminar es uno de los mejores ejercicios; **it's within walking distance** se puede ir caminando *or* andando

'walk·ing stick bastón *m*

'walk·ing tour visita *f* a pie

'Walk·man® walkman *m*

'walk·out *n* (*strike*) huelga *f*

'walk·over (*easy win*) paseo *m*

'walk-up *n* apartamento en un edificio sin ascensor

wall [wɔːl] *external, fig* muro *m*; *of room* pared *m*; **go to the wall** *of company* quebrar; **drive s.o. up the wall** F hacer que alguien se suba por las paredes

wal·let ['wɑːlɪt] cartera *f*

wal·lop ['wɑːləp] **1** *n* F *blow* tortazo *m* F, galletazo *m* F **2** *v/t* F dar un golpetazo a F; *opponent* dar una paliza a F

'wall·pa·per 1 *n* papel *m* pintado **2** *v/t* empapelar

wall-to-wall 'car·pet *Span* moqueta *f*, *L.Am.* alfombra *f*

wal·nut ['wɔːlnʌt] nuez *f*; *tree, wood* nogal *m*

waltz [wɔːlts] *n* vals *m*

wan [wɑːn] *adj face* pálido *m*

wan·der ['wɑːndər] *v/i* (*roam*) vagar, deambular; (*stray*) extraviarse; **my attention began to wander** empecé a distraerme
◆ **wander around** *v/i* deambular, pasear

wane [weɪn] *v/i of interest, enthusiasm* decaer, menguar

wan·gle ['wæŋgl] *v/t* F agenciarse F

want [wɑːnt] **1** *n*: **for want of** por falta de **2** *v/t* querer; (*need*) necesitar; **want to do sth** querer hacer algo; **I want to stay here** quiero quedarme aquí; **do you want to come too?** - **no, I don't want to** ¿quieres venir tú también? - no, no quiero; **you can have whatever you want** toma lo que quieras; **it's not what I wanted** no es lo que quería; **she wants you to go back** quiere que vuelvas; **he wants a haircut** necesita un corte de pelo **3** *v/i*: **he wants for nothing** no le falta nada

'want ad anuncio *m* por palabras (*buscando algo*)

want·ed ['wɑːntɪd] *adj by police* buscado por la policía

want·ing ['wɑːntɪŋ] *adj*: **the team is wanting in experience** al equipo le falta experiencia

wan·ton ['wɑːntən] *adj* gratuito

water polution

war [wɔːr] *n also fig* guerra *f*; **be at war** estar en guerra

war·ble ['wɔːrbl] *v/i of bird* trinar

ward [wɔːrd] *n in hospital* sala *f*; *child* pupilo(-a) *m(f)*

◆ **ward off** *v/t blow* parar; *attacker* rechazar; *cold* evitar

war·den ['wɔːrdn] *of prison* director(-a) *m(f)*, alcaide(sa) *m(f)*; *Br of hostel* vigilante *m/f*

ward·robe *for clothes* armario *m*; (*clothes*) guardarropa *m*

ware·house ['werhaus] almacén *m*

war·fare guerra *f*

war·head ojiva *f*

war·i·ly ['werɪlɪ] *adv* cautelosamente

warm [wɔːrm] 1 *adj hands, room, water* caliente; *weather, welcome* cálido; *coat* de abrigo; **it's warmer than yesterday** hace más calor que ayer 2 *v/t* → **warm up**

◆ **warm up** 1 *v/t* calentar 2 *v/i* calentarse; *of athlete etc* calentar

warm-heart·ed ['wɔːrmhɑːrtɪd] *adj* cariñoso, simpático

warm·ly ['wɔːrmlɪ] *adv welcome* calurosamente; **warmly dressed** abrigado

warmth [wɔːrmθ] calor *m*; *of welcome, smile* calor *m*, calidez *f*

warm-up SP calentamiento *m*

warn [wɔːrn] *v/t* advertir, avisar

warn·ing ['wɔːrnɪŋ] *n* advertencia *f*, aviso *m*; **without warning** sin previo aviso

warp [wɔːrp] 1 *v/t wood* combar; *character* corromper 2 *v/i of wood* combarse

warped [wɔːrpt] *adj fig* retorcido

war·plane avión *m* de guerra

war·rant ['wɔːrənt] 1 *n* orden *f* judicial 2 *v/t* (*deserve, call for*) justificar

war·ran·ty ['wɔːrəntɪ] (*guarantee*) garantía *f*; **be under warranty** estar en garantía

war·ri·or ['wɔːrɪər] guerrero(-a) *m(f)*

war·ship buque *m* de guerra

wart [wɔːrt] verruga *f*

war·time tiempos *mpl* de guerra

war·y ['werɪ] *adj* cauto, precavido; **be wary of** desconfiar de

was [wʌz] *pret* → **be**

wash [wɑːʃ] 1 *n* lavado *m*; **have a wash** lavarse; **that shirt needs a wash** hay que lavar esa camisa 2 *v/t* lavar 3 *v/i* lavarse

◆ **wash up** *v/i* (*wash one's hands and face*) lavarse

wash·a·ble ['wɑːʃəbl] *adj* lavable

wash·ba·sin, **wash·bowl** lavabo *m*

wash·cloth toallita *f*

washed out [wɑːʃt'aut] *adj* agotado

wash·er ['wɑːʃər] *for faucet etc* arandela *f*; → **washing machine**

wash·ing ['wɑːʃɪŋ] (*clothes washed*) ropa *f* limpia; (*dirty clothes*) ropa *f* sucia; **do the washing** lavar la ropa, hacer la colada

wash·ing ma·chine lavadora *f*

wash·ing-'up liq·uid *Br* lavavajillas *m inv*

wash·room lavabo *m*, aseo *m*

wasp [wɑːsp] *insect* avispa *f*

waste [weɪst] 1 *n* desperdicio *m*; *from industrial process* desechos *mpl*; **it's a waste of time / money** es una pérdida de tiempo / dinero 2 *adj* residual; **waste land** erial *m* 3 *v/t* derrochar; *money* gastar; *time* perder

◆ **waste away** *v/i* consumirse

waste dis·pos·al (**unit**) trituradora *f* de basuras

waste·ful ['weɪstfəl] *adj* despilfarrador, derrochador

waste·land erial *m*

waste·pa·per papel *m* usado

waste·pa·per 'bas·ket papelera *f*

waste pipe tubería *f* de desagüe

waste prod·uct desecho *m*

watch [wɑːtʃ] 1 *n timepiece* reloj *m*; **keep watch** hacer la guardia, vigilar 2 *v/t film*, TV ver; (*look after*) vigilar 3 *v/i* mirar, observar

◆ **watch for** *v/t* esperar

◆ **watch out** *v/i* tener cuidado; **watch out!** ¡cuidado!

◆ **watch out for** *v/t* tener cuidado con

watch·ful ['wɑːtʃfəl] *adj* vigilante

watch·mak·er relojero(-a) *m(f)*

wa·ter ['wɔːtər] 1 *n* agua *f*; **waters** NAUT aguas *fpl* 2 *v/t plant* regar 3 *v/i*: **my eyes are watering** me lloran los ojos; **my mouth is watering** se me hace la boca agua

◆ **water down** *v/t drink* aguar, diluir

water can·non cañón *m* de agua

wa·ter·col·or, *Br* **wa·ter·col·our** acuarela *f*

wa·ter·cress berro *m*

watered 'down ['wɔːtərd] *adj fig* dulcificado

wa·ter·fall cascada *f*, catarata *f*

wa·ter·ing can ['wɔːtərɪŋ] regadera *f*

wa·ter·ing hole *hum* bar *m*

wa·ter lev·el nivel *m* del agua

wa·ter lil·y nenúfar *m*

wa·ter·line línea *f* de flotación

wa·ter·logged ['wɔːtərlɑːgd] *adj earth, field* anegado; *boat* lleno de agua

wa·ter main tubería *f* principal

wa·ter·mark filigrana *f*

wa·ter·mel·on sandía *f*

wa·ter pol·lu·tion contaminación *f* del agua

W

'wa·ter po·lo waterpolo *m*

'wa·ter·proof *adj* impermeable

'wa·ter·shed *fig* momento *m* clave

'wa·ter·side *n* orilla *f*; *at the waterside* en la orilla

'wa·ter·ski·ing esquí *m* acuático

'wa·ter·tight *adj compartment* estanco; *fig* irrefutable

'wa·ter·way curso *m* de agua navegable

'wa·ter·wings *npl* flotadores *mpl* (*para los brazos*)

wa·ter·works F: *turn on the waterworks* ponerse a llorar como una magdalena F

wa·ter·y ['wɒːtərɪ] *adj* aguado

watt [wɑːt] vatio *m*

wave¹ [weɪv] *n in sea* ola *f*

wave² [weɪv] **1** *n of hand* saludo *m* **2** *v/i with hand* saludar con la mano; *wave to s.o.* saludar con la mano a alguien **3** *v/t flag etc* agitar

'wave·length RAD longitud *f* de onda; *be on the same wavelength fig* estar en la misma onda

wa·ver ['weɪvər] *v/i* vacilar, titubear

wav·y ['weɪvɪ] *adj hair, line* ondulado

wax [wæks] *n for floor, furniture* cera *f*; *in ear* cera *f*, cerumen

way [weɪ] **1** *n* (*method*) manera *f*, forma *f*; (*manner*) manera *f*, modo *m*; (*route*) camino *m*; *I don't like the way he behaves* no me gusta cómo se comporta; *can you tell me the way to …?* ¿me podría decir cómo se va a …?; *this way* (*like this*) así; (*in this direction*) por aquí; *by the way* (*incidentally*) por cierto, a propósito; *by way of* (*via*) por; (*in the form of*) a modo de; *in a way* (*in certain respects*) en cierto sentido; *be under way* haber comenzado, estar en marcha; *give way* MOT ceder el paso; (*collapse*) ceder; *give way to* (*be replaced by*) ser reemplazado por; *have one's (own) way* salirse con la suya; *OK, we'll do it your way* de acuerdo, lo haremos a tu manera; *lead the way* abrir (el) camino; *fig* marcar la pauta; *lose one's way* perderse; *be in the way* (*be an obstruction*) estar en medio; *it's on the way to the station* está camino de la estación; *I was on my way to the station* iba camino de la estación; *no way!* ¡ni hablar!, ¡de ninguna manera!; *there's no way he can do it* es imposible que lo haga **2** *adv* F (*much*): *it's way too soon to decide* es demasiado pronto como para decidir; *they are way behind with their work* van atrasadísimos en el trabajo

way 'in entrada *f*

way of 'life modo *m* de vida

way 'out *n* salida *f*; *fig: from situation* salida *f*

we [wiː] *pron* nosotros *mpl*, nosotras *fpl*; *we are the best* somos los mejores; *they're going, but we're not* ellos van, pero nosotros no

weak [wiːk] *adj* débil; *tea, coffee* poco cargado

weak·en ['wiːkn] **1** *v/t* debilitar **2** *v/i* debilitarse

weak·ling ['wiːklɪŋ] *morally* cobarde *m/f*; *physically* enclenque *m/f*

weak·ness ['wiːknɪs] debilidad *f*; *have a weakness for sth* (*liking*) sentir debilidad por algo

wealth [welθ] riqueza *f*; *a wealth of* abundancia de

wealth·y ['welθɪ] *adj* rico

wean [wiːn] *v/t* destetar

weap·on ['wepən] arma *f*

wear [wer] **1** *n*: *wear (and tear)* desgaste *m*; *clothes for everyday / evening wear* ropa *f* de diario / de noche **2** *v/t* (*pret wore, pp worn*) (*have on*) llevar; (*damage*) desgastar **3** *v/i* (*pret wore, pp worn*) (*wear out*) desgastarse; (*last*) durar

◆ *wear away* **1** *v/i* desgastarse **2** *v/t* desgastar

◆ *wear down v/t* agotar

◆ *wear off v/i of effect, feeling* pasar

◆ *wear out* **1** *v/t* (*tire*) agotar; *shoes* desgastar **2** *v/i of shoes, carpet* desgastarse

wea·ri·ly ['wɪrɪlɪ] *adv* cansinamente

wear·ing ['werɪŋ] *adj* (*tiring*) agotador

wear·y ['wɪrɪ] *adj* cansado

weath·er ['weðər] **1** *n* tiempo *m*; *what's the weather like?* ¿qué tiempo hace?; *be feeling under the weather* estar pachucho **2** *v/t crisis* capear, superar

'weath·er-beat·en *adj* curtido

'weath·er chart mapa *m* del tiempo

'weath·er fore·cast pronóstico *m* del tiempo

'weath·er·man hombre *m* del tiempo

weave [wiːv] **1** *v/t* (*pret wove, pp woven*) tejer **2** *v/i* (*pret wove, pp woven*) *move* zigzaguear

web [web] *of spider* tela *f*; *the Web* COMPUT la Web

webbed 'feet patas *fpl* palmeadas

'web page página *f* web

'web site sitio *m* web

'wed·ding ['wedɪŋ] boda *f*

'wed·ding an·ni·ver·sa·ry aniversario *m* de boda

'wed·ding cake pastel *m or* tarta *f* de boda

'wed·ding day día *f* de la boda

'wed·ding dress vestido *m* de boda *or*

novia

'wed·ding ring anillo *m* de boda

wedge [wedʒ] **1** *n to hold sth in place* cuña *f*; *of cheese etc* trozo *m* **2** *v/t*: **wedge a door open** calzar una puerta para que se quede abierta

Wed·nes·day ['wenzdeɪ] miércoles *m inv*

weed [wiːd] **1** *n* mala hierba **2** *v/t* escardar

♦ **weed out** *v/t* (*remove*) eliminar; *candidates* descartar

'weed-kill·er herbicida *m*

weed·y ['wiːdɪ] *adj* F esmirriado, enclenque

week [wiːk] semana *f*; *a week tomorrow* dentro de una semana

'week·day día *m* de la semana

'week·end fin *m* de semana; *on the weekend* el fin de semana

week·ly ['wiːklɪ] **1** *adj* semanal **2** *n magazine* semanario *m* **3** *adv* semanalmente

weep [wiːp] *v/i* (*pret* & *pp* **wept**) llorar

'weep·ing wil·low sauce *m* llorón

weep·y ['wiːpɪ] *adj*: *be weepy* estar lloroso

wee-wee 1 *n* F pipí *m*; *do a wee-wee* hacer pipí **2** *v/i* F hacer pipí

weigh[1] [weɪ] **1** *v/t* pesar **2** *v/i* pesar; *how much do you weigh?* ¿cuánto pesas?

weigh[2] [weɪ] *v/t*: *weigh anchor* levar anclas

♦ **weigh down** *v/t* cargar; *be weighed down with* *bags* ir cargado con; *worries* estar abrumado por

♦ **weigh on** *v/t* preocupar

♦ **weigh up** *v/t* (*assess*) sopesar

weight [weɪt] peso *m*; *put on weight* engordar, ganar peso; *lose weight* adelgazar, perder peso

♦ **weight down** *v/t* sujetar (*con pesos*)

'weight·less ['weɪtləs] *adj* ingrávido

'weight·less·ness ['weɪtləsnəs] ingravidez *f*

'weight·lift·er levantador(a) *m(f)* de pesas

'weight·lift·ing halterofilia *f*, levantamiento *m* de pesas

weight·y ['weɪtɪ] *adj* (*fig: important*) serio

weir [wɪr] presa *f* (*rebasadero*)

weird [wɪrd] *adj* extraño, raro

weird·ly ['wɪrdlɪ] *adv* extrañamente

weird·o ['wɪrdou] *n* F bicho *m* raro F

wel·come ['welkəm] **1** *adj* bienvenido; *you're welcome!* ¡de nada!; *you're welcome to try some* prueba algunos, por favor **2** *n* bienvenida *f* **3** *v/t guests etc* dar la bienvenida a; *fig: decision etc* acoger positivamente

weld [weld] *v/t* soldar

weld·er ['weldər] soldador(a) *m(f)*

wel·fare ['welfer] bienestar *m*; *financial assistance* subsidio *m* estatal; *be on welfare* estar recibiendo subsidios del Estado

'wel·fare check cheque *m* con el importe del subsidio estatal

wel·fare 'state estado *m* del bienestar

'wel·fare work trabajo *m* social

'wel·fare work·er asistente *m/f* social

well[1] [wel] *n for water, oil* pozo *m*

well[2] **1** *adv* bien; *as well* (*too*) también; *as well as* (*in addition to*) así como; *it's just as well you told me* menos mal que me lo dijiste; *very well* muy bien; *well, well!* surprise ¡caramba!; *well ... uncertainty, thinking* bueno ...; *you might as well spend the night here* ya puestos quédate a pasar la noche aquí; *you might as well throw it out* yo de ti lo tiraría **2** *adj*: *be well* estar bien; *how are you? - I'm very well* ¿cómo estás? - muy bien; *feel well* sentirse bien; *get well soon!* ¡ponte bueno!, ¡que te mejores!

well-'bal·anced *adj person, diet* equilibrado

well-be'haved *adj* educado

well-'be·ing bienestar *m*

well-'built *adj also euph* fornido

well-'done *adj meat* muy hecho

well-'dressed *adj* bien vestido

well-'earned *adj* merecido

well-'heeled *adj* F adinerado, *Span* con pasta F

well-in'formed *adj* bien informado

well-'known *adj fact* conocido; *person* conocido, famoso

well-'made *adj* bien hecho

well-'man·nered *adj* educado

well-'mean·ing *adj* bienintencionado

well-'off *adj* acomodado

well-'paid *adj* bien pagado

well-'read *adj*: *be well-read* haber leído mucho

well-'timed *adj* oportuno

well-to-'do *adj* acomodado

'well-wish·er admirador(a) *m(f)*

well-'worn *adj* gastado

Welsh [welʃ] **1** *adj* galés **2** *n language* galés; *the Welsh* los galeses

went [went] *pret* → **go**

wept [wept] *pret* & *pp* → **weep**

were [wɜr] *pret* → **be**

west [west] **1** *n* oeste *m*; *the West* (*Western nations*) Occidente *m*; (*western part of a country*) el oeste **2** *adj* del oeste; *west Africa* África occidental **3** *adv travel* hacia el oeste; *west of* al oeste de

West 'Coast *of USA* Costa *f* Oeste

West In·di·an 1 adj antillano **2** n antillano(-a) m/f

West In·dies ['ɪndɪz] npl: **the West Indies** las Antillas

west·er·ly ['westərlɪ] adj wind del oeste; direction hacia el oeste

west·ern ['westərn] **1** adj occidental; **Western** occidental **2** n movie western m, película f del oeste

West·ern·er ['westərnər] occidental m/f

west·ern·ized ['westərnaɪzd] adj occidentalizado

west·ward ['westwərd] adv hacia el oeste

wet [wet] adj mojado; (damp) húmedo; (rainy) lluvioso; **get wet** mojarse; **wet paint** as sign recién pintado; **be wet through** estar empapado

wet 'blan·ket aguafiestas m/f inv

'wet suit for diving traje m de neopreno

whack [wæk] **1** n F (blow) porrazo m F; F (share) parte f **2** v/t F dar un porrazo a F

whacked [wækt] adj F hecho polvo F

whale [weɪl] ballena f

whal·ing ['weɪlɪŋ] caza f de ballenas

wharf [wɔːrf] n embarcadero m

what [wɑːt] **1** pron qué; **what is that?** ¿qué es eso?; **what is it?** (what do you want) ¿qué quieres?; **what?** (what do you want) ¿qué?; (what did you say) ¿qué?, ¿cómo?; astonishment ¿qué?; **what about some dinner?** ¿os apetece cenar?; **what about heading home?** ¿y si nos fuéramos a casa?; **what for?** (why) ¿para qué?; **so what?** ¿y qué?; **what is the book about?** ¿de qué trata el libro?; **take what you need** toma lo que te haga falta **2** adj qué; **what university are you at?** ¿en qué universidad estás?; **what color is the car?** ¿de qué color es el coche?

what·ev·er [wɑːt'evər] **1** pron: **I'll do whatever you want** haré lo que quieras; **whatever gave you that idea?** ¿se puede saber qué te ha dado esa idea?; **whatever the season** en cualquier estación; **whatever people say** diga lo que diga la gente **2** adj cualquier; **you have no reason whatever to worry** no tienes por qué preocuparte en absoluto

wheat [wiːt] trigo m

whee·dle ['wiːdl] v/t: **wheedle sth out of s.o.** camelar algo a alguien

wheel [wiːl] **1** n rueda f; (steering wheel) volante m **2** v/t bicycle empujar **3** v/i of birds volar en círculo

♦ **wheel around** v/i darse la vuelta

'wheel·bar·row carretilla f

'wheel·chair silla f de ruedas

'wheel clamp cepo m

wheeze [wiːz] n resoplido m

when [wen] **1** adv cuándo; **when do you open?** ¿a qué hora abren? **2** conj cuando; **when I was a child** cuando era niño

when·ev·er [wen'evər] adv (each time) cada vez que; **call me whenever you like** llámame cuando quieras; **I go to Paris whenever I can afford it** voy a París siempre que me lo puedo permitir

where [wer] **1** adv dónde; **where from?** ¿de dónde?; **where to?** ¿a dónde? **2** conj donde; **this is where I used to live** aquí es donde vivía antes

where·a·bouts [werə'bauts] **1** adv dónde **2** npl **nothing is known of his whereabouts** está en paradero desconocido

where·as conj mientras que

wher·ev·er [wer'evər] **1** conj dondequiera que; **sit wherever you like** siéntate donde prefieras **2** adv dónde

whet [wet] v/t (pret & pp **whetted**) appetite abrir

wheth·er ['weðər] conj si; **I don't know whether to tell him or not** no sé si decírselo o no; **whether you approve or not** te parezca bien o no

which [wɪtʃ] **1** adj qué; **which one is yours?** ¿cuál es tuyo? **2** pron interrogative cuál; relative que; **take one, it doesn't matter which** toma uno, no importa cuál

which·ev·er [wɪtʃ'evər] **1** adj: **whichever color you choose** elijas el color que elijas **2** pron: **whichever you like** el que quieras; **use whichever of the methods you prefer** utiliza el método que prefieras

whiff [wɪf] (smell) olorcillo m

while [waɪl] **1** conj mientras; (although) si bien **2** n rato m; **a long while** un rato largo; **for a while** durante un tiempo; **I lived in Tokyo for a while** viví en Tokio una temporada; **I'll wait a while longer** esperaré un rato más

♦ **while away** v/t pasar

whim [wɪm] capricho m

whim·per ['wɪmpər] **1** n gimoteo m **2** v/i gimotear

whine [waɪn] v/i of dog gimotear; F (complain) quejarse

whip [wɪp] **1** n látigo m **2** v/t (pret & pp **whipped**) (beat) azotar; cream batir, montar; F (defeat) dar una paliza a F

♦ **whip out** v/t F sacar rápidamente

♦ **whip up** v/t (arouse) agitar; F meal improvisar

'whipped cream [wɪpt] nata f montada

whip·ping ['wɪpɪŋ] (beating) azotes mpl; F (defeat) paliza f F

'whip·round F colecta *f*; **have a whip-round** hacer una colecta

whirl [wɜːrl] **1** *n*: **my mind is in a whirl** me da vueltas la cabeza **2** *v/i* dar vueltas

'whirl·pool *in river* remolino *m*; *for relaxation* bañera *f* de hidromasaje

whirr [wɜːr] *v/i* zumbar

whisk [wɪsk] **1** *n kitchen implement* **2** *v/t eggs* batir

◆ **whisk away** *v/t* retirar rápidamente

whis·kers ['wɪskərz] *npl of man* patillas *fpl*; *of animal* bigotes *mpl*

whis·key, whis·ky ['wɪskɪ] whisky *m*

whis·per ['wɪspər] **1** *n* susurro *m*; *(rumor)* rumor *m* **2** *v/i* susurrar **3** *v/t* susurrar

whis·tle ['wɪsl] **1** *n sound* silbido *m*; *device* silbato *m* **2** *v/t* & *v/i* silbar

white [waɪt] **1** *n color* blanco *m*; *of egg* clara *f*; *person* blanco(-a) *m(f)* **2** *adj* blanco; **her face went white** se puso blanca

white 'Christ·mas Navidades *fpl* blancas

white 'cof·fee *Br* café *m* con leche

white-col·lar 'work·er persona que trabaja en una oficina

'White House Casa *f* Blanca

white 'lie mentira *f* piadosa

white 'meat carne *f* blanca

'white·wash **1** *n* cal *f*; *fig* encubrimiento *m* **2** *v/t* encalar

white 'wine vino *m* blanco

whit·tle ['wɪtl] *v/t wood* tallar

◆ **whittle down** *v/t* reducir

whiz(z) [wɪz] *n*: **be a whiz(z) at** F ser un genio de

◆ **whizz by, whizz past** *v/i of time, car* pasar zumbando

'whiz·kid F joven *m/f* prodigio

who [huː] *pron interrogative* ¿quién?; *relative* que; **who do you want to speak to?** ¿con quién quieres hablar?; **I don't know who to believe?** no sé a quién creer

who·dun·(n)it [huː'dʌnɪt] libro o película centrados en la resolución de un caso

who·ev·er [huː'evər] *pron* quienquiera; **whoever can that be calling at this time of night?** ¿pero quién llama a estas horas de la noche?

whole [houl] **1** *adj* entero; **the whole town / country** toda la ciudad / todo el país; **he drank / ate the whole lot** se lo bebió / comió todo; **it's a whole lot easier / better** es mucho más fácil / mucho mejor **2** *n* totalidad *f*; **the whole of the United States** la totalidad de los Estados Unidos; **on the whole** en general

whole-heart·ed [houl'hɑːrtɪd] *adj* incondicional

whole-heart·ed·ly [houl'hɑːrtɪdlɪ] *adv* incondicionalmente

whole·meal 'bread pan *m* integral

'whole·sale **1** *adj* al por mayor; *fig* indiscriminado **2** *adv* al por mayor

whole·sal·er ['houlseɪlər] mayorista *m/f*

whole·some ['houlsəm] *adj* saludable, sano

whol·ly ['houlɪ] *adv* completamente

whol·ly owned 'sub·sid·i·ar·y subsidiaria *f* en propiedad absoluta

whom [huːm] *pron fml* quién; **whom did you see?** ¿a quién vio?; **the person to whom I was speaking** la persona con la que estaba hablando

whoop·ing cough ['huːpɪŋ] tos *f* ferina

whop·ping ['wɑːpɪŋ] *adj* F enorme

whore [hɔːr] *n* prostituta *f*

whose [huːz] **1** *pron interrogative* de quién; *relative* cuyo(-a); **whose is this?** ¿de quién es esto?; **a country whose economy is booming** un país cuya economía está experimentando un boom **2** *adj* de quién; **whose bike is that?** ¿de quién es esa bici?

why [waɪ] *adv interrogative* por qué; *relative* por qué; **that's why** por eso; **why not?** ¿por qué no?

wick [wɪk] pabilo *m*

wick·ed ['wɪkɪd] *adj* malvado, perverso

wick·er ['wɪkər] *adj* de mimbre

wick·er 'chair silla *f* de mimbre

wick·et ['wɪkɪt] *in station, bank etc* ventanilla *f*

wide [waɪd] *adj* ancho; *experience, range* amplio; **be 12 feet wide** tener 12 pies de ancho

wide a'wake *adj* completamente despierto

wide·ly ['waɪdlɪ] *adv used, known* ampliamente

wid·en ['waɪdn] **1** *v/t* ensanchar **2** *v/i* ensancharse

wide-'o·pen *adj* abierto de par en par

wide-'rang·ing *adj* amplio

'wide·spread *adj* extendido, muy difundido

wid·ow ['wɪdou] *n* viuda *f*

wid·ow·er ['wɪdouər] viudo *m*

width [wɪdθ] *n* anchura *f*, ancho *m*

wield [wiːld] *v/t weapon* empuñar; *power* detentar

wife [waɪf] (*pl* **wives** [waɪvz]) mujer *f*, esposa *f*

wig [wɪg] peluca *f*

wig·gle ['wɪgl] *v/t* menear

wild [waɪld] **1** *adj* animal salvaje; *flower* silvestre; *teenager, party* descontrolado; *(crazy: scheme)* descabellado; *applause*

W

arrebatado; **be wild about ...** (keen on) estar loco por ...; **go wild** (express enthusiasm) volverse loco; (become angry) ponerse hecho una furia; **run wild** of children descontrolarse **2** n: **the wilds** los parajes remotos

wil·der·ness ['wɪldərnɪs] (empty place) desierto m, yermo m; (fig: garden etc) jungla f

'wild-fire: **spread like wildfire** extenderse como un reguero de pólvora

wild-'goose chase búsqueda f infructuosa

'wild-life flora f y fauna; **wildlife program** TV documental m sobre la naturaleza

wild·ly ['waɪldlɪ] adv applaud enfervorizadamente; **I'm not wildly enthusiastic about the idea** la idea no me emociona demasiado

wil·ful Br → willful

will¹ [wɪl] n LAW testamento m

will² [wɪl] n (willpower) voluntad f

will³ [wɪl] v/aux: **I will let you know tomorrow** te lo diré mañana; **will you be there?** ¿estarás allí?; **I won't be back until late** volveré tarde; **you will call me, won't you?** me llamarás, ¿verdad?; **I'll pay for this - no you won't** esto lo pago yo - no, ni hablar; **the car won't start** el coche no arranca; **will you tell her that ...?** ¿le quieres decir que ...?; **will you have some more tea?** ¿quiere más té?; **will you stop that!** ¡basta ya!

will·ful ['wɪlfəl] adj person tozudo, obstinado; action deliberado, intencionado

will·ing ['wɪlɪŋ] adj dispuesto

will·ing·ly ['wɪlɪŋlɪ] adv gustosamente

will·ing·ness ['wɪlɪŋnɪs] buena disposición f

wil·low ['wɪloʊ] sauce m

'will-pow·er fuerza f de voluntad

wil·ly-nil·ly [wɪlɪ'nɪlɪ] adv (at random) a la buena de Dios

wilt [wɪlt] v/i of plant marchitarse

wi·ly ['waɪlɪ] adj astuto

wimp [wɪmp] F enclenque m/f F, blandengue m/f F

win [wɪn] **1** n victoria f, triunfo m **2** v/t & v/i (pret & pp **won**) ganar

◆ win back v/t recuperar

wince [wɪns] v/i hacer una mueca de dolor

winch [wɪntʃ] n torno m, cabestrante m

wind¹ [wɪnd] **1** n viento m; (flatulence) gases mpl; **get wind of ...** enterarse de ... **2** v/t: **be winded** quedarse sin respiración

wind² [waɪnd] **1** v/i (pret & pp **wound**) zigzaguear; serpentear; **wind around**

enrollarse en **2** v/t (pret & pp **wound**) enrollar

◆ wind down **1** v/i of party etc ir finalizando **2** v/t car window bajar, abrir; business ir reduciendo

◆ wind up **1** v/t clock dar cuerda a; car window subir, cerrar; speech, presentation finalizar; business, affairs concluir; company cerrar **2** v/i (finish) concluir; **wind up in hospital** acabar en el hospital

'wind-bag F cotorra f F

'wind-fall fig dinero m inesperado

wind-ing ['waɪndɪŋ] adj zigzagueante, serpenteante

'wind in·stru·ment instrumento m de viento

'wind-mill molino m de viento

win·dow ['wɪndoʊ] also COMPUT ventana f; of car ventana f, ventanilla f; **in the window** of store en el escaparate or L.Am. la vidriera

'win-dow box jardinera f

'win-dow clean·er person limpiacristales m/f inv

'win-dow-pane cristal f (de una ventana)

'win-dow seat on plane, train asiento m de ventana

'win-dow-shop v/i (pret & pp **window-shopping**): **go window-shopping** ir de escaparates or L.Am. vidrieras

win-dow-sill ['wɪndoʊsɪl] alféizar m

'wind-pipe tráquea f

'wind-screen Br, 'wind-shield parabrisas m inv

'wind-shield wip·er limpiaparabrisas m inv

'wind-surf·er person windsurfista m/f; board tabla f de windsurf

'wind-surf·ing el windsurf

wind·y ['wɪndɪ] adj ventoso; **a windy day** un día de mucho viento; **it's very windy today** hoy hace mucho viento; **it's getting windy** está empezando a soplar el viento

wine [waɪn] vino m

'wine bar bar especializado en vinos

'wine cel·lar bodega f

'wine glass copa f de vino

'wine list lista f de vinos

'wine mak·er viticultor(a) m(f)

'wine mer·chant comerciante m/f de vinos

win·er·y ['waɪnərɪ] bodega f

wing [wɪŋ] n ala f; SP lateral m/f, extremo m/f

'wing-span envergadura f

wink [wɪŋk] **1** n guiño m; **I didn't sleep a wink** F no pegué ojo **2** v/i of person guiñar, hacer un guiño; **wink at s.o.** guiñar *or* hacer un guiño a alguien

win·ner ['wɪnər] ganador(a) *m(f)*, vencedor(a) *m(f)*; *of lottery* acertante *m/f*

win·ning ['wɪnɪŋ] *adj* ganador

'win·ning post meta *f*

win·nings ['wɪnɪŋz] *npl* ganancias *fpl*

win·ter ['wɪntər] *n* invierno *m*

win·ter 'sports *npl* deportes *mpl* de invierno

win·try ['wɪntrɪ] *adj* invernal

wlpe [waɪp] *v/t* limpiar; *tape* borrar

◆ **wipe out** *v/t* (*kill, destroy*) eliminar; *debt* saldar

wip·er ['waɪpər] → **windshield wiper**

wire [waɪr] *n* alambre *m*; ELEC cable *m*

wire·less ['waɪrlɪs] radio *f*

wire 'net·ting tela *f* metálica

wir·ing ['waɪrɪŋ] *n* ELEC cableado *m*

wir·y ['waɪrɪ] *adj* person fibroso

wis·dom ['wɪzdəm] *of person* sabiduría *f*; *of action* prudencia *f*, sensatez *f*

'wis·dom tooth muela *f* del juicio

wise [waɪz] *adj* sabio; *action, decision* prudente, sensato

'wise·crack *n* F chiste *m*, comentario *m* gracioso

'wise guy *pej* sabelotodo *m*

wise·ly ['waɪzlɪ] *adv act* prudentemente, sensatamente

wish [wɪʃ] **1** *n* deseo *m*; **best wishes** un saludo cordial; **make a wish** pedir un deseo **2** *v/t* desear; *I wish that you could stay* ojalá te pudieras quedar; *wish s.o. well* desear a alguien lo mejor, *I wished him good luck* le deseé buena suerte **3** *v/i*: *wish for* desear

'wish·bone espoleta *f*

wish·ful 'think·ing ['wɪʃfəl] ilusiones *fpl*; *that's wishful thinking on her part* que no se haga ilusiones

wish·y-wash·y ['wɪʃɪwɑːʃɪ] *adj person* anodino; *color* pálido

wisp [wɪsp] *of hair* mechón *m*; *of smoke* voluta *f*

wist·ful ['wɪstfəl] *adj* nostálgico

wist·ful·ly ['wɪstfəlɪ] *adv* con nostalgia

wit [wɪt] (*humor*) ingenio *m*; *person* ingenioso(-a) *m(f)*; *be at one's wits' end* estar desesperado; *keep one's wits about one* mantener la calma; *be scared out of one's wits* estar aterrorizado

witch [wɪtʃ] bruja *f*

'witch·hunt *fig* caza *f* de brujas

with [wɪð] *prep* con; *shivering with fear* temblando de miedo; *a girl with brown eyes* una chica de ojos castaños; *are you with me?* (*do you understand?*) ¿me sigues?; *with no money* sin dinero

with·draw [wɪð'drɔː] **1** *v/t* (*pret* **withdrew**, *pp* **withdrawn**) *complaint, money, troops* retirar **2** *v/i* (*pret* **withdrew**, *pp* **withdrawn**) *of competitor, troops* retirarse

with·draw·al [wɪð'drɔːəl] *of complaint, application, troops* retirada *f*; *of money* reintegro *m*

with·draw·al symp·toms *npl* síndrome *m* de abstinencia

with·drawn [wɪð'drɔːn] *adj person* retraído

with·er ['wɪðər] *v/i* marchitarse

with·hold *v/t* (*pret & pp* **withheld**) *information* ocultar; *payment* retener; *consent* negar

with·in *prep* (*inside*) dentro de; *in expressions of time* en menos de; *within five miles of home* a cinco millas de casa; *we kept within the budget* no supramos el presupuesto; *it is well within your capabilities* lo puedes conseguir perfectamente; *within reach* al alcance de la mano

with·out *prep* sin; *without looking / asking* sin mirar / preguntar

with·stand *v/t* (*pret & pp* **withstood**) resistir, soportar

wit·ness ['wɪtnɪs] **1** *n* testigo *m/f* **2** *v/t* *accident, crime* ser testigo de; *signature* firmar en calidad de testigo

'wit·ness stand estrado *m* del testigo

wit·ti·cism ['wɪtɪsɪzm] comentario *m* gracioso *or* agudo

wit·ty ['wɪtɪ] *adj* ingenioso, agudo

wob·ble ['wɑːbl] *v/i* tambalearse

wob·bly ['wɑːblɪ] *adj* tambaleante

wok [wɑːk] wok *m*, sartén *típica de la cocina china*

woke [woʊk] *pret* → **wake¹**

wok·en ['woʊkn] *pp* → **wake¹**

wolf [wʊlf] **1** *n* (*pl* **wolves** [wʊlvz]) *animal* lobo *m*; (*fig: womanizer*) don juan *m* **2** *v/t*: *wolf (down)* engullir

'wolf whis·tle *n* silbido *m*

'wolf-whis·tle *v/i*: *wolf-whistle at s.o.* silbar a alguien (*como piropo*)

wom·an ['wʊmən] (*pl* **women** ['wɪmɪn]) mujer *f*

wom·an 'doc·tor médica *f*

wom·an 'driv·er conductora *f*

wom·an·iz·er ['wʊmənaɪzər] mujeriego(-a) *m(f)*

wom·an·ly ['wʊmənlɪ] *adj* femenino

wom·an 'priest mujer *f* sacerdote

womb [wuːm] matriz *f*, útero *m*

wom·en ['wɪmɪn] *pl* → **woman**

wom·en's lib [wɪmɪnz'lɪb] la liberación de la mujer

wom·en's lib·ber [wɪmɪnz'lɪbər] parti-

W

dario(-a) *m(f)* de la liberación de la mujer

won [wʌn] *pret & pp →* **win**

won·der ['wʌndər] **1** *n* (*amazement*) asombro *m*; **no wonder!** ¡no me sorprende!; **it's a wonder that ...** es increíble que ... **2** *v/i* preguntarse; **I've often wondered about that** me he preguntado eso a menudo **3** *v/t* preguntarse; **I wonder if you could help** ¿le importaría ayudarme?

won·der·ful ['wʌndərfəl] *adj* maravilloso

won·der·ful·ly ['wʌndərfəlɪ] *adv* (*extremely*) maravillosamente

won't [woʊnt] → **will**³

wood [wʊd] *n* madera *f*; *for fire* leña *f*; (*forest*) bosque *m*

wood·ed ['wʊdɪd] *adj* arbolado

wood·en ['wʊdn] *adj* (*made of wood*) de madera

wood·peck·er ['wʊdpekər] pájaro *m* carpintero

'wood·wind MUS sección *f* de viento de madera

'wood·work carpintería *f*

wool [wʊl] lana *f*

wool·en, *Br* **wool·len** ['wʊlən] **1** *adj* de lana **2** *n* prenda *f* de lana

word [wɜːrd] **1** *n* palabra *f*; **I didn't understand a word of what she said** no entendí nada de lo que dijo; **is there any word from ...?** ¿se sabe algo de ...?; **I've had word from my daughter** (*news*) he recibido noticias de mi hija; **you have my word** tienes mi palabra; **have words** (*argue*) discutir; **have a word with s.o.** hablar con alguien; **the words of song** la letra **2** *v/t article, letter* redactar

word·ing ['wɜːrdɪŋ]: **the wording of a letter** la redacción de una carta

word 'pro·cess·ing procesamiento *m* de textos

word 'pro·ces·sor *software* procesador *m* de textos

wore [wɔːr] *pret →* **wear**

work [wɜːrk] **1** *n* (*job*) trabajo *m*; (*employment*) trabajo *m*, empleo *m*; **out of work** desempleado, *Span* en el paro; **be at work** estar en el trabajo; **I go to work by bus** voy al trabajo en autobús **2** *v/i of person* trabajar; *of machine,* (*succeed*) funcionar; **how does it work?** *of device* ¿cómo funciona? **3** *v/t employee* hacer trabajar; *machine* hacer funcionar, utilizar

◆ **work off** *v/t bad mood, anger* desahogarse de; *flab* perder haciendo ejercicio

◆ **work out 1** *v/t problem, puzzle* resolver; *solution* encontrar, hallar **2** *v/i at gym* hacer ejercicios; *of relationship etc* funcionar, ir bien

◆ **work out to** *v/t* (*add up to*) sumar

◆ **work up** *v/t appetite* abrir; **work up enthusiasm** entusiasmarse; **get worked up** (*get angry*) alterarse; (*get nervous*) ponerse nervioso

work·a·ble ['wɜːrkəbl] *adj solution* viable

work·a·hol·ic [wɜːrkə'hɒːlɪk] *n* F *persona obsesionada con el trabajo*

work·er ['wɜːrkər] trabajador(a) *m(f)*; **she's a good worker** trabaja bien

'work·day (*hours of work*) jornada *f* laboral; (*not a holiday*) día *m* de trabajo

'work·force trabajadores *mpl*

'work hours *npl* horas *fpl* de trabajo

work·ing ['wɜːrkɪŋ] *n* funcionamiento *m*

'work·ing class clase *f* trabajadora

'work·ing-class *adj* de clase trabajadora

'work·ing con·di·tions *npl* condiciones *fpl* de trabajo

work·ing 'day → **workday**

work·ing hours → **work hours**

work·ing 'knowl·edge conocimientos *mpl* básicos

work·ing 'moth·er madre *f* que trabaja

'work·load cantidad *f* de trabajo

'work·man obrero *m*

'work·man·like *adj* competente

'work·man·ship factura *f*, confección *f*

work of 'art obra *f* de arte

'work·out sesión *f* de ejercicios

'work per·mit permiso *m* de trabajo

'work·shop (*also seminar*) taller *m*

'work sta·tion estación *f* de trabajo

'work·top encimera *f*

world [wɜːrld] *n* mundo *m*; **the world of computers / the theater** el mundo de la informática / del teatro; **out of this world** F sensacional

World 'Cup Mundial *m*, Copa *f* del Mundo

world·ly ['wɜːrldlɪ] *adj* mundano

world-'class *adj* de categoría mundial

world-'fa·mous *adj* mundialmente famoso

world 'pow·er potencia *f* mundial

world 're·cord récord *m* mundial *or* del mundo

world 'war guerra *f* mundial

'world·wide 1 *adj* mundial **2** *adv* en todo el mundo

worm [wɜːrm] *n* gusano *m*

worn [wɔːrn] *pp →* **wear**

worn-'out *adj shoes, carpet, part* gastado; *person* agotado

wor·ried ['wʌrɪd] *adj* preocupado

wor·ried·ly ['wʌrɪdlɪ] *adv* con preocupación

wor·ry ['wʌrɪ] **1** n preocupación f **2** v/t (pret & pp **worried**) preocupar **3** v/i (pret & pp **worried**) preocuparse; **don't worry, I'll get it!** ¡no te molestes, ya respondo yo!

wor·ry·ing ['wʌrɪɪŋ] adj preocupante

worse [wɜːrs] **1** adj peor; **get worse** empeorar **2** adv peor

wors·en ['wɜːrsn] v/i empeorar

wor·ship ['wɜːrʃɪp] **1** n culto m **2** v/t (pret & pp **worshipped**) adorar, rendir culto a; fig adorar

worst [wɜːrst] **1** adj & adv peor **2** n: **the worst** lo peor; **if the worst comes to the worst** en el peor de los casos

worst-case scen·a·ri·o el peor de los casos

worth [wɜːrθ] adj: **$20 worth of gas** 20 dólares de gasolina; **be worth ...** in monetary terms valer ...; **the book's worth reading** valer la pena leer el libro; **be worth it** valer la pena

worth·less ['wɜːrθlɪs] adj person inútil; **be worthless** of object no valer nada

worth·while adj que vale la pena; **be worthwhile** valer la pena

worth·y ['wɜːrðɪ] adj digno; cause justo; **be worthy of** (deserve) merecer

would [wʊd] v/aux: **I would help if I** te ayudaría si pudiera; **I said that I would go** dije que iría; **I told him I would not leave unless ...** le dije que no me iría a no ser que ...; **would you like to go to the movies?** ¿te gustaría ir al cine?; **would you mind if I smoked?** ¿le importa si fumo?; **would you tell her that ...?** ¿le podrías decir que ...?; **would you close the door?** ¿podrías cerrar la puerta?; **I would have told you but ...,** te lo habría dicho pero ...; **I would not have been so angry if ...** no me habría enfadado tanto si ...

wound¹ [wuːnd] **1** n herida f **2** v/t with weapon, remark herir

wound² [waʊnd] pret & pp → **wind²**

wove [woʊv] pret → **weave**

wov·en ['woʊvn] pp → **weave**

wow [waʊ] int ¡hala!

wrap [ræp] v/t (pret & pp **wrapped**) parcel, gift envolver; **he wrapped a scarf around his neck** se puso una bufanda al cuello

◆ **wrap up** v/i against the cold abrigarse

wrap·per ['ræpər] envoltorio m

wrap·ping ['ræpɪŋ] envoltorio m

wrap·ping pa·per papel m de envolver

wrath [ræθ] ira f

wreath [riːθ] corona f de flores

wreck [rek] **1** n restos mpl; **be a nervous wreck** ser un manojo de nervios **2** v/t ship hundir; car destrozar; plans, marriage arruinar

wreck·age ['rekɪdʒ] of car, plane restos mpl; of marriage, career ruina f

wreck·er ['rekər] grúa f

wreck·ing com·pa·ny ['rekɪŋ] empresa f de auxilio en carretera

wrench [rentʃ] **1** n tool llave f **2** v/t (pull) arrebatar; **wrench one's wrist** hacerse un esguince en la muñeca

wres·tle ['resl] v/i luchar

◆ **wrestle with** v/t problems combatir

wres·tler ['reslər] luchador(a) m(f) (de lucha libre)

wrest·ling ['reslɪŋ] lucha f libre

'wres·tling match combate m de lucha libre

wrig·gle ['rɪgl] v/i (squirm) menearse; along the ground arrastrarse; into small space escurrirse

◆ **wriggle out of** v/t librarse de

◆ **wring out** v/t (pret & pp **wrung**) cloth escurrir

wrin·kle ['rɪŋkl] **1** n arruga f **2** v/t clothes arrugar **3** v/i of clothes arrugarse

wrist [rɪst] muñeca f

'wrist·watch reloj m de pulsera

writ [rɪt] LAW mandato m judicial

write [raɪt] **1** v/t (pret **wrote**, pp **written**) escribir; check extender **2** v/i (pret **wrote**, pp **written**) escribir

◆ **write down** v/t escribir, tomar nota de

◆ **write off** v/t debt cancelar, anular; car destrozar

writ·er ['raɪtər] escritor(a) m(f); of book, song autor(a) m(f)

'write-up reseña f

writhe [raɪð] v/i retorcerse

writ·ing ['raɪtɪŋ] words, text escritura f; (hand-writing) letra f; **in writing** por escrito

'writ·ing desk escritorio m

'writ·ing pa·per papel m de escribir

writ·ten ['rɪtn] pp → **write**

wrong [rɒːŋ] **1** adj answer, information equivocado; decision, choice erróneo; **be wrong** of person estar equivocado; of answer ser incorrecto; morally ser injusto; **what's wrong?** ¿qué pasa?; **there is something wrong with the car** al coche le pasa algo; **you have the wrong number** TELEC se ha equivocado **2** adv mal; **go wrong** of person equivocarse; of marriage, plan etc fallar **3** n mal m; **right a wrong** deshacer un entuerto; **he knows right from wrong** sabe distinguir entre el bien y el mal; **be in the**

wrong tener la culpa
wrong·ful ['rɒːŋfəl] *adj* ilegal
wrong·ly ['rɒːŋlɪ] *adv* erróneamente
wrote [rout] *pret* → **write**

wrought 'i·ron [rɔːt] hierro *m* forjado
wrung [rʌŋ] *pret & pp* → **wring**
wry [raɪ] *adj* socarrón

X, Y

xen·o·pho·bi·a [zenou'foubɪə] xenofobia *f*
X-ray ['eksreɪ] **1** *n* rayo *m* X; *picture* radiografía *f* **2** *v/t* radiografiar, sacar un radiografía de
xy·lo·phone [zaɪlə'foun] xilofón *m*
yacht [jɑːt] yate *m*
yacht·ing ['jɑːtɪŋ] vela *f*
yachts·man ['jɑːtsmən] navegante *m/f* (*en embarcación de vela*)
Yank [jæŋk] F yanqui *m/f*
yank [jæŋk] *v/t* tirar de
yap [jæp] *v/i* (*pret & pp* **yapped**) *of small dog* ladrar (*con ladridos agudos*); F (*talk a lot*) parlotear F, largar F
yard[1] [jɑːrd] *of prison, institution etc* patio *m*; *behind house* jardín *m*; *for storage* almacén *m* (*al aire libre*)
yard[2] [jɑːrd] *measurement* yarda *f*
'yard·stick patrón *m*
yarn [jɑːrn] *n* (*thread*) hilo *m*; F (*story*) batallita *f* F
yawn [jɒːn] **1** *n* bostezo *m* **2** *v/i* bostezar
year [jɪr] año *m*; *I've know her for years* la conozco desde hace años; *we were in the same year* at school éramos del mismo curso; *be six years old* tener seis años (de edad)
year·ly ['jɪrlɪ] **1** *adj* anual **2** *adv* anualmente
yearn [jɜːrn] *v/i* anhelar
◆ **yearn for** *v/t* ansiar
yearn·ing ['jɜːrnɪŋ] *n* anhelo *m*
yeast [jiːst] levadura *f*
yell [jel] **1** *n* grito *m* **2** *v/i* gritar **3** *v/t* gritar
yel·low ['jelou] **1** *n* amarillo *m* **2** *adj* amarillo
yel·low 'pag·es *npl* páginas *fpl* amarillas
yelp [jelp] **1** *n* aullido *m* **2** *v/i* aullar
yes [jes] *int* sí; *she said yes* dijo que sí
'yes·man *pej* pelotillero *m*
yes·ter·day ['jestərdeɪ] **1** *adv* ayer; *the day before yesterday* anteayer; *yesterday afternoon* ayer por la tarde **2** *n* ayer *m*

yet [jet] **1** *adv* todavía, aún; *as yet* aún, todavía; *have you finished yet?* ¿has acabado ya?; *he hasn't arrived yet* todavía *or* aún no ha llegado; *is he here yet? - not yet* ¿ha llegado ya? - todavía *or* aún no; *yet bigger / longer* aún más grande / largo; *the fastest one yet* el más rápido hasta el momento **2** *conj* sin embargo; *yet I'm not sure* sin embargo no estoy seguro
yield [jiːld] **1** *n from fields etc* cosecha *f*; *from investment* rendimiento *m* **2** *v/t fruit, good harvest* proporcionar; *interest* rendir, devengar **3** *v/i* (*give way*) ceder; *of driver* ceder el paso
yo·ga ['jougə] yoga *m*
yog·hurt ['jougərt] yogur *m*
yolk [jouk] yema *f*
you [juː] *pron singular* tú, *L.Am.* usted, *Rpl, C.Am.* vos; *formal* usted; *plural: Span* vosotros, vosotras, *L.Am.* ustedes; *formal* ustedes; *you are clever* eres / sois inteligente; *do you know him?* ¿lo conoces / conocéis?; *you go, I'll stay* tú ve / usted vaya, yo me quedo; *never know* nunca se sabe; *you have to pay* hay que pagar; *exercise is good for you* es bueno hacer ejercicio
young [jʌŋ] *adj* joven
young·ster ['jʌŋstər] joven *m/f*
your [jʊr] *adj singular:* tu, *L.Am.* su; *formal* su; *plural: Span* vuestro, *L.Am.* su; *formal* su; *your house* tu / su casa; *your books* tus / sus libros
yours [jʊrz] *pron singular* el tuyo, la tuya, *L.Am.* el suyo, la suya; *formal* el suyo, la suya; *plural* el vuestro, la vuestra, *L.Am.* el suyo, la suya; *formal* el suyo, la suya; *a friend of yours* un amigo tuyo / vuestro; *yours ... at end of letter* un saludo
your·self [jʊr'self] *pron reflexive* te, *L.Am.* se; *formal* se; *emphatic* tú mismo *m*, tú misma *f*, *L.Am.* usted mismo, usted misma; *Rpl, C.Am.* vos mismo, vos mis-

ma; *formal* usted mismo, usted misma; *did you hurt yourself?* ¿te hiciste / se hizo daño?; *when you see yourself in the mirror* cuando te ves / se ve en el espejo; *by yourself* (*alone*) solo; (*without help*) tú solo, tú mismo, *Rpl, C.Am.* vos solo, vos mismo, *Am* usted solo, usted mismo; *formal* usted mismo, usted mismo

your·selves [jʊrˈselvz] *pron reflexive* os, *L.Am.* se; *formal* se; *emphatic* vosotros mismos *mpl*, vosotras mismas *fpl*, *Am* ustedes mismos, ustedes mismas; *formal* ustedes mismos, ustedes mismas; *did you hurt yourselves?* ¿os hicisteis / se hicieron daño?; *when you see your-

selves in the mirror cuando os veis / se ven en el espejo; *by yourselves* (*alone*) solos; (*without help*) vosotros solos, *Am* ustedes solos, ustedes mismos; *formal* ustedes solos, ustedes mismos

youth [juːθ] *n* juventud *f*; (*young man*) joven *m/f*

'**youth club** club *m* juvenil

youth·ful [ˈjuːθfəl] *adj* joven; *fashion, idealism* juvenil

'**youth hos·tel** albergue *m* juvenil

Yu·go·sla·vi·a [juːɡəˈslɑːvɪə] Yugoslavia

Yu·go·sla·vi·an [juːɡəˈslɑːvɪən] **1** *adj* yugoslavo **2** *n* yugoslavo(-a) *m(f)*

yup·pie [ˈjʌpɪ] F yupi *m/f*

Z

zap [zæp] *v/t* (*pret & pp* **zapped**) F (COMPUT: *delete*) borrar; (*kill*) liquidar F; (*hit*) golpear; (*send*) enviar

◆ **zap along** *v/i* F (*move fast*) volar F

zapped [zæpt] *adj* F (*exhausted*) hecho polvo F

zap·per [ˈzæpər] *for changing TV channels* telemando *m*, mando *m* a distancia

zap·py [ˈzæpɪ] *adj* F *car, pace* rápido; (*lively, energetic*) vivo

zeal [ziːl] *n* celo *m*

ze·bra [ˈzebrə] cebra *f*

ze·ro [ˈzɪrou] cero *m*; **10 degrees below zero** 10 bajo cero

ze·ro 'growth crecimiento *m* cero

◆ **zero in on** *v/t* (*identify*) centrarse en

zest [zest] entusiasmo *m*

zig·zag [ˈzɪgzæg] **1** *n* zigzag *m* **2** *v/i* (*pret & pp* **zigzagged**) zigzaguear

zilch [zɪltʃ] F nada de nada

zinc [zɪŋk] cinc *m*

zip [zɪp] *Br* cremallera *f*

◆ **zip up** *v/t* (*pret & pp* **zipped**) *dress, jacket* cerrar la cremallera de; COMPUT com-

pactar

'**zip code** código *m* postal

zip·per [ˈzɪpər] cremallera *f*

zit [zɪt] F *on face* grano *m*

zo·di·ac [ˈzoudɪæk] zodiaco *m*; *signs of the zodiac* signos *mpl* del zodiaco

zom·bie [ˈzɑːmbɪ] F (*idiot*) estúpido(-a) *m(f)* F; *feel like a zombie* (*exhausted*) sentirse como un zombi

zone [zoun] zona *f*

zonked [zɑːŋkt] *adj* P (*exhausted*) molido P

zoo [zuː] zoo *m*

zo·o·log·i·cal [zuːəˈlɑːdʒɪkl] *adj* zoológico

zo·ol·o·gist [zuːˈɑːlədʒɪst] zoólogo(-a) *m(f)*

zo·ol·o·gy [zuːˈɑːlədʒɪ] zoología *f*

zoom [zuːm] *v/i* F (*move fast*) ir zumbando F

◆ **zoom in on** *v/t* PHOT hacer un zoom sobre

zoom 'lens zoom *m*

zuc·chi·ni [zuːˈkiːnɪ] calabacín *m*

APPENDIX

Spanish verb conjugations

In the following conjugation patterns verb stems are shown in normal type and verb endings in *italic* type. Irregular forms are indicated by **bold** type.

Notes on the formation of tenses.

The following stems can be used to generate derived forms.

Stem forms	Derived forms
I. From the **Present indicative**, *3rd pers sg* (mand*a*, vend*e*, recib*e*)	**Imperative** *2nd pers. sg* (¡mand*a*! ¡vend*e*! ¡recib*e*!)
II. From the **Present subjunctive**, *2nd* and *3rd pers sg* and all plural forms (mand*es*, mand*e*, mand*emos*, mand*éis*, mand*en* – vend*as*, vend*a*, vend*amos*, vend*áis*, vend*an* – recib*as*, recib*a*, recib*amos*, recib*áis*, recib*an*)	**Imperative** *1st pers pl, 3rd pers sg* and *pl* as well as the negative imperative of the *2nd pers sg* and *pl* (no mand*es*, mand*e* Vd., mand*emos*, no mand*éis*, mand*en* Vds. – no vend*as*, vend*a* Vd., vend*amos*, no vend*áis*, vend*an* Vds. – no recib*as* etc)
III. From the **Preterite**, *3rd pers pl* (mand*aron*, vend*ieron*, recib*ieron*)	a) **Imperfect Subjunctive I** by changing …ron to …*ra* (mand*ara*, vend*iera*, recib*iera*) b) **Imperfect Subjunctive II** by changing …ron to …*se* (mand*ase*, vend*iese*, recib*iese*) c) **Future Subjunctive** by changing …ron to …*re* (mand*are*, vend*iere*, recib*iere*)
IV. From the **Infinitive** (mand*ar*, vend*er*, recib*ir*)	a) **Imperative** *2nd pers pl* by changing …r to …*d* (mand*ad*, vend*ed*, recib*id*) b) **Present participle** by changing …ar to …*undo*, …er and …ir to …*iendo* (or sometimes …*yendo*) (mand*ando*, vend*iendo*, recib*iendo*) c) **Future** by adding the *Present* tense endings of **haber** (mand*aré*, vend*eré*, recib*iré*) d) **Conditional** by adding the *Imperfect* endings of **haber** (mand*aría*, vend*ería*, recib*iría*)

V. From the **Past participle**
(mand*ado*, vend*ido*, recib*ido*)

all **compound tenses** by
placing a form of *haber* or *ser*
in front of the participle.

First Conjugation

⟨1a⟩ **mandar.** No change to the written or spoken form of the stem.

Simple tenses

Indicative

	Present	Imperfect	Preterite
sg	mand*o*	mand*aba*	mand*é*
	mand*as*	mand*abas*	mand*aste*
	mand*a*	mand*aba*	mand*ó*
pl	mand*amos*	mand*ábamos*	mand*amos*
	mand*áis*	mand*abais*	mand*asteis*
	mand*an*	mand*aban*	mand*aron*

	Future	Conditional
sg	mand*aré*	mand*aría*
	mand*arás*	mand*arías*
	mand*ará*	mand*aría*
pl	mand*aremos*	mand*aríamos*
	mand*aréis*	mand*aríais*
	mand*arán*	mand*arían*

Subjunctive

Present		Imperfect I	Imperfect II
sg	mand*e*	mand*ara*	mand*ase*
	mand*es*	mand*aras*	mand*ases*
	mand*e*	mand*ara*	mand*ase*
pl	mand*emos*	mand*áramos*	mand*ásemos*
	mand*éis*	mand*arais*	mand*aseis*
	mand*en*	mand*aran*	mand*asen*

	Future	Imperative
sg	mand*are*	—
	mand*ares*	mand*a* (no mand*es*)
	mand*are*	mand*e* Vd.
pl	mand*áremos*	mand*emos*
	mand*areis*	mand*ad* (no mand*éis*)
	mand*aren*	mand*en* Vds.

Infinitive: mand*ar*
Present participle: mand*ando*
Past participle: mand*ado*

Compound tenses

1. **Active forms:** the conjugated form of **haber** is placed before the *Past participle* (which does not change):

Indicative

Perfect	*he* mandado	**Future perfect**	*habré* mandado
Pluperfect	*había* mandado	**Past conditional**	*habría* mandado
Past anterior	*hube* mandado		
Past infinitive	*haber* mandado	**Past gerundive**	*habiendo* mandado

Subjunctive

Perfect	*haya* mandado	**Future perfect**	*hubiere* mandado
Pluperfect	*hubiera* mandado		
	hubiese mandado		

2. **Passive forms:** the conjugated form of **ser** (or **haber**) is placed before the *Past participle* (which does not change):

Indicative

Present	*soy* mandado	**Past anterior**	*hube sido* mandado
Imperfect	*era* mandado	**Future**	*seré* mandado
Preterite	*fui* mandado	**Future perfect**	*habré sido* mandado
Perfect	*he sido* mandado	**Conditional**	*sería* mandado
Pluperfect	*había sido* mandado	**Past conditional**	*habría sido* mandado

Infinitive / Gerundive

Present	*ser* mandado etc	**Present**	*siendo* mandado
Past	*haber sido* mandado	**Past**	*habiendo sido* mandado

Subjunctive

Present	*sea* mandado	**Pluperfect**	*hubiera sido* mandado
			hubiese sido mandado
Imperfect	*fuera* mandado		
	fuese mandado		
Future	*fuere* mandado	**Future perfect**	*hubiere sido* mandado
Past	*haya sido* mandado		

	Infinitive	Present Indicative	Present Subjunctive	Preterite
⟨1b⟩	**cambiar.** Model for all ...*iar* verbs, unless formed like *variar* ⟨1c⟩.			
		cambi*o*	cambi*e*	cambi*é*
		cambi*as*	cambi*es*	cambi*aste*
		cambi*a*	cambi*e*	cambi*ó*
		cambi*amos*	cambi*emos*	cambi*amos*
		cambi*áis*	cambi*éis*	cambi*asteis*
		cambi*an*	cambi*en*	cambi*aron*
⟨1c⟩	**variar.** *i* becomes *í* when the stem is stressed.			
		var*í*o	var*í*e	vari*é*
		var*í*as	var*í*es	vari*aste*
		var*í*a	var*í*e	vari*ó*
		vari*amos*	vari*emos*	vari*amos*
		vari*áis*	vari*éis*	vari*asteis*
		var*í*an	var*í*en	vari*aron*
⟨1d⟩	**evacuar.** Model for all ...*uar* verbs, unless formed like *acentuar* ⟨1e⟩.			
		evacu*o*	evacu*e*	evacu*é*
		evacu*as*	evacu*es*	evacu*aste*
		evacu*a*	evacu*e*	evacu*ó*
		evacu*amos*	evacu*emos*	evacu*amos*
		evacu*áis*	evacu*éis*	evacu*asteis*
		evacu*an*	evacu*en*	evacu*aron*
⟨1e⟩	**acentuar.** *u* becomes *ú* when the stem is stressed.			
		acent*ú*o	acent*ú*e	acentu*é*
		acent*ú*as	acent*ú*es	acentu*aste*
		acent*ú*a	acent*ú*e	acentu*ó*
		acentu*amos*	acentu*emos*	acentu*amos*
		acentu*áis*	acentu*éis*	acentu*asteis*
		acent*ú*an	acent*ú*en	acentu*aron*
⟨1f⟩	**cruzar.** Final *z* in the stem becomes *c* before *e*. Model for all ...*zar* verbs.			
		cruz*o*	cru*ce*s	cru*cé*
		cruz*as*	cru*ce*s	cruz*aste*
		cruz*a*	cru*ce*	cruz*ó*
		cruz*amos*	cru*cemos*	cruz*amos*
		cruz*áis*	cru*céis*	cruz*asteis*
		cruz*an*	cru*cen*	cruz*aron*

	Infinitive	Present Indicative	Present Subjunctive	Preterite

⟨1g⟩ **tocar.** Final *c* in the stem becomes *qu* before *e*. Model for all ...*car* verbs.

	toco	toque	toqué
	tocas	toques	tocaste
	toca	toque	tocó
	tocamos	toquemos	tocamos
	tocáis	toquéis	tocasteis
	tocan	toquen	tocaron

⟨1h⟩ **pagar.** Final *g* in the stem becomes *gu* (*u* is silent) before *e*. Model for all ...*gar* verbs.

	pago	pague	pagué
	pagas	pagues	pagaste
	paga	pague	pagó
	pagamos	paguemos	pagamos
	pagáis	paguéis	pagasteis
	pagan	paguen	pagaron

⟨1i⟩ **fraguar.** Final *gu* in the stem becomes *gü* before *e* (*u* with dieresis is pronounced). Model for all ...*guar* verbs.

	fraguo	fragüe	fragüé
	fraguas	fragües	fraguaste
	fragua	fragüe	fraguó
	fraguamos	fragüemos	fraguamos
	fraguáis	fragüéis	fraguasteis
	fraguan	fragüen	fraguaron

⟨1k⟩ **pensar.** Stressed *e* in the stem becomes *ie*.

	pienso	piense	pensé
	piensas	pienses	pensaste
	piensa	piense	pensó
	pensamos	pensemos	pensamos
	pensáis	penséis	pensasteis
	piensan	piensen	pensaron

⟨1l⟩ **errar.** Stressed *e* in the stem becomes *ye* (because it comes at the beginning of the word).

	yerro	yerre	erré
	yerras	yerres	erraste
	yerra	yerre	erró
	erramos	erremos	erramos
	erráis	erréis	errasteis
	yerran	yerren	erraron

	Infinitive	Present Indicative	Present Subjunctive	Preterite

⟨1m⟩ **contar.** Stressed *o* of the stem becomes *ue* (*u* is pronounced).

		cuento	cuente	conté
		cuentas	cuentes	contaste
		cuenta	cuente	contó
		contamos	contemos	contamos
		contáis	contéis	contasteis
		cuentan	cuenten	contaron

⟨1n⟩ **agorar.** Stressed *o* of the stem becomes *üe* (*u* with dieresis is pronounced).

		agüero	agüere	agoré
		agüeras	agüeres	agoraste
		agüera	agüere	agoró
		agoramos	agoremos	agoramos
		agoráis	agoréis	agorasteis
		agüeran	agüeren	agoraron

⟨1o⟩ **jugar.** Stressed *u* in the stem becomes *ue*; final *g* of the stem becomes *gu* before *e*: (see ⟨1h⟩); *conjugar, enjugar* and *enjugarse* are regular.

		juego	juegue	jugué
		juegas	juegues	jugaste
		juega	juegue	jugó
		jugamos	juguemos	jugamos
		jugáis	juguéis	jugasteis
		juegan	jueguen	jugaron

⟨1p⟩ **estar.** *Present indicative 1st pers sg* in *...oy*, otherwise regular, but note the stressed *a*; the *Present subjunctive* has a stress on the *e* in the endings (apart from *1st pers pl*); *Preterite etc* as ⟨21⟩. Otherwise regular.

		estoy	esté	estuve
		estás	estés	estuviste
		está	esté	estuvo
		estamos	estemos	estuvimos
		estáis	estéis	estuvisteis
		están	estén	estuvieron

⟨1q⟩ **andar.** *Preterite* and derived forms like *estar* as in ⟨21⟩. Otherwise regular.

		ando	ande	anduve
		andas	andes	anduviste
		anda	ande	anduvo
		andamos	andemos	anduvimos
		andáis	andéis	anduvisteis
		andan	anden	anduvieron

Infinitive	Present Indicative	Present Subjunctive	Preterite

⟨1r⟩ **dar.** *Present indicative 1st pers sg in …oy, otherwise regular. Present subjunctive 1st and 3rd pers sg takes an accent. Preterite etc follow the regular second conjugation.* Otherwise regular.

	Present Indicative	Present Subjunctive	Preterite
	doy	d**é**	d**i**
	d**as**	d**es**	d**iste**
	d**a**	d**é**	d**io**
	d**amos**	d**emos**	d**imos**
	d**áis**	d**eis**	d**isteis**
	d**an**	d**en**	d**ieron**

Second Conjugation

⟨2a⟩ **vender.** No change to the written or spoken form of the stem.

Simple tenses

Indicative

	Present	**Imperfect**	**Preterite**
sg	vend*o*	vend*ía*	vend*í*
	vend*es*	vend*ías*	vend*iste*
	vend*e*	vend*ía*	vend*ió*
pl	vend*emos*	vend*íamos*	vend*imos*
	vend*éis*	vend*íais*	vend*isteis*
	vend*en*	vend*ían*	vend*ieron*

	Future	**Conditional**
sg	vend*eré*	vend*ería*
	vend*erás*	vend*erías*
	vend*erá*	vend*ería*
pl	vend*eremos*	vend*eríamos*
	vend*eréis*	vend*eríais*
	vend*erán*	vend*erían*

Subjunctive

	Present	**Imperfect I**	**Imperfect II**
sg	vend*a*	vend*iera*	vend*iese*
	vend*as*	vend*ieras*	vend*ieses*
	vend*a*	vend*iera*	vend*iese*
pl	vend*amos*	vend*iéramos*	vend*iésemos*
	vend*áis*	vend*ierais*	vend*ieseis*
	vend*an*	vend*ieran*	vend*iesen*

	Future	**Imperative**
sg	vend*iere*	—
	vend*ieres*	vend*e* (no vend*as*)
	vend*iere*	vend*a* Vd.
pl	vend*iéremos*	vend*amos*
	vend*iereis*	vend*ed* (no vend*áis*)
	vend*ieren*	vend*an* Vds.

Infinitive: vend*er*
Present participle: vend*iendo*
Past participle: vend*ido*

Compound tenses

Formed with the *Past participle* together with **haber** and **ser**, see ⟨1a⟩.

	Infinitive	Present Indicative	Present Subjunctive	Preterite

⟨2b⟩ **vencer.** Final *c* of the stem becomes *z* bevore *a* and *o*. Model for all
...*cer* verbs where the ...*cer* is proceded by a consonant.

venzo	venza	vencí
vences	venzas	venciste
vence	venza	venció
vencemos	venzamos	vencimos
vencéis	venzáis	vencisteis
vencen	venzan	vencieron

⟨2c⟩ **coger.** Final *g* of the stem becomes *j* before *a* and *o*. Model for all
...*ger* verbs.

cojo	coja	cogí
coges	cojas	cogiste
coge	coja	cogió
cogemos	cojamos	cogimos
cogéis	cojáis	cogisteis
cogen	cojan	cogieron

⟨2d⟩ **merecer.** Final *c* of the stem becomes *zc* before *a* and *o*.

merezco	merezca	merecí
mereces	merezcas	mereciste
merece	merezca	mereció
merecemos	merezcamos	merecimos
merecéis	merezcáis	merecisteis
merecen	merezcan	merecieron

⟨2e⟩ **creer.** Unstressed *i* between two vowels becomes *y*. Past participle:
creído. Present participle: *creyendo*.

creo	crea	creí
crees	creas	creíste
cree	crea	creyó
creemos	creamos	creímos
creéis	creáis	creísteis
creen	crean	creyeron

⟨2f⟩ **tañer.** Unstressed *i* is omitted after *ñ* and *ll*; compare ⟨3h⟩ Present
participle: *tañendo*.

taño	taña	tañí
tañes	tañas	tañiste
tañe	taña	**tañó**
tañemos	tañamos	tañimos
tañéis	tañáis	tañisteis
tañen	tañan	tañeron

	Infinitive	Present Indicative	Present Subjunctive	Preterite

⟨2g⟩ **perder.** Stressed *e* in the stem becomes *ie*; model for many other verbs.

	pierd*o*	pierd*a*	perd*í*
	pierd*es*	pierd*as*	perd*iste*
	pierd*e*	pierd*a*	perd*ió*
	perd*emos*	perd*amos*	perd*imos*
	perd*éis*	perd*áis*	perd*isteis*
	pierd*en*	pierd*an*	perd*ieron*

⟨2h⟩ **mover.** Stressed *o* in the stem becomes *ue.* ...*olver* verbs form their *Past participle* with ...*uelto.*

	muev*o*	muev*a*	mov*í*
	muev*es*	muev*as*	mov*iste*
	muev*e*	muev*a*	mov*ió*
	mov*emos*	mov*amos*	mov*imos*
	mov*éis*	mov*áis*	mov*isteis*
	muev*en*	muev*an*	mov*ieron*

⟨2i⟩ **oler.** Stressed *o* in the stem becomes *hue...* (when it comes at the beginning of the word).

	huel*o*	huel*a*	ol*í*
	huel*es*	huel*as*	ol*iste*
	huel*e*	huel*a*	ol*ió*
	ol*emos*	ol*amos*	ol*imos*
	ol*éis*	ol*áis*	ol*isteis*
	huel*en*	huel*an*	ol*ieron*

⟨2k⟩ **haber.** Many irregular forms. In the *Future* and *Conditional* the *e* after the stem *hab...* is dropped. Future: *habré.* Imperative *2nd pers sg: he.*

	he	hay*a*	hub*e*
	ha*s*	hay*as*	hub*iste*
	ha	hay*a*	hub*o*
	he*mos*	hay*amos*	hub*imos*
	hab*éis*	hay*áis*	hub*isteis*
	ha*n*	hay*an*	hub*ieron*

⟨2l⟩ **tener.** Irregular in most forms. In the *Future* and *Conditional* the *e* coming after the stem is dropped and a *d* is inserted. Future: *tendré.* Imperative *2nd pers sg: ten.*

	teng*o*	teng*a*	**tuve**
	tien*es*	teng*as*	**tuv***iste*
	tien*e*	teng*a*	**tuv***o*
	ten*emos*	teng*amos*	**tuv***imos*
	ten*éis*	teng*áis*	**tuv***isteis*
	tien*en*	teng*an*	**tuv***ieron*

Infinitive	Present Indicative	Present Subjunctive	Preterite

⟨2m⟩ **caber.** Irregular in many forms. In the *Future* and *Conditional* the *e* coming after the stem is dropped. Future: *cabré*.

quepo	**quep**a	**cup**e
cab*es*	**quep**as	**cup**iste
cab*e*	**quep**a	**cup**o
cab*emos*	**quep**amos	**cup**imos
cab*éis*	**quep**áis	**cup**isteis
cab*en*	**quep**an	**cup**ieron

⟨2n⟩ **saber.** Irregular in many forms. In the *Future* and *Conditional* the *e* coming after the stem is dropped. Future: *sabré*.

sé	**sep**a	**sup**e
sab*es*	**sep**as	**sup**iste
sab*e*	**sep**a	**sup**o
sab*emos*	**sep**amos	**sup**imos
sab*éis*	**sep**áis	**sup**isteis
sab*en*	**sep**an	**sup**ieron

⟨2o⟩ **caer.** In the *Present* ...*ig*... is inserted after the stem. Unstressed *i* between vowels changes to *y* as with ⟨2e⟩. Past participle: *caído*. Present participle: *cayendo*.

ca**ig**o	ca**ig**a	caí
ca*es*	ca**ig**as	caíste
ca*e*	ca**ig**a	cayó
ca*emos*	ca**ig**amos	caímos
ca*éis*	ca**ig**áis	caísteis
ca*en*	ca**ig**an	cayeron

⟨2p⟩ **traer.** In the *Present* ...*ig*... is inserted after the stem. The *Preterite* ends in ...*je*. In the *Present participle i* changes to *y*. Past participle: *traído*. Present participle: *trayendo*.

tra**ig**o	tra**ig**a	tra**j**e
tra*es*	tra**ig**as	tra**j**iste
tra*e*	tra**ig**a	tra**j**o
tra*emos*	tra**ig**amos	tra**j**imos
tra*éis*	tra**ig**áis	tra**j**isteis
tra*en*	tra**ig**an	tra**j**eron

	Infinitive	Present Indicative	Present Subjunctive	Preterite

⟨2q⟩ **valer.** In the *Present* ...*g*... is inserted after the stem. In the *Future* and *Conditional* the *e* coming after the stem is dropped and a ...*d*... inserted. Future: *valdré.*

	valg*o*	valg*a*	val*í*
	val*es*	valg*as*	val*iste*
	val*e*	valg*a*	val*ió*
	val*emos*	valg*amos*	val*imos*
	val*éis*	valg*áis*	val*isteis*
	val*en*	valg*an*	val*ieron*

⟨2r⟩ **poner.** ...*g*... is inserted in the *Present*. Irregular in the *Preterite* and *Past participle*. In the *Future* and *Conditional* the *e* coming after the stem is dropped and a ...*d*... inserted. Future: *pondré*. Past participle: *puesto*. Imperative *2nd pers sg*: *pon*.

	pong*o*	pong*a*	**puse**
	pon*es*	pong*as*	**pusiste**
	pon*e*	pong*a*	**puso**
	pon*emos*	pong*amos*	**pusimos**
	pon*éis*	pong*áis*	**pusisteis**
	pon*en*	pong*an*	**pusieron**

⟨2s⟩ **hacer.** In the *1st* person of the *Present Indicative* and *Subjunctive g* replaces *c*. Irregular in the *Preterite* and *Past participle*. In the *Future* and *Conditional* the *ce* is dropped. In the *Imperative sg* just the stem is used with ...*c* changing to ...*z*. Future: *haré*. Imperative *2nd pers sg*: *haz*. Past participle: *hecho*.

	hag*o*	hag*a*	hic*e*
	hac*es*	hag*as*	hic*iste*
	hac*e*	hag*a*	hiz*o*
	hac*emos*	hag*amos*	hic*imos*
	hac*éis*	hag*áis*	hic*isteis*
	hac*en*	hag*an*	hic*ieron*

⟨2t⟩ **poder.** Stressed *o* in the stem changes to ...*ue*... in the *Present* and the *Imperative*. Irregular in the *Preterite* and *Present participle*. In the *Future* and *Conditional* the *e* coming after the stem is dropped. Future: *podré*. Present participle: *pudiendo*.

	pued*o*	pued*a*	**pude**
	pued*es*	pued*as*	**pudiste**
	pued*e*	pued*a*	**pudo**
	pod*emos*	pod*amos*	**pudimos**
	pod*éis*	pod*áis*	**pudisteis**
	pued*en*	pued*an*	**pudieron**

	Infinitive	Present Indicative	Present Subjunctive	Preterite

⟨2u⟩ **querer.** Stressed *e* in the stem changes to *ie* in the *Present* and *Imperative*. Irregular in the *Preterite*. In the *Future* and *Conditional* the *e* coming after the stem is dropped. Future: *querré*.

quiero	quiera	quise
quieres	quieras	quisiste
quiere	quiera	quiso
queremos	queramos	quisimos
queréis	queráis	quisisteis
quieren	quieran	quisieron

⟨2v⟩ **ver.** *Present indicative 1st pers sg, Present subjunctive* and *Imperfect* are formed on the stem *ve...*, otherwise formation is regular using the shortened stem *v...* Irregular in the *Past participle*. Past participle: *visto*.

veo	vea	vi
ves	veas	viste
ve	vea	vio
vemos	veamos	vimos
veis	veáis	visteis
ven	vean	vieron

	Infinitive	Present Indicative	Present Subjunctive	Imperfect Indicative	Preterite

⟨2w⟩ **ser.** Totally irregular with several different stems being used. Past participle: *sido*. Imperative *2nd pers sg*: *sé*. *2nd pers pl*: *sed*.

	soy	se*a*	*e*ra	**fu**i
	e*res*	se*as*	e*ras*	**fu**iste
	es	se*a*	e*ra*	**fu**e
	so*mos*	se*amos*	é*ramos*	**fu**imos
	so*is*	se*áis*	e*rais*	**fu**isteis
	so*n*	se*an*	e*ran*	**fu**eron

⟨2x⟩ **placer.** Used almost exclusively in the *3rd pers sg*. Irregular forms: *Present subjunctive* pl**e**ga and pl**e**gue egue as well as *plazca*; *Preterite* pl**ugo** (or *plació*), pl**ug**ieron (or *placieron*); *Imperfect subjunctive* pl**u**guiera, pl**u**guiese (or *placiera, placiese*); *Future subjunctive* pl**u**guiere (or *placiere*).

⟨2y⟩ **yacer.** Used mainly on gravestones and so used primarily in the *3rd pers*. The *Present indicative 1st pers sg* and *Present subjunctive* have three forms. The *Imperative* is regular; just the stem with *c* changing to *z*. *Present indicative*: ya**zc**o, ya**zg**o, ya**g**o, yaces etc; *Present subjunctive*: ya**zc**a, ya**zg**a, ya**g**a etc; *Imperative* yace and ya**z**.

⟨2z⟩ **raer.** The regular forms of the *Present indicative 1st pers sg* and *Present subjunctive* are less common than the forms with inserted *...ig...* as in ⟨2o⟩: ra**ig**o, ra**ig**a; but also *rayo, raya* (less common). Otherwise regular.

⟨2za⟩ **roer.** As well as their regular forms the *Present indicative 1st pers sg* and *Present subjunctive* have the less common forms: ro**ig**o, ro**ig**a, ro**y**o, ro**y**a.

Third Conjugation

⟨3a⟩ **recibir.** No change to the written or spoken form of the stem.

Simple tenses
Indicative

	Present	**Imperfect**	**Preterite**
sg	recib*o*	recib*ía*	recib*í*
	recib*es*	recib*ías*	recib*iste*
	recib*e*	recib*ía*	recib*ió*
pl	recib*imos*	recib*íamos*	recib*imos*
	recib*ís*	recib*íais*	recib*isteis*
	recib*en*	recib*ían*	recib*ieron*

	Future	**Conditional**
sg	recib*iré*	recib*iría*
	recib*irás*	recib*irías*
	recib*irá*	recib*iría*
pl	recib*iremos*	recib*iríamos*
	recib*iréis*	recib*iríais*
	recib*irán*	recib*irían*

Subjunctive

	Present	**Imperfect I**	**Imperfect II**
sg	recib*a*	recib*iera*	recib*iese*
	recib*as*	recib*ieras*	recib*ieses*
	recib*a*	recib*iera*	recib*iese*
pl	recib*amos*	recib*iéramos*	recib*iésemos*
	recib*áis*	recib*ierais*	recib*ieseis*
	recib*an*	recib*ieran*	recib*iesen*

	Future	**Imperative**
sg	recib*iere*	—
	recib*ieres*	recib*e* (no recib*as*)
	recib*iere*	recib*a* Vd.
pl	recib*iéremos*	recib*amos*
	recib*iereis*	recib*id* (no recib*áis*)
	recib*ieren*	recib*an* Vds.

Infinitive: recib*ir*
Present participle: recib*iendo*
Past participle: recib*ido*

Compound tenses

Formed with the *Past participle* together with **haber** and **ser**, see ⟨1a⟩.

	Infinitive	Present Indicative	Present Subjunctive	Preterite

⟨3b⟩ **esparcir.** Final *c* of the stem becomes *z* before *a* and *o*.

		esparzo	esparza	esparcí
		esparces	esparzas	esparciste
		esparce	esparza	esparció
		esparcimos	esparzamos	esparcimos
		esparcís	esparzáis	esparcisteis
		esparcen	esparzan	esparcieron

⟨3c⟩ **dirigir.** Final *g* of the stem becomes *j* before *a* and *o*.

		dirijo	dirija	dirigí
		diriges	dirijas	dirigiste
		dirige	dirija	dirigió
		dirigimos	dirijamos	dirigimos
		dirigís	dirijáis	dirigisteis
		dirigen	dirijan	dirigieron

⟨3d⟩ **distinguir.** Final *gu* of the stem becomes *g* before *a* and *o*.

		distingo	distinga	distinguí
		distingues	distingas	distinguiste
		distingue	distinga	distinguió
		distinguimos	distingamos	distinguimos
		distinguís	distingáis	distinguisteis
		distinguen	distingan	distinguieron

⟨3e⟩ **delinquir.** Final *qu* of the stem becomes *c* before *a* and *o*.

		delinco	delinca	delinquí
		delinques	delincas	delinquiste
		delinque	delinca	delinquió
		delinquimos	delincamos	delinquimos
		delinquís	delincáis	delinquisteis
		delinquen	delincan	delinquieron

⟨3f⟩ **lucir.** Final *c* of the stem becomes *zc* before *a* and *o*.

		luzco	luzca	lucí
		luces	luzcas	luciste
		luce	luzca	lució
		lucimos	luzcamos	lucimos
		lucís	luzcáis	lucisteis
		lucen	luzcan	lucieron

	Infinitive	Present Indicative	Present Subjunctive	Preterite

⟨3g⟩ **concluir.** A *y* is inserted after the stem unless the ending begins with *i*. Past participle: *concluido*. Present participle: *concluyendo*.

	concluyo	concluya	concluí
	concluyes	concluyas	concluiste
	concluye	concluya	concluyó
	concluimos	concluyamos	concluimos
	concluís	concluyáis	concluisteis
	concluyen	concluyan	concluyeron

⟨3h⟩ **gruñir.** Unstressed *i* is dropped after *ñ*, *ll* and *ch*. Likewise *mullir*: *mulló*, *mulleron*, *mullendo*; *henchir*: *hinchó*, *hincheron*, *hinchendo*. Present participle: *gruñendo*.

	gruño	gruñes	gruñe
	gruñimos	gruñís	gruñen
	gruña	gruñí	gruñas
	gruñiste	gruña	gruñó
	gruñamos	gruñimos	gruñáis
	gruñisteis	gruñan	gruñeron

⟨3i⟩ **sentir.** Stressed *e* of the stem becomes *ie*; unstressed *e* remains unchanged before endings starting with *i*, but before other endings it changes to *...i...*; likewise *adquirir*: stressed *i* of the stem becomes *ie*; unstressed *i* remains unchanged in all forms. Present participle: *sintiendo*.

	siento	sienta	sentí
	sientes	sientas	sentiste
	siente	sienta	sintió
	sentimos	sintamos	sentimos
	sentís	sintáis	sentisteis
	sienten	sientan	sintieron

⟨3k⟩ **dormir.** Stressed *o* of the stem becomes *ue*; unstressed *o* is unchanged when the ending starts with *i*; otherwise it changes to *...u...* Present participle: *durmiendo*.

	duermo	duerma	dormí
	duermes	duermas	dormiste
	duerme	duerma	durmió
	dormimos	durmamos	dormimos
	dormís	durmáis	dormisteis
	duermen	duerman	durmieron

Infinitive	Present Indicative	Present Subjunctive	Preterite

⟨3l⟩ **medir.** The *e* of the stem is kept if the ending contains an *i*. Otherwise it changes to ...*i*... whether stressed or unstressed. Present participle: *midiendo*.

mid*o*	mid*a*	med*í*
mid*es*	mid*as*	med*iste*
mid*e*	mid*a*	mid*ió*
med*imos*	mid*amos*	med*imos*
med*ís*	mid*áis*	med*isteis*
mid*en*	mid*an*	mid*ieron*

⟨3m⟩ **reír.** As *medir* ⟨3l⟩; when *e* changes to *i* any second *i* belonging to the ending is dropped. Past participle: *reído*. Present participle: *riendo*.

rí*o*	rí*a*	re*í*
rí*es*	rí*as*	re*íste*
rí*e*	rí*a*	ri*ó*
re*imos*	ri*amos*	re*ímos*
re*ís*	ri*áis*	re*ísteis*
rí*en*	rí*an*	ri*eron*

⟨3n⟩ **erguir.** As *medir* in the *Present indicative*, *Subjunctive* and *Imperative*. Other forms follow *sentir* with initial *ie*... changing to *ye*... Present participle: *irguiendo*. Imperative: *irgue, yergue*.

irg*o*, **yerg***o*	**irg***a*, **yerg***a*	ergu*í*
irg*ues*, **yerg***ues*	**irg***as*, **yerg***as*	ergu*iste*
irg*ue*, **yerg***ue*	**irg***a*, **yerg***a*	irgu*ió*
ergu*imos*	**irg***amos*, **yerg***amos*	ergu*imos*
ergu*ís*	**irg***áis*, **yerg***áis*	ergu*isteis*
irg*uen*, **yerg***uen*	**irg***an*, **yerg***an*	irgu*ieron*

⟨3o⟩ **conducir.** Final *c* of the stem, as with *lucir* ⟨3f⟩, becomes *zc* before *a* and *o*. *Preterite* is irregular with ...*je*.

conduz*co*	conduz*ca*	condu**je**
conduc*es*	conduz*cas*	conduj*iste*
conduc*e*	conduz*ca*	conduj*o*
conduc*imos*	conduz*camos*	conduj*imos*
conduc*ís*	conduz*cáis*	conduj*isteis*
conduc*en*	conduz*can*	conduj*eron*

Infinitive	Present Indicative	Present Subjunctive	Preterite

⟨3p⟩ **decir.** In the *Present* and *Imperative e* and *i* are changed, as with *medir*; in the *Present indicative 1st pers sg* and in the *Present subjunctive c* becomes *g*. Irregular *Future* and *Conditional* based on a shortened *Infinitive*. *Preterite* has *je*. Future: *diré*. Past participle: *dicho*. Present participle: *diciendo*. Imperative *2nd pers sg*: *di*.

di**go**	di**ga**	di**je**
di**ces**	di**gas**	di**j**iste
di**ce**	di**ga**	di**jo**
de**cimos**	di**gamos**	di**j**imos
de**cís**	di**gáis**	di**j**isteis
di**cen**	di**gan**	di**jeron**

⟨3q⟩ **oír.** In the *Present indicative 1st pers sg* and *Present subjunctive …ig…* is inserted after the *o…* of the stem. Unstressed *…i…* changes to *…y…* when coming between two vowels. Past participle: *oído*. Present participle: *oyendo*.

oi**go**	oi**ga**	oí
o**yes**	oi**gas**	oíste
o**ye**	oi**ga**	oyó
oímos	oi**gamos**	oímos
oís	oi**gáis**	oísteis
o**yen**	oi**gan**	o**yeron**

⟨3rk⟩ **salir.** In the *Present indicative 1st pers sg* and the *Present subjunctive a …g…* is inserted after the stem. In the *Future* and *Conditional* the *i* is replaced by *d*. Future: *saldré*. Imperative: *2nd pers sg*: *sal*.

sal**go**	sal**ga**	salí
sal**es**	sal**gas**	saliste
sal**e**	sal**ga**	salió
sal**imos**	sal**gamos**	salimos
sal**ís**	sal**gáis**	salisteis
sal**en**	sal**gan**	salieron

	Infinitive	Present Indicative	Present Subjunctive	Imperfect Indicative	Preterite

⟨3s⟩ **venir.** In the *Present* two changes: either a …*g*… is inserted after the stem or *e*, *ie* and *i* follow the same changes as *sentir*. In the *Future* and *Conditional* the *i* is dropped and replaced by *d*. Future: *vendré*. Present participle: *viniendo*. Imperative *2nd pers sg: ven*.

ven**go**	ven**ga**	ven**ía**	v**i**ne
vien**es**	ven**gs**	ven**ías**	v**i**n**iste**
vien**e**	ven**ga**	ven**ía**	v**i**no
ven**imos**	ven**gamos**	ven**íamos**	v**i**n**imos**
ven**ís**	ven**gáis**	ven**íais**	v**i**n**isteis**
vien**en**	ven**gan**	ven**ían**	v**i**n**ieron**

⟨3t⟩ **ir.** Totally irregular with several different stems being used. Present participle: *yendo*

voy	**vaya**	**ib**a	**fui**
vas	**vayas**	**ib**as	**fui**ste
va	**vaya**	**ib**a	**fue**
vamos	**vaya**mos	**íb**amos	**fui**mos
vais	**vayáis**	**ib**ais	**fui**steis
van	**vayan**	**ib**an	**fue**ron

Imperative: **ve** (no **vayas**), **vaya** Vd, **va**mos, *id* (no **vayáis**), **vayan** Vds.

Notas sobre el verbo inglés

a) Conjugación

1. **El tiempo presente** tiene la misma forma que el infinitivo en todas las personas menos la 3ª del singular; en ésta, se añade una *-s* al infinitivo, p.ej. *he brings*, o se añade *-es* si el infinitivo termina en sibilante (ch, sh, ss, zz), p.ej. *he passes*. Esta *s* tiene dos pronunciaciones distintas: tras consonante sorda se pronuncia sorda, p.ej. *he paints* [peɪnts]; tras consonante sonora se pronuncia sonora, *he sends* [sendz]; *-es* se pronuncia también sonora, sea la *e* parte de la desinencia o letra final del infinitivo, p.ej. *he washes* [wɑ:ʃɪz], *urges* ['ɜ:rdʒɪz]. Los verbos que terminan en *-y* la cambian en *-ies* en la tercera persona, p.ej. *he worries, he tries*, pero son regulares los verbos que en el infinitivo tienen una vocal delante de la *-y*, p.ej. *he plays*. El verbo *to be* es irregular en todas las personas: *I am, you are, he is, we are, you are, they are*. Tres verbos más tienen forma especial para la tercera persona del singular: *do-he does, go-he goes, have-he has*.

   En los demás tiempos, todas las personas son iguales. **El pretérito y el participio del pasado** se forman añadiendo *-ed* al infinitivo, p.ej. *I passed, passed*, o añadiendo *-d* a los infinitivos que terminan en *-e*, p.ej. *I faced, faced*. (Hay muchos verbos irregulares: v. abajo). Esta *-(e)d* se pronuncia generalmente como [t]: *passed* [pæst], *faced* [feɪst]; pero cuando se añade a un infinitivo que termina en consonante sonora o en sonido consonántico sonoro o en *r*, se pronuncia como [d]: *warmed* [wɔ:rmd], *moved* [mu:vd], *feared* [fɪrd]. Si el infinitivo termina en *-d* o *-t*, la desinencia *-ed* se pronuncia [ɪd]. Si el infinitivo termina en *-y*, ésta se cambia en *-ie*, antes de añadirse la *-d*: *try-tried* [traɪd], *pity-pitied* [pɪtɪd]. **Los tiempos compuestos del pasado** se forman con el verbo auxiliar *have* y el participio del pasado, como en español: **perfecto** *I have faced*, **pluscuamperfecto** *I had faced*. Con el verbo auxiliar *will* (*shall*) y el infinitivo se forma **el futuro**, p.ej. *I shall face*; y con el verbo auxiliar *would* (*should*) y el infinitivo se forma **el condicional**, p.ej. *I should face*. En cada tiempo existe además una forma continua que se forma con el verbo *be* (= estar) y el participio del presente (v. abajo): *I am going, I was writing, I had been staying, I shall be waiting*, etc.

2. **El subjuntivo** ha dejado casi de existir en inglés, salvo en algún caso especial (*if I were you, so be it, it is proposed that a vote be taken*, etc.). En el presente, tiene en todas las personas la misma forma que el infinitivo, *that I go, that he go*, etc.

3. **El participio del presente** y **el gerundio** tienen la misma forma en inglés, añadiéndose al infinitivo la desinencia *-ing*: *painting, sending*. Pero 1) Los verbos cuyo infinitivo termina en *-e* muda la pierden al añadir *-ing*, p.ej. *love-loving, write-writing* (excepciones que conservan la *-e*: *dye-dyeing, singe-singeing*); 2) El participio del presente de los verbos *die, lie, vie*, etc. se escribe *dying, lying, vying*, etc.

4. Existe una clase de verbos ligeramente irregulares, que terminan en consonante simple precedida de vocal simple acentuada; en éstos, antes de añadir la desinencia *-ing* o *-ed*, se dobla la consonante:

lob	lob*bed*	lob*bing*	compel	compel*led*	compel*ling*
wed	wed*ded*	wed*ding*	control	control*led*	control*ling*
beg	beg*ged*	beg*ging*	bar	bar*red*	bar*ring*
step	step*ped*	step*ping*	stir	stir*red*	stir*ring*
quit	quit*ted*	quit*ting*			

Los verbos que terminan en *-l, -p*, aunque precedida de vocal átona, tienen doblada la consonante en los dos participios en el inglés escrito en Gran Bretaña, aunque no en el de Estados Unidos:

travel	travel*ing*,	traveli*ng*
	Br travel*led*,	*Br* travel*led*

Los verbos que terminan en *-c* la cambian en *-ck* al añadirse las desinencias *-ed, -ing*:

traffic	traffic*ked*	traffic*king*

5. La voz pasiva se forma exactamente como en español, con el verbo *be* y el participio del pasado: *I am obliged, he was fined, they will be moved*, etc.

6. Cuando se dirige uno directamente a otra(s) persona(s) en inglés se emplea únicamente el pronombre *you*. *You* se traduce por el *tú*, *vosotros*, *usted* y *ustedes* del español.

b) Los verbos irregulares ingleses

Se citan las tres partes principales de cada verbo: infinitivo, pretérito, participio del pasado.

alight - alighted, alit - alighted, alit
arise - arose - arisen
awake - awoke - awoken, awaked
be (am, is, are) - was (were) been
bear - bore - borne
beat - beat - beaten
become - became become
begin - began - begun
behold - beheld - beheld
bend - bent - bent
beseech - besought, beseeched - besought, beseeched
bet - bet, betted - bet, betted
bid - bid - bid
bind - bound - bound
bite - bit - bitten
bleed - bled - bled

blow - blew - blown
break - broke - broken
breed - bred - bred
bring - brought - brought
broadcast - broadcast - broadcast
build - built - built
burn - burnt, burned - burnt, burned
burst - burst - burst
bust - bust(ed) - bust(ed)
buy - bought - bought
cast - cast - cast
catch - caught - caught
choose - chose - chosen
cleave (*cut*) - clove, cleft - cloven, cleft
cleave (*adhere*) - cleaved - cleaved
cling - clung - clung

come - came - come
cost (v/i) - cost - cost
creep - crept - crept
crow - crowed, crew - crowed
cut - cut - cut
deal - dealt - dealt
dig - dug - dug
do - did - done
draw - drew - drawn
dream - dreamt, dreamed - dreamt, dreamed
drink - drank - drunk
drive - drove - driven
dwell - dwelt, dwelled - dwelt, dwelled
eat - ate - eaten
fall - fell - fallen
feed - fed - fed
feel - felt - felt
fight - fought - fought
find - found - found
flee - fled - fled
fling - flung - flung
fly - flew - flown
forbear - forbore - forborne
forbid - forbad(e) - forbidden
forecast - forecast(ed) - forecast(ed)
forget - forgot - forgotten
forgive - forgave - forgiven
forsake - forsook - forsaken
freeze - froze - frozen
get - got - got, gotten
give - gave - given
go - went - gone
grind - ground - ground
grow - grew - grown
hang - hung, (v/t) hanged - hung, (v/t) hanged
have - had - had
hear - heard - heard
heave - heaved, NAUT hove - heaved, NAUT hove
hew - hewed - hewed, hewn
hide - hid - hidden
hit - hit - hit
hold - held - held
hurt - hurt - hurt

keep - kept - kept
kneel - knelt, kneeled - knelt, kneeled
know - knew - known
lay - laid - laid
lead - led - led
lean - leaned, leant - leaned, leant
leap - leaped, leapt - leaped, leapt
learn - learned, learnt - learned, learnt
leave - left - left
lend - lent - lent
let - let - let
lie - lay - lain
light - lighted, lit - lighted, lit
lose - lost - lost
make - made - made
mean - meant - meant
meet - met - met
mow - mowed - mowed, mown
pay - paid - paid
plead - pleaded, pled - pleaded, pled
prove - proved - proved, proven
put - put - put
quit - quit(ted) - quit(ted)
read - read [red] - read [red]
rend - rent - rent
rid - rid - rid
ride - rode - ridden
ring - rang - rung
rise - rose - risen
run - ran - run
saw - sawed - sawn, sawed
say - said - said
see - saw - seen
seek - sought - sought
sell - sold - sold
send - sent - sent
set - set - set
sew - sewed - sewed, sewn
shake - shook - shaken
shear - sheared - sheared, shorn
shed - shed - shed
shine - shone - shone
shit - shit(ted), shat - shit(ted), shat
shoe - shod - shod
shoot - shot - shot
show - showed - shown
shrink - shrank - shrunk

shut - shut - shut
sing - sang - sung
sink - sank - sunk
sit - sat - sat
slay - slew - slain
sleep - slept - slept
slide - slid - slid
sling - slung - slung
slink - slunk - slunk
slit - slit - slit
smell - smelt, smelled - smelt, smelled
smite - smote - smitten
sow - sowed - sown, sowed
speak - spoke - spoken
speed - sped, speeded - sped, speeded
spell - spelt, spelled - spelt, spelled
spend - spent - spent
spill - spilt, spilled - spilt, spilled
spin - spun, span - spun
spit - spat - spat
split - split - split
spoil - spoiled, spoilt - spoiled, spoilt
spread - spread - spread
spring - sprang, sprung - sprung
stand - stood - stood
stave - staved, stove - staved, stove
steal - stole - stolen
stick - stuck - stuck
sting - stung - stung

stink - stunk, stank - stunk
strew - strewed - strewed, strewn
stride - strode - stridden
strike - struck - struck
string - strung - strung
strive - strove - striven
swear - swore - sworn
sweep - swept - swept
swell - swelled - swollen
swim - swam - swum
swing - swung - swung
take - took - taken
teach - taught - taught
tear - tore - torn
tell - told - told
think - thought - thought
thrive - throve - thriven
throw - threw - thrown
thrust - thrust - thrust
tread - trod - trodden
understand - understood - understood
wake - woke, waked - woken, waked
wear - wore - worn
weave - wove - woven
wed - wed(ded) - wed(ded)
weep - wept - wept
wet - wet(ted) - wet(ted)
win - won - won
wind - wound - wound
wring - wrung - wrung
write - wrote - written

Numbers – Numerales

Cardinal Numbers – Números cardinales

0	*zero, Br tb nought* cero	40	*forty* cuarenta
1	*one* uno, una	50	*fifty* cincuenta
2	*two* dos	60	*sixty* sesenta
3	*three* tres	70	*seventy* setenta
4	*four* cuatro	80	*eighty* ochenta
5	*five* cinco	90	*ninety* noventa
6	*six* seis	100	*a hundred, one hundred* cien(to)
7	*seven* siete	101	*a hundred and one* ciento uno
8	*eight* ocho	110	*a hundred and ten* ciento diez
9	*nine* nueve	200	*two hundred* doscientos, -as
10	*ten* diez	300	*three hundred* trescientos, -as
11	*eleven* once	400	*four hundred* cuatrocientos, -as
12	*twelve* doce	500	*five hundred* quinientos, -as
13	*thirteen* trece	600	*six hundred* seiscientos, -as
14	*fourteen* catorce	700	*seven hundred* setecientos, -as
15	*fifteen* quince	800	*eight hundred* ochocientos, -as
16	*sixteen* dieciséis	900	*nine hundred* novecientos, -as
17	*seventeen* diecisiete	1000	*a thousand, one thousand* mil
18	*eighteen* dieciocho	1959	*one thousand nine hundred and fifty-nine* mil novecientos cincuenta y nueve
19	*nineteen* diecinueve		
20	*twenty* veinte	2000	*two thousand* dos mil
21	*twenty-one* veintiuno	1 000 000	*a million, one million* un millón
22	*twenty-two* veintidós	2 000 000	*two million* dos millones
30	*thirty* treinta		
31	*thirty-one* treinta y uno		

Notas:

i) In Spanish numbers a comma is used for decimals:

1.25 **one point two five** una coma veinticinco

ii) A period is used where, in English, we would use a comma:

1.000.000 = 1,000,000

Numbers like this can also be written using a space instead of a comma:

1 000 000 = 1,000,000

Ordinal Numbers – Números ordinales

1st	*first*	1°	primero
2nd	*second*	2°	segundo
3rd	*third*	3°	tercero
4th	*fourth*	4°	cuarto
5th	*fifth*	5°	quinto
6th	*sixth*	6°	sexto
7th	*seventh*	7°	séptimo
8th	*eighth*	8°	octavo
9th	*ninth*	9°	noveno, nono
10th	*tenth*	10°	décimo
11th	*eleventh*	11°	undécimo
12th	*twelfth*	12°	duodécimo
13th	*thirteenth*	13°	decimotercero
14th	*fourteenth*	14°	decimocuarto
15th	*fifteenth*	15°	decimoquinto
16th	*sixteenth*	16°	decimosexto
17th	*seventeenth*	17°	decimoséptimo
18th	*eighteenth*	18°	decimoctavo
19th	*nineteenth*	19°	decimonoveno, decimonono
20th	*twentieth*	20°	vigésimo
21st	*twenty-first*	21°	vigésimo prim(er)o
22nd	*twenty-second*	22°	vigésimo segundo
30th	*thirtieth*	30°	trigésimo
31st	*thirty-first*	31°	trigésimo prim(er)o
40th	*fortieth*	40°	cuadragésimo
50th	*fiftieth*	50°	quincuagésimo
60th	*sixtieth*	60°	sexagésimo
70th	*seventieth*	70°	septuagésimo
80th	*eightieth*	80°	octogésimo
90th	*ninetieth*	90°	nonagésimo
100th	*hundredth*	100°	centésimo
101st	*hundred and first*	101°	centésimo primero
110th	*hundred and tenth*	110°	centésimo décimo
200th	*two hundredth*	200°	ducentésimo
300th	*three hundredth*	300°	trecentésimo
400th	*four hundredth*	400°	cuadringentésimo
500th	*five hundredth*	500°	quingentésimo
600th	*six hundredth*	600°	sexcentésimo
700th	*seven hundredth*	700°	septingentésimo
800th	*eight hundredth*	800°	octingentésimo
900th	*nine hundredth*	900°	noningentésimo
1000th	*thousandth*	1000°	milésimo
2000th	*two thousandth*	2000°	dos milésimo
1,000,100th	*millionth*	1 000 100°	millonésimo
2,000,000th	*two millionth*	2 000 000°	dos millonésimo

Fractions and other Numerals –
Números quebrados y otros

¹/₂	*one half, a half*	medio, media
1¹/₂	*one and a half*	uno y medio
2¹/₂	*two and a half*	dos y medio
¹/₃	*one third, a third*	un tercio, la tercera parte
²/₃	*two thirds*	dos tercios, las dos terceras partes
¹/₄	*one quarter, a quarter*	un cuarto, la cuarta parte
³/₄	*three quarters*	tres cuartos, las tres cuartas partes
¹/₅	*one fifth, a fifth*	un quinto
3⁴/₅	*three and four fifths*	tres y cuatro quintos
¹/₁₁	*one eleventh, an eleventh*	un onzavo
⁵/₁₂	*five twelfths*	cinco dozavos
¹/₁₀₀₀	*one thousandth, a thousandth*	un milésimo
	seven times as big, seven times bigger	siete veces más grande
	twelve times more	doce veces más
	first(ly)	en primer lugar
	second(ly) etc	en segundo lugar
7 + 8 = 15	*seven and (or plus) eight are (or is) fifteen*	siete y (*or* más) ocho son quince
10 − 3 = 7	*ten minus three is seven, three from ten leaves seven*	diez menos tres resta siete, de tres a diez van siete
2 × 3 = 6	*two times three is six*	dos por tres son seis
20 4 = 5	*twenty divided by four is five*	veinte dividido por cuatro es cinco

Dates – Fechas

1996	*nineteen ninety-six*	mil novecientos noventa y seis
2005	*two thousand (and) five*	dos mil cinco

the 10th of November, November 10 (ten)
el diez de noviembre, el 10 de noviembre

the 1st of March, March 1 (first)
el uno de marzo, *L.Am.* **el primero de marzo, el 1o de marzo**

Headword in **blue**	**A·mer·i·ca** [əˈmerɪkə] *continent* América; *USA* Estados *mpl* Unidos
International Phonetic Alphabet	**in·sult 1** *n* [ˈɪnsʌlt] insulto *m* **2** *v/t* [ɪnˈsʌlt] insultar
Translation in normal characters with gender shown in *italics*	**break·down** *of vehicle, machine* avería *f*; *of talks* ruptura *f*; (*nervous breakdown*) crisis *f inv* nerviosa; *of figures* desglose *m*
Hyphenation points	**con·sum·er 'con·fi·dence** confianza *f* de los consumidores **con·sum·er goods** *npl* bienes *mpl* de consumo **con·sum·er so·ci·e·ty** sociedad *f* de consumo
Stress shown in headwords	**ˈmov·ie thea·ter** cine *m*, sala *f* de cine
Examples and phrases in ***bold italics***	**i·deal·ly** [aɪˈdiːəlɪ] *adv*: ***ideally situated*** en una posición ideal; ***ideally, we would do it like this*** lo ideal sería que lo hiciéramos así
Indicating words in *italics*	**stub·born** [ˈstʌbərn] *adj person* testarudo, terco; *defense, refusal, denial* tenaz, pertinaz **busi·ness** [ˈbɪznɪs] negocios *mpl*; (*company*) empresa *f*; (*sector*) sector *m*; (*affair, matter*) asunto *m*; *as subject of study* empresariales *fpl*; ***on business*** de negocios